America Votes™ 28

America Votes™ 28

ELECTION RETURNS BY STATE

RHODES COOK
ALICE V. McGILLIVRAY
RICHARD M. SCAMMON

2007–2008

CQ PRESS

A Division of SAGE
Washington, D.C.

CQ Press
2300 N Street, NW, Suite 800
Washington, DC 20037

Phone: 202-729-1900; toll-free, 1-866-4CQ-PRESS (1-866-427-7737)

Web: www.cqpress.com

Cover design: Anne Masters Design
Composition: C&M Digitals (P) Ltd.

♾ The paper used in this publication exceeds the requirements of the American National Standard for Information Sciences—Permanence of Paper for Printed Library Materials, ANSI Z39.48-1992.

Printed and bound in the United States of America

13 12 11 10 09   1 2 3 4 5

ISBN: 978-1-60426-534-7
ISSN: 0065-678X

Contents

List of Maps

Introduction

Borrowing from the parlance of the sporting world, the election of 2008 was an "instant classic." The campaign involved more money, more state-of-the-art technology, and more voters than ever before. And it ended on November 4 with the election of the first African American president in the nation's history.

In the process, America turned from a conservative Republican government that had recently controlled both ends of Pennsylvania Avenue to a more liberal Democratic government that starting in January 2009 dominated the White House and Capitol Hill.

Whether this election marks the beginning of a new era in American politics is an open question, one that only time will answer. But the 2008 election made clear that the political pendulum has swung once again.

So far this millennium, the nation has gone through several transformations—from a "50–50" nation after the 2000 election, to an electorate that clearly leaned Republican after 2004, to what is now a new political landscape that plainly favors the Democrats.

The Democrats' grip on the levers of power, however, could be tenuous. Barack Obama and his Democratic allies in Congress took office with wars continuing in Iraq and Afghanistan and the worst economic crisis since the Great Depression still unfolding. The same forces that fueled the Democratic success in 2008 could provide the seeds for failure in the years ahead.

But the current high-stakes environment also provides the opportunity for a long-term payoff for the Democrats if they prove able to provide creative solutions and competent government that also wins widespread voter approval.

Three of the presidents to whom Obama has been most often compared—Abraham Lincoln, Franklin D. Roosevelt, and Ronald Reagan—were able to do just that. In the process, they placed their personal stamp and that of their party on separate political eras that lasted well beyond their time in office.

Each of these three presidents came to the White House facing problems at least as trying as those confronting Obama. For Lincoln, it was the Civil War; for FDR, the Depression; for Reagan, a period of considerable economic unease during which analysts continued to use the "misery index."

2008: Democratic Hegemony

Democrats captured control of both ends of Pennsylvania Avenue in 2008, with Barack Obama winning the White House and Democrats extending their majorities in both the Senate and the House of Representatives. The results left the party with larger majorities in both chambers than Republicans enjoyed at any point during the presidency of George W. Bush. Democrats in 2008 also maintained their dominance of the nation's governorships.

The chart below reflects partisan totals immediately before and after the 2008 general election. The preelection House totals include a Democratic vacancy in Ohio that is credited to the Democrats in the preelection count. Two independent senators who caucus with the Democrats, Joseph I. Lieberman of Connecticut and Bernard Sanders of Vermont, are listed as independents. The postelection Senate totals also include Democrat Al Franken, whose narrow victory in Minnesota was not finally realized until late June 2009.

	Preelection			Postelection		
	Rep.	Dem.	Other	Rep.	Dem.	Other
Governor	22	28	0	21	29	0
Senate	49	49	2	41	57	2
House	199	236	0	178	257	0

And each of these presidents took office possessing political capital roughly similar to Obama's. In short, their triumph was not just a personal one, but it extended to their parties as well.

Lincoln was first elected in 1860 by a popular vote margin of 10 percentage points, and he was accompanied to Washington by a Republican Congress—the first time the fledgling party ever controlled both sides of Capitol Hill.

FDR was initially elected in 1932 by a hefty popular vote margin of 18 points, a win buttressed by the election of huge Democratic majorities in both the Senate and House.

Counting the 2008 Vote

For the second consecutive election cycle, Democrats in 2008 dominated the voting for federal offices. They had an aggregate advantage of 13 million votes in House races. Democrat Barack Obama prevailed in the presidential election by a margin exceeding 9.5 million votes. And in Senate contests, the nationwide vote favored the Democrats by more than 4.5 million.

No blank or void ballots are included in the totals below. They are based on official returns from 14 gubernatorial contests (11 held in 2008, 3 in 2007) and 35 Senate races, as well as two versions of the House vote. "All Races" feature the results from the districts in which a vote was taken in 2008, including those in which only one major party ran a candidate. "Contested Races" are those in which both the Democrats and Republicans fielded candidates. There were 380 contested House races in 2008, of which the Democrats won 216 compared to 164 for the Republicans.

Office	Total Vote	Republican	Democratic	Other	Rep.-Dem. Plurality	Percentage of Total Vote		
						Rep.	Dem.	Other
President	131,313,820	59,948,323	69,498,516	1,866,981	9,550,193 D	45.7%	52.9%	1.4%
Governor	19,801,733	9,466,043	9,726,126	609,564	260,083 D	47.8%	49.1%	3.1%
Senate	66,118,605	29,729,568	34,276,382	2,112,655	4,546,814 D	45.0%	51.8%	3.2%
House								
All Races	120,724,312	52,187,151	65,247,248	3,289,913	13,060,097 D	43.2%	54.0%	2.7%
Contested Races	109,604,158	49,472,908	57,907,264	2,223,986	8,434,356 D	45.1%	52.8%	2.0%

2008: Close House Races

The volume of highly competitive House races in 2008 dropped significantly from two years earlier, as the number of winners with less than 52 percent of the total vote fell from 42 in 2006 to 31 in 2008. In both elections, however, most of the sub–52 percent House winners were Republicans. An asterisk (*) indicates an incumbent.

Republicans (18)	2006 Winning Percentage	Democrats (13)	2006 Winning Percentage
Jean Schmidt, Ohio 2*	44.8%	Mary Jo Kilroy, Ohio 15	45.9%
Michele Bachmann, Minn. 6*	46.4%	Dina Titus, Nev. 3	47.4%
		Mark H. Schauer, Mich. 7	48.8%
Bill Cassidy, La. 6	48.1%	Frank Kratovil Jr., Md. 1	49.1%
John Fleming, La. 4	48.1%	Thomas S. P. Perriello, Va. 5	50.1%
Erik Paulsen, Minn. 3	48.5%	Bobby Bright, Ala. 2	50.2%
Anh "Joseph" Cao, La. 2	49.5%	Walt Minnick, Idaho 1	50.6%
Dan Lungren, Calif. 3*	49.5%	Eric J. J. Massa, N.Y. 29	51.0%
Blaine Luetkemeyer, Mo. 9	50.0%	Kathleen A. Dahlkemper, Pa. 3	51.2%
Don Young, Alaska*	50.1%	Jim Himes, Conn. 4	51.3%
Brian P. Bilbray, Calif. 50*	50.2%	Parker Griffith, Ala. 5	51.5%
Leonard Lance, N.J. 7	50.2%	Paul E. Kanjorski, Pa. 11*	51.6%
Tom McClintock, Calif. 4	50.2%	Carol Shea-Porter, N.H. 1*	51.7%
Lynn Jenkins, Kan. 2	50.6%		
Ken Calvert, Calif. 44*	51.2%		
Thaddeus McCotter, Mich. 11*	51.4%		
Dean Heller, Nev. 2*	51.8%		
Henry E. Brown Jr., S.C. 1*	51.9%		
Lee Terry, Neb. 2*	51.9%		

Reagan first won the White House in 1980 by nearly 10 percentage points, with his coattails helping to elect the first Republican Senate in more than a quarter century.

As for Obama, his margin of victory in 2008 was 7 points, less than the others, but a convincing margin nonetheless in an age when landslide victories have been replaced by a semblance of political parity. And Obama offered coattails of sorts as well, as his message of change fit a national mood that helped his party significantly strengthen its majorities on Capitol Hill.

In its scope, the Democratic victory in 2008 was almost identical to the one in 1992 led by another young politician, Bill Clinton. He won the popular vote that year by a margin of 6 percentage points and was joined by 258 Democrats in the House and 57 Democrats in the Senate.

In 2008 the Democrats elected 257 House members to the new 111th Congress to join 57 senators (a number that includes Al Franken of Minnesota, whose razor-thin victory over Republican incumbent Norm Coleman was not confirmed until late June 2009). That total grows to 59 if one includes Connecticut's Joseph I. Lieberman and Vermont's Bernard Sanders, who caucus with the Senate Democrats but were elected as independents. And Democrats found an important 60th Senate vote, the number needed to avoid filibusters, when Arlen Specter of Pennsylvania abruptly switched his party affiliation from Republican to Democrat in the spring of 2009.

The House Since 1990: From Democratic to Republican to Democratic

The House of Representatives went from Democratic to Republican control in 1994. After a succession of losses in both 2006 and 2008, however, Republicans have fallen back almost to where they were in 1992, before they won House control. Republicans still hold a majority of House seats in the South, but Democrats have a decided advantage in the other regions, most notably the East. Regions are defined below. An "I" indicates Independent.

	South				West			Midwest			East				Total House			
	R	D	I		R	D		R	D		R	D	I		R	D	I	
1990	44	85	0	D	37	48	D	45	68	D	41	66	1	D	167	267	1	D
1992	52	85	0	D	38	55	D	44	61	D	42	57	1	D	176	258	1	D
1994	73	64	0	R	53	40	R	59	46	R	45	54	1	D	230	204	1	R
1996	82	55	0	R	51	42	R	55	50	R	39	60	1	D	227	207	1	R
1998	82	55	0	R	49	44	R	54	51	R	38	61	1	D	223	211	1	R
2000	81	55	1	R	43	50	D	57	48	R	40	59	1	D	221	212	2	R
2002	85	57	0	R	46	52	D	61	39	R	37	57	1	D	229	205	1	R
2004	91	51	0	R	45	53	D	60	40	R	36	58	1	D	232	202	1	R
2006	85	57	0	R	41	57	D	51	49	R	25	70	0	D	202	233	0	D
2008	80	62	0	R	35	63	D	45	55	D	18	77	0	D	178	257	0	D
Net Change in GOP Seats, 1994–2008	+7				−18			−14			−27				−52			

EAST - Connecticut, Delaware, Maine, Maryland, Massachusetts, New Hampshire, New Jersey, New York, Pennsylvania, Rhode Island, Vermont, West Virginia.

MIDWEST - Illinois, Indiana, Iowa, Kansas, Michigan, Minnesota, Missouri, Nebraska, North Dakota, Ohio, South Dakota, Wisconsin.

SOUTH - Alabama, Arkansas, Florida, Georgia, Kentucky, Louisiana, Mississippi, North Carolina, Oklahoma, South Carolina, Tennessee, Texas, Virginia.

WEST - Alaska, Arizona, California, Colorado, Hawaii, Idaho, Montana, Nevada, New Mexico, Oregon, Utah, Washington, Wyoming.

Obama should have a stronger governing majority in Congress than Clinton did sixteen years earlier. Then, more than one quarter of all Senate Democrats and nearly one third of all House Democrats were from the South. Not only did a number of them occupy powerful committee chairmanships, but they also tended to be conservative in nature. As such, they represented a constant threat to defect from the more liberal party line to join congressional Republicans in an alliance that was widely known as the "conservative coalition."

That coalition, however, no longer exists, as conservative Southern Democrats are now almost an extinct species in Congress. Those Southern Democrats who remain comprise barely 10 percent of the party's membership in the Senate and less than one quarter in the House. They are not "old bulls" in the mold of James Eastland, Herman Talmadge, and Harry Byrd, but instead tend to be younger, more racially diverse individuals—a band of Southern Democrats at home in the national party. That does not mean they always march in lockstep with the party's liberal congressional leadership. Many number themselves among the fiscally conservative Blue Dog Democrats.

One thing is certain about Obama's victory: it cannot be credited to (or blamed on) third party interference.

Lincoln won the White House on the eve of the Civil War after the Democratic Party broke into Northern and Southern wings, each fielding its own presidential ticket in 1860. Lincoln was able to walk through the political rubble to an easy victory with just 40 percent of the popular vote.

In 1980 Reagan was helped a bit in his race against Democratic incumbent Jimmy Carter by the presence of a significant independent candidate in John Anderson. The latter was a Republican member of Congress from Illinois. But he offered himself as someone who wore "his wallet on the right and his heart on the left," and he ended up drawing roughly as many votes from Democratic as Republican voters. In the end, Reagan won easily, but his share of the vote represented a bare majority—50.7 percent—of all ballots cast.

In 1992 Clinton's path to victory over Republican president George H. W. Bush was made easier by the independent candidacy of Ross Perot. The wealthy Texan ran an expensive campaign that aimed much of its fire at the

2008: Defeated Incumbents

The election of 2008 was another bad one for the Republicans. Yet unlike 2006, the political carnage was not limited to the GOP side of the ballot. The Democrats lost 5 House incumbents in 2008, all freshman members with the exception of William J. Jefferson of Louisiana, a nine-term representative serving under an ethics cloud. Meanwhile, Republicans lost some congressional veterans of their own, including Sen. Ted Stevens of Alaska, who was appointed to his seat in 1968, and Rep. Christopher Shays of Connecticut, a ten-term House veteran who was the last Republican representative left in New England.

The chart lists the gubernatorial and Senate and House incumbents defeated in the 2008 primaries and general election, the number of full terms these incumbents had served in that office at the time of their loss in 2008, the percentage of the total vote they had received in the previous general election (2002 for senators, 2003 or 2004 for governors, and 2006 for House members), and their percentage of the total vote in the 2008 general election (for those who were not sidelined by the primaries).

	Number of Terms	Previous Election Percentage	2008 Election Percentage
GOVERNOR (1)			
General Election			
(1 Republican)			
Ernie Fletcher, R-Ky.*	1	55.0%	41.3%
SENATORS (5)			
General Election			
(5 Republicans)			
Norm Coleman, R-Minn.	1	49.5%	42.0%
Elizabeth Dole, R-N.C.	1	53.6%	44.2%
Gordon Smith, R-Ore.	2	56.2%	45.6%
Ted Stevens, R-Alaska	6	78.2%	46.5%
John E. Sununu, R-N.H.	1	50.8%	45.3%
REPRESENTATIVES (23)			
Primaries			
(3 Republicans, 1 Democrat)			
Chris Cannon, R-Utah 3	6	57.7%	—
David Davis, R-Tenn. 1	1	61.1%	—
Wayne T. Gilchrest, R-Md. 1	9	68.8%	—
Albert R. Wynn, D-Md. 4	8	80.7%	—
General Election			
(14 Republicans, 5 Democrats)			
Nancy Boyda, D-Kan. 2	1	50.6%	46.2%
Don Cazayoux, D-La. 6	@	—	40.3%
Steve Chabot, R-Ohio 1	7	52.2%	47.5%
Thelma Drake, R-Va. 2	2	51.3%	47.5%
Phil English, R-Pa. 3	7	53.6%	48.8%
Tom Feeney, R-Fla. 24	3	57.9%	41.1%
Virgil H. Goode Jr., R-Va. 5	6	59.1%	49.9%
Robin Hayes, R-N.C. 8	5	50.1%	44.6%
William J. Jefferson, D-La. 2#	9	56.5%	46.8%
Ric Keller, R-Fla. 8	4	52.8%	48.0%
Joe Knollenberg, R-Mich. 9	8	51.6%	42.6%
John R. "Randy" Kuhl Jr., R-N.Y. 29	2	51.5%	49.0%
Nick Lampson, D-Texas 22	1	51.8%	45.4%
Tim Mahoney, D-Fla. 16	1	49.5%	39.9%
Marilyn Musgrave, R-Colo. 4	3	45.6%	43.8%
Jon Porter, R-Nev. 3	3	48.5%	42.3%
Bill Sali, R-Idaho 1	1	49.9%	49.4%
Christopher Shays, R-Conn. 4	10	51.0%	47.6%
Tim Walberg, R-Mich. 7	1	49.9%	46.5%

Note: An asterisk (*) indicates that Gov. Ernie Fletcher was defeated in Kentucky's 2007 gubernatorial election. A pound sign (#) denotes that Rep. William J. Jefferson was defeated in an election that was delayed until December 2008. @ indicates that Rep. Don Cazayoux was first elected in a 2008 special election.

Republican incumbent. In essence, Perot ran as a blocking back for Clinton, who was elected with just 43 percent of the popular vote.

Independent candidates did not have much influence on FDR's victory over GOP incumbent Herbert Hoover in 1932, nor did they in Obama's win over John McCain in 2008. Like Republican George W. Bush's battle with Democrat John Kerry in 2004, the Obama-McCain contest was basically a straight-up Democratic versus Republican affair that left no room and no call for any significant third party options.

Obama received 69.5 million votes to McCain's 59.9 million. Independent Ralph Nader was the "best of the rest" in 2008, drawing just under 750,000 votes. Nader polled at least 1 percent of the vote in 14 far-flung states—Connecticut, Maine, Rhode Island, Vermont, and West Virginia in the Northeast; Minnesota and North and South Dakota in the Midwest; Arkansas in the South; and Alaska, Idaho, Oregon, Washington, and Wyoming in the West.

Libertarian candidate Bob Barr finished a distant fourth in the presidential balloting, with just over a half million votes. He reached 1 percent only in Indiana, where he was the lone independent or third party candidate to be listed on the ballot.

Barr's failure to make any headway elsewhere, including his home state of Georgia, was good news for McCain—although only in the sense that the Republican was able to hold a number of states that were habitually in the GOP column.

With the wind at his back in terms of money, issues, and voter registration, Obama was able to go on the offensive in the fall campaign. He did not have to worry about holding the Democratic base on the two coasts. By and large, these states were secure, which freed Obama to look expansively at the map.

He was able to throw his considerable resources into traditional battleground states such as Florida and Ohio, as well as an array of states that the Democrats had long conceded without much of a fight, such as Indiana, North Carolina, and Virginia.

In the end, Obama swept all 19 states that John Kerry had won in 2004 plus 9 others that had voted that year for President Bush. The latter was an eclectic group that included 3 states in the South (Florida, North Carolina, and Virginia), 3 in the Midwest (Indiana, Iowa, and Ohio), and 3 in the Mountain West (Colorado, Nevada, and New Mexico).

The Democratic share of the presidential vote rose in all parts of the country from 2004—with Obama posting an 18–percentage point increase in his boyhood home of Hawaii, an 11-point increase in Indiana (where he made a major effort in both the primary and general election), and 9-point increases in Delaware (home of Democratic vice-presidential candidate Joseph R. Biden Jr.), Vermont (the second best state for Obama behind Hawaii), Montana (where Obama spent the Fourth of July with his family), and the Plains states of North Dakota and Nebraska.

In the latter, Obama even won an electoral vote under Nebraska's unique system of awarding electors by congressional district (a format also favored by the state of Maine). Obama carried the single Nebraska district he realistically had a chance to win—the Second, which includes Omaha. There, he prevailed by barely 3,000 votes. McCain, meanwhile, swept the Lincoln-based First District by more than 25,000 votes and the vast rural western Nebraska Third District by nearly 100,000 votes.

In Maine, Obama handily carried the state's two congressional districts. The Portland-based First District went for the Democrat by a margin of nearly 90,000 votes, while the more rural northern Maine Second District produced a plurality of nearly 40,000 votes for Obama.

The only states where Obama was unable to improve the Democratic vote share from four years earlier were Massachusetts (Kerry's home state) and a band of states extending southwest out of Appalachia from West Virginia to Oklahoma. It was a part of the country where Obama had, by and large, run poorly in his closely contested Democratic primary battle with Hillary Clinton.

The 2008 election left the Republicans enjoying the upper hand in only one region of the country, the South. Dixie provided McCain with nearly two-thirds of his electoral votes and congressional Republicans with close to half their number on Capitol Hill.

But even in the South, the Democrats made significant inroads in 2008, none more notable than in Virginia. Obama pulled the electoral votes of the Old Dominion into the Democratic column for the first time since 1964. Former governor Mark Warner won an open Senate seat, two years after Democrat James Webb had won the other seat. And in the House, Democrats gained 3 seats to transform an 8 to 3 GOP advantage to 6 to 5 Democratic.

Elsewhere, Republicans continued the downward slide that had begun in 2006. In the Northeast, Democrats emerged from the 2008 election with a level of hegemony that was staggering. Obama won nearly 60 percent of the presidential vote across the region, outpolled McCain by close to 6 million votes, and easily carried every Northeastern state except West Virginia.

At the House level, the defeat of Christopher Shays in Connecticut left the GOP without a single seat in New England. And in New York, the Republicans were reduced to just 3 of the Empire State's 29 House seats.

Republicans fared better in the Midwest, but not by much. Obama swept virtually all of the vote-rich industrial states, losing only Missouri by a margin of less than 4,000 votes. At the congressional level, Democrats picked up 3 seats in Ohio and 2 in Michigan, swinging the majority in each state's House delegation from the Republicans to the Democrats.

The Republican carnage was also extensive in the West. Obama carried California, the nation's most populous state, by more than 3 million votes. That was nearly twice the margin rolled up by any previous presidential candidate in the Golden State, including Californians Richard Nixon and Ronald Reagan.

The West was also a prime source of new Senate seats for the Democrats, as they picked up a total of 4 from Alaska to New Mexico. In the latter, Democrats took full control of the congressional delegation, as they picked up 2 open Republican House seats as well as Pete Domenici's open Senate seat.

Stop here and 2008 was a terrible year for the Republicans, but it ended on a high note for the GOP, with a Senate runoff victory in Georgia December 2 and a pair of House wins in Louisiana four days later.

The Senate victory by incumbent Saxby Chambliss in Georgia was largely expected. Chambliss had nearly won the seat in November when he drew 49.8 percent of the vote, just short of the outright majority required by state law. In the lower-turnout runoff, which was short the large African American vote present in November, Chambliss scored a clear-cut victory with 57 percent of the vote.

Yet the win that was most heartening for the GOP came several days later in Democratic New Orleans, where political newcomer Anh "Joseph" Cao upset Democratic representative William J. Jefferson, who had represented the black-majority district for nine terms.

To be sure, Jefferson was ethically tainted several times over, and the turnout for the December election was extremely light—less than 70,000 voters. Yet Cao's late-inning win had symbolic value for the GOP. The first Vietnamese American ever elected to Congress, he was quickly embraced by Republican leaders as the perfect antidote for a party that had fared poorly among African American, Hispanic, and Asian voters in 2008.

The Methodology

The twenty-eighth volume of *America Votes* follows the general pattern used in recent editions of this series. There is an introduction with text and tables designed to help tie together various aspects of the 2008 election cycle. The front section that follows contains tables with the state-by-state voter turnout and the vote for presidential, gubernatorial, Senate, and House elections in the 2008 election cycle. There is also a summary of special elections held between the general elections of 2006 and 2008 to fill vacancies in the 110th Congress and a listing of changes in congressional membership in the 111th Congress that occurred between the 2008 general election and the end of July 2009.

Following this introductory material is the heart of the volume, 51 chapters—one for each state plus the District of Columbia. Each state chapter begins with a map showing its counties, major population centers, and congressional districts for members of the House in the 110th Congress. Next is a profile sheet listing the current governor, senators, and representatives, followed by tables of the statewide vote for president, governor, and senator from 1946 or 1948 to the present. After that are county-by-county tables of presidential, gubernatorial, and Senate elections. All these tables are for the 2008 general election except for the governorships in Kentucky, Louisiana, and Mississippi, where voting was conducted in 2007.

The county tables for presidential, gubernatorial, and Senate elections feature a three-column format (Republican, Democratic, Other). The only exceptions are for elections in which another candidate received at least 10 percent of the vote, in which case a column for that vote is added. All the county tables include 2000 population figures from the Census Bureau.

The county tables are followed by a listing of votes cast for candidates for the House of Representatives, arranged by congressional district. The implementation of the 2000 Census for redistricting purposes led to changes in all multimember states before the 2002 election, with the exception of Maine, which drew new congressional district lines after 2002. There were also post-2002 district line changes in Pennsylvania and Texas, although only those in Texas had major political ramifications, as well as significant post-2004 changes in Georgia and Texas. In the latter two states, the votes listed for House members are limited to the elections since the last round of line changes. Results for elections before 2002 are not included for any state except those with a single member in the House.

The conclusion of each state chapter consists of two parts. The first is the notes section containing a breakdown of votes cast in the general election for third party, independent, and write-in candidates. For those major party candidates who also ran on a third party ballot line, votes are aggregated as Democratic or Republican. Blank spaces by a contest indicate there were no votes cast in these categories.

The second part provides official results for the primary elections for president, governor, Senate, and House held in the 2008 election cycle, as well as the primary date or dates (where presidential and state primaries were held on different dates), registration data at the time of the state primary, and the rules on voter participation in the primary.

In the chapters for New England states, tables list the vote for president, governor, and senator by larger cities and towns as well as by counties. In Rhode Island, the results are listed for all cities and towns.

The America Votes series is compiled from official results obtained from election authorities in each state. While complete accuracy is always the goal, it can sometimes prove elusive in a work such as this. On occasion, states may belatedly report changes in their vote totals that occur after publication of this volume. And human nature being what it is, there is always an example or two (or three) of self-inflicted errors. The goal is always to keep these to a minimum.

Our wish is to make these reference volumes as useful as possible to readers and researchers. Suggestions for new materials, together with any corrections of data, are welcome.

As in the preparation of *America Votes 23, 24, 25, 26,* and *27,* heartfelt thanks are in order to Eileen Canavan, the deputy assistant staff director for disclosure at the Federal Election Commission, with whom the author consulted in an effort to reconcile discrepancies in vote totals. Curtis Gans, the director of the Center for the Study of the American Electorate (CSAE), a part of American University's Center for Democracy and Election Management, was again the source of voter turnout data. Richard Winger, the publisher of Ballot Access News, generously provided information on independent and third party presidential candidates.

Considerable thanks also to Andrea Cunningham and Joan Gossett at CQ Press, who shepherded the movement of copy over the long weeks and months of this project with skill and good humor. Their work, along with that of their colleagues, was invaluable in the completion of this volume.

And last, but certainly not least, a tip of the hat to my wife, Memrie McKay-Cook, who assumed a disproportionate role in maintaining the "home front" while work on this book unfolded. Without her forbearance, it would not have been possible.

Rhodes Cook
August 2009

Errata

America Votes 27

The following corrections should be made in the previous edition of *America Votes,* covering the 2005–2006 election cycle.

Page 215. Dave Heineman (R) in Nebraska was elected governor in 2006 for a four-year term.

Page 355. The first line of the Texas CD 13 returns are for 2006.

Page 376. The newly elected senator in Virginia was James Webb (D).

UNITED STATES
VOTER TURNOUT 2008

State	2008 Voting Age Population	Registration- 2008 General Election	Percentage Voting Age Registered	Presidential Vote	Presidential Vote as Percentage of Voting Age Population	Registered Voters	House Vote	Senate Vote	Governor Vote
Alabama	3,394,000	3,010,638	88.7%	2,099,819	61.9%	69.7%	1,855,268	2,060,191	—
Alaska	476,000	495,731	104.1%	326,197	68.5%	65.8%	316,978	317,723	
Arizona	4,117,000	3,441,141	83.6%	2,293,475	55.7%	66.6%	2,155,694	—	—
Arkansas	2,065,000	1,684,290	81.6%	1,086,617	52.6%	64.5%	787,193	1,011,754	—
California	22,319,000	17,304,091	77.5%	13,561,900	60.8%	78.4%	12,322,079	—	—
Colorado	3,219,000	3,203,583	99.5%	2,401,462	74.6%	75.0%	2,283,931	2,331,712	—
Connecticut	2,518,000	2,097,635	83.3%	1,646,797	65.4%	78.5%	1,527,399	—	—
Delaware	630,000	602,726	95.7%	412,412	65.5%	68.4%	385,457	398,134	395,204
Florida	12,923,000	11,247,634	87.0%	8,390,744	64.9%	74.6%	7,421,172	—	—
Georgia	6,302,000	5,755,750	91.3%	3,924,486	62.3%	68.2%	3,654,948	2,137,956*	—
Hawaii	918,000	691,356	75.3%	453,568	49.4%	65.6%	417,831	—	—
Idaho	1,024,000	861,869	84.2%	655,122	64.0%	76.0%	637,852	644,780	—
Illinois	8,540,000	8,849,117	103.6%	5,522,371	64.7%	62.4%	5,248,195	5,329,884	—
Indiana	4,586,000	4,514,804	98.4%	2,751,054	60.0%	60.9%	2,676,850	—	2,703,752
Iowa	2,201,000	2,169,682	98.6%	1,537,123	69.8%	70.8%	1,483,165	1,502,918	—
Kansas	1,968,000	1,749,756	88.9%	1,235,872	62.8%	70.6%	1,208,302	1,210,690	—
Kentucky	3,147,000	2,906,809	92.4%	1,826,620	58.0%	62.8%	1,749,840	1,800,821	1,055,325
Louisiana	3,338,000	2,945,619	88.2%	1,960,761	58.7%	66.6%	1,046,176	1,896,574	1,297,840
Maine	1,048,000	1,027,585	98.1%	731,163	69.8%	71.2%	710,101	724,430	—
Maryland	4,064,000	3,430,364	84.4%	2,631,596	64.8%	76.7%	2,497,952	—	—
Massachusetts	4,625,000	4,220,488	91.3%	3,080,985	66.6%	73.0%	2,605,114	2,994,247	—
Michigan	7,490,000	7,470,764	99.7%	5,001,766	66.8%	67.0%	4,810,690	4,848,620	—
Minnesota	3,824,000	3,203,835	83.8%	2,910,369	76.1%	90.8%	2,802,614	2,887,646	—
Mississippi	2,151,000	1,895,583	88.1%	1,289,865	60.0%	68.0%	1,264,747	2,490,499*	744,039
Missouri	4,328,000	4,205,774	97.2%	2,925,205	67.6%	69.6%	2,821,484	—	2,877,778
Montana	731,000	672,961	92.1%	490,302	67.1%	72.9%	480,900	477,658	486,734
Nebraska	1,243,000	1,157,034	93.1%	801,281	64.5%	69.3%	775,398	792,511	—
Nevada	1,642,000	1,446,027	88.1%	967,848	58.9%	66.9%	908,254	—	—
New Hampshire	1,016,000	954,913	94.0%	710,970	70.0%	74.5%	674,975	694,787	682,910
New Jersey	5,904,000	5,378,792	91.1%	3,868,237	65.5%	71.9%	3,437,980	3,482,445	—
New Mexico	1,346,000	1,192,969	88.6%	830,158	61.7%	69.6%	814,566	823,650	—
New York	12,653,000	12,031,312	95.1%	7,640,931	60.4%	63.5%	6,390,516	—	—
North Carolina	6,423,000	6,287,992	97.9%	4,310,789	67.1%	68.6%	4,215,093	4,271,970	4,268,941
North Dakota	485,000	—		316,621	65.3%	—	313,965	—	315,692
Ohio	8,562,000	8,302,900	97.0%	5,708,350	66.7%	68.8%	5,374,340	—	—
Oklahoma	2,561,000	2,184,084	85.3%	1,462,661	57.1%	67.0%	1,336,927	1,346,819	—
Oregon	2,615,000	2,166,866	82.9%	1,827,864	69.9%	84.4%	1,682,509	1,767,504	—
Pennsylvania	9,450,000	8,758,031	92.7%	6,013,272	63.6%	68.7%	5,791,284	—	—
Rhode Island	790,000	680,651	86.2%	471,766	59.7%	69.3%	438,232	438,812	—
South Carolina	3,224,000	2,553,923	79.2%	1,920,969	59.6%	75.2%	1,873,890	1,871,431	—
South Dakota	573,000	574,632	100.3%	381,975	66.7%	66.5%	379,007	380,673	—
Tennessee	4,512,000	3,977,586	88.2%	2,599,749	57.6%	65.4%	2,301,885	2,424,585	—
Texas	14,886,000	13,575,062	91.2%	8,077,795	54.3%	59.5%	7,528,622	7,912,075	—
Utah	1,578,000	1,432,525	90.8%	952,370	60.4%	66.5%	936,839	—	945,525
Vermont	495,000	454,466	91.8%	325,046	65.7%	71.5%	298,151	—	319,085
Virginia	5,560,000	5,034,660	90.6%	3,723,260	67.0%	74.0%	3,495,355	3,643,294	—
Washington	4,489,000	3,629,898	80.9%	3,036,878	67.7%	83.7%	2,914,463	—	3,002,862
West Virginia	1,428,000	1,212,117	84.9%	713,451	50.0%	58.9%	645,560	702,308	706,046
Wisconsin	4,183,000	3,502,196	83.7%	2,983,417	71.3%	85.2%	2,775,174	—	—
Wyoming	388,000	244,818	63.1%	254,658	65.6%	104.0%	249,395	499,504*	—
District of Columbia	371,000	426,761	115.0%	265,853	71.7%	62.3%	—	—	—
Total	208,323,000	186,819,800	89.7%	131,313,820	63.0%	70.3%	120,724,312	66,118,605	19,801,733

Source: Registration and voting age population figures were provided by the Committee for the Study of the American Electorate, a part of the American University Center for Democracy and Election Management. Voting age population figures are based on the estimated citizen voting age population in each state (and nationally) at the time of the November 2008 general election. Registration figures for virtually every state are as of the November 2008 general election. However, they must be viewed with caution. Some states limit their registration totals to active voters; some include inactive voters as well. In Alaska, Illinois, South Dakota, and the District of Columbia, the number of registered voters was more than 100 percent of the voting age population. North Dakota does not require voter registration.

Notes: The Senate vote in Georgia reflects the result of a runoff held December 2, 2008. No candidate received the majority of the vote required by Georgia law in the November general election. Mississippi and Wyoming held two Senate elections in 2008. The Senate vote for each state reflects the total vote cast in the two elections. The gubernatorial vote includes 2007 elections in Kentucky, Louisiana, and Mississippi.

GUBERNATORIAL ELECTIONS 2007 AND 2008

| | | Republican | | Democratic | | | | Total Vote | | Major Vote | |
State	Total Vote	Vote	Candidate	Vote	Candidate	Other Vote	Plurality	Rep.	Dem.	Rep.	Dem.
Delaware	395,204	126,662	Lee, William Swain	266,861	Markell, Jack	1,681	140,199 D	32.0%	67.5%	32.2%	67.8%
Indiana	2,703,752	1,563,885	Daniels, Mitch	1,082,463	Thompson, Jill Long	57,404	481,422 R	57.8%	40.0%	59.1%	40.9%
Kentucky	1,055,325	435,773	Fletcher, Ernie	619,552	Beshear, Steve		183,779 D	41.3%	58.7%	41.3%	58.7%
Louisiana*	1,297,840	699,275	Jindal, Bobby	397,755	Boasso, Walter J./Campbell, Foster	200,810	472,799 R	53.9%	30.6%	63.7%	36.3%
Mississippi	744,039	430,807	Barbour, Haley	313,232	Eaves, John A.		117,575 R	57.9%	42.1%	57.9%	42.1%
Missouri	2,877,778	1,136,364	Hulshof, Kenny	1,680,611	Nixon, Jeremiah W. "Jay"	60,803	544,247 D	39.5%	58.4%	40.3%	59.7%
Montana	486,734	158,268	Brown, Roy	318,670	Schweitzer, Brian	9,796	160,402 D	32.5%	65.5%	33.2%	66.8%
New Hampshire	682,910	188,555	Kenney, Joseph D.	479,042	Lynch, John	15,313	290,487 D	27.6%	70.1%	28.2%	71.8%
North Carolina	4,268,941	2,001,168	McCrory, Pat	2,146,189	Perdue, Bev	121,584	145,021 D	46.9%	50.3%	48.3%	51.7%
North Dakota	315,692	235,009	Hoeven, John	74,279	Mathern, Tim	6,404	160,730 R	74.4%	23.5%	76.0%	24.0%
Utah	945,525	734,049	Huntsman, Jon Jr.	186,503	Springmeyer, Bob	24,973	547,546 R	77.6%	19.7%	79.7%	20.3%
Vermont	319,085	170,492	Douglas, Jim	69,534	Symington, Gaye	79,059	100,701 R	53.4%	21.8%	71.0%	29.0%
Washington	3,002,862	1,404,124	Rossi, Dino	1,598,738	Gregoire, Christine		194,614 D	46.8%	53.2%	46.8%	53.2%
West Virginia	706,046	181,612	Weeks, Russ	492,697	Manchin, Joe III	31,737	311,085 D	25.7%	69.8%	26.9%	73.1%
Total	19,801,733	9,466,043		9,726,126		609,564	260,083 D	47.8%	49.1%	49.3%	50.7%

*Notes: The gubernatorial elections in Kentucky, Louisiana, and Mississippi were held in 2007. Louisiana has a unique election system for state offices such as governor. All candidates, regardless of party, ran together on the October 2007 ballot, and since Republican Bobby Jindal won a majority of the vote, he was elected. Jindal was the only Republican candidate on the ballot, while there were five Democrats who together collected 397,755 votes (30.6 percent of the total vote). The bulk of these votes were garnered by the party's top two vote-getters, who are listed in the Democratic column. Jindal's plurality is measured over the runner-up, Walter J. Boasso, who received 226,476 votes (17.5 percent of the total vote). The nationwide Democratic gubernatorial vote includes the combined vote for the five gubernatorial candidates in Louisiana who ran as Democrats. In Vermont, an independent candidate (Anthony Pollina) finished second with 69,791 votes (21.9% of the total vote). The plurality in Vermont represents the difference between the Republican winner and Pollina.

SENATE ELECTIONS 2008

State	Total Vote	Republican Vote	Republican Candidate	Democratic Vote	Democratic Candidate	Other Vote	Rep.-Dem. Plurality	Total Vote Rep.	Total Vote Dem.	Major Vote Rep.	Major Vote Dem.
Alabama	2,060,191	1,305,383	Sessions, Jeff	752,391	Figures, Vivian Davis	2,417	552,992 R	63.4%	36.5%	63.4%	36.6%
Alaska	317,723	147,814	Stevens, Ted	151,767	Begich, Mark	18,142	3,953 D	46.5%	47.8%	49.3%	50.7%
Arkansas	1,011,754		—	804,678	Pryor, Mark	207,076	804,678 D		79.5%		100.0%
Colorado	2,331,712	990,784	Schaffer, Bob	1,231,049	Udall, Mark	109,879	240,265 D	42.5%	52.8%	44.6%	55.4%
Delaware	398,134	140,595	O'Donnell, Christine	257,539	Biden, Joseph R. Jr.		116,944 D	35.3%	64.7%	35.3%	64.7%
Georgia*	2,137,956	1,228,033	Chambliss, Saxby	909,923	Martin, Jim		318,110 R	57.4%	42.6%	57.4%	42.6%
Idaho	644,780	371,744	Risch, Jim	219,903	LaRocco, Larry	53,133	151,841 R	57.7%	34.1%	62.8%	37.2%
Illinois	5,329,884	1,520,621	Sauerberg, Steve	3,615,844	Durbin, Richard J.	193,419	2,095,223 D	28.5%	67.8%	29.6%	70.4%
Iowa	1,502,918	560,006	Reed, Christopher	941,665	Harkin, Tom	1,247	381,659 D	37.3%	62.7%	37.3%	62.7%
Kansas	1,210,690	727,121	Roberts, Pat	441,399	Slattery, Jim	42,170	285,722 R	60.1%	36.5%	62.2%	37.8%
Kentucky	1,800,821	953,816	McConnell, Mitch	847,005	Lunsford, Bruce		106,811 R	53.0%	47.0%	53.0%	47.0%
Louisiana	1,896,574	867,177	Kennedy, John	988,298	Landrieu, Mary L.	41,099	121,121 D	45.7%	52.1%	46.7%	53.3%
Maine	724,430	444,300	Collins, Susan	279,510	Allen, Tom	620	164,790 R	61.3%	38.6%	61.4%	38.6%
Massachusetts	2,994,247	926,044	Beatty, Jeffrey K.	1,971,974	Kerry, John	96,229	1,045,930 D	30.9%	65.9%	32.0%	68.0%
Michigan	4,848,620	1,641,070	Hoogendyk, Jack Jr.	3,038,386	Levin, Carl	169,164	1,397,316 D	33.8%	62.7%	35.1%	64.9%
Minnesota	2,887,646	1,212,317	Coleman, Norm	1,212,629	Franken, Al	462,700	312 D	42.0%	42.0%	50.0%	50.0%
Mississippi	1,247,026	766,111	Cochran, Thad	480,915	Fleming, Erik R.		285,196 R	61.4%	38.6%	61.4%	38.6%
Mississippi (S)	1,243,473	683,409	Wicker, Roger	560,064	Musgrove, Ronnie		123,345 R	55.0%	45.0%	55.0%	45.0%
Montana	477,658	129,369	Kelleher, Bob	348,289	Baucus, Max		218,920 D	27.1%	72.9%	27.1%	72.9%
Nebraska	792,511	455,854	Johanns, Mike	317,456	Kleeb, Scott	19,201	138,398 R	57.5%	40.1%	58.9%	41.1%
New Hampshire	694,787	314,403	Sununu, John E.	358,438	Shaheen, Jeanne	21,946	44,035 D	45.3%	51.6%	46.7%	53.3%
New Jersey	3,482,445	1,461,025	Zimmer, Dick	1,951,218	Lautenberg, Frank R.	70,202	490,193 D	42.0%	56.0%	42.8%	57.2%
New Mexico	823,650	318,522	Pearce, Steve	505,128	Udall, Tom		186,606 D	38.7%	61.3%	38.7%	61.3%
North Carolina	4,271,970	1,887,510	Dole, Elizabeth	2,249,311	Hagan, Kay	135,149	361,801 D	44.2%	52.7%	45.6%	54.4%
Oklahoma	1,346,819	763,375	Inhofe, James M.	527,736	Rice, Andrew	55,708	235,639 R	56.7%	39.2%	59.1%	40.9%
Oregon	1,767,504	805,159	Smith, Gordon H.	864,392	Merkley, Jeff	97,953	59,233 D	45.6%	48.9%	48.2%	51.8%
Rhode Island	438,812	116,174	Tingle, Robert G.	320,644	Reed, Jack	1,994	204,470 D	26.5%	73.1%	26.6%	73.4%
South Carolina	1,871,431	1,076,534	Graham, Lindsey	790,621	Conley, Bob	4,276	285,913 R	57.5%	42.2%	57.7%	42.3%
South Dakota	380,673	142,784	Dykstra, Lenny	237,889	Johnson, Tim		95,105 D	37.5%	62.5%	37.5%	62.5%
Tennessee	2,424,585	1,579,477	Alexander, Lamar	767,236	Tuke, Robert D.	77,872	812,241 R	65.1%	31.6%	67.3%	32.7%
Texas	7,912,075	4,337,469	Cornyn, John	3,389,365	Noriega, Richard J. "Rick"	185,241	948,104 R	54.8%	42.8%	56.1%	43.9%
Virginia	3,643,294	1,228,830	Gilmore, James S. "Jim" III	2,369,327	Warner, Mark R.	45,137	1,140,497 D	33.7%	65.0%	34.2%	65.8%
West Virginia	702,308	254,629	Wolfe, Jay	447,560	Rockefeller, John D. IV	119	192,931 D	36.3%	63.7%	36.3%	63.7%
Wyoming	249,946	189,046	Enzi, Michael B.	60,631	Rothfuss, Chris	269	128,415 R	75.6%	24.3%	75.7%	24.3%
Wyoming (S)	249,558	183,063	Barrasso, John	66,202	Carter, Nick	293	116,861 R	73.4%	26.5%	73.4%	26.6%
Total	66,118,605	29,729,568		34,276,382		2,112,655	4,546,814 D	45.0%	51.8%	46.4%	53.6%

Notes: The Georgia vote reflects the results of a runoff held in December 2008. No candidate received the majority required by state law in the November general election. Then, the vote was 1,867,097 (49.8 percent of the total vote) Republican (Saxby Chambliss); 1,757,393 (46.8 percent) Democratic (Jim Martin); 127,995 (3.4 percent) Other, for a total of 3,752,485 votes. The nationwide Democratic and Republican Senate vote includes the results of the Georgia runoff, not the general election. Senate elections in Mississippi and Wyoming were for short terms.

HOUSE OF REPRESENTATIVES ELECTIONS 2008

State	Seats Won Republican	Seats Won Democratic	Total Vote	Republican	Democratic	Other	Rep.-Dem. Plurality	Total Vote Rep.	Total Vote Dem.	Major Vote Rep.	Major Vote Dem.
Alabama	4	3	1,855,268	1,120,903	718,367	15,998	402,536 R	60.4%	38.7%	60.9%	39.1%
Alaska	1		316,978	158,939	142,560	15,479	16,379 R	50.1%	45.0%	52.7%	47.3%
Arizona	3	5	2,155,694	1,021,798	1,055,305	78,591	33,507 D	47.4%	49.0%	49.2%	50.8%
Arkansas	1	3	787,193	215,196	415,481	156,516	200,285 D	27.3%	52.8%	34.1%	65.9%
California	19	34	12,322,079	4,515,372	7,377,725	428,982	2,862,353 D	36.6%	59.9%	38.0%	62.0%
Colorado	2	5	2,283,931	990,870	1,259,768	33,293	268,898 D	43.4%	55.2%	44.0%	56.0%
Connecticut		5	1,527,399	504,785	991,615	30,999	486,830 D	33.0%	64.9%	33.7%	66.3%
Delaware	1		385,457	235,437	146,434	3,586	89,003 R	61.1%	38.0%	61.7%	38.3%
Florida	15	10	7,421,172	3,792,167	3,434,831	194,174	357,336 R	51.1%	46.3%	52.5%	47.5%
Georgia	7	6	3,654,948	1,796,549	1,858,090	309	61,541 D	49.2%	50.8%	49.2%	50.8%
Hawaii		2	417,831	82,540	319,956	15,335	237,416 D	19.8%	76.6%	20.5%	79.5%
Idaho	1	1	637,852	377,464	259,776	612	117,688 R	59.2%	40.7%	59.2%	40.8%
Illinois	7	12	5,248,195	1,961,173	3,176,203	110,819	1,215,030 D	37.4%	60.5%	38.2%	61.8%
Indiana	4	5	2,676,850	1,240,577	1,388,963	47,310	148,386 D	46.3%	51.9%	47.2%	52.8%
Iowa	2	3	1,483,165	698,241	759,460	25,464	61,219 D	47.1%	51.2%	47.9%	52.1%
Kansas	3	1	1,208,302	690,005	470,031	48,266	219,974 R	57.1%	38.9%	59.5%	40.5%
Kentucky	4	2	1,749,840	955,182	761,209	33,449	193,973 R	54.6%	43.5%	55.7%	44.3%
Louisiana	6	1	1,046,176	594,306	398,474	53,396	195,832 R	56.8%	38.1%	59.9%	40.1%
Maine		2	710,101	278,198	431,903		153,705 D	39.2%	60.8%	39.2%	60.8%
Maryland	1	7	2,497,952	762,539	1,677,238	58,175	914,699 D	30.5%	67.1%	31.3%	68.7%
Massachusetts		10	2,605,114	318,461	2,245,778	40,875	1,927,317 D	12.2%	86.2%	12.4%	87.6%
Michigan	7	8	4,810,690	2,114,293	2,516,640	179,757	402,347 D	43.9%	52.3%	45.7%	54.3%
Minnesota	3	5	2,802,614	1,069,015	1,612,480	121,119	543,465 D	38.1%	57.5%	39.9%	60.1%
Mississippi	1	3	1,264,747	527,330	731,805	5,612	204,475 D	41.7%	57.9%	41.9%	58.1%
Missouri	5	4	2,821,484	1,313,018	1,413,016	95,450	99,998 D	46.5%	50.1%	48.2%	51.8%
Montana	1		480,900	308,470	155,930	16,500	152,540 R	64.1%	32.4%	66.4%	33.6%
Nebraska	3		775,398	510,513	264,885		245,628 R	65.8%	34.2%	65.8%	34.2%
Nevada	1	2	908,254	383,548	457,320	67,386	73,772 D	42.2%	50.4%	45.6%	54.4%
New Hampshire		2	674,975	294,560	364,767	15,648	70,207 D	43.6%	54.0%	44.7%	55.3%
New Jersey	5	8	3,437,980	1,461,820	1,911,827	64,333	450,007 D	42.5%	55.6%	43.3%	56.7%
New Mexico		3	814,566	321,083	457,135	36,348	136,052 D	39.4%	56.1%	41.3%	58.7%
New York	3	26	6,390,516	2,034,784	4,286,047	69,685	2,251,263 D	31.8%	67.1%	32.2%	67.8%
North Carolina	5	8	4,215,093	1,901,517	2,293,971	19,605	392,454 D	45.1%	54.4%	45.3%	54.7%
North Dakota		1	313,965	119,388	194,577		75,189 D	38.0%	62.0%	38.0%	62.0%
Ohio	8	10	5,374,340	2,491,498	2,752,111	130,731	260,613 D	46.4%	51.2%	47.5%	52.5%
Oklahoma	4	1	1,336,927	802,530	503,614	30,783	298,916 R	60.0%	37.7%	61.4%	38.6%
Oregon	1	4	1,682,509	435,920	1,036,171	210,418	600,251 D	25.9%	61.6%	29.6%	70.4%
Pennsylvania	7	12	5,791,284	2,520,805	3,209,168	61,311	688,363 D	43.5%	55.4%	44.0%	56.0%
Rhode Island		2	438,232	118,773	303,670	15,789	184,897 D	27.1%	69.3%	28.1%	71.9%
South Carolina	4	2	1,873,890	939,703	919,529	14,658	20,174 R	50.1%	49.1%	50.5%	49.5%
South Dakota		1	379,007	122,966	256,041		133,075 D	32.4%	67.6%	32.4%	67.6%
Tennessee	4	5	2,301,885	977,677	1,195,542	128,666	217,865 D	42.5%	51.9%	45.0%	55.0%
Texas	20	12	7,528,622	4,203,917	2,979,398	345,307	1,224,519 R	55.8%	39.6%	58.5%	41.5%
Utah	2	1	936,839	503,917	393,761	39,161	110,156 R	53.8%	42.0%	56.1%	43.9%
Vermont		1	298,151		248,203	49,948	248,203 D		83.2%		100.0%
Virginia	5	6	3,495,355	1,590,687	1,852,788	51,880	262,101 D	45.5%	53.0%	46.2%	53.8%
Washington	3	6	2,914,463	1,189,147	1,725,316		536,169 D	40.8%	59.2%	40.8%	59.2%
West Virginia	1	2	645,560	213,339	432,075	146	218,736 D	33.0%	66.9%	33.1%	66.9%
Wisconsin	3	5	2,775,174	1,274,987	1,383,536	116,651	108,549 D	45.9%	49.9%	48.0%	52.0%
Wyoming	1		249,395	131,244	106,758	11,393	24,486 R	52.6%	42.8%	55.1%	44.9%
Total	178	257	120,724,312	52,187,151	65,247,248	3,289,913	13,060,097 D	43.2%	54.0%	44.4%	55.6%

Notes: In states such as Connecticut and New York where third parties could endorse candidates of the major parties, all such votes are credited to the major party with which the candidates identified. In Louisiana, the vote totals include two House elections that were decided in December.

UNITED STATES
SPECIAL ELECTIONS, POSTELECTION CHANGES, AND PARTY SWITCHES, 2007–2008

SPECIAL ELECTIONS TO THE 110th CONGRESS

From the beginning of 2007 through 2008, two appointments were made to fill vacancies in the Senate and 13 special elections were held to fill vacancies in the House of Representatives. In addition, Democrat Barack Obama of Illinois resigned his Senate seat November 16, 2008, following his election November 4, 2008, as president of the United States. The Senate appointment to fill his vacancy was not made until late December 2008, on the eve of the start of the 111th Congress. The Senate appointments and House special elections held to fill vacancies in the 110th Congress are listed below.

SENATORS

MISSISSIPPI

Trent Lott (R) resigned December 18, 2007. Rep. Roger Wicker (R) was appointed to fill the vacancy and was sworn in as senator on December 31, 2007.

WYOMING

Craig Thomas (R) died June 4, 2007. John Barrasso (R) was appointed to fill the vacancy and was sworn into office on June 25, 2007.

REPRESENTATIVES

CALIFORNIA 12th CD

Tom Lantos (D) died February 11, 2008. Jackie Speier (D) was elected in the first round of voting on April 8, 2008, to fill the remainder of his term in the 110th Congress. Since she won a majority of the vote in round one, no second round was required.

April 8, 2008 Special Primary Election

66,279 Jackie Speier (D); 7,990 Greg Conlon (R); 4,546 Michelle T. McMurry (D); 4,517 Mike Moloney (R); 1,947 Barry Hermanson (Green); 2 Kevin Dempsey Peterson (write-in).

CALIFORNIA 37th CD

Juanita Millender-McDonald (D) died April 22, 2007. Laura Richardson (D) was elected August 21, 2007, to fill the remainder of her term in the 110th Congress. The highest vote-getter in each party in the June 26, 2007, special primary election qualified for the August 21 special general election.

June 26, 2007 Special Primary Election

11,956 Laura Richardson (D); 9,960 Jenny Oropeza (D); 3,027 Valerie McDonald (D); 2,425 John M. Kanaley (R); 1,125 Peter Mathews (D); 612 Teri Ramirez (R); 391 Daniel Abraham Brezenoff (Green); 386 Jeffrey "Lincoln" Leavitt (R); 363 Algbert Robles (D write-in); 362 Ed Wilson (D); 361 Leroy Joseph "L.J." Guillory (R); 342 Herb Peters (Libertarian); 242 George A. Parmer Jr. (D); 202 Lee Davis (D); 142 Jeffrey S. Price (D); 141 Bill Francisco Grisolia (D); 122 Felicia Ford (D); 29 Mervin Evans (D).

August 21, 2007 Special General Election

15,559 Laura Richardson (D); 5,837 John M. Kanaley (R); 1,274 Daniel Abraham Brezenoff (Green); 538 Herb Peters (Libertarian); 12 Lee Davis (write-in); 1 Christopher Remple (write-in).

GEORGIA 10th CD

Charlie Norwood (R) died February 13, 2007. Paul Broun (R) was elected July 17, 2007, to fill the remainder of his term in the 110th Congress. The highest two vote-getters, regardless of party, in the June 19, 2007, special election qualified for the July 17 special election runoff.

June 19, 2007 Special Election

23,555 Jim Whitehead (R); 11,208 Paul Broun (R); 11,010 James Marlow (D); 2,574 Denise Freeman (D); 1,778 Evita Paschall (D); 1,635 Bill Greene (R); 913 Nate Pulliam (R); 710 Jim Sendelbach (Libertarian); 378 Mark Myers (R); 376 Erik M. Underwood (R).

July 17, 2007 Special Election Runoff

23,529 Paul Broun (R); 23,135 Jim Whitehead (R).

ILLINOIS 14th CD

J. Dennis Hastert (R) resigned November 26, 2007. Bill Foster (D) was elected March 8, 2008, to fill the remainder of his term in the 110th Congress.

February 5, 2008 Special Democratic Primary

32,982 Bill Foster; 28,433 John Laesch; 5,082 Jotham Stein.

UNITED STATES
SPECIAL ELECTIONS TO THE 110th CONGRESS

ILLINOIS 14th CD (continued)

February 5, 2008 Special Republican Primary

41,980 Jim Oberweis; 32,955 Chris Lauzen.

March 8, 2008 Special General Election

52,205 Bill Foster (D); 47,180 Jim Oberweis (R).

INDIANA 7th CD

Julia Carson (D) died December 15, 2007. Andre Carson (D) was elected March 11, 2008, to fill the remainder of her term in the 110th Congress. No primary was held, as nominations were decided by party committees.

March 11, 2008 Special Election

45,668 Andre Carson (D); 36,415 Jon Elrod (R); 2,430 Sean Shepard (Libertarian).

LOUISIANA 1st CD

Bobby Jindal (R) resigned January 14, 2008, following his election as governor of Louisiana. Steve Scalise (R) was elected May 3, 2008, to fill the remainder of his term in the 110th Congress.

March 8, 2008 Special Democratic Primary

11,727 Gilda Reed; 5,086 M.V. "Vinny" Mendoza.

March 8, 2008 Special Republican Primary

16,799 Steve Scalise; 9,631 Tim Burns; 7,388 Ben Morris; 932 David Simpson.

April 5, 2008 Special Republican Primary Runoff

19,338 Steve Scalise; 13,958 Tim Burns.

May 3, 2008 Special General Election

33,867 Steve Scalise (R); 10,142 Gilda Reed (D); 786 R.A. "Skip" Galan (No Party); 280 Anthony "Tony G" Gentile (Other).

LOUISIANA 6th CD

Richard H. Baker (R) resigned February 2, 2008. Don Cazayoux (D) was elected May 3, 2008, to fill the remainder of his term in the 110th Congress.

March 8, 2008 Special Democratic Primary

16,636 Don Cazayoux; 12,941 Michael Jackson; 8,824 Jason DeCuir; 8,211 Andy Kopplin; 1,020 Joe Delatte.

March 8, 2008 Special Republican Primary

14,900 Louis "Woody" Jenkins; 7,609 Laurinda L. Calongne; 6,939 Paul Sawyer; 427 Michael Cloonan.

April 5, 2008 Special Democratic Primary Runoff

19,806 Don Cazayoux; 15,068 Michael Jackson.

April 5, 2008 Special Republican Primary Runoff

15,179 Louis "Woody" Jenkins; 9,327 Laurinda L. Calongne.

May 3, 2008 Special General Election

49,703 Don Cazayoux (D); 46,746 Louis "Woody" Jenkins (R); 3,718 Ashley Casey (No Party); 448 Peter J. Aranyosi (No Party); 402 Randall T. Hayes (Other).

MARYLAND 4th CD

Albert R. Wynn (D) resigned May 31, 2008. Donna F. Edwards (D) was elected June 17, 2008, to fill the remainder of his term in the 110th Congress. No primaries were held, as major party nominations were decided by party committees.

June 17, 2008 Special Election

16,481 Donna F. Edwards (D); 3,638 Peter James (R); 216 Thibeaux Lincecum (Libertarian); 15 Steve Schulin (Unaffiliated write-in); 1 Adrian Petrus (Unaffiliated write-in); 111 scattered write-in.

UNITED STATES
SPECIAL ELECTIONS TO THE 110th CONGRESS

MASSACHUSETTS 5th CD

Martin T. Meehan (D) resigned July 1, 2007, to become chancellor of the University of Massachusetts-Lowell. Niki Tsongas (D) was elected October 16, 2007, to fill the remainder of his term in the 110th Congress.

September 4, 2007 Special Democratic Primary

19,821 Niki Tsongas; 17,385 Eileen M. Donoghue; 8,042 James B. Eldridge; 6,999 Barry R. Finegold; 3,297 James R. Miceli; 99 scattered write-in.

September 4, 2007 Special Republican Primary

12,022 Jim Ogonowski; 1,471 Thomas P. Tierney; 96 scattered write-in.

October 16, 2007 Special General Election

54,359 Niki Tsongas (D); 47,782 Jim Ogonowski (R); 2,175 Patrick O. Murphy (Independent); 1,126 Kurt Hayes (Independent); 391 Kevin J. Thompson (Constitution); 103 scattered write-in.

MISSISSIPPI 1st CD

Roger Wicker (R) resigned December 31, 2007, to fill the Senate vacancy created by the resignation of Trent Lott (R). Travis W. Childers (D) was elected May 13, 2008, to fill his vacancy in the 110th Congress. The highest two vote-getters, regardless of party, in the April 22, 2008, special election qualified for the May 13 special election runoff.

April 22, 2008 Special Election

33,304 Travis W. Childers (D); 31,177 Greg Davis (R); 968 Glenn L. McCullouch Jr. (R); 789 Steve Holland (D); 725 Wally Pang (Independent); 398 John M. Wages Jr. (Green).

May 13, 2008 Special Election Runoff

58,037 Travis W. Childers (D); 49,877 Greg Davis (R).

OHIO 5th CD

Paul E. Gillmor (R) was found dead September 5, 2007. Robert E. Latta (R) was elected December 11, 2007, to fill his vacancy in the 110th Congress.

November 6, 2007 Special Democratic Primary

32,124 Robin Weirauch; 12,412 George Mays.

November 6, 2007 Special Republican Primary

32,392 Robert E. Latta; 29,850 Steve Buehrer; 4,955 Mark Hollenbaugh; 4,252 Fred Pieper; 2,742 Michael Smitley.

December 11, 2007 Special General Election

56,114 Robert E. Latta (R); 42,229 Robin Weirauch (D); 167 John Green (write-in).

OHIO 11th CD

Stephanie Tubbs Jones (D) died August 20, 2008. Marcia L. Fudge (D) was elected November 18, 2008, to fill her vacancy in the 110th Congress.

October 14, 2008 Special Democratic Primary

11,492 Marcia L. Fudge; 2,329 Jeffrey Johnson; 783 Carolyn R. Johnson; 256 Sean Ryan; 195 Isaac Powell; 191 Thomas J. Wheeler; 175 Frank Rives; 159 Gerald C. Henley; 156 Nathaniel Martin; 68 scattered write-in. (There were also four entries listed as "Candidate Withdrawn" who drew a total of 1,609 votes.)

November 18, 2008 Special General Election

8,597 Marcia L. Fudge (D).

VIRGINIA 1st CD

Jo Ann Davis (R) died October 6, 2007. Robert J. Wittman (R) was elected December 11, 2007, to fill her vacancy in the 110th Congress. No primaries were held, as major party nominations were decided by party conventions.

December 11, 2007 Special Election

42,772 Robert J. Wittman (R); 26,282 Philip R. Forgit (D); 1,253 Lucky R. Narain (Independent); 75 scattered write-in.

UNITED STATES

HOUSE SPECIAL ELECTIONS 2007 TO 2008: SUMMARY

Thirteen special House elections were held to fill vacancies in the 110th Congress. Three resulted in a change of party hands, with the Democrats winning all three. The partisan switches occurred in early 2008 in districts in Illinois, Louisiana, and Mississippi, and are indicated below in bold. All of the results are based on the decisive round of voting in each special election when the new member was elected to Congress. The special elections are listed in the chronological order in which they were held.

District	Former Member	New Member	Date Elected	Winning Percentage	Voter Turnout
Georgia 10th	Charlie Norwood (R)	Paul Broun (R)	July 17, 2007	50.4%	46,664
California 37th	Juanita Millender-McDonald (D)	Laura Richardson (D)	August 21, 2007	67.0%	23,221
Massachusetts 5th	Martin T. Meehan (D)	Niki Tsongas (D)	October 16, 2007	51.3%	105,936
Ohio 5th	Paul E. Gillmor (R)	Robert E. Latta (R)	December 11, 2007	57.0%	98,510
Virginia 1st	Jo Ann Davis (R)	Robert J. Wittman (R)	December 11, 2007	60.8%	70,382
Illinois 14th	**J. Dennis Hastert (R)**	**Bill Foster (D)**	**March 8, 2008**	**52.5%**	**99,385**
Indiana 7th	Julia Carson (D)	Andre Carson (D)	March 11, 2008	54.0%	84,513
California 12th	Tom Lantos (D)	Jackie Speier (D)	April 8, 2008	77.7%	85,281
Louisiana 1st	Bobby Jindal (R)	Steve Scalise (R)	May 3, 2008	75.1%	45,075
Louisiana 6th	**Richard H. Baker (R)**	**Don Cazayoux (D)**	**May 3, 2008**	**49.2%**	**101,017**
Mississippi 1st	**Roger Wicker (R)**	**Travis W. Childers (D)**	**May 13, 2008**	**53.8%**	**107,914**
Maryland 4th	Albert R. Wynn (D)	Donna F. Edwards (D)	June 17, 2008	80.5%	20,462
Ohio 11th	Stephanie Tubbs Jones (D)	Marcia L. Fudge (D)	November 18, 2008	100.0%	8,597

CHANGES FOLLOWING THE 2008 ELECTION

Following the 2008 general election, and through July 31, 2009, the following changes took place in the membership of the 111th Congress. In addition, Al Franken (D) emerged the winner of the 2008 Senate race in Minnesota on June 30, 2009, following a ruling in his favor by the Minnesota Supreme Court. He was sworn into office on July 7, 2009.

SENATORS

Colorado – Ken Salazar (D) resigned January 20, 2009, to become secretary of interior in the Obama administration. Michael Bennet (D) was sworn in January 22, 2009, to succeed him.

Delaware – Joseph R. Biden Jr. (D) resigned January 15, 2009, on the eve of his inauguration as vice president of the United States. Edward E. "Ted" Kaufman (D) was sworn in January 16, 2009, to succeed him.

Illinois – Barack Obama (D) resigned November 16, 2008, following his election as president of the United States. Roland Burris (D) was sworn in January 15, 2009, to succeed him.

New York – Hillary Rodham Clinton (D) resigned January 21, 2009, to become secretary of state in the Obama administration. Kirsten E. Gillibrand (D) was sworn in January 27, 2009, to succeed her.

PARTY SWITCH

Pennsylvania – Arlen Specter announced April 28, 2009, that he was switching his party affiliation from Republican to Democratic.

REPRESENTATIVES

California 10th District – Ellen O. Tauscher (D) resigned June 26, 2009, to become undersecretary of state for arms control and international security in the Obama administration. A special election was scheduled for November 3, 2009, to fill the seat.

California 32nd District – Hilda L. Solis (D) resigned February 24, 2009, to become secretary of labor in the Obama administration. Judy Chu (D) was elected July 14, 2009, to succeed her.

Illinois 5th District – Rahm Emanuel (D) resigned January 2, 2009, to become White House chief of staff. Mike Quigley (D) was elected April 7, 2009, to succeed him.

New York 20th District – Kirsten E. Gillibrand (D) resigned January 26, 2009, to fill the remainder of Hillary Rodham Clinton's Senate term. Scott Murphy (D) was elected March 31, 2009, to succeed her.

UNITED STATES
PRESIDENT 2008

The presidential candidates listed below include all who appeared on the ballot in at least one state. Write-in votes for independent and third party candidates are credited to their total below. See the minor parties table on page 11 for details. There, the state totals for all independent and third party candidates who received at least 100,000 votes in the 2008 presidential election are listed.

In New York the Democratic total includes Working Families votes and the Republican figures include Conservative and Independence votes.

In Minnesota the Democratic candidate appears on the ballot as Democratic-Farmer-Labor; in North Dakota as Democratic-Nonpartisan League. In many states various non-major party candidates appeared on the ballot with variations of the party designations, were carried with entirely different party labels, or were listed as "Independent."

69,498,516	Barack Obama and Joseph R. Biden Jr.	Democratic
59,948,323	John McCain and Sarah Palin	Republican
739,034	Ralph Nader and Matt Gonzalez	Independent
523,715	Bob Barr and Wayne A. Root	Libertarian
199,750	Chuck Baldwin and Darrell L. Castle	Constitution
161,797	Cynthia A. McKinney and Rosa A. Clemente	Green
47,746	Alan Keyes and Brian Rohrbough	America's Independent
42,426	Ron Paul and Barry Goldwater Jr./Michael Peroutka	Constitution/Louisiana Taxpayers
6,818	Gloria La Riva and Eugene Puryear/Robert Moses	Socialism and Liberation
6,538	Brian Moore and Stewart A. Alexander	Socialist
5,151	Roger Calero and Alyson Kennedy	Socialist Workers
3,905	Richard Duncan and Ricky Johnson	Independent
2,424	James Harris and Alyson Kennedy	Socialist Workers
2,422	Charles Jay and Dan Sallis Jr.	Boston Tea
1,149	John Polachek and "no candidate"	New
829	Frank McEnulty and David Mangan	New American Independent
764	Jeffrey Wamboldt and David J. Klimisch	Independent
755	Thomas Stevens and Alden Link	Objectivist
653	Gene Amondson and Leroy J. Pletten	Prohibition
639	Jeffrey Boss and Andrea Marie Psoras	Vote Here
531	George Phillies and Christopher Bennett	Libertarian
481	Ted Weill and Frank McEnulty	Reform
480	Jonathan Allen and Jeffrey D. Stath	HeartQuake '08
110	Bradford Lyttle and Abraham Bassford	U.S. Pacifist

Notes: In addition to the votes listed above, 112,597 scattered write-in votes were reported from various states, and 6,267 votes were cast for "None of These Candidates" in Nevada. In addition to Ron Paul and Gloria La Riva, Chuck Baldwin, Charles Jay, and Alan Keyes had a different vice-presidential candidate in at least one state.

UNITED STATES
PRESIDENT 2008

State	Electoral Vote Rep.	Electoral Vote Dem.	Total Vote	Republican	Democratic	Other	Rep.-Dem. Plurality	Percentage Total Vote Rep.	Total Vote Dem.	Major Vote Rep.	Major Vote Dem.
Alabama	9		2,099,819	1,266,546	813,479	19,794	453,067 R	60.3%	38.7%	60.9%	39.1%
Alaska	3		326,197	193,841	123,594	8,762	70,247 R	59.4%	37.9%	61.1%	38.9%
Arizona	10		2,293,475	1,230,111	1,034,707	28,657	195,404 R	53.6%	45.1%	54.3%	45.7%
Arkansas	6		1,086,617	638,017	422,310	26,290	215,707 R	58.7%	38.9%	60.2%	39.8%
California		55	13,561,900	5,011,781	8,274,473	275,646	3,262,692 D	37.0%	61.0%	37.7%	62.3%
Colorado		9	2,401,462	1,073,629	1,288,633	39,200	215,004 D	44.7%	53.7%	45.4%	54.6%
Connecticut		7	1,646,797	629,428	997,772	19,597	368,344 D	38.2%	60.6%	38.7%	61.3%
Delaware		3	412,412	152,374	255,459	4,579	103,085 D	36.9%	61.9%	37.4%	62.6%
Florida		27	8,390,744	4,045,624	4,282,074	63,046	236,450 D	48.2%	51.0%	48.6%	51.4%
Georgia	15		3,924,486	2,048,759	1,844,123	31,604	204,636 R	52.2%	47.0%	52.6%	47.4%
Hawaii		4	453,568	120,566	325,871	7,131	205,305 D	26.6%	71.8%	27.0%	73.0%
Idaho	4		655,122	403,012	236,440	15,670	166,572 R	61.5%	36.1%	63.0%	37.0%
Illinois		21	5,522,371	2,031,179	3,419,348	71,844	1,388,169 D	36.8%	61.9%	37.3%	62.7%
Indiana		11	2,751,054	1,345,648	1,374,039	31,367	28,391 D	48.9%	49.9%	49.5%	50.5%
Iowa		7	1,537,123	682,379	828,940	25,804	146,561 D	44.4%	53.9%	45.2%	54.8%
Kansas	6		1,235,872	699,655	514,765	21,452	184,890 R	56.6%	41.7%	57.6%	42.4%
Kentucky	8		1,826,620	1,048,462	751,985	26,173	296,477 R	57.4%	41.2%	58.2%	41.8%
Louisiana	9		1,960,761	1,148,275	782,989	29,497	365,286 R	58.6%	39.9%	59.5%	40.5%
Maine		4	731,163	295,273	421,923	13,967	126,650 D	40.4%	57.7%	41.2%	58.8%
Maryland		10	2,631,596	959,862	1,629,467	42,267	669,605 D	36.5%	61.9%	37.1%	62.9%
Massachusetts		12	3,080,985	1,108,854	1,904,097	68,034	795,243 D	36.0%	61.8%	36.8%	63.2%
Michigan		17	5,001,766	2,048,639	2,872,579	80,548	823,940 D	41.0%	57.4%	41.6%	58.4%
Minnesota		10	2,910,369	1,275,409	1,573,354	61,606	297,945 D	43.8%	54.1%	44.8%	55.2%
Mississippi	6		1,289,865	724,597	554,662	10,606	169,935 R	56.2%	43.0%	56.6%	43.4%
Missouri	11		2,925,205	1,445,814	1,441,911	37,480	3,903 R	49.4%	49.3%	50.1%	49.9%
Montana	3		490,302	242,763	231,667	15,872	11,096 R	49.5%	47.2%	51.2%	48.8%
Nebraska	4	1	801,281	452,979	333,319	14,983	119,660 R	56.5%	41.6%	57.6%	42.4%
Nevada		5	967,848	412,827	533,736	21,285	120,909 D	42.7%	55.1%	43.6%	56.4%
New Hampshire		4	710,970	316,534	384,826	9,610	68,292 D	44.5%	54.1%	45.1%	54.9%
New Jersey		15	3,868,237	1,613,207	2,215,422	39,608	602,215 D	41.7%	57.3%	42.1%	57.9%
New Mexico		5	830,158	346,832	472,422	10,904	125,590 D	41.8%	56.9%	42.3%	57.7%
New York		31	7,640,931	2,752,771	4,804,945	83,215	2,052,174 D	36.0%	62.9%	36.4%	63.6%
North Carolina		15	4,310,789	2,128,474	2,142,651	39,664	14,177 D	49.4%	49.7%	49.8%	50.2%
North Dakota	3		316,621	168,601	141,278	6,742	27,323 R	53.3%	44.6%	54.4%	45.6%
Ohio		20	5,708,350	2,677,820	2,940,044	90,486	262,224 D	46.9%	51.5%	47.7%	52.3%
Oklahoma	7		1,462,661	960,165	502,496		457,669 R	65.6%	34.4%	65.6%	34.4%
Oregon		7	1,827,864	738,475	1,037,291	52,098	298,816 D	40.4%	56.7%	41.6%	58.4%
Pennsylvania		21	6,013,272	2,655,885	3,276,363	81,024	620,478 D	44.2%	54.5%	44.8%	55.2%
Rhode Island		4	471,766	165,391	296,571	9,804	131,180 D	35.1%	62.9%	35.8%	64.2%
South Carolina	8		1,920,969	1,034,896	862,449	23,624	172,447 R	53.9%	44.9%	54.5%	45.5%
South Dakota	3		381,975	203,054	170,924	7,997	32,130 R	53.2%	44.7%	54.3%	45.7%
Tennessee	11		2,599,749	1,479,178	1,087,437	33,134	391,741 R	56.9%	41.8%	57.6%	42.4%
Texas	34		8,077,795	4,479,328	3,528,633	69,834	950,695 R	55.5%	43.7%	55.9%	44.1%
Utah	5		952,370	596,030	327,670	28,670	268,360 R	62.6%	34.4%	64.5%	35.5%
Vermont		3	325,046	98,974	219,262	6,810	120,288 D	30.4%	67.5%	31.1%	68.9%
Virginia		13	3,723,260	1,725,005	1,959,532	38,723	234,527 D	46.3%	52.6%	46.8%	53.2%
Washington		11	3,036,878	1,229,216	1,750,848	56,814	521,632 D	40.5%	57.7%	41.2%	58.8%
West Virginia	5		713,451	397,466	303,857	12,128	93,609 R	55.7%	42.6%	56.7%	43.3%
Wisconsin		10	2,983,417	1,262,393	1,677,211	43,813	414,818 D	42.3%	56.2%	42.9%	57.1%
Wyoming	3		254,658	164,958	82,868	6,832	82,090 R	64.8%	32.5%	66.6%	33.4%
District of Columbia		3	265,853	17,367	245,800	2,686	228,433 D	6.5%	92.5%	6.6%	93.4%
Total	173	365	131,313,820	59,948,323	69,498,516	1,866,981	9,550,193 D	45.7%	52.9%	46.3%	53.7%

UNITED STATES
PRESIDENT 2008 MINOR PARTIES

State	Total	Nader (Independent)	Barr (Libertarian)	Baldwin (Constitution)	McKinney (Green)	Other Candidates and Scattered Write-ins	Nader (Ind.)	Barr (Libert.)	Baldwin (Const.)	McKinney (Green)
Alabama	19,794	6,788	4,991	4,310		3,705	0.3%	0.2%	0.2%	
Alaska	8,762	3,783	1,589	1,660		1,730	1.2%	0.5%	0.5%	
Arizona	28,657	11,301	12,555	1,371*	3,406	24	0.5%	0.5%	0.1%	0.1%
Arkansas	26,290	12,882	4,776	4,023	3,470	1,139	1.2%	0.4%	0.4%	0.3%
California	275,646	108,381	67,582	3,145*	38,774	57,764	0.8%	0.5%		0.3%
Colorado	39,200	13,352	10,898	6,233	2,822	5,895	0.6%	0.5%	0.3%	0.1%
Connecticut	19,597	19,162		311*	90*	34	1.2%			
Delaware	4,579	2,401	1,109	626	385	58	0.6%	0.3%	0.2%	0.1%
Florida	63,046	28,124	17,218	7,915	2,887	6,902	0.3%	0.2%	0.1%	0.0%
Georgia	31,604	1,158*	28,731	1,402*	250*	63	0.0%	0.7%		
Hawaii	7,131	3,825	1,314	1,013	979		0.8%	0.3%	0.2%	0.2%
Idaho	15,670	7,175	3,658	4,747	39*	51	1.1%	0.6%	0.7%	
Illinois	71,844	30,948	19,642	8,256	11,838	1,160	0.6%	0.4%	0.1%	0.2%
Indiana	31,367	909*	29,257	1,024*	87*	90		1.1%		
Iowa	25,804	8,014	4,590	4,445	1,423	7,332	0.5%	0.3%	0.3%	0.1%
Kansas	21,452	10,527	6,706	4,148	35*	36	0.9%	0.5%	0.3%	
Kentucky	26,173	15,378	5,989	4,694		112	0.8%	0.3%	0.3%	
Louisiana	29,497	6,997		2,581	9,187	10,732	0.4%		0.1%	0.5%
Maine	13,967	10,636	251*	177*	2,900	3	1.5%			0.4%
Maryland	42,267	14,713	9,842	3,760	4,747	9,205	0.6%	0.4%	0.1%	0.2%
Massachusetts	68,034	28,841	13,189	4,971	6,550	14,483	0.9%	0.4%	0.2%	0.2%
Michigan	80,548	33,085	23,716	14,685	8,892	170	0.7%	0.5%	0.3%	0.2%
Minnesota	61,606	30,152	9,174	6,787	5,174	10,319	1.0%	0.3%	0.2%	0.2%
Mississippi	10,606	4,011	2,529	2,551	1,034	481	0.3%	0.2%	0.2%	0.1%
Missouri	37,480	17,813	11,386	8,201	80*		0.6%	0.4%	0.3%	
Montana	15,872	3,686	1,355	143*	23*	10,665	0.8%	0.3%		
Nebraska	14,983	5,406	2,740	2,972	1,028	2,837	0.7%	0.3%	0.4%	0.1%
Nevada	21,285	6,150	4,263	3,194	1,411	6,267	0.6%	0.4%	0.3%	0.1%
New Hampshire	9,610	3,503	2,217	226*	40*	3,624	0.5%	0.3%		
New Jersey	39,608	21,298	8,441	3,956	3,636	2,277	0.6%	0.2%	0.1%	0.1%
New Mexico	10,904	5,327	2,428	1,597	1,552		0.6%	0.3%	0.2%	0.2%
New York	83,215	41,249	19,596	634*	12,801	8,935	0.5%	0.3%		0.2%
North Carolina	39,664	1,448*	25,722		158*	12,336		0.6%		
North Dakota	6,742	4,189	1,354	1,199			1.3%	0.4%	0.4%	
Ohio	90,486	42,337	19,917	12,565	8,518	7,149	0.7%	0.3%	0.2%	0.1%
Oklahoma										
Oregon	52,098	18,614	7,635	7,693	4,543	13,613	1.0%	0.4%	0.4%	0.2%
Pennsylvania	81,024	42,977	19,912	1,092*		17,043	0.7%	0.3%		
Rhode Island	9,804	4,829	1,382	675	797	2,121	1.0%	0.3%	0.1%	0.2%
South Carolina	23,624	5,053	7,283	6,827	4,461		0.3%	0.4%	0.4%	0.2%
South Dakota	7,997	4,267	1,835	1,895			1.1%	0.5%	0.5%	
Tennessee	33,134	11,560	8,547	8,191	2,499	2,337	0.4%	0.3%	0.3%	0.1%
Texas	69,834	5,751*	56,116	5,708*	909*	1,350	0.1%	0.7%	0.1%	
Utah	28,670	8,416	6,966	12,012	982	294	0.9%	0.7%	1.3%	0.1%
Vermont	6,810	3,339	1,067	500	66*	1,838	1.0%	0.3%	0.2%	
Virginia	38,723	11,483	11,067	7,474	2,344	6,355	0.3%	0.3%	0.2%	0.1%
Washington	56,814	29,489	12,728	9,432	3,819	1,346	1.0%	0.4%	0.3%	0.1%
West Virginia	12,128	7,219		2,465	2,355	89	1.0%		0.3%	0.3%
Wisconsin	43,813	17,605	8,858	5,072	4,216	8,062	0.6%	0.3%	0.2%	0.1%
Wyoming	6,832	2,525	1,594	1,192		1,521	1.0%	0.6%	0.5%	
District of Columbia	2,686	958			590	1,138	0.4%			0.2%
Total	1,866,981	739,034	523,715	199,750	161,797	242,685	0.6%	0.4%	0.2%	0.1%

Note: An asterisk (*) indicates write-in votes.

UNITED STATES

POPULAR VOTE FOR PRESIDENT 1920 TO 2008

| | | Republican | | Democratic | | Other | | Percentage | | | |
| | | | | | | | | Total Vote | | Major Vote | |
Year	Total Vote	Vote	Candidate	Vote	Candidate	Vote	Plurality	Rep.	Dem.	Rep.	Dem.
2008	131,313,820	59,948,323	McCain, John	69,498,516	Obama, Barack	1,866,981	9,550,193 D	45.7%	52.9%	46.3%	53.7%
2004	122,295,345	62,040,610	Bush, George W.	59,028,439	Kerry, John	1,226,296	3,012,171 R	50.7%	48.3%	51.2%	48.8%
2000	105,396,627	50,455,156	Bush, George W.	50,992,335	Gore, Al	3,949,136	537,179 D	47.9%	48.4%	49.7%	50.3%
1996	96,277,872	39,198,755	Dole, Bob	47,402,357	Clinton, Bill	9,676,760	8,203,602 D	40.7%	49.2%	45.3%	54.7%
1992	104,425,014	39,103,882	Bush, George	44,909,326	Clinton, Bill	20,411,806	5,805,444 D	37.4%	43.0%	46.5%	53.5%
1988	91,594,809	48,886,097	Bush, George	41,809,074	Dukakis, Michael S.	899,638	7,077,023 R	53.4%	45.6%	53.9%	46.1%
1984	92,652,842	54,455,075	Reagan, Ronald	37,577,185	Mondale, Walter F.	620,582	16,877,890 R	58.8%	40.6%	59.2%	40.8%
1980	86,515,221	43,904,153	Reagan, Ronald	35,483,883	Carter, Jimmy	7,127,185	8,420,270 R	50.7%	41.0%	55.3%	44.7%
1976	81,555,889	39,147,793	Ford, Gerald R.	40,830,763	Carter, Jimmy	1,577,333	1,682,970 D	48.0%	50.1%	48.9%	51.1%
1972	77,718,554	47,169,911	Nixon, Richard M.	29,170,383	McGovern, George S.	1,378,260	17,999,528 R	60.7%	37.5%	61.8%	38.2%
1968	73,211,875	31,785,480	Nixon, Richard M.	31,275,166	Humphrey, Hubert H.	10,151,229	510,314 R	43.4%	42.7%	50.4%	49.6%
1964	70,644,592	27,178,188	Goldwater, Barry M.	43,129,566	Johnson, Lyndon B.	336,838	15,951,378 D	38.5%	61.1%	38.7%	61.3%
1960	68,838,219	34,108,157	Nixon, Richard M.	34,226,731	Kennedy, John F.	503,331	118,574 D	49.5%	49.7%	49.9%	50.1%
1956	62,026,908	35,590,472	Eisenhower, Dwight D.	26,022,752	Stevenson, Adlai E.	413,684	9,567,720 R	57.4%	42.0%	57.8%	42.2%
1952	61,550,918	33,936,234	Eisenhower, Dwight D.	27,314,992	Stevenson, Adlai E.	299,692	6,621,242 R	55.1%	44.4%	55.4%	44.6%
1948	48,793,826	21,991,291	Dewey, Thomas E.	24,179,345	Truman, Harry S.	2,623,190	2,188,054 D	45.1%	49.6%	47.6%	52.4%
1944	47,976,670	22,017,617	Dewey, Thomas E.	25,612,610	Roosevelt, Franklin D.	346,443	3,594,993 D	45.9%	53.4%	46.2%	53.8%
1940	49,900,418	22,348,480	Willkie, Wendell	27,313,041	Roosevelt, Franklin D.	238,897	4,964,561 D	44.8%	54.7%	45.0%	55.0%
1936	45,654,763	16,684,231	Landon, Alfred M.	27,757,333	Roosevelt, Franklin D.	1,213,199	11,073,102 D	36.5%	60.8%	37.5%	62.5%
1932	39,758,759	15,760,684	Hoover, Herbert C.	22,829,501	Roosevelt, Franklin D.	1,168,574	7,068,817 D	39.6%	57.4%	40.8%	59.2%
1928	36,805,951	21,437,277	Hoover, Herbert C.	15,007,698	Smith, Alfred E.	360,976	6,429,579 R	58.2%	40.8%	58.8%	41.2%
1924	29,095,023	15,719,921	Coolidge, Calvin	8,386,704	Davis, John W.	4,988,398	7,333,217 R	54.0%	28.8%	65.2%	34.8%
1920	26,768,613	16,153,115	Harding, Warren G.	9,133,092	Cox, James M.	1,482,406	7,020,023 R	60.3%	34.1%	63.9%	36.1%

For detail of other vote, see note section included with each U.S. summary table that follows.

ELECTORAL COLLEGE VOTE 1920 TO 2008

Year	Total	Republican	Democratic	Other	
2008	538	173	365	—	
2004	538	286	251	1	EDWARDS
2000	538	271	266	1	(Blank)
1996	538	159	379	—	
1992	538	168	370	—	
1988	538	426	111	1	BENTSEN
1984	538	525	13	—	
1980	538	489	49	—	
1976	538	240	297	1	REAGAN
1972	538	520	17	1	LIBERTARIAN
1968	538	301	191	46	AIP
1964	538	52	486	—	
1960	537	219	303	15	BYRD
1956	531	457	73	1	JONES
1952	531	442	89	—	
1948	531	189	303	39	SR
1944	531	99	432	—	
1940	531	82	449	—	
1936	531	8	523	—	
1932	531	59	472	—	
1928	531	444	87	—	
1924	531	382	136	13	PROGRESSIVE
1920	531	404	127	—	

PRESIDENT 2004

In New York the Republican total includes votes for their candidate on the Conservative line and the Democratic total includes votes for their candidate on the Working Families line.

In Minnesota the Democratic candidate appears on the ballot as Democratic-Farmer-Labor; in North Dakota as Democratic-Nonpartisan League. In many states various third party candidates appeared on the ballot with variations of the party designations, were carried with entirely different party labels, or were listed as "Independent." The state notes sections list the party labels used by the third party candidates.

The candidates listed below include all who appeared on the ballot in at least one state. Write-in votes for third party candidates are credited to their total below. See the third party chart on page 15 for details.

62,040,610	George W. Bush and Richard B. Cheney	Republican
59,028,439	John Kerry and John Edwards	Democratic
465,650	Ralph Nader and Peter Miguel Camejo	Independent
397,265	Michael Badnarik and Richard V. Campagna	Libertarian
143,630	Michael Peroutka and Chuck Baldwin	Constitution
119,859	David Cobb and Patricia LaMarche	Green
27,607	Leonard Peltier and Janice Jordan	Peace and Freedom
10,837	Walter F. Brown and Mary Alice Herbert	Socialist
7,102	James Harris and Margaret Trowe	Socialist Workers
3,689	Roger Calero and Arrin Hawkins	Socialist Workers
2,387	Thomas J. Harens and Jennifer A. Ryan	Christian Freedom
1,944	Gene Amondson and Leroy Pletten	Concerns of People
1,861	Bill Van Auken and Jim Lawrence	Socialist Equality
1,646	John Parker and Teresa Gutierrez	Workers World
946	Charles Jay and Marilyn Chambers Taylor	Personal Choice
804	Stanford E. "Andy" Andress and Irene M. Deasy	Unaffiliated
140	Earl F. Dodge and Howard F. Lydick	Prohibition

Notes: In addition to the votes listed above, 37,241 scattered write-in votes were reported from various states, and 3,688 votes were cast for "None of these Candidates" in Nevada.

UNITED STATES
PRESIDENT 2004

State	Electoral Vote Rep.	Dem.	Other	Total Vote	Republican	Democratic	Other	Rep.-Dem. Plurality	Total Vote Rep.	Dem.	Major Vote Rep.	Dem.
Alabama	9			1,883,449	1,176,394	693,933	13,122	482,461 R	62.5%	36.8%	62.9%	37.1%
Alaska	3			312,598	190,889	111,025	10,684	79,864 R	61.1%	35.5%	63.2%	36.8%
Arizona	10			2,012,585	1,104,294	893,524	14,767	210,770 R	54.9%	44.4%	55.3%	44.7%
Arkansas	6			1,054,945	572,898	469,953	12,094	102,945 R	54.3%	44.5%	54.9%	45.1%
California		55		12,421,852	5,509,826	6,745,485	166,541	1,235,659 D	44.4%	54.3%	45.0%	55.0%
Colorado	9			2,130,330	1,101,255	1,001,732	27,343	99,523 R	51.7%	47.0%	52.4%	47.6%
Connecticut		7		1,578,769	693,826	857,488	27,455	163,662 D	43.9%	54.3%	44.7%	55.3%
Delaware		3		375,190	171,660	200,152	3,378	28,492 D	45.8%	53.3%	46.2%	53.8%
Florida	27			7,609,810	3,964,522	3,583,544	61,744	380,978 R	52.1%	47.1%	52.5%	47.5%
Georgia	15			3,301,875	1,914,254	1,366,149	21,472	548,105 R	58.0%	41.4%	58.4%	41.6%
Hawaii		4		429,013	194,191	231,708	3,114	37,517 D	45.3%	54.0%	45.6%	54.4%
Idaho	4			598,447	409,235	181,098	8,114	228,137 R	68.4%	30.3%	69.3%	30.7%
Illinois		21		5,274,322	2,345,946	2,891,550	36,826	545,604 D	44.5%	54.8%	44.8%	55.2%
Indiana	11			2,468,002	1,479,438	969,011	19,553	510,427 R	59.9%	39.3%	60.4%	39.6%
Iowa	7			1,506,908	751,957	741,898	13,053	10,059 R	49.9%	49.2%	50.3%	49.7%
Kansas	6			1,187,756	736,456	434,993	16,307	301,463 R	62.0%	36.6%	62.9%	37.1%
Kentucky	8			1,795,882	1,069,439	712,733	13,710	356,706 R	59.5%	39.7%	60.0%	40.0%
Louisiana	9			1,943,106	1,102,169	820,299	20,638	281,870 R	56.7%	42.2%	57.3%	42.7%
Maine		4		740,752	330,201	396,842	13,709	66,641 D	44.6%	53.6%	45.4%	54.6%
Maryland		10		2,386,678	1,024,703	1,334,493	27,482	309,790 D	42.9%	55.9%	43.4%	56.6%
Massachusetts		12		2,912,388	1,071,109	1,803,800	37,479	732,691 D	36.8%	61.9%	37.3%	62.7%
Michigan		17		4,839,252	2,313,746	2,479,183	46,323	165,437 D	47.8%	51.2%	48.3%	51.7%
Minnesota		9	1	2,828,387	1,346,695	1,445,014	36,678	98,319 D	47.6%	51.1%	48.2%	51.8%
Mississippi	6			1,152,145	684,981	458,094	9,070	226,887 R	59.5%	39.8%	59.9%	40.1%
Missouri	11			2,731,364	1,455,713	1,259,171	16,480	196,542 R	53.3%	46.1%	53.6%	46.4%
Montana	3			450,445	266,063	173,710	10,672	92,353 R	59.1%	38.6%	60.5%	39.5%
Nebraska	5			778,186	512,814	254,328	11,044	258,486 R	65.9%	32.7%	66.8%	33.2%
Nevada	5			829,587	418,690	397,190	13,707	21,500 R	50.5%	47.9%	51.3%	48.7%
New Hampshire		4		677,738	331,237	340,511	5,990	9,274 D	48.9%	50.2%	49.3%	50.7%
New Jersey		15		3,611,691	1,670,003	1,911,430	30,258	241,427 D	46.2%	52.9%	46.6%	53.4%
New Mexico	5			756,304	376,930	370,942	8,432	5,988 R	49.8%	49.0%	50.4%	49.6%
New York		31		7,391,036	2,962,567	4,314,280	114,189	1,351,713 D	40.1%	58.4%	40.7%	59.3%
North Carolina	15			3,501,007	1,961,166	1,525,849	13,992	435,317 R	56.0%	43.6%	56.2%	43.8%
North Dakota	3			312,833	196,651	111,052	5,130	85,599 R	62.9%	35.5%	63.9%	36.1%
Ohio	20			5,627,908	2,859,768	2,741,167	26,973	118,601 R	50.8%	48.7%	51.1%	48.9%
Oklahoma	7			1,463,758	959,792	503,966		455,826 R	65.6%	34.4%	65.6%	34.4%
Oregon		7		1,836,782	866,831	943,163	26,788	76,332 D	47.2%	51.3%	47.9%	52.1%
Pennsylvania		21		5,769,590	2,793,847	2,938,095	37,648	144,248 D	48.4%	50.9%	48.7%	51.3%
Rhode Island		4		437,134	169,046	259,760	8,328	90,714 D	38.7%	59.4%	39.4%	60.6%
South Carolina	8			1,617,730	937,974	661,699	18,057	276,275 R	58.0%	40.9%	58.6%	41.4%
South Dakota	3			388,215	232,584	149,244	6,387	83,340 R	59.9%	38.4%	60.9%	39.1%
Tennessee	11			2,437,319	1,384,375	1,036,477	16,467	347,898 R	56.8%	42.5%	57.2%	42.8%
Texas	34			7,410,765	4,526,917	2,832,704	51,144	1,694,213 R	61.1%	38.2%	61.5%	38.5%
Utah	5			927,844	663,742	241,199	22,903	422,543 R	71.5%	26.0%	73.3%	26.7%
Vermont		3		312,309	121,180	184,067	7,062	62,887 D	38.8%	58.9%	39.7%	60.3%
Virginia	13			3,198,367	1,716,959	1,454,742	26,666	262,217 R	53.7%	45.5%	54.1%	45.9%
Washington		11		2,859,084	1,304,894	1,510,201	43,989	205,307 D	45.6%	52.8%	46.4%	53.6%
West Virginia	5			755,887	423,778	326,541	5,568	97,237 R	56.1%	43.2%	56.5%	43.5%
Wisconsin		10		2,997,007	1,478,120	1,489,504	29,383	11,384 D	49.3%	49.7%	49.8%	50.2%
Wyoming	3			243,428	167,629	70,776	5,023	96,853 R	68.9%	29.1%	70.3%	29.7%
District of Columbia		3		227,586	21,256	202,970	3,360	181,714 D	9.3%	89.2%	9.5%	90.5%
Total	286	251	1	122,295,345	62,040,610	59,028,439	1,226,296	3,012,171 R	50.7%	48.3%	51.2%	48.8%

Note: A Democratic elector in Minnesota cast a vote for Edwards rather than Kerry.

UNITED STATES
PRESIDENT 2004 MINOR PARTIES

State	Total	Nader	Badnarik	Peroutka	Cobb	Other Candidates and Scattered Write-ins
Alabama	13,122	6,701	3,529	1,994		898
Alaska	10,684	5,069	1,675	2,092	1,058	790
Arizona	14,767	2,773*	11,856		138*	
Arkansas	12,094	6,171	2,352	2,083	1,488	
California	166,541	21,213*	50,165	26,645	40,771	27,747
Colorado	27,343	12,718	7,664	2,562	1,591	2,808
Connecticut	27,455	12,969	3,367	1,543	9,564	12
Delaware	3,378	2,153	586	289	250	100
Florida	61,744	32,971	11,996	6,626	3,917	6,234
Georgia	21,472	2,231*	18,387	580*	228*	46
Hawaii	3,114		1,377		1,737	
Idaho	8,114	1,115*	3,844	3,084	58*	13
Illinois	36,826	3,571*	32,442	440*	241*	132
Indiana	19,553	1,328*	18,058		102*	65
Iowa	13,053	5,973	2,992	1,304	1,141	1,643
Kansas	16,307	9,348	4,013	2,899	33*	14
Kentucky	13,710	8,856	2,619	2,213		22
Louisiana	20,638	7,032	2,781	5,203	1,276	4,346
Maine	13,709	8,069	1,965	735	2,936	4
Maryland	27,482	11,854	6,094	3,421	3,632	2,481
Massachusetts	37,479	4,806*	15,022		10,623	7,028
Michigan	46,323	24,035	10,552	4,980	5,325	1,431
Minnesota	36,678	18,683	4,639	3,074	4,408	5,874
Mississippi	9,070	3,177	1,793	1,759	1,073	1,268
Missouri	16,480	1,294*	9,831	5,355		
Montana	10,672	6,168	1,733	1,764	996	11
Nebraska	11,044	5,698	2,041	1,314	978	1,013
Nevada	13,707	4,838	3,176	1,152	853	3,688
New Hampshire	5,990	4,479	372*	161*		978
New Jersey	30,258	19,418	4,514	2,750	1,807	1,769
New Mexico	8,432	4,053	2,382	771	1,226	
New York	114,189	99,873	11,607	207*	87*	2,415
North Carolina	13,992	1,805*	11,731		108*	348
North Dakota	5,130	3,756	851	514		9
Ohio	26,973		14,676	11,939	192*	166
Oklahoma						
Oregon	26,788		7,260	5,257	5,315	8,956
Pennsylvania	37,648	2,656*	21,185	6,318	6,319	1,170
Rhode Island	8,328	4,651	907	339	1,333	1,098
South Carolina	18,057	5,520	3,608	5,317	1,488	2,124
South Dakota	6,387	4,320	964	1,103		
Tennessee	16,467	8,992	4,866	2,570	33*	6
Texas	51,144	9,159*	38,787	1,636*	1,014*	548
Utah	22,903	11,305	3,375	6,841	39*	1,343
Vermont	7,062	4,494	1,102			1,466
Virginia	26,666	2,393*	11,032	10,161	104*	2,976
Washington	43,989	23,283	11,955	3,922	2,974	1,855
West Virginia	5,568	4,063	1,405	82*	5*	13
Wisconsin	29,383	16,390	6,464		2,661	3,868
Wyoming	5,023	2,741	1,171	631		480
District of Columbia	3,360	1,485	502		737	636
Total	1,226,296	465,650	397,265	143,630	119,859	99,892

Note: An asterisk (*) indicates write-in votes.

UNITED STATES
VOTER TURNOUT 2004

State	2004 Voting Age Population	Registration: 2004 General Election	Percentage Voting Age Registered	Presidential Vote	Presidential Vote as Percentage of Voting Age Population	Presidential Vote as Percentage of Registered Voters	U.S. House Vote	Senate Vote	Governor Vote
Alabama	3,419,000	2,842,985	83.2%	1,883,449	55.1%	66.2%	1,792,759	1,839,066	—
Alaska	447,000	473,927	106.0%	312,598	69.9%	66.0%	299,996	308,315	—
Arizona	3,768,000	2,643,331	70.2%	2,012,585	53.4%	76.1%	1,871,445	1,961,677	—
Arkansas	2,057,000	1,684,684	81.9%	1,054,945	51.3%	62.6%	791,240	1,039,349	—
California	20,754,000	16,557,273	79.8%	12,421,852	59.9%	75.0%	11,623,753	12,053,295	8,657,915
Colorado	3,275,000	3,114,566	95.1%	2,130,330	65.0%	68.4%	2,039,011	2,107,554	—
Connecticut	2,390,000	2,044,181	85.5%	1,578,769	66.1%	77.2%	1,428,738	1,424,726	—
Delaware	601,000	553,885	92.2%	375,190	62.4%	67.7%	356,045	—	365,008
Florida	11,904,000	10,301,290	86.5%	7,609,810	63.9%	73.9%	5,627,494	7,429,894	—
Georgia	6,135,000	4,951,955	80.7%	3,301,875	53.8%	66.7%	2,960,763	3,220,981	—
Hawaii	877,000	647,238	73.8%	429,013	48.9%	66.3%	416,570	415,347	—
Idaho	985,000	798,015	81.0%	598,447	60.8%	75.0%	572,426	503,932	—
Illinois	8,544,000	7,499,488	87.8%	5,274,322	61.7%	70.3%	4,988,665	5,141,520	—
Indiana	4,572,000	4,296,602	94.0%	2,468,002	54.0%	57.4%	2,416,251	2,428,233	2,448,498
Iowa	2,190,000	2,106,658	96.2%	1,506,908	68.8%	71.5%	1,458,161	1,479,228	—
Kansas	1,954,000	1,591,428	81.4%	1,187,756	60.8%	74.6%	1,156,383	1,129,022	—
Kentucky	3,134,000	2,794,286	89.2%	1,795,882	57.3%	64.3%	1,635,243	1,724,362	1,083,443
Louisiana	3,310,000	2,923,395	88.3%	1,943,106	58.7%	66.5%	1,545,982	1,848,056	1,407,842
Maine	984,000	1,023,956	104.1%	740,752	75.3%	72.3%	710,176	—	—
Maryland	3,804,000	3,074,889	80.8%	2,386,678	62.7%	77.6%	2,255,955	2,323,183	—
Massachusetts	4,501,000	4,098,634	91.1%	2,912,388	64.7%	71.1%	2,580,955	—	—
Michigan	7,289,000	7,164,047	98.3%	4,839,252	66.4%	67.5%	4,631,058	—	—
Minnesota	3,658,000	3,559,400	97.3%	2,828,387	77.3%	79.5%	2,721,681	—	—
Mississippi	2,155,000	1,791,666	83.1%	1,152,145	53.5%	64.3%	1,116,203	—	894,487
Missouri	4,242,000	4,194,146	98.9%	2,731,364	64.4%	65.1%	2,667,023	2,706,402	2,719,599
Montana	709,000	638,474	90.1%	450,445	63.5%	70.6%	444,230	—	446,146
Nebraska	1,256,000	1,160,199	92.4%	778,186	62.0%	67.1%	764,972	—	—
Nevada	1,528,000	1,071,101	70.1%	829,587	54.3%	77.5%	791,433	810,068	—
New Hampshire	942,000	855,861	90.9%	677,738	71.9%	79.2%	651,566	657,086	667,020
New Jersey	5,702,000	5,005,959	87.8%	3,611,691	63.3%	72.1%	3,284,595	—	—
New Mexico	1,322,000	1,105,372	83.6%	756,304	57.2%	68.4%	742,899	—	—
New York	12,496,000	11,837,068	94.7%	7,391,036	59.1%	62.4%	6,222,418	6,702,875	—
North Carolina	6,208,000	5,519,992	88.9%	3,501,007	56.4%	63.4%	3,413,071	3,472,082	3,486,688
North Dakota	483,000	—		312,833	64.8%	—	310,814	310,696	309,873
Ohio	8,486,000	7,972,826	94.0%	5,627,908	66.3%	70.6%	5,183,508	5,426,196	—
Oklahoma	2,581,000	2,143,978	83.1%	1,463,758	56.7%	68.3%	1,374,610	1,446,846	—
Oregon	2,581,000	2,141,243	83.0%	1,836,782	71.2%	85.8%	1,772,306	1,780,550	—
Pennsylvania	9,230,000	8,366,663	90.6%	5,769,590	62.5%	69.0%	5,152,274	5,559,105	—
Rhode Island	752,000	651,950	86.7%	437,134	58.1%	67.1%	402,175	—	—
South Carolina	3,120,000	2,315,462	74.2%	1,617,730	51.9%	69.9%	1,439,118	1,597,221	—
South Dakota	569,000	552,441	97.1%	388,215	68.2%	70.3%	389,468	391,188	—
Tennessee	4,462,000	3,742,829	83.9%	2,437,319	54.6%	65.1%	2,218,738	—	—
Texas	14,197,000	13,098,329	92.3%	7,410,765	52.2%	56.6%	6,958,603	—	—
Utah	1,587,000	1,278,251	80.5%	927,844	58.5%	72.6%	908,857	911,726	919,960
Vermont	470,000	444,077	94.5%	312,309	66.4%	70.3%	305,008	307,208	309,285
Virginia	5,290,000	4,517,980	85.4%	3,198,367	60.5%	70.8%	3,004,007	—	—
Washington	4,370,000	3,508,208	80.3%	2,859,084	65.4%	81.5%	2,729,995	2,818,651	2,810,058
West Virginia	1,423,000	1,168,694	82.1%	755,887	53.1%	64.7%	721,656	—	744,433
Wisconsin	4,057,000	—		2,997,007	73.9%	—	2,821,613	2,949,743	—
Wyoming	380,000	232,396	61.2%	243,428	64.1%	104.7%	239,034	—	—
District of Columbia	391,000	383,919	98.2%	227,586	58.2%	59.3%	—	—	—
Total	201,541,000	172,445,197	85.6%	122,295,345	60.7%	70.9%	111,910,944	86,225,383	27,270,255

Sources: Voting age population figures were compiled by the Committee for the Study of the American Electorate (CSAE) and represent the estimated citizen voting age population in each state (and nationally) at the time of the November 2004 general election. CSAE employs a more conservative methodology than does the Census Bureau, which no longer provides election-year voting age population estimates. Registration figures are as of the November 2004 general election and were obtained from state election officials. In some cases, the registration totals are suspect as a number of states include inactive voters in their totals. In Alaska and Wyoming, for instance, the number of registered voters was more than 100 percent of the voting age population. The Minnesota total includes election-day registrations. The Mississippi total was as of April 2004. North Dakota and Wisconsin did not compile statewide registration figures.

Notes: Votes are from the November 2004 general election, with the exception of gubernatorial elections in California, Kentucky, Louisiana, and Mississippi, which were held in 2003. The California gubernatorial contest was a special recall election.

PRESIDENT 2000

In New York the Republican figures include Conservative votes and the Democratic figures include Liberal and Working Families votes.

In Minnesota the Democratic candidate appears on the ballot as Democratic-Farmer-Labor. In many states various non-major party candidates appeared on the ballot with variations of the party designations, were carried with entirely different party labels, or were listed as "Independent."

The candidates listed below include all those who appeared on the ballot in at least one state. Write-in votes for minor party candidates are credited to their total below. See the minor parties table on page 19 for details.

50,455,156	George W. Bush and Richard B. Cheney	Republican
50,992,335	Al Gore and Joseph I. Lieberman	Democratic
2,882,738	Ralph Nader and Winona LaDuke	Green
449,077	Pat Buchanan and Ezola Foster	Reform
384,429	Harry Browne and Art Olivier	Libertarian
98,020	Howard Phillips and J. Curtis Frazier	Constitution
83,525	John Hagelin and Nat Goldhaber	Natural Law
7,378	James E. Harris Jr. and Margaret Trowe	Socialist Worker
5,775	L. Neil Smith and Vin Suprynowicz	Arizona Libertarian
5,602	David McReynolds and Mary Cal Hollis	Socialist
4,795	Monica Moorehead and Gloria La Riva	Workers World
1,606	Cathy Gordon Brown and Sabrina R. Allen	Independent
1,044	Denny Lane and Dale Wilkinson	Vermont Grassroots
535	Randall Venson and Gene Kelly	Independent
208	Earl F. Dodge and W. Dean Watkins	Prohibition
161	Louie G. Youngkeit and Robert Leo Beck	Unaffiliated

Notes: In addition to the votes listed above, 20,928 scattered write-in votes were reported from various states, and 3,315 votes were cast for "None of These Candidates" in Nevada.

UNITED STATES
PRESIDENT 2000

| | Electoral Vote | | | Total | | | Green | | Rep.-Dem. | Percentage | | |
State	Rep.	Dem.	Other	Vote	Republican	Democratic	(Nader)	Other	Plurality	Rep.	Dem.	Green
Alabama	9			1,666,272	941,173	692,611	18,323	14,165	248,562 R	56.5%	41.6%	1.1%
Alaska	3			285,560	167,398	79,004	28,747	10,411	88,394 R	58.6%	27.7%	10.1%
Arizona	8			1,532,016	781,652	685,341	45,645	19,378	96,311 R	51.0%	44.7%	3.0%
Arkansas	6			921,781	472,940	422,768	13,421	12,652	50,172 R	51.3%	45.9%	1.5%
California		54		10,965,856	4,567,429	5,861,203	418,707	118,517	1,293,774 D	41.7%	53.4%	3.8%
Colorado	8			1,741,368	883,748	738,227	91,434	27,959	145,521 R	50.8%	42.4%	5.3%
Connecticut		8		1,459,525	561,094	816,015	64,452	17,964	254,921 D	38.4%	55.9%	4.4%
Delaware		3		327,622	137,288	180,068	8,307	1,959	42,780 D	41.9%	55.0%	2.5%
Florida	25			5,963,110	2,912,790	2,912,253	97,488	40,579	537 R	48.8%	48.8%	1.6%
Georgia	13			2,596,645	1,419,720	1,116,230	13,273	47,422	303,490 R	54.7%	43.0%	0.5%
Hawaii		4		367,951	137,845	205,286	21,623	3,197	67,441 D	37.5%	55.8%	5.9%
Idaho	4			501,621	336,937	138,637	12,292	13,755	198,300 R	67.2%	27.6%	2.5%
Illinois		22		4,742,123	2,019,421	2,589,026	103,759	29,917	569,605 D	42.6%	54.6%	2.2%
Indiana	12			2,199,302	1,245,836	901,980	18,531	32,955	343,856 R	56.6%	41.0%	0.8%
Iowa		7		1,315,563	634,373	638,517	29,374	13,299	4,144 D	48.2%	48.5%	2.2%
Kansas	6			1,072,218	622,332	399,276	36,086	14,524	223,056 R	58.0%	37.2%	3.4%
Kentucky	8			1,544,187	872,492	638,898	23,192	9,605	233,594 R	56.5%	41.4%	1.5%
Louisiana	9			1,765,656	927,871	792,344	20,473	24,968	135,527 R	52.6%	44.9%	1.2%
Maine		4		651,817	286,616	319,951	37,127	8,123	33,335 D	44.0%	49.1%	5.7%
Maryland		10		2,020,480	813,797	1,140,782	53,768	12,133	326,985 D	40.3%	56.5%	2.7%
Massachusetts		12		2,702,984	878,502	1,616,487	173,564	34,431	737,985 D	32.5%	59.8%	6.4%
Michigan		18		4,232,711	1,953,139	2,170,418	84,165	24,989	217,279 D	46.1%	51.3%	2.0%
Minnesota		10		2,438,685	1,109,659	1,168,266	126,696	34,064	58,607 D	45.5%	47.9%	5.2%
Mississippi	7			994,184	572,844	404,614	8,122	8,604	168,230 R	57.6%	40.7%	0.8%
Missouri	11			2,359,892	1,189,924	1,111,138	38,515	20,315	78,786 R	50.4%	47.1%	1.6%
Montana	3			410,997	240,178	137,126	24,437	9,256	103,052 R	58.4%	33.4%	5.9%
Nebraska	5			697,019	433,862	231,780	24,540	6,837	202,082 R	62.2%	33.3%	3.5%
Nevada	4			608,970	301,575	279,978	15,008	12,409	21,597 R	49.5%	46.0%	2.5%
New Hampshire	4			569,081	273,559	266,348	22,198	6,976	7,211 R	48.1%	46.8%	3.9%
New Jersey		15		3,187,226	1,284,173	1,788,850	94,554	19,649	504,677 D	40.3%	56.1%	3.0%
New Mexico		5		598,605	286,417	286,783	21,251	4,154	366 D	47.8%	47.9%	3.6%
New York		33		6,821,999	2,403,374	4,107,697	244,030	66,898	1,704,323 D	35.2%	60.2%	3.6%
North Carolina	14			2,911,262	1,631,163	1,257,692	—	22,407	373,471 R	56.0%	43.2%	—
North Dakota	3			288,256	174,852	95,284	9,486	8,634	79,568 R	60.7%	33.1%	3.3%
Ohio	21			4,701,998	2,350,363	2,183,628	117,799	50,208	166,735 R	50.0%	46.4%	2.5%
Oklahoma	8			1,234,229	744,337	474,276		15,616	270,061 R	60.3%	38.4%	—
Oregon		7		1,533,968	713,577	720,342	77,357	22,692	6,765 D	46.5%	47.0%	5.0%
Pennsylvania		23		4,913,119	2,281,127	2,485,967	103,392	42,633	204,840 D	46.4%	50.6%	2.1%
Rhode Island		4		409,047	130,555	249,508	25,052	3,932	118,953 D	31.9%	61.0%	6.1%
South Carolina	8			1,382,717	785,937	565,561	20,200	11,019	220,376 R	56.8%	40.9%	1.5%
South Dakota	3			316,269	190,700	118,804	—	6,765	71,896 R	60.3%	37.6%	—
Tennessee	11			2,076,181	1,061,949	981,720	19,781	12,731	80,229 R	51.1%	47.3%	1.0%
Texas	32			6,407,637	3,799,639	2,433,746	137,994	36,258	1,365,893 R	59.3%	38.0%	2.2%
Utah	5			770,754	515,096	203,053	35,850	16,755	312,043 R	66.8%	26.3%	4.7%
Vermont		3		294,308	119,775	149,022	20,374	5,137	29,247 D	40.7%	50.6%	6.9%
Virginia	13			2,739,447	1,437,490	1,217,290	59,398	25,269	220,200 R	52.5%	44.4%	2.2%
Washington		11		2,487,433	1,108,864	1,247,652	103,002	27,915	138,788 D	44.6%	50.2%	4.1%
West Virginia	5			648,124	336,475	295,497	10,680	5,472	40,978 R	51.9%	45.6%	1.6%
Wisconsin		11		2,598,607	1,237,279	1,242,987	94,070	24,271	5,708 D	47.6%	47.8%	3.6%
Wyoming	3			218,351	147,947	60,481	4,625	5,298	87,466 R	67.8%	27.7%	2.1%
District of Columbia		2	1	201,894	18,073	171,923	10,576	1,322	153,850 D	9.0%	85.2%	5.2%
Total	271	266	1	105,396,627	50,455,156	50,992,335	2,882,738	1,066,398	537,179 D	47.9%	48.4%	2.7%

UNITED STATES
PRESIDENT 2000 MINOR PARTIES

State	Total	Buchanan	Browne	Phillips	Hagelin	Other Candidates and Scattered Write-ins
Alabama	14,165	6,351	5,893	775	447	699
Alaska	10,411	5,192	2,636	596	919	1,068
Arizona	19,378	12,373		110	1,120	5,775
Arkansas	12,652	7,358	2,781	1,415	1,098	—
California	118,517	44,987	45,520	17,042	10,934	34
Colorado	27,959	10,465	12,799	1,319	2,240	1,136
Connecticut	17,964	4,731	3,484	9,695	40	14
Delaware	1,959	777	774	208	107	93
Florida	40,579	17,484	16,415	1,371	2,281	3,028
Georgia	47,422	10,926	36,332	140		24
Hawaii	3,197	1,071	1,477	343	306	—
Idaho	13,755	7,615	3,488	1,469	1,177	6
Illinois	29,917	16,106	11,623	57	2,127	4
Indiana	32,955	16,959	15,530	200	167	99
Iowa	13,299	5,731	3,209	613	2,281	1,465
Kansas	14,524	7,370	4,525	1,254	1,375	—
Kentucky	9,605	4,173	2,896	923	1,533	80
Louisiana	24,968	14,356	2,951	5,483	1,075	1,103
Maine	8,123	4,443	3,074	579		27
Maryland	12,133	4,248	5,310	919	176	1,480
Massachusetts	34,431	11,149	16,366		2,884	4,032
Michigan	24,989	2061	16,711	3,791	2,426	—
Minnesota	34,064	22,166	5,282	3,272	2,294	1,050
Mississippi	8,604	2,265	2,009	3,267	450	613
Missouri	20,315	9,818	7,436	1,957	1,104	—
Montana	9,256	5,697	1,718	1,155	675	11
Nebraska	6,837	3,646	2,245	468	478	—
Nevada	12,409	4,747	3,311	621	415	3,315
New Hampshire	6,976	2,615	2,757	328		1,276
New Jersey	19,649	6,989	6,312	1,409	2,215	2,724
New Mexico	4,154	1,392	2,058	343	361	—
New York	66,898	31,599	7,649	1,498	24,361	1,791
North Carolina	22,407	8,874	12,307			1,226
North Dakota	8,634	7,288	660	373	313	—
Ohio	50,208	26,721	13,473	3,823	6,181	10
Oklahoma	15,616	9,014	6,602			—
Oregon	22,692	7,063	7,447	2,189	2,574	3,419
Pennsylvania	42,633	16,023	11,248	14,428		934
Rhode Island	3,932	2,273	742	97	271	549
South Carolina	11,019	3,519	4,876	1,682	942	—
South Dakota	6,765	3,322	1,662	1,781		—
Tennessee	12,731	4,250	4,284	1,015	613	2,569
Texas	36,258	12,394	23,160	567		137
Utah	16,755	9,319	3,616	2,709	763	348
Vermont	5,137	2,192	784	153	219	1,789
Virginia	25,269	5,455	15,198	1,809		2,807
Washington	27,915	7,171	13,135	1,989	2,927	2,693
West Virginia	5,472	3,169	1,912	23	367	1
Wisconsin	24,271	11,446	6,640	2,042	878	3,265
Wyoming	5,298	2,724	1,443	720	411	—
District of Columbia	1,322		669			653
Total	1,066,398	449,077	384,429	98,020	83,525	51,347

UNITED STATES
VOTER TURNOUT 2000

State	2000 Voting Age Population Est.	November 2000 Registration	Percentage Voting Age Registered	Presidential Vote	Presidential Vote as Percentage of Voting Age Population	Presidential Vote as Percentage of Registered Voters	House Vote	Senate Vote	Governor Vote
Alabama	3,333,000	2,528,963	75.9%	1,666,272	50.0%	65.9%	1,438,994		
Alaska	430,000	473,648	110.2%	285,560	66.4%	60.3%	274,393		
Arizona	3,625,000	2,654,700	73.2%	1,532,016	42.3%	57.7%	1,465,656	1,397,076	
Arkansas	1,929,000	1,555,809	80.7%	921,781	47.8%	59.2%	632,765		
California	24,873,000	15,707,307	63.2%	10,965,856	44.1%	69.8%	10,437,665	10,623,614	
Colorado	3,067,000	2,858,239	93.2%	1,741,368	56.8%	60.9%	1,623,882		
Connecticut	2,499,000	2,031,626	81.3%	1,459,525	58.4%	71.8%	1,313,490	1,311,261	
Delaware	582,000	503,672	86.5%	327,622	56.3%	65.0%	313,171	327,017	323,688
Florida	11,774,000	8,752,717	74.3%	5,963,110	50.6%	68.1%	5,011,372	5,856,731	
Georgia	5,893,000	4,648,205	78.9%	2,596,645	44.1%	55.9%	2,416,622	2,428,510	
Hawaii	909,000	637,349	70.1%	367,951	40.5%	57.7%	340,424	345,623	
Idaho	921,000	728,085	79.1%	501,621	54.5%	68.9%	492,835		
Illinois	8,983,000	7,117,449	79.2%	4,742,123	52.8%	66.6%	4,393,352		
Indiana	4,448,000	4,000,809	89.9%	2,199,302	49.4%	55.0%	2,156,744	2,145,209	2,179,413
Iowa	2,165,000	1,969,199	91.0%	1,315,563	60.8%	66.8%	1,275,934		
Kansas	1,983,000	1,623,623	81.9%	1,072,218	54.1%	66.0%	1,038,379		
Kentucky	2,993,000	2,556,815	85.4%	1,544,187	51.6%	60.4%	1,435,409		580,074
Louisiana	3,255,000	2,782,929	85.5%	1,765,656	54.2%	63.4%	1,202,171		1,295,205
Maine	968,000	947,189	97.9%	651,817	67.3%	68.8%	638,399	634,872	
Maryland	3,925,000	2,715,366	69.2%	2,020,480	51.5%	74.4%	1,926,764	1,946,898	
Massachusetts	4,749,000	4,000,218	84.2%	2,702,984	56.9%	67.6%	2,347,375	2,599,420	
Michigan	7,358,000	6,861,342	93.3%	4,232,711	56.6%	60.7%	4,069,736	4,167,685	
Minnesota	3,547,000	2,801,077	79.0%	2,438,685	68.8%	87.1%	2,363,738	2,419,520	
Mississippi	2,047,000			994,184	48.6%		986,139	994,144	763,938
Missouri	4,105,000	3,676,664	89.6%	2,359,892	57.5%	64.2%	2,325,788	2,361,586	2,346,830
Montana	668,000	698,260	104.5%	410,997	61.5%	58.9%	410,523	411,601	410,192
Nebraska	1,234,000	1,085,272	87.9%	697,019	56.5%	64.2%	683,071	692,344	
Nevada	1,390,000	878,970	63.2%	608,970	43.8%	69.3%	585,204	600,250	
New Hampshire	911,000	856,519	94.0%	569,081	62.5%	66.4%	556,417		564,953
New Jersey	6,245,000	4,710,768	75.4%	3,187,226	51.0%	67.7%	2,988,233	3,015,662	
New Mexico	1,263,000	928,931	73.5%	598,605	47.4%	64.4%	587,514	589,526	
New York	13,805,000	11,262,816	81.6%	6,821,999	49.4%	60.6%	5,823,850	6,779,839	
North Carolina	5,797,000	5,186,094	89.5%	2,911,262	50.2%	56.1%	2,779,800		2,942,062
North Dakota	477,000			288,256	60.4%		285,658	287,539	289,412
Ohio	8,433,000	7,537,822	89.4%	4,701,998	55.8%	62.4%	4,517,838	4,448,801	
Oklahoma	2,531,000	2,233,602	88.2%	1,234,229	48.8%	55.3%	1,087,515		
Oregon	2,530,000	1,950,902	77.1%	1,533,968	60.6%	78.6%	1,440,002		
Pennsylvania	9,155,000	7,781,997	85.0%	4,913,119	53.7%	63.1%	4,554,347	4,735,504	
Rhode Island	753,000	655,107	87.0%	409,047	54.3%	62.4%	384,127	391,537	
South Carolina	2,977,000	2,266,200	76.1%	1,382,717	46.4%	61.0%	1,321,312		
South Dakota	542,000	520,881	96.1%	316,269	58.4%	60.7%	314,761		
Tennessee	4,221,000	3,400,487	80.6%	2,076,181	49.2%	61.1%	1,854,378	1,928,613	
Texas	14,850,000	12,365,235	83.3%	6,407,637	43.1%	51.8%	5,985,763	6,276,652	
Utah	1,465,000	1,120,129	76.5%	770,754	52.6%	68.8%	758,754	769,704	761,806
Vermont	460,000	427,354	92.9%	294,308	64.0%	68.9%	283,366	288,500	293,473
Virginia	5,263,000	4,071,471	77.4%	2,739,447	52.1%	67.3%	2,421,729	2,718,301	
Washington	4,368,000	3,335,714	76.4%	2,487,433	56.9%	74.6%	2,382,411	2,461,379	2,469,852
West Virginia	1,416,000	1,067,822	75.4%	648,124	45.8%	60.7%	579,872	603,477	648,047
Wisconsin	3,930,000			2,598,607	66.1%		2,506,314	2,540,083	
Wyoming	358,000	220,012	61.5%	218,351	61.0%	99.2%	212,312	213,659	
District of Columbia	411,000	354,410		201,894	49.1%	57.0%			
Total	205,814,000	159,049,775	77.3%	105,396,627	51.2%	66.3%	97,226,268	79,312,137	15,868,945

Sources: Registration figures—Committee for the Study of the American Electorate; voting age population—U.S. Census Bureau

Notes: Voting age population excluding states without registration: 199,360,000. Wisconsin and North Dakota do not maintain registration systems. Figures for Mississippi were unavailable. Excluding these states, the percentage of the voting age population that was registered was 79.8 percent. The presidential vote as a percentage of the voting age population was 50.9 percent and as a percentage of registered voters was 63.8 percent.

PRESIDENT 1996

In New York the Republican figures include Conservative, Freedom, and Right to Life votes and the Democratic figures include Liberal votes.

In Minnesota the Democratic candidate appears on the ballot as Democratic-Farmer-Labor. In many states various non-major party candidates appeared on the ballot with variations of the party designations, were carried with entirely different party labels, or were listed as "Independent."

The candidates listed below include all those who appeared on the ballot in at least one state. Write-in votes for minor party candidates are credited to their total below. See the minor parties table on page 23 for details.

47,402,357	Bill Clinton and Al Gore	Democratic
39,198,755	Bob Dole and Jack Kemp	Republican
8,085,402	Ross Perot and Pat Choate	Reform
685,040	Ralph Nader and Winona LaDuke	Green
485,798	Harry Browne and Jo Jorgensen	Libertarian
184,658	Howard Phillips and Herbert W. Titus	U.S. Taxpayers
113,668	John Hagelin and Mike Tompkins	Natural Law
29,083	Monica Moorehead and Gloria La Riva	Workers World
25,332	Marsha Feinland and Kate McClatchy	Peace and Freedom
8,930	Charles Collins and Rosemary Giumarra	Independent
8,476	James Harris and Laura Garza	Socialist Workers
5,378	Dennis Peron and Arlin D. Troutt Jr.	Grassroots
4,706	Mary Cal Hollis and Eric Chester	Socialist
2,438	Jerome White and Fred Mazelis	Socialist Equality
1,847	Diane Beall Templin and Gary Van Horn	American
1,298	Earl F. Dodge and Rachel B. Kelly	Prohibition
1,101	A. Peter Crane and Connie Chandler	Independent
932	Ralph Forbes and "Pro-Life" Anderson	America First
787	John Birrenbach and George McMahon	Independent Grassroots
752	Isabell Masters and Shirley Jean Masters	Looking Back
408	Steve Michael and Ann Northrop	Independent

Notes: In addition to the votes listed above, 25,118 scattered write-in votes were reported from various states, and 5,608 votes were cast for "None of These Candidates" in Nevada.

UNITED STATES
PRESIDENT 1996

State	Electoral Vote Rep.	Electoral Vote Dem.	Electoral Vote Other	Total Vote	Republican	Democratic	Reform	Other	Plurality		Percentage Rep.	Percentage Dem.	Percentage Reform
Alabama	9			1,534,349	769,044	662,165	92,149	10,991	106,879	R	50.1%	43.2%	6.0%
Alaska	3			241,620	122,746	80,380	26,333	12,161	42,366	R	50.8%	33.3%	10.9%
Arizona		8		1,404,405	622,073	653,288	112,072	16,972	31,215	D	44.3%	46.5%	8.0%
Arkansas		6		884,262	325,416	475,171	69,884	13,791	149,755	D	36.8%	53.7%	7.9%
California		54		10,019,484	3,828,380	5,119,835	697,847	373,422	1,291,455	D	38.2%	51.1%	7.0%
Colorado	8			1,510,704	691,848	671,152	99,629	48,075	20,696	R	45.8%	44.4%	6.6%
Connecticut		8		1,392,614	483,109	735,740	139,523	34,242	252,631	D	34.7%	52.8%	10.0%
Delaware		3		271,084	99,062	140,355	28,719	2,948	41,293	D	36.5%	51.8%	10.6%
Florida		25		5,303,794	2,244,536	2,546,870	483,870	28,518	302,334	D	42.3%	48.0%	9.1%
Georgia	13			2,299,071	1,080,843	1,053,849	146,337	18,042	26,994	R	47.0%	45.8%	6.4%
Hawaii		4		360,120	113,943	205,012	27,358	13,807	91,069	D	31.6%	56.9%	7.6%
Idaho	4			491,719	256,595	165,443	62,518	7,163	91,152	R	52.2%	33.6%	12.7%
Illinois		22		4,311,391	1,587,021	2,341,744	346,408	36,218	754,723	D	36.8%	54.3%	8.0%
Indiana	12			2,135,842	1,006,693	887,424	224,299	17,426	119,269	R	47.1%	41.5%	10.5%
Iowa		7		1,234,075	492,644	620,258	105,159	16,014	127,614	D	39.9%	50.3%	8.5%
Kansas	6			1,074,300	583,245	387,659	92,639	10,757	195,586	R	54.3%	36.1%	8.6%
Kentucky		8		1,388,708	623,283	636,614	120,396	8,415	13,331	D	44.9%	45.8%	8.7%
Louisiana		9		1,783,959	712,586	927,837	123,293	20,243	215,251	D	39.9%	52.0%	6.9%
Maine		4		605,897	186,378	312,788	85,970	20,761	126,410	D	30.8%	51.6%	14.2%
Maryland		10		1,780,870	681,530	966,207	115,812	17,321	284,677	D	38.3%	54.3%	6.5%
Massachusetts		12		2,556,785	718,107	1,571,763	227,217	39,698	853,656	D	28.1%	61.5%	8.9%
Michigan		18		3,848,844	1,481,212	1,989,653	336,670	41,309	508,441	D	38.5%	51.7%	8.7%
Minnesota		10		2,192,640	766,476	1,120,438	257,704	48,022	353,962	D	35.0%	51.1%	11.8%
Mississippi	7			893,857	439,838	394,022	52,222	7,775	45,816	R	49.2%	44.1%	5.8%
Missouri		11		2,158,065	890,016	1,025,935	217,188	24,926	135,919	D	41.2%	47.5%	10.1%
Montana	3			407,261	179,652	167,922	55,229	4,458	11,730	R	44.1%	41.2%	13.6%
Nebraska	5			677,415	363,467	236,761	71,278	5,909	126,706	R	53.7%	35.0%	10.5%
Nevada		4		464,279	199,244	203,974	43,986	17,075	4,730	D	42.9%	43.9%	9.5%
New Hampshire		4		499,175	196,532	246,214	48,390	8,039	49,682	D	39.4%	49.3%	9.7%
New Jersey		15		3,075,807	1,103,078	1,652,329	262,134	58,266	549,251	D	35.9%	53.7%	8.5%
New Mexico		5		556,074	232,751	273,495	32,257	17,571	40,744	D	41.9%	49.2%	5.8%
New York		33		6,316,129	1,933,492	3,756,177	503,458	123,002	1,822,685	D	30.6%	59.5%	8.0%
North Carolina	14			2,515,807	1,225,938	1,107,849	168,059	13,961	118,089	R	48.7%	44.0%	6.7%
North Dakota	3			266,411	125,050	106,905	32,515	1,941	18,145	R	46.9%	40.1%	12.2%
Ohio		21		4,534,434	1,859,883	2,148,222	483,207	43,122	288,339	D	41.0%	47.4%	10.7%
Oklahoma	8			1,206,713	582,315	488,105	130,788	5,505	94,210	R	48.3%	40.4%	10.8%
Oregon		7		1,377,760	538,152	649,641	121,221	68,746	111,489	D	39.1%	47.2%	8.8%
Pennsylvania		23		4,506,118	1,801,169	2,215,819	430,984	58,146	414,650	D	40.0%	49.2%	9.6%
Rhode Island		4		390,284	104,683	233,050	43,723	8,828	128,367	D	26.8%	59.7%	11.2%
South Carolina	8			1,151,689	573,458	506,283	64,386	7,562	67,175	R	49.8%	44.0%	5.6%
South Dakota	3			323,826	150,543	139,333	31,250	2,700	11,210	R	46.5%	43.0%	9.7%
Tennessee		11		1,894,105	863,530	909,146	105,918	15,511	45,616	D	45.6%	48.0%	5.6%
Texas	32			5,611,644	2,736,167	2,459,683	378,537	37,257	276,484	R	48.8%	43.8%	6.7%
Utah	5			665,629	361,911	221,633	66,461	15,624	140,278	R	54.4%	33.3%	10.0%
Vermont		3		258,449	80,352	137,894	31,024	9,179	57,542	D	31.1%	53.4%	12.0%
Virginia	13			2,416,642	1,138,350	1,091,060	159,861	27,371	47,290	R	47.1%	45.1%	6.6%
Washington		11		2,253,837	840,712	1,123,323	201,003	88,799	282,611	D	37.3%	49.8%	8.9%
West Virginia		5		636,459	233,946	327,812	71,639	3,062	93,866	D	36.8%	51.5%	11.3%
Wisconsin		11		2,196,169	845,029	1,071,971	227,339	51,830	226,942	D	38.5%	48.8%	10.4%
Wyoming	3			211,571	105,388	77,934	25,928	2,321	27,454	R	49.8%	36.8%	12.3%
District of Columbia		3		185,726	17,339	158,220	3,611	6,556	140,881	D	9.3%	85.2%	1.9%
Total	159	379		96,277,872	39,198,755	47,402,357	8,085,402	1,591,358	8,203,602	D	40.7%	49.2%	8.4%

UNITED STATES
PRESIDENT 1996 MINOR PARTIES

State	Total	Nader	Browne	Phillips	Hagelin	Moorehead	Feinland	Other Candidates and Scattered Write-ins
Alabama	10,991		5,290	2,365	1,697			1,639
Alaska	12,161	7,597	2,276	925	729			634
Arizona	16,972	2,062*	14,358	347*	153*			52
Arkansas	13,791	3,649	3,076	2,065	729	747		3,525
California	373,422	237,016	73,600	21,202	15,403		25,332	869
Colorado	48,075	25,070	12,392	2,813	2,547	599		4,654
Connecticut	34,242	24,321	5,788	2,425	1,703			5
Delaware	2,948	156*	2,052	348	274			118
Florida	28,518	4,101*	23,965		418*			34
Georgia	18,042		17,870	145*				27
Hawaii	13,807	10,386	2,493	358	570			
Idaho	7,163		3,325	2,230	1,600			8
Illinois	36,218	1,447*	22,548	7,606	4,606			11
Indiana	17,426	895*	15,632	291*	118*			490
Iowa	16,014	6,550	2,315	2,229	3,349			1,571
Kansas	10,757	914*	4,557	3,519	1,655			112
Kentucky	8,415	701*	4,009	2,204	1,493			8
Louisiana	20,243	4,719	7,499	3,366	2,981	1,678		
Maine	20,761	15,279	2,996	1,517	825			144
Maryland	17,321	2,606*	8,765	3,402	2,517			31
Massachusetts	39,698	4,565*	20,426		5,184	3,277		6,246
Michigan	41,309	2,322*	27,670	539*	4,254	3,153		3,371
Minnesota	48,022	24,908	8,271	3,416	1,808			9,619
Mississippi	7,775		2,809	2,314	1,447			1,205
Missouri	24,926	534*	10,522	11,521	2,287			62
Montana	4,458		2,526	152*	1,754			26
Nebraska	5,909		2,792	1,928	1,189			
Nevada	17,075	4,730	4,460	1,732	545			5,608
New Hampshire	8,039		4,237	1,346				2,456
New Jersey	58,266	32,465	14,763	3,440	3,887	1,337		2,374
New Mexico	17,571	13,218	2,996	713	644			
New York	123,002	75,956	12,220	23,580	5,011	3,473		2,762
North Carolina	13,961	2,108*	8,740	258*	2,771			84
North Dakota	1,941		847	745	349			
Ohio	43,122	2,962*	12,851	7,361	9,120	10,813		15
Oklahoma	5,505		5,505					
Oregon	68,746	49,415	8,903	3,379	2,798			4,251
Pennsylvania	58,146	3,086*	28,000	19,552	5,783			1,725
Rhode Island	8,828	6,040	1,109	1,021	435	186		37
South Carolina	7,562		4,271	2,043	1,248			
South Dakota	2,700		1,472	912	316			
Tennessee	15,511	6,427	5,020	1,818	636			1,610
Texas	37,257	4,810*	20,256	7,472	4,422			297
Utah	15,624	4,615	4,129	2,601	1,085	298		2,896
Vermont	9,179	5,585	1,183	382	498			1,531
Virginia	27,371		9,174	13,687	4,510			
Washington	88,799	60,322	12,522	4,578	6,076	2,189		3,112
West Virginia	3,062		3,062					
Wisconsin	51,830	28,723	7,929	8,811	1,879	1,333		3,655
Wyoming	2,321		1,739		582			
District of Columbia	6,556	4,780	588		283			905
Total	1,591,358	685,040	485,798	184,658	113,668	29,083	25,332	67,779

Notes: An asterisk (*) indicates write-in votes. The vote, including write-ins, for other minor party candidates who were listed on the ballot in at least one state: 8,930 Collins (Arizona, Arkansas, California, Colorado, Georgia, Idaho, Kansas, Maryland, Mississippi, Missouri, Montana, Tennessee, Utah, Washington); 8,476 Harris (Alabama, California, Colorado, Connecticut, Florida, Georgia, Iowa, Minnesota, New Jersey, New York, North Carolina, Utah, Vermont, Washington, Wisconsin, District of Columbia); 5,378 Peron (Minnesota, Vermont); 4,706 Holllis (Arkansas, Colorado, Florida, Maryland, Massachusetts, Montana, Oregon, Texas, Utah, Vermont, Wisconsin); 2,438 White (Michigan, Minnesota, New Jersey); 1,847 Templin (Colorado, Utah); 1,298 Dodge (Arkansas, Colorado, Illinois, Massachusetts, Tennessee, Utah); 1,101 Crane (Utah); 932 Forbes (Arkansas); 787 Birrenbach (Minnesota); 752 Masters (Arkansas, California, Maryland); 408 Michael (Tennessee). The Other Candidates and Scattered Write-ins column includes 5,608 votes cast in Nevada for "None of These Candidates" and 25,118 scattered write-ins.

UNITED STATES
VOTER TURNOUT 1996

State	1996 Census Voting Age Pop. Est.	November 1996 Registration	Percentage Voting Age Registered	Total Valid Vote President	Percentage Voting Age Voted	Percentage Registered Voted
Alabama	3,218,000	2,470,766	76.8%	1,534,349	47.7%	62.1%
Alaska	425,000	414,817	97.6%	241,620	56.9%	58.2%
Arizona	3,094,000	2,244,672	72.5%	1,404,405	45.4%	62.6%
Arkansas	1,860,000	1,396,459	75.1%	884,262	47.5%	63.3%
California	23,133,000	15,662,075	67.7%	10,019,484	43.3%	64.0%
Colorado	2,843,000	2,285,503	80.4%	1,510,704	53.1%	66.1%
Connecticut	2,468,000	1,975,000	80.0%	1,392,614	56.4%	70.5%
Delaware	547,000	419,695	76.7%	271,084	49.6%	64.6%
Florida	11,043,000	8,077,877	73.1%	5,303,794	48.0%	65.7%
Georgia	5,396,000	3,811,284	70.6%	2,299,071	42.6%	60.3%
Hawaii	882,000	544,916	61.8%	360,120	40.8%	66.1%
Idaho	845,000	700,430	82.9%	491,719	58.2%	70.2%
Illinois	8,764,000	6,663,301	76.0%	4,311,391	49.2%	64.7%
Indiana	4,369,000	3,484,033	79.7%	2,135,842	48.9%	61.3%
Iowa	2,138,000	1,776,433	83.1%	1,234,075	57.7%	69.5%
Kansas	1,898,000	1,436,418	75.7%	1,074,300	56.6%	74.8%
Kentucky	2,924,000	2,396,086	81.9%	1,388,708	47.5%	58.0%
Louisiana	3,137,000	2,539,240	80.9%	1,783,959	56.9%	70.3%
Maine	939,000	1,001,292	106.6%	605,897	64.5%	60.5%
Maryland	3,811,000	2,587,977	67.9%	1,780,870	46.7%	68.8%
Massachusetts	4,623,000	3,459,193	74.8%	2,556,785	55.3%	73.9%
Michigan	7,067,000	6,688,893	94.6%	3,848,844	54.5%	57.5%
Minnesota	3,412,000	2,730,505	80.0%	2,192,640	64.3%	80.3%
Mississippi	1,961,000			893,857	45.6%	
Missouri	3,980,000	3,339,852	83.9%	2,158,065	54.2%	64.6%
Montana	647,000	590,749	91.3%	407,261	62.9%	68.9%
Nebraska	1,208,000	1,015,056	84.0%	677,415	56.1%	66.7%
Nevada	1,180,000	778,298	66.0%	464,279	39.3%	59.7%
New Hampshire	860,000	713,236	82.9%	499,175	58.0%	70.0%
New Jersey	6,005,000	4,320,866	72.0%	3,075,807	51.2%	71.2%
New Mexico	1,210,000	837,794	69.2%	556,074	46.0%	66.4%
New York	13,579,000	10,162,156	74.8%	6,316,129	46.5%	62.2%
North Carolina	5,499,000	4,315,723	78.5%	2,515,807	45.8%	58.3%
North Dakota	473,000			266,411	56.3%	
Ohio	8,358,000	6,879,687	82.3%	4,534,434	54.3%	65.9%
Oklahoma	2,419,000	1,979,017	81.8%	1,206,713	49.9%	61.0%
Oregon	2,396,000	1,962,155	81.9%	1,377,760	57.5%	70.2%
Pennsylvania	9,196,000	6,799,637	73.9%	4,506,118	49.0%	66.3%
Rhode Island	750,000	602,692	80.4%	390,284	52.0%	64.8%
South Carolina	2,777,000	1,814,777	65.4%	1,151,689	41.5%	63.5%
South Dakota	530,000	476,422	89.9%	323,826	61.1%	68.0%
Tennessee	4,021,000	3,097,336	77.0%	1,894,105	47.1%	61.2%
Texas	13,622,000	10,520,379	77.2%	5,611,644	41.2%	53.3%
Utah	1,323,000	1,050,452	79.4%	665,629	50.3%	63.4%
Vermont	441,000	385,328	87.4%	258,449	58.6%	67.1%
Virginia	5,089,000	3,322,740	65.3%	2,416,642	47.5%	72.7%
Washington	4,122,000	3,081,971	74.8%	2,253,837	54.7%	73.1%
West Virginia	1,414,000	970,745	68.7%	636,459	45.0%	65.6%
Wisconsin	3,824,000			2,196,169	57.4%	
Wyoming	352,000			211,571	60.1%	
District of Columbia	435,000	361,419	83.1%	185,726	42.7%	51.4%
Total	196,507,000	144,145,352	73.4%	96,277,872	49.0%	66.8%

Source: Registration figures—Committee for the Study of the American Electorate.

Notes: Mississippi, North Dakota, Wisconsin, and Wyoming do not maintain formal voter registration systems or had no figures readily available. Excluding these four states, the percentage of the voting age population registered in the remaining states was 75.9 percent, and the percentage of registered that voted was 64.3 percent.

PRESIDENT 1992

In New York the Republican figures include Conservative and Right to Life votes and the Democratic figures include Liberal votes.

In Minnesota the Republican candidates appear on the ballot as Independent-Republican, the Democratic as Democratic-Farmer-Labor. In many states various non-major party candidates appeared on the ballot with variations of the party designations, were carried with entirely different party labels, or were listed as "Independent." In several states minor party vice-presidential candidates were different from those listed below.

The candidates listed below include all those who appeared on the ballot in at least one state. Write-in votes for minor party candidates are credited to their total below.

44,909,326	Bill Clinton and Al Gore	Democratic
39,103,882	George Bush and J. Danforth Quayle	Republican
19,741,657	Ross Perot and James Stockdale	Independent
291,627	Andre V. Marrou and Nancy Lord	Libertarian
107,014	James Gritz and Cyril Minett	America First
73,714	Lenora B. Fulani and Maria E. Munoz	New Alliance
43,434	Howard Phillips and Albion W. Knight	Taxpayers
39,179	John Hagelin and Mike Tompkins	Natural Law
27,961	Ron Daniels and Asiba Tupahache	Peace and Freedom
26,333	Lyndon H. LaRouche Jr. and James L. Bevel	Economic Recovery
23,096	James Warren and Willie Mae Reid	Socialist Workers
4,749	Drew Bradford and no vice-presidential candidate	Independent
3,875	Jack Herer and Derrick P. Grimmer	Grassroots
3,057	J. Quinn Brisben and Barbara Garson	Socialist
3,050	Helen Halyard and Fred Mazelis	Workers League
2,199	John Yiamouyiannis and Allen C. McCone	Take Back America
1,149	Delbert L. Ehlers and Rick Wendt	Independent
961	Earl F. Dodge and George Ormsby	Prohibition
956	Jim Boren and Will Weidman	Apathy
405	Eugene A. Hem and Joanne Roland	Third Party
339	Isabell Masters and Walter Masters	Looking Back
292	Robert J. Smith and Doris Feimer	American
181	Gloria La Riva and Larry Holmes	Workers World

Notes: In addition to the votes listed above, 14,041 scattered write-in votes were reported from various states, and 2,537 votes were cast for "None of These Candidates" in Nevada.

UNITED STATES
PRESIDENT 1992

State	Electoral Vote Rep.	Dem.	Other	Total Vote	Republican	Democratic	Independent	Other	Plurality		Percentage Rep.	Dem.	Ind.
Alabama	9			1,688,060	804,283	690,080	183,109	10,588	114,203	R	47.6%	40.9%	10.8%
Alaska	3			258,506	102,000	78,294	73,481	4,731	23,706	R	39.5%	30.3%	28.4%
Arizona	8			1,486,975	572,086	543,050	353,741	18,098	29,036	R	38.5%	36.5%	23.8%
Arkansas		6		950,653	337,324	505,823	99,132	8,374	168,499	D	35.5%	53.2%	10.4%
California		54		11,131,721	3,630,574	5,121,325	2,296,006	83,816	1,490,751	D	32.6%	46.0%	20.6%
Colorado		8		1,569,180	562,850	629,681	366,010	10,639	66,831	D	35.9%	40.1%	23.3%
Connecticut		8		1,616,332	578,313	682,318	348,771	6,930	104,005	D	35.8%	42.2%	21.6%
Delaware		3		289,735	102,313	126,054	59,213	2,155	23,741	D	35.3%	43.5%	20.4%
Florida	25			5,314,392	2,173,310	2,072,698	1,053,067	15,317	100,612	R	40.9%	39.0%	19.8%
Georgia		13		2,321,125	995,252	1,008,966	309,657	7,250	13,714	D	42.9%	43.5%	13.3%
Hawaii		4		372,842	136,822	179,310	53,003	3,707	42,488	D	36.7%	48.1%	14.2%
Idaho	4			482,142	202,645	137,013	130,395	12,089	65,632	R	42.0%	28.4%	27.0%
Illinois		22		5,050,157	1,734,096	2,453,350	840,515	22,196	719,254	D	34.3%	48.6%	16.6%
Indiana	12			2,305,871	989,375	848,420	455,934	12,142	140,955	R	42.9%	36.8%	19.8%
Iowa		7		1,354,607	504,891	586,353	253,468	9,895	81,462	D	37.3%	43.3%	18.7%
Kansas	6			1,157,335	449,951	390,434	312,358	4,592	59,517	R	38.9%	33.7%	27.0%
Kentucky		8		1,492,900	617,178	665,104	203,944	6,674	47,926	D	41.3%	44.6%	13.7%
Louisiana		9		1,790,017	733,386	815,971	211,478	29,182	82,585	D	41.0%	45.6%	11.8%
Maine		4		679,499	206,504	263,420	206,820	2,755	56,600	D	30.4%	38.8%	30.4%
Maryland		10		1,985,046	707,094	988,571	281,414	7,967	281,477	D	35.6%	49.8%	14.2%
Massachusetts		12		2,773,700	805,049	1,318,662	630,731	19,258	513,613	D	29.0%	47.5%	22.7%
Michigan		18		4,274,673	1,554,940	1,871,182	824,813	23,738	316,242	D	36.4%	43.8%	19.3%
Minnesota		10		2,347,948	747,841	1,020,997	562,506	16,604	273,156	D	31.9%	43.5%	24.0%
Mississippi	7			981,793	487,793	400,258	85,626	8,116	87,535	R	49.7%	40.8%	8.7%
Missouri		11		2,391,565	811,159	1,053,873	518,741	7,792	242,714	D	33.9%	44.1%	21.7%
Montana		3		410,611	144,207	154,507	107,225	4,672	10,300	D	35.1%	37.6%	26.1%
Nebraska	5			737,546	343,678	216,864	174,104	2,900	126,814	R	46.6%	29.4%	23.6%
Nevada		4		506,318	175,828	189,148	132,580	8,762	13,320	D	34.7%	37.4%	26.2%
New Hampshire		4		537,943	202,484	209,040	121,337	5,082	6,556	D	37.6%	38.9%	22.6%
New Jersey		15		3,343,594	1,356,865	1,436,206	521,829	28,694	79,341	D	40.6%	43.0%	15.6%
New Mexico		5		569,986	212,824	261,617	91,895	3,650	48,793	D	37.3%	45.9%	16.1%
New York		33		6,926,925	2,346,649	3,444,450	1,090,721	45,105	1,097,801	D	33.9%	49.7%	15.7%
North Carolina	14			2,611,850	1,134,661	1,114,042	357,864	5,283	20,619	R	43.4%	42.7%	13.7%
North Dakota	3			308,133	136,244	99,168	71,084	1,637	37,076	R	44.2%	32.2%	23.1%
Ohio		21		4,939,967	1,894,310	1,984,942	1,036,426	24,289	90,632	D	38.3%	40.2%	21.0%
Oklahoma	8			1,390,359	592,929	473,066	319,878	4,486	119,863	R	42.6%	34.0%	23.0%
Oregon		7		1,462,643	475,757	621,314	354,091	11,481	145,557	D	32.5%	42.5%	24.2%
Pennsylvania		23		4,959,810	1,791,841	2,239,164	902,667	26,138	447,323	D	36.1%	45.1%	18.2%
Rhode Island		4		453,477	131,601	213,299	105,045	3,532	81,698	D	29.0%	47.0%	23.2%
South Carolina	8			1,202,527	577,507	479,514	138,872	6,634	97,993	R	48.0%	39.9%	11.5%
South Dakota	3			336,254	136,718	124,888	73,295	1,353	11,830	R	40.7%	37.1%	21.8%
Tennessee		11		1,982,638	841,300	933,521	199,968	7,849	92,221	D	42.4%	47.1%	10.1%
Texas	32			6,154,018	2,496,071	2,281,815	1,354,781	21,351	214,256	R	40.6%	37.1%	22.0%
Utah	5			743,999	322,632	183,429	203,400	34,538	119,232	R	43.4%	24.7%	27.3%
Vermont		3		289,701	88,122	133,592	65,991	1,996	45,470	D	30.4%	46.1%	22.8%
Virginia	13			2,558,665	1,150,517	1,038,650	348,639	20,859	111,867	R	45.0%	40.6%	13.6%
Washington		11		2,288,230	731,234	993,037	541,780	22,179	261,803	D	32.0%	43.4%	23.7%
West Virginia		5		683,762	241,974	331,001	108,829	1,958	89,027	D	35.4%	48.4%	15.9%
Wisconsin		11		2,531,114	930,855	1,041,066	544,479	14,714	110,211	D	36.8%	41.1%	21.5%
Wyoming	3			200,598	79,347	68,160	51,263	1,828	11,187	R	39.6%	34.0%	25.6%
District of Columbia		3		227,572	20,698	192,619	9,681	4,574	171,921	D	9.1%	84.6%	4.3%
Total	168	370		104,425,014	39,103,882	44,909,326	19,741,657	670,149	5,805,444	D	37.4%	43.0%	18.9%

PRESIDENT 1988

In West Virginia one Democratic elector voted in the electoral college for Lloyd Bentsen for president and Michael S. Dukakis for vice president.

In New York the Republican figures include Conservative votes and the Democratic figures include Liberal votes.

In Minnesota the Republican candidates appear on the ballot as Independent-Republican, the Democratic as Democratic-Farmer-Labor. In many states various non-major party candidates appeared on the ballot with variations of the party designations, were listed as "Independent," or were carried with entirely different party labels.

In several states minor party vice-presidential candidates were different from those listed below. The full list of candidates for president and vice president was:

48,886,097	George Bush and J. Danforth Quayle	Republican
41,809,074	Michael S. Dukakis and Lloyd Bentsen	Democratic
432,179	Ron Paul and Andre V. Marrou	Libertarian
217,219	Lenora B. Fulani and Joyce Dattner	New Alliance
47,047	David E. Duke and Floyd C. Parker	Populist
30,905	Eugene J. McCarthy and Florence Rice	Consumer
27,818	James C. Griffin and Charles J. Morsa	American Independent
25,562	Lyndon H. LaRouche and Debra H. Freeman	National Economic Recovery
20,504	William A. Matra and Joan Andrews	Right to Life
18,693	Ed Winn and Barry Porster	Workers League
15,604	James Warren and Kathleen Mickells	Socialist Workers
10,370	Herbert Lewin and Vikki Murdock	Peace and Freedom
8,002	Earl F. Dodge and George Ormsby	Prohibition
7,846	Larry Holmes and Gloria LaRiva	Workers World
3,882	Willa Kenoyer and Ron Ehrenreich	Socialist
3,475	Delmar Dennis and Earl Jeppson	American
1,949	Jack Herer and Dana Beal	Grassroots
372	Louie G. Youngkeit with no vice presidential candidate	Independent
236	John G. Martin and Cleveland Sparrow	Third World Assembly

Notes: The candidates listed above are those who appeared on the ballot in at least one state. Republican, Democratic, and New Alliance candidates appeared on the ballot in all fifty-one jurisdictions. The Libertarian nominees were on the ballot in 47 jurisdictions. Where identified by state authorities, write-in votes for minor party candidates were credited to their total above. In addition to the votes listed, 21,041 scattered write-in votes were reported from various states, and 6,934 votes were cast for "None of These Candidates" in Nevada.

UNITED STATES
PRESIDENT 1988

State	Electoral Vote Rep.	Dem.	Other	Total Vote	Republican	Democratic	Other	Plurality		Percentage Total Vote Rep.	Dem.	Major Vote Rep.	Dem.
Alabama	9			1,378,476	815,576	549,506	13,394	266,070	R	59.2%	39.9%	59.7%	40.3%
Alaska	3			200,116	119,251	72,584	8,281	46,667	R	59.6%	36.3%	62.2%	37.8%
Arizona	7			1,171,873	702,541	454,029	15,303	248,512	R	60.0%	38.7%	60.7%	39.3%
Arkansas	6			827,738	466,578	349,237	11,923	117,341	R	56.4%	42.2%	57.2%	42.8%
California	47			9,887,065	5,054,917	4,702,233	129,915	352,684	R	51.1%	47.6%	51.8%	48.2%
Colorado	8			1,372,394	728,177	621,453	22,764	106,724	R	53.1%	45.3%	54.0%	46.0%
Connecticut	8			1,443,394	750,241	676,584	16,569	73,657	R	52.0%	46.9%	52.6%	47.4%
Delaware	3			249,891	139,639	108,647	1,605	30,992	R	55.9%	43.5%	56.2%	43.8%
Florida	21			4,302,313	2,618,885	1,656,701	26,727	962,184	R	60.9%	38.5%	61.3%	38.7%
Georgia	12			1,809,672	1,081,331	714,792	13,549	366,539	R	59.8%	39.5%	60.2%	39.8%
Hawaii		4		354,461	158,625	192,364	3,472	33,739	D	44.8%	54.3%	45.2%	54.8%
Idaho	4			408,968	253,881	147,272	7,815	106,609	R	62.1%	36.0%	63.3%	36.7%
Illinois	24			4,559,120	2,310,939	2,215,940	32,241	94,999	R	50.7%	48.6%	51.0%	49.0%
Indiana	12			2,168,621	1,297,763	860,643	10,215	437,120	R	59.8%	39.7%	60.1%	39.9%
Iowa		8		1,225,614	545,355	670,557	9,702	125,202	D	44.5%	54.7%	44.9%	55.1%
Kansas	7			993,044	554,049	422,636	16,359	131,413	R	55.8%	42.6%	56.7%	43.3%
Kentucky	9			1,322,517	734,281	580,368	7,868	153,913	R	55.5%	43.9%	55.9%	44.1%
Louisiana	10			1,628,202	883,702	717,460	27,040	166,242	R	54.3%	44.1%	55.2%	44.8%
Maine	4			555,035	307,131	243,569	4,335	63,562	R	55.3%	43.9%	55.8%	44.2%
Maryland	10			1,714,358	876,167	826,304	11,887	49,863	R	51.1%	48.2%	51.5%	48.5%
Massachusetts		13		2,632,805	1,194,635	1,401,415	36,755	206,780	D	45.4%	53.2%	46.0%	54.0%
Michigan	20			3,669,163	1,965,486	1,675,783	27,894	289,703	R	53.6%	45.7%	54.0%	46.0%
Minnesota		10		2,096,790	962,337	1,109,471	24,982	147,134	D	45.9%	52.9%	46.4%	53.6%
Mississippi	7			931,527	557,890	363,921	9,716	193,969	R	59.9%	39.1%	60.5%	39.5%
Missouri	11			2,093,713	1,084,953	1,001,619	7,141	83,334	R	51.8%	47.8%	52.0%	48.0%
Montana	4			365,674	190,412	168,936	6,326	21,476	R	52.1%	46.2%	53.0%	47.0%
Nebraska	5			661,465	397,956	259,235	4,274	138,721	R	60.2%	39.2%	60.6%	39.4%
Nevada	4			350,067	206,040	132,738	11,289	73,302	R	58.9%	37.9%	60.8%	39.2%
New Hampshire	4			451,074	281,537	163,696	5,841	117,841	R	62.4%	36.3%	63.2%	36.8%
New Jersey	16			3,099,553	1,743,192	1,320,352	36,009	422,840	R	56.2%	42.6%	56.9%	43.1%
New Mexico	5			521,287	270,341	244,497	6,449	25,844	R	51.9%	46.9%	52.5%	47.5%
New York		36		6,485,683	3,081,871	3,347,882	55,930	266,011	D	47.5%	51.6%	47.9%	52.1%
North Carolina	13			2,134,370	1,237,258	890,167	6,945	347,091	R	58.0%	41.7%	58.2%	41.8%
North Dakota	3			297,261	166,559	127,739	2,963	38,820	R	56.0%	43.0%	56.6%	43.4%
Ohio	23			4,393,699	2,416,549	1,939,629	37,521	476,920	R	55.0%	44.1%	55.5%	44.5%
Oklahoma	8			1,171,036	678,367	483,423	9,246	194,944	R	57.9%	41.3%	58.4%	41.6%
Oregon		7		1,201,694	560,126	616,206	25,362	56,080	D	46.6%	51.3%	47.6%	52.4%
Pennsylvania	25			4,536,251	2,300,087	2,194,944	41,220	105,143	R	50.7%	48.4%	51.2%	48.8%
Rhode Island		4		404,620	177,761	225,123	1,736	47,362	D	43.9%	55.6%	44.1%	55.9%
South Carolina	8			986,009	606,443	370,554	9,012	235,889	R	61.5%	37.6%	62.1%	37.9%
South Dakota	3			312,991	165,415	145,560	2,016	19,855	R	52.8%	46.5%	53.2%	46.8%
Tennessee	11			1,636,250	947,233	679,794	9,223	267,439	R	57.9%	41.5%	58.2%	41.8%
Texas	29			5,427,410	3,036,829	2,352,748	37,833	684,081	R	56.0%	43.3%	56.3%	43.7%
Utah	5			647,008	428,442	207,343	11,223	221,099	R	66.2%	32.0%	67.4%	32.6%
Vermont	3			243,328	124,331	115,775	3,222	8,556	R	51.1%	47.6%	51.8%	48.2%
Virginia	12			2,191,609	1,309,162	859,799	22,648	449,363	R	59.7%	39.2%	60.4%	39.6%
Washington		10		1,865,253	903,835	933,516	27,902	29,681	D	48.5%	50.0%	49.2%	50.8%
West Virginia		5	1	653,311	310,065	341,016	2,230	30,951	D	47.5%	52.2%	47.6%	52.4%
Wisconsin		11		2,191,608	1,047,499	1,126,794	17,315	79,295	D	47.8%	51.4%	48.2%	51.8%
Wyoming	3			176,551	106,867	67,113	2,571	39,754	R	60.5%	38.0%	61.4%	38.6%
District of Columbia		3		192,877	27,590	159,407	5,880	131,817	D	14.3%	82.6%	14.8%	85.2%
Total	*426*	*111*	*1*	*91,594,809*	*48,886,097*	*41,809,074*	*899,638*	*7,077,023*	*R*	*53.4%*	*45.6%*	*53.9%*	*46.1%*

PRESIDENT 1984

In New York the Republican figures include Conservative votes and the Democratic figures include Liberal votes.

In Minnesota the Republican candidates appear on the ballot as Independent-Republican, the Democratic as Democratic-Farmer-Labor. In many states various non-major party candidates appeared on the ballot with variations of the party designations, were listed as "Independent" or "Non-Party," or were carried with entirely different party labels.

The Workers World candidate for president was Gavrielle Holmes in Ohio and Rhode Island; in several states minor party vice-presidential candidates were different from those listed below.

The full list of candidates for president and vice president was:

54,455,075	Ronald Reagan and George Bush	Republican
37,577,185	Walter F. Mondale and Geraldine A. Ferraro	Democratic
228,314	David Bergland and James A. Lewis	Libertarian
78,807	Lyndon H. LaRouche Jr. and Billy M. Davis	Independent
72,200	Sonia Johnson and Richard Walton	Citizens
66,336	Bob Richards and Maureen Salaman	Populist
46,868	Dennis L. Serrette and Nancy Ross	Alliance
36,386	Gus Hall and Angela Davis	Communist
24,706	Mel Mason and Matilde Zimmermann	Socialist Workers
17,985	Larry Holmes and Gloria La Riva	Workers World
13,161	Delmar Dennis and Traves Brownlee	American
10,801	Ed Winn and Helen Halyard	Workers League
4,242	Earl F. Dodge and Warren C. Martin	Prohibition
1,486	John B. Anderson and Grace Pierce	National Unity
892	Gerald Baker and Ferris Alger	Big Deal
825	Arthur J. Lowery and Raymond L. Garland	United Sovereign Citizens

Notes: The candidates listed above are those who appeared on the ballot in at least one state. Where identified by state authorities, write-in votes for minor party candidates are credited to their total above. In addition to the votes listed above, 13,623 scattered write-in votes were reported from various states, and 3,950 votes were cast for "None of These Candidates" in Nevada.

UNITED STATES
PRESIDENT 1984

State	Electoral Vote Rep.	Dem.	Other	Total Vote	Republican	Democratic	Other	Plurality		Percentage Total Vote Rep.	Dem.	Major Vote Rep.	Dem.
Alabama	9			1,441,713	872,849	551,899	16,965	320,950	R	60.5%	38.3%	61.3%	38.7%
Alaska	3			207,605	138,377	62,007	7,221	76,370	R	66.7%	29.9%	69.1%	30.9%
Arizona	7			1,025,897	681,416	333,854	10,627	347,562	R	66.4%	32.5%	67.1%	32.9%
Arkansas	6			884,406	534,774	338,646	10,986	196,128	R	60.5%	38.3%	61.2%	38.8%
California	47			9,505,423	5,467,009	3,922,519	115,895	1,544,490	R	57.5%	41.3%	58.2%	41.8%
Colorado	8			1,295,380	821,817	454,975	18,588	366,842	R	63.4%	35.1%	64.4%	35.6%
Connecticut	8			1,466,900	890,877	569,597	6,426	321,280	R	60.7%	38.8%	61.0%	39.0%
Delaware	3			254,572	152,190	101,656	726	50,534	R	59.8%	39.9%	60.0%	40.0%
Florida	21			4,180,051	2,730,350	1,448,816	885	1,281,534	R	65.3%	34.7%	65.3%	34.7%
Georgia	12			1,776,120	1,068,722	706,628	770	362,094	R	60.2%	39.8%	60.2%	39.8%
Hawaii	4			335,846	185,050	147,154	3,642	37,896	R	55.1%	43.8%	55.7%	44.3%
Idaho	4			411,144	297,523	108,510	5,111	189,013	R	72.4%	26.4%	73.3%	26.7%
Illinois	24			4,819,088	2,707,103	2,086,499	25,486	620,604	R	56.2%	43.3%	56.5%	43.5%
Indiana	12			2,233,069	1,377,230	841,481	14,358	535,749	R	61.7%	37.7%	62.1%	37.9%
Iowa	8			1,319,805	703,088	605,620	11,097	97,468	R	53.3%	45.9%	53.7%	46.3%
Kansas	7			1,021,991	677,296	333,149	11,546	344,147	R	66.3%	32.6%	67.0%	33.0%
Kentucky	9			1,369,345	821,702	539,539	8,104	282,163	R	60.0%	39.4%	60.4%	39.6%
Louisiana	10			1,706,822	1,037,299	651,586	17,937	385,713	R	60.8%	38.2%	61.4%	38.6%
Maine	4			553,144	336,500	214,515	2,129	121,985	R	60.8%	38.8%	61.1%	38.9%
Maryland	10			1,675,873	879,918	787,935	8,020	91,983	R	52.5%	47.0%	52.8%	47.2%
Massachusetts	13			2,559,453	1,310,936	1,239,606	8,911	71,330	R	51.2%	48.4%	51.4%	48.6%
Michigan	20			3,801,658	2,251,571	1,529,638	20,449	721,933	R	59.2%	40.2%	59.5%	40.5%
Minnesota		10		2,084,449	1,032,603	1,036,364	15,482	3,761	D	49.5%	49.7%	49.9%	50.1%
Mississippi	7			941,104	582,377	352,192	6,535	230,185	R	61.9%	37.4%	62.3%	37.7%
Missouri	11			2,122,783	1,274,188	848,583	12	425,605	R	60.0%	40.0%	60.0%	40.0%
Montana	4			384,377	232,450	146,742	5,185	85,708	R	60.5%	38.2%	61.3%	38.7%
Nebraska	5			652,090	460,054	187,866	4,170	272,188	R	70.6%	28.8%	71.0%	29.0%
Nevada	4			286,667	188,770	91,655	6,242	97,115	R	65.8%	32.0%	67.3%	32.7%
New Hampshire	4			389,066	267,051	120,395	1,620	146,656	R	68.6%	30.9%	68.9%	31.1%
New Jersey	16			3,217,862	1,933,630	1,261,323	22,909	672,307	R	60.1%	39.2%	60.5%	39.5%
New Mexico	5			514,370	307,101	201,769	5,500	105,332	R	59.7%	39.2%	60.3%	39.7%
New York	36			6,806,810	3,664,763	3,119,609	22,438	545,154	R	53.8%	45.8%	54.0%	46.0%
North Carolina	13			2,175,361	1,346,481	824,287	4,593	522,194	R	61.9%	37.9%	62.0%	38.0%
North Dakota	3			308,971	200,336	104,429	4,206	95,907	R	64.8%	33.8%	65.7%	34.3%
Ohio	23			4,547,619	2,678,560	1,825,440	43,619	853,120	R	58.9%	40.1%	59.5%	40.5%
Oklahoma	8			1,255,676	861,530	385,080	9,066	476,450	R	68.6%	30.7%	69.1%	30.9%
Oregon	7			1,226,527	685,700	536,479	4,348	149,221	R	55.9%	43.7%	56.1%	43.9%
Pennsylvania	25			4,844,903	2,584,323	2,228,131	32,449	356,192	R	53.3%	46.0%	53.7%	46.3%
Rhode Island	4			410,492	212,080	197,106	1,306	14,974	R	51.7%	48.0%	51.8%	48.2%
South Carolina	8			968,529	615,539	344,459	8,531	271,080	R	63.6%	35.6%	64.1%	35.9%
South Dakota	3			317,867	200,267	116,113	1,487	84,154	R	63.0%	36.5%	63.3%	36.7%
Tennessee	11			1,711,994	990,212	711,714	10,068	278,498	R	57.8%	41.6%	58.2%	41.8%
Texas	29			5,397,571	3,433,428	1,949,276	14,867	1,484,152	R	63.6%	36.1%	63.8%	36.2%
Utah	5			629,656	469,105	155,369	5,182	313,736	R	74.5%	24.7%	75.1%	24.9%
Vermont	3			234,561	135,865	95,730	2,966	40,135	R	57.9%	40.8%	58.7%	41.3%
Virginia	12			2,146,635	1,337,078	796,250	13,307	540,828	R	62.3%	37.1%	62.7%	37.3%
Washington	10			1,883,910	1,051,670	807,352	24,888	244,318	R	55.8%	42.9%	56.6%	43.4%
West Virginia	6			735,742	405,483	328,125	2,134	77,358	R	55.1%	44.6%	55.3%	44.7%
Wisconsin	11			2,211,689	1,198,584	995,740	17,365	202,844	R	54.2%	45.0%	54.6%	45.4%
Wyoming	3			188,968	133,241	53,370	2,357	79,871	R	70.5%	28.2%	71.4%	28.6%
District of Columbia		3		211,288	29,009	180,408	1,871	151,399	D	13.7%	85.4%	13.9%	86.1%
Total	525	13		92,652,842	54,455,075	37,577,185	620,582	16,877,890	R	58.8%	40.6%	59.2%	40.8%

PRESIDENT 1980

In New York the Republican figures include Conservative votes. In many states various non-major party candidates appeared on the ballot with variations of the party designations, without any party designation, or with entirely different party names.

In several cases vice presidential nominees were different from those listed for most states. The Socialist Workers Party nominee for president varied from state to state.

43,904,153	Ronald Reagan and George Bush	Republican
35,483,883	Jimmy Carter and Walter F. Mondale	Democratic
5,720,060	John B. Anderson and Patrick J. Lucey	Independent
921,299	Edward E. Clark and David Koch	Libertarian
234,294	Barry Commoner and LaDonna Harris	Citizens
45,023	Gus Hall and Angela Davis	Communist
41,268	John R. Rarick and Eileen M. Shearer	American Independent
38,737	Clifton DeBerry and Matilde Zimmermann	Socialist Workers
32,327	Ellen McCormack and Carroll Driscoll	Right to Life
18,116	Maureen Smith and Elizabeth Barron	Peace and Freedom
13,300	Deirdre Griswold and Larry Holmes	Workers World
7,212	Benjamin C. Bubar and Earl F. Dodge	Statesman
6,898	David McReynolds and Diane Drufenbrock	Socialist
6,647	Percy L. Greaves and Frank L. Varnum	American
6,272	Andrew Pulley and Matilde Zimmermann	Socialist Workers
4,029	Richard Congress and Matilde Zimmermann	Socialist Workers
3,694	Kurt Lynen and Harry Kieve	Middle Class
1,718	Bill Gahres and J. F. Loughlin	Down With Lawyers
1,555	Frank W. Shelton and George E. Jackson	American
923	Martin E. Wendelken with no vice-presidential candidate	Independent
296	Harley McLain and Jewelie Goeller	Natural Peoples

Notes: In addition to the votes listed above, 13,185 scattered write-in votes were reported from various states, 6,139 votes were cast in Minnesota for American Party electors without designated national nominees, and 4,193 votes were cast for "None of These Candidates" in Nevada.

UNITED STATES
PRESIDENT 1980

State	Electoral Vote Rep.	Electoral Vote Dem.	Electoral Vote Other	Total Vote	Republican	Democratic	Other	Plurality		Percentage Total Vote Rep.	Percentage Total Vote Dem.	Major Vote Rep.	Major Vote Dem.
Alabama	9			1,341,929	654,192	636,730	51,007	17,462	R	48.8%	47.4%	50.7%	49.3%
Alaska	3			158,445	86,112	41,842	30,491	44,270	R	54.3%	26.4%	67.3%	32.7%
Arizona	6			873,945	529,688	246,843	97,414	282,845	R	60.6%	28.2%	68.2%	31.8%
Arkansas	6			837,582	403,164	398,041	36,377	5,123	R	48.1%	47.5%	50.3%	49.7%
California	45			8,587,063	4,524,858	3,083,661	978,544	1,441,197	R	52.7%	35.9%	59.5%	40.5%
Colorado	7			1,184,415	652,264	367,973	164,178	284,291	R	55.1%	31.1%	63.9%	36.1%
Connecticut	8			1,406,285	677,210	541,732	187,343	135,478	R	48.2%	38.5%	55.6%	44.4%
Delaware	3			235,900	111,252	105,754	18,894	5,498	R	47.2%	44.8%	51.3%	48.7%
Florida	17			3,686,930	2,046,951	1,419,475	220,504	627,476	R	55.5%	38.5%	59.1%	40.9%
Georgia		12		1,596,695	654,168	890,733	51,794	236,565	D	41.0%	55.8%	42.3%	57.7%
Hawaii		4		303,287	130,112	135,879	37,296	5,767	D	42.9%	44.8%	48.9%	51.1%
Idaho	4			437,431	290,699	110,192	36,540	180,507	R	66.5%	25.2%	72.5%	27.5%
Illinois	26			4,749,721	2,358,049	1,981,413	410,259	376,636	R	49.6%	41.7%	54.3%	45.7%
Indiana	13			2,242,033	1,255,656	844,197	142,180	411,459	R	56.0%	37.7%	59.8%	40.2%
Iowa	8			1,317,661	676,026	508,672	132,963	167,354	R	51.3%	38.6%	57.1%	42.9%
Kansas	7			979,795	566,812	326,150	86,833	240,662	R	57.9%	33.3%	63.5%	36.5%
Kentucky	9			1,294,627	635,274	616,417	42,936	18,857	R	49.1%	47.6%	50.8%	49.2%
Louisiana	10			1,548,591	792,853	708,453	47,285	84,400	R	51.2%	45.7%	52.8%	47.2%
Maine	4			523,011	238,522	220,974	63,515	17,548	R	45.6%	42.3%	51.9%	48.1%
Maryland		10		1,540,496	680,606	726,161	133,729	45,555	D	44.2%	47.1%	48.4%	51.6%
Massachusetts	14			2,524,298	1,057,631	1,053,802	412,865	3,829	R	41.9%	41.7%	50.1%	49.9%
Michigan	21			3,909,725	1,915,225	1,661,532	332,968	253,693	R	49.0%	42.5%	53.5%	46.5%
Minnesota		10		2,051,980	873,268	954,174	224,538	80,906	D	42.6%	46.5%	47.8%	52.2%
Mississippi	7			892,620	441,089	429,281	22,250	11,808	R	49.4%	48.1%	50.7%	49.3%
Missouri	12			2,099,824	1,074,181	931,182	94,461	142,999	R	51.2%	44.3%	53.6%	46.4%
Montana	4			363,952	206,814	118,032	39,106	88,782	R	56.8%	32.4%	63.7%	36.3%
Nebraska	5			640,854	419,937	166,851	54,066	253,086	R	65.5%	26.0%	71.6%	28.4%
Nevada	3			247,885	155,017	66,666	26,202	88,351	R	62.5%	26.9%	69.9%	30.1%
New Hampshire	4			383,990	221,705	108,864	53,421	112,841	R	57.7%	28.4%	67.1%	32.9%
New Jersey	17			2,975,684	1,546,557	1,147,364	281,763	399,193	R	52.0%	38.6%	57.4%	42.6%
New Mexico	4			456,971	250,779	167,826	38,366	82,953	R	54.9%	36.7%	59.9%	40.1%
New York	41			6,201,959	2,893,831	2,728,372	579,756	165,459	R	46.7%	44.0%	51.5%	48.5%
North Carolina	13			1,855,833	915,018	875,635	65,180	39,383	R	49.3%	47.2%	51.1%	48.9%
North Dakota	3			301,545	193,695	79,189	28,661	114,506	R	64.2%	26.3%	71.0%	29.0%
Ohio	25			4,283,603	2,206,545	1,752,414	324,644	454,131	R	51.5%	40.9%	55.7%	44.3%
Oklahoma	8			1,149,708	695,570	402,026	52,112	293,544	R	60.5%	35.0%	63.4%	36.6%
Oregon	6			1,181,516	571,044	456,890	153,582	114,154	R	48.3%	38.7%	55.6%	44.4%
Pennsylvania	27			4,561,501	2,261,872	1,937,540	362,089	324,332	R	49.6%	42.5%	53.9%	46.1%
Rhode Island		4		416,072	154,793	198,342	62,937	43,549	D	37.2%	47.7%	43.8%	56.2%
South Carolina	8			894,071	441,841	430,385	21,845	11,456	R	49.4%	48.1%	50.7%	49.3%
South Dakota	4			327,703	198,343	103,855	25,505	94,488	R	60.5%	31.7%	65.6%	34.4%
Tennessee	10			1,617,616	787,761	783,051	46,804	4,710	R	48.7%	48.4%	50.1%	49.9%
Texas	26			4,541,636	2,510,705	1,881,147	149,784	629,558	R	55.3%	41.4%	57.2%	42.8%
Utah	4			604,222	439,687	124,266	40,269	315,421	R	72.8%	20.6%	78.0%	22.0%
Vermont	3			213,299	94,628	81,952	36,719	12,676	R	44.4%	38.4%	53.6%	46.4%
Virginia	12			1,866,032	989,609	752,174	124,249	237,435	R	53.0%	40.3%	56.8%	43.2%
Washington	9			1,742,394	865,244	650,193	226,957	215,051	R	49.7%	37.3%	57.1%	42.9%
West Virginia		6		737,715	334,206	367,462	36,047	33,256	D	45.3%	49.8%	47.6%	52.4%
Wisconsin	11			2,273,221	1,088,845	981,584	202,792	107,261	R	47.9%	43.2%	52.6%	47.4%
Wyoming	3			176,713	110,700	49,427	16,586	61,273	R	62.6%	28.0%	69.1%	30.9%
District of Columbia		3		175,237	23,545	131,113	20,579	107,568	D	13.4%	74.8%	15.2%	84.8%
Total	489	49		86,515,221	43,904,153	35,483,883	7,127,185	8,420,270	R	50.7%	41.0%	55.3%	44.7%

PRESIDENT 1976

In Washington one Republican elector voted in the electoral college for Ronald Reagan for president and Robert Dole for vice president.

In New York the Republican figures include Conservative votes, and the Democratic figures include Liberal votes; in Vermont the Democratic figures include votes cast on the Independent Vermonters Party ticket.

In many states various non-major party candidates appeared on the ballot with variations of the party designations and in several states with entirely different party names.

The ballot designations for electors for Eugene J. McCarthy for president varied from state to state, as did the names of vice-presidential candidates running with him. In New Jersey the Maddox vice-presidential candidate was Edmund O. Matzal.

The full list of candidates for president and vice president was:

40,830,763	Jimmy Carter and Walter F. Mondale	Democratic
39,147,793	Gerald R. Ford and Robert Dole	Republican
756,691	Eugene J. McCarthy with various vice-presidential candidates	Independent
173,011	Roger L. MacBride and David D. Bergland	Libertarian
170,531	Lester G. Maddox and William D. Dyke	American Independent
160,773	Thomas J. Anderson and Rufus Shackelford	American
91,314	Peter Camejo and Willie Mae Reid	Socialist Workers
58,992	Gus Hall and Jarvis Tyner	Communist
49,024	Margaret Wright and Benjamin Spock	People's
40,043	Lyndon H. LaRouche Jr. and R. W. Evans	United States Labor
15,934	Benjamin C. Bubar and Earl F. Dodge	Prohibition
9,616	Julius Levin and Constance Blomen	Socialist Labor
6,038	Frank P. Zeidler and J. Q. Brisben	Socialist
361	Ernest L. Miller and Roy N. Eddy	Restoration
36	Frank Taylor and Henry Swan	United American

Notes: In addition to the votes listed above, 39,861 scattered write-in votes were reported from various states, and 5,108 votes were cast for "None of These Candidates" in Nevada.

UNITED STATES
PRESIDENT 1976

| | Electoral Vote | | | | | | | | | Percentage | | | |
| | | | | Total | | | | | | Total Vote | | Major Vote | |
State	Rep.	Dem.	Other	Vote	Republican	Democratic	Other	Plurality		Rep.	Dem.	Rep.	Dem.
Alabama		9		1,182,850	504,070	659,170	19,610	155,100	D	42.6%	55.7%	43.3%	56.7%
Alaska	3			123,574	71,555	44,058	7,961	27,497	R	57.9%	35.7%	61.9%	38.1%
Arizona	6			742,719	418,642	295,602	28,475	123,040	R	56.4%	39.8%	58.6%	41.4%
Arkansas		6		767,535	267,903	498,604	1,028	230,701	D	34.9%	65.0%	35.0%	65.0%
California	45			7,867,117	3,882,244	3,742,284	242,589	139,960	R	49.3%	47.6%	50.9%	49.1%
Colorado	7			1,081,554	584,367	460,353	36,834	124,014	R	54.0%	42.6%	55.9%	44.1%
Connecticut	8			1,381,526	719,261	647,895	14,370	71,366	R	52.1%	46.9%	52.6%	47.4%
Delaware		3		235,834	109,831	122,596	3,407	12,765	D	46.6%	52.0%	47.3%	52.7%
Florida		17		3,150,631	1,469,531	1,636,000	45,100	166,469	D	46.6%	51.9%	47.3%	52.7%
Georgia		12		1,467,458	483,743	979,409	4,306	495,666	D	33.0%	66.7%	33.1%	66.9%
Hawaii		4		291,301	140,003	147,375	3,923	7,372	D	48.1%	50.6%	48.7%	51.3%
Idaho	4			344,071	204,151	126,549	13,371	77,602	R	59.3%	36.8%	61.7%	38.3%
Illinois	26			4,718,914	2,364,269	2,271,295	83,350	92,974	R	50.1%	48.1%	51.0%	49.0%
Indiana	13			2,220,362	1,183,958	1,014,714	21,690	169,244	R	53.3%	45.7%	53.8%	46.2%
Iowa	8			1,279,306	632,863	619,931	26,512	12,932	R	49.5%	48.5%	50.5%	49.5%
Kansas	7			957,845	502,752	430,421	24,672	72,331	R	52.5%	44.9%	53.9%	46.1%
Kentucky		9		1,167,142	531,852	615,717	19,573	83,865	D	45.6%	52.8%	46.3%	53.7%
Louisiana		10		1,278,439	587,446	661,365	29,628	73,919	D	46.0%	51.7%	47.0%	53.0%
Maine	4			483,216	236,320	232,279	14,617	4,041	R	48.9%	48.1%	50.4%	49.6%
Maryland		10		1,439,897	672,661	759,612	7,624	86,951	D	46.7%	52.8%	47.0%	53.0%
Massachusetts		14		2,547,558	1,030,276	1,429,475	87,807	399,199	D	40.4%	56.1%	41.9%	58.1%
Michigan	21			3,653,749	1,893,742	1,696,714	63,293	197,028	R	51.8%	46.4%	52.7%	47.3%
Minnesota		10		1,949,931	819,395	1,070,440	60,096	251,045	D	42.0%	54.9%	43.4%	56.6%
Mississippi		7		769,361	366,846	381,309	21,206	14,463	D	47.7%	49.6%	49.0%	51.0%
Missouri		12		1,953,600	927,443	998,387	27,770	70,944	D	47.5%	51.1%	48.2%	51.8%
Montana	4			328,734	173,703	149,259	5,772	24,444	R	52.8%	45.4%	53.8%	46.2%
Nebraska	5			607,668	359,705	233,692	14,271	126,013	R	59.2%	38.5%	60.6%	39.4%
Nevada	3			201,876	101,273	92,479	8,124	8,794	R	50.2%	45.8%	52.3%	47.7%
New Hampshire	4			339,618	185,935	147,635	6,048	38,300	R	54.7%	43.5%	55.7%	44.3%
New Jersey	17			3,014,472	1,509,688	1,444,653	60,131	65,035	R	50.1%	47.9%	51.1%	48.9%
New Mexico	4			418,409	211,419	201,148	5,842	10,271	R	50.5%	48.1%	51.2%	48.8%
New York		41		6,534,170	3,100,791	3,389,558	43,821	288,767	D	47.5%	51.9%	47.8%	52.2%
North Carolina		13		1,678,914	741,960	927,365	9,589	185,405	D	44.2%	55.2%	44.4%	55.6%
North Dakota	3			297,188	153,470	136,078	7,640	17,392	R	51.6%	45.8%	53.0%	47.0%
Ohio		25		4,111,873	2,000,505	2,011,621	99,747	11,116	D	48.7%	48.9%	49.9%	50.1%
Oklahoma	8			1,092,251	545,708	532,442	14,101	13,266	R	50.0%	48.7%	50.6%	49.4%
Oregon	6			1,029,876	492,120	490,407	47,349	1,713	R	47.8%	47.6%	50.1%	49.9%
Pennsylvania		27		4,620,787	2,205,604	2,328,677	86,506	123,073	D	47.7%	50.4%	48.6%	51.4%
Rhode Island		4		411,170	181,249	227,636	2,285	46,387	D	44.1%	55.4%	44.3%	55.7%
South Carolina		8		802,583	346,149	450,807	5,627	104,658	D	43.1%	56.2%	43.4%	56.6%
South Dakota	4			300,678	151,505	147,068	2,105	4,437	R	50.4%	48.9%	50.7%	49.3%
Tennessee		10		1,476,345	633,969	825,879	16,497	191,910	D	42.9%	55.9%	43.4%	56.6%
Texas		26		4,071,884	1,953,300	2,082,319	36,265	129,019	D	48.0%	51.1%	48.4%	51.6%
Utah	4			541,198	337,908	182,110	21,180	155,798	R	62.4%	33.6%	65.0%	35.0%
Vermont	3			187,765	102,085	80,954	4,726	21,131	R	54.4%	43.1%	55.8%	44.2%
Virginia	12			1,697,094	836,554	813,896	46,644	22,658	R	49.3%	48.0%	50.7%	49.3%
Washington	8		1	1,555,534	777,732	717,323	60,479	60,409	R	50.0%	46.1%	52.0%	48.0%
West Virginia		6		750,964	314,760	435,914	290	121,154	D	41.9%	58.0%	41.9%	58.1%
Wisconsin		11		2,104,175	1,004,987	1,040,232	58,956	35,245	D	47.8%	49.4%	49.1%	50.9%
Wyoming	3			156,343	92,717	62,239	1,387	30,478	R	59.3%	39.8%	59.8%	40.2%
District of Columbia		3		168,830	27,873	137,818	3,139	109,945	D	16.5%	81.6%	16.8%	83.2%
Total	240	297	1	81,555,889	39,147,793	40,830,763	1,577,333	1,682,970	D	48.0%	50.1%	48.9%	51.1%

PRESIDENT 1972

In Virginia one Republican elector voted in the electoral college for the Libertarian candidates for president and vice president.

In New York the Republican figures include Conservative votes, and the Democratic figures include Liberal votes. In Alabama the Democratic figures include votes cast on the National Democratic Party of Alabama ticket, and in South Carolina they include United Citizens Party votes.

In many states various non-major party candidates appeared on the ballot under party names other than those used below; for the Socialist Workers Party the votes listed for Jenness and Pulley were actually cast for substitute candidates (Reed and DeBerry) or without named candidates in several states.

The Democratic vice-presidential candidate originally was Sen. Thomas F. Eagleton; upon his withdrawal shortly after the party convention, R. Sargent Shriver was named by the Democratic National Committee as the candidate.

The full list of candidates for president and vice president was:

47,169,911	Richard M. Nixon and Spiro T. Agnew	Republican
29,170,383	George S. McGovern and R. Sargent Shriver	Democratic
1,099,482	John G. Schmitz and Thomas J. Anderson	American
78,756	Benjamin Spock and Julius Hobson	People's
66,677	Linda Jenness and Andrew Pulley	Socialist Workers
53,814	Louis Fisher and Genevieve Gunderson	Socialist Labor
25,595	Gus Hall and Jarvis Tyner	Communist
13,505	E. Harold Munn and Marshall E. Uncapher	Prohibition
3,673	John Hospers and Theodora Nathan	Libertarian
1,743	John V. Mahalchik and Irving Homer	America First
220	Gabriel Green and Daniel Fry	Universal

Notes: In addition to the votes listed above, 34,795 scattered write-in votes were reported from various states. Vice President Agnew resigned in October 1973 and Rep. Gerald R. Ford of Michigan was nominated by President Nixon to fill the vacancy. In November (Senate) and December (House of Representatives) this action was approved by Congress. In August 1974 President Nixon resigned and was succeeded by Vice President Ford. In the same month Nelson A. Rockefeller, former governor of New York, was nominated to be vice president and was confirmed by Congress in December 1974.

UNITED STATES
PRESIDENT 1972

State	Electoral Vote Rep.	Electoral Vote Dem.	Electoral Vote Other	Total Vote	Republican	Democratic	Other	Plurality		Percentage Total Vote Rep.	Percentage Total Vote Dem.	Percentage Major Vote Rep.	Percentage Major Vote Dem.
Alabama	9			1,006,111	728,701	256,923	20,487	471,778	R	72.4%	25.5%	73.9%	26.1%
Alaska	3			95,219	55,349	32,967	6,903	22,382	R	58.1%	34.6%	62.7%	37.3%
Arizona	6			622,926	402,812	198,540	21,574	204,272	R	64.7%	31.9%	67.0%	33.0%
Arkansas	6			651,320	448,541	199,892	2,887	248,649	R	68.9%	30.7%	69.2%	30.8%
California	45			8,367,862	4,602,096	3,475,847	289,919	1,126,249	R	55.0%	41.5%	57.0%	43.0%
Colorado	7			953,884	597,189	329,980	26,715	267,209	R	62.6%	34.6%	64.4%	35.6%
Connecticut	8			1,384,277	810,763	555,498	18,016	255,265	R	58.6%	40.1%	59.3%	40.7%
Delaware	3			235,516	140,357	92,283	2,876	48,074	R	59.6%	39.2%	60.3%	39.7%
Florida	17			2,583,283	1,857,759	718,117	7,407	1,139,642	R	71.9%	27.8%	72.1%	27.9%
Georgia	12			1,174,772	881,496	289,529	3,747	591,967	R	75.0%	24.6%	75.3%	24.7%
Hawaii	4			270,274	168,865	101,409		67,456	R	62.5%	37.5%	62.5%	37.5%
Idaho	4			310,379	199,384	80,826	30,169	118,558	R	64.2%	26.0%	71.2%	28.8%
Illinois	26			4,723,236	2,788,179	1,913,472	21,585	874,707	R	59.0%	40.5%	59.3%	40.7%
Indiana	13			2,125,529	1,405,154	708,568	11,807	696,586	R	66.1%	33.3%	66.5%	33.5%
Iowa	8			1,225,944	706,207	496,206	23,531	210,001	R	57.6%	40.5%	58.7%	41.3%
Kansas	7			916,095	619,812	270,287	25,996	349,525	R	67.7%	29.5%	69.6%	30.4%
Kentucky	9			1,067,499	676,446	371,159	19,894	305,287	R	63.4%	34.8%	64.6%	35.4%
Louisiana	10			1,051,491	686,852	298,142	66,497	388,710	R	65.3%	28.4%	69.7%	30.3%
Maine	4			417,042	256,458	160,584		95,874	R	61.5%	38.5%	61.5%	38.5%
Maryland	10			1,353,812	829,305	505,781	18,726	323,524	R	61.3%	37.4%	62.1%	37.9%
Massachusetts		14		2,458,756	1,112,078	1,332,540	14,138	220,462	D	45.2%	54.2%	45.5%	54.5%
Michigan	21			3,489,727	1,961,721	1,459,435	68,571	502,286	R	56.2%	41.8%	57.3%	42.7%
Minnesota	10			1,741,652	898,269	802,346	41,037	95,923	R	51.6%	46.1%	52.8%	47.2%
Mississippi	7			645,963	505,125	126,782	14,056	378,343	R	78.2%	19.6%	79.9%	20.1%
Missouri	12			1,855,803	1,153,852	697,147	4,804	456,705	R	62.2%	37.6%	62.3%	37.7%
Montana	4			317,603	183,976	120,197	13,430	63,779	R	57.9%	37.8%	60.5%	39.5%
Nebraska	5			576,289	406,298	169,991		236,307	R	70.5%	29.5%	70.5%	29.5%
Nevada	3			181,766	115,750	66,016		49,734	R	63.7%	36.3%	63.7%	36.3%
New Hampshire	4			334,055	213,724	116,435	3,896	97,289	R	64.0%	34.9%	64.7%	35.3%
New Jersey	17			2,997,229	1,845,502	1,102,211	49,516	743,291	R	61.6%	36.8%	62.6%	37.4%
New Mexico	4			386,241	235,606	141,084	9,551	94,522	R	61.0%	36.5%	62.5%	37.5%
New York	41			7,165,919	4,192,778	2,951,084	22,057	1,241,694	R	58.5%	41.2%	58.7%	41.3%
North Carolina	13			1,518,612	1,054,889	438,705	25,018	616,184	R	69.5%	28.9%	70.6%	29.4%
North Dakota	3			280,514	174,109	100,384	6,021	73,725	R	62.1%	35.8%	63.4%	36.6%
Ohio	25			4,094,787	2,441,827	1,558,889	94,071	882,938	R	59.6%	38.1%	61.0%	39.0%
Oklahoma	8			1,029,900	759,025	247,147	23,728	511,878	R	73.7%	24.0%	75.4%	24.6%
Oregon	6			927,946	486,686	392,760	48,500	93,926	R	52.4%	42.3%	55.3%	44.7%
Pennsylvania	27			4,592,106	2,714,521	1,796,951	80,634	917,570	R	59.1%	39.1%	60.2%	39.8%
Rhode Island	4			415,808	220,383	194,645	780	25,738	R	53.0%	46.8%	53.1%	46.9%
South Carolina	8			673,960	477,044	186,824	10,092	290,220	R	70.8%	27.7%	71.9%	28.1%
South Dakota	4			307,415	166,476	139,945	994	26,531	R	54.2%	45.5%	54.3%	45.7%
Tennessee	10			1,201,182	813,147	357,293	30,742	455,854	R	67.7%	29.7%	69.5%	30.5%
Texas	26			3,471,281	2,298,896	1,154,289	18,096	1,144,607	R	66.2%	33.3%	66.6%	33.4%
Utah	4			478,476	323,643	126,284	28,549	197,359	R	67.6%	26.4%	71.9%	28.1%
Vermont	3			186,947	117,149	68,174	1,624	48,975	R	62.7%	36.5%	63.2%	36.8%
Virginia	11		1	1,457,019	988,493	438,887	29,639	549,606	R	67.8%	30.1%	69.3%	30.7%
Washington	9			1,470,847	837,135	568,334	65,378	268,801	R	56.9%	38.6%	59.6%	40.4%
West Virginia	6			762,399	484,964	277,435		207,529	R	63.6%	36.4%	63.6%	36.4%
Wisconsin	11			1,852,890	989,430	810,174	53,286	179,256	R	53.4%	43.7%	55.0%	45.0%
Wyoming	3			145,570	100,464	44,358	748	56,106	R	69.0%	30.5%	69.4%	30.6%
District of Columbia		3		163,421	35,226	127,627	568	92,401	D	21.6%	78.1%	21.6%	78.4%
Total	520	17	1	77,718,554	47,169,911	29,170,383	1,378,260	17,999,528	R	60.7%	37.5%	61.8%	38.2%

PRESIDENT 1968

In North Carolina one Republican elector voted in the electoral college for the American Independent candidates for president and vice president.

In New York the Democratic figure includes Liberal votes, and in Alabama the Democratic vote is the total of the Alabama Independent Democratic and National Democratic Party of Alabama vote. In many states various non-major party candidates appeared on the ballot with variations of the party designations, and n most states the vice-presidential candidate of the American Independent party was listed as Marvin Griffin rather than Curtis E. LeMay.

The full list of candidates for president and vice president was:

31,785,480	Richard M. Nixon and Spiro T. Agnew	Republican
31,275,166	Hubert H. Humphrey and Edmund S. Muskie	Democratic
9,906,473	George C. Wallace and Curtis E. LeMay	American Independent
52,588	Henning A. Blomen and George S. Taylor	Socialist Labor
47,133	Dick Gregory	Peace and Freedom, with various vice-presidential candidates
41,388	Fred Halstead and Paul Boutelle	Socialist Workers
36,563	Eldridge Cleaver	Peace and Freedom, with various vice-presidential candidates
25,552	Eugene J. McCarthy	Under various titles and written-in, but without indication of vice-presidential candidates
15,123	E. Harold Munn and Rolland E. Fisher	Prohibition
1,519	Ventura Chavez and Adelicio Moya	People's Constitutional
1,075	Charlene Mitchell and Michael Zagarell	Communist
142	James Hensley and Roscoe B. MacKenna	Universal
34	Richard K. Troxell and Merle Thayer	Constitution
7	Kent M. Soeters and James P. Powers	Berkeley Defense Group

Notes: In addition to the votes listed above, 11,192 scattered write-in votes were reported from various states, and 12,430 were cast for elector tickets for which there were no formal presidential or vice-presidential candidates. In the vote listed above for Eldridge Cleaver, two states are included (California and Utah) in which only the party vice-presidential candidate appeared on the ballot.

UNITED STATES
PRESIDENT 1968

State	Electoral Vote Rep.	Dem.	Other	Total Vote	Republican	Democratic	American Independent	Other	Plurality		Rep.	Dem.	Amer. Ind.
Alabama			10	1,049,922	146,923	196,579	691,425	14,995	494,846	A	14.0%	18.7%	65.9%
Alaska	3			83,035	37,600	35,411	10,024		2,189	R	45.3%	42.6%	12.1%
Arizona	5			486,936	266,721	170,514	46,573	3,128	96,207	R	54.8%	35.0%	9.6%
Arkansas			6	619,969	190,759	188,228	240,982		50,223	A	30.8%	30.4%	38.9%
California	40			7,251,587	3,467,664	3,244,318	487,270	52,335	223,346	R	47.8%	44.7%	6.7%
Colorado	6			811,199	409,345	335,174	60,813	5,867	74,171	R	50.5%	41.3%	7.5%
Connecticut		8		1,256,232	556,721	621,561	76,650	1,300	64,840	D	44.3%	49.5%	6.1%
Delaware	3			214,367	96,714	89,194	28,459		7,520	R	45.1%	41.6%	13.3%
Florida	14			2,187,805	886,804	676,794	624,207		210,010	R	40.5%	30.9%	28.5%
Georgia			12	1,250,266	380,111	334,440	535,550	165	155,439	A	30.4%	26.7%	42.8%
Hawaii				236,218	91,425	141,324	3,469		49,899	D	38.7%	59.8%	1.5%
Idaho	4	4		291,183	165,369	89,273	36,541		76,096	R	56.8%	30.7%	12.5%
Illinois	26			4,619,749	2,174,774	2,039,814	390,958	14,203	134,960	R	47.1%	44.2%	8.5%
Indiana	13			2,123,597	1,067,885	806,659	243,108	5,945	261,226	R	50.3%	38.0%	11.4%
Iowa	9			1,167,931	619,106	476,699	66,422	5,704	142,407	R	53.0%	40.8%	5.7%
Kansas	7			872,783	478,674	302,996	88,921	2,192	175,678	R	54.8%	34.7%	10.2%
Kentucky	9			1,055,893	462,411	397,541	193,098	2,843	64,870	R	43.8%	37.6%	18.3%
Louisiana			10	1,097,450	257,535	309,615	530,300		220,685	A	23.5%	28.2%	48.3%
Maine		4		392,936	169,254	217,312	6,370		48,058	D	43.1%	55.3%	1.6%
Maryland		10		1,235,039	517,995	538,310	178,734		20,315	D	41.9%	43.6%	14.5%
Massachusetts		14		2,331,752	766,844	1,469,218	87,088	8,602	702,374	D	32.9%	63.0%	3.7%
Michigan		21		3,306,250	1,370,665	1,593,082	331,968	10,535	222,417	D	41.5%	48.2%	10.0%
Minnesota		10		1,588,506	658,643	857,738	68,931	3,194	199,095	D	41.5%	54.0%	4.3%
Mississippi			7	654,509	88,516	150,644	415,349		264,705	A	13.5%	23.0%	63.5%
Missouri	12			1,809,502	811,932	791,444	206,126		20,488	R	44.9%	43.7%	11.4%
Montana	4			274,404	138,835	114,117	20,015	1,437	24,718	R	50.6%	41.6%	7.3%
Nebraska	5			536,851	321,163	170,784	44,904		150,379	R	59.8%	31.8%	8.4%
Nevada	3			154,218	73,188	60,598	20,432		12,590	R	47.5%	39.3%	13.2%
New Hampshire	4			297,298	154,903	130,589	11,173	633	24,314	R	52.1%	43.9%	3.8%
New Jersey	17			2,875,395	1,325,467	1,264,206	262,187	23,535	61,261	R	46.1%	44.0%	9.1%
New Mexico	4			327,350	169,692	130,081	25,737	1,840	39,611	R	51.8%	39.7%	7.9%
New York		43		6,791,688	3,007,932	3,378,470	358,864	46,422	370,538	D	44.3%	49.7%	5.3%
North Carolina	12		1	1,587,493	627,192	464,113	496,188		131,004	R	39.5%	29.2%	31.3%
North Dakota	4			247,882	138,669	94,769	14,244	200	43,900	R	55.9%	38.2%	5.7%
Ohio	26			3,959,698	1,791,014	1,700,586	467,495	603	90,428	R	45.2%	42.9%	11.8%
Oklahoma	8			943,086	449,697	301,658	191,731		148,039	R	47.7%	32.0%	20.3%
Oregon	6			819,622	408,433	358,866	49,683	2,640	49,567	R	49.8%	43.8%	6.1%
Pennsylvania		29		4,747,928	2,090,017	2,259,405	378,582	19,924	169,388	D	44.0%	47.6%	8.0%
Rhode Island		4		385,000	122,359	246,518	15,678	445	124,159	D	31.8%	64.0%	4.1%
South Carolina	8			666,978	254,062	197,486	215,430		38,632	R	38.1%	29.6%	32.3%
South Dakota	4			281,264	149,841	118,023	13,400		31,818	R	53.3%	42.0%	4.8%
Tennessee	11			1,248,617	472,592	351,233	424,792		47,800	R	37.8%	28.1%	34.0%
Texas		25		3,079,216	1,227,844	1,266,804	584,269	299	38,960	D	39.9%	41.1%	19.0%
Utah	4			422,568	238,728	156,665	26,906	269	82,063	R	56.5%	37.1%	6.4%
Vermont	3			161,404	85,142	70,255	5,104	903	14,887	R	52.8%	43.5%	3.2%
Virginia	12			1,361,491	590,319	442,387	321,833	6,952	147,932	R	43.4%	32.5%	23.6%
Washington		9		1,304,281	588,510	616,037	96,990	2,744	27,527	D	45.1%	47.2%	7.4%
West Virginia		7		754,206	307,555	374,091	72,560		66,536	D	40.8%	49.6%	9.6%
Wisconsin	12			1,691,538	809,997	748,804	127,835	4,902	61,193	R	47.9%	44.3%	7.6%
Wyoming	3			127,205	70,927	45,173	11,105		25,754	R	55.8%	35.5%	8.7%
District of Columbia		3		170,578	31,012	139,566			108,554	D	18.2%	81.8%	
Total	*301*	*191*	*46*	*73,211,875*	*31,785,480*	*31,275,166*	*9,906,473*	*244,756*	*510,314*	*R*	*43.4%*	*42.7%*	*13.5%*

PRESIDENT 1964

In New York the Democratic figure includes Liberal votes.

The full list of candidates for president and vice president was:

43,129,566	Lyndon B. Johnson and Hubert H. Humphrey	Democratic
27,178,188	Barry M. Goldwater and William E. Miller	Republican
45,219	Eric Hass and Henning A. Blomen	Socialist Labor
32,720	Clifton DeBerry and Edward Shaw	Socialist Workers
23,267	E. Harold Munn and Mark R. Shaw	Prohibition
6,953	John Kasper and J. B. Stoner	National States Rights
5,060	Joseph B. Lightburn and T. C. Billings	Constitution
19	James Hensley and John O. Hopkins	Universal

Notes: In addition to the votes listed above, 12,868 scattered write-in votes were reported from various states, and 210,732 votes were cast in Alabama for an unpledged Democratic elector ticket.

UNITED STATES
PRESIDENT 1964

State	Electoral Vote Rep.	Dem.	Other	Total Vote	Republican	Democratic	Other	Plurality		Percentage Total Vote Rep.	Dem.	Major Vote Rep.	Dem.
Alabama	10			689,818	479,085		210,733	479,085	R	69.5%		100.0%	
Alaska		3		67,259	22,930	44,329		21,399	D	34.1%	65.9%	34.1%	65.9%
Arizona	5			480,770	242,535	237,753	482	4,782	R	50.4%	49.5%	50.5%	49.5%
Arkansas		6		560,426	243,264	314,197	2,965	70,933	D	43.4%	56.1%	43.6%	56.4%
California		40		7,057,586	2,879,108	4,171,877	6,601	1,292,769	D	40.8%	59.1%	40.8%	59.2%
Colorado		6		776,986	296,767	476,024	4,195	179,257	D	38.2%	61.3%	38.4%	61.6%
Connecticut		8		1,218,578	390,996	826,269	1,313	435,273	D	32.1%	67.8%	32.1%	67.9%
Delaware		3		201,320	78,078	122,704	538	44,626	D	38.8%	60.9%	38.9%	61.1%
Florida		14		1,854,481	905,941	948,540		42,599	D	48.9%	51.1%	48.9%	51.1%
Georgia	12			1,139,335	616,584	522,556	195	94,028	R	54.1%	45.9%	54.1%	45.9%
Hawaii		4		207,271	44,022	163,249		119,227	D	21.2%	78.8%	21.2%	78.8%
Idaho		4		292,477	143,557	148,920		5,363	D	49.1%	50.9%	49.1%	50.9%
Illinois		26		4,702,841	1,905,946	2,796,833	62	890,887	D	40.5%	59.5%	40.5%	59.5%
Indiana		13		2,091,606	911,118	1,170,848	9,640	259,730	D	43.6%	56.0%	43.8%	56.2%
Iowa		9		1,184,539	449,148	733,030	2,361	283,882	D	37.9%	61.9%	38.0%	62.0%
Kansas		7		857,901	386,579	464,028	7,294	77,449	D	45.1%	54.1%	45.4%	54.6%
Kentucky		9		1,046,105	372,977	669,659	3,469	296,682	D	35.7%	64.0%	35.8%	64.2%
Louisiana	10			896,293	509,225	387,068		122,157	R	56.8%	43.2%	56.8%	43.2%
Maine		4		380,965	118,701	262,264		143,563	D	31.2%	68.8%	31.2%	68.8%
Maryland		10		1,116,457	385,495	730,912	50	345,417	D	34.5%	65.5%	34.5%	65.5%
Massachusetts		14		2,344,798	549,727	1,786,422	8,649	1,236,695	D	23.4%	76.2%	23.5%	76.5%
Michigan		21		3,203,102	1,060,152	2,136,615	6,335	1,076,463	D	33.1%	66.7%	33.2%	66.8%
Minnesota		10		1,554,462	559,624	991,117	3,721	431,493	D	36.0%	63.8%	36.1%	63.9%
Mississippi	7			409,146	356,528	52,618		303,910	R	87.1%	12.9%	87.1%	12.9%
Missouri		12		1,817,879	653,535	1,164,344		510,809	D	36.0%	64.0%	36.0%	64.0%
Montana		4		278,628	113,032	164,246	1,350	51,214	D	40.6%	58.9%	40.8%	59.2%
Nebraska		5		584,154	276,847	307,307		30,460	D	47.4%	52.6%	47.4%	52.6%
Nevada		3		135,433	56,094	79,339		23,245	D	41.4%	58.6%	41.4%	58.6%
New Hampshire		4		288,093	104,029	184,064		80,035	D	36.1%	63.9%	36.1%	63.9%
New Jersey		17		2,847,663	964,174	1,868,231	15,258	904,057	D	33.9%	65.6%	34.0%	66.0%
New Mexico		4		328,645	132,838	194,015	1,792	61,177	D	40.4%	59.0%	40.6%	59.4%
New York		43		7,166,275	2,243,559	4,913,102	9,614	2,669,543	D	31.3%	68.6%	31.3%	68.7%
North Carolina		13		1,424,983	624,844	800,139		175,295	D	43.8%	56.2%	43.8%	56.2%
North Dakota		4		258,389	108,207	149,784	398	41,577	D	41.9%	58.0%	41.9%	58.1%
Ohio		26		3,969,196	1,470,865	2,498,331		1,027,466	D	37.1%	62.9%	37.1%	62.9%
Oklahoma		8		932,499	412,665	519,834		107,169	D	44.3%	55.7%	44.3%	55.7%
Oregon		6		786,305	282,779	501,017	2,509	218,238	D	36.0%	63.7%	36.1%	63.9%
Pennsylvania		29		4,822,690	1,673,657	3,130,954	18,079	1,457,297	D	34.7%	64.9%	34.8%	65.2%
Rhode Island		4		390,091	74,615	315,463	13	240,848	D	19.1%	80.9%	19.1%	80.9%
South Carolina	8			524,779	309,048	215,723	8	93,325	R	58.9%	41.1%	58.9%	41.1%
South Dakota		4		293,118	130,108	163,010		32,902	D	44.4%	55.6%	44.4%	55.6%
Tennessee		11		1,143,946	508,965	634,947	34	125,982	D	44.5%	55.5%	44.5%	55.5%
Texas		25		2,626,811	958,566	1,663,185	5,060	704,619	D	36.5%	63.3%	36.6%	63.4%
Utah		4		401,413	181,785	219,628		37,843	D	45.3%	54.7%	45.3%	54.7%
Vermont		3		163,089	54,942	108,127	20	53,185	D	33.7%	66.3%	33.7%	66.3%
Virginia		12		1,042,267	481,334	558,038	2,895	76,704	D	46.2%	53.5%	46.3%	53.7%
Washington		9		1,258,556	470,366	779,881	8,309	309,515	D	37.4%	62.0%	37.6%	62.4%
West Virginia		7		792,040	253,953	538,087		284,134	D	32.1%	67.9%	32.1%	67.9%
Wisconsin		12		1,691,815	638,495	1,050,424	2,896	411,929	D	37.7%	62.1%	37.8%	62.2%
Wyoming		3		142,716	61,998	80,718		18,720	D	43.4%	56.6%	43.4%	56.6%
District of Columbia		3		198,597	28,801	169,796		140,995	D	14.5%	85.5%	14.5%	85.5%
Total	*52*	*486*		*70,644,592*	*27,178,188*	*43,129,566*	*336,838*	*15,951,378*	*D*	*38.5%*	*61.1%*	*38.7%*	*61.3%*

PRESIDENT 1960

Sen. Harry Flood Byrd received 15 votes for president in the electoral college; these were the votes of 6 of the 11 Democratic electors in Alabama, all 8 unpledged Democratic electors in Mississippi, and 1 of the 8 Republican electors in Oklahoma. The Alabama and Mississippi electors also cast 14 votes for Sen. Strom Thurmond for vice president; the single Oklahoma elector voted for Sen. Barry M. Goldwater for vice president.

In New York the Democratic figure includes Liberal votes.

The full list of candidates for president and vice president was:

34,226,731	John F. Kennedy and Lyndon B. Johnson	Democratic
34,108,157	Richard M. Nixon and Henry Cabot Lodge	Republican
47,522	Eric Hass and Georgia Cozzini	Socialist Labor
46,203	Rutherford L. Decker and E. Harold Munn	Prohibition
44,977	Orval E. Faubus and John G. Crommelin	National States Rights
40,165	Farrell Dobbs and Myra Tanner Weiss	Socialist Workers
18,162	Charles L. Sullivan and Merritt B. Curtis	Constitution
8,708	J. Bracken Lee and Kent H. Courtney	Conservative
4,204	C. Benton Coiner and Edward J. Silverman	Conservative
1,767	Lar Daly and B. M. Miller	Tax Cut
1,485	Clennon King and Reginald Carter	Independent Afro-American
1,401	Merritt B. Curtis and B. M. Miller	Constitution

Notes: In addition to the votes listed above, 2,378 scattered write-in votes were reported from various states, 169,572 votes were cast in Louisiana for Independent electors, and 116,248 votes were cast in Mississippi for an unpledged Democratic elector ticket. Another 539 votes were cast in Michigan for an Independent American ticket.

UNITED STATES
PRESIDENT 1960

State	Electoral Vote Rep.	Electoral Vote Dem.	Electoral Vote Other	Total Vote	Republican	Democratic	Other	Plurality		Total Vote Rep.	Total Vote Dem.	Major Vote Rep.	Major Vote Dem.
Alabama		5	6	570,225	237,981	324,050	8,194	86,069	D	41.7%	56.8%	42.3%	57.7%
Alaska	3			60,762	30,953	29,809		1,144	R	50.9%	49.1%	50.9%	49.1%
Arizona	4			398,491	221,241	176,781		44,460	R	55.5%	44.4%	55.6%	44.4%
Arkansas		8		428,509	184,508	215,049	28,952	30,541	D	43.1%	50.2%	46.2%	53.8%
California	32			6,506,578	3,259,722	3,224,099	22,757	35,623	R	50.1%	49.6%	50.3%	49.7%
Colorado	6			736,236	402,242	330,629	3,365	71,613	R	54.6%	44.9%	54.9%	45.1%
Connecticut		8		1,222,883	565,813	657,055	15	91,242	D	46.3%	53.7%	46.3%	53.7%
Delaware		3		196,683	96,373	99,590	720	3,217	D	49.0%	50.6%	49.2%	50.8%
Florida	10			1,544,176	795,476	748,700		46,776	R	51.5%	48.5%	51.5%	48.5%
Georgia		12		733,349	274,472	458,638	239	184,166	D	37.4%	62.5%	37.4%	62.6%
Hawaii		3		184,705	92,295	92,410		115	D	50.0%	50.0%	50.0%	50.0%
Idaho	4			300,450	161,597	138,853		22,744	R	53.8%	46.2%	53.8%	46.2%
Illinois		27		4,757,409	2,368,988	2,377,846	10,575	8,858	D	49.8%	50.0%	49.9%	50.1%
Indiana	13			2,135,360	1,175,120	952,358	7,882	222,762	R	55.0%	44.6%	55.2%	44.8%
Iowa	10			1,273,810	722,381	550,565	864	171,816	R	56.7%	43.2%	56.7%	43.3%
Kansas	8			928,825	561,474	363,213	4,138	198,261	R	60.4%	39.1%	60.7%	39.3%
Kentucky	10			1,124,462	602,607	521,855		80,752	R	53.6%	46.4%	53.6%	46.4%
Louisiana		10		807,891	230,980	407,339	169,572	176,359	D	28.6%	50.4%	36.2%	63.8%
Maine	5			421,767	240,608	181,159		59,449	R	57.0%	43.0%	57.0%	43.0%
Maryland		9		1,055,349	489,538	565,808	3	76,270	D	46.4%	53.6%	46.4%	53.6%
Massachusetts		16		2,469,480	976,750	1,487,174	5,556	510,424	D	39.6%	60.2%	39.6%	60.4%
Michigan		20		3,318,097	1,620,428	1,687,269	10,400	66,841	D	48.8%	50.9%	49.0%	51.0%
Minnesota		11		1,541,887	757,915	779,933	4,039	22,018	D	49.2%	50.6%	49.3%	50.7%
Mississippi			8	298,171	73,561	108,362	116,248	34,801	D	24.7%	36.3%	40.4%	59.6%
Missouri		13		1,934,422	962,221	972,201		9,980	D	49.7%	50.3%	49.7%	50.3%
Montana	4			277,579	141,841	134,891	847	6,950	R	51.1%	48.6%	51.3%	48.7%
Nebraska	6			613,095	380,553	232,542		148,011	R	62.1%	37.9%	62.1%	37.9%
Nevada		3		107,267	52,387	54,880		2,493	D	48.8%	51.2%	48.8%	51.2%
New Hampshire	4			295,761	157,989	137,772		20,217	R	53.4%	46.6%	53.4%	46.6%
New Jersey		16		2,773,111	1,363,324	1,385,415	24,372	22,091	D	49.2%	50.0%	49.6%	50.4%
New Mexico		4		311,107	153,733	156,027	1,347	2,294	D	49.4%	50.2%	49.6%	50.4%
New York		45		7,291,079	3,446,419	3,830,085	14,575	383,666	D	47.3%	52.5%	47.4%	52.6%
North Carolina		14		1,368,556	655,420	713,136		57,716	D	47.9%	52.1%	47.9%	52.1%
North Dakota	4			278,431	154,310	123,963	158	30,347	R	55.4%	44.5%	55.5%	44.5%
Ohio	25			4,161,859	2,217,611	1,944,248		273,363	R	53.3%	46.7%	53.3%	46.7%
Oklahoma	7		1	903,150	533,039	370,111		162,928	R	59.0%	41.0%	59.0%	41.0%
Oregon	6			776,421	408,060	367,402	959	40,658	R	52.6%	47.3%	52.6%	47.4%
Pennsylvania		32		5,006,541	2,439,956	2,556,282	10,303	116,326	D	48.7%	51.1%	48.8%	51.2%
Rhode Island		4		405,535	147,502	258,032	1	110,530	D	36.4%	63.6%	36.4%	63.6%
South Carolina		8		386,688	188,558	198,129	1	9,571	D	48.8%	51.2%	48.8%	51.2%
South Dakota	4			306,487	178,417	128,070		50,347	R	58.2%	41.8%	58.2%	41.8%
Tennessee	11			1,051,792	556,577	481,453	13,762	75,124	R	52.9%	45.8%	53.6%	46.4%
Texas		24		2,311,084	1,121,310	1,167,567	22,207	46,257	D	48.5%	50.5%	49.0%	51.0%
Utah	4			374,709	205,361	169,248	100	36,113	R	54.8%	45.2%	54.8%	45.2%
Vermont	3			167,324	98,131	69,186	7	28,945	R	58.6%	41.3%	58.6%	41.4%
Virginia	12			771,449	404,521	362,327	4,601	42,194	R	52.4%	47.0%	52.8%	47.2%
Washington	9			1,241,572	629,273	599,298	13,001	29,975	R	50.7%	48.3%	51.2%	48.8%
West Virginia		8		837,781	395,995	441,786		45,791	D	47.3%	52.7%	47.3%	52.7%
Wisconsin	12			1,729,082	895,175	830,805	3,102	64,370	R	51.8%	48.0%	51.9%	48.1%
Wyoming	3			140,782	77,451	63,331		14,120	R	55.0%	45.0%	55.0%	45.0%
Total	219	303	15	68,838,219	34,108,157	34,226,731	503,331	118,574	D	49.5%	49.7%	49.9%	50.1%

2008 PRESIDENTIAL PRIMARIES

In 2008, 40 states and the District of Columbia held presidential primaries, in which at least one of the parties held contests where voters balloted directly for candidates or for a statewide slate of delegates that was pledged to a candidate. The Democratic presidential primary in Puerto Rico in June 2008 is not included. The list is limited to those jurisdictions that vote for president in November—namely, the 50 states and the District of Columbia. States not listed in this table held a caucus rather than a primary.

At the time they were held, the January Democratic primaries in Florida and Michigan were not sanctioned by the Democratic National Committee (DNC) and were not allowed to elect delegates. Only New Hampshire and South Carolina were permitted by DNC rules to hold their 2008 primaries in January, although the contests in Florida and Michigan proceeded anyway.

The list below, alphabetical by state, gives primary vote totals for all candidates who were listed on the ballot or received write-in votes. The tables on pages 49–52 give a chronological summary of the primary votes for those candidates in the Democratic and Republican parties who received at least 200,000 votes nationwide.

Republican candidates on the ballot in at least one primary were: Sam Brownback, Michael Burzynski, Hugh Cort, John H. Cox, Jerry Curry, H. Neal Fendig Jr., John Michael Fitzpatrick, Bob Forthan, Daniel Gilbert, Rudolph Giuliani, Albert Howard, Mike Huckabee, Duncan Hunter, Alan Keyes, Mark Klein, Stephen W. Marchuk, John McCain, Frank McEnulty, John R. McGrath, James Creighton Mitchell Jr., Sean "Cf" Murphy, Cornelius Edward O'Connor, Rick Outzen, Ron Paul, Mitt Romney, David Ruben, Michael P. Shaw, Jack Shepard, Charles Skelley, Rhett R. Smith, Vermin Supreme, Tom Tancredo, Fred Thompson, Hoa Tran, Virgil L.R.Wiles, Vern Wuensche.

Democratic candidates on the ballot in at least one primary were: Joseph R. Biden Jr., Peter "Simon" Bollander, Richard Edward Caligiuri, William Campbell, Kenneth A. Capalbo, Hillary Rodham Clinton, Randy Crow, Orion Daley, Edward Dobson, Christopher J. Dodd, John Edwards, Loti Gest, Mike Gravel, Richardson Grayson, Tish Haymer, Henry Hewes, Libby Hubbard, William C. Hughes, D.R. Hunter, Keith Russell Judd, William "Bill" Keefe, Caroline P. Killeen, Tom Koos, Karl Krueger, Dennis J. Kucinich, Dal LaMagna, Tom Laughlin, Rich Lee, Frank Lynch, Leland Montell, Michael Oatman, Barack Obama, Bill Richardson, Jim Rogers, O. Savior, Chuck See, Michael Skok, Ralph Spelbring, Philip Tanner, Evelyn L. Vitullo, Sandy Whitehouse.

ALABAMA   February 5

Republican
227,766 Huckabee; 204,867 McCain; 98,019 Romney; 14,810 Paul; 2,134 Giuliani; 1,835 Thompson; 1,234 Uncommitted; 778 Keyes; 391 Hunter; 228 Cort; 93 Tancredo.

Democratic
300,319 Obama; 223,089 Clinton; 7,841 Edwards; 2,663 Uncommitted; 1,174 Biden; 1,017 Richardson; 523 Dodd.

ARIZONA   February 5

Republican
255,197 McCain; 186,838 Romney; 48,849 Huckabee; 22,692 Paul; 13,658 Giuliani; 9,492 Thompson; 1,082 Hunter; 970 Keyes; 490 McGrath; 333 McEnulty; 269 Murphy; 199 Fitzpatrick; 193 Mitchell; 104 Ruben; 98 Burzynski; 98 Curry; 78 Shepard; 75 Forthan; 62 Shaw; 58 Cort; 53 Gilbert; 53 Outzen; 50 Skelley; 44 Smith.

Democratic
229,501 Clinton; 193,126 Obama; 23,621 Edwards; 2,842 Richardson; 1,973 Kucinich; 632 Whitehouse; 484 Dodd; 398 Dobson; 340 Gravel; 322 Grayson; 291 Krueger; 249 See; 248 Campbell; 248 Lynch; 209 Hubbard; 192 Oatman; 162 Lee; 154 Bollander; 132 Vitullo; 130 Tanner; 107 Haymer; 98 Daley; 94 Montell; 82 Gest.

ARKANSAS   February 5

Republican
138,557 Huckabee; 46,343 McCain; 30,997 Romney; 10,983 Paul; 987 Uncommitted; 658 Giuliani; 628 Thompson.

Democratic
220,136 Clinton; 82,476 Obama; 5,873 Edwards; 3,398 Uncommitted; 810 Richardson; 515 Biden; 393 Kucinich; 325 Gravel; 308 Dodd.

CALIFORNIA   February 5

Republican
1,238,988 McCain; 1,013,471 Romney; 340,669 Huckabee; 128,681 Giuliani; 125,365 Paul; 50,275 Thompson; 14,021 Hunter; 11,742 Keyes; 3,884 Tancredo; 3,219 Cox; 2,486 Brownback; 6 Irish (write-in); 2 Shaw (write-in); 1 Marshall (write-in); 1 Neuberg (write-in).

2008 PRESIDENTIAL PRIMARIES

CALIFORNIA (continued)

Democratic   2,608,184 Clinton; 2,186,662 Obama; 193,617 Edwards; 24,126 Kucinich; 19,939 Richardson; 18,261 Biden; 8,184 Gravel; 8,005 Dodd; 4 Carter (write-in); 4 Hinzman (write-in); 3 Epstein (write-in); 2 Calef (write-in); 1 Frey (write-in); 1 McAndrew (write-in).

CONNECTICUT   February 5

Republican   78,836 McCain; 49,891 Romney; 10,607 Huckabee; 6,287 Paul; 2,470 Giuliani; 2,462 Uncommitted; 538 Thompson; 376 Keyes; 137 Hunter.

Democratic   179,742 Obama; 165,426 Clinton; 3,424 Edwards; 3,038 Uncommitted; 912 Dodd; 846 Kucinich; 440 Biden; 436 Richardson; 275 Gravel.

DELAWARE   February 5

Republican   22,628 McCain; 16,344 Romney; 7,706 Huckabee; 2,131 Paul; 1,255 Giuliani; 175 Tancredo.

Democratic   51,148 Obama; 40,760 Clinton; 2,863 Biden; 1,241 Edwards; 192 Kucinich; 170 Dodd.

DISTRICT OF COLUMBIA   February 12

Republican   4,198 McCain; 1,020 Huckabee; 494 Paul; 398 Romney; 101 Giuliani.

Democratic   93,386 Obama; 29,470 Clinton; 347 Edwards; 339 Uncommitted; 193 Kucinich; 145 Richardson; 114 scattered write-in.

FLORIDA   January 29

Republican   701,761 McCain; 604,932 Romney; 286,089 Giuliani; 262,681 Huckabee; 62,887 Paul; 22,668 Thompson; 4,060 Keyes; 2,847 Hunter; 1,573 Tancredo.

Democratic   870,986 Clinton; 576,214 Obama; 251,562 Edwards; 15,704 Biden; 14,999 Richardson; 9,703 Kucinich; 5,477 Dodd; 5,275 Gravel.

GEORGIA   February 5

Republican   326,874 Huckabee; 304,751 McCain; 290,707 Romney; 28,096 Paul; 7,162 Giuliani; 3,414 Thompson; 1,458 Keyes; 755 Hunter; 324 Tancredo.

Democratic   704,247 Obama; 330,026 Clinton; 18,209 Edwards; 2,538 Biden; 2,096 Kucinich; 1,879 Richardson; 952 Gravel; 904 Dodd.

IDAHO   May 27

Republican   87,460 McCain; 29,785 Paul; 8,325 None of the Names Shown.

Democratic   23,980 Obama; 16,122 Clinton; 1,966 None of the Names Shown; 734 Judd.

ILLINOIS   February 5

Republican   426,777 McCain; 257,265 Romney; 148,053 Huckabee; 45,055 Paul; 11,837 Giuliani; 7,259 Thompson; 2,318 Keyes; 483 Mitchell; 375 Tancredo.

Democratic   1,318,234 Obama; 667,930 Clinton; 39,719 Edwards; 4,234 Kucinich; 3,788 Biden; 3,538 Richardson; 1,171 Dodd.

2008 PRESIDENTIAL PRIMARIES

INDIANA May 6

Republican   320,318 McCain; 41,173 Huckabee; 31,612 Paul; 19,581 Romney.

Democratic   646,282 Clinton; 632,073 Obama.

KENTUCKY May 20

Republican   142,918 McCain; 16,388 Huckabee; 13,427 Paul; 10,755 Uncommitted; 9,206 Romney; 3,055 Giuliani; 2,044 Keyes.

Democratic   459,511 Clinton; 209,954 Obama; 18,091 Uncommitted; 14,212 Edwards.

LOUISIANA February 9

Republican   69,594 Huckabee; 67,551 McCain; 10,222 Romney; 8,590 Paul; 1,603 Thompson; 1,593 Giuliani; 837 Keyes; 521 Curry; 368 Hunter; 183 Gilbert; 107 Tancredo.

Democratic   220,632 Obama; 136,925 Clinton; 13,026 Edwards; 6,178 Biden; 4,257 Richardson; 1,924 Dodd; 1,404 Kucinich.

MARYLAND February 12

Republican   176,046 McCain; 91,608 Huckabee; 22,426 Romney; 19,196 Paul; 4,548 Giuliani; 3,386 Keyes; 2,901 Thompson; 522 Hunter; 356 Tancredo.

Democratic   532,665 Obama; 314,211 Clinton; 11,417 Uncommitted; 10,506 Edwards; 3,776 Biden; 2,098 Richardson; 1,909 Kucinich; 804 Gravel; 788 Dodd.

MASSACHUSETTS February 5

Republican   255,892 Romney; 204,779 McCain; 19,103 Huckabee; 13,251 Paul; 2,707 Giuliani; 1,959 No Preference; 916 Thompson; 258 Hunter; 153 Tancredo; 1,532 scattered write-in.

Democratic   705,185 Clinton; 511,680 Obama; 20,101 Edwards; 8,041 No Preference; 3,216 Biden; 2,992 Kucinich; 1,846 Richardson; 1,463 Gravel; 1,120 Dodd; 3,279 scattered write-in.

MICHIGAN January 15

Republican   338,316 Romney; 257,985 McCain; 139,764 Huckabee; 54,475 Paul; 32,159 Thompson; 24,725 Giuliani; 18,118 Uncommitted; 2,819 Hunter; 457 Tancredo; 351 Brownback.

Democratic   328,309 Clinton; 238,168 Uncommitted; 21,715 Kucinich; 3,845 Dodd; 2,361 Gravel.

MISSISSIPPI March 11

Republican   113,074 McCain; 17,943 Huckabee; 5,510 Paul; 2,177 Romney; 2,160 Thompson; 945 Giuliani; 842 Keyes; 414 Hunter; 221 Tancredo.

Democratic   265,502 Obama; 159,221 Clinton; 3,933 Edwards; 1,816 Biden; 1,396 Richardson; 912 Kucinich; 739 Dodd; 591 Gravel; 42 Undecided.

2008 PRESIDENTIAL PRIMARIES

MISSOURI   February 5

Republican   194,053 McCain; 185,642 Huckabee; 172,329 Romney; 26,464 Paul; 3,593 Giuliani; 3,102 Thompson; 2,097 Uncommitted; 892 Keyes; 307 Hunter; 124 Wiles; 107 Tancredo; 88 Gilbert; 46 Cort.

Democratic   406,917 Obama; 395,185 Clinton; 16,763 Edwards; 3,142 Uncommitted; 820 Kucinich; 689 Richardson; 626 Biden; 438 Gravel; 250 Dodd; 220 Spelbring.

MONTANA   June 3

Republican   72,791 McCain; 20,606 Paul; 2,333 No Preference.

Democratic   103,174 Obama; 74,889 Clinton; 4,358 No Preference.

NEBRASKA   May 13

Republican   118,876 McCain; 17,772 Paul.

Democratic   46,670 Obama; 43,979 Clinton; 3,886 Gravel.

NEW HAMPSHIRE   January 8

Republican   88,713 McCain; 75,675 Romney; 26,916 Huckabee; 20,344 Giuliani; 18,346 Paul; 2,956 Thompson; 1,192 Hunter; 205 Keyes; 127 Marchuk; 63 Tancredo; 46 O'Connor; 43 Howard; 43 Supreme; 39 Cox; 36 Wuensche; 35 Cort; 35 Gilbert; 28 Shepard; 26 Mitchell; 16 Klein; 13 Fendig; 4,896 scattered write-in.

Democratic   112,404 Clinton; 104,815 Obama; 48,699 Edwards; 13,269 Richardson; 3,891 Kucinich; 638 Biden; 404 Gravel; 253 Caligiuri; 205 Dodd; 108 Capalbo; 95 D.R. Hunter; 51 Keefe; 47 Laughlin; 37 Crow; 32 Skok; 30 Savior; 17 Hewes; 16 Hughes; 11 Killeen; 10 Koos; 8 LaMagna; 2,517 scattered write-in.

NEW JERSEY   February 5

Republican   313,459 McCain; 160,388 Romney; 46,284 Huckabee; 27,301 Paul; 15,516 Giuliani; 3,253 Thompson.

Democratic   613,500 Clinton; 501,372 Obama; 15,728 Edwards; 4,081 Biden; 3,366 Richardson; 3,152 Kucinich.

NEW MEXICO   June 3

Republican   95,378 McCain; 15,561 Paul.

Democratic   No presidential primary.

NEW YORK   February 5

Republican   333,001 McCain; 178,043 Romney; 68,477 Huckabee; 40,113 Paul; 23,260 Giuliani.

Democratic   1,068,496 Clinton; 751,019 Obama; 21,924 Edwards; 8,458 Kucinich; 8,227 Richardson; 4,321 Biden.

NORTH CAROLINA   May 6

Republican   383,085 McCain; 63,018 Huckabee; 37,260 Paul; 20,624 No Preference; 13,596 Keyes.

Democratic   887,391 Obama; 657,669 Clinton; 23,214 No Preference; 12,452 Gravel.

2008 PRESIDENTIAL PRIMARIES

OHIO   March 4

Republican   656,687 McCain; 335,356 Huckabee; 50,964 Paul; 36,031 Romney; 16,879 Thompson.

Democratic   1,259,620 Clinton; 1,055,769 Obama; 39,332 Edwards.

OKLAHOMA   February 5

Republican   122,772 McCain; 111,899 Huckabee; 83,030 Romney; 11,183 Paul; 2,412 Giuliani; 1,924 Thompson; 817 Keyes; 387 Curry; 317 Hunter; 189 Tancredo; 124 Gilbert.

Democratic   228,480 Clinton; 130,130 Obama; 42,725 Edwards; 7,078 Richardson; 3,905 Rogers; 2,511 Dodd; 2,378 Kucinich.

OREGON   May 20

Republican   285,881 McCain; 51,100 Paul; 16,495 scattered write-in.

Democratic   375,385 Obama; 259,825 Clinton; 6,289 scattered write-in.

PENNSYLVANIA   April 22

Republican   595,175 McCain; 129,323 Paul; 92,430 Huckabee.

Democratic   1,275,039 Clinton; 1,061,441 Obama.

RHODE ISLAND   March 4

Republican   17,480 McCain; 5,847 Huckabee; 1,777 Paul; 1,181 Romney; 570 Uncommitted; 117 Keyes; 24 Cort.

Democratic   108,949 Clinton; 75,316 Obama; 1,133 Edwards; 1,041 Uncommitted.

SOUTH CAROLINA   January 19 (R), January 26 (D)

Republican   147,686 McCain; 132,943 Huckabee; 69,651 Thompson; 68,142 Romney; 16,154 Paul; 9,557 Giuliani; 1,051 Hunter; 121 Tancredo; 88 Cort; 83 Cox; 23 Fendig.

Democratic   294,898 Obama; 140,990 Clinton; 93,801 Edwards; 726 Richardson; 693 Biden; 551 Kucinich; 247 Dodd; 245 Gravel.

SOUTH DAKOTA   June 3

Republican   42,788 McCain; 10,072 Paul; 4,328 Huckabee; 1,990 Romney; 1,786 Uncommitted.

Democratic   54,128 Clinton; 43,669 Obama.

TENNESSEE   February 5

Republican   190,904 Huckabee; 176,091 McCain; 130,632 Romney; 31,026 Paul; 16,263 Thompson; 5,159 Giuliani; 1,830 Uncommitted; 978 Keyes; 738 Hunter; 194 Tancredo.

Democratic   336,245 Clinton; 252,874 Obama; 27,820 Edwards; 3,158 Uncommitted; 1,531 Biden; 1,178 Richardson; 971 Kucinich; 526 Dodd; 461 Gravel.

2008 PRESIDENTIAL PRIMARIES

TEXAS   March 4

Republican   697,767 McCain; 518,002 Huckabee; 66,360 Paul; 27,264 Romney; 17,574 Uncommitted; 11,503 Thompson; 8,260 Keyes; 8,222 Hunter; 6,038 Giuliani; 728 Cort; 604 Tran.

Democratic   1,462,734 Clinton; 1,362,476 Obama; 29,936 Edwards; 10,773 Richardson; 5,290 Biden; 3,777 Dodd.

UTAH   February 5

Republican   264,956 Romney; 15,931 McCain; 8,846 Paul; 4,252 Huckabee; 988 Giuliani; 613 Thompson; 261 Keyes; 211 Hunter; 3 Tancredo.

Democratic   74,538 Obama; 51,333 Clinton; 3,758 Edwards; 549 Richardson; 462 Biden; 408 Kucinich; 166 Gravel; 117 Dodd; 72 Lynch.

VERMONT   March 4

Republican   28,417 McCain; 5,698 Huckabee; 2,635 Paul; 1,809 Romney; 931 Giuliani; 353 scattered write-in.

Democratic   91,901 Obama; 59,806 Clinton; 1,936 Edwards; 1,010 Kucinich; 307 scattered write-in.

VIRGINIA   February 12

Republican   244,829 McCain; 199,003 Huckabee; 21,999 Paul; 18,002 Romney; 3,395 Thompson; 2,024 Giuliani.

Democratic   627,820 Obama; 349,766 Clinton; 5,206 Edwards; 1,625 Kucinich; 991 Richardson; 795 Biden.

WASHINGTON   February 19

Republican   262,304 McCain; 127,657 Huckabee; 86,140 Romney; 40,539 Paul; 5,145 Giuliani; 4,865 Thompson; 2,226 Keyes; 1,056 Hunter.

Democratic   354,112 Obama; 315,744 Clinton; 11,892 Edwards; 4,021 Kucinich; 2,040 Richardson; 1,883 Biden; 1,071 Gravel; 618 Dodd.

WEST VIRGINIA   May 13

Republican   90,469 McCain; 12,310 Huckabee; 5,969 Paul; 5,242 Romney; 2,875 Giuliani; 1,441 Keyes; 728 Curry.

Democratic   240,890 Clinton; 92,736 Obama; 26,284 Edwards.

WISCONSIN   February 19

Republican   224,755 McCain; 151,707 Huckabee; 19,090 Paul; 8,080 Romney; 2,709 Thompson; 1,935 Giuliani; 850 Uninstructed Delegation; 799 Hunter; 185 Tancredo; 497 scattered write-in.

Democratic   646,851 Obama; 453,954 Clinton; 6,693 Edwards; 2,625 Kucinich; 861 Uninstructed Delegation; 755 Biden; 528 Richardson; 517 Gravel; 501 Dodd; 468 scattered write-in.

DEMOCRATIC PRESIDENTIAL PRIMARIES 2008

Date	State	Total Vote	Clinton	Edwards	Obama	Other
Jan. 8	New Hampshire	287,557	112,404 **39.1%**	48,699 **16.9%**	104,815 **36.5%**	21,639 **7.5%**
Jan. 15	Michigan	594,398	328,309 **55.2%**			266,089 **44.8%**
Jan. 26	South Carolina	532,151	140,990 **26.5%**	93,801 **17.6%**	294,898 **55.4%**	2,462 **0.5%**
Jan. 29	Florida	1,749,920	870,986 **49.8%**	251,562 **14.4%**	576,214 **32.9%**	51,158 **2.9%**
Feb. 5	Alabama	536,626	223,089 **41.6%**	7,841 **1.5%**	300,319 **56.0%**	5,377 **1.0%**
Feb. 5	Arizona	455,635	229,501 **50.4%**	23,621 **5.2%**	193,126 **42.4%**	9,387 **2.1%**
Feb. 5	Arkansas	314,234	220,136 **70.1%**	5,873 **1.9%**	82,476 **26.2%**	5,749 **1.8%**
Feb. 5	California	5,066,993	2,608,184 **51.5%**	193,617 **3.8%**	2,186,662 **43.2%**	78,530 **1.5%**
Feb. 5	Connecticut	354,539	165,426 **46.7%**	3,424 **1.0%**	179,742 **50.7%**	5,947 **1.7%**
Feb. 5	Delaware	96,374	40,760 **42.3%**	1,241 **1.3%**	51,148 **53.1%**	3,225 **3.3%**
Feb. 5	Georgia	1,060,851	330,026 **31.1%**	18,209 **1.7%**	704,247 **66.4%**	8,369 **0.8%**
Feb. 5	Illinois	2,038,614	667,930 **32.8%**	39,719 **1.9%**	1,318,234 **64.7%**	12,731 **0.6%**
Feb. 5	Massachusetts	1,258,923	705,185 **56.0%**	20,101 **1.6%**	511,680 **40.6%**	21,957 **1.7%**
Feb. 5	Missouri	825,050	395,185 **47.9%**	16,763 **2.0%**	406,917 **49.3%**	6,185 **0.7%**
Feb. 5	New Jersey	1,141,199	613,500 **53.8%**	15,728 **1.4%**	501,372 **43.9%**	10,599 **0.9%**
Feb. 5	New York	1,862,445	1,068,496 **57.4%**	21,924 **1.2%**	751,019 **40.3%**	21,006 **1.1%**
Feb. 5	Oklahoma	417,207	228,480 **54.8%**	42,725 **10.2%**	130,130 **31.2%**	15,872 **3.8%**
Feb. 5	Tennessee	624,764	336,245 **53.8%**	27,820 **4.5%**	252,874 **40.5%**	7,825 **1.3%**
Feb. 5	Utah	131,403	51,333 **39.1%**	3,758 **2.9%**	74,538 **56.7%**	1,774 **1.4%**
Feb. 9	Louisiana	384,346	136,925 **35.6%**	13,026 **3.4%**	220,632 **57.4%**	13,763 **3.6%**
Feb. 12	District of Columbia	123,994	29,470 **23.8%**	347 **0.3%**	93,386 **75.3%**	791 **0.6%**
Feb. 12	Maryland	878,174	314,211 **35.8%**	10,506 **1.2%**	532,665 **60.7%**	20,792 **2.4%**
Feb. 12	Virginia	986,203	349,766 **35.5%**	5,206 **0.5%**	627,820 **63.7%**	3,411 **0.3%**
Feb. 19	Washington	691,381	315,744 **45.7%**	11,892 **1.7%**	354,112 **51.2%**	9,633 **1.4%**
Feb. 19	Wisconsin	1,113,753	453,954 **40.8%**	6,693 **0.6%**	646,851 **58.1%**	6,255 **0.6%**
March 4	Ohio	2,354,721	1,259,620 **53.5%**	39,332 **1.7%**	1,055,769 **44.8%**	
March 4	Rhode Island	186,439	108,949 **58.4%**	1,133 **0.6%**	75,316 **40.4%**	1,041 **0.6%**
March 4	Texas	2,874,986	1,462,734 **50.9%**	29,936 **1.0%**	1,362,476 **47.4%**	19,840 **0.7%**
March 4	Vermont	154,960	59,806 **38.6%**	1,936 **1.2%**	91,901 **59.3%**	1,317 **0.8%**
March 11	Mississippi	434,152	159,221 **36.7%**	3,933 **0.9%**	265,502 **61.2%**	5,496 **1.3%**
April 22	Pennsylvania	2,336,480	1,275,039 **54.6%**		1,061,441 **45.4%**	
May 6	Indiana	1,278,355	646,282 **50.6%**		632,073 **49.4%**	

DEMOCRATIC PRESIDENTIAL PRIMARIES 2008

Date	State	Total Vote	Clinton	Edwards	Obama	Other
May 6	North Carolina	1,580,726	657,669 **41.6%**		887,391 **56.1%**	35,666 **2.3%**
May 13	Nebraska	94,535	43,979 **46.5%**		46,670 **49.4%**	3,886 **4.1%**
May 13	West Virginia	359,910	240,890 **66.9%**	26,284 **7.3%**	92,736 **25.8%**	
May 20	Kentucky	701,768	459,511 **65.5%**	14,212 **2.0%**	209,954 **29.9%**	18,091 **2.6%**
May 20	Oregon	641,499	259,825 **40.5%**		375,385 **58.5%**	6,289 **1.0%**
May 27	Idaho	42,802	16,122 **37.7%**		23,980 **56.0%**	2,700 **6.3%**
June 3	Montana	182,421	74,889 **41.1%**		103,174 **56.6%**	4,358 **2.4%**
June 3	South Dakota	97,797	54,128 **55.3%**		43,669 **44.7%**	
	Total	*36,848,285*	*17,714,899* **2.7%**	*1,000,862* **2.7%**	*17,423,314* **47.3%**	*709,210* **1.9%**
	Total without Florida and Michigan	*34,503,967*	*16,515,604* **47.9%**	*749,300* **2.2%**	*16,847,100* **48.8%**	*391,963* **1.1%**

Notes: The January primaries in Florida and Michigan were not sanctioned by the Democratic National Committee and did not elect delegates. Democratic candidates were not allowed to campaign in either state and Barack Obama did not permit his name to be listed on the Michigan primary ballot. The first Total line includes the results from the Democratic primaries in Florida and Michigan. The second Total line does not include the results from either primary. Neither Total line includes the results from the June 1 Democratic primary in Puerto Rico, where the complete but unofficial vote was: 263,120 Clinton; 121,458 Obama. The table is limited to the jurisdictions that vote for president in November—namely, the 50 states and the District of Columbia. States not listed in the primary table held caucuses rather than primaries.

Candidates who received at least 200,000 votes in the Democratic primaries are included in the table above. Other vote for names that were on the ballot in at least one primary: 322,937 Uncommitted; 104,616 Richardson; 102,598 Kucinich; 81,344 Biden; 40,210 Gravel; 35,122 Dodd; 3,905 Rogers; 734 Judd; 632 Whitehouse; 398 Dobson; 322 Grayson; 320 Lynch; 291 Krueger; 253 Caligiuri; 249 See; 248 Campbell; 220 Spelbring; 209 Hubbard; 192 Oatman; 162 Lee; 154 Bollander; 132 Vitullo; 130 Tanner; 108 Capalbo; 107 Haymer; 98 Daley; 95 D.R. Hunter; 94 Montell; 82 Gest; 51 Keefe; 47 Laughlin; 37 Crow; 32 Skok; 30 Savior; 17 Hewes; 16 Hughes; 11 Killeen; 10 Koos; 8 LaMagna; 12,989 scattered write-in. The Uncommitted total includes votes cast on the following ballot lines: Uncommitted, No Preference, None of the Names Shown, Uninstructed Delegation.

REPUBLICAN PRESIDENTIAL PRIMARIES 2008

Date	State	Total Vote	Giuliani	Huckabee	McCain	Paul	Romney	Thompson	Other
Jan. 8	New Hampshire	239,793	20,344 8.5%	26,916 11.2%	88,713 37.0%	18,346 7.7%	75,675 31.6%	2,956 1.2%	6,843 2.9%
Jan. 15	Michigan	869,169	24,725 2.8%	139,764 16.1%	257,985 29.7%	54,475 6.3%	338,316 38.9%	32,159 3.7%	21,745 2.5%
Jan. 19	South Carolina	445,499	9,557 2.1%	132,943 29.8%	147,686 33.2%	16,154 3.6%	68,142 15.3%	69,651 15.6%	1,366 0.3%
Jan. 29	Florida	1,949,498	286,089 14.7%	262,681 13.5%	701,761 36.0%	62,887 3.2%	604,932 31.0%	22,668 1.2%	8,480 0.4%
Feb. 5	Alabama	552,155	2,134 0.4%	227,766 41.3%	204,867 37.1%	14,810 2.7%	98,019 17.8%	1,835 0.3%	2,724 0.5%
Feb. 5	Arizona	541,035	13,658 2.5%	48,849 9.0%	255,197 47.2%	22,692 4.2%	186,838 34.5%	9,492 1.8%	4,309 0.8%
Feb. 5	Arkansas	229,153	658 0.3%	138,557 60.5%	46,343 20.2%	10,983 4.8%	30,997 13.5%	628 0.3%	987 0.4%
Feb. 5	California	2,932,811	128,681 4.4%	340,669 11.6%	1,238,988 42.2%	125,365 4.3%	1,013,471 34.6%	50,275 1.7%	35,362 1.2%
Feb. 5	Connecticut	151,604	2,470 1.6%	10,607 7.0%	78,836 52.0%	6,287 4.1%	49,891 32.9%	538 0.4%	2,975 2.0%
Feb. 5	Delaware	50,239	1,255 2.5%	7,706 15.3%	22,628 45.0%	2,131 4.2%	16,344 32.5%		175 0.3%
Feb. 5	Georgia	963,541	7,162 0.7%	326,874 33.9%	304,751 31.6%	28,096 2.9%	290,707 30.2%	3,414 0.4%	2,537 0.3%
Feb. 5	Illinois	899,422	11,837 1.3%	148,053 16.5%	426,777 47.5%	45,055 5.0%	257,265 28.6%	7,259 0.8%	3,176 0.4%
Feb. 5	Massachusetts	500,550	2,707 0.5%	19,103 3.8%	204,779 40.9%	13,251 2.6%	255,892 51.1%	916 0.2%	3,902 0.8%
Feb. 5	Missouri	588,844	3,593 0.6%	185,642 31.5%	194,053 33.0%	26,464 4.5%	172,329 29.3%	3,102 0.5%	3,661 0.6%
Feb. 5	New Jersey	566,201	15,516 2.7%	46,284 8.2%	313,459 55.4%	27,301 4.8%	160,388 28.3%	3,253 0.6%	
Feb. 5	New York	642,894	23,260 3.6%	68,477 10.7%	333,001 51.8%	40,113 6.2%	178,043 27.7%		
Feb. 5	Oklahoma	335,054	2,412 0.7%	111,899 33.4%	122,772 36.6%	11,183 3.3%	83,030 24.8%	1,924 0.6%	1,834 0.5%
Feb. 5	Tennessee	553,815	5,159 0.9%	190,904 34.5%	176,091 31.8%	31,026 5.6%	130,632 23.6%	16,263 2.9%	3,740 0.7%
Feb. 5	Utah	296,061	988 0.3%	4,252 1.4%	15,931 5.4%	8,846 3.0%	264,956 89.5%	613 0.2%	475 0.2%
Feb. 9	Louisiana	161,169	1,593 1.0%	69,594 43.2%	67,551 41.9%	8,590 5.3%	10,222 6.3%	1,603 1.0%	2,016 1.3%
Feb. 12	District of Columbia	6,211	101 1.6%	1,020 16.4%	4,198 67.6%	494 8.0%	398 6.4%		
Feb. 12	Maryland	320,989	4,548 1.4%	91,608 28.5%	176,046 54.8%	19,196 6.0%	22,426 7.0%	2,901 0.9%	4,264 1.3%
Feb. 12	Virginia	489,252	2,024 0.4%	199,003 40.7%	244,829 50.0%	21,999 4.5%	18,002 3.7%	3,395 0.7%	
Feb. 19	Washington	529,932	5,145 1.0%	127,657 24.1%	262,304 49.5%	40,539 7.6%	86,140 16.3%	4,865 0.9%	3,282 0.6%
Feb. 19	Wisconsin	410,607	1,935 0.5%	151,707 36.9%	224,755 54.7%	19,090 4.6%	8,080 2.0%	2,709 0.7%	2,331 0.6%
March 4	Ohio	1,095,917		335,356 30.6%	656,687 59.9%	50,964 4.7%	36,031 3.3%	16,879 1.5%	
March 4	Rhode Island	26,996		5,847 21.7%	17,480 64.8%	1,777 6.6%	1,181 4.4%		711 2.6%
March 4	Texas	1,362,322	6,038 0.4%	518,002 38.0%	697,767 51.2%	66,360 4.9%	27,264 2.0%	11,503 0.8%	35,388 2.6%
March 4	Vermont	39,843	931 2.3%	5,698 14.3%	28,417 71.3%	2,635 6.6%	1,809 4.5%		353 0.9%
March 11	Mississippi	143,286	945 0.7%	17,943 12.5%	113,074 78.9%	5,510 3.8%	2,177 1.5%	2,160 1.5%	1,477 1.0%
April 22	Pennsylvania	816,928		92,430 11.3%	595,175 72.9%	129,323 15.8%			

REPUBLICAN PRESIDENTIAL PRIMARIES 2008

Date	State	Total Vote	Giuliani	Huckabee	McCain	Paul	Romney	Thompson	Other
May 6	Indiana	412,684		41,173 10.0%	320,318 77.6%	31,612 7.7%	19,581 4.7%		
May 6	North Carolina	517,583		63,018 12.2%	383,085 74.0%	37,260 7.2%			34,220 6.6%
May 13	Nebraska	136,648			118,876 87.0%	17,772 13.0%			
May 13	West Virginia	119,034	2,875 2.4%	12,310 10.3%	90,469 76.0%	5,969 5.0%	5,242 4.4%		2,169 1.8%
May 20	Kentucky	197,793	3,055 1.5%	16,388 8.3%	142,918 72.3%	13,427 6.8%	9,206 4.7%		12,799 6.5%
May 20	Oregon	353,476			285,881 80.9%	51,100 14.5%			16,495 4.7%
May 27	Idaho	125,570			87,460 69.7%	29,785 23.7%			8,325 6.6%
June 3	Montana	95,730			72,791 76.0%	20,606 21.5%			2,333 2.4%
June 3	New Mexico	110,939			95,378 86.0%	15,561 14.0%			
June 3	South Dakota	60,964		4,328 7.1%	42,788 70.2%	10,072 16.5%	1,990 3.3%		1,786 2.9%
	Total	20,841,211	591,395 2.8%	4,191,028 20.1%	9,862,865 47.3%	1,165,106 5.6%	4,525,616 21.7%	272,961 1.3%	232,240 1.1%

Notes: Candidates who received at least 200,000 votes in the Republican primaries are included in the table above. Other vote for names that were on the ballot in at least one primary: 91,504 Uncommitted; 57,604 Keyes; 37,507 Hunter; 8,580 Tancredo; 3,341 Cox; 2,837 Brownback; 1,734 Curry; 1,207 Cort; 702 Mitchell; 604 Tran; 490 McGrath; 483 Gilbert; 333 McEnulty; 269 Murphy; 199 Fitzpatrick; 127 Marchuk; 124 Wiles; 106 Shepard; 104 Ruben; 98 Burzynski; 75 Forthan; 62 Shaw; 53 Outzen; 50 Skelley; 46 O'Connor; 44 Smith; 43 Howard; 43 Supreme; 36 Fendig; 36 Wuensche; 16 Klein; 23,783 scattered write-in.

The Uncommitted total includes votes cast on the following ballot lines: Uncommitted, No Preference, None of the Names Shown, Uninstructed Delegation.

ALABAMA

Congressional districts first established for elections held in 2002
7 members

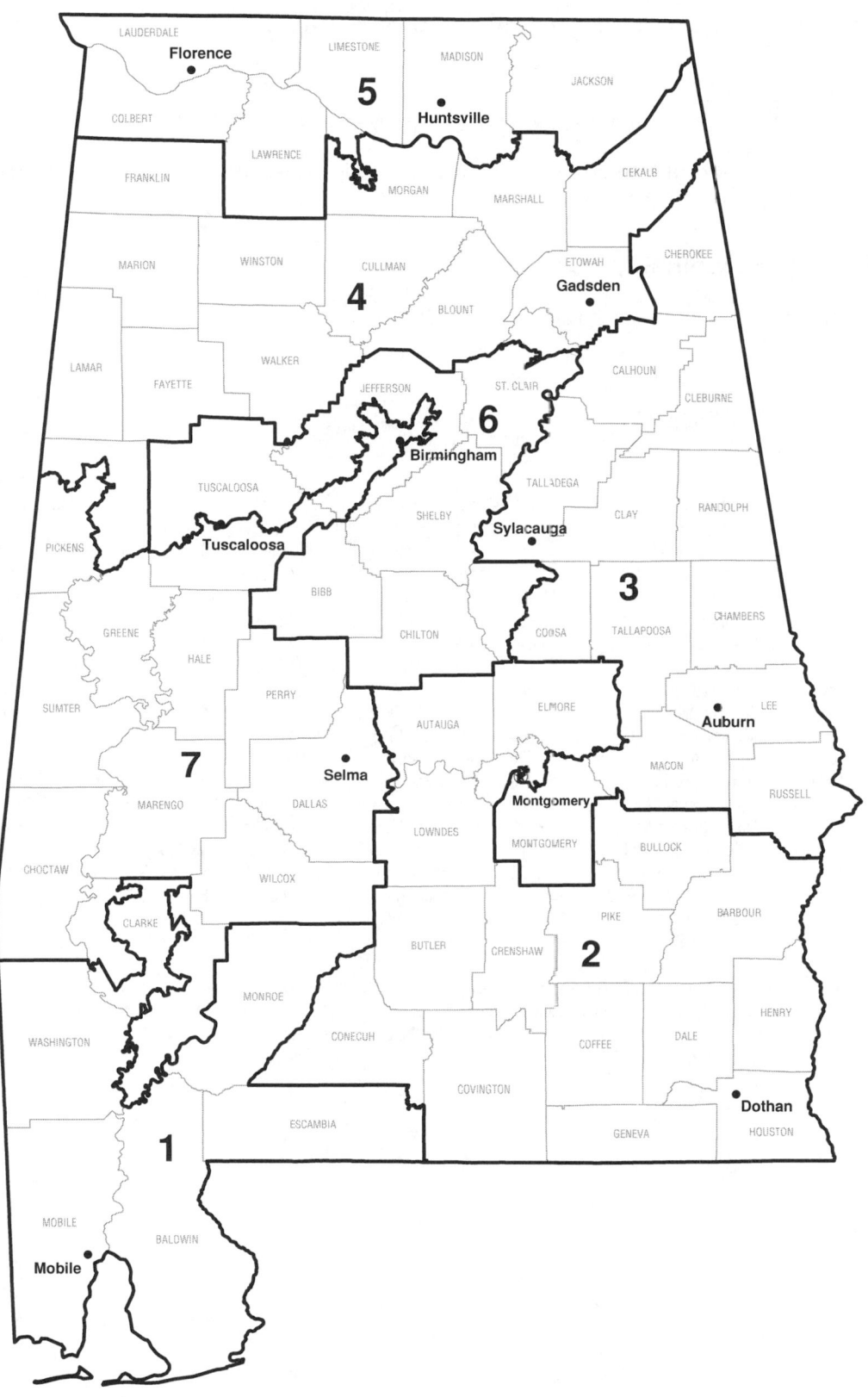

ALABAMA

GOVERNOR
Bob Riley (R). Reelected 2006 to a four-year term. Previously elected 2002.

SENATORS (2 Republicans)
Jeff Sessions (R). Reelected 2008 to a six-year term. Previously elected 2002, 1996.

Richard C. Shelby (R). Reelected 2004 to a six-year term. Previously elected 1998, 1992, 1986. Changed party affiliation from Democratic to Republican in November 1994.

REPRESENTATIVES (4 Republicans, 3 Democrats)
1. Jo Bonner (R)
2. Bobby Bright (D)
3. Mike D. Rogers (R)
4. Robert B. Aderholt (R)
5. Parker Griffith (D)
6. Spencer Bachus (R)
7. Artur Davis (D)

POSTWAR VOTE FOR PRESIDENT

		Republican		Democratic		Other		Total Vote		Major Vote	
Year	Total Vote	Vote	Candidate	Vote	Candidate	Vote	Plurality	Rep.	Dem.	Rep.	Dem
2008	2,099,819	1,266,546	McCain, John	813,479	Obama, Barack	19,794	453,067 R	60.3%	38.7%	60.9%	39.1%
2004	1,883,415	1,176,394	Bush, George W.	693,933	Kerry, John	13,088	482,461 R	62.5%	36.8%	62.9%	37.1%
2000**	1,666,272	941,173	Bush, George W.	692,611	Gore, Al	32,488	248,562 R	56.5%	41.6%	57.6%	42.4%
1996**	1,534,349	769,044	Dole, Bob	662,165	Clinton, Bill	103,140	106,879 R	50.1%	43.2%	53.7%	46.3%
1992**	1,688,060	804,283	Bush, George	690,080	Clinton, Bill	193,697	114,203 R	47.6%	40.9%	53.8%	46.2%
1988	1,378,476	815,576	Bush, George	549,506	Dukakis, Michael S.	13,394	266,070 R	59.2%	39.9%	59.7%	40.3%
1984	1,441,713	872,849	Reagan, Ronald	551,899	Mondale, Walter F.	16,965	320,950 R	60.5%	38.3%	61.3%	38.7%
1980**	1,341,929	654,192	Reagan, Ronald	636,730	Carter, Jimmy	51,007	17,462 R	48.8%	47.4%	50.7%	49.3%
1976	1,182,850	504,070	Ford, Gerald R.	659,170	Carter, Jimmy	19,610	155,100 D	42.6%	55.7%	43.3%	56.7%
1972	1,006,111	728,701	Nixon, Richard M.	256,923	McGovern, George S.	20,487	471,778 R	72.4%	25.5%	73.9%	26.1%
1968**	1,049,922	146,923	Nixon, Richard M.	196,579	Humphrey, Hubert H.	706,420	494,846 A	14.0%	18.7%	42.8%	57.2%
1964**	689,818	479,085	Goldwater, Barry M.	—	Johnson, Lyndon B.	210,733	268,353 R	69.5%		100.0%	
1960	570,225	237,981	Nixon, Richard M.	324,050	Kennedy, John F.	8,194	86,069 D	41.7%	56.8%	42.3%	57.7%
1956	496,861	195,694	Eisenhower, Dwight D.	280,844	Stevenson, Adlai E.	20,323	85,150 D	39.4%	56.5%	41.1%	58.9%
1952	426,120	149,231	Eisenhower, Dwight D.	275,075	Stevenson, Adlai E.	1,814	125,844 D	35.0%	64.6%	35.2%	64.8%
1948**	214,980	40,930	Dewey, Thomas E.	—	Truman, Harry S.	174,050	130,513 SR	19.0%		100.0%	

**In past elections, the other vote included: 2000 - 18,323 Green (Ralph Nader); 1996 - 92,149 Reform (Ross Perot); 1992 - 183,109 Independent (Perot); 1980 - 16,481 Independent (John Anderson); 1968 - 691,425 American Independent (George Wallace); 1964 - 210,732 Unpledged Democratic; 1948 - 171,443 States' Rights (Strom Thurmond). In 1948 and 1964, the Democratic presidential candidate was not listed on the ballot. Wallace carried Alabama in 1968 with 65.9 percent of the vote. Thurmond won the state in 1948 with 79.7 percent.

ALABAMA

POSTWAR VOTE FOR GOVERNOR

Year	Total Vote	Republican Vote	Candidate	Democratic Vote	Candidate	Other Vote	Rep.-Dem. Plurality	Total Vote Rep.	Dem.	Major Vote Rep.	Dem.
2006	1,250,401	718,327	Riley, Bob	519,827	Baxley, Lucy	12,247	198,500 R	57.4%	41.6%	58.0%	42.0%
2002	1,367,053	672,225	Riley, Bob	669,105	Siegelman, Don	25,723	3,120 R	49.2%	48.9%	50.1%	49.9%
1998	1,317,842	554,746	James, Forrest H.	760,155	Siegelman, Don	2,941	205,409 D	42.1%	57.7%	42.2%	57.8%
1994	1,201,969	604,926	James, Forrest H.	594,169	Folsom, James E.	2,874	10,757 R	50.3%	49.4%	50.4%	49.6%
1990	1,216,250	633,519	Hunt, Guy	582,106	Hubbert, Paul R.	625	51,413 R	52.1%	47.9%	52.1%	47.9%
1986	1,236,230	696,203	Hunt, Guy	537,163	Baxley, Bill	2,864	159,040 R	56.3%	43.5%	56.4%	43.6%
1982	1,128,725	440,815	Folmar, Emory	650,538	Wallace, George C.	37,372	209,723 D	39.1%	57.6%	40.4%	59.6%
1978	760,474	196,963	Hunt, Guy	551,886	James, Forrest H.	11,625	354,923 D	25.9%	72.6%	26.3%	73.7%
1974	598,305	88,381	McCary, Elvin	497,574	Wallace, George C.	12,350	409,193 D	14.8%	83.2%	15.1%	84.9%
1970**	854,952		—	637,046	Wallace, George C.	217,906	637,046 D		74.5%		100.0%
1966	848,101	262,943	Martin, James D.	537,505	Wallace, Mrs. George C.	47,653	274,562 D	31.0%	63.4%	32.8%	67.2%
1962	315,776		—	303,987	Wallace, George C.	11,789	303,987 D		96.3%		100.0%
1958	270,952	30,415	Longshore, W. L.	239,633	Patterson, John	904	209,218 D	11.2%	88.4%	11.3%	88.7%
1954	333,090	88,688	Amernethy, Tom	244,401	Folsom, James E.	1	155,713 D	26.6%	73.4%	26.6%	73.4%
1950	170,541	15,127	Crowder, John S.	155,414	Persons, Gordon		140,287 D	8.9%	91.1%	8.9%	91.1%
1946	197,324	22,362	Ward, Lyman	174,962	Folsom, James E.		152,600 D	11.3%	88.7%	11.3%	88.7%

**In past elections, the other vote included: 1970 - 125,491 National Democratic Party of Alabama (John Logan Cashin). The Republican Party did not run a candidate in the 1962 and 1970 gubernatorial elections.

POSTWAR VOTE FOR SENATOR

Year	Total Vote	Republican Vote	Candidate	Democratic Vote	Candidate	Other Vote	Rep.-Dem. Plurality	Total Vote Rep.	Dem.	Major Vote Rep.	Dem.
2008	2,060,191	1,305,383	Sessions, Jeff	752,391	Figures, Vivian Davis	2,417	552,992 R	63.4%	36.5%	63.4%	36.6%
2004	1,839,066	1,242,200	Shelby, Richard C.	595,018	Sowell, Wayne	1,848	647,182 R	67.5%	32.4%	67.6%	32.4%
2002	1,353,023	792,561	Sessions, Jeff	538,878	Parker, Susan	21,584	253,683 R	58.6%	39.8%	59.5%	40.5%
1998	1,293,405	817,973	Shelby, Richard C.	474,568	Suddith, Clayton	864	343,405 R	63.2%	36.7%	63.3%	36.7%
1996	1,499,393	786,436	Sessions, Jeff	681,651	Bedford, Roger	31,306	104,785 R	52.5%	45.5%	53.6%	46.4%
1992	1,577,799	522,015	Sellers, Richard	1,022,698	Shelby, Richard C.	33,086	500,683 D	33.1%	64.8%	33.8%	66.2%
1990	1,185,563	467,190	Cabaniss, Bill	717,814	Heflin, Howell	559	250,624 D	39.4%	60.5%	39.4%	60.6%
1986	1,211,953	602,537	Denton, Jeremiah	609,360	Shelby, Richard C.	56	6,823 D	49.7%	50.3%	49.7%	50.3%
1984	1,371,238	498,508	Smith, Albert L.	860,535	Heflin, Howell	12,195	362,027 D	36.4%	62.8%	36.7%	63.3%
1980	1,296,757	650,362	Denton, Jeremiah	610,175	Folsom, James E., Jr.	36,220	40,187 R	50.2%	47.1%	51.6%	48.4%
1978	582,025		—	547,054	Heflin, Howell	34,971	547,054 D		94.0%		100.0%
1978S	731,614	316,170	Martin, James D.	401,852	Stewart, Donald W.	13,592	85,682 D	43.2%	54.9%	44.0%	56.0%
1974	523,290		—	501,541	Allen, James B.	21,749	501,541 D		95.8%		100.0%
1972	1,051,099	347,523	Blount, Winston M.	654,491	Sparkman, John J.	49,085	306,968 D	33.1%	62.3%	34.7%	65.3%
1968	912,708	201,227	Hooper, Perry	638,774	Allen, James B.	72,707	437,547 D	22.0%	70.0%	24.0%	76.0%
1966	802,608	313,018	Grenier, John	482,138	Sparkman, John J.	7,452	169,120 D	39.0%	60.1%	39.4%	60.6%
1962	397,079	195,134	Martin, James D.	201,937	Hill, Lister	8	6,803 D	49.1%	50.9%	49.1%	50.9%
1960	554,081	164,868	Elgin, Julian	389,196	Sparkman, John J.	17	224,328 D	29.8%	70.2%	29.8%	70.2%
1956	330,191		—	330,182	Hill, Lister	9	330,182 D		100.0%		100.0%
1954	314,459	55,110	Guin, J. Foy	259,348	Sparkman, John J.	1	204,238 D	17.5%	82.5%	17.5%	82.5%
1950	164,011		—	125,534	Hill, Lister	38,477	125,534 D		76.5%		100.0%
1948	220,875	35,341	Parsons, Paul G.	185,534	Sparkman, John J.		150,193 D	16.0%	84.0%	16.0%	84.0%
1946S	163,217		—	163,217	Sparkman, John J.		163,217 D		100.0%		100.0%

Notes: The 1946 election and one of the 1978 elections were for short terms to fill vacancies. The Republican Party did not run a candidate in Senate elections in 1946, 1950, 1956, 1974, and 1978.

ALABAMA

PRESIDENT 2008

2000 Census Population	County	Total Vote	Republican	Democratic	Other	Rep.-Dem. Plurality	Percentage			
							Total Vote		Major Vote	
							Rep.	Dem.	Rep.	Dem.
43,671	AUTAUGA	23,641	17,403	6,093	145	11,310 R	73.6%	25.8%	74.1%	25.9%
140,415	BALDWIN	81,413	61,271	19,386	756	41,885 R	75.3%	23.8%	76.0%	24.0%
29,038	BARBOUR	11,630	5,866	5,697	67	169 R	50.4%	49.0%	50.7%	49.3%
20,826	BIBB	8,644	6,262	2,299	83	3,963 R	72.4%	26.6%	73.1%	26.9%
51,024	BLOUNT	24,267	20,389	3,522	356	16,867 R	84.0%	14.5%	85.3%	14.7%
11,714	BULLOCK	5,415	1,391	4,011	13	2,620 D	25.7%	74.1%	25.7%	74.3%
21,399	BUTLER	9,709	5,485	4,188	36	1,297 R	56.5%	43.1%	56.7%	43.3%
112,249	CALHOUN	49,242	32,348	16,334	560	16,014 R	65.7%	33.2%	66.4%	33.6%
36,583	CHAMBERS	14,956	8,067	6,799	90	1,268 R	53.9%	45.5%	54.3%	45.7%
23,988	CHEROKEE	9,745	7,298	2,306	141	4,992 R	74.9%	23.7%	76.0%	24.0%
39,593	CHILTON	17,785	13,960	3,674	151	10,286 R	78.5%	20.7%	79.2%	20.8%
15,922	CHOCTAW	7,894	4,223	3,636	35	587 R	53.5%	46.1%	53.7%	46.3%
27,867	CLARKE	13,435	7,466	5,914	55	1,552 R	55.6%	44.0%	55.8%	44.2%
14,254	CLAY	6,819	4,984	1,760	75	3,224 R	73.1%	25.8%	73.9%	26.1%
14,123	CLEBURNE	6,492	5,216	1,168	108	4,048 R	80.3%	18.0%	81.7%	18.3%
43,615	COFFEE	20,128	14,919	5,079	130	9,840 R	74.1%	25.2%	74.6%	25.4%
54,984	COLBERT	24,843	14,739	9,703	401	5,036 R	59.3%	39.1%	60.3%	39.7%
14,089	CONECUH	6,943	3,470	3,429	44	41 R	50.0%	49.4%	50.3%	49.7%
12,202	COOSA	5,563	3,248	2,273	42	975 R	58.4%	40.9%	58.8%	41.2%
37,631	COVINGTON	15,787	12,444	3,240	103	9,204 R	78.8%	20.5%	79.3%	20.7%
13,665	CRENSHAW	6,291	4,319	1,938	34	2,381 R	68.7%	30.8%	69.0%	31.0%
77,483	CULLMAN	35,305	28,896	5,864	545	23,032 R	81.8%	16.6%	83.1%	16.9%
49,129	DALE	19,320	13,886	5,270	164	8,616 R	71.9%	27.3%	72.5%	27.5%
46,365	DALLAS	20,852	6,798	13,986	68	7,188 D	32.6%	67.1%	32.7%	67.3%
64,452	DE KALB	24,015	17,957	5,658	400	12,299 R	74.8%	23.6%	76.0%	24.0%
65,874	ELMORE	34,315	25,777	8,301	237	17,476 R	75.1%	24.2%	75.6%	24.4%
38,440	ESCAMBIA	14,674	9,375	5,188	111	4,187 R	63.9%	35.4%	64.4%	35.6%
103,459	ETOWAH	44,737	30,595	13,497	645	17,098 R	68.4%	30.2%	69.4%	30.6%
18,495	FAYETTE	7,957	5,883	1,994	80	3,889 R	73.9%	25.1%	74.7%	25.3%
31,223	FRANKLIN	11,693	8,048	3,469	176	4,579 R	68.8%	29.7%	69.9%	30.1%
25,764	GENEVA	11,657	9,417	2,134	106	7,283 R	80.8%	18.3%	81.5%	18.5%
9,974	GREENE	5,305	876	4,408	21	3,532 D	16.5%	83.1%	16.6%	83.4%
17,185	HALE	8,214	3,200	4,982	32	1,782 D	39.0%	60.7%	39.1%	60.9%
16,310	HENRY	8,648	5,585	3,018	45	2,567 R	64.6%	34.9%	64.9%	35.1%
88,787	HOUSTON	41,735	29,254	12,225	256	17,029 R	70.1%	29.3%	70.5%	29.5%
53,926	JACKSON	20,874	14,083	6,374	417	7,709 R	67.5%	30.5%	68.8%	31.2%
662,047	JEFFERSON	318,524	149,921	166,121	2,482	16,200 D	47.1%	52.2%	47.4%	52.6%
15,904	LAMAR	7,075	5,419	1,614	42	3,805 R	76.6%	22.8%	77.1%	22.9%
87,966	LAUDERDALE	38,104	24,068	13,329	707	10,739 R	63.2%	35.0%	64.4%	35.6%
34,803	LAWRENCE	14,680	9,277	5,164	239	4,113 R	63.2%	35.2%	64.2%	35.8%
115,092	LEE	54,325	32,230	21,498	597	10,732 R	59.3%	39.6%	60.0%	40.0%
65,676	LIMESTONE	33,551	23,598	9,536	417	14,062 R	70.3%	28.4%	71.2%	28.8%
13,473	LOWNDES	7,278	1,809	5,449	20	3,640 D	24.9%	74.9%	24.9%	75.1%
24,105	MACON	10,877	1,396	9,450	31	8,054 D	12.8%	86.9%	12.9%	87.1%
276,700	MADISON	152,899	86,965	64,117	1,817	22,848 R	56.9%	41.9%	57.6%	42.4%
22,539	MARENGO	11,471	5,516	5,926	29	410 D	48.1%	51.7%	48.2%	51.8%
31,214	MARION	12,355	9,536	2,600	219	6,936 R	77.2%	21.0%	78.6%	21.4%
82,231	MARSHALL	33,166	25,727	7,038	401	18,689 R	77.6%	21.2%	78.5%	21.5%
399,843	MOBILE	181,424	98,049	82,181	1,194	15,868 R	54.0%	45.3%	54.4%	45.6%
24,324	MONROE	11,252	6,175	5,025	52	1,150 R	54.9%	44.7%	55.1%	44.9%
223,510	MONTGOMERY	104,743	42,031	62,166	546	20,135 D	40.1%	59.4%	40.3%	59.7%
111,064	MORGAN	50,542	36,014	13,895	633	22,119 R	71.3%	27.5%	72.2%	27.8%
11,861	PERRY	6,159	1,679	4,457	23	2,778 D	27.3%	72.4%	27.4%	72.6%
20,949	PICKENS	10,067	5,434	4,594	39	840 R	54.0%	45.6%	54.2%	45.8%
29,605	PIKE	13,955	8,004	5,879	72	2,125 R	57.4%	42.1%	57.7%	42.3%
22,380	RANDOLPH	10,384	7,175	3,064	145	4,111 R	69.1%	29.5%	70.1%	29.9%
49,756	RUSSELL	18,915	8,705	10,085	125	1,380 D	46.0%	53.3%	46.3%	53.7%
64,742	ST. CLAIR	34,088	27,649	6,091	348	21,558 R	81.1%	17.9%	81.9%	18.1%
143,293	SHELBY	90,643	69,060	20,625	958	48,435 R	76.2%	22.8%	77.0%	23.0%
14,798	SUMTER	7,020	1,731	5,264	25	3,533 D	24.7%	75.0%	24.7%	75.3%

ALABAMA

PRESIDENT 2008

2000 Census Population	County	Total Vote	Republican	Democratic	Other	Rep.-Dem. Plurality	Percentage			
							Total Vote		Major Vote	
							Rep.	Dem.	Rep.	Dem.
80,321	TALLADEGA	34,204	20,112	13,779	313	6,333 R	58.8%	40.3%	59.3%	40.7%
41,475	TALLAPOOSA	19,311	13,116	6,063	132	7,053 R	67.9%	31.4%	68.4%	31.6%
164,875	TUSCALOOSA	78,912	45,405	32,796	711	12,609 R	57.5%	41.6%	58.1%	41.9%
70,713	WALKER	28,652	20,722	7,420	510	13,302 R	72.3%	25.9%	73.6%	26.4%
18,097	WASHINGTON	8,775	5,654	3,067	54	2,587 R	64.4%	35.0%	64.8%	35.2%
13,183	WILCOX	6,494	1,868	4,612	14	2,744 D	28.8%	71.0%	28.8%	71.2%
24,843	WINSTON	10,031	8,103	1,757	171	6,346 R	80.8%	17.5%	82.2%	17.8%
4,447,100	TOTAL	2,099,819	1,266,546	813,479	19,794	453,067 R	60.3%	38.7%	60.9%	39.1%

ALABAMA

SENATOR 2008

2000 Census Population	County	Total Vote	Republican	Democratic	Other	Rep.-Dem. Plurality	Percentage			
							Total Vote		Major Vote	
							Rep.	Dem.	Rep.	Dem.
43,671	AUTAUGA	23,288	17,941	5,316	31	12,625 R	77.0%	22.8%	77.1%	22.9%
140,415	BALDWIN	80,273	63,685	16,456	132	47,229 R	79.3%	20.5%	79.5%	20.5%
29,038	BARBOUR	11,227	5,772	5,435	20	337 R	51.4%	48.4%	51.5%	48.5%
20,826	BIBB	8,548	6,276	2,267	5	4,009 R	73.4%	26.5%	73.5%	26.5%
51,024	BLOUNT	23,890	20,286	3,558	46	16,728 R	84.9%	14.9%	85.1%	14.9%
11,714	BULLOCK	5,203	1,466	3,734	3	2,268 D	28.2%	71.8%	28.2%	71.8%
21,399	BUTLER	9,504	5,600	3,895	9	1,705 R	58.9%	41.0%	59.0%	41.0%
112,249	CALHOUN	48,258	32,461	15,733	64	16,728 R	67.3%	32.6%	67.4%	32.6%
36,583	CHAMBERS	14,451	7,759	6,683	9	1,076 R	53.7%	46.2%	53.7%	46.3%
23,988	CHEROKEE	9,449	6,820	2,616	13	4,204 R	72.2%	27.7%	72.3%	27.7%
39,593	CHILTON	17,461	13,733	3,698	30	10,035 R	78.6%	21.2%	78.8%	21.2%
15,922	CHOCTAW	7,635	4,103	3,530	2	573 R	53.7%	46.2%	53.8%	46.2%
27,867	CLARKE	13,144	7,532	5,605	7	1,927 R	57.3%	42.6%	57.3%	42.7%
14,254	CLAY	6,609	4,827	1,780	2	3,047 R	73.0%	26.9%	73.1%	26.9%
14,123	CLEBURNE	6,161	4,823	1,326	12	3,497 R	78.3%	21.5%	78.4%	21.6%
43,615	COFFEE	19,758	15,109	4,616	33	10,493 R	76.5%	23.4%	76.6%	23.4%
54,984	COLBERT	24,182	14,864	9,297	21	5,567 R	61.5%	38.4%	61.5%	38.5%
14,089	CONECUH	6,760	3,519	3,234	7	285 R	52.1%	47.8%	52.1%	47.9%
12,202	COOSA	5,425	3,250	2,169	6	1,081 R	59.9%	40.0%	60.0%	40.0%
37,631	COVINGTON	15,411	12,413	2,979	19	9,434 R	80.5%	19.3%	80.6%	19.4%
13,665	CRENSHAW	6,131	4,319	1,809	3	2,510 R	70.4%	29.5%	70.5%	29.5%
77,483	CULLMAN	34,882	28,704	6,112	66	22,592 R	82.3%	17.5%	82.4%	17.6%
49,129	DALE	18,894	14,026	4,843	25	9,183 R	74.2%	25.6%	74.3%	25.7%
46,365	DALLAS	20,460	7,281	13,168	11	5,887 D	35.6%	64.4%	35.6%	64.4%
64,452	DE KALB	23,357	17,777	5,565	15	12,212 R	76.1%	23.8%	76.2%	23.8%
65,874	ELMORE	33,779	26,458	7,283	38	19,175 R	78.3%	21.6%	78.4%	21.6%
38,440	ESCAMBIA	14,279	9,446	4,816	17	4,630 R	66.2%	33.7%	66.2%	33.8%
103,459	ETOWAH	44,117	30,128	13,925	64	16,203 R	68.3%	31.6%	68.4%	31.6%
18,495	FAYETTE	7,790	5,700	2,090		3,610 R	73.2%	26.8%	73.2%	26.8%
31,223	FRANKLIN	11,351	8,091	3,248	12	4,843 R	71.3%	28.6%	71.4%	28.6%
25,764	GENEVA	11,423	9,441	1,960	22	7,481 R	82.6%	17.2%	82.8%	17.2%
9,974	GREENE	5,168	994	4,172	2	3,178 D	19.2%	80.7%	19.2%	80.8%
17,185	HALE	7,976	3,286	4,678	12	1,392 D	41.2%	58.7%	41.3%	58.7%
16,310	HENRY	8,396	5,543	2,840	13	2,703 R	66.0%	33.8%	66.1%	33.9%
88,787	HOUSTON	40,948	29,686	11,192	70	18,494 R	72.5%	27.3%	72.6%	27.4%
53,926	JACKSON	19,934	13,838	6,060	36	7,778 R	69.4%	30.4%	69.5%	30.5%
662,047	JEFFERSON	313,801	159,091	154,495	215	4,596 R	50.7%	49.2%	50.7%	49.3%
15,904	LAMAR	6,739	4,955	1,784		3,171 R	73.5%	26.5%	73.5%	26.5%
87,966	LAUDERDALE	37,343	25,249	12,012	82	13,237 R	67.6%	32.2%	67.8%	32.2%
34,803	LAWRENCE	14,282	9,315	4,936	31	4,379 R	65.2%	34.6%	65.4%	34.6%

ALABAMA

SENATOR 2008

2000 Census Population	County	Total Vote	Republican	Democratic	Other	Rep.-Dem. Plurality		Percentage			
								Total Vote		Major Vote	
								Rep.	Dem.	Rep.	Dem.
115,092	LEE	53,092	33,168	19,806	118	13,362 R		62.5%	37.3%	62.6%	37.4%
65,676	LIMESTONE	32,834	24,567	8,198	69	16,369 R		74.8%	25.0%	75.0%	25.0%
13,473	LOWNDES	7,008	2,009	4,993	6	2,984 D		28.7%	71.2%	28.7%	71.3%
24,105	MACON	10,625	1,876	8,745	4	6,869 D		17.7%	82.3%	17.7%	82.3%
276,700	MADISON	149,744	97,185	52,363	196	44,822 R		64.9%	35.0%	65.0%	35.0%
22,539	MARENGO	11,150	5,613	5,528	9	85 R		50.3%	49.6%	50.4%	49.6%
31,214	MARION	12,037	9,200	2,817	20	6,383 R		76.4%	23.4%	76.6%	23.4%
82,231	MARSHALL	32,559	26,752	5,754	53	20,998 R		82.2%	17.7%	82.3%	17.7%
399,843	MOBILE	179,416	102,043	77,292	81	24,751 R		56.9%	43.1%	56.9%	43.1%
24,324	MONROE	11,095	6,457	4,626	12	1,831 R		58.2%	41.7%	58.3%	41.7%
223,510	MONTGOMERY	102,988	45,962	56,956	70	10,994 D		44.6%	55.3%	44.7%	55.3%
111,064	MORGAN	49,691	37,987	11,630	74	26,357 R		76.4%	23.4%	76.6%	23.4%
11,861	PERRY	6,035	1,808	4,223	4	2,415 D		30.0%	70.0%	30.0%	70.0%
20,949	PICKENS	9,806	5,387	4,415	4	972 R		54.9%	45.0%	55.0%	45.0%
29,605	PIKE	13,670	8,298	5,363	9	2,935 R		60.7%	39.2%	60.7%	39.3%
22,380	RANDOLPH	9,807	6,684	3,116	7	3,568 R		68.2%	31.8%	68.2%	31.8%
49,756	RUSSELL	18,208	8,263	9,901	44	1,638 D		45.4%	54.4%	45.5%	54.5%
64,742	ST. CLAIR	33,594	27,538	6,001	55	21,537 R		82.0%	17.9%	82.1%	17.9%
143,293	SHELBY	89,468	71,691	17,609	168	54,082 R		80.1%	19.7%	80.3%	19.7%
14,798	SUMTER	6,867	1,823	5,042	2	3,219 D		26.5%	73.4%	26.6%	73.4%
80,321	TALLADEGA	33,689	20,184	13,449	56	6,735 R		59.9%	39.9%	60.0%	40.0%
41,475	TALLAPOOSA	18,831	12,997	5,806	28	7,191 R		69.0%	30.8%	69.1%	30.9%
164,875	TUSCALOOSA	77,377	46,642	30,663	72	15,979 R		60.3%	39.6%	60.3%	39.7%
70,713	WALKER	28,222	20,021	8,177	24	11,844 R		70.9%	29.0%	71.0%	29.0%
18,097	WASHINGTON	8,585	5,587	2,990	8	2,597 R		65.1%	34.8%	65.1%	34.9%
13,183	WILCOX	6,293	1,983	4,309	1	2,326 D		31.5%	68.5%	31.5%	68.5%
24,843	WINSTON	9,813	8,091	1,704	18	6,387 R		82.5%	17.4%	82.6%	17.4%
4,447,100	TOTAL	2,060,191	1,305,383	752,391	2,417	552,992 R		63.4%	36.5%	63.4%	36.6%

ALABAMA

HOUSE OF REPRESENTATIVES

CD	Year	Total Vote	Republican		Democratic		Other Vote	Rep.-Dem. Plurality	Percentage			
			Vote	Candidate	Vote	Candidate			Total Vote		Major Vote	
									Rep.	Dem.	Rep.	Dem.
1	2008	214,367	210,660	BONNER, JO*	—		3,707	210,660 R	98.3%		100.0%	
1	2006	165,841	112,944	BONNER, JO*	52,770	BECKERLE, VIVIAN SHEFFIELD	127	60,174 R	68.1%	31.8%	68.2%	31.8%
1	2004	255,164	161,067	BONNER, JO*	93,938	BELK, JUDY McCAIN	159	67,129 R	63.1%	36.8%	63.2%	36.8%
1	2002	178,687	108,102	BONNER, JO	67,507	BELK, JUDY McCAIN	3,078	40,595 R	60.5%	37.8%	61.6%	38.4%
2	2008	287,394	142,578	LOVE, JAY	144,368	BRIGHT, BOBBY	448	1,790 D	49.6%	50.2%	49.7%	50.3%
2	2006	178,919	124,302	EVERETT, TERRY*	54,450	JAMES, CHARLES "CHUCK" DEAN	167	69,852 R	69.5%	30.4%	69.5%	30.5%
2	2004	247,947	177,086	EVERETT, TERRY*	70,562	JAMES, CHARLES "CHUCK" DEAN	299	106,524 R	71.4%	28.5%	71.5%	28.5%
2	2002	187,965	129,233	EVERETT, TERRY*	55,495	WOODS, CHARLES	3,237	73,738 R	68.8%	29.5%	70.0%	30.0%
3	2008	264,120	142,708	ROGERS, MIKE D.*	121,080	SEGALL, JOSHUA	332	21,628 R	54.0%	45.8%	54.1%	45.9%
3	2006	165,301	98,257	ROGERS, MIKE D.*	63,559	PIERCE, GREG A.	3,485	34,698 R	59.4%	38.5%	60.7%	39.3%
3	2004	245,784	150,411	ROGERS, MIKE D.*	95,240	FULLER, BILL	133	55,171 R	61.2%	38.7%	61.2%	38.8%
3	2002	181,223	91,169	ROGERS, MIKE D.	87,351	TURNHAM, JOE	2,703	3,818 R	50.3%	48.2%	51.1%	48.9%
4	2008	263,167	196,741	ADERHOLT, ROBERT B.*	66,077	SPARKS, NICHOLAS B.	349	130,664 R	74.8%	25.1%	74.9%	25.1%
4	2006	183,072	128,484	ADERHOLT, ROBERT B.*	54,382	BOBO, BARBARA	206	74,102 R	70.2%	29.7%	70.3%	29.7%
4	2004	255,724	191,110	ADERHOLT, ROBERT B.*	64,278	COLE, CARL	336	126,832 R	74.7%	25.1%	74.8%	25.2%
4	2002	161,101	139,705	ADERHOLT, ROBERT B.*	—		21,396	139,705 R	86.7%		100.0%	

ALABAMA

HOUSE OF REPRESENTATIVES

CD	Year	Total Vote	Republican Vote	Candidate	Democratic Vote	Candidate	Other Vote	Rep.-Dem. Plurality	Total Vote Rep.	Total Vote Dem.	Major Vote Rep.	Major Vote Dem.
5	2008	307,282	147,314	PARKER, WAYNE	158,324	GRIFFITH, PARKER	1,644	11,010 D	47.9%	51.5%	48.2%	51.8%
5	2006	145,555		—	143,015	CRAMER, ROBERT E. "BUD"*	2,540	143,015 D		98.3%		100.0%
5	2004	275,459	74,145	WALLACE, GERALD "GERRY"	200,999	CRAMER, ROBERT E. "BUD"*	315	126,854 D	26.9%	73.0%	26.9%	73.1%
5	2002	195,171	48,226	ENGEL, STEPHEN P.	143,029	CRAMER, ROBERT E. "BUD"*	3,916	94,803 D	24.7%	73.3%	25.2%	74.8%
6	2008	287,237	280,902	BACHUS, SPENCER*		—	6,335	280,902 R	97.8%		100.0%	
6	2006	166,300	163,514	BACHUS, SPENCER*		—	2,786	163,514 R	98.3%		100.0%	
6	2004	268,043	264,819	BACHUS, SPENCER*		—	3,224	264,819 R	98.8%		100.0%	
6	2002	198,346	178,171	BACHUS, SPENCER*		—	20,175	178,171 R	89.8%		100.0%	
7	2008	231,701		—	228,518	DAVIS, ARTUR*	3,183	228,518 D		98.6%		100.0%
7	2006	135,164		—	133,870	DAVIS, ARTUR*	1,294	133,870 D		99.0%		100.0%
7	2004	244,638	61,019	CAMERON, STEVE F.	183,408	DAVIS, ARTUR*	211	122,389 D	24.9%	75.0%	25.0%	75.0%
7	2002	166,309		—	153,735	DAVIS, ARTUR	12,574	153,735 D		92.4%		100.0%
TOTAL	2008	1,855,268	1,120,903		718,367		15,998	402,536 R	60.4%	38.7%	60.9%	39.1%
TOTAL	2006	1,140,152	627,501		502,046		10,605	125,455 R	55.0%	44.0%	55.6%	44.4%
TOTAL	2004	1,792,759	1,079,657		708,425		4,677	371,232 R	60.2%	39.5%	60.4%	39.6%
TOTAL	2002	1,268,802	694,606		507,117		67,079	187,489 R	54.7%	40.0%	57.8%	42.2%

Note: An asterisk (*) denotes incumbent.

ALABAMA

GENERAL AND PRIMARY ELECTIONS

2008 GENERAL ELECTIONS

President   Other vote was 6,788 Independent (Ralph Nader); 4,991 Independent (Bob Barr); 4,310 Independent (Chuck Baldwin); 3,705 scattered write-in.

Senator   Other vote was 2,417 scattered write-in.

House   Other vote was:

CD 1   3,707 scattered write-in.
CD 2   448 scattered write-in.
CD 3   332 scattered write-in.
CD 4   349 scattered write-in.
CD 5   1,644 scattered write-in.
CD 6   6,335 scattered write-in.
CD 7   3,183 scattered write-in.

2008 PRIMARY ELECTIONS

Primary   February 5, 2008 (President)   **Registration**   2,786,824   No Party
June 3, 2008 (Congress)   (as of May 30, 2008;   Registration
includes 189,743
inactive registrants)

Primary Runoff   July 15, 2008

Primary Type   Open—Any registered voter could vote in either the Democratic or Republican primary, although any voter who participated in the Republican primary could not vote in the Democratic runoff. There was no such restriction on participation in the Republican runoff.

ALABAMA

GENERAL AND PRIMARY ELECTIONS

	REPUBLICAN PRIMARIES			DEMOCRATIC PRIMARIES		
President	Mike Huckabee	227,766	41.3%	Barack Obama	300,319	56.0%
	John McCain	204,867	37.1%	Hillary Clinton	223,089	41.6%
	Mitt Romney	98,019	17.8%	John Edwards	7,841	1.5%
	Ron Paul	14,810	2.7%	Uncommitted	2,663	0.5%
	Rudolph Giuliani	2,134	0.4%	Joseph R. Biden Jr.	1,174	0.2%
	Fred Thompson	1,835	0.3%	Bill Richardson	1,017	0.2%
	Uncommitted	1,234	0.2%	Christopher J. Dodd	523	0.1%
	Alan Keyes	778	0.1%			
	Duncan Hunter	391	0.1%			
	Hugh Cort	228				
	Tom Tancredo	93				
	TOTAL	*552,155*		*TOTAL*	*536,626*	
Senator	Jeff Sessions*	Unopposed		Vivian Davis Figures	112,074	63.7%
				Johnny Swanson III	38,757	22.0%
				Mark 'No NCAA' Townsend	25,058	14.2%
				TOTAL	*175,889*	
Congressional District 1	Jo Bonner*	Unopposed		*No Democratic candidate. Thomas E. Fuller filed for the Democratic primary but subsequently withdrew from the race.*		
Congressional District 2	Jay Love	20,131	35.5%	Bobby Bright	19,456	66.6%
	Harri Anne Smith	12,349	21.8%	Cendie Crawley	5,110	17.5%
	Craig D. Schmidtke	11,350	20.0%	Cheryl Sabel	4,631	15.9%
	David Woods	9,757	17.2%			
	David Grimes	2,324	4.1%			
	John W. Martin	824	1.5%			
	TOTAL	*56,735*		*TOTAL*	*29,197*	
	PRIMARY RUNOFF					
	Jay Love	24,725	53.1%			
	Harri Anne Smith	21,827	46.9%			
	TOTAL	*46,552*				
Congressional District 3	Mike D. Rogers*	Unopposed		Joshua Segall	Unopposed	
Congressional District 4	Robert B. Aderholt*	Unopposed		Nicholas B. Sparks	15,777	58.1%
				Greg Warren	11,381	41.9%
				TOTAL	*27,158*	
Congressional District 5	Wayne Parker	18,515	48.8%	Parker Griffith	34,543	89.9%
	Cheryl Baswell Guthrie	6,942	18.3%	David Maker	3,874	10.1%
	Angelo 'Doc' Mancuso	6,161	16.2%			
	Ray McKee	3,342	8.8%			
	George C. Barry	2,274	6.0%			
	Mark Huff	707	1.9%			
	TOTAL	*37,941*		*TOTAL*	*38,417*	
	PRIMARY RUNOFF					
	Wayne Parker	16,031	78.7%			
	Cheryl Baswell Guthrie	4,330	21.3%			
	TOTAL	*20,361*				
Congressional District 6	Spencer Bachus*	Unopposed		No Democratic candidate		
Congressional District 7	No Republican candidate			Artur Davis*	Unopposed	

Note: An asterisk (*) denotes incumbent.

ALASKA

One member At Large

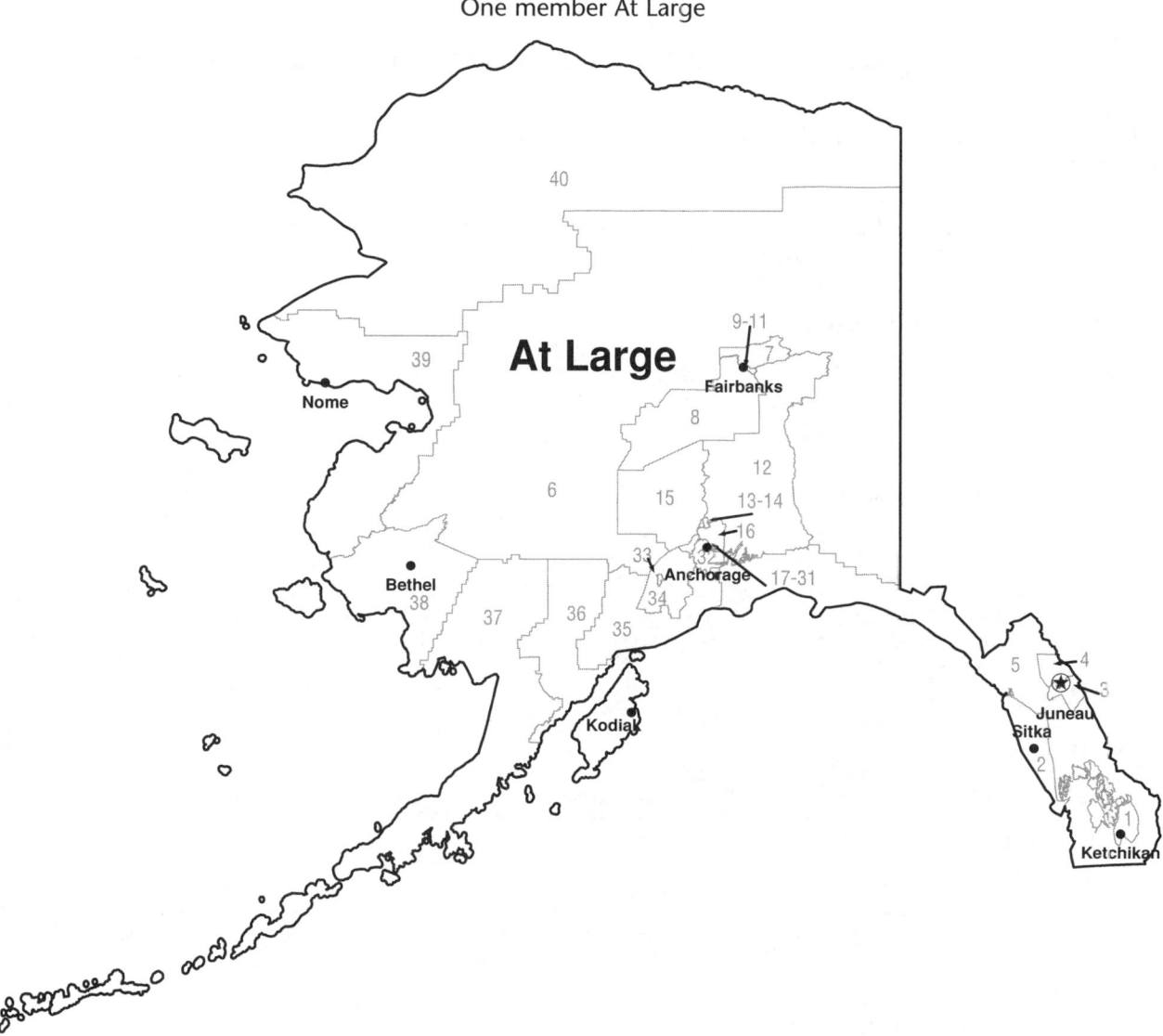

ALASKA

GOVERNOR

Sean R. Parnell (R). Assumed office July 26, 2009, upon the resignation of Sarah H. Palin (R).

SENATORS (1 Democrat, 1 Republican)

Mark Begich (D). Elected 2008 to a six-year term.

Lisa Murkowski (R). Elected 2004 to a six-year term. Had been appointed in December 2002 to fill the vacancy created by the resignation of her father, Frank H. Murkowski (R), to become governor of Alaska.

REPRESENTATIVE (1 Republican)

At Large. Don Young (R)

POSTWAR VOTE FOR PRESIDENT

| | | Republican | | Democratic | | Other | | Percentage | | | |
| | Total | | | | | | | Total Vote | | Major Vote | |
Year	Vote	Vote	Candidate	Vote	Candidate	Vote	Plurality	Rep.	Dem.	Rep.	Dem.
2008	326,197	193,841	McCain, John	123,594	Obama, Barack	8,762	70,247 R	59.4%	37.9%	61.1%	38.9%
2004	312,598	190,889	Bush, George W.	111,025	Kerry, John	10,684	79,864 R	61.1%	35.5%	63.2%	36.8%
2000**	285,560	167,398	Bush, George W.	79,004	Gore, Al	39,158	88,394 R	58.6%	27.7%	67.9%	32.1%
1996**	241,620	122,746	Dole, Bob	80,380	Clinton, Bill	38,494	42,366 R	50.8%	33.3%	60.4%	39.6%
1992**	258,506	102,000	Bush, George	78,294	Clinton, Bill	78,212	23,706 R	39.5%	30.3%	56.6%	43.4%
1988	200,116	119,251	Bush, George	72,584	Dukakis, Michael S.	8,281	46,667 R	59.6%	36.3%	62.2%	37.8%
1984	207,605	138,377	Reagan, Ronald	62,007	Mondale, Walter F.	7,221	76,370 R	66.7%	29.9%	69.1%	30.9%
1980**	158,445	86,112	Reagan, Ronald	41,842	Carter, Jimmy	30,491	44,270 R	54.3%	26.4%	67.3%	32.7%
1976	123,574	71,555	Ford, Gerald R.	44,058	Carter, Jimmy	7,961	27,497 R	57.9%	35.7%	61.9%	38.1%
1972	95,219	55,349	Nixon, Richard M.	32,967	McGovern, George S.	6,903	22,382 R	58.1%	34.6%	62.7%	37.3%
1968**	83,035	37,600	Nixon, Richard M.	35,411	Humphrey, Hubert H.	10,024	2,189 R	45.3%	42.6%	51.5%	48.5%
1964	67,259	22,930	Goldwater, Barry M.	44,329	Johnson, Lyndon B.		21,399 D	34.1%	65.9%	34.1%	65.9%
1960	60,762	30,953	Nixon, Richard M.	29,809	Kennedy, John F.		1,144 R	50.9%	49.1%	50.9%	49.1%

Notes: **In past elections, the other vote included: 2000 - 28,747 Green (Ralph Nader); 1996 - 26,333 Reform (Ross Perot); 1992 - 73,481 Independent (Perot); 1980 - 18,479 Libertarian (Ed Clark) and 11,155 Independent (John Anderson); 1968 - 10,024 American Independent (George Wallace). Alaska was formally admitted as a state in January 1959.

POSTWAR VOTE FOR GOVERNOR

| | | Republican | | Democratic | | Other | | Percentage | | | |
| | Total | | | | | | | Total Vote | | Major Vote | |
Year	Vote	Vote	Candidate	Vote	Candidate	Vote	Plurality	Rep.	Dem.	Rep.	Dem.
2006	237,322	114,697	Palin, Sarah H.	97,238	Knowles, Tony	25,387	17,459 R	48.3%	41.0%	54.1%	45.9%
2002	231,484	129,279	Murkowski, Frank H.	94,216	Ulmer, Fran	7,989	35,063 R	55.8%	40.7%	57.8%	42.2%
1998**	220,177	39,331	Lindauer, John	112,879	Knowles, Tony	67,967	72,670 D	17.9%	51.3%	25.8%	74.2%
1994**	213,435	87,157	Campbell, James O.	87,693	Knowles, Tony	38,585	536 D	40.8%	41.1%	49.8%	50.2%
1990**	194,750	50,991	Sturgulewski, Arliss	60,201	Knowles, Tony	83,558	15,520 AI	26.2%	30.9%	45.9%	54.1%
1986	179,555	76,515	Sturgulewski, Arliss	84,943	Cowper, Steve	18,097	8,428 D	42.6%	47.3%	47.4%	52.6%
1982**	194,885	72,291	Fink, Tom	89,918	Sheffield, Bill	32,676	17,627 D	37.1%	46.1%	44.6%	55.4%
1978**	126,910	49,580	Hammond, Jay S.	25,656	Croft, Chancy	51,674	16,025 R	39.1%	20.2%	65.9%	34.1%
1974	96,163	45,840	Hammond, Jay S.	45,553	Egan, William A.	4,770	287 R	47.7%	47.4%	50.2%	49.8%
1970	80,779	37,264	Miller, Keith	42,309	Egan, William A.	1,206	5,045 D	46.1%	52.4%	46.8%	53.2%
1966	66,294	33,145	Hickel, Walter J.	32,065	Egan, William A.	1,084	1,080 R	50.0%	48.4%	50.8%	49.2%
1962	56,681	27,054	Stepovich, Mike	29,627	Egan, William A.		2,573 D	47.7%	52.3%	47.7%	52.3%
1958	48,968	19,299	Butrovich, John	29,189	Egan, William A.	480	9,890 D	39.4%	59.6%	39.8%	60.2%

Notes: **In past elections, the other vote included: 1998 - 40,209 write-in (Robin Taylor), who finished second; 1994 - 27,838 Alaskan Independence (John B. "Jack" Coghill); 1990 - 75,721 Alaskan Independence (Walter J. Hickel); 1982 - 29,067 Libertarian (Richard L. Randolph); 1978 - 33,555 write-in (Walter J. Hickel) and 15,656 Alaskans for Kelly (Tom Kelly). Hickel won the 1990 election with 38.9 percent of the total vote and finished second in 1978.

ALASKA

POSTWAR VOTE FOR SENATOR

Year	Total Vote	Republican Vote	Republican Candidate	Democratic Vote	Democratic Candidate	Other Vote	Plurality	Percentage Total Vote Rep.	Percentage Total Vote Dem.	Percentage Major Vote Rep.	Percentage Major Vote Dem.
2008	317,723	147,814	Stevens, Ted	151,767	Begich, Mark	18,142	3,953 D	46.5%	47.8%	49.3%	50.7%
2004	308,315	149,773	Murkowski, Lisa	140,424	Knowles, Tony	18,118	9,349 R	48.6%	45.5%	51.6%	48.4%
2002	229,548	179,438	Stevens, Ted	24,133	Vondersaar, Frank	25,977	155,305 R	78.2%	10.5%	88.1%	11.9%
1998	221,807	165,227	Murkowski, Frank H.	43,743	Sonneman, Joseph	12,837	121,484 R	74.5%	19.7%	79.1%	20.9%
1996**	231,916	177,893	Stevens, Ted	23,977	Obermeyer, Theresa	30,046	148,856 R	76.7%	10.3%	88.1%	11.9%
1992	239,714	127,163	Murkowski, Frank H.	92,065	Smith, Tony	20,486	35,098 R	53.0%	38.4%	58.0%	42.0%
1990	189,957	125,806	Stevens, Ted	61,152	Beasley, Michael	2,999	64,654 R	66.2%	32.2%	67.3%	32.7%
1986	180,801	97,674	Murkowski, Frank H.	79,727	Olds, Glenn	3,400	17,947 R	54.0%	44.1%	55.1%	44.9%
1984	206,438	146,919	Stevens, Ted	58,804	Havelock, John E.	715	88,115 R	71.2%	28.5%	71.4%	28.6%
1980	156,762	84,159	Murkowski, Frank H.	72,007	Gruening, Clark S.	596	12,152 R	53.7%	45.9%	53.9%	46.1%
1978	122,741	92,783	Stevens, Ted	29,574	Hobbs, Donald W.	384	63,209 R	75.6%	24.1%	75.8%	24.2%
1974	93,275	38,914	Lewis, C. R.	54,361	Gravel, Mike		15,447 D	41.7%	58.3%	41.7%	58.3%
1972	96,007	74,216	Stevens, Ted	21,791	Guess, Gene		52,425 R	77.3%	22.7%	77.3%	22.7%
1970S	80,364	47,908	Stevens, Ted	32,456	Kay, Wendell P.		15,452 R	59.6%	40.4%	59.6%	40.4%
1968	80,931	30,286	Rasmuson, Elmer	36,527	Gravel, Mike	14,118	6,241 D	37.4%	45.1%	45.3%	54.7%
1966	65,250	15,961	McKinley, Lee L.	49,289	Bartlett, E. L.		33,328 D	24.5%	75.5%	24.5%	75.5%
1962	58,181	24,354	Stevens, Ted	33,827	Gruening, Ernest		9,473 D	41.9%	58.1%	41.9%	58.1%
1960	59,978	21,937	McKinley, Lee L.	38,041	Bartlett, E. L.		16,104 D	36.6%	63.4%	36.6%	63.4%
1958S	49,525	23,462	Stepovich, Mike	26,063	Gruening, Ernest		2,601 D	47.4%	52.6%	47.4%	52.6%
1958S	48,837	7,299	Robertson, R. E.	40,939	Bartlett, E. L.	599	33,640 D	14.9%	83.8%	15.1%	84.9%

Notes: **In past elections, the other vote included: 1996 - 29,037 Green (Jed Whittaker), who finished second. S = The 1970 election was for a short term to fill a vacancy. The two 1958 elections were held to indeterminate terms and the Senate later determined by lot that Senator Gruening would serve four years, Senator Bartlett two.

ALASKA

PRESIDENT 2008

2000 Census Population	District	Total Vote	Republican	Democratic	Other	Rep.-Dem. Plurality	Percentage			
							Total Vote		Major Vote	
							Rep.	Dem.	Rep.	Dem.
15,031	DISTRICT 1	6,970	4,149	2,597	224	1,552 R	59.5%	37.3%	61.5%	38.5%
14,991	DISTRICT 2	7,735	4,029	3,468	238	561 R	52.1%	44.8%	53.7%	46.3%
15,203	DISTRICT 3	8,767	2,829	5,657	281	2,828 D	32.3%	64.5%	33.3%	66.7%
15,508	DISTRICT 4	8,736	4,302	4,161	273	141 R	49.2%	47.6%	50.8%	49.2%
15,048	DISTRICT 5	7,123	3,426	3,393	304	33 R	48.1%	47.6%	50.2%	49.8%
14,905	DISTRICT 6	6,824	4,234	2,351	239	1,883 R	62.0%	34.5%	64.3%	35.7%
15,494	DISTRICT 7	10,894	6,297	4,283	314	2,014 R	57.8%	39.3%	59.5%	40.5%
15,552	DISTRICT 8	10,320	4,983	4,995	342	12 D	48.3%	48.4%	49.9%	50.1%
15,723	DISTRICT 9	7,143	4,141	2,805	197	1,336 R	58.0%	39.3%	59.6%	40.4%
15,599	DISTRICT 10	5,615	3,392	2,074	149	1,318 R	60.4%	36.9%	62.1%	37.9%
15,904	DISTRICT 11	9,866	7,736	1,924	206	5,812 R	78.4%	19.5%	80.1%	19.9%
16,303	DISTRICT 12	7,589	5,467	1,914	208	3,553 R	72.0%	25.2%	74.1%	25.9%
16,231	DISTRICT 13	11,526	8,432	2,800	294	5,632 R	73.2%	24.3%	75.1%	24.9%
16,119	DISTRICT 14	10,456	8,108	2,132	216	5,976 R	77.5%	20.4%	79.2%	20.8%
16,137	DISTRICT 15	11,086	8,227	2,510	349	5,717 R	74.2%	22.6%	76.6%	23.4%
16,104	DISTRICT 16	10,697	7,774	2,636	287	5,138 R	72.7%	24.6%	74.7%	25.3%
15,819	DISTRICT 17	9,448	6,621	2,645	182	3,976 R	70.1%	28.0%	71.5%	28.5%
15,639	DISTRICT 18	6,411	4,252	2,046	113	2,206 R	66.3%	31.9%	67.5%	32.5%
15,841	DISTRICT 19	7,372	4,106	3,095	171	1,011 R	55.7%	42.0%	57.0%	43.0%
15,837	DISTRICT 20	5,138	2,536	2,474	128	62 R	49.4%	48.2%	50.6%	49.4%
15,850	DISTRICT 21	8,675	4,837	3,647	191	1,190 R	55.8%	42.0%	57.0%	43.0%
15,831	DISTRICT 22	6,634	3,109	3,337	188	228 D	46.9%	50.3%	48.2%	51.8%
15,847	DISTRICT 23	7,082	2,808	4,075	199	1,267 D	39.6%	57.5%	40.8%	59.2%
15,812	DISTRICT 24	7,688	4,127	3,380	181	747 R	53.7%	44.0%	55.0%	45.0%
15,836	DISTRICT 25	6,443	3,042	3,233	168	191 D	47.2%	50.2%	48.5%	51.5%
15,823	DISTRICT 26	8,695	4,037	4,472	186	435 D	46.4%	51.4%	47.4%	52.6%
15,820	DISTRICT 27	8,498	5,159	3,130	209	2,029 R	60.7%	36.8%	62.2%	37.8%
15,839	DISTRICT 28	9,792	5,953	3,642	197	2,311 R	60.8%	37.2%	62.0%	38.0%
15,846	DISTRICT 29	6,962	4,127	2,684	151	1,443 R	59.3%	38.6%	60.6%	39.4%
15,839	DISTRICT 30	9,183	5,500	3,486	197	2,014 R	59.9%	38.0%	61.2%	38.8%
15,811	DISTRICT 31	10,220	6,419	3,596	205	2,823 R	62.8%	35.2%	64.1%	35.9%
15,329	DISTRICT 32	12,307	6,867	5,176	264	1,691 R	55.8%	42.1%	57.0%	43.0%
16,466	DISTRICT 33	8,909	6,571	2,089	249	4,482 R	73.8%	23.4%	75.9%	24.1%
16,409	DISTRICT 34	9,548	7,358	1,920	270	5,438 R	77.1%	20.1%	79.3%	20.7%
16,436	DISTRICT 35	9,503	4,959	4,254	290	705 R	52.2%	44.8%	53.8%	46.2%
14,928	DISTRICT 36	6,673	4,201	2,264	208	1,937 R	63.0%	33.9%	65.0%	35.0%
15,150	DISTRICT 37	4,665	2,661	1,868	136	793 R	57.0%	40.0%	58.8%	41.2%
14,921	DISTRICT 38	4,820	2,056	2,549	215	493 D	42.7%	52.9%	44.6%	55.4%
14,996	DISTRICT 39	5,184	2,323	2,695	166	372 D	44.8%	52.0%	46.3%	53.7%
15,155	DISTRICT 40	5,000	2,686	2,137	177	549 R	53.7%	42.7%	55.7%	44.3%
626,932	TOTAL	326,197	193,841	123,594	8,762	70,247 R	59.4%	37.9%	61.1%	38.9%

ALASKA
SENATOR 2008

2000 Census Population	District	Total Vote	Republican	Democratic	Other	Rep.-Dem. Plurality	Percentage Total Vote Rep.	Dem.	Major Vote Rep.	Dem.
15,031	DISTRICT 1	6,730	3,352	2,912	466	440 R	49.8%	43.3%	53.5%	46.5%
14,991	DISTRICT 2	7,499	3,003	4,091	405	1,088 D	40.0%	54.6%	42.3%	57.7%
15,203	DISTRICT 3	8,578	2,202	6,081	295	3,879 D	25.7%	70.9%	26.6%	73.4%
15,508	DISTRICT 4	8,516	3,094	5,050	372	1,956 D	36.3%	59.3%	38.0%	62.0%
15,048	DISTRICT 5	6,962	2,581	3,890	491	1,309 D	37.1%	55.9%	39.9%	60.1%
14,905	DISTRICT 6	6,641	3,060	3,114	467	54 D	46.1%	46.9%	49.6%	50.4%
15,494	DISTRICT 7	10,660	4,804	5,068	788	264 D	45.1%	47.5%	48.7%	51.3%
15,552	DISTRICT 8	10,088	3,807	5,573	708	1,766 D	37.7%	55.2%	40.6%	59.4%
15,723	DISTRICT 9	6,921	3,085	3,370	466	285 D	44.6%	48.7%	47.8%	52.2%
15,599	DISTRICT 10	5,355	2,354	2,524	477	170 D	44.0%	47.1%	48.3%	51.7%
15,904	DISTRICT 11	9,483	5,274	3,246	963	2,028 R	55.6%	34.2%	61.9%	38.1%
16,303	DISTRICT 12	7,289	3,852	2,813	624	1,039 R	52.8%	38.6%	57.8%	42.2%
16,231	DISTRICT 13	11,263	6,279	4,302	682	1,977 R	55.7%	38.2%	59.3%	40.7%
16,119	DISTRICT 14	10,163	5,957	3,600	606	2,357 R	58.6%	35.4%	62.3%	37.7%
16,137	DISTRICT 15	10,842	6,290	3,865	687	2,425 R	58.0%	35.6%	61.9%	38.1%
16,104	DISTRICT 16	10,544	6,166	3,790	588	2,376 R	58.5%	35.9%	61.9%	38.1%
15,819	DISTRICT 17	9,176	4,982	3,717	477	1,265 R	54.3%	40.5%	57.3%	42.7%
15,639	DISTRICT 18	5,918	2,526	2,894	498	368 D	42.7%	48.9%	46.6%	53.4%
15,841	DISTRICT 19	7,195	3,134	3,729	332	595 D	43.6%	51.8%	45.7%	54.3%
15,837	DISTRICT 20	4,977	1,942	2,814	221	872 D	39.0%	56.5%	40.8%	59.2%
15,850	DISTRICT 21	8,506	3,817	4,357	332	540 D	44.9%	51.2%	46.7%	53.3%
15,831	DISTRICT 22	6,469	2,404	3,783	282	1,379 D	37.2%	58.5%	38.9%	61.1%
15,847	DISTRICT 23	6,930	2,398	4,266	266	1,868 D	34.6%	61.6%	36.0%	64.0%
15,812	DISTRICT 24	7,501	3,323	3,857	321	534 D	44.3%	51.4%	46.3%	53.7%
15,836	DISTRICT 25	6,291	2,523	3,490	278	967 D	40.1%	55.5%	42.0%	58.0%
15,823	DISTRICT 26	8,553	3,642	4,644	267	1,002 D	42.6%	54.3%	44.0%	56.0%
15,820	DISTRICT 27	8,356	4,274	3,738	344	536 R	51.1%	44.7%	53.3%	46.7%
15,839	DISTRICT 28	9,626	5,038	4,186	402	852 R	52.3%	43.5%	54.6%	45.4%
15,846	DISTRICT 29	6,789	3,238	3,278	273	40 D	47.7%	48.3%	49.7%	50.3%
15,839	DISTRICT 30	9,024	4,467	4,215	342	252 R	49.5%	46.7%	51.5%	48.5%
15,811	DISTRICT 31	10,070	5,480	4,221	369	1,259 R	54.4%	41.9%	56.5%	43.5%
15,329	DISTRICT 32	12,122	6,050	5,652	420	398 R	49.9%	46.6%	51.7%	48.3%
16,466	DISTRICT 33	8,662	4,493	3,321	848	1,172 R	51.9%	38.3%	57.5%	42.5%
16,409	DISTRICT 34	9,325	5,077	3,107	1,141	1,970 R	54.4%	33.3%	62.0%	38.0%
16,436	DISTRICT 35	9,242	3,818	4,979	445	1,161 D	41.3%	53.9%	43.4%	56.6%
14,928	DISTRICT 36	6,359	2,701	3,208	450	507 D	42.5%	50.4%	45.7%	54.3%
15,150	DISTRICT 37	4,532	2,076	2,253	203	177 D	45.8%	49.7%	48.0%	52.0%
14,921	DISTRICT 38	4,729	1,464	3,072	193	1,608 D	31.0%	65.0%	32.3%	67.7%
14,996	DISTRICT 39	5,072	1,944	2,958	170	1,014 D	38.3%	58.3%	39.7%	60.3%
15,155	DISTRICT 40	4,765	1,843	2,739	183	896 D	38.7%	57.5%	40.2%	59.8%
626,932	TOTAL	317,723	147,814	151,767	18,142	3,953 D	46.5%	47.8%	49.3%	50.7%

ALASKA

HOUSE OF REPRESENTATIVES

| | | | Republican | | | Democratic | | | | Percentage | | | |
| | | | | | | | | | | Total Vote | | Major Vote | |
CD	Year	Total Vote	Vote	Candidate	Vote	Candidate	Other Vote	Rep.-Dem. Plurality		Rep.	Dem.	Rep.	Dem.
AL	2008	316,978	158,939	YOUNG, DON*	142,560	BERKOWITZ, ETHAN A.	15,479	16,379	R	50.1%	45.0%	52.7%	47.3%
AL	2006	234,645	132,743	YOUNG, DON*	93,879	BENSON, DIANE E.	8,023	38,864	R	56.6%	40.0%	58.6%	41.4%
AL	2004	299,996	213,216	YOUNG, DON*	67,074	HIGGINS, THOMAS M.	19,706	146,142	R	71.1%	22.4%	76.1%	23.9%
AL	2002	227,725	169,685	YOUNG, DON*	39,357	GREENE, CLIFFORD	18,683	130,328	R	74.5%	17.3%	81.2%	18.8%
AL	2000	274,393	190,862	YOUNG, DON*	45,372	GREENE, CLIFFORD	38,159	145,490	R	69.6%	16.5%	80.8%	19.2%
AL	1998	223,300	139,676	YOUNG, DON*	77,232	DUNCAN, JIM	6,392	62,444	R	62.6%	34.6%	64.4%	35.6%
AL	1996	233,700	138,834	YOUNG, DON*	85,114	LINCOLN, GEORGIANNA	9,752	53,720	R	59.4%	36.4%	62.0%	38.0%
AL	1994	208,240	118,537	YOUNG, DON*	68,172	SMITH, TONY	21,531	50,365	R	56.9%	32.7%	63.5%	36.5%
AL	1992	239,116	111,849	YOUNG, DON*	102,378	DEVENS, JOHN S.	24,889	9,471	R	46.8%	42.8%	52.2%	47.8%
AL	1990	191,647	99,003	YOUNG, DON*	91,677	DEVENS, JOHN S.	967	7,326	R	51.7%	47.8%	51.9%	48.1%
AL	1988	192,955	120,595	YOUNG, DON*	71,881	GRUENSTEIN, PETER	479	48,714	R	62.5%	37.3%	62.7%	37.3%
AL	1986	180,277	101,799	YOUNG, DON*	74,053	BEGICH, PEGGE	4,425	27,746	R	56.5%	41.1%	57.9%	42.1%
AL	1984	206,437	113,582	YOUNG, DON*	86,052	BEGICH, PEGGE	6,803	27,530	R	55.0%	41.7%	56.9%	43.1%
AL	1982	181,084	128,274	YOUNG, DON*	52,011	CARLSON, DAVE	799	76,263	R	70.8%	28.7%	71.2%	28.8%
AL	1980	154,618	114,089	YOUNG, DON*	39,922	PARNELL, KEVIN	607	74,167	R	73.8%	25.8%	74.1%	25.9%
AL	1978	124,187	68,811	YOUNG, DON*	55,176	RODNEY, PATRICK	200	13,635	R	55.4%	44.4%	55.5%	44.5%
AL	1976	118,208	83,722	YOUNG, DON*	34,194	HOPSON, EBEN	292	49,528	R	70.8%	28.9%	71.0%	29.0%
AL	1974	95,921	51,641	YOUNG, DON*	44,280	HENSLEY, WILLIAM L.		7,361	R	53.8%	46.2%	53.8%	46.2%
AL	1972	95,401	41,750	YOUNG, DON	53,651	BEGICH, NICK*		11,901	D	43.8%	56.2%	43.8%	56.2%
AL	1970	80,084	35,947	MURKOWSKI, FRANK H.	44,137	BEGICH, NICK		8,190	D	44.9%	55.1%	44.9%	55.1%
AL	1968	80,362	43,577	POLLOCK, HOWARD W.*	36,785	BEGICH, NICK		6,792	R	54.2%	45.8%	54.2%	45.8%
AL	1966	65,907	34,040	POLLOCK, HOWARD W.	31,867	RIVERS, RALPH J.*		2,173	R	51.6%	48.4%	51.6%	48.4%
AL	1964	67,146	32,556	THOMAS, LOWELL	34,590	RIVERS, RALPH J.*		2,034	D	48.5%	51.5%	48.5%	51.5%
AL	1962	58,591	26,638	THOMAS, LOWELL	31,953	RIVERS, RALPH J.*		5,315	D	45.5%	54.5%	45.5%	54.5%
AL	1960	59,063	25,517	RETTIG, R.L.	33,546	RIVERS, RALPH J.*		8,029	D	43.2%	56.8%	43.2%	56.8%
AL	1958	48,647	20,699	BENSON, HENRY A.	27,948	RIVERS, RALPH J.		7,249	D	42.5%	57.5%	42.5%	57.5%

Note: An asterisk (*) denotes incumbent.

ALASKA

GENERAL AND PRIMARY ELECTIONS

2008 GENERAL ELECTIONS

President Other vote was 3,783 Independent (Ralph Nader); 1,660 Alaskan Independence (Chuck Baldwin); 1,589 Libertarian (Bob Barr); 1,730 scattered write-in.

Senator Other vote was 13,197 Alaskan Independence (Bob Bird); 2,483 Libertarian (Fredrick D. "David" Haase); 1,385 None (Ted Gianoutsos); 1,077 scattered write-in.

House Other vote was:

 At Large 14,274 Alaskan Independence (Don R. Wright); 1,205 scattered write-in.

2008 PRIMARY ELECTIONS

Primary August 26, 2008

Registration (as of August 26, 2008)

Republican	127,447
Democratic	77,019
Alaskan Independence	13,788
Libertarian	6,810
Republican Moderate	3,823
Green	2,895
Veterans	1,915
Other	24
Nonpartisan	77,349
Undeclared	184,480
TOTAL	*495,550*

ALASKA

GENERAL AND PRIMARY ELECTIONS

2008 PRIMARY ELECTIONS

Primary Type   Any registered voter could participate in the Democratic primary. The Republican primary was restricted to registered Republican, Undeclared, and Nonpartisan voters. (Undeclared voters may be associated with a party, but do not wish to declare which one. Nonpartisan voters are not associated with any party.) Democratic candidates were listed on the primary ballot together with candidates of the Alaskan Independence and Libertarian parties. The high vote-getter of each party went on to the general election ballot. Republican candidates were listed on a primary ballot of their own.

	REPUBLICAN PRIMARIES			DEMOCRATIC PRIMARIES		
Senator	Ted Stevens*	66,900	63.5%	Mark Begich	63,747	90.8%
	David W. Cuddy	28,364	26.9%	Ray Metcalfe	5,480	7.8%
	Vic Vickers	6,102	5.8%	Frank J. Vondersaar	965	1.4%
	Michael D. Corey	1,496	1.4%			
	Roderic H. Sikma	1,133	1.1%			
	Rich M. Wanda	732	0.7%			
	Gerald L. Heikes	599	0.6%			
	TOTAL	*105,326*		*TOTAL*	*70,192*	
House	Don Young*	48,195	45.5%	Ethan A. Berkowitz	39,784	58.4%
At Large	Sean R. Parnell	47,891	45.2%	Diane E. Benson	28,347	41.6%
	Gabrielle LeDoux	9,901	9.3%			
	TOTAL	*105,987*		*TOTAL*	*68,131*	

Note: An asterisk (*) denotes incumbent.

ARIZONA

Congressional districts first established for elections held in 2002
8 members

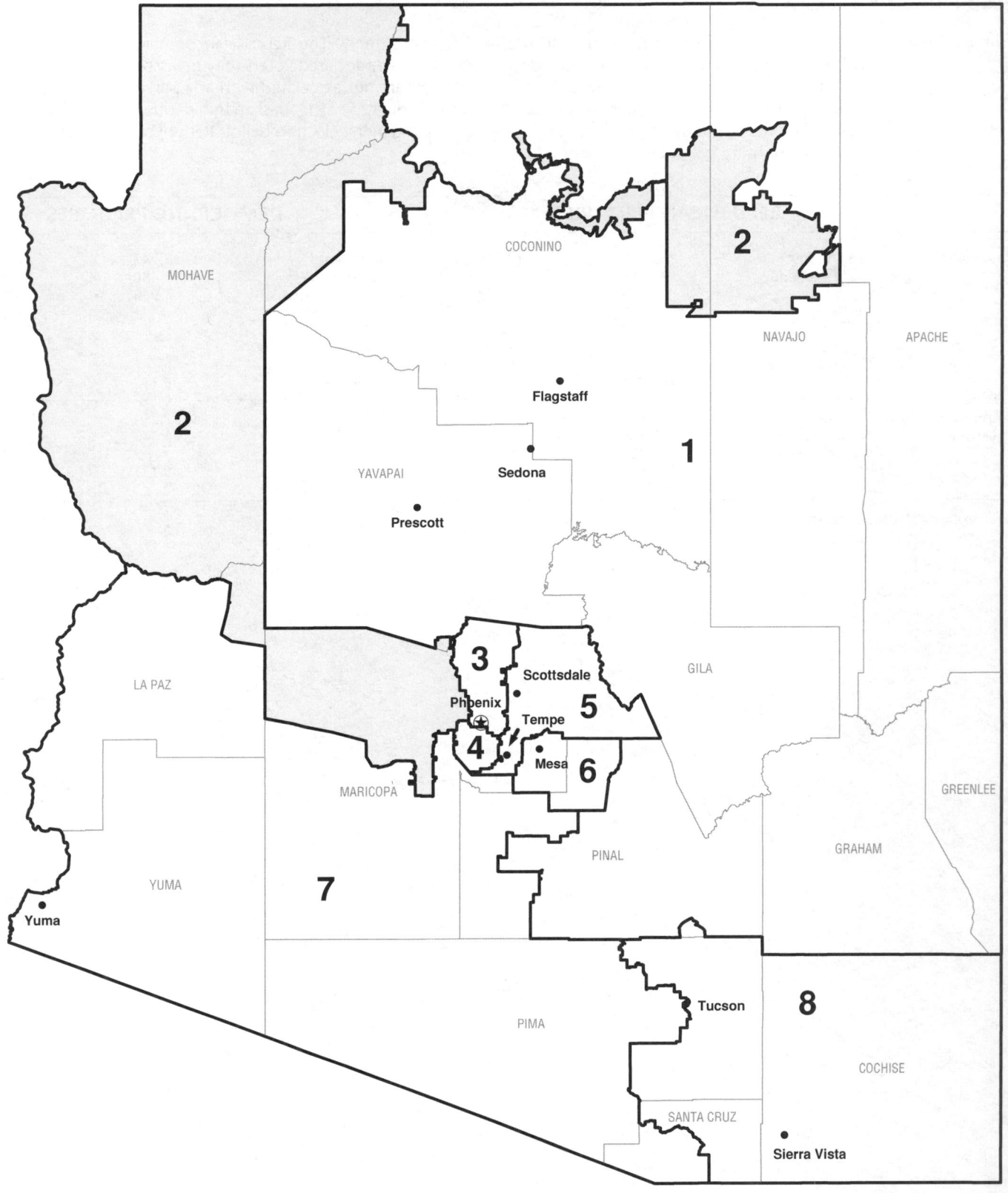

ARIZONA

GOVERNOR

Jan Brewer (R). Sworn in as governor January 21, 2009, to fill the vacancy created by the resignation of Janet Napolitano (D) to become U.S. Secretary of Homeland Security.

SENATORS (2 Republicans)

Jon Kyl (R). Reelected 2006 to a six-year term. Previously elected 2000, 1994.

John McCain (R). Reelected 2004 to a six-year term. Previously elected 1998, 1992, 1986.

REPRESENTATIVES (5 Democrats, 3 Republicans)

1. Ann Kirkpatrick (D)
2. Trent Franks (R)
3. John Shadegg (R)
4. Ed Pastor (D)
5. Harry Mitchell (D)
6. Jeff Flake (R)
7. Raul M. Grijalva (D)
8. Gabrielle Giffords (D)

POSTWAR VOTE FOR PRESIDENT

| | | Republican | | Democratic | | Other | | Percentage Total Vote | | Major Vote | |
| | Total | | | | | | | | | | |
Year	Vote	Vote	Candidate	Vote	Candidate	Vote	Plurality	Rep.	Dem.	Rep.	Dem.
2008	2,293,475	1,230,111	McCain, John	1,034,707	Obama, Barack	28,657	195,404 R	53.6%	45.1%	54.3%	45.7%
2004	2,012,585	1,104,294	Bush, George W.	893,524	Kerry, John	14,767	210,770 R	54.9%	44.4%	55.3%	44.7%
2000**	1,532,016	781,652	Bush, George W.	685,341	Gore, Al	65,023	96,311 R	51.0%	44.7%	53.3%	46.7%
1996**	1,404,405	622,073	Dole, Bob	653,288	Clinton, Bill	129,044	31,215 D	44.3%	46.5%	48.8%	51.2%
1992**	1,486,975	572,086	Bush, George	543,050	Clinton, Bill	371,839	29,036 R	38.5%	36.5%	51.3%	48.7%
1988	1,171,873	702,541	Bush, George	454,029	Dukakis, Michael S.	15,303	248,512 R	60.0%	38.7%	60.7%	39.3%
1984	1,025,897	681,416	Reagan, Ronald	333,854	Mondale, Walter F.	10,627	347,562 R	66.4%	32.5%	67.1%	32.9%
1980**	873,945	529,688	Reagan, Ronald	246,843	Carter, Jimmy	97,414	282,845 R	60.6%	28.2%	68.2%	31.8%
1976	742,719	418,642	Ford, Gerald R.	295,602	Carter, Jimmy	28,475	123,040 R	56.4%	39.8%	58.6%	41.4%
1972	622,926	402,812	Nixon, Richard M.	198,540	McGovern, George S.	21,574	204,272 R	64.7%	31.9%	67.0%	33.0%
1968**	486,936	266,721	Nixon, Richard M.	170,514	Humphrey, Hubert H.	49,701	96,207 R	54.8%	35.0%	61.0%	39.0%
1964	480,770	242,535	Goldwater, Barry M.	237,753	Johnson, Lyndon B.	482	4,782 R	50.4%	49.5%	50.5%	49.5%
1960	398,491	221,241	Nixon, Richard M.	176,781	Kennedy, John F.	469	44,460 R	55.5%	44.4%	55.6%	44.4%
1956	290,173	176,990	Eisenhower, Dwight D.	112,880	Stevenson, Adlai E.	303	64,110 R	61.0%	38.9%	61.1%	38.9%
1952	260,570	152,042	Eisenhower, Dwight D.	108,528	Stevenson, Adlai E.		43,514 R	58.3%	41.7%	58.3%	41.7%
1948	177,065	77,597	Dewey, Thomas E.	95,251	Truman, Harry S.	4,217	17,654 D	43.8%	53.8%	44.9%	55.1%

Note: **In past elections, the other vote included: 2000 - 45,645 Green (Ralph Nader); 1996 - 112,072 Reform (Ross Perot); 1992 - 353,741 Independent (Perot); 1980 - 76,952 Independent (John Anderson); 1968 - 46,573 American Independent (George Wallace).

ARIZONA

POSTWAR VOTE FOR GOVERNOR

Year	Total Vote	Republican		Democratic		Other Vote	Rep.-Dem. Plurality	Percentage			
								Total Vote		Major Vote	
		Vote	Candidate	Vote	Candidate			Rep.	Dem.	Rep.	Dem.
2006	1,533,645	543,528	Munsil, Len	959,830	Napolitano, Janet	30,287	416,302 D	35.4%	62.6%	36.2%	63.8%
2002	1,226,111	554,465	Salmon, Matt	566,284	Napolitano, Janet	105,362	11,819 D	45.2%	46.2%	49.5%	50.5%
1998	1,017,616	620,188	Hull, Jane Dee	361,552	Johnson, Paul	35,876	258,636 R	60.9%	35.5%	63.2%	36.8%
1994	1,129,607	593,492	Symington, Fife	500,702	Basha, Eddie	35,413	92,790 R	52.5%	44.3%	54.2%	45.8%
1990**	940,737	492,569	Symington, Fife	448,168	Goddard, Terry		44,401 R	52.4%	47.6%	52.4%	47.6%
1986**	866,984	343,913	Mecham, Evan	298,986	Warner, Carolyn	224,085	44,927 R	39.7%	34.5%	53.5%	46.5%
1982	726,364	235,877	Corbet, Leo	453,795	Babbitt, Bruce	36,692	217,918 D	32.5%	62.5%	34.2%	65.8%
1978	538,556	241,093	Mecham, Evan	282,605	Babbitt, Bruce	14,858	41,512 D	44.8%	52.5%	46.0%	54.0%
1974	552,202	273,674	Williams, Russell	278,375	Castro, Raul H.	153	4,701 D	49.6%	50.4%	49.6%	50.4%
1970**	411,409	209,522	Williams, John R.	201,887	Castro, Raul H.		7,635 R	50.9%	49.1%	50.9%	49.1%
1968	483,998	279,923	Williams, John R.	204,075	Goddard, Sam		75,848 R	57.8%	42.2%	57.8%	42.2%
1966	378,342	203,438	Williams, John R.	174,904	Goddard, Sam		28,534 R	53.8%	46.2%	53.8%	46.2%
1964	473,502	221,404	Kleindienst, Richard	252,098	Goddard, Sam		30,694 D	46.8%	53.2%	46.8%	53.2%
1962	365,841	200,578	Fannin, Paul	165,263	Goddard, Sam		35,315 R	54.8%	45.2%	54.8%	45.2%
1960	397,107	235,502	Fannin, Paul	161,605	Ackerman, Lee		73,897 R	59.3%	40.7%	59.3%	40.7%
1958	290,465	160,136	Fannin, Paul	130,329	Morrison, Robert		29,807 R	55.1%	44.9%	55.1%	44.9%
1956	288,592	116,744	Griffen, Horace B.	171,848	McFarland, Ernest W.		55,104 D	40.5%	59.5%	40.5%	59.5%
1954	243,970	115,866	Pyle, Howard	128,104	McFarland, Ernest W.		12,238 D	47.5%	52.5%	47.5%	52.5%
1952	260,285	156,592	Pyle, Howard	103,693	Haldiman, Joe C.		52,899 R	60.2%	39.8%	60.2%	39.8%
1950	195,227	99,109	Pyle, Howard	96,118	Frohmiller, Ana		2,991 R	50.8%	49.2%	50.8%	49.2%
1948	175,767	70,419	Brockett, Bruce	104,008	Garvey, Dan E.	1,340	33,589 D	40.1%	59.2%	40.4%	59.6%
1946	122,462	48,867	Brockett, Bruce	73,595	Osborn, Sidney P.		24,728 D	39.9%	60.1%	39.9%	60.1%

Notes: **In 1990 neither major party candidate won an absolute majority, therefore a runoff election was held February 26, 1991; the vote above is for the February runoff. In the November 1990 election, a total of 1,055,406 votes were cast as follows: 523,984 (49.6 percent) Republican (Fife Symington); 519,691 (49.2 percent) Democratic (Terry Goddard); 11,731 (1.1 percent) Other. In past elections, the other vote included: 1986 - 224,085 Independent (Bill Schulz). The term of office for governor was increased from two to four years effective with the 1970 election.

POSTWAR VOTE FOR SENATOR

Year	Total Vote	Republican		Democratic		Other Vote	Rep.-Dem. Plurality	Percentage			
								Total Vote		Major Vote	
		Vote	Candidate	Vote	Candidate			Rep.	Dem.	Rep.	Dem.
2006	1,526,782	814,398	Kyl, Jon	664,141	Pederson, Jim	48,243	150,257 R	53.3%	43.5%	55.1%	44.9%
2004	1,961,677	1,505,372	McCain, John	404,507	Starky, Stuart	51,798	1,100,865 R	76.7%	20.6%	78.8%	21.2%
2000	1,397,076	1,108,196	Kyl, Jon	—		288,880	1,108,196 R	79.3%		100.0%	
1998	1,013,280	696,577	McCain, John	275,224	Ranger, Ed	41,479	421,353 R	68.7%	27.2%	71.7%	28.3%
1994	1,119,060	600,999	Kyl, Jon	442,510	Coppersmith, Sam	75,551	158,489 R	53.7%	39.5%	57.6%	42.4%
1992**	1,382,051	771,395	McCain, John	436,321	Sargent, Claire	174,335	335,074 R	55.8%	31.6%	63.9%	36.1%
1988	1,164,539	478,060	DeGreen, Keith	660,403	DeConcini, Dennis	26,076	182,343 D	41.1%	56.7%	42.0%	58.0%
1986	862,921	521,850	McCain, John	340,965	Kimball, Richard	106	180,885 R	60.5%	39.5%	60.5%	39.5%
1982	723,885	291,749	Dunn, Pete	411,970	DeConcini, Dennis	20,166	120,221 D	40.3%	56.9%	41.5%	58.5%
1980	874,238	432,371	Goldwater, Barry M.	422,972	Schulz, Bill	18,895	9,399 R	49.5%	48.4%	50.5%	49.5%
1976	741,210	321,236	Steiger, Sam	400,334	DeConcini, Dennis	19,640	79,098 D	43.3%	54.0%	44.5%	55.5%
1974	549,919	320,396	Goldwater, Barry M.	229,523	Marshall, Jonathan		90,873 R	58.3%	41.7%	58.3%	41.7%
1970	407,796	228,284	Fannin, Paul	179,512	Grossman, Sam		48,772 R	56.0%	44.0%	56.0%	44.0%
1968	479,945	274,607	Goldwater, Barry M.	205,338	Elson, Roy L.		69,269 R	57.2%	42.8%	57.2%	42.8%
1964	468,801	241,089	Fannin, Paul	227,712	Elson, Roy L.		13,377 R	51.4%	48.6%	51.4%	48.6%
1962	362,605	163,388	Mecham, Evan	199,217	Hayden, Carl		35,829 D	45.1%	54.9%	45.1%	54.9%
1958	293,623	164,593	Goldwater, Barry M.	129,030	McFarland, Ernest W.		35,563 R	56.1%	43.9%	56.1%	43.9%
1956	278,263	107,447	Jones, Ross F.	170,816	Hayden, Carl		63,369 D	38.6%	61.4%	38.6%	61.4%
1952	257,401	132,063	Goldwater, Barry M.	125,338	McFarland, Ernest W.		6,725 R	51.3%	48.7%	51.3%	48.7%
1950	185,092	68,846	Brockett, Bruce	116,246	Hayden, Carl		47,400 D	37.2%	62.8%	37.2%	62.8%
1946	116,239	35,022	Powers, Ward S.	80,415	McFarland, Ernest W.	802	45,393 D	30.1%	69.2%	30.3%	69.7%

Notes: **In past elections, the other vote included: 1992 - 145,361 Independent (Evan Mecham). The Democratic Party did not run a candidate in the 2000 Senate election.

ARIZONA

PRESIDENT 2008

2000 Census Population	County	Total Vote	Republican	Democratic	Other	Rep.-Dem. Plurality		Percentage			
								Total Vote		Major Vote	
								Rep.	Dem.	Rep.	Dem.
69,423	APACHE	24,262	8,551	15,390	321	6,839	D	35.2%	63.4%	35.7%	64.3%
117,755	COCHISE	48,820	29,026	18,943	851	10,083	R	59.5%	38.8%	60.5%	39.5%
116,320	COCONINO	54,344	22,186	31,433	725	9,247	D	40.8%	57.8%	41.4%	58.6%
51,335	GILA	22,333	14,095	7,884	354	6,211	R	63.1%	35.3%	64.1%	35.9%
33,489	GRAHAM	12,007	8,376	3,487	144	4,889	R	69.8%	29.0%	70.6%	29.4%
8,547	GREENLEE	2,913	1,712	1,165	36	547	R	58.8%	40.0%	59.5%	40.5%
19,715	LA PAZ	5,552	3,509	1,929	114	1,580	R	63.2%	34.7%	64.5%	35.5%
3,072,149	MARICOPA	1,364,962	746,448	602,166	16,348	144,282	R	54.7%	44.1%	55.3%	44.7%
155,032	MOHAVE	67,605	44,333	22,092	1,180	22,241	R	65.6%	32.7%	66.7%	33.3%
97,470	NAVAJO	35,800	19,761	15,579	460	4,182	R	55.2%	43.5%	55.9%	44.1%
843,746	PIMA	393,428	182,406	206,254	4,768	23,848	D	46.4%	52.4%	46.9%	53.1%
179,727	PINAL	104,883	59,421	44,254	1,208	15,167	R	56.7%	42.2%	57.3%	42.7%
38,381	SANTA CRUZ	13,303	4,518	8,683	102	4,165	D	34.0%	65.3%	34.2%	65.8%
167,517	YAVAPAI	99,648	61,192	36,889	1,567	24,303	R	61.4%	37.0%	62.4%	37.6%
160,026	YUMA	43,615	24,577	18,559	479	6,018	R	56.3%	42.6%	57.0%	43.0%
5,130,632	TOTAL	2,293,475	1,230,111	1,034,707	28,657	195,404	R	53.6%	45.1%	54.3%	45.7%

ARIZONA

HOUSE OF REPRESENTATIVES

		Total Vote	Republican		Democratic		Other Vote	Rep.-Dem. Plurality	Percentage			
									Total Vote		Major Vote	
CD	Year		Vote	Candidate	Vote	Candidate			Rep.	Dem.	Rep.	Dem.
1	2008	278,787	109,924	HAY, SYDNEY	155,791	KIRKPATRICK, ANN	13,072	45,867 D	39.4%	55.9%	41.4%	58.6%
1	2006	204,139	105,646	RENZI, RICK*	88,691	SIMON, ELLEN	9,802	16,955 R	51.8%	43.4%	54.4%	45.6%
1	2004	253,351	148,315	RENZI, RICK*	91,776	BABBITT, PAUL	13,260	56,539 R	58.5%	36.2%	61.8%	38.2%
1	2002	174,687	85,967	RENZI, RICK	79,730	CORDOVA, GEORGE	8,990	6,237 R	49.2%	45.6%	51.9%	48.1%
2	2008	338,023	200,914	FRANKS, TRENT*	125,611	THRASHER, JOHN	11,498	75,303 R	59.4%	37.2%	61.5%	38.5%
2	2006	230,560	135,150	FRANKS, TRENT*	89,671	THRASHER, JOHN	5,739	45,479 R	58.6%	38.9%	60.1%	39.9%
2	2004	279,303	165,260	FRANKS, TRENT*	107,406	CAMACHO, RANDY	6,637	57,854 R	59.2%	38.5%	60.6%	39.4%
2	2002	167,502	100,359	FRANKS, TRENT	61,217	CAMACHO, RANDY	5,926	39,142 R	59.9%	36.5%	62.1%	37.9%
3	2008	275,161	148,800	SHADEGG, JOHN*	115,759	LORD, BOB	10,602	33,041 R	54.1%	42.1%	56.2%	43.8%
3	2006	189,849	112,519	SHADEGG, JOHN*	72,586	PAINE, HERB	4,744	39,933 R	59.3%	38.2%	60.8%	39.2%
3	2004	225,974	181,012	SHADEGG, JOHN*	—		44,962	181,012 R	80.1%		100.0%	
3	2002	155,751	104,847	SHADEGG, JOHN*	47,173	HILL, CHARLES	3,731	57,674 R	67.3%	30.3%	69.0%	31.0%
4	2008	124,427	26,435	KARG, DON	89,721	PASTOR, ED*	8,271	63,286 D	21.2%	72.1%	22.8%	77.2%
4	2006	77,861	18,627	KARG, DON	56,464	PASTOR, ED*	2,770	37,837 D	23.9%	72.5%	24.8%	75.2%
4	2004	110,027	28,238	KARG, DON	77,150	PASTOR, ED*	4,639	48,912 D	25.7%	70.1%	26.8%	73.2%
4	2002	66,065	18,381	BARNETT, JONATHAN	44,517	PASTOR, ED*	3,167	26,136 D	27.8%	67.4%	29.2%	70.8%
5	2008	280,365	122,165	SCHWEIKERT, DAVID	149,033	MITCHELL, HARRY*	9,167	26,868 D	43.6%	53.2%	45.0%	55.0%
5	2006	202,010	93,815	HAYWORTH, J.D.*	101,838	MITCHELL, HARRY	6,357	8,023 D	46.4%	50.4%	47.9%	52.1%
5	2004	268,007	159,455	HAYWORTH, J.D.*	102,363	ROGERS, ELIZABETH	6,189	57,092 R	59.5%	38.2%	60.9%	39.1%
5	2002	169,812	103,870	HAYWORTH, J.D.*	61,559	COLUMBUS, CRAIG	4,383	42,311 R	61.2%	36.3%	62.8%	37.2%
6	2008	334,176	208,582	FLAKE, JEFF*	115,457	SCHNEIDER, REBECCA	10,137	93,125 R	62.4%	34.5%	64.4%	35.6%
6	2006	203,486	152,201	FLAKE, JEFF*	—		51,285	152,201 R	74.8%		100.0%	
6	2004	255,577	202,882	FLAKE, JEFF*	—		52,695	202,882 R	79.4%		100.0%	
6	2002	156,337	103,094	FLAKE, JEFF*	49,355	THOMAS, DEBORAH	3,888	53,739 R	65.9%	31.6%	67.6%	32.4%
7	2008	196,489	64,425	SWEENEY, JOSEPH	124,304	GRIJALVA, RAUL M.*	7,760	59,879 D	32.8%	63.3%	34.1%	65.9%
7	2006	131,525	46,498	DRAKE, RON	80,354	GRIJALVA, RAUL M.*	4,673	33,856 D	35.4%	61.1%	36.7%	63.3%
7	2004	175,437	59,066	SWEENEY, JOSEPH	108,868	GRIJALVA, RAUL M.*	7,503	49,802 D	33.7%	62.1%	35.2%	64.8%
7	2002	103,818	38,474	HIEB, ROSS	61,256	GRIJALVA, RAUL M.	4,088	22,782 D	37.1%	59.0%	38.6%	61.4%
8	2008	328,266	140,553	BEE, TIM	179,629	GIFFORDS, GABRIELLE*	8,084	39,076 D	42.8%	54.7%	43.9%	56.1%
8	2006	253,720	106,790	GRAF, RANDY	137,655	GIFFORDS, GABRIELLE	9,275	30,865 D	42.1%	54.3%	43.7%	56.3%
8	2004	303,769	183,363	KOLBE, JIM*	109,963	BACAL, EVA	10,443	73,400 R	60.4%	36.2%	62.5%	37.5%
8	2002	200,428	126,930	KOLBE, JIM*	67,328	RYAN, MARY JUDGE	6,170	59,602 R	63.3%	33.6%	65.3%	34.7%
TOTAL	2008	2,155,694	1,021,798		1,055,305		78,591	33,507 D	47.4%	49.0%	49.2%	50.8%
TOTAL	2006	1,493,150	771,246		627,259		94,645	143,987 R	51.7%	42.0%	55.1%	44.9%
TOTAL	2004	1,871,445	1,127,591		597,526		146,328	530,065 R	60.3%	31.9%	65.4%	34.6%
TOTAL	2002	1,194,400	681,922		472,135		40,343	209,787 R	57.1%	39.5%	59.1%	40.9%

Note: An asterisk (*) denotes incumbent.

ARIZONA

GENERAL AND PRIMARY ELECTIONS

2008 GENERAL ELECTIONS

President — Other vote was 12,555 Libertarian (Bob Barr); 11,301 None (Ralph Nader); 3,406 Green (Cynthia A. McKinney); 1,371 write-in (Chuck Baldwin); 16 write-in (Charles Jay); 8 write-in (Jonathan Allen).

House — Other vote was:

- **CD 1** 9,394 Independent (Brent Maupin); 3,678 Libertarian (Thane Eichenauer).
- **CD 2** 7,882 Libertarian (Powell Gammill); 3,616 Green (William Crum).
- **CD 3** 10,602 Libertarian (Michael Schoen).
- **CD 4** 4,464 Green (Rebecca DeWitt); 3,807 Libertarian (Joe Cobb).
- **CD 5** 9,158 Libertarian (Warren Severin); 9 write-in (Ralph Hughes).
- **CD 6** 10,137 Libertarian (Rick Biondi).
- **CD 7** 7,755 Libertarian (Raymond Patrick Petrulsky); 5 write-in (Harley Meyer).
- **CD 8** 8,081 Libertarian (Paul Davis); 3 write-in (Paul Price).

ARIZONA

GENERAL AND PRIMARY ELECTIONS

2008 PRIMARY ELECTIONS

Primary	February 5, 2008 (President) September 2, 2008 (Congress)	Registration (as of September 2, 2008)	Republican	1,061,591
			Democratic	957,895
			Libertarian	17,278
			Green	3,467
			Other	759,159
			TOTAL	*2,799,390*

Primary Type The presidential primary was "closed." Only registered Democrats and Republicans could cast a ballot in their party's primary for president. The congressional primary was "semi-open." Registered Democrats and Republicans could vote only in their party's primary. But voters not registered with any political party could participate in the primary of their choice.

	REPUBLICAN PRIMARIES			DEMOCRATIC PRIMARIES		
President	John McCain	255,197	47.2%	Hillary Clinton	229,501	50.4%
	Mitt Romney	186,838	34.5%	Barack Obama	193,126	42.4%
	Mike Huckabee	48,849	9.0%	John Edwards	23,621	5.2%
	Ron Paul	22,692	4.2%	Bill Richardson	2,842	0.6%
	Rudolph Giuliani	13,658	2.5%	Dennis J. Kucinich	1,973	0.4%
	Fred Thompson	9,492	1.8%	Sandy Whitehouse	632	0.1%
	Duncan Hunter	1,082	0.2%	Christopher J. Dodd	484	0.1%
	Alan Keyes	970	0.2%	Edward Dobson	398	0.1%
	John R. McGrath	490	0.1%	Mike Gravel	340	0.1%
	Frank McEnulty	333	0.1%	Richardson Grayson	322	0.1%
	Sean "Cf" Murphy	269		Karl Krueger	291	0.1%
	John Michael Fitzpatrick	199		Chuck See	249	0.1%
	James Creighton Mitchell Jr.	193		William Campbell	248	0.1%
	David Ruben	104		Frank Lynch	248	0.1%
	Michael Burzynski	98		Libby Hubbard	209	
	Jerry Curry	98		Michael Oatman	192	
	Jack Shepard	78		Rich Lee	162	
	Bob Forthan	75		Peter "Simon" Bollander	154	
	Michael P. Shaw	62		Evelyn L. Vitullo	132	
	Hugh Cort	58		Philip Tanner	130	
	Daniel Gilbert	53		Tish Haymer	107	
	Rick Outzen	53		Orion Daley	98	
	Charles Skelley	50		Leland Montell	94	
	Rhett R. Smith	44		Loti Gest	82	
	TOTAL	*541,035*		*TOTAL*	*455,635*	
Congressional District 1	Sydney Hay	17,825	39.1%	Ann Kirkpatrick	26,734	47.2%
	Sandra L. B. Livingstone	15,621	34.2%	Mary Kim Titla	18,428	32.6%
	Tom Hansen	7,847	17.2%	Howard Shanker	8,056	14.2%
	Barry Hall	2,743	6.0%	Jeffrey Brown	3,376	6.0%
	Preston Korn	1,596	3.5%			
	TOTAL	*45,632*		*TOTAL*	*56,594*	

ARIZONA

GENERAL AND PRIMARY ELECTIONS

	REPUBLICAN PRIMARIES			DEMOCRATIC PRIMARIES		
Congressional District 2	Trent Franks*	58,707	100.0%	John Thrasher	27,711	100.0%
Congressional District 3	John Shadegg*	43,538	100.0%	Bob Lord	22,554	100.0%
Congressional District 4	Don Karg Richard Grayson (write-in) TOTAL	8,073 8 8,081	99.9% 0.1%	Ed Pastor*	18,660	100.0%
Congressional District 5	David Schweikert Susan Bitter Smith Laura Knaperek Jim Ogsbury Lee Gentry TOTAL	14,233 13,212 7,523 6,042 706 41,716	34.1% 31.7% 18.0% 14.5% 1.7%	Harry Mitchell*	25,174	100.0%
Congressional District 6	Jeff Flake*	51,562	100.0%	Rebecca Schneider Chris Gramazio TOTAL	15,644 5,568 21,212	73.8% 26.2%
Congressional District 7	Joseph Sweeney Gene Chewning TOTAL	11,011 5,464 16,475	66.8% 33.2%	Raul M. Grijalva*	30,630	100.0%
Congressional District 8	Tim Bee	52,671	100.0%	Gabrielle Giffords*	46,223	100.0%

Note: An asterisk (*) denotes incumbent.

ARKANSAS

Congressional districts first established for elections held in 2002
4 members

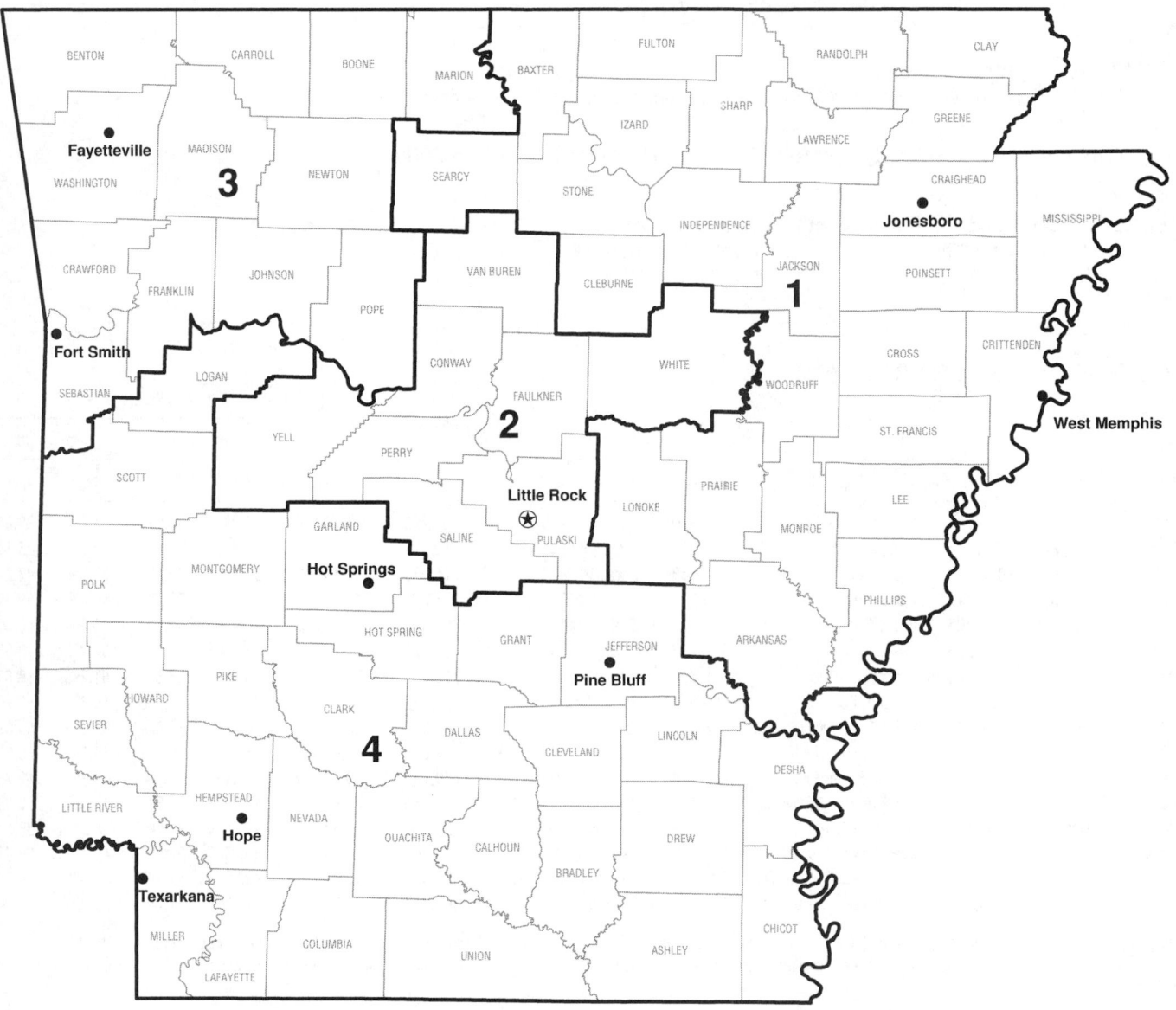

ARKANSAS

GOVERNOR
Mike D. Beebe (D). Elected 2006 to a four-year term.

SENATORS (2 Democrats)
Blanche Lincoln (D). Reelected 2004 to a six-year term. Previously elected 1998.

Mark Pryor (D). Reelected 2008 to a six-year term. Previously elected 2002.

REPRESENTATIVES (3 Democrats, 1 Republican)
1. Marion Berry (D)
2. Vic Snyder (D)
3. John Boozman (R)
4. Mike Ross (D)

POSTWAR VOTE FOR PRESIDENT

		Republican		Democratic				Total Vote		Major Vote	
Year	Total Vote	Vote	Candidate	Vote	Candidate	Other Vote	Plurality	Rep.	Dem.	Rep.	Dem.
2008	1,086,617	638,017	McCain, John	422,310	Obama, Barack	26,290	215,707 R	58.7%	38.9%	60.2%	39.8%
2004	1,054,945	572,898	Bush, George W.	469,953	Kerry, John	12,094	102,945 R	54.3%	44.5%	54.9%	45.1%
2000**	921,781	472,940	Bush, George W.	422,768	Gore, Al	26,073	50,172 R	51.3%	45.9%	52.8%	47.2%
1996**	884,262	325,416	Dole, Bob	475,171	Clinton, Bill	83,675	149,755 D	36.8%	53.7%	40.6%	59.4%
1992**	950,653	337,324	Bush, George	505,823	Clinton, Bill	107,506	168,499 D	35.5%	53.2%	40.0%	60.0%
1988	827,738	466,578	Bush, George	349,237	Dukakis, Michael S.	11,923	117,341 R	56.4%	42.2%	57.2%	42.8%
1984	884,406	534,774	Reagan, Ronald	338,646	Mondale, Walter F.	10,986	196,128 R	60.5%	38.3%	61.2%	38.8%
1980**	837,582	403,164	Reagan, Ronald	398,041	Carter, Jimmy	36,377	5,123 R	48.1%	47.5%	50.3%	49.7%
1976	767,535	267,903	Ford, Gerald R.	498,604	Carter, Jimmy	1,028	230,701 D	34.9%	65.0%	35.0%	65.0%
1972	651,320	448,541	Nixon, Richard M.	199,892	McGovern, George S.	2,887	248,649 R	68.9%	30.7%	69.2%	30.8%
1968**	619,969	190,759	Nixon, Richard M.	188,228	Humphrey, Hubert H.	240,982	50,223 A	30.8%	30.4%	50.3%	49.7%
1964	560,426	243,264	Goldwater, Barry M.	314,197	Johnson, Lyndon B.	2,965	70,933 D	43.4%	56.1%	43.6%	56.4%
1960	428,509	184,508	Nixon, Richard M.	215,049	Kennedy, John F.	28,952	30,541 D	43.1%	50.2%	46.2%	53.8%
1956	406,572	186,287	Eisenhower, Dwight D.	213,277	Stevenson, Adlai E.	7,008	26,990 D	45.8%	52.5%	46.6%	53.4%
1952	404,800	177,155	Eisenhower, Dwight D.	226,300	Stevenson, Adlai E.	1,345	49,145 D	43.8%	55.9%	43.9%	56.1%
1948**	242,475	50,959	Dewey, Thomas E.	149,659	Truman, Harry S.	41,857	98,700 D	21.0%	61.7%	25.4%	74.6%

**In past elections, the other vote included: 2000 - 13,421 Green (Ralph Nader); 1996 - 69,884 Reform (Ross Perot); 1992 - 99,132 Independent (Perot); 1980 - 22,468 Independent (John Anderson); 1968 - 240,982 American Independent (George Wallace); 1948 - 40,068 States' Rights (Strom Thurmond). Wallace carried Arkansas in 1968 with 38.9 percent of the vote.

ARKANSAS

POSTWAR VOTE FOR GOVERNOR

| | | Republican | | Democratic | | | | Percentage | | | |
| | Total | | | | | Other | Rep.-Dem. | Total Vote | | Major Vote | |
Year	Vote	Vote	Candidate	Vote	Candidate	Vote	Plurality	Rep.	Dem.	Rep.	Dem.
2006	774,680	315,040	Hutchinson, Asa	430,765	Beebe, Mike D.	28,875	115,725 D	40.7%	55.6%	42.2%	57.8%
2002	805,696	427,082	Huckabee, Mike	378,250	Fisher, Jimmie Lou	364	48,832 R	53.0%	46.9%	53.0%	47.0%
1998	706,011	421,989	Huckabee, Mike	272,923	Bristow, Bill	11,099	149,066 R	59.8%	38.7%	60.7%	39.3%
1994	716,840	287,904	Nelson, Sheffield	428,936	Tucker, Jim Guy		141,032 D	40.2%	59.8%	40.2%	59.8%
1990	696,412	295,925	Nelson, Sheffield	400,386	Clinton, Bill	101	104,461 D	42.5%	57.5%	42.5%	57.5%
1986**	688,551	248,427	White, Frank D.	439,882	Clinton, Bill	242	191,455 D	36.1%	63.9%	36.1%	63.9%
1984	886,548	331,987	Freeman, Woody	554,561	Clinton, Bill		222,574 D	37.4%	62.6%	37.4%	62.6%
1982	789,351	357,496	White, Frank D.	431,855	Clinton, Bill		74,359 D	45.3%	54.7%	45.3%	54.7%
1980	838,925	435,684	White, Frank D.	403,241	Clinton, Bill		32,443 R	51.9%	48.1%	51.9%	48.1%
1978	528,912	193,746	Lowe, A. Lynn	335,101	Clinton, Bill	65	141,355 D	36.6%	63.4%	36.6%	63.4%
1976	726,949	121,716	Griffith, Leon	605,083	Pryor, David H.	150	483,367 D	16.7%	83.2%	16.7%	83.3%
1974	545,974	187,872	Coon, Ken	358,018	Pryor, David H.	84	170,146 D	34.4%	65.6%	34.4%	65.6%
1972	648,069	159,177	Blaylock, Len E.	488,892	Bumpers, Dale		329,715 D	24.6%	75.4%	24.6%	75.4%
1970	609,198	197,418	Rockefeller, Winthrop	375,648	Bumpers, Dale	36,132	178,230 D	32.4%	61.7%	34.4%	65.6%
1968	615,595	322,782	Rockefeller, Winthrop	292,813	Crank, Marion		29,969 R	52.4%	47.6%	52.4%	47.6%
1966	563,527	306,324	Rockefeller, Winthrop	257,203	Johnson, James D.		49,121 R	54.4%	45.6%	54.4%	45.6%
1964	592,113	254,561	Rockefeller, Winthrop	337,489	Faubus, Orval E.	63	82,928 D	43.0%	57.0%	43.0%	57.0%
1962	308,092	82,349	Ricketts, Willis	225,743	Faubus, Orval E.		143,394 D	26.7%	73.3%	26.7%	73.3%
1960	421,985	129,921	Britt, Henry M.	292,064	Faubus, Orval E.		162,143 D	30.8%	69.2%	30.8%	69.2%
1958	286,886	50,288	Johnson, George W.	236,598	Faubus, Orval E.		186,310 D	17.5%	82.5%	17.5%	82.5%
1956	399,012	77,215	Mitchell, Roy	321,797	Faubus, Orval E.		244,582 D	19.4%	80.6%	19.4%	80.6%
1954	335,176	127,004	Remmel, Pratt C.	208,121	Faubus, Orval E.	51	81,117 D	37.9%	62.1%	37.9%	62.1%
1952	391,592	49,292	Speck, Jefferson W.	342,292	Cherry, Francis	8	293,000 D	12.6%	87.4%	12.6%	87.4%
1950	317,087	50,309	Speck, Jefferson W.	266,778	McMath, Sidney S.		216,469 D	15.9%	84.1%	15.9%	84.1%
1948	249,301	26,500	Black, Charles R.	222,801	McMath, Sidney S.		196,301 D	10.6%	89.4%	10.6%	89.4%
1946	152,162	24,133	Mills, W. T.	128,029	Laney, Ben T.		103,896 D	15.9%	84.1%	15.9%	84.1%

**The term of office for governor was increased from two to four years effective with the 1986 election.

POSTWAR VOTE FOR SENATOR

| | | Republican | | Democratic | | | | Percentage | | | |
| | | | | | | Other | Rep.-Dem. | Total Vote | | Major Vote | |
Year	Total Vote	Vote	Candidate	Vote	Candidate	Vote	Plurality	Rep.	Dem.	Rep.	Dem.
2008**	1,011,754		—	804,678	Pryor, Mark	207,076	804,678 D		79.5%		100.0%
2004	1,039,349	458,036	Holt, Jim	580,973	Lincoln, Blanche	340	122,937 D	44.1%	55.9%	44.1%	55.9%
2002	803,959	370,653	Hutchinson, Tim	433,306	Pryor, Mark		62,653 D	46.1%	53.9%	46.1%	53.9%
1998	700,644	295,870	Boozman, Fay	385,878	Lincoln, Blanche	18,895	90,008 D	42.2%	55.1%	43.4%	56.6%
1996	846,183	445,942	Hutchinson, Tim	400,241	Bryant, Winston		45,701 R	52.7%	47.3%	52.7%	47.3%
1992	920,008	366,373	Huckabee, Mike	553,635	Bumpers, Dale		187,262 D	39.8%	60.2%	39.8%	60.2%
1990**	494,735		—	493,910	Pryor, David H.	825	493,910 D		99.8%		100.0%
1986	695,487	262,313	Hutchinson, Asa	433,122	Bumpers, Dale	52	170,809 D	37.7%	62.3%	37.7%	62.3%
1984	875,956	373,615	Bethune, Ed	502,341	Pryor, David H.		128,726 D	42.7%	57.3%	42.7%	57.3%
1980	808,812	330,576	Clark, Bill	477,905	Bumpers, Dale	331	147,329 D	40.9%	59.1%	40.9%	59.1%
1978	522,239	84,722	Kelly, Tom	399,916	Pryor, David H.	37,601	315,194 D	16.2%	76.6%	17.5%	82.5%
1974	543,082	82,026	Jones, John H.	461,056	Bumpers, Dale		379,030 D	15.1%	84.9%	15.1%	84.9%
1972	634,636	248,238	Babbitt, Wayne H.	386,398	McClellan, John L.		138,160 D	39.1%	60.9%	39.1%	60.9%
1968	591,704	241,739	Bernard, Charles T.	349,965	Fulbright, J. W.		108,226 D	40.9%	59.1%	40.9%	59.1%
1966**			—		McClellan, John L.		D				
1962	312,880	98,013	Jones, Kenneth	214,867	Fulbright, J. W.		116,854 D	31.3%	68.7%	31.3%	68.7%
1960**			—		McClellan, John L.		D				
1956	399,695	68,016	Henley, Ben C.	331,679	Fulbright, J. W.		263,663 D	17.0%	83.0%	17.0%	83.0%
1954	291,058		—	291,058	McClellan, John L.		291,058 D		100.0%		100.0%
1950	302,582		—	302,582	Fulbright, J. W.		302,582 D		100.0%		100.0%
1948	216,401		—	216,401	McClellan, John L.		216,401 D		100.0%		100.0%

Notes: **In past elections, the other vote included: 2008 - 207,076 Green (Rebekah Kennedy), who finished second. In 1990 the vote for Senator David H. Pryor was not canvassed in seven counties because he was unopposed. Senator John L. McClellan was reelected in 1960 and in 1966, but his vote was not canvassed in many counties. The Republican Party did not run a candidate in the 1948, 1950, 1954, 1960, 1966, 1990, and 2008 Senate elections.

ARKANSAS

PRESIDENT 2008

2000 Census Population	County	Total Vote	Republican	Democratic	Other	Rep.-Dem. Plurality	Percentage			
							Total Vote		Major Vote	
							Rep.	Dem.	Rep.	Dem.
20,749	ARKANSAS	6,978	4,185	2,619	174	1,566 R	60.0%	37.5%	61.5%	38.5%
24,209	ASHLEY	8,642	5,406	2,976	260	2,430 R	62.6%	34.4%	64.5%	35.5%
38,386	BAXTER	19,981	12,852	6,539	590	6,313 R	64.3%	32.7%	66.3%	33.7%
153,406	BENTON	76,073	51,124	23,331	1,618	27,793 R	67.2%	30.7%	68.7%	31.3%
33,948	BOONE	15,474	10,575	4,435	464	6,140 R	68.3%	28.7%	70.5%	29.5%
12,600	BRADLEY	4,041	2,262	1,680	99	582 R	56.0%	41.6%	57.4%	42.6%
5,744	CALHOUN	2,217	1,462	691	64	771 R	65.9%	31.2%	67.9%	32.1%
25,357	CARROLL	10,579	6,083	4,172	324	1,911 R	57.5%	39.4%	59.3%	40.7%
14,117	CHICOT	5,208	2,119	3,043	46	924 D	40.7%	58.4%	41.0%	59.0%
23,546	CLARK	9,094	4,608	4,267	219	341 R	50.7%	46.9%	51.9%	48.1%
17,609	CLAY	5,511	3,032	2,244	235	788 R	55.0%	40.7%	57.5%	42.5%
24,046	CLEBURNE	11,338	7,962	2,951	425	5,011 R	70.2%	26.0%	73.0%	27.0%
8,571	CLEVELAND	3,505	2,451	911	143	1,540 R	69.9%	26.0%	72.9%	27.1%
25,603	COLUMBIA	9,558	5,861	3,554	143	2,307 R	61.3%	37.2%	62.3%	37.7%
20,336	CONWAY	8,138	4,691	3,149	298	1,542 R	57.6%	38.7%	59.8%	40.2%
82,148	CRAIGHEAD	30,968	18,881	11,294	793	7,587 R	61.0%	36.5%	62.6%	37.4%
53,247	CRAWFORD	20,532	14,688	5,238	606	9,450 R	71.5%	25.5%	73.7%	26.3%
50,866	CRITTENDEN	18,255	7,650	10,330	275	2,680 D	41.9%	56.6%	42.5%	57.5%
19,526	CROSS	7,130	4,393	2,580	157	1,813 R	61.6%	36.2%	63.0%	37.0%
9,210	DALLAS	3,318	1,757	1,471	90	286 R	53.0%	44.3%	54.4%	45.6%
15,341	DESHA	4,678	1,999	2,569	110	570 D	42.7%	54.9%	43.8%	56.2%
18,723	DREW	6,610	3,860	2,598	152	1,262 R	58.4%	39.3%	59.8%	40.2%
86,014	FAULKNER	41,179	25,362	14,955	862	10,407 R	61.6%	36.3%	62.9%	37.1%
17,771	FRANKLIN	6,475	4,411	1,869	195	2,542 R	68.1%	28.9%	70.2%	29.8%
11,642	FULTON	4,676	2,702	1,819	155	883 R	57.8%	38.9%	59.8%	40.2%
88,068	GARLAND	43,719	26,825	15,899	995	10,926 R	61.4%	36.4%	62.8%	37.2%
16,464	GRANT	6,793	5,023	1,562	208	3,461 R	73.9%	23.0%	76.3%	23.7%
37,331	GREENE	13,612	8,578	4,541	493	4,037 R	63.0%	33.4%	65.4%	34.6%
23,587	HEMPSTEAD	7,349	4,273	2,869	207	1,404 R	58.1%	39.0%	59.8%	40.2%
30,353	HOT SPRING	11,955	7,209	4,288	458	2,921 R	60.3%	35.9%	62.7%	37.3%
14,300	HOWARD	4,846	2,957	1,746	143	1,211 R	61.0%	36.0%	62.9%	37.1%
34,233	INDEPENDENCE	12,299	8,255	3,688	356	4,567 R	67.1%	30.0%	69.1%	30.9%
13,249	IZARD	5,218	3,193	1,792	233	1,401 R	61.2%	34.3%	64.1%	35.9%
18,418	JACKSON	5,582	3,118	2,207	257	911 R	55.9%	39.5%	58.6%	41.4%
84,278	JEFFERSON	29,689	10,655	18,465	569	7,810 D	35.9%	62.2%	36.6%	63.4%
22,781	JOHNSON	8,180	4,922	3,034	224	1,888 R	60.2%	37.1%	61.9%	38.1%
8,559	LAFAYETTE	2,902	1,685	1,133	84	552 R	58.1%	39.0%	59.8%	40.2%
17,774	LAWRENCE	5,830	3,357	2,138	335	1,219 R	57.6%	36.7%	61.1%	38.9%
12,580	LEE	3,763	1,454	2,263	46	809 D	38.6%	60.1%	39.1%	60.9%
14,492	LINCOLN	4,406	2,513	1,710	183	803 R	57.0%	38.8%	59.5%	40.5%
13,628	LITTLE RIVER	5,152	3,247	1,753	152	1,494 R	63.0%	34.0%	64.9%	35.1%
22,486	LOGAN	7,907	5,350	2,286	271	3,064 R	67.7%	28.9%	70.1%	29.9%
52,828	LONOKE	23,741	17,242	5,968	531	11,274 R	72.6%	25.1%	74.3%	25.7%
14,243	MADISON	6,328	3,972	2,144	212	1,828 R	62.8%	33.9%	64.9%	35.1%
16,140	MARION	7,162	4,524	2,384	254	2,140 R	63.2%	33.3%	65.5%	34.5%
40,443	MILLER	15,063	9,913	4,869	281	5,044 R	65.8%	32.3%	67.1%	32.9%
51,979	MISSISSIPPI	14,010	6,976	6,667	367	309 R	49.8%	47.6%	51.1%	48.9%
10,254	MONROE	3,449	1,754	1,615	80	139 R	50.9%	46.8%	52.1%	47.9%
9,245	MONTGOMERY	3,622	2,365	1,092	165	1,273 R	65.3%	30.1%	68.4%	31.6%
9,955	NEVADA	3,635	2,062	1,474	99	588 R	56.7%	40.6%	58.3%	41.7%
8,608	NEWTON	3,960	2,588	1,182	190	1,406 R	65.4%	29.8%	68.6%	31.4%
28,790	OUACHITA	9,960	5,427	4,346	187	1,081 R	54.5%	43.6%	55.5%	44.5%
10,209	PERRY	4,279	2,743	1,352	184	1,391 R	64.1%	31.6%	67.0%	33.0%
26,445	PHILLIPS	8,969	3,097	5,695	177	2,598 D	34.5%	63.5%	35.2%	64.8%
11,303	PIKE	3,966	2,727	1,089	150	1,638 R	68.8%	27.5%	71.5%	28.5%
25,614	POINSETT	7,928	4,903	2,742	283	2,161 R	61.8%	34.6%	64.1%	35.9%
20,229	POLK	7,681	5,473	1,957	251	3,516 R	71.3%	25.5%	73.7%	26.3%
54,469	POPE	22,079	15,568	6,002	509	9,566 R	70.5%	27.2%	72.2%	27.8%
9,539	PRAIRIE	3,381	2,223	1,048	110	1,175 R	65.7%	31.0%	68.0%	32.0%
361,474	PULASKI	161,343	70,212	88,854	2,277	18,642 D	43.5%	55.1%	44.1%	55.9%

ARKANSAS

PRESIDENT 2008

2000 Census Population	County	Total Vote	Republican	Democratic	Other	Rep.-Dem. Plurality	Percentage Total Vote Rep	Percentage Total Vote Dem.	Percentage Major Vote Rep	Percentage Major Vote Dem.
18,195	RANDOLPH	6,319	3,615	2,469	235	1,146 R	57.2%	39.1%	59.4%	40.6%
29,329	ST. FRANCIS	9,505	3,917	5,486	102	1,569 D	41.2%	57.7%	41.7%	58.3%
83,529	SALINE	44,653	30,981	12,695	977	18,286 R	69.4%	28.4%	70.9%	29.1%
10,996	SCOTT	3,995	2,791	1,053	151	1,738 R	69.9%	26.4%	72.6%	27.4%
8,261	SEARCY	3,847	2,726	961	160	1,765 R	70.9%	25.0%	73.9%	26.1%
115,071	SEBASTIAN	43,212	28,637	13,673	902	14,964 R	66.3%	31.6%	67.7%	32.3%
15,757	SEVIER	4,580	3,125	1,291	164	1,834 R	68.2%	28.2%	70.8%	29.2%
17,119	SHARP	7,252	4,535	2,436	281	2,099 R	62.5%	33.6%	65.1%	34.9%
11,499	STONE	5,324	3,534	1,598	192	1,936 R	66.4%	30.0%	68.9%	31.1%
45,629	UNION	17,179	10,677	6,190	312	4,487 R	62.2%	36.0%	63.3%	36.7%
16,192	VAN BUREN	6,703	4,276	2,151	276	2,125 R	63.8%	32.1%	66.5%	33.5%
157,715	WASHINGTON	68,380	37,963	29,021	1,396	8,942 R	55.5%	42.4%	56.7%	43.3%
67,165	WHITE	26,955	19,467	6,732	756	12,735 R	72.2%	25.0%	74.3%	25.7%
8,741	WOODRUFF	2,761	1,206	1,412	143	206 D	43.7%	51.1%	46.1%	53.9%
21,139	YELL	6,036	3,808	2,003	225	1,805 R	63.1%	33.2%	65.5%	34.5%
2,673,400	TOTAL	1,086,617	638,017	422,310	26,290	215,707 R	58.7%	38.9%	60.2%	39.8%

ARKANSAS

SENATOR 2008

2000 Census Population	County	Total Vote	Republican	Democratic	Other	Rep.-Dem. Plurality	Percentage Total Vote Rep.	Percentage Total Vote Dem.	Percentage Major Vote Rep.	Percentage Major Vote Dem.
20,749	ARKANSAS	6,609		5,814	795	5,814 D		88.0%		100.0%
24,209	ASHLEY	7,959		6,759	1,200	6,759 D		84.9%		100.0%
38,386	BAXTER	18,180		12,288	5,892	12,288 D		67.6%		100.0%
153,406	BENTON	68,888		48,459	20,429	48,459 D		70.3%		100.0%
33,948	BOONE	13,695		9,583	4,112	9,583 D		70.0%		100.0%
12,600	BRADLEY	3,793		3,381	412	3,381 D		89.1%		100.0%
5,744	CALHOUN	2,081		1,747	334	1,747 D		84.0%		100.0%
25,357	CARROLL	10,075		7,355	2,720	7,355 D		73.0%		100.0%
14,117	CHICOT	5,084		4,553	531	4,553 D		89.6%		100.0%
23,546	CLARK	8,610		7,268	1,342	7,268 D		84.4%		100.0%
17,609	CLAY	5,145		4,296	849	4,296 D		83.5%		100.0%
24,046	CLEBURNE	9,838		7,266	2,572	7,266 D		73.9%		100.0%
8,571	CLEVELAND	3,301		2,788	513	2,788 D		84.5%		100.0%
25,603	COLUMBIA	8,379		6,726	1,653	6,726 D		80.3%		100.0%
20,336	CONWAY	7,790		6,430	1,360	6,430 D		82.5%		100.0%
82,148	CRAIGHEAD	29,359		24,192	5,167	24,192 D		82.4%		100.0%
53,247	CRAWFORD	19,184		14,791	4,393	14,791 D		77.1%		100.0%
50,866	CRITTENDEN	16,421		13,895	2,526	13,895 D		84.6%		100.0%
19,526	CROSS	6,683		5,565	1,118	5,565 D		83.3%		100.0%
9,210	DALLAS	3,172		2,797	375	2,797 D		88.2%		100.0%

ARKANSAS
SENATOR 2008

2000 Census Population	County	Total Vote	Republican	Democratic	Other	Rep.-Dem. Plurality	Percentage Total Vote Rep.	Dem.	Major Vote Rep.	Dem.
15,341	DESHA	4,359		3,972	387	3,972 D		91.1%		100.0%
18,723	DREW	6,145		5,388	757	5,388 D		87.7%		100.0%
86,014	FAULKNER	37,527		28,582	8,945	28,582 D		76.2%		100.0%
17,771	FRANKLIN	6,155		5,014	1,141	5,014 D		81.5%		100.0%
11,642	FULTON	4,188		3,252	936	3,252 D		77.7%		100.0%
88,068	GARLAND	41,189		31,793	9,396	31,793 D		77.2%		100.0%
16,464	GRANT	6,428		5,160	1,268	5,160 D		80.3%		100.0%
37,331	GREENE	12,609		9,909	2,700	9,909 D		78.6%		100.0%
23,587	HEMPSTEAD	6,866		5,949	917	5,949 D		86.6%		100.0%
30,353	HOT SPRING	11,556		9,560	1,996	9,560 D		82.7%		100.0%
14,300	HOWARD	4,583		4,039	544	4,039 D		88.1%		100.0%
34,233	INDEPENDENCE	11,543		9,609	1,934	9,609 D		83.2%		100.0%
13,249	IZARD	4,852		3,647	1,205	3,647 D		75.2%		100.0%
18,418	JACKSON	5,157		4,410	747	4,410 D		85.5%		100.0%
84,278	JEFFERSON	28,239		25,368	2,871	25,368 D		89.8%		100.0%
22,781	JOHNSON	7,649		6,118	1,531	6,118 D		80.0%		100.0%
8,559	LAFAYETTE	2,642		2,190	452	2,190 D		82.9%		100.0%
17,774	LAWRENCE	5,645		4,803	842	4,803 D		85.1%		100.0%
12,580	LEE	3,653		3,364	289	3,364 D		92.1%		100.0%
14,492	LINCOLN	4,203		3,638	565	3,638 D		86.6%		100.0%
13,628	LITTLE RIVER	4,719		4,048	671	4,048 D		85.8%		100.0%
22,486	LOGAN	7,709		6,422	1,287	6,422 D		83.3%		100.0%
52,828	LONOKE	22,326		16,668	5,658	16,668 D		74.7%		100.0%
14,243	MADISON	5,890		4,688	1,202	4,688 D		79.6%		100.0%
16,140	MARION	5,537		4,254	1,283	4,254 D		76.8%		100.0%
40,443	MILLER	13,450		10,203	3,247	10,203 D		75.9%		100.0%
51,979	MISSISSIPPI	12,386		10,415	1,971	10,415 D		84.1%		100.0%
10,254	MONROE	3,267		2,909	358	2,909 D		89.0%		100.0%
9,245	MONTGOMERY	3,414		2,698	716	2,698 D		79.0%		100.0%
9,955	NEVADA	3,395		2,995	400	2,995 D		88.2%		100.0%
8,608	NEWTON	3,581		2,631	950	2,631 D		73.5%		100.0%
28,790	OUACHITA	9,309		7,984	1,325	7,984 D		85.8%		100.0%
10,209	PERRY	4,064		3,090	974	3,090 D		76.0%		100.0%
26,445	PHILLIPS	8,522		7,592	930	7,592 D		89.1%		100.0%
11,303	PIKE	3,847		3,143	704	3,143 D		81.7%		100.0%
25,614	POINSETT	7,680		6,458	1,222	6,458 D		84.1%		100.0%
20,229	POLK	7,067		5,427	1,640	5,427 D		76.8%		100.0%
54,469	POPE	21,148		16,265	4,883	16,265 D		76.9%		100.0%
9,539	PRAIRIE	3,219		2,814	405	2,814 D		87.4%		100.0%
361,474	PULASKI	153,294		124,291	29,003	124,291 D		81.1%		100.0%
18,195	RANDOLPH	5,640		4,525	1,115	4,525 D		80.2%		100.0%
29,329	ST. FRANCIS	9,048		7,958	1,090	7,958 D		88.0%		100.0%
83,529	SALINE	42,481		32,157	10,324	32,157 D		75.7%		100.0%
10,996	SCOTT	3,849		3,185	664	3,185 D		82.7%		100.0%
8,261	SEARCY	3,457		2,531	926	2,531 D		73.2%		100.0%
115,071	SEBASTIAN	40,356		32,101	8,255	32,101 D		79.5%		100.0%
15,757	SEVIER	4,293		3,553	740	3,553 D		82.8%		100.0%
17,119	SHARP	6,572		5,171	1,401	5,171 D		78.7%		100.0%
11,499	STONE	5,038		3,773	1,265	3,773 D		74.9%		100.0%
45,629	UNION	14,883		11,668	3,215	11,668 D		78.4%		100.0%
16,192	VAN BUREN	6,356		4,846	1,510	4,846 D		76.2%		100.0%
157,715	WASHINGTON	64,044		50,398	13,646	50,398 D		78.7%		100.0%
67,165	WHITE	24,116		18,928	5,188	18,928 D		78.5%		100.0%
8,741	WOODRUFF	2,639		2,403	236	2,403 D		91.1%		100.0%
21,139	YELL	5,724		4,768	956	4,768 D		83.3%		100.0%
2,673,400	TOTAL	1,011,754		804,678	207,076	804,678 D		79.5%		100.0%

ARKANSAS

HOUSE OF REPRESENTATIVES

CD	Year	Total Vote	Republican		Democratic		Other Vote	Rep.-Dem. Plurality	Percentage			
									Total Vote		Major Vote	
			Vote	Candidate	Vote	Candidate			Rep.	Dem.	Rep.	Dem.
1	2008			—		BERRY, MARION*		D				
1	2006	184,188	56,611	STUMBAUGH, MICKEY	127,577	BERRY, MARION*		70,966 D	30.7%	69.3%	30.7%	69.3%
1	2004	243,944	81,556	HUMPHREY, VERNON	162,388	BERRY, MARION*		80,832 D	33.4%	66.6%	33.4%	66.6%
1	2002	194,058	64,357	ROBINSON, TOMMY F.	129,701	BERRY, MARION*		65,344 D	33.2%	66.8%	33.2%	66.8%
2	2008	277,366		—	212,303	SNYDER, VIC*	65,063	212,303 D		76.5%		100.0%
2	2006	206,303	81,432	MAYBERRY, ANDY	124,871	SNYDER, VIC*		43,439 D	39.5%	60.5%	39.5%	60.5%
2	2004	276,493	115,655	PARKS, MARVIN	160,834	SNYDER, VIC*	4	45,179 D	41.8%	58.2%	41.8%	58.2%
2	2002	153,626		—	142,752	SNYDER, VIC*	10,874	142,752 D		92.9%		100.0%
3	2008	274,046	215,196	BOOZMAN, JOHN*		—	58,850	215,196 R	78.5%		100.0%	
3	2006	200,924	125,039	BOOZMAN, JOHN*	75,885	ANDERSON, WOODROW		49,154 R	62.2%	37.8%	62.2%	37.8%
3	2004	270,803	160,629	BOOZMAN, JOHN*	103,158	JUDY, JAN	7,016	57,471 R	59.3%	38.1%	60.9%	39.1%
3	2002	143,055	141,478	BOOZMAN, JOHN*		—	1,577	141,478 R	98.9%		100.0%	
4	2008	235,781		—	203,178	ROSS, MIKE*	32,603	203,178 D		86.2%		100.0%
4	2006	171,596	43,360	ROSS, JOE	128,236	ROSS, MIKE*		84,876 D	25.3%	74.7%	25.3%	74.7%
4	2004			—		ROSS, MIKE*		D				
4	2002	197,537	77,904	DICKEY, JAY	119,633	ROSS, MIKE*		41,729 D	39.4%	60.6%	39.4%	60.6%
Total	2008	787,193	215,196		415,481		155,516	200,285 D	27.3%	52.8%	34.1%	65.9%
Total	2006	763,011	306,442		456,569			150,127 D	40.2%	59.8%	40.2%	59.8%
Total	2004	791,240	357,840		426,380		7,020	68,540 D	45.2%	53.9%	45.6%	54.4%
Total	2002	688,276	283,739		392,086		12,451	108,347 D	41.2%	57.0%	42.0%	58.0%

ARKANSAS

GENERAL AND PRIMARY ELECTIONS

2008 GENERAL ELECTIONS

President Other vote was 12,882 Independent (Ralph Nader); 4,776 Libertarian (Bob Barr); 4,023 Constitution (Chuck Baldwin); 3,470 Green (Cynthia A. McKinney); 1,139 Socialism & Liberation (Gloria La Riva).

Senator Other vote was 207,076 Green (Rebekah Kennedy).

House Other vote was:

CD 1
CD 2 64,398 Green (Deb McFarland); 665 write-in (Danial Suits).
CD 3 58,850 Green (Abel Noah Tomlinson).
CD 4 32,603 Green (Joshua Drake).

2008 PRIMARY ELECTIONS

Primary February 5, 2008 (President)   **Registration**   1,598,763   No Party Registration
May 20, 2008 (Congress)   (as of May 20, 2008)

Primary Runoff June 10, 2008

Primary Type Open—Any registered voter could participate in either the Democratic or Republican primary.

ARKANSAS

GENERAL AND PRIMARY ELECTIONS

	REPUBLICAN PRIMARIES			DEMOCRATIC PRIMARIES		
President	Mike Huckabee	138,557	60.5%	Hillary Clinton	220,136	70.1%
	John McCain	46,343	20.2%	Barack Obama	82,476	26.2%
	Mitt Romney	30,997	13.5%	John Edwards	5,873	1.9%
	Ron Paul	10,983	4.8%	Uncommitted	3,398	1.1%
	Uncommitted	987	0.4%	Bill Richardson	810	0.3%
	Rudolph Giuliani	658	0.3%	Joseph R. Biden Jr.	515	0.2%
	Fred Thompson	628	0.3%	Dennis J. Kucinich	393	0.1%
				Mike Gravel	325	0.1%
				Christopher J. Dodd	308	0.1%
	TOTAL	*229,153*		*TOTAL*	*314,234*	
Senator	No Republican candidate			Mark Pryor*	Unopposed	
Congressional District 1	No Republican candidate			Marion Berry*	Unopposed	
Congressional District 2	No Republican candidate			Vic Snyder*	Unopposed	
Congressional District 3	John Boozman*	Unopposed		No Democratic candidate		
Congressional District 4	No Republican candidate			Mike Ross*	Unopposed	

Note: An asterisk (*) denotes incumbent. No votes were tallied in contests where a candidate ran unopposed.

CALIFORNIA

Congressional districts first established for elections held in 2002
53 members

CALIFORNIA

San Francisco Bay Area

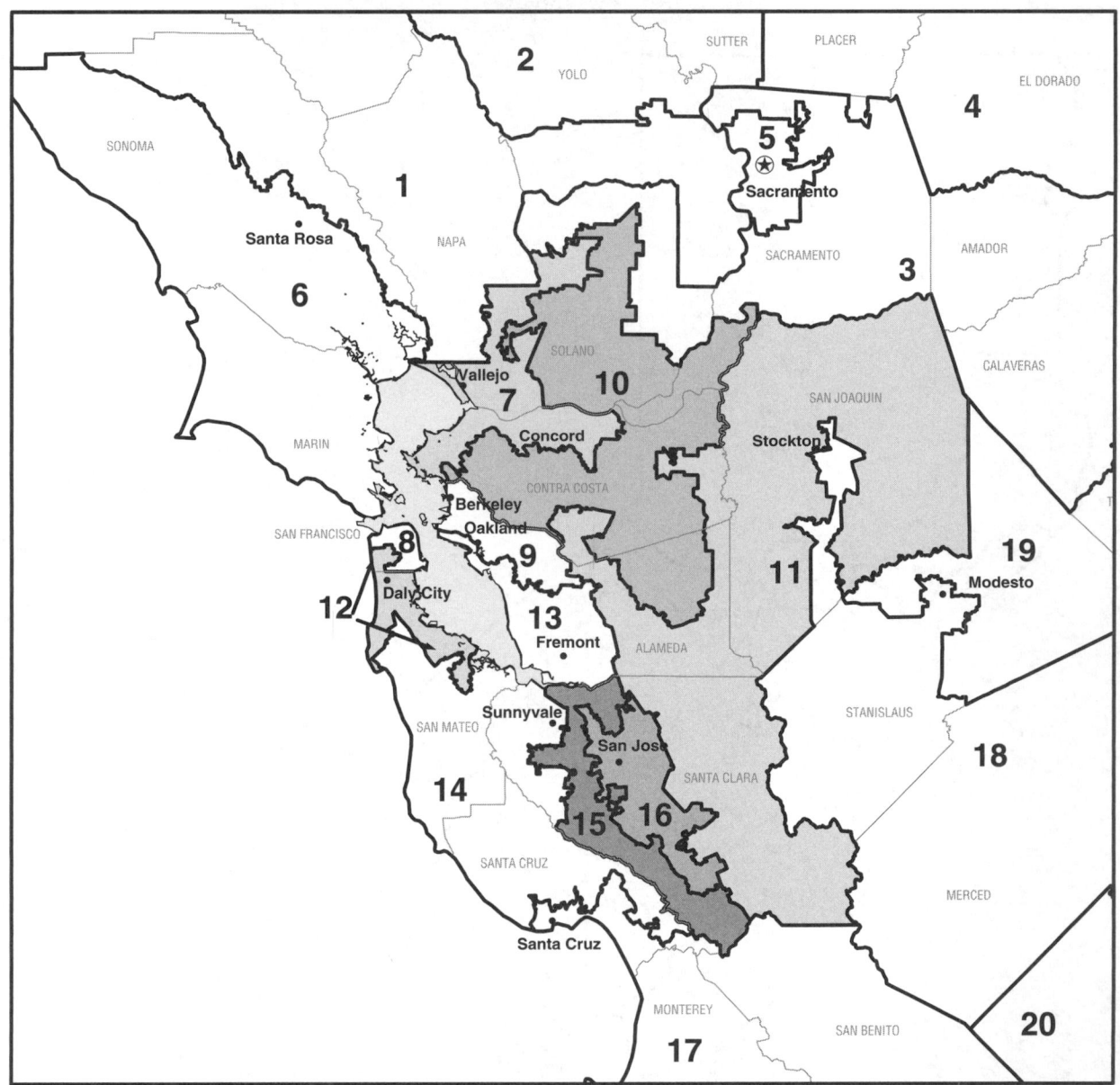

CALIFORNIA

Los Angeles, San Diego Areas

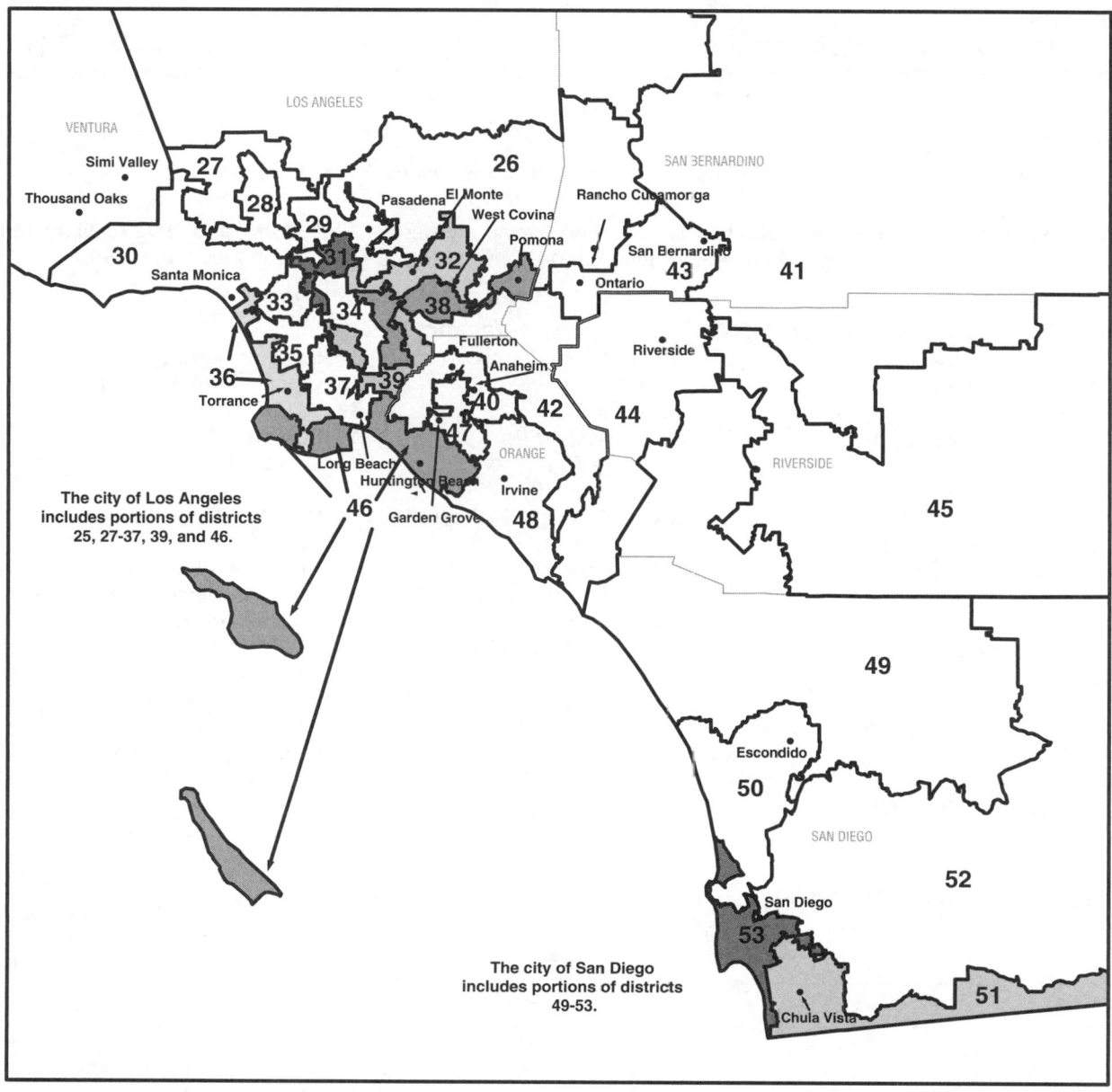

The city of Los Angeles includes portions of districts 25, 27-37, 39, and 46.

The city of San Diego includes portions of districts 49-53.

CALIFORNIA

GOVERNOR

Arnold Schwarzenegger (R). Reelected 2006 to a four-year term. Previously elected in October 2003 to fill the remaining three years of the term vacated when Governor Gray Davis (D) lost a recall vote in the same special election.

SENATORS (2 Democrats)

Barbara Boxer (D). Reelected 2004 to a six-year term. Previously elected 1998, 1992.

Dianne Feinstein (D). Reelected 2006 to a six-year term. Previously elected 2000, 1994, and 1992 to fill the remaining two years of the term vacated when Senator Pete Wilson (R) was elected governor in November 1990.

REPRESENTATIVES (33 Democrats, 19 Republicans, 1 Vacancy)

1. Mike Thompson (D)
2. Wally Herger (R)
3. Dan Lungren (R)
4. Tom McClintock (R)
5. Doris Matsui (D)
6. Lynn Woolsey (D)
7. George Miller (D)
8. Nancy Pelosi (D)
9. Barbara Lee (D)
10. Vacancy
11. Jerry McNerney (D)
12. Jackie Speier (D)
13. Pete Stark (D)
14. Anna G. Eshoo (D)
15. Michael M. Honda (D)
16. Zoe Lofgren (D)
17. Sam Farr (D)
18. Dennis Cardoza (D)
19. George P. Radanovich (R)
20. Jim Costa (D)
21. Devin Nunes (R)
22. Kevin McCarthy (R)
23. Lois Capps (D)
24. Elton Gallegly (R)
25. Howard P. "Buck" McKeon (R)
26. David Dreier (R)
27. Brad Sherman (D)
28. Howard L. Berman (D)
29. Adam B. Schiff (D)
30. Henry A. Waxman (D)
31. Xavier Becerra (D)
32. Judy Chu (D)
33. Diane Watson (D)
34. Lucille Roybal-Allard (D)
35. Maxine Waters (D)
36. Jane Harman (D)
37. Laura Richardson (D)
38. Grace F. Napolitano (D)
39. Linda T. Sanchez (D)
40. Ed Royce (R)
41. Jerry Lewis (R)
42. Gary G. Miller (R)
43. Joe Baca (D)
44. Ken Calvert (R)
45. Mary Bono Mack (R)
46. Dana Rohrabacher (R)
47. Loretta Sanchez (D)
48. John Campbell (R)
49. Darrell Issa (R)
50. Brian P. Bilbray (R)
51. Bob Filner (D)
52. Duncan D. Hunter (R)
53. Susan A. Davis (D)

POSTWAR VOTE FOR PRESIDENT

Year	Total Vote	Republican Vote	Republican Candidate	Democratic Vote	Democratic Candidate	Other Vote	Plurality	Total Vote Rep.	Total Vote Dem.	Major Vote Rep.	Major Vote Dem.
2008	13,561,900	5,011,781	McCain, John	8,274,473	Obama, Barack	275,646	3,262,692 D	37.0%	61.0%	37.7%	62.3%
2004	12,421,852	5,509,826	Bush, George W.	6,745,485	Kerry, John	166,541	1,235,659 D	44.4%	54.3%	45.0%	55.0%
2000**	10,965,856	4,567,429	Bush, George W.	5,861,203	Gore, Al	537,224	1,293,774 D	41.7%	53.4%	43.8%	56.2%
1996**	10,019,484	3,828,380	Dole, Bob	5,119,835	Clinton, Bill	1,071,269	1,291,455 D	38.2%	51.1%	42.8%	57.2%
1992**	11,131,721	3,630,574	Bush, George	5,121,325	Clinton, Bill	2,379,822	1,490,751 D	32.6%	46.0%	41.5%	58.5%
1988	9,887,065	5,054,917	Bush, George	4,702,233	Dukakis, Michael S.	129,915	352,684 R	51.1%	47.6%	51.8%	48.2%
1984	9,505,423	5,467,009	Reagan, Ronald	3,922,519	Mondale, Walter F.	115,895	1,544,490 R	57.5%	41.3%	58.2%	41.8%
1980**	8,587,063	4,524,858	Reagan, Ronald	3,083,661	Carter, Jimmy	978,544	1,441,197 R	52.7%	35.9%	59.5%	40.5%
1976	7,867,117	3,882,244	Ford, Gerald R.	3,742,284	Carter, Jimmy	242,589	139,960 R	49.3%	47.6%	50.9%	49.1%
1972	8,367,862	4,602,096	Nixon, Richard M.	3,475,847	McGovern, George S.	289,919	1,126,249 R	55.0%	41.5%	57.0%	43.0%
1968**	7,251,587	3,467,664	Nixon, Richard M.	3,244,318	Humphrey, Hubert H.	539,605	223,346 R	47.8%	44.7%	51.7%	48.3%
1964	7,057,586	2,879,108	Goldwater, Barry M.	4,171,877	Johnson, Lyndon B.	6,601	1,292,769 D	40.8%	59.1%	40.8%	59.2%
1960	6,506,578	3,259,722	Nixon, Richard M.	3,224,099	Kennedy, John F.	22,757	35,623 R	50.1%	49.6%	50.3%	49.7%
1956	5,466,355	3,027,668	Eisenhower, Dwight D.	2,420,135	Stevenson, Adlai E.	18,552	607,533 R	55.4%	44.3%	55.6%	44.4%
1952	5,141,849	2,897,310	Eisenhower, Dwight D.	2,197,548	Stevenson, Adlai E.	46,991	699,762 R	56.3%	42.7%	56.9%	43.1%
1948	4,021,538	1,895,269	Dewey, Thomas E.	1,913,134	Truman, Harry S.	213,135	17,865 D	47.1%	47.6%	49.8%	50.2%

**In past elections, the other vote included: 2000 - 418,707 Green (Ralph Nader); 1996 - 697,847 Reform (Ross Perot); 1992 - 2,296,006 Independent (Perot); 1980 - 739,833 Independent (John Anderson); 1968 - 487,270 American Independent (George Wallace).

CALIFORNIA

POSTWAR VOTE FOR GOVERNOR

Year	Total Vote	Republican		Democratic		Other Vote	Rep.-Dem. Plurality	Percentage			
								Total Vote		Major Vote	
		Vote	Candidate	Vote	Candidate			Rep.	Dem.	Rep.	Dem.
2006	8,679,416	4,850,157	Schwarzenegger, Arnold	3,376,732	Angelides, Phil	452,527	1,473,425 R	55.9%	38.9%	59.0%	41.0%
2003S	8,657,915	4,206,284	Schwarzenegger, Arnold	2,724,874	Bustamante, Cruz	1,726,757	1,481,410 R	48.6%	31.5%	—	—
2002	7,476,311	3,169,801	Simon, Bill	3,533,490	Davis, Gray	773,020	363,689 D	42.4%	47.3%	47.3%	52.7%
1998	8,385,196	3,218,030	Lungren, Dan	4,860,702	Davis, Gray	306,464	1,642,672 D	38.4%	58.0%	39.8%	60.2%
1994	8,665,375	4,781,766	Wilson, Pete	3,519,799	Brown, Kathleen	363,810	1,261,967 R	55.2%	40.6%	57.6%	42.4%
1990	7,699,467	3,791,904	Wilson, Pete	3,525,197	Feinstein, Dianne	382,366	266,707 R	49.2%	45.8%	51.8%	48.2%
1986	7,443,551	4,506,601	Deukmejian, George	2,781,714	Bradley, Tom	155,236	1,724,887 R	60.5%	37.4%	61.8%	38.2%
1982	7,876,698	3,881,014	Deukmejian, George	3,787,669	Bradley, Tom	208,015	93,345 R	49.3%	48.1%	50.6%	49.4%
1978	6,922,378	2,526,534	Younger, Evelle J.	3,878,812	Brown, Edmund G., Jr.	517,032	1,352,278 D	36.5%	56.0%	39.4%	60.6%
1974	6,248,070	2,952,954	Flournoy, Houston I.	3,131,648	Brown, Edmund G., Jr.	163,468	178,694 D	47.3%	50.1%	48.5%	51.5%
1970	6,510,072	3,439,664	Reagan, Ronald	2,938,607	Unruh, Jess	131,801	501,057 R	52.8%	45.1%	53.9%	46.1%
1966	6,503,445	3,742,913	Reagan, Ronald	2,749,174	Brown, Edmund G.	11,358	993,739 R	57.6%	42.3%	57.7%	42.3%
1962	5,853,270	2,740,351	Nixon, Richard M.	3,037,109	Brown, Edmund G.	75,810	296,758 D	46.8%	51.9%	47.4%	52.6%
1958	5,255,777	2,110,911	Knowland, William F.	3,140,076	Brown, Edmund G.	4,790	1,029,165 D	40.2%	59.7%	40.2%	59.8%
1954	4,030,368	2,290,519	Knight, Goodwin J.	1,739,368	Graves, Richard P.	481	551,151 R	56.8%	43.2%	56.8%	43.2%
1950	3,796,090	2,461,754	Warren, Earl	1,333,856	Roosevelt, James	480	1,127,898 R	64.8%	35.1%	64.9%	35.1%
1946**	2,558,399	2,344,542	Warren, Earl	—		213,857	2,344,542 R	91.6%		100.0%	

Notes: **The 2003 election was for a short term to fill a vacancy created by voter approval of a measure to remove Governor Gray Davis (D) from office. The measure passed by a vote of 4,976,274 votes (55.4 percent) for recall to 4,007,783 (44.6 percent) against recall. In the same election, more than 100 candidates ran for the right to succeed Davis. No primary election was held to cull the field. All candidates, regardless of party, ran together on the same ballot. The winner, Arnold Schwarzenegger, is listed as the Republican candidate. The leading Democratic vote-getter, Cruz Bustamante, is listed as the Democratic candidate. The percentages given are for Schwarzenegger and Bustamante. The leading "Other" candidate was Republican Tom McClintock, who received 1,161,287 votes (13.4 percent of the total). In 1946 the Republican candidate won both major party nominations.

POSTWAR VOTE FOR SENATOR

Year	Total Vote	Republican		Democratic		Other Vote	Rep.-Dem. Plurality	Percentage			
								Total Vote		Major Vote	
		Vote	Candidate	Vote	Candidate			Rep.	Dem.	Rep.	Dem.
2006	8,541,476	2,990,822	Mountjoy, Richard "Dick"	5,076,289	Feinstein, Dianne	474,365	2,085,467 D	35.0%	59.4%	37.1%	62.9%
2004	12,053,295	4,555,922	Jones, Bill	6,955,728	Boxer, Barbara	541,645	2,399,806 D	37.8%	57.7%	39.6%	60.4%
2000	10,623,614	3,886,853	Campbell, Tom	5,932,522	Feinstein, Dianne	804,239	2,045,669 D	36.6%	55.8%	39.6%	60.4%
1998	8,314,953	3,576,351	Fong, Matt	4,411,705	Boxer, Barbara	326,897	835,354 D	43.0%	53.1%	44.8%	55.2%
1994	8,514,089	3,817,025	Huffington, Michael	3,979,152	Feinstein, Dianne	717,912	162,127 D	44.8%	46.7%	49.0%	51.0%
1992	10,799,703	4,644,182	Herschensohn, Bruce	5,173,467	Boxer, Barbara	982,054	529,285 D	43.0%	47.9%	47.3%	52.7%
1992S	10,782,743	4,093,501	Seymour, John	5,853,651	Feinstein, Dianne	835,591	1,760,150 D	38.0%	54.3%	41.2%	58.8%
1988	9,743,598	5,143,409	Wilson, Pete	4,287,253	McCarthy, Leo	312,936	856,156 R	52.8%	44.0%	54.5%	45.5%
1986	7,398,549	3,541,804	Zschau, Ed	3,646,672	Cranston, Alan	210,073	104,868 D	47.9%	49.3%	49.3%	50.7%
1982	7,805,538	4,022,565	Wilson, Pete	3,494,968	Brown, Edmund G., Jr.	288,005	527,597 R	51.5%	44.8%	53.5%	46.5%
1980	8,327,481	3,093,426	Gann, Paul	4,705,399	Cranston, Alan	528,656	1,611,973 D	37.1%	56.5%	39.7%	60.3%
1976	7,472,268	3,748,973	Hayakawa, S. I.	3,502,862	Tunney, John V.	220,433	246,111 R	50.2%	46.9%	51.7%	48.3%
1974	6,102,432	2,210,267	Richardson, H. L.	3,693,160	Cranston, Alan	199,005	1,482,893 D	36.2%	60.5%	37.4%	62.6%
1970	6,492,157	2,877,617	Murphy, George	3,496,558	Tunney, John V.	117,982	618,941 D	44.3%	53.9%	45.1%	54.9%
1968	7,102,465	3,329,148	Rafferty, Max	3,680,352	Cranston, Alan	92,965	351,204 D	46.9%	51.8%	47.5%	52.5%
1964	7,041,821	3,628,555	Murphy, George	3,411,912	Salinger, Pierre	1,354	216,643 R	51.5%	48.5%	51.5%	48.5%
1962	5,647,952	3,180,483	Kuchel, Thomas H.	2,452,839	Richards, Richard	14,630	727,644 R	56.3%	43.4%	56.5%	43.5%
1958	5,135,221	2,204,337	Knight, Goodwin J.	2,927,693	Engle, Clair	3,191	723,356 D	42.9%	57.0%	43.0%	57.0%
1956	5,361,467	2,892,918	Kuchel, Thomas H.	2,445,816	Richards, Richard	22,733	447,102 R	54.0%	45.6%	54.2%	45.8%
1954S	3,929,668	2,090,836	Kuchel, Thomas H.	1,788,071	Yorty, Samuel W.	50,761	302,765 R	53.2%	45.5%	53.9%	46.1%
1952**	4,542,548	3,982,448	Knowland, William F.	—		560,100	3,982,448 R	87.7%		100.0%	
1950	3,686,315	2,183,454	Nixon, Richard M.	1,502,507	Douglas, Helen	354	680,947 R	59.2%	40.8%	59.2%	40.8%
1946	2,639,465	1,428,067	Knowland, William F.	1,167,161	Rogers, Will, Jr.	44,237	260,906 R	54.1%	44.2%	55.0%	45.0%

Notes: **In past elections, the other vote included: 1952 - 542,270 Progressive (Reuben W. Borough), who finished second. The Republican candidate that year won both major party nominations. The 1954 election was for a short term to fill a vacancy, as was one of the 1992 elections.

CALIFORNIA

PRESIDENT 2008

2000 Census Population	County	Total Vote	Republican	Democratic	Other	Rep.-Dem. Plurality	Percentage			
							Total Vote		Major Vote	
							Rep.	Dem.	Rep.	Dem.
1,443,741	ALAMEDA	621,029	119,555	489,106	12,368	369,551 D	19.3%	78.8%	19.6%	80.4%
1,208	ALPINE	692	252	422	18	170 D	36.4%	61.0%	37.4%	62.6%
35,100	AMADOR	18,810	10,561	7,813	436	2,748 R	56.1%	41.5%	57.5%	42.5%
203,171	BUTTE	98,325	46,706	49,013	2,606	2,307 D	47.5%	49.8%	48.8%	51.2%
40,554	CALAVERAS	23,306	12,835	9,813	658	3,022 R	55.1%	42.1%	56.7%	43.3%
18,804	COLUSA	6,429	3,733	2,569	127	1,164 R	58.1%	40.0%	59.2%	40.8%
948,816	CONTRA COSTA	451,650	136,436	306,983	8,231	170,547 D	30.2%	68.0%	30.8%	69.2%
27,507	DEL NORTE	9,531	4,967	4,323	241	644 R	52.1%	45.4%	53.5%	46.5%
156,299	EL DORADO	92,926	50,314	40,529	2,083	9,785 R	54.1%	43.6%	55.4%	44.6%
799,407	FRESNO	272,289	131,015	136,706	4,568	5,691 D	48.1%	50.2%	48.9%	51.1%
26,453	GLENN	9,879	5,910	3,734	235	2,176 R	59.8%	37.8%	61.3%	38.7%
126,518	HUMBOLDT	63,727	21,713	39,692	2,322	17,979 D	34.1%	62.3%	35.4%	64.6%
142,361	IMPERIAL	38,820	14,008	24,162	650	10,154 D	36.1%	62.2%	36.7%	63.3%
17,945	INYO	8,533	4,523	3,743	267	780 R	53.0%	43.9%	54.7%	45.3%
661,645	KERN	232,850	134,793	93,457	4,600	41,336 R	57.9%	40.1%	59.1%	40.9%
129,461	KINGS	35,108	19,710	14,747	651	4,963 R	56.1%	42.0%	57.2%	42.8%
58,309	LAKE	25,542	9,935	14,854	753	4,919 D	38.9%	58.2%	40.1%	59.9%
33,828	LASSEN	11,387	7,483	3,586	318	3,897 R	65.7%	31.5%	67.6%	32.4%
9,519,338	LOS ANGELES	3,318,248	956,425	2,295,853	65,970	1,339,428 D	28.8%	69.2%	29.4%	70.6%
123,109	MADERA	42,355	23,583	17,952	820	5,631 R	55.7%	42.4%	56.8%	43.2%
247,289	MARIN	140,197	28,384	109,320	2,493	80,936 D	20.2%	78.0%	20.6%	79.4%
17,130	MARIPOSA	9,651	5,298	4,100	253	1,198 R	54.9%	42.5%	56.4%	43.6%
86,265	MENDOCINO	40,016	10,721	27,843	1,452	17,122 D	26.8%	69.6%	27.8%	72.2%
210,554	MERCED	63,808	28,704	34,031	1,073	5,327 D	45.0%	53.3%	45.8%	54.2%
9,449	MODOC	4,420	2,981	1,313	126	1,668 R	67.4%	29.7%	69.4%	30.6%
12,853	MONO	5,571	2,354	3,093	124	739 D	42.3%	55.5%	43.2%	56.8%
401,762	MONTEREY	129,783	38,797	88,453	2,533	49,656 D	29.9%	68.2%	30.5%	69.5%
124,279	NAPA	59,642	19,484	38,849	1,309	19,365 D	32.7%	65.1%	33.4%	66.6%
92,033	NEVADA	55,647	25,663	28,617	1,367	2,954 D	46.1%	51.4%	47.3%	52.7%
2,846,289	ORANGE	1,153,687	579,064	549,558	25,065	29,506 R	50.2%	47.6%	51.3%	48.7%
248,399	PLACER	173,107	94,647	75,112	3,348	19,535 R	54.7%	43.4%	55.8%	44.2%
20,824	PLUMAS	11,028	6,035	4,715	278	1,320 R	54.7%	42.8%	56.1%	43.9%
1,545,387	RIVERSIDE	647,299	310,041	325,017	12,241	14,976 D	47.9%	50.2%	48.8%	51.2%
1,223,499	SACRAMENTO	541,101	213,583	316,506	11,012	102,923 D	39.5%	58.5%	40.3%	59.7%
53,234	SAN BENITO	19,705	7,425	11,917	363	4,492 D	37.7%	60.5%	38.4%	61.6%
1,709,434	SAN BERNARDINO	606,334	277,408	315,720	13,206	38,312 D	45.8%	52.1%	46.8%	53.2%
2,813,833	SAN DIEGO	1,231,047	541,032	666,581	23,434	125,549 D	43.9%	54.1%	44.8%	55.2%
776,733	SAN FRANCISCO	382,865	52,292	322,220	8,353	269,928 D	13.7%	84.2%	14.0%	86.0%
563,598	SAN JOAQUIN	209,349	91,607	113,974	3,768	22,367 D	43.8%	54.4%	44.6%	55.4%
246,681	SAN LUIS OBISPO	132,653	61,055	68,176	3,422	7,121 D	46.0%	51.4%	47.2%	52.8%
707,161	SAN MATEO	303,292	75,057	222,826	5,409	147,769 D	24.7%	73.5%	25.2%	74.8%
399,347	SANTA BARBARA	174,912	65,585	105,614	3,713	40,029 D	37.5%	60.4%	38.3%	61.7%
1,682,585	SANTA CLARA	665,589	190,039	462,241	13,309	272,202 D	28.6%	69.4%	29.1%	70.9%
255,602	SANTA CRUZ	127,483	25,244	98,745	3,494	73,501 D	19.8%	77.5%	20.4%	79.6%
163,256	SHASTA	80,390	49,588	28,867	1,935	20,721 R	61.7%	35.9%	63.2%	36.8%
3,555	SIERRA	1,991	1,158	743	90	415 R	58.2%	37.3%	60.9%	39.1%
44,301	SISKIYOU	21,470	11,520	9,292	658	2,228 R	53.7%	43.3%	55.4%	44.6%
394,542	SOLANO	160,973	56,035	102,095	2,843	46,060 D	34.8%	63.4%	35.4%	64.6%
458,614	SONOMA	229,351	55,127	168,888	5,336	113,761 D	24.0%	73.6%	24.6%	75.4%
446,997	STANISLAUS	161,015	77,497	80,279	3,239	2,782 D	48.1%	49.9%	49.1%	50.9%
78,930	SUTTER	32,941	18,911	13,412	618	5,499 R	57.4%	40.7%	58.5%	41.5%
56,039	TEHAMA	24,436	14,843	8,945	648	5,898 R	60.7%	36.6%	62.4%	37.6%
13,022	TRINITY	6,374	2,940	3,233	201	293 D	46.1%	50.7%	47.6%	52.4%
368,021	TULARE	105,206	59,765	43,634	1,807	16,131 R	56.8%	41.5%	57.8%	42.2%
54,501	TUOLUMNE	27,181	14,988	11,532	661	3,456 R	55.1%	42.4%	56.5%	43.5%
753,197	VENTURA	339,800	145,853	187,601	6,346	41,748 D	42.9%	55.2%	43.7%	56.3%
168,660	YOLO	79,749	24,592	53,488	1,669	28,896 D	30.8%	67.1%	31.5%	68.5%
60,219	YUBA	21,401	12,007	8,866	528	3,141 R	56.1%	41.4%	57.5%	42.5%
33,871,648	*TOTAL*	*13,561,900*	*5,011,781*	*8,274,473*	*275,646*	*3,262,692 D*	*37.0%*	*61.0%*	*37.7%*	*62.3%*

CALIFORNIA

HOUSE OF REPRESENTATIVES

CD	Year	Total Vote	Republican Vote	Republican Candidate	Democratic Vote	Democratic Candidate	Other Vote	Rep.-Dem. Plurality	Total Vote Rep.	Total Vote Dem.	Major Vote Rep.	Major Vote Dem.
1	2008	290,472	67,853	STARKEWOLF, ZANE	197,812	THOMPSON, MIKE*	24,807	129,959 D	23.4%	68.1%	25.5%	74.5%
1	2006	218,044	63,194	JONES, JOHN W.	144,409	THOMPSON, MIKE*	10,441	81,215 D	29.0%	66.2%	30.4%	69.6%
1	2004	282,971	79,970	WIESNER, LAWRENCE R.	189,366	THOMPSON, MIKE*	13,635	109,396 D	28.3%	66.9%	29.7%	70.3%
1	2002	185,216	60,013	WIESNER, LAWRENCE R.	118,669	THOMPSON, MIKE*	6,534	58,656 D	32.4%	64.1%	33.6%	66.4%
2	2008	282,337	163,459	HERGER, WALLY*	118,878	MORRIS, JEFF		44,581 R	57.9%	42.1%	57.9%	42.1%
2	2006	210,202	134,911	HERGER, WALLY*	68,234	SEKHON, A.J.	7,057	66,677 R	64.2%	32.5%	66.4%	33.6%
2	2004	272,429	182,119	HERGER, WALLY*	90,310	JOHNSON, MIKE		91,809 R	66.9%	33.1%	66.9%	33.1%
2	2002	178,985	117,747	HERGER, WALLY*	52,455	JOHNSON, MIKE	8,783	65,292 R	65.8%	29.3%	69.2%	30.8%
3	2008	314,046	155,424	LUNGREN, DAN*	137,971	DURSTON, BILL	20,651	17,453 R	49.5%	43.9%	53.0%	47.0%
3	2006	228,169	135,709	LUNGREN, DAN*	86,318	DURSTON, BILL	6,142	49,391 R	59.5%	37.8%	61.1%	38.9%
3	2004	287,073	177,738	LUNGREN, DAN	100,025	CASTILLO, GABE	9,310	77,713 R	61.9%	34.8%	64.0%	36.0%
3	2002	194,918	121,732	OSE, DOUG*	67,136	BEEMAN, HOWARD	6,050	54,596 R	62.5%	34.4%	64.5%	35.5%
4	2008	369,780	185,790	McCLINTOCK, TOM	183,990	BROWN, CHARLIE		1,800 R	50.2%	49.8%	50.2%	49.8%
4	2006	276,893	135,818	DOOLITTLE, JOHN T.*	126,999	BROWN, CHARLIE	14,076	8,819 R	49.1%	45.9%	51.7%	48.3%
4	2004	339,369	221,926	DOOLITTLE, JOHN T.*	117,443	WINTERS, DAVID I.		104,483 R	65.4%	34.6%	65.4%	34.6%
4	2002	228,506	147,997	DOOLITTLE, JOHN T.*	72,860	NORBERG, MARK A.	7,649	75,137 R	64.8%	31.9%	67.0%	33.0%
5	2008	221,155	46,002	SMITH, PAUL A.	164,242	MATSUI, DORIS*	10,911	118,240 D	20.8%	74.3%	21.9%	78.1%
5	2006	149,266	35,106	YAN, CLAIRE	105,676	MATSUI, DORIS*	8,484	70,570 D	23.5%	70.8%	24.9%	75.1%
5	2004	193,387	45,120	DUGAS, MIKE	138,004	MATSUI, ROBERT T.*	10,263	92,884 D	23.3%	71.4%	24.6%	75.4%
5	2002	131,578	34,749	FRANKHUIZEN, RICHARD	92,726	MATSUI, ROBERT T.*	4,103	57,977 D	26.4%	70.5%	27.3%	72.7%
6	2008	320,362	77,073	HALLIWELL, MIKE	229,672	WOOLSEY, LYNN*	13,617	152,599 D	24.1%	71.7%	25.1%	74.9%
6	2006	246,628	64,405	HOOPER, TODD	173,190	WOOLSEY, LYNN*	9,033	108,785 D	26.1%	70.2%	27.1%	72.9%
6	2004	311,667	85,244	ERICKSON, PAUL L.	226,423	WOOLSEY, LYNN*		141,179 D	27.4%	72.6%	27.4%	72.6%
6	2002	209,563	62,052	ERICKSON, PAUL L.	139,750	WOOLSEY, LYNN*	7,761	77,698 D	29.6%	66.7%	30.7%	69.3%
7	2008	234,773	51,166	PETERSEN, ROGER ALLEN	170,962	MILLER, GEORGE*	12,645	119,796 D	21.8%	72.8%	23.0%	77.0%
7	2006	140,486		—	118,000	MILLER, GEORGE*	22,486	118,000 D		84.0%		100.0%
7	2004	219,277	52,446	HARGRAVE, CHARLES	166,831	MILLER, GEORGE*		114,385 D	23.9%	76.1%	23.9%	76.1%
7	2002	138,376	36,584	HARGRAVE, CHARLES	97,849	MILLER, GEORGE*	3,943	61,265 D	26.4%	70.7%	27.2%	72.8%
8	2008	285,247	27,614	WALSH, DANA	204,996	PELOSI, NANCY*	52,637	177,382 D	9.7%	71.9%	11.9%	88.1%
8	2006	184,639	19,800	DeNUNZIO, MIKE	148,435	PELOSI, NANCY*	16,404	128,635 D	10.7%	80.4%	11.8%	88.2%
8	2004	270,064	31,074	DEPALMA, JENNIFER	224,017	PELOSI, NANCY*	14,973	192,943 D	11.5%	82.9%	12.2%	87.8%
8	2002	160,441	20,063	GERMAN, G. MICHAEL	127,684	PELOSI, NANCY*	12,694	107,621 D	12.5%	79.6%	13.6%	86.4%
9	2008	277,600	26,917	HARGRAVE, CHARLES	238,915	LEE, BARBARA*	11,768	211,998 D	9.7%	86.1%	10.1%	89.9%
9	2006	193,686	20,786	den DULK, JOHN "J.D."	167,245	LEE, BARBARA*	5,655	146,459 D	10.7%	86.3%	11.1%	88.9%
9	2004	255,039	31,278	BERMUDEZ, CLAUDIA	215,630	LEE, BARBARA*	8,131	184,352 D	12.3%	84.5%	12.7%	87.3%
9	2002	166,917	25,333	UDINSKY, JERRY	135,893	LEE, BARBARA*	5,691	110,560 D	15.2%	81.4%	15.7%	84.3%
10	2008	295,165	91,877	GERBER, NICHOLAS	192,226	TAUSCHER, ELLEN O.*	11,062	100,349 D	31.1%	65.1%	32.3%	67.7%
10	2006	196,978	66,069	LINN, DARCY	130,859	TAUSCHER, ELLEN O.*	50	64,790 D	33.5%	66.4%	33.5%	66.5%
10	2004	278,099	95,349	KETELSON, JEFF	182,750	TAUSCHER, ELLEN O.*		87,401 D	34.3%	65.7%	34.3%	65.7%
10	2002	167,197		—	126,390	TAUSCHER, ELLEN O.*	40,807	126,390 D		75.6%		100.0%
11	2008	297,616	133,104	ANDAL, DEAN	164,500	McNERNEY, JERRY*	12	31,396 D	44.7%	55.3%	44.7%	55.3%
11	2006	206,264	96,396	POMBO, RICHARD W.*	109,868	McNERNEY, JERRY		13,472 D	46.7%	53.3%	46.7%	53.3%
11	2004	267,169	163,582	POMBO, RICHARD W.*	103,587	McNERNEY, JERRY		59,995 R	61.2%	38.8%	61.2%	38.8%
11	2002	173,956	104,921	POMBO, RICHARD W.*	69,035	SHAW, ELAINE DUGGER		35,886 R	60.3%	39.7%	60.3%	39.7%
12	2008	266,853	49,258	CONLON, GREG	200,442	SPEIER, JACKIE*	17,153	151,184 D	18.5%	75.1%	19.7%	80.3%
12	2006	182,324	43,674	MOLONEY, MIKE	138,650	LANTOS, TOM*		94,976 D	24.0%	76.0%	24.0%	76.0%
12	2004	252,599	52,593	GARZA, MIKE	171,852	LANTOS, TOM*	28,154	119,259 D	20.8%	68.0%	23.4%	76.6%
12	2002	154,984	38,381	MOLONEY, MIKE	105,597	LANTOS, TOM*	11,006	67,216 D	24.8%	68.1%	26.7%	73.3%
13	2008	218,276	51,447	CHUI, RAYMOND	166,829	STARK, PETE*		115,382 D	23.6%	76.4%	23.6%	76.4%
13	2006	147,897	37,141	BRUNO, GEORGE I.	110,756	STARK, PETE*		73,615 D	25.1%	74.9%	25.1%	74.9%
13	2004	201,921	48,439	BRUNO, GEORGE I.	144,605	STARK, PETE*	8,877	96,166 D	24.0%	71.6%	25.1%	74.9%
13	2002	121,723	26,852	MAHMOOD, SYED R.	86,495	STARK, PETE*	8,376	59,643 D	22.1%	71.1%	23.7%	76.3%
14	2008	272,766	60,610	SANTANA, RONNY	190,301	ESHOO, ANNA G.*	21,855	129,691 D	22.2%	69.8%	24.2%	75.8%
14	2006	198,575	48,097	SMITH, ROB	141,153	ESHOO, ANNA G.*	9,325	93,056 D	24.2%	71.1%	25.4%	74.6%

CALIFORNIA

HOUSE OF REPRESENTATIVES

CD	Year	Total Vote	Republican Vote	Republican Candidate	Democratic Vote	Democratic Candidate	Other Vote	Rep.-Dem. Plurality	Total Vote Rep.	Total Vote Dem.	Major Vote Rep.	Major Vote Dem.
14	2004	261,888	69,564	HAUGEN, CHRIS	182,712	ESHOO, ANNA G.*	9,612	113,148 D	26.6%	69.8%	27.6%	72.4%
14	2002	171,678	48,346	NIXON, JOSEPH H.	117,055	ESHOO, ANNA G.*	6,277	68,709 D	28.2%	68.2%	29.2%	70.8%
15	2008	238,589	55,489	CORDI, JOYCE STOER	170,977	HONDA, MICHAEL M.*	12,123	115,488 D	23.3%	71.7%	24.5%	75.5%
15	2006	159,718	44,186	CHUCKWU, RAYMOND L.	115,532	HONDA, MICHAEL M.*		71,346 D	27.7%	72.3%	27.7%	72.3%
15	2004	214,338	59,953	CHUCKWU, RAYMOND L.	154,385	HONDA, MICHAEL M.*		94,432 D	28.0%	72.0%	28.0%	72.0%
15	2002	133,022	41,251	HERMANN, LINDA RAE	87,482	HONDA, MICHAEL M.*	4,289	46,231 D	31.0%	65.8%	32.0%	68.0%
16	2008	205,327	49,399	WINSTON, CHAREL	146,481	LOFGREN, ZOE*	9,447	97,082 D	24.1%	71.3%	25.2%	74.8%
16	2006	136,059	37,130	WINSTON, CHAREL	98,929	LOFGREN, ZOE*		61,799 D	27.3%	72.7%	27.3%	72.7%
16	2004	182,281	47,992	McNEA, DOUGLAS ADAMS	129,222	LOFGREN, ZOE*	5,067	81,230 D	26.3%	70.9%	27.1%	72.9%
16	2002	107,986	32,182	McNEA, DOUGLAS ADAMS	72,370	LOFGREN, ZOE*	3,434	40,188 D	29.8%	67.0%	30.8%	69.2%
17	2008	228,626	59,037	TAYLOR, JEFF	168,907	FARR, SAM*	682	109,870 D	25.8%	73.9%	25.9%	74.1%
17	2006	159,293	35,932	DE MAIO, ANTHONY R.	120,750	FARR, SAM*	2,611	84,818 D	22.6%	75.8%	22.9%	77.1%
17	2004	223,225	65,117	RISLEY, MARK	148,958	FARR, SAM*	9,150	83,841 D	29.2%	66.7%	30.4%	69.6%
17	2002	149,296	40,334	ENGLER, CLINT C.	101,632	FARR, SAM*	7,330	61,298 D	27.0%	68.1%	28.4%	71.6%
18	2008	130,192		—	130,192	CARDOZA, DENNIS*		130,192 D		100.0%		100.0%
18	2006	108,713	37,531	KANNO, JOHN A.	71,182	CARDOZA, DENNIS*		33,651 D	34.5%	65.5%	34.5%	65.5%
18	2004	153,705	49,973	PRINGLE, CHARLES F.	103,732	CARDOZA, DENNIS*		53,759 D	32.5%	67.5%	32.5%	67.5%
18	2002	109,593	47,528	MONTEITH, DICK	56,181	CARDOZA, DENNIS	5,884	8,653 D	43.4%	51.3%	45.8%	54.2%
19	2008	182,101	179,245	RADANOVICH, GEORGE P.*		—	2,856	179,245 R	98.4%		100.0%	
19	2006	181,994	110,246	RADANOVICH, GEORGE P.*	71,748	COX, T.J.		38,498 R	60.6%	39.4%	60.6%	39.4%
19	2004	235,264	155,354	RADANOVICH, GEORGE P.*	64,047	BUFFORD, JAMES LEX	15,863	91,307 R	66.0%	27.2%	70.8%	29.2%
19	2002	157,802	106,209	RADANOVICH, GEORGE P.*	47,403	VEEN, JOHN	4,190	58,806 R	67.3%	30.0%	69.1%	30.9%
20	2008	125,141	32,118	LOPEZ, JIM	93,023	COSTA, JIM*		60,905 D	25.7%	74.3%	25.7%	74.3%
20	2006	61,120		—	61,120	COSTA, JIM*		61,120 D		100.0%		100.0%
20	2004	114,236	53,231	ASHBURN, ROY	61,005	COSTA, JIM		7,774 D	46.6%	53.4%	46.6%	53.4%
20	2002	74,770	25,628	MINUTH, ANDRE	47,627	DOOLEY, CAL*	1,515	21,999 D	34.3%	63.7%	35.0%	65.0%
21	2008	209,815	143,498	NUNES, DEVIN*	66,317	JOHNSON, LARRY		77,181 R	68.4%	31.6%	68.4%	31.6%
21	2006	142,661	95,214	NUNES, DEVIN*	42,718	HAZE, STEVEN	4,729	52,496 R	66.7%	29.9%	69.0%	31.0%
21	2004	192,315	140,721	NUNES, DEVIN*	51,594	DAVIS, FRED B.		89,127 R	73.2%	26.8%	73.2%	26.8%
21	2002	124,198	87,544	NUNES, DEVIN	32,584	LaPERE, DAVID G.	4,070	54,960 R	70.5%	26.2%	72.9%	27.1%
22	2008	224,549	224,549	McCARTHY, KEVIN*		—		224,549 R	100.0%		100.0%	
22	2006	188,504	133,278	McCARTHY, KEVIN	55,226	BEERY, SHARON M.		78,052 R	70.7%	29.3%	70.7%	29.3%
22	2004	209,384	209,384	THOMAS, BILL*		—		209,384 R	100.0%		100.0%	
22	2002	164,285	120,473	THOMAS, BILL*	38,988	CORVERA, JAIME	4,824	81,485 R	73.3%	23.7%	75.6%	24.4%
23	2008	251,788	80,385	KOKKONEN, MATT T.	171,403	CAPPS, LOIS*		91,018 D	31.9%	68.1%	31.9%	68.1%
23	2006	175,951	61,272	TOGNAZZINI, VICTOR D.	114,661	CAPPS, LOIS*	18	53,389 D	34.8%	65.2%	34.8%	65.2%
23	2004	244,297	83,926	REGAN, DON	153,980	CAPPS, LOIS*	6,391	70,054 D	34.4%	63.0%	35.3%	64.7%
23	2002	162,222	62,604	ROGERS, BETH	95,752	CAPPS, LOIS*	3,866	33,148 D	38.6%	59.0%	39.5%	60.5%
24	2008	300,052	174,492	GALLEGLY, ELTON*	125,560	JORGENSEN, MARTA ANN		48,932 R	58.2%	41.8%	58.2%	41.8%
24	2006	209,292	129,812	GALLEGLY, ELTON*	79,461	MARTINEZ, JILL M.	19	50,351 R	62.0%	38.0%	62.0%	38.0%
24	2004	284,378	178,660	GALLEGLY, ELTON*	96,397	WAGNER, BRETT	9,321	82,263 R	62.8%	33.9%	65.0%	35.0%
24	2002	185,006	120,585	GALLEGLY, ELTON*	58,755	RUDIN, FERN	5,666	61,830 R	65.2%	31.8%	67.2%	32.8%
25	2008	250,589	144,660	McKEON, HOWARD P. "BUCK"*	105,929	CONAWAY, JACKIE		38,731 R	57.7%	42.3%	57.7%	42.3%
25	2006	156,773	93,987	McKEON, HOWARD P. "BUCK"*	55,913	RODRIGUEZ, ROBERT	6,873	38,074 R	60.0%	35.7%	62.7%	37.3%
25	2004	225,970	145,575	McKEON, HOWARD P. "BUCK"*	80,395	WILLOUGHBY, FRED "TIM"		65,180 R	64.4%	35.6%	64.4%	35.6%
25	2002	124,336	80,775	McKEON, HOWARD P. "BUCK"*	38,674	CONAWAY, BOB	4,887	42,101 R	65.0%	31.1%	67.6%	32.4%
26	2008	267,130	140,615	DREIER, DAVID*	108,039	WARNER, RUSS	18,476	32,576 R	52.6%	40.4%	56.6%	43.4%
26	2006	179,144	102,028	DREIER, DAVID*	67,878	MATTHEWS, CYNTHIA	9,238	34,150 R	57.0%	37.9%	60.0%	40.0%
26	2004	251,207	134,596	DREIER, DAVID*	107,522	MATTHEWS, CYNTHIA	9,089	27,074 R	53.6%	42.8%	55.6%	44.4%
26	2002	149,530	95,360	DREIER, DAVID*	50,081	MIKELS, MARJORIE MUSSER	4,089	45,279 R	63.8%	33.5%	65.6%	34.4%
27	2008	212,835	52,852	SINGH, NAVRAJ	145,812	SHERMAN, BRAD*	14,171	92,960 D	24.8%	68.5%	26.6%	73.4%
27	2006	134,724	42,074	HANKWITZ, PETER	92,650	SHERMAN, BRAD*		50,576 D	31.2%	68.8%	31.2%	68.8%
27	2004	201,198	66,946	LEVY, ROBERT M.	125,296	SHERMAN, BRAD*	8,956	58,350 D	33.3%	62.3%	34.8%	65.2%
27	2002	128,811	48,996	LEVY, ROBERT M.	79,815	SHERMAN, BRAD*		30,819 D	38.0%	62.0%	38.0%	62.0%

CALIFORNIA

HOUSE OF REPRESENTATIVES

| | | | Republican | | Democratic | | | | Percentage | | | |
| | | Total | | | | | Other | Rep.-Dem. | Total Vote | | Major Vote | |
CD	Year	Vote	Vote	Candidate	Vote	Candidate	Vote	Plurality	Rep.	Dem.	Rep.	Dem.
28	2008	137,621	—		137,471	BERMAN, HOWARD L.*	150	137,471 D		99.9%		100.0%
28	2006	108,042	20,629	KESSELMAN, STANLEY KIMMEL	79,866	BERMAN, HOWARD L.*	7,547	59,237 D	19.1%	73.9%	20.5%	79.5%
28	2004	162,510	37,868	HERNANDEZ, DAVID	115,303	BERMAN, HOWARD L.*	9,339	77,435 D	23.3%	71.0%	24.7%	75.3%
28	2002	103,326	23,926	HERNANDEZ, DAVID	73,771	BERMAN, HOWARD L.*	5,629	49,845 D	23.2%	71.4%	24.5%	75.5%
29	2008	212,144	56,727	HAHN, CHARLES	146,198	SCHIFF, ADAM B.*	9,219	89,471 D	26.7%	68.9%	28.0%	72.0%
29	2006	143,404	39,321	BODELL, WILLIAM J.	91,014	SCHIFF, ADAM B.*	13,069	51,693 D	27.4%	63.5%	30.2%	69.8%
29	2004	206,832	62,871	SCOLINOS, HARRY FRANK	133,670	SCHIFF, ADAM B.*	10,291	70,799 D	30.4%	64.6%	32.0%	68.0%
29	2002	121,541	40,616	SCILEPPI, JIM	76,036	SCHIFF, ADAM B.*	4,889	35,420 D	33.4%	62.6%	34.8%	65.2%
30	2008	242,792	—		242,792	WAXMAN, HENRY A.*		242,792 D		100.0%		100.0%
30	2006	211,734	55,904	JONES, DAVID NELSON	151,284	WAXMAN, HENRY A.*	4,546	95,380 D	26.4%	71.5%	27.0%	73.0%
30	2004	304,147	87,465	ELIZALDE, VICTOR	216,682	WAXMAN, HENRY A.*		129,217 D	28.8%	71.2%	28.8%	71.2%
30	2002	185,593	54,989	GOSS, TONY, D.	130,604	WAXMAN, HENRY A.*		75,615 D	29.6%	70.4%	29.6%	70.4%
31	2008	110,955		—	110,955	BECERRA, XAVIER*		110,955 D		100.0%		100.0%
31	2006	64,952		—	64,952	BECERRA, XAVIER*		64,952 D		100.0%		100.0%
31	2004	111,411	22,048	VEGA, LUIS	89,363	BECERRA, XAVIER*		67,315 D	19.8%	80.2%	19.8%	30.2%
31	2002	67,243	12,674	VEGA, LUIS	54,569	BECERRA, XAVIER*		41,895 D	18.8%	81.2%	18.8%	81.2%
32	2008	130,150		—	130,142	SOLIS, HILDA L.*	8	130,142 D		100.0%		100.0%
32	2006	91,686		—	76,059	SOLIS, HILDA L.*	15,627	76,059 D		83.0%		100.0%
32	2004	140,146		—	119,144	SOLIS, HILDA L.*	21,002	119,144 D		85.0%		100.0%
32	2002	85,079	23,366	FISCHBECK, EMMA E.	58,530	SOLIS, HILDA L.*	3,183	35,164 D	27.5%	68.8%	28.5%	71.5%
33	2008	213,460	26,536	CROWLEY, DAVID C. II	186,924	WATSON, DIANE*		160,388 D	12.4%	87.6%	12.4%	87.6%
33	2004	113,715		—	113,715	WATSON, DIANE*		113,715 D		100.0%		100.0%
33	2004	188,314		—	166,801	WATSON, DIANE*	21,513	166,801 D		88.6%		100.0%
33	2002	118,449	16,699	KIM, ANDREW	97,779	WATSON, DIANE*	3,971	81,080 D	14.1%	82.5%	14.6%	85.4%
34	2008	127,769	29,266	BALDING, CHRISTOPHER	98,503	ROYBAL-ALLARD, LUCILLE*		69,237 D	22.9%	77.1%	22.9%	77.1%
34	2006	74,819	17,359	MILLER, WAYNE	57,459	ROYBAL-ALLARD, LUCILLE*	1	40,100 D	23.2%	76.8%	23.2%	76.8%
34	2004	110,457	28,175	MILLER, WAYNE	82,282	ROYBAL-ALLARD, LUCILLE*		54,107 D	25.5%	74.5%	25.5%	74.5%
34	2002	65,824	17,090	MILLER, WAYNE	48,734	ROYBAL-ALLARD, LUCILLE*		31,644 D	26.0%	74.0%	26.0%	74.0%
35	2008	182,579	24,169	HAYES, TED	150,778	WATERS, MAXINE*	7,632	126,609 D	13.2%	82.6%	13.8%	86.2%
35	2006	98,506		—	82,498	WATERS, MAXINE*	16,008	82,498 D		83.7%		100.0%
35	2004	156,407	23,591	MOEN, ROSS	125,949	WATERS, MAXINE*	6,867	102,358 D	15.1%	80.5%	15.8%	84.2%
35	2002	93,407	18,094	MOEN, ROSS	72,401	WATERS, MAXINE*	2,912	54,307 D	19.4%	77.5%	20.0%	80.0%
36	2008	250,491	78,543	GIBSON, BRIAN	171,948	HARMAN, JANE*		93,405 D	31.4%	68.6%	31.4%	68.6%
36	2006	166,153	53,068	GIBSON, BRIAN	105,323	HARMAN, JANE*	7,762	52,255 D	31.9%	63.4%	33.5%	66.5%
36	2004	244,044	81,666	WHITEHEAD, PAUL	151,208	HARMAN, JANE*	11,170	69,542 D	33.5%	62.0%	35.1%	64.9%
36	2002	143,751	50,328	JOHNSON, STUART	88,198	HARMAN, JANE*	5,225	37,870 D	35.0%	61.4%	36.3%	63.7%
37	2008	175,252		—	131,342	RICHARDSON, LAURA*	43,910	131,342 D		74.9%		100.0%
37	2006	97,962		—	80,716	MILLENDER-McDONALD, JUANITA*	17,246	80,716 D		82.4%		100.0%
37	2004	158,318	31,960	VAN, VERNON	118,823	MILLENDER-McDONALD, JUANITA*	7,535	86,863 D	20.2%	75.1%	21.2%	78.8%
37	2002	87,012	20,154	VELASCO, OSCAR A.	63,445	MILLENDER-McDONALD, JUANITA*	3,413	43,291 D	23.2%	72.9%	24.1%	75.9%
38	2008	159,324		—	130,211	NAPOLITANO, GRACE F.*	29,113	130,211 D		81.7%		100.0%
38	2006	99,801	24,620	STREET, SIDNEY W.	75,181	NAPOLITANO, GRACE F.*		50,561 D	24.7%	75.3%	24.7%	75.3%
38	2004	116,851		—	116,851	NAPOLITANO, GRACE F.*		116,851 D		100.0%		100.0%
38	2002	88,027	23,126	BURROLA, ALEX A.	62,600	NAPOLITANO, GRACE F.*	2,301	39,474 D	26.3%	71.1%	27.0%	73.0%
39	2008	179,822	54,533	LENNING, DIANE A.	125,289	SANCHEZ, LINDA T.*		70,756 D	30.3%	69.7%	30.3%	69.7%
39	2006	109,533	37,384	ANDION, JAMES L.	72,149	SANCHEZ, LINDA T.*		34,765 D	34.1%	65.9%	34.1%	65.9%
39	2004	164,964	64,832	ESCOBAR, TIM	100,132	SANCHEZ, LINDA T.*		35,300 D	39.3%	60.7%	39.3%	60.7%
39	2002	95,346	38,925	ESCOBAR, TIM	52,256	SANCHEZ, LINDA T.	4,165	13,331 D	40.8%	54.8%	42.7%	57.3%
40	2008	231,695	144,923	ROYCE, ED*	86,772	AVALOS, CHRISTINA		58,151 R	62.5%	37.5%	62.5%	37.5%
40	2006	151,289	100,995	ROYCE, ED*	46,418	HOFFMAN, FLORICE OREA	3,876	54,577 R	66.8%	30.7%	68.5%	31.5%
40	2004	217,301	147,617	ROYCE, ED*	69,684	WILLIAMS, J. TILMAN		77,933 R	67.9%	32.1%	67.9%	32.1%
40	2002	136,642	92,422	ROYCE, ED*	40,265	AVALOS, CHRISTINA	3,955	52,157 R	67.6%	29.5%	69.7%	30.3%
41	2008	258,700	159,486	LEWIS, JERRY*	99,214	PRINCE, TIM		60,272 R	61.6%	38.4%	61.6%	38.4%
41	2006	164,044	109,761	LEWIS, JERRY*	54,235	CONTRERAS, LOUIE A.	48	55,526 R	66.9%	33.1%	66.9%	33.1%
41	2004	218,937	181,605	LEWIS, JERRY*		—	37,332	181,605 R	82.9%		100.0%	
41	2002	135,533	91,326	LEWIS, JERRY*	40,155	JOHNSON, KEITH A.	4,052	51,171 R	67.4%	29.6%	69.5%	30.5%

CALIFORNIA

HOUSE OF REPRESENTATIVES

| | | | Republican | | Democratic | | | | Percentage | | | |
| | | | | | | | | | Total Vote | | Major Vote | |
CD	Year	Total Vote	Vote	Candidate	Vote	Candidate	Other Vote	Rep.-Dem. Plurality	Rep.	Dem.	Rep.	Dem.
42	2008	263,313	158,404	MILLER, GARY G.*	104,909	CHAU, EDWIN "ED"		53,495 R	60.2%	39.8%	60.2%	39.8%
42	2006	129,720	129,720	MILLER, GARY G.*	—			129,720 R	¨00.0%		100.0%	
42	2004	246,025	167,632	MILLER, GARY G.*	78,393	MYERS, LEWIS		89,239 R	68.1%	31.9%	68.1%	31.9%
42	2002	145,246	98,476	MILLER, GARY G.*	42,090	WALDRON, RICHARD	4,680	56,386 R	67.8%	29.0%	70.1%	29.9%
43	2008	156,571	48,312	ROBERTS, JOHN	108,259	BACA, JOE*		59,947 D	30.9%	69.1%	30.9%	69.1%
43	2006	81,860	29,069	FOLKENS, SCOTT	52,791	BACA, JOE*		23,722 D	35.5%	64.5%	35.5%	64.5%
43	2004	130,834	44,004	LANING, ED	86,830	BACA, JOE*		42,826 D	33.6%	66.4%	33.6%	66.4%
43	2002	68,340	20,821	NEIGHBOR, WENDY C.	45,374	BACA, JOE*	2,145	24,553 D	30.5%	66.4%	31.5%	68.5%
44	2008	253,827	129,937	CALVERT, KEN*	123,890	HEDRICK, BILL		6,047 R	51.2%	48.8%	51.2%	48.8%
44	2006	149,316	89,555	CALVERT, KEN*	55,275	VANDENBERG, LOUIS	4,486	34,280 R	60.0%	37.0%	61.8%	38.2%
44	2004	225,123	138,768	CALVERT, KEN*	78,796	VANDENBERG, LOUIS	7,559	59,972 R	61.6%	35.0%	63.8%	36.2%
44	2002	120,463	76,686	CALVERT, KEN*	38,021	VANDENBERG, LOUIS	5,756	38,665 R	63.7%	31.6%	66.9%	33.1%
45	2008	266,192	155,166	BONO MACK, MARY*	111,026	BORNSTEIN, JULIE		44,140 R	58.3%	41.7%	58.3%	41.7%
45	2006	164,251	99,638	BONO, MARY*	64,613	ROTH, DAVID		35,025 R	60.7%	39.3%	60.7%	39.3%
45	2004	230,490	153,523	BONO, MARY*	76,967	MEYER, RICHARD J.		76,556 R	66.6%	33.4%	66.6%	33.4%
45	2002	133,533	87,101	BONO, MARY*	43,692	KURPIEWSKI, ELLE K.	2,740	43,409 R	65.2%	32.7%	66.6%	33.4%
46	2008	285,277	149,818	ROHRABACHER, DANA*	122,891	COOK, DEBBIE	12,568	26,927 R	52.5%	43.1%	54.9%	45.1%
46	2006	195,052	116,176	ROHRABACHER, DANA*	71,573	BRANDT, JIM	7,303	44,603 R	59.6%	36.7%	61.9%	38.1%
46	2004	276,690	171,318	ROHRABACHER, DANA*	90,129	BRANDT, JIM	15,243	81,189 R	61.9%	32.6%	65.5%	34.5%
46	2002	176,265	108,807	ROHRABACHER, DANA*	60,890	SCHIPSKE, GERRIE	6,568	47,917 R	61.7%	34.5%	64.1%	35.9%
47	2008	123,584	31,432	AVILA, ROSEMARIE "ROSIE"	85,878	SANCHEZ, LORETTA*	6,274	54,446 D	25.4%	69.5%	26.8%	73.2%
47	2006	75,619	28,485	NGUYEN, TAN	47,134	SANCHEZ, LORETTA*		18,649 D	37.7%	62.3%	37.7%	62.3%
47	2004	108,783	43,099	CORONADO, ALEXANDRIA A. "ALEX"	65,684	SANCHEZ, LORETTA*		22,585 D	39.6%	60.4%	39.6%	60.4%
47	2002	70,178	24,346	CHAVEZ, JEFF	42,501	SANCHEZ, LORETTA*	3,331	18,155 D	34.7%	60.6%	36.4%	63.6%
48	2008	308,702	171,658	CAMPBELL, JOHN*	125,537	YOUNG, STEVE	11,507	46,121 R	55.6%	40.7%	57.8%	42.2%
48	2006	200,527	120,130	CAMPBELL, JOHN*	74,647	YOUNG, STEVE	5,750	45,483 R	59.9%	37.2%	61.7%	38.3%
48	2004	290,872	189,004	COX, CHRISTOPHER*	93,525	GRAHAM, JOHN	8,343	95,479 R	65.0%	32.2%	66.9%	33.1%
48	2002	179,549	122,884	COX, CHRISTOPHER*	51,058	GRAHAM, JOHN	5,607	71,826 R	68.4%	28.4%	70.6%	29.4%
49	2008	240,670	140,300	ISSA, DARRELL*	90,138	HAMILTON, ROBERT	10,232	50,162 R	58.3%	37.5%	60.9%	39.1%
49	2006	156,137	98,831	ISSA, DARRELL*	52,227	CRISCENZO, JEENI	5,079	46,604 R	63.3%	33.4%	65.4%	34.6%
49	2004	226,466	141,658	ISSA, DARRELL*	79,057	BYRON, MIKE	5,751	62,601 R	62.6%	34.9%	64.2%	35.8%
49	2002	122,497	94,594	ISSA, DARRELL*	—		27,903	94,594 R	77.2%		100.0%	
50	2008	313,502	157,502	BILBRAY, BRIAN P.*	141,635	LEIBHAM, NICK	14,365	15,867 R	50.2%	45.2%	52.7%	47.3%
50	2006	222,102	118,018	BILBRAY, BRIAN P.*	96,612	BUSBY, FRANCINE	7,472	21,406 R	53.1%	43.5%	55.0%	45.0%
50	2004	289,328	169,025	CUNNINGHAM, RANDY "DUKE"*	105,590	BUSBY, FRANCINE	14,713	63,435 R	58.4%	36.5%	61.5%	38.5%
50	2002	172,701	111,095	CUNNINGHAM, RANDY "DUKE"*	55,855	STEWART, DEL G.	5,751	55,240 R	64.3%	32.3%	66.5%	33.5%
51	2008	203,825	49,345	JOY, DAVID LEE	148,281	FILNER, BOB*	6,199	98,936 D	24.2%	72.7%	25.0%	75.0%
51	2006	115,839	34,931	MILES, BLAKE L.	78,114	FILNER, BOB*	2,794	43,183 D	30.2%	67.4%	30.9%	69.1%
51	2004	180,879	63,526	GIORGINO, MICHAEL	111,441	FILNER, BOB*	5,912	47,915 D	35.1%	61.6%	36.3%	63.7%
51	2002	102,787	40,430	GARCIA, MARIA GUADALUPE	59,541	FILNER, BOB*	2,816	19,111 D	39.3%	57.9%	40.4%	59.6%
52	2008	285,138	160,724	HUNTER, DUNCAN D.	111,051	LUMPKIN, MIKE	13,363	49,673 R	56.4%	38.9%	59.1%	40.9%
52	2006	191,369	123,696	HUNTER, DUNCAN*	61,208	RINALDI, JOHN	6,465	62,488 R	64.6%	32.0%	66.9%	33.1%
52	2004	271,438	187,799	HUNTER, DUNCAN*	74,857	KELIHER, BRIAN S.	8,782	112,942 R	69.2%	27.6%	71.5%	28.5%
52	2002	169,010	118,561	HUNTER, DUNCAN*	43,526	MOORE-KOCHLACS, PETER	6,923	75,035 R	70.2%	25.8%	73.1%	26.9%
53	2008	235,542	64,658	CRIMMINS, MICHAEL	161,315	DAVIS, SUSAN A.*	9,569	96,657 D	27.5%	68.5%	28.6%	71.4%
53	2006	144,387	43,312	WOODRUM, JOHN "WOODY"	97,541	DAVIS, SUSAN A.*	3,534	54,229 D	30.0%	67.6%	30.7%	69.3%
53	2004	221,436	63,897	HUNZEKER, DARIN	146,449	DAVIS, SUSAN A.*	11,090	82,552 D	28.9%	66.1%	30.4%	69.6%
53	2002	116,180	43,891	VanDeWEGHE, BILL	72,252	DAVIS, SUSAN A.*	37	28,361 D	37.8%	62.2%	37.8%	62.2%
TOTAL	2008	12,322,079	4,515,372		7,377,725		428,982	2,862,353 D	36.6%	59.9%	38.0%	62.0%
TOTAL	2006	8,295,816	3,314,398		4,720,164		261,254	1,405,766 D	40.0%	56.9%	41.3%	58.7%
TOTAL	2004	11,623,753	5,030,821		6,223,698		369,234	1,192,877 D	43.3%	53.5%	44.7%	55.3%
TOTAL	2002	7,258,417	3,225,666		3,731,081		301,670	505,415 D	44.4%	51.4%	46.4%	53.6%

CALIFORNIA

GENERAL AND PRIMARY ELECTIONS

2008 GENERAL ELECTIONS

President Other vote was 108,381 Peace and Freedom (Ralph Nader); 67,582 Libertarian (Bob Barr); 40,673 American Independent (Alan Keyes); 38,774 Green (Cynthia A. McKinney); 17,006 Independent write-in (Ron Paul); 3,145 Independent write-in (Chuck Baldwin); 49 Independent write-in (James Harris); 36 Independent write-in (Frank Moore).

House Other vote was:

CD 1   24,793 Green (Carol Wolman); 14 Green write-in (Pamela Elizondo).

CD 2

CD 3   13,378 Peace and Freedom (Dina J. Padilla); 7,273 Libertarian (Douglas Arthur Tuma).

CD 4

CD 5   10,731 Peace and Freedom (L.R. Roberts); 180 Independent write-in (David B. Lynch).

CD 6   13,617 Libertarian (Joel R. Smolen).

CD 7   6,695 Peace and Freedom (Bill Callison); 5,950 Libertarian (Camden McConnell).

CD 8   46,118 Independent (Cindy Sheehan); 6,504 Libertarian (Philip Z. Berg); 11 Independent write-in (Lea Sherman); 4 Independent write-in (Michelle Wong Clay).

CD 9   11,704 Libertarian (James M. Eyer); 37 Green write-in (David Heller); 27 Republican write-in (Christopher Kula).

CD 10   11,062 Peace and Freedom (Eugene E. Ruyle).

CD 11   12 American Independent write-in (David Christensen).

CD 12   5,793 Peace and Freedom (Nathalie Hrizi); 5,776 Green (Barry Hermanson); 5,584 Libertarian (Kevin Dempsey Peterson).

CD 13

CD 14   11,929 Libertarian (Brian Holtz); 9,926 Green (Carol Brouillet).

CD 15   12,123 Green (Peter Myers).

CD 16   9,447 Libertarian (Steven Wells).

CD 17   682 Independent write-in (Peter Andresen).

CD 18

CD 19   2,490 Democratic write-in (Peter Leinau); 366 Independent write-in (Phil Rockey).

CD 20

CD 21

CD 22

CD 23

CD 24

CD 25

CD 26   18,476 Libertarian (Ted Brown).

CD 27   14,171 Libertarian (Tim Denton).

CD 28   150 Independent write-in (Michael J. Koch).

CD 29   9,219 Libertarian (Alan Pyeatt).

CD 30

CD 31

CD 32   8 Independent write-in (Innocent O. Osunwa).

CD 33

CD 34

CD 35   7,632 Libertarian (Herb Peters).

CD 36

CD 37   42,774 Independent (Nicholas "Nick" Dibs); 600 Democratic write-in (Peter Mathews); 526 Republican write-in (June Viena Pouesi); 10 Democratic write-in (Lee Davis).

CD 38   29,113 Libertarian (Christopher M. Agrella).

CD 39

CD 40

CD 41

CD 42

CD 43

CALIFORNIA

GENERAL AND PRIMARY ELECTIONS

CD 44
CD 45
CD 46   8,257 Green (Thomas Lash); 4,311 Libertarian (Ernst P. Gasteiger).
CD 47   6,274 American Independent (Robert Lauten).
CD 48   11,507 Libertarian (Don Patterson).
CD 49   10,232 Libertarian (Lars R. Grossmith).
CD 50   14,365 Libertarian (Wayne Dunlap).
CD 51   6,199 Libertarian (Dan "Frodo" Litwin).
CD 52   13,316 Libertarian (Michael Benoit); 47 Independent write-in (Joseph M. Ryan).
CD 53   9,569 Libertarian (Edward M. Teyssier).

2008 PRIMARY ELECTIONS

Primary	February 5, 2008 (President) June 3, 2008 (Congress)	Registration (as of May 19, 2008)	Democratic	7,053,860
			Republican	5,244,394
			American Independent	331,619
			Green	120,725
			Libertarian	79,711
			Peace and Freedom	56,364
			Other	108,430
			Decline to State	3,128,684
			TOTAL	*16,123,787*

Primary Type The Democrats held "semi-open" primaries for president and Congress. In them, registered Democrats could vote only in their party's primary. So too could voters not registered with a recognized party (i.e., Decline to State). Republicans also held a "semi-open" congressional primary in which voters registered as "Decline to State" could cast ballots. But participation in the Republican presidential primary was limited to registered Republicans.

	REPUBLICAN PRIMARIES			**DEMOCRATIC PRIMARIES**		
President	John McCain	1,238,988	42.2%	Hillary Clinton	2,608,184	51.5%
	Mitt Romney	1,013,471	34.6%	Barack Obama	2,186,662	43.2%
	Mike Huckabee	340,669	11.6%	John Edwards	193,617	3.8%
	Rudolph Giuliani	128,681	4.4%	Dennis J. Kucinich	24,126	0.5%
	Ron Paul	125,365	4.3%	Bill Richardson	19,939	0.4%
	Fred Thompson	50,275	1.7%	Joseph R. Biden Jr.	18,261	0.4%
	Duncan Hunter	14,021	0.5%	Mike Gravel	8,184	0.2%
	Alan Keyes	11,742	0.4%	Christopher J. Dodd	8,005	0.2%
	Tom Tancredo	3,884	0.1%	Willie Felix Carter (write-in)	4	
	John H. Cox	3,219	0.1%	Eric Hinzman (write-in)	4	
	Sam Brownback	2,486	0.1%	Phil Epstein (write-in)	3	
	Karen Irish (write-in)	6		Brian F. Calef (write-in)	2	
	Michael P. Shaw (write-in)	2		David Robert Frey (write-in)	1	
	Edward Marshall (write-in)	1		Joseph McAndrew (write-in)	1	
	Joel Gary Neuberg (write-in)	1				
	TOTAL	*2,932,811*		*TOTAL*	*5,066,993*	
Congressional District 1	Zane Starkewolf	18,346	54.0%	Mike Thompson*	69,622	87.7%
	Douglas Pharr	15,628	46.0%	Mitchell Clogg	9,752	12.3%
	TOTAL	*33,974*		*TOTAL*	*79,374*	
Congressional District 2	Wally Herger*	62,394	100.0%	Jeff Morris	14,750	34.7%
				A. J. Sekhon	14,340	33.7%
				John Jacobson	13,470	31.6%
				TOTAL	*42,560*	
Congressional District 3	Dan Lungren*	50,532	100.0%	Bill Durston	37,318	100.0%

CALIFORNIA

GENERAL AND PRIMARY ELECTIONS

	REPUBLICAN PRIMARIES			DEMOCRATIC PRIMARIES		
Congressional District 4	Tom McClintock	51,655	53.5%	Charlie Brown	51,028	88.0%
	Doug Ose	37,802	39.1%	John "Wolf" Wolfgram	6,962	12.0%
	Suzanne Jones	4,920	5.1%			
	Theodore Terbolizard	2,249	2.3%			
	TOTAL	96,626		TOTAL	57,990	
Congressional District 5	Paul A. Smith	18,232	100.0%	Doris Matsui*	51,006	100.0%
Congressional District 6	Mike Halliwell	29,527	100.0%	Lynn Woolsey*	88,969	100.0%
				Edward K. Newman (write-in)	26	
				TOTAL	88,995	
Congressional District 7	Roger Allen Petersen	9,658	55.8%	George Miller*	49,260	100.0%
	Virginia Fuller	7,660	44.2%			
	TOTAL	17,318				
Congressional District 8	Dana Walsh	7,903	100.0%	Nancy Pelosi*	83,510	89.2%
				Shirley Golub	10,105	10.8%
				TOTAL	93,615	
Congressional District 9	Charles Hargrave	7,893	100.0%	Barbara Lee*	80,466	99.9%
				Brad Newsham (write-in)	79	0.1%
				TOTAL	80,545	
Congressional District 10	Nicholas Gerber	30,324	100.0%	Ellen O. Tauscher*	55,427	100.0%
Congressional District 11	Dean Andal	41,879	100.0%	Jerry McNerney*	40,403	100.0%
Congressional District 12	Greg Conlon	12,060	65.0%	Jackie Speier*	60,393	89.5%
	Mike Moloney	6,498	35.0%	Michelle T. McMurry	3,827	5.7%
				Frank Henry Wade	1,652	2.4%
				Robert M. Barrows	1,594	2.4%
	TOTAL	18,558		TOTAL	67,466	
Congressional District 13	Raymond Chui	12,706	100.0%	Pete Stark*	42,897	100.0%
Congressional District 14	Ronny Santana	22,812	100.0%	Anna G. Eshoo*	60,856	100.0%
Congressional District 15	Joyce Stoer Cordi	19,750	100.0%	Michael M. Honda*	46,652	100.0%
Congressional District 16	Charel Winston	16,836	100.0%	Zoe Lofgren*	39,616	100.0%
Congressional District 17	Jeff Taylor	23,188	100.0%	Sam Farr*	53,057	100.0%
Congressional District 18	No Republican candidate			Dennis Cardoza*	26,392	100.0%
Congressional District 19	George P. Radanovich*	51,645	100.0%	No Democratic candidate		
Congressional District 20	Jim Lopez	11,257	100.0%	Jim Costa*	22,042	100.0%
Congressional District 21	Devin Nunes*	41,638	100.0%	Larry Johnson	21,738	100.0%

CALIFORNIA

GENERAL AND PRIMARY ELECTIONS

	REPUBLICAN PRIMARIES			DEMOCRATIC PRIMARIES		
Congressional District 22	Kevin McCarthy*	61,915	100.0%	No Democratic candidate		
Congressional District 23	Matt T. Kokkonen	30,094	100.0%	Lois Capps* Sandra Marshall-Eminger (write-in) *TOTAL*	50,385 164 *50,549*	99.7% 0.3%
Congressional District 24	Elton Gallegly* Michael Tenenbaum *TOTAL*	45,124 13,446 *58,570*	77.0% 23.0%	Marta Ann Jorgensen Jill Martinez Mary Pallant *TOTAL*	17,640 12,324 8,733 *38,697*	45.6% 31.8% 22.6%
Congressional District 25	Howard P. "Buck" McKeon*	30,937	100.0%	Jackie Conaway	18,054	100.0%
Congressional District 26	David Dreier* Sonny Sardo *TOTAL*	29,627 10,158 *39,785*	74.5% 25.5%	Russ Warner Cynthia Rodriguez Matthews *TOTAL*	17,165 8,327 *25,492*	67.3% 32.7%
Congressional District 27	Navraj Singh	13,354	100.0%	Brad Sherman*	25,591	100.0%
Congressional District 28	No Republican candidate			Howard L. Berman*	23,265	100.0%
Congressional District 29	Charles Hahn	16,241	100.0%	Adam B. Schiff*	24,486	100.0%
Congressional District 30	Keith H. Fichtelman (write-in) *Keith H. Fichtelman did not qualify for the general election ballot. As a write-in candidate in the primary, he needed to receive more than 2,100 votes, or 1 percent of the number cast for the U.S. House in the 30th District in the previous general election.*	121	100.0%	Henry A. Waxman*	52,980	100.0%
Congressional District 31	No Republican candidate			Xavier Becerra*	18,127	100.0%
Congressional District 32	No Republican candidate			Hilda L. Solis*	17,345	100.0%
Congressional District 33	David C. Crowley II	4,680	100.0%	Diane Watson* Felicia Ford Mervin Leon Evans *TOTAL*	44,934 3,738 2,315 *50,987*	88.1% 7.3% 4.5%
Congressional District 34	Christopher Balding Wayne Miller *TOTAL*	2,948 2,027 *4,975*	59.3% 40.7%	Lucille Roybal-Allard* Kevin M. Moreau (write-in) *TOTAL*	12,622 2 *12,624*	100.0%
Congressional District 35	Ted Hayes	5,686	100.0%	Maxine Waters*	36,685	100.0%
Congressional District 36	Brian Gibson	20,109	100.0%	Jane Harman*	32,009	100.0%
Congressional District 37	No Republican candidate			Laura Richardson* Peter Mathews Lee Davis *TOTAL*	25,713 5,860 2,983 *34,556*	74.4% 17.0% 8.6%
Congressional District 38	No Republican candidate			Grace F. Napolitano*	16,140	100.0%

CALIFORNIA

GENERAL AND PRIMARY ELECTIONS

	REPUBLICAN PRIMARIES			DEMOCRATIC PRIMARIES		
Congressional District 39	Diane A. Lenning	10,485	100.0%	Linda T. Sanchez*	18,949	100.0%
Congressional District 40	Ed Royce*	39,565	100.0%	Christina Avalos	11,481	56.3%
				Tom Kennedy	8,908	43.7%
				TOTAL	*20,389*	
Congressional District 41	Jerry Lewis*	36,663	82.5%	Tim Prince	8,335	31.9%
	Eric R. Stone	4,330	9.7%	Rita Ramirez-Dean	7,435	28.4%
	Pamela Zander	3,455	7.8%	Pat Meagher	6,952	26.6%
				Beverly Bruins	3,441	13.2%
	TOTAL	*44,448*		*TOTAL*	*26,163*	
Congressional District 42	Gary G. Miller*	39,168	100.0%	Edwin "Ed" Chau	8,935	47.7%
				Michael Williamson	5,217	27.9%
				Ron Shepston	4,568	24.4%
				TOTAL	*18,720*	
Congressional District 43	John Roberts	5,406	59.6%	Joe Baca*	13,177	66.3%
	Scott Folkens	3,670	40.4%	Joanne T. Gilbert	6,701	33.7%
	TOTAL	*9,076*		*TOTAL*	*19,878*	
Congressional District 44	Ken Calvert*	32,702	100.0%	Bill Hedrick	20,074	100.0%
Congressional District 45	Mary Bono Mack*	38,726	89.3%	Julie Bornstein	18,479	61.0%
	George Pearne	4,618	10.7%	Paul Clay	8,697	28.7%
				David E. Hunsicker	3,127	10.3%
	TOTAL	*43,344*		*TOTAL*	*30,303*	
Congressional District 46	Dana Rohrabacher*	43,693	86.6%	Debbie Cook	24,238	80.8%
	Ronald R. St. John	6,751	13.4%	Dan Kalmick	5,759	19.2%
	TOTAL	*50,444*		*TOTAL*	*29,997*	
Congressional District 47	Rosemarie "Rosie" Avila	12,245	100.0%	Loretta Sanchez*	16,430	100.0%
Congressional District 48	John Campbell*	50,101	100.0%	Steve Young	22,959	100.0%
Congressional District 49	Darrell Issa*	41,369	100.0%	Robert Hamilton	21,571	100.0%
Congressional District 50	Brian P. Bilbray*	58,511	100.0%	Nick Leibham	23,874	57.7%
				Cheryl Martin Ede	17,523	42.3%
				TOTAL	*41,397*	
Congressional District 51	David Lee Joy	13,417	65.0%	Bob Filner*	31,690	75.7%
	Dan Felzer	7,234	35.0%	Daniel C. "Danny" Ramirez	10,182	24.3%
	TOTAL	*20,651*		*TOTAL*	*41,872*	
Congressional District 52	Duncan D. Hunter	47,930	72.2%	Mike Lumpkin	22,460	58.0%
	Brian Jones	10,862	16.4%	Vickie Butcher	16,294	42.0%
	Bob Watkins	5,539	8.3%			
	Rick L. Powell	2,074	3.1%			
	TOTAL	*66,405*		*TOTAL*	*38,754*	
Congressional District 53	Michael Crimmins	19,819	74.9%	Susan A. Davis*	43,171	87.6%
	Naomi Bar-Lev	6,642	25.1%	Mike Copass	6,113	12.4%
	TOTAL	*26,461*		*TOTAL*	*49,284*	

Note: An asterisk (*) denotes incumbent.

COLORADO

Congressional districts first established for elections held in 2002
7 members

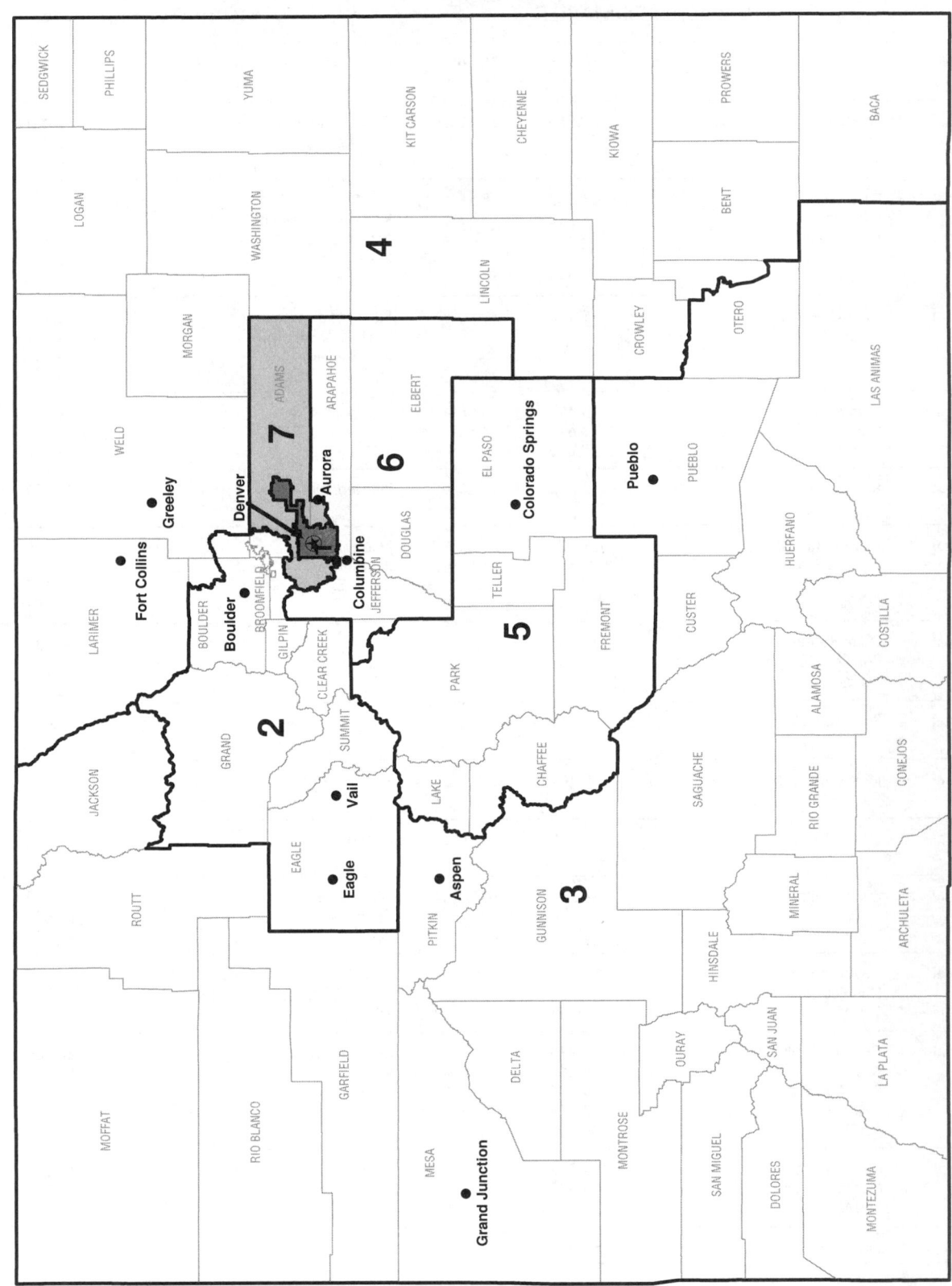

COLORADO

Denver Area

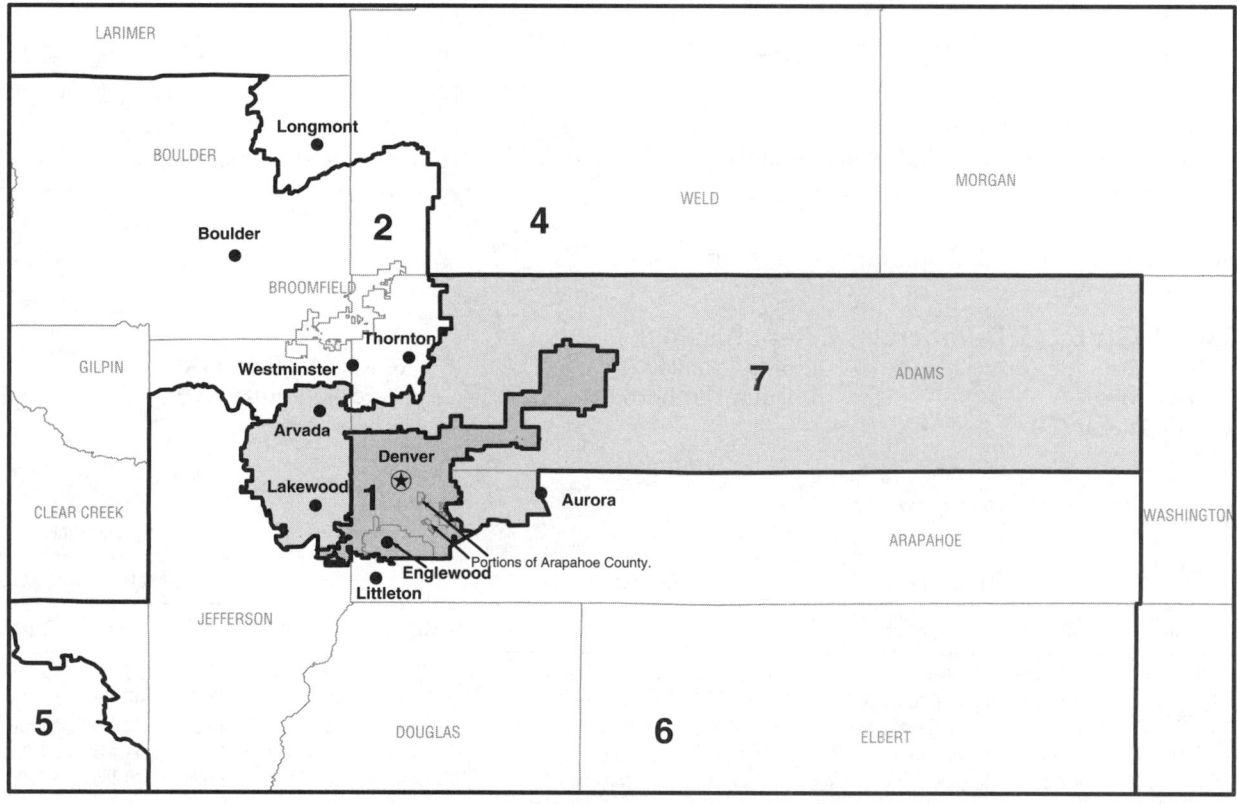

COLORADO

GOVERNOR
Bill Ritter Jr. (D). Elected 2006 to a four-year term.

SENATORS (2 Democrats)
Michael Bennet (D). Sworn in as senator January 22, 2009, to fill the vacancy created by the resignation of Ken Salazar (D) to become U.S. Secretary of Interior.

Mark Udall (D). Elected 2008 to a six-year term.

REPRESENTATIVES (5 Democrats, 2 Republicans)
1. Diana DeGette (D)
2. Jared Polis (D)
3. John Salazar (D)
4. Betsy Markey (D)
5. Doug Lamborn (R)
6. Mike Coffman (R)
7. Ed Perlmutter (D)

POSTWAR VOTE FOR PRESIDENT

		Republican		Democratic				Total Vote		Major Vote	
Year	Total Vote	Vote	Candidate	Vote	Candidate	Other Vote	Plurality	Rep.	Dem.	Rep.	Dem.
2008	2,401,462	1,073,629	McCain, John	1,288,633	Obama, Barack	39,200	215,004 D	44.7%	53.7%	45.4%	54.6%
2004	2,130,330	1,101,255	Bush, George W.	1,001,732	Kerry, John	27,343	99,523 R	51.7%	47.0%	52.4%	47.6%
2000**	1,741,368	883,748	Bush, George W.	738,227	Gore, Al	119,393	145,521 R	50.8%	42.4%	54.5%	45.5%
1996**	1,510,704	691,848	Dole, Bob	671,152	Clinton, Bill	147,704	20,696 R	45.8%	44.4%	50.8%	49.2%
1992**	1,569,180	562,850	Bush, George	629,681	Clinton, Bill	376,649	66,831 D	35.9%	40.1%	47.2%	52.8%
1988	1,372,394	728,177	Bush, George	621,453	Dukakis, Michael S.	22,764	106,724 R	53.1%	45.3%	54.0%	46.0%
1984	1,295,380	821,817	Reagan, Ronald	454,975	Mondale, Walter F.	18,588	366,842 R	63.4%	35.1%	64.4%	35.6%
1980**	1,184,415	652,264	Reagan, Ronald	367,973	Carter, Jimmy	164,178	284,291 R	55.1%	31.1%	63.9%	36.1%
1976	1,081,554	584,367	Ford, Gerald R.	460,353	Carter, Jimmy	36,834	124,014 R	54.0%	42.6%	55.9%	44.1%
1972	953,884	597,189	Nixon, Richard M.	329,980	McGovern, George S.	26,715	267,209 R	62.6%	34.6%	64.4%	35.6%
1968**	811,199	409,345	Nixon, Richard M.	335,174	Humphrey, Hubert H.	66,680	74,171 R	50.5%	41.3%	55.0%	45.0%
1964	776,986	296,767	Goldwater, Barry M.	476,024	Johnson, Lyndon B.	4,195	179,257 D	38.2%	61.3%	38.4%	61.6%
1960	736,236	402,242	Nixon, Richard M.	330,629	Kennedy, John F.	3,365	71,613 R	54.6%	44.9%	54.9%	45.1%
1956	657,074	394,479	Eisenhower, Dwight D.	257,997	Stevenson, Adlai E.	4,598	136,482 R	60.0%	39.3%	60.5%	39.5%
1952	630,103	379,782	Eisenhower, Dwight D.	245,504	Stevenson, Adlai E.	4,817	134,278 R	60.3%	39.0%	60.7%	39.3%
1948	515,237	239,714	Dewey, Thomas E.	267,288	Truman, Harry S.	8,235	27,574 D	46.5%	51.9%	47.3%	52.7%

**In past elections, the other vote included: 2000 - 91,434 Green (Ralph Nader); 1996 - 99,629 Reform (Ross Perot); 1992 - 366,010 Independent (Perot); 1980 - 130,633 Independent (John Anderson); 1968 - 60,813 American Independent (George Wallace).

COLORADO

POSTWAR VOTE FOR GOVERNOR

Year	Total Vote	Republican Vote	Republican Candidate	Democratic Vote	Democratic Candidate	Other Vote	Rep.-Dem. Plurality	Total Vote Rep.	Total Vote Dem.	Major Vote Rep.	Major Vote Dem.
2006	1,558,387	625,886	Beauprez, Bob	888,096	Ritter, Bill Jr.	44,405	262,210 D	40.2%	57.0%	41.3%	58.7%
2002	1,412,602	884,583	Owens, Bill	475,373	Heath, Rollie	52,646	409,210 R	62.6%	33.7%	65.0%	35.0%
1998	1,321,307	648,202	Owens, Bill	639,905	Schoettler, Gail	33,200	8,297 R	49.1%	48.4%	50.3%	49.7%
1994	1,116,307	432,042	Benson, Bruce	619,205	Romer, Roy	65,060	187,163 D	38.7%	55.5%	41.1%	58.9%
1990	1,011,272	358,403	Andrews, John	626,032	Romer, Roy	26,837	267,629 D	35.4%	61.9%	36.4%	63.6%
1986	1,058,928	434,420	Strickland, Ted	616,325	Romer, Roy	8,183	181,905 D	41.0%	58.2%	41.3%	58.7%
1982	956,021	302,740	Fuhr, John D.	627,960	Lamm, Richard D.	25,321	325,220 D	31.7%	65.7%	32.5%	67.5%
1978	823,807	317,292	Strickland, Ted	483,985	Lamm, Richard D.	22,530	166,693 D	38.5%	58.7%	39.6%	60.4%
1974	828,968	378,698	Vanderhoof, John D.	441,408	Lamm, Richard D.	8,862	62,710 D	45.7%	53.2%	46.2%	53.8%
1970	668,496	350,690	Love, John A.	302,432	Hogan, Mark	15,374	48,258 R	52.5%	45.2%	53.7%	46.3%
1966	660,063	356,730	Love, John A.	287,132	Knous, Robert L.	16,201	69,598 R	54.0%	43.5%	55.4%	44.6%
1962	616,481	349,342	Love, John A.	262,890	McNichols, Stephen	4,249	86,452 R	56.7%	42.6%	57.1%	42.9%
1958**	549,808	228,643	Burch, Palmer L.	321,165	McNichols, Stephen		92,522 D	41.6%	58.4%	41.6%	58.4%
1956	645,233	313,950	Brotzman, Donald G.	331,283	McNichols, Stephen		17,333 D	48.7%	51.3%	48.7%	51.3%
1954	489,540	227,335	Brotzman, Donald G.	262,205	Johnson, Ed C.		34,870 D	46.4%	53.6%	46.4%	53.6%
1952	613,034	349,924	Thornton, Dan	260,044	Metzger, John W.	3,066	89,880 R	57.1%	42.4%	57.4%	42.6%
1950	450,994	236,472	Thornton, Dan	212,976	Johnson, Walter	1,546	23,496 R	52.4%	47.2%	52.6%	47.4%
1948	501,680	168,928	Hamil, David A.	332,752	Knous, William Lee		163,824 D	33.7%	66.3%	33.7%	66.3%
1946	335,087	160,483	Lavington, Leon E.	174,604	Knous, William Lee		14,121 D	47.9%	52.1%	47.9%	52.1%

**The term of office of Colorado's governor was increased from two to four years effective with the 1958 election.

POSTWAR VOTE FOR SENATOR

Year	Total Vote	Republican Vote	Republican Candidate	Democratic Vote	Democratic Candidate	Other Vote	Rep.-Dem. Plurality	Total Vote Rep.	Total Vote Dem.	Major Vote Rep.	Major Vote Dem.
2008	2,331,712	990,784	Schaffer, Bob	1,231,049	Udall, Mark	109,879	240,265 D	42.5%	52.8%	44.6%	55.4%
2004	2,107,554	980,668	Coors, Pete	1,081,188	Salazar, Ken	45,698	100,520 D	46.5%	51.3%	47.6%	52.4%
2002	1,416,082	717,893	Allard, Wayne	648,130	Strickland, Tom	50,059	69,763 R	50.7%	45.8%	52.6%	47.4%
1998	1,327,235	829,370	Campbell, Ben Nighthorse	464,754	Lamm, Dottie	33,111	364,616 R	62.5%	35.0%	64.1%	35.9%
1996	1,469,611	750,325	Allard, Wayne	677,600	Strickland, Tom	41,686	72,725 R	51.1%	46.1%	52.5%	47.5%
1992	1,552,289	662,893	Considine, Terry	803,725	Campbell, Ben Nighthorse	85,671	140,832 D	42.7%	51.8%	45.2%	54.8%
1990	1,022,027	569,048	Brown, Hank	425,746	Heath, Josie	27,233	143,302 R	55.7%	41.7%	57.2%	42.8%
1986	1,060,765	512,994	Kramer, Ken	529,449	Wirth, Timothy E.	18,322	16,455 D	48.4%	49.9%	49.2%	50.8%
1984	1,297,809	833,821	Armstrong, William L.	449,327	Dick, Nancy	14,661	384,494 R	64.2%	34.6%	65.0%	35.0%
1980	1,173,646	571,295	Buchanan, Mary E.	590,501	Hart, Gary W.	11,850	19,206 D	48.7%	50.3%	49.2%	50.8%
1978	819,150	480,596	Armstrong, William L.	330,247	Haskell, Floyd K.	8,307	150,349 R	58.7%	40.3%	59.3%	40.7%
1974	824,166	325,508	Dominick, Peter H.	471,691	Hart, Gary W.	26,967	146,183 D	39.5%	57.2%	40.8%	59.2%
1972	926,093	447,957	Allott, Gordon	457,545	Haskell, Floyd K.	20,591	9,588 D	48.4%	49.4%	49.5%	50.5%
1968	785,536	459,952	Dominick, Peter H.	325,584	McNichols, Stephen		134,368 R	58.6%	41.4%	58.6%	41.4%
1966	634,898	368,307	Allott, Gordon	266,259	Romer, Roy	332	102,048 R	58.0%	41.9%	58.0%	42.0%
1962	613,444	328,655	Dominick, Peter H.	279,586	Carroll, John A.	5,203	49,069 R	53.6%	45.6%	54.0%	46.0%
1960	727,633	389,428	Allott, Gordon	334,854	Knous, Robert L.	3,351	54,574 R	53.5%	46.0%	53.8%	46.2%
1956	636,974	317,102	Thornton, Dan	319,872	Carroll, John A.		2,770 D	49.8%	50.2%	49.8%	50.2%
1954	484,188	248,502	Allott, Gordon	235,686	Carroll, John A.		12,816 R	51.3%	48.7%	51.3%	48.7%
1950	450,176	239,734	Millikin, Eugene D.	210,442	Carroll, John A.		29,292 R	53.3%	46.7%	53.3%	46.7%
1948	510,121	165,069	Nicholson, W. F.	340,719	Johnson, Ed C.	4,333	175,650 D	32.4%	66.8%	32.6%	67.4%

COLORADO

PRESIDENT 2008

2000 Census Population	County	Total Vote	Republican	Democratic	Other	Rep.-Dem. Plurality	Total Vote Rep.	Total Vote Dem.	Major Vote Rep.	Major Vote Dem.
348,618	ADAMS	160,501	63,976	93,445	3,080	29,469 D	39.9%	58.2%	40.6%	59.4%
14,966	ALAMOSA	6,286	2,635	3,521	130	886 D	41.9%	56.0%	42.8%	57.2%
487,967	ARAPAHOE	266,156	113,868	148,224	4,064	34,356 D	42.8%	55.7%	43.4%	56.6%
9,898	ARCHULETA	6,625	3,638	2,836	151	802 R	54.9%	42.8%	56.2%	43.8%
4,517	BACA	2,175	1,572	536	67	1,036 R	72.3%	24.6%	74.6%	25.4%
5,998	BENT	1,920	1,077	799	44	278 R	56.1%	41.6%	57.4%	42.6%
269,814	BOULDER	171,763	44,904	124,159	2,700	79,255 D	26.1%	72.3%	26.6%	73.4%
38,272	BROOMFIELD*	29,453	12,757	16,168	528	3,411 D	43.3%	54.9%	44.1%	55.9%
16,242	CHAFFEE	9,921	4,873	4,862	186	11 R	49.1%	49.0%	50.1%	49.9%
2,231	CHEYENNE	1,111	890	198	23	692 R	80.1%	17.8%	81.8%	18.2%
9,322	CLEAR CREEK	5,767	2,300	3,332	135	1,032 D	39.9%	57.8%	40.8%	59.2%
8,400	CONEJOS	3,874	1,653	2,154	67	501 D	42.7%	55.6%	43.4%	56.6%
3,663	COSTILLA	1,697	415	1,245	37	830 D	24.5%	73.4%	25.0%	75.0%
5,518	CROWLEY	1,558	976	552	30	424 R	62.6%	35.4%	63.9%	36.1%
3,503	CUSTER	2,629	1,672	912	45	760 R	63.6%	34.7%	64.7%	35.3%
27,834	DELTA	15,434	10,067	5,084	283	4,983 R	65.2%	32.9%	66.4%	33.6%
554,636	DENVER	271,533	62,567	204,882	4,084	142,315 D	23.0%	75.5%	23.4%	76.6%
1,844	DOLORES	1,217	818	369	30	449 R	67.2%	30.3%	68.9%	31.1%
175,766	DOUGLAS	151,819	88,108	61,960	1,751	26,148 R	58.0%	40.8%	58.7%	41.3%
41,659	EAGLE	21,658	8,181	13,191	286	5,010 D	37.8%	60.9%	38.3%	61.7%
19,872	ELBERT	13,206	9,108	3,819	279	5,289 R	69.0%	28.9%	70.5%	29.5%
516,929	EL PASO	273,175	160,318	108,899	3,958	51,419 R	58.7%	39.9%	59.5%	40.5%
46,145	FREMONT	19,919	12,668	6,844	407	5,824 R	63.6%	34.4%	64.9%	35.1%
43,791	GARFIELD	23,082	11,359	11,357	366	2 R	49.2%	49.2%	50.0%	50.0%
4,757	GILPIN	3,369	1,283	1,990	96	707 D	38.1%	59.1%	39.2%	60.8%
12,442	GRAND	8,309	4,128	4,037	144	91 R	49.7%	48.6%	50.6%	49.4%
13,956	GUNNISON	8,871	3,131	5,557	183	2,426 D	35.3%	62.6%	36.0%	64.0%
790	HINSDALE	599	344	240	15	104 R	57.4%	40.1%	58.9%	41.1%
7,862	HUERFANO	3,643	1,580	1,989	74	409 D	43.4%	54.6%	44.3%	55.7%
1,577	JACKSON	914	624	277	13	347 R	68.3%	30.3%	69.3%	30.7%
525,507	JEFFERSON	295,068	131,628	158,158	5,282	26,530 D	44.6%	53.6%	45.4%	54.6%
1,622	KIOWA	852	650	178	24	472 R	76.3%	20.9%	78.5%	21.5%
8,011	KIT CARSON	3,442	2,455	912	75	1,543 R	71.3%	26.5%	72.9%	27.1%
7,812	LAKE	3,002	1,078	1,859	65	781 D	35.9%	61.9%	36.7%	63.3%
43,941	LA PLATA	27,979	11,503	16,057	419	4,554 D	41.1%	57.4%	41.7%	58.3%
251,494	LARIMER	166,375	73,642	89,823	2,910	16,181 D	44.3%	54.0%	45.1%	54.9%
15,207	LAS ANIMAS	6,761	3,086	3,562	113	476 D	45.6%	52.7%	46.4%	53.6%
6,087	LINCOLN	2,304	1,717	546	41	1,171 R	74.5%	23.7%	75.9%	24.1%
20,504	LOGAN	8,977	6,002	2,846	129	3,156 R	66.9%	31.7%	67.8%	32.2%
116,255	MESA	69,631	44,578	24,008	1,045	20,570 R	64.0%	34.5%	65.0%	35.0%
831	MINERAL	623	334	270	19	64 R	53.6%	43.3%	55.3%	44.7%
13,184	MOFFAT	5,871	4,135	1,582	154	2,553 R	70.4%	26.9%	72.3%	27.7%
23,830	MONTEZUMA	11,825	6,961	4,661	203	2,300 R	58.9%	39.4%	59.9%	40.1%
33,432	MONTROSE	19,153	12,199	6,495	459	5,704 R	63.7%	33.9%	65.3%	34.7%
27,171	MORGAN	10,234	6,272	3,813	149	2,459 R	61.3%	37.3%	62.2%	37.8%
20,311	OTERO	8,065	4,393	3,547	125	846 R	54.5%	44.0%	55.3%	44.7%
3,742	OURAY	3,060	1,367	1,636	57	269 D	44.7%	53.5%	45.5%	54.5%
14,523	PARK	9,383	4,896	4,250	237	646 R	52.2%	45.3%	53.5%	46.5%
4,480	PHILLIPS	2,261	1,613	622	26	991 R	71.3%	27.5%	72.2%	27.8%
14,872	PITKIN	9,966	2,484	7,349	133	4,865 D	24.9%	73.7%	25.3%	74.7%

88

88

COLORADO

PRESIDENT 2008

2000 Census Population	County	Total Vote	Republican	Democratic	Other	Rep.-Dem. Plurality	Total Vote Rep.	Total Vote Dem.	Major Vote Rep.	Major Vote Dem.
14,483	PROWERS	4,615	3,043	1,487	85	1,556 R	65.9%	32.2%	67.2%	32.8%
141,472	PUEBLO	72,427	30,257	41,097	1,073	10,840 D	41.8%	56.7%	42.4%	57.6%
5,986	RIO BLANCO	3,147	2,437	655	55	1,782 R	77.4%	20.8%	78.8%	21.2%
12,413	RIO GRANDE	5,444	2,930	2,448	66	482 R	53.8%	45.0%	54.5%	45.5%
19,690	ROUTT	13,199	4,725	8,270	204	3,545 D	35.8%	62.7%	36.4%	63.6%
5,917	SAGUACHE	2,750	956	1,730	64	774 D	34.8%	62.9%	35.6%	64.4%
558	SAN JUAN	496	218	264	14	46 D	44.0%	53.2%	45.2%	54.8%
6,594	SAN MIGUEL	4,350	933	3,349	68	2,416 D	21.4%	77.0%	21.8%	78.2%
2,747	SEDGWICK	1,351	857	468	26	389 R	63.4%	34.6%	64.7%	35.3%
23,548	SUMMIT	14,899	4,883	9,802	214	4,919 D	32.8%	65.8%	33.3%	66.7%
20,555	TELLER	12,906	8,146	4,513	247	3,633 R	63.1%	35.0%	64.3%	35.7%
4,926	WASHINGTON	2,513	1,949	529	35	1,420 R	77.6%	21.1%	78.7%	21.3%
180,926	WELD	105,866	56,526	47,292	2,048	9,234 R	53.4%	44.7%	54.4%	45.6%
9,841	YUMA	4,483	3,286	1,117	80	2,169 R	73.3%	24.9%	74.6%	25.4%
4,301,261	TOTAL	2,401,462	1,073,629	1,288,633	39,200	215,004 D	44.7%	53.7%	45.4%	54.6%

*Broomfield County was created effective 2001 out of portions of Adams, Boulder, Jefferson, and Weld counties. The population figures in this table have been adjusted for each county using 2000 census data.

COLORADO

SENATOR 2008

2000 Census Population	County	Total Vote	Republican	Democratic	Other	Rep.-Dem. Plurality	Total Vote Rep.	Total Vote Dem.	Major Vote Rep.	Major Vote Dem.
348,618	ADAMS	155,121	56,195	89,542	9,384	33,347 D	36.2%	57.7%	38.6%	61.4%
14,966	ALAMOSA	6,127	2,252	3,410	465	1,158 D	36.8%	55.7%	39.8%	60.2%
487,967	ARAPAHOE	257,436	106,555	139,115	11,766	32,560 D	41.4%	54.0%	43.4%	55.6%
9,898	ARCHULETA	6,450	3,210	2,787	453	423 R	49.8%	43.2%	53.5%	46.5%
4,517	BACA	2,122	1,360	635	127	725 R	64.1%	29.9%	68.2%	31.8%
5,998	BENT	1,892	932	861	99	71 R	49.3%	45.5%	52.0%	48.0%
269,814	BOULDER	166,096	43,375	117,042	5,679	73,667 D	26.1%	70.5%	27.0%	73.0%
38,272	BROOMFIELD*	28,669	12,034	15,451	1,184	3,417 D	42.0%	53.9%	43.8%	56.2%
16,242	CHAFFEE	9,585	4,369	4,664	552	295 D	45.6%	48.7%	48.4%	51.6%
2,231	CHEYENNE	1,074	766	247	61	519 R	71.3%	23.0%	75.6%	24.4%
9,322	CLEAR CREEK	5,635	2,113	3,216	306	1,103 D	37.5%	57.1%	39.7%	60.3%
8,400	CONEJOS	3,781	1,469	2,142	170	673 D	38.9%	56.7%	40.7%	59.3%
3,663	COSTILLA	1,646	369	1,185	92	816 D	22.4%	72.0%	23.7%	76.3%
5,518	CROWLEY	1,533	850	582	101	268 R	55.4%	38.0%	59.4%	40.6%
3,503	CUSTER	2,550	1,528	900	122	628 R	59.9%	35.3%	62.9%	37.1%
27,834	DELTA	15,107	8,856	5,401	850	3,455 R	58.6%	35.8%	62.1%	37.9%
554,636	DENVER	267,039	60,199	196,252	10,588	136,053 D	22.5%	73.5%	23.5%	76.5%
1,844	DOLORES	1,164	658	445	61	213 R	56.5%	38.2%	59.7%	40.3%
175,766	DOUGLAS	147,159	84,552	57,587	5,020	26,965 R	57.5%	39.1%	59.5%	40.5%
41,659	EAGLE	21,003	7,759	12,433	811	4,674 D	36.9%	59.2%	38.4%	61.6%

COLORADO
SENATOR 2008

2000 Census Population	County	Total Vote	Republican	Democratic	Other	Rep.-Dem. Plurality	Percentage			
							Total Vote		Major Vote	
							Rep.	Dem.	Rep.	Dem.
19,872	ELBERT	12,826	8,403	3,694	729	4,709 R	65.5%	28.8%	69.5%	30.5%
516,929	EL PASO	262,850	148,716	100,876	13,258	47,840 R	56.6%	38.4%	59.6%	40.4%
46,145	FREMONT	19,335	10,896	7,198	1,241	3,698 R	56.4%	37.2%	60.2%	39.8%
43,791	GARFIELD	22,636	10,376	11,192	1,068	816 D	45.8%	49.4%	48.1%	51.9%
4,757	GILPIN	3,272	1,126	1,891	255	765 D	34.4%	57.8%	37.3%	62.7%
12,442	GRAND	8,134	3,820	3,967	347	147 D	47.0%	48.8%	49.1%	50.9%
13,956	GUNNISON	8,480	2,859	5,182	439	2,323 D	33.7%	61.1%	35.6%	64.4%
790	HINSDALE	557	294	229	34	65 R	52.8%	41.1%	56.2%	43.8%
7,862	HUERFANO	3,635	1,376	2,015	244	639 D	37.9%	55.4%	40.6%	59.4%
1,577	JACKSON	874	530	284	60	246 R	60.6%	32.5%	65.1%	34.9%
525,507	JEFFERSON	288,053	121,889	151,616	14,548	29,727 D	42.3%	52.6%	44.6%	55.4%
1,622	KIOWA	828	585	201	42	384 R	70.7%	24.3%	74.4%	25.6%
8,011	KIT CARSON	3,288	2,081	1,004	203	1,077 R	63.3%	30.5%	67.5%	32.5%
7,812	LAKE	2,916	918	1,792	206	874 D	31.5%	61.5%	33.9%	66.1%
43,941	LA PLATA	26,872	10,551	15,550	771	4,999 D	39.3%	57.9%	40.4%	59.6%
251,494	LARIMER	160,733	70,269	82,728	7,736	12,459 D	43.7%	51.5%	45.9%	54.1%
15,207	LAS ANIMAS	6,549	2,492	3,642	415	1,150 D	38.1%	55.6%	40.6%	59.4%
6,087	LINCOLN	2,221	1,534	554	133	980 R	69.1%	24.9%	73.5%	26.5%
20,504	LOGAN	8,693	5,190	3,031	472	2,159 R	59.7%	34.9%	63.1%	36.9%
116,255	MESA	67,202	38,582	25,591	3,029	12,991 R	57.4%	38.1%	60.1%	39.9%
831	MINERAL	614	269	297	48	28 D	43.8%	48.4%	47.5%	52.5%
13,184	MOFFAT	5,734	3,549	1,773	412	1,776 R	61.9%	30.9%	66.7%	33.3%
23,830	MONTEZUMA	11,521	6,165	4,905	451	1,260 R	53.5%	42.6%	55.7%	44.3%
33,432	MONTROSE	18,792	10,852	6,963	977	3,889 R	57.7%	37.1%	60.9%	39.1%
27,171	MORGAN	9,907	5,420	3,952	535	1,468 R	54.7%	39.9%	57.8%	42.2%
20,311	OTERO	7,911	3,853	3,626	432	227 R	48.7%	45.8%	51.5%	48.5%
3,742	OURAY	2,991	1,312	1,581	98	269 D	43.9%	52.9%	45.4%	54.6%
14,523	PARK	9,118	4,522	3,991	605	531 R	49.6%	43.8%	53.1%	46.9%
4,480	PHILLIPS	2,193	1,437	667	89	770 R	65.5%	30.4%	68.3%	31.7%
14,872	PITKIN	9,605	2,375	6,899	331	4,524 D	24.7%	71.8%	25.6%	74.4%
14,483	PROWERS	4,517	2,545	1,731	241	814 R	56.3%	38.3%	59.5%	40.5%
141,472	PUEBLO	71,217	26,566	41,290	3,361	14,724 D	37.3%	58.0%	39.2%	60.8%
5,986	RIO BLANCO	3,082	2,217	709	156	1,508 R	71.9%	23.0%	75.8%	24.2%
12,413	RIO GRANDE	5,327	2,609	2,381	337	228 R	49.0%	44.7%	52.3%	47.7%
19,690	ROUTT	12,850	4,536	7,799	515	3,263 D	35.3%	60.7%	36.8%	63.2%
5,917	SAGUACHE	2,661	831	1,630	200	799 D	31.2%	61.3%	33.8%	66.2%
558	SAN JUAN	486	183	274	29	91 D	37.7%	56.4%	40.0%	60.0%
6,594	SAN MIGUEL	4,157	918	3,035	204	2,117 D	22.1%	73.0%	23.2%	76.8%
2,747	SEDGWICK	1,318	741	486	91	255 R	56.2%	36.9%	60.4%	39.6%
23,548	SUMMIT	14,407	4,575	9,275	557	4,700 D	31.8%	64.4%	33.0%	67.0%
20,555	TELLER	12,532	7,575	4,275	682	3,300 R	60.4%	34.1%	63.9%	36.1%
4,926	WASHINGTON	2,443	1,727	604	112	1,123 R	70.7%	24.7%	74.1%	25.9%
180,926	WELD	102,879	51,253	45,522	6,104	5,731 R	49.8%	44.2%	53.0%	47.0%
9,841	YUMA	4,307	2,866	1,250	191	1,616 R	66.5%	29.0%	69.6%	30.4%
4,301,261	TOTAL	2,331,712	990,784	1,231,049	109,879	240,265 D	42.5%	52.8%	44.6%	55.4%

*Broomfield County was created effective 2001 out of portions of Adams, Boulder, Jefferson, and Weld counties. The population figures in this table have been adjusted for each county using 2000 census data.

COLORADO

HOUSE OF REPRESENTATIVES

CD	Year	Total Vote	Republican		Democratic		Other Vote	Rep.-Dem. Plurality	Percentage Total Vote		Major Vote	
			Vote	Candidate	Vote	Candidate			Rep.	Dem.	Rep.	Dem.
1	2008	283,249	67,346	LILLY, GEORGE C.	203,756	DeGETTE, DIANA*	12,147	136,410 D	23.8%	71.9%	24.8%	75.2%
1	2006	162,271		—	129,446	DeGETTE, DIANA*	32,825	129,446 D		79.8%		100.0%
1	2004	240,929	58,659	CHICAS, ROLAND	177,077	DeGETTE, DIANA*	5,193	118,418 D	24.3%	73.5%	24.9%	75.1%
1	2002	168,564	49,884	CHLOUBER, KEN	111,718	DeGETTE, DIANA*	6,962	61,834 D	29.6%	66.3%	30.9%	69.1%
2	2008	344,428	116,619	STARIN, SCOTT	215,602	POLIS, JARED	12,207	98,983 D	33.9%	62.6%	35.1%	64.9%
2	2006	231,307	65,481	MANCUSO, RICH	157,850	UDALL, MARK*	7,976	92,369 D	28.3%	68.2%	29.3%	70.7%
2	2004	309,364	94,160	HACKMAN, STEPHEN M.	207,900	UDALL, MARK*	7,304	113,740 D	30.4%	67.2%	31.2%	68.8%
2	2002	205,522	75,564	HUME, SANDY	123,504	UDALL, MARK*	6,454	47,940 D	36.8%	60.1%	38.0%	62.0%
3	2008	330,219	126,762	WOLF, WAYNE	203,457	SALAZAR, JOHN*		76,695 D	38.4%	61.6%	38.4%	61.6%
3	2006	237,858	86,930	TIPTON, SCOTT	146,488	SALAZAR, JOHN*	4,440	59,558 D	36.5%	61.6%	37.2%	62.8%
3	2004	303,646	141,376	WALCHER, GREG	153,500	SALAZAR, JOHN	8,770	12,124 D	46.6%	50.6%	47.9%	52.1%
3	2002	217,972	143,433	McINNIS, SCOTT*	68,160	BERCKEFELDT, DENIS	6,379	75,273 R	65.8%	31.3%	67.8%	32.2%
4	2008	333,378	146,030	MUSGRAVE, MARILYN*	187,348	MARKEY, BETSY		41,318 D	43.8%	56.2%	43.8%	56.2%
4	2006	240,613	109,732	MUSGRAVE, MARILYN*	103,748	PACCIONE, ANGIE	27,133	5,984 R	45.6%	43.1%	51.4%	48.6%
4	2004	305,509	155,958	MUSGRAVE, MARILYN*	136,812	MATSUNAKA, STAN	12,739	19,146 R	51.0%	44.8%	53.3%	46.7%
4	2002	209,955	115,359	MUSGRAVE, MARILYN	87,499	MATSUNAKA, STAN	7,097	27,860 R	54.9%	41.7%	56.9%	43.1%
5	2008	305,145	183,179	LAMBORN, DOUG*	113,027	BIDLACK, HAL	8,939	70,152 R	60.0%	37.0%	61.8%	38.2%
5	2006	206,756	123,264	LAMBORN, DOUG	83,431	FAWCETT, JAY	61	39,833 R	59.6%	40.4%	59.6%	40.4%
5	2004	274,058	193,333	HEFLEY, JOEL*	74,098	HARDEE, FRED	6,627	119,235 R	70.5%	27.0%	72.3%	27.7%
5	2002	184,677	128,118	HEFLEY, JOEL*	45,587	IMRIE, CURTIS	10,972	82,531 R	69.4%	24.7%	73.8%	26.2%
6	2008	413,518	250,877	COFFMAN, MIKE	162,641	ENG, HANK		88,236 R	60.7%	39.3%	60.7%	39.3%
6	2006	270,931	158,806	TANCREDO, TOM*	108,007	WINTER, BILL	4,118	50,799 R	58.6%	39.9%	59.5%	40.5%
6	2004	357,741	212,778	TANCREDO, TOM*	139,870	CONTI, JOANNA L.	5,093	72,908 R	59.5%	39.1%	60.3%	39.7%
6	2002	237,501	158,851	TANCREDO, TOM*	71,327	WRIGHT, LANCE	7,323	87,524 R	66.9%	30.0%	69.0%	31.0%
7	2008	273,994	100,057	LEREW, JOHN W.	173,937	PERLMUTTER, ED*		73,880 D	36.5%	63.5%	36.5%	63.5%
7	2006	189,172	79,571	O'DONNELL, RICK	103,918	PERLMUTTER, ED	5,683	24,347 D	42.1%	54.9%	43.4%	56.6%
7	2004	247,764	135,571	BEAUPREZ, BOB*	106,026	THOMAS, DAVE	6,167	29,545 R	54.7%	42.8%	56.1%	43.9%
7	2002	172,879	81,789	BEAUPREZ, BOB	81,668	FEELEY, MIKE	9,422	121 R	47.3%	47.2%	50.0%	50.0%
TOTAL	2008	2,283,931	990,870		1,259,768		33,293	268,898 D	43.4%	55.2%	44.0%	56.0%
TOTAL	2006	1,538,908	623,784		832,888		82,236	209,104 D	40.5%	54.1%	42.8%	57.2%
TOTAL	2004	2,039,011	991,835		995,283		51,893	3,448 D	48.6%	48.8%	49.9%	50.1%
TOTAL	2002	1,397,070	752,998		589,463		54,609	163,535 R	53.9%	42.2%	56.1%	43.9%

Note: An asterisk (*) denotes incumbent.

COLORADO

GENERAL AND PRIMARY ELECTIONS

2008 GENERAL ELECTIONS

President Other vote was 13,352 Unaffiliated (Ralph Nader); 10,898 Libertarian (Bob Barr); 6,233 Constitution (Chuck Baldwin); 3,051 America's Independent (Alan Keyes); 2,822 Green (Cynthia A. McKinney); 829 Unaffiliated (Frank Edward McEnulty); 598 Boston Tea Party (Charles Jay); 348 HeartQuake '08 (Jonathan E. Allen); 336 Objectivist (Thomas Robert Stevens); 226 Socialist (Brian Moore); 158 Socialism and Liberalism (Gloria La Riva); 154 Socialist Workers (James Harris); 110 U.S. Pacifist (Bradford Lyttle); 85 Prohibition (Gene C. Amondson).

Senator Other vote was 59,736 American Constitution (Douglas "Dayhorse" Campbell); 50,008 Green (Bob Kinsey); 116 Unaffiliated write-in (Buddy Moore); 10 Unaffiliated write-in (Gary Cooper); 9 Green write-in (Bruce E. Lohmiller).

COLORADO

GENERAL AND PRIMARY ELECTIONS

House   Other vote was:

CD 1   12,136 Libertarian (Martin L. Buchanan); 11 Unaffiliated write-in (Gary Swing).
CD 2   10,031 Green (J.A. Calhoun); 2,176 Unity (William Robert "Bill" Hammons).
CD 3
CD 4
CD 5   8,894 American Constitution (Brian X. Scott); 45 Unaffiliated write-in (Rich Hand).
CD 6
CD 7

2008 PRIMARY ELECTIONS

Primary	August 12, 2008	Registration (as of July 31, 2008—includes 781,462 inactive registrants)		
		Republican		1,024,504
		Democratic		946,277
		Libertarian		8,274
		Green		5,425
		American Constitution		918
		Others		9
		Unaffiliated		1,022,376
		TOTAL		*3,007,783*

Primary Type   Semi-open—Registered Democrats and Republicans could vote only in their party's primary. "Unaffiliated" voters could participate in either primary, but in the process had to declare their affiliation with that party.

	REPUBLICAN PRIMARIES			DEMOCRATIC PRIMARIES		
Senator	Bob Schaffer	239,212	100.0%	Mark Udall	194,227	100.0%
Congressional District 1	George C. Lilly	6,300	58.2%	Diana DeGette*	35,804	100.0%
	Charles R. Crain	4,533	41.8%			
	TOTAL	*10,833*				
Congressional District 2	Scott Starin	19,293	100.0%	Jared Polis	20,493	41.7%
				Joan Fitz-Gerald	18,599	37.8%
				Will Shafroth	10,075	20.5%
				TOTAL	*49,167*	
Congressional District 3	Wayne Wolf	24,263	100.0%	John Salazar*	22,192	100.0%
Congressional District 4	Marilyn Musgrave*	31,822	100.0%	Betsy Markey	19,010	100.0%
Congressional District 5	Doug Lamborn*	24,995	44.0%	Hal Bidlack	13,146	100.0%
	Jeff Crank	16,794	29.6%			
	Bentley Rayburn	14,986	26.4%			
	TOTAL	*56,775*				
Congressional District 6	Mike Coffman	28,509	40.1%	Hank Eng	27,661	100.0%
	Wil Armstrong	23,213	32.7%			
	Ted Harvey	10,886	15.3%			
	Steve Ward	8,452	11.9%			
	TOTAL	*71,060*				
Congressional District 7	John W. Lerew	25,155	100.0%	Ed Perlmutter*	29,704	100.0%

Note: An asterisk (*) denotes incumbent.

CONNECTICUT

Congressional districts first established for elections held in 2002
5 members

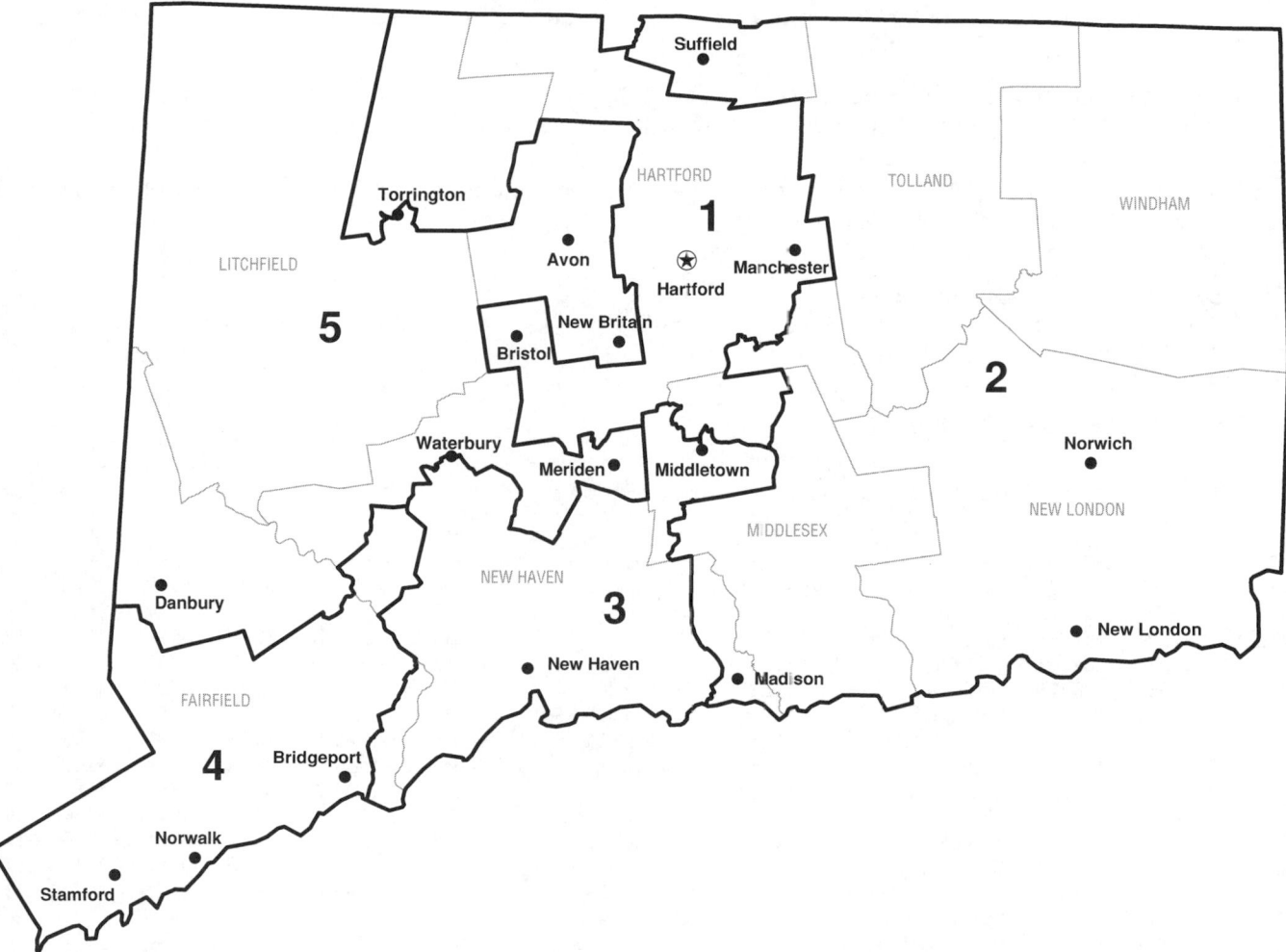

CONNECTICUT

GOVERNOR

M. Jodi Rell (R). Elected 2006 to a four-year term. Assumed office July 1, 2004, following the resignation of John Rowland (R), who was under threat of impeachment for accepting gifts from state employees and contractors.

SENATORS (1 Democrat, 1 Independent Democrat)

Christopher J. Dodd (D). Reelected 2004 to a six-year term. Previously elected 1998, 1992, 1986, 1980.

Joseph I. Lieberman (ID). Reelected 2006 to a six-year term on the Connecticut for Lieberman ballot line. Previously elected 2000, 1994, and 1988 as a Democrat.

REPRESENTATIVES (5 Democrats)

1. John B. Larson (D)
2. Joe Courtney (D)
3. Rosa DeLauro (D)
4. Jim Himes (D)
5. Chris Murphy (D)

POSTWAR VOTE FOR PRESIDENT

| Year | Total Vote | Republican | | Democratic | | Other Vote | Plurality | Percentage | | | |
| | | Vote | Candidate | Vote | Candidate | | | Total Vote | | Major Vote | |
								Rep.	Dem.	Rep.	Dem.
2008	1,646,797	629,428	McCain, John	997,772	Obama, Barack	19,597	368,344 D	38.2%	60.6%	38.7%	61.3%
2004	1,578,769	693,826	Bush, George W.	857,488	Kerry, John	27,455	163,662 D	43.9%	54.3%	44.7%	55.3%
2000**	1,459,525	561,094	Bush, George W.	816,015	Gore, Al	82,416	254,921 D	38.4%	55.9%	40.7%	59.3%
1996**	1,392,614	483,109	Dole, Bob	735,740	Clinton, Bill	173,765	252,631 D	34.7%	52.8%	39.6%	60.4%
1992**	1,616,332	578,313	Bush, George	682,318	Clinton, Bill	355,701	104,005 D	35.8%	42.2%	45.9%	54.1%
1988	1,443,394	750,241	Bush, George	676,584	Dukakis, Michael S.	16,569	73,657 R	52.0%	46.9%	52.6%	47.4%
1984	1,466,900	890,877	Reagan, Ronald	569,597	Mondale, Walter F.	6,426	321,280 R	60.7%	38.8%	61.0%	39.0%
1980**	1,406,285	677,210	Reagan, Ronald	541,732	Carter, Jimmy	187,343	135,478 R	48.2%	38.5%	55.6%	44.4%
1976	1,381,526	719,261	Ford, Gerald R.	647,895	Carter, Jimmy	14,370	71,366 R	52.1%	46.9%	52.6%	47.4%
1972	1,384,277	810,763	Nixon, Richard M.	555,498	McGovern, George S.	18,016	255,265 R	58.6%	40.1%	59.3%	40.7%
1968**	1,256,232	556,721	Nixon, Richard M.	621,561	Humphrey, Hubert H.	77,950	64,840 D	44.3%	49.5%	47.2%	52.8%
1964	1,218,578	390,996	Goldwater, Barry M.	826,269	Johnson, Lyndon B.	1,313	435,273 D	32.1%	67.8%	32.1%	67.9%
1960	1,222,883	565,813	Nixon, Richard M.	657,055	Kennedy, John F.	15	91,242 D	46.3%	53.7%	46.3%	53.7%
1956	1,117,121	711,837	Eisenhower, Dwight D.	405,079	Stevenson, Adlai E.	205	306,758 R	63.7%	36.3%	63.7%	36.3%
1952	1,096,911	611,012	Eisenhower, Dwight D.	481,649	Stevenson, Adlai E.	4,250	129,363 R	55.7%	43.9%	55.9%	44.1%
1948	883,518	437,754	Dewey, Thomas E.	423,297	Truman, Harry S.	22,467	14,457 R	49.5%	47.9%	50.8%	49.2%

**In past elections, the other vote included: 2000 - 64,452 Green (Ralph Nader); 1996 - 139,523 Reform (Ross Perot); 1992 - 348,771 Independent (Perot); 1980 - 171,807 Independent (John Anderson); 1968 - 76,650 American Independent (George Wallace).

CONNECTICUT

POSTWAR VOTE FOR GOVERNOR

Year	Total Vote	Republican Vote	Republican Candidate	Democratic Vote	Democratic Candidate	Other Vote	Plurality	Total Vote Rep.	Total Vote Dem.	Major Vote Rep.	Major Vote Dem.
2006	1,123,466	710,048	Rell, M. Jodi	398,220	DeStefano, John	15,198	311,828 R	63.2%	35.4%	64.1%	35.9%
2002	1,022,998	573,958	Rowland, John G.	448,984	Curry, Bill	56	124,974 R	56.1%	43.9%	56.1%	43.9%
1998	999,537	628,707	Rowland, John G.	354,187	Kennelly, Barbara B.	16,643	274,520 R	62.9%	35.4%	64.0%	36.0%
1994**	1,147,084	415,201	Rowland, John G.	375,133	Curry, Bill	356,750	40,068 R	36.2%	32.7%	52.5%	47.5%
1990**	1,141,122	427,840	Rowland, John G.	236,641	Morrison, Bruce A.	476,641	32,736 C	37.5%	20.7%	64.4%	35.6%
1986	993,692	408,489	Belaga, Julie D.	575,638	O'Neill, William A.	9,565	167,149 D	41.1%	57.9%	41.5%	58.5%
1982	1,084,156	497,773	Rome, Lewis B.	578,264	O'Neill, William A.	8,119	80,491 D	45.9%	53.3%	46.3%	53.7%
1978	1,036,608	422,316	Sarasin, Ronald A.	613,109	Grasso, Ella T.	1,183	190,793 D	40.7%	59.1%	40.8%	59.2%
1974	1,102,773	440,169	Steele, Robert H.	643,490	Grasso, Ella T.	19,114	203,321 D	39.9%	58.4%	40.6%	59.4%
1970	1,082,797	582,160	Meskill, Thomas J.	500,561	Daddario, Emilio	76	81,599 R	53.8%	46.2%	53.8%	46.2%
1966	1,008,557	446,536	Gengras, E. Clayton	561,599	Dempsey, John N.	422	115,063 D	44.3%	55.7%	44.3%	55.7%
1962	1,031,902	482,852	Alsop, John	549,027	Dempsey, John N.	23	66,175 D	46.8%	53.2%	46.8%	53.2%
1958	974,509	360,644	Zeller, Fred R.	607,012	Ribicoff, Abraham A.	6,853	246,368 D	37.0%	62.3%	37.3%	62.7%
1954	936,753	460,528	Lodge, John D.	463,643	Ribicoff, Abraham A.	12,582	3,115 D	49.2%	49.5%	49.8%	50.2%
1950**	878,735	436,418	Lodge, John D.	419,404	Bowles, Chester	22,913	17,014 R	49.7%	47.7%	51.0%	49.0%
1948	875,170	429,071	Shannon, James C.	431,296	Bowles, Chester	14,803	2,225 D	49.0%	49.3%	49.9%	50.1%
1946	683,831	371,852	McConaughy, J. L.	276,335	Snow, Wilbert	35,644	95,517 R	54.4%	40.4%	57.4%	42.6%

Notes: **In past elections, the other vote included: 1994 - 216,585 A Connecticut Party (Elaine Strong Groark) and 130,128 Independent (Tom Scott); 1990 - 460,576 A Connecticut Party (Lowell P. Weicker Jr.). Weicker won the 1990 election with 40.4 percent of the total vote. The term of office for Connecticut's governor was increased from two to four years effective with the 1950 election.

POSTWAR VOTE FOR SENATOR

Year	Total Vote	Republican Vote	Republican Candidate	Democratic Vote	Democratic Candidate	Other Vote	Plurality	Total Vote Rep.	Total Vote Dem.	Major Vote Rep.	Major Vote Dem.
2006**	1,134,780	109,198	Schlesinger, Alan	450,844	Lamont, Ned	574,738	113,251 I	9.6%	39.7%	19.5%	80.5%
2004	1,424,726	457,749	Orchulli, Jack	945,347	Dodd, Christopher J.	21,630	487,598 D	32.1%	66.4%	32.6%	67.4%
2000	1,311,261	448,077	Giordano, Philip A.	828,902	Lieberman, Joseph I.	34,282	380,825 D	34.2%	63.2%	35.1%	64.9%
1998	964,457	312,177	Franks, Gary A.	628,306	Dodd, Christopher J.	23,974	316,129 D	32.4%	65.1%	33.2%	66.8%
1994	1,079,767	334,833	Labriola, Jerry	723,842	Lieberman, Joseph I.	21,092	389,009 D	31.0%	67.0%	31.6%	68.4%
1992	1,500,709	572,036	Johnson, Brook	882,569	Dodd, Christopher J.	46,104	310,533 D	38.1%	58.8%	39.3%	60.7%
1988	1,383,526	678,454	Weicker, Lowell P.	688,499	Lieberman, Joseph I.	16,573	10,045 D	49.0%	49.8%	49.6%	50.4%
1986	976,933	340,438	Eddy, Roger W.	632,695	Dodd, Christopher J.	3,800	292,257 D	34.8%	64.8%	35.0%	65.0%
1982	1,083,613	545,987	Weicker, Lowell P.	499,146	Moffett, Anthony T.	38,480	46,841 R	50.4%	46.1%	52.2%	47.8%
1980	1,356,075	581,884	Buckley, James L.	763,969	Dodd, Christopher J.	10,222	182,085 D	42.9%	56.3%	43.2%	56.8%
1976	1,361,666	785,683	Weicker, Lowell P.	561,018	Schaffer, Gloria	14,965	224,665 R	57.7%	41.2%	58.3%	41.7%
1974	1,084,918	372,055	Brannen, James H.	690,820	Ribicoff, Abraham A.	22,043	318,765 D	34.3%	63.7%	35.0%	65.0%
1970**	1,089,353	454,721	Weicker, Lowell P.	368,111	Duffey, Joseph D.	266,521	86,610 R	41.7%	33.8%	55.3%	44.7%
1968	1,206,537	551,455	May, Edwin H.	655,043	Ribicoff, Abraham A.	39	103,588 D	45.7%	54.3%	45.7%	54.3%
1964	1,208,163	426,939	Lodge, John D.	781,008	Dodd, Thomas J.	216	354,069 D	35.3%	64.6%	35.3%	64.7%
1962	1,029,301	501,694	Seely-Brown, Horace	527,522	Ribicoff, Abraham A.	85	25,828 D	48.7%	51.3%	48.7%	51.3%
1958	965,463	410,622	Purtell, William A.	554,841	Dodd, Thomas J.		144,219 D	42.5%	57.5%	42.5%	57.5%
1956	1,113,819	610,829	Bush, Prescott	479,460	Dodd, Thomas J.	23,530	131,369 R	54.8%	43.0%	56.0%	44.0%
1952	1,093,467	573,854	Purtell, William A.	485,066	Benton, William	34,547	88,788 R	52.5%	44.4%	54.2%	45.8%
1952S	1,093,268	559,465	Bush, Prescott	530,505	Ribicoff, Abraham A.	3,298	28,960 R	51.2%	48.5%	51.3%	48.7%
1950	877,827	409,053	Talbot, Joseph E.	453,646	McMahon, Brien	15,128	44,593 D	46.6%	51.7%	47.4%	52.6%
1950S	877,135	430,311	Bush, Prescott	431,413	Benton, William	15,411	1,102 D	49.1%	49.2%	49.9%	50.1%
1946	682,921	381,328	Baldwin, Raymond	276,424	Tone, Joseph M.	25,169	104,904 R	55.8%	40.5%	58.0%	42.0%

Notes: **In past elections, the other vote included: 2006 - 564,095 Connecticut for Lieberman (Joseph I. Lieberman); 1970 - 266,497 Independent (Thomas J. Dodd). Lieberman won the 2006 election with 49.7 percent of the vote. S = One of the two elections held in both 1950 and 1952 of the 1950 and 1952 elections was for a short term to fill a vacancy.

CONNECTICUT

PRESIDENT 2008

2000 Census Population	County	Total Vote	Republican	Democratic	Other	Rep.-Dem. Plurality		Percentage			
								Total Vote		Major Vote	
								Rep.	Dem.	Rep.	Dem.
882,567	FAIRFIELD	413,741	167,736	242,936	3,069	75,200	D	40.5%	58.7%	40.8%	59.2%
857,183	HARTFORD	412,728	138,984	268,721	5,023	129,737	D	33.7%	65.1%	34.1%	65.9%
182,193	LITCHFIELD	98,966	46,173	51,041	1,752	4,868	D	46.7%	51.6%	47.5%	52.5%
155,071	MIDDLESEX	87,252	32,918	52,983	1,351	20,065	D	37.7%	60.7%	38.3%	61.7%
824,008	NEW HAVEN	382,886	144,650	233,589	4,647	88,939	D	37.8%	61.0%	38.2%	61.8%
259,088	NEW LONDON	124,874	48,491	74,776	1,607	26,285	D	38.8%	59.9%	39.3%	60.7%
136,364	TOLLAND	75,501	29,266	45,053	1,182	15,787	D	38.8%	59.7%	39.4%	60.6%
109,091	WINDHAM	50,844	21,210	28,673	961	7,463	D	41.7%	56.4%	42.5%	57.5%
3,405,565	*TOTAL*	1,646,797	629,428	997,772	19,597	368,344	D	38.2%	60.6%	38.7%	61.3%

2000 Census Population	City/Town	Total Vote	Republican	Democratic	Other	Rep.-Dem. Plurality		Percentage			
								Total Vote		Major Vote	
								Rep.	Dem.	Rep.	Dem.
18,554	ANSONIA	7,658	2,918	4,616	124	1,698	D	38.1%	60.3%	38.7%	61.3%
19,587	BLOOMFIELD	12,222	1,778	10,384	60	8,606	D	14.5%	85.0%	14.6%	85.4%
28,683	BRANFORD	15,144	5,906	9,062	176	3,156	D	39.0%	59.8%	39.5%	60.5%
139,529	BRIDGEPORT	40,682	6,507	33,976	199	27,469	D	16.0%	83.5%	16.1%	83.9%
60,062	BRISTOL	26,566	10,203	15,966	397	5,763	D	38.4%	60.1%	39.0%	61.0%
28,543	CHESHIRE	15,162	6,839	8,177	146	1,338	D	45.1%	53.9%	45.5%	54.5%
74,848	DANBURY	26,979	10,732	16,028	219	5,296	D	39.8%	59.4%	40.1%	59.9%
19,607	DARIEN	10,960	5,949	4,943	68	1,006	R	54.3%	45.1%	54.6%	45.4%
49,575	EAST HARTFORD	20,236	5,195	14,811	230	9,616	D	25.7%	73.2%	26.0%	74.0%
28,289	EAST HAVEN	12,350	5,287	6,878	185	1,591	D	42.8%	55.7%	43.5%	56.5%
45,212	ENFIELD	19,557	7,656	11,584	317	3,928	D	39.1%	59.2%	39.8%	60.2%
57,340	FAIRFIELD	30,537	13,071	17,236	230	4,165	D	42.8%	56.4%	43.1%	56.9%
23,641	FARMINGTON	14,071	5,822	8,088	161	2,266	D	41.4%	57.5%	41.9%	58.1%
31,876	GLASTONBURY	19,778	7,755	11,767	256	4,012	D	39.2%	59.5%	39.7%	60.3%
61,101	GREENWICH	30,374	13,937	16,233	204	2,296	D	45.9%	53.4%	46.2%	53.8%
39,907	GROTON	14,937	5,814	8,953	170	3,139	D	38.9%	59.9%	39.4%	60.6%
21,398	GUILFORD	13,330	5,073	8,134	123	3,061	D	38.1%	61.0%	38.4%	61.6%
56,913	HAMDEN	28,772	8,531	19,960	281	11,429	D	29.7%	69.4%	29.9%	70.1%
121,578	HARTFORD	34,597	2,686	31,741	170	29,055	D	7.8%	91.7%	7.8%	92.2%
54,740	MANCHESTER	26,602	8,457	17,782	363	9,325	D	31.8%	66.8%	32.2%	67.8%
20,720	MANSFIELD	10,306	2,235	7,874	197	5,639	D	21.7%	76.4%	22.1%	77.9%
58,244	MERIDEN	23,577	7,363	15,913	301	8,550	D	31.2%	67.5%	31.6%	68.4%
43,167	MIDDLETOWN	21,392	5,907	15,143	342	9,236	D	27.6%	70.8%	28.1%	71.9%
52,305	MILFORD	26,994	11,772	14,873	349	3,101	D	43.6%	55.1%	44.2%	55.8%
30,989	NAUGATUCK	13,345	6,148	7,034	163	886	D	46.1%	52.7%	46.6%	53.4%
71,538	NEW BRITAIN	22,460	5,442	16,742	276	11,300	D	24.2%	74.5%	24.5%	75.5%
123,626	NEW HAVEN	44,569	5,098	39,112	359	34,014	D	11.4%	87.8%	11.5%	88.5%
25,671	NEW LONDON	10,434	1,982	8,358	94	6,376	D	19.0%	80.1%	19.2%	80.8%
27,121	NEW MILFORD	13,763	6,255	7,364	144	1,109	D	45.4%	53.5%	45.9%	54.1%
29,306	NEWINGTON	15,831	5,726	9,875	230	4,149	D	36.2%	62.4%	36.7%	63.3%
25,031	NEWTOWN	15,182	7,270	7,764	148	494	D	47.9%	51.1%	48.4%	51.6%
23,035	NORTH HAVEN	13,430	6,298	6,982	150	684	D	46.9%	52.0%	47.4%	52.6%
82,951	NORWALK	37,384	12,651	24,489	244	11,838	D	33.8%	65.5%	34.1%	65.9%
36,117	NORWICH	13,591	4,505	8,896	190	4,391	D	33.1%	65.5%	33.6%	66.4%
23,643	RIDGEFIELD	14,337	6,786	7,480	71	694	D	47.3%	52.2%	47.6%	52.4%
38,101	SHELTON	20,342	10,428	9,655	259	773	R	51.3%	47.5%	51.9%	48.1%
23,234	SIMSBURY	14,027	5,928	7,964	135	2,036	D	42.3%	56.8%	42.7%	57.3%
24,412	SOUTH WINDSOR	14,380	5,421	8,773	186	3,352	D	37.7%	61.0%	38.2%	61.8%
39,728	SOUTHINGTON	22,230	9,845	12,066	319	2,221	D	44.3%	54.3%	44.9%	55.1%
117,083	STAMFORD	49,534	17,510	31,733	291	14,223	D	35.3%	64.1%	35.6%	64.4%

CONNECTICUT

PRESIDENT 2008

2000 Census Population	City/Town	Total Vote	Republican	Democratic	Other	Rep.-Dem. Plurality	Percentage			
							Total Vote		Major Vote	
							Rep.	Dem.	Rep.	Dem.
49,976	STRATFORD	25,090	10,199	14,626	265	4,427 D	40.6%	58.3%	41.1%	58.9%
35,202	TORRINGTON	15,970	7,424	8,159	387	735 D	46.5%	51.1%	47.6%	52.4%
34,243	TRUMBULL	19,842	9,927	9,757	158	170 R	50.0%	49.2%	50.4%	49.6%
28,063	VERNON	13,936	5,098	8,645	193	3,547 D	36.6%	62.0%	37.1%	62.9%
43,026	WALLINGFORD	22,544	9,372	12,833	339	3,461 D	41.6%	56.9%	42.2%	57.8%
107,271	WATERBURY	35,954	12,821	22,599	534	9,778 D	35.7%	62.9%	36.2%	63.8%
21,661	WATERTOWN	11,694	6,601	4,914	179	1,687 R	56.4%	42.0%	57.3%	42.7%
63,589	WEST HARTFORD	33,997	10,021	23,576	400	13,555 D	29.5%	69.3%	29.8%	70.2%
52,360	WEST HAVEN	21,450	7,005	14,186	259	7,181 D	32.7%	66.1%	33.1%	66.9%
25,749	WESTPORT	15,475	5,342	10,067	66	4,725 D	34.5%	65.1%	34.7%	65.3%
26,271	WETHERSFIELD	14,713	5,890	8,642	181	2,752 D	40.0%	58.7%	40.5%	59.5%
22,857	WINDHAM	8,798	2,341	6,312	145	3,971 D	26.6%	71.7%	27.1%	72.9%
28,237	WINDSOR	16,454	4,305	11,956	193	7,651 D	26.2%	72.7%	26.5%	73.5%

Note: The presidential vote was amended to include 5 more write-in votes. They are included in the total statewide vote, but are not part of the county or city/town tables.

CONNECTICUT

HOUSE OF REPRESENTATIVES

CD	Year	Total Vote	Republican		Democratic		Other Vote	Rep.-Dem. Plurality	Percentage			
			Vote	Candidate	Vote	Candidate			Total Vote		Major Vote	
									Rep.	Dem.	Rep.	Dem.
1	2008	295,557	76,860	VISCONTI, JOE	211,493	LARSON, JOHN B.*	7,204	134,633 D	26.0%	71.6%	26.7%	73.3%
1	2006	207,592	53,010	MacLEAN, SCOTT	154,539	LARSON, JOHN B.*	43	101,529 D	25.5%	74.4%	25.5%	74.5%
1	2004	272,403	73,601	HALSTEAD, JOHN M.	198,802	LARSON, JOHN B.*		125,201 D	27.0%	73.0%	27.0%	73.0%
1	2002	201,688	66,968	STEELE, PHIL	134,698	LARSON, JOHN B.*	22	67,730 D	33.2%	66.8%	33.2%	66.8%
2	2008	323,041	104,574	SULLIVAN, SEAN	212,148	COURTNEY, JOE*	6,319	107,574 D	32.4%	65.7%	33.0%	67.0%
2	2006	242,413	121,165	SIMMONS, ROB*	121,248	COURTNEY, JOE		83 D	50.0%	50.0%	50.0%	50.0%
2	2004	307,078	166,412	SIMMONS, ROB*	140,536	SULLIVAN, JIM	130	25,876 R	54.2%	45.8%	54.2%	45.8%
2	2002	217,108	117,434	SIMMONS, ROB*	99,674	COURTNEY, JOE		17,760 R	54.1%	45.9%	54.1%	45.9%
3	2008	297,368	58,583	ITSHAKY, BO	230,172	DeLAURO, ROSA*	8,613	171,589 D	19.7%	77.4%	20.3%	79.7%
3	2006	197,911	44,386	VOLLANO, JOSEPH	150,436	DeLAURO, ROSA*	3,089	106,050 D	22.4%	76.0%	22.8%	77.2%
3	2004	276,980	69,160	ELSER, RICHTER	200,638	DeLAURO, ROSA*	7,182	131,478 D	25.0%	72.4%	25.6%	74.4%
3	2002	185,364	54,757	ELSER, RICHTER	121,557	DeLAURO, ROSA*	9,050	66,800 D	29.5%	65.6%	31.1%	68.9%
4	2008	308,776	146,854	SHAYS, CHRISTOPHER*	158,475	HIMES, JIM	3,447	11,621 D	47.6%	51.3%	48.1%	51.9%
4	2006	209,019	106,510	SHAYS, CHRISTOPHER*	99,450	FARRELL, DIANE	3,059	7,060 R	51.0%	47.6%	51.7%	48.3%
4	2004	290,830	152,493	SHAYS, CHRISTOPHER*	138,333	FARRELL, DIANE	4	14,160 R	52.4%	47.6%	52.4%	47.6%
4	2002	175,695	113,197	SHAYS, CHRISTOPHER*	62,491	SANCHEZ, STEPHANIE H.	7	50,706 R	64.4%	35.6%	64.4%	35.6%
5	2008	302,657	117,914	CAPPIELLO, DAVID J.	179,327	MURPHY, CHRIS*	5,416	61,413 D	39.0%	59.3%	39.7%	60.3%
5	2006	217,804	94,824	JOHNSON, NANCY L.*	122,980	MURPHY, CHRIS		28,156 D	43.5%	56.5%	43.5%	56.5%
5	2004	278,251	168,268	JOHNSON, NANCY L.*	107,438	GERRATANA, THERESA B.	2,545	60,830 R	60.5%	38.6%	61.0%	39.0%
5	2002	209,454	113,626	JOHNSON, NANCY L.*	90,616	MALONEY, JIM*	5,212	23,010 R	54.2%	43.3%	55.6%	44.4%
TOTAL	2008	1,527,399	504,785		991,615		30,999	486,830 D	33.0%	64.9%	33.7%	66.3%
TOTAL	2006	1,074,739	419,895		648,653		6,191	228,758 D	39.1%	60.4%	39.3%	60.7%
TOTAL	2004	1,425,542	629,934		785,747			155,813 D	44.2%	55.1%	44.5%	55.5%
TOTAL	2002	989,309	465,982		509,036		14,291	43,054 D	47.1%	51.5%	47.8%	52.2%

Note: An asterisk (*) denotes incumbent.

CONNECTICUT

GENERAL AND PRIMARY ELECTIONS

2008 GENERAL ELECTIONS

President	Other vote was 19,162 Independent (Ralph Nader); 311 write-in (Chuck Baldwin); 90 write-in (Cynthia A. McKinney); 19 write-in (Brian Moore); 15 write-in (Roger Calero).
House	Other vote was:
CD 1	7,201 Green (Stephen E.D. Fournier); 3 write-in (Matthew Coleman). Democrat John B. Larson received 17,000 votes on the Working Families ballot line that was included in his total vote.
CD 2	6,300 Green (G. Scott Deshefy); 19 write-in (Todd Vachon). Democrat Joe Courtney received 13,164 votes on the Working Families ballot line that was included in her total vote.
CD 3	8,613 Green (Ralph A. Ferrucci). Democrat Rosa DeLauro received 25,411 votes on the Working Families ballot line that was included in her total vote.
CD 4	2,049 Libertarian (Michael Anthony Carrano); 1,388 Green (Richard Z. Duffee); 10 write-in (Eugene Flanagan). Democrat Jim Himes received 9,130 votes on the Working Families ballot line that was included in his total vote.
CD 5	3,082 Independent (Thomas L. Winn); 2,324 Green (Harold H. Burbank II); 10 write-in (Walter Gengarelly). Democrat Chris Murphy received 18,149 votes on the Working Families ballot line that was included in his total vote.

2008 PRIMARY ELECTIONS

Primary   February 5, 2008 (President)
August 12, 2008
(Congress)

Registration
(as of October 31, 2007—
includes 126,787 inactive
registrants)

Democratic	707,431
Republican	427,138
Other Parties	7,718
Unaffiliated	902,224
TOTAL	*2,044,511*

Primary Type   Closed—Only registered Democrats and Republicans could vote in their party's primary.

	REPUBLICAN PRIMARIES			DEMOCRATIC PRIMARIES		
President	John McCain	78,836	52.0%	Barack Obama	179,742	50.7%
	Mitt Romney	49,891	32.9%	Hillary Clinton	165,426	46.7%
	Mike Huckabee	10,607	7.0%	John Edwards	3,424	1.0%
	Ron Paul	6,287	4.1%	Uncommitted	3,038	0.9%
	Rudolph Giuliani	2,470	1.6%	Christopher J. Dodd	912	0.3%
	Uncommitted	2,462	1.6%	Dennis J. Kucinich	846	0.2%
	Fred Thompson	538	0.4%	Joseph R. Biden Jr.	440	0.1%
	Alan Keyes	376	0.2%	Bill Richardson	436	0.1%
	Duncan Hunter	137	0.1%	Mike Gravel	275	0.1%
	TOTAL	*151,604*		*TOTAL*	*354,539*	
Congressional District 1	Joe Visconti	Nominated by convention		John B. Larson*	Nominated by convention	
Congressional District 2	Sean Sullivan	Nominated by convention		Joe Courtney*	Nominated by convention	
Congressional District 3	Bo Itshaky	Nominated by convention		Rosa DeLauro*	Nominated by convention	
Congressional District 4	Christopher Shays*	Nominated by convention		Jim Himes	12,260	87.0%
				L. Lee Whitnum	1,840	13.0%
				TOTAL	*14,100*	
Congressional District 5	David J. Cappiello	Nominated by convention		Chris Murphy*	Nominated by convention	

Notes: An asterisk (*) denotes incumbent. A Senate or House candidate had to receive at least 15 percent of the vote in a pre-primary convention to force a primary or had to petition to appear on the primary ballot.

DELAWARE

One member At Large

Wilmington

Newark

NEW CASTLE

Dover

KENT

At Large

Rehoboth Beach

SUSSEX

Bethany Beach

DELAWARE

GOVERNOR
Jack Markell (D). Elected 2008 to a four-year term.

SENATORS (2 Democrats)
Thomas R. Carper (D). Reelected 2006 to a six-year term. Previously elected 2000.

Edward E. "Ted" Kaufman (D). Sworn in as senator January 16, 2009, to fill the vacancy created by the resignation of Joseph R. Biden Jr. (D) after his election as vice president of the United States.

REPRESENTATIVE (1 Republican)
At Large. Michael N. Castle (R)

POSTWAR VOTE FOR PRESIDENT

		Republican		Democratic		Other		Total Vote		Major Vote	
Year	Total Vote	Vote	Candidate	Vote	Candidate	Vote	Plurality	Rep.	Dem.	Rep.	Dem.
2008	412,412	152,374	McCain, John	255,459	Obama, Barack	4,579	103,085 D	36.9%	61.9%	37.4%	62.6%
2004	375,190	171,660	Bush, George W.	200,152	Kerry, John	3,378	28,492 D	45.8%	53.3%	46.2%	53.8%
2000**	327,622	137,288	Bush, George W.	180,068	Gore, Al	10,266	42,780 D	41.9%	55.0%	43.3%	56.7%
1996**	271,084	99,062	Dole, Bob	140,355	Clinton, Bill	31,667	41,293 D	36.5%	51.8%	41.4%	58.6%
1992**	289,735	102,313	Bush, George	126,054	Clinton, Bill	61,368	23,741 D	35.3%	43.5%	44.8%	55.2%
1988	249,891	139,639	Bush, George	108,647	Dukakis, Michael S.	1,605	30,992 R	55.9%	43.5%	56.2%	43.8%
1984	254,572	152,190	Reagan, Ronald	101,656	Mondale, Walter F.	726	50,534 R	59.8%	39.9%	60.0%	40.0%
1980**	235,900	111,252	Reagan, Ronald	105,754	Carter, Jimmy	18,894	5,498 R	47.2%	44.8%	51.3%	48.7%
1976	235,834	109,831	Ford, Gerald R.	122,596	Carter, Jimmy	3,407	12,765 D	46.6%	52.0%	47.3%	52.7%
1972	235,516	140,357	Nixon, Richard M.	92,283	McGovern, George S.	2,876	48,074 R	59.6%	39.2%	60.3%	39.7%
1968**	214,367	96,714	Nixon, Richard M.	89,194	Humphrey, Hubert H.	28,459	7,520 R	45.1%	41.6%	52.0%	48.0%
1964	201,320	78,078	Goldwater, Barry M.	122,704	Johnson, Lyndon B.	538	44,626 D	38.8%	60.9%	38.9%	61.1%
1960	196,683	96,373	Nixon, Richard M.	99,590	Kennedy, John F.	720	3,217 D	49.0%	50.6%	49.2%	50.8%
1956	177,988	98,057	Eisenhower, Dwight D.	79,421	Stevenson, Adlai E.	510	18,636 R	55.1%	44.6%	55.3%	44.7%
1952	174,025	90,059	Eisenhower, Dwight D.	83,315	Stevenson, Adlai E.	651	6,744 R	51.8%	47.9%	51.9%	48.1%
1948	139,073	69,588	Dewey, Thomas E.	67,813	Truman, Harry S.	1,672	1,775 R	50.0%	48.8%	50.6%	49.4%

**In past elections, the other vote included: 2000 - 8,307 Green (Ralph Nader); 1996 - 28,719 Reform (Ross Perot); 1992 - 59,213 Independent (Perot); 1980 - 16,288 Independent (John Anderson); 1968 - 28,459 American Independent (George Wallace).

POSTWAR VOTE FOR GOVERNOR

		Republican		Democratic		Other	Rep.-Dem.	Total Vote		Major Vote	
Year	Total Vote	Vote	Candidate	Vote	Candidate	Vote	Plurality	Rep.	Dem.	Rep.	Dem.
2008	395,204	126,662	Lee, William Swain	266,861	Markell, Jack	1,681	140,199 D	32.0%	67.5%	32.2%	67.8%
2004	365,008	167,115	Lee, William Swain	185,687	Minner, Ruth Ann	12,206	18,572 D	45.8%	50.9%	47.4%	52.6%
2000	323,688	128,603	Burris, John M.	191,695	Minner, Ruth Ann	3,390	63,092 D	39.7%	59.2%	40.2%	59.8%
1996	271,122	82,654	Rzewnicki, Janet	188,300	Carper, Thomas R.	168	105,646 D	30.5%	69.5%	30.5%	69.5%
1992	277,058	90,725	Scott, B. Gary	179,365	Carper, Thomas R.	6,968	88,640 D	32.7%	64.7%	33.6%	66.4%
1988	239,969	169,733	Castle, Michael N.	70,236	Kreshtoll, Jacob		99,497 R	70.7%	29.3%	70.7%	29.3%
1984	243,565	135,250	Castle, Michael N.	108,315	Quillen, William T.		26,935 R	55.5%	44.5%	55.5%	44.5%
1980	225,081	159,004	duPont, Pierre	64,217	Gordy, William J.	1,860	94,787 R	70.6%	28.5%	71.2%	28.8%
1976	229,563	130,531	duPont, Pierre	97,480	Tribbitt, Sherman W.	1,552	33,051 R	56.9%	42.5%	57.2%	42.8%
1972	228,722	109,583	Peterson, Russell W.	117,274	Tribbitt, Sherman W.	1,865	7,691 D	47.9%	51.3%	48.3%	51.7%
1968	206,834	104,474	Peterson, Russell W.	102,360	Terry, Charles L.		2,114 R	50.5%	49.5%	50.5%	49.5%
1964	200,171	97,374	Buckson, David P.	102,797	Terry, Charles L.		5,423 D	48.6%	51.4%	48.6%	51.4%
1960	194,835	94,043	Rollins, John W.	100,792	Carvel, Elbert N.		6,749 D	48.3%	51.7%	48.3%	51.7%
1956	177,012	91,965	Boggs, J. Caleb	85,047	McConnell, J. H. T.		6,918 R	52.0%	48.0%	52.0%	48.0%
1952	170,749	88,977	Boggs, J. Caleb	81,772	Carvel, Elbert N.		7,205 R	52.1%	47.9%	52.1%	47.9%
1948	140,335	64,996	George, Hyland P.	75,339	Carvel, Elbert N.		10,343 D	46.3%	53.7%	46.3%	53.7%

DELAWARE

POSTWAR VOTE FOR SENATOR

Year	Total Vote	Republican Vote	Republican Candidate	Democratic Vote	Democratic Candidate	Other Vote	Rep.-Dem. Plurality		Percentage Total Vote Rep.	Dem.	Major Vote Rep.	Dem.
2008	398,134	140,595	O'Donnell, Christine	257,539	Biden, Joseph R. Jr.		116,944	D	35.3%	64.7%	35.3%	64.7%
2006	254,099	69,734	Ting, Jan	170,567	Carper, Thomas R.	13,798	100,833	D	27.4%	67.1%	29.0%	71.0%
2002	232,314	94,793	Clatworthy, Raymond J.	135,253	Biden, Joseph R. Jr.	2,268	40,460	D	40.8%	58.2%	41.2%	58.8%
2000	327,017	142,891	Roth, William V.	181,566	Carper, Thomas R.	2,560	38,675	D	43.7%	55.5%	44.0%	56.0%
1996	275,605	105,088	Clatworthy, Raymond J.	165,465	Biden, Joseph R. Jr.	5,052	60,377	D	38.1%	60.0%	38.8%	61.2%
1994	199,029	111,088	Roth, William V.	84,554	Oberly, Charles M.	3,387	26,534	R	55.8%	42.5%	56.8%	43.2%
1990	180,152	64,554	Brady, M. Jane	112,918	Biden, Joseph R. Jr.	2,680	48,364	D	35.8%	62.7%	36.4%	63.6%
1988	243,493	151,115	Roth, William V.	92,378	Woo, S. B.		58,737	R	62.1%	37.9%	62.1%	37.9%
1984	245,932	98,101	Burris, John M.	147,831	Biden, Joseph R. Jr.		49,730	D	39.9%	60.1%	39.9%	60.1%
1982	190,960	105,357	Roth, William V.	84,413	Levinson, David N.	1,190	20,944	R	55.2%	44.2%	55.5%	44.5%
1978	162,072	66,479	Baxter, James H.	93,930	Biden, Joseph R. Jr.	1,663	27,451	D	41.0%	58.0%	41.4%	58.6%
1976	224,859	125,502	Roth, William V.	98,055	Maloney, Thomas C.	1,302	27,447	R	55.8%	43.6%	56.1%	43.9%
1972	229,828	112,844	Boggs, J. Caleb	116,006	Biden, Joseph R. Jr.	978	3,162	D	49.1%	50.5%	49.3%	50.7%
1970	161,439	94,979	Roth, William V.	64,740	Zimmerman, Jacob	1,720	30,239	R	58.8%	40.1%	59.5%	40.5%
1966	164,549	97,268	Boggs, J. Caleb	67,281	Tunnell, James M., Jr.		29,987	R	59.1%	40.9%	59.1%	40.9%
1964	200,703	103,782	Williams, John J.	96,850	Carvel, Elbert N.	71	6,932	R	51.7%	48.3%	51.7%	48.3%
1960	194,964	98,874	Boggs, J. Caleb	96,090	Frear, J. Allen		2,784	R	50.7%	49.3%	50.7%	49.3%
1958	154,432	82,280	Williams, John J.	72,152	Carvel, Elbert N.		10,128	R	53.3%	46.7%	53.3%	46.7%
1954	144,900	62,389	Warburton, H. B.	82,511	Frear, J. Allen		20,122	D	43.1%	56.9%	43.1%	56.9%
1952	170,705	93,020	Williams, John J.	77,685	Bayard, A. I. duP.		15,335	R	54.5%	45.5%	54.5%	45.5%
1948	141,362	68,246	Buck, C. Douglas	71,888	Frear, J. Allen	1,228	3,642	D	48.3%	50.9%	48.7%	51.3%
1946	113,513	62,603	Williams, John J.	50,910	Tunnell, James M.		11,693	R	55.2%	44.8%	55.2%	44.8%

DELAWARE

PRESIDENT 2008

2000 Census Population	County	Total Vote	Republican	Democratic	Other	Rep.-Dem. Plurality		Percentage Total Vote Rep.	Dem.	Major Vote Rep.	Dem.
126,697	KENT	66,925	29,827	36,392	706	6,565	D	44.6%	54.4%	45.0%	55.0%
500,265	NEW CASTLE	256,417	74,608	178,768	3,041	104,160	D	29.1%	69.7%	29.4%	70.6%
156,638	SUSSEX	89,070	47,939	40,299	832	7,640	R	53.8%	45.2%	54.3%	45.7%
783,600	TOTAL	412,412	152,374	255,459	4,579	103,085	D	36.9%	61.9%	37.4%	62.6%

DELAWARE

GOVERNOR 2008

2000 Census Population	County	Total Vote	Republican	Democratic	Other	Rep.-Dem. Plurality		Percentage Total Vote Rep.	Dem.	Major Vote Rep.	Dem.
126,697	KENT	64,940	23,646	41,076	218	17,430	D	36.4%	63.3%	36.5%	63.5%
500,265	NEW CASTLE	243,884	62,432	180,240	1,212	117,808	D	25.6%	73.9%	25.7%	74.3%
156,638	SUSSEX	86,380	40,584	45,545	251	4,961	D	47.0%	52.7%	47.1%	52.9%
783,600	TOTAL	395,204	126,662	266,861	1,681	140,199	D	32.0%	67.5%	32.2%	67.8%

DELAWARE

SENATOR 2008

2000 Census Population	County	Total Vote	Republican	Democratic	Other	Rep.-Dem. Plurality	Percentage Total Vote Rep.	Dem.	Major Vote Rep.	Dem.
126,697	KENT	65,055	27,981	37,074		9,093 D	43.0%	57.0%	43.0%	57.0%
500,265	NEW CASTLE	246,561	69,491	177,070		107,579 D	28.2%	71.8%	28.2%	71.8%
156,638	SUSSEX	86,518	43,123	43,395		272 D	49.8%	50.2%	49.8%	50.2%
783,600	TOTAL	398,134	140,595	257,539		116,944 D	35.3%	64.7%	35.3%	64.7%

DELAWARE

HOUSE OF REPRESENTATIVES

CD	Year	Total Vote	Republican Vote	Republican Candidate	Democratic Vote	Democratic Candidate	Other Vote	Rep.-Dem. Plurality	Total Vote Rep.	Dem.	Major Vote Rep.	Dem.
AL	2008	385,457	235,437	CASTLE, MICHAEL N.*	146,434	HARTLEY-NAGLE, KAREN	3,586	89,003 R	61.1%	38.0%	61.7%	38.3%
AL	2006	251,694	143,897	CASTLE, MICHAEL N.*	97,565	SPIVACK, DENNIS	10,232	46,332 R	57.2%	38.8%	59.6%	40.4%
AL	2004	356,045	245,978	CASTLE, MICHAEL N.*	105,716	DONNELLY, PAUL	4,351	140,262 R	69.1%	29.7%	69.9%	30.1%
AL	2002	228,405	164,605	CASTLE, MICHAEL N.*	61,011	MILLER, MICHEAL C.	2,789	103,594 R	72.1%	26.7%	73.0%	27.0%
AL	2000	313,126	211,797	CASTLE, MICHAEL N.*	96,488	MILLER, MICHEAL C.	4,841	115,309 R	67.6%	30.8%	68.7%	31.3%
AL	1998	180,527	119,811	CASTLE, MICHAEL N.*	57,446	WILLIAMS, DENNIS E.	3,270	62,365 R	66.4%	31.8%	67.6%	32.4%
AL	1996	266,836	185,576	CASTLE, MICHAEL N.*	73,253	WILLIAMS, DENNIS E.	8,007	112,323 R	69.5%	27.5%	71.7%	28.3%
AL	1994	195,037	137,960	CASTLE, MICHAEL N.*	51,803	DESANTIS, CAROL ANN	5,274	86,157 R	70.7%	26.6%	72.7%	27.3%
AL	1992	276,157	153,037	CASTLE, MICHAEL N.	117,426	WOO, S.B.	5,694	35,611 R	55.4%	42.5%	56.6%	43.4%
AL	1990	177,432	58,037	WILLIAMS, RALPH O.	116,274	CARPER, THOMAS R.*	3,121	58,237 D	32.7%	65.5%	33.3%	66.7%
AL	1988	234,517	76,179	KRAPF, JAMES P.	158,338	CARPER, THOMAS R.*		82,159 D	32.5%	67.5%	32.5%	67.5%
AL	1986	160,757	53,767	NEUBERGER, THOMAS S.	106,351	CARPER, THOMAS R.*	639	52,584 D	33.4%	66.2%	33.6%	66.4%
AL	1984	243,014	100,650	duPONT, ELISE	142,070	CARPER, THOMAS R.*	294	41,420 D	41.4%	58.5%	41.5%	58.5%
AL	1982	188,064	87,153	EVANS, THOMAS B.*	98,533	CARPER, THOMAS R.	2,378	11,380 D	46.3%	52.4%	46.9%	53.1%
AL	1980	216,629	133,842	EVANS, THOMAS B.*	81,227	MAXWELL, ROBERT L.	1,560	52,615 R	61.8%	37.5%	62.2%	37.8%
AL	1978	157,566	91,689	EVANS, THOMAS B.*	64,863	HINDES, GARY E.	1,014	26,826 R	58.2%	41.2%	58.6%	41.4%
AL	1976	214,799	110,677	EVANS, THOMAS B.	102,431	SHIPLEY, SAMUEL L.	1,691	8,246 R	51.5%	47.7%	51.9%	48.1%
AL	1974	160,328	93,826	duPONT, PIERRE*	63,490	SOLES, JAMES	3,012	30,336 R	58.5%	39.6%	59.6%	40.4%
AL	1972	225,851	141,237	duPONT, PIERRE*	83,230	HANDLOFF, NORMA	1,384	58,007 R	62.5%	36.9%	62.9%	37.1%
AL	1970	160,313	86,125	duPONT, PIERRE	71,429	DANIELLO, JOHN D.	2,759	14,696 R	53.7%	44.6%	54.7%	45.3%
AL	1968	200,820	117,827	ROTH, WILLIAM V.*	82,993	McDOWELL, HARRIS B.		34,834 R	58.7%	41.3%	58.7%	41.3%
AL	1966	163,103	90,961	ROTH, WILLIAM V.	72,142	McDOWELL, HARRIS B.*		18,819 R	55.8%	44.2%	55.8%	44.2%
AL	1964	198,691	86,254	SNOWDEN, JAMES H.	112,361	McDOWELL, HARRIS B.*	76	26,107 D	43.4%	56.6%	43.4%	56.6%
AL	1962	153,356	71,934	WILLIAMS, WILMER F.	81,166	McDOWELL, HARRIS B.*	256	9,232 D	46.9%	52.9%	47.0%	53.0%
AL	1960	194,564	96,337	McKINSTRY, JAMES T.	98,227	McDOWELL, HARRIS B.*		1,890 D	49.5%	50.5%	49.5%	50.5%
AL	1958	152,896	76,099	HASKELL, HARRY G.*	76,797	McDOWELL, HARRIS B.		698 D	49.8%	50.2%	49.8%	50.2%
AL	1956	176,182	91,538	HASKELL, HARRY G.	84,644	McDOWELL, HARRIS B.*	6,894	6,894 R	52.0%	48.0%	52.0%	48.0%
AL	1954	144,236	65,035	MARTIN, LILLIAN	79,201	McDOWELL, HARRIS B.		14,166 D	45.1%	54.9%	45.1%	54.9%
AL	1952	170,015	88,285	WARBURTON, H.B.	81,730	SCANNELL, JOSEPH S.		6,555 R	51.9%	48.1%	51.9%	48.1%
AL	1950	129,404	73,313	BOGGS, J. CALEB*	56,091	WINCHESTER, H.M.		17,222 R	56.7%	43.3%	56.7%	43.3%
AL	1948	140,535	71,127	BOGGS, J. CALEB*	68,909	McGUIGAN, J. CARL	499	2,218 R	50.6%	49.0%	50.8%	49.2%
AL	1946	112,621	63,516	BOGGS, J. CALEB	49,105	TRAYNOR, PHILIP A.*		14,411 R	56.4%	43.6%	56.4%	43.6%

Note: An asterisk (*) denotes incumbent.

DELAWARE
GENERAL AND PRIMARY ELECTIONS

2008 GENERAL ELECTIONS

President Other vote was 2,401 Independent Party of Delaware (Ralph Nader); 1,109 Libertarian (Bob Barr); 626 Constitution (Chuck Baldwin); 385 Green (Cynthia A. McKinney); 58 Socialist Workers (Roger Calero).

Governor Other vote was 1,681 Blue Enigma (Jeffrey Brown).

Senator

House Other vote was:

At Large 3,586 Libertarian (Mark Anthony Parks).

2008 PRIMARY ELECTIONS

Primary February 5, 2008 (President) **Registration** Democratic 266,381
September 9, 2008 (Congress) (as of September 1, 2008) Republican 179,808
Others 137,509

TOTAL 583,698

Primary Type Closed—Only registered Democrats and Republicans could vote in their party's primary.

	REPUBLICAN PRIMARIES			DEMOCRATIC PRIMARIES		
President	John McCain	22,628	45.0%	Barack Obama	51,148	53.1%
	Mitt Romney	16,344	32.5%	Hillary Clinton	40,760	42.3%
	Mike Huckabee	7,706	15.3%	Joseph R. Biden Jr.	2,863	3.0%
	Ron Paul	2,131	4.2%	John Edwards	1,241	1.3%
	Rudolph Giuliani	1,255	2.5%	Dennis J. Kucinich	192	0.2%
	Tom Tancredo	175	0.3%	Christopher J. Dodd	170	0.2%
	TOTAL	50,239		TOTAL	96,374	
Governor	William Swain Lee	20,826	71.9%	Jack Markell	37,849	51.2%
	Michael D. Protack	8,146	28.1%	John Carney	36,112	48.8%
	TOTAL	28,972		TOTAL	73,961	
Senator	Christine O'Donnell	Unopposed		Joseph R. Biden Jr.*	Unopposed	
House At Large	Michael N. Castle*	Unopposed		Karen Hartley-Nagle	35,995	55.4%
				Micheal Miller	22,393	34.5%
				Jerry W. Northington	6,609	10.2%
				TOTAL	64,997	

Note: An asterisk (*) denotes incumbent. The names of unopposed candidates did not appear on the primary ballot; therefore, no votes were cast for these candidates.

FLORIDA

Congressional districts first established for elections held in 2002
25 members

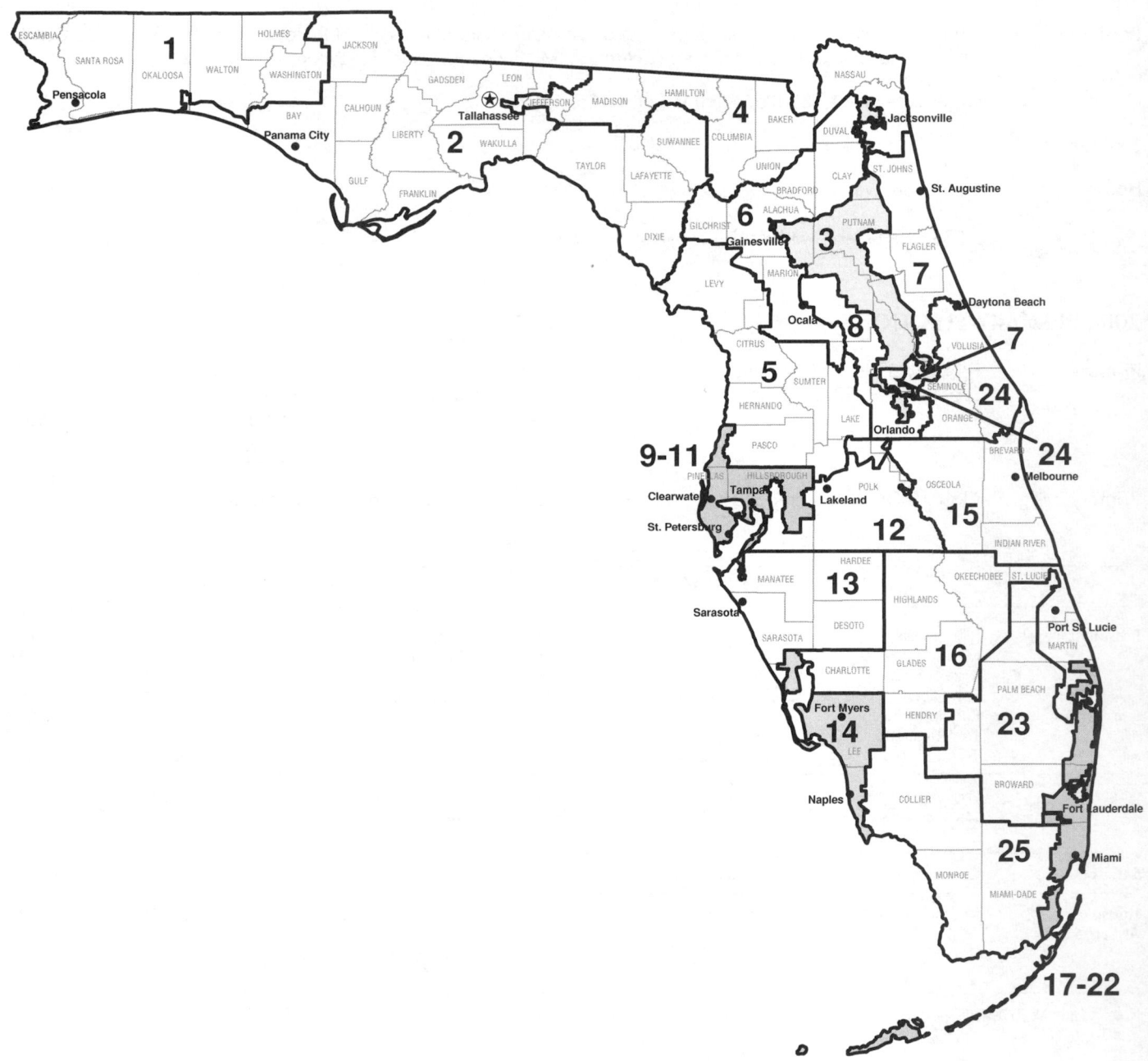

FLORIDA

St. Petersburg, Tampa, Fort Myers Areas

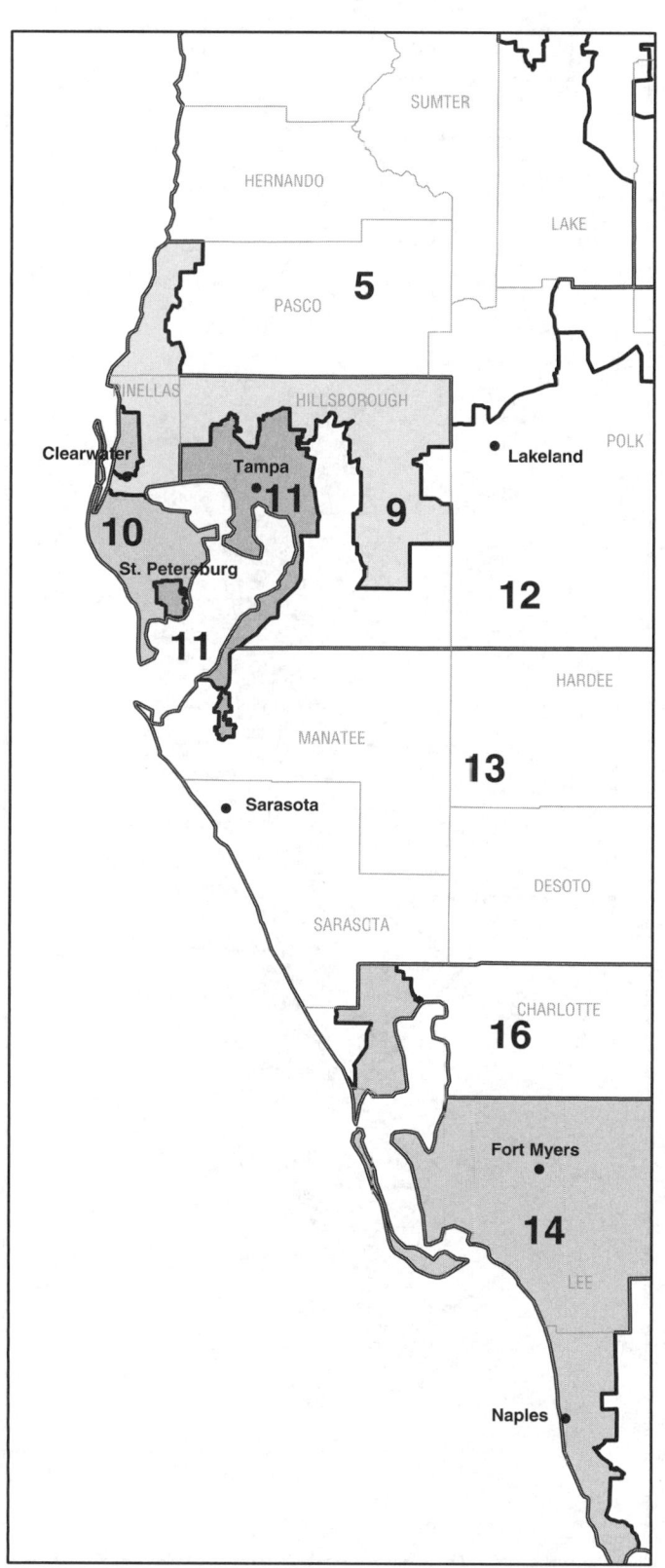

FLORIDA

Miami, Fort Lauderdale Areas

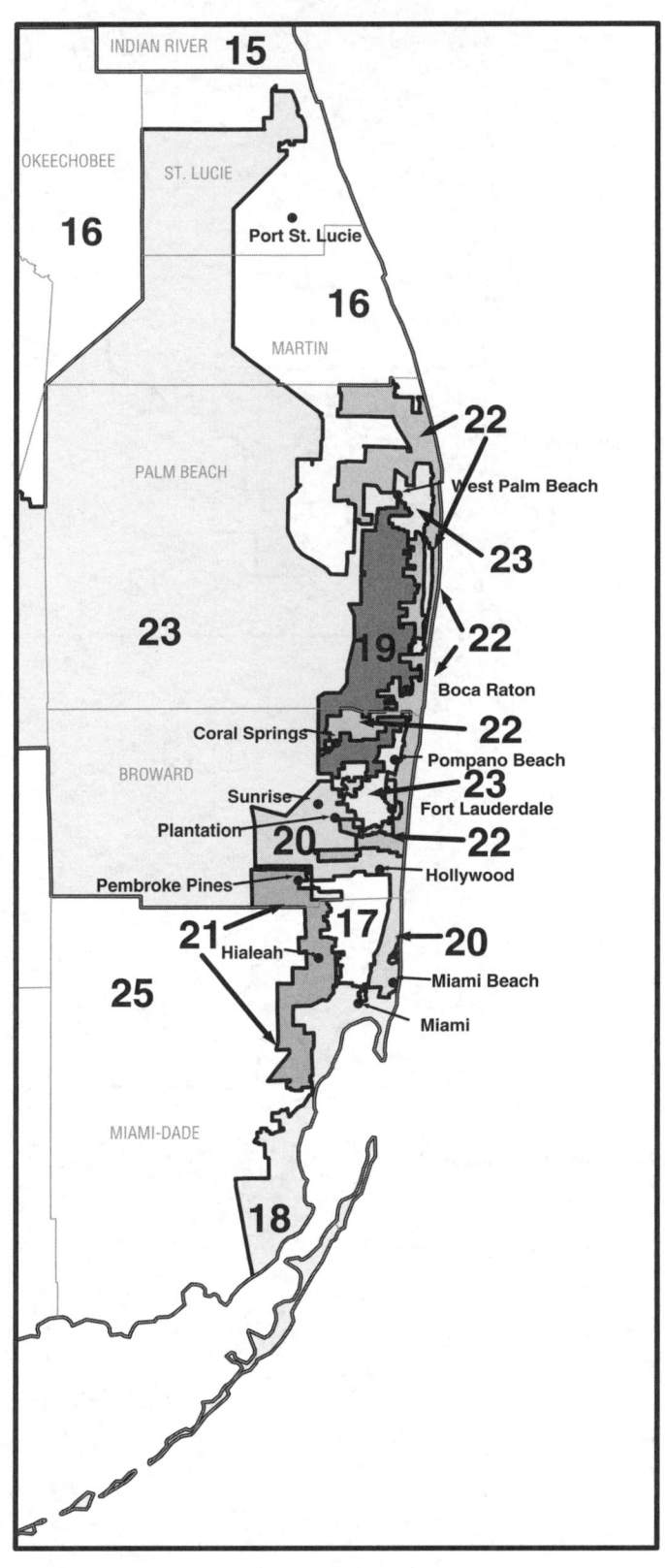

FLORIDA

GOVERNOR
Charlie Crist (R). Elected 2006 to a four-year term.

SENATORS (1 Democrat, 1 Republican)
Mel Martinez (R). Elected 2004 to a six-year term.

Bill Nelson (D). Reelected 2006 to a six-year term. Previously elected 2000.

REPRESENTATIVES (15 Republicans, 10 Democrats)
1. Jeff Miller (R)
2. Allen Boyd (D)
3. Corrine Brown (D)
4. Ander Crenshaw (R)
5. Ginny Brown-Waite (R)
6. Cliff Stearns (R)
7. John L. Mica (R)
8. Alan Grayson (D)
9. Gus Michael Bilirakis (R)
10. C.W. Bill Young (R)
11. Kathy Castor (D)
12. Adam H. Putnam (R)
13. Vern Buchanan (R)
14. Connie Mack (R)
15. Bill Posey (R)
16. Tom Rooney (R)
17. Kendrick B. Meek (D)
18. Ileana Ros-Lehtinen (R)
19. Robert Wexler (D)
20. Debbie Wasserman Schultz (D)
21. Lincoln Diaz-Balart (R)
22. Ron Klein (D)
23. Alcee L. Hastings (D)
24. Suzanne Kosmas (D)
25. Mario Diaz-Balart (R)

POSTWAR VOTE FOR PRESIDENT

Year	Total Vote	Republican Vote	Republican Candidate	Democratic Vote	Democratic Candidate	Other Vote	Plurality	Total Vote Rep.	Total Vote Dem.	Major Vote Rep.	Major Vote Dem.
2008	8,390,744	4,045,624	McCain, John	4,282,074	Obama, Barack	63,046	236,450 D	48.2%	51.0%	48.6%	51.4%
2004	7,609,810	3,964,522	Bush, George W.	3,583,544	Kerry, John	61,744	380,978 R	52.1%	47.1%	52.5%	47.5%
2000**	5,963,110	2,912,790	Bush, George W.	2,912,253	Gore, Al	138,067	537 R	48.8%	48.8%	50.0%	50.0%
1996**	5,303,794	2,244,536	Dole, Bob	2,546,870	Clinton, Bill	512,388	302,334 D	42.3%	48.0%	46.8%	53.2%
1992**	5,314,392	2,173,310	Bush, George	2,072,698	Clinton, Bill	1,068,384	100,612 R	40.9%	39.0%	51.2%	48.8%
1988	4,302,313	2,618,885	Bush, George	1,656,701	Dukakis, Michael S.	26,727	962,184 R	60.9%	38.5%	61.3%	38.7%
1984	4,180,051	2,730,350	Reagan, Ronald	1,448,816	Mondale, Walter F.	885	1,281,534 R	65.3%	34.7%	65.3%	34.7%
1980**	3,686,930	2,046,951	Reagan, Ronald	1,419,475	Carter, Jimmy	220,504	627,476 R	55.5%	38.5%	59.1%	40.9%
1976	3,150,631	1,469,531	Ford, Gerald R.	1,636,000	Carter, Jimmy	45,100	166,469 D	46.6%	51.9%	47.3%	52.7%
1972	2,583,283	1,857,759	Nixon, Richard M.	718,117	McGovern, George S.	7,407	1,139,642 R	71.9%	27.8%	72.1%	27.9%
1968**	2,187,805	886,804	Nixon, Richard M.	676,794	Humphrey, Hubert H.	624,207	210,010 R	40.5%	30.9%	56.7%	43.3%
1964	1,854,481	905,941	Goldwater, Barry M.	948,540	Johnson, Lyndon B.		42,599 D	48.9%	51.1%	48.9%	51.1%
1960	1,544,176	795,476	Nixon, Richard M.	748,700	Kennedy, John F.		46,776 R	51.5%	48.5%	51.5%	48.5%
1956	1,125,762	643,849	Eisenhower, Dwight D.	480,371	Stevenson, Adlai E.	1,542	163,478 R	57.2%	42.7%	57.3%	42.7%
1952	989,337	544,036	Eisenhower, Dwight D.	444,950	Stevenson, Adlai E.	351	99,086 R	55.0%	45.0%	55.0%	45.0%
1948**	577,643	194,280	Dewey, Thomas E.	281,988	Truman, Harry S.	101,375	87,708 D	33.6%	48.8%	40.8%	59.2%

**In past elections, the other vote included: 2000 - 97,488 Green (Ralph Nader); 1996 - 483,870 Reform (Ross Perot); 1992 - 1,053,067 Independent (Perot); 1980 - 189,692 Independent (John Anderson); 1968 - 624,207 American Independent (George Wallace); 1948 - 89,755 States' Rights (Strom Thurmond).

FLORIDA

POSTWAR VOTE FOR GOVERNOR

Year	Total Vote	Republican Vote	Republican Candidate	Democratic Vote	Democratic Candidate	Other Vote	Rep.-Dem. Plurality	Total Vote Rep.	Total Vote Dem.	Major Vote Rep.	Major Vote Dem.
2006	4,829,270	2,519,845	Crist, Charlie	2,178,289	Davis, Jim	131,136	341,556 R	52.2%	45.1%	53.6%	46.4%
2002	5,100,581	2,856,845	Bush, Jeb	2,201,427	McBride, Bill	42,309	655,418 R	56.0%	43.2%	56.5%	43.5%
1998	3,964,441	2,191,105	Bush, Jeb	1,773,054	MacKay, Buddy	282	418,051 R	55.3%	44.7%	55.3%	44.7%
1994	4,206,659	2,071,068	Bush, Jeb	2,135,008	Chiles, Lawton	583	63,940 D	49.2%	50.8%	49.2%	50.8%
1990	3,530,871	1,535,068	Martinez, Bob	1,995,206	Chiles, Lawton	597	460,138 D	43.5%	56.5%	43.5%	56.5%
1986	3,386,171	1,847,525	Martinez, Bob	1,538,620	Pajcic, Steve	26	308,905 R	54.6%	45.4%	54.6%	45.4%
1982	2,688,566	949,013	Bafalis, L. A. "Skip"	1,739,553	Graham, Bob		790,540 D	35.3%	64.7%	35.3%	64.7%
1978	2,530,468	1,123,888	Eckerd, Jack M.	1,406,580	Graham, Bob		282,692 D	44.4%	55.6%	44.4%	55.6%
1974	1,828,392	709,438	Thomas, Jerry	1,118,954	Askew, Reubin		409,516 D	38.8%	61.2%	38.8%	61.2%
1970	1,730,813	746,243	Kirk, Claude R.	984,305	Askew, Reubin	265	238,062 D	43.1%	56.9%	43.1%	56.9%
1966	1,489,661	821,190	Kirk, Claude R.	668,233	High, Robert King	238	152,957 R	55.1%	44.9%	55.1%	44.9%
1964S	1,663,481	686,297	Holley, Charles R.	933,554	Burns, Haydon	43,630	247,257 D	41.3%	56.1%	42.4%	57.6%
1960	1,419,343	569,936	Petersen, George C.	849,407	Bryant, Farris		279,471 D	40.2%	59.8%	40.2%	59.8%
1956	1,014,733	266,980	Washburne, W. A.	747,753	Collins, LeRoy		480,773 D	26.3%	73.7%	26.3%	73.7%
1954S	357,783	69,852	Watson, J. Tom	287,769	Collins, LeRoy	162	217,917 D	19.5%	80.4%	19.5%	80.5%
1952	834,518	210,009	Swan, Harry S.	624,463	McCarty, Dan	46	414,454 D	25.2%	74.8%	25.2%	74.8%
1948	457,638	76,153	Acker, Bert Lee	381,459	Warren, Fuller	26	305,306 D	16.6%	83.4%	16.6%	83.4%

Notes: The 1964 election was for a two-year term to permit shifting the vote for governor to non-presidential years. The 1954 election was for a short term to fill a vacancy.

POSTWAR VOTE FOR SENATOR

Year	Total Vote	Republican Vote	Republican Candidate	Democratic Vote	Democratic Candidate	Other Vote	Rep.-Dem. Plurality	Total Vote Rep.	Total Vote Dem.	Major Vote Rep.	Major Vote Dem.
2006	4,793,534	1,826,127	Harris, Katherine	2,890,548	Nelson, Bill	76,859	1,064,421 D	38.1%	60.3%	38.7%	61.3%
2004	7,429,894	3,672,864	Martinez, Mel	3,590,201	Castor, Betty	166,829	82,663 R	49.4%	48.3%	50.6%	49.4%
2000	5,856,731	2,705,348	McCollum, Bill	2,989,487	Nelson, Bill	161,896	284,139 D	46.2%	51.0%	47.5%	52.5%
1998	3,900,162	1,463,755	Crist, Charlie	2,436,407	Graham, Bob		972,652 D	37.5%	62.5%	37.5%	62.5%
1994	4,106,176	2,894,726	Mack, Connie	1,210,412	Rodham, Hugh E.	1,038	1,684,314 R	70.5%	29.5%	70.5%	29.5%
1992	4,962,290	1,716,505	Grant, Bill	3,245,565	Graham, Bob	220	1,529,060 D	34.6%	65.4%	34.6%	65.4%
1988	4,068,209	2,051,071	Mack, Connie	2,016,553	MacKay, Buddy	585	34,518 R	50.4%	49.6%	50.4%	49.6%
1986	3,429,996	1,552,376	Hawkins, Paula	1,877,543	Graham, Bob	77	325,167 D	45.3%	54.7%	45.3%	54.7%
1982	2,653,419	1,015,330	Poole, Van B.	1,637,667	Chiles, Lawton	422	622,337 D	38.3%	61.7%	38.3%	61.7%
1980	3,528,028	1,822,460	Hawkins, Paula	1,705,409	Gunter, Bill	159	117,051 R	51.7%	48.3%	51.7%	48.3%
1976	2,857,534	1,057,886	Grady, John	1,799,518	Chiles, Lawton	130	741,632 D	37.0%	63.0%	37.0%	63.0%
1974**	1,800,539	736,674	Eckerd, Jack M.	781,031	Stone, Richard	282,834	44,357 D	40.9%	43.4%	48.5%	51.5%
1970	1,675,378	772,817	Cramer, William C.	902,438	Chiles, Lawton	123	129,621 D	46.1%	53.9%	46.1%	53.9%
1968	2,024,136	1,131,499	Gurney, Edward J.	892,637	Collins, LeRoy		238,862 R	55.9%	44.1%	55.9%	44.1%
1964	1,560,337	562,212	Kirk, Claude R.	997,585	Holland, Spessard L.	540	435,373 D	36.0%	63.9%	36.0%	64.0%
1962	939,207	281,381	Rupert, Emerson H.	657,633	Smathers, George A.	193	376,252 D	30.0%	70.0%	30.0%	70.0%
1958	542,069	155,956	Hyzer, Leland	386,113	Holland, Spessard L.		230,157 D	28.8%	71.2%	28.8%	71.2%
1956**	655,418		—	655,418	Smathers, George A.		655,418 D		100.0%		100.0%
1952**	617,800		—	616,665	Holland, Spessard L.	1,135	616,665 D		99.8%		100.0%
1950	313,487	74,228	Booth, John P.	238,987	Smathers, George A.	272	164,759 D	23.7%	76.2%	23.7%	76.3%
1946	198,640	42,408	Schad, J. Harry	156,232	Holland, Spessard L.		113,824 D	21.3%	78.7%	21.3%	78.7%

Notes: **In past elections, the other vote included: 1974 - 282,659 American (John Grady). The Republican Party did not run a candidate in the 1952 and 1956 Senate elections.

FLORIDA

PRESIDENT 2008

2000 Census Population	County	Total Vote	Republican	Democratic	Other	Rep.-Dem. Plurality		Percentage Total Vote Rep.	Dem.	Major Vote Rep.	Dem.
217,955	ALACHUA	125,519	48,513	75,565	1,441	27,052	D	38.6%	60.2%	39.1%	60.9%
22,259	BAKER	11,059	8,672	2,327	60	6,345	R	78.4%	21.0%	78.8%	21.2%
148,217	BAY	81,127	56,683	23,653	791	33,030	R	69.9%	29.2%	70.6%	29.4%
26,088	BRADFORD	11,676	8,136	3,430	110	4,706	R	69.7%	29.4%	70.3%	29.7%
476,230	BREVARD	287,859	157,589	127,620	2,650	29,969	R	54.7%	44.3%	55.3%	44.7%
1,623,018	BROWARD	733,899	237,729	492,640	3,530	254,911	D	32.4%	67.1%	32.5%	67.5%
13,017	CALHOUN	6,244	4,345	1,821	78	2,524	R	69.6%	29.2%	70.5%	29.5%
141,627	CHARLOTTE	85,158	45,205	39,031	922	6,174	R	53.1%	45.8%	53.7%	46.3%
118,085	CITRUS	76,158	43,706	31,460	992	12,246	R	57.4%	41.3%	58.1%	41.9%
140,814	CLAY	94,577	67,203	26,697	677	40,506	R	71.1%	28.2%	71.6%	28.4%
251,377	COLLIER	141,988	86,379	54,450	1,159	31,929	R	60.8%	38.3%	61.3%	38.7%
56,513	COLUMBIA	28,128	18,670	9,171	287	9,499	R	66.4%	32.6%	67.1%	32.9%
32,209	DESOTO	10,131	5,632	4,383	116	1,249	R	55.6%	43.3%	56.2%	43.8%
13,827	DIXIE	7,264	5,194	1,925	145	3,269	R	71.5%	26.5%	73.0%	27.0%
778,879	DUVAL	415,761	210,537	202,618	2,606	7,919	R	50.6%	48.7%	51.0%	49.0%
294,410	ESCAMBIA	154,447	91,411	61,572	1,464	29,839	R	59.2%	39.9%	59.8%	40.2%
49,832	FLAGLER	49,031	23,951	24,726	354	775	D	48.8%	50.4%	49.2%	50.8%
11,057	FRANKLIN	6,029	3,818	2,134	77	1,684	R	63.3%	35.4%	64.1%	35.9%
45,087	GADSDEN	22,510	6,811	15,582	117	8,771	D	30.3%	69.2%	30.4%	69.6%
14,437	GILCHRIST	7,819	5,656	1,996	167	3,660	R	72.3%	25.5%	73.9%	26.1%
10,576	GLADES	3,358	1,938	1,381	39	557	R	57.7%	41.1%	58.4%	41.6%
13,332	GULF	7,205	4,980	2,149	76	2,831	R	69.1%	29.8%	69.9%	30.1%
13,327	HAMILTON	5,587	3,179	2,364	44	815	R	56.9%	42.3%	57.4%	42.6%
26,938	HARDEE	7,412	4,763	2,568	81	2,195	R	64.3%	34.6%	65.0%	35.0%
36,210	HENDRY	10,879	5,780	4,998	101	782	R	53.1%	45.9%	53.6%	46.4%
130,802	HERNANDO	87,901	45,021	41,886	994	3,135	R	51.2%	47.7%	51.8%	48.2%
87,366	HIGHLANDS	44,783	26,221	18,135	427	8,086	R	58.6%	40.5%	59.1%	40.9%
998,948	HILLSBOROUGH	513,312	236,355	272,963	3,994	36,608	D	46.0%	53.2%	46.4%	53.6%
18,564	HOLMES	8,589	7,033	1,446	110	5,587	R	81.9%	16.8%	82.9%	17.1%
112,947	INDIAN RIVER	70,591	40,176	29,710	705	10,466	R	56.9%	42.1%	57.5%	42.5%
46,755	JACKSON	21,565	13,717	7,671	177	6,046	R	63.6%	35.6%	64.1%	35.9%
12,902	JEFFERSON	7,957	3,797	4,088	72	291	D	47.7%	51.4%	48.2%	51.8%
7,022	LAFAYETTE	3,359	2,679	642	38	2,037	R	79.8%	19.1%	80.7%	19.3%
210,528	LAKE	146,926	82,802	62,948	1,176	19,854	R	56.4%	42.8%	56.8%	43.2%
440,888	LEE	269,276	147,608	119,701	1,967	27,907	R	54.8%	44.5%	55.2%	44.8%
239,452	LEON	148,608	55,705	91,747	1,156	36,042	D	37.5%	61.7%	37.8%	62.2%
34,450	LEVY	18,725	11,754	6,711	260	5,043	R	62.8%	35.8%	63.7%	36.3%
7,021	LIBERTY	3,278	2,339	895	44	1,444	R	71.4%	27.3%	72.3%	27.7%
18,733	MADISON	8,907	4,544	4,270	93	274	R	51.0%	47.9%	51.6%	48.4%
264,002	MANATEE	151,994	80,721	70,034	1,239	10,687	R	53.1%	46.1%	53.5%	46.5%
258,916	MARION	162,022	89,628	70,839	1,555	18,789	R	55.3%	43.7%	55.9%	44.1%
126,731	MARTIN	78,294	44,143	33,508	643	10,635	R	56.4%	42.8%	56.8%	43.2%
2,253,362	MIAMI-DADE	863,486	360,551	499,831	3,104	139,280	D	41.8%	57.9%	41.9%	58.1%
79,589	MONROE	40,272	18,933	20,907	432	1,974	D	47.0%	51.9%	47.5%	52.5%
57,663	NASSAU	38,304	27,403	10,618	283	16,785	R	71.5%	27.7%	72.1%	27.9%
170,498	OKALOOSA	95,529	68,789	25,872	868	42,917	R	72.0%	27.1%	72.7%	27.3%
35,910	OKEECHOBEE	12,786	7,561	5,108	117	2,453	R	59.1%	39.9%	59.7%	40.3%
896,344	ORANGE	462,711	186,832	273,009	2,870	86,177	D	40.4%	59.0%	40.6%	59.4%
172,493	OSCEOLA	100,670	40,086	59,962	622	19,876	D	39.8%	59.6%	40.1%	59.9%
1,131,184	PALM BEACH	590,500	226,037	361,271	3,192	135,234	D	38.3%	61.2%	38.5%	61.5%
344,765	PASCO	214,866	110,104	102,417	2,345	7,687	R	51.2%	47.7%	51.8%	48.2%
921,482	PINELLAS	463,282	210,066	248,299	4,917	38,233	D	45.3%	53.6%	45.8%	54.2%
483,924	POLK	244,833	128,878	113,865	2,090	15,013	R	52.6%	46.5%	53.1%	46.9%
70,423	PUTNAM	33,171	19,637	13,236	298	6,401	R	59.2%	39.9%	59.7%	40.3%
123,135	ST. JOHNS	105,844	69,222	35,791	831	33,431	R	65.4%	33.8%	65.9%	34.1%
192,695	ST. LUCIE	120,579	52,512	67,125	942	14,613	D	43.5%	55.7%	43.9%	56.1%
117,743	SANTA ROSA	76,185	55,972	19,470	743	36,502	R	73.5%	25.6%	74.2%	25.8%
325,957	SARASOTA	207,353	102,897	102,686	1,770	211	R	49.6%	49.5%	50.1%	49.9%
365,196	SEMINOLE	205,895	105,070	99,335	1,490	5,735	R	51.0%	48.2%	51.4%	48.6%
53,345	SUMTER	48,868	30,866	17,655	347	13,211	R	63.2%	36.1%	63.6%	36.4%

FLORIDA

PRESIDENT 2008

2000 Census Population	County	Total Vote	Republican	Democratic	Other	Rep.-Dem. Plurality	Total Vote Rep.	Dem.	Major Vote Rep.	Dem.
34,844	SUWANNEE	17,662	12,534	4,916	212	7,618 R	71.0%	27.8%	71.8%	28.2%
19,256	TAYLOR	9,366	6,457	2,803	106	3,654 R	68.9%	29.9%	69.7%	30.3%
13,442	UNION	5,293	3,940	1,300	53	2,640 R	74.4%	24.6%	75.2%	24.8%
443,343	VOLUSIA	243,824	113,938	127,795	2,091	13,857 D	46.7%	52.4%	47.1%	52.9%
22,863	WAKULLA	14,376	8,877	5,311	188	3,566 R	61.7%	36.9%	62.6%	37.4%
40,601	WALTON	27,046	19,561	7,174	311	12,387 R	72.3%	26.5%	73.2%	26.8%
20,973	WASHINGTON	11,131	8,178	2,863	90	5,315 R	73.5%	25.7%	74.1%	25.9%
15,982,378	TOTAL	8,390,744	4,045,624	4,282,074	63,046	236,450 D	48.2%	51.0%	48.6%	51.4%

FLORIDA

HOUSE OF REPRESENTATIVES

CD	Year	Total Vote	Republican Vote	Candidate	Democratic Vote	Candidate	Other Vote	Rep.-Dem. Plurality	Total Vote Rep.	Dem.	Major Vote Rep.	Dem.
1	2008	331,356	232,559	MILLER, JEFF*	98,797	BRYAN, JAMES JIM		133,762 R	70.2%	29.8%	70.2%	29.8%
1	2006	198,126	135,786	MILLER, JEFF*	62,340	ROBERTS, JOE		73,446 R	68.5%	31.5%	68.5%	31.5%
1	2004	309,110	236,604	MILLER, JEFF*	72,506	COUTO, MARK S.		164,098 R	76.5%	23.5%	76.5%	23.5%
1	2002	204,626	152,635	MILLER, JEFF*	51,972	ORAM, BERT	19	100,663 R	74.6%	25.4%	74.6%	25.4%
2	2008	350,367	133,404	MULLIGAN, MARK	216,804	BOYD, ALLEN*	159	83,400 D	38.1%	61.9%	38.1%	61.9%
2	2006					BOYD, ALLEN*		D				
2	2004	326,987	125,399	KILMER, BEV	201,577	BOYD, ALLEN*	11	76,178 D	38.3%	61.6%	38.4%	61.6%
2	2002	227,439	75,275	McGURK, TOM	152,164	BOYD, ALLEN*		76,889 D	33.1%	66.9%	33.1%	66.9%
3	2008			—		BROWN, CORRINE*		D				
3	2006			—		BROWN, CORRINE*		D				
3	2004	174,156		—	172,833	BROWN, CORRINE*	1,323	172,833 D		99.2%		100.0%
3	2002	149,213	60,747	CARROLL, JENIFER	88,462	BROWN, CORRINE*	4	27,715 D	40.7%	59.3%	40.7%	59.3%
4	2008	343,442	224,112	CRENSHAW, ANDER*	119,330	McGOVERN, JAY		104,782 R	65.3%	34.7%	65.3%	34.7%
4	2006	203,479	141,759	CRENSHAW, ANDER*	61,704	HARMS, ROBERT J.	16	80,055 R	69.7%	30.3%	69.7%	30.3%
4	2004	257,327	256,157	CRENSHAW, ANDER*		—	1,170	256,157 R	99.5%		100.0%	
4	2002	171,661	171,152	CRENSHAW, ANDER*		—	509	171,152 R	99.7%		100.0%	
5	2008	433,632	265,186	BROWN-WAITE, GINNY*	168,446	RUSSELL, JOHN		96,740 R	61.2%	38.8%	61.2%	38.8%
5	2006	271,380	162,421	BROWN-WAITE, GINNY*	108,959	RUSSELL, JOHN		53,462 R	59.9%	40.1%	59.9%	40.1%
5	2004	364,488	240,315	BROWN-WAITE, GINNY*	124,140	WHITTEL, ROBERT G.	33	116,175 R	65.9%	34.1%	65.9%	34.1%
5	2002	254,671	121,998	BROWN-WAITE, GINNY	117,758	THURMAN, KAREN L.*	14,915	4,240 R	47.9%	46.2%	50.9%	49.1%
6	2008	374,957	228,302	STEARNS, CLIFF*	146,655	CUNHA, TIM		81,647 R	60.9%	39.1%	60.9%	39.1%
6	2006	228,129	136,601	STEARNS, CLIFF*	91,528	BRUDERLY, DAVID E.		45,073 R	59.9%	40.1%	59.9%	40.1%
6	2004	327,853	211,137	STEARNS, CLIFF*	116,680	BRUDERLY, DAVID E.	36	94,457 R	64.4%	35.6%	64.4%	35.6%
6	2002	216,616	141,570	STEARNS, CLIFF*	75,046	BRUDERLY, DAVID E.		66,524 R	65.4%	34.6%	65.4%	34.6%
7	2008	385,013	238,721	MICA, JOHN L.*	146,292	ARMITAGE, FAYE		92,429 R	62.0%	38.0%	62.0%	38.0%
7	2006	237,240	149,656	MICA, JOHN L.*	87,584	CHAGNON, JOHN F.		62,072 R	63.1%	36.9%	63.1%	36.9%
7	2004			MICA, JOHN L.*		—		R				
7	2002	238,591	142,147	MICA, JOHN L.*	96,444	HOGAN, WAYNE		45,703 R	59.6%	40.4%	59.6%	40.4%

FLORIDA

HOUSE OF REPRESENTATIVES

| | | | Republican | | Democratic | | | | Percentage | | | |
| | | | | | | | | | Total Vote | | Major Vote | |
CD	Year	Total Vote	Vote	Candidate	Vote	Candidate	Other Vote	Rep.-Dem. Plurality	Rep.	Dem.	Rep.	Dem.
8	2008	332,344	159,490	KELLER, RIC*	172,854	GRAYSON, ALAN		13,364 D	48.0%	52.0%	48.0%	52.0%
8	2006	180,444	95,258	KELLER, RIC*	82,526	STUART, CHARLIE	2,660	12,732 R	52.8%	45.7%	53.6%	46.4%
8	2004	284,575	172,232	KELLER, RIC*	112,343	MURRAY, STEPHEN		59,889 R	60.5%	39.5%	60.5%	39.5%
8	2002	189,596	123,497	KELLER, RIC*	66,099	DIAZ, EDDIE		57,398 R	65.1%	34.9%	65.1%	34.9%
9	2008	348,378	216,591	BILIRAKIS, GUS MICHAEL*	126,346	MITCHELL, BILL	5,441	90,245 R	62.2%	36.3%	63.2%	36.8%
9	2006	220,013	123,016	BILIRAKIS, GUS MICHAEL	96,978	BUSANSKY, PHYLLIS	19	26,038 R	55.9%	44.1%	55.9%	44.1%
9	2004	284,278	284,035	BILIRAKIS, MICHAEL*	—		243	284,035 R	99.9%		100.0%	
9	2002	237,008	169,369	BILIRAKIS, MICHAEL*	67,623	KALOGIANIS, CHUCK	16	101,746 R	71.5%	28.5%	71.5%	28.5%
10	2008	301,220	182,781	YOUNG, C.W. BILL*	118,430	HACKWORTH, BOB	9	64,351 R	60.7%	39.3%	60.7%	39.3%
10	2006	199,445	131,488	YOUNG, C.W. BILL*	67,950	SIMPSON, SAMM	7	63,538 R	65.9%	34.1%	65.9%	34.1%
10	2004	298,833	207,175	YOUNG, C.W. BILL*	91,658	DERRY, ROBERT D. "BOB"		115,517 R	69.3%	30.7%	69.3%	30.7%
10	2002			YOUNG, C.W. BILL*		—		R				
11	2008	256,931	72,825	ADAMS, EDDIE JR.	184,106	CASTOR, KATHY*		111,281 D	28.3%	71.7%	28.3%	71.7%
11	2006	139,942	42,454	ADAMS, EDDIE JR.	97,470	CASTOR, KATHY	18	55,016 D	30.3%	69.7%	30.3%	69.7%
11	2004	223,481		—	191,780	DAVIS, JIM*	31,701	191,780 D		85.8%		100.0%
11	2002			—		DAVIS, JIM*		D				
12	2008	323,163	185,698	PUTNAM, ADAM H.*	137,465	TUDOR, DOUG		48,233 R	57.5%	42.5%	57.5%	42.5%
12	2006	180,064	124,452	PUTNAM, ADAM H.*	—		55,612	124,452 R	69.1%		100.0%	
12	2004	276,169	179,204	PUTNAM, ADAM H.*	96,965	HAGENMAIER, BOB		82,239 R	64.9%	35.1%	64.9%	35.1%
12	2002			PUTNAM, ADAM H.*		—		R				
13	2008	367,996	204,382	BUCHANAN, VERN*	137,967	JENNINGS, CHRISTINE	25,647	66,415 R	55.5%	37.5%	59.7%	40.3%
13	2006	238,249	119,309	BUCHANAN, VERN	118,940	JENNINGS, CHRISTINE		369 R	50.1%	49.9%	50.1%	49.9%
13	2004	344,438	190,477	HARRIS, KATHERINE*	153,961	SCHNEIDER, JAN		36,516 R	55.3%	44.7%	55.3%	44.7%
13	2002	253,809	139,048	HARRIS, KATHERINE	114,739	SCHNEIDER, JAN	22	24,309 R	54.8%	45.2%	54.8%	45.2%
14	2008	377,891	224,602	MACK, CONNIE*	93,590	NEELD, ROBERT M.	59,699	131,012 R	59.4%	24.8%	70.6%	29.4%
14	2006	235,539	151,615	MACK, CONNIE*	83,920	NEELD, ROBERT M.	4	67,695 R	64.4%	35.6%	64.4%	35.6%
14	2004	335,334	226,662	MACK, CONNIE	108,672	NEELD, ROBERT M.		117,990 R	67.6%	32.4%	67.6%	32.4%
14	2002			GOSS, PORTER J.*		—		R				
15	2008	361,871	192,151	POSEY, BILL	151,951	BLYTHE, STEPHEN	17,769	40,200 R	53.1%	42.0%	55.8%	44.2%
15	2006	223,799	125,965	WELDON, DAVE*	97,834	BOWMAN, BOB		28,131 R	56.3%	43.7%	56.3%	43.7%
15	2004	321,926	210,388	WELDON, DAVE*	111,538	PRISTOOP, SIMON		98,850 R	65.4%	34.6%	65.4%	34.6%
15	2002	231,857	146,414	WELDON, DAVE*	85,433	TSO, JIM	10	60,981 R	63.1%	36.8%	63.2%	36.8%
16	2008	349,247	209,874	ROONEY, TOM	139,373	MAHONEY, TIM*		70,501 R	60.1%	39.9%	60.1%	39.9%
16	2006	233,773	111,415	NEGRON, JOE#	115,832	MAHONEY, TIM	6,526	4,417 D	47.7%	49.5%	49.0%	51.0%
16	2004	316,810	215,563	FOLEY, MARK*	101,247	FISHER, JEFF		114,316 R	68.0%	32.0%	68.0%	32.0%
16	2002	223,340	176,171	FOLEY, MARK*	—		47,169	176,171 R	78.9%		100.0%	
17	2008			—		MEEK, KENDRICK B.*		D				
17	2006	90,686		—	90,663	MEEK, KENDRICK B.*	23	90,663 D		100.0%		100.0%
17	2004	179,424		—	178,690	MEEK, KENDRICK B.*	734	178,690 D		99.6%		100.0%
17	2002	113,822		—	113,749	MEEK, KENDRICK B.	73	113,749 D		99.9%		100.0%
18	2008	242,989	140,617	ROS-LEHTINEN, ILEANA*	102,372	TADDEO, ANNETTE		38,245 R	57.9%	42.1%	57.9%	42.1%
18	2006	128,132	79,631	ROS-LEHTINEN, ILEANA*	48,499	PATLAK, DAVID "BIG DAVE"	2	31,132 R	62.1%	37.9%	62.1%	37.9%
18	2004	221,928	143,647	ROS-LEHTINEN, ILEANA*	78,281	SHELDON, SAM		65,366 R	64.7%	35.3%	64.7%	35.3%
18	2002	149,787	103,512	ROS-LEHTINEN, ILEANA*	42,852	CHOTE, RAY	3,423	60,660 R	69.1%	28.6%	70.7%	29.3%
19	2008	306,036	83,357	LYNCH, EDWARD J.	202,465	WEXLER, ROBERT*	20,214	119,108 D	27.2%	66.2%	29.2%	70.8%
19	2006			—		WEXLER, ROBERT*		D				
19	2004			—		WEXLER, ROBERT*		D				
19	2002	217,224	60,477	MERKL, JACK	156,747	WEXLER, ROBERT*		96,270 D	27.8%	72.2%	27.8%	72.2%

FLORIDA

HOUSE OF REPRESENTATIVES

CD	Year	Total Vote	Republican Vote	Republican Candidate	Democratic Vote	Democratic Candidate	Other Vote	Rep.-Dem. Plurality	Total Vote Rep.	Total Vote Dem.	Major Vote Rep.	Major Vote Dem.
20	2008	261,799		—	202,832	WASSERMAN SCHULTZ, DEBBIE*	58,967	202,832 D		77.5%		100.0%
20	2006			—		WASSERMAN SCHULTZ, DEBBIE*		D				
20	2004	272,408	81,213	HOSTETTER, MARGARET	191,195	WASSERMAN-SCHULTZ, DEBBIE		109,982 D	29.8%	70.2%	29.8%	70.2%
20	2002			—		DEUTSCH, PETER*		D				
21	2008	237,002	137,226	DIAZ-BALART, LINCOLN*	99,776	MARTINEZ, RAUL L.		37,450 R	57.9%	42.1%	57.9%	42.1%
21	2006	112,306	66,784	DIAZ-BALART, LINCOLN*	45,522	GONZALEZ, FRANK J.		21,262 R	59.5%	40.5%	59.5%	40.5%
21	2004	201,243	146,507	DIAZ-BALART, LINCOLN*		—	54,736	146,507 R	72.8%		100.0%	
21	2002			DIAZ-BALART, LINCOLN*		—		R				
22	2008	309,151	140,104	WEST, ALLEN	169,041	KLEIN, RON*	6	28,937 D	45.3%	54.7%	45.3%	54.7%
22	2006	213,605	100,663	SHAW, E. CLAY JR.*	108,688	KLEIN, RON	4,254	8,025 D	47.1%	50.9%	48.1%	51.9%
22	2004	306,726	192,581	SHAW, E. CLAY JR.*	108,258	RORAPAUGH, ROBIN	5,887	84,323 R	62.8%	35.3%	64.0%	36.0%
22	2002	217,115	131,930	SHAW, E. CLAY JR.*	83,265	ROBERTS, CAROL A.	1,920	48,665 R	60.8%	38.4%	61.3%	38.7%
23	2008	210,306	37,431	THORPE, MARION D. JR.	172,835	HASTINGS, ALCEE L.*	40	135,404 D	17.8%	82.2%	17.8%	82.2%
23	2006			—		HASTINGS, ALCEE L.*		D				
23	2004			—		HASTINGS, ALCEE L.*		D				
23	2002	124,338	27,986	LAURIE, CHARLES	96,347	HASTINGS, ALCEE L.*	5	68,361 D	22.5%	77.5%	22.5%	77.5%
24	2008	369,370	151,863	FEENEY, TOM*	211,284	KOSMAS, SUZANNE M.	6,223	59,421 D	41.1%	57.2%	41.8%	58.2%
24	2006	213,658	123,795	FEENEY, TOM*	89,863	CURTIS, CLINT		33,932 R	57.9%	42.1%	57.9%	42.1%
24	2004			FEENEY, TOM*		—		R				
24	2002	219,243	135,576	FEENEY, TOM	83,667	JACOBS, HARRY		51,909 R	61.8%	38.2%	61.8%	38.2%
25	2008	246,711	130,891	DIAZ-BALART, MARIO*	115,820	GARCIA, JOE		15,071 R	53.1%	46.9%	53.1%	46.9%
25	2006	103,933	60,765	DIAZ-BALART, MARIO*	43,168	CALDERIN, MICHAEL		17,597 R	58.5%	41.5%	58.5%	41.5%
25	2004			DIAZ-BALART, MARIO*		—		R				
25	2002	126,602	81,845	DIAZ-BALART, MARIO	44,757	BETANCOURT, ANNIE		37,088 R	64.6%	35.4%	64.6%	35.4%
TOTAL	2008	7,421,172	3,792,167		3,434,831		194,174	357,336 R	51.1%	46.3%	52.5%	47.5%
TOTAL	2006	3,851,942	2,182,833		1,599,968		69,141	582,865 R	56.7%	41.5%	57.7%	42.3%
TOTAL	2004	5,627,494	3,319,296		2,212,324		95,874	1,106,972 R	59.0%	39.3%	60.0%	40.0%
TOTAL	2002	3,766,558	2,161,349		1,537,124		68,085	624,225 R	57.4%	40.8%	58.4%	41.6%

Notes: In Florida districts where a candidate had no opposition, including write-ins, no vote was taken. An asterisk (*) denotes incumbent. A pound sign (#) indicates that Republican Rep. Mark Foley resigned from the House in late September 2006, too late to have his name removed from the general election ballot. Votes cast for Foley were credited to Joe Negron, the candidate selected by the Republican Party to replace Foley.

FLORIDA
GENERAL AND PRIMARY ELECTIONS

2008 GENERAL ELECTIONS

President   Other vote was 28,124 Ecology Party of Florida (Ralph Nader); 17,218 Libertarian (Bob Barr); 7,915 Constitution (Chuck Baldwin); 2,887 Green (Cynthia A. McKinney); 2,550 America's Independent Party of Florida (Alan Keyes); 1,516 Party for Socialism and Liberation–Florida (Gloria La Riva); 795 Boston Tea Party of Florida (Charles Jay); 533 Socialist Workers (James Harris); 419 Objectivist Party of Florida (Thomas Robert Stevens); 405 Socialist (Brian Moore); 391 write-in (Gary Nettles); 293 Prohibition (Gene Amondson).

House   Other vote was:

CD 1
CD 2   159 write-in (Robert Ortiz).
CD 3
CD 4
CD 5
CD 6
CD 7
CD 8
CD 9   3,394 No Party Affiliation (John "Johnny K" Kalimnios); 2,042 Term Limits for the
          United States Congress (Richard O. Emmons); 5 write-in (Andrew Pasayan).
CD 10   9 write-in (Don Callahan).
CD 11
CD 12
CD 13   20,289 No Party Affiliation (Jan Schneider); 5,358 No Party Affiliation (Don Baldauf).
CD 14   54,750 No Party Affiliation (Burt Saunders); 4,949 No Party Affiliation (Jeff George).
CD 15   14,274 No Party Affiliation (Frank Zilaitis); 3,495 No Party Affiliation (Trevor Lowing).
CD 16
CD 17
CD 18
CD 19   20,214 No Party Affiliation (Ben Graber).
CD 20   58,958 No Party Affiliation (Margaret Hostetter); 9 write-in (Marc Luzietti).
CD 21
CD 22   6 write-in (Piotr Blass).
CD 23   40 write-in (April Cook).
CD 24   6,223 No Party Affiliation (Gaurav Bhola).
CD 25

2008 PRIMARY ELECTIONS

Primary   January 29, 2008 (President)   **Registration**

Democratic	4,389,698
Republican	3,924,081
Independepdent Party of Florida	241,752
Independence Party of Florida	64,057
Libertarian	15,384
Independent Democrats of Florida	7,165
Green	5,734
Other Parties	10,575
No Party Affiliation	1,960,073
TOTAL	*10,618,519*

August 26, 2008 (Congress) (as of July 28, 2008)

Primary Type   Closed—Only registered Democrats and Republicans could vote in their party's primary, with the exception of races where there were to be no other candidates (including write-ins) on the general election ballot. Then, the contested primary would be open to all voters.

FLORIDA

GENERAL AND PRIMARY ELECTIONS

	REPUBLICAN PRIMARIES			DEMOCRATIC PRIMARIES		
President	John McCain	701,761	36.0%	Hillary Clinton	870,986	49.8%
	Mitt Romney	604,932	31.0%	Barack Obama	576,214	32.9%
	Rudolph Giuliani	286,089	14.7%	John Edwards	251,562	14.4%
	Mike Huckabee	262,681	13.5%	Joseph R. Biden Jr.	15,704	0.9%
	Ron Paul	62,887	3.2%	Bill Richardson	14,999	0.9%
	Fred Thompson	22,668	1.2%	Dennis J. Kucinich	9,703	0.6%
	Alan Keyes	4,060	0.2%	Christopher J. Dodd	5,477	0.3%
	Duncan Hunter	2,847	0.1%	Mike Gravel	5,275	0.3%
	Tom Tancredo	1,573	0.1%			
	TOTAL	*1,949,498*		*TOTAL*	*1,749,920*	
Congressional District 1	Jeff Miller*	Unopposed		James Jim Bryan	Unopposed	
Congressional District 2	Mark Mulligan	28,734	68.0%	Allen Boyd*	Unopposed	
	Eddie Hendry	13,505	32.0%			
	TOTAL	*42,239*				
Congressional District 3	No Republican candidate			Corrine Brown*	Unopposed	
Congressional District 4	Ander Crenshaw*	Unopposed		Jay McGovern	Unopposed	
Congressional District 5	Ginny Brown-Waite*	49,134	80.1%	John Russell	16,900	50.8%
	Jim King	12,232	19.9%	Carol Castagnero	12,854	38.6%
				H. David Werder	3,532	10.6%
	TOTAL	*61,366*		*TOTAL*	*33,286*	
Congressional District 6	Cliff Stearns*	Unopposed		Tim Cunha	Unopposed	
Congressional District 7	John L. Mica*	Unopposed		Faye Armitage	18,018	63.9%
				Clyde Malloy	10,159	36.1%
				TOTAL	*28,177*	
Congressional District 8	Ric Keller*	22,198	53.1%	Alan Grayson	16,104	48.5%
	Todd Long	19,640	46.9%	Charlie Stuart	9,146	27.5%
				Mike Smith	5,727	17.2%
				Quoc Ba Van	1,219	3.7%
				Alexander Fry	1,030	3.1%
	TOTAL	*41,838*		*TOTAL*	*33,226*	
Congressional District 9	Gus Michael Bilirakis*	Unopposed		Bill Mitchell	7,726	37.4%
				John Dicks	7,039	34.1%
				Anita de Palma	5,902	28.6%
				TOTAL	*20,667*	
Congressional District 10	C.W. Bill Young*	Unopposed		Bob Hackworth	10,420	46.7%
				Samm "Denise" Simpson	6,445	28.9%
				Max Linn	5,424	24.3%
				TOTAL	*22,289*	
Congressional District 11	Eddie Adams Jr.	Unopposed		Kathy Castor*	Unopposed	
Congressional District 12	Adam H. Putnam*	Unopposed		Doug Tudor	Unopposed	
Congressional District 13	Vern Buchanan*	Unopposed		Christine Jennings	Unopposed	
Congressional District 14	Connie Mack*	Unopposed		Robert M. Neeld	Unopposed	

FLORIDA

GENERAL AND PRIMARY ELECTIONS

	REPUBLICAN PRIMARIES			DEMOCRATIC PRIMARIES		
Congressional District 15	Bill Posey	40,892	76.8%	Stephen Blythe	19,281	65.6%
	Alan Bergman	7,809	14.7%	Paul Rancatore	10,089	34.4%
	Kevin Lehoullier	4,519	8.5%			
	TOTAL	53,220		TOTAL	29,370	
Congressional District 16	Tom Rooney	20,637	36.7%	Tim Mahoney*	Unopposed	
	Gayle Harrell	19,626	34.9%			
	Hal Valeche	15,916	28.3%			
	TOTAL	56,179				
Congressional District 17	No Republican candidate			Kendrick B. Meek*	Unopposed	
Congressional District 18	Ileana Ros-Lehtinen*	Unopposed		Annette Taddeo	Unopposed	
Congressional District 19	Edward J. Lynch	Unopposed		Robert Wexler*	Unopposed	
Congressional District 20	No Republican candidate			Debbie Wasserman Schultz*	Unopposed	
Congressional District 21	Lincoln Diaz-Balart*	Unopposed		Raul L. Martinez	Unopposed	
Congressional District 22	Allen West	Unopposed		Ron Klein*	20,507	85.1%
				Paul Francis Renneisen	3,603	14.9%
				TOTAL	24,110	
Congressional District 23	Marion D. Thorpe Jr.	Unopposed		Alcee L. Hastings*	31,182	88.0%
				Ray Torres Sanchez	4,235	12.0%
				TOTAL	35,417	
Congressional District 24	Tom Feeney*	27,048	76.6%	Suzanne M. Kosmas	18,672	72.3%
	Jason Paul Davis	8,277	23.4%	Clint Curtis	7,137	27.7%
	TOTAL	35,325		TOTAL	25,809	
Congressional District 25	Mario Diaz-Balart*	Unopposed		Joe Garcia	Unopposed	

Notes: An asterisk (*) denotes incumbent. The names of unopposed candidates did not appear on the primary ballot; therefore, no votes were cast for these candidates.

130

GEORGIA

Congressional districts first established for elections held in 2002
13 members

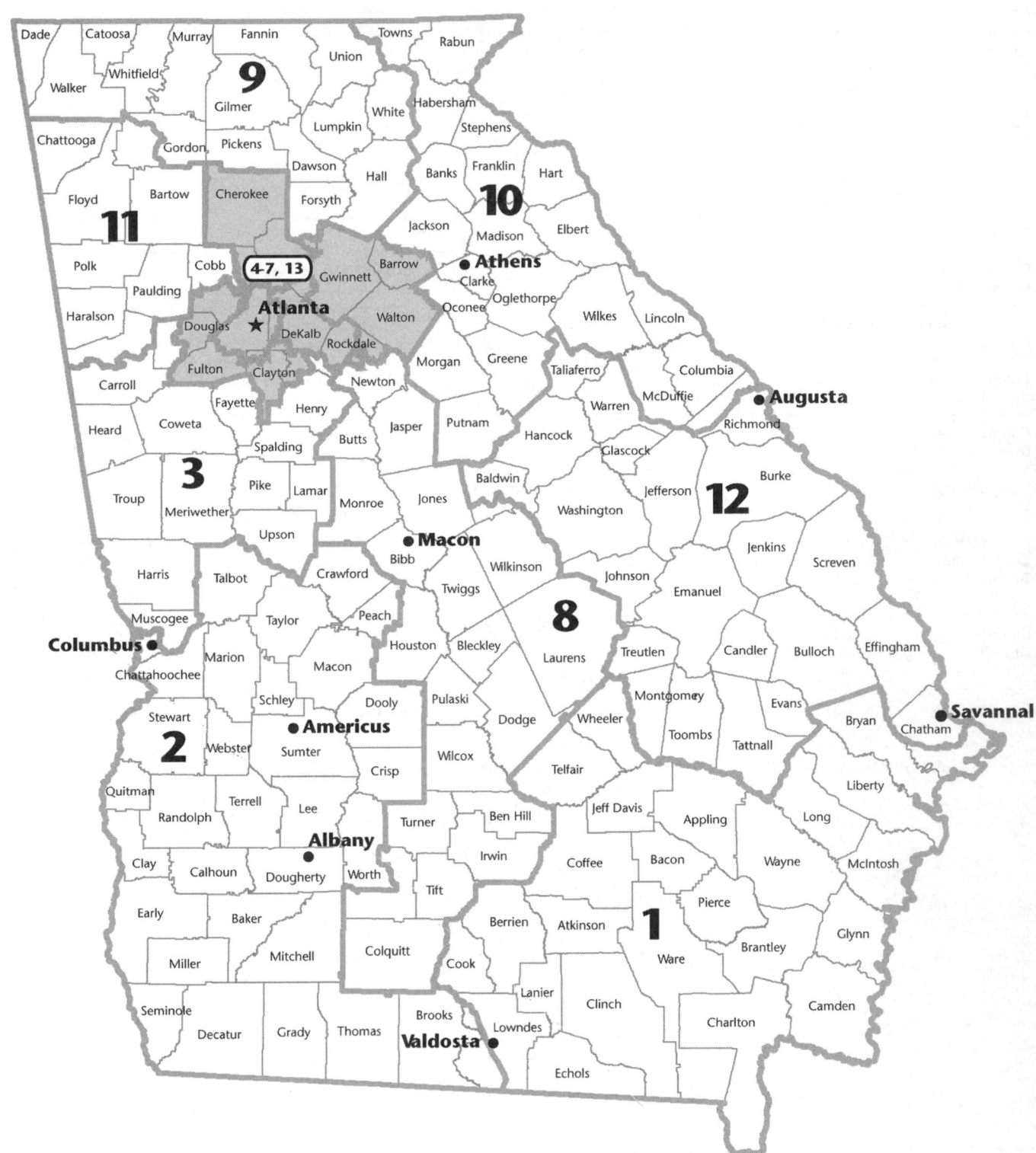

GEORGIA

Atlanta Area

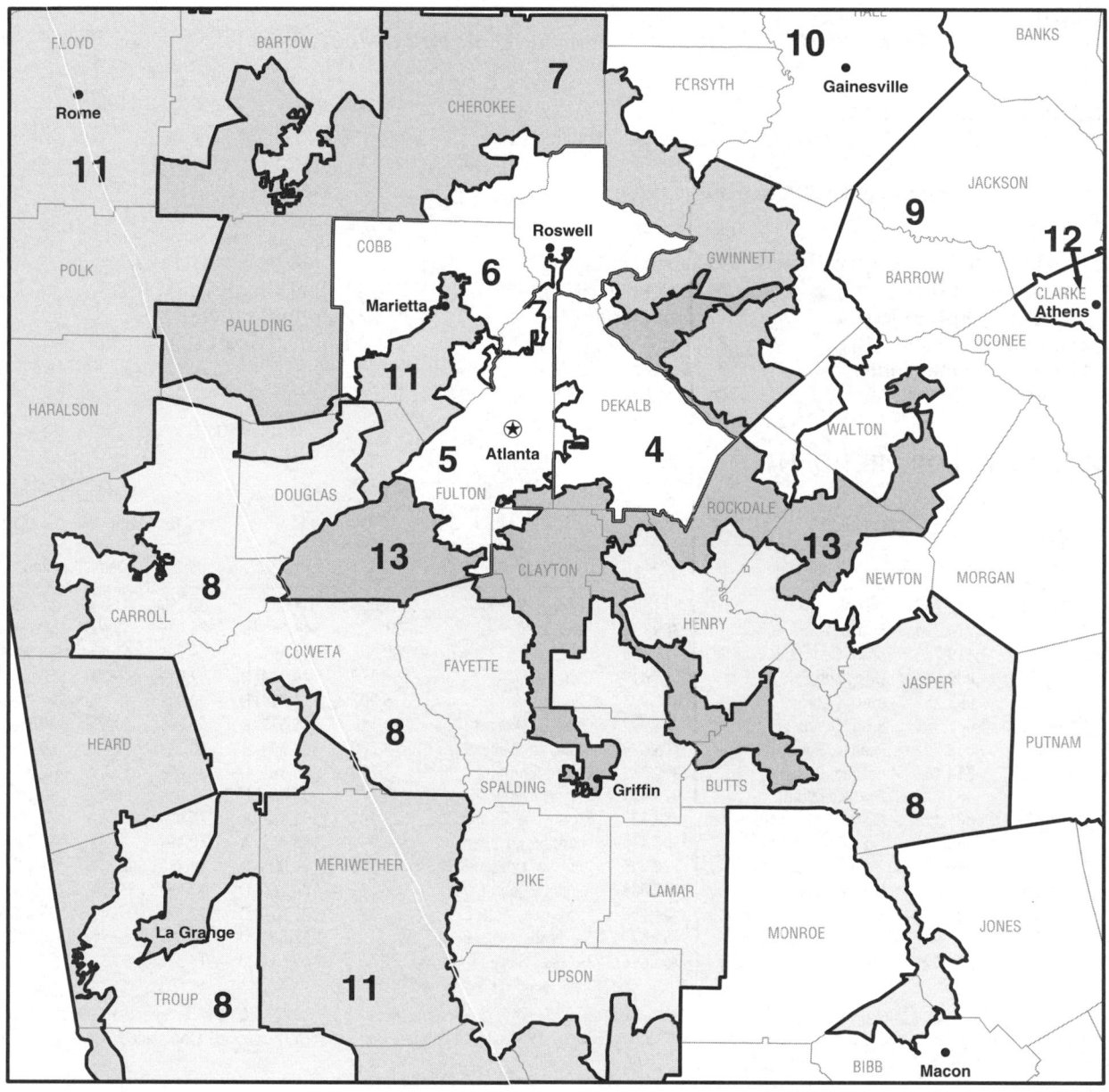

GEORGIA

GOVERNOR
Sonny Perdue (R). Reelected 2006 to a four-year term. Previously elected 2002.

SENATORS (2 Republicans)
Saxby Chambliss (R). Reelected 2008 to a six-year term. Previously elected 2002.

Johnny Isakson (R). Elected 2004 to a six-year term.

REPRESENTATIVES (7 Republicans, 6 Democrats)
1. Jack Kingston (R)
2. Sanford D. Bishop Jr. (D)
3. Lynn Westmoreland (R)
4. Henry C. "Hank" Johnson Jr. (D)
5. John Lewis (D)
6. Tom Price (R)
7. John Linder (R)
8. Jim Marshall (D)
9. Nathan Deal (R)
10. Paul Broun (R)
11. Phil Gingrey (R)
12. John Barrow (D)
13. David Scott (D)

POSTWAR VOTE FOR PRESIDENT

		Republican		Democratic				Total Vote		Major Vote	
Year	Total Vote	Vote	Candidate	Vote	Candidate	Other Vote	Plurality	Rep.	Dem.	Rep.	Dem.
2008	3,924,486	2,048,759	McCain, John	1,844,123	Obama, Barack	31,604	204,636 R	52.2%	47.0%	52.6%	47.4%
2004	3,301,875	1,914,254	Bush, George W.	1,366,149	Kerry, John	21,472	548,105 R	58.0%	41.4%	58.4%	41.6%
2000**	2,596,645	1,419,720	Bush, George W.	1,116,230	Gore, Al	60,695	303,490 R	54.7%	43.0%	56.0%	44.0%
1996**	2,299,071	1,080,843	Dole, Bob	1,053,849	Clinton, Bill	164,379	26,994 R	47.0%	45.8%	50.6%	49.4%
1992**	2,321,125	995,252	Bush, George	1,008,966	Clinton, Bill	316,907	13,714 D	42.9%	43.5%	49.7%	50.3%
1988	1,809,672	1,081,331	Bush, George	714,792	Dukakis, Michael S.	13,549	366,539 R	59.8%	39.5%	60.2%	39.8%
1984	1,776,120	1,068,722	Reagan, Ronald	706,628	Mondale, Walter F.	770	362,094 R	60.2%	39.8%	60.2%	39.8%
1980**	1,596,695	654,168	Reagan, Ronald	890,733	Carter, Jimmy	51,794	236,565 D	41.0%	55.8%	42.3%	57.7%
1976	1,467,458	483,743	Ford, Gerald R.	979,409	Carter, Jimmy	4,306	495,666 D	33.0%	66.7%	33.1%	66.9%
1972	1,174,772	881,496	Nixon, Richard M.	289,529	McGovern, George S.	3,747	591,967 R	75.0%	24.6%	75.3%	24.7%
1968**	1,250,266	380,111	Nixon, Richard M.	334,440	Humphrey, Hubert H.	535,715	155,439 A	30.4%	26.7%	53.2%	46.8%
1964	1,139,335	616,584	Goldwater, Barry M.	522,556	Johnson, Lyndon B.	195	94,028 R	54.1%	45.9%	54.1%	45.9%
1960	733,349	274,472	Nixon, Richard M.	458,638	Kennedy, John F.	239	184,166 D	37.4%	62.5%	37.4%	62.6%
1956	669,655	222,778	Eisenhower, Dwight D.	444,688	Stevenson, Adlai E.	2,189	221,910 D	33.3%	66.4%	33.4%	66.6%
1952	655,785	198,961	Eisenhower, Dwight D.	456,823	Stevenson, Adlai E.	1	257,862 D	30.3%	69.7%	30.3%	69.7%
1948**	418,844	76,691	Dewey, Thomas E.	254,646	Truman, Harry S.	87,507	169,511 D	18.3%	60.8%	23.1%	76.9%

**In past elections, the other vote included: 2000 - 13,273 Green (Ralph Nader); 1996 - 146,337 Reform (Ross Perot); 1992 - 309,657 Independent (Perot); 1980 - 36,055 Independent (John Anderson); 1968 - 535,550 American Independent (George Wallace); 1948 - 85,135 States' Rights (Strom Thurmond), who placed second statewide. Wallace carried Georgia in 1968 with 42.8 percent of the vote.

GEORGIA

POSTWAR VOTE FOR GOVERNOR

Year	Total Vote	Republican Vote	Republican Candidate	Democratic Vote	Democratic Candidate	Other Vote	Rep.-Dem. Plurality	Total Vote Rep.	Total Vote Dem.	Major Vote Rep.	Major Vote Dem.
2006	2,122,258	1,229,724	Perdue, Sonny	811,049	Taylor, Mark	81,485	418,675 R	57.9%	38.2%	60.3%	39.7%
2002	2,027,177	1,041,700	Perdue, Sonny	937,070	Barnes, Roy	48,407	104,630 R	51.4%	46.2%	52.6%	47.4%
1998	1,792,808	790,201	Millner, Guy	941,076	Barnes, Roy	61,531	150,875 D	44.1%	52.5%	45.6%	54.4%
1994	1,545,328	756,371	Millner, Guy	788,926	Miller, Zell	31	32,555 D	48.9%	51.1%	48.9%	51.1%
1990	1,449,682	645,625	Isakson, Johnny	766,662	Miller, Zell	37,395	121,037 D	44.5%	52.9%	45.7%	54.3%
1986	1,175,114	346,512	Davis, Guy	828,465	Harris, Joe Frank	137	481,953 D	29.5%	70.5%	29.5%	70.5%
1982	1,169,041	434,496	Bell, Robert H.	734,090	Harris, Joe Frank	455	299,594 D	37.2%	62.8%	37.2%	62.8%
1978	662,862	128,139	Cook, Rodney M.	534,572	Busbee, George	151	406,433 D	19.3%	80.6%	19.3%	80.7%
1974	936,438	289,113	Thompson, Ronnie	646,777	Busbee, George	548	357,664 D	30.9%	69.1%	30.9%	69.1%
1970	1,046,663	424,983	Suit, Hal	620,419	Carter, Jimmy	1,261	195,436 D	40.6%	59.3%	40.7%	59.3%
1966**	975,019	453,665	Callaway, Howard H.	450,626	Maddox, Lester	70,728	3,039 R	46.5%	46.2%	50.2%	49.8%
1962	311,691		—	311,524	Sanders, Carl E.	167	311,524 D		99.9%		100.0%
1958	168,497		—	168,414	Vandiver, Ernest	83	168,414 D		100.0%		100.0%
1954	331,966		—	331,899	Griffin, Marvin	67	331,899 D		100.0%		100.0%
1950	234,430		—	230,771	Talmadge, Herman	3,659	230,771 D		98.4%		100.0%
1948S	363,763		—	354,711	Talmadge, Herman	9,052	354,711 D		97.5%		100.0%
1946	145,403		—	143,279	Talmadge, Herman	2,124	143,279 D		98.5%		100.0%

Notes: In 1966 in the absence of a majority for any candidate, the state legislature elected Democrat Lester Maddox to a four-year term. The 1948 election was for a short term to fill a vacancy. The Republican Party did not run a candidate in the 1946, 1948, 1950, 1954, 1958, and 1962 gubernatorial elections.

POSTWAR VOTE FOR SENATOR

Year	Total Vote	Republican Vote	Republican Candidate	Democratic Vote	Democratic Candidate	Other Vote	Rep.-Dem. Plurality	Total Vote Rep.	Total Vote Dem.	Major Vote Rep.	Major Vote Dem.
2008**	2,137,956	1,228,033	Chambliss, Saxby	909,923	Martin, Jim		318,110 R	57.4%	42.6%	57.4%	42.6%
2004	3,220,981	1,864,202	Isakson, Johnny	1,287,690	Majette, Denise L.	69,089	576,512 R	57.9%	40.0%	59.1%	40.9%
2002	2,030,608	1,071,464	Chambliss, Saxby	932,156	Cleland, Max	26,988	139,308 R	52.8%	45.9%	53.5%	46.5%
2000S	2,428,510	920,478	Mattingly, Mack	1,413,224	Miller, Zell	94,808	492,746 D	37.9%	58.2%	39.4%	60.6%
1998	1,753,911	918,540	Coverdell, Paul	791,904	Coles, Michael	43,467	126,636 R	52.4%	45.2%	53.7%	46.3%
1996	2,259,232	1,073,969	Millner, Guy	1,103,993	Cleland, Max	81.270	30,024 D	47.5%	48.9%	49.3%	50.7%
1992**	1,253,991	635,114	Coverdell, Paul	618,877	Fowler, Wyche		16,237 R	50.6%	49.4%	50.6%	49.4%
1990	1,033,517		—	1,033,439	Nunn, Sam	78	1,033,439 D		100.0%		100.0%
1986	1,225,008	601,241	Mattingly, Mack	623,707	Fowler, Wyche	60	22,466 D	49.1%	50.9%	49.1%	50.9%
1984	1,681,344	337,196	Hicks, Jon Michael	1,344,104	Nunn, Sam	44	1,006,908 D	20.1%	79.9%	20.1%	79.9%
1980	1,580,340	803,686	Mattingly, Mack	776,143	Talmadge, Herman	511	27,543 R	50.9%	49.1%	50.9%	49.1%
1978	645,164	108,808	Stokes, John W.	536,320	Nunn, Sam	36	427,512 D	16.9%	83.1%	16.9%	83.1%
1974	874,555	246,866	Johnson, Jerry R.	627,376	Talmadge, Herman	313	380,510 D	28.2%	71.7%	28.2%	71.8%
1972	1,178,708	542,331	Thompson, Fletcher	635,970	Nunn, Sam	407	93,639 D	46.0%	54.0%	46.0%	54.0%
1968	1,141,889	256,796	Patton, E. Earl	885,093	Talmadge, Herman		628,297 D	22.5%	77.5%	22.5%	77.5%
1966	622,371		—	622,043	Russell, Richard B.	328	622,043 D		99.9%		100.0%
1962	306,250		—	306,250	Talmadge, Herman		306,250 D		100.0%		100.0%
1960	576,495		—	576,140	Russell, Richard B.	355	576,140 D		99.9%		100.0%
1956	541,267		—	541,094	Talmadge, Herman	173	541,094 D		100.0%		100.0%
1954	333,936		—	333,917	Russell, Richard B.	19	333,917 D		100.0%		100.0%
1950	261,293		—	261,290	George, Walter F.	3	261,290 D		100.0%		100.0%
1948	362,504		—	362,104	Russell, Richard B.	400	362,104 D		99.9%		100.0%

Notes: **In 1992 and 2008, no candidate drew a majority of the general election vote required by state law, forcing runoff elections whose results are listed above for each year. In 2008 the November general election vote was 1,867,097 (49.8 percent) Republican (Saxby Chambliss); 1,757,393 (46.8 percent) Democratic (Jim Martin); and 127,995 (3.4 percent) Other. In 1992 the November general election vote was 1,073,282 (47.7 percent) Republican (Paul Coverdell); 1,108,416 (49.2 percent) Democratic (Wyche Fowler); and 69,889 (3.1 percent) Other. The 2008 runoff was held December 2; the 1992 runoff took place on November 24. The 2000 election was for a short term to fill a vacancy. The Republican Party did not run a candidate in the 1948–1966 or 1990 Senate elections.

GEORGIA

PRESIDENT 2008

2000 Census Population	County	Total Vote	Republican	Democratic	Other	Rep.-Dem. Plurality	Total Vote Rep.	Total Vote Dem.	Major Vote Rep.	Major Vote Dem.
17,419	APPLING	6,996	5,085	1,846	65	3,239 R	72.7%	26.4%	73.4%	26.6%
7,609	ATKINSON	2,904	1,941	938	25	1,003 R	66.8%	32.3%	67.4%	32.6%
10,103	BACON	3,938	3,089	817	32	2,272 R	78.4%	20.7%	79.1%	20.9%
4,074	BAKER	1,687	828	846	13	18 D	49.1%	50.1%	49.5%	50.5%
44,700	BALDWIN	16,537	7,823	8,587	127	764 D	47.3%	51.9%	47.7%	52.3%
14,422	BANKS	6,241	5,120	1,027	94	4,093 R	82.0%	16.5%	83.3%	16.7%
46,144	BARROW	24,582	17,625	6,657	300	10,968 R	71.7%	27.1%	72.6%	27.4%
76,019	BARTOW	36,093	25,976	9,662	455	16,314 R	72.0%	26.8%	72.9%	27.1%
17,484	BEN HILL	6,036	3,417	2,590	29	827 R	56.6%	42.9%	56.9%	43.1%
16,235	BERRIEN	6,449	4,901	1,471	77	3,430 R	76.0%	22.8%	76.9%	23.1%
153,887	BIBB	66,368	27,037	38,987	344	11,950 D	40.7%	58.7%	41.0%	59.0%
11,666	BLECKLEY	5,071	3,657	1,380	34	2,277 R	72.1%	27.2%	72.6%	27.4%
14,629	BRANTLEY	6,277	5,080	1,119	78	3,961 R	80.9%	17.8%	81.9%	18.1%
16,450	BROOKS	6,201	3,507	2,669	25	838 R	56.6%	43.0%	56.8%	43.2%
23,417	BRYAN	12,845	9,112	3,636	97	5,476 R	70.9%	28.3%	71.5%	28.5%
55,983	BULLOCH	23,920	14,174	9,586	160	4,588 R	59.3%	40.1%	59.7%	40.3%
22,243	BURKE	9,626	4,344	5,233	49	889 D	45.1%	54.4%	45.4%	54.6%
19,522	BUTTS	9,091	5,947	3,065	79	2,882 R	65.4%	33.7%	66.0%	34.0%
6,320	CALHOUN	2,211	862	1,342	7	480 D	39.0%	60.7%	39.1%	60.9%
43,664	CAMDEN	17,084	10,502	6,482	100	4,020 R	61.5%	37.9%	61.8%	38.2%
9,577	CANDLER	3,518	2,286	1,209	23	1,077 R	65.0%	34.4%	65.4%	34.6%
87,268	CARROLL	43,498	28,661	14,334	503	14,327 R	65.9%	33.0%	66.7%	33.3%
53,282	CATOOSA	24,496	18,218	6,025	253	12,193 R	74.4%	24.6%	75.1%	24.9%
10,282	CHARLTON	3,685	2,466	1,197	22	1,269 R	66.9%	32.5%	67.3%	32.7%
232,048	CHATHAM	110,238	46,829	62,755	654	15,926 D	42.5%	56.9%	42.7%	57.3%
14,882	CHATTAHOOCHEE	1,653	811	830	12	19 D	49.1%	50.2%	49.4%	50.6%
25,470	CHATTOOGA	8,307	5,572	2,596	139	2,976 R	67.1%	31.3%	68.2%	31.8%
141,903	CHEROKEE	93,772	70,279	22,350	1,143	47,929 R	74.9%	23.8%	75.9%	24.1%
101,489	CLARKE	45,510	15,333	29,591	586	14,258 D	33.7%	65.0%	34.1%	65.9%
3,357	CLAY	1,440	558	879	3	321 D	38.8%	61.0%	38.8%	61.2%
236,517	CLAYTON	99,438	16,506	82,527	405	66,021 D	16.6%	83.0%	16.7%	83.3%
6,878	CLINCH	2,696	1,678	989	29	689 R	62.2%	36.7%	62.9%	37.1%
607,751	COBB	315,444	170,957	141,216	3,271	29,741 R	54.2%	44.8%	54.8%	45.2%
37,413	COFFEE	13,747	8,872	4,811	64	4,061 R	64.5%	35.0%	64.8%	35.2%
42,053	COLQUITT	13,435	9,185	4,139	111	5,046 R	68.4%	30.8%	68.9%	31.1%
89,288	COLUMBIA	55,351	39,322	15,703	326	23,619 R	71.0%	28.4%	71.5%	28.5%
15,771	COOK	5,903	3,782	2,075	46	1,707 R	64.1%	35.2%	64.6%	35.4%
89,215	COWETA	53,549	37,571	15,521	457	22,050 R	70.2%	29.0%	70.8%	29.2%
12,495	CRAWFORD	5,240	3,358	1,832	50	1,526 R	64.1%	35.0%	64.7%	35.3%
21,996	CRISP	7,550	4,424	3,085	41	1,339 R	58.6%	40.9%	58.9%	41.1%
15,154	DADE	6,408	4,703	1,612	93	3,091 R	73.4%	25.2%	74.5%	25.5%
15,999	DAWSON	9,974	8,242	1,632	100	6,610 R	82.6%	16.4%	83.5%	16.5%
28,240	DECATUR	10,374	5,890	4,424	60	1,466 R	56.8%	42.6%	57.1%	42.9%
665,865	DEKALB	322,301	65,581	254,594	2,126	189,013 D	20.3%	79.0%	20.5%	79.5%
19,171	DODGE	8,212	5,543	2,595	74	2,948 R	67.5%	31.6%	68.1%	31.9%
11,525	DOOLY	4,160	1,991	2,138	31	147 D	47.9%	51.4%	48.2%	51.8%
96,065	DOUGHERTY	38,846	12,547	26,135	164	13,588 D	32.3%	67.3%	32.4%	67.6%
92,174	DOUGLAS	55,083	26,812	27,825	446	1,013 D	48.7%	50.5%	49.1%	50.9%
12,354	EARLY	5,335	2,711	2,603	21	108 R	50.8%	48.8%	51.0%	49.0%
3,754	ECHOLS	1,187	981	201	5	780 R	82.6%	16.9%	83.0%	17.0%
37,535	EFFINGHAM	20,316	15,230	4,936	150	10,294 R	75.0%	24.3%	75.5%	24.5%
20,511	ELBERT	8,317	4,868	3,366	83	1,502 R	58.5%	40.5%	59.1%	40.9%
21,837	EMANUEL	8,242	5,110	3,068	64	2,042 R	62.0%	37.2%	62.5%	37.5%
10,495	EVANS	3,855	2,462	1,374	19	1,088 R	63.9%	35.6%	64.2%	35.8%
19,798	FANNIN	10,584	7,807	2,611	166	5,196 R	73.8%	24.7%	74.9%	25.1%

GEORGIA

PRESIDENT 2008

2000 Census Population	County	Total Vote	Republican	Democratic	Other	Rep.-Dem. Plurality	Percentage			
							Total Vote		Major Vote	
							Rep.	Dem.	Rep.	Dem.
91,263	FAYETTE	59,321	38,501	20,313	507	18,188 R	64.9%	34.2%	65.5%	34.5%
90,565	FLOYD	34,213	23,132	10,691	390	12,441 R	67.6%	31.2%	68.4%	31.6%
98,407	FORSYTH	75,376	59,166	15,406	804	43,760 R	78.5%	20.4%	79.3%	20.7%
20,285	FRANKLIN	8,073	6,069	1,914	90	4,155 R	75.2%	23.7%	76.0%	24.0%
816,006	FULTON	404,941	130,136	272,000	2,805	141,864 D	32.1%	67.2%	32.4%	67.6%
23,456	GILMER	11,149	8,408	2,614	127	5,794 R	75.4%	23.4%	76.3%	23.7%
2,556	GLASCOCK	1,428	1,202	210	16	992 R	84.2%	14.7%	85.1%	14.9%
67,568	GLYNN	33,341	20,479	12,676	186	7,803 R	61.4%	38.0%	61.8%	38.2%
44,104	GORDON	17,607	13,113	4,268	226	8,845 R	74.5%	24.2%	75.4%	24.6%
23,659	GRADY	9,365	5,775	3,539	51	2,236 R	61.7%	37.8%	62.0%	38.0%
14,406	GREENE	7,919	4,532	3,339	48	1,193 R	57.2%	42.2%	57.6%	42.4%
588,448	GWINNETT	290,271	158,746	129,025	2,500	29,721 R	54.7%	44.4%	55.2%	44.8%
35,902	HABERSHAM	14,808	11,766	2,900	142	8,866 R	79.5%	19.6%	80.2%	19.8%
139,277	HALL	59,928	44,962	14,457	509	30,505 R	75.0%	24.1%	75.7%	24.3%
10,076	HANCOCK	4,344	795	3,535	14	2,740 D	18.3%	81.4%	18.4%	81.6%
25,690	HARALSON	11,097	8,658	2,248	191	6,410 R	78.0%	20.3%	79.4%	20.6%
23,695	HARRIS	14,908	10,648	4,184	76	6,464 R	71.4%	28.1%	71.8%	28.2%
22,997	HART	10,002	6,537	3,365	100	3,172 R	65.4%	33.6%	66.0%	34.0%
11,012	HEARD	4,225	3,133	1,042	50	2,091 R	74.2%	24.7%	75.0%	25.0%
119,341	HENRY	88,311	47,157	40,567	587	6,590 R	53.4%	45.9%	53.8%	46.2%
110,765	HOUSTON	55,931	33,392	22,094	445	11,298 R	59.7%	39.5%	60.2%	39.8%
9,931	IRWIN	3,828	2,605	1,197	26	1,408 R	68.1%	31.3%	68.5%	31.5%
41,589	JACKSON	22,960	17,776	4,950	234	12,826 R	77.4%	21.6%	78.2%	21.8%
11,426	JASPER	5,904	3,916	1,935	53	1,981 R	66.3%	32.8%	66.9%	33.1%
12,684	JEFF DAVIS	5,278	3,867	1,356	55	2,511 R	73.3%	25.7%	74.0%	26.0%
17,266	JEFFERSON	7,234	3,061	4,149	24	1,088 D	42.3%	57.4%	42.5%	57.5%
8,575	JENKINS	3,440	1,936	1,482	22	454 R	56.3%	43.1%	56.6%	43.4%
8,560	JOHNSON	3,647	2,426	1,198	23	1,228 R	66.5%	32.8%	66.9%	33.1%
23,639	JONES	12,438	7,782	4,572	84	3,210 R	62.6%	36.8%	63.0%	37.0%
15,912	LAMAR	7,688	4,873	2,752	63	2,121 R	63.4%	35.8%	63.9%	36.1%
7,241	LANIER	2,873	1,787	1,062	24	725 R	62.2%	37.0%	62.7%	37.3%
44,874	LAURENS	19,937	12,052	7,769	116	4,283 R	60.5%	39.0%	60.8%	39.2%
24,757	LEE	13,087	9,925	3,100	62	6,825 R	75.8%	23.7%	76.2%	23.8%
61,610	LIBERTY	16,376	5,828	10,474	74	4,646 D	35.6%	64.0%	35.8%	64.2%
8,348	LINCOLN	4,416	2,731	1,650	35	1,081 R	61.8%	37.4%	62.3%	37.7%
10,304	LONG	3,450	2,119	1,288	43	831 R	61.4%	37.3%	62.2%	37.8%
92,115	LOWNDES	39,078	21,269	17,597	212	3,672 R	54.4%	45.0%	54.7%	45.3%
21,016	LUMPKIN	11,075	8,326	2,586	163	5,740 R	75.2%	23.3%	76.3%	23.7%
21,231	MCDUFFIE	9,440	5,400	3,989	51	1,411 R	57.2%	42.3%	57.5%	42.5%
10,847	MCINTOSH	6,229	3,282	2,905	42	377 R	52.7%	46.6%	53.0%	47.0%
14,074	MACON	4,981	1,712	3,251	18	1,539 D	34.4%	65.3%	34.5%	65.5%
25,730	MADISON	11,334	8,226	2,965	143	5,261 R	72.6%	26.2%	73.5%	26.5%
7,144	MARION	3,184	1,772	1,381	31	391 R	55.7%	43.4%	56.2%	43.8%
22,534	MERIWETHER	9,504	4,982	4,465	57	517 R	52.4%	47.0%	52.7%	47.3%
6,383	MILLER	2,738	1,899	818	21	1,081 R	69.4%	29.9%	69.9%	30.1%
23,932	MITCHELL	8,120	4,201	3,872	47	329 R	51.7%	47.7%	52.0%	48.0%
21,757	MONROE	12,131	7,933	4,106	92	3,827 R	65.4%	33.8%	65.9%	34.1%
8,270	MONTGOMERY	3,590	2,521	1,045	24	1,476 R	70.2%	29.1%	70.7%	29.3%
15,457	MORGAN	9,151	5,987	3,091	73	2,896 R	65.4%	33.8%	66.0%	34.0%
36,506	MURRAY	11,382	8,180	3,026	176	5,154 R	71.9%	26.6%	73.0%	27.0%
186,291	MUSCOGEE	74,065	29,568	44,158	339	14,590 D	39.9%	59.6%	40.1%	59.9%
62,001	NEWTON	41,435	20,337	20,827	271	490 D	49.1%	50.3%	49.4%	50.6%
26,225	OCONEE	17,132	12,120	4,825	187	7,295 R	70.7%	28.2%	71.5%	28.5%
12,635	OGLETHORPE	6,447	4,144	2,232	71	1,912 R	64.3%	34.6%	65.0%	35.0%
81,678	PAULDING	56,985	39,192	17,229	564	21,963 R	68.8%	30.2%	69.5%	30.5%

GEORGIA

PRESIDENT 2008

2000 Census Population	County	Total Vote	Republican	Democratic	Other	Rep.-Dem. Plurality	Percentage Total Vote Rep.	Dem.	Major Vote Rep.	Dem.
23,668	PEACH	11,165	5,173	5,927	65	754 D	46.3%	53.1%	46.6%	53.4%
22,983	PICKENS	12,786	10,004	2,595	187	7,409 R	78.2%	20.3%	79.4%	20.6%
15,636	PIERCE	6,791	5,500	1,253	38	4,247 R	81.0%	18.5%	81.4%	18.6%
13,688	PIKE	8,203	6,547	1,575	81	4,972 R	79.8%	19.2%	80.6%	19.4%
38,127	POLK	14,113	9,850	4,052	211	5,798 R	69.8%	28.7%	70.9%	29.1%
9,588	PULASKI	3,953	2,553	1,377	23	1,176 R	64.6%	34.8%	65.0%	35.0%
18,812	PUTNAM	9,132	5,966	3,102	64	2,864 R	65.3%	34.0%	65.8%	34.2%
2,598	QUITMAN	1,114	509	597	8	88 D	45.7%	53.6%	46.0%	54.0%
15,050	RABUN	7,599	5,487	2,001	111	3,486 R	72.2%	26.3%	73.3%	26.7%
7,791	RANDOLPH	3,215	1,370	1,833	12	463 D	42.6%	57.0%	42.8%	57.2%
199,775	RICHMOND	79,333	26,842	52,100	391	25,258 D	33.8%	65.7%	34.0%	66.0%
70,111	ROCKDALE	37,706	16,921	20,526	259	3,605 D	44.9%	54.4%	45.2%	54.8%
3,766	SCHLEY	1,738	1,252	479	7	773 R	72.0%	27.6%	72.3%	27.7%
15,374	SCREVEN	6,481	3,423	3,024	34	399 R	52.8%	46.7%	53.1%	46.9%
9,369	SEMINOLE	3,996	2,315	1,660	21	655 R	57.9%	41.5%	58.2%	41.8%
58,417	SPALDING	25,255	14,885	10,141	229	4,744 R	58.9%	40.2%	59.5%	40.5%
25,435	STEPHENS	10,517	7,689	2,705	123	4,984 R	73.1%	25.7%	74.0%	26.0%
5,252	STEWART	2,105	783	1,305	17	522 D	37.2%	62.0%	37.5%	62.5%
33,200	SUMTER	12,235	5,717	6,454	64	737 D	46.7%	52.8%	47.0%	53.0%
6,498	TALBOT	3,700	1,301	2,369	30	1,068 D	35.2%	64.0%	35.4%	64.6%
2,077	TALIAFERRO	990	339	643	8	304 D	34.2%	64.9%	34.5%	65.5%
22,305	TATTNALL	6,714	4,730	1,932	52	2,798 R	70.4%	28.8%	71.0%	29.0%
8,815	TAYLOR	3,583	2,021	1,536	26	485 R	56.4%	42.9%	56.8%	43.2%
11,794	TELFAIR	4,374	2,486	1,862	26	624 R	56.8%	42.6%	57.2%	42.8%
10,970	TERRELL	4,416	1,890	2,501	25	611 D	42.8%	56.6%	43.0%	57.0%
42,737	THOMAS	18,459	10,642	7,720	97	2,922 R	57.7%	41.8%	58.0%	42.0%
38,407	TIFT	14,257	9,431	4,749	77	4,682 R	66.1%	33.3%	66.5%	33.5%
26,067	TOOMBS	9,688	6,658	2,964	66	3,694 R	68.7%	30.6%	69.2%	30.8%
9,319	TOWNS	5,739	4,292	1,391	56	2,901 R	74.8%	24.2%	75.5%	24.5%
6,854	TREUTLEN	2,954	1,826	1,112	16	714 R	61.8%	37.6%	62.2%	37.8%
58,779	TROUP	26,028	15,391	10,455	182	4,936 R	59.1%	40.2%	59.5%	40.5%
9,504	TURNER	3,553	2,096	1,427	30	669 R	59.0%	40.2%	59.5%	40.5%
10,590	TWIGGS	4,519	2,087	2,402	30	315 D	46.2%	53.2%	46.5%	53.5%
17,289	UNION	10,634	8,013	2,486	135	5,527 R	75.4%	23.4%	76.3%	23.7%
27,597	UPSON	11,421	7,291	4,061	69	3,230 R	63.8%	35.6%	64.2%	35.8%
61,053	WALKER	23,542	17,110	6,095	337	11,015 R	72.7%	25.9%	73.7%	26.3%
60,687	WALTON	36,026	27,253	8,469	304	18,784 R	75.6%	23.5%	76.3%	23.7%
35,483	WARE	12,416	8,311	4,034	71	4,277 R	66.9%	32.5%	67.3%	32.7%
6,336	WARREN	2,660	1,087	1,554	19	467 D	40.9%	58.4%	41.2%	58.8%
21,176	WASHINGTON	8,863	4,216	4,607	40	391 D	47.6%	52.0%	47.8%	52.2%
26,565	WAYNE	10,560	7,601	2,858	101	4,743 R	72.0%	27.1%	72.7%	27.3%
2,390	WEBSTER	1,111	588	515	8	73 R	52.9%	46.4%	53.3%	46.7%
6,179	WHEELER	2,210	1,408	794	8	614 R	63.7%	35.9%	63.9%	36.1%
19,944	WHITE	10,761	8,467	2,174	120	6,293 R	78.7%	20.2%	79.6%	20.4%
83,525	WHITFIELD	27,677	19,230	8,167	280	11,063 R	69.5%	29.5%	70.2%	29.8%
8,577	WILCOX	3,163	2,159	978	26	1,181 R	68.3%	30.9%	68.8%	31.2%
10,687	WILKES	5,052	2,705	2,315	32	390 R	53.5%	45.8%	53.9%	46.1%
10,220	WILKINSON	4,673	2,349	2,298	26	51 R	50.3%	49.2%	50.5%	49.5%
21,967	WORTH	8,370	5,780	2,542	48	3,238 R	69.1%	30.4%	69.5%	30.5%
8,186,453	TOTAL	3,924,486	2,048,759	1,844,123	31,604	204,636 R	52.2%	47.0%	52.6%	47.4%

GEORGIA

SENATOR 2008 (General Election)

2000 Census Population	County	Total Vote	Republican	Democratic	Other	Rep.-Dem. Plurality	Percentage			
							Total Vote		Major Vote	
							Rep.	Dem.	Rep.	Dem.
17,419	APPLING	6,601	4,312	2,111	178	2,201 R	65.3%	32.0%	67.1%	32.9%
7,609	ATKINSON	2,694	1,530	1,090	74	440 R	56.8%	40.5%	58.4%	41.6%
10,103	BACON	3,642	2,542	1,024	76	1,518 R	69.8%	28.1%	71.3%	28.7%
4,074	BAKER	1,616	750	833	33	83 D	46.4%	51.5%	47.4%	52.6%
44,700	BALDWIN	15,603	6,948	8,244	411	1,296 D	44.5%	52.8%	45.7%	54.3%
14,422	BANKS	6,078	4,268	1,513	297	2,755 R	70.2%	24.9%	73.8%	26.2%
46,144	BARROW	23,740	15,684	6,821	1,235	8,863 R	66.1%	28.7%	69.7%	30.3%
76,019	BARTOW	34,653	22,591	10,469	1,593	12,122 R	65.2%	30.2%	68.3%	31.7%
17,484	BEN HILL	5,724	2,868	2,716	140	152 R	50.1%	47.4%	51.4%	48.6%
16,235	BERRIEN	6,172	3,925	1,994	253	1,931 R	63.6%	32.3%	66.3%	33.7%
153,887	BIBB	63,447	26,422	35,850	1,175	9,428 D	41.6%	56.5%	42.4%	57.6%
11,666	BLECKLEY	4,920	3,134	1,677	109	1,457 R	63.7%	34.1%	65.1%	34.9%
14,629	BRANTLEY	5,895	4,221	1,464	210	2,757 R	71.6%	24.8%	74.2%	25.8%
16,450	BROOKS	5,692	3,239	2,316	137	923 R	56.9%	40.7%	58.3%	41.7%
23,417	BRYAN	12,192	7,957	3,737	498	4,220 R	65.3%	30.7%	68.0%	32.0%
55,983	BULLOCH	22,876	12,690	9,514	672	3,176 R	55.5%	41.6%	57.2%	42.8%
22,243	BURKE	8,875	3,864	4,841	170	977 D	43.5%	54.5%	44.4%	55.6%
19,522	BUTTS	8,671	5,165	3,222	284	1,943 R	59.6%	37.2%	61.6%	38.4%
6,320	CALHOUN	2,138	809	1,307	22	498 D	37.8%	61.1%	38.2%	61.8%
43,664	CAMDEN	15,827	9,689	5,640	498	4,049 R	61.2%	35.6%	63.2%	36.8%
9,577	CANDLER	3,301	1,851	1,342	108	509 R	56.1%	40.7%	58.0%	42.0%
87,268	CARROLL	41,737	25,221	14,739	1,777	10,482 R	60.4%	35.3%	63.1%	36.9%
53,282	CATOOSA	22,977	16,122	6,163	692	9,959 R	70.2%	26.8%	72.3%	27.7%
10,282	CHARLTON	3,315	2,180	1,062	73	1,118 R	65.8%	32.0%	67.2%	32.8%
232,048	CHATHAM	103,455	43,554	56,596	3,305	13,042 D	42.1%	54.7%	43.5%	56.5%
14,882	CHATTAHOOCHEE	1,548	614	889	45	275 D	39.7%	57.4%	40.9%	59.1%
25,470	CHATTOOGA	7,918	4,251	3,408	259	843 R	53.7%	43.0%	55.5%	44.5%
141,903	CHEROKEE	90,772	64,464	21,599	4,709	42,865 R	71.0%	23.8%	74.9%	25.1%
101,489	CLARKE	43,269	15,279	26,202	1,788	10,923 D	35.3%	60.6%	36.8%	63.2%
3,357	CLAY	1,296	478	800	18	322 D	36.9%	61.7%	37.4%	62.6%
236,517	CLAYTON	94,119	15,893	76,122	2,104	60,229 D	16.9%	80.9%	17.3%	82.7%
6,878	CLINCH	2,445	1,420	963	62	457 R	58.1%	39.4%	59.6%	40.4%
607,751	COBB	304,437	162,249	129,133	13,055	33,116 R	53.3%	42.4%	55.7%	44.3%
37,413	COFFEE	13,021	7,554	5,119	348	2,435 R	58.0%	39.3%	59.6%	40.4%
42,053	COLQUITT	13,017	8,389	4,274	354	4,115 R	64.4%	32.8%	66.2%	33.8%
89,288	COLUMBIA	52,493	36,022	14,896	1,575	21,126 R	68.6%	28.4%	70.7%	29.3%
15,771	COOK	5,589	3,249	2,195	145	1,054 R	58.1%	39.3%	59.7%	40.3%
89,215	COWETA	51,363	33,988	15,311	2,064	18,677 R	66.2%	29.8%	68.9%	31.1%
12,495	CRAWFORD	5,048	2,945	1,957	146	988 R	58.3%	38.8%	60.1%	39.9%
21,996	CRISP	7,022	4,010	2,862	150	1,148 R	57.1%	40.8%	58.4%	41.6%
15,154	DADE	5,954	3,858	1,852	244	2,006 R	64.8%	31.1%	67.6%	32.4%
15,999	DAWSON	9,671	7,259	1,896	516	5,363 R	75.1%	19.6%	79.3%	20.7%
28,240	DECATUR	9,612	5,502	3,947	163	1,555 R	57.2%	41.1%	58.2%	41.8%
665,865	DEKALB	307,929	65,531	233,727	8,671	168,196 D	21.3%	75.9%	21.9%	78.1%
19,171	DODGE	7,730	4,548	3,026	156	1,522 R	58.8%	39.1%	60.0%	40.0%
11,525	DOOLY	3,920	1,859	1,990	71	131 D	47.4%	50.8%	48.3%	51.7%
96,065	DOUGHERTY	36,678	12,534	23,523	621	10,989 D	34.2%	64.1%	34.8%	65.2%
92,174	DOUGLAS	52,464	24,241	26,410	1,813	2,169 D	46.2%	50.3%	47.9%	52.1%
12,354	EARLY	4,970	2,490	2,418	62	72 R	50.1%	48.7%	50.7%	49.3%
3,754	ECHOLS	1,067	731	296	40	435 R	68.5%	27.7%	71.2%	28.8%

GEORGIA

SENATOR 2008 (General Election)

2000 Census Population	County	Total Vote	Republican	Democratic	Other	Rep.-Dem. Plurality	Percentage			
							Total Vote		Major Vote	
							Rep.	Dem.	Rep.	Dem.
37,535	EFFINGHAM	19,462	13,066	5,634	762	7,432 R	67.1%	28.9%	69.9%	30.1%
20,511	ELBERT	7,631	4,213	3,227	191	986 R	55.2%	42.3%	56.6%	43.4%
21,837	EMANUEL	7,545	4,295	3,079	171	1,216 R	56.9%	40.8%	58.2%	41.8%
10,495	EVANS	3,687	2,078	1,507	102	571 R	56.4%	40.9%	58.0%	42.0%
19,798	FANNIN	10,079	6,497	3,097	485	3,400 R	64.5%	30.7%	67.7%	32.3%
91,263	FAYETTE	57,257	35,528	19,420	2,309	16,108 R	62.1%	33.9%	64.7%	35.3%
90,565	FLOYD	32,636	19,425	11,962	1,249	7,463 R	59.5%	36.7%	61.9%	38.1%
98,407	FORSYTH	73,170	54,928	14,601	3,641	40,327 R	75.1%	20.0%	79.0%	21.0%
20,285	FRANKLIN	7,699	4,951	2,431	317	2,520 R	64.3%	31.6%	67.1%	32.9%
816,006	FULTON	393,073	131,438	249,201	12,434	117,763 D	33.4%	63.4%	34.5%	65.5%
23,456	GILMER	10,682	7,022	3,069	591	3,953 R	65.7%	28.7%	69.6%	30.4%
2,556	GLASCOCK	1,313	894	384	35	510 R	68.1%	29.2%	70.0%	30.0%
67,568	GLYNN	31,177	18,690	11,553	934	7,137 R	59.9%	37.1%	61.8%	38.2%
44,104	GORDON	16,802	10,892	5,077	833	5,815 R	64.8%	30.2%	68.2%	31.8%
23,659	GRADY	8,554	5,158	3,196	200	1,962 R	60.3%	37.4%	61.7%	38.3%
14,406	GREENE	7,555	4,209	3,168	178	1,041 R	55.7%	41.9%	57.1%	42.9%
588,448	GWINNETT	282,939	150,433	121,015	11,491	29,418 R	53.2%	42.8%	55.4%	44.6%
35,902	HABERSHAM	14,406	10,164	3,532	710	6,632 R	70.6%	24.5%	74.2%	25.8%
139,277	HALL	57,865	39,539	15,250	3,076	24,289 R	68.3%	26.4%	72.2%	27.8%
10,076	HANCOCK	4,002	762	3,177	63	2,415 D	19.0%	79.4%	19.3%	80.7%
25,690	HARALSON	10,782	7,145	3,039	598	4,106 R	66.3%	28.2%	70.2%	29.8%
23,695	HARRIS	14,185	9,344	4,404	437	4,940 R	65.9%	31.0%	68.0%	32.0%
22,997	HART	9,214	5,352	3,575	287	1,777 R	58.1%	38.8%	60.0%	40.0%
11,012	HEARD	4,031	2,589	1,271	171	1,318 R	64.2%	31.5%	67.1%	32.9%
119,341	HENRY	83,961	42,537	38,466	2,958	4,071 R	50.7%	45.8%	52.5%	47.5%
110,765	HOUSTON	53,696	30,750	21,631	1,315	9,119 R	57.3%	40.3%	58.7%	41.3%
9,931	IRWIN	3,673	2,107	1,467	99	640 R	57.4%	39.9%	59.0%	41.0%
41,589	JACKSON	22,234	15,769	5,417	1,048	10,352 R	70.9%	24.4%	74.4%	25.6%
11,426	JASPER	5,696	3,399	2,093	204	1,306 R	59.7%	36.7%	61.9%	38.1%
12,684	JEFF DAVIS	5,004	3,286	1,555	163	1,731 R	65.7%	31.1%	67.9%	32.1%
17,266	JEFFERSON	6,586	2,698	3,784	104	1,086 D	41.0%	57.5%	41.6%	58.4%
8,575	JENKINS	3,207	1,526	1,627	54	101 D	47.6%	50.7%	48.4%	51.6%
8,560	JOHNSON	3,416	2,015	1,331	70	684 R	59.0%	39.0%	60.2%	39.8%
23,639	JONES	12,004	6,917	4,790	297	2,127 R	57.6%	39.9%	59.1%	40.9%
15,912	LAMAR	7,435	4,316	2,877	242	1,439 R	58.0%	38.7%	60.0%	40.0%
7,241	LANIER	2,682	1,612	1,004	66	608 R	60.1%	37.4%	61.6%	38.4%
44,874	LAURENS	18,981	10,653	7,936	392	2,717 R	56.1%	41.8%	57.3%	42.7%
24,757	LEE	12,665	8,803	3,509	353	5,294 R	69.5%	27.7%	71.5%	28.5%
61,610	LIBERTY	15,310	5,108	9,810	392	4,702 D	33.4%	64.1%	34.2%	65.8%
8,348	LINCOLN	4,105	2,351	1,655	99	696 R	57.3%	40.3%	58.7%	41.3%
10,304	LONG	3,264	1,692	1,451	121	241 R	51.8%	44.5%	53.8%	46.2%
92,115	LOWNDES	36,683	19,825	16,000	858	3,825 R	54.0%	43.6%	55.3%	44.7%
21,016	LUMPKIN	10,790	7,039	3,060	691	3,979 R	65.2%	28.4%	69.7%	30.3%
21,231	MCDUFFIE	8,852	4,838	3,829	185	1,009 R	54.7%	43.3%	55.8%	44.2%
10,847	MCINTOSH	5,920	2,863	2,895	162	32 D	48.4%	48.9%	49.7%	50.3%
14,074	MACON	4,645	1,598	2,984	63	1,386 D	34.4%	64.2%	34.9%	65.1%
25,730	MADISON	10,914	7,028	3,447	439	3,581 R	64.4%	31.6%	67.1%	32.9%
7,144	MARION	3,029	1,419	1,509	101	90 D	46.8%	49.8%	48.5%	51.5%
22,534	MERIWETHER	9,098	4,296	4,497	305	201 D	47.2%	49.4%	48.9%	51.1%
6,383	MILLER	2,542	1,621	853	68	768 R	63.8%	33.6%	65.5%	34.5%

GEORGIA

SENATOR 2008 (General Election)

2000 Census Population	County	Total Vote	Republican	Democratic	Other	Rep.-Dem. Plurality	Total Vote Rep.	Total Vote Dem.	Major Vote Rep.	Major Vote Dem.
23,932	MITCHELL	7,741	3,821	3,821	99		49.4%	49.4%	50.0%	50.0%
21,757	MONROE	11,860	7,150	4,376	334	2,774 R	60.3%	36.9%	62.0%	38.0%
8,270	MONTGOMERY	3,412	2,047	1,281	84	766 R	60.0%	37.5%	61.5%	38.5%
15,457	MORGAN	8,801	5,469	3,078	254	2,391 R	62.1%	35.0%	64.0%	36.0%
36,506	MURRAY	10,727	6,636	3,653	438	2,983 R	61.9%	34.1%	64.5%	35.5%
186,291	MUSCOGEE	69,371	26,256	41,324	1,791	15,068 D	37.8%	59.6%	38.9%	61.1%
62,001	NEWTON	39,629	18,195	20,197	1,237	2,002 D	45.9%	51.0%	47.4%	52.6%
26,225	OCONEE	16,660	11,443	4,583	634	6,860 R	68.7%	27.5%	71.4%	28.6%
12,635	OGLETHORPE	6,181	3,614	2,335	232	1,279 R	58.5%	37.8%	60.7%	39.3%
81,678	PAULDING	54,918	35,242	17,335	2,341	17,907 R	64.2%	31.6%	67.0%	33.0%
23,668	PEACH	10,728	4,849	5,679	200	830 D	45.2%	52.9%	46.1%	53.9%
22,983	PICKENS	12,345	8,617	3,086	642	5,531 R	69.8%	25.0%	73.6%	26.4%
15,636	PIERCE	6,348	4,942	1,294	112	3,648 R	77.9%	20.4%	79.2%	20.8%
13,688	PIKE	8,039	5,816	1,906	317	3,910 R	72.3%	23.7%	75.3%	24.7%
38,127	POLK	13,512	7,942	5,056	514	2,886 R	58.8%	37.4%	61.1%	38.9%
9,588	PULASKI	3,800	2,116	1,598	86	518 R	55.7%	42.1%	57.0%	43.0%
18,812	PUTNAM	8,758	5,361	3,146	251	2,215 R	61.2%	35.9%	63.0%	37.0%
2,598	QUITMAN	990	400	565	25	165 D	40.4%	57.1%	41.5%	58.5%
15,050	RABUN	7,297	4,418	2,530	349	1,888 R	60.5%	34.7%	63.6%	36.4%
7,791	RANDOLPH	2,956	1,236	1,675	45	439 D	41.8%	56.7%	42.5%	57.5%
199,775	RICHMOND	73,086	24,709	46,767	1,610	22,058 D	33.8%	64.0%	34.6%	65.4%
70,111	ROCKDALE	36,105	15,491	19,524	1,090	4,033 D	42.9%	54.1%	44.2%	55.8%
3,766	SCHLEY	1,647	1,092	515	40	577 R	66.3%	31.3%	68.0%	32.0%
15,374	SCREVEN	6,031	2,863	3,029	139	166 D	47.5%	50.2%	48.6%	51.4%
9,369	SEMINOLE	3,694	2,008	1,590	96	418 R	54.4%	43.0%	55.8%	44.2%
58,417	SPALDING	23,729	13,087	9,868	774	3,219 R	55.2%	41.6%	57.0%	43.0%
25,435	STEPHENS	9,913	6,337	3,273	303	3,064 R	63.9%	33.0%	65.9%	34.1%
5,252	STEWART	1,903	687	1,184	32	497 D	36.1%	62.2%	36.7%	63.3%
33,200	SUMTER	11,625	5,430	5,971	224	541 D	46.7%	51.4%	47.6%	52.4%
6,498	TALBOT	3,437	1,095	2,238	104	1,143 D	31.9%	65.1%	32.9%	67.1%
2,077	TALIAFERRO	869	290	563	16	273 D	33.4%	64.8%	34.0%	66.0%
22,305	TATTNALL	6,332	3,867	2,295	170	1,572 R	61.1%	36.2%	62.8%	37.2%
8,815	TAYLOR	3,416	1,769	1,589	58	180 R	51.8%	46.5%	52.7%	47.3%
11,794	TELFAIR	4,211	1,980	2,170	61	190 D	47.0%	51.5%	47.7%	52.3%
10,970	TERRELL	4,218	1,850	2,302	66	452 D	43.9%	54.6%	44.6%	55.4%
42,737	THOMAS	17,052	9,771	6,827	454	2,944 R	57.3%	40.0%	58.9%	41.1%
38,407	TIFT	13,675	8,398	4,973	304	3,425 R	61.4%	36.4%	62.8%	37.2%
26,067	TOOMBS	9,141	5,609	3,241	291	2,368 R	61.4%	35.5%	63.4%	36.6%
9,319	TOWNS	5,492	3,559	1,689	244	1,870 R	64.8%	30.8%	67.8%	32.2%
6,854	TREUTLEN	2,766	1,500	1,206	60	294 R	54.2%	43.6%	55.4%	44.6%
58,779	TROUP	24,524	13,595	10,153	776	3,442 R	55.4%	41.4%	57.2%	42.8%
9,504	TURNER	3,337	1,732	1,521	84	211 R	51.9%	45.6%	53.2%	46.8%
10,590	TWIGGS	4,323	1,753	2,468	102	715 D	40.6%	57.1%	41.5%	58.5%
17,289	UNION	10,229	6,483	3,292	454	3,191 R	63.4%	32.2%	66.3%	33.7%
27,597	UPSON	10,910	6,536	4,112	262	2,424 R	59.9%	37.7%	61.4%	38.6%
61,053	WALKER	22,143	14,785	6,656	702	8,129 R	66.8%	30.1%	69.0%	31.0%
60,687	WALTON	34,704	24,619	8,765	1,320	15,854 R	70.9%	25.3%	73.7%	26.3%
35,483	WARE	11,628	7,677	3,724	227	3,953 R	66.0%	32.0%	67.3%	32.7%
6,336	WARREN	2,408	940	1,407	61	467 D	39.0%	58.4%	40.1%	59.9%
21,176	WASHINGTON	8,356	3,679	4,556	121	877 D	44.0%	54.5%	44.7%	55.3%

GEORGIA

SENATOR 2008 (General Election)

2000 Census Population	County	Total Vote	Republican	Democratic	Other	Rep.-Dem. Plurality	Total Vote Rep.	Total Vote Dem.	Major Vote Rep.	Major Vote Dem.
26,565	WAYNE	9,995	6,099	3,535	361	2,564 R	61.0%	35.4%	63.3%	36.7%
2,390	WEBSTER	1,057	496	544	17	48 D	46.9%	51.5%	47.7%	52.3%
6,179	WHEELER	2,123	1,184	908	31	276 R	55.8%	42.8%	56.6%	43.4%
19,944	WHITE	10,493	7,234	2,676	583	4,558 R	68.9%	25.5%	73.0%	27.0%
83,525	WHITFIELD	26,369	16,805	8,542	1,022	8,263 R	63.7%	32.4%	66.3%	33.7%
8,577	WILCOX	3,045	1,778	1,219	48	559 R	58.4%	40.0%	59.3%	40.7%
10,687	WILKES	4,626	2,282	2,252	92	30 R	49.3%	48.7%	50.3%	49.7%
10,220	WILKINSON	4,456	1,980	2,403	73	423 D	44.4%	53.9%	45.2%	54.8%
21,967	WORTH	8,013	4,906	2,882	225	2,024 R	61.2%	36.0%	63.0%	37.0%
8,186,453	TOTAL	3,752,485	1,867,097	1,757,393	127,995	109,704 R	49.8%	46.8%	51.5%	48.5%

GEORGIA

SENATOR 2008 (Runoff)

2000 Census Population	County	Total Vote	Republican	Democratic	Other	Rep.-Dem. Plurality	Total Vote Rep.	Total Vote Dem.	Major Vote Rep.	Major Vote Dem.
17,419	APPLING	3,655	2,635	1,020		1,615 R	72.1%	27.9%	72.1%	27.9%
7,609	ATKINSON	1,276	847	429		418 R	66.4%	33.6%	66.4%	33.6%
10,103	BACON	1,760	1,402	358		1,044 R	79.7%	20.3%	79.7%	20.3%
4,074	BAKER	929	455	474		19 D	49.0%	51.0%	49.0%	51.0%
44,700	BALDWIN	8,935	4,452	4,483		31 D	49.8%	50.2%	49.8%	50.2%
14,422	BANKS	3,565	2,966	599		2,367 R	83.2%	16.8%	83.2%	16.8%
46,144	BARROW	12,886	10,035	2,851		7,184 R	77.9%	22.1%	77.9%	22.1%
76,019	BARTOW	18,234	13,807	4,427		9,380 R	75.7%	24.3%	75.7%	24.3%
17,484	BEN HILL	3,021	1,694	1,327		367 R	56.1%	43.9%	56.1%	43.9%
16,235	BERRIEN	3,257	2,398	859		1,539 R	73.6%	26.4%	73.6%	26.4%
153,887	BIBB	35,923	17,036	18,887		1,851 D	47.4%	52.6%	47.4%	52.6%
11,666	BLECKLEY	2,818	2,089	729		1,360 R	74.1%	25.9%	74.1%	25.9%
14,629	BRANTLEY	2,608	2,160	448		1,712 R	82.8%	17.2%	82.8%	17.2%
16,450	BROOKS	3,260	1,992	1,268		724 R	61.1%	38.9%	61.1%	38.9%
23,417	BRYAN	6,227	4,580	1,647		2,933 R	73.6%	26.4%	73.6%	26.4%
55,983	BULLOCH	11,405	7,555	3,850		3,705 R	66.2%	33.8%	66.2%	33.8%
22,243	BURKE	5,065	2,532	2,533		1 D	50.0%	50.0%	50.0%	50.0%
19,522	BUTTS	5,072	3,448	1,624		1,824 R	68.0%	32.0%	68.0%	32.0%
6,320	CALHOUN	1,264	540	724		184 D	42.7%	57.3%	42.7%	57.3%
43,664	CAMDEN	6,897	4,848	2,049		2,799 R	70.3%	29.7%	70.3%	29.7%
9,577	CANDLER	1,781	1,166	615		551 R	65.5%	34.5%	65.5%	34.5%
87,268	CARROLL	23,347	16,451	6,896		9,555 R	70.5%	29.5%	70.5%	29.5%
53,282	CATOOSA	11,661	8,652	3,009		5,643 R	74.2%	25.8%	74.2%	25.8%
10,282	CHARLTON	1,501	1,066	435		631 R	71.0%	29.0%	71.0%	29.0%
232,048	CHATHAM	58,619	28,287	30,332		2,045 D	48.3%	51.7%	48.3%	51.7%
14,882	CHATTAHOOCHEE	686	357	329		28 R	52.0%	48.0%	52.0%	48.0%
25,470	CHATTOOGA	3,780	2,419	1,361		1,058 R	64.0%	36.0%	64.0%	36.0%
141,903	CHEROKEE	52,425	42,860	9,565		33,295 R	81.8%	18.2%	81.8%	18.2%
101,489	CLARKE	24,350	9,331	15,019		5,688 D	38.3%	61.7%	38.3%	61.7%
3,357	CLAY	743	315	428		113 D	42.4%	57.6%	42.4%	57.6%

GEORGIA

SENATOR 2008 (Runoff)

2000 Census Population	County	Total Vote	Republican	Democratic	Other	Rep.-Dem. Plurality		Percentage			
								Total Vote		Major Vote	
								Rep.	Dem.	Rep.	Dem.
236,517	CLAYTON	51,633	10,368	41,265		30,897	D	20.1%	79.9%	20.1%	79.9%
6,878	CLINCH	1,096	705	391		314	R	64.3%	35.7%	64.3%	35.7%
607,751	COBB	184,124	117,116	67,008		50,108	R	63.6%	36.4%	63.6%	36.4%
37,413	COFFEE	6,654	4,386	2,268		2,118	R	65.9%	34.1%	65.9%	34.1%
42,053	COLQUITT	7,814	5,683	2,131		3,552	R	72.7%	27.3%	72.7%	27.3%
89,288	COLUMBIA	30,220	23,016	7,204		15,812	R	76.2%	23.8%	76.2%	23.8%
15,771	COOK	3,782	2,445	1,337		1,108	R	64.6%	35.4%	64.6%	35.4%
89,215	COWETA	30,062	22,536	7,526		15,010	R	75.0%	25.0%	75.0%	25.0%
12,495	CRAWFORD	2,878	1,850	1,028		822	R	64.3%	35.7%	64.3%	35.7%
21,996	CRISP	3,791	2,443	1,348		1,095	R	64.4%	35.6%	64.4%	35.6%
15,154	DADE	3,500	2,446	1,054		1,392	R	69.9%	30.1%	69.9%	30.1%
15,999	DAWSON	5,863	4,993	870		4,123	R	85.2%	14.8%	85.2%	14.8%
28,240	DECATUR	4,634	2,718	1,916		802	R	58.7%	41.3%	58.7%	41.3%
665,865	DEKALB	186,760	47,643	139,117		91,474	D	25.5%	74.5%	25.5%	74.5%
19,171	DODGE	6,395	4,092	2,303		1,789	R	64.0%	36.0%	64.0%	35.0%
11,525	DOOLY	2,421	1,274	1,147		127	R	52.6%	47.4%	52.6%	47.4%
96,065	DOUGHERTY	21,524	7,776	13,748		5,972	D	36.1%	63.9%	36.1%	63.9%
92,174	DOUGLAS	29,373	16,359	13,014		3,345	R	55.7%	44.3%	55.7%	44.3%
12,354	EARLY	3,302	1,643	1,659		16	D	49.8%	50.2%	49.8%	50.2%
3,754	ECHOLS	486	379	107		272	R	78.0%	22.0%	78.0%	22.0%
37,535	EFFINGHAM	10,721	8,123	2,598		5,525	R	75.8%	24.2%	75.8%	24.2%
20,511	ELBERT	3,691	2,309	1,382		927	R	62.6%	37.4%	62.6%	37.4%
21,837	EMANUEL	3,840	2,466	1,374		1,092	R	64.2%	35.8%	64.2%	35.8%
10,495	EVANS	2,041	1,302	739		563	R	63.8%	36.2%	63.8%	36.2%
19,798	FANNIN	5,657	4,204	1,453		2,751	R	74.3%	25.7%	74.3%	25.7%
91,263	FAYETTE	37,418	25,884	11,534		14,350	R	69.2%	30.8%	69.2%	30.8%
90,565	FLOYD	17,330	12,118	5,212		6,906	R	69.9%	30.1%	69.9%	30.1%
98,407	FORSYTH	43,837	37,232	6,605		30,627	R	84.9%	15.1%	84.9%	15.1%
20,285	FRANKLIN	3,836	2,995	841		2,154	R	78.1%	21.9%	78.1%	21.9%
816,006	FULTON	222,876	88,270	134,606		46,336	D	39.6%	60.4%	39.6%	60.4%
23,456	GILMER	6,536	5,056	1,480		3,576	R	77.4%	22.6%	77.4%	22.6%
2,556	GLASCOCK	833	682	151		531	R	81.9%	18.1%	81.9%	18.1%
67,568	GLYNN	16,615	11,317	5,298		6,019	R	68.1%	31.9%	68.1%	31.9%
44,104	GORDON	9,753	7,451	2,302		5,149	R	76.4%	23.6%	76.4%	23.6%
23,659	GRADY	4,292	2,880	1,412		1,468	R	67.1%	32.9%	67.1%	32.9%
14,406	GREENE	5,246	3,357	1,889		1,468	R	64.0%	36.0%	64.0%	36.0%
588,448	GWINNETT	165,607	105,931	59,676		46,255	R	64.0%	36.0%	64.0%	36.0%
35,902	HABERSHAM	8,580	6,934	1,646		5,288	R	80.8%	19.2%	80.8%	19.2%
139,277	HALL	34,054	27,343	6,711		20,632	R	80.3%	19.7%	80.3%	19.7%
10,076	HANCOCK	2,183	428	1,755		1,327	D	19.6%	80.4%	19.6%	80.4%
25,690	HARALSON	5,781	4,538	1,243		3,295	R	78.5%	21.5%	78.5%	21.5%
23,695	HARRIS	7,978	5,712	2,266		3,446	R	71.6%	28.4%	71.6%	28.4%
22,997	HART	4,368	3,042	1,326		1,716	R	69.6%	30.4%	69.6%	30.4%
11,012	HEARD	2,192	1,586	606		980	R	72.4%	27.6%	72.4%	27.6%
119,341	HENRY	47,196	27,263	19,933		7,330	R	57.8%	42.2%	57.8%	42.2%
110,765	HOUSTON	28,842	18,781	10,061		8,720	R	65.1%	34.9%	65.1%	34.9%
9,931	IRWIN	2,202	1,451	751		700	R	65.9%	34.1%	65.9%	34.1%
41,589	JACKSON	12,939	10,542	2,397		8,145	R	81.5%	18.5%	81.5%	18.5%
11,426	JASPER	3,640	2,428	1,212		1,216	R	66.7%	33.3%	66.7%	33.3%
12,684	JEFF DAVIS	4,384	3,069	1,315		1,754	R	70.0%	30.0%	70.0%	30.0%

GEORGIA

SENATOR 2008 (Runoff)

2000 Census Population	County	Total Vote	Republican	Democratic	Other	Rep.-Dem. Plurality	Percentage			
							Total Vote		Major Vote	
							Rep.	Dem.	Rep.	Dem.
17,266	JEFFERSON	3,927	1,819	2,108		289 D	46.3%	53.7%	46.3%	53.7%
8,575	JENKINS	1,685	968	717		251 R	57.4%	42.6%	57.4%	42.6%
8,560	JOHNSON	1,944	1,388	556		832 R	71.4%	28.6%	71.4%	28.6%
23,639	JONES	6,775	4,232	2,543		1,689 R	62.5%	37.5%	62.5%	37.5%
15,912	LAMAR	4,394	2,932	1,462		1,470 R	66.7%	33.3%	66.7%	33.3%
7,241	LANIER	1,148	748	400		348 R	65.2%	34.8%	65.2%	34.8%
44,874	LAURENS	10,749	6,623	4,126		2,497 R	61.6%	38.4%	61.6%	38.4%
24,757	LEE	7,190	5,466	1,724		3,742 R	76.0%	24.0%	76.0%	24.0%
61,610	LIBERTY	6,826	2,651	4,175		1,524 D	38.8%	61.2%	38.8%	61.2%
8,348	LINCOLN	2,162	1,461	701		760 R	67.6%	32.4%	67.6%	32.4%
10,304	LONG	1,352	816	536		280 R	60.4%	39.6%	60.4%	39.6%
92,115	LOWNDES	17,876	10,673	7,203		3,470 R	59.7%	40.3%	59.7%	40.3%
21,016	LUMPKIN	6,365	4,832	1,533		3,299 R	75.9%	24.1%	75.9%	24.1%
21,231	MCDUFFIE	5,107	3,208	1,899		1,309 R	62.8%	37.2%	62.8%	37.2%
10,847	MCINTOSH	3,010	1,608	1,402		206 R	53.4%	46.6%	53.4%	46.6%
14,074	MACON	2,686	976	1,710		734 D	36.3%	63.7%	36.3%	63.7%
25,730	MADISON	6,492	4,834	1,658		3,176 R	74.5%	25.5%	74.5%	25.5%
7,144	MARION	1,486	822	664		158 R	55.3%	44.7%	55.3%	44.7%
22,534	MERIWETHER	5,380	2,934	2,446		488 R	54.5%	45.5%	54.5%	45.5%
6,383	MILLER	1,232	906	326		580 R	73.5%	26.5%	73.5%	26.5%
23,932	MITCHELL	4,581	2,411	2,170		241 R	52.6%	47.4%	52.6%	47.4%
21,757	MONROE	7,156	4,945	2,211		2,734 R	69.1%	30.9%	69.1%	30.9%
8,270	MONTGOMERY	1,954	1,353	601		752 R	69.2%	30.8%	69.2%	30.8%
15,457	MORGAN	5,514	3,817	1,697		2,120 R	69.2%	30.8%	69.2%	30.8%
36,506	MURRAY	4,397	3,117	1,280		1,837 R	70.9%	29.1%	70.9%	29.1%
186,291	MUSCOGEE	35,247	15,237	20,010		4,773 D	43.2%	56.8%	43.2%	56.8%
62,001	NEWTON	22,546	12,232	10,314		1,918 R	54.3%	45.7%	54.3%	45.7%
26,225	OCONEE	10,800	8,078	2,722		5,356 R	74.8%	25.2%	74.8%	25.2%
12,635	OGLETHORPE	3,772	2,485	1,287		1,198 R	65.9%	34.1%	65.9%	34.1%
81,678	PAULDING	26,929	19,864	7,065		12,799 R	73.8%	26.2%	73.8%	26.2%
23,668	PEACH	5,320	2,770	2,550		220 R	52.1%	47.9%	52.1%	47.9%
22,983	PICKENS	7,285	5,835	1,450		4,385 R	80.1%	19.9%	80.1%	19.9%
15,636	PIERCE	3,455	2,912	543		2,369 R	84.3%	15.7%	84.3%	15.7%
13,688	PIKE	4,833	3,882	951		2,931 R	80.3%	19.7%	80.3%	19.7%
38,127	POLK	6,970	4,829	2,141		2,688 R	69.3%	30.7%	69.3%	30.7%
9,588	PULASKI	2,423	1,537	886		651 R	63.4%	36.6%	63.4%	36.6%
18,812	PUTNAM	5,472	3,850	1,622		2,228 R	70.4%	29.6%	70.4%	29.6%
2,598	QUITMAN	482	234	248		14 D	48.5%	51.5%	48.5%	51.5%
15,050	RABUN	4,222	3,057	1,165		1,892 R	72.4%	27.6%	72.4%	27.6%
7,791	RANDOLPH	1,833	851	982		131 D	46.4%	53.6%	46.4%	53.6%
199,775	RICHMOND	39,599	16,089	23,510		7,421 D	40.6%	59.4%	40.6%	59.4%
70,111	ROCKDALE	21,712	11,006	10,706		300 R	50.7%	49.3%	50.7%	49.3%
3,766	SCHLEY	921	663	258		405 R	72.0%	28.0%	72.0%	28.0%
15,374	SCREVEN	3,303	1,807	1,496		311 R	54.7%	45.3%	54.7%	45.3%
9,369	SEMINOLE	1,753	1,086	667		419 R	62.0%	38.0%	62.0%	38.0%
58,417	SPALDING	13,544	8,703	4,841		3,862 R	64.3%	35.7%	64.3%	35.7%
25,435	STEPHENS	4,675	3,538	1,137		2,401 R	75.7%	24.3%	75.7%	24.3%
5,252	STEWART	1,026	403	623		220 D	39.3%	60.7%	39.3%	60.7%
33,200	SUMTER	6,473	3,286	3,187		99 R	50.8%	49.2%	50.8%	49.2%
6,498	TALBOT	1,818	678	1,140		462 D	37.3%	62.7%	37.3%	62.7%

GEORGIA

SENATOR 2008 (Runoff)

2000 Census Population	County	Total Vote	Republican	Democratic	Other	Rep.-Dem. Plurality	Percentage Total Vote Rep.	Percentage Total Vote Dem.	Percentage Major Vote Rep.	Percentage Major Vote Dem.
2,077	TALIAFERRO	542	190	352		162 D	35.1%	64.9%	35.1%	64.9%
22,305	TATTNALL	3,947	2,791	1,156		1,635 R	70.7%	29.3%	70.7%	29.3%
8,815	TAYLOR	1,988	1,153	835		318 R	58.0%	42.0%	58.0%	42.0%
11,794	TELFAIR	2,513	1,309	1,204		105 R	52.1%	47.9%	52.1%	47.9%
10,970	TERRELL	2,567	1,209	1,358		149 D	47.1%	52.9%	47.1%	52.9%
42,737	THOMAS	8,755	5,644	3,111		2,533 R	64.5%	35.5%	64.5%	35.5%
38,407	TIFT	8,262	5,818	2,444		3,374 R	70.4%	29.6%	70.4%	29.6%
26,067	TOOMBS	5,046	3,676	1,370		2,306 R	72.8%	27.2%	72.8%	27.2%
9,319	TOWNS	3,485	2,566	919		1,647 R	73.6%	26.4%	73.6%	26.4%
6,854	TREUTLEN	1,393	869	524		345 R	62.4%	37.6%	62.4%	37.6%
58,779	TROUP	12,875	8,242	4,633		3,609 R	64.0%	36.0%	64.0%	36.0%
9,504	TURNER	1,877	1,171	706		465 R	62.4%	37.6%	62.4%	37.6%
10,590	TWIGGS	2,448	1,112	1,336		224 D	45.4%	54.6%	45.4%	54.6%
17,289	UNION	6,172	4,625	1,547		3,078 R	74.9%	25.1%	74.9%	25.1%
27,597	UPSON	6,094	4,004	2,090		1,914 R	65.7%	34.3%	65.7%	34.3%
61,053	WALKER	10,903	7,876	3,027		4,849 R	72.2%	27.8%	72.2%	27.8%
60,687	WALTON	21,222	16,952	4,270		12,682 R	79.9%	20.1%	79.9%	20.1%
35,483	WARE	6,582	4,798	1,784		3,014 R	72.9%	27.1%	72.9%	27.1%
6,336	WARREN	1,347	665	682		17 D	49.4%	50.6%	49.4%	50.6%
21,176	WASHINGTON	4,634	2,308	2,326		18 D	49.8%	50.2%	49.8%	50.2%
26,565	WAYNE	5,662	3,994	1,668		2,326 R	70.5%	29.5%	70.5%	29.5%
2,390	WEBSTER	589	330	259		71 R	56.0%	44.0%	56.0%	44.0%
6,179	WHEELER	1,359	847	512		335 R	62.3%	37.7%	62.3%	37.7%
19,944	WHITE	6,311	4,975	1,336		3,639 R	78.8%	21.2%	78.8%	21.2%
83,525	WHITFIELD	13,272	9,738	3,534		6,204 R	73.4%	26.6%	73.4%	26.6%
8,577	WILCOX	1,754	1,189	565		624 R	67.8%	32.2%	67.8%	32.2%
10,687	WILKES	3,350	1,917	1,433		484 R	57.2%	42.8%	57.2%	42.8%
10,220	WILKINSON	2,606	1,296	1,310		14 D	49.7%	50.3%	49.7%	50.3%
21,967	WORTH	4,870	3,377	1,493		1,884 R	69.3%	30.7%	69.3%	30.7%
8,186,453	TOTAL	2,137,956	1,228,033	909,923		318,110 R	57.4%	42.6%	57.4%	42.6%

GEORGIA

HOUSE OF REPRESENTATIVES

CD	Year	Total Vote	Republican Vote	Republican Candidate	Democratic Vote	Democratic Candidate	Other Vote	Rep.-Dem. Plurality		Total Vote Rep.	Total Vote Dem.	Major Vote Rep.	Major Vote Dem.
1	2008	249,334	165,890	KINGSTON, JACK*	83,444	GILLESPIE, BILL		82,446	R	66.5%	33.5%	66.5%	33.5%
1	2006	138,629	94,961	KINGSTON, JACK*	43,668	NELSON, JIM		51,293	R	68.5%	31.5%	68.5%	31.5%
2	2008	229,786	71,351	FERRELL, LEE	158,435	BISHOP, SANFORD D. JR.*		87,084	D	31.1%	68.9%	31.1%	68.9%
2	2006	130,629	41,967	HUGHES, BRADLEY C.	88,662	BISHOP, SANFORD D. JR.*		46,695	D	32.1%	67.9%	32.1%	67.9%
3	2008	342,580	225,055	WESTMORELAND, LYNN*	117,522	CAMP, STEPHEN	3	107,533	R	65.7%	34.3%	65.7%	34.3%
3	2006	192,799	130,428	WESTMORELAND, LYNN*	62,371	McGRAW, MIKE		68,057	R	67.6%	32.4%	67.6%	32.4%
4	2008	224,694		—	224,494	JOHNSON, HENRY C. "HANK" JR.*	200	224,494	D		99.9%		100.0%
4	2006	141,194	34,778	DAVIS, CATHERINE	106,352	JOHNSON, HENRY C. "HANK" JR.	64	71,574	D	24.6%	75.3%	24.6%	75.4%
5	2008	231,474		—	231,368	LEWIS, JOHN*	106	231,368	D		100.0%		100.0%
5	2006	122,428		—	122,380	LEWIS, JOHN*	48	122,380	D		100.0%		100.0%
6	2008	338,071	231,520	PRICE, TOM*	106,551	JONES, BILL		124,969	R	68.5%	31.5%	68.5%	31.5%
6	2006	200,252	144,958	PRICE, TOM*	55,294	SINTON, STEVE		89,664	R	72.4%	27.6%	72.4%	27.6%
7	2008	337,513	209,354	LINDER, JOHN*	128,159	HECKMAN, DOUG		81,195	R	62.0%	38.0%	62.0%	38.0%
7	2006	184,114	130,561	LINDER, JOHN*	53,553	BURNS, ALLAN		77,008	R	70.9%	29.1%	70.9%	29.1%
8	2008	274,687	117,446	GODDARD, RICK	157,241	MARSHALL, JIM*		39,795	D	42.8%	57.2%	42.8%	57.2%
8	2006	159,568	78,908	COLLINS, MAC	80,660	MARSHALL, JIM*		1,752	D	49.5%	50.5%	49.5%	50.5%
9	2008	288,030	217,493	DEAL, NATHAN*	70,537	SCOTT, JEFF		146,956	R	75.5%	24.5%	75.5%	24.5%
9	2006	167,926	128,685	DEAL, NATHAN*	39,240	BRADBURY, JOHN D.	1	89,445	R	76.6%	23.4%	76.6%	23.4%
10	2008	291,903	177,265	BROUN, PAUL*	114,638	SAXON, BOBBY		62,627	R	60.7%	39.3%	60.7%	39.3%
10	2006	174,753	117,721	NORWOOD, CHARLIE*	57,032	HOLLEY, TERRY		60,689	R	67.4%	32.6%	67.4%	32.6%
11	2008	299,302	204,082	GINGREY, PHIL*	95,220	GAMMON, HUGH "BUD"		108,862	R	68.2%	31.8%	68.2%	31.8%
11	2006	166,788	118,524	GINGREY, PHIL*	48,261	PILLION, PATRICK SAMUEL	3	70,263	R	71.1%	28.9%	71.1%	28.9%
12	2008	249,335	84,773	STONE, JOHN	164,562	BARROW, JOHN*		79,789	D	34.0%	66.0%	34.0%	66.0%
12	2006	142,438	70,787	BURNS, MAX	71,651	BARROW, JOHN*		864	D	49.7%	50.3%	49.7%	50.3%
13	2008	298,239	92,320	HONEYCUTT, DEBORAH	205,919	SCOTT, DAVID*		113,599	D	31.0%	69.0%	31.0%	69.0%
13	2006	148,789	45,770	HONEYCUTT, DEBORAH	103,019	SCOTT, DAVID*		57,249	D	30.8%	69.2%	30.8%	69.2%
TOTAL	2008	3,654,948	1,796,549		1,858,090		309	61,541	D	49.2%	50.8%	49.2%	50.8%
TOTAL	2006	2,070,307	1,138,048		932,143		116	205,905	R	55.0%	45.0%	55.0%	45.0%
TOTAL	2004	2,960,763	1,819,817		1,140,869		77	678,948	R	61.5%	38.5%	61.5%	38.5%
TOTAL	2002	1,918,297	1,104,162		814,024		111	290,138	R	57.6%	42.4%	57.6%	42.4%

Note: An asterisk (*) denotes incumbent. Georgia's congressional district lines were changed between the 2004 and 2006 elections. For general election results for 2002 and 2004, see America Votes 26, p. 139.

GEORGIA

GENERAL AND PRIMARY ELECTIONS

2008 GENERAL ELECTIONS

President   Other vote was 28,731 Libertarian (Bob Barr); 1,402 write-in (Chuck Baldwin); 1,158 write-in (Ralph Nader); 250 write-in (Cynthia A. McKinney); 23 write-in (Michael A. Peroutka); 20 write-in (James Harris); 8 write-in (Jonathan Allen); 6 write-in (Frank Moore); 4 write-in (David C. Byrne); 2 write-in (Brian Russell Brown).

Senator   Other vote was 127,923 Libertarian (Allen Buckley); 43 write-in (Eleanor Garcia); 29 write-in (William Salomone Jr.).

House   Other vote was:

CD 1
CD 2
CD 3   3 write-in (Loretta VanPelt).
CD 4   159 write-in (Loren Christopher Collins); 35 write-in (Faye Coffield); 6 write-in (Jacob Perasso).
CD 5   81 write-in (Shira Kash); 25 write-in (Jeanne Fitzmaurice).
CD 6
CD 7
CD 8
CD 9
CD 10
CD 11
CD 12
CD 13

2008 PRIMARY ELECTIONS

Primary   February 5, 2008 (President)   **Registration**   5,410,967   No Party Registration
July 15, 2008 (Congress)   (includes 669,469 inactive
registrants as of June 16, 2008)

Primary Runoff   August 5, 2008

Primary Type   Open—Any registered voter could participate in either the Democratic or Republican primary, although if they voted in one party's primary they could not participate in a primary runoff of the other party. Voters who did not participate in the primary could vote in either party's runoff.

GEORGIA

GENERAL AND PRIMARY ELECTIONS

	REPUBLICAN PRIMARIES			DEMOCRATIC PRIMARIES		
President	Mike Huckabee	326,874	33.9%	Barack Obama	704,247	66.4%
	John McCain	304,751	31.6%	Hillary Clinton	330,026	31.1%
	Mitt Romney	290,707	30.2%	John Edwards	18,209	1.7%
	Ron Paul	28,096	2.9%	Joseph R. Biden Jr.	2,538	0.2%
	Rudolph Giuliani	7,162	0.7%	Dennis J. Kucinich	2,096	0.2%
	Fred Thompson	3,414	0.4%	Bill Richardson	1,879	0.2%
	Alan Keyes	1,458	0.2%	Mike Gravel	952	0.1%
	Duncan Hunter	755	0.1%	Christopher J. Dodd	904	0.1%
	Tom Tancredo	324				
	TOTAL	*963,541*		*TOTAL*	*1,060,851*	
Senator	Saxby Chambliss*	392,902		Vernon Jones	199,026	40.4%
				Jim Martin	169,635	34.4%
				Dale Cardwell	79,181	16.1%
				Rand Knight	25,667	5.2%
				Josh Lanier	19,717	4.0%
				TOTAL	*493,226*	
				PRIMARY RUNOFF		
				Jim Martin	191,061	59.9%
				Vernon Jones	127,993	40.1%
				TOTAL	*319,054*	
Congressional District 1	Jack Kingston*	32,470	100.0%	Bill Gillespie	32,802	100.0%
Congressional District 2	Lee Ferrell	11,430	100.0%	Sanford D. Bishop Jr.*	59,384	100.0%
Congressional District 3	Lynn Westmoreland*	55,128	100.0%	Stephen Camp	18,984	100.0%
Congressional District 4	No Republican candidate			Henry C. "Hank" Johnson Jr.*	47,439	100.0%
Congressional District 5	No Republican candidate			John Lewis*	36,713	69.0%
				Markel Hutchins	8,287	15.6%
				"Able" Mable Thomas	8,185	15.4%
				TOTAL	*53,185*	
Congressional District 6	Tom Price*	30,957	100.0%	Bill Jones	10,920	100.0%
Congressional District 7	John Linder*	48,668	100.0%	Doug Heckman	13,318	100.0%
Congressional District 8	Rick Goddard	25,420	100.0%	Jim Marshall*	44,211	85.7%
				Robert Nowak	7,396	14.3%
				TOTAL	*51,607*	
Congressional District 9	Nathan Deal*	54,653	100.0%	Jeff Scott	12,596	100.0%
Congressional District 10	Paul Broun*	44,956	71.0%	Bobby Saxon	24,001	100.0%
	Barry Fleming	18,372	29.0%			
	TOTAL	*63,328*				
Congressional District 11	Phil Gingrey*	29,155	100.0%	Hugh "Bud" Gammon	15,099	100.0%
Congressional District 12	John Stone	9,462	56.7%	John Barrow*	45,235	76.4%
	Ray McKinney	5,316	31.9%	Regina D. Thomas	13,955	23.6%
	Ben Crystal	1,908	11.4%			
	TOTAL	*16,686*		*TOTAL*	*59,190*	
Congressional District 13	Deborah Honeycutt	11,478	100.0%	David Scott*	30,719	63.7%
				Donzella James	17,526	36.3%
				TOTAL	*48,245*	

Note: An asterisk (*) denotes incumbent.

HAWAII

Congressional districts first established for elections held in 2002
2 members

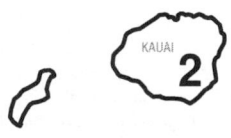

HAWAII

GOVERNOR
Linda Lingle (R). Reelected 2006 to a four-year term. Previously elected 2002.

SENATORS (2 Democrats)
Daniel K. Akaka (D). Reelected 2006 to a six-year term. Previously elected 2000, 1994, and 1990 to fill out the remaining four years of the term vacated by the death of Senator Spark M. Matsunaga (D); Akaka had been appointed in May 1990 to fill this vacancy.

Daniel K. Inouye (D). Reelected 2004 to a six-year term. Previously elected 1998, 1992, 1986, 1980, 1974, 1968, 1962.

REPRESENTATIVES (2 Democrats)
1. Neil Abercrombie (D)　　　　　2. Mazie K. Hirono (D)

POSTWAR VOTE FOR PRESIDENT

| | | Republican | | Democratic | | Other | | Percentage | | | |
| | | | | | | | | Total Vote | | Major Vote | |
Year	Total Vote	Vote	Candidate	Vote	Candidate	Vote	Plurality	Rep.	Dem.	Rep.	Dem.
2008	453,568	120,566	McCain, John	325,871	Obama, Barack	7,131	205,305 D	26.6%	71.8%	27.0%	73.0%
2004	429,013	194,191	Bush, George W.	231,708	Kerry, John	3,114	37,517 D	45.3%	54.0%	45.6%	54.4%
2000**	367,951	137,845	Bush, George W.	205,286	Gore, Al	24,820	67,441 D	37.5%	55.8%	40.2%	59.8%
1996**	360,120	113,943	Dole, Bob	205,012	Clinton, Bill	41,165	91,069 D	31.6%	56.9%	35.7%	64.3%
1992**	372,842	136,822	Bush, George	179,310	Clinton, Bill	56,710	42,488 D	36.7%	48.1%	43.3%	56.7%
1988	354,461	158,625	Bush, George	192,364	Dukakis, Michael S.	3,472	33,739 D	44.8%	54.3%	45.2%	54.8%
1984	335,846	185,050	Reagan, Ronald	147,154	Mondale, Walter F.	3,642	37,896 R	55.1%	43.8%	55.7%	44.3%
1980**	303,287	130,112	Reagan, Ronald	135,879	Carter, Jimmy	37,296	5,767 D	42.9%	44.8%	48.9%	51.1%
1976	291,301	140,003	Ford, Gerald R.	147,375	Carter, Jimmy	3,923	7,372 D	48.1%	50.6%	48.7%	51.3%
1972	270,274	168,865	Nixon, Richard M.	101,409	McGovern, George S.		67,456 R	62.5%	37.5%	62.5%	37.5%
1968**	236,218	91,425	Nixon, Richard M.	141,324	Humphrey, Hubert H.	3,469	49,899 D	38.7%	59.8%	39.3%	60.7%
1964	207,271	44,022	Goldwater, Barry M.	163,249	Johnson, Lyndon B.		119,227 D	21.2%	78.8%	21.2%	78.8%
1960	184,705	92,295	Nixon, Richard M.	92,410	Kennedy, John F.		115 D	50.0%	50.0%	50.0%	50.0%

Notes: **In past elections, the other vote included: 2000 - 21,623 Green (Ralph Nader); 1996 - 27,358 Reform (Ross Perot); 1992 - 53,003 Independent (Perot); 1980 - 32,021 Independent (John Anderson); 1968 - 3,469 American Independent (George Wallace). Hawaii was formally admitted as a state in August 1959.

HAWAII

POSTWAR VOTE FOR GOVERNOR

Year	Total Vote	Republican Vote	Republican Candidate	Democratic Vote	Democratic Candidate	Other Vote	Plurality	Total Vote Rep.	Total Vote Dem.	Major Vote Rep.	Major Vote Dem.
2006	344,315	215,313	Lingle, Linda	121,717	Iwase, Randy	7,285	93,596 R	62.5%	35.4%	63.9%	36.1%
2002	382,110	197,009	Lingle, Linda	179,647	Hirono, Mazie K.	5,454	17,362 R	51.6%	47.0%	52.3%	47.7%
1998	407,556	198,952	Lingle, Linda	204,206	Cayetano, Benjamin J.	4,398	5,254 D	48.8%	50.1%	49.3%	50.7%
1994**	369,013	107,908	Saiki, Patricia	134,978	Cayetano, Benjamin J.	126,127	21,820 D	29.2%	36.6%	44.4%	55.6%
1990	340,132	131,310	Hemmings, Fred	203,491	Waihee, John	5,331	72,181 D	38.6%	59.8%	39.2%	60.8%
1986	334,115	160,460	Anderson, D. G.	173,655	Waihee, John		13,195 D	48.0%	52.0%	48.0%	52.0%
1982**	311,853	81,507	Anderson, D. G.	141,043	Ariyoshi, George R.	89,303	51,740 D	26.1%	45.2%	36.6%	63.4%
1978	281,587	124,610	Leopold, John	153,394	Ariyoshi, George R.	3,583	28,784 D	44.3%	54.5%	44.8%	55.2%
1974	249,650	113,388	Crossley, Randolph	136,262	Ariyoshi, George R.		22,874 D	45.4%	54.6%	45.4%	54.6%
1970	239,061	101,249	King, Samuel P.	137,812	Burns, John A.		36,563 D	42.4%	57.6%	42.4%	57.6%
1966	213,164	104,324	Crossley, Randolph	108,840	Burns, John A.		4,516 D	48.9%	51.1%	48.9%	51.1%
1962	196,015	81,707	Quinn, William F.	114,308	Burns, John A.		32,601 D	41.7%	58.3%	41.7%	58.3%
1959S	168,662	86,213	Quinn, William F.	82,074	Burns, John A.	375	4,139 R	51.1%	48.7%	51.2%	48.8%

Notes: **In past elections, the other vote included: 1994 - 113,158 Best Party (Frank F. Fasi); 1982 - 89,303 Independent Democrat (Fasi). In both 1982 and 1994, Fasi finished second. The 1959 election was for a short term pending the regular vote in 1962.

POSTWAR VOTE FOR SENATOR

Year	Total Vote	Republican Vote	Republican Candidate	Democratic Vote	Democratic Candidate	Other Vote	Rep.-Dem. Plurality	Total Vote Rep.	Total Vote Dem.	Major Vote Rep.	Major Vote Dem.
2006	342,842	126,097	Thielen, Cynthia	210,330	Akaka, Daniel K.	6,415	84,233 D	36.8%	61.3%	37.5%	62.5%
2004	415,347	87,172	Cavasso, Cam	313,629	Inouye, Daniel K.	14,546	226,457 D	21.0%	75.5%	21.7%	78.3%
2000	345,623	84,701	Carroll, John S.	251,215	Akaka, Daniel K.	9,707	166,514 D	24.5%	72.7%	25.2%	74.8%
1998	398,124	70,964	Young, Crystal	315,252	Inouye, Daniel K.	11,908	244,288 D	17.8%	79.2%	18.4%	81.6%
1994	356,902	86,320	Hustace, Maria M.	256,189	Akaka, Daniel K.	14,393	169,869 D	24.2%	71.8%	25.2%	74.8%
1992**	363,662	97,928	Reed, Rick	208,266	Inouye, Daniel K.	57,468	110,338 D	26.9%	57.3%	32.0%	68.0%
1990S	349,666	155,978	Saiki, Patricia	188,901	Akaka, Daniel K.	4,787	32,923 D	44.6%	54.0%	45.2%	54.8%
1988	323,876	66,987	Hustace, Maria M.	247,941	Matsunaga, Spark M.	8,948	180,954 D	20.7%	76.6%	21.3%	78.7%
1986	328,797	86,910	Hutchinson, Frank	241,887	Inouye, Daniel K.		154,977 D	26.4%	73.6%	26.4%	73.6%
1982	306,410	52,071	Brown, Clarence J.	245,386	Matsunaga, Spark M.	8,953	193,315 D	17.0%	80.1%	17.5%	82.5%
1980	288,006	53,068	Brown, Cooper	224,485	Inouye, Daniel K.	10,453	171,417 D	18.4%	77.9%	19.1%	80.9%
1976	302,092	122,724	Quinn, William F.	162,305	Matsunaga, Spark M.	17,063	39,581 D	40.6%	53.7%	43.1%	56.9%
1974**	250,221		—	207,454	Inouye, Daniel K.	42,767	207,454 D		82.9%		100.0%
1970	240,760	124,163	Fong, Hiram L.	116,597	Heftel, Cecil		7,566 R	51.6%	48.4%	51.6%	48.4%
1968	226,927	34,008	Thiessen, Wayne C.	189,248	Inouye, Daniel K.	3,671	155,240 D	15.0%	83.4%	15.2%	84.8%
1964	208,814	110,747	Fong, Hiram L.	96,789	Gill, Thomas P.	1,278	13,958 R	53.0%	46.4%	53.4%	46.6%
1962	196,361	60,067	Dillingham, Ben F.	136,294	Inouye, Daniel K.		76,227 D	30.6%	69.4%	30.6%	69.4%
1959S	164,808	87,161	Fong, Hiram L.	77,647	Fasi, Frank F.		9,514 R	52.9%	47.1%	52.9%	47.1%
1959S	163,875	79,123	Tsukiyama, W. C.	83,700	Long, Oren E.	1,052	4,577 D	48.3%	51.1%	48.6%	51.4%

Notes: **In past elections, the other vote was: 1992 - 49,921 Green (Linda B. Martin); 1974 - 42,767 Peoples (James D. Kimmel). The 1990 election was for a short term to fill a vacancy. The two 1959 elections were held to indeterminate terms and the Senate later determined by lot that Senator Long would serve a short term and Senator Fong a long term. The Republican Party did not run a candidate in the 1974 Senate election.

HAWAII

PRESIDENT 2008

2000 Census Population	County	Total Vote	Republican	Democratic	Other	Rep.-Dem. Plurality	Percentage			
							Total Vote		Major Vote	
							Rep.	Dem.	Rep.	Dem.
148,677	HAWAII	66,916	14,866	50,819	1,231	35,953 D	22.2%	75.9%	22.6%	77.4%
876,156	HONOLULU	306,813	88,164	214,239	4,410	126,075 D	28.7%	69.8%	29.2%	70.8%
58,463	KAUAI	27,224	6,245	20,416	563	14,171 D	22.9%	75.0%	23.4%	76.6%
128,094	MAUI	51,789	11,154	39,727	908	28,573 D	21.5%	76.7%	21.9%	78.1%
	Overseas Ballots	826	137	670	19	533 D	16.6%	81.1%	17.0%	83.0%
1,211,537	TOTAL	453,568	120,566	325,871	7,131	205,305 D	26.6%	71.8%	27.0%	73.0%

Note: The 2000 Census included 147 people in Kalawao County; their votes are part of the Maui County returns.

HAWAII

HOUSE OF REPRESENTATIVES

CD	Year	Total Vote	Republican		Democratic		Other Vote	Rep.-Dem. Plurality	Percentage			
			Vote	Candidate	Vote	Candidate			Total Vote		Major Vote	
									Rep.	Dem.	Rep.	Dem.
1	2008	199,917	38,115	TATAII, STEVE	154,208	ABERCROMBIE, NEIL*	7,594	116,093 D	19.1%	77.1%	19.8%	80.2%
1	2006	162,794	49,890	HOUGH, RICHARD "NOAH"	112,904	ABERCROMBIE, NEIL*		63,014 D	30.6%	69.4%	30.6%	69.4%
1	2004	204,181	69,371	TANONAKA, DALTON	128,567	ABERCROMBIE, NEIL*	6,243	59,196 D	34.0%	63.0%	35.0%	65.0%
1	2002	180,733	45,032	TERRY, MARK	131,673	ABERCROMBIE, NEIL*	4,028	86,641 D	24.9%	72.9%	25.5%	74.5%
2	2008	217,914	44,425	EVANS, ROGER B.	165,748	HIRONO, MAZIE K.*	7,741	121,323 D	20.4%	76.1%	21.1%	78.9%
2	2006	175,150	68,244	HOGUE, BOB	106,906	HIRONO, MAZIE K.		38,662 D	39.0%	61.0%	39.0%	61.0%
2	2004	212,389	79,072	GABBARD, MIKE	133,317	CASE, ED*		54,245 D	37.2%	62.8%	37.2%	62.8%
2	2002	179,251	71,661	McDERMOTT, BOB	100,671	MINK, PATSY T.*	6,919	29,010 D	40.0%	56.2%	41.6%	58.4%
TOTAL	2008	417,831	82,540		319,956		15,335	237,416 D	19.8%	76.6%	20.5%	79.5%
TOTAL	2006	337,944	118,134		219,810		—	101,676 D	35.0%	65.0%	35.0%	65.0%
TOTAL	2004	416,570	148,443		261,884		6,243	113,441 D	35.6%	62.9%	36.2%	63.8%
TOTAL	2002	359,984	116,693		232,344		10,947	115,651 D	32.4%	64.5%	33.4%	66.6%

Note: An asterisk (*) denotes incumbent.

HAWAII

GENERAL AND PRIMARY ELECTIONS

2008 GENERAL ELECTIONS

President   Other vote was 3,825 Independent (Ralph Nader); 1,314 Libertarian (Bob Barr); 1,013 Constitution (Chuck Baldwin); 979 Green (Cynthia A. McKinney).

House   Other vote was:

CD 1   7,594 Libertarian (Li Zhao).
CD 2   4,042 Independent (Shaun Stenshol); 3,699 Libertarian (Lloyd J. "Jeff" Mallan).

2008 PRIMARY ELECTIONS

Primary   September 20, 2008   **Registration**   667,647   No Party Registration
                                            (as of September 20, 2008)

Primary Type   Open—Any registered voter could participate in the party primary of their choice.

	REPUBLICAN PRIMARIES			DEMOCRATIC PRIMARIES		
Congressional District 1	Steve Tataii	13,088	100.0%	Neil Abercrombie*	76,140	100.0%
Congressional District 2	Roger B. Evans	12,750	100.0%	Mazie K. Hirono*	73,822	100.0%

Note: An asterisk (*) denotes incumbent.

IDAHO

Congressional districts first established for elections held in 2002
2 members

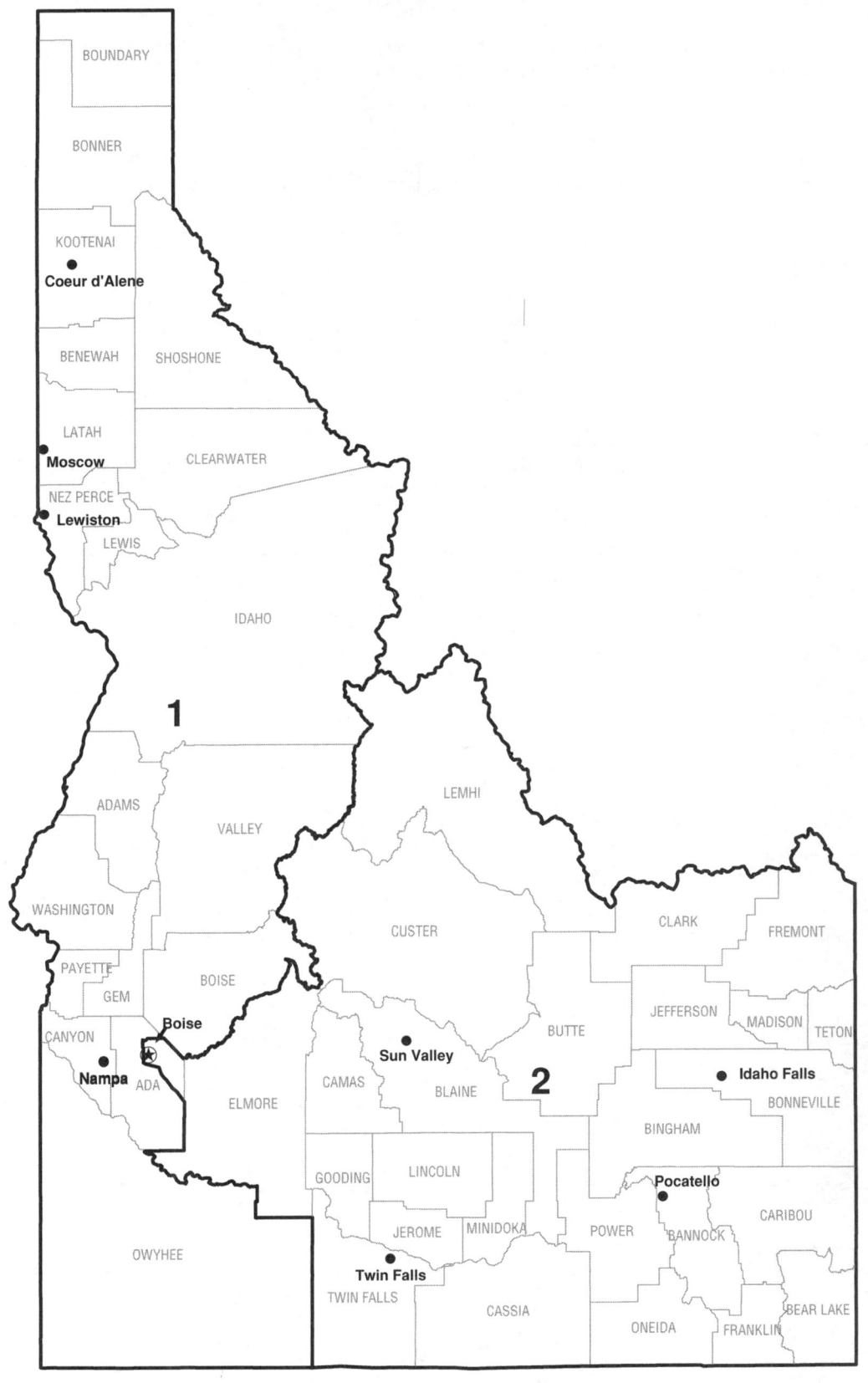

IDAHO

GOVERNOR
C. L. "Butch" Otter (R). Elected 2006 to a four-year term.

SENATORS (2 Republicans)
Michael D. Crapo (R). Reelected 2004 to a six-year term. Previously e ected 1998.

Jim Risch (R). Elected 2008 to a six-year term.

REPRESENTATIVES (1 Democrat, 1 Republican)
1. Walt Minnick (D)   2. Mike Simpson (R)

POSTWAR VOTE FOR PRESIDENT

Year	Total Vote	Republican Vote	Republican Candidate	Democratic Vote	Democratic Candidate	Other Vote	Plurality	Total Vote Rep.	Total Vote Dem.	Major Vote Rep.	Major Vote Dem.
2008	655,122	403,122	McCain, John	236,440	Obama, Barack	15,670	166,572 R	61.5%	36.1%	63.0%	37.0%
2004	598,447	409,235	Bush, George W.	181,098	Kerry, John	8,114	228,137 R	68.4%	30.3%	69.3%	30.7%
2000**	501,621	336,937	Bush, George W.	138,637	Gore, Al	26,047	198,300 R	67.2%	27.6%	70.8%	29.2%
1996**	491,719	256,595	Dole, Bob	165,443	Clinton, Bill	69,681	91,152 R	52.2%	33.6%	60.8%	39.2%
1992**	482,142	202,645	Bush, George	137,013	Clinton, Bill	142,484	65,632 R	42.0%	28.4%	59.7%	40.3%
1988	408,968	253,881	Bush, George	147,272	Dukakis, Michael S.	7,815	106,609 R	62.1%	36.0%	63.3%	36.7%
1984	411,144	297,523	Reagan, Ronald	108,510	Mondale, Walter F.	5,111	189,013 R	72.4%	26.4%	73.3%	26.7%
1980**	437,431	290,699	Reagan, Ronald	110,192	Carter, Jimmy	36,540	180,507 R	66.5%	25.2%	72.5%	27.5%
1976	344,071	204,151	Ford, Gerald R.	126,549	Carter, Jimmy	13,371	77,602 R	59.3%	36.8%	61.7%	38.3%
1972	310,379	199,384	Nixon, Richard M.	80,826	McGovern, George S.	30,169	118,558 R	64.2%	26.0%	71.2%	28.8%
1968**	291,183	165,369	Nixon, Richard M.	89,273	Humphrey, Hubert H.	36,541	76,096 R	56.8%	30.7%	64.9%	35.1%
1964	292,477	143,557	Goldwater, Barry M.	148,920	Johnson, Lyndon B.		5,363 D	49.1%	50.9%	49.1%	50.9%
1960	300,450	161,597	Nixon, Richard M.	138,853	Kennedy, John F.		22,744 R	53.8%	46.2%	53.8%	46.2%
1956	272,989	166,979	Eisenhower, Dwight D.	105,868	Stevenson, Adlai E.	142	61,111 R	61.2%	38.8%	61.2%	38.8%
1952	276,254	180,707	Eisenhower, Dwight D.	95,081	Stevenson, Adlai E.	466	85,626 R	65.4%	34.4%	65.5%	34.5%
1948	214,816	101,514	Dewey, Thomas E.	107,370	Truman, Harry S.	5,932	5,856 D	47.3%	50.0%	48.6%	51.4%

**In past elections, the other vote included: 2000–12,292 - Green (Ralph Nader); 1996 - 62,518 Reform (Ross Perot); 1992 - 130,395 Independent (Perot); 1980 - 27,058 Independent (John Anderson); 1968 - 36,541 American Independent (George Wallace).

IDAHO

POSTWAR VOTE FOR GOVERNOR

Year	Total Vote	Republican		Democratic		Other Vote	Rep.-Dem. Plurality	Percentage			
								Total Vote		Major Vote	
		Vote	Candidate	Vote	Candidate			Rep.	Dem.	Rep.	Dem.
2006	450,850	237,437	Otter, C.L. "Butch"	198,845	Brady, Jerry M.	14,568	38,592 R	52.7%	44.1%	54.4%	45.6%
2002	411,477	231,566	Kempthorne, Dirk	171,711	Brady, Jerry M.	8,200	59,855 R	56.3%	41.7%	57.4%	42.6%
1998	381,248	258,095	Kempthorne, Dirk	110,815	Huntley, Robert C.	12,338	147,280 R	67.7%	29.1%	70.0%	30.0%
1994	413,346	216,123	Batt, Phil	181,363	EchoHawk, Larry	15,860	34,760 R	52.3%	43.9%	54.4%	45.6%
1990	320,610	101,937	Fairchild, Roger	218,673	Andrus, Cecil D.		116,736 D	31.8%	68.2%	31.8%	68.2%
1986	387,426	189,794	Leroy, David H.	193,429	Andrus, Cecil D.	4,203	3,635 D	49.0%	49.9%	49.5%	50.5%
1982	326,522	161,157	Batt, Philip	165,365	Evans, John V.		4,208 D	49.4%	50.6%	49.4%	50.6%
1978	288,566	114,149	Larsen, Allan	169,540	Evans, John V.	4,877	55,391 D	39.6%	58.8%	40.2%	59.8%
1974	259,632	68,731	Murphy, Jack M.	184,142	Andrus, Cecil D.	6,759	115,411 D	26.5%	70.9%	27.2%	72.8%
1970	245,112	117,108	Samuelson, Don	128,004	Andrus, Cecil D.		10,896 D	47.8%	52.2%	47.8%	52.2%
1966**	252,593	104,586	Samuelson, Don	93,744	Andrus, Cecil D.	54,263	10,842 R	41.4%	37.1%	52.7%	47.3%
1962	255,454	139,578	Smylie, Robert E.	115,876	Smith, Vernon K.		23,702 R	54.6%	45.4%	54.6%	45.4%
1958	239,046	121,810	Smylie, Robert E.	117,236	Derr, A. M.		4,574 R	51.0%	49.0%	51.0%	49.0%
1954	228,685	124,038	Smylie, Robert E.	104,647	Hamilton, Clark		19,391 R	54.2%	45.8%	54.2%	45.8%
1950	204,792	107,642	Jordan, Len B.	97,150	Wright, Calvin E.		10,492 R	52.6%	47.4%	52.6%	47.4%
1946	181,364	102,233	Robins, C. A.	79,131	Williams, Arnold		23,102 R	56.4%	43.6%	56.4%	43.6%

**In past elections, the other vote included: 1966 - 30,913 Independent (Perry Swisher).

POSTWAR VOTE FOR SENATOR

Year	Total Vote	Republican		Democratic		Other Vote	Rep.-Dem. Plurality	Percentage			
								Total Vote		Major Vote	
		Vote	Candidate	Vote	Candidate			Rep.	Dem.	Rep.	Dem.
2008	644,780	371,744	Risch, Jim	219,903	LaRocco, Larry	53,133	151,841 R	57.7%	34.1%	62.8%	37.2%
2004**	503,932	499,796	Crapo, Michael D.	—		4,136	499,796 R	99.2%		100.0%	
2002	408,544	266,215	Craig, Larry E.	132,975	Blinken, Alan	9,354	133,240 R	65.2%	32.5%	66.7%	33.3%
1998	378,174	262,966	Crapo, Michael D.	107,375	Mauk, Bill	7,833	155,591 R	69.5%	28.4%	71.0%	29.0%
1996	497,233	283,532	Craig, Larry E.	198,422	Minnick, Walt	15,279	85,110 R	57.0%	39.9%	58.8%	41.2%
1992	478,522	270,468	Kempthorne, Dirk	208,036	Stallings, Richard	18	62,432 R	56.5%	43.5%	56.5%	43.5%
1990	315,936	193,641	Craig, Larry E.	122,295	Twilegar, Ron J.		71,346 R	61.3%	38.7%	61.3%	38.7%
1986	382,024	196,958	Symms, Steven D.	185,066	Evans, John V.		11,892 R	51.6%	48.4%	51.6%	48.4%
1984	406,168	293,193	McClure, James A.	105,591	Busch, Peter M.	7,384	187,602 R	72.2%	26.0%	73.5%	26.5%
1980	439,647	218,701	Symms, Steven D.	214,439	Church, Frank	6,507	4,262 R	49.7%	48.8%	50.5%	49.5%
1978	284,047	194,412	McClure, James A.	89,635	Jensen, Dwight		104,777 R	68.4%	31.6%	68.4%	31.6%
1974	258,847	109,072	Smith, Robert L.	145,140	Church, Frank	4,635	36,068 D	42.1%	56.1%	42.9%	57.1%
1972	309,602	161,804	McClure, James A.	140,913	Davis, William E.	6,885	20,891 R	52.3%	45.5%	53.5%	46.5%
1968	287,876	114,394	Hansen, George V.	173,482	Church, Frank		59,088 D	39.7%	60.3%	39.7%	60.3%
1966	252,456	139,819	Jordan, Len B.	112,637	Harding, Ralph R.		27,182 R	55.4%	44.6%	55.4%	44.6%
1962	258,786	117,129	Hawley, Jack	141,657	Church, Frank		24,528 D	45.3%	54.7%	45.3%	54.7%
1962S	257,677	131,279	Jordan, Len B.	126,398	Pfost, Gracie		4,881 R	50.9%	49.1%	50.9%	49.1%
1960	292,096	152,648	Dworshak, Henry C.	139,448	McLaughlin, Bob		13,200 R	52.3%	47.7%	52.3%	47.7%
1956	265,292	102,781	Welker, Herman	149,096	Church, Frank	13,415	46,315 D	38.7%	56.2%	40.8%	59.2%
1954	226,408	142,269	Dworshak, Henry C.	84,139	Taylor, Glen H.		58,130 R	62.8%	37.2%	62.8%	37.2%
1950	201,417	124,237	Welker, Herman	77,180	Clark, D. Worth		47,057 R	61.7%	38.3%	61.7%	38.3%
1950S	201,970	104,068	Dworshak, Henry C.	97,902	Burtenshaw, Claude		6,166 R	51.5%	48.5%	51.5%	48.5%
1948	214,188	103,868	Dworshak, Henry C.	107,000	Miller, Bert H.	3,320	3,132 D	48.5%	50.0%	49.3%	50.7%
1946S	180,152	105,523	Dworshak, Henry C.	74,629	Donart, George E.		30,894 R	58.6%	41.4%	58.6%	41.4%

Notes: In 2004 there was no Democratic candidate. A write-in candidate, who was a Democrat, received 4,136 votes, which are listed in the Other Vote column. The 1946 election and one each of the 1950 and 1962 elections were for short terms to fill vacancies.

IDAHO

PRESIDENT 2008

2000 Census Population	County	Total Vote	Republican	Democratic	Other	Rep.-Dem. Plurality	Total Vote Rep.	Total Vote Dem.	Major Vote Rep.	Major Vote Dem.
300,904	ADA	179,402	93,328	82,236	3,838	11,092 R	52.0%	45.8%	53.2%	46.8%
3,476	ADAMS	2,320	1,517	728	75	789 R	65.4%	31.4%	67.6%	32.4%
75,565	BANNOCK	35,105	19,356	14,792	957	4,564 R	55.1%	42.1%	56.7%	43.3%
6,411	BEAR LAKE	2,943	2,377	502	64	1,875 R	80.8%	17.1%	82.6%	17.4%
9,171	BENEWAH	4,164	2,646	1,407	111	1,239 R	63.5%	33.8%	65.3%	34.7%
41,735	BINGHAM	17,155	12,230	4,424	501	7,806 R	71.3%	25.8%	73.4%	26.6%
18,991	BLAINE	10,571	3,439	6,947	185	3,508 D	32.5%	65.7%	33.1%	66.9%
6,670	BOISE	3,773	2,433	1,240	100	1,193 R	64.5%	32.9%	66.2%	33.8%
36,835	BONNER	19,547	11,145	7,840	562	3,305 R	57.0%	40.1%	58.7%	41.3%
82,522	BONNEVILLE	41,703	29,334	11,417	952	17,917 R	70.3%	27.4%	72.0%	28.0%
9,871	BOUNDARY	4,733	3,078	1,484	171	1,594 R	65.0%	31.4%	67.5%	32.5%
2,899	BUTTE	1,410	1,056	318	36	738 R	74.9%	22.6%	76.9%	23.1%
991	CAMAS	618	422	187	9	235 R	68.3%	30.3%	69.3%	30.7%
131,441	CANYON	64,246	42,752	20,147	1,347	22,605 R	66.5%	31.4%	68.0%	32.0%
7,304	CARIBOU	3,302	2,656	553	93	2,103 R	80.4%	16.7%	82.8%	17.2%
21,416	CASSIA	7,842	6,309	1,332	201	4,977 R	80.5%	17.0%	82.6%	17.4%
1,022	CLARK	375	305	64	6	241 R	81.3%	17.1%	82.7%	17.3%
8,930	CLEARWATER	3,906	2,569	1,211	126	1,358 R	65.8%	31.0%	68.0%	32.0%
4,342	CUSTER	2,352	1,694	611	47	1,083 R	72.0%	26.0%	73.5%	26.5%
29,130	ELMORE	8,436	5,665	2,591	180	3,074 R	67.2%	30.7%	68.6%	31.4%
11,329	FRANKLIN	5,073	4,246	600	227	3,646 R	83.7%	11.8%	87.6%	12.4%
11,819	FREMONT	5,880	4,700	1,065	115	3,635 R	79.9%	18.1%	81.5%	18.5%
15,181	GEM	7,947	5,585	2,166	196	3,419 R	70.3%	27.3%	72.1%	27.9%
14,155	GOODING	5,391	3,765	1,489	137	2,276 R	69.8%	27.6%	71.7%	28.3%
15,511	IDAHO	8,210	5,895	2,017	298	3,878 R	71.8%	24.6%	74.5%	25.5%
19,155	JEFFERSON	10,441	8,540	1,641	260	6,899 R	81.8%	15.7%	83.9%	16.1%
18,342	JEROME	6,847	4,897	1,794	156	3,103 R	71.5%	26.2%	73.2%	26.8%
108,685	KOOTENAI	61,932	38,387	22,120	1,425	16,267 R	62.0%	35.7%	63.4%	36.6%
34,935	LATAH	17,714	7,988	9,195	531	1,207 D	45.1%	51.9%	46.5%	53.5%
7,806	LEMHI	4,105	2,938	1,061	106	1,877 R	71.6%	25.8%	73.5%	26.5%
3,747	LEWIS	1,804	1,275	479	50	796 R	70.7%	26.6%	72.7%	27.3%
4,044	LINCOLN	1,870	1,232	545	93	687 R	65.9%	29.1%	69.3%	30.7%
27,467	MADISON	13,057	11,131	1,627	299	9,504 R	85.2%	12.5%	87.2%	12.8%
20,174	MINIDOKA	6,890	5,087	1,630	173	3,457 R	73.8%	23.7%	75.7%	24.3%
37,410	NEZ PERCE	17,823	10,357	7,123	343	3,234 R	58.1%	40.0%	59.3%	40.7%
4,125	ONEIDA	2,162	1,724	381	57	1,343 R	79.7%	17.6%	81.9%	18.1%
10,644	OWYHEE	4,058	3,024	944	90	2,080 R	74.5%	23.3%	76.2%	23.8%
20,578	PAYETTE	8,613	5,988	2,415	210	3,573 R	69.5%	28.0%	71.3%	28.7%
7,538	POWER	2,842	1,754	1,027	61	727 R	61.7%	36.1%	63.1%	36.9%
13,771	SHOSHONE	5,666	2,953	2,521	192	432 R	52.1%	44.5%	53.9%	46.1%
5,999	TETON	4,658	2,263	2,302	93	39 D	48.6%	49.4%	49.6%	50.4%
64,284	TWIN FALLS	28,344	19,032	8,621	691	10,411 R	67.1%	30.4%	68.8%	31.2%
7,651	VALLEY	5,296	2,772	2,405	119	367 R	52.3%	45.4%	53.5%	46.5%
9,977	WASHINGTON	4,506	3,168	1,241	97	1,927 R	70.3%	27.5%	71.9%	28.1%
1,293,953	TOTAL	655,122	403,012	236,440	15,670	156,572 R	61.5%	36.1%	63.0%	37.0%

Note: The presidential vote was amended to include 90 write-in votes. They are included in the total statewide vote, but are not part of the county table.

IDAHO

SENATOR 2008

2000 Census Population	County	Total Vote	Republican	Democratic	Other	Rep.-Dem. Plurality	Percentage Total Vote Rep.	Dem.	Major Vote Rep.	Dem.
300,904	ADA	175,450	91,425	73,722	10,303	17,703 R	52.1%	42.0%	55.4%	44.6%
3,476	ADAMS	2,224	1,268	698	258	570 R	57.0%	31.4%	64.5%	35.5%
75,565	BANNOCK	35,008	18,313	13,600	3,095	4,713 R	52.3%	38.8%	57.4%	42.6%
6,411	BEAR LAKE	2,894	2,162	525	207	1,637 R	74.7%	18.1%	80.5%	19.5%
9,171	BENEWAH	3,950	2,376	1,377	197	999 R	60.2%	34.9%	63.3%	36.7%
41,735	BINGHAM	17,105	10,455	4,058	2,592	6,397 R	61.1%	23.7%	72.0%	28.0%
18,991	BLAINE	10,293	3,782	6,126	385	2,344 D	36.7%	59.5%	38.2%	61.8%
6,670	BOISE	3,712	2,218	1,196	298	1,022 R	59.8%	32.2%	65.0%	35.0%
36,835	BONNER	18,810	10,779	6,970	1,061	3,809 R	57.3%	37.1%	60.7%	39.3%
82,522	BONNEVILLE	41,337	25,201	10,702	5,434	14,499 R	61.0%	25.9%	70.2%	29.8%
9,871	BOUNDARY	4,551	2,798	1,406	347	1,392 R	61.5%	30.9%	66.6%	33.4%
2,899	BUTTE	1,397	880	326	191	554 R	63.0%	23.3%	73.0%	27.0%
991	CAMAS	599	372	174	53	198 R	62.1%	29.0%	68.1%	31.9%
131,441	CANYON	63,436	39,213	18,804	5,419	20,409 R	61.8%	29.6%	67.6%	32.4%
7,304	CARIBOU	3,273	2,399	534	340	1,865 R	73.3%	16.3%	81.8%	18.2%
21,416	CASSIA	7,795	5,553	1,316	926	4,237 R	71.2%	16.9%	80.8%	19.2%
1,022	CLARK	366	229	70	67	159 R	62.6%	19.1%	76.6%	23.4%
8,930	CLEARWATER	3,838	2,278	1,330	230	948 R	59.4%	34.7%	63.1%	36.9%
4,342	CUSTER	2,302	1,389	567	346	822 R	60.3%	24.6%	71.0%	29.0%
29,130	ELMORE	8,269	5,124	2,561	584	2,563 R	62.0%	31.0%	66.7%	33.3%
11,329	FRANKLIN	5,067	4,023	660	384	3,363 R	79.4%	13.0%	85.9%	14.1%
11,819	FREMONT	5,875	3,993	944	938	3,049 R	68.0%	16.1%	80.9%	19.1%
15,181	GEM	7,879	5,013	2,139	727	2,874 R	63.6%	27.1%	70.1%	29.9%
14,155	GOODING	5,398	3,402	1,444	552	1,958 R	63.0%	26.8%	70.2%	29.8%
15,511	IDAHO	8,016	5,433	2,106	477	3,327 R	67.8%	26.3%	72.1%	27.9%
19,155	JEFFERSON	10,470	7,197	1,511	1,762	5,686 R	68.7%	14.4%	82.6%	17.4%
18,342	JEROME	6,852	4,343	1,786	723	2,557 R	63.4%	26.1%	70.9%	29.1%
108,685	KOOTENAI	60,533	36,185	20,558	3,790	15,627 R	59.8%	34.0%	63.8%	36.2%
34,935	LATAH	17,404	7,706	8,854	844	1,148 D	44.3%	50.9%	46.5%	53.5%
7,806	LEMHI	4,054	2,570	986	498	1,584 R	63.4%	24.3%	72.3%	27.7%
3,747	LEWIS	1,776	1,150	492	134	658 R	64.8%	27.7%	70.0%	30.0%
4,044	LINCOLN	1,794	1,068	521	205	547 R	59.5%	29.0%	67.2%	32.8%
27,467	MADISON	12,871	9,552	1,282	2,037	8,270 R	74.2%	10.0%	88.2%	11.8%
20,174	MINIDOKA	6,943	4,446	1,581	916	2,865 R	64.0%	22.8%	73.8%	26.2%
37,410	NEZ PERCE	17,706	9,241	7,600	865	1,641 R	52.2%	42.9%	54.9%	45.1%
4,125	ONEIDA	2,091	1,523	385	183	1,138 R	72.8%	18.4%	79.8%	20.2%
10,644	OWYHEE	4,008	2,743	918	347	1,825 R	68.4%	22.9%	74.9%	25.1%
20,578	PAYETTE	8,551	5,554	2,332	665	3,222 R	65.0%	27.3%	70.4%	29.6%
7,538	POWER	2,798	1,641	904	253	737 R	58.6%	32.3%	64.5%	35.5%
13,771	SHOSHONE	5,617	2,552	2,694	371	142 D	45.4%	48.0%	48.6%	51.4%
5,999	TETON	4,520	1,812	2,072	636	260 D	40.1%	45.8%	46.7%	53.3%
64,284	TWIN FALLS	28,285	16,963	8,487	2,835	8,476 R	60.0%	30.0%	66.7%	33.3%
7,651	VALLEY	5,219	2,694	2,265	260	429 R	51.6%	43.4%	54.3%	45.7%
9,977	WASHINGTON	4,441	2,726	1,320	395	1,406 R	61.4%	29.7%	67.4%	32.6%
1,293,953	TOTAL	644,780	371,744	219,903	53,133	151,841 R	57.7%	34.1%	62.8%	37.2%

Note: The Senate vote was amended to include 3 write-in votes. They are included in the total statewide vote, but are not part of the county table.

IDAHO

HOUSE OF REPRESENTATIVES

CD	Year	Total Vote	Republican		Democratic		Other Vote	Rep.-Dem. Plurality	Percentage			
									Total Vote		Major Vote	
			Vote	Candidate	Vote	Candidate			Rep.	Dem.	Rep.	Dem.
1	2008	347,585	171,687	SALI, BILL*	175,898	MINNICK, WALT		4,211 D	49.4%	50.6%	49.4%	50.6%
1	2006	231,974	115,843	SALI, BILL	103,935	GRANT, LARRY	12,196	11,908 R	49.9%	44.8%	52.7%	47.3%
1	2004	298,589	207,662	OTTER, C.L. "BUTCH"*	90,927	PRESTON, NAOMI		116,735 R	69.5%	30.5%	69.5%	30.5%
1	2002	206,141	120,743	OTTER, C.L. "BUTCH"*	80,269	RICHARDSON, BETTY	5,129	40,474 R	58.6%	38.9%	60.1%	39.9%
2	2008	290,267	205,777	SIMPSON, MIKE*	83,878	HOLMES, DEBORAH	612	121,899 R	70.9%	28.9%	70.9%	28.9%
2	2006	213,332	132,262	SIMPSON, MIKE*	73,441	HANSEN, JIM	7,629	58,821 R	62.0%	34.4%	64.3%	35.7%
2	2004	273,837	193,704	SIMPSON, MIKE*	80,133	WITWORTH, LIN		113,571 R	70.7%	29.3%	70.7%	29.3%
2	2002	198,882	135,605	SIMPSON, MIKE*	57,769	KINGHORN, EDWARD	5,508	77,836 R	68.2%	29.0%	70.1%	29.9%
TOTAL	2008	637,852	377,464		259,776		612	117,688 R	59.2%	40.7%	59.2%	40.7%
TOTAL	2006	445,306	248,105		177,376		19,825	70,729 R	55.7%	39.8%	58.3%	41.7%
TOTAL	2004	572,426	401,366		171,060			230,306 R	70.1%	29.9%	70.1%	29.9%
TOTAL	2002	405,023	256,348		138,038		10,637	118,310 R	63.3%	34.1%	65.0%	35.0%

Note: An asterisk (*) denotes incumbent.

IDAHO

GENERAL AND PRIMARY ELECTIONS

2008 GENERAL ELECTIONS

President Other vote was 7,175 Independent (Ralph Nader); 4,747 Constitution (Chuck Baldwin); 3,658 Libertarian (Bob Barr); 40 write-in (Alan Keys); write-in (Cynthia A. McKinney), 6 write-in (Santa Claus); 3 write-in (Brian Moore); 1 write-in (Lawson Mitchell Bone); 1 write-in (Reverend MerePeace-MsMere).

Senator Other vote was 34,510 Independent (Rex Rammell); 9,958 Libertarian (Kent A. Marmon); 8,662 Independent (Pro-Life); 3 write-in (Kevin Volkmann).

House Other vote was:

CD 1
CD 2 612 write-in (Gregory Nemitz).

2008 PRIMARY ELECTIONS

Primary May 27, 2008 **Registration** (as of May 27, 2008) 721,269 No Party Registration

Primary Type Open—Any registered voter could participate in either the Democratic or Republican primary.

IDAHO

GENERAL AND PRIMARY ELECTIONS

	REPUBLICAN PRIMARIES			DEMOCRATIC PRIMARIES		
President	John McCain	87,460	69.7%	Barack Obama	23,980	56.0%
	Ron Paul	29,785	23.7%	Hillary Clinton	16,122	37.7%
	None of the Names Shown	8,325	6.6%	None of the Names Shown	1,966	4.6%
				Keith Russell Judd	734	1.7%
	TOTAL	*125,570*		*TOTAL*	*42,802*	
Senator	Jim Risch	80,743	65.3%	Larry LaRocco	29,023	72.3%
	Scott A. Syme	16,660	13.5%	David J. Archuleta	11,074	27.6%
	Richard Phenneger	6,532	5.3%	Kevin Volkmann (write-in)	20	
	Neal Thompson	5,375	4.3%			
	Fred M. Adams	4,987	4.0%			
	Bill Hunter	4,280	3.5%			
	Brian E. Hefner	2,915	2.4%			
	Hal James Styles Jr.	2,082	1.7%			
	TOTAL	*123,574*		*TOTAL*	*40,117*	
Congressional District 1	Bill Sali*	41,073	60.1%	Walt Minnick	19,449	100.0%
	Matthew Salisbury	27,267	39.9%			
	TOTAL	*68,340*				
Congressional District 2	Mike Simpson*	49,586	85.2%	Deborah Holmes	11,578	69.5%
	Jack Wayne Chappell	4,900	8.4%	David Sneddon	5,074	30.5%
	Gregory Nemitz	3,747	6.4%			
	TOTAL	*58,233*		*TOTAL*	*16,652*	

Note: An asterisk (*) denotes incumbent.

ILLINOIS

Congressional districts first established for elections held in 2002
19 members

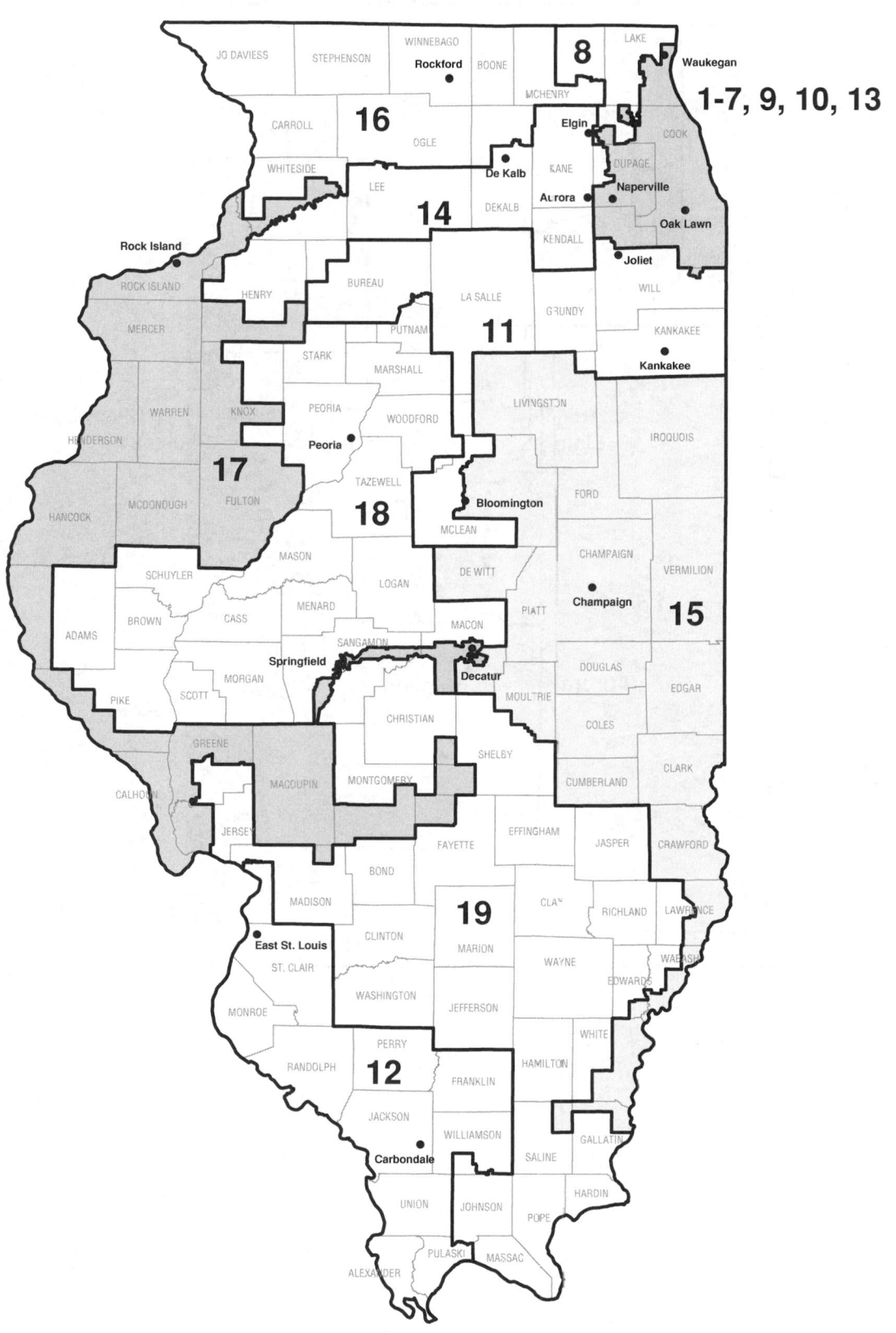

1-7, 9, 10, 13

ILLINOIS

Chicago Area

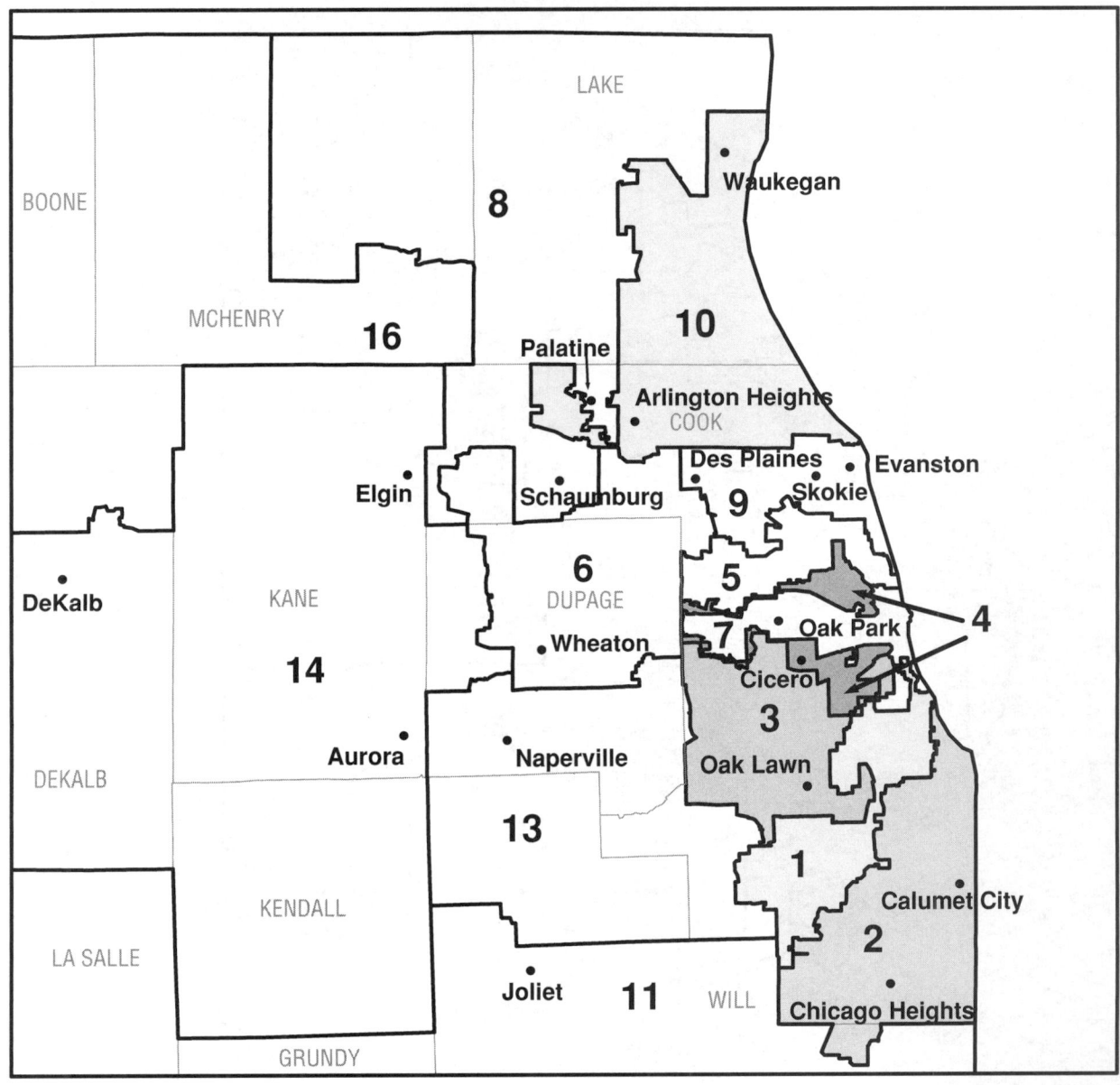

LAKE

BOONE

8

Waukegan

MCHENRY   16

10

Palatine

Arlington Heights

COOK

Des Plaines   Evanston

Elgin   Schaumburg   Skokie

9

DeKalb   KANE   6   5

DUPAGE   7   Oak Park   4

14   Wheaton   Cicero

3

Oak Lawn

DEKALB   Aurora   Naperville

1   Calumet City

13   2

KENDALL

LA SALLE   Chicago Heights

Joliet   11   WILL

GRUNDY

ILLINOIS

GOVERNOR

Pat Quinn (D). Sworn in as governor January 29, 2009, upon the impeachment and expulsion from office of Rod R. Blagojevich (D).

SENATORS (2 Democrats)

Roland Burris (D). Sworn in as senator January 15, 2009, to fill the vacancy created by the resignation of Barack Obama (D) following his election as president of the United States.

Richard J. Durbin (D). Reelected 2008 to a six-year term. Previously elected 2002, 1996.

REPRESENTATIVES (12 Democrats, 7 Republicans)

1. Bobby L. Rush (D)
2. Jesse L. Jackson Jr. (D)
3. Daniel Lipinski (D)
4. Luis V. Gutierrez (D)
5. Mike Quigley (D)
6. Peter J. Roskam (R)
7. Danny K. Davis (D)
8. Melissa Bean (D)
9. Jan Schakowsky (D)
10. Mark Steven Kirk (R)
11. Deborah L. Halvorson (D)
12. Jerry F. Costello (D)
13. Judy Biggert (R)
14. Bill Foster (D)
15. Timothy V. Johnson (R)
16. Donald Manzullo (R)
17. Phil Hare (D)
18. Aaron Schock (R)
19. John Shimkus (R)

POSTWAR VOTE FOR PRESIDENT

Year	Total Vote	Republican Vote	Republican Candidate	Democratic Vote	Democratic Candidate	Other Vote	Plurality	Total Vote Rep.	Total Vote Dem.	Major Vote Rep.	Major Vote Dem.
2008	5,522,371	2,031,179	McCain, John	3,419,348	Obama, Barack	71,844	1,388,169 D	36.8%	61.9%	37.3%	62.7%
2004	5,274,322	2,345,946	Bush, George W.	2,891,550	Kerry, John	36,826	545,604 D	44.5%	54.8%	44.8%	55.2%
2000**	4,742,123	2,019,421	Bush, George W.	2,589,026	Gore, Al	133,676	569,605 D	42.6%	54.6%	43.8%	56.2%
1996**	4,311,391	1,587,021	Dole, Bob	2,341,744	Clinton, Bill	332,626	754,723 D	36.8%	54.3%	40.4%	59.6%
1992**	5,050,157	1,734,096	Bush, George	2,453,350	Clinton, Bill	852,711	719,254 D	34.3%	48.6%	41.4%	58.6%
1988	4,559,120	2,310,939	Bush, George	2,215,940	Dukakis, Michael S.	32,241	94,999 R	50.7%	48.6%	51.0%	49.0%
1984	4,819,088	2,707,103	Reagan, Ronald	2,086,499	Mondale, Walter F.	25,486	620,604 R	56.2%	43.3%	56.5%	43.5%
1980**	4,749,721	2,358,049	Reagan, Ronald	1,981,413	Carter, Jimmy	410,259	376,636 R	49.6%	41.7%	54.3%	45.7%
1976	4,718,914	2,364,269	Ford, Gerald R.	2,271,295	Carter, Jimmy	83,350	92,974 R	50.1%	48.1%	51.0%	49.0%
1972	4,723,236	2,788,179	Nixon, Richard M.	1,913,472	McGovern, George S.	21,585	874,707 R	59.0%	40.5%	59.3%	40.7%
1968**	4,619,749	2,174,774	Nixon, Richard M.	2,039,814	Humphrey, Hubert H.	405,161	134,960 R	47.1%	44.2%	51.6%	48.4%
1964	4,702,841	1,905,946	Goldwater, Barry M.	2,796,833	Johnson, Lyndon B.	62	890,887 D	40.5%	59.5%	40.5%	59.5%
1960	4,757,409	2,368,988	Nixon, Richard M.	2,377,846	Kennedy, John F.	10,575	8,858 D	49.8%	50.0%	49.9%	50.1%
1956	4,407,407	2,623,327	Eisenhower, Dwight D.	1,775,682	Stevenson, Adlai E.	8,398	847,645 R	59.5%	40.3%	59.6%	40.4%
1952	4,481,058	2,457,327	Eisenhower, Dwight D.	2,013,920	Stevenson, Adlai E.	9,811	443,407 R	54.8%	44.9%	55.0%	45.0%
1948	3,984,046	1,961,103	Dewey, Thomas E.	1,994,715	Truman, Harry S.	28,228	33,612 D	49.2%	50.1%	49.6%	50.4%

**In past elections, the other vote included: 2000 - 103,759 Green (Ralph Nader); 1996 - 346,408 Reform (Ross Perot); 1992 - 840,515 Independent (Perot); 1980 - 346,754 Independent (John Anderson); 1968 - 390,958 American Independent (George Wallace).

ILLINOIS

POSTWAR VOTE FOR GOVERNOR

Year	Total Vote	Republican Vote	Republican Candidate	Democratic Vote	Democratic Candidate	Other Vote	Plurality	Total Vote Rep.	Total Vote Dem.	Major Vote Rep.	Major Vote Dem.
2006**	3,487,989	1,369,315	Topinka, Judy Baar	1,736,731	Blagojevich, Rod R.	381,943	367,416 D	39.3%	49.8%	44.1%	55.9%
2002	3,538,891	1,594,960	Ryan, Jim	1,847,040	Blagojevich, Rod R.	96,891	252,080 D	45.1%	52.2%	46.3%	53.7%
1998	3,358,705	1,714,094	Ryan, George H.	1,594,191	Poshard, Glenn	50,420	119,903 R	51.0%	47.5%	51.8%	48.2%
1994	3,106,566	1,984,318	Edgar, Jim	1,069,850	Netsch, Dawn C.	52,398	914,468 R	63.9%	34.4%	65.0%	35.0%
1990	3,257,410	1,653,126	Edgar, Jim	1,569,217	Hartigan, Neil F.	35,067	83,909 R	50.7%	48.2%	51.3%	48.7%
1986**	3,143,978	1,655,849	Thompson, James R.	208,830	—	1,279,299	399,223 R	52.7%	6.6%	88.8%	11.2%
1982	3,673,681	1,816,101	Thompson, James R.	1,811,027	Stevenson, Adlai E., III	46,553	5,074 R	49.4%	49.3%	50.1%	49.9%
1978	3,150,095	1,859,684	Thompson, James R.	1,263,134	Bakalis, Michael	27,277	596,550 R	59.0%	40.1%	59.6%	40.4%
1976S	4,638,997	3,000,395	Thompson, James R.	1,610,258	Howlett, Michael J.	28,344	1,390,137 R	64.7%	34.7%	65.1%	34.9%
1972	4,678,804	2,293,809	Ogilvie, Richard B.	2,371,303	Walker, Daniel	13,692	77,494 D	49.0%	50.7%	49.2%	50.8%
1968	4,506,000	2,307,295	Ogilvie, Richard B.	2,179,501	Shapiro, Samuel H.	19,204	127,794 R	51.2%	48.4%	51.4%	48.6%
1964	4,657,500	2,239,095	Percy, Charles H.	2,418,394	Kerner, Otto	11	179,299 D	48.1%	51.9%	48.1%	51.9%
1960	4,674,187	2,070,479	Stratton, William G.	2,594,731	Kerner, Otto	8,977	524,252 D	44.3%	55.5%	44.4%	55.6%
1956	4,314,611	2,171,786	Stratton, William G.	2,134,909	Austin, Richard B.	7,916	36,877 R	50.3%	49.5%	50.4%	49.6%
1952	4,415,864	2,317,363	Stratton, William G.	2,089,721	Dixon, Sherwood	8,780	227,642 R	52.5%	47.3%	52.6%	47.4%
1948	3,940,257	1,678,007	Green, Dwight H.	2,250,074	Stevenson, Adlai E.	12,176	572,067 D	42.6%	57.1%	42.7%	57.3%

Notes: **In past elections, the other vote included: 2006 - 361,336 Green (Rich Whitney); 1986 - 1,256,626 Illinois Solidarity (Adlai E. Stevenson III). In 1986 there was no Democratic candidate for governor on the ballot. Mark Fairchild, a supporter of Lyndon H. LaRouche Jr., was the "paired" Democratic candidate for lieutenant governor and the Democratic vote was cast for this "no name" ticket and Fairchild. Running on the Illinois Solidarity ticket, Stevenson finished second with 40.0 percent of the vote. The 1976 vote was for a two-year term to permit shifting the election for governor to non-presidential years.

POSTWAR VOTE FOR SENATOR

Year	Total Vote	Republican Vote	Republican Candidate	Democratic Vote	Democratic Candidate	Other Vote	Rep.-Dem. Plurality	Total Vote Rep.	Total Vote Dem.	Major Vote Rep.	Major Vote Dem.
2008	5,329,884	1,520,621	Sauerberg, Steve	3,615,844	Durbin, Richard J.	193,419	2,095,223 D	28.5%	67.8%	29.6%	70.4%
2004	5,141,520	1,390,690	Keyes, Alan	3,597,456	Obama, Barack	153,374	2,206,766 D	27.0%	70.0%	27.9%	72.1%
2002	3,486,851	1,325,703	Durkin, Jim	2,103,766	Durbin, Richard J.	57,382	778,063 D	38.0%	60.3%	38.7%	61.3%
1998	3,394,521	1,709,041	Fitzgerald, Peter G.	1,610,496	Moseley-Braun, Carol	74,984	98,545 R	50.3%	47.4%	51.5%	48.5%
1996	4,250,722	1,728,824	Salvi, Al	2,384,028	Durbin, Richard J.	137,870	655,204 D	40.7%	56.1%	42.0%	58.0%
1992	4,939,558	2,126,833	Williamson, Richard S.	2,631,229	Moseley-Braun, Carol	181,496	504,396 D	43.1%	53.3%	44.7%	55.3%
1990	3,251,005	1,135,628	Martin, Lynn	2,115,377	Simon, Paul		979,749 D	34.9%	65.1%	34.9%	65.1%
1986	3,122,883	1,053,734	Koehler, Judy	2,033,783	Dixon, Alan J.	35,366	980,049 D	33.7%	65.1%	34.1%	65.9%
1984	4,787,473	2,308,039	Percy, Charles H.	2,397,303	Simon, Paul	82,131	89,264 D	48.2%	50.1%	49.1%	50.9%
1980	4,580,029	1,946,296	O'Neal, David C.	2,565,302	Dixon, Alan J.	68,431	619,006 D	42.5%	56.0%	43.1%	56.9%
1978	3,184,764	1,698,711	Percy, Charles H.	1,448,187	Seith, Alex	37,866	250,524 R	53.3%	45.5%	54.0%	46.0%
1974	2,914,666	1,084,884	Burditt, George M.	1,811,496	Stevenson, Adlai E., III	18,286	726,612 D	37.2%	62.2%	37.5%	62.5%
1972	4,608,380	2,867,078	Percy, Charles H.	1,721,031	Pucinski, Roman C.	20,271	1,146,047 R	62.2%	37.3%	62.5%	37.5%
1970S	3,599,272	1,519,718	Smith, Ralph T.	2,065,054	Stevenson, Adlai E., III	14,500	545,336 D	42.2%	57.4%	42.4%	57.6%
1968	4,449,757	2,358,947	Dirksen, Everett M.	2,073,242	Clark, William G.	17,568	285,705 R	53.0%	46.6%	53.2%	46.8%
1966	3,822,725	2,100,449	Percy, Charles H.	1,678,147	Douglas, Paul H.	44,129	422,302 R	54.9%	43.9%	55.6%	44.4%
1962	3,709,216	1,961,202	Dirksen, Everett M.	1,748,007	Yates, Sidney R.	7	213,195 R	52.9%	47.1%	52.9%	47.1%
1960	4,632,796	2,093,846	Witwer, Samuel W.	2,530,943	Douglas, Paul H.	8,007	437,097 D	45.2%	54.6%	45.3%	54.7%
1956	4,264,830	2,307,352	Dirksen, Everett M.	1,949,883	Stengel, Richard	7,595	357,469 R	54.1%	45.7%	54.2%	45.8%
1954	3,368,025	1,563,683	Meek, Joseph T.	1,804,338	Douglas, Paul H.	4	240,655 D	46.4%	53.6%	46.4%	53.6%
1950	3,622,673	1,951,984	Dirksen, Everett M.	1,657,630	Lucas, Scott W.	13,059	294,354 R	53.9%	45.8%	54.1%	45.9%
1948	3,900,285	1,740,026	Brooks, C. Wayland	2,147,754	Douglas, Paul H.	12,505	407,728 D	44.6%	55.1%	44.8%	55.2%

Note: The 1970 election was for a short term to fill a vacancy.

ILLINOIS

PRESIDENT 2008

2000 Census Population	County	Total Vote	Republican	Democratic	Other	Rep.-Dem. Plurality	Percentage Total Vote Rep.	Dem.	Major Vote Rep.	Dem.
68,277	ADAMS	30,823	18,711	11,794	318	6,917 R	60.7%	38.3%	61.3%	38.7%
9,590	ALEXANDER	3,937	1,692	2,189	56	497 D	43.0%	55.6%	43.6%	56.4%
17,633	BOND	7,924	3,947	3,843	134	104 R	49.8%	48.5%	50.7%	49.3%
41,786	BOONE	22,157	10,403	11,333	421	930 D	47.0%	51.1%	47.9%	52.1%
6,950	BROWN	2,569	1,544	986	39	558 R	60.1%	38.4%	61.0%	39.0%
35,503	BUREAU	17,113	7,911	8,889	313	978 D	46.2%	51.9%	47.1%	52.9%
5,084	CALHOUN	2,699	1,221	1,423	55	202 D	45.2%	52.7%	46.2%	53.8%
16,674	CARROLL	7,674	3,596	3,965	113	369 D	46.9%	51.7%	47.6%	52.4%
13,695	CASS	5,408	2,617	2,690	101	73 D	48.4%	49.7%	49.3%	50.7%
179,669	CHAMPAIGN	84,143	33,871	48,597	1,675	14,726 D	40.3%	57.8%	41.1%	58.9%
35,372	CHRISTIAN	15,100	7,872	6,918	310	954 R	52.1%	45.8%	53.2%	46.8%
17,008	CLARK	8,288	4,409	3,742	137	667 R	53.2%	45.1%	54.1%	45.9%
14,560	CLAY	6,454	3,926	2,425	103	1,501 R	60.8%	37.6%	61.8%	38.2%
35,535	CLINTON	17,314	9,357	7,657	300	1,700 R	54.0%	44.2%	55.0%	45.0%
53,196	COLES	23,076	10,978	11,716	382	738 D	47.6%	50.8%	48.4%	51.6%
5,376,741	COOK	2,137,466	487,736	1,629,024	20,706	1,141,288 D	22.8%	76.2%	23.0%	77.0%
20,452	CRAWFORD	9,129	5,070	3,883	176	1,187 R	55.5%	42.5%	56.6%	43.4%
11,253	CUMBERLAND	5,321	3,156	2,055	110	1,101 R	59.3%	38.6%	60.6%	39.4%
88,969	DE KALB	44,818	18,266	25,784	768	7,518 D	40.8%	57.5%	41.5%	58.5%
16,798	DE WITT	7,801	4,348	3,308	145	1,040 R	55.7%	42.4%	56.8%	43.2%
19,922	DOUGLAS	8,356	5,005	3,228	123	1,777 R	59.9%	38.6%	60.8%	39.2%
904,161	DU PAGE	417,973	183,626	228,698	5,649	45,072 D	43.9%	54.7%	44.5%	55.5%
19,704	EDGAR	8,255	4,398	3,743	114	655 R	53.3%	45.3%	54.0%	46.0%
6,971	EDWARDS	3,350	2,137	1,140	73	997 R	63.8%	34.0%	65.2%	34.8%
34,264	EFFINGHAM	16,835	11,323	5,262	250	6,061 R	67.3%	31.3%	68.3%	31.7%
21,802	FAYETTE	9,680	5,499	3,967	214	1,532 R	56.8%	41.0%	58.1%	41.9%
14,241	FORD	6,386	4,079	2,227	80	1,852 R	63.9%	34.9%	64.7%	35.3%
39,018	FRANKLIN	18,641	9,404	8,880	357	524 R	50.4%	47.6%	51.4%	48.6%
38,250	FULTON	16,323	6,251	9,732	340	3,481 D	38.3%	59.6%	39.1%	60.9%
6,445	GALLATIN	2,859	1,212	1,587	60	375 D	42.4%	55.5%	43.3%	56.7%
14,761	GREENE	5,807	3,053	2,619	135	434 R	52.6%	45.1%	53.8%	46.2%
37,535	GRUNDY	22,171	10,687	11,063	421	376 D	48.2%	49.9%	49.1%	50.9%
8,621	HAMILTON	4,264	2,353	1,796	115	557 R	55.2%	42.1%	56.7%	43.3%
20,121	HANCOCK	9,469	5,161	4,141	167	1,020 R	54.5%	43.7%	55.5%	44.5%
4,800	HARDIN	2,255	1,330	892	33	438 R	59.0%	39.6%	59.9%	40.1%
8,213	HENDERSON	3,814	1,541	2,215	58	674 D	40.4%	58.1%	41.0%	59.0%
51,020	HENRY	24,785	11,263	13,181	341	1,918 D	45.4%	53.2%	46.1%	53.9%
31,334	IROQUOIS	13,596	8,695	4,643	258	4,052 R	64.0%	34.1%	65.2%	34.8%
59,612	JACKSON	25,532	9,687	15,248	597	5,561 D	37.9%	59.7%	38.8%	61.2%
10,117	JASPER	5,131	2,964	2,063	104	901 R	57.8%	40.2%	59.0%	41.0%
40,045	JEFFERSON	17,141	9,302	7,462	377	1,840 R	54.3%	43.5%	55.5%	44.5%
21,668	JERSEY	10,583	5,329	5,042	212	287 R	50.4%	47.6%	51.4%	48.6%
22,289	JO DAVIESS	11,750	5,170	6,403	177	1,233 D	44.0%	54.5%	44.7%	55.3%
12,878	JOHNSON	5,901	3,912	1,871	118	2,041 R	66.3%	31.7%	67.6%	32.4%
404,119	KANE	193,299	83,963	106,756	2,580	22,793 D	43.4%	55.2%	44.0%	56.0%
103,833	KANKAKEE	48,016	22,527	24,750	739	2,223 D	46.9%	51.5%	47.6%	52.4%
54,544	KENDALL	46,631	21,380	24,742	509	3,362 D	45.8%	53.1%	46.4%	53.6%
55,836	KNOX	23,988	9,419	14,191	378	4,772 D	39.3%	59.2%	39.9%	60.1%
644,356	LAKE	299,105	118,545	177,242	3,318	58,697 D	39.6%	59.3%	40.1%	59.9%
111,509	LA SALLE	50,185	21,872	27,443	870	5,571 D	43.6%	54.7%	44.4%	55.6%
15,452	LAWRENCE	6,536	3,403	3,016	117	387 R	52.1%	46.1%	53.0%	47.0%
36,062	LEE	16,318	8,258	7,765	295	493 R	50.6%	47.6%	51.5%	48.5%
39,678	LIVINGSTON	15,625	9,191	6,189	245	3,002 R	58.8%	39.6%	59.8%	40.2%
31,183	LOGAN	12,896	7,429	5,250	217	2,179 R	57.6%	40.7%	58.6%	41.4%
32,913	MCDONOUGH	13,042	6,055	6,783	204	728 D	46.4%	52.0%	47.2%	52.8%

ILLINOIS

PRESIDENT 2008

2000 Census Population	County	Total Vote	Republican	Democratic	Other	Rep.-Dem. Plurality		Percentage Total Vote Rep.	Dem.	Major Vote Rep.	Dem.
260,077	MCHENRY	139,268	64,845	72,288	2,135	7,443	D	46.6%	51.9%	47.3%	52.7%
150,433	MCLEAN	75,750	36,767	37,689	1,294	922	D	48.5%	49.8%	49.4%	50.6%
114,706	MACON	51,216	24,948	25,487	781	539	D	48.7%	49.8%	49.5%	50.5%
49,019	MACOUPIN	22,373	9,891	12,090	392	2,199	D	44.2%	54.0%	45.0%	55.0%
258,941	MADISON	128,334	57,177	68,979	2,178	11,802	D	44.6%	53.7%	45.3%	54.7%
41,691	MARION	17,364	8,691	8,345	328	346	R	50.1%	48.1%	51.0%	49.0%
13,180	MARSHALL	6,333	3,145	3,081	107	64	R	49.7%	48.6%	50.5%	49.5%
16,038	MASON	6,808	3,141	3,542	125	401	D	46.1%	52.0%	47.0%	53.0%
15,161	MASSAC	7,186	4,371	2,693	122	1,678	R	60.8%	37.5%	61.9%	38.1%
12,486	MENARD	6,464	3,672	2,706	86	966	R	56.8%	41.9%	57.6%	42.4%
16,957	MERCER	8,848	3,833	4,887	128	1,054	D	43.3%	55.2%	44.0%	56.0%
27,619	MONROE	18,083	9,881	7,953	249	1,928	R	54.6%	44.0%	55.4%	44.6%
30,652	MONTGOMERY	12,871	6,150	6,491	230	341	D	47.8%	50.4%	48.7%	51.3%
36,616	MORGAN	15,353	7,591	7,467	295	124	R	49.4%	48.6%	50.4%	49.6%
14,287	MOULTRIE	6,260	3,471	2,668	121	803	R	55.4%	42.6%	56.5%	43.5%
51,032	OGLE	24,850	13,144	11,253	453	1,891	R	52.9%	45.3%	53.9%	46.1%
183,433	PEORIA	81,704	34,579	45,906	1,219	11,327	D	42.3%	56.2%	43.0%	57.0%
23,094	PERRY	9,995	5,086	4,701	208	385	R	50.9%	47.0%	52.0%	48.0%
16,365	PIATT	8,999	4,991	3,859	149	1,132	R	55.5%	42.9%	56.4%	43.6%
17,384	PIKE	7,616	4,457	3,024	135	1,433	R	58.5%	39.7%	59.6%	40.4%
4,413	POPE	2,231	1,343	845	43	498	R	60.2%	37.9%	61.4%	38.6%
7,348	PULASKI	3,270	1,593	1,638	39	45	D	48.7%	50.1%	49.3%	50.7%
6,086	PUTNAM	3,337	1,378	1,900	59	522	D	41.3%	56.9%	42.0%	58.0%
33,893	RANDOLPH	15,202	7,538	7,395	269	143	R	49.6%	48.6%	50.5%	49.5%
16,149	RICHLAND	7,650	4,329	3,181	140	1,148	R	56.6%	41.6%	57.6%	42.4%
149,374	ROCK ISLAND	68,401	25,364	42,210	827	16,846	D	37.1%	61.7%	37.5%	62.5%
256,082	ST. CLAIR	125,744	47,958	76,160	1,626	28,202	D	38.1%	60.6%	38.6%	61.4%
26,733	SALINE	11,428	6,099	5,083	246	1,016	R	53.4%	44.5%	54.5%	45.5%
188,951	SANGAMON	99,828	46,945	51,300	1,583	4,355	D	47.0%	51.4%	47.8%	52.2%
7,189	SCHUYLER	3,823	1,833	1,900	90	67	D	47.9%	49.7%	49.1%	50.9%
5,537	SCOTT	2,600	1,455	1,090	55	365	R	56.0%	41.9%	57.2%	42.8%
22,893	SHELBY	10,868	6,396	4,245	227	2,151	R	58.9%	39.1%	60.1%	39.9%
6,332	STARK	2,907	1,513	1,357	37	156	R	52.0%	46.7%	52.7%	47.3%
48,979	STEPHENSON	21,605	9,909	11,349	347	1,440	D	45.9%	52.5%	46.6%	53.4%
128,485	TAZEWELL	63,854	33,247	29,384	1,223	3,863	R	52.1%	46.0%	53.1%	46.9%
18,293	UNION	9,116	5,003	3,918	195	1,085	R	54.9%	43.0%	56.1%	43.9%
83,919	VERMILION	32,872	16,054	16,246	572	192	D	48.8%	49.4%	49.7%	50.3%
12,937	WABASH	5,782	3,254	2,462	66	792	R	56.3%	42.6%	56.9%	43.1%
18,735	WARREN	8,029	3,637	4,286	106	649	D	45.3%	53.4%	45.9%	54.1%
15,148	WASHINGTON	7,932	4,473	3,342	117	1,131	R	56.4%	42.1%	57.2%	42.8%
17,151	WAYNE	8,071	5,390	2,547	134	2,843	R	66.8%	31.6%	67.9%	32.1%
15,371	WHITE	7,453	3,987	3,315	151	672	R	53.5%	44.5%	54.6%	45.4%
60,653	WHITESIDE	26,906	10,883	15,607	416	4,724	D	40.4%	58.0%	41.1%	58.9%
502,266	WILL	286,420	122,597	160,406	3,417	37,809	D	42.8%	56.0%	43.3%	56.7%
61,296	WILLIAMSON	30,141	17,039	12,589	513	4,450	R	56.5%	41.8%	57.5%	42.5%
278,418	WINNEBAGO	126,031	53,886	70,034	2,111	16,148	D	42.8%	55.6%	43.5%	56.5%
35,469	WOODFORD	19,483	12,191	6,999	293	5,192	R	62.6%	35.9%	63.5%	36.5%
12,419,293	TOTAL	5,522,371	2,031,179	3,419,348	71,844	1,388,169	D	36.8%	61.9%	37.3%	62.7%

ILLINOIS

SENATOR 2008

2000 Census Population	County	Total Vote	Republican	Democratic	Other	Rep.-Dem. Plurality	Total Vote Rep.	Total Vote Dem.	Major Vote Rep.	Major Vote Dem.
68,277	ADAMS	30,117	12,955	16,328	834	3,373 D	43.0%	54.2%	44.2%	55.8%
9,590	ALEXANDER	3,610	1,082	2,321	207	1,239 D	30.0%	64.3%	31.8%	68.2%
17,633	BOND	7,759	2,996	4,525	238	1,529 D	38.6%	58.3%	39.8%	60.2%
41,786	BOONE	21,643	8,412	12,065	1,166	3,653 D	38.9%	55.7%	41.1%	58.9%
6,950	BROWN	2,444	881	1,458	105	577 D	36.0%	59.7%	37.7%	62.3%
35,503	BUREAU	16,710	5,846	10,291	573	4,445 D	35.0%	61.6%	36.2%	63.8%
5,084	CALHOUN	2,604	728	1,783	93	1,055 D	28.0%	68.5%	29.0%	71.0%
16,674	CARROLL	7,468	2,828	4,274	366	1,446 D	37.9%	57.2%	39.8%	60.2%
13,695	CASS	5,318	1,628	3,547	143	1,919 D	30.6%	66.7%	31.5%	68.5%
179,669	CHAMPAIGN	81,138	25,603	51,612	3,923	26,009 D	31.6%	63.6%	33.2%	66.8%
35,372	CHRISTIAN	14,827	4,929	9,314	584	4,385 D	33.2%	62.8%	34.6%	65.4%
17,008	CLARK	8,088	3,677	4,141	270	464 D	45.5%	51.2%	47.0%	53.0%
14,560	CLAY	6,130	2,711	3,184	235	473 D	44.2%	51.9%	46.0%	54.0%
35,535	CLINTON	16,777	6,678	9,372	727	2,694 D	39.8%	55.9%	41.6%	58.4%
53,196	COLES	22,722	6,954	14,797	971	7,843 D	30.6%	65.1%	32.0%	68.0%
5,376,741	COOK	2,038,397	347,434	1,629,347	61,616	1,281,913 D	17.0%	79.9%	17.6%	82.4%
20,452	CRAWFORD	8,882	3,911	4,495	476	584 D	44.0%	50.6%	46.5%	53.5%
11,253	CUMBERLAND	5,213	2,053	2,895	265	842 D	39.4%	55.5%	41.5%	58.5%
88,969	DE KALB	43,602	13,918	27,467	2,217	13,549 D	31.9%	63.0%	33.6%	66.4%
16,798	DE WITT	7,664	2,824	4,595	245	1,771 D	36.8%	60.0%	38.1%	61.9%
19,922	DOUGLAS	8,205	3,399	4,586	220	1,187 D	41.4%	55.9%	42.6%	57.4%
904,161	DU PAGE	409,638	154,134	240,521	14,983	86,387 D	37.6%	58.7%	39.1%	60.9%
19,704	EDGAR	8,070	3,107	4,730	233	1,623 D	38.5%	58.6%	39.6%	60.4%
6,971	EDWARDS	3,137	1,693	1,292	152	401 R	54.0%	41.2%	56.7%	43.3%
34,264	EFFINGHAM	16,435	7,714	8,266	455	552 D	46.9%	50.3%	48.3%	51.7%
21,802	FAYETTE	9,414	4,067	4,960	387	893 D	43.2%	52.7%	45.1%	54.9%
14,241	FORD	6,274	2,955	3,122	197	167 D	47.1%	49.8%	48.6%	51.4%
39,018	FRANKLIN	18,242	5,541	11,967	734	6,426 D	30.4%	65.6%	31.6%	68.4%
38,250	FULTON	16,036	4,240	11,067	729	6,827 D	26.4%	69.0%	27.7%	72.3%
6,445	GALLATIN	2,661	651	1,844	166	1,193 D	24.5%	69.3%	26.1%	73.9%
14,761	GREENE	5,646	2,052	3,343	251	1,291 D	36.3%	59.2%	38.0%	62.0%
37,535	GRUNDY	21,705	7,867	12,835	1,003	4,968 D	36.2%	59.1%	38.0%	62.0%
8,621	HAMILTON	3,970	1,338	2,438	194	1,100 D	33.7%	61.4%	35.4%	64.6%
20,121	HANCOCK	9,043	3,653	5,043	347	1,390 D	40.4%	55.8%	42.0%	58.0%
4,800	HARDIN	2,135	807	1,212	116	405 D	37.8%	56.8%	40.0%	60.0%
8,213	HENDERSON	3,624	1,089	2,387	148	1,298 D	30.0%	65.9%	31.3%	68.7%
51,020	HENRY	23,769	8,689	14,158	922	5,469 D	36.6%	59.6%	38.0%	62.0%
31,334	IROQUOIS	13,260	6,229	6,424	607	195 D	47.0%	48.4%	49.2%	50.8%
59,612	JACKSON	24,945	7,282	15,986	1,677	8,704 D	29.2%	64.1%	31.3%	68.7%
10,117	JASPER	4,997	2,107	2,711	179	604 D	42.2%	54.3%	43.7%	56.3%
40,045	JEFFERSON	16,146	5,717	9,475	954	3,758 D	35.4%	58.7%	37.6%	62.4%
21,668	JERSEY	10,249	3,718	6,018	513	2,300 D	36.3%	58.7%	38.2%	61.8%
22,289	JO DAVIESS	11,307	4,294	6,489	524	2,195 D	38.0%	57.4%	39.8%	60.2%
12,878	JOHNSON	5,700	2,693	2,667	340	26 R	47.2%	46.8%	50.2%	49.8%
404,119	KANE	188,073	70,521	109,917	7,635	39,396 D	37.5%	58.4%	39.1%	60.9%
103,833	KANKAKEE	46,748	15,283	29,242	2,223	13,959 D	32.7%	62.6%	34.3%	65.7%
54,544	KENDALL	44,844	17,475	25,759	1,610	8,284 D	39.0%	57.4%	40.4%	59.6%
55,836	KNOX	23,559	6,702	16,075	782	9,373 D	28.4%	68.2%	29.4%	70.6%
644,356	LAKE	289,685	95,989	184,254	9,442	88,265 D	33.1%	63.6%	34.3%	65.7%
111,509	LA SALLE	48,395	14,269	31,900	2,226	17,631 D	29.5%	65.9%	30.9%	69.1%
15,452	LAWRENCE	6,195	2,576	3,247	372	671 D	41.6%	52.4%	44.2%	55.8%
36,062	LEE	15,936	6,205	8,979	752	2,774 D	38.9%	56.3%	40.9%	59.1%
39,678	LIVINGSTON	15,106	6,840	7,718	548	878 D	45.3%	51.1%	47.0%	53.0%
31,183	LOGAN	12,331	5,181	6,695	455	1,514 D	42.0%	54.3%	43.6%	56.4%
32,913	MCDONOUGH	12,678	4,562	7,584	532	3,022 D	36.0%	59.8%	37.6%	62.4%

ILLINOIS

SENATOR 2008

2000 Census Population	County	Total Vote	Republican	Democratic	Other	Rep.-Dem. Plurality	Percentage			
							Total Vote		Major Vote	
							Rep.	Dem.	Rep.	Dem.
260,077	MCHENRY	135,058	54,635	73,846	6,577	19,211 D	40.5%	54.7%	42.5%	57.5%
150,433	MCLEAN	73,960	29,611	41,250	3,099	11,639 D	40.0%	55.8%	41.8%	58.2%
114,706	MACON	50,473	15,713	33,232	1,528	17,519 D	31.1%	65.8%	32.1%	67.9%
49,019	MACOUPIN	21,907	7,003	14,148	756	7,145 D	32.0%	64.6%	33.1%	66.9%
258,941	MADISON	123,884	43,863	74,043	5,978	30,180 D	35.4%	59.8%	37.2%	62.8%
41,691	MARION	17,003	5,794	10,587	622	4,793 D	34.1%	62.3%	35.4%	64.6%
13,180	MARSHALL	6,103	2,252	3,634	217	1,382 D	36.9%	59.5%	38.3%	61.7%
16,038	MASON	6,694	1,898	4,601	195	2,703 D	28.4%	68.7%	29.2%	70.8%
15,161	MASSAC	6,831	2,911	3,619	301	708 D	42.6%	53.0%	44.6%	55.4%
12,486	MENARD	6,299	2,705	3,440	154	735 D	42.9%	54.6%	44.0%	56.0%
16,957	MERCER	8,377	2,773	5,233	371	2,460 D	33.1%	62.5%	34.6%	65.4%
27,619	MONROE	17,594	8,078	8,931	585	853 D	45.9%	50.8%	47.5%	52.5%
30,652	MONTGOMERY	12,551	4,482	7,655	414	3,173 D	35.7%	61.0%	36.9%	63.1%
36,616	MORGAN	15,110	4,801	9,813	496	5,012 D	31.8%	64.9%	32.9%	67.1%
14,287	MOULTRIE	6,143	2,211	3,749	183	1,538 D	36.0%	61.0%	37.1%	62.9%
51,032	OGLE	24,015	10,044	12,910	1,061	2,866 D	41.8%	53.8%	43.8%	56.2%
183,433	PEORIA	78,988	26,027	50,081	2,880	24,054 D	33.0%	63.4%	34.2%	65.8%
23,094	PERRY	9,727	3,249	6,038	440	2,789 D	33.4%	62.1%	35.0%	65.0%
16,365	PIATT	8,884	3,381	5,245	258	1,864 D	38.1%	59.0%	39.2%	60.8%
17,384	PIKE	7,485	2,782	4,458	245	1,676 D	37.2%	59.6%	38.4%	61.6%
4,413	POPE	2,149	921	1,135	93	214 D	42.9%	52.8%	44.8%	55.2%
7,348	PULASKI	3,133	1,067	1,971	95	904 D	34.1%	62.9%	35.1%	64.9%
6,086	PUTNAM	3,218	908	2,219	91	1,311 D	28.2%	69.0%	29.0%	71.0%
33,893	RANDOLPH	14,711	5,251	8,937	523	3,686 D	35.7%	60.8%	37.0%	63.0%
16,149	RICHLAND	7,386	3,485	3,584	317	99 D	47.2%	48.5%	49.3%	50.7%
149,374	ROCK ISLAND	66,830	20,172	44,418	2,240	24,246 D	30.2%	66.5%	31.2%	68.8%
256,082	ST. CLAIR	120,819	37,319	77,920	5,580	40,601 D	30.9%	64.5%	32.4%	67.6%
26,733	SALINE	10,590	3,461	6,466	663	3,005 D	32.7%	61.1%	34.9%	65.1%
188,951	SANGAMON	98,938	33,589	62,050	3,299	28,461 D	33.9%	62.7%	35.1%	64.9%
7,189	SCHUYLER	3,749	1,258	2,325	166	1,067 D	33.6%	62.0%	35.1%	64.9%
5,537	SCOTT	2,517	890	1,519	108	629 D	35.4%	60.3%	36.9%	63.1%
22,893	SHELBY	10,699	4,027	6,307	365	2,280 D	37.6%	58.9%	39.0%	61.0%
6,332	STARK	2,782	1,043	1,637	102	594 D	37.5%	58.8%	38.9%	61.1%
48,979	STEPHENSON	20,526	7,703	12,033	790	4,330 D	37.5%	58.6%	39.0%	61.0%
128,485	TAZEWELL	62,373	24,386	35,388	2,599	11,002 D	39.1%	56.7%	40.8%	59.2%
18,293	UNION	8,881	3,116	5,236	529	2,120 D	35.1%	59.0%	37.3%	62.7%
83,919	VERMILION	32,521	10,066	21,463	992	11,397 D	31.0%	66.0%	31.9%	68.1%
12,937	WABASH	5,448	2,563	2,608	277	45 D	47.0%	47.9%	49.6%	50.4%
18,735	WARREN	7,744	2,701	4,803	240	2,102 D	34.9%	62.0%	36.0%	64.0%
15,148	WASHINGTON	7,659	3,294	4,077	288	783 D	43.0%	53.2%	44.7%	55.3%
17,151	WAYNE	7,561	3,958	3,177	426	781 R	52.3%	42.0%	55.5%	44.5%
15,371	WHITE	7,188	2,886	4,021	281	1,135 D	40.2%	55.9%	41.8%	58.2%
60,653	WHITESIDE	26,254	8,285	16,917	1,052	8,632 D	31.6%	64.4%	32.9%	67.1%
502,266	WILL	279,334	91,183	178,525	9,626	87,342 D	32.6%	63.9%	33.8%	66.2%
61,296	WILLIAMSON	29,020	11,564	16,002	1,454	4,438 D	39.8%	55.1%	42.0%	58.0%
278,418	WINNEBAGO	122,921	43,066	73,518	6,337	30,452 D	35.0%	59.8%	36.9%	63.1%
35,469	WOODFORD	18,576	9,559	8,353	664	1,206 R	51.5%	45.0%	53.4%	46.6%
12,419,293	TOTAL	5,329,884	1,520,621	3,615,844	193,419	2,095,223 D	28.5%	67.8%	29.6%	70.4%

ILLINOIS

HOUSE OF REPRESENTATIVES

| | | | Republican | | Democratic | | | | Percentage | | | |
| | | | | | | | | | Total Vote | | Major Vote | |
CD	Year	Total Vote	Vote	Candidate	Vote	Candidate	Other Vote	Rep.-Dem. Plurality	Rep.	Dem.	Rep.	Dem.
1	2008	271,397	38,361	MEMBERS, ANTOINE	233,036	RUSH, BOBBY L.*		194,675 D	14.1%	85.9%	14.1%	85.9%
1	2006	174,427	27,804	TABOUR, JASON E.	146,623	RUSH, BOBBY L.*		118,819 D	15.9%	84.1%	15.9%	84.1%
1	2004	249,949	37,840	WARDINGLEY, RAYMOND G.	212,109	RUSH, BOBBY L.*		174,269 D	15.1%	84.9%	15.1%	84.9%
1	2002	183,656	29,776	WARDINGLEY, RAYMOND G.	149,068	RUSH, BOBBY L.*	4,812	119,292 D	16.2%	81.2%	16.6%	83.4%
2	2008	280,776	29,721	WILLIAMS, ANTHONY W.	251,052	JACKSON, JESSE L. JR.*	3	221,331 D	10.6%	89.4%	10.6%	89.4%
2	2006	172,490	20,395	BELIN, ROBERT	146,347	JACKSON, JESSE L. JR.*	5,748	125,952 D	11.8%	84.8%	12.2%	87.8%
2	2004	234,525		—	207,535	JACKSON, JESSE L. JR.*	26,990	207,535 D		88.5%		100.0%
2	2002	184,010	32,567	NELSON, DOUG	151,443	JACKSON, JESSE L. JR.*		118,876 D	17.7%	82.3%	17.7%	82.3%
3	2008	235,524	50,336	HAWKINS, MICHAEL	172,581	LIPINSKI, DANIEL*	12,607	122,245 D	21.4%	73.3%	22.6%	77.4%
3	2006	165,722	37,954	WARDINGLEY, RAYMOND G.	127,768	LIPINSKI, DANIEL*		89,814 D	22.9%	77.1%	22.9%	77.1%
3	2004	229,956	57,845	CHLADA, RYAN	167,034	LIPINSKI, DANIEL	5,077	109,189 D	25.2%	72.6%	25.7%	74.3%
3	2002	156,042		—	156,042	LIPINSKI, WILLIAM O.*		156,042 D		100.0%		100.0%
4	2008	139,606	16,024	CUNNINGHAM, DANIEL	112,529	GUTIERREZ, LUIS V*	11,053	96,505 D	11.5%	80.6%	12.5%	87.5%
4	2006	81,442	11,532	MELICHAR, ANN	69,910	GUTIERREZ, LUIS V*		58,378 D	14.2%	85.8%	14.2%	85.8%
4	2004	125,142	15,536	CISNEROS, TONY	104,761	GUTIERREZ, LUIS V*	4,845	89,225 D	12.4%	83.7%	12.9%	87.1%
4	2002	84,513	12,778	LOPEZ-CISNEROS, ANTHONY J. "TONY"	67,339	GUTIERREZ, LUIS V*	4,396	54,561 D	15.1%	79.7%	15.9%	84.1%
5	2008	230,892	50,881	HANSON, TOM	170,728	EMANUEL, RAHM*	9,283	119,847 D	22.0%	73.9%	23.0%	77.0%
5	2006	146,581	32,250	WHITE, KEVIN EDWARD	114,319	EMANUEL, RAHM*	12	82,069 D	22.0%	78.0%	22.0%	78.0%
5	2004	207,930	49,530	BEST, BRUCE	158,400	EMANUEL, RAHM*		108,870 D	23.8%	76.2%	23.8%	76.2%
5	2002	159,435	46,008	AUGUSTI, MARK A.	106,514	EMANUEL, RAHM	6,913	60,506 D	28.9%	66.8%	30.2%	69.8%
6	2008	256,913	147,906	ROSKAM, PETER J.*	109,007	MORGENTHALER, JILL		38,899 R	57.6%	42.4%	57.6%	42.4%
6	2006	177,957	91,382	ROSKAM, PETER J.	86,572	DUCKWORTH, L. TAMMY	3	4,810 R	51.4%	48.6%	51.4%	48.6%
6	2004	250,097	139,627	HYDE, HENRY J.*	110,470	CEGELIS, CHRISTINE		29,157 R	55.8%	44.2%	55.8%	44.2%
6	2002	173,872	113,174	HYDE, HENRY J.*	60,698	BERRY, TOM		52,476 R	65.1%	34.9%	65.1%	34.9%
7	2008	276,817	41,474	MILLER, STEVE	235,343	DAVIS, DANNY K.*		193,869 D	15.0%	85.0%	15.0%	85.0%
7	2006	165,011	21,939	HUTCHINSON, CHARLES	143,071	DAVIS, DANNY K.*	1	121,132 D	13.3%	86.7%	13.3%	86.7%
7	2004	256,736	35,603	DAVIS-FAIRMAN, ANTONIO	221,133	DAVIS, DANNY K.*		185,530 D	13.9%	86.1%	13.9%	86.1%
7	2002	165,756	25,280	TUNNEY, MARK	137,933	DAVIS, DANNY K.*	2,543	112,653 D	15.3%	83.2%	15.5%	84.5%
8	2008	295,525	116,081	GREENBERG, STEVE	179,444	BEAN, MELISSA*		63,363 D	39.3%	60.7%	39.3%	60.7%
8	2006	183,394	80,720	McSWEENEY, DAVID	93,355	BEAN, MELISSA*	9,319	12,635 D	44.0%	50.9%	46.4%	53.6%
8	2004	270,393	130,601	CRANE, PHILIP M.*	139,792	BEAN, MELISSA		9,191 D	48.3%	51.7%	48.3%	51.7%
8	2002	165,926	95,275	CRANE, PHILIP M.*	70,626	BEAN, MELISSA	25	24,649 R	57.4%	42.6%	57.4%	42.6%
9	2008	243,694	53,593	YOUNAN, MICHAEL BENJAMIN	181,948	SCHAKOWSKY, JAN*	8,153	128,355 D	22.0%	74.7%	22.8%	77.2%
9	2006	164,713	41,858	SHANNON, MICHAEL P.	122,852	SCHAKOWSKY, JAN*	3	80,994 D	25.4%	74.6%	25.4%	74.6%
9	2004	231,417	56,135	ECKHARDT, KURT J.	175,282	SCHAKOWSKY, JAN*		119,147 D	24.3%	75.7%	24.3%	75.7%
9	2002	168,836	45,307	DURIC, NICHOLAS M.	118,642	SCHAKOWSKY, JAN*	4,887	73,335 D	26.8%	70.3%	27.6%	72.4%
10	2008	291,258	153,082	KIRK, MARK STEVEN*	138,176	SEALS, DANIEL J.		14,906 R	52.6%	47.4%	52.6%	47.4%
10	2006	202,208	107,929	KIRK, MARK STEVEN*	94,278	SEALS, DANIEL J.	1	13,651 R	53.4%	46.6%	53.4%	46.6%
10	2004	276,711	177,493	KIRK, MARK STEVEN*	99,218	GOODMAN, LEE		78,275 R	64.1%	35.9%	64.1%	35.9%
10	2002	186,911	128,611	KIRK, MARK STEVEN*	58,300	PERRITT, HENRY H. "HANK"		70,311 R	68.8%	31.2%	68.8%	31.2%
11	2008	317,895	109,608	OZINGA, MARTY	185,652	HALVORSON, DEBORAH L.	22,635	76,044 D	34.5%	58.4%	37.1%	62.9%
11	2006	197,856	109,009	WELLER, JERRY*	88,846	PAVICH, JOHN	1	20,163 R	55.1%	44.9%	55.1%	44.9%
11	2004	294,960	173,057	WELLER, JERRY*	121,903	RENNER, TARI		51,154 R	58.7%	41.3%	58.7%	41.3%
11	2002	193,085	124,192	WELLER, JERRY*	68,893	VAN DUYNE, KEITH S.		55,299 R	64.3%	35.7%	64.3%	35.7%
12	2008	298,181	74,382	TIMOTHY JAY RICHARDSON JR.	212,891	COSTELLO, JERRY F.*	10,908	138,509 D	24.9%	71.4%	25.9%	74.1%
12	2006	157,809		—	157,802	COSTELLO, JERRY F.*	7	157,802 D		100.0%		100.0%
12	2004	286,435	82,677	ZWEIGART, ERIN R.	198,962	COSTELLO, JERRY F.*	4,796	116,285 D	28.9%	69.5%	29.4%	70.6%
12	2002	190,020	58,440	SADLER, DAVID	131,580	COSTELLO, JERRY F.*		73,140 D	30.8%	69.2%	30.8%	69.2%

ILLINOIS

HOUSE OF REPRESENTATIVES

CD	Year	Total Vote	Republican		Democratic		Other Vote	Rep.-Dem. Plurality	Percentage			
			Vote	Candidate	Vote	Candidate			Total Vote		Major Vote	
									Rep.	Dem.	Rep.	Dem.
13	2004	337,771	180,888	BIGGERT, JUDY*	147,430	HARPER, SCOTT	9,453	33,458 R	53.6%	43.6%	55.1%	44.9%
13	2006	205,234	119,720	BIGGERT, JUDY*	85,507	SHANNON, JOSEPH	7	34,213 R	58.3%	41.7%	58.3%	41.7%
13	2004	308,312	200,472	BIGGERT, JUDY*	107,836	ANDERSEN, GLORIA SCHOR	4	92,636 R	65.0%	35.0%	65.0%	35.0%
13	2002	198,615	139,546	BIGGERT, JUDY*	59,069	MASON, TOM		80,477 R	70.3%	29.7%	70.3%	29.7%
14	2008	321,057	135,653	OBERWEIS, JIM	185,404	FOSTER, BILL*		49,751 D	42.3%	57.7%	42.3%	57.7%
14	2006	197,144	117,870	HASTERT, J. DENNIS*	79,274	LAESCH, JONATHAN "JOHN"		38,596 R	59.8%	40.2%	59.8%	40.2%
14	2004	279,208	191,618	HASTERT, J. DENNIS*	87,590	ZAMORA, RUBEN		104,028 R	68.6%	31.4%	68.6%	31.4%
14	2002	182,363	135,198	HASTERT, J. DENNIS*	47,165	QUICK, LAURENCE J.		88,033 R	74.1%	25.9%	74.1%	25.9%
15	2008	291,514	187,121	JOHNSON, TIMOTHY V.*	104,393	COX, STEVE		82,728 R	64.2%	35.8%	64.2%	35.8%
15	2006	202,835	116,810	JOHNSON, TIMOTHY V.*	86,025	GILL, DAVID		30,785 R	57.6%	42.4%	57.6%	42.4%
15	2004	291,739	178,114	JOHNSON, TIMOTHY V.*	113,625	GILL, DAVID		64,489 R	61.1%	38.9%	61.1%	38.9%
15	2002	206,617	134,650	JOHNSON, TIMOTHY V.*	64,131	HARTKE, JOSHUA T.	7,836	70,519 R	65.2%	31.0%	67.7%	32.3%
16	2008	312,220	190,039	MANZULLO, DONALD*	112,648	ABBOUD, ROBERT G.	9,533	77,391 R	60.9%	36.1%	62.8%	37.2%
16	2006	198,101	125,951	MANZULLO, DONALD*	63,627	AUMAN, RICHARD D.	8,523	62,324 R	63.6%	32.1%	66.4%	33.6%
16	2004	295,806	204,350	MANZULLO, DONALD*	91,452	KUTSCH, JOHN H.	4	112,898 R	69.1%	30.9%	69.1%	30.9%
16	2002	188,827	133,339	MANZULLO, DONALD*	55,488	KUTSCH, JOHN H.		77,851 R	70.6%	29.4%	70.6%	29.4%
17	2008	221,478		—	220,961	HARE, PHIL*	517	220,961 D		99.8%		100.0%
17	2006	201,186	86,161	ZINGA, ANDREA	115,025	HARE, PHIL		28,864 D	42.8%	57.2%	42.8%	57.2%
17	2004	284,000	111,680	ZINGA, ANDREA	172,320	EVANS, LANE*		60,640 D	39.3%	60.7%	39.3%	60.7%
17	2002	203,612	76,519	CALDERONE, PETER	127,093	EVANS, LANE*		50,574 D	37.6%	62.4%	37.6%	62.4%
18	2008	310,088	182,589	SCHOCK, AARON	117,642	CALLAHAN, COLLEEN	9,857	64,947 R	58.9%	37.9%	60.8%	39.2%
18	2006	223,246	150,194	LaHOOD, RAY*	73,052	WATERWORTH, STEVE		77,142 R	67.3%	32.7%	67.3%	32.7%
18	2004	307,595	216,047	LaHOOD, RAY*	91,548	WATERWORTH, STEVE		124,499 R	70.2%	29.8%	70.2%	29.8%
18	2002	192,567	192,567	LaHOOD, RAY*		—		192,567 R	100.0%		100.0%	
19	2008	315,589	203,434	SHIMKUS, JOHN*	105,338	DAVIS, DANIEL	6,817	98,096 R	64.5%	33.4%	65.9%	34.1%
19	2006	236,352	143,491	SHIMKUS, JOHN*	92,861	STOVER, DANNY L.		50,630 R	60.7%	39.3%	60.7%	39.3%
19	2004	307,754	213,451	SHIMKUS, JOHN*	94,303	BAGWELL, TIM		119,148 R	69.4%	30.6%	69.4%	30.6%
19	2002	244,473	133,956	SHIMKUS, JOHN*	110,517	PHELPS, DAVID*		23,439 R	54.8%	45.2%	54.8%	45.2%
TOTAL	2008	5,248,195	1,961,173		3,176,203		110,819	1,215,030 D	37.4%	60.5%	38.2%	61.8%
TOTAL	2006	3,453,708	1,442,969		1,987,114		23,625	544,145 D	41.8%	57.5%	42.1%	57.9%
TOTAL	2004	4,988,665	2,271,676		2,675,273		41,716	403,597 D	45.5%	53.6%	45.9%	54.1%
TOTAL	2002	3,429,136	1,657,183		1,740,541		31,412	83,358 D	48.3%	50.8%	48.8%	51.2%

Note: An asterisk (*) denotes incumbent.

ILLINOIS

GENERAL AND PRIMARY ELECTIONS

2008 GENERAL ELECTIONS

President   Other vote was 30,948 Independent (Ralph Nader); 19,642 Libertarian (Bob Barr); 11,838 Green (Cynthia A. McKinney); 8,256 Constitution (Chuck Baldwin); 1,149 New (John Joseph Polachek); 4 write-in (Ronald G. Hobbs); 3 write-in (Frank James Moore); 3 write-in (Donald K. Allen); 1 write-in (Ron Paul).

Senator   Other vote was 119,135 Green (Kathy Cummings); 50,224 Libertarian (Larry A. Stafford); 24,059 Constitution (Chad N. Koppie); 1 write-in (Patricia Elaine Beard).

House   Other vote was:

CD 1
CD 2   3 write-in (Nathan Peoples).
CD 3   12,607 Green (Jerome Pohlen).
CD 4   11,053 Green (Omar N. Lopez).
CD 5   9,283 Green (Alan Augustson).
CD 6
CD 7
CD 8
CD 9   8,140 Green (Morris Shanfield); 13 write-in (Susanne Atanus).
CD 10
CD 11   22,635 Green (Jason M. Wallace).
CD 12   10,907 Green (Rodger W. Jennings); 1 write-in (Harold Wiegand).
CD 13   9,402 Green (Steve Alesch); 51 write-in (Theodore Knapp).
CD 14
CD 15
CD 16   9,533 Green (Scott Summers).
CD 17   517 write-in (Mark Edward Lioen).
CD 18   9,857 Green (Sheldon Schafer).
CD 19   6,817 Green (Troy Dennis).

2008 PRIMARY ELECTIONS

Primary   February 5, 2008   **Registration** (as of February 5, 2008)   7,304,563   No Party Registration

Primary Type   Open—Any registered voter could participate in the primary of either party.

ILLINOIS

GENERAL AND PRIMARY ELECTIONS

	REPUBLICAN PRIMARIES			DEMOCRATIC PRIMARIES		
President	John McCain	426,777	47.5%	Barack Obama	1,318,234	64.7%
	Mitt Romney	257,265	28.6%	Hillary Clinton	667,930	32.8%
	Mike Huckabee	148,053	16.5%	John Edwards	39,719	1.9%
	Ron Paul	45,055	5.0%	Dennis J. Kucinich	4,234	0.2%
	Rudolph Giuliani	11,837	1.3%	Joseph R. Biden Jr.	3,788	0.2%
	Fred Thompson	7,259	0.8%	Bill Richardson	3,538	0.2%
	Alan Keyes	2,318	0.3%	Christopher J. Dodd	1,171	0.1%
	James Creighton Mitchell Jr.	483	0.1%			
	Tom Tancredo	375				
	TOTAL	899,422		TOTAL	2,038,614	
Senator	Steve Sauerberg	395,199	55.6%	Richard J. Durbin*	1,653,833	100.0%
	Andy Martin	240,548	33.9%			
	Mike Psak	74,829	10.5%			
	TOTAL	710,576				
Congressional District 1	Antoine Members	7,987	100.0%	Bobby L. Rush*	134,343	87.5%
				William Walls III	19,272	12.5%
				TOTAL	153,615	
Congressional District 2	No Republican candidate filed for the primary. Anthony W. Williams was subsequently named to fill the vacancy on the general election ballot.			Jesse L. Jackson Jr.*	149,760	100.0%
Congressional District 3	Michael Hawkins	13,722	66.9%	Daniel Lipinksi*	62,439	53.8%
	Arthur J. Jones	6,804	33.1%	Mark N. Pera	29,544	25.5%
				Jim Capparelli	13,312	11.5%
				Jerry Bennett	10,742	9.3%
	TOTAL	20,526		TOTAL	116,037	
Congressional District 4	No Republican candidate filed for the primary. Daniel Cunningham was subsequently named to fill the vacancy on the general election ballot.			Luis V. Gutierrez*	63,436	100.0%
Congressional District 5	No Republican candidate filed for the primary. Tom Hanson was subsequently named to fill the vacancy on the general election ballot.			Rahm Emanuel*	94,406	100.0%
Congressional District 6	Peter J. Roskam*	57,612	100.0%	Jill Morgenthaler	52,690	77.0%
				Stan Jagla	15,767	23.0%
				TOTAL	68,457	
Congressional District 7	No Republican candidate filed for the primary. Steve Miller was subsequently named to fill the vacancy on the general election ballot.			Danny K. Davis*	129,865	91.1%
				Robert Dallas	12,629	8.9%
				TOTAL	142,494	
Congressional District 8	Steve Greenberg	29,261	57.2%	Melissa Bean*	64,255	83.2%
	Kirk Morris	11,640	22.7%	Randi Scheurer	12,968	16.8%
	Kenneth W. Arnold	10,289	20.1%			
	TOTAL	51,190		TOTAL	77,223	
Congressional District 9	Michael Benjamin Younan	16,587	100.0%	Jan Schakowsky*	98,374	87.9%
				John Nocita	13,485	12.1%
				TOTAL	111,859	
Congressional District 10	Mark Steven Kirk*	44,967	100.0%	Daniel J. Seals	75,877	81.5%
				Jay K. Footlik	17,271	18.5%
				TOTAL	93,148	

ILLINOIS

GENERAL AND PRIMARY ELECTIONS

	REPUBLICAN PRIMARIES			DEMOCRATIC PRIMARIES		
Congressional District 11	Timothy A. Baldermann	32,767	61.9%	Deborah L. Halvorson	74,194	100.0%
	Terry Heenan	10,938	20.7%			
	Jimmy Lee	9,206	17.4%			
	TOTAL	52,911				
	Timothy A. Baldermann quit the race after the primary and was replaced on the general election ballot by Marty Ozinga.					
Congressional District 12	Timmy Jay Richardson Jr.	31,780		Jerry F. Costello*	91,636	100.0%
Congressional District 13	Judy Biggert*	58,533	77.3%	Scott Harper	85,787	100.0%
	Sean O'Kane	17,206	22.7%			
	TOTAL	75,739				
Congressional District 14	Jim Oberweis	44,462	56.4%	Bill Foster	32,410	42.5%
	Chris Lauzen	32,584	41.3%	John Laesch	32,012	41.9%
	Michael J. Dilger	1,847	2.3%	Joe Serra	6,033	7.9%
				Jotham Stein	5,865	7.7%
	TOTAL	78,893		TOTAL	76,320	
Congressional District 15	Timothy V. Johnson*	64,635	100.0%	Steve Cox	54,898	100.0%
Congressional District 16	Donald Manzullo*	65,804	100.0%	Robert G. Abboud	56,951	100.0%
Congressional District 17	No Republican candidate			Phil Hare*	75,567	100.0%
Congressional District 18	Aaron Schock	55,610	71.2%	*No Democratic candidate filed for the primary. Colleen Callahan was subsequently named to fill the vacancy on the general election ballot.*		
	Jim McConoughey	13,363	17.1%			
	John D. Morris	9,160	11.7%			
	TOTAL	78,133				
Congressional District 19	John Shimkus*	60,014	100.0%	Daniel Davis	40,773	59.5%
				Joe McMenamin	27,700	40.5%
				TOTAL	68,473	

Note: An asterisk (*) denotes incumbent.

INDIANA

Congressional districts first established for elections held in 2002
9 members

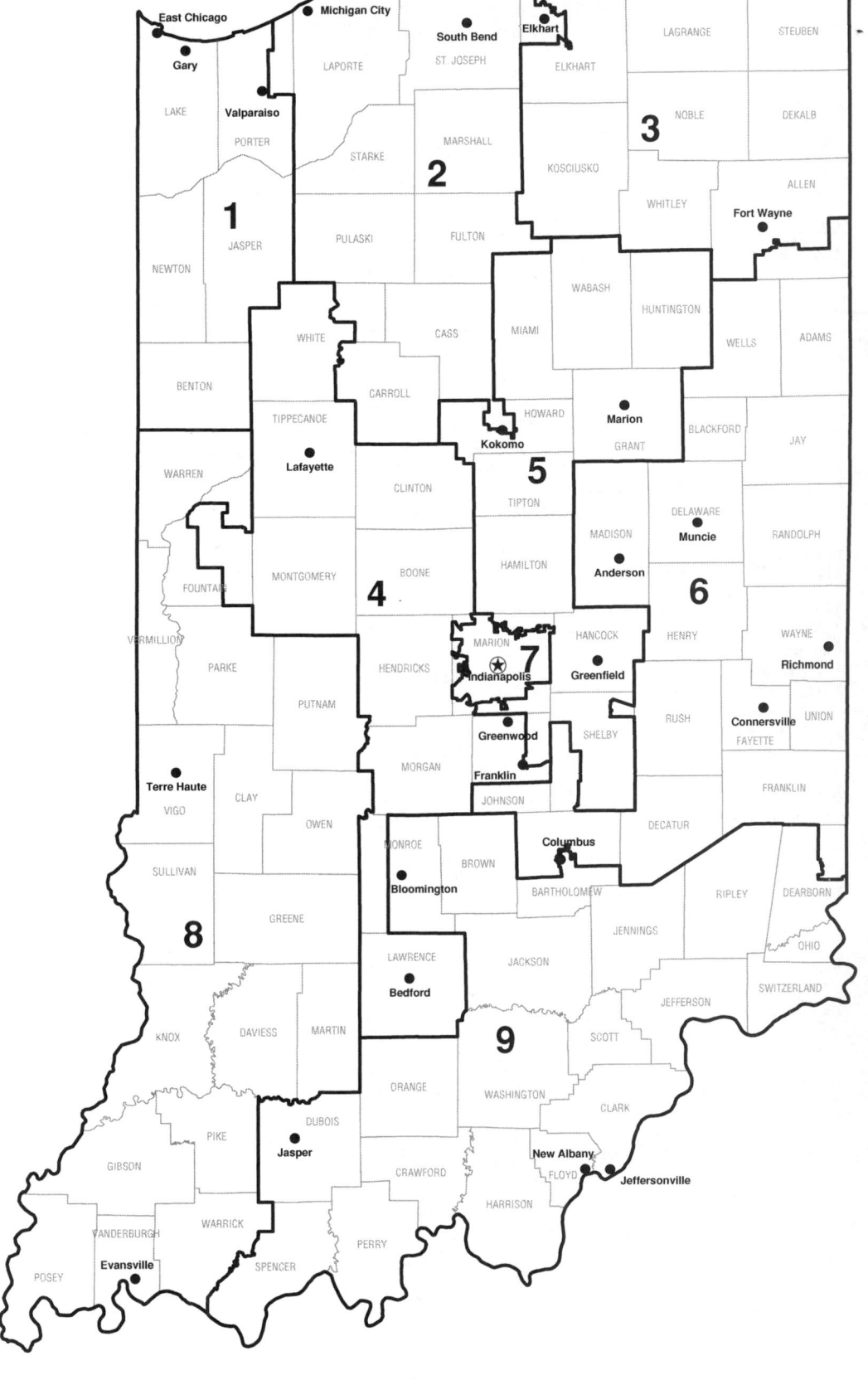

INDIANA

GOVERNOR
Mitch Daniels (R). Reelected 2008 to a four-year term. Previously elected 2004.

SENATORS (1 Democrat, 1 Republican)
Evan Bayh (D). Reelected 2004 to a six-year term. Previously elected 1998.

Richard G. Lugar (R). Reelected 2006 to a six-year term. Previously elected 2000, 1994, 1988, 1982, 1976.

REPRESENTATIVES (5 Democrats, 4 Republicans)
1. Peter J. Visclosky (D)
2. Joseph S. Donnelly (D)
3. Mark Souder (R)
4. Steve Buyer (R)
5. Dan Burton (R)
6. Mike Pence (R)
7. Andre Carson (D)
8. Brad Ellsworth (D)
9. Baron P. Hill (D)

POSTWAR VOTE FOR PRESIDENT

Year	Total Vote	Republican Vote	Republican Candidate	Democratic Vote	Democratic Candidate	Other Vote	Plurality	Total Vote Rep.	Total Vote Dem.	Major Vote Rep.	Major Vote Dem.
2008	2,751,054	1,345,648	McCain, John	1,374,039	Obama, Barack	31,367	28,391 D	48.9%	49.9%	49.5%	50.5%
2004	2,468,002	1,479,438	Bush, George W.	969,011	Kerry, John	19,553	510,427 R	59.9%	39.3%	60.4%	39.6%
2000**	2,199,302	1,245,836	Bush, George W.	901,980	Gore, Al	51,486	343,856 R	56.6%	41.0%	58.0%	42.0%
1996**	2,135,842	1,006,693	Dole, Bob	887,424	Clinton, Bill	241,725	119,269 R	47.1%	41.5%	53.1%	46.9%
1992**	2,305,871	989,375	Bush, George	848,420	Clinton, Bill	468,076	140,955 R	42.9%	36.8%	53.8%	46.2%
1988	2,168,621	1,297,763	Bush, George	860,643	Dukakis, Michael S.	10,215	437,120 R	59.8%	39.7%	60.1%	39.9%
1984	2,233,069	1,377,230	Reagan, Ronald	841,481	Mondale, Walter F.	14,358	535,749 R	61.7%	37.7%	62.1%	37.9%
1980**	2,242,033	1,255,656	Reagan, Ronald	844,197	Carter, Jimmy	142,180	411,459 R	56.0%	37.7%	59.8%	40.2%
1976	2,220,362	1,183,958	Ford, Gerald R.	1,014,714	Carter, Jimmy	21,690	169,244 R	53.3%	45.7%	53.8%	46.2%
1972	2,125,529	1,405,154	Nixon, Richard M.	708,568	McGovern, George S.	11,807	696,586 R	66.1%	33.3%	66.5%	33.5%
1968**	2,123,597	1,067,885	Nixon, Richard M.	806,659	Humphrey, Hubert H.	249,053	261,226 R	50.3%	38.0%	57.0%	43.0%
1964	2,091,606	911,118	Goldwater, Barry M.	1,170,848	Johnson, Lyndon B.	9,640	259,730 D	43.6%	56.0%	43.8%	56.2%
1960	2,135,360	1,175,120	Nixon, Richard M.	952,358	Kennedy, John F.	7,882	222,762 R	55.0%	44.6%	55.2%	44.8%
1956	1,974,607	1,182,811	Eisenhower, Dwight D.	783,908	Stevenson, Adlai E.	7,888	398,903 R	59.9%	39.7%	60.1%	39.9%
1952	1,955,049	1,136,259	Eisenhower, Dwight D.	801,530	Stevenson, Adlai E.	17,260	334,729 R	58.1%	41.0%	58.6%	41.4%
1948	1,656,212	821,079	Dewey, Thomas E.	807,831	Truman, Harry S.	27,302	13,248 R	49.6%	48.8%	50.4%	49.6%

**In past elections, the other vote included: 2000 - 18,531 Green (Ralph Nader); 1996 - 224,299 Reform (Ross Perot); 1992 - 455,934 Independent (Perot); 1980 - 111,639 Independent (John Anderson); 1968 - 243,108 American Independent (George Wallace).

INDIANA

POSTWAR VOTE FOR GOVERNOR

Year	Total Vote	Republican Vote	Republican Candidate	Democratic Vote	Democratic Candidate	Other Vote	Rep.-Dem. Plurality	Total Vote Rep.	Total Vote Dem.	Major Vote Rep.	Major Vote Dem.
2008	2,703,752	1,563,885	Daniels, Mitch	1,082,463	Thompson, Jill Long	57,404	481,422 R	57.8%	40.0%	59.1%	40.9%
2004	2,448,498	1,302,912	Daniels, Mitch	1,113,900	Kernan, Joseph E.	31,686	189,012 R	53.2%	45.5%	53.9%	46.1%
2000	2,179,413	908,285	McIntosh, David M.	1,232,525	O'Bannon, Frank L.	38,603	324,240 D	41.7%	56.6%	42.4%	57.6%
1996	2,110,047	986,982	Goldsmith, Stephen	1,087,128	O'Bannon, Frank L.	35,937	100,146 D	46.8%	51.5%	47.6%	52.4%
1992	2,229,116	822,533	Pearson, Linley E.	1,382,151	Bayh, Evan	24,432	559,618 D	36.9%	62.0%	37.3%	62.7%
1988	2,140,781	1,002,207	Mutz, John M.	1,138,574	Bayh, Evan		136,367 D	46.8%	53.2%	46.8%	53.2%
1984	2,197,988	1,146,497	Orr, Robert D.	1,036,922	Townsend, W. Wayne	14,569	109,575 R	52.2%	47.2%	52.5%	47.5%
1980	2,178,403	1,257,383	Orr, Robert D.	913,116	Hillenbrand, John A.	7,904	344,267 R	57.7%	41.9%	57.9%	42.1%
1976	2,175,324	1,236,555	Bowen, Otis R.	927,243	Conrad, Larry A.	11,526	309,312 R	56.8%	42.6%	57.1%	42.9%
1972	2,120,847	1,203,903	Bowen, Otis R.	900,489	Welsh, Matthew E.	16,455	303,414 R	56.8%	42.5%	57.2%	42.8%
1968	2,049,072	1,080,271	Whitcomb, Edgar D.	965,816	Rock, Robert L.	2,985	114,455 R	52.7%	47.1%	52.8%	47.2%
1964	2,072,915	901,342	Ristine, Richard O.	1,164,620	Branigin, Roger D.	6,953	263,278 D	43.5%	56.2%	43.6%	56.4%
1960	2,128,965	1,049,540	Parker, Crawford F.	1,072,717	Welsh, Matthew E.	6,708	23,177 D	49.3%	50.4%	49.5%	50.5%
1956	1,954,290	1,086,868	Handley, Harold W.	859,393	Tucker, Ralph	8,029	227,475 R	55.6%	44.0%	55.8%	44.2%
1952	1,931,869	1,075,685	Craig, George N.	841,984	Watkins, John A.	14,200	233,701 R	55.7%	43.6%	56.1%	43.9%
1948	1,652,321	745,892	Creighton, Hobart	884,995	Schricker, Henry F.	21,434	139,103 D	45.1%	53.6%	45.7%	54.3%

POSTWAR VOTE FOR SENATOR

Year	Total Vote	Republican Vote	Republican Candidate	Democratic Vote	Democratic Candidate	Other Vote	Rep.-Dem. Plurality	Total Vote Rep.	Total Vote Dem.	Major Vote Rep.	Major Vote Dem.
2006**	1,341,111	1,171,553	Lugar, Richard G.	—		169,558	1,171,553 R	87.4%		100.0%	
2004	2,428,233	903,913	Scott, Marvin	1,496,976	Bayh, Evan	27,344	593,063 D	37.2%	61.6%	37.6%	62.4%
2000	2,145,209	1,427,944	Lugar, Richard G.	683,273	Johnson, David L.	33,992	744,671 R	66.6%	31.9%	67.6%	32.4%
1998	1,588,617	552,732	Helmke, Paul	1,012,244	Bayh, Evan	23,641	459,512 D	34.8%	63.7%	35.3%	64.7%
1994	1,543,568	1,039,625	Lugar, Richard G.	470,799	Jontz, Jim	33,144	568,826 R	67.4%	30.5%	68.8%	31.2%
1992	2,211,426	1,267,972	Coats, Daniel R.	900,148	Hogsett, Joseph H.	43,306	367,824 R	57.3%	40.7%	58.5%	41.5%
1990S	1,504,302	806,048	Coats, Daniel R.	696,639	Hill, Baron P.	1,615	109,409 R	53.6%	46.3%	53.6%	46.4%
1988	2,099,303	1,430,525	Lugar, Richard G.	668,778	Wickes, Jack		761,747 R	68.1%	31.9%	68.1%	31.9%
1986	1,545,563	936,143	Quayle, J. Danforth	595,192	Long, Jill L.	14,228	340,951 R	60.6%	38.5%	61.1%	38.9%
1982	1,817,287	978,301	Lugar, Richard G.	828,400	Fithian, Floyd	10,586	149,901 R	53.8%	45.6%	54.1%	45.9%
1980	2,198,376	1,182,414	Quayle, J. Danforth	1,015,962	Bayh, Birch		166,452 R	53.8%	46.2%	53.8%	46.2%
1976	2,171,187	1,275,833	Lugar, Richard G.	878,522	Hartke, R. Vance	16,832	397,311 R	58.8%	40.5%	59.2%	40.8%
1974	1,752,978	814,117	Lugar, Richard G.	889,269	Bayh, Birch	49,592	75,152 D	46.4%	50.7%	47.8%	52.2%
1970	1,737,697	866,707	Roudebush, Richard	870,990	Hartke, R. Vance		4,283 D	49.9%	50.1%	49.9%	50.1%
1968	2,053,118	988,571	Ruckelshaus, William	1,060,456	Bayh, Birch	4,091	71,885 D	48.1%	51.7%	48.2%	51.8%
1964	2,076,963	941,519	Bontrager, D. Russell	1,128,505	Hartke, R. Vance	6,939	186,986 D	45.3%	54.3%	45.5%	54.5%
1962	1,800,038	894,547	Capehart, Homer E.	905,491	Bayh, Birch		10,944 D	49.7%	50.3%	49.7%	50.3%
1958	1,724,598	731,635	Handley, Harold W.	973,636	Hartke, R. Vance	19,327	242,001 D	42.4%	56.5%	42.9%	57.1%
1956	1,963,986	1,084,262	Capehart, Homer E.	871,781	Wickard, Claude	7,943	212,481 R	55.2%	44.4%	55.4%	44.6%
1952	1,946,118	1,020,605	Jenner, William E.	911,169	Schricker, Henry F.	14,344	109,436 R	52.4%	46.8%	52.8%	47.2%
1950	1,598,724	844,303	Capehart, Homer E.	741,025	Campbell, Alex M.	13,396	103,278 R	52.8%	46.4%	53.3%	46.7%
1946	1,347,434	739,809	Jenner, William E.	584,288	Townsend, M. Clifford	23,337	155,521 R	54.9%	43.4%	55.9%	44.1%

Notes: **In past elections, the other vote included: 2006 - 168,820 Libertarian (Steve Osborn). The Democratic Party did not run a candidate in the 2006 Senate election. The 1990 election was for a short term to fill a vacancy.

INDIANA

PRESIDENT 2008

2000 Census Population	County	Total Vote	Republican	Democratic	Other	Rep.-Dem. Plurality	Percentage			
							Total Vote		Major Vote	
							Rep.	Dem.	Rep.	Dem.
33,625	ADAMS	13,513	8,404	4,928	181	3,476 R	62.2%	36.5%	63.0%	37.0%
331,849	ALLEN	150,324	77,793	71,263	1,268	6,530 R	51.8%	47.4%	52.2%	47.8%
71,435	BARTHOLOMEW	31,043	17,067	13,567	409	3,500 R	55.0%	43.7%	55.7%	44.3%
9,421	BENTON	3,814	2,183	1,563	68	620 R	57.2%	41.0%	58.3%	41.7%
14,048	BLACKFORD	5,441	2,690	2,677	74	13 R	49.4%	49.2%	50.1%	49.9%
46,107	BOONE	26,647	16,622	9,752	273	6,870 R	62.4%	36.6%	63.0%	37.0%
14,957	BROWN	8,055	4,060	3,854	141	206 R	50.4%	47.8%	51.3%	48.7%
20,165	CARROLL	8,736	4,858	3,736	142	1,122 R	55.6%	42.8%	56.5%	43.5%
40,930	CASS	15,653	8,346	7,011	296	1,335 R	53.3%	44.8%	54.3%	45.7%
96,472	CLARK	47,725	25,326	21,953	446	3,373 R	53.1%	46.0%	53.6%	46.4%
26,556	CLAY	11,395	6,267	4,954	174	1,313 R	55.0%	43.5%	55.9%	44.1%
33,866	CLINTON	12,392	6,919	5,307	166	1,612 R	55.8%	42.8%	56.6%	43.4%
10,743	CRAWFORD	4,744	2,393	2,286	65	107 R	50.4%	48.2%	51.1%	48.9%
29,820	DAVIESS	10,586	7,098	3,370	118	3,728 R	67.1%	31.8%	67.8%	32.2%
46,109	DEARBORN	22,217	14,886	7,123	208	7,763 R	67.0%	32.1%	67.6%	32.4%
24,555	DECATUR	10,488	6,449	3,892	147	2,557 R	61.5%	37.1%	62.4%	37.6%
40,285	DE KALB	17,149	9,780	7,175	194	2,605 R	57.0%	41.8%	57.7%	42.3%
118,769	DELAWARE	49,863	20,916	28,384	563	7,468 D	41.9%	56.9%	42.4%	57.6%
39,674	DUBOIS	18,565	9,526	8,748	291	778 R	51.3%	47.1%	52.1%	47.9%
182,791	ELKHART	71,458	39,396	31,398	664	7,998 R	55.1%	43.9%	55.6%	44.4%
25,588	FAYETTE	9,462	4,917	4,389	156	528 R	52.0%	46.4%	52.8%	47.2%
70,823	FLOYD	36,537	19,957	16,263	317	3,694 R	54.6%	44.5%	55.1%	44.9%
17,954	FOUNTAIN	7,410	4,158	3,094	158	1,064 R	56.1%	41.8%	57.3%	42.7%
22,151	FRANKLIN	10,610	7,018	3,404	188	3,614 R	66.1%	32.1%	67.3%	32.7%
20,511	FULTON	9,006	5,147	3,702	157	1,445 R	57.2%	41.1%	58.2%	41.8%
32,500	GIBSON	15,095	8,449	6,455	191	1,994 R	56.0%	42.8%	56.7%	43.3%
73,403	GRANT	26,299	14,734	11,293	272	3,441 R	56.0%	42.9%	56.6%	43.4%
33,157	GREENE	13,629	7,691	5,709	229	1,982 R	56.4%	41.9%	57.4%	42.6%
182,740	HAMILTON	129,064	78,401	49,704	959	28,697 R	60.7%	38.5%	61.2%	38.8%
55,391	HANCOCK	34,253	22,008	11,874	371	10,134 R	64.3%	34.7%	65.0%	35.0%
34,325	HARRISON	18,091	10,551	7,288	252	3,263 R	58.3%	40.3%	59.1%	40.9%
104,093	HENDRICKS	64,955	39,728	24,548	679	15,180 R	61.2%	37.8%	61.8%	38.2%
48,508	HENRY	21,319	10,896	10,059	364	837 R	51.1%	47.2%	52.0%	48.0%
84,964	HOWARD	38,624	20,248	17,871	505	2,377 R	52.4%	46.3%	53.1%	46.9%
38,075	HUNTINGTON	16,328	10,291	5,843	194	4,448 R	63.0%	35.8%	63.8%	36.2%
41,335	JACKSON	17,374	9,726	7,354	294	2,372 R	56.0%	42.3%	56.9%	43.1%
30,043	JASPER	12,875	7,669	5,044	162	2,625 R	59.6%	39.2%	60.3%	39.7%
21,806	JAY	8,315	4,401	3,748	166	653 R	52.9%	45.1%	54.0%	46.0%
31,705	JEFFERSON	13,490	7,053	6,255	182	798 R	52.3%	46.4%	53.0%	47.0%
27,554	JENNINGS	11,839	6,261	5,312	266	949 R	52.9%	44.9%	54.1%	45.9%
115,209	JOHNSON	58,644	36,487	21,553	604	14,934 R	62.2%	36.8%	62.9%	37.1%
39,256	KNOX	16,424	8,639	7,569	216	1,070 R	52.6%	46.1%	53.3%	46.7%
74,057	KOSCIUSKO	30,134	20,488	9,236	410	11,252 R	68.0%	30.6%	68.9%	31.1%
34,909	LAGRANGE	9,491	5,702	3,663	126	2,039 R	60.1%	38.6%	60.9%	39.1%
484,564	LAKE	208,757	67,742	139,301	1,714	71,559 D	32.5%	66.7%	32.7%	67.3%
110,106	LA PORTE	46,919	17,918	28,258	743	10,340 D	38.2%	60.2%	38.8%	61.2%
45,922	LAWRENCE	18,534	11,018	7,208	308	3,810 R	59.4%	38.9%	60.5%	39.5%
133,358	MADISON	57,340	26,403	30,152	785	3,749 D	46.0%	52.6%	46.7%	53.3%
860,454	MARION	379,362	134,313	241,987	3,062	107,674 D	35.4%	63.8%	35.7%	64.3%
45,128	MARSHALL	18,550	10,406	7,889	255	2,517 R	56.1%	42.5%	56.9%	43.1%

INDIANA

PRESIDENT 2008

2000 Census Population	County	Total Vote	Republican	Democratic	Other	Rep.-Dem. Plurality	Percentage Total Vote Rep.	Dem.	Major Vote Rep.	Dem.
10,369	MARTIN	4,903	3,122	1,706	75	1,416 R	63.7%	34.8%	64.7%	35.3%
36,082	MIAMI	14,113	8,312	5,564	237	2,748 R	58.9%	39.4%	59.9%	40.1%
120,563	MONROE	63,215	21,118	41,450	647	20,332 D	33.4%	65.6%	33.8%	66.2%
37,629	MONTGOMERY	15,285	9,060	6,013	212	3,047 R	59.3%	39.3%	60.1%	39.9%
66,689	MORGAN	28,811	18,129	10,330	352	7,799 R	62.9%	35.9%	63.7%	36.3%
14,566	NEWTON	6,045	3,301	2,625	119	676 R	54.6%	43.4%	55.7%	44.3%
46,275	NOBLE	16,974	9,673	7,064	237	2,609 R	57.0%	41.6%	57.8%	42.2%
5,623	OHIO	2,918	1,713	1,158	47	555 R	58.7%	39.7%	59.7%	40.3%
19,306	ORANGE	8,086	4,536	3,390	160	1,146 R	56.1%	41.9%	57.2%	42.8%
21,786	OWEN	8,170	4,415	3,570	185	845 R	54.0%	43.7%	55.3%	44.7%
17,241	PARKE	6,964	3,909	2,924	131	985 R	56.1%	42.0%	57.2%	42.8%
18,899	PERRY	8,490	3,202	5,141	147	1,939 D	37.7%	60.6%	38.4%	61.6%
12,837	PIKE	6,028	3,221	2,700	107	521 R	53.4%	44.8%	54.4%	45.6%
146,798	PORTER	73,916	33,857	39,178	881	5,321 D	45.8%	53.0%	46.4%	53.6%
27,061	POSEY	12,771	6,804	5,828	139	976 R	53.3%	45.6%	53.9%	46.1%
13,755	PULASKI	5,964	3,388	2,466	110	922 R	56.8%	41.3%	57.9%	42.1%
36,019	PUTNAM	14,646	8,086	6,334	226	1,752 R	55.2%	43.2%	56.1%	43.9%
27,401	RANDOLPH	10,808	5,788	4,839	181	949 R	53.6%	44.8%	54.5%	45.5%
26,523	RIPLEY	12,188	7,794	4,187	207	3,607 R	63.9%	34.4%	65.1%	34.9%
18,261	RUSH	7,629	4,271	3,229	129	1,042 R	56.0%	42.3%	56.9%	43.1%
265,559	ST. JOSEPH	118,389	48,510	68,710	1,169	20,200 D	41.0%	58.0%	41.4%	58.6%
22,960	SCOTT	8,877	4,445	4,271	161	174 R	50.1%	48.1%	51.0%	49.0%
43,445	SHELBY	17,574	10,333	6,987	254	3,346 R	58.8%	39.8%	59.7%	40.3%
20,391	SPENCER	10,181	5,001	5,039	141	38 D	49.1%	49.5%	49.8%	50.2%
23,556	STARKE	9,466	4,473	4,778	215	305 D	47.3%	50.5%	48.4%	51.6%
33,214	STEUBEN	14,146	7,674	6,284	188	1,390 R	54.2%	44.4%	55.0%	45.0%
21,751	SULLIVAN	8,782	4,343	4,284	155	59 R	49.5%	48.8%	50.3%	49.7%
9,065	SWITZERLAND	3,640	1,940	1,638	62	302 R	53.3%	45.0%	54.2%	45.8%
148,955	TIPPECANOE	68,436	29,822	37,781	833	7,959 D	43.6%	55.2%	44.1%	55.9%
16,577	TIPTON	7,827	4,452	3,250	125	1,202 R	56.9%	41.5%	57.8%	42.2%
7,349	UNION	3,348	2,061	1,224	63	837 R	61.6%	36.6%	62.7%	37.3%
171,922	VANDERBURGH	77,656	37,512	39,423	721	1,911 D	48.3%	50.8%	48.8%	51.2%
16,788	VERMILLION	7,135	3,010	4,003	122	993 D	42.2%	56.1%	42.9%	57.1%
105,848	VIGO	43,706	18,121	25,040	545	6,919 D	41.5%	57.3%	42.0%	58.0%
34,960	WABASH	13,871	8,238	5,456	177	2,782 R	59.4%	39.3%	60.2%	39.8%
8,419	WARREN	3,998	2,166	1,755	77	411 R	54.2%	43.9%	55.2%	44.8%
52,383	WARRICK	28,665	16,013	12,329	323	3,684 R	55.9%	43.0%	56.5%	43.5%
27,223	WASHINGTON	11,305	6,519	4,562	224	1,957 R	57.7%	40.4%	58.8%	41.2%
71,097	WAYNE	28,562	14,558	13,459	545	1,099 R	51.0%	47.1%	52.0%	48.0%
27,600	WELLS	13,073	8,504	4,403	166	4,101 R	65.1%	33.7%	65.9%	34.1%
25,267	WHITE	10,767	5,731	4,839	197	892 R	53.2%	44.9%	54.2%	45.8%
30,707	WHITLEY	15,188	9,124	5,862	202	3,262 R	60.1%	38.6%	60.9%	39.1%
6,080,485	TOTAL	2,751,054	1,345,648	1,374,039	31,367	28,391 D	48.9%	49.9%	49.5%	50.5%

INDIANA

GOVERNOR 2008

2000 Census Population	County	Total Vote	Republican	Democratic	Other	Rep.-Dem. Plurality		Rep.	Dem.	Rep.	Dem.
								Total Vote		Major Vote	
33,625	ADAMS	13,523	8,291	4,938	294	3,353	R	61.3%	36.5%	62.7%	37.3%
331,849	ALLEN	147,414	89,938	55,027	2,449	34,911	R	61.0%	37.3%	62.0%	38.0%
71,435	BARTHOLOMEW	30,527	21,547	8,447	533	13,100	R	70.6%	27.7%	71.8%	28.2%
9,421	BENTON	3,815	2,398	1,308	109	1,090	R	62.9%	34.3%	64.7%	35.3%
14,048	BLACKFORD	5,416	3,098	2,221	97	877	R	57.2%	41.0%	58.2%	41.8%
46,107	BOONE	26,525	21,352	4,633	540	16,719	R	80.5%	17.5%	82.2%	17.8%
14,957	BROWN	8,097	4,967	2,880	250	2,087	R	61.3%	35.6%	63.3%	36.7%
20,165	CARROLL	8,752	5,586	2,925	241	2,661	R	63.8%	33.4%	65.6%	34.4%
40,930	CASS	15,682	8,831	6,418	433	2,413	R	56.3%	40.9%	57.9%	42.1%
96,472	CLARK	47,125	28,622	17,821	682	10,801	R	60.7%	37.8%	61.6%	38.4%
26,556	CLAY	11,353	5,986	5,055	312	931	R	52.7%	44.5%	54.2%	45.8%
33,866	CLINTON	12,286	8,322	3,658	306	4,664	R	67.7%	29.8%	69.5%	30.5%
10,743	CRAWFORD	4,806	1,869	2,869	68	1,000	D	38.9%	59.7%	39.4%	60.6%
29,820	DAVIESS	10,331	6,043	3,978	310	2,065	R	58.5%	38.5%	60.3%	39.7%
46,109	DEARBORN	21,595	14,536	6,540	519	7,996	R	67.3%	30.3%	69.0%	31.0%
24,555	DECATUR	10,290	7,486	2,534	270	4,952	R	72.8%	24.6%	74.7%	25.3%
40,285	DE KALB	16,738	9,562	6,752	424	2,810	R	57.1%	40.3%	58.6%	41.4%
118,769	DELAWARE	49,359	27,876	20,588	895	7,288	R	56.5%	41.7%	57.5%	42.5%
39,674	DUBOIS	18,329	9,946	7,938	445	2,008	R	54.3%	43.3%	55.6%	44.4%
182,791	ELKHART	70,837	40,983	28,114	1,740	12,869	R	57.9%	39.7%	59.3%	40.7%
25,588	FAYETTE	9,223	5,373	3,670	180	1,703	R	58.3%	39.8%	59.4%	40.6%
70,823	FLOYD	36,067	22,471	13,020	576	9,451	R	62.3%	36.1%	63.3%	36.7%
17,954	FOUNTAIN	7,435	4,350	2,816	269	1,534	R	58.5%	37.9%	60.7%	39.3%
22,151	FRANKLIN	10,454	6,443	3,674	337	2,769	R	61.6%	35.1%	63.7%	36.3%
20,511	FULTON	9,049	5,309	3,493	247	1,816	R	58.7%	38.6%	60.3%	39.7%
32,500	GIBSON	15,114	9,087	5,757	270	3,330	R	60.1%	38.1%	61.2%	38.8%
73,403	GRANT	25,899	16,006	9,431	462	6,575	R	61.8%	36.4%	62.9%	37.1%
33,157	GREENE	13,481	6,756	6,261	464	495	R	50.1%	46.4%	51.9%	48.1%
182,740	HAMILTON	127,879	106,574	19,442	1,863	87,132	R	83.3%	15.2%	84.6%	15.4%
55,391	HANCOCK	34,248	26,395	7,053	800	19,342	R	77.1%	20.6%	78.9%	21.1%
34,325	HARRISON	18,066	10,277	7,447	342	2,830	R	56.9%	41.2%	58.0%	42.0%
104,093	HENDRICKS	64,172	49,490	13,381	1,301	36,109	R	77.1%	20.9%	78.7%	21.3%
48,508	HENRY	21,250	12,142	8,519	589	3,623	R	57.1%	40.1%	58.8%	41.2%
84,964	HOWARD	38,750	23,852	14,143	755	9,709	R	61.6%	36.5%	62.8%	37.2%
38,075	HUNTINGTON	16,071	10,555	5,139	377	5,416	R	65.7%	32.0%	67.3%	32.7%
41,335	JACKSON	17,380	9,729	7,218	433	2,511	R	56.0%	41.5%	57.4%	42.6%
30,043	JASPER	12,452	6,737	5,419	296	1,318	R	54.1%	43.5%	55.4%	44.6%
21,806	JAY	8,347	4,763	3,404	180	1,359	R	57.1%	40.8%	58.3%	41.7%
31,705	JEFFERSON	13,040	6,671	6,127	242	544	R	51.2%	47.0%	52.1%	47.9%
27,554	JENNINGS	11,770	6,016	5,373	381	643	R	51.1%	45.6%	52.8%	47.2%
115,209	JOHNSON	57,835	44,743	11,813	1,279	32,930	R	77.4%	20.4%	79.1%	20.9%
39,256	KNOX	15,660	7,119	8,165	376	1,046	D	45.5%	52.1%	46.6%	53.4%
74,057	KOSCIUSKO	29,477	19,901	8,825	751	11,076	R	67.5%	29.9%	69.3%	30.7%
34,909	LAGRANGE	9,490	5,441	3,727	322	1,714	R	57.3%	39.3%	59.3%	40.7%
484,564	LAKE	191,004	66,145	122,111	2,748	55,966	D	34.6%	63.9%	35.1%	64.9%
110,106	LA PORTE	45,658	15,495	28,922	1,241	13,427	D	33.9%	63.3%	34.9%	65.1%
45,922	LAWRENCE	18,280	10,504	7,281	495	3,223	R	57.5%	39.8%	59.1%	40.9%
133,358	MADISON	56,924	34,028	21,776	1,120	12,252	R	59.8%	38.3%	61.0%	39.0%
860,454	MARION	377,650	209,955	160,318	7,377	49,637	R	55.6%	42.5%	56.7%	43.3%
45,128	MARSHALL	18,155	10,314	7,447	394	2,867	R	56.8%	41.0%	58.1%	41.9%

INDIANA
GOVERNOR 2008

2000 Census Population	County	Total Vote	Republican	Democratic	Other	Rep.-Dem. Plurality	Percentage Total Vote Rep.	Percentage Total Vote Dem.	Percentage Major Vote Rep.	Percentage Major Vote Dem.
10,369	MARTIN	4,897	2,714	2,030	153	684 R	55.4%	41.5%	57.2%	42.8%
36,082	MIAMI	13,459	7,816	5,174	469	2,642 R	58.1%	38.4%	60.2%	39.8%
120,563	MONROE	60,272	28,482	30,026	1,764	1,544 D	47.3%	49.8%	48.7%	51.3%
37,629	MONTGOMERY	15,226	11,304	3,605	317	7,699 R	74.2%	23.7%	75.8%	24.2%
66,689	MORGAN	28,296	19,818	7,570	908	12,248 R	70.0%	26.8%	72.4%	27.6%
14,566	NEWTON	6,007	2,999	2,822	186	177 R	49.9%	47.0%	51.5%	48.5%
46,275	NOBLE	16,812	9,408	6,951	453	2,457 R	56.0%	41.3%	57.5%	42.5%
5,623	OHIO	2,867	1,590	1,197	80	393 R	55.5%	41.8%	57.1%	42.9%
19,306	ORANGE	7,998	4,046	3,760	192	286 R	50.6%	47.0%	51.8%	48.2%
21,786	OWEN	8,138	4,717	3,074	347	1,643 R	58.0%	37.8%	60.5%	39.5%
17,241	PARKE	7,029	3,553	3,240	236	313 R	50.5%	46.1%	52.3%	47.7%
18,899	PERRY	8,400	3,169	5,133	98	1,964 D	37.7%	61.1%	38.2%	61.8%
12,837	PIKE	5,931	2,850	2,924	157	74 D	48.1%	49.3%	49.4%	50.6%
146,798	PORTER	72,709	31,388	39,519	1,802	8,131 D	43.2%	54.4%	44.3%	55.7%
27,061	POSEY	12,739	7,983	4,592	164	3,391 R	62.7%	36.0%	63.5%	36.5%
13,755	PULASKI	5,773	3,096	2,524	153	572 R	53.6%	43.7%	55.1%	44.9%
36,019	PUTNAM	14,386	9,443	4,597	346	4,846 R	65.6%	32.0%	67.3%	32.7%
27,401	RANDOLPH	10,535	6,268	3,987	280	2,281 R	59.5%	37.8%	61.1%	38.9%
26,523	RIPLEY	12,091	7,347	4,342	402	3,005 R	60.8%	35.9%	62.9%	37.1%
18,261	RUSH	7,619	5,071	2,311	237	2,760 R	66.6%	30.3%	68.7%	31.3%
265,559	ST. JOSEPH	117,413	56,176	59,259	1,978	3,083 D	47.8%	50.5%	48.7%	51.3%
22,960	SCOTT	8,924	4,414	4,330	180	84 R	49.5%	48.5%	50.5%	49.5%
43,445	SHELBY	17,522	11,774	5,259	489	6,515 R	67.2%	30.0%	69.1%	30.9%
20,391	SPENCER	10,079	5,527	4,418	134	1,109 R	54.8%	43.8%	55.6%	44.4%
23,556	STARKE	9,226	4,339	4,726	161	387 D	47.0%	51.2%	47.9%	52.1%
33,214	STEUBEN	14,120	7,896	5,822	402	2,074 R	55.9%	41.2%	57.6%	42.4%
21,751	SULLIVAN	8,553	3,463	4,779	311	1,316 D	40.5%	55.9%	42.0%	58.0%
9,065	SWITZERLAND	3,632	1,730	1,776	126	46 D	47.6%	48.9%	49.3%	50.7%
148,955	TIPPECANOE	67,430	41,740	23,980	1,710	17,760 R	61.9%	35.6%	63.5%	36.5%
16,577	TIPTON	7,824	5,244	2,376	204	2,868 R	67.0%	30.4%	68.8%	31.2%
7,349	UNION	3,306	1,756	1,412	138	344 R	53.1%	42.7%	55.4%	44.6%
171,922	VANDERBURGH	77,117	48,033	28,090	994	19,943 R	62.3%	36.4%	63.1%	36.9%
16,788	VERMILLION	7,156	2,769	4,164	223	1,395 D	38.7%	58.2%	39.9%	60.1%
105,848	VIGO	43,400	21,941	20,448	1,011	1,493 R	50.6%	47.1%	51.8%	48.2%
34,960	WABASH	13,320	8,578	4,434	308	4,144 R	64.4%	33.3%	65.9%	34.1%
8,419	WARREN	3,980	2,057	1,804	119	253 R	51.7%	45.3%	53.3%	46.7%
52,383	WARRICK	28,415	18,498	9,531	386	8,967 R	65.1%	33.5%	66.0%	34.0%
27,223	WASHINGTON	11,284	6,141	4,894	249	1,247 R	54.4%	43.4%	55.7%	44.3%
71,097	WAYNE	28,233	14,832	12,203	1,198	2,629 R	52.5%	43.2%	54.9%	45.1%
27,600	WELLS	12,863	8,418	4,153	292	4,265 R	65.4%	32.3%	67.0%	33.0%
25,267	WHITE	10,808	6,620	3,845	343	2,775 R	61.3%	35.6%	63.3%	36.7%
30,707	WHITLEY	14,883	8,997	5,566	320	3,431 R	60.5%	37.4%	61.8%	38.2%
6,080,485	TOTAL	2,703,752	1,563,885	1,082,463	57,404	481,422 R	57.8%	40.0%	59.1%	40.9%

INDIANA

HOUSE OF REPRESENTATIVES

CD	Year	Total Vote	Republican Vote	Republican Candidate	Democratic Vote	Democratic Candidate	Other Vote	Rep.-Dem. Plurality	Total Vote Rep.	Total Vote Dem.	Major Vote Rep.	Major Vote Dem.
1	2008	282,022	76,647	LEYVA, MARK J.	199,954	VISCLOSKY, PETER J.*	5,421	123,307 D	27.2%	70.9%	27.7%	72.3%
1	2006	149,607	40,146	LEYVA, MARK J.	104,195	VISCLOSKY, PETER J.*	5,266	64,049 D	26.8%	69.6%	27.8%	72.2%
1	2004	261,264	82,858	LEYVA, MARK J.	178,406	VISCLOSKY, PETER J.*		95,548 D	31.7%	68.3%	31.7%	68.3%
1	2002	135,111	41,909	LEYVA, MARK J.	90,443	VISCLOSKY, PETER J.*	2,759	48,534 D	31.0%	66.9%	31.7%	68.3%
2	2008	279,346	84,455	PUCKETT, LUKE WAYNE	187,416	DONNELLY, JOSEPH S.*	7,475	102,961 D	30.2%	67.1%	31.1%	68.9%
2	2006	191,861	88,300	CHOCOLA, CHRIS*	103,561	DONNELLY, JOSEPH S.		15,261 D	46.0%	54.0%	46.0%	54.0%
2	2004	259,355	140,496	CHOCOLA, CHRIS*	115,513	DONNELLY, JOSEPH S.	3,346	24,983 R	54.2%	44.5%	54.9%	45.1%
2	2002	188,458	95,081	CHOCOLA, CHRIS	86,253	THOMPSON, JILL LONG	7,124	8,828 R	50.5%	45.8%	52.4%	47.6%
3	2008	282,879	155,693	SOUDER, MARK*	112,309	MONTAGANO, MICHAEL A.	14,877	43,384 R	55.0%	39.7%	58.1%	41.9%
3	2006	175,778	95,421	SOUDER, MARK*	80,357	HAYHURST, THOMAS E.		15,064 R	54.3%	45.7%	54.3%	45.7%
3	2004	247,621	171,389	SOUDER, MARK*	76,232	PARRA, MARIA M.		95,157 R	69.2%	30.8%	69.2%	30.8%
3	2002	146,606	92,566	SOUDER, MARK*	50,509	RIGDON, JAY	3,531	42,057 R	63.1%	34.5%	64.7%	35.3%
4	2008	321,564	192,526	BUYER, STEVE*	129,038	ACKERSON, NELS		63,488 R	59.9%	40.1%	59.9%	40.1%
4	2006	178,043	111,057	BUYER, STEVE*	66,986	SANDERS, DAVID AVRAM		44,071 R	62.4%	37.6%	62.4%	37.6%
4	2004	274,136	190,445	BUYER, STEVE*	77,574	SANDERS, DAVID AVRAM	6,117	112,871 R	69.5%	28.3%	71.1%	28.9%
4	2002	158,008	112,760	BUYER, STEVE*	41,314	ABBOTT, BILL	3,934	71,446 R	71.4%	26.1%	73.2%	26.8%
5	2008	358,062	234,705	BURTON, DAN*	123,357	RULEY, MARY ETTA		111,348 R	65.5%	34.5%	65.5%	34.5%
5	2006	204,929	133,118	BURTON, DAN*	64,362	CARR, KATHERINE FOX	7,449	68,756 R	65.0%	31.4%	67.4%	32.6%
5	2004	318,363	228,718	BURTON, DAN*	82,637	CARR, KATHERINE FOX	7,008	146,081 R	71.8%	26.0%	73.5%	26.5%
5	2002	179,855	129,442	BURTON, DAN*	45,283	CARR, KATHERINE FOX	5,130	84,159 R	72.0%	25.2%	74.1%	25.9%
6	2008	282,412	180,608	PENCE, MIKE*	94,265	WELSH, BARRY A.	7,539	86,343 R	64.0%	33.4%	65.7%	34.3%
6	2006	192,078	115,266	PENCE, MIKE*	76,812	WELSH, BARRY A.		38,454 R	60.0%	40.0%	60.0%	40.0%
6	2004	272,049	182,529	PENCE, MIKE*	85,123	FOX, MELINA ANN	4,397	97,406 R	67.1%	31.3%	68.2%	31.8%
6	2002	185,653	118,436	PENCE, MIKE*	63,871	FOX, MELINA ANN	3,346	54,565 R	63.8%	34.4%	65.0%	35.0%
7	2008	265,299	92,645	CAMPO, GABRIELLE	172,650	CARSON, ANDRE*	4	80,005 D	34.9%	65.1%	34.9%	65.1%
7	2006	139,054	64,304	DICKERSON, ERIC	74,750	CARSON, JULIA*		10,446 D	46.2%	53.8%	46.2%	53.8%
7	2004	223,175	97,491	HORNING, ANDREW	121,303	CARSON, JULIA*	4,381	23,812 D	43.7%	54.4%	44.6%	55.4%
7	2002	145,840	64,379	McVEY, BROSE A.	77,478	CARSON, JULIA*	3,983	13,099 D	44.1%	53.1%	45.4%	54.6%
8	2008	291,462	102,769	GOODE, GREGORY J.	188,693	ELLSWORTH, BRAD*		85,924 D	35.3%	64.7%	35.3%	64.7%
8	2006	214,723	83,704	HOSTETTLER, JOHN*	131,019	ELLSWORTH, BRAD		47,315 D	39.0%	61.0%	39.0%	61.0%
8	2004	272,778	145,576	HOSTETTLER, JOHN*	121,522	JENNINGS, JON P.	5,680	24,054 R	53.4%	44.5%	54.5%	45.5%
8	2002	192,865	98,952	HOSTETTLER, JOHN*	88,763	HARTKE, BRYAN L.	5,150	10,189 R	51.3%	46.0%	52.7%	47.3%
9	2008	313,804	120,529	SODREL, MIKE	181,281	HILL, BARON P.*	11,994	60,752 D	38.4%	57.8%	39.9%	60.1%
9	2006	220,849	100,469	SODREL, MIKE*	110,454	HILL, BARON P.	9,926	9,985 D	45.5%	50.0%	47.6%	52.4%
9	2004	287,510	142,197	SODREL, MIKE	140,772	HILL, BARON P.*	4,541	1,425 R	49.5%	49.0%	50.3%	49.7%
9	2002	188,957	87,169	SODREL, MIKE	96,654	HILL, BARON P.*	5,134	9,485 D	46.1%	51.2%	47.4%	52.6%
TOTAL	2008	2,676,850	1,240,577		1,388,963		47,310	148,386 D	46.3%	51.9%	47.2%	52.8%
TOTAL	2006	1,666,922	831,785		812,496		22,641	19,289 R	49.9%	48.7%	50.6%	49.4%
TOTAL	2004	2,416,251	1,381,699		999,082		35,470	382,617 R	57.2%	41.3%	58.0%	42.0%
TOTAL	2002	1,521,353	840,694		640,568		40,091	200,126 R	55.3%	42.1%	56.8%	43.2%

Note: An asterisk (*) denotes incumbent.

INDIANA

GENERAL AND PRIMARY ELECTIONS

2008 GENERAL ELECTIONS

President	Other vote was 29,257 Libertarian (Bob Barr); 1,024 Independent write-in (Chuck Baldwin); 909 Independent write-in (Ralph Nader); 87 Green write-in (Cynthia A. McKinney); 51 Constitution write-in (Darrell L. Castle); 14 Socialist write-in (Brian Moore); 12 America's Independence write-in (Michael L. Faith); 9 Independent write-in (Kevin Mottus); 2 Independent write-in (Lawson Mitchell Bone); 1 Republican write-in ("Lou" Kujawski); 1 Independent write-in (John Leroy Plemons).
Governor	Other vote was 57,376 Libertarian (Andy Horning); 19 Independent write-in (Christopher Stried); 9 Independent write-in (Timothy Lee Frye).
House	Other vote was:

CD 1	5,421 Libertarian (Jeff Duensing).
CD 2	7,475 Libertarian (Mark Vogel).
CD 3	14,877 Libertarian (William R. Larsen).
CD 4	
CD 5	
CD 6	7,539 Libertarian (George T. Holland).
CD 7	4 Republican write-in (Delbert Suits).
CD 8	
CD 9	11,994 Libertarian (D. Eric Schansberg).

2008 PRIMARY ELECTIONS

Primary	May 6, 2008	**Registration** (as of May 6, 2008)	4,318,663	No Party Registration

Primary Type	Open—Any registered voter could participate in the primary of either party.

	REPUBLICAN PRIMARIES			DEMOCRATIC PRIMARIES		
President	John McCain	320,318	77.6%	Hillary Clinton	646,282	50.6%
	Mike Huckabee	41,173	10.0%	Barack Obama	632,073	49.4%
	Ron Paul	31,612	7.7%			
	Mitt Romney	19,581	4.7%			
	TOTAL	*412,684*		*TOTAL*	*1,278,355*	
Governor	Mitch Daniels*	350,390	100.0%	Jill Long Thompson	582,860	50.6%
				Jim Schellinger	569,091	49.4%
				TOTAL	*1,151,951*	
Congressional District 1	Mark J. Leyva	7,278	36.2%	Peter J. Visclosky*	134,505	100.0%
	Mark E. Coleman	3,940	19.6%			
	Richard "Ric" Holtz	3,791	18.8%			
	Chuck Barman	2,945	14.6%			
	Jayson Reeves	2,170	10.8%			
	TOTAL	*20,124*				
Congressional District 2	Luke Wayne Puckett	14,327	50.3%	Joseph S. Donnelly*	119,217	100.0%
	Joseph Roush	9,073	31.8%			
	Tony Zirkle	5,092	17.9%			
	TOTAL	*28,492*				

INDIANA

GENERAL AND PRIMARY ELECTIONS

	REPUBLICAN PRIMARIES			DEMOCRATIC PRIMARIES		
Congressional District 3	Mark Souder*	40,161	77.1%	Michael A. Montagano	76,428	100.0%
	Scott Wise	11,946	22.9%			
	TOTAL	*52,107*				
Congressional District 4	Steve Buyer*	45,538	71.6%	Nels Ackerson	83,638	100.0%
	Mike Campbell	9,541	15.0%			
	LaRon Keith	8,545	13.4%			
	TOTAL	*63,624*				
Congressional District 5	Dan Burton*	45,682	51.8%	Mary Etta Ruley	46,606	46.7%
	John McGoff	39,701	45.1%	Kenny Stall	29,513	29.5%
	Clayton L. Alfred	2,742	3.1%	Chester Kelsey	23,768	23.8%
	TOTAL	*88,125*		*TOTAL*	*99,887*	
Congressional District 6	Mike Pence*	46,488	100.0%	Barry A. Welsh	94,002	100.0%
Congressional District 7	Jon Elrod	19,135	84.6%	Andre Carson*	66,659	46.5%
	Catherine "Cat" Ping	2,574	11.4%	Woodrow A. "Woody" Myers Jr.	33,683	23.5%
	Lawrence B. "Larry" Shouse	921	4.1%	David Orentlicher	29,231	20.4%
	TOTAL	*22,630*		Carolene Mays	11,011	7.7%
				Joseph C. Stockett III "Hippie Joe"	1,125	0.8%
	Jon Elrod quit the race after the primary and was replaced			Frances Nelson Williams	708	0.5%
	on the general election ballot by Gabrielle Campo.			Larry Lamont Ledford	648	0.5%
				Pierre Quincy Pullins	240	0.2%
				TOTAL	*143,305*	
Congressional District 8	Gregory J. Goode	27,147	100.0%	Brad Ellsworth*	134,796	100.0%
Congressional District 9	Mike Sodrel	32,101	100.0%	Baron P. Hill*	99,332	67.6%
				Gretchen Clearwater	23,157	15.8%
				John R. Bottorff	18,963	12.9%
				Lendall B. Terry	5,429	3.7%
				TOTAL	*146,881*	

Note: An asterisk (*) denotes incumbent.

IOWA

Congressional districts first established for elections held in 2002
5 members

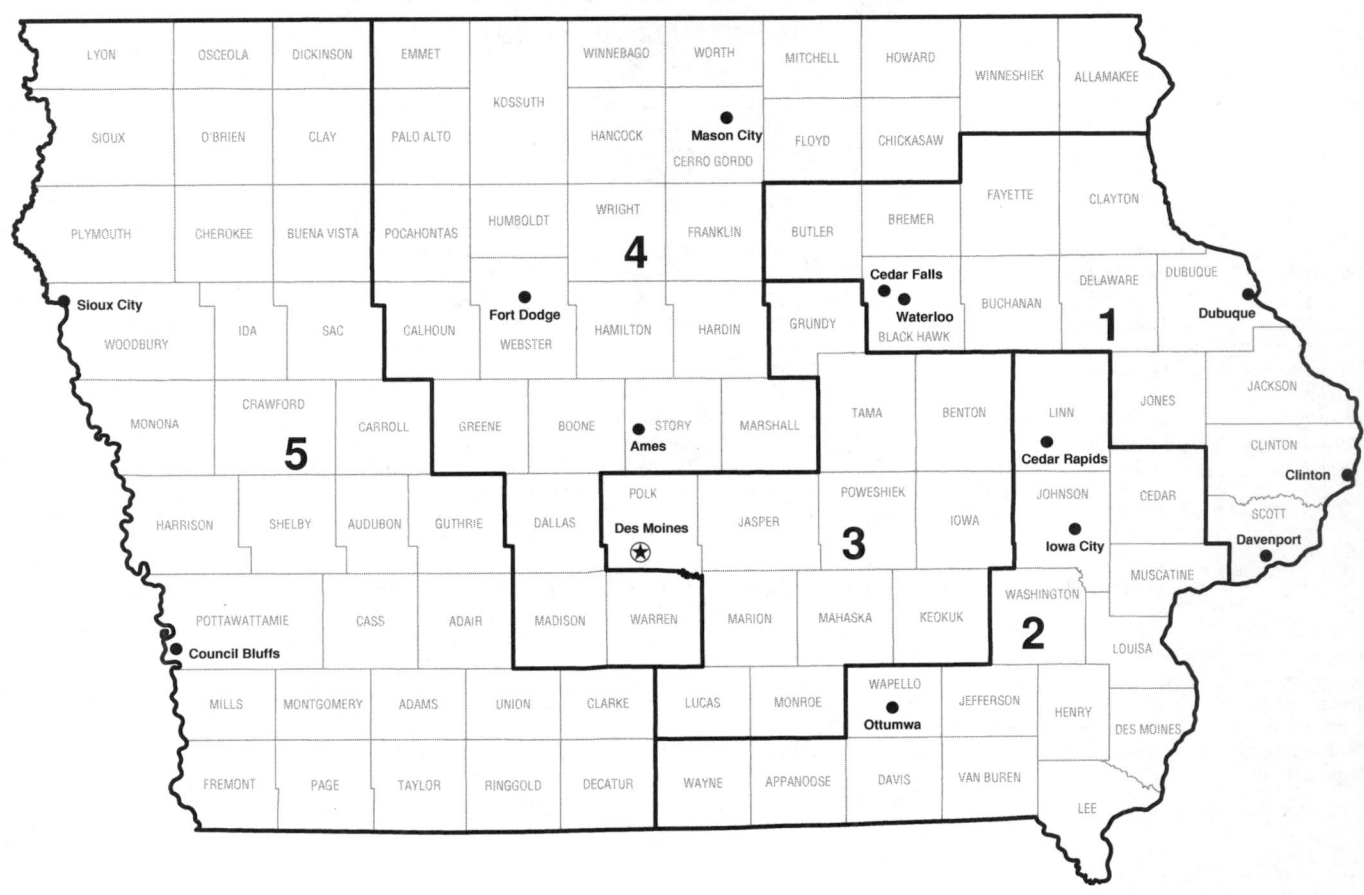

IOWA

GOVERNOR

Chet Culver (D). Elected 2006 to a four-year term.

SENATORS (1 Democrat, 1 Republican)

Charles E. Grassley (R). Reelected 2004 to a six-year term. Previously elected 1998, 1992, 1986, 1980.

Tom Harkin (D). Reelected 2008 to a six-year term. Previously elected 2002, 1996, 1990, 1984.

REPRESENTATIVES (3 Democrats, 2 Republicans)

1. Bruce Braley (D)
2. Dave Loebsack (D)
3. Leonard L. Boswell (D)
4. Tom Latham (R)
5. Steve King (R)

POSTWAR VOTE FOR PRESIDENT

Year	Total Vote	Republican Vote	Republican Candidate	Democratic Vote	Democratic Candidate	Other Vote	Plurality		Total Vote Rep.	Total Vote Dem.	Major Vote Rep.	Major Vote Dem.
2008	1,537,123	682,379	McCain, John	828,940	Obama, Barack	25,804	146,561	D	44.4%	53.9%	45.2%	54.8%
2004	1,506,908	751,957	Bush, George W.	741,898	Kerry, John	13,053	10,059	R	49.9%	49.2%	50.3%	49.7%
2000**	1,315,563	634,373	Bush, George W.	638,517	Gore, Al	42,673	4,144	D	48.2%	48.5%	49.8%	50.2%
1996**	1,234,075	492,644	Dole, Bob	620,258	Clinton, Bill	121,173	127,614	D	39.9%	50.3%	44.3%	55.7%
1992**	1,354,607	504,891	Bush, George	586,353	Clinton, Bill	263,363	81,462	D	37.3%	43.3%	46.3%	53.7%
1988	1,225,614	545,355	Bush, George	670,557	Dukakis, Michael S.	9,702	125,202	D	44.5%	54.7%	44.9%	55.1%
1984	1,319,805	703,088	Reagan, Ronald	605,620	Mondale, Walter F.	11,097	97,468	R	53.3%	45.9%	53.7%	46.3%
1980**	1,317,661	676,026	Reagan, Ronald	508,672	Carter, Jimmy	132,963	167,354	R	51.3%	38.6%	57.1%	42.9%
1976	1,279,306	632,863	Ford, Gerald R.	619,931	Carter, Jimmy	26,512	12,932	R	49.5%	48.5%	50.5%	49.5%
1972	1,225,944	706,207	Nixon, Richard M.	496,206	McGovern, George S.	23,531	210,001	R	57.6%	40.5%	58.7%	41.3%
1968**	1,167,931	619,106	Nixon, Richard M.	476,699	Humphrey, Hubert H.	72,126	142,407	R	53.0%	40.8%	56.5%	43.5%
1964	1,184,539	449,148	Goldwater, Barry M.	733,030	Johnson, Lyndon B.	2,361	283,882	D	37.9%	61.9%	38.0%	62.0%
1960	1,273,810	722,381	Nixon, Richard M.	550,565	Kennedy, John F.	864	171,816	R	56.7%	43.2%	56.7%	43.3%
1956	1,234,564	729,187	Eisenhower, Dwight D.	501,858	Stevenson, Adlai E.	3,519	227,329	R	59.1%	40.7%	59.2%	40.8%
1952	1,268,773	808,906	Eisenhower, Dwight D.	451,513	Stevenson, Adlai E.	8,354	357,393	R	63.8%	35.6%	64.2%	35.8%
1948	1,038,264	494,018	Dewey, Thomas E.	522,380	Truman, Harry S.	21,866	28,362	D	47.6%	50.3%	48.6%	51.4%

**In past elections, the other vote included: 2000 - 29,374 Green (Ralph Nader); 1996 - 105,159 Reform (Ross Perot); 1992 - 253,468 Independent (Perot); 1980 - 115,633 Independent (John Anderson); 1968 - 66,422 American Independent (George Wallace).

IOWA

POSTWAR VOTE FOR GOVERNOR

Year	Total Vote	Republican Vote	Republican Candidate	Democratic Vote	Democratic Candidate	Other Vote	Rep.-Dem. Plurality	Total Vote Rep.	Total Vote Dem.	Major Vote Rep.	Major Vote Dem.
2006	1,053,255	467,425	Nussle, Jim	569,021	Culver, Chet	16,809	101,596 D	44.4%	54.0%	45.1%	54.9%
2002	1,025,802	456,612	Gross, Doug	540,449	Vilsack, Tom	28,741	83,837 D	44.5%	52.7%	45.8%	54.2%
1998	956,418	444,787	Lightfoot, Jim Ross	500,231	Vilsack, Tom	11,400	55,444 D	46.5%	52.3%	47.1%	52.9%
1994	997,248	566,395	Branstad, Terry E.	414,453	Campbell, Bonnie J.	16,400	151,942 R	56.8%	41.6%	57.7%	42.3%
1990	976,483	591,852	Branstad, Terry E.	379,372	Avenson, Donald D.	5,259	212,480 R	60.6%	38.9%	60.9%	39.1%
1986	910,623	472,712	Branstad, Terry E.	436,987	Junkins, Lowell L.	924	35,725 R	51.9%	48.0%	52.0%	48.0%
1982	1,038,229	548,313	Branstad, Terry E.	483,291	Conlin, Roxanne	6,625	65,022 R	52.8%	46.5%	53.2%	46.8%
1978	843,190	491,713	Ray, Robert	345,519	Fitzgerald, Jerome D.	5,958	146,194 R	58.3%	41.0%	58.7%	41.3%
1974**	920,458	534,518	Ray, Robert	377,553	Schaben, James, F.	8,387	156,965 R	58.1%	41.0%	58.6%	41.4%
1972	1,210,222	707,177	Ray, Robert	487,282	Franzenburg, Paul	15,763	219,895 R	58.4%	40.3%	59.2%	40.8%
1970	791,241	403,394	Ray, Robert	368,911	Fulton, Robert	18,936	34,483 R	51.0%	46.6%	52.2%	47.8%
1968	1,136,489	614,328	Ray, Robert	521,216	Franzenburg, Paul	945	93,112 R	54.1%	45.9%	54.1%	45.9%
1966	893,175	394,518	Murray, William G.	494,259	Hughes, Harold E.	4,398	99,741 D	44.2%	55.3%	44.4%	55.6%
1964	1,167,734	365,131	Hultman, Evan	794,610	Hughes, Harold E.	7,993	429,479 D	31.3%	68.0%	31.5%	68.5%
1962	819,854	388,955	Erbe, Norman A.	430,899	Hughes, Harold E.		41,944 D	47.4%	52.6%	47.4%	52.6%
1960	1,237,089	645,026	Erbe, Norman A.	592,063	McManus, E. J.		52,963 R	52.1%	47.9%	52.1%	47.9%
1958	859,095	394,071	Murray, William G.	465,024	Loveless, Herschel C.		70,953 D	45.9%	54.1%	45.9%	54.1%
1956	1,204,235	587,383	Hoegh, Leo A.	616,852	Loveless, Herschel C.		29,469 D	48.8%	51.2%	48.8%	51.2%
1954	848,592	435,944	Hoegh, Leo A.	410,255	Herring, Clyde E.	2,393	25,689 R	51.4%	48.3%	51.5%	48.5%
1952	1,230,045	638,388	Beardsley, William	587,671	Loveless, Herschel C.	3,986	50,717 R	51.9%	47.8%	52.1%	47.9%
1950	857,213	506,642	Beardsley, William	347,176	Gillette, Lester S.	3,395	159,466 R	59.1%	40.5%	59.3%	40.7%
1948	994,833	553,900	Beardsley, William	434,432	Switzer, Carroll O.	6,501	119,468 R	55.7%	43.7%	56.0%	44.0%
1946	631,681	362,592	Blue, Robert D.	266,190	Miles, Frank	2,899	96,402 R	57.4%	42.1%	57.7%	42.3%

**The term of office of Iowa's governor was increased from two to four years effective with the 1974 election.

POSTWAR VOTE FOR SENATOR

Year	Total Vote	Republican Vote	Republican Candidate	Democratic Vote	Democratic Candidate	Other Vote	Rep.-Dem. Plurality	Total Vote Rep.	Total Vote Dem.	Major Vote Rep.	Major Vote Dem.
2008	1,502,918	560,006	Reed, Christopher	941,665	Harkin, Tom	1,247	381,659 D	37.3%	62.7%	37.3%	62.7%
2004	1,479,228	1,038,175	Grassley, Charles E.	412,365	Small, Arthur	28,688	625,810 R	70.2%	27.9%	71.6%	28.4%
2002	1,023,075	447,892	Ganske, Greg	554,278	Harkin, Tom	20,905	106,386 D	43.8%	54.2%	44.7%	55.3%
1998	947,907	648,480	Grassley, Charles E.	289,049	Osterberg, David	10,378	359,431 R	68.4%	30.5%	69.2%	30.8%
1996	1,224,054	571,807	Lightfoot, Jim Ross	634,166	Harkin, Tom	18,081	62,359 D	46.7%	51.8%	47.4%	52.6%
1992	1,292,494	899,761	Grassley, Charles E.	351,561	Lloyd-Jones, Jean	41,172	548,200 R	69.6%	27.2%	71.9%	28.1%
1990	983,933	446,869	Tauke, Tom	535,975	Harkin, Tom	1,089	89,106 D	45.4%	54.5%	45.5%	54.5%
1986	891,762	588,880	Grassley, Charles E.	299,406	Roehrick, John P.	3,476	289,474 R	66.0%	33.6%	66.3%	33.7%
1984	1,292,700	564,381	Jepsen, Roger W.	716,883	Harkin, Tom	11,436	152,502 D	43.7%	55.5%	44.0%	56.0%
1980	1,277,034	683,014	Grassley, Charles E.	581,545	Culver, John C.	12,475	101,469 R	53.5%	45.5%	54.0%	46.0%
1978	824,654	421,598	Jepsen, Roger W.	395,066	Clark, Richard	7,990	26,532 R	51.1%	47.9%	51.6%	48.4%
1974	889,561	420,546	Stanley, David M.	462,947	Culver, John C.	6,068	42,401 D	47.3%	52.0%	47.6%	52.4%
1972	1,203,333	530,525	Miller, Jack	662,637	Clark, Richard	10,171	132,112 D	44.1%	55.1%	44.5%	55.5%
1968	1,144,086	568,469	Stanley, David M.	574,884	Hughes, Harold E.	733	6,415 D	49.7%	50.2%	49.7%	50.3%
1966	857,496	522,339	Miller, Jack	324,114	Smith, E. B.	11,043	198,225 R	60.9%	37.8%	61.7%	38.3%
1962	807,972	431,364	Hickenlooper, Bourke B.	376,602	Smith, E. B.	6	54,762 R	53.4%	46.6%	53.4%	46.6%
1960	1,237,582	642,463	Miller, Jack	595,119	Loveless, Herschel C.		47,344 R	51.9%	48.1%	51.9%	48.1%
1956	1,178,655	635,499	Hickenlooper, Bourke B.	543,156	Evans, R. M.		92,343 R	53.9%	46.1%	53.9%	46.1%
1954	847,355	442,409	Martin, Thomas E.	402,712	Gillette, Guy	2,234	39,697 R	52.2%	47.5%	52.3%	47.7%
1950	858,523	470,613	Hickenlooper, Bourke B.	383,766	Loveland, A. J.	4,144	86,847 R	54.8%	44.7%	55.1%	44.9%
1948	1,000,412	415,778	Wilson, George A.	578,226	Gillette, Guy	6,408	162,448 D	41.6%	57.8%	41.8%	58.2%

IOWA

PRESIDENT 2008

2000 Census Population	County	Total Vote	Republican	Democratic	Other	Rep.-Dem. Plurality	Total Vote Rep.	Total Vote Dem.	Major Vote Rep.	Major Vote Dem.
8,243	ADAIR	4,053	2,060	1,924	69	136 R	50.8%	47.5%	51.7%	48.3%
4,482	ADAMS	2,206	1,046	1,118	42	72 D	47.4%	50.7%	48.3%	51.7%
14,675	ALLAMAKEE	7,062	2,965	3,971	126	1,006 D	42.0%	56.2%	42.7%	57.3%
13,721	APPANOOSE	6,179	3,086	2,970	123	116 R	49.9%	48.1%	51.0%	49.0%
6,830	AUDUBON	3,436	1,634	1,739	63	105 D	47.6%	50.6%	48.4%	51.6%
25,308	BENTON	13,717	6,447	7,058	212	611 D	47.0%	51.5%	47.7%	52.3%
128,012	BLACK HAWK	64,787	24,662	39,184	941	14,522 D	38.1%	60.5%	38.6%	61.4%
26,224	BOONE	13,931	6,293	7,356	282	1,063 D	45.2%	52.8%	46.1%	53.9%
23,325	BREMER	12,872	5,741	6,940	191	1,199 D	44.6%	53.9%	45.3%	54.7%
21,093	BUCHANAN	10,342	4,139	6,050	153	1,911 D	40.0%	58.5%	40.6%	59.4%
20,411	BUENA VISTA	8,420	4,223	4,075	122	148 R	50.2%	48.4%	50.9%	49.1%
15,305	BUTLER	7,166	3,700	3,364	102	336 R	51.6%	46.9%	52.4%	47.6%
11,115	CALHOUN	5,195	2,741	2,341	113	400 R	52.8%	45.1%	53.9%	46.1%
21,421	CARROLL	10,395	4,922	5,302	171	380 D	47.3%	51.0%	48.1%	51.9%
14,684	CASS	7,352	4,006	3,211	135	795 R	54.5%	43.7%	55.5%	44.5%
18,187	CEDAR	9,665	4,289	5,221	155	932 D	44.4%	54.0%	45.1%	54.9%
46,447	CERRO GORDO	24,143	9,375	14,405	363	5,030 D	38.8%	59.7%	39.4%	60.6%
13,035	CHEROKEE	6,368	3,372	2,890	106	482 R	53.0%	45.4%	53.8%	46.2%
13,095	CHICKASAW	6,586	2,557	3,923	106	1,366 D	38.8%	59.6%	39.5%	60.5%
9,133	CLARKE	4,445	2,118	2,218	109	100 D	47.6%	49.9%	48.8%	51.2%
17,372	CLAY	8,402	4,355	3,925	122	430 R	51.8%	46.7%	52.6%	47.4%
18,678	CLAYTON	8,990	3,651	5,195	144	1,544 D	40.6%	57.8%	41.3%	58.7%
50,149	CLINTON	24,722	9,324	15,018	380	5,694 D	37.7%	60.7%	38.3%	61.7%
16,942	CRAWFORD	7,191	3,345	3,715	131	370 D	46.5%	51.7%	47.4%	52.6%
40,750	DALLAS	32,643	16,954	15,149	540	1,805 R	51.9%	46.4%	52.8%	47.2%
8,541	DAVIS	3,818	2,029	1,680	109	349 R	53.1%	44.0%	54.7%	45.3%
8,689	DECATUR	4,106	2,020	1,986	100	34 R	49.2%	48.4%	50.4%	49.6%
18,404	DELAWARE	8,903	4,113	4,649	141	536 D	46.2%	52.2%	46.9%	53.1%
42,351	DES MOINES	20,574	7,721	12,462	391	4,741 D	37.5%	60.6%	38.3%	61.7%
16,424	DICKINSON	9,907	5,162	4,625	120	537 R	52.1%	46.7%	52.7%	47.3%
89,143	DUBUQUE	47,963	18,651	28,611	701	9,960 D	38.9%	59.7%	39.5%	60.5%
11,027	EMMET	5,015	2,373	2,570	72	197 D	47.3%	51.2%	48.0%	52.0%
22,008	FAYETTE	10,262	4,205	5,908	149	1,703 D	41.0%	57.6%	41.6%	58.4%
16,900	FLOYD	8,093	3,051	4,822	220	1,771 D	37.7%	59.6%	38.8%	61.2%
10,704	FRANKLIN	5,149	2,501	2,575	73	74 D	48.6%	50.0%	49.3%	50.7%
8,010	FREMONT	3,896	1,989	1,848	59	141 R	51.1%	47.4%	51.8%	48.2%
10,366	GREENE	4,804	2,349	2,371	84	22 D	48.9%	49.4%	49.8%	50.2%
12,369	GRUNDY	6,829	3,945	2,790	94	1,155 R	57.8%	40.9%	58.6%	41.4%
11,353	GUTHRIE	5,849	3,074	2,625	150	449 R	52.6%	44.9%	53.9%	46.1%
16,438	HAMILTON	8,081	3,913	4,018	150	105 D	48.4%	49.7%	49.3%	50.7%
12,100	HANCOCK	5,930	3,016	2,805	109	211 R	50.9%	47.3%	51.8%	48.2%
18,812	HARDIN	8,861	4,315	4,393	153	78 D	48.7%	49.6%	49.6%	50.4%
15,666	HARRISON	7,583	3,909	3,555	119	354 R	51.5%	46.9%	52.4%	47.6%
20,336	HENRY	9,380	4,822	4,349	209	473 R	51.4%	46.4%	52.6%	47.4%
9,932	HOWARD	4,729	1,722	2,941	66	1,219 D	36.4%	62.2%	36.9%	63.1%
10,381	HUMBOLDT	5,123	2,895	2,160	68	735 R	56.5%	42.2%	57.3%	42.7%
7,837	IDA	3,547	2,036	1,454	57	582 R	57.4%	41.0%	58.3%	41.7%
15,671	IOWA	8,548	4,188	4,202	158	14 D	49.0%	49.2%	49.9%	50.1%
20,296	JACKSON	9,957	3,673	6,102	182	2,429 D	36.9%	61.3%	37.6%	62.4%
37,213	JASPER	19,422	8,794	10,250	378	1,456 D	45.3%	52.8%	46.2%	53.8%

IOWA

PRESIDENT 2008

2000 Census Population	County	Total Vote	Republican	Democratic	Other	Rep.-Dem. Plurality	Percentage Total Vote Rep.	Dem.	Major Vote Rep.	Dem.
16,181	JEFFERSON	8,632	3,324	5,070	238	1,746 D	38.5%	58.7%	39.6%	60.4%
111,006	JOHNSON	72,989	20,732	51,027	1,230	30,295 D	28.4%	69.9%	28.9%	71.1%
20,221	JONES	10,008	4,405	5,446	157	1,041 D	44.0%	54.4%	44.7%	55.3%
11,400	KEOKUK	5,362	2,712	2,518	132	194 R	50.6%	47.0%	51.9%	48.1%
17,163	KOSSUTH	9,100	4,329	4,625	146	296 D	47.6%	50.8%	48.3%	51.7%
38,052	LEE	17,230	7,062	9,821	347	2,759 D	41.0%	57.0%	41.8%	58.2%
191,701	LINN	113,369	43,626	68,037	1,706	24,411 D	38.5%	60.0%	39.1%	60.9%
12,183	LOUISA	4,921	2,314	2,523	84	209 D	47.0%	51.3%	47.8%	52.2%
9,422	LUCAS	4,476	2,330	2,029	117	301 R	52.1%	45.3%	53.5%	46.5%
11,763	LYON	6,220	4,471	1,675	74	2,796 R	71.9%	26.9%	72.7%	27.3%
14,019	MADISON	8,481	4,579	3,733	169	846 R	54.0%	44.0%	55.1%	44.9%
22,335	MAHASKA	10,934	6,271	4,464	199	1,807 R	57.4%	40.8%	58.4%	41.6%
32,052	MARION	17,032	9,256	7,421	355	1,835 R	54.3%	43.6%	55.5%	44.5%
39,311	MARSHALL	18,663	8,278	10,023	362	1,745 D	44.4%	53.7%	45.2%	54.8%
14,547	MILLS	7,283	4,183	2,976	124	1,207 R	57.4%	40.9%	58.4%	41.6%
10,874	MITCHELL	5,766	2,469	3,179	118	710 D	42.8%	55.1%	43.7%	56.3%
10,020	MONONA	4,797	2,411	2,295	91	116 R	50.3%	47.8%	51.2%	48.8%
8,016	MONROE	3,874	2,000	1,798	76	202 R	51.6%	46.4%	52.7%	47.3%
11,771	MONTGOMERY	5,289	2,887	2,326	76	561 R	54.6%	44.0%	55.4%	44.6%
41,722	MUSCATINE	19,120	7,929	10,920	271	2,991 D	41.5%	57.1%	42.1%	57.9%
15,102	O'BRIEN	7,333	4,894	2,338	101	2,556 R	66.7%	31.9%	67.7%	32.3%
7,003	OSCEOLA	3,129	2,027	1,037	65	990 R	64.8%	33.1%	66.2%	33.8%
16,976	PAGE	7,359	4,351	2,900	108	1,451 R	59.1%	39.4%	60.0%	40.0%
10,147	PALO ALTO	4,808	2,294	2,428	86	134 D	47.7%	50.5%	48.6%	51.4%
24,849	PLYMOUTH	12,515	7,765	4,629	121	3,136 R	62.0%	37.0%	62.7%	37.3%
8,662	POCAHONTAS	4,012	2,138	1,800	74	338 R	53.3%	44.9%	54.3%	45.7%
374,601	POLK	214,409	89,668	120,984	3,757	31,316 D	41.8%	56.4%	42.6%	57.4%
87,704	POTTAWATTAMIE	42,324	21,237	20,436	651	801 R	50.2%	48.3%	51.0%	49.0%
18,815	POWESHIEK	10,033	4,340	5,519	174	1,179 D	43.3%	55.0%	44.0%	56.0%
5,469	RINGGOLD	2,689	1,401	1,236	52	165 R	52.1%	46.0%	53.1%	46.9%
11,529	SAC	5,053	2,705	2,256	92	449 R	53.5%	44.6%	54.5%	45.5%
158,668	SCOTT	86,378	36,365	48,927	1,086	12,562 D	42.1%	56.6%	42.6%	57.4%
13,173	SHELBY	6,455	3,488	2,863	104	625 R	54.0%	44.4%	54.9%	45.1%
31,589	SIOUX	16,665	13,490	3,030	145	10,460 R	80.9%	18.2%	81.7%	18.3%
79,981	STORY	46,581	18,995	26,548	1,038	7,553 D	40.8%	57.0%	41.7%	58.3%
18,103	TAMA	8,852	3,820	4,899	133	1,079 D	43.2%	55.3%	43.8%	56.2%
6,958	TAYLOR	3,026	1,607	1,347	72	260 R	53.1%	44.5%	54.4%	45.6%
12,309	UNION	5,914	2,781	3,000	133	219 D	47.0%	50.7%	48.1%	51.9%
7,809	VAN BUREN	3,612	1,986	1,546	80	440 R	55.0%	42.8%	56.2%	43.8%
36,051	WAPELLO	15,940	6,663	8,820	457	2,157 D	41.8%	55.3%	43.0%	57.0%
40,671	WARREN	24,889	12,144	12,299	446	155 D	48.8%	49.4%	49.7%	50.3%
20,670	WASHINGTON	10,629	5,247	5,170	212	77 R	49.4%	48.6%	50.4%	49.6%
6,730	WAYNE	2,981	1,565	1,357	59	208 R	52.5%	45.5%	53.6%	46.4%
40,235	WEBSTER	18,556	8,337	9,917	302	1,580 D	44.9%	53.4%	45.7%	54.3%
11,723	WINNEBAGO	6,085	2,730	3,254	101	524 D	44.9%	53.5%	45.6%	54.4%
21,310	WINNESHIEK	11,284	4,273	6,829	182	2,556 D	37.9%	60.5%	38.5%	61.5%
103,877	WOODBURY	44,815	22,219	21,983	613	236 R	49.6%	49.1%	50.3%	49.7%
7,909	WORTH	4,259	1,612	2,567	80	955 D	37.8%	60.3%	38.6%	61.4%
14,334	WRIGHT	6,395	3,198	3,102	95	96 R	50.0%	48.5%	50.8%	49.2%
2,926,324	TOTAL	1,537,123	682,379	828,940	25,804	146,561 D	44.4%	53.9%	45.2%	54.8%

IOWA

SENATOR 2008

2000 Census Population	County	Total Vote	Republican	Democratic	Other	Rep.-Dem. Plurality	Percentage			
							Total Vote		Major Vote	
							Rep.	Dem.	Rep.	Dem.
8,243	ADAIR	4,019	1,648	2,367	4	719 D	41.0%	58.9%	41.0%	59.0%
4,482	ADAMS	2,173	885	1,288		403 D	40.7%	59.3%	40.7%	59.3%
14,675	ALLAMAKEE	6,886	2,453	4,429	4	1,976 D	35.6%	64.3%	35.6%	64.4%
13,721	APPANOOSE	6,070	2,524	3,541	5	1,017 D	41.6%	58.3%	41.6%	58.4%
6,830	AUDUBON	3,365	1,406	1,958	1	552 D	41.8%	58.2%	41.8%	58.2%
25,308	BENTON	13,512	4,985	8,519	8	3,534 D	36.9%	63.0%	36.9%	63.1%
128,012	BLACK HAWK	62,770	20,043	42,681	46	22,638 D	31.9%	68.0%	32.0%	68.0%
26,224	BOONE	13,734	5,361	8,365	8	3,004 D	39.0%	60.9%	39.1%	60.9%
23,325	BREMER	12,617	4,835	7,778	4	2,943 D	38.3%	61.6%	38.3%	61.7%
21,093	BUCHANAN	10,180	3,226	6,952	2	3,726 D	31.7%	68.3%	31.7%	68.3%
20,411	BUENA VISTA	8,202	3,129	5,071	2	1,942 D	38.1%	61.8%	38.2%	61.8%
15,305	BUTLER	7,066	3,030	4,031	5	1,001 D	42.9%	57.0%	42.9%	57.1%
11,115	CALHOUN	5,096	2,096	2,994	6	898 D	41.1%	58.8%	41.2%	58.8%
21,421	CARROLL	10,104	4,194	5,905	5	1,711 D	41.5%	58.4%	41.5%	58.5%
14,684	CASS	7,161	3,230	3,928	3	698 D	45.1%	54.9%	45.1%	54.9%
18,187	CEDAR	9,470	3,343	6,123	4	2,780 D	35.3%	64.7%	35.3%	64.7%
46,447	CERRO GORDO	23,776	7,449	16,314	13	8,865 D	31.3%	68.6%	31.3%	68.7%
13,035	CHEROKEE	6,282	2,398	3,883	1	1,485 D	38.2%	61.8%	38.2%	61.8%
13,095	CHICKASAW	6,451	2,005	4,445	1	2,440 D	31.1%	68.9%	31.1%	68.9%
9,133	CLARKE	4,409	1,727	2,680	2	953 D	39.2%	60.8%	39.2%	60.8%
17,372	CLAY	8,201	3,297	4,898	6	1,601 D	40.2%	59.7%	40.2%	59.8%
18,678	CLAYTON	8,841	2,916	5,907	18	2,991 D	33.0%	66.8%	33.0%	67.0%
50,149	CLINTON	24,272	7,025	17,238	9	10,213 D	28.9%	71.0%	29.0%	71.0%
16,942	CRAWFORD	6,894	2,420	4,469	5	2,049 D	35.1%	64.8%	35.1%	64.9%
40,750	DALLAS	32,030	15,248	16,765	17	1,517 D	47.6%	52.3%	47.6%	52.4%
8,541	DAVIS	3,794	1,556	2,236	2	680 D	41.0%	58.9%	41.0%	59.0%
8,689	DECATUR	4,025	1,577	2,448		871 D	39.2%	60.8%	39.2%	60.8%
18,404	DELAWARE	8,748	3,234	5,513	1	2,279 D	37.0%	63.0%	37.0%	63.0%
42,351	DES MOINES	20,088	6,343	13,721	24	7,378 D	31.6%	68.3%	31.6%	68.4%
16,424	DICKINSON	9,692	3,846	5,843	3	1,997 D	39.7%	60.3%	39.7%	60.3%
89,143	DUBUQUE	46,595	14,482	32,086	27	17,604 D	31.1%	68.9%	31.1%	68.9%
11,027	EMMET	4,893	1,554	3,337	2	1,783 D	31.8%	68.2%	31.8%	68.2%
22,008	FAYETTE	10,139	3,326	6,810	3	3,484 D	32.8%	67.2%	32.8%	67.2%
16,900	FLOYD	7,991	2,360	5,629	2	3,269 D	29.5%	70.4%	29.5%	70.5%
10,704	FRANKLIN	5,070	2,075	2,993	2	918 D	40.9%	59.0%	40.9%	59.1%
8,010	FREMONT	3,801	1,537	2,260	4	723 D	40.4%	59.5%	40.5%	59.5%
10,366	GREENE	4,723	1,977	2,743	3	766 D	41.9%	58.1%	41.9%	58.1%
12,369	GRUNDY	6,718	3,325	3,389	4	64 D	49.5%	50.4%	49.5%	50.5%
11,353	GUTHRIE	5,788	2,635	3,147	6	512 D	45.5%	54.4%	45.6%	54.4%
16,438	HAMILTON	7,945	3,178	4,765	2	1,587 D	40.0%	60.0%	40.0%	60.0%
12,100	HANCOCK	5,846	2,326	3,518	2	1,192 D	39.8%	60.2%	39.8%	60.2%
18,812	HARDIN	8,749	3,611	5,131	7	1,520 D	41.3%	58.6%	41.3%	58.7%
15,666	HARRISON	7,359	2,928	4,422	9	1,494 D	39.8%	60.1%	39.8%	60.2%
20,336	HENRY	9,150	3,950	5,193	7	1,243 D	43.2%	56.8%	43.2%	56.8%
9,932	HOWARD	4,642	1,281	3,361		2,080 D	27.6%	72.4%	27.6%	72.4%
10,381	HUMBOLDT	5,056	2,275	2,777	4	502 D	45.0%	54.9%	45.0%	55.0%
7,837	IDA	3,436	1,447	1,987	2	540 D	42.1%	57.8%	42.1%	57.9%
15,671	IOWA	8,375	3,318	5,051	6	1,733 D	39.6%	60.3%	39.6%	60.4%
20,296	JACKSON	9,686	2,813	6,871	2	4,058 D	29.0%	70.9%	29.0%	71.0%
37,213	JASPER	19,138	7,759	11,368	11	3,609 D	40.5%	59.4%	40.6%	59.4%

IOWA

SENATOR 2008

2000 Census Population	County	Total Vote	Republican	Democratic	Other	Rep.-Dem. Plurality	Percentage Total Vote Rep.	Dem.	Major Vote Rep.	Dem.
16,181	JEFFERSON	8,400	2,700	5,690	10	2,990 D	32.1%	67.7%	32.2%	67.8%
111,006	JOHNSON	70,413	17,537	52,741	135	35,204 D	24.9%	74.9%	25.0%	75.0%
20,221	JONES	9,856	3,543	6,306	7	2,763 D	35.9%	64.0%	36.0%	64.0%
11,400	KEOKUK	5,206	2,035	3,170	1	1,135 D	39.1%	60.9%	39.1%	60.9%
17,163	KOSSUTH	8,982	3,100	5,880	2	2,780 D	34.5%	65.5%	34.5%	65.5%
38,052	LEE	16,813	5,327	11,473	13	6,146 D	31.7%	68.2%	31.7%	68.3%
191,701	LINN	111,176	36,662	74,373	141	37,711 D	33.0%	66.9%	33.0%	67.0%
12,183	LOUISA	4,825	1,656	3,167	2	1,511 D	34.3%	65.6%	34.3%	65.7%
9,422	LUCAS	4,400	2,039	2,360	1	321 D	46.3%	53.6%	46.4%	53.6%
11,763	LYON	5,938	3,614	2,318	6	1,296 R	60.9%	39.0%	60.9%	39.1%
14,019	MADISON	8,348	3,953	4,386	9	433 D	47.4%	52.5%	47.4%	52.6%
22,335	MAHASKA	10,743	5,248	5,490	5	242 D	48.9%	51.1%	48.9%	51.1%
32,052	MARION	16,787	8,168	8,609	10	441 D	48.7%	51.3%	48.7%	51.3%
39,311	MARSHALL	18,360	7,327	11,023	10	3,696 D	39.9%	60.0%	39.9%	60.1%
14,547	MILLS	7,024	3,303	3,715	6	412 D	47.0%	52.9%	47.1%	52.9%
10,874	MITCHELL	5,645	1,761	3,881	3	2,120 D	31.2%	68.8%	31.2%	68.8%
10,020	MONONA	4,701	1,671	3,026	4	1,355 D	35.5%	64.4%	35.6%	64.4%
8,016	MONROE	3,810	1,549	2,260	1	711 D	40.7%	59.3%	40.7%	59.3%
11,771	MONTGOMERY	5,156	2,343	2,812	1	469 D	45.4%	54.5%	45.5%	54.5%
41,722	MUSCATINE	18,607	6,242	12,348	17	6,106 D	33.5%	66.4%	33.6%	66.4%
15,102	O'BRIEN	7,143	3,881	3,259	3	622 R	54.3%	45.6%	54.4%	45.6%
7,003	OSCEOLA	3,038	1,570	1,465	3	105 R	51.7%	48.2%	51.7%	48.3%
16,976	PAGE	7,186	3,618	3,565	3	53 R	50.3%	49.6%	50.4%	49.6%
10,147	PALO ALTO	4,680	1,665	3,012	3	1,347 D	35.6%	64.4%	35.6%	64.4%
24,849	PLYMOUTH	12,126	5,886	6,240		354 D	48.5%	51.5%	48.5%	51.5%
8,662	POCAHONTAS	3,960	1,666	2,291	3	625 D	42.1%	57.9%	42.1%	57.9%
374,601	POLK	211,235	80,051	130,928	256	50,877 D	37.9%	62.0%	37.9%	62.1%
87,704	POTTAWATTAMIE	41,031	17,017	23,980	34	6,963 D	41.5%	58.4%	41.5%	58.5%
18,815	POWESHIEK	9,851	3,647	6,196	8	2,549 D	37.0%	62.9%	37.1%	62.9%
5,469	RINGGOLD	2,672	1,023	1,648	1	625 D	38.3%	61.7%	38.3%	61.7%
11,529	SAC	4,942	2,088	2,850	4	762 D	42.3%	57.7%	42.3%	57.7%
158,668	SCOTT	83,847	28,642	55,129	76	26,487 D	34.2%	65.7%	34.2%	65.8%
13,173	SHELBY	6,241	2,787	3,449	5	662 D	44.7%	55.3%	44.7%	55.3%
31,589	SIOUX	16,240	11,945	4,291	4	7,654 R	73.6%	26.4%	73.6%	26.4%
79,981	STORY	45,199	16,802	28,351	46	11,549 D	37.2%	62.7%	37.2%	62.8%
18,103	TAMA	8,713	3,163	5,547	3	2,384 D	36.3%	63.7%	36.3%	63.7%
6,958	TAYLOR	2,956	1,209	1,745	2	536 D	40.9%	59.0%	40.9%	59.1%
12,309	UNION	5,797	2,336	3,458	3	1,122 D	40.3%	59.7%	40.3%	59.7%
7,809	VAN BUREN	3,519	1,492	2,022	5	530 D	42.4%	57.5%	42.5%	57.5%
36,051	WAPELLO	15,536	5,336	10,184	16	4,848 D	34.3%	65.6%	34.4%	65.6%
40,671	WARREN	24,467	10,471	13,979	17	3,508 D	42.8%	57.1%	42.8%	57.2%
20,670	WASHINGTON	10,337	4,209	6,122	6	1,913 D	40.7%	59.2%	40.7%	59.3%
6,730	WAYNE	2,937	1,340	1,596	1	256 D	45.6%	54.3%	45.6%	54.4%
40,235	WEBSTER	18,244	6,460	11,773	11	5,313 D	35.4%	64.5%	35.4%	64.6%
11,723	WINNEBAGO	5,967	2,055	3,912		1,857 D	34.4%	65.6%	34.4%	65.6%
21,310	WINNESHIEK	10,921	3,303	7,612	6	4,309 D	30.2%	69.7%	30.3%	69.7%
103,877	WOODBURY	43,423	17,358	26,038	27	8,680 D	40.0%	60.0%	40.0%	60.0%
7,909	WORTH	4,196	1,113	3,081	2	1,968 D	26.5%	73.4%	26.5%	73.5%
14,334	WRIGHT	6,296	2,509	3,786	1	1,277 D	39.9%	60.1%	39.9%	60.1%
2,926,324	TOTAL	1,502,918	560,006	941,665	1,247	381,659 D	37.3%	62.7%	37.3%	62.7%

IOWA

HOUSE OF REPRESENTATIVES

		Total	Republican		Democratic		Other	Rep.-Dem.	Percentage			
									Total Vote		Major Vote	
CD	Year	Vote	Vote	Candidate	Vote	Candidate	Vote	Plurality	Rep.	Dem.	Rep.	Dem.
1	2008	289,629	102,439	HARTSUCH, DAVID	186,991	BRALEY, BRUCE*	199	84,552 D	35.4%	64.6%	35.4%	64.6%
1	2006	207,621	89,729	WHALEN, MIKE	114,322	BRALEY, BRUCE	3,570	24,593 D	43.2%	55.1%	44.0%	56.0%
1	2004	290,054	159,993	NUSSLE, JIM*	125,490	GLUBA, BILL	4,571	34,503 R	55.2%	43.3%	56.0%	44.0%
1	2002	196,455	112,280	NUSSLE, JIM*	83,779	HUTCHINSON, ANN	396	28,501 R	57.2%	42.6%	57.3%	42.7%
2	2008	306,358	118,778	MILLER-MEEKS, MARIANNETTE	175,218	LOEBSACK, DAVE*	12,362	56,440 D	38.8%	57.2%	40.4%	59.6%
2	2006	209,586	101,707	LEACH, JIM*	107,683	LOEBSACK, DAVE	196	5,976 D	48.5%	51.4%	48.6%	51.4%
2	2004	299,881	176,684	LEACH, JIM*	117,405	FRANKER, DAVE	5,792	59,279 R	58.9%	39.2%	60.1%	39.9%
2	2002	207,171	108,130	LEACH, JIM*	94,767	THOMAS, JULIE	4,274	13,363 R	52.2%	45.7%	53.3%	46.7%
3	2008	314,160	132,136	SCHMETT, KIM	176,904	BOSWELL, LEONARD L.*	5,120	44,768 D	42.1%	56.3%	42.8%	57.2%
3	2006	223,287	103,722	LAMBERTI, JEFF	115,769	BOSWELL, LEONARD L.*	3,796	12,047 D	46.5%	51.8%	47.3%	52.7%
3	2004	304,319	136,099	THOMPSON, STAN	168,007	BOSWELL, LEONARD L.*	213	31,908 D	44.7%	55.2%	44.8%	55.2%
3	2002	215,985	97,285	THOMPSON, STAN	115,367	BOSWELL, LEONARD L.*	3,333	18,082 D	45.0%	53.4%	45.7%	54.3%
4	2008	306,401	185,458	LATHAM, TOM*	120,746	GREENWALD, BECKY	197	64,712 R	60.5%	39.4%	60.6%	39.4%
4	2006	212,730	121,650	LATHAM, TOM*	90,982	SPENCER, SELDEN E.	98	30,668 R	57.2%	42.8%	57.2%	42.8%
4	2004	297,566	181,294	LATHAM, TOM*	116,121	JOHNSON, PAUL W.	151	65,173 R	60.9%	39.0%	61.0%	39.0%
4	2002	210,774	115,430	LATHAM, TOM*	90,784	NORRIS, JOHN	4,560	24,646 R	54.8%	43.1%	56.0%	44.0%
5	2008	266,617	159,430	KING, STEVE*	99,601	HUBLER, ROB	7,586	59,829 R	59.8%	37.4%	61.5%	38.5%
5	2006	180,464	105,580	KING, STEVE*	64,181	SCHULTE, JOYCE	10,703	41,399 R	58.5%	35.6%	62.2%	37.8%
5	2004	266,341	168,583	KING, STEVE*	97,597	SCHULTE, JOYCE	161	70,986 R	63.3%	36.6%	63.3%	36.7%
5	2002	182,237	113,257	KING, STEVE	68,853	SHOMSHOR, PAUL	127	44,404 R	62.1%	37.8%	62.2%	37.8%
TOTAL	2008	1,483,165	698,241		759,460		25,464	61,219 D	47.1%	51.2%	47.9%	52.1%
TOTAL	2006	1,033,688	522,388		492,937		18,363	29,451 R	50.5%	47.7%	51.5%	48.5%
TOTAL	2004	1,458,161	822,653		624,620		10,888	198,033 R	56.4%	42.8%	56.8%	43.2%
TOTAL	2002	1,012,622	546,382		453,550		12,690	92,832 R	54.0%	44.8%	54.6%	45.4%

Note: An asterisk (*) denotes incumbent.

IOWA

GENERAL AND PRIMARY ELECTIONS

2008 GENERAL ELECTIONS

President — Other vote was 8,014 Peace and Freedom (Ralph Nader); 4,590 Libertarian (Bob Barr); 4,445 Constitution (Chuck Baldwin); 1,423 Green (Cynthia A. McKinney); 292 Socialist Workers (James Harris); 182 Socialist (Brian Moore); 121 Party for Socialism and Liberation (Gloria La Riva); 6,737 scattered write-in.

Senator — Other vote was 1,247 scattered write-in.

House — Other vote was:

CD 1 — 199 scattered write-in.
CD 2 — 6,664 Green (Wendy Barth); 5,437 Nominated by Petition (Brian White); 261 scattered write-in.
CD 3 — 4,599 Socialist Workers (Frank V. Forrestal); 521 scattered write-in.
CD 4 — 197 scattered write-in.
CD 5 — 7,406 Independent (Victor Vara); 180 scattered write-in.

IOWA

GENERAL AND PRIMARY ELECTIONS

2008 PRIMARY ELECTIONS

Primary	June 3, 2008	**Registration** (as of June 2, 2008— includes 151,710 inactive registrants)		Democratic Republican Other No Party		704,321 613,522 194 760,917
				TOTAL		*2,078,954*

Primary Type   Semi-open—Registered Democrats and Republicans could vote only in their party's primary, although any registered voter (including those not affiliated with either party) could participate in either party's primary by changing their registration to that party on primary day.

	REPUBLICAN PRIMARIES			DEMOCRATIC PRIMARIES		
President (Precinct caucuses)	Mike Huckabee	40,954	34.4%	Barack Obama	—	37.6%
	Mitt Romney	30,021	25.2%	John Edwards	—	29.8%
	Fred Thompson	15,960	13.4%	Hillary Clinton	—	29.5%
	John McCain	15,536	13.0%	Bill Richardson	—	2.1%
	Ron Paul	11,841	9.9%	Joseph R. Biden Jr.	—	0.9%
	Rudolph Giuliani	4,099	3.4%	Uncommitted	—	0.1%
	Duncan Hunter	506	0.4%	Christopher J. Dodd	—	
	Alan Keyes	247	0.2%			
	John Cox	10				
	Hugh Cort	5				
	Tom Tancredo	5				
	TOTAL	*119,184*				
Senator	Christopher Reed	24,964	35.3%	Tom Harkin*	90,785	98.8%
	George S. Eichhorn	24,390	34.5%	Scattered write-in	1,074	1.2%
	Steve Rathje	21,062	29.8%			
	Scattered write-in	256	0.4%			
	TOTAL	*70,672*		*TOTAL*	*91,859*	
Congressional District 1	David Hartsuch	8,865	99.3%	Bruce Braley*	10,596	99.4%
	Scattered write-in	59	0.7%	Scattered write-in	62	0.6%
	TOTAL	*8,924*		*TOTAL*	*10,658*	
Congressional District 2	Mariannette Miller-Meeks	7,372	43.6%	Dave Loebsack*	21,084	98.9%
	Peter Teahen	7,258	42.9%	Scattered write-in	231	1.1%
	Lee Harder	2,258	13.4%			
	Scattered write-in	22	0.1%			
	TOTAL	*16,910*		*TOTAL*	*21,315*	
Congressional District 3	Kim Schmett	10,666	98.6%	Leonard L. Boswell*	20,401	60.9%
	Scattered write-in	150	1.4%	Ed Fallon	13,035	38.9%
				Scattered write-in	37	0.1%
	TOTAL	*10,816*		*TOTAL*	*33,473*	
Congressional District 4	Tom Latham*	13,144	99.6%	Becky Greenwald	9,247	50.5%
	Scattered write-in	47	0.4%	Kurt Meyer	5,041	27.6%
				William J. Meyers	2,086	11.4%
				Kevin Miskell	1,885	10.3%
				Scattered write-in	36	0.2%
	TOTAL	*13,191*		*TOTAL*	*18,295*	
Congressional District 5	Steve King*	22,663	99.3%	Rob Hubler	8,052	99.5%
	Scattered write-in	160	0.7%	Scattered write-in	43	0.5%
	TOTAL	*22,823*		*TOTAL*	*8,095*	

Note: An asterisk (*) denotes incumbent. Rather than holding a presidential primary, both the Democratic and Republican parties in Iowa elected national convention delegates through a caucus process that began with precinct caucuses on the night of January 3, 2008. Given their importance to the nominating process in both parties, the results from the precinct caucuses are listed above, as compiled by the state parties. Democratic results are given in the form of a measurement used by the Iowa Democratic Party called state delegate equivalents; there was no direct vote for presidential candidates on the Democratic side. Republican results reflect a statewide preference vote taken at the GOP precinct caucuses that was not binding on the selection of delegates.

KANSAS

Congressional districts first established for elections held in 2002
4 members

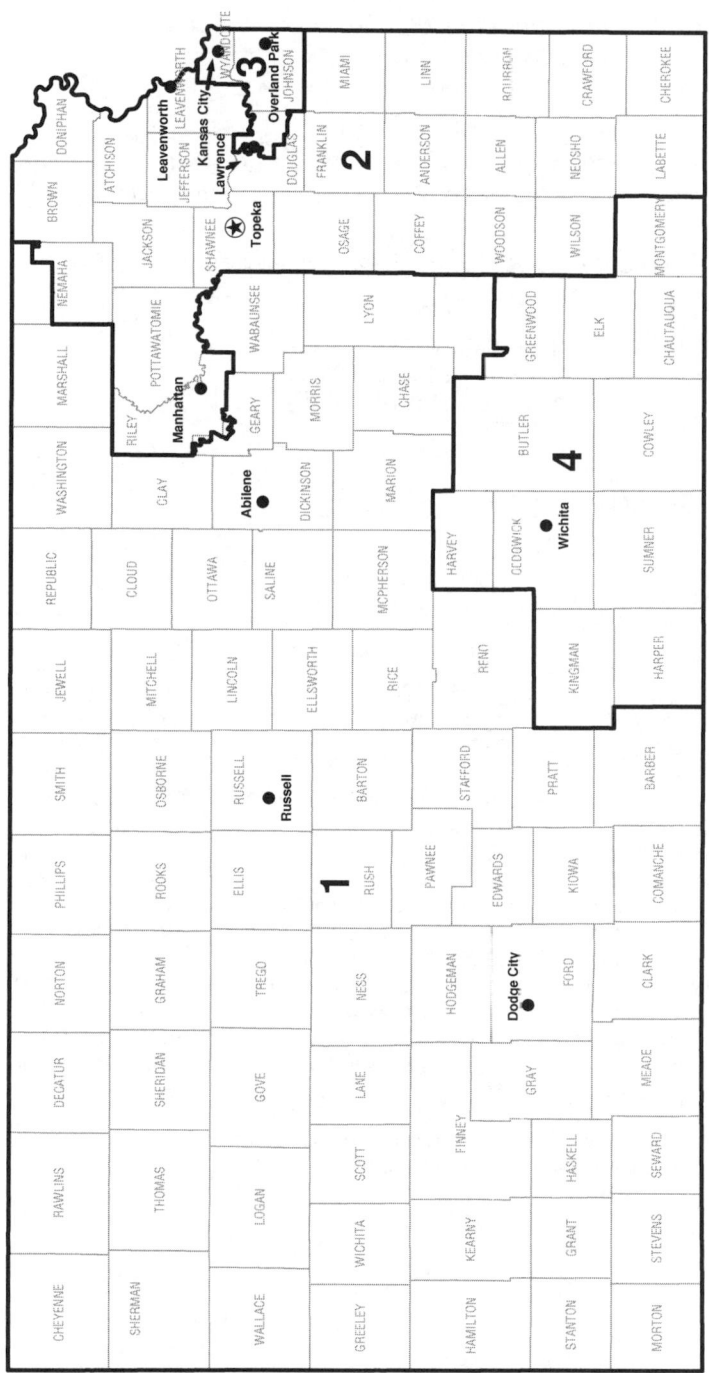

KANSAS

GOVERNOR

Mark Parkinson (D). Sworn in as governor April 28, 2009, upon the resignation of Kathleen Sebelius (D) to become U.S. Secretary of Health and Human Services.

SENATORS (2 Republicans)

Sam Brownback (R). Reelected 2004 to a six-year term. Previously elected 1998 and 1996 to fill out the remaining two years of the term vacated when Senator Robert Dole (R) resigned to run for president.

Pat Roberts (R). Reelected 2008 to a six-year term. Previously elected 2002, 1996.

REPRESENTATIVES (3 Republicans, 1 Democrat)

1. Jerry Moran (R)
2. Lynn Jenkins (R)
3. Dennis Moore (D)
4. Todd Tiahrt (R)

POSTWAR VOTE FOR PRESIDENT

Year	Total Vote	Republican Vote	Candidate	Democratic Vote	Candidate	Other Vote	Plurality	Total Vote Rep.	Total Vote Dem.	Major Vote Rep.	Major Vote Dem.
2008	1,235,872	699,655	McCain, John	514,765	Obama, Barack	21,452	184,890 R	56.6%	41.7%	57.6%	42.4%
2004	1,187,756	736,456	Bush, George W.	434,993	Kerry, John	16,307	301,463 R	62.0%	36.6%	62.9%	37.1%
2000**	1,072,218	622,332	Bush, George W.	399,276	Gore, Al	50,610	223,056 R	58.0%	37.2%	60.9%	39.1%
1996**	1,074,300	583,245	Dole, Bob	387,659	Clinton, Bill	103,396	195,586 R	54.3%	36.1%	60.1%	39.9%
1992**	1,157,335	449,951	Bush, George	390,434	Clinton, Bill	316,950	59,517 R	38.9%	33.7%	53.5%	46.5%
1988	993,044	554,049	Bush, George	422,636	Dukakis, Michael S.	16,359	131,413 R	55.8%	42.6%	56.7%	43.3%
1984	1,021,991	677,296	Reagan, Ronald	333,149	Mondale, Walter F.	11,546	344,147 R	66.3%	32.6%	67.0%	33.0%
1980**	979,795	566,812	Reagan, Ronald	326,150	Carter, Jimmy	86,833	240,662 R	57.9%	33.3%	63.5%	36.5%
1976	957,845	502,752	Ford, Gerald R.	430,421	Carter, Jimmy	24,672	72,331 R	52.5%	44.9%	53.9%	46.1%
1972	916,095	619,812	Nixon, Richard M.	270,287	McGovern, George S.	25,996	349,525 R	67.7%	29.5%	69.6%	30.4%
1968**	872,783	478,674	Nixon, Richard M.	302,996	Humphrey, Hubert H.	91,113	175,678 R	54.8%	34.7%	61.2%	38.8%
1964	857,901	386,579	Goldwater, Barry M.	464,028	Johnson, Lyndon B.	7,294	77,449 D	45.1%	54.1%	45.4%	54.6%
1960	928,825	561,474	Nixon, Richard M.	363,213	Kennedy, John F.	4,138	198,261 R	60.4%	39.1%	60.7%	39.3%
1956	866,243	566,878	Eisenhower, Dwight D.	296,317	Stevenson, Adlai E.	3,048	270,561 R	65.4%	34.2%	65.7%	34.3%
1952	896,166	616,302	Eisenhower, Dwight D.	273,296	Stevenson, Adlai E.	6,568	343,006 R	68.8%	30.5%	69.3%	30.7%
1948	788,819	423,039	Dewey, Thomas E.	351,902	Truman, Harry S.	13,878	71,137 R	53.6%	44.6%	54.6%	45.4%

**In past elections, the other vote included: 2000 - 36,086 Green (Ralph Nader); 1996 - 92,639 Reform (Ross Perot); 1992 - 312,358 Independent (Perot); 1980 - 68,231 Independent (John Anderson); 1968 - 88,921 American Independent (George Wallace).

KANSAS

POSTWAR VOTE FOR GOVERNOR

Year	Total Vote	Republican Vote	Candidate	Democratic Vote	Candidate	Other Vote	Rep.-Dem. Plurality	Rep.	Dem.	Rep.	Dem.
2006	849,700	343,586	Barnett, Jim	491,993	Sebelius, Kathleen	14,121	148,407 D	40.4%	57.9%	41.1%	58.9%
2002	835,692	376,830	Shallenburger, Tim	441,858	Sebelius, Kathleen	17,004	65,028 D	45.1%	52.9%	46.0%	54.0%
1998	742,665	544,882	Graves, Bill	168,243	Sawyer, Tom	29,540	376,639 R	73.4%	22.7%	76.4%	23.6%
1994	821,030	526,113	Graves, Bill	294,733	Slattery, Jim	184	231,380 R	64.1%	35.9%	64.1%	35.9%
1990	783,325	333,589	Hayden, Mike	380,609	Finney, Joan	69,127	47,020 D	42.6%	48.6%	46.7%	53.3%
1986	840,605	436,267	Hayden, Mike	404,338	Docking, Thomas R.		31,929 R	51.9%	48.1%	51.9%	48.1%
1982	763,263	339,356	Hardage, Sam	405,772	Carlin, John	18,135	66,416 D	44.5%	53.2%	45.5%	54.5%
1978	736,246	348,015	Bennett, Robert F.	363,835	Carlin, John	24,396	15,820 D	47.3%	49.4%	48.9%	51.1%
1974**	783,875	387,792	Bennett, Robert F.	384,115	Miller, Vern	11,968	3,677 R	49.5%	49.0%	50.2%	49.8%
1972	921,552	341,440	Kay, Morris	571,256	Docking, Robert	8,856	229,816 D	37.1%	62.0%	37.4%	62.6%
1970	745,196	333,227	Frizzell, Kent	404,611	Docking, Robert	7,358	71,384 D	44.7%	54.3%	45.2%	54.8%
1968	862,473	410,673	Harman, Rick	447,269	Docking, Robert	4,531	36,596 D	47.6%	51.9%	47.9%	52.1%
1966	692,955	304,325	Avery, William H.	380,030	Docking, Robert	8,600	75,705 D	43.9%	54.8%	44.5%	55.5%
1964	850,414	432,667	Avery, William H.	400,264	Wiles, Harry G.	17,483	32,403 R	50.9%	47.1%	51.9%	48.1%
1962	638,798	341,257	Anderson, John	291,285	Saffels, Dale E.	6,256	49,972 R	53.4%	45.6%	54.0%	46.0%
1960	922,522	511,534	Anderson, John	402,261	Docking, George	8,727	109,273 R	55.4%	43.6%	56.0%	44.0%
1958	735,939	313,036	Reed, Clyde M.	415,506	Docking, George	7,397	102,470 D	42.5%	56.5%	43.0%	57.0%
1956	864,935	364,340	Shaw, Warren W.	479,701	Docking, George	20,894	115,361 D	42.1%	55.5%	43.2%	56.8%
1954	622,633	329,868	Hall, Fred	286,218	Docking, George	6,547	43,650 R	53.0%	46.0%	53.5%	46.5%
1952	872,139	491,338	Arn, Edward F.	363,482	Rooney, Charles	17,319	127,856 R	56.3%	41.7%	57.5%	42.5%
1950	619,310	333,001	Arn, Edward F.	275,494	Anderson, Kenneth	10,815	57,507 R	53.8%	44.5%	54.7%	45.3%
1948	760,407	433,396	Carlson, Frank	307,485	Carpenter, Randolph	19,526	125,911 R	57.0%	40.4%	58.5%	41.5%
1946	577,694	309,064	Carlson, Frank	254,283	Woodring, Harry H.	14,347	54,781 R	53.5%	44.0%	54.9%	45.1%

**The term of office of Kansas's governor was increased from two to four years effective with the 1974 election.

POSTWAR VOTE FOR SENATOR

Year	Total Vote	Republican Vote	Candidate	Democratic Vote	Candidate	Other Vote	Rep.-Dem. Plurality	Rep.	Dem.	Rep.	Dem.
2008	1,210,690	727,121	Roberts, Pat	441,399	Slattery, Jim	42,170	285,722 R	60.1%	36.5%	62.2%	37.8%
2004	1,129,022	780,863	Brownback, Sam	310,337	Jones, Lee	37,822	470,526 R	69.2%	27.5%	71.6%	28.4%
2002	776,850	641,075	Roberts, Pat	—		135,775	641,075 R	82.5%		100.0%	
1998	727,236	474,639	Brownback, Sam	229,718	Feleciano, Paul, Jr.	22,879	244,921 R	65.3%	31.6%	67.4%	32.6%
1996	1,052,300	652,677	Roberts, Pat	362,380	Thompson, Sally	37,243	290,297 R	62.0%	34.4%	64.3%	35.7%
1996S	1,064,716	574,021	Brownback, Sam	461,344	Docking, Jill	29,351	112,677 R	53.9%	43.3%	55.4%	44.6%
1992	1,126,447	706,246	Dole, Robert	349,525	O'Dell, Gloria	70,676	356,721 R	62.7%	31.0%	66.9%	33.1%
1990	786,235	578,605	Kassebaum, Nancy Landon	207,491	Williams, Dick	139	371,114 R	73.6%	26.4%	73.6%	26.4%
1986	823,566	576,902	Dole, Robert	246,664	MacDonald, Guy		330,238 R	70.0%	30.0%	70.0%	30.0%
1984	996,729	757,402	Kassebaum, Nancy Landon	211,664	Maher, James	27,663	545,738 R	76.0%	21.2%	78.2%	21.8%
1980	938,957	598,686	Dole, Robert	340,271	Simpson, John		258,415 R	63.8%	36.2%	63.8%	36.2%
1978	748,839	403,354	Kassebaum, Nancy Landon	317,602	Roy, William R.	27,883	85,752 R	53.9%	42.4%	55.9%	44.1%
1974	794,437	403,983	Dole, Robert	390,451	Roy, William R.	3	13,532 R	50.9%	49.1%	50.9%	49.1%
1972	871,722	622,591	Pearson, James B.	200,764	Tetzlaff, Arch O.	48,367	421,827 R	71.4%	23.0%	75.6%	24.4%
1968	817,096	490,911	Dole, Robert	315,911	Robinson, William I.	10,274	175,000 R	60.1%	38.7%	60.8%	39.2%
1966	671,345	350,077	Pearson, James B.	303,223	Breeding, J. Floyd	18,045	46,854 R	52.1%	45.2%	53.6%	46.4%
1962	622,232	388,500	Carlson, Frank	223,630	Smith, K. L.	10,102	164,870 R	62.4%	35.9%	63.5%	36.5%
1962S	613,250	344,689	Pearson, James B.	260,756	Aylward, Paul L.	7,805	83,933 R	56.2%	42.5%	56.9%	43.1%
1960	888,592	485,499	Schoeppel, Andrew F.	388,895	Theis, Frank	14,198	96,604 R	54.6%	43.8%	55.5%	44.5%
1956	825,280	477,822	Carlson, Frank	333,939	Hart, George	13,519	143,883 R	57.9%	40.5%	58.9%	41.1%
1954	618,063	348,144	Schoeppel, Andrew F.	258,575	McGill, George	11,344	89,569 R	56.3%	41.8%	57.4%	42.6%
1950	619,104	335,880	Carlson, Frank	271,365	Aiken, Paul	11,859	64,515 R	54.3%	43.8%	55.3%	44.7%
1948	716,342	393,412	Schoeppel, Andrew F.	305,987	McGill, George	16,943	87,425 R	54.9%	42.7%	56.3%	43.7%

Notes: One of the 1996 and 1962 elections was for a short term to fill a vacancy. The Democratic Party did not run a candidate in the 2002 Senate election.

KANSAS

PRESIDENT 2008

2000 Census Population	County	Total Vote	Republican	Democratic	Other	Rep.-Dem. Plurality	Percentage Total Vote Rep.	Dem.	Major Vote Rep.	Dem.
14,385	ALLEN	5,855	3,552	2,189	114	1,363 R	60.7%	37.4%	61.9%	38.1%
8,110	ANDERSON	3,626	2,362	1,175	89	1,187 R	65.1%	32.4%	66.8%	33.2%
16,774	ATCHISON	7,191	3,791	3,241	159	550 R	52.7%	45.1%	53.9%	46.1%
5,307	BARBER	2,462	1,833	598	31	1,235 R	74.5%	24.3%	75.4%	24.6%
28,205	BARTON	11,057	7,802	3,027	228	4,775 R	70.6%	27.4%	72.0%	28.0%
15,379	BOURBON	6,781	4,240	2,394	147	1,846 R	62.5%	35.3%	63.9%	36.1%
10,724	BROWN	4,376	2,985	1,317	74	1,668 R	68.2%	30.1%	69.4%	30.6%
59,482	BUTLER	27,873	18,155	9,159	559	8,996 R	65.1%	32.9%	66.5%	33.5%
3,030	CHASE	1,384	976	383	25	593 R	70.5%	27.7%	71.8%	28.2%
4,359	CHAUTAUQUA	1,852	1,418	401	33	1,017 R	76.6%	21.7%	78.0%	22.0%
22,605	CHEROKEE	9,665	5,886	3,594	185	2,292 R	60.9%	37.2%	62.1%	37.9%
3,165	CHEYENNE	1,498	1,148	323	27	825 R	76.6%	21.6%	78.0%	22.0%
2,390	CLARK	1,159	897	245	17	652 R	77.4%	21.1%	78.5%	21.5%
8,822	CLAY	4,054	2,998	1,009	47	1,989 R	74.0%	24.9%	74.8%	25.2%
10,268	CLOUD	4,451	3,121	1,233	97	1,888 R	70.1%	27.7%	71.7%	28.3%
8,865	COFFEY	4,232	3,054	1,121	57	1,933 R	72.2%	26.5%	73.1%	26.9%
1,967	COMANCHE	974	765	194	15	571 R	78.5%	19.9%	79.8%	20.2%
36,291	COWLEY	13,787	8,492	5,012	283	3,480 R	61.6%	36.4%	62.9%	37.1%
38,242	CRAWFORD	16,075	7,735	7,957	383	222 D	48.1%	49.5%	49.3%	50.7%
3,472	DECATUR	1,548	1,189	343	16	846 R	76.8%	22.2%	77.6%	22.4%
19,344	DICKINSON	8,667	6,081	2,422	164	3,659 R	70.2%	27.9%	71.5%	28.5%
8,249	DONIPHAN	3,564	2,372	1,115	77	1,257 R	66.6%	31.3%	68.0%	32.0%
99,962	DOUGLAS	53,398	17,929	34,398	1,071	16,469 D	33.6%	64.4%	34.3%	65.7%
3,449	EDWARDS	1,357	995	333	29	662 R	73.3%	24.5%	74.9%	25.1%
3,261	ELK	1,434	1,042	363	29	679 R	72.7%	25.3%	74.2%	25.8%
27,507	ELLIS	12,447	8,207	4,010	230	4,197 R	65.9%	32.2%	67.2%	32.8%
6,525	ELLSWORTH	2,938	2,021	851	66	1,170 R	68.8%	29.0%	70.4%	29.6%
40,523	FINNEY	10,354	6,926	3,275	153	3,651 R	66.9%	31.6%	67.9%	32.1%
32,458	FORD	8,864	5,730	2,991	143	2,739 R	64.6%	33.7%	65.7%	34.3%
24,784	FRANKLIN	11,739	7,079	4,433	227	2,646 R	60.3%	37.8%	61.5%	38.5%
27,947	GEARY	8,094	4,492	3,491	111	1,001 R	55.5%	43.1%	56.3%	43.7%
3,068	GOVE	1,418	1,136	261	21	875 R	80.1%	18.4%	81.3%	18.7%
2,946	GRAHAM	1,423	1,060	325	38	735 R	74.5%	22.8%	76.5%	23.5%
7,909	GRANT	2,661	1,995	635	31	1,360 R	75.0%	23.9%	75.9%	24.1%
5,904	GRAY	2,119	1,643	436	40	1,207 R	77.5%	20.6%	79.0%	21.0%
1,534	GREELEY	745	591	151	3	440 R	79.3%	20.3%	79.6%	20.4%
7,673	GREENWOOD	2,279	1,619	622	38	997 R	71.0%	27.3%	72.2%	27.8%
2,670	HAMILTON	1,096	844	233	19	611 R	77.0%	21.3%	78.4%	21.6%
6,536	HARPER	2,796	1,999	736	61	1,263 R	71.5%	26.3%	73.1%	26.9%
32,869	HARVEY	15,613	9,006	6,318	289	2,688 R	57.7%	40.5%	58.8%	41.2%
4,307	HASKELL	1,570	1,277	278	15	999 R	81.3%	17.7%	82.1%	17.9%
2,085	HODGEMAN	1,096	865	211	20	654 R	78.9%	19.3%	80.4%	19.6%
12,657	JACKSON	6,253	3,811	2,308	134	1,503 R	60.9%	36.9%	62.3%	37.7%
18,426	JEFFERSON	8,950	5,220	3,542	188	1,678 R	58.3%	39.6%	59.6%	40.4%
3,791	JEWELL	1,584	1,231	313	40	918 R	77.7%	19.8%	79.7%	20.3%
451,086	JOHNSON	283,432	152,627	127,091	3,714	25,536 R	53.8%	44.8%	54.6%	45.4%
4,531	KEARNY	1,482	1,159	309	14	850 R	78.2%	20.9%	79.0%	21.0%
8,673	KINGMAN	3,664	2,603	963	98	1,640 R	71.0%	26.3%	73.0%	27.0%
3,278	KIOWA	1,135	912	200	23	712 R	80.4%	17.6%	82.0%	18.0%
22,835	LABETTE	9,031	5,001	3,839	191	1,162 R	55.4%	42.5%	56.6%	43.4%
2,155	LANE	1,027	814	193	20	621 R	79.3%	18.8%	80.8%	19.2%
68,691	LEAVENWORTH	30,591	16,791	13,255	545	3,536 R	54.9%	43.3%	55.9%	44.1%
3,578	LINCOLN	1,586	1,204	347	35	857 R	75.9%	21.9%	77.6%	22.4%
9,570	LINN	4,617	3,086	1,425	106	1,661 R	66.8%	30.9%	68.4%	31.6%
3,046	LOGAN	1,440	1,187	225	28	962 R	82.4%	15.6%	84.1%	15.9%

KANSAS

PRESIDENT 2008

2000 Census Population	County	Total Vote	Republican	Democratic	Other	Rep.-Dem. Plurality	Percentage Total Vote Rep.	Percentage Total Vote Dem.	Percentage Major Vote Rep.	Percentage Major Vote Dem.
35,935	LYON	12,911	6,698	5,924	289	774 R	51.9%	45.9%	53.1%	46.9%
29,554	MCPHERSON	13,386	8,937	4,218	231	4,719 R	66.8%	31.5%	67.9%	32.1%
13,361	MARION	6,059	4,159	1,801	99	2,358 R	68.6%	29.7%	69.8%	30.2%
10,965	MARSHALL	5,036	3,157	1,784	95	1,373 R	62.7%	35.4%	63.9%	36.1%
4,631	MEADE	1,931	1,540	357	34	1,183 R	79.8%	18.5%	81.2%	18.8%
28,351	MIAMI	15,377	9,382	5,742	253	3,640 R	61.0%	37.3%	62.0%	38.0%
6,932	MITCHELL	3,203	2,440	701	62	1,739 R	76.2%	21.9%	77.7%	22.3%
36,252	MONTGOMERY	13,907	9,309	4,338	260	4,971 R	66.9%	31.2%	68.2%	31.8%
6,104	MORRIS	2,841	1,875	907	59	968 R	66.0%	31.9%	67.4%	32.6%
3,496	MORTON	1,402	1,153	229	20	924 R	82.2%	16.3%	83.4%	16.6%
10,717	NEMAHA	5,359	3,817	1,432	110	2,385 R	71.2%	26.7%	72.7%	27.3%
16,997	NEOSHO	7,192	4,473	2,563	156	1,910 R	62.2%	35.6%	63.6%	36.4%
3,454	NESS	1,525	1,207	289	29	918 R	79.1%	19.0%	80.7%	19.3%
5,953	NORTON	2,415	1,878	497	40	1,381 R	77.8%	20.6%	79.1%	20.9%
16,712	OSAGE	7,544	4,820	2,534	190	2,286 R	63.9%	33.6%	65.5%	34.5%
4,452	OSBORNE	1,930	1,490	403	37	1,087 R	77.2%	20.9%	78.7%	21.3%
6,163	OTTAWA	3,086	2,323	704	59	1,619 R	75.3%	22.8%	76.7%	23.3%
7,233	PAWNEE	2,879	1,946	882	51	1,064 R	67.6%	30.6%	68.8%	31.2%
6,001	PHILLIPS	2,667	2,105	525	37	1,580 R	78.9%	19.7%	80.0%	20.0%
18,209	POTTAWATOMIE	9,837	6,929	2,599	309	4,330 R	70.4%	26.4%	72.7%	27.3%
9,647	PRATT	4,190	2,822	1,294	74	1,528 R	67.4%	30.9%	68.6%	31.4%
2,966	RAWLINS	1,549	1,247	273	29	974 R	80.5%	17.6%	82.0%	18.0%
64,790	RENO	26,512	16,112	9,916	484	6,196 R	60.8%	37.4%	61.9%	38.1%
5,835	REPUBLIC	2,671	1,978	640	53	1,338 R	74.1%	24.0%	75.6%	24.4%
10,761	RICE	4,021	2,780	1,163	78	1,617 R	69.1%	28.9%	70.5%	29.5%
62,843	RILEY	22,997	12,111	10,495	391	1,616 R	52.7%	45.6%	53.6%	46.4%
5,685	ROOKS	2,588	2,068	468	52	1,600 R	79.9%	18.1%	81.5%	18.5%
3,551	RUSH	1,781	1,225	504	52	721 R	68.8%	28.3%	70.9%	29.1%
7,370	RUSSELL	3,293	2,509	736	48	1,773 R	76.2%	22.4%	77.3%	22.7%
53,597	SALINE	22,788	14,165	8,186	437	5,979 R	62.2%	35.9%	63.4%	36.6%
5,120	SCOTT	2,179	1,823	321	35	1,502 R	83.7%	14.7%	85.0%	15.0%
452,869	SEDGWICK	192,733	106,849	82,337	3,547	24,512 R	55.4%	42.7%	56.5%	43.5%
22,510	SEWARD	5,336	3,791	1,493	52	2,298 R	71.0%	28.0%	71.7%	28.3%
169,871	SHAWNEE	84,177	41,476	41,235	1,466	241 R	49.3%	49.0%	50.1%	49.9%
2,813	SHERIDAN	1,376	1,108	254	14	854 R	80.5%	18.5%	81.4%	18.6%
6,760	SHERMAN	2,704	1,959	688	57	1,271 R	72.4%	25.4%	74.0%	26.0%
4,536	SMITH	2,204	1,719	446	39	1,273 R	78.0%	20.2%	79.4%	20.6%
4,789	STAFFORD	2,074	1,495	542	37	953 R	72.1%	26.1%	73.4%	26.6%
2,406	STANTON	827	628	188	11	440 R	75.9%	22.7%	77.0%	23.0%
5,463	STEVENS	2,127	1,815	283	29	1,532 R	85.3%	13.3%	86.5%	13.5%
25,946	SUMNER	10,337	6,737	3,353	247	3,384 R	65.2%	32.4%	66.8%	33.2%
8,180	THOMAS	3,673	2,837	787	49	2,050 R	77.2%	21.4%	78.3%	21.7%
3,319	TREGO	1,671	1,225	420	26	805 R	73.3%	25.1%	74.5%	25.5%
6,885	WABAUNSEE	3,521	2,395	1,036	90	1,359 R	68.0%	29.4%	69.8%	30.2%
1,749	WALLACE	804	690	96	18	594 R	85.8%	11.9%	87.8%	12.2%
6,483	WASHINGTON	2,980	2,248	659	73	1,589 R	75.4%	22.1%	77.3%	22.7%
2,531	WICHITA	1,019	840	163	16	677 R	82.4%	16.0%	83.7%	16.3%
10,332	WILSON	4,121	2,850	1,170	101	1,680 R	69.2%	28.4%	70.9%	29.1%
3,788	WOODSON	1,599	1,055	512	32	543 R	66.0%	32.0%	67.3%	32.7%
157,882	WYANDOTTE	57,169	16,506	39,865	798	23,359 D	28.9%	69.7%	29.3%	70.7%
2,688,418	TOTAL	1,235,872	699,655	514,765	21,452	184,890 R	56.6%	41.7%	57.6%	42.4%

KANSAS

SENATOR 2008

2000 Census Population	County	Total Vote	Republican	Democratic	Other	Rep.-Dem. Plurality	Percentage Total Vote Rep.	Percentage Total Vote Dem.	Percentage Major Vote Rep.	Percentage Major Vote Dem.
14,385	ALLEN	5,802	3,448	2,159	195	1,289 R	59.4%	37.2%	61.5%	38.5%
8,110	ANDERSON	3,537	2,291	1,079	167	1,212 R	64.8%	30.5%	68.0%	32.0%
16,774	ATCHISON	7,152	3,383	3,535	234	152 D	47.3%	49.4%	48.9%	51.1%
5,307	BARBER	2,433	1,871	504	58	1,367 R	76.9%	20.7%	78.8%	21.2%
28,205	BARTON	10,944	8,362	2,283	299	6,079 R	76.4%	20.9%	78.6%	21.4%
15,379	BOURBON	6,738	4,263	2,287	188	1,976 R	63.3%	33.9%	65.1%	34.9%
10,724	BROWN	4,358	2,872	1,376	110	1,496 R	65.9%	31.6%	67.6%	32.4%
59,482	BUTLER	27,495	18,561	7,975	959	10,586 R	67.5%	29.0%	69.9%	30.1%
3,030	CHASE	1,374	967	366	41	601 R	70.4%	26.6%	72.5%	27.5%
4,359	CHAUTAUQUA	1,793	1,375	344	74	1,031 R	76.7%	19.2%	80.0%	20.0%
22,605	CHEROKEE	9,575	5,525	3,718	332	1,807 R	57.7%	38.8%	59.8%	40.2%
3,165	CHEYENNE	1,479	1,232	215	32	1,017 R	83.3%	14.5%	85.1%	14.9%
2,390	CLARK	1,153	940	198	15	742 R	81.5%	17.2%	82.6%	17.4%
8,822	CLAY	4,017	3,128	803	86	2,325 R	77.9%	20.0%	79.6%	20.4%
10,268	CLOUD	4,404	3,229	1,057	118	2,172 R	73.3%	24.0%	75.3%	24.7%
8,865	COFFEY	4,186	3,077	974	135	2,103 R	73.5%	23.3%	76.0%	24.0%
1,967	COMANCHE	969	797	153	19	644 R	82.2%	15.8%	83.9%	16.1%
36,291	COWLEY	13,531	8,499	4,551	481	3,948 R	62.8%	33.6%	65.1%	34.9%
38,242	CRAWFORD	15,983	7,828	7,561	594	267 R	49.0%	47.3%	50.9%	49.1%
3,472	DECATUR	1,544	1,278	240	26	1,038 R	82.8%	15.5%	84.2%	15.8%
19,344	DICKINSON	8,593	6,338	1,982	273	4,356 R	73.8%	23.1%	76.2%	23.8%
8,249	DONIPHAN	3,504	2,192	1,193	119	999 R	62.6%	34.0%	64.8%	35.2%
99,962	DOUGLAS	52,011	20,861	28,908	2,242	8,047 D	40.1%	55.6%	41.9%	58.1%
3,449	EDWARDS	1,363	1,070	254	39	816 R	78.5%	18.6%	80.8%	19.2%
3,261	ELK	1,407	981	389	37	592 R	69.7%	27.6%	71.6%	28.4%
27,507	ELLIS	12,316	8,566	3,402	348	5,164 R	69.6%	27.6%	71.6%	28.4%
6,525	ELLSWORTH	2,937	2,174	681	82	1,493 R	74.0%	23.2%	76.1%	23.9%
40,523	FINNEY	10,248	7,430	2,532	286	4,898 R	72.5%	24.7%	74.6%	25.4%
32,458	FORD	8,764	6,706	1,851	207	4,855 R	76.5%	21.1%	78.4%	21.6%
24,784	FRANKLIN	11,550	7,152	3,894	504	3,258 R	61.9%	33.7%	64.7%	35.3%
27,947	GEARY	7,764	4,502	2,966	296	1,536 R	58.0%	38.2%	60.3%	39.7%
3,068	GOVE	1,413	1,201	192	20	1,009 R	85.0%	13.6%	86.2%	13.8%
2,946	GRAHAM	1,411	1,091	273	47	818 R	77.3%	19.3%	80.0%	20.0%
7,909	GRANT	2,623	2,086	465	72	1,621 R	79.5%	17.7%	81.8%	18.2%
5,904	GRAY	2,102	1,762	304	36	1,458 R	83.8%	14.5%	85.3%	14.7%
1,534	GREELEY	739	621	105	13	516 R	84.0%	14.2%	85.5%	14.5%
7,673	GREENWOOD	2,265	1,565	602	98	963 R	69.1%	26.6%	72.2%	27.8%
2,670	HAMILTON	1,080	886	171	23	715 R	82.0%	15.8%	83.8%	16.2%
6,536	HARPER	2,767	2,036	644	87	1,392 R	73.6%	23.3%	76.0%	24.0%
32,869	HARVEY	15,477	9,762	5,195	520	4,567 R	63.1%	33.6%	65.3%	34.7%
4,307	HASKELL	1,549	1,339	184	26	1,155 R	86.4%	11.9%	87.9%	12.1%
2,085	HODGEMAN	1,097	935	147	15	788 R	85.2%	13.4%	86.4%	13.6%
12,657	JACKSON	6,235	3,908	2,095	232	1,813 R	62.7%	33.6%	65.1%	34.9%
18,426	JEFFERSON	8,914	5,385	3,234	295	2,151 R	60.4%	36.3%	62.5%	37.5%
3,791	JEWELL	1,550	1,245	247	58	998 R	80.3%	15.9%	83.4%	16.6%
451,086	JOHNSON	274,291	158,312	106,297	9,682	52,015 R	57.7%	38.8%	59.8%	40.2%
4,531	KEARNY	1,469	1,221	219	29	1,002 R	83.1%	14.9%	84.8%	15.2%
8,673	KINGMAN	3,610	2,625	853	132	1,772 R	72.7%	23.6%	75.5%	24.5%
3,278	KIOWA	1,120	965	135	20	830 R	86.2%	12.1%	87.7%	12.3%
22,835	LABETTE	8,951	5,024	3,639	288	1,385 R	56.1%	40.7%	58.0%	42.0%
2,155	LANE	1,021	862	143	16	719 R	84.4%	14.0%	85.8%	14.2%
68,691	LEAVENWORTH	29,798	16,643	11,933	1,222	4,710 R	55.9%	40.0%	58.2%	41.8%
3,578	LINCOLN	1,583	1,277	258	48	1,019 R	80.7%	16.3%	83.2%	16.8%
9,570	LINN	4,557	2,925	1,447	185	1,478 R	64.2%	31.8%	66.9%	33.1%
3,046	LOGAN	1,435	1,224	185	26	1,039 R	85.3%	12.9%	86.9%	13.1%

KANSAS

SENATOR 2008

2000 Census Population	County	Total Vote	Republican	Democratic	Other	Rep.-Dem. Plurality	Total Vote Rep.	Total Vote Dem.	Major Vote Rep.	Major Vote Dem.
35,935	LYON	12,635	7,125	5,064	446	2,061 R	56.4%	40.1%	58.5%	41.5%
29,554	MCPHERSON	13,256	9,545	3,322	389	6,223 R	72.0%	25.1%	74.2%	25.8%
13,361	MARION	6,049	4,406	1,504	139	2,902 R	72.8%	24.9%	74.6%	25.4%
10,965	MARSHALL	4,999	3,239	1,627	133	1,612 R	64.8%	32.5%	66.6%	33.4%
4,631	MEADE	1,922	1,598	287	37	1,311 R	83.1%	14.9%	84.8%	15.2%
28,351	MIAMI	14,977	9,601	4,780	596	4,821 R	64.1%	31.9%	66.8%	33.2%
6,932	MITCHELL	3,170	2,558	541	71	2,017 R	80.7%	17.1%	82.5%	17.5%
36,252	MONTGOMERY	13,756	8,855	4,488	413	4,367 R	64.4%	32.6%	66.4%	33.6%
6,104	MORRIS	2,813	1,985	746	82	1,239 R	70.6%	26.5%	72.7%	27.3%
3,496	MORTON	1,381	1,177	181	23	996 R	85.2%	13.1%	86.7%	13.3%
10,717	NEMAHA	5,330	3,582	1,628	120	1,954 R	67.2%	30.5%	68.8%	31.2%
16,997	NEOSHO	7,097	4,286	2,634	177	1,652 R	60.4%	37.1%	61.9%	38.1%
3,454	NESS	1,517	1,276	214	27	1,062 R	84.1%	14.1%	85.6%	14.4%
5,953	NORTON	2,404	1,947	397	60	1,550 R	81.0%	16.5%	83.1%	16.9%
16,712	OSAGE	7,478	4,738	2,435	305	2,303 R	63.4%	32.6%	66.1%	33.9%
4,452	OSBORNE	1,932	1,499	395	38	1,104 R	77.6%	20.4%	79.1%	20.9%
6,163	OTTAWA	3,077	2,426	551	100	1,875 R	78.8%	17.9%	81.5%	18.5%
7,233	PAWNEE	2,852	2,103	694	55	1,409 R	73.7%	24.3%	75.2%	24.8%
6,001	PHILLIPS	2,646	2,187	407	52	1,780 R	82.7%	15.4%	84.3%	15.7%
18,209	POTTAWATOMIE	9,771	6,990	2,253	528	4,737 R	71.5%	23.1%	75.6%	24.4%
9,647	PRATT	4,149	2,983	1,050	116	1,933 R	71.9%	25.3%	74.0%	26.0%
2,966	RAWLINS	1,555	1,305	213	37	1,092 R	83.9%	13.7%	86.0%	14.0%
64,790	RENO	26,307	16,922	8,380	1,005	8,542 R	64.3%	31.9%	66.9%	33.1%
5,835	REPUBLIC	2,658	2,088	509	61	1,579 R	78.6%	19.1%	80.4%	19.6%
10,761	RICE	3,983	2,855	1,000	128	1,855 R	71.7%	25.1%	74.1%	25.9%
62,843	RILEY	22,463	13,821	7,870	772	5,951 R	61.5%	35.0%	63.7%	36.3%
5,685	ROOKS	2,579	2,113	396	70	1,717 R	81.9%	15.4%	84.2%	15.8%
3,551	RUSH	1,753	1,317	391	45	926 R	75.1%	22.3%	77.1%	22.9%
7,370	RUSSELL	3,282	2,566	652	64	1,914 R	78.2%	19.9%	79.7%	20.3%
53,597	SALINE	22,516	15,016	6,596	904	8,420 R	66.7%	29.3%	69.5%	30.5%
5,120	SCOTT	2,171	1,849	286	36	1,563 R	85.2%	13.2%	86.6%	13.4%
452,869	SEDGWICK	188,399	112,784	68,808	6,807	43,976 R	59.9%	36.5%	62.1%	37.9%
22,510	SEWARD	5,122	3,874	1,099	149	2,775 R	75.6%	21.5%	77.9%	22.1%
169,871	SHAWNEE	83,362	43,931	36,418	3,013	7,513 R	52.7%	43.7%	54.7%	45.3%
2,813	SHERIDAN	1,364	1,120	224	20	896 R	82.1%	16.4%	83.3%	16.7%
6,760	SHERMAN	2,675	2,125	501	49	1,624 R	79.4%	18.7%	80.9%	19.1%
4,536	SMITH	2,178	1,708	427	43	1,281 R	78.4%	19.6%	80.0%	20.0%
4,789	STAFFORD	2,062	1,584	422	56	1,162 R	76.8%	20.5%	79.0%	21.0%
2,406	STANTON	804	687	99	18	588 R	85.4%	12.3%	87.4%	12.6%
5,463	STEVENS	2,093	1,818	231	44	1,587 R	86.9%	11.0%	88.7%	11.3%
25,946	SUMNER	10,208	6,714	3,040	454	3,674 R	65.8%	29.8%	68.8%	31.2%
8,180	THOMAS	3,640	2,927	651	62	2,276 R	80.4%	17.9%	81.8%	18.2%
3,319	TREGO	1,659	1,322	313	24	1,009 R	79.7%	18.9%	80.9%	19.1%
6,885	WABAUNSEE	3,504	2,461	893	150	1,568 R	70.2%	25.5%	73.4%	26.6%
1,749	WALLACE	806	732	64	10	668 R	90.8%	7.9%	92.0%	8.0%
6,483	WASHINGTON	2,947	2,318	549	80	1,769 R	78.7%	18.6%	80.9%	19.1%
2,531	WICHITA	1,015	866	138	11	728 R	85.3%	13.6%	86.3%	13.7%
10,332	WILSON	4,085	2,823	1,101	161	1,722 R	69.1%	27.0%	71.9%	28.1%
3,788	WOODSON	1,580	1,037	482	61	555 R	65.6%	30.5%	68.3%	31.7%
157,882	WYANDOTTE	54,728	16,534	36,051	2143	19,517 D	30.2%	65.9%	31.4%	68.6%
2,688,418	TOTAL	1,210,690	727,121	441,399	42,170	285,722 R	60.1%	36.5%	62.2%	37.8%

KANSAS

HOUSE OF REPRESENTATIVES

CD	Year	Total Vote	Republican		Democratic		Other Vote	Rep.-Dem. Plurality	Percentage			
			Vote	Candidate	Vote	Candidate			Total Vote		Major Vote	
									Rep.	Dem.	Rep.	Dem.
1	2008	262,027	214,549	MORAN, JERRY*	34,771	BORDONARO, JAMES	12,707	179,778 R	81.9%	13.3%	86.1%	13.9%
1	2006	199,378	156,728	MORAN, JERRY*	39,781	DOLL, JOHN	2,869	116,947 R	78.6%	20.0%	79.8%	20.2%
1	2004	264,293	239,776	MORAN, JERRY*		—	24,517	239,776 R	90.7%		100.0%	
1	2002	208,561	189,976	MORAN, JERRY*		—	18,585	189,976 R	91.1%		100.0%	
2	2008	307,308	155,532	JENKINS, LYNN	142,013	BOYDA, NANCY*	9,763	13,519 R	50.6%	46.2%	52.3%	47.7%
2	2006	225,562	106,329	RYUN, JIM*	114,139	BOYDA, NANCY	5,094	7,810 D	47.1%	50.6%	48.2%	51.8%
2	2004	294,436	165,325	RYUN, JIM*	121,532	BOYDA, NANCY	7,579	43,793 R	56.1%	41.3%	57.6%	42.4%
2	2002	210,977	127,477	RYUN, JIM*	79,160	LYKINS, DAN	4,340	48,317 R	60.4%	37.5%	61.7%	38.3%
3	2008	358,858	142,307	JORDAN, NICK	202,541	MOORE, DENNIS*	14,010	60,234 D	39.7%	56.4%	41.3%	58.7%
3	2006	236,980	79,824	AHNER, CHUCK	153,105	MOORE, DENNIS*	4,051	73,281 D	33.7%	64.6%	34.3%	65.7%
3	2004	335,739	145,542	KOBACH, KRIS	184,050	MOORE, DENNIS*	6,147	38,508 D	43.3%	54.8%	44.2%	55.8%
3	2002	219,389	102,882	TAFF, ADAM	110,095	MOORE, DENNIS*	6,412	7,213 D	46.9%	50.2%	48.3%	51.7%
4	2008	280,109	177,617	TIAHRT, TODD*	90,706	BETTS, DONALD JR.	11,786	86,911 R	63.4%	32.4%	66.2%	33.8%
4	2006	183,207	116,386	TIAHRT, TODD*	62,166	McGINN, GARTH J.	4,655	54,220 R	63.5%	33.9%	65.2%	34.8%
4	2004	261,915	173,151	TIAHRT, TODD*	81,388	KINARD, MICHAEL	7,376	91,763 R	66.1%	31.1%	68.0%	32.0%
4	2002	190,963	115,691	TIAHRT, TODD*	70,656	NOLLA, CARLOS	4,616	45,035 R	60.6%	37.0%	62.1%	37.9%
TOTAL	2008	1,208,302	690,005		470,031		48,266	219,974 R	57.1%	38.9%	59.5%	40.5%
TOTAL	2006	845,127	459,267		369,191		16,669	90,076 R	54.3%	43.7%	55.4%	44.6%
TOTAL	2004	1,156,383	723,794		386,970		45,619	336,824 R	62.6%	33.5%	65.2%	34.8%
TOTAL	2002	829,890	536,026		259,911		33,953	276,115 R	64.6%	31.3%	67.3%	32.7%

Note: An asterisk (*) denotes incumbent.

KANSAS

GENERAL AND PRIMARY ELECTIONS

2008 GENERAL ELECTIONS

President Other vote was 10,527 Independent (Ralph Nader); 6,706 Libertarian (Bob Barr); 4,148 Reform (Chuck Baldwin); 35 write-in (Cynthia A. McKinney); 31 write-in (Alan Keyes); 2 write-in (Jonathan E. Allen); 2 write-in (Frank Moore); 1 write-in (Keith Russell Judd).

Senator Other vote was 25,727 Libertarian (Randall L. Hodgkinson); 16,443 Reform (Joseph L. Martin).

House Other vote was:

CD 1 7,145 Reform (Kathleen M. Burton); 5,562 Libertarian (Jack Warner).
CD 2 5,080 Reform (Leslie S. Martin); 4,683 Libertarian (Robert Garrard).
CD 3 10,073 Libertarian (Joe Bellis); 3,937 Reform (Roger D. Tucker).
CD 4 6,441 Reform (Susan G. Ducey); 5,345 Libertarian (Steven A. Rosile).

KANSAS

GENERAL AND PRIMARY ELECTIONS

2008 PRIMARY ELECTIONS

Primary	August 5, 2008	**Registration** (as of July 21, 2008)		
		Republican	741,786
		Democratic	449,058
		Libertarian	9,152
		Reform	1,344
		Unaffiliated	451,633
		TOTAL	*1,652,973*

Primary Type   Semi-open—Registered Democrats and Republicans could vote only in their party's primary. "Unaffiliated" voters could participate in either primary, although if they voted in the Republican primary they had to change their registration to Republican on primary day.

	REPUBLICAN PRIMARIES			DEMOCRATIC PRIMARIES		
Senator	Pat Roberts*	214,911	100.0%	Jim Slattery	68,106	68.9%
				Lee Jones	30,699	31.1%
				TOTAL	*98,805*	
Congressional District 1	Jerry Moran*	67,978	100.0%	James Bordonaro	13,580	100.0%
Congressional District 2	Lynn Jenkins	34,278	51.0%	Nancy Boyda*	32,395	100.0%
	Jim Ryun	32,966	49.0%			
	TOTAL	*67,244*				
Congressional District 3	Nick Jordan	39,091	76.0%	Dennis Moore*	27,431	100.0%
	Paul V. Showen	12,338	24.0%			
	TOTAL	*51,429*				
Congressional District 4	Todd Tiahrt*	39,494	100.0%	Donald Betts Jr.	15,448	100.0%

Note: An asterisk (*) denotes incumbent.

KENTUCKY

Congressional districts first established for elections held in 2002
6 members

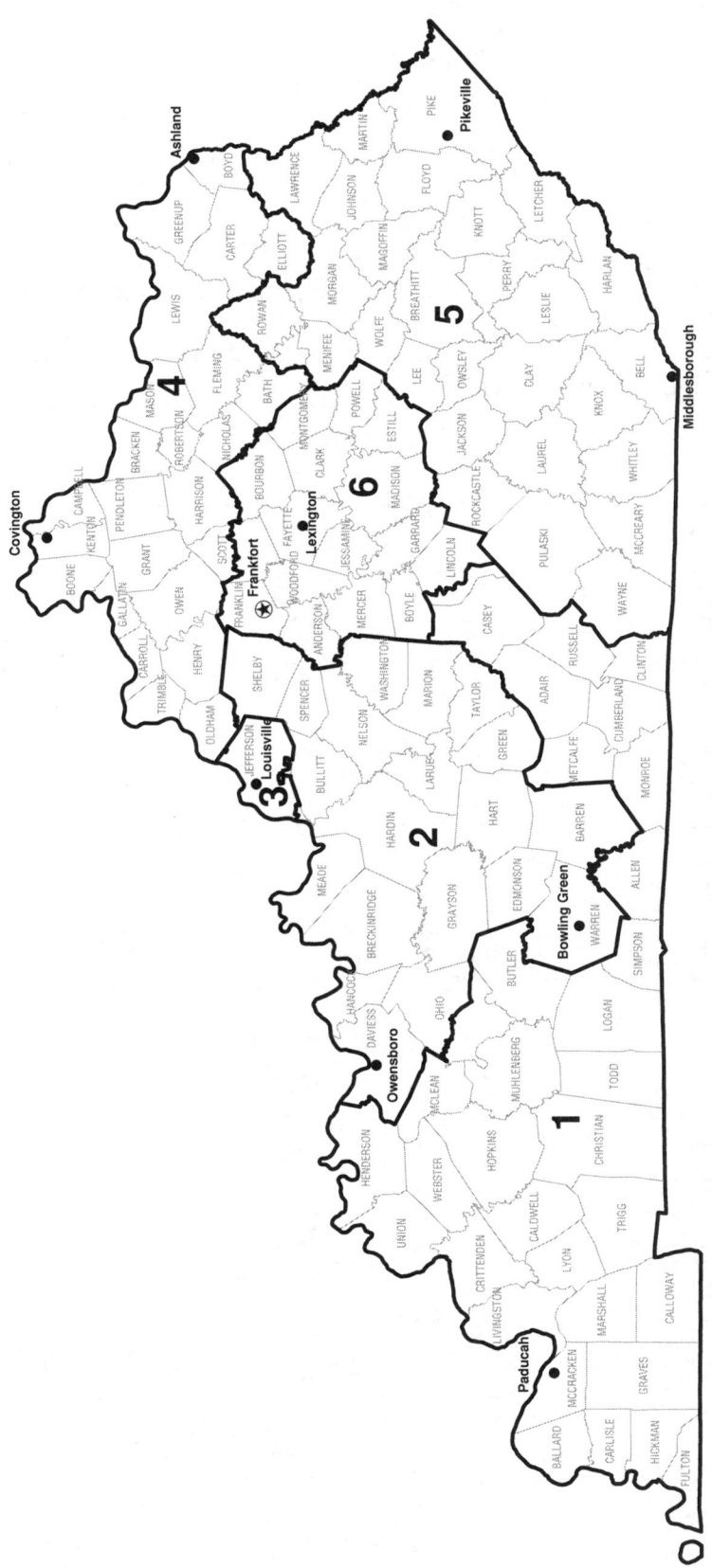

KENTUCKY

GOVERNOR

Steven L. Beshear (D). Elected 2007 to a four-year term.

SENATORS (2 Republicans)

Jim Bunning (R). Reelected 2004 to a six-year term. Previously elected 1998.

Mitch McConnell (R). Reelected 2008 to a six-year term. Previously elected 2002, 1996, 1990, 1984.

REPRESENTATIVES (4 Republicans, 2 Democrats)

1. Edward Whitfield (R)
2. Brett Guthrie (R)
3. John Yarmuth (D)
4. Geoff Davis (R)
5. Harold Rogers (R)
6. Ben Chandler (D)

POSTWAR VOTE FOR PRESIDENT

Year	Total Vote	Republican Vote	Republican Candidate	Democratic Vote	Democratic Candidate	Other Vote	Plurality	Total Vote Rep.	Total Vote Dem.	Major Vote Rep.	Major Vote Dem.
2008	1,826,620	1,048,462	McCain, John	751,985	Obama, Barack	26,173	296,477 R	57.4%	41.2%	58.2%	41.8%
2004	1,795,860	1,069,439	Bush, George W.	712,733	Kerry, John	13,688	356,706 R	59.6%	39.7%	60.0%	40.0%
2000**	1,544,187	872,492	Bush, George W.	638,898	Gore, Al	32,797	233,594 R	56.5%	41.4%	57.7%	42.3%
1996**	1,388,708	623,283	Dole, Bob	636,614	Clinton, Bill	128,811	13,331 D	44.9%	45.8%	49.5%	50.5%
1992**	1,492,900	617,178	Bush, George	665,104	Clinton, Bill	210,618	47,926 D	41.3%	44.6%	48.1%	51.9%
1988	1,322,517	734,281	Bush, George	580,368	Dukakis, Michael S.	7,868	153,913 R	55.5%	43.9%	55.9%	44.1%
1984	1,369,345	821,702	Reagan, Ronald	539,539	Mondale, Walter F.	8,104	282,163 R	60.0%	39.4%	60.4%	39.6%
1980**	1,294,627	635,274	Reagan, Ronald	616,417	Carter, Jimmy	42,936	18,857 R	49.1%	47.6%	50.8%	49.2%
1976	1,167,142	531,852	Ford, Gerald R.	615,717	Carter, Jimmy	19,573	83,865 D	45.6%	52.8%	46.3%	53.7%
1972	1,067,499	676,446	Nixon, Richard M.	371,159	McGovern, George S.	19,894	305,287 R	63.4%	34.8%	64.6%	35.4%
1968**	1,055,893	462,411	Nixon, Richard M.	397,541	Humphrey, Hubert H.	95,941	64,870 R	43.8%	37.6%	53.8%	46.2%
1964	1,046,105	372,977	Goldwater, Barry M.	669,659	Johnson, Lyndon B.	3,469	296,682 D	35.7%	64.0%	35.8%	64.2%
1960	1,124,462	602,607	Nixon, Richard M.	521,855	Kennedy, John F.		80,752 R	53.6%	46.4%	53.6%	46.4%
1956	1,053,805	572,192	Eisenhower, Dwight D.	476,453	Stevenson, Adlai E.	5,160	95,739 R	54.3%	45.2%	54.6%	45.4%
1952	993,148	495,029	Eisenhower, Dwight D.	495,729	Stevenson, Adlai E.	2,390	700 D	49.8%	49.9%	50.0%	50.0%
1948	822,658	341,210	Dewey, Thomas E.	466,756	Truman, Harry S.	14,692	125,546 D	41.5%	56.7%	42.2%	57.8%

**In past elections, the other vote included: 2000 - 23,192 Green (Ralph Nader); 1996 - 120,396 Reform (Ross Perot); 1992 - 203,944 Independent (Perot); 1980 - 31,127 Independent (John Anderson); 1968 - 193,098 American Independent (George Wallace).

KENTUCKY

POSTWAR VOTE FOR GOVERNOR

		Republican		Democratic		Other	Rep.-Dem.	Total Vote		Major Vote	
								Percentage			
Year	Total Vote	Vote	Candidate	Vote	Candidate	Vote	Plurality	Rep.	Dem.	Rep.	Dem.
2007	1,055,325	435,773	Fletcher, Ernie	619,552	Beshear, Steven L.		183,779 D	41.3%	58.7%	41.3%	58.7%
2003	1,083,443	596,284	Fletcher, Ernie	487,159	Chandler, Ben		109,125 R	55.0%	45.0%	55.0%	45.0%
1999**	580,074	128,788	Martin, Peppy	352,099	Patton, Paul E.	99,187	223,311 D	22.2%	60.7%**	26.8%	73.2%
1995	983,979	479,227	Forgy, Larry	500,787	Patton, Paul E.	3,965	21,560 D	48.7%	50.9%	48.9%	51.1%
1991	834,920	294,452	Hopkins, Larry J.	540,468	Jones, Brereton C.		246,016 D	35.3%	64.7%	35.3%	64.7%
1987	777,815	273,141	Harper, John	504,674	Wilkinson, Wallace G.		231,533 D	35.1%	64.9%	35.1%	64.9%
1983	1,030,671	454,650	Bunning, Jim	561,674	Collins, Martha Layne	14,347	107,024 D	44.1%	54.5%	44.7%	55.3%
1979	939,366	381,278	Nunn, Louie B.	558,088	Brown, J. Y., Jr.		176,810 D	40.6%	59.4%	40.6%	59.4%
1975	748,157	277,998	Gable, Robert E.	470,159	Carroll, Julian		192,161 D	37.2%	62.8%	37.2%	62.8%
1971	930,790	412,653	Emberton, Thomas	470,720	Ford, Wendell H.	47,417	58,067 D	44.3%	50.6%	46.7%	53.3%
1967	886,946	454,123	Nunn, Louie B.	425,674	Ward, Henry	7,149	28,449 R	51.2%	48.0%	51.6%	48.4%
1963	886,047	436,496	Nunn, Louie B.	449,551	Breathitt, Edward T.		13,055 D	49.3%	50.7%	49.3%	50.7%
1959	853,005	336,456	Robsion, John M.	516,549	Combs, Bert T.		180,093 D	39.4%	60.6%	39.4%	60.6%
1955	778,488	322,671	Denney, Edwin R.	451,647	Chandler, Albert B.	4,170	128,976 D	41.4%	58.0%	41.7%	58.3%
1951	634,359	288,014	Siler, Eugene	346,345	Wetherby, Lawrence		58,331 D	45.4%	54.6%	45.4%	54.6%
1947	672,372	287,130	Dummit, Eldon S.	385,242	Clements, Earle C.		98,112 D	42.7%	57.3%	42.7%	57.3%

**In past elections, the other vote included: 1999 - 88,930 Reform (Gatewood Galbraith).

POSTWAR VOTE FOR SENATOR

		Republican		Democratic		Other	Rep.-Dem.	Total Vote		Major Vote	
								Percentage			
Year	Total Vote	Vote	Candidate	Vote	Candidate	Vote	Plurality	Rep.	Dem.	Rep.	Dem.
2008	1,800,821	953,816	McConnell, Mitch	847,005	Lunsford, Bruce		106,811 R	53.0%	47.0%	53.0%	47.0%
2004	1,724,362	873,507	Bunning, Jim	850,855	Mongiardo, Daniel		22,652 R	50.7%	49.3%	50.7%	49.3%
2002	1,131,475	731,679	McConnell, Mitch	399,634	Weinberg, Lois Combs	162	332,045 R	64.7%	35.3%	64.7%	35.3%
1998	1,145,414	569,817	Bunning, Jim	563,051	Baesler, Scotty	12,546	6,766 R	49.7%	49.2%	50.3%	49.7%
1996	1,307,046	724,794	McConnell, Mitch	560,012	Beshear, Steven L.	22,240	164,782 R	55.5%	42.8%	56.4%	43.6%
1992	1,330,858	476,604	Williams, David L.	836,888	Ford, Wendell H.	17,366	360,284 D	35.8%	62.9%	36.3%	63.7%
1990	916,010	478,034	McConnell, Mitch	437,976	Sloane, Harvey		40,058 R	52.2%	47.8%	52.2%	47.8%
1986	677,280	173,330	Andrews, Jackson M.	503,775	Ford, Wendell H.	175	330,445 D	25.6%	74.4%	25.6%	74.4%
1984	1,292,407	644,990	McConnell, Mitch	639,721	Huddleston, Walter	7,696	5,269 R	49.9%	49.5%	50.2%	49.8%
1980	1,106,890	386,029	Foust, Mary Louise	720,861	Ford, Wendell H.		334,832 D	34.9%	65.1%	34.9%	65.1%
1978	476,783	175,766	Guenthner, Louie	290,730	Huddleston, Walter	10,287	114,964 D	36.9%	61.0%	37.7%	62.3%
1974	745,994	328,982	Cook, Marlow W.	399,406	Ford, Wendell H.	17,606	70,424 D	44.1%	53.5%	45.2%	54.8%
1972	1,037,861	494,337	Nunn, Louie B.	528,550	Huddleston, Walter	14,974	34,213 D	47.6%	50.9%	48.3%	51.7%
1968	942,865	484,260	Cook, Marlow W.	448,960	Peden, Katherine	9,645	35,300 R	51.4%	47.6%	51.9%	48.1%
1966	749,884	483,805	Cooper, John Sherman	266,079	Brown, J. Y.		217,726 R	64.5%	35.5%	64.5%	35.5%
1962	820,088	432,648	Morton, Thruston B.	387,440	Wyatt, Wilson W.		45,208 R	52.8%	47.2%	52.8%	47.2%
1960	1,088,377	644,087	Cooper, John Sherman	444,290	Johnson, Keen		199,797 R	59.2%	40.8%	59.2%	40.8%
1956	1,006,825	506,903	Morton, Thruston B.	499,922	Clements, Earle C.		6,981 R	50.3%	49.7%	50.3%	49.7%
1956S	1,011,645	538,505	Cooper, John Sherman	473,140	Wetherby, Lawrence		65,365 R	53.2%	46.8%	53.2%	46.8%
1954	797,057	362,948	Cooper, John Sherman	434,109	Barkley, Alben W.		71,161 D	45.5%	54.5%	45.5%	54.5%
1952S	960,228	494,576	Cooper, John Sherman	465,652	Underwood, Thomas R.		28,924 R	51.5%	48.5%	51.5%	48.5%
1950	612,617	278,368	Dawson, Charles L.	334,249	Clements, Earle C.		55,881 D	45.4%	54.6%	45.4%	54.6%
1948	794,469	383,776	Cooper, John Sherman	408,256	Chapman, Virgil	2,437	24,480 D	48.3%	51.4%	48.5%	51.5%
1946S	615,119	327,652	Cooper, John Sherman	285,829	Brown, J. Y.	1,638	41,823 R	53.3%	46.5%	53.4%	46.6%

Note: The elections in 1946, 1952, and 1956 were for short terms to fill vacancies.

KENTUCKY

PRESIDENT 2008

2000 Census Population	County	Total Vote	Republican	Democratic	Other	Rep.-Dem. Plurality	Percentage Total Vote Rep.	Dem.	Major Vote Rep.	Dem.
17,244	ADAIR	7,298	5,512	1,668	118	3,844 R	75.5%	22.9%	76.8%	23.2%
17,800	ALLEN	7,390	5,258	2,024	108	3,234 R	71.2%	27.4%	72.2%	27.8%
19,111	ANDERSON	10,552	6,885	3,462	205	3,423 R	65.2%	32.8%	66.5%	33.5%
8,286	BALLARD	4,060	2,537	1,427	96	1,110 R	62.5%	35.1%	64.0%	36.0%
38,033	BARREN	16,808	11,133	5,434	241	5,699 R	66.2%	32.3%	67.2%	32.8%
11,085	BATH	4,543	2,234	2,210	99	24 R	49.2%	48.6%	50.3%	49.7%
30,060	BELL	9,598	6,681	2,782	135	3,899 R	69.6%	29.0%	70.6%	29.4%
85,991	BOONE	50,775	33,812	16,292	671	17,520 R	66.6%	32.1%	67.5%	32.5%
19,360	BOURBON	8,330	4,820	3,385	125	1,435 R	57.9%	40.6%	58.7%	41.3%
49,752	BOYD	20,670	11,430	8,886	354	2,544 R	55.3%	43.0%	56.3%	43.7%
27,697	BOYLE	12,635	7,701	4,769	165	2,932 R	60.9%	37.7%	61.8%	38.2%
8,279	BRACKEN	3,400	2,066	1,241	93	825 R	60.8%	36.5%	62.5%	37.5%
16,100	BREATHITT	5,030	2,671	2,205	154	466 R	53.1%	43.8%	54.8%	45.2%
18,648	BRECKINRIDGE	8,523	5,281	3,110	132	2,171 R	62.0%	36.5%	62.9%	37.1%
61,236	BULLITT	30,726	20,102	10,177	447	9,925 R	65.4%	33.1%	66.4%	33.6%
13,010	BUTLER	5,318	3,696	1,555	67	2,141 R	69.5%	29.2%	70.4%	29.6%
13,060	CALDWELL	6,199	3,866	2,212	121	1,654 R	62.4%	35.7%	63.6%	36.4%
34,177	CALLOWAY	15,405	8,991	6,165	249	2,826 R	58.4%	40.0%	59.3%	40.7%
88,616	CAMPBELL	40,298	24,046	15,622	630	8,424 R	59.7%	38.8%	60.6%	39.4%
5,351	CARLISLE	2,617	1,699	879	39	820 R	64.9%	33.6%	65.9%	34.1%
10,155	CARROLL	3,835	2,032	1,716	87	316 R	53.0%	44.7%	54.2%	45.8%
26,889	CARTER	9,813	5,252	4,316	245	936 R	53.5%	44.0%	54.9%	45.1%
15,447	CASEY	5,957	4,679	1,219	59	3,460 R	78.5%	20.5%	79.3%	20.7%
72,265	CHRISTIAN	22,782	13,699	8,880	203	4,819 R	60.1%	39.0%	60.7%	39.3%
33,144	CLARK	15,628	9,664	5,749	215	3,915 R	61.8%	36.8%	62.7%	37.3%
24,556	CLAY	7,364	5,710	1,552	102	4,158 R	77.5%	21.1%	78.6%	21.4%
9,634	CLINTON	4,172	3,366	761	45	2,605 R	80.7%	18.2%	81.6%	18.4%
9,384	CRITTENDEN	3,930	2,604	1,254	72	1,350 R	66.3%	31.9%	67.5%	32.5%
7,147	CUMBERLAND	2,797	2,056	697	44	1,359 R	73.5%	24.9%	74.7%	25.3%
91,545	DAVIESS	43,624	23,692	19,282	650	4,410 R	54.3%	44.2%	55.1%	44.9%
11,644	EDMONSON	5,270	3,562	1,652	56	1,910 R	67.6%	31.3%	68.3%	31.7%
6,748	ELLIOTT	2,515	902	1,535	78	633 D	35.9%	61.0%	37.0%	63.0%
15,307	ESTILL	5,314	3,685	1,555	74	2,130 R	69.3%	29.3%	70.3%	29.7%
260,512	FAYETTE	127,648	59,884	66,042	1,722	6,158 D	46.9%	51.7%	47.6%	52.4%
13,792	FLEMING	5,832	3,432	2,279	121	1,153 R	58.8%	39.1%	60.1%	39.9%
42,441	FLOYD	15,659	7,741	7,530	388	211 R	49.4%	48.1%	50.7%	49.3%
47,687	FRANKLIN	24,082	11,911	11,767	404	144 R	49.5%	48.9%	50.3%	49.7%
7,752	FULTON	2,825	1,530	1,238	57	292 R	54.2%	43.8%	55.3%	44.7%
7,870	GALLATIN	3,193	1,840	1,278	75	562 R	57.6%	40.0%	59.0%	41.0%
14,792	GARRARD	7,210	5,118	2,012	80	3,106 R	71.0%	27.9%	71.8%	28.2%
22,384	GRANT	8,755	5,510	3,112	133	2,398 R	62.9%	35.5%	63.9%	36.1%
37,028	GRAVES	16,208	10,056	5,843	309	4,213 R	62.0%	36.1%	63.2%	36.8%
24,053	GRAYSON	9,903	6,605	3,154	144	3,451 R	66.7%	31.8%	67.7%	32.3%
11,518	GREEN	5,079	3,785	1,204	90	2,581 R	74.5%	23.7%	75.9%	24.1%
36,891	GREENUP	15,799	8,849	6,621	329	2,228 R	56.0%	41.9%	57.2%	42.8%
8,392	HANCOCK	4,144	1,928	2,135	81	207 D	46.5%	51.5%	47.5%	52.5%
94,174	HARDIN	39,990	23,896	15,650	444	8,246 R	59.8%	39.1%	60.4%	39.6%
33,202	HARLAN	9,914	7,165	2,586	163	4,579 R	72.3%	26.1%	73.5%	26.5%
17,983	HARRISON	7,590	4,520	2,916	154	1,604 R	59.6%	38.4%	60.8%	39.2%
17,445	HART	6,818	4,397	2,290	131	2,107 R	64.5%	33.6%	65.8%	34.2%

KENTUCKY

PRESIDENT 2008

2000 Census Population	County	Total Vote	Republican	Democratic	Other	Rep.-Dem. Plurality		Total Vote Rep.	Dem.	Major Vote Rep.	Dem.
44,829	HENDERSON	19,862	9,523	10,049	290	526	D	47.9%	50.6%	48.7%	51.3%
15,060	HENRY	6,919	4,081	2,725	113	1,356	R	59.0%	39.4%	60.0%	40.0%
5,262	HICKMAN	2,250	1,406	812	32	594	R	62.5%	36.1%	63.4%	36.6%
46,519	HOPKINS	19,349	11,916	7,104	329	4,812	R	61.6%	36.7%	62.6%	37.4%
13,495	JACKSON	5,224	4,407	743	74	3,664	R	84.4%	14.2%	85.6%	14.4%
693,604	JEFFERSON	353,900	153,957	196,435	3,508	42,478	D	43.5%	55.5%	43.9%	56.1%
39,041	JESSAMINE	20,215	13,711	6,236	268	7,475	R	67.8%	30.8%	68.7%	31.3%
23,445	JOHNSON	8,517	5,948	2,407	162	3,541	R	69.8%	28.3%	71.2%	28.8%
151,464	KENTON	68,214	40,714	26,480	1,020	14,234	R	59.7%	38.8%	60.6%	39.4%
17,649	KNOTT	5,820	3,070	2,612	138	458	R	52.7%	44.9%	54.0%	46.0%
31,795	KNOX	11,389	8,150	3,074	165	5,076	R	71.6%	27.0%	72.6%	27.4%
13,373	LARUE	6,178	4,153	1,913	112	2,240	R	67.2%	31.0%	68.5%	31.5%
52,715	LAUREL	22,500	17,660	4,618	222	13,042	R	78.5%	20.5%	79.3%	20.7%
15,569	LAWRENCE	5,649	3,503	2,036	110	1,467	R	62.0%	36.0%	63.2%	36.8%
7,916	LEE	2,773	1,978	752	43	1,226	R	71.3%	27.1%	72.5%	27.5%
12,401	LESLIE	4,397	3,574	766	57	2,808	R	81.3%	17.4%	82.4%	17.6%
25,277	LETCHER	8,235	5,367	2,623	245	2,744	R	65.2%	31.9%	67.2%	32.8%
14,092	LEWIS	4,791	3,213	1,510	68	1,703	R	67.1%	31.5%	68.0%	32.0%
23,361	LINCOLN	9,151	6,273	2,752	126	3,521	R	68.5%	30.1%	69.5%	30.5%
9,804	LIVINGSTON	4,593	2,890	1,622	81	1,268	R	62.9%	35.3%	64.1%	35.9%
26,573	LOGAN	10,891	6,925	3,811	155	3,114	R	63.6%	35.0%	64.5%	35.5%
8,080	LYON	3,855	2,220	1,577	58	643	R	57.6%	40.9%	58.5%	41.5%
65,514	MCCRACKEN	30,754	19,043	11,285	426	7,758	R	61.9%	36.7%	62.8%	37.2%
17,080	MCCREARY	5,407	4,078	1,258	71	2,820	R	75.4%	23.3%	76.4%	23.6%
9,938	MCLEAN	4,423	2,386	1,963	74	423	R	53.9%	44.4%	54.9%	45.1%
70,872	MADISON	32,537	19,694	12,392	451	7,302	R	60.5%	38.1%	61.4%	38.6%
13,332	MAGOFFIN	4,651	2,434	2,105	112	329	R	52.3%	45.3%	53.6%	46.4%
18,212	MARION	7,615	3,842	3,596	177	246	R	50.5%	47.2%	51.7%	48.3%
30,125	MARSHALL	15,487	9,512	5,683	292	3,829	R	61.4%	36.7%	62.6%	37.4%
12,578	MARTIN	3,692	2,824	808	60	2,016	R	76.5%	21.9%	77.8%	22.2%
16,800	MASON	7,121	4,102	2,891	128	1,211	R	57.6%	40.6%	58.7%	41.3%
26,349	MEADE	11,206	6,691	4,343	172	2,348	R	59.7%	38.8%	60.6%	39.4%
6,556	MENIFEE	2,489	1,155	1,276	58	121	D	46.4%	51.3%	47.5%	52.5%
20,817	MERCER	10,060	6,781	3,159	120	3,622	R	67.4%	31.4%	68.2%	31.8%
10,037	METCALFE	4,199	2,734	1,350	115	1,384	R	65.1%	32.2%	66.9%	33.1%
11,756	MONROE	4,665	3,537	1,067	61	2,470	R	75.8%	22.9%	76.8%	23.2%
22,554	MONTGOMERY	10,331	5,947	4,234	150	1,713	R	57.6%	41.0%	58.4%	41.6%
13,948	MORGAN	4,379	2,396	1,879	104	517	R	54.7%	42.9%	56.0%	44.0%
31,839	MUHLENBERG	12,889	6,447	6,221	221	226	R	50.0%	48.3%	50.9%	49.1%
37,477	NELSON	18,146	10,139	7,654	353	2,485	R	55.9%	42.2%	57.0%	43.0%
6,813	NICHOLAS	2,970	1,634	1,272	64	362	R	55.0%	42.8%	56.2%	43.8%
22,916	OHIO	9,939	5,687	4,059	193	1,628	R	57.2%	40.8%	58.4%	41.6%
46,178	OLDHAM	29,316	18,997	10,000	319	8,997	R	64.8%	34.1%	65.5%	34.5%
10,547	OWEN	4,752	2,969	1,694	89	1,275	R	62.5%	35.6%	63.7%	36.3%
4,858	OWSLEY	1,686	1,279	381	26	898	R	75.9%	22.6%	77.0%	23.0%
14,390	PENDLETON	5,802	3,676	2,027	99	1,649	R	63.4%	34.9%	64.5%	35.5%
29,390	PERRY	10,375	6,762	3,444	169	3,318	R	65.2%	33.2%	66.3%	33.7%
68,736	PIKE	22,643	12,655	9,525	463	3,130	R	55.9%	42.1%	57.1%	42.9%
13,237	POWELL	4,972	2,837	2,065	70	772	R	57.1%	41.5%	57.9%	42.1%
56,217	PULASKI	25,766	19,862	5,590	314	14,272	R	77.1%	21.7%	78.0%	22.0%

KENTUCKY

PRESIDENT 2008

2000 Census Population	County	Total Vote	Republican	Democratic	Other	Rep.-Dem. Plurality	Percentage Total Vote Rep.	Dem.	Major Vote Rep.	Dem.
2,266	ROBERTSON	1,015	533	451	31	82 R	52.5%	44.4%	54.2%	45.8%
16,582	ROCKCASTLE	6,274	4,757	1,410	107	3,347 R	75.8%	22.5%	77.1%	22.9%
22,094	ROWAN	8,154	3,907	4,074	173	167 D	47.9%	50.0%	49.0%	51.0%
16,315	RUSSELL	7,475	5,779	1,569	127	4,210 R	77.3%	21.0%	78.6%	21.4%
33,061	SCOTT	19,734	11,782	7,712	240	4,070 R	59.7%	39.1%	60.4%	39.6%
33,337	SHELBY	18,540	11,451	6,871	218	4,580 R	61.8%	37.1%	62.5%	37.5%
16,405	SIMPSON	7,309	4,437	2,775	97	1,662 R	60.7%	38.0%	61.5%	38.5%
11,766	SPENCER	8,050	5,378	2,519	153	2,859 R	66.8%	31.3%	68.1%	31.9%
22,927	TAYLOR	10,860	7,568	3,165	127	4,403 R	69.7%	29.1%	70.5%	29.5%
11,971	TODD	4,941	3,336	1,543	62	1,793 R	67.5%	31.2%	68.4%	31.6%
12,597	TRIGG	6,527	4,189	2,246	92	1,943 R	64.2%	34.4%	65.1%	34.9%
8,125	TRIMBLE	3,812	2,239	1,484	89	755 R	58.7%	38.9%	60.1%	39.9%
15,637	UNION	6,034	3,120	2,804	110	316 R	51.7%	46.5%	52.7%	47.3%
92,522	WARREN	44,146	25,993	17,669	484	8,324 R	58.9%	40.0%	59.5%	40.5%
10,916	WASHINGTON	5,275	3,305	1,890	80	1,415 R	62.7%	35.8%	63.6%	36.4%
19,923	WAYNE	7,196	4,868	2,201	127	2,667 R	67.6%	30.6%	68.9%	31.1%
14,120	WEBSTER	5,540	3,037	2,390	113	647 R	54.8%	43.1%	56.0%	44.0%
35,865	WHITLEY	13,704	10,015	3,484	205	6,531 R	73.1%	25.4%	74.2%	25.8%
7,065	WOLFE	2,968	1,408	1,493	67	85 D	47.4%	50.3%	48.5%	51.5%
23,208	WOODFORD	12,297	7,130	5,027	140	2,103 R	58.0%	40.9%	58.6%	41.4%
4,041,769	TOTAL	1,826,620	1,048,462	751,985	26,173	296,477 R	57.4%	41.2%	58.2%	41.8%

KENTUCKY

GOVERNOR 2007

2000 Census Population	County	Total Vote	Republican	Democratic	Other	Rep.-Dem. Plurality	Percentage Total Vote Rep.	Dem.	Major Vote Rep.	Dem.
17,244	ADAIR	4,632	3,138	1,494		1,644 R	67.7%	32.3%	67.7%	32.3%
17,800	ALLEN	3,775	1,955	1,820		135 R	51.8%	48.2%	51.8%	48.2%
19,111	ANDERSON	7,207	2,844	4,363		1,519 D	39.5%	60.5%	39.5%	60.5%
8,286	BALLARD	2,719	927	1,792		865 D	34.1%	65.9%	34.1%	65.9%
38,033	BARREN	11,135	5,279	5,856		577 D	47.4%	52.6%	47.4%	52.6%
11,085	BATH	3,433	1,136	2,297		1,161 D	33.1%	66.9%	33.1%	66.9%
30,060	BELL	5,009	2,003	3,006		1,003 D	40.0%	60.0%	40.0%	60.0%
85,991	BOONE	19,992	10,147	9,845		302 R	50.8%	49.2%	50.8%	49.2%
19,360	BOURBON	5,250	2,214	3,036		822 D	42.2%	57.8%	42.2%	57.8%
49,752	BOYD	10,962	3,723	7,239		3,516 D	34.0%	66.0%	34.0%	66.0%
27,697	BOYLE	7,184	3,329	3,855		526 D	46.3%	53.7%	46.3%	53.7%
8,279	BRACKEN	1,931	797	1,134		337 D	41.3%	58.7%	41.3%	58.7%
16,100	BREATHITT	4,122	1,065	3,057		1,992 D	25.8%	74.2%	25.8%	74.2%
18,648	BRECKINRIDGE	5,351	2,492	2,859		367 D	46.6%	53.4%	46.6%	53.4%
61,236	BULLITT	16,682	7,384	9,298		1,914 D	44.3%	55.7%	44.3%	55.7%
13,010	BUTLER	2,796	1,565	1,231		334 R	56.0%	44.0%	56.0%	44.0%
13,060	CALDWELL	3,791	1,335	2,456		1,121 D	35.2%	64.8%	35.2%	64.8%
34,177	CALLOWAY	8,720	3,861	4,859		998 D	44.3%	55.7%	44.3%	55.7%
88,616	CAMPBELL	19,564	8,690	10,874		2,184 D	44.4%	55.6%	44.4%	55.6%
5,351	CARLISLE	1,884	743	1,141		398 D	39.4%	60.6%	39.4%	60.6%

KENTUCKY
GOVERNOR 2007

2000 Census Population	County	Total Vote	Republican	Democratic	Other	Rep.-Dem. Plurality	Percentage Total Vote Rep.	Dem.	Major Vote Rep.	Dem.
10,155	CARROLL	2,181	708	1,473		765 D	32.5%	67.5%	32.5%	67.5%
26,889	CARTER	5,833	1,809	4,024		2,215 D	31.0%	69.0%	31.0%	69.0%
15,447	CASEY	3,637	2,509	1,128		1,381 R	69.0%	31.0%	69.0%	31.0%
72,265	CHRISTIAN	8,865	4,279	4,586		307 D	48.3%	51.7%	48.3%	51.7%
33,144	CLARK	9,483	4,300	5,183		883 D	45.3%	54.7%	45.3%	54.7%
24,556	CLAY	4,755	2,713	2,042		671 R	57.1%	42.9%	57.1%	42.9%
9,634	CLINTON	2,062	1,366	696		670 R	66.2%	33.8%	66.2%	33.8%
9,384	CRITTENDEN	2,403	1,121	1,282		161 D	46.7%	53.3%	46.7%	53.3%
7,147	CUMBERLAND	1,654	1,071	583		488 R	64.8%	35.2%	64.8%	35.2%
91,545	DAVIESS	24,828	8,845	15,983		7,138 D	35.6%	64.4%	35.6%	64.4%
11,644	EDMONSON	3,670	1,752	1,918		166 D	47.7%	52.3%	47.7%	52.3%
6,748	ELLIOTT	1,836	205	1,631		1,426 D	11.2%	88.8%	11.2%	88.8%
15,307	ESTILL	3,649	1,970	1,679		291 R	54.0%	46.0%	54.0%	46.0%
260,512	FAYETTE	71,758	29,456	42,302		12,846 D	41.0%	59.0%	41.0%	59.0%
13,792	FLEMING	4,020	1,826	2,194		368 D	45.4%	54.6%	45.4%	54.6%
42,441	FLOYD	9,880	1,912	7,968		6,056 D	19.4%	80.6%	19.4%	80.6%
47,687	FRANKLIN	18,900	5,022	13,878		8,856 D	26.6%	73.4%	26.6%	73.4%
7,752	FULTON	1,488	539	949		410 D	36.2%	63.8%	36.2%	63.8%
7,870	GALLATIN	1,480	481	999		518 D	32.5%	67.5%	32.5%	67.5%
14,792	GARRARD	4,231	2,433	1,798		635 R	57.5%	42.5%	57.5%	42.5%
22,384	GRANT	4,196	1,695	2,501		806 D	40.4%	59.6%	40.4%	59.6%
37,028	GRAVES	9,922	3,848	6,074		2,226 D	38.8%	61.2%	38.8%	61.2%
24,053	GRAYSON	5,966	3,060	2,906		154 R	51.3%	48.7%	51.3%	48.7%
11,518	GREEN	2,943	1,681	1,262		419 R	57.1%	42.9%	57.1%	42.9%
36,891	GREENUP	8,424	2,686	5,738		3,052 D	31.9%	68.1%	31.9%	68.1%
8,392	HANCOCK	2,503	825	1,678		853 D	33.0%	67.0%	33.0%	67.0%
94,174	HARDIN	20,837	10,042	10,795		753 D	48.2%	51.8%	48.2%	51.8%
33,202	HARLAN	5,578	1,805	3,773		1,968 D	32.4%	67.6%	32.4%	67.6%
17,983	HARRISON	4,709	1,947	2,762		815 D	41.3%	58.7%	41.3%	58.7%
17,445	HART	4,060	1,894	2,166		272 D	46.7%	53.3%	46.7%	53.3%
44,829	HENDERSON	12,310	4,071	8,239		4,168 D	33.1%	66.9%	33.1%	66.9%
15,060	HENRY	4,379	1,633	2,746		1,113 D	37.3%	62.7%	37.3%	62.7%
5,262	HICKMAN	1,516	629	887		258 D	41.5%	58.5%	41.5%	58.5%
46,519	HOPKINS	11,583	4,194	7,389		3,195 D	36.2%	63.8%	36.2%	63.8%
13,495	JACKSON	3,413	2,641	772		1,869 R	77.4%	22.6%	77.4%	22.6%
693,604	JEFFERSON	216,013	74,542	141,471		66,929 D	34.5%	65.5%	34.5%	65.5%
39,041	JESSAMINE	11,770	6,455	5,315		1,140 R	54.8%	45.2%	54.8%	45.2%
23,445	JOHNSON	4,853	2,247	2,606		359 D	46.3%	53.7%	46.3%	53.7%
151,464	KENTON	32,502	14,643	17,859		3,216 D	45.1%	54.9%	45.1%	54.9%
17,649	KNOTT	4,401	1,429	2,972		1,543 D	32.5%	67.5%	32.5%	67.5%
31,795	KNOX	6,041	3,140	2,901		239 R	52.0%	48.0%	52.0%	48.0%
13,373	LARUE	3,794	1,860	1,934		74 D	49.0%	51.0%	49.0%	51.0%
52,715	LAUREL	12,448	7,551	4,897		2,654 R	60.7%	39.3%	60.7%	39.3%
15,569	LAWRENCE	3,205	1,055	2,150		1,095 D	32.9%	67.1%	32.9%	67.1%
7,916	LEE	1,898	1,053	845		208 R	55.5%	44.5%	55.5%	44.5%
12,401	LESLIE	2,762	1,263	1,499		236 D	45.7%	54.3%	45.7%	54.3%
25,277	LETCHER	4,815	1,420	3,395		1,975 D	29.5%	70.5%	29.5%	70.5%
14,092	LEWIS	2,504	1,260	1,244		16 R	50.3%	49.7%	50.3%	49.7%
23,361	LINCOLN	5,307	2,733	2,574		159 R	51.5%	48.5%	51.5%	48.5%
9,804	LIVINGSTON	2,958	1,020	1,938		918 D	34.5%	65.5%	34.5%	65.5%

KENTUCKY

GOVERNOR 2007

2000 Census Population	County	Total Vote	Republican	Democratic	Other	Rep.-Dem. Plurality	Total Vote Rep.	Total Vote Dem.	Major Vote Rep.	Major Vote Dem.
26,573	LOGAN	5,199	2,316	2,883		567 D	44.5%	55.5%	44.5%	55.5%
8,080	LYON	2,762	913	1,849		936 D	33.1%	66.9%	33.1%	66.9%
65,514	MCCRACKEN	17,437	7,569	9,868		2,299 D	43.4%	56.6%	43.4%	56.6%
17,080	MCCREARY	2,569	1,469	1,100		369 R	57.2%	42.8%	57.2%	42.8%
9,938	MCLEAN	2,665	825	1,840		1,015 D	31.0%	69.0%	31.0%	69.0%
70,872	MADISON	18,689	8,849	9,840		991 D	47.3%	52.7%	47.3%	52.7%
13,332	MAGOFFIN	3,253	952	2,301		1,349 D	29.3%	70.7%	29.3%	70.7%
18,212	MARION	4,789	1,439	3,350		1,911 D	30.0%	70.0%	30.0%	70.0%
30,125	MARSHALL	10,127	3,577	6,550		2,973 D	35.3%	64.7%	35.3%	64.7%
12,578	MARTIN	1,740	771	969		198 D	44.3%	55.7%	44.3%	55.7%
16,800	MASON	4,121	1,834	2,287		453 D	44.5%	55.5%	44.5%	55.5%
26,349	MEADE	6,581	2,809	3,772		963 D	42.7%	57.3%	42.7%	57.3%
6,556	MENIFEE	1,704	554	1,150		596 D	32.5%	67.5%	32.5%	67.5%
20,817	MERCER	6,535	3,021	3,514		493 D	46.2%	53.8%	46.2%	53.8%
10,037	METCALFE	2,497	1,094	1,403		309 D	43.8%	56.2%	43.8%	56.2%
11,756	MONROE	2,922	1,947	975		972 R	66.6%	33.4%	66.6%	33.4%
22,554	MONTGOMERY	6,325	2,717	3,608		891 D	43.0%	57.0%	43.0%	57.0%
13,948	MORGAN	3,390	1,029	2,361		1,332 D	30.4%	69.6%	30.4%	69.6%
31,839	MUHLENBERG	7,492	1,947	5,545		3,598 D	26.0%	74.0%	26.0%	74.0%
37,477	NELSON	10,543	3,971	6,572		2,601 D	37.7%	62.3%	37.7%	62.3%
6,813	NICHOLAS	1,959	706	1,253		547 D	36.0%	64.0%	36.0%	64.0%
22,916	OHIO	5,963	2,637	3,326		689 D	44.2%	55.8%	44.2%	55.8%
46,178	OLDHAM	16,224	8,350	7,874		476 R	51.5%	48.5%	51.5%	48.5%
10,547	OWEN	2,818	1,107	1,711		604 D	39.3%	60.7%	39.3%	60.7%
4,858	OWSLEY	1,147	571	576		5 D	49.8%	50.2%	49.8%	50.2%
14,390	PENDLETON	2,954	1,318	1,636		318 D	44.6%	55.4%	44.6%	55.4%
29,390	PERRY	6,693	1,870	4,823		2,953 D	27.9%	72.1%	27.9%	72.1%
68,736	PIKE	13,150	3,780	9,370		5,590 D	28.7%	71.3%	28.7%	71.3%
13,237	POWELL	3,284	1,227	2,057		830 D	37.4%	62.6%	37.4%	62.6%
56,217	PULASKI	14,732	9,180	5,552		3,628 R	62.3%	37.7%	62.3%	37.7%
2,266	ROBERTSON	621	274	347		73 D	44.1%	55.9%	44.1%	55.9%
16,582	ROCKCASTLE	3,582	2,384	1,198		1,186 R	66.6%	33.4%	66.6%	33.4%
22,094	ROWAN	4,913	1,549	3,364		1,815 D	31.5%	68.5%	31.5%	68.5%
16,315	RUSSELL	4,832	2,936	1,896		1,040 R	60.8%	39.2%	60.8%	39.2%
33,061	SCOTT	11,542	5,209	6,333		1,124 D	45.1%	54.9%	45.1%	54.9%
33,337	SHELBY	11,456	5,143	6,313		1,170 D	44.9%	55.1%	44.9%	55.1%
16,405	SIMPSON	3,686	1,590	2,096		506 D	43.1%	56.9%	43.1%	56.9%
11,766	SPENCER	4,465	2,088	2,377		289 D	46.8%	53.2%	46.8%	53.2%
22,927	TAYLOR	6,241	3,312	2,929		383 R	53.1%	46.9%	53.1%	46.9%
11,971	TODD	1,943	865	1,078		213 D	44.5%	55.5%	44.5%	55.5%
12,597	TRIGG	3,718	1,718	2,000		282 D	46.2%	53.8%	46.2%	53.8%
8,125	TRIMBLE	2,274	836	1,438		602 D	36.8%	63.2%	36.8%	63.2%
15,637	UNION	3,518	1,068	2,450		1,382 D	30.4%	69.6%	30.4%	69.6%
92,522	WARREN	22,150	9,954	12,196		2,242 D	44.9%	55.1%	44.9%	55.1%
10,916	WASHINGTON	3,409	1,600	1,809		209 D	46.9%	53.1%	46.9%	53.1%
19,923	WAYNE	4,668	2,336	2,332		4 R	50.0%	50.0%	50.0%	50.0%
14,120	WEBSTER	3,122	919	2,203		1,284 D	29.4%	70.6%	29.4%	70.6%
35,865	WHITLEY	8,240	4,576	3,664		912 R	55.5%	44.5%	55.5%	44.5%
7,065	WOLFE	2,307	568	1,739		1,171 D	24.6%	75.4%	24.6%	75.4%
23,208	WOODFORD	8,012	3,233	4,779		1,546 D	40.4%	59.6%	40.4%	59.6%
4,041,769	TOTAL	1,055,325	435,773	619,552		183,779 D	41.3%	58.7%	41.3%	58.7%

KENTUCKY

SENATOR 2008

2000 Census Population	County	Total Vote	Republican	Democratic	Other	Rep.-Dem. Plurality	Percentage Total Vote Rep.	Dem.	Major Vote Rep.	Dem.
17,244	ADAIR	7,118	4,920	2,198		2,722 R	69.1%	30.9%	69.1%	30.9%
17,800	ALLEN	7,318	4,987	2,331		2,656 R	68.1%	31.9%	68.1%	31.9%
19,111	ANDERSON	10,347	5,559	4,788		771 R	53.7%	46.3%	53.7%	46.3%
8,286	BALLARD	4,055	2,162	1,893		269 R	53.3%	46.7%	53.3%	46.7%
38,033	BARREN	16,365	9,630	6,735		2,895 R	58.8%	41.2%	58.8%	41.2%
11,085	BATH	4,477	1,730	2,747		1,017 D	38.6%	61.4%	38.6%	61.4%
30,060	BELL	9,241	5,649	3,592		2,057 R	61.1%	38.9%	61.1%	38.9%
85,991	BOONE	49,509	34,285	15,224		19,061 R	69.3%	30.7%	69.3%	30.7%
19,360	BOURBON	8,276	3,951	4,325		374 D	47.7%	52.3%	47.7%	52.3%
49,752	BOYD	20,605	9,430	11,175		1,745 D	45.8%	54.2%	45.8%	54.2%
27,697	BOYLE	12,487	6,629	5,858		771 R	53.1%	46.9%	53.1%	46.9%
8,279	BRACKEN	3,357	1,975	1,382		593 R	58.8%	41.2%	58.8%	41.2%
16,100	BREATHITT	5,066	1,955	3,111		1,156 D	38.6%	61.4%	38.6%	61.4%
18,648	BRECKINRIDGE	8,488	4,752	3,736		1,016 R	56.0%	44.0%	56.0%	44.0%
61,236	BULLITT	30,226	17,579	12,647		4,932 R	58.2%	41.8%	58.2%	41.8%
13,010	BUTLER	5,272	3,501	1,771		1,730 R	66.4%	33.6%	66.4%	33.6%
13,060	CALDWELL	6,093	3,272	2,821		451 R	53.7%	46.3%	53.7%	46.3%
34,177	CALLOWAY	15,136	8,266	6,870		1,396 R	54.6%	45.4%	54.6%	45.4%
88,616	CAMPBELL	39,381	24,592	14,789		9,803 R	62.4%	37.6%	62.4%	37.6%
5,351	CARLISLE	2,623	1,403	1,220		183 R	53.5%	46.5%	53.5%	46.5%
10,155	CARROLL	3,769	1,612	2,157		545 D	42.8%	57.2%	42.8%	57.2%
26,889	CARTER	9,716	4,494	5,222		728 D	46.3%	53.7%	46.3%	53.7%
15,447	CASEY	5,836	4,053	1,783		2,270 R	69.4%	30.6%	69.4%	30.6%
72,265	CHRISTIAN	22,384	13,278	9,106		4,172 R	59.3%	40.7%	59.3%	40.7%
33,144	CLARK	15,334	7,898	7,436		462 R	51.5%	48.5%	51.5%	48.5%
24,556	CLAY	7,262	4,804	2,458		2,346 R	66.2%	33.8%	66.2%	33.8%
9,634	CLINTON	4,048	3,019	1,029		1,990 R	74.6%	25.4%	74.6%	25.4%
9,384	CRITTENDEN	3,883	2,268	1,615		653 R	58.4%	41.6%	58.4%	41.6%
7,147	CUMBERLAND	2,666	1,903	763		1,140 R	71.4%	28.6%	71.4%	28.6%
91,545	DAVIESS	43,342	22,563	20,779		1,784 R	52.1%	47.9%	52.1%	47.9%
11,644	EDMONSON	5,245	3,249	1,996		1,253 R	61.9%	38.1%	61.9%	38.1%
6,748	ELLIOTT	2,542	712	1,830		1,118 D	28.0%	72.0%	28.0%	72.0%
15,307	ESTILL	5,227	3,065	2,162		903 R	58.6%	41.4%	58.6%	41.4%
260,512	FAYETTE	125,636	57,605	68,031		10,426 D	45.9%	54.1%	45.9%	54.1%
13,792	FLEMING	5,786	2,841	2,945		104 D	49.1%	50.9%	49.1%	50.9%
42,441	FLOYD	15,703	5,598	10,105		4,507 D	35.6%	64.4%	35.6%	64.4%
47,687	FRANKLIN	23,539	9,651	13,888		4,237 D	41.0%	59.0%	41.0%	59.0%
7,752	FULTON	2,797	1,281	1,516		235 D	45.8%	54.2%	45.8%	54.2%
7,870	GALLATIN	3,143	1,708	1,435		273 R	54.3%	45.7%	54.3%	45.7%
14,792	GARRARD	7,127	4,269	2,858		1,411 R	59.9%	40.1%	59.9%	40.1%
22,384	GRANT	8,673	5,265	3,408		1,857 R	60.7%	39.3%	60.7%	39.3%
37,028	GRAVES	16,073	8,234	7,839		395 R	51.2%	48.8%	51.2%	48.8%
24,053	GRAYSON	9,846	5,983	3,863		2,120 R	60.8%	39.2%	60.8%	39.2%
11,518	GREEN	4,974	3,197	1,777		1,420 R	64.3%	35.7%	64.3%	35.7%
36,891	GREENUP	15,632	7,374	8,258		884 D	47.2%	52.8%	47.2%	52.8%
8,392	HANCOCK	4,108	1,802	2,306		504 D	43.9%	56.1%	43.9%	56.1%
94,174	HARDIN	39,644	22,326	17,318		5,008 R	56.3%	43.7%	56.3%	43.7%
33,202	HARLAN	9,669	5,229	4,440		789 R	54.1%	45.9%	54.1%	45.9%
17,983	HARRISON	7,557	3,743	3,814		71 D	49.5%	50.5%	49.5%	50.5%
17,445	HART	6,642	3,680	2,962		718 R	55.4%	44.6%	55.4%	44.6%

KENTUCKY

SENATOR 2008

2000 Census Population	County	Total Vote	Republican	Democratic	Other	Rep.-Dem. Plurality	Percentage			
							Total Vote		Major Vote	
							Rep.	Dem.	Rep.	Dem.
44,829	HENDERSON	19,707	8,659	11,048		2,389 D	43.9%	56.1%	43.9%	56.1%
15,060	HENRY	6,867	3,672	3,195		477 R	53.5%	46.5%	53.5%	46.5%
5,262	HICKMAN	2,209	1,160	1,049		111 R	52.5%	47.5%	52.5%	47.5%
46,519	HOPKINS	18,900	10,419	8,481		1,938 R	55.1%	44.9%	55.1%	44.9%
13,495	JACKSON	5,039	3,794	1,245		2,549 R	75.3%	24.7%	75.3%	24.7%
693,604	JEFFERSON	350,897	155,333	195,564		40,231 D	44.3%	55.7%	44.3%	55.7%
39,041	JESSAMINE	19,817	11,970	7,847		4,123 R	60.4%	39.6%	60.4%	39.6%
23,445	JOHNSON	8,451	5,199	3,252		1,947 R	61.5%	38.5%	61.5%	38.5%
151,464	KENTON	66,516	41,351	25,165		16,186 R	62.2%	37.8%	62.2%	37.8%
17,649	KNOTT	5,834	2,217	3,617		1,400 D	38.0%	62.0%	38.0%	62.0%
31,795	KNOX	11,096	6,767	4,329		2,438 R	61.0%	39.0%	61.0%	39.0%
13,373	LARUE	6,012	3,489	2,523		966 R	58.0%	42.0%	58.0%	42.0%
52,715	LAUREL	22,111	15,223	6,888		8,335 R	68.8%	31.2%	68.8%	31.2%
15,569	LAWRENCE	5,564	2,923	2,641		282 R	52.5%	47.5%	52.5%	47.5%
7,916	LEE	2,698	1,625	1,073		552 R	60.2%	39.8%	60.2%	39.8%
12,401	LESLIE	4,307	3,224	1,083		2,141 R	74.9%	25.1%	74.9%	25.1%
25,277	LETCHER	8,100	3,902	4,198		296 D	48.2%	51.8%	48.2%	51.8%
14,092	LEWIS	4,671	2,884	1,787		1,097 R	61.7%	38.3%	61.7%	38.3%
23,361	LINCOLN	9,058	4,939	4,119		820 R	54.5%	45.5%	54.5%	45.5%
9,804	LIVINGSTON	4,524	2,382	2,142		240 R	52.7%	47.3%	52.7%	47.3%
26,573	LOGAN	10,758	6,379	4,379		2,000 R	59.3%	40.7%	59.3%	40.7%
8,080	LYON	3,810	1,989	1,821		168 R	52.2%	47.8%	52.2%	47.8%
65,514	MCCRACKEN	30,309	17,303	13,006		4,297 R	57.1%	42.9%	57.1%	42.9%
17,080	MCCREARY	5,182	3,606	1,576		2,030 R	69.6%	30.4%	69.6%	30.4%
9,938	MCLEAN	4,402	2,177	2,225		48 D	49.5%	50.5%	49.5%	50.5%
70,872	MADISON	31,894	17,237	14,657		2,580 R	54.0%	46.0%	54.0%	46.0%
13,332	MAGOFFIN	4,623	1,904	2,719		815 D	41.2%	58.8%	41.2%	58.8%
18,212	MARION	7,462	3,158	4,304		1,146 D	42.3%	57.7%	42.3%	57.7%
30,125	MARSHALL	15,430	8,067	7,363		704 R	52.3%	47.7%	52.3%	47.7%
12,578	MARTIN	3,625	2,422	1,203		1,219 R	66.8%	33.2%	66.8%	33.2%
16,800	MASON	6,942	3,847	3,095		752 R	55.4%	44.6%	55.4%	44.6%
26,349	MEADE	11,054	5,905	5,149		756 R	53.4%	46.6%	53.4%	46.6%
6,556	MENIFEE	2,471	951	1,520		569 D	38.5%	61.5%	38.5%	61.5%
20,817	MERCER	9,822	5,484	4,338		1,146 R	55.8%	44.2%	55.8%	44.2%
10,037	METCALFE	4,011	2,245	1,766		479 R	56.0%	44.0%	56.0%	44.0%
11,756	MONROE	4,555	3,318	1,237		2,081 R	72.8%	27.2%	72.8%	27.2%
22,554	MONTGOMERY	10,186	4,660	5,526		866 D	45.7%	54.3%	45.7%	54.3%
13,948	MORGAN	4,378	1,881	2,497		616 D	43.0%	57.0%	43.0%	57.0%
31,839	MUHLENBERG	12,842	5,406	7,436		2,030 D	42.1%	57.9%	42.1%	57.9%
37,477	NELSON	17,788	8,965	8,823		142 R	50.4%	49.6%	50.4%	49.6%
6,813	NICHOLAS	2,921	1,184	1,737		553 D	40.5%	59.5%	40.5%	59.5%
22,916	OHIO	9,901	5,242	4,659		583 R	52.9%	47.1%	52.9%	47.1%
46,178	OLDHAM	28,952	18,746	10,206		8,540 R	64.7%	35.3%	64.7%	35.3%
10,547	OWEN	4,702	2,683	2,019		664 R	57.1%	42.9%	57.1%	42.9%
4,858	OWSLEY	1,622	1,063	559		504 R	65.5%	34.5%	65.5%	34.5%
14,390	PENDLETON	5,675	3,520	2,155		1,365 R	62.0%	38.0%	62.0%	38.0%
29,390	PERRY	10,237	5,211	5,026		185 R	50.9%	49.1%	50.9%	49.1%
68,736	PIKE	22,591	9,679	12,912		3,233 D	42.8%	57.2%	42.8%	57.2%
13,237	POWELL	4,944	2,081	2,863		782 D	42.1%	57.9%	42.1%	57.9%
56,217	PULASKI	25,180	17,072	8,108		8,964 R	67.8%	32.2%	67.8%	32.2%

KENTUCKY
SENATOR 2008

2000 Census Population	County	Total Vote	Republican	Democratic	Other	Rep.-Dem. Plurality	Percentage			
							Total Vote		Major Vote	
							Rep.	Dem.	Rep.	Dem.
2,266	ROBERTSON	1,012	514	498		16 R	50.8%	49.2%	50.8%	49.2%
16,582	ROCKCASTLE	6,014	4,177	1,837		2,340 R	69.5%	30.5%	69.5%	30.5%
22,094	ROWAN	8,022	3,312	4,710		1,398 D	41.3%	58.7%	41.3%	58.7%
16,315	RUSSELL	7,223	4,783	2,440		2,343 R	66.2%	33.8%	66.2%	33.8%
33,061	SCOTT	19,505	10,267	9,238		1,029 R	52.6%	47.4%	52.6%	47.4%
33,337	SHELBY	18,336	10,790	7,546		3,244 R	58.8%	41.2%	58.8%	41.2%
16,405	SIMPSON	7,040	3,922	3,118		804 R	55.7%	44.3%	55.7%	44.3%
11,766	SPENCER	7,970	4,811	3,159		1,652 R	60.4%	39.6%	60.4%	39.6%
22,927	TAYLOR	10,807	6,644	4,163		2,481 R	61.5%	38.5%	61.5%	38.5%
11,971	TODD	4,804	3,032	1,772		1,260 R	63.1%	36.9%	63.1%	36.9%
12,597	TRIGG	6,470	3,833	2,637		1,196 R	59.2%	40.8%	59.2%	40.8%
8,125	TRIMBLE	3,788	1,861	1,927		66 D	49.1%	50.9%	49.1%	50.9%
15,637	UNION	6,013	2,678	3,335		657 D	44.5%	55.5%	44.5%	55.5%
92,522	WARREN	43,763	24,579	19,184		5,395 R	56.2%	43.8%	56.2%	43.8%
10,916	WASHINGTON	5,142	2,826	2,316		510 R	55.0%	45.0%	55.0%	45.0%
19,923	WAYNE	7,032	3,987	3,045		942 R	56.7%	43.3%	56.7%	43.3%
14,120	WEBSTER	5,516	2,516	3,000		484 D	45.6%	54.4%	45.6%	54.4%
35,865	WHITLEY	13,334	8,485	4,849		3,636 R	63.6%	36.4%	63.6%	36.4%
7,065	WOLFE	3,006	1,120	1,886		766 D	37.3%	62.7%	37.3%	62.7%
23,208	WOODFORD	12,134	6,231	5,903		328 R	51.4%	48.6%	51.4%	48.6%
4,041,769	TOTAL	1,800,821	953,816	847,005		106,811 R	53.0%	47.0%	53.0%	47.0%

KENTUCKY

HOUSE OF REPRESENTATIVES

CD	Year	Total Vote	Republican Vote	Republican Candidate	Democratic Vote	Democratic Candidate	Other Vote	Rep.-Dem. Plurality	Total Vote Rep.	Total Vote Dem.	Major Vote Rep.	Major Vote Dem.
1	2008	276,786	178,107	WHITFIELD, EDWARD*	98,674	RYAN, HEATHER A.	5	79,433 R	64.3%	35.6%	64.3%	35.7%
1	2006	207,483	123,618	WHITFIELD, EDWARD*	83,865	BARLOW, TOM		39,753 R	59.6%	40.4%	59.6%	40.4%
1	2004	261,201	175,972	WHITFIELD, EDWARD*	85,229	CARTWRIGHT, BILLY R.		90,743 R	67.4%	32.6%	67.4%	32.6%
1	2002	180,217	117,600	WHITFIELD, EDWARD*	62,617	ALEXANDER, KLINT		54,983 R	65.3%	34.7%	65.3%	34.7%
2	2008	302,315	158,936	GUTHRIE, BRETT	143,379	BOSWELL, DAVID E.		15,557 R	52.6%	47.4%	52.6%	47.4%
2	2006	213,963	118,548	LEWIS, RON*	95,415	WEAVER, MIKE		23,133 R	55.4%	44.6%	55.4%	44.6%
2	2004	272,979	185,394	LEWIS, RON*	87,585	SMITH, ADAM		97,809 R	67.9%	32.1%	67.9%	32.1%
2	2002	176,288	122,773	LEWIS, RON*	51,431	WILLIAMS, DAVID L.	2,084	71,342 R	69.6%	29.2%	70.5%	29.5%
3	2008	343,370	139,527	NORTHUP, ANNE M.	203,843	YARMUTH, JOHN*		64,316 D	40.6%	59.4%	40.6%	59.4%
3	2006	241,965	116,568	NORTHUP, ANNE M.*	122,489	YARMUTH, JOHN	2,908	5,921 D	48.2%	50.6%	48.8%	51.2%
3	2004	328,139	197,736	NORTHUP, ANNE M.*	124,040	MILLER, TONY	6,363	73,696 R	60.3%	37.8%	61.5%	38.5%
3	2002	229,074	118,228	NORTHUP, ANNE M.*	110,846	CONWAY, JACK		7,382 R	51.6%	48.4%	51.6%	48.4%
4	2008	301,759	190,210	DAVIS, GEOFF*	111,549	KELLEY, MICHAEL		78,661 R	63.0%	37.0%	63.0%	37.0%
4	2006	204,767	105,845	DAVIS, GEOFF*	88,822	LUCAS, KEN	10,100	17,023 R	51.7%	43.4%	54.4%	45.6%
4	2004	295,927	160,982	DAVIS, GEOFF	129,876	CLOONEY, NICK	5,069	31,106 R	54.4%	43.9%	55.3%	44.7%
4	2002	171,735	81,651	DAVIS, GEOFF	87,776	LUCAS, KEN*	2,308	6,125 D	47.5%	51.1%	48.2%	51.8%
5	2008	210,468	177,024	ROGERS, HAROLD*	—		33,444	177,024 R	84.1%		100.0%	
5	2006	199,568	147,201	ROGERS, HAROLD*	52,367	STEPP, KENNETH		94,834 R	73.8%	26.2%	73.8%	26.2%
5	2004	177,579	177,579	ROGERS, HAROLD*	—			177,579 R	100.0%		100.0%	
5	2002	176,240	137,986	ROGERS, HAROLD*	38,254	BAILEY, SIDNEY JANE		99,732 R	78.3%	21.7%	78.3%	21.7%
6	2008	315,142	111,378	LARSON, JON	203,764	CHANDLER, BEN*		92,386 D	35.3%	64.7%	35.3%	64.7%
6	2006	185,780		—	158,765	CHANDLER, BEN*	27,015	158,765 D		85.5%		100.0%
6	2004	299,217	119,716	BUFORD, TOM	175,355	CHANDLER, BEN*	4,146	55,639 D	40.0%	58.6%	40.6%	59.4%
6	2002	160,688	115,622	FLETCHER, ERNIE*	—		45,066	115,622 R	72.0%		100.0%	
TOTAL	2008	1,749,840	955,182		761,209		33,449	193,973 R	54.6%	43.5%	55.7%	44.3%
TOTAL	2006	1,253,526	611,780		601,723		40,023	10,057 R	48.8%	48.0%	50.4%	49.6%
TOTAL	2004	1,635,042	1,017,379		602,085		15,578	415,294 R	62.2%	36.8%	62.8%	37.2%
TOTAL	2002	1,094,242	693,860		350,924		49,458	342,936 R	63.4%	32.1%	66.4%	33.6%

Note: An asterisk (*) denotes incumbent.

KENTUCKY

GENERAL AND PRIMARY ELECTIONS

2008 GENERAL ELECTIONS

President Other vote was 15,378 Independent (Ralph Nader); 5,989 Libertarian (Bob Barr); 4,694 Constitution (Chuck Baldwin); 57 write-in (Leonard C. Habermehl); 27 write-in (Alan Keyes); 18 write-in (Billy Mills); 7 write-in (Brian Moore); 1 write-in (Shelley Renee Upchurch); 1 write-in (Jonathan Allen); 1 write-in (Keith Russell Judd).

Governor (2007)

Senator

House Other vote was:

CD 1 5 write-in (Charles K. Hatchett).
CD 2
CD 3
CD 4
CD 5 33,444 Independent (Jim Holbert).
CD 6

KENTUCKY

GENERAL AND PRIMARY ELECTIONS

2008 PRIMARY ELECTIONS

Primary	May 22, 2007 (Governor) May 20, 2008	**Registration** (as of May 20, 2008)	Democratic Republican Other	1,629,845 1,040,438 186,948
			TOTAL	*2,857,231*

Primary Type   Closed—Only registered Democrats and Republicans could vote in their party's primary.

	REPUBLICAN PRIMARIES			**DEMOCRATIC PRIMARIES**		
President	John McCain	142,918	72.3%	Hillary Clinton	459,511	65.5%
	Mike Huckabee	16,388	8.3%	Barack Obama	209,954	29.9%
	Ron Paul	13,427	6.8%	Uncommitted	18,091	2.6%
	Uncommitted	10,755	5.4%	John Edwards	14,212	2.0%
	Mitt Romney	9,206	4.7%			
	Rudolph Giuliani	3,055	1.5%			
	Alan Keyes	2,044	1.0%			
	TOTAL	*197,793*		*TOTAL*	*701,768*	
Governor (2007)	Ernie Fletcher*	101,328	50.1%	Steven L. Beshear	142,838	41.0%
	Anne M. Northup	73,919	36.5%	Bruce Lunsford	74,578	21.4%
	Billy Harper	27,092	13.4%	Steve Henry	60,893	17.5%
				Jody Richards	45,433	13.0%
				Gatewood Galbraith	20,704	5.9%
				Otis Hensley	3,792	1.1%
	TOTAL	*202,339*		*TOTAL*	*348,238*	
Senator	Mitch McConnell*	168,127	86.1%	Bruce Lunsford	316,992	51.1%
	Daniel Essek	27,170	13.9%	Greg Fischer	209,827	33.8%
				David L. Williams	34,363	5.5%
				James E. Rice	20,403	3.3%
				Michael Cassaro	17,340	2.8%
				Kenneth Stepp	13,451	2.2%
				David Wylie	7,528	1.2%
	TOTAL	*195,297*		*TOTAL*	*619,904*	
Congressional District 1	Edward Whitfield*	Unopposed		Heather A. Ryan	Unopposed	
Congressional District 2	Brett Guthrie	Unopposed		David E. Boswell	61,007	58.6%
				Reid Haire	43,100	41.4%
				TOTAL	*104,107*	
Congressional District 3	Anne M. Northup	32,570	76.9%	John Yarmuth*	Unopposed	
	Chris Thieneman	9,080	21.4%			
	Bob DeVore Jr.	713	1.7%			
	TOTAL	*42,363*				
Congressional District 4	Geoff Davis*	30,189	85.2%	Michael Kelley	Unopposed	
	Warren O. Stone	2,831	8.0%			
	G.E. Puckett	2,427	6.8%			
	TOTAL	*35,447*				
Congressional District 5	Harold Rogers*	Unopposed		No Democratic candidate		
Congressional District 6	Jon Larson	12,647	51.5%	Ben Chandler*	Unopposed	
	Tony McCurdy	11,906	48.5%			
	TOTAL	*24,553*				

Note: An asterisk (*) denotes incumbent. The names of unopposed candidates did not appear on the primary ballot; therefore, no votes were cast for these candidates.

LOUISIANA

Congressional districts first established for elections held in 2002
7 members

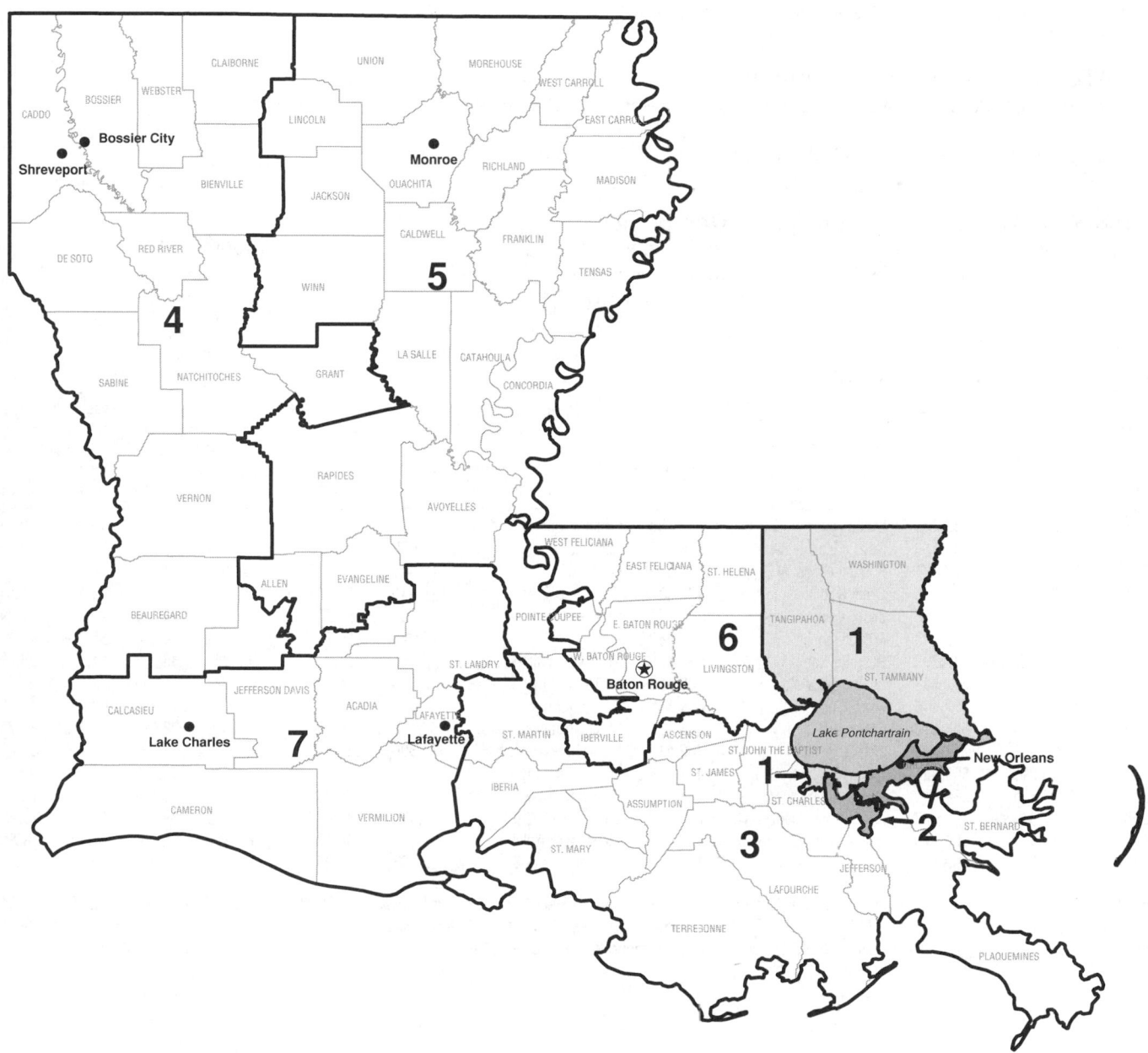

LOUISIANA

GOVERNOR
Bobby Jindal (R). Elected 2007 to a four-year term.

SENATORS (1 Democrat, 1 Republican)
Mary L. Landrieu (D). Reelected 2008 to a six-year term. Previously elected 2002, 1996.

David Vitter (R). Elected 2004 to a six-year term.

REPRESENTATIVES (6 Republicans, 1 Democrat)
1. Steve Scalise (R)
2. Anh "Joseph" Cao (R)
3. Charlie Melancon (D)
4. John Fleming (R)
5. Rodney Alexander (R)
6. Bill Cassidy (R)
7. Charles Boustany Jr. (R)

POSTWAR VOTE FOR PRESIDENT

Year	Total Vote	Republican Vote	Republican Candidate	Democratic Vote	Democratic Candidate	Other Vote	Plurality		Total Vote Rep.	Total Vote Dem.	Major Vote Rep.	Major Vote Dem.
2008	1,960,761	1,148,275	McCain, John	782,989	Obama, Barack	29,497	365,286	R	58.6%	39.9%	59.5%	40.5%
2004	1,943,106	1,102,169	Bush, George W.	820,299	Kerry, John	20,638	281,870	R	56.7%	42.2%	57.3%	42.7%
2000**	1,765,656	927,871	Bush, George W.	792,344	Gore, Al	45,441	135,527	R	52.6%	44.9%	53.9%	46.1%
1996**	1,783,959	712,586	Dole, Bob	927,837	Clinton, Bill	143,536	215,251	D	39.9%	52.0%	43.4%	56.6%
1992**	1,790,017	733,386	Bush, George	815,971	Clinton, Bill	240,660	82,585	D	41.0%	45.6%	47.3%	52.7%
1988	1,628,202	883,702	Bush, George	717,460	Dukakis, Michael S.	27,040	166,242	R	54.3%	44.1%	55.2%	44.8%
1984	1,706,822	1,037,299	Reagan, Ronald	651,586	Mondale, Walter F.	17,937	385,713	R	60.8%	38.2%	61.4%	38.6%
1980**	1,548,591	792,853	Reagan, Ronald	708,453	Carter, Jimmy	47,285	84,400	R	51.2%	45.7%	52.8%	47.2%
1976	1,278,439	587,446	Ford, Gerald R.	661,365	Carter, Jimmy	29,628	73,919	D	46.0%	51.7%	47.0%	53.0%
1972	1,051,491	686,852	Nixon, Richard M.	298,142	McGovern, George S.	66,497	388,710	R	65.3%	28.4%	69.7%	30.3%
1968**	1,097,450	257,535	Nixon, Richard M.	309,615	Humphrey, Hubert H.	530,300	220,685	A	23.5%	28.2%	45.4%	54.6%
1964	896,293	509,225	Goldwater, Barry M.	387,068	Johnson, Lyndon B.		122,157	R	56.8%	43.2%	56.8%	43.2%
1960**	807,891	230,980	Nixon, Richard M.	407,339	Kennedy, John F.	169,572	176,359	D	28.6%	50.4%	36.2%	63.8%
1956	617,544	329,047	Eisenhower, Dwight D.	243,977	Stevenson, Adlai E.	44,520	85,070	R	53.3%	39.5%	57.4%	42.6%
1952	651,952	306,925	Eisenhower, Dwight D.	345,027	Stevenson, Adlai E.		38,102	D	47.1%	52.9%	47.1%	52.9%
1948**	416,336	72,657	Dewey, Thomas E.	136,344	Truman, Harry S.	207,335	67,946	SR	17.5%	32.7%	34.8%	65.2%

Notes: **In past elections, the other vote included: 2000 - 20,473 Green (Ralph Nader); 1996 - 123,293 Reform (Ross Perot); 1992 - 211,478 Independent (Perot); 1980 - 26,345 Independent (John Anderson); 1968 - 530,300 American Independent (George Wallace); 1960 - 169,572 Unpledged Independent Electors; 1948 - 204,290 States' Rights (Strom Thurmond). Wallace carried Louisiana in 1968 with 48.3% of the vote. Thurmond won the state in 1948 with 49.1%.

LOUISIANA

POSTWAR VOTE FOR GOVERNOR

Year	Total Vote	Republican Vote	Republican Candidate	Democratic Vote	Democratic Candidate	Other Vote	Plurality	Total Vote Rep.	Total Vote Dem.	Major Vote Rep.	Major Vote Dem.
2007**	1,297,840	699,275	Jindal, Bobby	226,476	Boasso, Walter J.	372,089	472,799 R	53.9%	17.5%		
2003*	1,407,842	676,484	Jindal, Bobby	731,358	Blanco, Kathleen Babineaux		54,874 D	48.1%	51.9%	48.1%	51.9%
1999	1,295,205	805,203	Foster, Mike	382,445	Jefferson, William J.	107,557	422,758 R	62.2%	29.5%		
1995*	1,550,360	984,499	Foster, Mike	565,861	Fields, Cleo		418,638 R	63.5%	36.5%	63.5%	36.5%
1991*	1,728,040	671,009	Duke, David E.	1,057,031	Edwards, Edwin W.		386,022 D	38.8%	61.2%	38.8%	61.2%
1987**	1,558,730	287,780	Livingston, Robert L.	516,078	Roemer, Charles	754,872	78,277 D	18.5%	33.1%		
1983	1,615,905	588,508	Treen, David C.	1,006,561	Edwards, Edwin W.	20,836	418,053 D	36.4%	62.3%		
1979*	1,371,825	690,691	Treen, David C.	681,134	Lambert, Louis		9,557 R	50.3%	49.7%	50.3%	49.7%
1975	430,095		—	430,095	Edwards, Edwin W.		430,095 D		100.0%		100.0%
1972	1,121,570	480,424	Treen, David C.	641,146	Edwards, Edwin W.		160,722 D	42.8%	57.2%	42.8%	57.2%
1968	372,762		—	372,762	McKeithen, John J.		372,762 D		100.0%		100.0%
1964	773,390	297,753	Lyons, C. H.	469,589	McKeithen, John J.	6,048	171,836 D	38.5%	60.7%	38.8%	61.2%
1960	506,562	86,135	Grevemberg, F. C.	407,907	Davis, Jimmie H.	12,520	321,772 D	17.0%	80.5%	17.4%	82.6%
1956	172,291		—	172,291	Long, Earl K.		172,291 D		100.0%		100.0%
1952	123,681	4,958	Bagwell, Harrison G.	118,723	Kennon, Robert F.		113,765 D	4.0%	96.0%	4.0%	96.0%
1948	76,566		—	76,566	Long, Earl K.		76,566 D		100.0%		100.0%

Notes: Since the 1970s, Louisiana has had a two-tier election system for governor in which all candidates, regardless of party, run together in an open election. A candidate that wins a majority of the vote is elected. If no candidate receives 50 percent, a runoff is held between the top two finishers. An asterisk (*) indicates gubernatorial elections that were decided in a runoff, with the results of the runoff listed in this table. In elections that did not require a runoff, the leading Democratic and Republican candidates are listed with their votes from the first-round, open election. The votes for other candidates are listed in the "Other" column (**), regardless of whether they were Democratic, Republican, or independent. In past elections, the other vote included: 2007 - 186,682 No Party (John Georges), and 161,665 Democrat (Foster Campbell); 1987 - 437,801 Democrat (Edwin W. Edwards). In 1987, Edwards withdrew after finishing second in the initial round of voting. Democrat Charles Roemer finished first with 33.1 percent and with Edwards's withdrawal, no runoff was held. The major party vote percentages are given for those elections where there was no more than one Democratic and one Republican candidate. The Republican candidate did not run a candidate in the 1948, 1956, 1968, and 1975 gubernatorial elections.

POSTWAR VOTE FOR SENATOR

Year	Total Vote	Republican Vote	Republican Candidate	Democratic Vote	Democratic Candidate	Other Vote	Plurality	Total Vote Rep.	Total Vote Dem.	Major Vote Rep.	Major Vote Dem.
2008	1,896,574	867,177	Kennedy, John	988,298	Landrieu, Mary L.	41,099	121,121 D	45.7%	52.1%	46.7%	53.3%
2004**	1,848,056	943,014	Vitter, David	542,150	John, Chris	362,892	400,864 R	51.0%	29.3%		
2002*	1,235,296	596,642	Terrell, Suzanne Haik	638,654	Landrieu, Mary L.		42,012 D	48.3%	51.7%	48.3%	51.7%
1998	969,165	306,616	Donelon, Jim	620,502	Breaux, John B.	42,047	313,886 D	31.6%	64.0%		
1996*	1,700,102	847,157	Jenkins, Louis	852,945	Landrieu, Mary L.		5,788 D	49.8%	50.2%	49.8%	50.2%
1992	843,037	69,986	Stockstill, Lyle	616,021	Breaux, John B.	157,030	541,236 D	8.3%	73.1%		
1990	1,396,113	607,391	Duke, David E.	752,902	Johnston, J. Bennett	35,820	145,511 D	43.5%	53.9%		
1986*	1,369,897	646,311	Moore, W. Henson	723,586	Breaux, John B.		77,275 D	47.2%	52.8%	47.2%	52.8%
1984	977,473	86,546	Robert M. Ross	838,181	Johnston, J. Bennett	52,746	751,635 D	8.9%	85.7%		
1980**	841,013	13,739	Bardwell, Jerry C.	484,770	Long, Russell B.	342,504	158,848 D	1.6%	57.6%		
1978**	839,669		—	498,773	Johnston, J. Bennett	340,896	157,877 D		59.4%		
1974	434,643		—	434,643	Long, Russell B.		434,643 D		100.0%		100.0%
1972**	1,084,904	206,846	Toledano, Ben C.	598,987	Johnston, J. Bennett	279,071	348,826 D	19.1%	55.2%	25.7%	74.3%
1968	518,586		—	518,586	Long, Russell B.		518,586 D		100.0%		100.0%
1966	437,695		—	437,695	Ellender, Allen J.		437,695 D		100.0%		100.0%
1962	421,904	103,066	O'Hearn, Taylor W.	318,838	Long, Russell B.		215,772 D	24.4%	75.6%	24.4%	75.6%
1960	541,928	109,698	Reese, George W.	432,228	Ellender, Allen J.	2	322,530 D	20.2%	79.8%	20.2%	79.8%
1956	335,564		—	335,564	Long, Russell B.		335,564 D		100.0%		100.0%
1954	207,115		—	207,115	Ellender, Allen J.		207,115 D		100.0%		100.0%
1950	251,838	30,931	Gerth, Charles S.	220,907	Long, Russell B.		189,976 D	12.3%	87.7%	12.3%	87.7%
1948	330,124		—	330,115	Ellender, Allen J.	9	330,115 D		100.0%		100.0%
1948S	408,667	102,331	Clarke, Clem S.	306,336	Long, Russell B.		204,005 D	25.0%	75.0%	25.0%	75.0%

Notes: In 2008 Louisiana returned to the traditional system of party primaries followed by a general election to fill seats in Congress. From 1978 through 2004, Senate seats were decided in open elections in which candidates of all parties ran together on the same ballot. If no candidate won a majority of the vote in the first round, a runoff was held between the top two vote-getters, regardless of party. An asterisk (*) indicates Senate elections that were decided in a runoff, with the results of the runoff listed in this table. In elections that did not require a runoff, the leading Democratic and Republican candidates are listed with their votes in the first-round, open election. The votes for other candidates are listed in the "Other" column (**), regardless of whether they were Democratic, Republican, or independent. In past elections, the other vote included: 2004 - 275,821 Democrat (John Kennedy); 1980 - 325,922 Democrat (Louis Jenkins); 1978 - 340,896 Democrat (Louis Jenkins); 1972 - 250,161 Independent (John J. McKeithen). One of the 1948 elections was for a short term to fill a vacancy. The major party vote percentages are given for those elections where there was no more than one Democratic and one Republican candidate. The Republican Party did not run a candidate in 1948, 1954, 1956, 1966, 1968, 1974, and 1978.

LOUISIANA

PRESIDENT 2008

2000 Census Population	Parish	Total Vote	Republican	Democratic	Other	Rep.-Dem. Plurality		Percentage			
								Total Vote		Major Vote	
								Rep.	Dem.	Rep.	Dem.
58,861	ACADIA	26,711	19,229	7,028	454	12,201	R	72.0%	26.3%	73.2%	26.8%
25,440	ALLEN	9,467	6,333	2,891	243	3,442	R	66.9%	30.5%	68.7%	31.3%
76,627	ASCENSION	46,571	31,239	14,625	707	16,614	R	67.1%	31.4%	68.1%	31.9%
23,388	ASSUMPTION	10,960	5,981	4,756	223	1,225	R	54.6%	43.4%	55.7%	44.3%
41,481	AVOYELLES	16,938	10,236	6,327	375	3,909	R	60.4%	37.4%	61.8%	38.2%
32,986	BEAUREGARD	14,074	10,718	3,071	285	7,647	R	76.2%	21.8%	77.7%	22.3%
15,752	BIENVILLE	7,430	3,776	3,589	65	187	R	50.8%	48.3%	51.3%	48.7%
98,310	BOSSIER	45,835	32,713	12,703	419	20,010	R	71.4%	27.7%	72.0%	28.0%
252,161	CADDO	108,660	52,228	55,536	896	3,308	D	48.1%	51.1%	48.5%	51.5%
183,577	CALCASIEU	82,131	50,449	30,244	1,438	20,205	R	61.4%	36.8%	62.5%	37.5%
10,560	CALDWELL	4,893	3,696	1,118	79	2,578	R	75.5%	22.8%	76.8%	23.2%
9,991	CAMERON	3,793	3,089	613	91	2,476	R	81.4%	16.2%	83.4%	16.6%
10,920	CATAHOULA	5,225	3,486	1,659	80	1,827	R	66.7%	31.8%	67.8%	32.2%
16,851	CLAIBORNE	6,841	3,750	3,025	66	725	R	54.8%	44.2%	55.4%	44.6%
20,247	CONCORDIA	9,527	5,668	3,766	93	1,902	R	59.5%	39.5%	60.1%	39.9%
25,494	DE SOTO	12,257	6,883	5,242	132	1,641	R	56.2%	42.8%	56.8%	43.2%
412,852	EAST BATON ROUGE	197,349	95,390	99,652	2,307	4,262	D	48.3%	50.5%	48.9%	51.1%
9,421	EAST CARROLL	3,559	1,254	2,267	38	1,013	D	35.2%	63.7%	35.6%	64.4%
21,360	EAST FELICIANA	9,947	5,432	4,383	132	1,049	R	54.6%	44.1%	55.3%	44.7%
35,434	EVANGELINE	15,976	9,793	5,853	330	3,940	R	61.3%	36.6%	62.6%	37.4%
21,263	FRANKLIN	9,358	6,278	2,961	119	3,317	R	67.1%	31.6%	68.0%	32.0%
18,698	GRANT	8,558	6,907	1,474	177	5,433	R	80.7%	17.2%	82.4%	17.6%
73,266	IBERIA	33,168	20,127	12,492	549	7,635	R	60.7%	37.7%	61.7%	38.3%
33,320	IBERVILLE	16,421	7,185	9,023	213	1,838	D	43.8%	54.9%	44.3%	55.7%
15,397	JACKSON	7,736	5,190	2,456	90	2,734	R	67.1%	31.7%	67.9%	32.1%
455,466	JEFFERSON	181,120	113,191	65,096	2,833	48,095	R	62.5%	35.9%	63.5%	36.5%
31,435	JEFFERSON DAVIS	13,501	9,278	3,923	300	5,355	R	68.7%	29.1%	70.3%	29.7%
190,503	LAFAYETTE	95,642	62,055	32,145	1,442	29,910	R	64.9%	33.6%	65.9%	34.1%
89,974	LAFOURCHE	37,893	27,089	9,662	1,142	17,427	R	71.5%	25.5%	73.7%	26.3%
14,282	LA SALLE	6,553	5,602	860	91	4,742	R	85.5%	13.1%	86.7%	13.3%
42,509	LINCOLN	19,179	10,680	8,292	207	2,388	R	55.7%	43.2%	56.3%	43.7%
91,814	LIVINGSTON	50,892	43,269	6,681	942	36,588	R	85.0%	13.1%	86.6%	13.4%
13,728	MADISON	5,300	2,152	3,100	48	948	D	40.6%	58.5%	41.0%	59.0%
31,021	MOREHOUSE	13,200	7,258	5,792	150	1,466	R	55.0%	43.9%	55.6%	44.4%
39,080	NATCHITOCHES	17,067	9,054	7,801	212	1,253	R	53.0%	45.7%	53.7%	46.3%
484,674	ORLEANS	147,439	28,130	117,102	2,207	88,972	D	19.1%	79.4%	19.4%	80.6%
147,250	OUACHITA	67,244	41,741	24,813	690	16,928	R	62.1%	36.9%	62.7%	37.3%
26,757	PLAQUEMINES	10,449	6,894	3,380	175	3,514	R	66.0%	32.3%	67.1%	32.9%
22,763	POINTE COUPEE	12,435	6,702	5,516	217	1,186	R	53.9%	44.4%	54.9%	45.1%
126,337	RAPIDES	57,521	36,611	20,127	783	16,484	R	63.6%	35.0%	64.5%	35.5%
9,622	RED RIVER	4,629	2,484	2,080	65	404	R	53.7%	44.9%	54.4%	45.6%
20,981	RICHLAND	9,181	5,751	3,311	119	2,440	R	62.6%	36.1%	63.5%	36.5%
23,459	SABINE	9,652	7,226	2,245	181	4,981	R	74.9%	23.3%	76.3%	23.7%
67,229	ST. BERNARD	13,541	9,643	3,491	407	6,152	R	71.2%	25.8%	73.4%	26.6%
48,072	ST. CHARLES	25,397	16,457	8,522	418	7,935	R	64.8%	33.6%	65.9%	34.1%
10,525	ST. HELENA	6,184	2,522	3,567	95	1,045	D	40.8%	57.7%	41.4%	58.6%
21,216	ST. JAMES	12,564	5,432	6,994	138	1,562	D	43.2%	55.7%	43.7%	56.3%
43,044	ST. JOHN THE BAPTIST	21,656	8,912	12,424	320	3,512	D	41.2%	57.4%	41.8%	58.2%
87,700	ST. LANDRY	42,493	21,650	20,268	575	1,382	R	50.9%	47.7%	51.6%	48.4%
48,583	ST. MARTIN	24,252	14,443	9,419	390	5,024	R	59.6%	38.8%	60.5%	39.5%
53,500	ST. MARY	22,903	13,183	9,345	375	3,838	R	57.6%	40.8%	58.5%	41.5%
191,268	ST. TAMMANY	109,542	83,078	24,596	1,868	58,482	R	75.8%	22.5%	77.2%	22.8%
100,588	TANGIPAHOA	48,602	31,434	16,438	730	14,996	R	64.7%	33.8%	65.7%	34.3%
6,618	TENSAS	3,040	1,367	1,646	27	279	D	45.0%	54.1%	45.4%	54.6%
104,503	TERREBONNE	40,696	28,210	11,581	905	16,629	R	69.3%	28.5%	70.9%	29.1%

LOUISIANA

PRESIDENT 2008

2000 Census Population	Parish	Total Vote	Republican	Democratic	Other	Rep.-Dem. Plurality	Percentage			
							Total Vote		Major Vote	
							Rep.	Dem.	Rep.	Dem.
22,803	UNION	10,868	7,619	3,103	146	4,516 R	70.1%	28.6%	71.1%	28.9%
53,807	VERMILION	24,833	18,069	6,266	498	11,803 R	72.8%	25.2%	74.3%	25.7%
52,531	VERNON	15,769	11,946	3,534	289	8,412 R	75.8%	22.4%	77.2%	22.8%
43,926	WASHINGTON	18,624	12,215	6,122	287	6,093 R	65.6%	32.9%	66.6%	33.4%
41,831	WEBSTER	18,270	11,417	6,610	243	4,807 R	62.5%	36.2%	63.3%	36.7%
21,601	WEST BATON ROUGE	11,866	6,654	5,043	169	1,611 R	56.1%	42.5%	56.9%	43.1%
12,314	WEST CARROLL	4,987	4,045	878	64	3,167 R	81.1%	17.6%	82.2%	17.8%
15,111	WEST FELICIANA	5,620	3,150	2,415	55	735 R	56.0%	43.0%	56.6%	43.4%
16,894	WINN	6,772	4,632	2,047	93	2,585 R	68.4%	30.2%	69.4%	30.6%
4,468,976	TOTAL	1,960,761	1,148,275	782,989	29,497	365,286 R	58.6%	39.9%	59.5%	40.5%

LOUISIANA

GOVERNOR 2007

2000 Census Population	Parish	Total Vote	Jindal (R)	Boasso (D)	Georges (I)	Campbell (D)	Other	Plurality	Winner	Percentage of Total Vote			
										Jindal (R)	Boasso (D)	Georges (I)	Campbell (D)
58,861	ACADIA	19,377	10,443	4,099	2,796	1,693	346	6,344	Jindal	53.9%	21.2%	14.4%	8.7%
25,440	ALLEN	7,870	3,317	2,206	766	1,299	282	1,111	Jindal	42.1%	28.0%	9.7%	16.5%
76,627	ASCENSION	29,705	18,455	4,311	2,684	3,817	438	14,144	Jindal	62.1%	14.5%	9.0%	12.8%
23,388	ASSUMPTION	9,220	4,228	2,336	1,280	1,098	278	1,892	Jindal	45.9%	25.3%	13.9%	11.9%
41,481	AVOYELLES	15,121	6,256	4,404	1,700	2,198	563	1,852	Jindal	41.4%	29.1%	11.2%	14.5%
32,986	BEAUREGARD	10,016	5,424	1,492	1,194	1,629	277	3,795	Jindal	54.2%	14.9%	11.9%	16.3%
15,752	BIENVILLE	5,727	1,970	967	427	2,211	152	241	Campbell	34.4%	16.9%	7.5%	38.6%
98,310	BOSSIER	26,914	16,200	2,615	2,577	5,305	217	10,895	Jindal	60.2%	9.7%	9.6%	19.7%
252,161	CADDO	65,143	30,559	13,281	6,592	14,045	666	16,514	Jindal	46.9%	20.4%	10.1%	21.6%
183,577	CALCASIEU	46,503	24,515	9,669	5,633	5,813	873	14,846	Jindal	52.7%	20.8%	12.1%	12.5%
10,560	CALDWELL	4,433	2,091	818	648	754	122	1,273	Jindal	47.2%	18.5%	14.6%	17.0%
9,991	CAMERON	3,622	1,812	763	567	384	96	1,049	Jindal	50.0%	21.1%	15.7%	10.6%
10,920	CATAHOULA	4,564	1,940	876	508	1,062	178	878	Jindal	42.5%	19.2%	11.1%	23.3%
16,851	CLAIBORNE	4,799	2,150	722	443	1,394	90	756	Jindal	44.8%	15.0%	9.2%	29.0%
20,247	CONCORDIA	7,525	3,454	1,416	708	1,692	255	1,762	Jindal	45.9%	18.8%	9.4%	22.5%
25,494	DE SOTO	8,881	4,065	1,574	871	2,203	168	1,862	Jindal	45.8%	17.7%	9.8%	24.8%
412,852	EAST BATON ROUGE	124,547	67,237	21,574	15,147	18,979	1,610	45,663	Jindal	54.0%	17.3%	12.2%	15.2%
9,421	EAST CARROLL	3,074	1,039	761	306	769	199	270	Jindal	33.8%	24.8%	10.0%	25.0%
21,360	EAST FELICIANA	7,598	3,445	1,288	674	2,042	149	1,403	Jindal	45.3%	17.0%	8.9%	26.9%
35,434	EVANGELINE	12,062	4,902	3,412	1,583	1,746	419	1,490	Jindal	40.6%	28.3%	13.1%	14.5%
21,263	FRANKLIN	7,587	3,809	1,252	988	1,312	226	2,497	Jindal	50.2%	16.5%	13.0%	17.3%
18,698	GRANT	6,673	3,656	1,129	809	888	191	2,527	Jindal	54.8%	16.9%	12.1%	13.3%
73,266	IBERIA	22,878	12,716	4,242	3,158	2,235	527	8,474	Jindal	55.6%	18.5%	13.8%	9.8%
33,320	IBERVILLE	13,372	5,406	3,390	1,556	2,473	547	2,016	Jindal	40.4%	25.4%	11.6%	18.5%
15,397	JACKSON	5,264	2,716	859	629	968	92	1,748	Jindal	51.6%	16.3%	11.9%	18.4%
455,466	JEFFERSON	116,154	76,591	12,438	21,401	4,489	1,235	55,190	Jindal	65.9%	10.7%	18.4%	3.9%
31,435	JEFFERSON DAVIS	10,076	5,262	1,983	1,646	951	234	3,279	Jindal	52.2%	19.7%	16.3%	9.4%
190,503	LAFAYETTE	57,292	33,721	8,020	8,161	6,567	823	25,560	Jindal	58.9%	14.0%	14.2%	11.5%
89,974	LAFOURCHE	27,535	15,726	4,196	4,990	2,066	557	10,736	Jindal	57.1%	15.2%	18.1%	7.5%
14,282	LA SALLE	5,665	3,125	833	751	803	153	2,292	Jindal	55.2%	14.7%	13.3%	14.2%

LOUISIANA

GOVERNOR 2007

2000 Census Population	Parish	Total Vote	Jindal (R)	Boasso (D)	Georges (I)	Campbell (D)	Other	Plurality	Winner	Percentage of Total Vote Jindal (R)	Boasso (D)	Georges (I)	Campbell (D)
42,509	LINCOLN	10,448	5,531	1,889	1,208	1,647	173	3,642	Jindal	52.9%	18.1%	11.6%	15.8%
91,814	LIVINGSTON	33,117	22,091	3,671	2,901	4,119	335	17,972	Jindal	66.7%	11.1%	8.8%	12.4%
13,728	MADISON	3,800	1,392	1,000	437	723	248	392	Jindal	36.6%	26.3%	11.5%	19.0%
31,021	MOREHOUSE	8,477	4,294	1,968	814	1,216	185	2,326	Jindal	50.7%	23.2%	9.6%	14.3%
39,080	NATCHITOCHES	13,209	6,209	2,491	1,102	3,058	349	3,151	Jindal	47.0%	18.9%	8.3%	23.2%
484,674	ORLEANS	75,882	26,278	15,359	27,370	5,739	1,136	1,092	Georges	34.6%	20.2%	36.1%	7.6%
147,250	OUACHITA	43,322	24,554	6,983	4,908	6,226	651	17,571	Jindal	56.7%	16.1%	11.3%	14.4%
26,757	PLAQUEMINES	7,858	4,831	1,527	1,023	338	139	3,304	Jindal	61.5%	19.4%	13.0%	4.3%
22,763	POINTE COUPEE	10,833	4,657	2,687	1,274	1,929	286	1,970	Jindal	43.0%	24.8%	11.8%	17.8%
126,337	RAPIDES	39,348	21,253	7,805	5,431	4,139	720	13,448	Jindal	54.0%	19.8%	13.8%	10.5%
9,622	RED RIVER	3,706	1,192	574	249	1,594	97	402	Campbell	32.2%	15.5%	6.7%	43.0%
20,981	RICHLAND	7,197	3,876	1,218	703	1,247	153	2,629	Jindal	53.9%	16.9%	9.8%	17.3%
23,459	SABINE	7,776	3,990	1,523	797	1,304	162	2,467	Jindal	51.3%	19.6%	10.2%	16.8%
67,229	ST. BERNARD	11,589	4,542	5,449	1,067	404	127	907	Boasso	39.2%	47.0%	9.2%	3.5%
48,072	ST. CHARLES	18,206	11,144	1,866	4,039	853	304	7,105	Jindal	61.2%	10.2%	22.2%	4.7%
10,525	ST. HELENA	5,355	1,818	1,328	921	1,054	234	490	Jindal	33.9%	24.8%	17.2%	19.7%
21,216	ST. JAMES	10,106	4,415	2,038	1,789	1,550	314	2,377	Jindal	43.7%	20.2%	17.7%	15.3%
43,044	ST. JOHN THE BAPTIST	15,028	7,157	2,965	3,283	1,139	484	3,874	Jindal	47.6%	19.7%	21.8%	7.6%
87,700	ST. LANDRY	33,208	13,741	8,622	4,331	5,589	925	5,119	Jindal	41.4%	26.0%	13.0%	16.8%
48,583	ST. MARTIN	16,630	8,097	3,395	2,227	2,515	396	4,702	Jindal	48.7%	20.4%	13.4%	15.1%
53,500	ST. MARY	15,296	8,002	4,000	1,910	896	488	4,002	Jindal	52.3%	26.2%	12.5%	5.9%
191,268	ST. TAMMANY	68,531	51,000	6,981	7,498	2,439	613	43,502	Jindal	74.4%	10.2%	10.9%	3.6%
100,588	TANGIPAHOA	32,292	19,807	4,701	4,307	2,856	621	15,106	Jindal	61.3%	14.6%	13.3%	8.8%
6,618	TENSAS	2,753	1,103	560	371	592	127	511	Jindal	40.1%	20.3%	13.5%	21.5%
104,503	TERREBONNE	28,078	16,763	4,423	4,889	1,399	604	11,874	Jindal	59.7%	15.8%	17.4%	5.0%
22,803	UNION	7,616	4,280	962	915	1,317	142	2,963	Jindal	56.2%	12.6%	12.0%	17.3%
53,807	VERMILION	20,281	10,101	4,284	3,433	2,070	393	5,817	Jindal	49.8%	21.1%	16.9%	10.2%
52,531	VERNON	10,498	5,585	1,443	1,150	1,943	377	3,642	Jindal	53.2%	13.7%	11.0%	18.5%
43,926	WASHINGTON	13,077	7,859	1,857	1,736	1,288	337	6,002	Jindal	60.1%	14.2%	13.3%	9.8%
41,831	WEBSTER	12,073	5,511	1,669	1,013	3,715	165	1,796	Jindal	45.6%	13.8%	8.4%	30.8%
21,601	WEST BATON ROUGE	8,673	4,505	1,631	958	1,439	140	2,874	Jindal	51.9%	18.8%	11.0%	16.6%
12,314	WEST CARROLL	3,937	2,242	497	477	627	94	1,615	Jindal	56.9%	12.6%	12.1%	15.9%
15,111	WEST FELICIANA	4,473	2,120	1,120	434	717	82	1,000	Jindal	47.4%	25.0%	9.7%	16.0%
16,894	WINN	5,970	3,105	1,064	524	1,099	178	2,006	Jindal	52.0%	17.8%	8.8%	18.4%
4,468,976	TOTAL	1,297,840	699,275	226,476	186,682	161,665	23,742	472,799	Jindal	53.9%	17.5%	14.4%	12.5%

Note: The plurality is based on the difference between the vote for the leading vote-getter in each parish and the runner-up in that parish.

LOUISIANA

SENATOR 2008

2000 Census Population	Parish	Total Vote	Republican	Democratic	Other	Rep.-Dem. Plurality	Percentage			
							Total Vote		Major Vote	
							Rep.	Dem.	Rep.	Dem.
58,861	ACADIA	26,117	14,090	11,383	644	2,707 R	53.9%	43.6%	55.3%	44.7%
25,440	ALLEN	9,091	4,134	4,665	292	531 D	45.5%	51.3%	47.0%	53.0%
76,627	ASCENSION	45,300	24,039	20,269	992	3,770 R	53.1%	44.7%	54.3%	45.7%
23,388	ASSUMPTION	10,373	3,793	6,401	179	2,608 D	36.6%	61.7%	37.2%	62.8%
41,481	AVOYELLES	16,301	7,086	8,737	478	1,651 D	43.5%	53.6%	44.8%	55.2%
32,986	BEAUREGARD	13,342	7,500	5,297	545	2,203 R	56.2%	39.7%	58.6%	41.4%
15,752	BIENVILLE	7,201	2,796	4,143	262	1,347 D	38.8%	57.5%	40.3%	59.7%
98,310	BOSSIER	43,922	25,700	17,232	990	8,468 R	58.5%	39.2%	59.9%	40.1%
252,161	CADDO	103,631	41,348	60,558	1,725	19,210 D	39.9%	58.4%	40.6%	59.4%
183,577	CALCASIEU	80,239	36,855	41,183	2,201	4,328 D	45.9%	51.3%	47.2%	52.8%
10,560	CALDWELL	4,689	2,835	1,732	122	1,103 R	60.5%	36.9%	62.1%	37.9%
9,991	CAMERON	3,704	1,738	1,863	103	125 D	46.9%	50.3%	48.3%	51.7%
10,920	CATAHOULA	5,012	2,482	2,411	119	71 R	49.5%	48.1%	50.7%	49.3%
16,851	CLAIBORNE	6,578	2,883	3,468	227	585 D	43.8%	52.7%	45.4%	54.6%
20,247	CONCORDIA	9,095	4,175	4,687	233	512 D	45.9%	51.5%	47.1%	52.9%
25,494	DE SOTO	11,737	5,352	6,134	251	782 D	45.6%	52.3%	46.6%	53.4%
412,852	EAST BATON ROUGE	193,960	80,222	110,694	3,044	30,472 D	41.4%	57.1%	42.0%	58.0%
9,421	EAST CARROLL	3,337	993	2,296	48	1,303 D	29.8%	68.8%	30.2%	69.8%
21,360	EAST FELICIANA	9,742	4,402	5,175	165	773 D	45.2%	53.1%	46.0%	54.0%
35,434	EVANGELINE	15,315	6,852	8,082	381	1,230 D	44.7%	52.8%	45.9%	54.1%
21,263	FRANKLIN	8,988	5,032	3,784	172	1,248 R	56.0%	42.1%	57.1%	42.9%
18,698	GRANT	8,201	5,230	2,702	269	2,528 R	63.8%	32.9%	65.9%	34.1%
73,266	IBERIA	31,390	14,858	15,895	637	1,037 D	47.3%	50.6%	48.3%	51.7%
33,320	IBERVILLE	15,713	4,936	10,532	245	5,596 D	31.4%	67.0%	31.9%	68.1%
15,397	JACKSON	7,528	4,183	3,157	188	1,026 R	55.6%	41.9%	57.0%	43.0%
455,466	JEFFERSON	175,605	79,965	91,966	3,674	12,001 D	45.5%	52.4%	46.5%	53.5%
31,435	JEFFERSON DAVIS	12,846	6,487	6,028	331	459 R	50.5%	46.9%	51.8%	48.2%
190,503	LAFAYETTE	93,078	50,054	40,826	2,198	9,228 R	53.8%	43.9%	55.1%	44.9%
89,974	LAFOURCHE	36,187	17,513	17,778	896	265 D	48.4%	49.1%	49.6%	50.4%
14,282	LA SALLE	6,365	4,542	1,599	224	2,943 R	71.4%	25.1%	74.0%	26.0%
42,509	LINCOLN	18,144	8,840	8,960	344	120 D	48.7%	49.4%	49.7%	50.3%
91,814	LIVINGSTON	49,977	33,401	15,295	1,281	18,106 R	66.8%	30.6%	68.6%	31.4%
13,728	MADISON	4,972	1,722	3,165	85	1,443 D	34.6%	63.7%	35.2%	64.8%
31,021	MOREHOUSE	12,656	5,763	6,647	246	884 D	45.5%	52.5%	46.4%	53.6%
39,080	NATCHITOCHES	16,541	7,084	9,016	441	1,932 D	42.8%	54.5%	44.0%	56.0%
484,674	ORLEANS	143,038	20,434	119,991	2,613	99,557 D	14.3%	83.9%	14.5%	85.4%
147,250	OUACHITA	64,402	35,075	28,323	1,004	6,752 R	54.5%	44.0%	55.3%	44.7%
26,757	PLAQUEMINES	10,110	4,547	5,361	202	814 D	45.0%	53.0%	45.9%	54.1%
22,763	POINTE COUPEE	12,118	3,979	7,937	202	3,958 D	32.8%	65.5%	33.4%	66.6%
126,337	RAPIDES	56,241	29,414	25,511	1,316	3,903 R	52.3%	45.4%	53.6%	46.4%
9,622	RED RIVER	4,439	1,734	2,601	104	867 D	39.1%	58.6%	40.0%	60.0%
20,981	RICHLAND	8,824	4,688	3,983	153	705 R	53.1%	45.1%	54.1%	45.9%
23,459	SABINE	9,148	5,338	3,480	330	1,858 R	58.4%	38.0%	60.5%	39.5%
67,229	ST. BERNARD	13,133	5,119	7,628	386	2,509 D	39.0%	58.1%	40.2%	59.8%
48,072	ST. CHARLES	24,407	12,097	11,785	525	312 R	49.6%	48.3%	50.7%	49.3%
10,525	ST. HELENA	6,052	1,892	4,063	97	2,171 D	31.3%	67.1%	31.8%	68.2%
21,216	ST. JAMES	11,913	3,743	8,011	159	4,268 D	31.4%	67.2%	31.8%	68.2%
43,044	ST. JOHN THE BAPTIST	20,568	6,458	13,754	356	7,296 D	31.4%	66.9%	32.0%	68.0%
87,700	ST. LANDRY	41,041	16,580	23,762	699	7,182 D	40.4%	57.9%	41.1%	58.9%
48,583	ST. MARTIN	22,915	10,515	11,990	410	1,475 D	45.9%	52.3%	46.7%	53.3%

LOUISIANA
SENATOR 2008

2000 Census Population	Parish	Total Vote	Republican	Democratic	Other	Rep.-Dem. Plurality		Percentage			
								Total Vote		Major Vote	
								Rep.	Dem.	Rep.	Dem.
53,500	ST. MARY	21,622	9,458	11,633	531	2,175 D		43.7%	53.8%	44.8%	55.2%
191,268	ST. TAMMANY	107,095	65,150	39,429	2,516	25,721 R		60.8%	36.8%	62.3%	37.7%
100,588	TANGIPAHOA	47,419	23,714	22,475	1,230	1,239 R		50.0%	47.4%	51.3%	48.7%
6,618	TENSAS	2,795	979	1,771	45	792 D		35.0%	63.4%	35.6%	64.4%
104,503	TERREBONNE	39,147	19,542	18,625	980	917 R		49.9%	47.6%	51.2%	48.8%
22,803	UNION	10,345	6,175	3,966	204	2,209 R		59.7%	38.3%	60.9%	39.1%
53,807	VERMILION	24,145	12,356	11,148	641	1,208 R		51.2%	46.2%	52.6%	47.4%
52,531	VERNON	14,847	8,266	5,961	620	2,305 R		55.7%	40.1%	58.1%	41.9%
43,926	WASHINGTON	18,142	8,743	8,852	547	109 D		48.2%	48.8%	49.7%	50.3%
41,831	WEBSTER	17,419	8,468	8,516	435	48 D		48.6%	48.9%	49.9%	50.1%
21,601	WEST BATON ROUGE	11,667	4,760	6,712	195	1,952 D		40.8%	57.5%	41.5%	58.5%
12,314	WEST CARROLL	4,744	3,138	1,502	104	1,636 R		66.1%	31.7%	67.6%	32.4%
15,111	WEST FELICIANA	5,494	2,452	2,953	89	501 D		44.6%	53.7%	45.4%	54.6%
16,894	WINN	6,467	3,478	2,815	174	663 R		53.8%	43.5%	55.3%	44.7%
4,468,976	TOTAL	1,896,574	867,177	988,298	41,099	121,121 D		45.7%	52.1%	46.7%	53.3%

LOUISIANA

HOUSE OF REPRESENTATIVES

| | | | Republican | | Democratic | | | | Percentage | | | |
| | | | | | | | | | Total Vote | | Major Vote | |
CD	Year	Total Vote	Vote	Candidate	Vote	Candidate	Other Vote	Rep.-Dem. Plurality	Rep.	Dem.	Rep.	Dem.
1	2008	288,007	189,168	SCALISE, STEVE*	98,839	HARLAN, JIM		90,329 R	65.7%	34.3%		
1	2006	148,128	130,508	JINDAL, BOBBY*	10,919	GEREIGHTY, DAVID	6,701	119,589 R	88.1%	7.4%		
1	2004	287,897	225,708	JINDAL, BOBBY	19,266	ARMSTRONG, ROY	42,923	206,442 R	78.4%	6.7%		
1	2002	180,570	147,117	VITTER, DAVID*		—	33,453	147,117 R	81.5%			
2	2008@	66,882	33,132	CAO, ANH "JOSEPH"	31,318	JEFFERSON, WILLIAM J.*	2,432	1,814 R	49.5%	46.8%	51.4%	48.6%
2	2006#	62,164		—	62,164	JEFFERSON*/CARTER		8,142 D		100.0%		100.0%
2	2004	219,607	46,097	SCHWERTZ, ARTHUR L. "ART"	173,510	JEFFERSON, WILLIAM J.*		127,413 D	21.0%	79.0%	21.0%	79.0%
2	2002	142,156	15,440	SULLIVAN, "SILKY"	90,310	JEFFERSON, WILLIAM J.*	36,406	74,870 D	10.9%	63.5%		
3	2008			—		MELANCON, CHARLIE*		D				
3	2006	136,331	54,950	ROMERO, CRAIG	75,023	MELANCON, CHARLIE*	6,358	20,073 D	40.3%	55.0%		
3	2004#	114,653	57,042	TAUZIN, W.J. "BILLY" III	57,611	MELANCON, CHARLIE		569 D	49.8%	50.2%	49.8%	50.2%
3	2002	150,342	130,323	TAUZIN, BILLY*		—	20,019	130,323 R	86.7%		100.0%	
4	2008@	92,572	44,501	FLEMING, JOHN	44,151	CARMOUCHE, PAUL J.	3,920	350 R	48.1%	47.7%	50.2%	49.8%
4	2006	134,272	77,078	McCRERY, JIM*	22,757	CASH, ARTIS R. SR.	34,437	54,321 R	57.4%	16.9%		
4	2004			McCRERY, JIM*		—		R				
4	2002	160,093	114,649	McCRERY, JIM*	42,340	MILKOVICH, JOHN	3,104	72,309 R	71.6%	26.4%	73.0%	27.0%
5	2008			ALEXANDER, RODNEY*		—		R				
5	2006	114,582	78,211	ALEXANDER, RODNEY*	33,233	HEARN, GLORIA WILLIAMS	3,138	44,978 R	68.3%	29.0%	70.2%	29.8%
5	2004	238,057	141,495	ALEXANDER, RODNEY*	58,591	BLAKES, ZELMA "TISA"	37,971	82,904 R	59.4%	24.6%		
5	2002#	172,462	85,744	FLETCHER, LEE	86,718	ALEXANDER, RODNEY		974 D	49.7%	50.3%	49.7%	50.3%
6	2008	312,416	150,332	CASSIDY, BILL	125,886	CAZAYOUX, DON*	36,198	24,446 R	48.1%	40.3%	54.4%	45.6%
6	2006	114,306	94,658	BAKER, RICHARD H.*		—	19,648	94,658 R	82.8%		100.0%	
6	2004	261,869	189,106	BAKER, RICHARD H.*	50,732	CRAIG, RUFUS HOLT JR.	22,031	138,374 R	72.2%		100.0%	
6	2002	174,830	146,932	BAKER, RICHARD H.*		—	27,898	146,932 R	84.0%		100.0%	
7	2008	286,299	177,173	BOUSTANY, CHARLES JR.*	98,280	CRAVINS, DONALD JR.	10,846	78,893 R	61.9%	34.3%	64.3%	35.7%
7	2006	160,853	113,720	BOUSTANY, CHARLES JR.*	47,133	STAGG, MIKE		66,587 R	70.7%	29.3%	70.7%	29.3%
7	2004#	136,532	75,039	BOUSTANY, CHARLES JR.	61,493	MOUNT, WILLIE LANDRY		13,546 R	55.0%	45.0%	55.0%	45.0%
7	2002	159,710		—	138,659	JOHN, CHRIS*	21,051	138,659 D		86.8%		100.0%
TOTAL	2008	1,046,176	594,306		398,474		53,396	195,832 R	56.8%	38.1%	59.9%	40.1%
TOTAL	2006	902,498	579,702		295,762		27,034	283,940 R	64.2%	32.8%	66.2%	33.8%
TOTAL	2004	1,545,982	936,801		609,181			327,620 R	60.6%	39.4%	60.6%	39.4%
TOTAL	2002	1,152,358	707,923		361,473		82,962	346,450 R	61.4%	31.4%	66.2%	33.8%

Notes: In 2008, three of the general elections for House seats in Louisiana were held on November 4. Two others were held December 6 (following primary runoffs on November 4), and are indicated by "@." In the other two districts, no election was held as one candidate in each district ran unopposed. Previously, Louisiana had a unique two-tier electoral system for House seats, with a first round of voting that featured candidates from all parties running together on the same ballot. A candidate who won a majority of the vote in the first round was elected. Otherwise, the top two finishers met in a runoff. In 2002 and again in 2006, one runoff for the House of Representatives was required; in 2004 there were two runoffs. They are indicated by a pound sign (#). In elections that did not require a runoff, the leading Democratic and Republican candidates are listed with their first-round votes. The votes for other candidates are listed in the "Other" column, regardless of whether they were Democratic, Republican, or unaffiliated with either party. However, the statewide vote totals represent the aggregate vote for all House candidates of each party in the decisive round of balloting, not just the top finishers. The major party vote percentages are given for those individual House elections where there was no more than one Democratic and one Republican candidate.

An asterisk (*) denotes incumbent. In 2006, the runoff in the 2nd District featured two Democrats: William J. Jefferson 35,153 (56.5 percent) and Karen Carter 27,011 (43.5 percent), resulting in a Jefferson plurality of 8,142 votes.

LOUISIANA

GENERAL AND PRIMARY ELECTIONS

2008 GENERAL ELECTIONS

President   Other vote was 9,368 Louisiana Taxpayers (Ron Paul); 9,187 Green (Cynthia A. McKinney); 6,997 Independent (Ralph Nader); 2,581 Constitution (Chuck Baldwin); 735 Socialist Workers (James Harris); 354 Socialism and Liberation (Gloria La Riva); 275 Prohibition (Gene Amondson).

Governor   Other vote was 5,868 Democrat (Mary Volentine Smith); 4,791 Other (B. Alexandrenko); 3,372 Other
(2007)   (Anthony "Tony G" Gentile); 2,648 Libertarian (T. Lee Horne III); 2,323 No Party (Sheldon Forest); 2,080 Democrat (M.V. "Vinny" Mendoza); 1,666 Democrat (Hardy Parkerson); 994 No Party (Arthur D. "Jim" Nichols).

Senator   Other vote was 18,590 Libertarian (Richard Fontanesi); 13,729 No Party (Jay Patel); 8,780 Other (Robert Stewart).

House   Other vote was:

    CD 1
    CD 2   1,883 Green (Malik Rahim); 549 Libertarian (Gregory W. Kahn).
    CD 3
    CD 4   3,245 No Party (Chester T. "Catfish" Kelley); 675 Other (Gerald J. Bowen Jr.)
    CD 5
    CD 6   36,198 No Party (Michael Jackson).
    CD 7   10,846 Other (Peter Vidrine).

Note: Candidates are listed as "Other" if they did not belong to a recognized political party in Louisiana.

2007–2008 PRIMARY ELECTIONS

Open Election	October 20, 2007 (Governor)	**Registration**	Democratic	1,517,436
	February 9, 2008 (President)	(as of September 15, 2008—	Republican	728,705
		includes active and	Other	642,723
		inactive registrants)		
			TOTAL	*2,888,864*

Primary   October 4, 2008 (Congress)

Primary Runoff   November 4, 2008

Primary Type   For federal offices, Republicans held a closed primary limited to registered Republican voters only. Democrats held a semi-open primary, in which registered Democrats and registered voters not affiliated with any recognized party could participate. For governor, Louisiana has a two-tier electoral system in which all voters can participate. The first round is an open election that features candidates from all parties running together on the same ballot. A candidate who wins a majority of the vote in the first round is elected. Otherwise, there is a runoff held several weeks later between the top two finishers.

LOUISIANA

GENERAL AND PRIMARY ELECTIONS

	REPUBLICAN PRIMARIES			DEMOCRATIC PRIMARIES		
President	Mike Huckabee	69,594	43.2%	Barack Obama	220,632	57.4%
	John McCain	67,551	41.9%	Hillary Clinton	136,925	35.6%
	Mitt Romney	10,222	6.3%	John Edwards	13,026	3.4%
	Ron Paul	8,590	5.3%	Joseph R. Biden Jr.	6,178	1.6%
	Fred Thompson	1,603	1.0%	Bill Richardson	4,257	1.1%
	Rudolph Giuliani	1,593	1.0%	Christopher J. Dodd	1,924	0.5%
	Alan Keyes	837	0.5%	Dennis J. Kucinich	1,404	0.4%
	Jerry Curry	521	0.3%			
	Duncan Hunter	368	0.2%			
	Daniel Gilbert	183	0.1%			
	Tom Tancredo	107	0.1%			
	TOTAL	161,169		TOTAL	384,346	
Senator	John Kennedy	Unopposed		Mary L. Landrieu*	Unopposed	
Congressional District 1	Steve Scalise*	Unopposed		Jim Harlan	37,883	72.7%
				M.V. "Vinny" Mendoza	14,254	27.3%
				TOTAL	52,137	
Congressional District 2	Anh "Joseph" Cao	Unopposed		William J. Jefferson*	17,510	25.3%
				Helena Moreno	13,795	19.9%
				Cedric Richmond	12,095	17.5%
				James Carter	9,286	13.4%
				Byron L. Lee	8,979	13.0%
				Troy "C" Carter	5,797	8.4%
				Kenya J.H. Smith	1,749	2.5%
				TOTAL	69,211	
				PRIMARY RUNOFF		
				William J. Jefferson*	92,921	56.8%
				Helena Moreno	70,705	43.2%
				TOTAL	163,626	
Congressional District 3	No Republican candidate			Charlie Melancon*	Unopposed	
Congressional District 4	John Fleming	14,500	35.1%	Paul J. Carmouche	36,936	48.1%
	Chris Gorman	14,072	34.1%	Willie Banks	17,621	23.0%
	Jeff Thompson	12,693	30.8%	John Milkovich	16,137	21.0%
				Artis "Doc" Cash	6,065	7.9%
	TOTAL	41,265		TOTAL	76,759	
	PRIMARY RUNOFF			PRIMARY RUNOFF		
	John Fleming	43,012	55.6%	Paul J. Carmouche	93,093	62.0%
	Chris Gorman	34,405	44.4%	Willie Banks	57,078	38.0%
	TOTAL	77,417		TOTAL	150,171	
Congressional District 5	Rodney Alexander*	27,819	89.7%	No Democratic candidate		
	Andrew Clack	3,203	10.3%			
	TOTAL	31,022				
Congressional District 6	Bill Cassidy	Unopposed		Don Cazayoux*	Unopposed	
Congressional District 7	Charles Boustany Jr.*	Unopposed		Donald Cravins Jr.	Unopposed	

Notes: An asterisk (*) denotes incumbent. The names of unopposed candidates did not appear on the primary ballot; therefore, no votes were cast for these candidates.

MAINE

Congressional districts first established for elections held in 2004
2 members

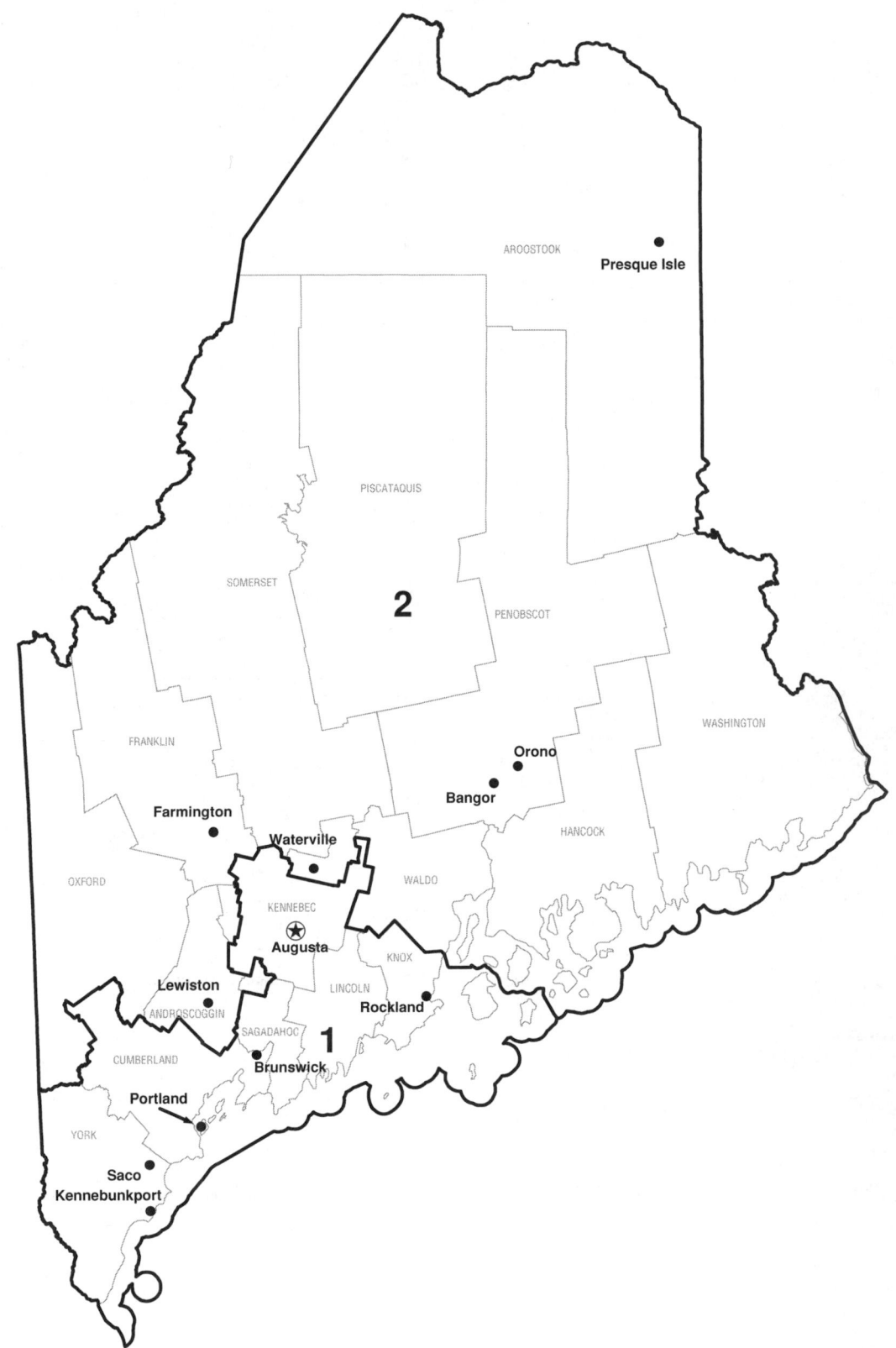

MAINE

GOVERNOR
John Baldacci (D). Reelected 2006 to a four-year term. Previously elected 2002.

SENATORS (2 Republicans)
Susan Collins (R). Reelected 2008 to a six-year term. Previously elected 2002, 1996.

Olympia J. Snowe (R). Reelected 2006 to a six-year term. Previously elected 2000, 1994.

REPRESENTATIVES (2 Democrats)
1. Chellie Pingree (D)   2. Michael H. Michaud (D)

POSTWAR VOTE FOR PRESIDENT

| Year | Total Vote | Republican | | Democratic | | Other Vote | Plurality | Percentage | | | |
| | | Vote | Candidate | Vote | Candidate | | | Total Vote | | Major Vote | |
								Rep.	Dem.	Rep.	Dem.
2008	731,163	295,273	McCain, John	421,923	Obama, Barack	13,967	126,650 D	40.4%	57.7%	41.2%	58.8%
2004	740,752	330,201	Bush, George W.	396,842	Kerry, John	13,709	66,641 D	44.6%	53.6%	45.4%	54.6%
2000**	651,817	286,616	Bush, George W.	319,951	Gore, Al	45,250	33,335 D	44.0%	49.1%	47.3%	52.7%
1996**	605,897	186,378	Dole, Bob	312,788	Clinton, Bill	106,731	126,410 D	30.8%	51.6%	37.3%	62.7%
1992**	679,499	206,504	Bush, George	263,420	Clinton, Bill	209,575	56,600 D	30.4%	38.8%	43.9%	56.1%
1988	555,035	307,131	Bush, George	243,569	Dukakis, Michael S.	4,335	63,562 R	55.3%	43.9%	55.8%	44.2%
1984	553,144	336,500	Reagan, Ronald	214,515	Mondale, Walter F.	2,129	121,985 R	60.8%	38.8%	61.1%	38.9%
1980**	523,011	238,522	Reagan, Ronald	220,974	Carter, Jimmy	63,515	17,548 R	45.6%	42.3%	51.9%	48.1%
1976	483,216	236,320	Ford, Gerald R.	232,279	Carter, Jimmy	14,617	4,041 R	48.9%	48.1%	50.4%	49.6%
1972	417,042	256,458	Nixon, Richard M.	160,584	McGovern, George S.		95,874 R	61.5%	38.5%	61.5%	38.5%
1968**	392,936	169,254	Nixon, Richard M.	217,312	Humphrey, Hubert H.	6,370	48,058 D	43.1%	55.3%	43.8%	56.2%
1964	380,965	118,701	Goldwater, Barry M.	262,264	Johnson, Lyndon B.		143,563 D	31.2%	68.8%	31.2%	68.8%
1960	421,767	240,608	Nixon, Richard M.	181,159	Kennedy, John F.		59,449 R	57.0%	43.0%	57.0%	43.0%
1956	351,706	249,238	Eisenhower, Dwight D.	102,468	Stevenson, Adlai E.		146,770 R	70.9%	29.1%	70.9%	29.1%
1952	351,786	232,353	Eisenhower, Dwight D.	118,806	Stevenson, Adlai E.	627	113,547 R	66.0%	33.8%	66.2%	33.8%
1948	264,787	150,234	Dewey, Thomas E.	111,916	Truman, Harry S.	2,637	38,318 R	56.7%	42.3%	57.3%	42.7%

**In past elections, the other vote included: 2000 - 37,127 Green (Ralph Nader); 1996 - 85,970 Reform (Ross Perot); 1992 - 206,820 Independent (Perot), who placed second statewide; 1980 - 53,327 Independent (John Anderson); 1968 - 6,370 American Independent (George Wallace).

MAINE

POSTWAR VOTE FOR GOVERNOR

Year	Total Vote	Republican Vote	Republican Candidate	Democratic Vote	Democratic Candidate	Other Vote	Plurality	Total Vote Rep.	Total Vote Dem.	Major Vote Rep.	Major Vote Dem.
2006**	550,865	166,425	Woodcock, Chandler E.	209,927	Baldacci, John	174,513	43,502 D	30.2%	38.1%	44.2%	55.8%
2002	505,190	209,496	Cianchette, Peter E.	238,179	Baldacci, John	57,515	28,683 D	41.5%	47.1%	46.8%	53.2%
1998**	421,009	79,716	Longley, James B., Jr.	50,506	Connolly, Thomas J.	290,787	167,056 I	18.9%	12.0%	61.2%	38.8%
1994**	511,308	117,990	Collins, Susan	172,951	Brennan, Joseph E.	220,367	7,878 I	23.1%	33.8%	40.6%	59.4%
1990	522,492	243,766	McKernan, John R.	230,038	Brennan, Joseph E.	48,688	13,728 R	46.7%	44.0%	51.4%	48.6%
1986**	426,861	170,312	McKernan, John R.	128,744	Tierney, James	127,805	41,568 R	39.9%	30.2%	56.9%	43.1%
1982	460,295	172,949	Cragin, Charles L.	281,066	Brennan, Joseph E.	6,280	108,117 D	37.6%	61.1%	38.1%	61.9%
1978**	370,258	126,862	Palmer, Linwood E.	176,493	Brennan, Joseph E.	66,903	49,631 D	34.3%	47.7%	41.8%	58.2%
1974**	363,945	84,176	Erwin, James S.	132,219	Mitchell, George J.	147,550	10,245 I	23.1%	36.3%	38.9%	61.1%
1970	325,386	162,248	Erwin, James S.	163,138	Curtis, Kenneth M.		890 D	49.9%	50.1%	49.9%	50.1%
1966	323,838	151,802	Reed, John H.	172,036	Curtis, Kenneth M.		20,234 D	46.9%	53.1%	46.9%	53.1%
1962	292,725	146,604	Reed, John H.	146,121	Dolloff, Maynard C.		483 R	50.1%	49.9%	50.1%	49.9%
1960S	417,315	219,768	Reed, John H.	197,547	Coffin, Frank M.		22,221 R	52.7%	47.3%	52.7%	47.3%
1958**	280,295	134,572	Hildreth, Horace A.	145,723	Clauson, Clinton A.		11,151 D	48.0%	52.0%	48.0%	52.0%
1956	304,649	124,395	Trafton, Willis A.	180,254	Muskie, Edmund S.		55,859 D	40.8%	59.2%	40.8%	59.2%
1954	248,971	113,298	Cross, Burton M.	135,673	Muskie, Edmund S.		22,375 D	45.5%	54.5%	45.5%	54.5%
1952	248,441	128,532	Cross, Burton M.	82,538	Oliver, James C.	37,371	45,994 R	51.7%	33.2%	60.9%	39.1%
1950	241,177	145,823	Payne, Frederick G.	94,304	Grant, Earl S.	1,050	51,519 R	60.5%	39.1%	60.7%	39.3%
1948	222,500	145,956	Payne, Frederick G.	76,544	Lausier, Louis B.		69,412 R	65.6%	34.4%	65.6%	34.4%
1946	179,951	110,327	Hildreth, Horace A.	69,624	Clark, F. Davis		40,703 R	61.3%	38.7%	61.3%	38.7%

Notes: **In past elections, the other vote included: 2006 - 118,715 Independent Maine Course (Barbara Merrill); 1998 - 246,772 Independent (Angus King), who was reelected with 58.6 percent of the total vote; 1994 - 180,829 Independent (King), who was elected with 35.4 percent of the total vote; 1986 - 64,317 Independent (Sherry F. Huber) and 63,474 Independent (John E. Menario); 1978 - 65,889 Independent (Herman C. Frankland); 1974 - 142,464 Independent (James B. Longley), who was elected with 39.1 percent of the total vote. The 1960 election was for a short term to fill a vacancy. The term of office of Maine's governor was increased from two to four years effective with the 1958 election.

POSTWAR VOTE FOR SENATOR

Year	Total Vote	Republican Vote	Republican Candidate	Democratic Vote	Democratic Candidate	Other Vote	Rep.-Dem. Plurality	Total Vote Rep.	Total Vote Dem.	Major Vote Rep.	Major Vote Dem.
2008	724,430	444,300	Collins, Susan	279,510	Allen, Tom	620	164,790 R	61.3%	38.6%	61.4%	38.6%
2006	543,981	402,598	Snowe, Olympia J.	111,984	Hay Bright, Jean	29,399	290,614 R	74.0%	20.6%	78.2%	21.8%
2002	504,899	295,041	Collins, Susan	209,858	Pingree, Chellie		85,183 R	58.4%	41.6%	58.4%	41.6%
2000	634,872	437,689	Snowe, Olympia J.	197,183	Lawrence, Mark		240,506 R	68.9%	31.1%	68.9%	31.1%
1996	606,777	298,422	Collins, Susan	266,226	Brennan, Joseph E.	42,129	32,196 R	49.2%	43.9%	52.9%	47.1%
1994	511,733	308,244	Snowe, Olympia J.	186,042	Andrews, Thomas H.	17,447	122,202 R	60.2%	36.4%	62.4%	37.6%
1990	520,320	319,167	Cohen, William S.	201,053	Rolde, Neil	100	118,114 R	61.3%	38.6%	61.4%	38.6%
1988	557,375	104,758	Wyman, Jasper S.	452,590	Mitchell, George J.	27	347,832 D	18.8%	81.2%	18.8%	81.2%
1984	551,406	404,414	Cohen, William S.	142,626	Mitchell, Elizabeth H.	4,366	261,788 R	73.3%	25.9%	73.9%	26.1%
1982	459,715	179,882	Emery, David F.	279,819	Mitchell, George J.	14	99,937 D	39.1%	60.9%	39.1%	60.9%
1978	375,172	212,294	Cohen, William S.	127,327	Hathaway, William D.	35,551	84,967 R	56.6%	33.9%	62.5%	37.5%
1976	486,254	193,489	Monks, Robert A. G.	292,704	Muskie, Edmund S.	61	99,215 D	39.8%	60.2%	39.8%	60.2%
1972	421,310	197,040	Smith, Margaret Chase	224,270	Hathaway, William D.		27,230 D	46.8%	53.2%	46.8%	53.2%
1970	323,860	123,906	Bishop, Neil S.	199,954	Muskie, Edmund S.		76,048 D	38.3%	61.7%	38.3%	61.7%
1966	319,535	188,291	Smith, Margaret Chase	131,136	Violette, Elmer H.	108	57,155 R	58.9%	41.0%	58.9%	41.1%
1964	380,551	127,040	McIntire, Clifford	253,511	Muskie, Edmund S.		126,471 D	33.4%	66.6%	33.4%	66.6%
1960	416,699	256,890	Smith, Margaret Chase	159,809	Cormier, Lucia M.		97,081 R	61.6%	38.4%	61.6%	38.4%
1958	284,226	111,522	Payne, Frederick G.	172,704	Muskie, Edmund S.		61,182 D	39.2%	60.8%	39.2%	60.8%
1954	246,605	144,530	Smith, Margaret Chase	102,075	Fullam, Paul A.		42,455 R	58.6%	41.4%	58.6%	41.4%
1952	237,164	139,205	Payne, Frederick G.	82,665	Dube, Roger P.	15,294	56,540 R	58.7%	34.9%	62.7%	37.3%
1948	223,256	159,182	Smith, Margaret Chase	64,074	Scolten, Adrian H.		95,108 R	71.3%	28.7%	71.3%	28.7%
1946	175,014	111,215	Brewster, Owen	63,799	MacDonald, Peter		47,416 R	63.5%	36.5%	63.5%	36.5%

MAINE

PRESIDENT 2008

2000 Census Population	County	Total Vote	Republican	Democratic	Other	Rep.-Dem. Plurality	Percentage			
							Total Vote		Major Vote	
							Rep.	Dem.	Rep.	Dem.
103,793	ANDROSCOGGIN	54,850	22,671	31,017	1,162	8,346 D	41.3%	56.5%	42.2%	57.8%
73,938	AROOSTOOK	35,994	15,898	19,345	751	3,447 D	44.2%	53.7%	45.1%	54.9%
265,612	CUMBERLAND	164,151	56,186	105,218	2,747	49,032 D	34.2%	64.1%	34.8%	65.2%
29,467	FRANKLIN	17,178	6,627	10,113	438	3,486 D	38.6%	58.9%	39.6%	60.4%
51,791	HANCOCK	32,165	12,686	18,895	584	6,209 D	39.4%	58.7%	40.2%	59.8%
117,114	KENNEBEC	65,986	27,482	37,238	1,266	9,756 D	41.6%	56.4%	42.5%	57.5%
39,618	KNOX	22,980	8,816	13,728	436	4,912 D	38.4%	59.7%	39.1%	60.9%
33,616	LINCOLN	21,584	9,287	11,886	411	2,599 D	43.0%	55.1%	43.9%	56.1%
54,755	OXFORD	31,650	12,863	17,940	847	5,077 D	40.6%	56.7%	41.8%	58.2%
144,919	PENOBSCOT	80,467	37,495	41,614	1,358	4,119 D	46.6%	51.7%	47.4%	52.6%
17,235	PISCATAQUIS	9,434	4,785	4,430	219	355 R	50.7%	47.0%	51.9%	48.1%
35,214	SAGADAHOC	21,301	8,721	12,152	428	3,431 D	40.9%	57.0%	41.8%	58.2%
50,888	SOMERSET	25,758	11,867	13,335	556	1,468 D	46.1%	51.8%	47.1%	52.9%
36,280	WALDO	21,850	9,423	11,967	460	2,544 D	43.1%	54.8%	44.1%	55.9%
33,941	WASHINGTON	16,654	8,077	8,246	331	169 D	48.5%	49.5%	49.5%	50.5%
186,742	YORK	109,161	42,389	64,799	1,973	22,410 D	38.8%	59.4%	39.5%	60.5%
1,274,923	TOTAL	731,163	295,273	421,923	13,967	126,650 D	40.4%	57.7%	41.2%	58.8%

2000 Census Population	City/Town	Total Vote	Republican	Democratic	Other	Rep.-Dem. Plurality	Percentage			
							Total Vote		Major Vote	
							Rep.	Dem.	Rep.	Dem.
23,203	AUBURN	11,783	4,686	6,866	231	2,180 D	39.8%	58.3%	40.6%	59.4%
18,560	AUGUSTA	9,454	3,662	5,556	236	1,894 D	38.7%	58.8%	39.7%	60.3%
31,473	BANGOR	15,916	6,258	9,406	252	3,148 D	39.3%	59.1%	40.0%	60.0%
9,266	BATH	4,796	1,678	3,025	93	1,347 D	35.0%	63.1%	35.7%	64.3%
6,381	BELFAST	3,798	1,339	2,375	84	1,036 D	35.3%	62.5%	36.1%	63.9%
6,353	BERWICK	3,706	1,719	1,931	56	212 D	46.4%	52.1%	47.1%	52.9%
20,942	BIDDEFORD	9,959	2,903	6,840	216	3,937 D	29.1%	68.7%	29.8%	70.2%
8,987	BREWER	5,129	2,600	2,446	83	154 R	50.7%	47.7%	51.5%	48.5%
21,172	BRUNSWICK	11,722	3,692	7,845	185	4,153 D	31.5%	66.9%	32.0%	68.0%
7,452	BUXTON	4,534	2,008	2,432	94	424 D	44.3%	53.6%	45.2%	54.8%
5,254	CAMDEN	3,331	910	2,377	44	1,467 D	27.3%	71.4%	27.7%	72.3%
9,068	CAPE ELIZABETH	6,339	2,118	4,164	57	2,046 D	33.4%	65.7%	33.7%	66.3%
8,312	CARIBOU	3,903	1,681	2,148	74	467 D	43.1%	55.0%	43.9%	56.1%
7,159	CUMBERLAND TOWN	4,843	1,956	2,812	75	856 D	40.4%	58.1%	41.0%	59.0%
5,954	ELIOT	3,919	1,594	2,276	49	682 D	40.7%	58.1%	41.2%	58.8%
6,456	ELLSWORTH	4,105	1,897	2,158	50	261 D	46.2%	52.6%	46.8%	53.2%
6,573	FAIRFIELD	3,387	1,394	1,907	86	513 D	41.2%	56.3%	42.2%	57.8%
10,310	FALMOUTH	7,141	2,861	4,189	91	1,328 D	40.1%	58.7%	40.6%	59.4%
7,410	FARMINGTON	4,342	1,422	2,819	101	1,397 D	32.7%	64.9%	33.5%	66.5%
7,800	FREEPORT	4,990	1,599	3,289	102	1,690 D	32.0%	65.9%	32.7%	67.3%

MAINE

PRESIDENT 2008

2000 Census Population	City/Town	Total Vote	Republican	Democratic	Other	Rep.-Dem. Plurality		Percentage			
								Total Vote		Major Vote	
								Rep.	Dem.	Rep.	Dem.
6,198	GARDINER	3,150	1,248	1,836	66	588	D	39.6%	58.3%	40.5%	59.5%
14,141	GORHAM	8,946	3,600	5,196	150	1,596	D	40.2%	58.1%	40.9%	59.1%
6,820	GRAY	4,553	1,994	2,454	105	460	D	43.8%	53.9%	44.8%	55.2%
6,327	HAMPDEN	4,372	2,152	2,159	61	7	D	49.2%	49.4%	49.9%	50.1%
5,239	HARPSWELL	3,471	1,413	2,000	58	587	D	40.7%	57.6%	41.4%	58.6%
6,476	HOULTON	2,735	1,462	1,221	52	241	R	53.5%	44.6%	54.5%	45.5%
4,985	JAY	2,672	865	1,737	70	872	D	32.4%	65.0%	33.2%	66.8%
10,476	KENNEBUNK	7,019	2,685	4,237	97	1,552	D	38.3%	60.4%	38.8%	61.2%
9,543	KITTERY	5,386	1,811	3,511	64	1,700	D	33.6%	65.2%	34.0%	66.0%
35,690	LEWISTON	16,914	5,961	10,629	324	4,668	D	35.2%	62.8%	35.9%	64.1%
2,361	LIMESTONE	976	367	587	22	220	D	37.6%	60.1%	38.5%	61.5%
5,221	LINCOLN TOWN	2,451	1,332	1,067	52	265	R	54.3%	43.5%	55.5%	44.5%
9,077	LISBON	4,831	2,293	2,428	110	135	D	47.5%	50.3%	48.6%	51.4%
5,203	MILLINOCKET	2,630	1,086	1,487	57	401	D	41.3%	56.5%	42.2%	57.8%
5,959	OAKLAND	3,324	1,459	1,809	56	350	D	43.9%	54.4%	44.6%	55.4%
8,856	OLD ORCHARD BEACH	5,306	1,817	3,384	105	1,567	D	34.2%	63.8%	34.9%	65.1%
8,130	OLD TOWN	4,213	1,464	2,686	63	1,222	D	34.7%	63.8%	35.3%	64.7%
9,112	ORONO	5,749	1,416	4,244	89	2,828	D	24.6%	73.8%	25.0%	75.0%
62,249	PORTLAND	36,840	7,844	28,317	679	20,473	D	21.3%	76.9%	21.7%	78.3%
9,511	PRESQUE ISLE	4,613	2,094	2,420	99	326	D	45.4%	52.5%	46.4%	53.6%
7,609	ROCKLAND	3,541	1,248	2,215	78	967	D	35.2%	62.6%	36.0%	64.0%
6,472	RUMFORD	3,025	949	1,977	99	1,028	D	31.4%	65.4%	32.4%	67.6%
16,822	SACO	9,998	3,374	6,457	167	3,083	D	33.7%	64.6%	34.3%	65.7%
20,806	SANFORD	9,781	3,607	5,953	221	2,346	D	36.9%	60.9%	37.7%	62.3%
16,970	SCARBOROUGH	11,788	4,866	6,750	172	1,884	D	41.3%	57.3%	41.9%	58.1%
8,824	SKOWHEGAN	4,117	1,572	2,480	65	908	D	38.2%	60.2%	38.8%	61.2%
6,671	SOUTH BERWICK	4,085	1,608	2,416	61	808	D	39.4%	59.1%	40.0%	60.0%
23,324	SOUTH PORTLAND	14,211	4,017	9,942	252	5,925	D	28.3%	70.0%	28.8%	71.2%
9,285	STANDISH	5,490	2,515	2,896	79	381	D	45.8%	52.8%	46.5%	53.5%
9,100	TOPSHAM	5,490	2,269	3,127	94	858	D	41.3%	57.0%	42.0%	58.0%
15,605	WATERVILLE	7,311	2,109	5,080	122	2,971	D	28.8%	69.5%	29.3%	70.7%
9,400	WELLS	5,931	2,476	3,353	102	877	D	41.7%	56.5%	42.5%	57.5%
16,142	WESTBROOK	8,783	3,030	5,590	163	2,560	D	34.5%	63.6%	35.2%	64.8%
14,904	WINDHAM	9,252	4,000	5,086	166	1,086	D	43.2%	55.0%	44.0%	56.0%
7,743	WINSLOW	4,329	1,766	2,490	73	724	D	40.8%	57.5%	41.5%	58.5%
6,232	WINTHROP	3,645	1,569	2,006	70	437	D	43.0%	55.0%	43.9%	56.1%
8,360	YARMOUTH	5,463	1,898	3,513	52	1,615	D	34.7%	64.3%	35.1%	64.9%
12,854	YORK TOWN	8,537	3,314	5,107	116	1,793	D	38.8%	59.8%	39.4%	60.6%

MAINE

SENATOR 2008

2000 Census Population	County	Total Vote	Republican	Democratic	Other	Rep.-Dem. Plurality	Percentage Total Vote Rep.	Dem.	Major Vote Rep.	Dem.
103,793	ANDROSCOGGIN	54,658	33,714	20,941	3	12,773 R	61.7%	38.3%	61.7%	38.3%
73,938	AROOSTOOK	35,150	25,324	9,812	14	15,512 R	72.0%	27.9%	72.1%	27.9%
265,612	CUMBERLAND	162,056	88,050	73,658	348	14,392 R	54.3%	45.5%	54.4%	45.6%
29,467	FRANKLIN	17,005	10,471	6,534		3,937 R	61.6%	38.4%	61.6%	38.4%
51,791	HANCOCK	31,937	19,152	12,771	14	6,381 R	60.0%	40.0%	60.0%	40.0%
117,114	KENNEBEC	65,793	41,794	23,977	22	17,817 R	63.5%	36.4%	63.5%	36.5%
39,618	KNOX	22,738	13,139	9,578	21	3,561 R	57.8%	42.1%	57.8%	42.2%
33,616	LINCOLN	21,565	13,691	7,847	27	5,844 R	63.5%	36.4%	63.6%	36.4%
54,755	OXFORD	31,535	19,621	11,903	11	7,718 R	62.2%	37.7%	62.2%	37.8%
144,919	PENOBSCOT	80,196	53,619	26,543	34	27,076 R	66.9%	33.1%	66.9%	33.1%
17,235	PISCATAQUIS	9,394	6,494	2,896	4	3,598 R	69.1%	30.8%	69.2%	30.8%
35,214	SAGADAHOC	21,175	13,166	7,993	16	5,173 R	62.2%	37.7%	62.2%	37.8%
50,888	SOMERSET	25,733	16,635	9,095	3	7,540 R	64.6%	35.3%	64.7%	35.3%
36,280	WALDO	21,661	13,347	8,288	26	5,059 R	61.6%	38.3%	61.7%	38.3%
33,941	WASHINGTON	16,728	11,215	5,507	6	5,708 R	67.0%	32.9%	67.1%	32.9%
186,742	YORK	107,106	64,868	42,167	71	22,701 R	60.6%	39.4%	60.6%	39.4%
1,274,923	TOTAL	724,430	444,300	279,510	620	164,790 R	61.3%	38.6%	61.4%	38.6%

2000 Census Population	City/Town	Total Vote	Republican	Democratic	Other	Rep.-Dem. Plurality	Percentage Total Vote Rep.	Dem.	Major Vote Rep.	Dem.
23,203	AUBURN	11,675	7,166	4,509		2,657 R	61.4%	38.6%	61.4%	38.6%
18,560	AUGUSTA	9,476	5,772	3,704		2,068 R	60.9%	39.1%	60.9%	39.1%
31,473	BANGOR	15,961	9,870	6,080	11	3,790 R	61.8%	38.1%	61.9%	38.1%
9,266	BATH	4,813	2,755	2,054	4	701 R	57.2%	42.7%	57.3%	42.7%
6,381	BELFAST	3,717	2,024	1,693		331 R	54.5%	45.5%	54.5%	45.5%
6,353	BERWICK	3,582	2,329	1,251	2	1,078 R	65.0%	34.9%	65.1%	34.9%
20,942	BIDDEFORD	9,848	5,208	4,638	2	570 R	52.9%	47.1%	52.9%	47.1%
8,987	BREWER	5,075	3,624	1,451		2,173 R	71.4%	28.6%	71.4%	28.6%
21,172	BRUNSWICK	11,622	5,924	5,664	34	260 R	51.0%	48.7%	51.1%	48.9%
7,452	BUXTON	4,501	2,952	1,546	3	1,406 R	65.6%	34.3%	65.6%	34.4%
5,254	CAMDEN	3,300	1,595	1,705		110 D	48.3%	51.7%	48.3%	51.7%
9,068	CAPE ELIZABETH	6,270	3,316	2,950	4	366 R	52.9%	47.0%	52.9%	47.1%
8,312	CARIBOU	2,875	2,034	841		1,193 R	70.7%	29.3%	70.7%	29.3%
7,159	CUMBERLAND TOWN	4,806	3,097	1,708	1	1,389 R	64.4%	35.5%	64.5%	35.5%
5,954	ELIOT	3,824	2,324	1,495	5	829 R	60.8%	39.1%	60.9%	39.1%
6,456	ELLSWORTH	4,048	2,755	1,289	4	1,466 R	68.1%	31.8%	68.1%	31.9%
6,573	FAIRFIELD	3,362	2,054	1,308		746 R	61.1%	38.9%	61.1%	38.9%
10,310	FALMOUTH	7,078	4,409	2,663	5	1,746 R	62.3%	37.6%	62.3%	37.7%
7,410	FARMINGTON	4,278	2,560	1,718		842 R	59.8%	40.2%	59.8%	40.2%
7,800	FREEPORT	4,910	2,614	2,283	13	331 R	53.2%	46.5%	53.4%	46.6%
6,198	GARDINER	3,150	2,017	1,127	5	890 R	64.0%	35.8%	64.2%	35.8%
14,141	GORHAM	8,834	5,443	3,367	24	2,076 R	61.6%	38.1%	61.8%	38.2%
6,820	GRAY	4,480	3,002	1,474	4	1,528 R	67.0%	32.9%	67.1%	32.9%
6,327	HAMPDEN	4,335	3,011	1,324		1,687 R	69.5%	30.5%	69.5%	30.5%
5,239	HARPSWELL	3,440	2,066	1,363	11	703 R	60.1%	39.6%	60.3%	39.7%

MAINE

SENATOR 2008

2000 Census Population	City/Town	Total Vote	Republican	Democratic	Other	Rep.-Dem. Plurality		Percentage			
								Total Vote		Major	Vote
								Rep.	Dem.	Rep.	Dem.
6,476	HOULTON	2,779	2,153	625	1	1,528	R	77.5%	22.5%	77.5%	22.5%
4,985	JAY	2,664	1,411	1,253		158	R	53.0%	47.0%	53.0%	47.0%
10,476	KENNEBUNK	6,879	4,217	2,659	3	1,558	R	61.3%	38.7%	61.3%	38.7%
9,543	KITTERY	5,060	2,724	2,332	4	392	R	53.8%	46.1%	53.9%	46.1%
35,690	LEWISTON	16,874	9,267	7,604	3	1,663	R	54.9%	45.1%	54.9%	45.1%
2,361	LIMESTONE	966	695	271		424	R	71.9%	28.1%	71.9%	28.1%
5,221	LINCOLN TOWN	2,470	1,792	676	2	1,116	R	72.6%	27.4%	72.6%	27.4%
9,077	LISBON	4,806	3,244	1,562		1,682	R	67.5%	32.5%	67.5%	32.5%
5,203	MILLINOCKET	2,611	1,634	977		657	R	62.6%	37.4%	62.6%	37.4%
5,959	OAKLAND	3,312	2,214	1,098		1,116	R	66.8%	33.2%	66.8%	33.2%
8,856	OLD ORCHARD BEACH	5,225	2,826	2,391	8	435	R	54.1%	45.8%	54.2%	45.8%
8,130	OLD TOWN	4,164	2,453	1,709	2	744	R	58.9%	41.0%	58.9%	41.1%
9,112	ORONO	5,628	2,827	2,795	6	32	R	50.2%	49.7%	50.3%	49.7%
62,249	PORTLAND	36,127	13,689	22,237	201	8,548	D	37.9%	61.6%	38.1%	61.9%
9,511	PRESQUE ISLE	4,595	3,398	1,197		2,201	R	73.9%	26.1%	73.9%	26.1%
7,609	ROCKLAND	3,555	1,915	1,636	4	279	R	53.9%	46.0%	53.9%	46.1%
6,472	RUMFORD	3,017	1,589	1,428		161	R	52.7%	47.3%	52.7%	47.3%
16,822	SACO	9,832	5,537	4,295		1,242	R	56.3%	43.7%	56.3%	43.7%
20,806	SANFORD	9,581	5,712	3,869		1,843	R	59.6%	40.4%	59.6%	40.4%
16,970	SCARBOROUGH	11,604	7,390	4,214		3,176	R	63.7%	36.3%	63.7%	36.3%
8,824	SKOWHEGAN	4,136	2,441	1,695		746	R	59.0%	41.0%	59.0%	41.0%
6,671	SOUTH BERWICK	3,976	2,400	1,576		824	R	60.4%	39.6%	60.4%	39.6%
23,324	SOUTH PORTLAND	14,060	6,724	7,311	25	587	D	47.8%	52.0%	47.9%	52.1%
9,285	STANDISH	5,422	3,587	1,835		1,752	R	66.2%	33.8%	66.2%	33.8%
9,100	TOPSHAM	5,383	3,404	1,979		1,425	R	63.2%	36.8%	63.2%	36.8%
15,605	WATERVILLE	7,202	3,572	3,628	2	56	D	49.6%	50.4%	49.6%	50.4%
9,400	WELLS	5,826	3,836	1,982	8	1,854	R	65.8%	34.0%	65.9%	34.1%
16,142	WESTBROOK	8,772	4,879	3,892	1	987	R	55.6%	44.4%	55.6%	44.4%
14,904	WINDHAM	9,144	5,921	3,217	6	2,704	R	64.8%	35.2%	64.8%	35.2%
7,743	WINSLOW	4,350	2,714	1,636		1,078	R	62.4%	37.6%	62.4%	37.6%
6,232	WINTHROP	3,646	2,468	1,178		1,290	R	67.7%	32.3%	67.7%	32.3%
8,360	YARMOUTH	5,392	3,137	2,250	5	887	R	58.2%	41.7%	58.2%	41.8%
12,854	YORK TOWN	8,337	4,935	3,390	12	1,545	R	59.2%	40.7%	59.3%	40.7%

MAINE

HOUSE OF REPRESENTATIVES

			Republican		Democratic		Other	Rep.-Dem.	Percentage			
		Total							Total Vote		Major Vote	
CD	Year	Vote	Vote	Candidate	Vote	Candidate	Vote	Plurality	Rep.	Dem.	Rep.	Dem.
1	2008	374,559	168,930	SUMMERS, CHARLES E.	205,629	PINGREE, CHELLIE		36,699 D	45.1%	54.9%	45.1%	54.9%
1	2006	280,987	88,009	CURLEY, DARLENE J.	170,949	ALLEN, TOM*	22,029	82,940 D	31.3%	60.8%	34.0%	66.0%
1	2004	366,740	147,663	SUMMERS, CHARLES E.	219,077	ALLEN, TOM*		71,414 D	40.3%	59.7%	40.3%	59.7%
2	2008	335,542	109,268	FRARY, JOHN N.	226,274	MICHAUD, MICHAEL H.*		117,006 D	32.6%	67.4%	32.6%	67.4%
2	2006	254,878	75,146	D'AMBOISE, LAURENCE S.	179,732	MICHAUD, MICHAEL H.*		104,586 D	29.5%	70.5%	29.5%	70.5%
2	2004	343,436	135,547	HAMEL, BRIAN N.	199,303	MICHAUD, MICHAEL H.*	8,586	63,756 D	39.5%	58.0%	40.5%	59.5%
TOTAL	2008	710,101	278,198		431,903			153,705 D	39.2%	60.8%	39.2%	60.8%
TOTAL	2006	535,865	163,155		350,681		22,029	187,526 D	30.4%	65.4%	31.8%	68.2%
TOTAL	2004	710,176	283,210		418,380		8,586	135,170 D	39.9%	58.9%	40.4%	59.6%
TOTAL	2002	495,294	205,780		289,514		—	83,734 D	41.5%	58.5%	41.5%	58.5%

Note: An asterisk (*) denotes incumbent.

MAINE

GENERAL AND PRIMARY ELECTIONS

2008 GENERAL ELECTIONS

President　　Other vote was 10,636 Independent (Ralph Nader); 2,900 Green Independent (Cynthia A. McKinney); 251 Libertarian write-in (Bob Barr); 177 Constitution write-in (Chuck Baldwin); 3 HeartQuake '08 write-in (Jonathan Allen).

Senator　　Other vote was 620 write-in.

House　　Other vote was:

　CD 1
　CD 2

2008 PRIMARY ELECTIONS

Primary　　June 10, 2008　　**Registration**
　　　　　　　　　　　　　　　　(as of November 2006)

Democratic	309,525
Republican	279,641
Green Independent	29,347
Unenrolled	375,235
TOTAL	993,748

Primary Type　　Semi-open—Registered voters in a political party could participate only in their party's primary. "Unenrolled" and new voters could vote in either party's primary by enrolling in that party on primary day.

MAINE

GENERAL AND PRIMARY ELECTIONS

	REPUBLICAN PRIMARIES			DEMOCRATIC PRIMARIES		
Senator	Susan Collins*	56,304	100.0%	Tom Allen	69,932	85.6%
	Edward L. Cohen (write-in)	19		Thomas J. Ledue	11,795	14.4%
	TOTAL	56,323		TOTAL	81,727	
Congressional District 1	Charles E. Summers	21,154	59.8%	Chellie Pingree	24,324	43.9%
	C. Peter Scontras	14,248	40.2%	Adam Roland Cote	15,706	28.4%
				Michael F. Brennan	6,040	10.9%
				Ethan King Strimling	5,833	10.5%
				Mark W. Lawrence	2,726	4.9%
				Stephen J. Meister	753	1.4%
	TOTAL	35,402		TOTAL	55,382	
Congressional District 2	John N. Frary	17,741	100.0%	Michael H. Michaud*	27,873	100.0%

Note: An asterisk (*) denotes incumbent.

MARYLAND

Congressional districts first established for elections held in 2002
8 members

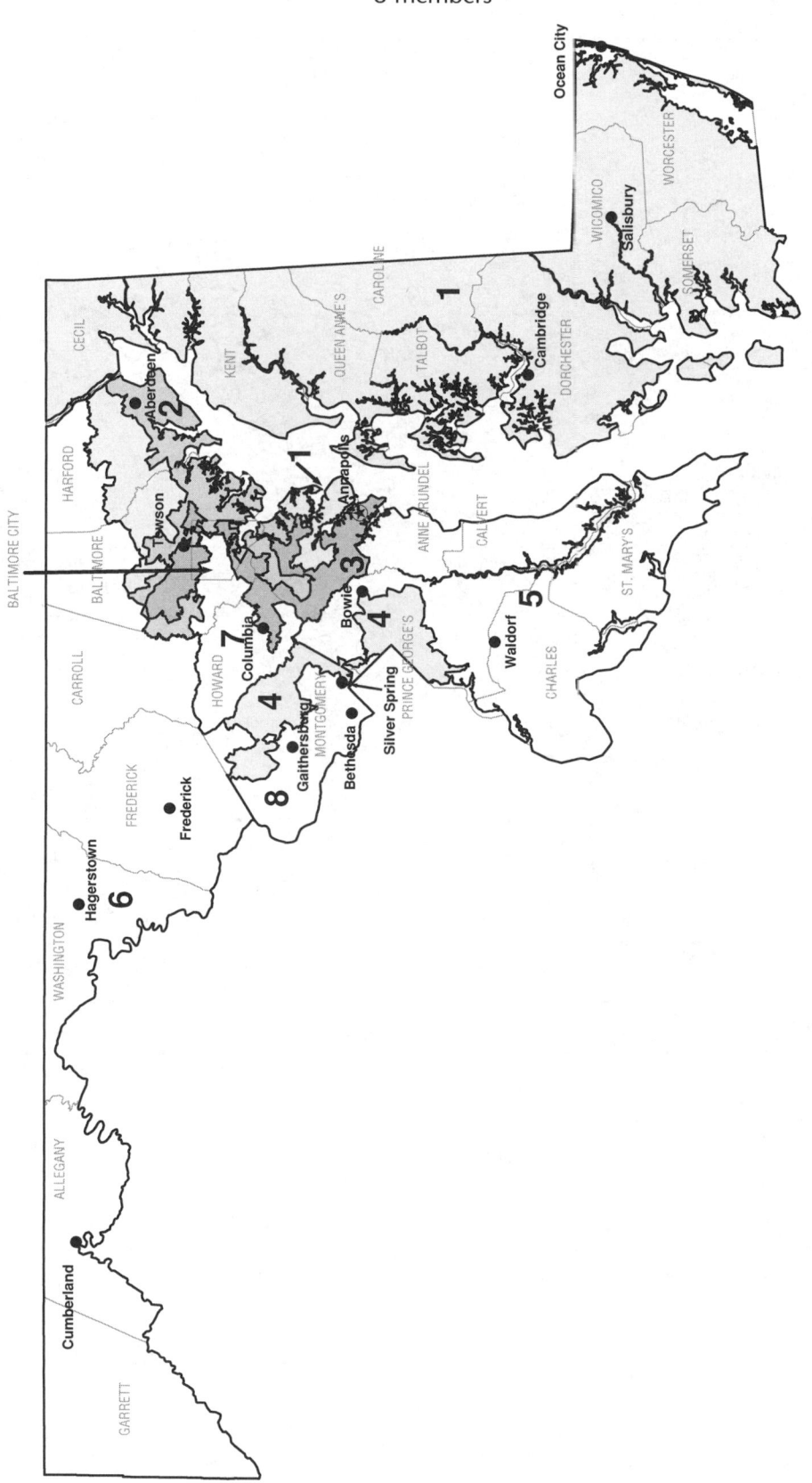

MARYLAND

Baltimore, Washington, D.C., Areas

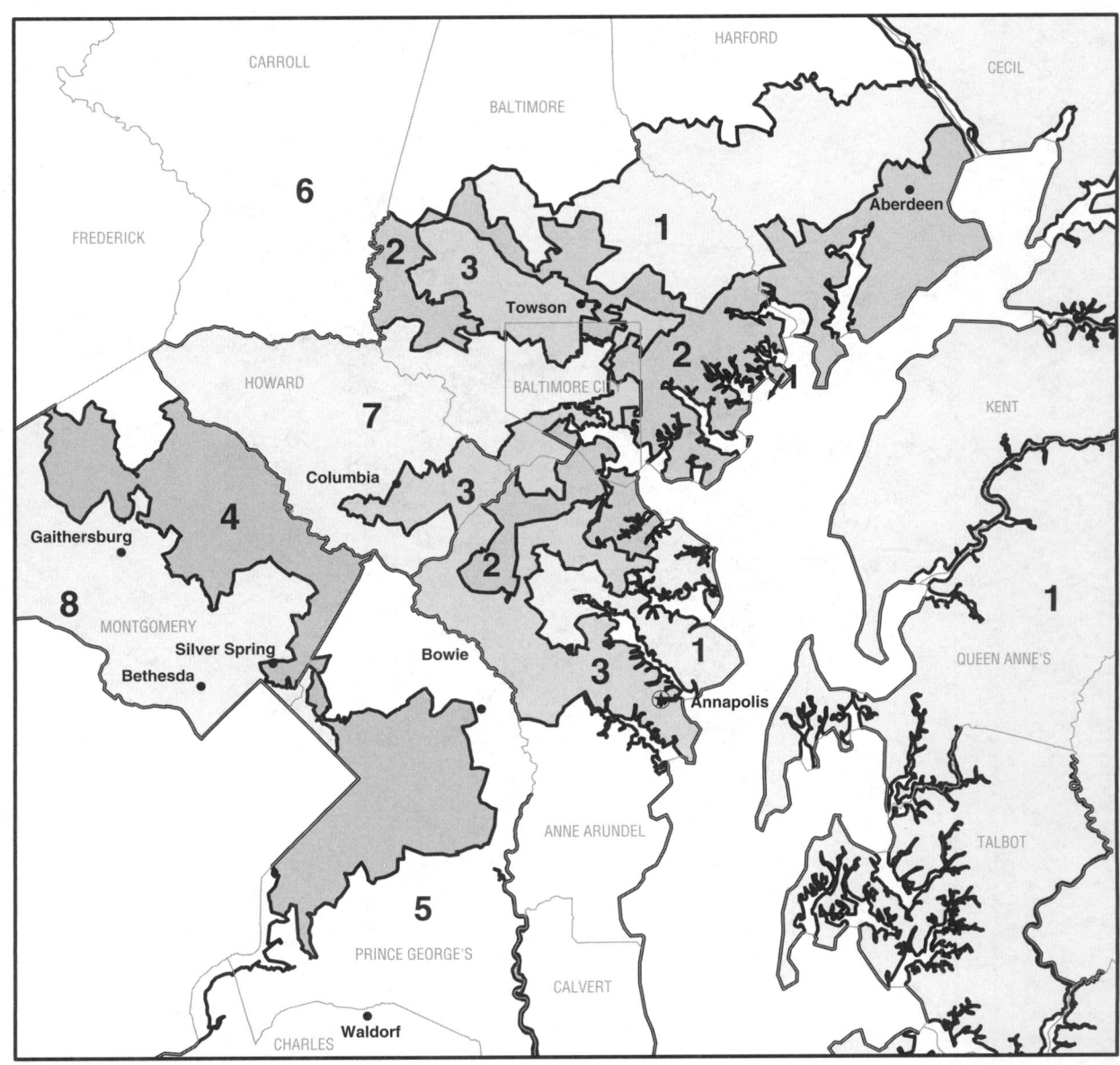

MARYLAND

GOVERNOR
Martin O'Malley (D). Elected 2006 to a four-year term.

SENATORS (2 Democrats)
Benjamin L. Cardin (D). Elected 2006 to a six-year term.

Barbara A. Mikulski (D). Reelected 2004 to a six-year term. Previously elected 1998, 1992, 1986.

REPRESENTATIVES (7 Democrats, 1 Republican)
1. Frank Kratovil Jr. (D)
2. C.A. Dutch Ruppersberger (D)
3. John P. Sarbanes (D)
4. Donna F. Edwards (D)
5. Steny H. Hoyer (D)
6. Roscoe G. Bartlett (R)
7. Elijah E. Cummings (D)
8. Chris Van Hollen (D)

POSTWAR VOTE FOR PRESIDENT

Year	Total Vote	Republican Vote	Republican Candidate	Democratic Vote	Democratic Candidate	Other Vote	Plurality	Total Vote Rep.	Total Vote Dem.	Major Vote Rep.	Major Vote Dem.
2008	2,631,596	959,862	McCain, John	1,629,467	Obama, Barack	42,267	669,605 D	36.5%	61.9%	37.1%	62.9%
2004	2,386,678	1,024,703	Bush, George W.	1,334,493	Kerry, John	27,482	309,790 D	42.9%	55.9%	43.4%	56.6%
2000**	2,020,480	813,797	Bush, George W.	1,140,782	Gore, Al	65,901	326,985 D	40.3%	56.5%	41.6%	58.4%
1996**	1,780,870	681,530	Dole, Bob	966,207	Clinton, Bill	133,133	284,677 D	38.3%	54.3%	41.4%	58.6%
1992**	1,985,046	707,094	Bush, George	988,571	Clinton, Bill	289,381	281,477 D	35.6%	49.8%	41.7%	58.3%
1988	1,714,358	876,167	Bush, George	826,304	Dukakis, Michael S.	11,887	49,863 R	51.1%	48.2%	51.5%	48.5%
1984	1,675,873	879,918	Reagan, Ronald	787,935	Mondale, Walter F.	8,020	91,983 R	52.5%	47.0%	52.8%	47.2%
1980**	1,540,496	680,606	Reagan, Ronald	726,161	Carter, Jimmy	133,729	45,555 D	44.2%	47.1%	48.4%	51.6%
1976	1,439,897	672,661	Ford, Gerald R.	759,612	Carter, Jimmy	7,624	86,951 D	46.7%	52.8%	47.0%	53.0%
1972	1,353,812	829,305	Nixon, Richard M.	505,781	McGovern, George S.	18,726	323,524 R	61.3%	37.4%	62.1%	37.9%
1968**	1,235,039	517,995	Nixon, Richard M.	538,310	Humphrey, Hubert H.	178,734	20,315 D	41.9%	43.6%	49.0%	51.0%
1964	1,116,457	385,495	Goldwater, Barry M.	730,912	Johnson, Lyndon B.	50	345,417 D	34.5%	65.5%	34.5%	65.5%
1960	1,055,349	489,538	Nixon, Richard M.	565,808	Kennedy, John F.	3	76,270 D	46.4%	53.6%	46.4%	53.6%
1956	932,827	559,738	Eisenhower, Dwight D.	372,613	Stevenson, Adlai E.	476	187,125 R	60.0%	39.9%	60.0%	40.0%
1952	902,074	499,424	Eisenhower, Dwight D.	395,337	Stevenson, Adlai E.	7,313	104,087 R	55.4%	43.8%	55.8%	44.2%
1948	596,748	294,814	Dewey, Thomas E.	286,521	Truman, Harry S.	15,413	8,293 R	49.4%	48.0%	50.7%	49.3%

**In past elections, the other vote included: 2000 - 53,768 Green (Ralph Nader); 1996 - 115,812 Reform (Ross Perot); 1992 - 281,414 Independent (Perot); 1980 - 119,537 Independent (John Anderson); 1968 - 178,734 American Independent (George Wallace).

MARYLAND

POSTWAR VOTE FOR GOVERNOR

Year	Total Vote	Republican Vote	Republican Candidate	Democratic Vote	Democratic Candidate	Other Vote	Rep.-Dem. Plurality	Total Vote Rep.	Total Vote Dem.	Major Vote Rep.	Major Vote Dem.
2006	1,788,316	825,464	Ehrlich, Robert L. Jr.	942,279	O'Malley, Martin	20,573	116,815 D	46.2%	52.7%	46.7%	53.3%
2002	1,706,179	879,592	Ehrlich, Robert L. Jr.	813,422	Townsend, Kathleen Kennedy	13,165	66,170 R	51.6%	47.7%	52.0%	48.0%
1998	1,535,978	688,357	Sauerbrey, Ellen R.	846,972	Glendening, Parris N.	649	158,615 D	44.8%	55.1%	44.8%	55.2%
1994	1,410,300	702,101	Sauerbrey, Ellen R.	708,094	Glendening, Parris N.	105	5,993 D	49.8%	50.2%	49.8%	50.2%
1990	1,111,088	446,980	Shepard, William S.	664,015	Schaefer, William D.	93	217,035 D	40.2%	59.8%	40.2%	59.8%
1986	1,101,476	194,185	Mooney, Thomas J.	907,291	Schaefer, William D.		713,106 D	17.6%	82.4%	17.6%	82.4%
1982	1,139,149	432,826	Pascal, Robert A.	705,910	Hughes, Harry	413	273,084 D	38.0%	62.0%	38.0%	62.0%
1978	1,011,963	293,635	Beall, J. Glenn, Jr.	718,328	Hughes, Harry		424,693 D	29.0%	71.0%	29.0%	71.0%
1974	949,097	346,449	Gore, Louise	602,648	Mandel, Marvin		256,199 D	36.5%	63.5%	36.5%	63.5%
1970	973,099	314,336	Blain, C. Stanley	639,579	Mandel, Marvin	19,184	325,243 D	32.3%	65.7%	33.0%	67.0%
1966	918,761	455,318	Agnew, Spiro T.	373,543	Mahoney, George P.	89,900	81,775 R	49.6%	40.7%	54.9%	45.1%
1962	775,101	343,051	Small, Frank	432,045	Tawes, J. Millard	5	88,994 D	44.3%	55.7%	44.3%	55.7%
1958	763,234	278,173	Devereux, James	485,061	Tawes, J. Millard		206,888 D	36.4%	63.6%	36.4%	63.6%
1954	700,484	381,451	McKeldin, Theodore	319,033	Byrd, Harry C.		62,418 R	54.5%	45.5%	54.5%	45.5%
1950	645,631	369,807	McKeldin, Theodore	275,824	Lane, William P.		93,983 R	57.3%	42.7%	57.3%	42.7%
1946	489,836	221,752	McKeldin, Theodore	268,084	Lane, William P.		46,332 D	45.3%	54.7%	45.3%	54.7%

POSTWAR VOTE FOR SENATOR

Year	Total Vote	Republican Vote	Republican Candidate	Democratic Vote	Democratic Candidate	Other Vote	Rep.-Dem. Plurality	Total Vote Rep.	Total Vote Dem.	Major Vote Rep.	Major Vote Dem.
2006	1,781,139	787,182	Steele, Michael S.	965,477	Cardin, Benjamin L.	28,480	178,295 D	44.2%	54.2%	44.9%	55.1%
2004	2,323,183	783,055	Pipkin, E.J.	1,504,691	Mikulski, Barbara A.	35,437	721,636 D	33.7%	64.8%	34.2%	65.8%
2000	1,946,898	715,178	Rappaport, Paul	1,230,013	Sarbanes, Paul S.	1,707	514,835 D	36.7%	63.2%	36.8%	63.2%
1998	1,507,447	444,637	Pierpont, Ross Z.	1,062,810	Mikulski, Barbara A.		618,173 D	29.5%	70.5%	29.5%	70.5%
1994	1,369,104	559,908	Brock, William E.	809,125	Sarbanes, Paul S.	71	249,217 D	40.9%	59.1%	40.9%	59.1%
1992	1,841,735	533,688	Keyes, Alan L.	1,307,610	Mikulski, Barbara A.	437	773,922 D	29.0%	71.0%	29.0%	71.0%
1988	1,617,065	617,537	Keyes, Alan L.	999,166	Sarbanes, Paul S.	362	381,629 D	38.2%	61.8%	38.2%	61.8%
1986	1,112,637	437,411	Chavez, Linda	675,225	Mikulski, Barbara A.	1	237,814 D	39.3%	60.7%	39.3%	60.7%
1982	1,114,690	407,334	Hogan, Lawrence J.	707,356	Sarbanes, Paul S.		300,022 D	36.5%	63.5%	36.5%	63.5%
1980	1,286,088	850,970	Mathias, Charles	435,118	Conroy, Edward T.		415,852 R	66.2%	33.8%	66.2%	33.8%
1976	1,365,568	530,439	Beall, J. Glenn, Jr.	772,101	Sarbanes, Paul S.	63,028	241,662 D	38.8%	56.5%	40.7%	59.3%
1974	877,786	503,223	Mathias, Charles	374,563	Mikulski, Barbara A.		128,660 R	57.3%	42.7%	57.3%	42.7%
1970	956,370	484,960	Beall, J. Glenn, Jr.	460,422	Tydings, Joseph D.	10,988	24,538 R	50.7%	48.1%	51.3%	48.7%
1968**	1,133,727	541,893	Mathias, Charles	443,367	Brewster, Daniel B.	148,467	98,526 R	47.8%	39.1%	55.0%	45.0%
1964	1,081,049	402,393	Beall, J. Glenn	678,649	Tydings, Joseph D.	7	276,256 D	37.2%	62.8%	37.2%	62.8%
1962	714,248	270,312	Miller, Edward T.	443,935	Brewster, Daniel B.	1	173,623 D	37.8%	62.2%	37.8%	62.2%
1958	749,291	382,021	Beall, J. Glenn	367,270	D'Alesandro, Thomas		14,751 R	51.0%	49.0%	51.0%	49.0%
1956	892,167	473,059	Butler, John Marshall	419,108	Mahoney, George P.		53,951 R	53.0%	47.0%	53.0%	47.0%
1952	856,193	449,823	Beall, J. Glenn	406,370	Mahoney, George P.		43,453 R	52.5%	47.5%	52.5%	47.5%
1950	615,614	326,291	Butler, John Marshall	283,180	Tydings, Millard E.	6,143	43,111 R	53.0%	46.0%	53.5%	46.5%
1946	472,232	235,000	Markey, David John	237,232	O'Conor, Herbert R.		2,232 D	49.8%	50.2%	49.8%	50.2%

**In past elections, the other vote included: 1968 - 148,467 Independent (George P. Mahoney).

MARYLAND

PRESIDENT 2008

2000 Census Population	County	Total Vote	Republican	Democratic	Other	Rep.-Dem. Plurality	Percentage Total Vote Rep.	Dem.	Major Vote Rep.	Dem.
74,930	ALLEGANY	29,742	18,405	10,693	644	7,712 R	61.9%	36.0%	63.3%	36.7%
489,656	ANNE ARUNDEL	259,619	129,682	125,015	4,922	4,667 R	50.0%	48.2%	50.9%	49.1%
651,154	BALTIMORE CITY	245,968	28,681	214,385	2,902	185,704 D	11.7%	87.2%	11.8%	88.2%
754,292	BALTIMORE COUNTY	380,938	158,714	214,151	8,073	55,437 D	41.7%	56.2%	42.6%	57.4%
74,563	CALVERT	44,057	23,095	20,299	663	2,796 R	52.4%	46.1%	53.2%	46.8%
29,772	CAROLINE	13,218	8,015	4,971	232	3,044 R	60.6%	37.6%	61.7%	38.3%
150,897	CARROLL	84,760	54,503	28,060	2,197	26,443 R	64.3%	33.1%	66.0%	34.0%
85,951	CECIL	42,494	23,855	17,665	974	6,190 R	56.1%	41.6%	57.5%	42.5%
120,546	CHARLES	70,127	25,732	43,635	760	17,903 D	36.7%	62.2%	37.1%	62.9%
30,674	DORCHESTER	15,274	8,168	6,912	194	1,256 R	53.5%	45.3%	54.2%	45.8%
195,277	FREDERICK	111,186	55,170	54,013	2,003	1,157 R	49.6%	48.6%	50.5%	49.5%
29,846	GARRETT	12,872	8,903	3,736	233	5,167 R	69.2%	29.0%	70.4%	29.6%
218,590	HARFORD	123,295	71,751	48,552	2,992	23,199 R	58.2%	39.4%	59.6%	40.4%
247,842	HOWARD	145,233	55,393	87,120	2,720	31,727 D	38.1%	60.0%	38.9%	61.1%
19,197	KENT	10,020	4,905	4,953	162	48 D	49.0%	49.4%	49.8%	50.2%
873,341	MONTGOMERY	439,261	118,608	314,444	6,209	195,836 D	27.0%	71.6%	27.4%	72.6%
801,515	PRINCE GEORGES	374,026	38,833	332,396	2,797	293,563 D	10.4%	88.9%	10.5%	89.5%
40,563	QUEEN ANNES	24,045	15,087	8,575	383	6,512 R	62.7%	35.7%	63.8%	36.2%
86,211	ST. MARYS	44,409	24,705	19,023	681	5,682 R	55.6%	42.8%	56.5%	43.5%
24,747	SOMERSET	9,924	5,037	4,779	108	258 R	50.8%	48.2%	51.3%	48.7%
33,812	TALBOT	20,328	10,995	9,035	298	1,960 R	54.1%	44.4%	54.9%	45.1%
131,923	WASHINGTON	61,600	34,169	26,245	1,186	7,924 R	55.5%	42.6%	56.6%	43.4%
84,644	WICOMICO	41,854	21,849	19,436	569	2,413 R	52.2%	46.4%	52.9%	47.1%
46,543	WORCESTER	27,346	15,607	11,374	365	4,233 R	57.1%	41.6%	57.8%	42.2%
5,296,486	TOTAL	2,631,596	959,862	1,629,467	42,267	669,605 D	36.5%	61.9%	37.1%	62.9%

MARYLAND

HOUSE OF REPRESENTATIVES

			Republican		Democratic		Other	Rep.-Dem.	Percentage			
									Total Vote		Major Vote	
CD	Year	Total Vote	Vote	Candidate	Vote	Candidate	Vote	Plurality	Rep.	Dem.	Rep.	Dem.
1	2008	360,480	174,213	HARRIS, ANDY	177,065	KRATOVIL, FRANK JR.	9,202	2,852 D	48.3%	49.1%	49.6%	50.4%
1	2006	269,147	185,177	GILCHREST, WAYNE T.*	83,738	CORWIN, JIM	232	101,439 R	68.8%	31.1%	68.9%	31.1%
1	2004	323,526	245,149	GILCHREST, WAYNE T.*	77,872	ALEXAKIS, KOSTAS	505	167,277 R	75.8%	24.1%	75.9%	24.1%
1	2002	250,413	192,004	GILCHREST, WAYNE T.*	57,986	TAMLYN, ANN D.	423	134,018 R	76.7%	23.2%	76.8%	23.2%
2	2008	276,333	68,561	MATTHEWS, RICHARD PRYCE	198,578	RUPPERSBERGER, C.A. DUTCH*	9,194	130,017 D	24.8%	71.9%	25.7%	74.3%
2	2006	196,228	60,195	MATHIS, JIMMY	135,818	RUPPERSBERGER, C.A. DUTCH*	215	75,623 D	30.7%	69.2%	30.7%	69.3%
2	2004	247,295	75,812	BROOKS, JANE	164,751	RUPPERSBERGER, C.A. DUTCH*	6,732	88,939 D	30.7%	66.6%	31.5%	68.5%
2	2002	195,202	88,954	BENTLEY, HELEN DELICH	105,718	RUPPERSBERGER, C.A. DUTCH	530	16,764 D	45.6%	54.2%	45.7%	54.3%
3	2008	292,448	87,971	HARRIS, THOMAS E. "PINKSTON"	203,711	SARBANES, JOHN P.*	766	115,740 D	30.1%	69.7%	30.2%	69.8%
3	2006	234,486	79,174	WHITE, JOHN	150,142	SARBANES, JOHN P.	5,170	70,968 D	33.8%	64.0%	34.5%	65.5%
3	2004	287,219	97,008	DUCKWORTH, ROBERT P.	182,066	CARDIN, BENJAMIN L.*	8,145	85,058 D	33.8%	63.4%	34.8%	65.2%
3	2002	221,543	75,721	CONWELL, SCOTT	145,589	CARDIN, BENJAMIN L.*	233	69,868 D	34.2%	65.7%	34.2%	65.8%
4	2008	301,431	38,739	JAMES, PETER	258,704	EDWARDS, DONNA F.*	3,988	219,965 D	12.9%	85.8%	13.0%	87.0%
4	2006	175,903	32,792	STARKMAN, MICHAEL MOSHE	141,897	WYNN, ALBERT R.*	1,214	109,105 D	18.6%	80.7%	18.8%	81.2%
4	2004	261,860	52,907	McKINNIS, JOHN	196,809	WYNN, ALBERT R.*	12,144	143,902 D	20.2%	75.2%	21.2%	78.8%
4	2002	167,555	34,890	KIMBLE, JOHN B.	131,644	WYNN, ALBERT R.*	1,021	96,754 D	20.8%	78.6%	21.0%	79.0%
5	2008	344,691	82,631	BAILEY, COLLINS	253,854	HOYER, STENY H.*	8,206	171,223 D	24.0%	73.6%	24.6%	75.4%
5	2006	203,323			168,114	HOYER, STENY H.*	35,209	168,114 D		82.7%		100.0%
5	2004	298,335	87,189	JEWITT, BRAD	204,867	HOYER, STENY H.*	6,279	117,678 D	29.2%	68.7%	29.9%	70.1%
5	2002	199,087	60,758	CRAWFORD, JOSEPH T.	137,903	HOYER, STENY H.*	426	77,145 D	30.5%	69.3%	30.6%	69.4%
6	2008	330,535	190,926	BARTLETT, ROSCOE G.*	128,207	DOUGHERTY, JENNIFER P.	11,402	62,719 R	57.8%	38.8%	59.8%	40.2%
6	2006	239,453	141,200	BARTLETT, ROSCOE G.*	92,030	DUCK, ANDREW	6,223	49,170 R	59.0%	38.4%	60.5%	39.5%
6	2004	305,857	206,076	BARTLETT, ROSCOE G.*	90,108	BOSLEY, KENNETH T.	9,673	115,968 R	67.4%	29.5%	69.6%	30.4%
6	2002	223,611	147,825	BARTLETT, ROSCOE G.*	75,575	DeARMON, DONALD M.	211	72,250 R	66.1%	33.8%	66.2%	33.8%
7	2008	286,020	53,147	HARGADON, MICHAEL T.	227,379	CUMMINGS, ELIJAH E.*	5,494	174,232 D	18.6%	79.5%	18.9%	81.1%
7	2006	161,977		—	158,830	CUMMINGS, ELIJAH E.*	3,147	158,830 D		98.1%		100.0%
7	2004	244,183	60,102	SALAZAR, TONY	179,189	CUMMINGS, ELIJAH E.*	4,892	119,087 D	24.6%	73.4%	25.1%	74.9%
7	2002	186,394	49,172	WARD, JOSEPH E.	137,047	CUMMINGS, ELIJAH E.*	175	87,875 D	26.4%	73.5%	26.4%	73.6%
8	2008	306,014	66,351	HUDSON, STEVE	229,740	VAN HOLLEN, CHRIS*	9,923	163,389 D	21.7%	75.1%	22.4%	77.6%
8	2006	220,685	48,324	STEIN, JEFFREY M.	168,872	VAN HOLLEN, CHRIS*	3,489	120,548 D	21.9%	76.5%	22.2%	77.8%
8	2004	287,680	71,989	FLOYD, CHUCK	215,129	VAN HOLLEN, CHRIS*	562	143,140 D	25.0%	74.8%	25.1%	74.9%
8	2002	218,113	103,587	MORELLA, CONSTANCE A.*	112,788	VAN HOLLEN, CHRIS	1,738	9,201 D	47.5%	51.7%	47.9%	52.1%
TOTAL	2008	2,497,952	762,539		1,677,238		58,175	914,699 D	30.5%	67.1%	31.3%	68.7%
TOTAL	2006	1,701,202	546,862		1,099,441		54,899	552,579 D	32.1%	64.6%	33.2%	66.8%
TOTAL	2004	2,255,955	896,232		1,310,791		48,932	414,559 D	39.7%	58.1%	40.6%	59.4%
TOTAL	2002	1,661,918	752,911		904,250		4,757	151,339 D	45.3%	54.4%	45.4%	54.6%

Note: An asterisk (*) denotes incumbent.

MARYLAND

GENERAL AND PRIMARY ELECTIONS

2008 GENERAL ELECTIONS

President Other vote was 14,713 Independent (Ralph Nader); 9,842 Libertarian (Bob Barr); 4,747 Green (Cynthia A. McKinney); 3,760 Constitution (Chuck Baldwin); 103 write-in (Alan Keyes); 17 write-in (Donald K. Allen); 12 write-in (Blaine Taylor); 10 write-in (Brian Moore); 8 write-in (Joe Schriner); 4 write-in (Lynne A. Starr); 2 write-in (RaeDeen R. Heupel); 2 write-in (Frank Moore); 1 write-in (Jose M. Aparicio); 1 write-in (Theodis "Ted" Brown Sr.); 1 write-in (Ronald G. Hobbs); 1 write-in (Charles Jay); 9,043 scattered write-in.

House Other vote was:

CD 1 8,873 Libertarian (Richard James Davis); 329 scattered write-in.
CD 2 8,786 Libertarian (Lorenzo Gaztanaga); 408 scattered write-in.
CD 3 766 scattered write-in.
CD 4 3,384 Libertarian (Thibeaux Lincecum); 75 write-in (Steve Schulin); 48 write-in (Bobby Broadus); 28 write-in (Darryn O'Shea Jackson Sr.); 453 scattered write-in.
CD 5 7,829 Libertarian (Darlene H. Nicholas); 377 scattered write-in.
CD 6 11,060 Libertarian (Gary W. Hoover Sr.); 342 scattered write-in.
CD 7 5,214 Libertarian (Ronald M. Owens-Bey); 13 write-in (Ray Bly); 8 write-in (Charles U. Smith); 259 scattered write-in.
CD 8 6,828 Green (Gordon Clark); 2,562 Libertarian (Ian Thomas); 188 write-in (Deborah A. Vollmer); 28 write-in (Lih Young); 317 scattered write-in.

2008 PRIMARY ELECTIONS

Primary February 12, 2008

Registration (active registrants as of January 22, 2008)

Democratic	1,733,102
Republican	889,849
Green	8,048
Libertarian	5,279
Unaffiliated & Other	499,495
TOTAL	3,135,773

Primary Type Closed—Only registered Democrats and Republicans could vote in their party's primary.

	REPUBLICAN PRIMARIES			DEMOCRATIC PRIMARIES		
President	John McCain	176,046	54.8%	Barack Obama	532,665	60.7%
	Mike Huckabee	91,608	28.5%	Hillary Clinton	314,211	35.8%
	Mitt Romney	22,426	7.0%	Uncommitted	11,417	1.3%
	Ron Paul	19,196	6.0%	John Edwards	10,506	1.2%
	Rudolph Giuliani	4,548	1.4%	Joseph R. Biden Jr.	3,776	0.4%
	Alan Keyes	3,386	1.1%	Bill Richardson	2,098	0.2%
	Fred Thompson	2,901	0.9%	Dennis J. Kucinich	1,909	0.2%
	Duncan Hunter	522	0.2%	Mike Gravel	804	0.1%
	Tom Tancredo	356	0.1%	Christopher J. Dodd	788	0.1%
	TOTAL	320,989		TOTAL	878,174	
Congressional District 1	Andy Harris	33,627	43.4%	Frank Kratovil Jr.	28,566	40.2%
	Wayne T. Gilchrest*	25,624	33.1%	Christopher Robert Robinson	21,892	30.8%
	E.J. Pipken	15,700	20.3%	Steve Harper	11,904	16.7%
	Joe Arminio	1,277	1.6%	Joseph Werner	8,753	12.3%
	Robert Joseph Banks	1,186	1.5%			
	TOTAL	77,414		TOTAL	71,115	

MARYLAND

GENERAL AND PRIMARY ELECTIONS

REPUBLICAN PRIMARIES			DEMOCRATIC PRIMARIES		
Congressional District 2	Richard Pryce Matthews	15,451	100.0%	C.A. Dutch Ruppersberger*	60,631	100.0%
Congressional District 3	Thomas E. "Pinkston" Harris	10,346	38.9%	John P. Sarbanes*	86,598	89.1%
	John Stafford	8,576	32.2%	John M. Rea	10,614	10.9%
	Christopher Panasuk	3,953	14.9%			
	Paul Spause	3,721	14.0%			
	TOTAL	26,596		TOTAL	97,212	
Congressional District 4	Peter James	4,912	39.0%	Donna F. Edwards	78,008	58.9%
	Michael Moshe Starkman	3,200	25.4%	Albert R. Wynn*	48,885	36.9%
	Robert Broadus	2,748	21.8%	George E. Mitchell	1,737	1.3%
	Vincent Martorano	1,722	13.7%	Michael Babula	1,429	1.1%
				Jason Jennings	1,429	1.1%
				George E. McDermott	1,046	0.8%
	TOTAL	12,582		TOTAL	132,534	
Congressional District 5	Collins Bailey	12,382	44.0%	Steny H. Hoyer*	90,513	82.6%
	Mike Hethmon	8,126	28.9%	James Patrick Cusick Sr.	19,067	17.4%
	Jesse James Dann	7,619	27.1%			
	TOTAL	28,127		TOTAL	109,580	
Congressional District 6	Roscoe G. Bartlett*	51,635	77.6%	Jennifer P. Dougherty	25,967	44.2%
	Joseph T. Krysztoforski	5,686	8.5%	Andrew Duck	21,629	36.8%
	Tom Croft	4,895	7.4%	Robin L. Deibert	5,800	9.9%
	John B. Kimble	3,433	5.2%	Larry John Smith	4,162	7.1%
	Frank K. Nethken	857	1.3%	Rick Lank	1,222	2.1%
	TOTAL	66,506		TOTAL	58,780	
Congressional District 7	Michael T. Hargadon	10,588	73.2%	Elijah E. Cummings*	98,027	93.0%
	Ray Bly	3,875	26.8%	Charles Ulysses Smith	7,322	7.0%
	TOTAL	14,463		TOTAL	105,349	
Congressional District 8	Steve Hudson	8,683	37.4%	Chris Van Hollen*	104,108	87.8%
	Bruce Stern	5,763	24.8%	Deborah A. Vollmer	11,052	9.3%
	Brian Mezger	4,533	19.5%	Lih Young	3,391	2.9%
	Jay Roberts	2,843	12.3%			
	Meyer F. Marks	1,375	5.9%			
	TOTAL	23,197		TOTAL	118,551	

Note: An asterisk (*) denotes incumbent.

MASSACHUSETTS

Congressional districts first established for elections held in 2002
10 members

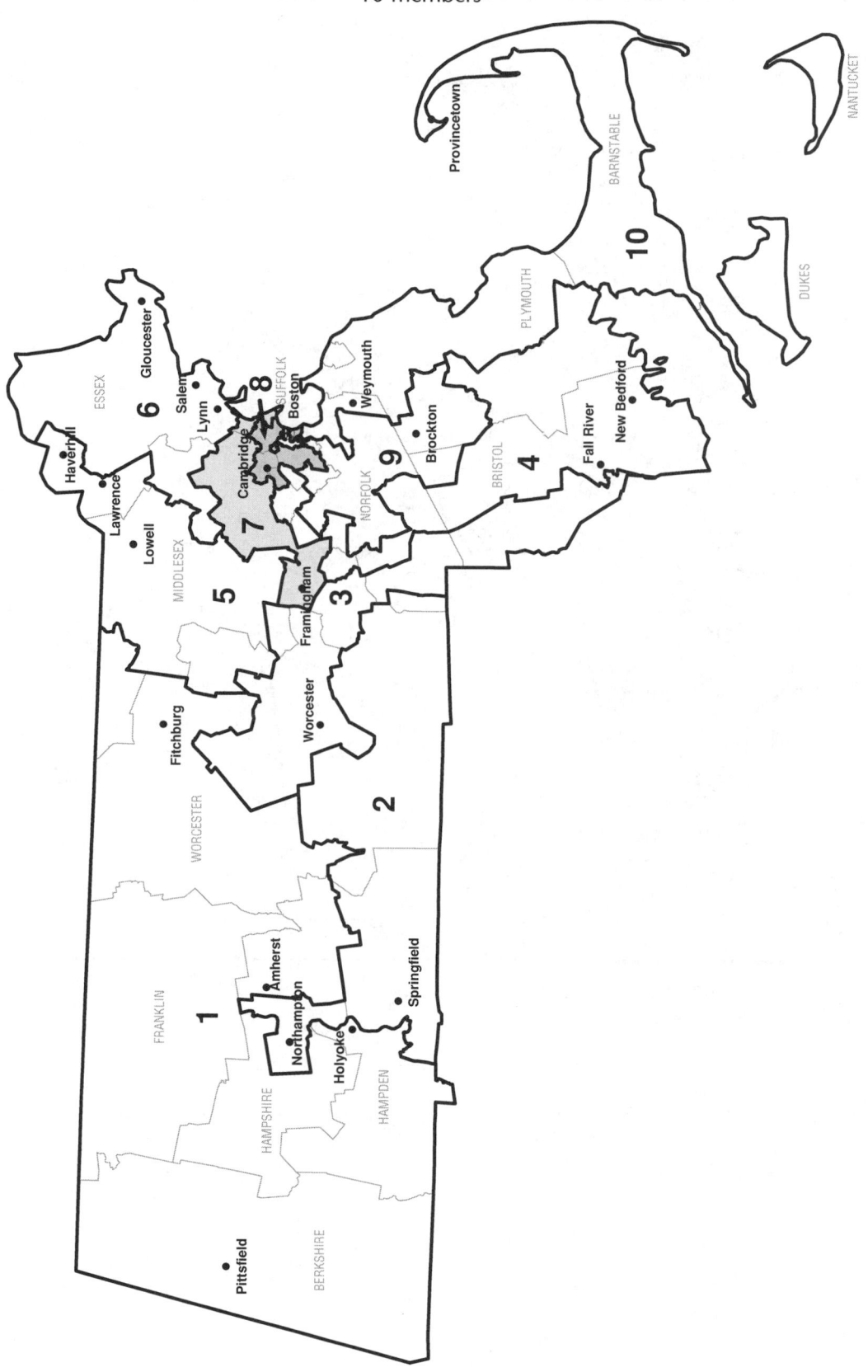

MASSACHUSETTS

Boston Area

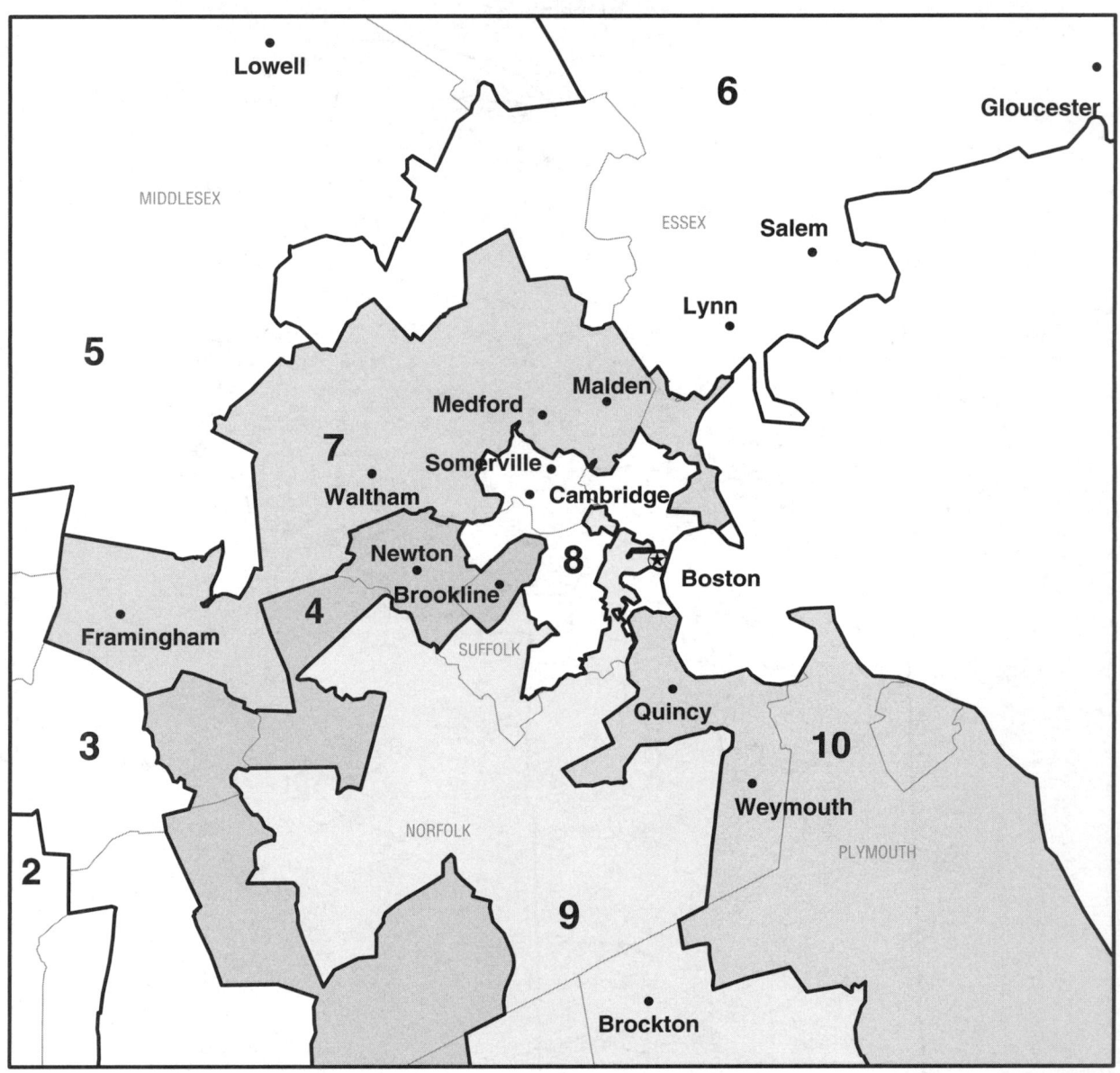

MASSACHUSETTS

GOVERNOR
Deval L. Patrick (D). Elected 2006 to a four-year term.

SENATORS (2 Democrats)
Edward M. Kennedy (D). Reelected 2006 to a six-year term. Previously elected 2000, 1994, 1988, 1982, 1976, 1970, 1964, and in 1962 to fill out the term vacated by the December 1960 resignation of Senator John F. Kennedy, who was elected President in November 1960.

John Kerry (D). Reelected 2008 to a six-year term. Previously elected 2002, 1996, 1990, 1984.

REPRESENTATIVES (10 Democrats)
1. John W. Olver (D)
2. Richard E. Neal (D)
3. Jim McGovern (D)
4. Barney Frank (D)
5. Niki Tsongas (D)
6. John F. Tierney (D)
7. Edward J. Markey (D)
8. Michael E. Capuano (D)
9. Stephen F. Lynch (D)
10. Bill Delahunt (D)

POSTWAR VOTE FOR PRESIDENT

Year	Total Vote	Republican Vote	Republican Candidate	Democratic Vote	Democratic Candidate	Other Vote	Plurality	Total Vote Rep.	Total Vote Dem.	Major Vote Rep.	Major Vote Dem.
2008	3,080,985	1,108,854	McCain, John	1,904,097	Obama, Barack	68,034	795,243 D	36.0%	61.8%	36.8%	63.2%
2004	2,912,388	1,071,109	Bush, George W.	1,803,800	Kerry, John	37,479	732,691 D	36.8%	61.9%	37.3%	62.7%
2000**	2,702,984	878,502	Bush, George W.	1,616,487	Gore, Al	207,995	737,985 D	32.5%	59.8%	35.2%	64.8%
1996**	2,556,785	718,107	Dole, Bob	1,571,763	Clinton, Bill	266,915	853,656 D	28.1%	61.5%	31.4%	68.6%
1992**	2,773,700	805,049	Bush, George	1,318,662	Clinton, Bill	649,989	513,613 D	29.0%	47.5%	37.9%	62.1%
1988	2,632,805	1,194,635	Bush, George	1,401,415	Dukakis, Michael S.	36,755	206,780 D	45.4%	53.2%	46.0%	54.0%
1984	2,559,453	1,310,936	Reagan, Ronald	1,239,606	Mondale, Walter F.	8,911	71,330 R	51.2%	48.4%	51.4%	48.6%
1980**	2,524,298	1,057,631	Reagan, Ronald	1,053,802	Carter, Jimmy	412,865	3,829 R	41.9%	41.7%	50.1%	49.9%
1976	2,547,558	1,030,276	Ford, Gerald R.	1,429,475	Carter, Jimmy	87,807	399,199 D	40.4%	56.1%	41.9%	58.1%
1972	2,458,756	1,112,078	Nixon, Richard M.	1,332,540	McGovern, George S.	14,138	220,462 D	45.2%	54.2%	45.5%	54.5%
1968**	2,331,752	766,844	Nixon, Richard M.	1,469,218	Humphrey, Hubert H.	95,690	702,374 D	32.9%	63.0%	34.3%	65.7%
1964	2,344,798	549,727	Goldwater, Barry M.	1,786,422	Johnson, Lyndon B.	8,649	1,236,695 D	23.4%	76.2%	23.5%	76.5%
1960	2,469,480	976,750	Nixon, Richard M.	1,487,174	Kennedy, John F.	5,556	510,424 D	39.6%	60.2%	39.6%	60.4%
1956	2,348,506	1,393,197	Eisenhower, Dwight D.	948,190	Stevenson, Adlai E.	7,119	445,007 R	59.3%	40.4%	59.5%	40.5%
1952	2,383,398	1,292,325	Eisenhower, Dwight D.	1,083,525	Stevenson, Adlai E.	7,548	208,800 R	54.2%	45.5%	54.4%	45.6%
1948	2,107,146	909,370	Dewey, Thomas E.	1,151,788	Truman, Harry S.	45,988	242,418 D	43.2%	54.7%	44.1%	55.9%

**In past elections, the other vote included: 2000 - 173,564 - Green (Ralph Nader); 1996 - 227,217 Reform (Ross Perot); 1992 - 630,731 Independent (Perot); 1980 - 382,539 Independent (John Anderson); 1968 - 87,088 American Independent (George Wallace).

MASSACHUSETTS

POSTWAR VOTE FOR GOVERNOR

Year	Total Vote	Republican Vote	Republican Candidate	Democratic Vote	Democratic Candidate	Other Vote	Rep.-Dem. Plurality	Percentage Total Vote Rep.	Dem.	Major Vote Rep.	Dem.
2006	2,219,779	784,342	Healey, Kerry	1,234,984	Patrick, Deval L.	200,453	450,642 D	35.3%	55.6%	38.8%	61.2%
2002	2,194,179	1,091,988	Romney, Mitt	985,981	O'Brien, Shannon P.	116,210	106,007 R	49.8%	44.9%	52.6%	47.4%
1998	1,903,336	967,160	Cellucci, Paul	901,843	Harshbarger, Scott	34,333	65,317 R	50.8%	47.4%	51.7%	48.3%
1994	2,164,318	1,533,430	Weld, William F.	611,650	Roosevelt, Mark	19,238	921,780 R	70.9%	28.3%	71.5%	28.5%
1990	2,342,927	1,175,817	Weld, William F.	1,099,878	Silber, John	67,232	75,939 R	50.2%	46.9%	51.7%	48.3%
1986	1,684,079	525,364	Kariotis, George	1,157,786	Dukakis, Michael S.	929	632,422 D	31.2%	68.7%	31.2%	68.8%
1982	2,050,254	749,679	Sears, John W.	1,219,109	Dukakis, Michael S.	81,466	469,430 D	36.6%	59.5%	38.1%	61.9%
1978	1,962,251	926,072	Hatch, Francis W.	1,030,294	King, Edward J.	5,885	104,222 D	47.2%	52.5%	47.3%	52.7%
1974	1,854,798	784,353	Sargent, Francis W.	992,284	Dukakis, Michael S.	78,161	207,931 D	42.3%	53.5%	44.1%	55.9%
1970	1,867,906	1,058,623	Sargent, Francis W.	799,269	White, Kevin H.	10,014	259,354 R	56.7%	42.8%	57.0%	43.0%
1966**	2,041,177	1,277,358	Volpe, John A.	752,720	McCormack, Edward J.	11,099	524,638 R	62.6%	36.9%	62.9%	37.1%
1964	2,340,130	1,176,462	Volpe, John A.	1,153,416	Bellotti, Francis X.	10,252	23,046 R	50.3%	49.3%	50.5%	49.5%
1962	2,109,089	1,047,891	Volpe, John A.	1,053,322	Peabody, Endicott	7,876	5,431 D	49.7%	49.9%	49.9%	50.1%
1960	2,417,133	1,269,295	Volpe, John A.	1,130,810	Ward, Joseph D.	17,028	138,485 R	52.5%	46.8%	52.9%	47.1%
1958	1,899,117	818,463	Gibbons, Charles	1,067,020	Furcolo, Foster	13,634	248,557 D	43.1%	56.2%	43.4%	56.6%
1956	2,339,884	1,096,759	Whittier, Sumner G.	1,234,618	Furcolo, Foster	8,507	137,859 D	46.9%	52.8%	47.0%	53.0%
1954	1,903,774	985,339	Herter, Christian A.	910,087	Murphy, Robert F.	8,348	75,252 R	51.8%	47.8%	52.0%	48.0%
1952	2,356,298	1,175,955	Herter, Christian A.	1,161,499	Dever, Paul A.	18,844	14,456 R	49.9%	49.3%	50.3%	49.7%
1950	1,910,180	824,069	Coolidge, Arthur W.	1,074,570	Dever, Paul A.	11,541	250,501 D	43.1%	56.3%	43.4%	56.6%
1948	2,099,250	849,895	Bradford, Robert F.	1,239,247	Dever, Paul A.	10,108	389,352 D	40.5%	59.0%	40.7%	59.3%
1946	1,683,452	911,152	Bradford, Robert F.	762,743	Tobin, Maurice	9,557	148,409 R	54.1%	45.3%	54.4%	45.6%

**The term of office of Massachusetts's governor was increased from two to four years effective with the 1966 election.

POSTWAR VOTE FOR SENATOR

Year	Total Vote	Republican Vote	Republican Candidate	Democratic Vote	Democratic Candidate	Other Vote	Rep.-Dem. Plurality	Percentage Total Vote Rep.	Dem.	Major Vote Rep.	Dem.
2008	2,994,247	926,044	Beatty, Jeffrey K.	1,971,974	Kerry, John	96,229	1,045,930 D	30.9%	65.9%	32.0%	68.0%
2006	2,165,490	661,532	Chase, Kenneth G.	1,500,738	Kennedy, Edward M.	3,220	839,206 D	30.5%	69.3%	30.6%	69.4%
2002**	2,006,758	—		1,605,976	Kerry, John	400,782	1,605,976 D		80.0%		100.0%
2000**	2,599,420	334,341	Robinson, Jack E.	1,889,494	Kennedy, Edward M.	375,585	1,555,153 D	12.9%	72.7%	15.0%	85.0%
1996	2,555,886	1,142,837	Weld, William F.	1,334,345	Kerry, John	78,704	191,508 D	44.7%	52.2%	46.1%	53.9%
1994	2,179,964	894,005	Romney, Mitt	1,266,011	Kennedy, Edward M.	19,948	372,006 D	41.0%	58.1%	41.4%	58.6%
1990	2,316,212	992,917	Rappaport, Jim	1,321,712	Kerry, John	1,583	328,795 D	42.9%	57.1%	42.9%	57.1%
1988	2,606,225	884,267	Malone, Joseph	1,693,344	Kennedy, Edward M.	28,614	809,077 D	33.9%	65.0%	34.3%	65.7%
1984	2,530,195	1,136,806	Shamie, Raymond	1,392,981	Kerry, John	408	256,175 D	44.9%	55.1%	44.9%	55.1%
1982	2,050,769	784,602	Shamie, Raymond	1,247,084	Kennedy, Edward M.	19,083	462,482 D	38.3%	60.8%	38.6%	61.4%
1978	1,985,700	890,584	Brooke, Edward W.	1,093,283	Tsongas, Paul E.	1,833	202,699 D	44.8%	55.1%	44.9%	55.1%
1976	2,491,255	722,641	Robertson, Michael	1,726,657	Kennedy, Edward M.	41,957	1,004,016 D	29.0%	69.3%	29.5%	70.5%
1972	2,370,676	1,505,932	Brooke, Edward W.	823,278	Droney, John J.	41,466	682,654 R	63.5%	34.7%	64.7%	35.3%
1970	1,935,607	715,978	Spaulding, Josiah A.	1,202,856	Kennedy, Edward M.	16,773	486,878 D	37.0%	62.1%	37.3%	62.7%
1966	1,999,949	1,213,473	Brooke, Edward W.	774,761	Peabody, Endicott	11,715	438,712 R	60.7%	38.7%	61.0%	39.0%
1964	2,312,028	587,663	Whitmore, Howard	1,716,907	Kennedy, Edward M.	7,458	1,129,244 D	25.4%	74.3%	25.5%	74.5%
1962S	2,097,085	877,669	Lodge, George C.	1,162,611	Kennedy, Edward M.	56,805	284,942 D	41.9%	55.4%	43.0%	57.0%
1960	2,417,813	1,358,556	Saltonstall, Leverett	1,050,725	O'Connor, Thomas J.	8,532	307,831 R	56.2%	43.5%	56.4%	43.6%
1958	1,862,041	488,318	Celeste, Vincent J.	1,362,926	Kennedy, John F.	10,797	874,608 D	26.2%	73.2%	26.4%	73.6%
1954	1,892,710	956,605	Saltonstall, Leverett	927,899	Furcolo, Foster	8,206	28,706 R	50.5%	49.0%	50.8%	49.2%
1952	2,360,425	1,141,247	Lodge, Henry Cabot	1,211,984	Kennedy, John F.	7,194	70,737 D	48.3%	51.3%	48.5%	51.5%
1948	2,055,798	1,088,475	Saltonstall, Leverett	954,398	Fitzgerald, John I.	12,925	134,077 R	52.9%	46.4%	53.3%	46.7%
1946	1,662,063	989,736	Lodge, Henry Cabot	660,200	Walsh, David I.	12,127	329,536 R	59.5%	39.7%	60.0%	40.0%

Notes: ** In past elections, the other vote included: 2002 - 369,807 Libertarian (Michael E. Cloud); 2000 - 308,748 Libertarian (Carla Howell). The Republican Party did not run a candidate in the 2002 Senate election. The 1962 election was for a short term to fill a vacancy.

MASSACHUSETTS

PRESIDENT 2008

2000 Census Population	County	Total Vote	Republican	Democratic	Other	Rep.-Dem. Plurality	Percentage			
							Total Vote		Major Vote	
							Rep.	Dem.	Rep.	Dem.
222,230	BARNSTABLE	132,270	55,694	74,264	2,312	18,570 D	42.1%	56.1%	42.9%	57.1%
134,953	BERKSHIRE	66,130	14,876	49,558	1,696	34,682 D	22.5%	74.9%	23.1%	76.9%
534,678	BRISTOL	243,120	90,531	146,861	5,728	56,330 D	37.2%	60.4%	38.1%	61.9%
14,987	DUKES	10,553	2,442	7,913	198	5,471 D	23.1%	75.0%	23.6%	76.4%
723,419	ESSEX	353,462	137,129	208,976	7,357	71,847 D	38.8%	59.1%	39.6%	60.4%
71,535	FRANKLIN	38,529	9,545	27,919	1,065	18,374 D	24.8%	72.5%	25.5%	74.5%
456,228	HAMPDEN	197,720	71,350	121,454	4,916	50,104 D	36.1%	61.4%	37.0%	63.0%
152,251	HAMPSHIRE	79,570	20,618	56,869	2,083	36,251 D	25.9%	71.5%	26.6%	73.4%
1,465,396	MIDDLESEX	726,031	245,766	464,484	15,781	218,718 D	33.9%	64.0%	34.6%	65.4%
9,520	NANTUCKET	6,052	1,863	4,073	116	2,210 D	30.8%	67.3%	31.4%	68.6%
650,308	NORFOLK	344,916	136,841	200,675	7,400	63,834 D	39.7%	58.2%	40.5%	59.5%
472,822	PLYMOUTH	249,817	112,904	131,817	5,096	18,913 D	45.2%	52.8%	46.1%	53.9%
689,807	SUFFOLK	269,221	57,194	207,127	4,900	149,933 D	21.2%	76.9%	21.6%	78.4%
750,963	WORCESTER	363,594	152,101	202,107	9,386	50,006 D	41.8%	55.6%	42.9%	57.1%
6,349,097	TOTAL	3,080,985	1,108,854	1,904,097	68,034	795,243 D	36.0%	61.8%	36.8%	63.2%

2000 Census Population	City/Town	Total Vote	Republican	Democratic	Other	Rep.-Dem. Plurality	Percentage			
							Total Vote		Major Vote	
							Rep.	Dem.	Rep.	Dem.
20,331	ACTON	11,601	3,477	7,894	230	4,417 D	30.0%	68.0%	30.6%	69.4%
28,144	AGAWAM	14,436	6,428	7,595	413	1,167 D	44.5%	52.6%	45.8%	54.2%
34,874	AMHERST	12,880	1,307	11,198	375	9,891 D	10.1%	86.9%	10.5%	89.5%
31,247	ANDOVER	18,291	7,798	10,177	316	2,379 D	42.6%	55.6%	43.4%	56.6%
42,389	ARLINGTON	25,365	6,407	18,365	593	11,958 D	25.3%	72.4%	25.9%	74.1%
42,068	ATTLEBORO	19,018	8,003	10,523	492	2,520 D	42.1%	55.3%	43.2%	56.8%
47,821	BARNSTABLE	25,028	11,084	13,559	385	2,475 D	44.3%	54.2%	45.0%	55.0%
24,194	BELMONT	13,702	3,982	9,404	316	5,422 D	29.1%	68.6%	29.7%	70.3%
39,862	BEVERLY	20,383	7,780	12,247	356	4,467 D	38.2%	60.1%	38.8%	61.2%
38,981	BILLERICA	19,448	9,280	9,700	468	420 D	47.7%	49.9%	48.9%	51.1%
589,141	BOSTON	235,578	45,548	185,976	4,054	140,428 D	19.3%	78.9%	19.7%	80.3%
33,828	BRAINTREE	18,700	8,964	9,298	438	334 D	47.9%	49.7%	49.1%	50.9%
94,304	BROCKTON	33,528	9,646	23,299	583	13,653 D	28.8%	69.5%	29.3%	70.7%
57,107	BROOKLINE	27,848	4,842	22,484	522	17,642 D	17.4%	80.7%	17.7%	82.3%
22,876	BURLINGTON	12,786	5,703	6,822	261	1,119 D	44.6%	53.4%	45.5%	54.5%
101,355	CAMBRIDGE	46,531	4,697	40,876	958	36,179 D	10.1%	87.8%	10.3%	89.7%
20,775	CANTON	12,071	5,396	6,460	215	1,064 D	44.7%	53.5%	45.5%	54.5%
33,858	CHELMSFORD	19,486	8,712	10,360	414	1,648 D	44.7%	53.2%	45.7%	54.3%
54,653	CHICOPEE	23,236	8,268	14,172	796	5,904 D	35.6%	61.0%	36.8%	63.2%
16,993	CONCORD	10,534	2,903	7,435	196	4,532 D	27.6%	70.6%	28.1%	71.9%
25,212	DANVERS	13,980	6,093	7,558	329	1,465 D	43.6%	54.1%	44.6%	55.4%
30,666	DARTMOUTH	16,737	5,876	10,442	419	4,566 D	35.1%	62.4%	36.0%	64.0%
23,464	DEDHAM	12,763	5,361	7,108	294	1,747 D	42.0%	55.7%	43.0%	57.0%
28,562	DRACUT	14,730	7,284	7,216	230	68 R	49.5%	49.0%	50.2%	49.8%
22,299	EASTON	11,991	5,667	6,111	213	444 D	47.3%	51.0%	48.1%	51.9%
38,037	EVERETT	12,842	4,140	8,338	364	4,198 D	32.2%	64.9%	33.2%	66.8%
91,938	FALL RIVER	31,202	7,933	22,591	678	14,658 D	25.4%	72.4%	26.0%	74.0%
32,660	FALMOUTH	19,599	7,503	11,725	371	4,222 D	38.3%	59.8%	39.0%	61.0%
39,102	FITCHBURG	14,340	5,378	8,596	366	3,218 D	37.5%	59.9%	38.5%	61.5%
66,910	FRAMINGHAM	26,932	8,464	17,839	629	9,375 D	31.4%	66.2%	32.2%	67.8%

MASSACHUSETTS

PRESIDENT 2008

2000 Census Population	City/Town	Total Vote	Republican	Democratic	Other	Rep.-Dem. Plurality		Total Vote Rep.	Dem.	Major Vote Rep.	Dem.
29,560	FRANKLIN	16,728	7,535	8,800	393	1,265	D	45.0%	52.6%	46.1%	53.9%
30,273	GLOUCESTER	15,444	5,113	9,967	364	4,854	D	33.1%	64.5%	33.9%	66.1%
58,969	HAVERHILL	26,854	10,814	15,552	488	4,738	D	40.3%	57.9%	41.0%	59.0%
19,882	HINGHAM	13,381	6,099	7,129	153	1,030	D	45.6%	53.3%	46.1%	53.9%
39,838	HOLYOKE	15,394	4,000	11,034	360	7,034	D	26.0%	71.7%	26.6%	73.4%
72,043	LAWRENCE	19,578	3,624	15,632	322	12,008	D	18.5%	79.8%	18.8%	81.2%
41,303	LEOMINSTER	18,184	7,709	10,063	412	2,354	D	42.4%	55.3%	43.4%	56.6%
30,355	LEXINGTON	17,884	4,593	12,984	307	8,391	D	25.7%	72.6%	26.1%	73.9%
105,167	LOWELL	31,700	10,393	20,646	661	10,253	D	32.8%	65.1%	33.5%	66.5%
89,050	LYNN	29,739	8,719	20,276	744	11,557	D	29.3%	68.2%	30.1%	69.9%
56,340	MALDEN	20,476	6,075	13,865	536	7,790	D	29.7%	67.7%	30.5%	69.5%
20,377	MARBLEHEAD	12,397	4,659	7,513	225	2,854	D	37.6%	60.6%	38.3%	61.7%
36,255	MARLBOROUGH	16,292	6,520	9,367	405	2,847	D	40.0%	57.5%	41.0%	59.0%
24,324	MARSHFIELD	14,554	7,026	7,255	273	229	D	48.3%	49.8%	49.2%	50.8%
55,765	MEDFORD	26,882	8,655	17,598	629	8,943	D	32.2%	65.5%	33.0%	67.0%
27,134	MELROSE	15,325	5,846	9,139	340	3,293	D	38.1%	59.6%	39.0%	61.0%
43,789	METHUEN	20,956	9,303	11,263	390	1,960	D	44.4%	53.7%	45.2%	54.8%
26,799	MILFORD	12,316	4,958	7,073	285	2,115	D	40.3%	57.4%	41.2%	58.8%
26,062	MILTON	15,510	5,753	9,486	271	3,733	D	37.1%	61.2%	37.8%	62.2%
32,170	NATICK	17,858	6,050	11,406	402	5,356	D	33.9%	63.9%	34.7%	65.3%
28,911	NEEDHAM	17,241	5,652	11,331	258	5,679	D	32.8%	65.7%	33.3%	66.7%
93,768	NEW BEDFORD	33,890	8,201	24,881	808	16,680	D	24.2%	73.4%	24.8%	75.2%
83,829	NEWTON	44,508	10,283	33,360	865	23,077	D	23.1%	75.0%	23.6%	76.4%
27,202	NORTH ANDOVER	14,945	6,939	7,777	229	838	D	46.4%	52.0%	47.2%	52.8%
27,143	NORTH ATTLEBOROUGH	14,134	6,713	7,099	322	386	D	47.5%	50.2%	48.6%	51.4%
28,978	NORTHAMPTON	16,225	2,387	13,412	426	11,025	D	14.7%	82.7%	15.1%	84.9%
28,587	NORWOOD	14,324	6,033	7,944	347	1,911	D	42.1%	55.5%	43.2%	56.8%
48,129	PEABODY	26,250	10,800	14,818	632	4,018	D	41.1%	56.4%	42.2%	57.8%
45,793	PITTSFIELD	20,581	4,404	15,665	512	11,261	D	21.4%	76.1%	21.9%	78.1%
51,701	PLYMOUTH	28,900	13,139	15,180	581	2,041	D	45.5%	52.5%	46.4%	53.6%
88,025	QUINCY	39,386	15,546	22,810	1,030	7,264	D	39.5%	57.9%	40.5%	59.5%
30,963	RANDOLPH	14,516	3,811	10,424	281	6,613	D	26.3%	71.8%	26.8%	73.2%
23,708	READING	13,744	5,831	7,694	219	1,863	D	42.4%	56.0%	43.1%	56.9%
47,283	REVERE	16,685	6,242	9,941	502	3,699	D	37.4%	59.6%	38.6%	61.4%
40,407	SALEM	19,213	5,601	13,080	532	7,479	D	29.2%	68.1%	30.0%	70.0%
26,078	SAUGUS	13,390	6,314	6,769	307	455	D	47.2%	50.6%	48.3%	51.7%
17,863	SCITUATE	11,177	5,121	5,850	206	729	D	45.8%	52.3%	46.7%	53.3%
31,640	SHREWSBURY	17,682	7,296	10,000	386	2,704	D	41.3%	56.6%	42.2%	57.8%
77,478	SOMERVILLE	32,762	5,215	26,665	882	21,450	D	15.9%	81.4%	16.4%	83.6%
152,082	SPRINGFIELD	51,788	11,331	39,516	941	28,185	D	21.9%	76.3%	22.3%	77.7%
22,219	STONEHAM	12,100	5,231	6,625	244	1,394	D	43.2%	54.8%	44.1%	55.9%
27,149	STOUGHTON	13,544	5,296	7,915	333	2,619	D	39.1%	58.4%	40.1%	59.9%
55,976	TAUNTON	22,535	8,677	13,243	615	4,566	D	38.5%	58.8%	39.6%	60.4%
28,851	TEWKSBURY	15,659	7,683	7,628	348	55	R	49.1%	48.7%	50.2%	49.8%
24,804	WAKEFIELD	14,176	6,118	7,743	315	1,625	D	43.2%	54.6%	44.1%	55.9%
22,824	WALPOLE	13,585	6,712	6,600	273	112	R	49.4%	48.6%	50.4%	49.6%
59,226	WALTHAM	24,284	8,383	15,276	625	6,893	D	34.5%	62.9%	35.4%	64.6%
32,986	WATERTOWN	16,124	4,249	11,520	355	7,271	D	26.4%	71.4%	26.9%	73.1%
26,613	WELLESLEY	14,387	4,885	9,270	232	4,385	D	34.0%	64.4%	34.5%	65.5%
27,899	WEST SPRINGFIELD	12,215	5,128	6,751	336	1,623	D	42.0%	55.3%	43.2%	56.8%
40,072	WESTFIELD	17,545	7,762	9,304	479	1,542	D	44.2%	53.0%	45.5%	54.5%
53,988	WEYMOUTH	27,757	12,358	14,727	672	2,369	D	44.5%	53.1%	45.6%	54.4%
20,810	WINCHESTER	12,410	4,846	7,381	183	2,535	D	39.0%	59.5%	39.6%	60.4%
37,258	WOBURN	19,075	8,466	10,237	372	1,771	D	44.4%	53.7%	45.3%	54.7%
172,648	WORCESTER	61,374	18,474	41,352	1,548	22,878	D	30.1%	67.4%	30.9%	69.1%
24,807	YARMOUTH	14,003	6,187	7,547	269	1,360	D	44.2%	53.9%	45.0%	55.0%

MASSACHUSETTS

SENATOR 2008

2000 Census Population	County	Total Vote	Republican	Democratic	Other	Rep.-Dem. Plurality	Percentage			
							Total Vote		Major Vote	
							Rep.	Dem.	Rep.	Dem.
222,230	BARNSTABLE	129,981	55,673	71,509	2,799	15,836 D	42.8%	55.0%	43.8%	56.2%
134,953	BERKSHIRE	64,682	11,863	50,364	2,455	38,501 D	18.3%	77.9%	19.1%	80.9%
534,678	BRISTOL	235,747	68,449	158,827	8,471	90,378 D	29.0%	67.4%	30.1%	69.9%
14,987	DUKES	10,310	2,501	7,491	318	4,990 D	24.3%	72.7%	25.0%	75.0%
723,419	ESSEX	344,115	115,312	218,583	10,220	103,271 D	33.5%	63.5%	34.5%	65.5%
71,535	FRANKLIN	37,853	8,079	27,944	1,830	19,865 D	21.3%	73.8%	22.4%	77.6%
456,228	HAMPDEN	191,164	56,212	125,283	9,669	69,071 D	29.4%	65.5%	31.0%	69.0%
152,251	HAMPSHIRE	77,763	17,221	57,053	3,489	39,832 D	22.1%	73.4%	23.2%	76.8%
1,465,396	MIDDLESEX	707,620	209,940	476,434	21,246	266,494 D	29.7%	67.3%	30.6%	69.4%
9,520	NANTUCKET	5,916	1,717	3,991	208	2,274 D	29.0%	67.5%	30.1%	69.9%
650,308	NORFOLK	335,357	112,229	214,071	9,057	101,842 D	33.5%	63.8%	34.4%	65.6%
472,822	PLYMOUTH	243,716	94,567	142,223	6,926	47,656 D	38.8%	58.4%	39.9%	60.1%
689,807	SUFFOLK	255,813	44,308	204,753	6,752	160,445 D	17.3%	80.0%	17.8%	82.2%
750,963	WORCESTER	354,210	127,973	213,448	12,789	85,475 D	36.1%	60.3%	37.5%	62.5%
6,349,097	TOTAL	2,994,247	926,044	1,971,974	96,229	1,045,930 D	30.9%	65.9%	32.0%	68.0%

2000 Census Population	City/Town	Total Vote	Republican	Democratic	Other	Rep.-Dem. Plurality	Percentage			
							Total Vote		Major Vote	
							Rep.	Dem.	Rep.	Dem.
20,331	ACTON	11,361	3,382	7,681	298	4,299 D	29.8%	67.6%	30.6%	69.4%
28,144	AGAWAM	14,048	4,999	8,415	634	3,416 D	35.6%	59.9%	37.3%	62.7%
34,874	AMHERST	12,426	1,142	10,794	490	9,652 D	9.2%	86.9%	9.6%	90.4%
31,247	ANDOVER	17,823	7,066	10,316	441	3,250 D	39.6%	57.9%	40.7%	59.3%
42,389	ARLINGTON	24,845	5,538	18,584	723	13,046 D	22.3%	74.8%	23.0%	77.0%
42,068	ATTLEBORO	18,531	6,153	11,733	645	5,580 D	33.2%	63.3%	34.4%	65.6%
47,821	BARNSTABLE	24,654	10,956	13,171	527	2,215 D	44.4%	53.4%	45.4%	54.6%
24,194	BELMONT	13,381	3,753	9,244	384	5,491 D	28.0%	69.1%	28.9%	71.1%
39,862	BEVERLY	20,026	6,568	12,866	592	6,298 D	32.8%	64.2%	33.8%	66.2%
38,981	BILLERICA	19,000	7,391	10,885	724	3,494 D	38.9%	57.3%	40.4%	59.6%
589,141	BOSTON	223,772	36,180	181,868	5724	145,688 D	16.2%	81.3%	16.6%	83.4%
33,828	BRAINTREE	18,161	6,869	10,800	492	3,931 D	37.8%	59.5%	38.9%	61.1%
94,304	BROCKTON	32,348	7,485	24,092	771	16,607 D	23.1%	74.5%	23.7%	76.3%
57,107	BROOKLINE	27,036	4,386	22,004	646	17,618 D	16.2%	81.4%	16.6%	83.4%
22,876	BURLINGTON	12,468	4,661	7,446	361	2,785 D	37.4%	59.7%	38.5%	61.5%
101,355	CAMBRIDGE	45,198	4,627	39,183	1388	34,556 D	10.2%	86.7%	10.6%	89.4%
20,775	CANTON	11,721	4,279	7,150	292	2,871 D	36.5%	61.0%	37.4%	62.6%
33,858	CHELMSFORD	18,932	7,870	10,485	577	2,615 D	41.6%	55.4%	42.9%	57.1%
54,653	CHICOPEE	22,781	6,151	15,239	1391	9,088 D	27.0%	66.9%	28.8%	71.2%
16,993	CONCORD	10,326	3,099	7,029	198	3,930 D	30.0%	68.1%	30.6%	69.4%
25,212	DANVERS	13,698	5,123	8,203	372	3,080 D	37.4%	59.9%	38.4%	61.6%
30,666	DARTMOUTH	16,267	4,636	11,057	574	6,421 D	28.5%	68.0%	29.5%	70.5%
23,464	DEDHAM	12,386	4,326	7,707	353	3,381 D	34.9%	62.2%	36.0%	64.0%
28,562	DRACUT	14,480	6,066	7,895	519	1,829 D	41.9%	54.5%	43.4%	56.6%
22,299	EASTON	11,634	4,687	6,625	322	1,938 D	40.3%	56.9%	41.4%	58.6%
38,037	EVERETT	12,400	2,832	9,214	354	6,382 D	22.8%	74.3%	23.5%	76.5%
91,938	FALL RIVER	29,899	5,482	23,287	1130	17,805 D	18.3%	77.9%	19.1%	80.9%
32,660	FALMOUTH	19,204	7,222	11,523	459	4,301 D	37.6%	60.0%	38.5%	61.5%
39,102	FITCHBURG	14,024	4,350	9,147	527	4,797 D	31.0%	65.2%	32.2%	67.8%
66,910	FRAMINGHAM	26,340	7,309	18,293	738	10,984 D	27.7%	69.4%	28.5%	71.5%

MASSACHUSETTS

SENATOR 2008

2000 Census Population	City/Town	Total Vote	Republican	Democratic	Other	Rep.-Dem. Plurality	Percentage			
							Total Vote		Major Vote	
							Rep.	Dem.	Rep.	Dem.
29,560	FRANKLIN	16,250	6,214	9,600	436	3,386 D	38.2%	59.1%	39.3%	60.7%
30,273	GLOUCESTER	14,970	4,280	10,113	577	5,833 D	28.6%	67.6%	29.7%	70.3%
58,969	HAVERHILL	26,151	8,773	16,433	945	7,660 D	33.5%	62.8%	34.8%	65.2%
19,882	HINGHAM	13,111	5,450	7,402	259	1,952 D	41.6%	56.5%	42.4%	57.6%
39,838	HOLYOKE	14,579	3,164	10,782	633	7,618 D	21.7%	74.0%	22.7%	77.3%
72,043	LAWRENCE	17,938	2,798	14,682	458	11,884 D	15.6%	81.8%	16.0%	84.0%
41,303	LEOMINSTER	17,832	6,208	11,037	587	4,829 D	34.8%	61.9%	36.0%	64.0%
30,355	LEXINGTON	17,407	4,293	12,753	361	8,460 D	24.7%	73.3%	25.2%	74.8%
105,167	LOWELL	30,469	8,332	21,038	1099	12,706 D	27.3%	69.0%	28.4%	71.6%
89,050	LYNN	29,000	6,396	21,767	837	15,371 D	22.1%	75.1%	22.7%	77.3%
56,340	MALDEN	19,858	4,639	14,579	640	9,940 D	23.4%	73.4%	24.1%	75.9%
20,377	MARBLEHEAD	12,181	4,369	7,542	270	3,173 D	35.9%	61.9%	36.7%	63.3%
36,255	MARLBOROUGH	15,957	5,384	10,028	545	4,644 D	33.7%	62.8%	34.9%	65.1%
24,324	MARSHFIELD	14,206	5,910	7,909	387	1,999 D	41.6%	55.7%	42.8%	57.2%
55,765	MEDFORD	26,267	6,682	18,729	856	12,047 D	25.4%	71.3%	26.3%	73.7%
27,134	MELROSE	14,934	4,895	9,619	420	4,724 D	32.8%	64.4%	33.7%	66.3%
43,789	METHUEN	20,336	7,426	12,279	631	4,853 D	36.5%	60.4%	37.7%	62.3%
26,799	MILFORD	11,941	4,047	7,520	374	3,473 D	33.9%	63.0%	35.0%	65.0%
26,062	MILTON	14,969	4,676	9,954	339	5,278 D	31.2%	66.5%	32.0%	68.0%
32,170	NATICK	17,435	5,424	11,509	502	6,085 D	31.1%	66.0%	32.0%	68.0%
28,911	NEEDHAM	16,823	5,102	11,352	369	6,250 D	30.3%	67.5%	31.0%	69.0%
93,768	NEW BEDFORD	32,788	6,137	25,505	1146	19,368 D	18.7%	77.8%	19.4%	80.6%
83,829	NEWTON	43,260	8,777	33,394	1089	24,617 D	20.3%	77.2%	20.8%	79.2%
27,202	NORTH ANDOVER	14,674	6,041	8,256	377	2,215 D	41.2%	56.3%	42.3%	57.7%
27,143	NORTH ATTLEBOROUGH	13,740	5,340	7,917	483	2,577 D	38.9%	57.6%	40.3%	59.7%
28,978	NORTHAMPTON	15,815	2,062	13,120	633	11,058 D	13.0%	83.0%	13.6%	86.4%
28,587	NORWOOD	13,905	4,754	8,724	427	3,970 D	34.2%	62.7%	35.3%	64.7%
48,129	PEABODY	25,636	8,403	16,533	700	8,130 D	32.8%	64.5%	33.7%	66.3%
45,793	PITTSFIELD	20,048	3,502	15,869	677	12,367 D	17.5%	79.2%	18.1%	81.9%
51,701	PLYMOUTH	28,317	11,265	16,319	733	5,054 D	39.8%	57.6%	40.8%	59.2%
88,025	QUINCY	38,139	12,192	24,801	1146	12,609 D	32.0%	65.0%	33.0%	67.0%
30,963	RANDOLPH	14,125	2,970	10,824	331	7,854 D	21.0%	76.6%	21.5%	78.5%
23,708	READING	13,384	4,955	8,124	305	3,169 D	37.0%	60.7%	37.9%	62.1%
47,283	REVERE	15,855	4,135	11,221	499	7,086 D	26.1%	70.8%	26.9%	73.1%
40,407	SALEM	18,744	4,600	13,540	604	8,940 D	24.5%	72.2%	25.4%	74.6%
26,078	SAUGUS	13,073	4,800	7,852	421	3,052 D	36.7%	60.1%	37.9%	62.1%
17,863	SCITUATE	10,947	4,651	5,993	303	1,342 D	42.5%	54.7%	43.7%	56.3%
31,640	SHREWSBURY	17,251	6,483	10,372	396	3,889 D	37.6%	60.1%	38.5%	61.5%
77,478	SOMERVILLE	31,839	4,308	26,360	1171	22,052 D	13.5%	82.8%	14.0%	86.0%
152,082	SPRINGFIELD	49,287	8,351	38,411	2525	30,060 D	16.9%	77.9%	17.9%	82.1%
22,219	STONEHAM	11,746	4,134	7,300	312	3,166 D	35.2%	62.1%	36.2%	63.8%
27,149	STOUGHTON	13,153	4,130	8,719	304	4,589 D	31.4%	66.3%	32.1%	67.9%
55,976	TAUNTON	21,760	6,200	14,807	753	8,607 D	28.5%	68.0%	29.5%	70.5%
28,851	TEWKSBURY	15,257	6,098	8,647	512	2,549 D	40.0%	56.7%	41.4%	58.6%
24,804	WAKEFIELD	13,789	5,027	8,391	371	3,364 D	36.5%	60.9%	37.5%	62.5%
22,824	WALPOLE	13,194	5,380	7,448	366	2,068 D	40.8%	56.4%	41.9%	58.1%
59,226	WALTHAM	23,459	6,628	16,096	735	9,468 D	28.3%	68.6%	29.2%	70.8%
32,986	WATERTOWN	15,710	3,564	11,656	490	8,092 D	22.7%	74.2%	23.4%	76.6%
26,613	WELLESLEY	13,993	4,746	8,924	323	4,178 D	33.9%	63.8%	34.7%	65.3%
27,899	WEST SPRINGFIELD	11,874	4,061	7,247	566	3,186 D	34.2%	61.0%	35.9%	64.1%
40,072	WESTFIELD	17,129	6,394	9,874	861	3,480 D	37.3%	57.6%	39.3%	60.7%
53,988	WEYMOUTH	27,105	9,756	16,578	771	6,822 D	36.0%	61.2%	37.0%	63.0%
20,810	WINCHESTER	12,094	4,417	7,383	294	2,966 D	36.5%	61.0%	37.4%	62.6%
37,258	WOBURN	18,563	6,597	11,387	579	4,790 D	35.5%	61.3%	36.7%	63.3%
172,648	WORCESTER	58,841	14,379	42,249	2213	27,870 D	24.4%	71.8%	25.4%	74.6%
24,807	YARMOUTH	13,768	6,243	7,260	265	1,017 D	45.3%	52.7%	46.2%	53.8%

MASSACHUSETTS
HOUSE OF REPRESENTATIVES

| | | | Republican | | Democratic | | | | Percentage | | | |
| | | | | | | | | | Total Vote | | Major Vote | |
CD	Year	Total Vote	Vote	Candidate	Vote	Candidate	Other Vote	Rep.-Dem. Plurality	Rep.	Dem.	Rep.	Dem.
1	2008	296,099	80,067	BECH, NATHAN A.	215,696	OLVER, JOHN W.*	336	135,629 D	27.0%	72.8%	27.1%	72.9%
1	2006	206,884		—	158,057	OLVER, JOHN W.*	48,827	158,057 D		76.4%		100.0%
1	2004	231,747		—	229,465	OLVER, JOHN W.*	2,282	229,465 D		99.0%		100.0%
1	2002	204,019	66,061	KINNAMAN, MATTHEW W.	137,841	OLVER, JOHN W.*	117	71,780 D	32.4%	67.6%	32.4%	67.6%
2	2008	238,000		—	234,369	NEAL, RICHARD E.*	3,631	234,369 D		98.5%		100.0%
2	2006	167,193		—	164,939	NEAL, RICHARD E.*	2,254	164,939 D		98.7%		100.0%
2	2004	220,484		—	217,682	NEAL, RICHARD E.*	2,802	217,682 D		98.7%		100.0%
2	2002	154,728		—	153,387	NEAL, RICHARD E.*	1,341	153,387 D		99.1%		100.0%
3	2008	231,107		—	227,619	McGOVERN, JIM*	3,488	227,619 D		98.5%		100.0%
3	2006	168,956		—	166,973	McGOVERN, JIM*	1,983	166,973 D		98.8%		100.0%
3	2004	272,412	80,197	CREWS, RONALD A.	192,036	McGOVERN, JIM*	179	111,839 D	29.4%	70.5%	29.5%	70.5%
3	2002	157,545		—	155,697	McGOVERN, JIM*	1,848	155,697 D		98.8%		100.0%
4	2008	298,788	75,571	SHOLLEY, EARL HENRY	203,032	FRANK, BARNEY*	20,185	127,461 D	25.3%	68.0%	27.1%	72.9%
4	2006	179,243		—	176,513	FRANK, BARNEY*	2,730	176,513 D		98.5%		100.0%
4	2004	282,039		—	219,260	FRANK, BARNEY*	62,779	219,260 D		77.7%		100.0%
4	2002	167,816		—	166,125	FRANK, BARNEY*	1,691	166,125 D		99.0%		100.0%
5	2008	228,907		—	225,947	TSONGAS, NIKI*	2,960	225,947 D		98.7%		100.0%
5	2006	162,272		—	159,120	MEEHAN, MARTIN T.*	3,152	159,120 D		98.1%		100.0%
5	2004	268,189	88,232	TIERNEY, THOMAS P.	179,652	MEEHAN, MARTIN T.*	305	91,420 D	32.9%	67.0%	32.9%	67.1%
5	2002	203,777	69,337	McCARTHY, CHARLES	122,562	MEEHAN, MARTIN T.*	11,878	53,225 D	34.0%	60.1%	36.1%	63.9%
6	2008	321,312	94,845	BAKER, RICHARD A.	226,216	TIERNEY, JOHN F.*	251	131,371 D	29.5%	70.4%	29.5%	70.5%
6	2006	241,625	72,997	BARTON, RICHARD W.	168,056	TIERNEY, JOHN F.*	572	95,059 D	30.2%	69.6%	30.3%	69.7%
6	2004	305,522	91,597	O'MALLEY, STEPHEN P. JR.	213,458	TIERNEY, JOHN F.*	467	121,861 D	30.0%	69.9%	30.0%	70.0%
6	2002	238,615	75,462	SMITH, MARK C.	162,900	TIERNEY, JOHN F.*	253	87,438 D	31.6%	68.3%	31.7%	68.3%
7	2008	280,682	67,978	CUNNINGHAM, JOHN	212,304	MARKEY, EDWARD J.*	400	144,326 D	24.2%	75.6%	24.3%	75.7%
7	2006	174,791		—	171,902	MARKEY, EDWARD J.*	2,889	171,902 D		98.3%		100.0%
7	2004	275,099	60,334	CHASE, KENNETH G.	202,399	MARKEY, EDWARD J.*	12,366	142,065 D	21.9%	73.6%	23.0%	77.0%
7	2002	174,037		—	170,968	MARKEY, EDWARD J.*	3,069	170,968 D		98.2%		100.0%
8	2008	188,252		—	185,530	CAPUANO, MICHAEL E.*	2,722	185,530 D		98.6%		100.0%
8	2006	138,455		—	125,515	CAPUANO, MICHAEL E.*	12,940	125,515 D		90.7%		100.0%
8	2004	168,081		—	165,852	CAPUANO, MICHAEL E.*	2,229	165,852 D		98.7%		100.0%
8	2002	112,356		—	111,861	CAPUANO, MICHAEL E.*	495	111,861 D		99.6%		100.0%
9	2008	245,294		—	242,166	LYNCH, STEPHEN F.*	3,128	242,166 D		98.7%		100.0%
9	2006	217,036	47,114	ROBINSON, JACK E.	169,420	LYNCH, STEPHEN F.*	502	122,306 D	21.7%	78.1%	21.8%	78.2%
9	2004	220,312		—	218,167	LYNCH, STEPHEN F.*	2,145	218,167 D		99.0%		100.0%
9	2002	168,976		—	168,055	LYNCH, STEPHEN F.*	921	168,055 D		99.5%		100.0%
10	2008	276,673		—	272,899	DELAHUNT, BILL*	3,774	272,899 D		98.6%		100.0%
10	2006	267,202	78,439	BEATTY, JEFFREY K.	171,812	DELAHUNT, BILL*	16,951	93,373 D	29.4%	64.3%	31.3%	68.7%
10	2004	337,070	114,879	JONES, MICHAEL J.	222,013	DELAHUNT, BILL*	178	107,134 D	34.1%	65.9%	34.1%	65.9%
10	2002	259,002	79,624	GONZAGA, LUIS	179,238	DELAHUNT, BILL*	140	99,614 D	30.7%	69.2%	30.8%	69.2%
TOTAL	2008	2,605,114	318,461		2,245,778		40,875	1,927,317 D	12.2%	86.2%	12.4%	87.6%
TOTAL	2006	1,923,657	198,550		1,632,307		92,800	1,433,757 D	10.3%	84.9%	10.8%	89.2%
TOTAL	2004	2,580,955	435,239		2,059,984		85,732	1,624,745 D	16.9%	79.8%	17.4%	82.6%
TOTAL	2002	1,840,871	290,484		1,528,634		21,753	1,238,150 D	15.8%	83.0%	16.0%	84.0%

An asterisk (*) denotes incumbent.

MASSACHUSETTS
GENERAL AND PRIMARY ELECTIONS

2008 GENERAL ELECTIONS

President   Other vote was 28,841 Independent (Ralph Nader); 13,189 Libertarian (Bob Barr); 6,550 Green-Rainbow (Cynthia A. McKinney); 4,971 Constitution (Chuck Baldwin); 14,483 scattered write-in.

Senator   Other vote was 93,713 Libertarian (Robert J. Underwood); 2,516 scattered write-in.

House   Other vote was:

CD 1	336 scattered write-in.
CD 2	3,631 scattered write-in.
CD 3	3,488 scattered write-in.
CD 4	19,848 Independent (Susan Allen); 337 scattered write-in.
CD 5	2,960 scattered write-in.
CD 6	251 scattered write-in.
CD 7	400 scattered write-in.
CD 8	2,722 scattered write-in.
CD 9	3,128 scattered write-in.
CD 10	3,774 scattered write-in.

2008 PRIMARY ELECTIONS

Primary	February 5, 2008 (President) September 16, 2008 (Congress)	**Registration** (as of January 16, 2008)	Democratic	1,475,769
			Republican	485,959
			Green-Rainbow	6,611
			Working Families	2,755
			Other Parties	20,473
			Unenrolled	2,018,746
			TOTAL	*4,010,313*

Primary Type   Semi-open—Registered Democrats and Republicans could vote only in their party's primary. "Unenrolled" voters could participate in either party's primary.

MASSACHUSETTS

GENERAL AND PRIMARY ELECTIONS

	REPUBLICAN PRIMARIES			DEMOCRATIC PRIMARIES		
President	Mitt Romney	255,892	51.1%	Hillary Clinton	705,185	56.0%
	John McCain	204,779	40.9%	Barack Obama	511,680	40.6%
	Mike Huckabee	19,103	3.8%	John Edwards	20,101	1.6%
	Ron Paul	13,251	2.6%	No Preference	8,041	0.6%
	Rudolph Giuliani	2,707	0.5%	Joseph R. Biden Jr.	3,216	0.3%
	No Preference	1,959	0.4%	Dennis J. Kucinich	2,992	0.2%
	Fred Thompson	916	0.2%	Bill Richardson	1,846	0.1%
	Duncan Hunter	258	0.1%	Mike Gravel	1,463	0.1%
	Tom Tancredo	153		Christopher J. Dodd	1,120	0.1%
	Scattered write-in	1,532	0.3%	Scattered write-in	3,279	0.3%
	TOTAL	*500,550*		*TOTAL*	*1,258,923*	
Senator	Jeffrey K. Beatty	51,788	98.0%	John Kerry*	342,446	68.9%
	Scattered write-in	1,043	2.0%	Edward J. O'Reilly	154,395	31.0%
				Scattered write-in	538	0.1%
	TOTAL	*52,831*		*TOTAL*	*497,379*	
Congressional District 1	Nathan A. Bech	3,659	98.9%	John W. Olver*	33,513	79.2%
	Scattered write-in	42	1.1%	Robert A. Feuer	8,765	20.7%
				Scattered write-in	34	0.1%
	TOTAL	*3,701*		*TOTAL*	*42,312*	
Congressional District 2	*No Republican candidate filed for the primary. There were 390 scattered write-in votes.*			Richard E. Neal*	30,017	98.8%
				Scattered write-in	360	1.2%
				TOTAL	*30,377*	
Congressional District 3	*No Republican candidate filed for the primary. There were 548 scattered write-in votes.*			Jim McGovern*	37,041	99.2%
				Scattered write-in	284	0.8%
				TOTAL	*37,325*	
Congressional District 4	Earl Henry Sholley	4,087	99.0%	Barney Frank*	38,642	99.0%
	Scattered write-in	41	1.0%	Scattered write-in	381	1.0%
	TOTAL	*4,128*		*TOTAL*	*39,023*	
Congressional District 5	*No Republican candidate filed for the primary. There were 114 write-in votes cast for Theodore J. Gaiero Jr., as well as 618 scattered write-in votes.*			Niki Tsongas*	40,248	98.7%
				Scattered write-in	521	1.3%
				TOTAL	*40,769*	
Congressional District 6	Richard A. Baker	5,160	99.1%	John F. Tierney*	36,646	98.7%
	Scattered write-in	49	0.9%	Scattered write-in	478	1.3%
	TOTAL	*5,209*		*TOTAL*	*37,124*	
Congressional District 7	John Cunningham	4,825	98.1%	Edward J. Markey*	56,210	98.6%
	Scattered write-in	95	1.9%	Scattered write-in	805	1.4%
	TOTAL	*4,920*		*TOTAL*	*57,015*	
Congressional District 8	*No Republican candidate filed for the primary. There were 302 scattered write-in votes.*			Michael E. Capuano*	35,189	98.6%
				Scattered write-in	497	1.4%
				TOTAL	*35,686*	
Congressional District 9	*No Republican candidate filed for the primary. There were 587 scattered write-in votes.*			Stephen F. Lynch*	40,332	98.9%
				Scattered write-in	468	1.1%
				TOTAL	*40,800*	
Congressional District 10	*No Republican candidate filed for the primary. There were 856 scattered write-in votes.*			Bill Delahunt*	45,587	98.4%
				Scattered write-in	722	1.6%
				TOTAL	*46,309*	

Note: An asterisk (*) denotes incumbent.

MICHIGAN

Congressional districts first established for elections held in 2002
15 members

MICHIGAN

Detroit Area

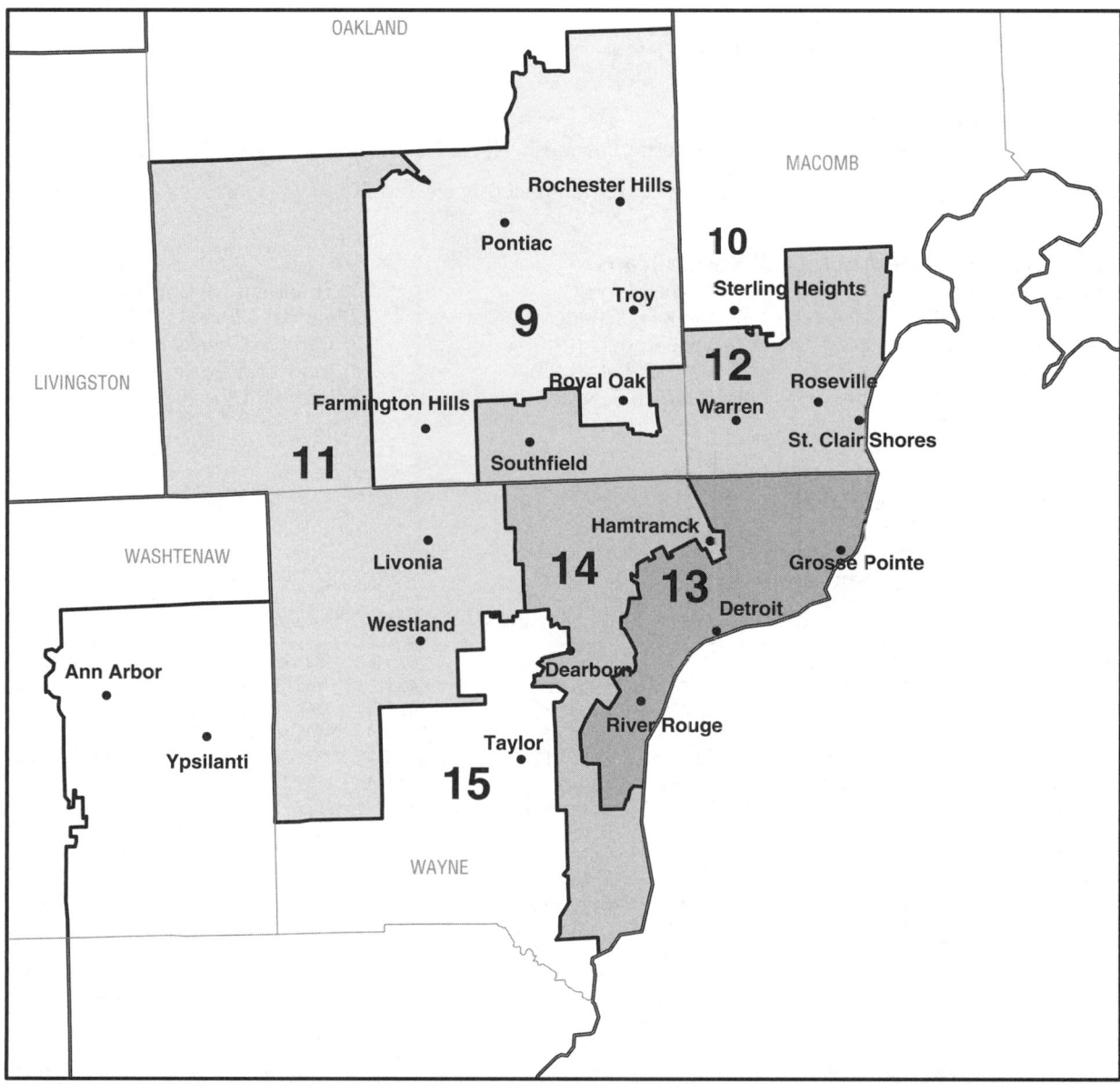

MICHIGAN

GOVERNOR

Jennifer M. Granholm (D). Reelected 2006 to a four-year term. Previously elected 2002.

SENATORS (2 Democrats)

Carl Levin (D). Reelected 2008 to a six-year term. Previously elected 2002, 1996, 1990, 1984, 1978.

Debbie Stabenow (D). Elected 2006 to a six-year term. Previously elected 2000.

REPRESENTATIVES (8 Democrats, 7 Republicans)

1. Bart Stupak (D)
2. Peter Hoekstra (R)
3. Vernon J. Ehlers (R)
4. Dave Camp (R)
5. Dale E. Kildee (D)
6. Fred Upton (R)
7. Mark H. Schauer (D)
8. Mike Rogers (R)
9. Gary C. Peters (D)
10. Candice S. Miller (R)
11. Thaddeus McCotter (R)
12. Sander M. Levin (D)
13. Carolyn Cheeks Kilpatrick (D)
14. John Conyers Jr. (D)
15. John D. Dingell (D)

POSTWAR VOTE FOR PRESIDENT

Year	Total Vote	Republican Vote	Republican Candidate	Democratic Vote	Democratic Candidate	Other Vote	Plurality	Total Vote Rep.	Total Vote Dem.	Major Vote Rep.	Major Vote Dem.
2008	5,001,766	2,048,639	McCain, John	2,872,579	Obama, Barack	80,548	823,940 D	41.0%	57.4%	41.6%	58.4%
2004	4,839,252	2,313,746	Bush, George W.	2,479,183	Kerry, John	46,323	165,437 D	47.8%	51.2%	48.3%	51.7%
2000**	4,232,711	1,953,139	Bush, George W.	2,170,418	Gore, Al	109,154	217,279 D	46.1%	51.3%	47.4%	52.6%
1996**	3,848,844	1,481,212	Dole, Bob	1,989,653	Clinton, Bill	377,979	508,441 D	38.5%	51.7%	42.7%	57.3%
1992**	4,274,673	1,554,940	Bush, George	1,871,182	Clinton, Bill	848,551	316,242 D	36.4%	43.8%	45.4%	54.6%
1988	3,669,163	1,965,486	Bush, George	1,675,783	Dukakis, Michael S.	27,894	289,703 R	53.6%	45.7%	54.0%	46.0%
1984	3,801,658	2,251,571	Reagan, Ronald	1,529,638	Mondale, Walter F.	20,449	721,933 R	59.2%	40.2%	59.5%	40.5%
1980**	3,909,725	1,915,225	Reagan, Ronald	1,661,532	Carter, Jimmy	332,968	253,693 R	49.0%	42.5%	53.5%	46.5%
1976	3,653,749	1,893,742	Ford, Gerald R.	1,696,714	Carter, Jimmy	63,293	197,028 R	51.8%	46.4%	52.7%	47.3%
1972	3,489,727	1,961,721	Nixon, Richard M.	1,459,435	McGovern, George S.	68,571	502,286 R	56.2%	41.8%	57.3%	42.7%
1968**	3,306,250	1,370,665	Nixon, Richard M.	1,593,082	Humphrey, Hubert H.	342,503	222,417 D	41.5%	48.2%	46.2%	53.8%
1964	3,203,102	1,060,152	Goldwater, Barry M.	2,136,615	Johnson, Lyndon B.	6,335	1,076,463 D	33.1%	66.7%	33.2%	66.8%
1960	3,318,097	1,620,428	Nixon, Richard M.	1,687,269	Kennedy, John F.	10,400	66,841 D	48.8%	50.9%	49.0%	51.0%
1956	3,080,468	1,713,647	Eisenhower, Dwight D.	1,359,898	Stevenson, Adlai E.	6,923	353,749 R	55.6%	44.1%	55.8%	44.2%
1952	2,798,592	1,551,529	Eisenhower, Dwight D.	1,230,657	Stevenson, Adlai E.	16,406	320,872 R	55.4%	44.0%	55.8%	44.2%
1948	2,109,609	1,038,595	Dewey, Thomas E.	1,003,448	Truman, Harry S.	67,566	35,147 R	49.2%	47.6%	50.9%	49.1%

**In past elections, the other vote included: 2000 - 84,165 Green (Ralph Nader); 1996 - 336,670 Reform (Ross Perot); 1992 - 824,813 Independent (Perot); 1980 - 275,223 Independent (John Anderson); 1968 - 331,968 American Independent (George Wallace).

MICHIGAN

POSTWAR VOTE FOR GOVERNOR

Year	Total Vote	Republican Vote	Republican Candidate	Democratic Vote	Democratic Candidate	Other Vote	Rep.-Dem. Plurality	Total Vote Rep.	Total Vote Dem.	Major Vote Rep.	Major Vote Dem.
2006	3,801,256	1,608,086	DeVos, Dick	2,142,513	Granholm, Jennifer M.	50,657	534,427 D	42.3%	56.4%	42.9%	57.1%
2002	3,177,565	1,506,104	Posthumus, Dick	1,633,796	Granholm, Jennifer M.	37,665	127,692 D	47.4%	51.4%	48.0%	52.0%
1998	3,027,104	1,883,005	Engler, John	1,143,574	Fieger, Geoffrey	525	739,431 R	62.2%	37.8%	62.2%	37.8%
1994	3,089,077	1,899,101	Engler, John	1,188,438	Wolpe, Howard	1,538	710,663 R	61.5%	38.5%	61.5%	38.5%
1990	2,564,563	1,276,134	Engler, John	1,258,539	Blanchard, James J.	29,890	17,595 R	49.8%	49.1%	50.3%	49.7%
1986	2,396,564	753,647	Lucas, William	1,632,138	Blanchard, James J.	10,779	878,491 D	31.4%	68.1%	31.6%	68.4%
1982	3,040,008	1,369,582	Headlee, Richard H.	1,561,291	Blanchard, James J.	109,135	191,709 D	45.1%	51.4%	46.7%	53.3%
1978	2,867,212	1,628,485	Milliken, William G.	1,237,256	Fitzgerald, William	1,471	391,229 R	56.8%	43.2%	56.8%	43.2%
1974	2,657,017	1,356,865	Milliken, William G.	1,242,247	Levin, Sander	57,905	114,618 R	51.1%	46.8%	52.2%	47.8%
1970	2,656,162	1,339,047	Milliken, William G.	1,294,638	Levin, Sander	22,477	44,409 R	50.4%	48.7%	50.8%	49.2%
1966**	2,461,909	1,490,430	Romney, George W.	963,383	Ferency, Zolton A.	8,096	527,047 R	60.5%	39.1%	60.7%	39.3%
1964	3,158,102	1,764,355	Romney, George W.	1,381,442	Staebler, Neil	12,305	382,913 R	55.9%	43.7%	56.1%	43.9%
1962	2,764,839	1,420,086	Romney, George W.	1,339,513	Swainson, John B.	5,240	80,573 R	51.4%	48.4%	51.5%	48.5%
1960	3,255,991	1,602,022	Bagwell, Paul D.	1,643,634	Swainson, John B.	10,335	41,612 D	49.2%	50.5%	49.4%	50.6%
1958	2,312,184	1,078,089	Bagwell, Paul D.	1,225,533	Williams, G. Mennen	8,562	147,444 D	46.6%	53.0%	46.8%	53.2%
1956	3,049,651	1,376,376	Cobo, Albert E.	1,666,689	Williams, G. Mennen	6,586	290,313 D	45.1%	54.7%	45.2%	54.8%
1954	2,187,027	963,300	Leonard, Donald S.	1,216,308	Williams, G. Mennen	7,419	253,008 D	44.0%	55.6%	44.2%	55.8%
1952	2,865,980	1,423,275	Alger, Fred M.	1,431,893	Williams, G. Mennen	10,812	8,618 D	49.7%	50.0%	49.8%	50.2%
1950	1,879,382	933,998	Kelly, Harry F.	935,152	Williams, G. Mennen	10,232	1,154 D	49.7%	49.8%	50.0%	50.0%
1948	2,113,122	964,810	Sigler, Kim	1,128,664	Williams, G. Mennen	19,648	163,854 D	45.7%	53.4%	46.1%	53.9%
1946	1,665,475	1,003,878	Sigler, Kim	644,540	Van Wagoner, Murray	17,057	359,338 R	60.3%	38.7%	60.9%	39.1%

**The term of office of Michigan's governor was increased from two to four years effective with the 1966 election.

POSTWAR VOTE FOR SENATOR

Year	Total Vote	Republican Vote	Republican Candidate	Democratic Vote	Democratic Candidate	Other Vote	Rep.-Dem. Plurality	Total Vote Rep.	Total Vote Dem.	Major Vote Rep.	Major Vote Dem.
2008	4,848,620	1,641,070	Hoogendyk, Jack Jr.	3,038,386	Levin, Carl	169,164	1,397,316 D	33.8%	62.7%	35.1%	64.9%
2006	3,780,142	1,559,597	Bouchard, Michael	2,151,278	Stabenow, Debbie	69,267	591,681 D	41.3%	56.9%	42.0%	58.0%
2002	3,129,287	1,185,545	Raczkowski, Andrew	1,896,614	Levin, Carl	47,128	711,069 D	37.9%	60.6%	38.5%	61.5%
2000	4,167,685	1,994,693	Abraham, Spencer	2,061,952	Stabenow, Debbie	111,040	67,259 D	47.9%	49.5%	49.2%	50.8%
1996	3,762,575	1,500,106	Romney, Ronna	2,195,738	Levin, Carl	66,731	695,632 D	39.9%	58.4%	40.6%	59.4%
1994	3,043,385	1,578,770	Abraham, Spencer	1,300,960	Carr, M. Robert	163,655	277,810 R	51.9%	42.7%	54.8%	45.2%
1990	2,560,494	1,055,695	Schuette, Bill	1,471,753	Levin, Carl	33,046	416,058 D	41.2%	57.5%	41.8%	58.2%
1988	3,505,985	1,348,219	Dunn, Jim	2,116,865	Riegle, Donald W.	40,901	768,646 D	38.5%	60.4%	38.9%	61.1%
1984	3,700,938	1,745,302	Lousma, Jack	1,915,831	Levin, Carl	39,805	170,529 D	47.2%	51.8%	47.7%	52.3%
1982	2,994,334	1,223,288	Ruppe, Philip E.	1,728,793	Riegle, Donald W.	42,253	505,505 D	40.9%	57.7%	41.4%	58.6%
1978	2,846,630	1,362,165	Griffin, Robert P.	1,484,193	Levin, Carl	272	122,028 D	47.9%	52.1%	47.9%	52.1%
1976	3,490,664	1,635,087	Esch, Marvin L.	1,831,031	Riegle, Donald W.	24,546	195,944 D	46.8%	52.5%	47.2%	52.8%
1972	3,406,906	1,781,065	Griffin, Robert P.	1,577,178	Kelley, Frank J.	48,663	203,887 R	52.3%	46.3%	53.0%	47.0%
1970	2,610,839	858,470	Romney, Lenore	1,744,716	Hart, Philip A.	7,653	886,246 D	32.9%	66.8%	33.0%	67.0%
1966	2,439,365	1,363,530	Griffin, Robert P.	1,069,484	Williams, G. Mennen	6,351	294,046 R	55.9%	43.8%	56.0%	44.0%
1964	3,101,667	1,096,272	Peterson, Elly M.	1,996,912	Hart, Philip A.	8,483	900,640 D	35.3%	64.4%	35.4%	64.6%
1960	3,226,647	1,548,873	Bentley, Alvin M.	1,669,179	McNamara, Patrick V.	8,595	120,306 D	48.0%	51.7%	48.1%	51.9%
1958	2,271,644	1,046,963	Potter, Charles E.	1,216,966	Hart, Philip A.	7,715	170,003 D	46.1%	53.6%	46.2%	53.8%
1954	2,144,840	1,049,420	Ferguson, Homer	1,088,550	McNamara, Patrick V.	6,870	39,130 D	48.9%	50.8%	49.1%	50.9%
1952	2,821,133	1,428,352	Potter, Charles E.	1,383,416	Moody, Blair	9,365	44,936 R	50.6%	49.0%	50.8%	49.2%
1948	2,062,097	1,045,156	Ferguson, Homer	1,000,329	Hook, Frank E.	16,612	44,827 R	50.7%	48.5%	51.1%	48.9%
1946	1,618,720	1,085,570	Vandenberg, Arthur	517,923	Lee, James H.	15,227	567,647 R	67.1%	32.0%	67.7%	32.3%

MICHIGAN
PRESIDENT 2008

2000 Census Population	County	Total Vote	Republican	Democratic	Other	Rep.-Dem. Plurality	Percentage Total Vote Rep.	Dem.	Major Vote Rep.	Dem.
11,719	ALCONA	6,420	3,404	2,896	120	508 R	53.0%	45.1%	54.0%	46.0%
9,862	ALGER	4,750	2,188	2,472	90	284 D	46.1%	52.0%	47.0%	53.0%
105,665	ALLEGAN	55,279	30,061	24,165	1,053	5,896 R	54.4%	43.7%	55.4%	44.6%
31,314	ALPENA	15,085	7,125	7,705	255	580 D	47.2%	51.1%	48.0%	52.0%
23,110	ANTRIM	13,852	7,506	6,079	267	1,427 R	54.2%	43.9%	55.3%	44.7%
17,269	ARENAC	8,128	3,807	4,155	166	348 D	46.8%	51.1%	47.8%	52.2%
8,746	BARAGA	3,644	1,846	1,725	73	121 R	50.7%	47.3%	51.7%	48.3%
56,755	BARRY	30,565	16,431	13,449	685	2,982 R	53.8%	44.0%	55.0%	45.0%
110,157	BAY	57,428	23,795	32,589	1,044	8,794 D	41.4%	56.7%	42.2%	57.8%
15,998	BENZIE	10,309	4,687	5,451	171	764 D	45.5%	52.9%	46.2%	53.8%
162,453	BERRIEN	77,666	36,130	40,381	1,155	4,251 D	46.5%	52.0%	47.2%	52.8%
45,787	BRANCH	18,285	9,534	8,413	338	1,121 R	52.1%	46.0%	53.1%	46.9%
137,985	CALHOUN	64,196	28,553	34,561	1,082	6,008 D	44.5%	53.8%	45.2%	54.8%
51,104	CASS	23,576	11,114	12,083	379	969 D	47.1%	51.3%	47.9%	52.1%
26,090	CHARLEVOIX	14,367	7,306	6,817	244	489 R	50.9%	47.4%	51.7%	48.3%
26,448	CHEBOYGAN	13,901	6,920	6,720	261	200 R	49.8%	48.3%	50.7%	49.3%
38,543	CHIPPEWA	16,708	8,267	8,184	257	83 R	49.5%	49.0%	50.3%	49.7%
31,252	CLARE	14,567	6,793	7,496	278	703 D	46.6%	51.5%	47.5%	52.5%
64,753	CLINTON	40,381	19,726	20,005	650	279 D	48.8%	49.5%	49.6%	50.4%
14,273	CRAWFORD	7,178	3,561	3,441	176	120 R	49.6%	47.9%	50.9%	49.1%
38,520	DELTA	19,064	8,763	9,974	327	1,211 D	46.0%	52.3%	46.8%	53.2%
27,472	DICKINSON	13,311	7,049	5,995	267	1,054 R	53.0%	45.0%	54.0%	46.0%
103,655	EATON	57,616	25,900	30,742	974	4,842 D	45.0%	53.4%	45.7%	54.3%
31,437	EMMET	18,149	9,314	8,515	320	799 R	51.3%	46.9%	52.2%	47.8%
436,141	GENESEE	219,896	72,451	143,927	3,518	71,476 D	32.9%	65.5%	33.5%	66.5%
26,023	GLADWIN	13,241	6,391	6,590	260	199 D	48.3%	49.8%	49.2%	50.8%
17,370	GOGEBIC	8,264	3,330	4,757	177	1,427 D	40.3%	57.6%	41.2%	58.8%
77,654	GRAND TRAVERSE	48,733	24,716	23,258	759	1,458 R	50.7%	47.7%	51.5%	48.5%
42,285	GRATIOT	17,738	8,322	9,105	311	783 D	46.9%	51.3%	47.8%	52.2%
46,527	HILLSDALE	20,449	11,221	8,765	463	2,456 R	54.9%	42.9%	56.1%	43.9%
36,016	HOUGHTON	15,972	8,101	7,476	395	625 R	50.7%	46.8%	52.0%	48.0%
36,079	HURON	17,135	8,434	8,367	334	67 R	49.2%	48.8%	50.2%	49.8%
279,320	INGHAM	142,729	46,483	93,994	2,252	47,511 D	32.6%	65.9%	33.1%	66.9%
61,518	IONIA	27,319	14,156	12,565	598	1,591 R	51.8%	46.0%	53.0%	47.0%
27,339	IOSCO	14,187	6,583	7,309	295	726 D	46.4%	51.5%	47.4%	52.6%
13,138	IRON	6,162	2,947	3,080	135	133 D	47.8%	50.0%	48.9%	51.1%
63,351	ISABELLA	28,350	11,220	16,679	451	5,459 D	39.6%	58.8%	40.2%	59.8%
158,422	JACKSON	74,503	35,692	37,480	1,331	1,788 D	47.9%	50.3%	48.8%	51.2%
238,603	KALAMAZOO	130,781	51,554	77,051	2,176	25,497 D	39.4%	58.9%	40.1%	59.9%
16,571	KALKASKA	8,499	4,527	3,780	192	747 R	53.3%	44.5%	54.5%	45.5%
574,335	KENT	303,235	148,336	149,909	4,990	1,573 D	48.9%	49.4%	49.7%	50.3%
2,301	KEWEENAW	1,410	756	610	44	146 R	53.6%	43.3%	55.3%	44.7%
11,333	LAKE	5,292	2,269	2,919	104	650 D	42.9%	55.2%	43.7%	56.3%
87,904	LAPEER	45,362	22,831	21,457	1,074	1,374 R	50.3%	47.3%	51.6%	48.4%
21,119	LEELANAU	14,464	6,938	7,355	171	417 D	48.0%	50.9%	48.5%	51.5%
98,890	LENAWEE	47,734	22,225	24,640	869	2,415 D	46.6%	51.6%	47.4%	52.6%
156,951	LIVINGSTON	99,638	55,592	42,349	1,697	13,243 R	55.8%	42.5%	56.8%	43.2%
7,024	LUCE	2,740	1,490	1,191	59	299 R	54.4%	43.5%	55.6%	44.4%
11,943	MACKINAC	6,396	3,268	3,027	101	241 R	51.1%	47.3%	51.9%	48.1%
788,149	MACOMB	419,216	187,663	223,784	7,769	36,121 D	44.8%	53.4%	45.6%	54.4%

MICHIGAN

PRESIDENT 2008

2000 Census Population	County	Total Vote	Republican	Democratic	Other	Rep.-Dem. Plurality	Percentage Total Vote Rep.	Dem.	Major Vote Rep.	Dem.
24,527	MANISTEE	13,009	5,510	7,235	264	1,725 D	42.4%	55.6%	43.2%	56.8%
64,634	MARQUETTE	33,185	12,906	19,635	644	6,729 D	38.9%	59.2%	39.7%	60.3%
28,274	MASON	15,223	7,147	7,817	259	670 D	46.9%	51.3%	47.8%	52.2%
40,553	MECOSTA	18,664	9,238	9,101	325	137 R	49.5%	48.8%	50.4%	49.6%
25,326	MENOMINEE	11,072	4,855	5,981	236	1,126 D	43.8%	54.0%	44.8%	55.2%
82,874	MIDLAND	43,707	22,263	20,701	743	1,562 R	50.9%	47.4%	51.8%	48.2%
14,478	MISSAUKEE	7,492	4,469	2,898	125	1,571 R	59.7%	38.7%	60.7%	39.3%
145,945	MONROE	76,422	35,858	39,180	1,384	3,322 D	46.9%	51.3%	47.8%	52.2%
61,266	MONTCALM	27,051	13,291	13,208	552	83 R	49.1%	48.8%	50.2%	49.8%
10,315	MONTMORENCY	5,360	2,841	2,403	116	438 R	53.0%	44.8%	54.2%	45.8%
170,200	MUSKEGON	84,271	29,145	53,821	1,305	24,676 D	34.6%	63.9%	35.1%	64.9%
47,874	NEWAYGO	23,105	11,862	10,790	453	1,072 R	51.3%	46.7%	52.4%	47.6%
1,194,156	OAKLAND	659,068	276,956	372,566	9,546	95,610 D	42.0%	56.5%	42.6%	57.4%
26,873	OCEANA	12,509	5,860	6,405	244	545 D	46.8%	51.2%	47.8%	52.2%
21,645	OGEMAW	10,768	5,133	5,391	244	258 D	47.7%	50.1%	48.8%	51.2%
7,818	ONTONAGON	3,885	1,823	1,966	96	143 D	46.9%	50.6%	48.1%	51.9%
23,197	OSCEOLA	11,026	5,973	4,855	198	1,118 R	54.2%	44.0%	55.2%	44.8%
9,418	OSCODA	4,328	2,320	1,887	121	433 R	53.6%	43.6%	55.1%	44.9%
23,301	OTSEGO	12,616	6,752	5,634	230	1,118 R	53.5%	44.7%	54.5%	45.5%
238,314	OTTAWA	136,268	83,330	50,828	2,110	32,502 R	61.2%	37.3%	62.1%	37.9%
14,411	PRESQUE ISLE	7,505	3,606	3,722	177	116 D	48.0%	49.6%	49.2%	50.8%
25,469	ROSCOMMON	14,051	6,727	7,082	242	355 D	47.9%	50.4%	48.7%	51.3%
210,039	SAGINAW	104,090	42,225	60,276	1,589	18,051 D	40.6%	57.9%	41.2%	58.8%
164,235	ST. CLAIR	80,900	38,536	40,677	1,687	2,141 D	47.6%	50.3%	48.6%	51.4%
62,422	ST. JOSEPH	25,702	12,886	12,322	494	564 R	50.1%	47.9%	51.1%	48.9%
44,547	SANILAC	20,169	10,679	9,047	443	1,632 R	52.9%	44.9%	54.1%	45.9%
8,903	SCHOOLCRAFT	4,326	2,058	2,184	84	126 D	47.6%	50.5%	48.5%	51.5%
71,687	SHIAWASSEE	36,415	16,268	19,397	750	3,129 D	44.7%	53.3%	45.6%	54.4%
58,266	TUSCOLA	27,798	13,740	13,503	555	237 R	49.4%	48.6%	50.4%	49.6%
76,263	VAN BUREN	34,766	15,534	18,588	644	3,054 D	44.7%	53.5%	45.5%	54.5%
322,895	WASHTENAW	187,115	53,946	130,578	2,591	76,632 D	28.8%	69.8%	29.2%	70.8%
2,061,162	WAYNE	890,326	219,582	660,085	10,659	440,503 D	24.7%	74.1%	25.0%	75.0%
30,484	WEXFORD	15,704	8,044	7,379	281	665 R	51.2%	47.0%	52.2%	47.8%
9,938,444	TOTAL	5,001,766	2,048,639	2,872,579	80,548	823,940 D	41.0%	57.4%	41.6%	58.4%

MICHIGAN
SENATOR 2008

2000 Census Population	County	Total Vote	Republican	Democratic	Other	Rep.-Dem. Plurality	Percentage Total Vote Rep.	Dem.	Major Vote Rep.	Dem.
11,719	ALCONA	6,297	2,562	3,506	229	944 D	40.7%	55.7%	42.2%	57.8%
9,862	ALGER	4,630	1,446	3,045	139	1,599 D	31.2%	65.8%	32.2%	67.8%
105,665	ALLEGAN	54,007	27,402	24,697	1,908	2,705 R	50.7%	45.7%	52.6%	47.4%
31,314	ALPENA	14,791	4,278	10,037	476	5,759 D	28.9%	67.9%	29.9%	70.1%
23,110	ANTRIM	13,536	6,403	6,624	509	221 D	47.3%	48.9%	49.2%	50.8%
17,269	ARENAC	7,858	2,667	4,867	324	2,200 D	33.9%	61.9%	35.4%	64.6%
8,746	BARAGA	3,575	1,158	2,309	108	1,151 D	32.4%	64.6%	33.4%	66.6%
56,755	BARRY	29,838	14,409	14,211	1,218	198 R	48.3%	47.6%	50.3%	49.7%
110,157	BAY	55,592	16,766	36,807	2,019	20,041 D	30.2%	66.2%	31.3%	68.7%
15,998	BENZIE	10,047	4,101	5,597	349	1,496 D	40.8%	55.7%	42.3%	57.7%
162,453	BERRIEN	74,992	31,919	40,497	2,576	8,578 D	42.6%	54.0%	44.1%	55.9%
45,787	BRANCH	17,616	7,834	9,136	646	1,302 D	44.5%	51.9%	46.2%	53.8%
137,985	CALHOUN	62,504	23,060	37,323	2,121	14,263 D	36.9%	59.7%	38.2%	61.8%
51,104	CASS	22,619	9,612	12,138	869	2,526 D	42.5%	53.7%	44.2%	55.8%
26,090	CHARLEVOIX	14,060	6,060	7,471	529	1,411 D	43.1%	53.1%	44.8%	55.2%
26,448	CHEBOYGAN	13,524	5,264	7,742	518	2,478 D	38.9%	57.2%	40.5%	59.5%
38,543	CHIPPEWA	16,234	5,659	9,991	584	4,332 D	34.9%	61.5%	36.2%	63.8%
31,252	CLARE	14,148	5,103	8,429	616	3,326 D	36.1%	59.6%	37.7%	62.3%
64,753	CLINTON	38,926	16,708	20,996	1,222	4,288 D	42.9%	53.9%	44.3%	55.7%
14,273	CRAWFORD	6,935	2,661	3,951	323	1,290 D	38.4%	57.0%	40.2%	59.8%
38,520	DELTA	18,562	5,966	12,112	484	6,146 D	32.1%	65.3%	33.0%	67.0%
27,472	DICKINSON	12,959	4,773	7,759	427	2,986 D	36.8%	59.9%	38.1%	61.9%
103,655	EATON	55,832	21,540	32,378	1,914	10,838 D	38.6%	58.0%	39.9%	60.1%
31,437	EMMET	17,644	7,806	9,146	692	1,340 D	44.2%	51.8%	46.0%	54.0%
436,141	GENESEE	214,610	58,302	148,596	7,712	90,294 D	27.2%	69.2%	28.2%	71.8%
26,023	GLADWIN	12,905	4,844	7,570	491	2,726 D	37.5%	58.7%	39.0%	61.0%
17,370	GOGEBIC	7,986	2,205	5,503	278	3,298 D	27.6%	68.9%	28.6%	71.4%
77,654	GRAND TRAVERSE	47,384	21,489	24,105	1,790	2,616 D	45.4%	50.9%	47.1%	52.9%
42,285	GRATIOT	17,203	6,700	9,896	607	3,196 D	38.9%	57.5%	40.4%	59.6%
46,527	HILLSDALE	19,624	9,458	9,236	930	222 R	48.2%	47.1%	50.6%	49.4%
36,016	HOUGHTON	15,565	5,779	9,284	502	3,505 D	37.1%	59.6%	38.4%	61.6%
36,079	HURON	16,513	5,776	10,170	567	4,394 D	35.0%	61.6%	36.2%	63.8%
279,320	INGHAM	138,115	38,529	94,652	4,934	56,123 D	27.9%	68.5%	28.9%	71.1%
61,518	IONIA	26,435	11,528	13,779	1,128	2,251 D	43.6%	52.1%	45.6%	54.4%
27,339	IOSCO	13,854	4,879	8,447	528	3,568 D	35.2%	61.0%	36.6%	63.4%
13,138	IRON	6,010	1,907	3,922	181	2,015 D	31.7%	65.3%	32.7%	67.3%
63,351	ISABELLA	27,083	9,063	16,924	1,096	7,861 D	33.5%	62.5%	34.9%	65.1%
158,422	JACKSON	71,786	27,838	41,035	2,913	13,197 D	38.8%	57.2%	40.4%	59.6%
238,603	KALAMAZOO	126,830	47,663	74,977	4,190	27,314 D	37.6%	59.1%	38.9%	61.1%
16,571	KALKASKA	8,219	3,536	4,237	446	701 D	43.0%	51.6%	45.5%	54.5%
574,335	KENT	295,171	135,895	149,242	10,034	13,347 D	46.0%	50.6%	47.7%	52.3%
2,301	KEWEENAW	1,370	517	808	45	291 D	37.7%	59.0%	39.0%	61.0%
11,333	LAKE	5,150	1,813	3,137	200	1,324 D	35.2%	60.9%	36.6%	63.4%
87,904	LAPEER	43,892	18,720	23,108	2,064	4,388 D	42.7%	52.6%	44.8%	55.2%
21,119	LEELANAU	14,161	6,098	7,638	425	1,540 D	43.1%	53.9%	44.4%	55.6%
98,890	LENAWEE	45,839	17,769	26,208	1,862	8,439 D	38.8%	57.2%	40.4%	59.6%
156,951	LIVINGSTON	95,953	46,231	45,687	4,035	544 R	48.2%	47.6%	50.3%	49.7%
7,024	LUCE	2,627	956	1,566	105	610 D	36.4%	59.6%	37.9%	62.1%
11,943	MACKINAC	6,235	2,338	3,696	201	1,358 D	37.5%	59.3%	38.7%	61.3%
788,149	MACOMB	404,623	131,962	257,439	15,222	125,477 D	32.6%	63.6%	33.9%	66.1%

MICHIGAN
SENATOR 2008

2000 Census Population	County	Total Vote	Republican	Democratic	Other	Rep.-Dem. Plurality	Total Vote Rep.	Total Vote Dem.	Major Vote Rep.	Major Vote Dem.
24,527	MANISTEE	12,760	4,426	7,888	446	3,462 D	34.7%	61.8%	35.9%	64.1%
64,634	MARQUETTE	32,421	8,621	22,660	1,140	14,039 D	26.6%	69.9%	27.6%	72.4%
28,274	MASON	14,836	5,910	8,468	458	2,558 D	39.8%	57.1%	41.1%	58.9%
40,553	MECOSTA	18,120	7,793	9,718	609	1,925 D	43.0%	53.6%	44.5%	55.5%
25,326	MENOMINEE	10,529	3,570	6,599	360	3,029 D	33.9%	62.7%	35.1%	64.9%
82,874	MIDLAND	42,598	18,764	22,430	1,404	3,666 D	44.0%	52.7%	45.6%	54.4%
14,478	MISSAUKEE	7,317	3,786	3,286	245	500 R	51.7%	44.9%	53.5%	46.5%
145,945	MONROE	72,880	25,564	44,485	2,831	18,921 D	35.1%	61.0%	36.5%	63.5%
61,266	MONTCALM	26,283	10,848	14,380	1,055	3,532 D	41.3%	54.7%	43.0%	57.0%
10,315	MONTMORENCY	5,207	2,037	2,977	193	940 D	39.1%	57.2%	40.6%	59.4%
170,200	MUSKEGON	81,782	23,648	55,636	2,498	31,988 D	28.9%	68.0%	29.8%	70.2%
47,874	NEWAYGO	22,539	10,210	11,463	866	1,253 D	45.3%	50.9%	47.1%	52.9%
1,194,156	OAKLAND	639,062	220,597	396,862	21,603	176,265 D	34.5%	62.1%	35.7%	64.3%
26,873	OCEANA	12,195	4,932	6,844	419	1,912 D	40.4%	56.1%	41.9%	58.1%
21,645	OGEMAW	10,374	3,548	6,422	404	2,874 D	34.2%	61.9%	35.6%	64.4%
7,818	ONTONAGON	3,788	1,108	2,530	150	1,422 D	29.3%	66.8%	30.5%	69.5%
23,197	OSCEOLA	10,717	4,861	5,460	396	599 D	45.4%	50.9%	47.1%	52.9%
9,418	OSCODA	4,192	1,740	2,258	194	518 D	41.5%	53.9%	43.5%	56.5%
23,301	OTSEGO	12,231	5,334	6,429	468	1,095 D	43.6%	52.6%	45.3%	54.7%
238,314	OTTAWA	132,869	78,535	50,577	3,757	27,958 R	59.1%	38.1%	60.8%	39.2%
14,411	PRESQUE ISLE	7,339	2,386	4,668	285	2,282 D	32.5%	63.6%	33.8%	66.2%
25,469	ROSCOMMON	13,709	4,951	8,232	526	3,281 D	36.1%	60.0%	37.6%	62.4%
210,039	SAGINAW	100,869	31,099	67,025	2,745	35,926 D	30.8%	66.4%	31.7%	68.3%
164,235	ST. CLAIR	78,144	28,478	46,265	3,401	17,787 D	36.4%	59.2%	38.1%	61.9%
62,422	ST. JOSEPH	24,935	10,932	13,075	928	2,143 D	43.8%	52.4%	45.5%	54.5%
44,547	SANILAC	19,530	8,113	10,614	803	2,501 D	41.5%	54.3%	43.3%	56.7%
8,903	SCHOOLCRAFT	4,181	1,362	2,698	121	1,336 D	32.6%	64.5%	33.5%	66.5%
71,687	SHIAWASSEE	35,411	13,107	20,872	1,432	7,765 D	37.0%	58.9%	38.6%	61.4%
58,266	TUSCOLA	27,044	10,540	15,408	1,096	4,868 D	39.0%	57.0%	40.6%	59.4%
76,263	VAN BUREN	33,748	13,669	18,932	1,147	5,263 D	40.5%	56.1%	41.9%	58.1%
322,895	WASHTENAW	181,621	45,832	128,973	6,816	83,141 D	25.2%	71.0%	26.2%	73.8%
2,061,162	WAYNE	862,258	161,329	674,528	26,401	513,199 D	18.7%	78.2%	19.3%	80.7%
30,484	WEXFORD	15,262	6,488	8,093	681	1,605 D	42.5%	53.0%	44.5%	55.5%
9,938,444	TOTAL	4,848,620	1,641,070	3,038,386	169,164	1,397,316 D	33.8%	62.7%	35.1%	64.9%

MICHIGAN

HOUSE OF REPRESENTATIVES

CD	Year	Total Vote	Republican Vote	Republican Candidate	Democratic Vote	Democratic Candidate	Other Vote	Rep.-Dem. Plurality	Total Vote Rep.	Total Vote Dem.	Major Vote Rep.	Major Vote Dem.
1	2008	327,836	107,340	CASPERSON, TOM	213,216	STUPAK, BART*	7,280	105,876 D	32.7%	65.0%	33.5%	66.5%
1	2006	259,927	72,753	HOOPER, DON	180,448	STUPAK, BART*	6,726	107,695 D	28.0%	69.4%	28.7%	71.3%
1	2004	322,674	105,706	HOOPER, DON	211,571	STUPAK, BART*	5,397	105,865 D	32.8%	65.6%	33.3%	66.7%
1	2002	222,687	69,254	HOOPER, DON	150,701	STUPAK, BART*	2,732	81,447 D	31.1%	67.7%	31.5%	68.5%
2	2008	343,309	214,100	HOEKSTRA, PETER*	119,506	JOHNSON, FRED	9,703	94,594 R	62.4%	34.8%	64.2%	35.8%
2	2006	275,394	183,006	HOEKSTRA, PETER*	86,950	KOTOS, KIMON	5,438	96,056 R	66.5%	31.6%	67.8%	32.2%
2	2004	325,005	225,343	HOEKSTRA, PETER*	94,040	KOTOS, KIMON	5,622	131,303 R	69.3%	28.9%	70.6%	29.4%
2	2002	222,907	156,937	HOEKSTRA, PETER*	61,749	WRISLEY, JEFF	4,221	95,188 R	70.4%	27.7%	71.8%	28.2%
3	2008	333,518	203,799	EHLERS, VERNON J.*	117,961	SANCHEZ, HENRY	11,758	85,838 R	61.1%	35.4%	63.3%	36.7%
3	2006	271,352	171,212	EHLERS, VERNON J.*	93,846	RINCK, JAMES	6,294	77,366 R	63.1%	34.6%	64.6%	35.4%
3	2004	322,103	214,465	EHLERS, VERNON J.*	101,395	HICKEY, PETER	6,243	113,070 R	66.6%	31.5%	67.9%	32.1%
3	2002	218,855	153,131	EHLERS, VERNON J.*	61,987	LYNNES, KATHRYN	3,737	91,144 R	70.0%	28.3%	71.2%	28.8%
4	2008	329,764	204,259	CAMP, DAVE*	117,665	CONCANNON, ANDREW D.	7,840	86,594 R	61.9%	35.7%	63.4%	36.6%
4	2006	264,245	160,041	CAMP, DAVE*	100,260	HUCKLEBERRY, MIKE	3,944	59,781 R	60.6%	37.9%	61.5%	38.5%
4	2004	318,924	205,274	CAMP, DAVE*	110,885	HUCKLEBERRY, MIKE	2,765	94,389 R	64.4%	34.8%	64.9%	35.1%
4	2002	218,573	149,090	CAMP, DAVE*	65,950	HOLLENBECK, LAWRENCE	3,533	83,140 R	68.2%	30.2%	69.3%	30.7%
5	2008	315,295	85,017	SAWICKI, MATT	221,841	KILDEE, DALE E.*	8,437	136,824 D	27.0%	70.4%	27.7%	72.3%
5	2006	241,691	60,967	KLAMMER, ERIC	176,171	KILDEE, DALE E.*	4,553	115,204 D	25.2%	72.9%	25.7%	74.3%
5	2004	309,915	96,934	KIRKWOOD, MYRAH	208,163	KILDEE, DALE E.*	4,818	111,229 D	31.3%	67.2%	31.8%	68.2%
5	2002	173,339		—	158,709	KILDEE, DALE E.*	14,630	158,709 D		91.6%		100.0%
6	2008	319,646	188,157	UPTON, FRED*	123,257	COONEY, DON	8,232	64,900 R	58.9%	38.6%	60.4%	39.6%
6	2006	234,583	142,125	UPTON, FRED*	88,978	CLARK, KIM	3,480	53,147 R	60.6%	37.9%	61.5%	38.5%
6	2004	302,158	197,425	UPTON, FRED*	97,978	ELLIOTT, SCOTT	6,755	99,447 R	65.3%	32.4%	66.8%	33.2%
6	2002	183,517	126,936	UPTON, FRED*	53,793	GIGUERE, GARY JR.	2,788	73,143 R	69.2%	29.3%	70.2%	29.8%
7	2008	322,286	149,781	WALBERG, TIM*	157,213	SCHAUER, MARK H.	15,292	7,432 D	46.5%	48.8%	48.8%	51.2%
7	2006	245,026	122,348	WALBERG, TIM	112,665	RENIER, SHARON	10,013	9,683 R	49.9%	46.0%	52.1%	47.9%
7	2004	301,642	176,053	SCHWARZ, JOE	109,527	RENIER, SHARON	16,062	66,526 R	58.4%	36.3%	61.6%	38.4%
7	2002	203,069	121,142	SMITH, NICK*	78,412	SIMPSON, MIKE	3,515	42,730 R	59.7%	38.6%	60.7%	39.3%
8	2008	361,607	204,408	ROGERS, MIKE*	145,491	ALEXANDER, ROBERT	11,708	58,917 R	56.5%	40.2%	58.4%	41.6%
8	2006	284,471	157,237	ROGERS, MIKE*	122,107	MARCINKOWSKI, JIM	5,127	35,130 R	55.3%	42.9%	56.3%	43.7%
8	2004	340,423	207,925	ROGERS, MIKE*	125,619	ALEXANDER, ROBERT	6,879	82,306 R	61.1%	36.9%	62.3%	37.7%
8	2002	230,597	156,525	ROGERS, MIKE*	70,920	McALPINE, FRANK	3,152	85,605 R	67.9%	30.8%	68.8%	31.2%
9	2008	351,963	150,035	KNOLLENBERG, JOE*	183,311	PETERS, GARY C.	18,617	33,276 D	42.6%	52.1%	45.0%	55.0%
9	2006	276,180	142,390	KNOLLENBERG, JOE*	127,620	SKINNER, NANCY	6,170	14,770 R	51.6%	46.2%	52.7%	47.3%
9	2004	340,799	199,210	KNOLLENBERG, JOE*	134,764	REIFMAN, STEVEN	6,825	64,446 R	58.5%	39.5%	59.6%	40.4%
9	2002	242,880	141,102	KNOLLENBERG, JOE*	96,856	FINK, DAVID	4,922	44,246 R	58.1%	39.9%	59.3%	40.7%
10	2008	347,603	230,471	MILLER, CANDICE S.*	108,354	DENISON, ROBERT	8,778	122,117 R	66.3%	31.2%	68.0%	32.0%
10	2006	270,421	179,072	MILLER, CANDICE S.*	84,689	DENISON, ROBERT	6,660	94,383 R	66.2%	31.3%	67.9%	32.1%
10	2004	331,868	227,720	MILLER, CANDICE S.*	98,029	CASEY, ROB	6,119	129,691 R	68.6%	29.5%	69.9%	30.1%
10	2002	216,928	137,339	MILLER, CANDICE S.	77,053	MARLINGA, CARL	2,536	60,286 R	63.3%	35.5%	64.1%	35.9%
11	2008	345,182	177,461	McCOTTER, THADDEUS*	156,625	LARKIN, JOSEPH	11,096	20,836 R	51.4%	45.4%	53.1%	46.9%
11	2006	265,784	143,658	McCOTTER, THADDEUS*	114,248	TRUPIANO, TONY	7,878	29,410 R	54.1%	43.0%	55.7%	44.3%
11	2004	327,216	186,431	McCOTTER, THADDEUS*	134,301	TRURAN, PHILLIP	6,484	52,130 R	57.0%	41.0%	58.1%	41.9%
11	2002	220,405	126,050	McCOTTER, THADDEUS	87,402	KELLEY, KEVIN	6,953	38,648 R	57.2%	39.7%	59.1%	40.9%
12	2008	312,344	74,565	COPPLE, BERT	225,094	LEVIN, SANDER M.*	12,685	150,529 D	23.9%	72.1%	24.9%	75.1%
12	2006	240,115	62,689	SHAFER, RANDELL	168,494	LEVIN, SANDER M.*	8,932	105,805 D	26.1%	70.2%	27.1%	72.9%
12	2004	304,134	88,256	SHAFER, RANDELL	210,827	LEVIN, SANDER M.*	5,051	122,571 D	29.0%	69.3%	29.5%	70.5%
12	2002	206,528	61,502	DEAN, HARVEY	140,970	LEVIN, SANDER M.*	4,056	79,468 D	29.8%	68.3%	30.4%	69.6%

MICHIGAN

HOUSE OF REPRESENTATIVES

			Republican		Democratic				Total Vote		Major Vote	
CD	Year	Total Vote	Vote	Candidate	Vote	Candidate	Other Vote	Rep.-Dem. Plurality	Rep.	Dem.	Rep.	Dem.
13	2008	225,922	43,098	GUBICS, EDWARD J.	167,481	KILPATRICK, CAROLYN CHEEKS*	15,343	124,383 D	19.1%	74.1%	20.5%	79.5%
13	2006	126,323		—	126,308	KILPATRICK, CAROLYN CHEEKS*	15	126,308 D		100.0%		100.0%
13	2004	221,654	40,935	CASSELL, CYNTHIA	173,246	KILPATRICK, CAROLYN CHEEKS*	7,473	132,311 D	18.5%	78.2%	19.1%	80.9%
13	2002	131,941		—	120,869	KILPATRICK, CAROLYN CHEEKS*	11,072	120,869 D		91.6%		100.0%
14	2008	246,588		—	227,841	CONYERS, JOHN JR.*	18,747	227,841 D		92.4%		100.0%
14	2006	186,122	27,367	MILES, CHAD	158,755	CONYERS, JOHN JR.*		131,388 D	14.7%	85.3%	14.7%	85.3%
14	2004	254,580	35,089	PEDRAZA, VERONICA	213,681	CONYERS, JOHN JR.*	5,810	178,592 D	13.8%	83.9%	14.1%	85.9%
14	2002	174,608	26,544	STONE, DAVE	145,285	CONYERS, JOHN JR.*	2,779	118,741 D	15.2%	83.2%	15.4%	84.6%
15	2008	327,827	81,802	LYNCH, JOHN	231,784	DINGELL, JOHN D.*	14,241	149,982 D	25.0%	70.7%	26.1%	73.9%
15	2006	206,868		—	181,946	DINGELL, JOHN D.*	24,922	181,946 D		88.0%		100.0%
15	2004	307,963	81,828	REAMER, DAWN	218,409	DINGELL, JOHN D.*	7,726	136,581 D	26.6%	70.9%	27.3%	72.7%
15	2002	189,063	48,626	KALTENBACH, MARTIN	136,518	DINGELL, JOHN D.*	3,919	87,892 D	25.7%	72.2%	26.3%	73.7%
TOTAL	2008	4,810,690	2,114,293		2,516,640		179,757	402,347 D	43.9%	52.3%	45.7%	54.3%
TOTAL	2006	3,648,502	1,624,865		1,923,485		100,152	298,620 D	44.5%	52.7%	45.8%	54.2%
TOTAL	2004	4,631,058	2,288,594		2,242,435		100,029	46,159 R	49.4%	48.4%	50.5%	49.5%
TOTAL	2002	3,055,897	1,474,178		1,507,174		74,545	32,996 D	48.2%	49.3%	49.4%	50.6%

Note: An asterisk (*) denotes incumbent.

MICHIGAN

GENERAL AND PRIMARY ELECTIONS

2008 GENERAL ELECTIONS

Governor — Other vote was 33,085 Natural Law (Ralph Nader); 23,716 Libertarian (Bob Barr); 14,685 U.S. Taxpayers (Chuck Baldwin); 8,892 Green (Cynthia A. McKinney); 129 write-in (Alan Keyes); 41 write-in (Brian Moore).

Senator — Other vote was 76,347 Libertarian (Scotty Boman); 43,440 Green (Harley G. Mikkelson); 30,827 U.S. Taxpayers (Michael N. Nikitin); 18,550 Natural Law (Doug Dern).

House — Other vote was:

CD 1 — 2,669 Green (Jean Treacy); 2,533 Libertarian (Daniel W. Grow); 2,070 U.S. Taxpayers (Joshua J. Warren); 8 write-in (Don Hooper).

CD 2 — 5,496 Libertarian (Dan Johnson); 4,200 U.S. Taxpayers (Ronald E. Graeser); 7 write-in (William Bailey).

CD 3 — 11,758 Libertarian (Erwin J. Haas).

CD 4 — 4,055 U.S. Taxpayers (John Emerick); 3,785 Libertarian (Allitta Hren).

CD 5 — 4,293 Libertarian (Leonard Schwartz); 4,144 Green (Ken Mathenia).

CD 6 — 4,720 Libertarian (Greg Merle); 3,512 Green (Edward Pinkney).

CD 7 — 9,528 Green (Lynn Meadows); 5,675 Libertarian (Ken Proctor); 89 write-in (Sharon Renier).

CD 8 — 4,373 Libertarian (Will Tyler White); 3,836 Green (Aaron Stuttman); 3,499 - U.S. Taxpayers (George M. Zimmer).

CD 9 — 8,987 No Party Affiliation (Jack Kevorkian); 4,893 Libertarian (Adam Goodman); 4,737 Green (Douglas Campbell).

CD 10 — 4,632 Libertarian (Neil Kiernan Stephenson); 4,146 Green (Candace R. Caveny).

CD 11 — 6,001 Libertarian (John J. Tatar); 5,072 Green (Erik Shelley); 23 write-in (Bhagwan Dashairya).

CD 12 — 4,767 Libertarian (John Vico); 4,076 U.S. Taxpayers (Les Townsend); 3,842 Green (William J. Opalicky).

CD 13 — 9,579 Green (George L. Corsetti); 5,764 Libertarian (Gregory Creswell).

CD 14 — 10,732 Libertarian (Richard Secula); 8,015 Green (Clyde Shabazz).

CD 15 — 7,082 Green (Aimee Smith); 4,002 Libertarian (Gregory Scott Stempfle); 3,157 U.S. Taxpayers (James H. Wagner).

2008 PRIMARY ELECTIONS

Primary — January 15, 2008 (President); August 5, 2008 (Congress)

Registration (as of July 2008) — 7,243,261 — No Party Registration

Primary Type — Open—Any registered voter could participate in the primary of either party.

MICHIGAN

GENERAL AND PRIMARY ELECTIONS

	REPUBLICAN PRIMARIES			DEMOCRATIC PRIMARIES		
President	Mitt Romney	338,316	38.9%	Hillary Clinton	328,309	55.2%
	John McCain	257,985	29.7%	Uncommitted	238,168	40.1%
	Mike Huckabee	139,764	16.1%	Dennis J. Kucinich	21,715	3.7%
	Ron Paul	54,475	6.3%	Christopher J. Dodd	3,845	0.6%
	Fred Thompson	32,159	3.7%	Mike Gravel	2,361	0.4%
	Rudolph Giuliani	24,725	2.8%			
	Uncommitted	18,118	2.1%			
	Duncan Hunter	2,819	0.3%			
	Tom Tancredo	457	0.1%			
	Sam Brownback	351				
	TOTAL	869,169		TOTAL	594,398	
Senator	Jack Hoogendyk Jr.	495,467	100.0%	Carl Levin*	561,676	100.0%
Congressional District 1	Tom Casperson	17,433	46.2%	Bart Stupak*	51,114	100.0%
	Don Hooper	10,718	28.4%			
	Linda Goldthorpe	9,565	25.4%			
	TOTAL	37,716				
Congressional District 2	Peter Hoekstra*	53,322	100.0%	Fred Johnson	20,617	100.0%
Congressional District 3	Vernon J. Ehlers*	49,698	100.0%	Henry Sanchez	13,664	100.0%
Congressional District 4	Dave Camp*	57,136	100.0%	Andrew D. Concannon	23,441	100.0%
Congressional District 5	Matt Sawicki	14,682	100.0%	Dale E. Kildee*	41,697	100.0%
Congressional District 6	Fred Upton*	47,753	100.0%	Don Cooney	13,657	100.0%
Congressional District 7	Tim Walberg*	39,314	100.0%	Mark H. Schauer	17,270	65.7%
				Sharon Renier	9,034	34.3%
				TOTAL	26,304	
Congressional District 8	Mike Rogers*	45,850	100.0%	Robert Alexander	25,963	100.0%
Congressional District 9	Joe Knollenberg*	49,940	100.0%	Gary C. Peters	41,978	100.0%
Congressional District 10	Candice S. Miller*	66,003	100.0%	Robert Denison	25,040	100.0%
Congressional District 11	Thaddeus McCotter*	43,303	100.0%	Joseph Larkin	25,924	72.9%
				Edward Kriewall	9,635	27.1%
				TOTAL	35,559	
Congressional District 12	Bert Copple	18,561	100.0%	Sander M. Levin*	58,763	100.0%
Congressional District 13	Edward J. Gubics	7,016	100.0%	Carolyn Cheeks Kilpatrick*	21,089	39.2%
				Mary Waters	19,303	35.8%
				Martha Scott	13,471	25.0%
				TOTAL	53,863	
Congressional District 14	No Republican candidate			John Conyers Jr.*	51,511	100.0%
Congressional District 15	John Lynch	11,160	100.0%	John D. Dingell*	51,306	100.0%

Note: An asterisk (*) denotes incumbent.

MINNESOTA

Congressional districts first established for elections held in 2002
8 members

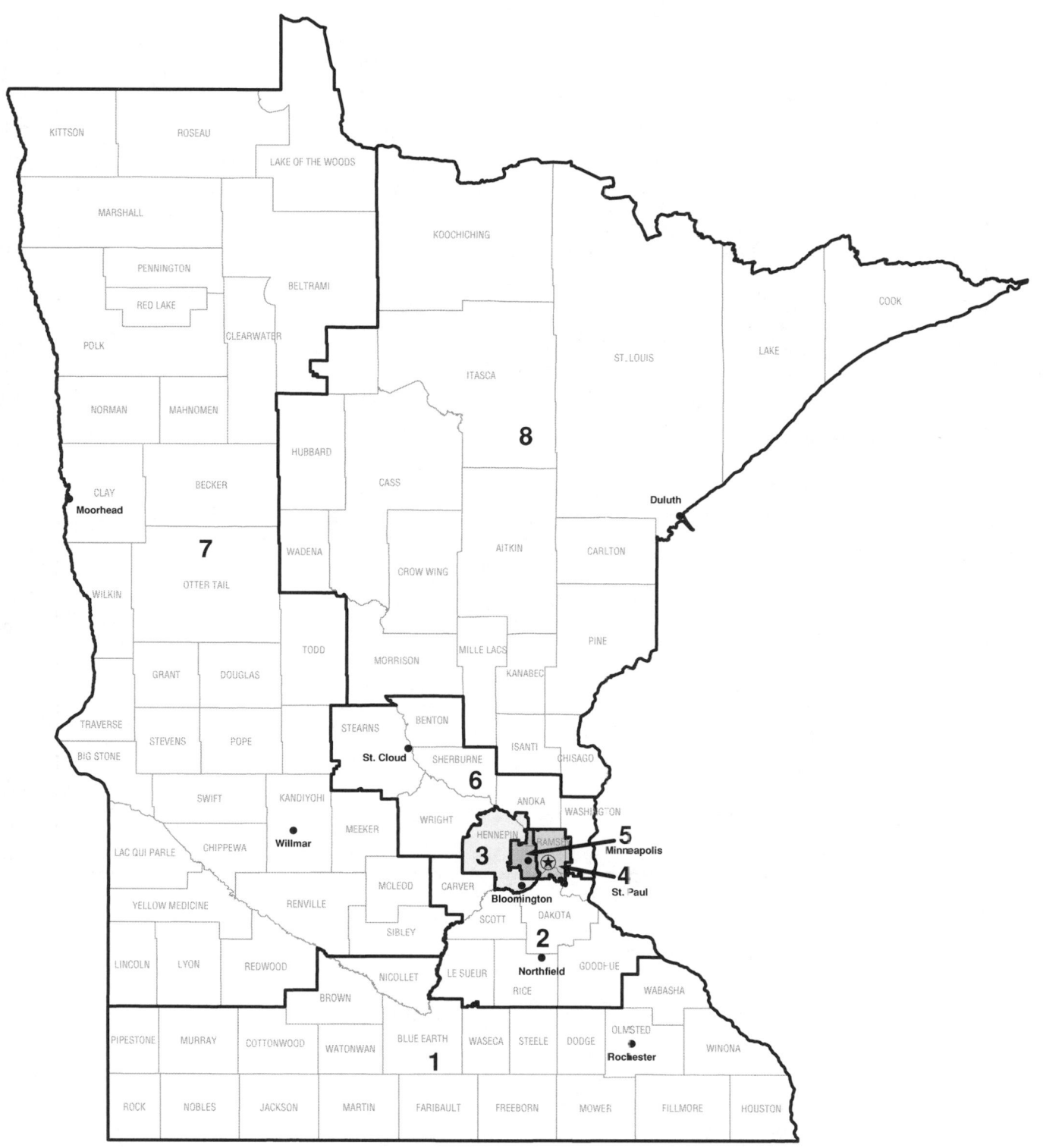

MINNESOTA

Minneapolis–St.Paul Area

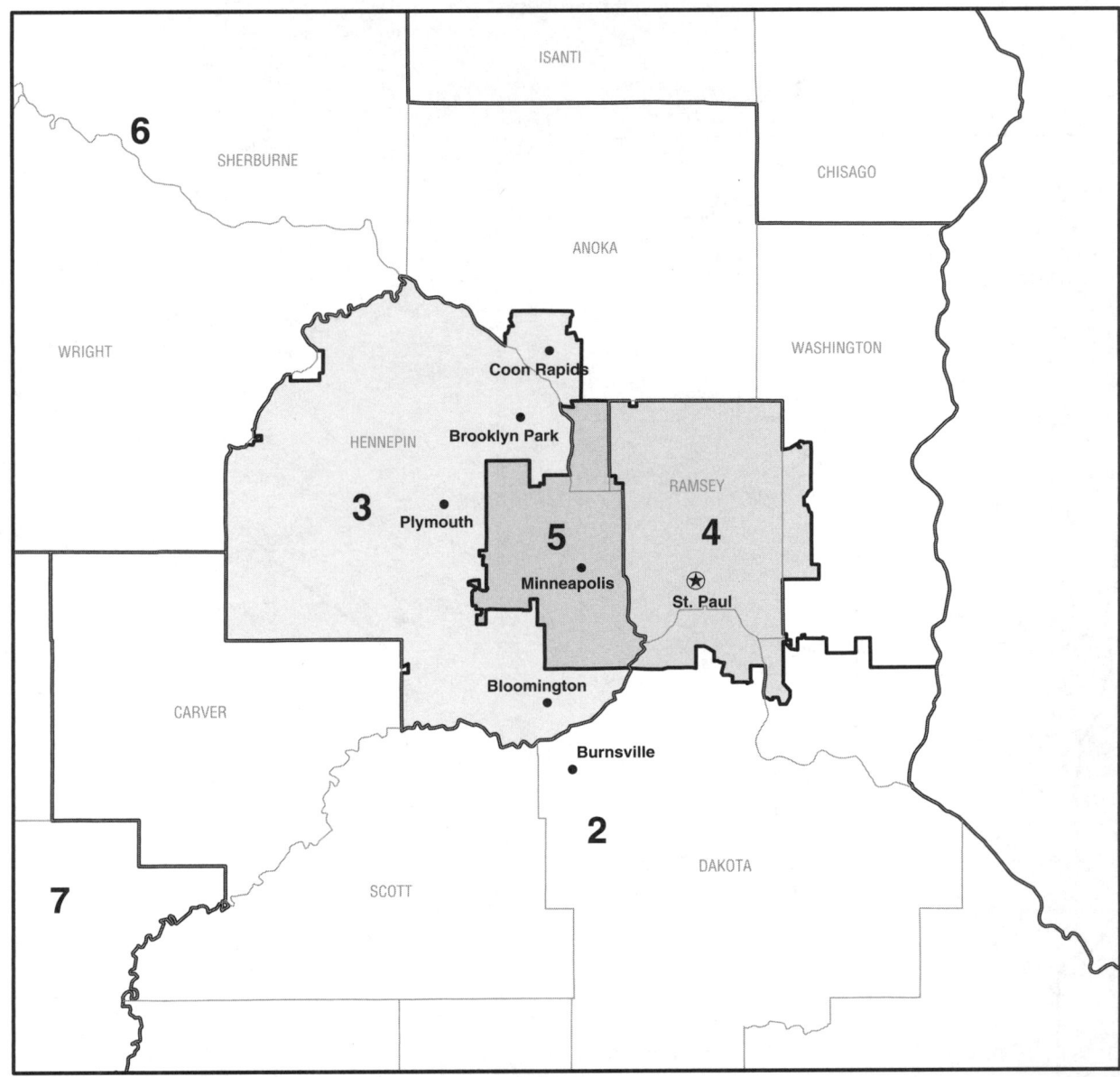

MINNESOTA

GOVERNOR
Tim Pawlenty (R). Reelected 2006 to a four-year term. Previously elected 2002.

SENATORS (2 Democrats)
Al Franken (D). Elected 2008 to a six-year term. He was not sworn in until July 7, 2009, because of a protracted legal challenge caused by the closeness of the election. Amy Klobuchar (D). Elected 2006 to a six-year term.

REPRESENTATIVES (5 Democrats, 3 Republicans)
1. Timothy J. Walz (D)
2. John Kline (R)
3. Erik Paulsen (R)
4. Betty McCollum (D)
5. Keith Ellison (D)
6. Michele Bachmann (R)
7. Collin C. Peterson (D)
8. James L. Oberstar (D)

POSTWAR VOTE FOR PRESIDENT

Year	Total Vote	Republican Vote	Candidate	Democratic Vote	Candidate	Other Vote	Plurality	Total Vote Rep.	Dem.	Major Vote Rep.	Dem.
2008	2,910,369	1,275,409	McCain, John	1,573,354	Obama, Barack	61,606	297,945 D	43.8%	54.1%	44.8%	55.2%
2004	2,828,387	1,346,695	Bush, George W.	1,445,014	Kerry, John	36,678	98,319 D	47.6%	51.1%	48.2%	51.8%
2000**	2,438,685	1,109,659	Bush, George W.	1,168,266	Gore, Al	160,760	58,607 D	45.5%	47.9%	48.7%	51.3%
1996**	2,192,640	766,476	Dole, Bob	1,120,438	Clinton, Bill	305,726	353,962 D	35.0%	51.1%	40.6%	59.4%
1992**	2,347,948	747,841	Bush, George	1,020,997	Clinton, Bill	579,110	273,156 D	31.9%	43.5%	42.3%	57.7%
1988	2,096,790	962,337	Bush, George	1,109,471	Dukakis, Michael S.	24,982	147,134 D	45.9%	52.9%	46.4%	53.6%
1984	2,084,449	1,032,603	Reagan, Ronald	1,036,364	Mondale, Walter F.	15,482	3,761 D	49.5%	49.7%	49.9%	50.1%
1980**	2,051,980	873,268	Reagan, Ronald	954,174	Carter, Jimmy	224,538	80,906 D	42.6%	46.5%	47.8%	52.2%
1976	1,949,931	819,395	Ford, Gerald R.	1,070,440	Carter, Jimmy	60,096	251,045 D	42.0%	54.9%	43.4%	56.6%
1972	1,741,652	898,269	Nixon, Richard M.	802,346	McGovern, George S.	41,037	95,923 R	51.6%	46.1%	52.8%	47.2%
1968**	1,588,506	658,643	Nixon, Richard M.	857,738	Humphrey, Hubert H.	72,125	199,095 D	41.5%	54.0%	43.4%	56.6%
1964	1,554,462	559,624	Goldwater, Barry M.	991,117	Johnson, Lyndon B.	3,721	431,493 D	36.0%	63.8%	36.1%	63.9%
1960	1,541,887	757,915	Nixon, Richard M.	779,933	Kennedy, John F.	4,039	22,018 D	49.2%	50.6%	49.3%	50.7%
1956	1,340,005	719,302	Eisenhower, Dwight D.	617,525	Stevenson, Adlai E.	3,178	101,777 R	53.7%	46.1%	53.8%	46.2%
1952	1,379,483	763,211	Eisenhower, Dwight D.	608,458	Stevenson, Adlai E.	7,814	154,753 R	55.3%	44.1%	55.6%	44.4%
1948	1,212,226	483,617	Dewey, Thomas E.	692,966	Truman, Harry S.	35,643	209,349 D	39.9%	57.2%	41.1%	58.9%

**In past elections, the other vote included: 2000 - 126,696 Green (Nader); 1996 - 257,704 Reform (Ross Perot); 1992 - 562,506 Independent (Perot); 1980 - 174,990 Independent (John Anderson); 1968 - 68,931 American Independent (George Wallace).

MINNESOTA

POSTWAR VOTE FOR GOVERNOR

Year	Total Vote	Republican Vote	Republican Candidate	Democratic Vote	Democratic Candidate	Other Vote	Plurality	Total Vote Rep.	Total Vote Dem.	Major Vote Rep.	Major Vote Dem.
2006	2,202,937	1,028,568	Pawlenty, Tim	1,007,460	Hatch, Mike	166,909	21,108 R	46.7%	45.7%	50.5%	49.5%
2002**	2,252,473	999,473	Pawlenty, Tim	821,268	Moe, Roger D.	431,732	178,205 R	44.4%	36.5%	54.9%	45.1%
1998**	2,090,518	716,880	Coleman, Norm	587,060	Humphrey, Hubert H., III	786,578	56,523 V	34.3%	28.1%	55.0%	45.0%
1994	1,765,590	1,094,165	Carlson, Arne	589,344	Marty, John	82,081	504,821 R	62.0%	33.4%	65.0%	35.0%
1990	1,806,777	895,988	Carlson, Arne	836,218	Perpich, Rudy	74,571	59,770 R	49.6%	46.3%	51.7%	48.3%
1986	1,415,989	606,755	Ludeman, Cal R.	790,138	Perpich, Rudy	19,096	183,383 D	42.9%	55.8%	43.4%	56.6%
1982	1,789,539	715,796	Whitney, Wheelock	1,049,104	Perpich, Rudy	24,639	333,308 D	40.0%	58.6%	40.6%	59.4%
1978	1,585,702	830,019	Quie, Albert H.	718,244	Perpich, Rudy	37,439	111,775 R	52.3%	45.3%	53.6%	46.4%
1974	1,252,898	367,722	Johnson, John W.	786,787	Anderson, Wendell R.	98,389	419,065 D	29.3%	62.8%	31.9%	68.1%
1970	1,365,443	621,780	Head, Douglas M.	737,921	Anderson, Wendell R.	5,742	116,141 D	45.5%	54.0%	45.7%	54.3%
1966	1,295,058	680,593	LeVander, Harold	607,943	Rolvaag, Karl F.	6,522	72,650 R	52.6%	46.9%	52.8%	47.2%
1962**	1,246,904	619,751	Andersen, Elmer L.	619,842	Rolvaag, Karl F.	7,311	91 D	49.7%	49.7%	50.0%	50.0%
1960	1,550,265	783,813	Andersen, Elmer L.	760,934	Freeman, Orville L.	5,518	22,879 R	50.6%	49.1%	50.7%	49.3%
1958	1,159,915	490,731	MacKinnon, George	658,326	Freeman, Orville L.	10,858	167,595 D	42.3%	56.8%	42.7%	57.3%
1956	1,422,161	685,196	Nelsen, Ancher	731,180	Freeman, Orville L.	5,785	45,984 D	48.2%	51.4%	48.4%	51.6%
1954	1,151,417	538,865	Anderson, C. Elmer	607,099	Freeman, Orville L.	5,453	68,234 D	46.8%	52.7%	47.0%	53.0%
1952	1,418,869	785,125	Anderson, C. Elmer	624,480	Freeman, Orville L.	9,264	160,645 R	55.3%	44.0%	55.7%	44.3%
1950	1,046,632	635,800	Youngdahl, Luther	400,637	Peterson, Harry H.	10,195	235,163 R	60.7%	38.3%	61.3%	38.7%
1948	1,210,894	643,572	Youngdahl, Luther	545,766	Halsted, Charles L.	21,556	97,806 R	53.1%	45.1%	54.1%	45.9%
1946	880,348	519,067	Youngdahl, Luther	349,565	Barker, Harold H.	11,716	169,502 R	59.0%	39.7%	59.8%	40.2%

**In past elections, the other vote included: 2002 - 364,534 Independence (Timothy J. Penny); 1998 - 773,403 Reform (Jesse Ventura), who was elected with 37.0 percent of the total vote. The term of office of Minnesota's governor was increased from two to four years effective with the 1962 election.

POSTWAR VOTE FOR SENATOR

Year	Total Vote	Republican Vote	Republican Candidate	Democratic Vote	Democratic Candidate	Other Vote	Rep.-Dem. Plurality	Total Vote Rep.	Total Vote Dem.	Major Vote Rep.	Major Vote Dem.
2008**	2,887,646	1,212,317	Coleman, Norm	1,212,629	Franken, Al	462,700	312 D	42.0%	42.0%	50.0%	50.0%
2006	2,202,772	835,653	Kennedy, Mark	1,278,849	Klobuchar, Amy	88,270	443,196 D	37.9%	58.1%	39.5%	60.5%
2002**	2,254,639	1,116,697	Coleman, Norm	1,067,246	Mondale, Walter F.	70,696	49,451 R	49.5%	47.3%	51.1%	48.9%
2000	2,419,520	1,047,474	Grams, Rod	1,181,553	Dayton, Mark	190,493	134,079 D	43.3%	48.8%	47.0%	53.0%
1996	2,183,062	901,282	Boschwitz, Rudy	1,098,493	Wellstone, Paul	183,287	197,211 D	41.3%	50.3%	45.1%	54.9%
1994	1,772,929	869,653	Grams, Rod	781,860	Wynia, Ann	121,416	87,793 R	49.1%	44.1%	52.7%	47.3%
1990	1,808,045	864,375	Boschwitz, Rudy	911,999	Wellstone, Paul	31,671	47,624 D	47.8%	50.4%	48.7%	51.3%
1988	2,093,953	1,176,210	Durenberger, David	856,694	Humphrey, Hubert H. III	61,049	319,516 R	56.2%	40.9%	57.9%	42.1%
1984	2,066,143	1,199,926	Boschwitz, Rudy	852,844	Growe, Joan Anderson	13,373	347,082 R	58.1%	41.3%	58.5%	41.5%
1982	1,804,675	949,207	Durenberger, David	840,401	Dayton, Mark	15,067	108,806 R	52.6%	46.6%	53.0%	47.0%
1978	1,580,778	894,092	Boschwitz, Rudy	638,375	Anderson, Wendell R.	48,311	255,717 R	56.6%	40.4%	58.3%	41.7%
1978S	1,560,724	957,908	Durenberger, David	538,675	Short, Robert E.	64,141	419,233 R	61.4%	34.5%	64.0%	36.0%
1976	1,912,068	478,611	Brekke, Gerald W.	1,290,736	Humphrey, Hubert H.	142,721	812,125 D	25.0%	67.5%	27.1%	72.9%
1972	1,731,653	742,121	Hansen, Philip	981,340	Mondale, Walter F.	8,192	239,219 D	42.9%	56.7%	43.1%	56.9%
1970	1,364,887	568,025	MacGregor, Clark	788,256	Humphrey, Hubert H.	8,606	220,231 D	41.6%	57.8%	41.9%	58.1%
1966	1,271,426	574,868	Forsythe, Robert A.	685,840	Mondale, Walter F.	10,718	110,972 D	45.2%	53.9%	45.6%	54.4%
1964	1,543,590	605,933	Whitney, Wheelock	931,353	McCarthy, Eugene J.	6,304	325,420 D	39.3%	60.3%	39.4%	60.6%
1960	1,536,839	648,586	Peterson, P. K.	884,168	Humphrey, Hubert H.	4,085	235,582 D	42.2%	57.5%	42.3%	57.7%
1958	1,150,883	536,629	Thye, Edward J.	608,847	McCarthy, Eugene J.	5,407	72,218 D	46.6%	52.9%	46.8%	53.2%
1954	1,138,952	479,619	Bjornson, Val	642,193	Humphrey, Hubert H.	17,140	162,574 D	42.1%	56.4%	42.8%	57.2%
1952	1,387,419	785,649	Thye, Edward J.	590,011	Carlson, William E.	11,759	195,638 R	56.6%	42.5%	57.1%	42.9%
1948	1,220,250	485,801	Ball, Joseph H.	729,494	Humphrey, Hubert H.	4,955	243,693 D	39.8%	59.8%	40.0%	60.0%
1946	878,731	517,775	Thye, Edward J.	349,520	Jorgenson, Theodore	11,436	168,255 R	58.9%	39.8%	59.7%	40.3%

Notes: **In past elections, the other vote included: 2008 - 437,505 Independence (Dean Barkley). In October 2002 the Democratic incumbent, Paul Wellstone, was killed in an airplane crash. Walter F. Mondale was named to replace him on the general election ballot. One of the 1978 elections was for a short term to fill a vacancy.

MINNESOTA

PRESIDENT 2008

2000 Census Population	County	Total Vote	Republican	Democratic	Other	Rep.-Dem. Plurality	Percentage Total Vote Rep.	Percentage Total Vote Dem.	Percentage Major Vote Rep.	Percentage Major Vote Dem.
15,301	AITKIN	9,410	4,589	4,595	226	6 D	48.8%	48.8%	50.0%	50.0%
298,084	ANOKA	182,224	91,357	86,976	3,891	4,381 R	50.1%	47.7%	51.2%	48.8%
30,000	BECKER	16,965	8,851	7,687	427	1,164 R	52.2%	45.3%	53.5%	46.5%
39,650	BELTRAMI	22,236	9,762	12,019	455	2,257 D	43.9%	54.1%	44.8%	55.2%
34,226	BENTON	19,339	10,338	8,454	547	1,884 R	53.5%	43.7%	55.0%	45.0%
5,820	BIG STONE	2,990	1,362	1,552	76	190 D	45.6%	51.9%	46.7%	53.3%
55,941	BLUE EARTH	35,070	14,782	19,325	963	4,543 D	42.1%	55.1%	43.3%	56.7%
26,911	BROWN	13,620	7,456	5,809	355	1,647 R	54.7%	42.7%	56.2%	43.8%
31,671	CARLTON	18,449	6,549	11,501	399	4,952 D	35.5%	62.3%	36.3%	63.7%
70,205	CARVER	49,683	28,156	20,654	873	7,502 R	56.7%	41.6%	57.7%	42.3%
27,150	CASS	16,307	8,660	7,276	371	1,384 R	53.1%	44.6%	54.3%	45.7%
13,088	CHIPPEWA	6,356	2,907	3,280	169	373 D	45.7%	51.6%	47.0%	53.0%
41,101	CHISAGO	29,305	15,789	12,783	733	3,006 R	53.9%	43.6%	55.3%	44.7%
51,229	CLAY	29,259	11,978	16,666	615	4,688 D	40.9%	57.0%	41.8%	58.2%
8,423	CLEARWATER	4,261	2,291	1,877	93	414 R	53.8%	44.1%	55.0%	45.0%
5,168	COOK	3,348	1,240	2,019	89	779 D	37.0%	60.3%	38.0%	62.0%
12,167	COTTONWOOD	6,036	3,157	2,759	120	398 R	52.3%	45.7%	53.4%	46.6%
55,099	CROW WING	35,165	18,567	15,859	739	2,708 R	52.8%	45.1%	53.9%	46.1%
355,904	DAKOTA	225,472	104,364	116,778	4.330	12,414 D	46.3%	51.8%	47.2%	52.8%
17,731	DODGE	10,213	5,468	4,463	282	1,005 R	53.5%	43.7%	55.1%	44.9%
32,821	DOUGLAS	20,918	11,241	9,256	421	1,985 R	53.7%	44.2%	54.8%	45.2%
16,181	FARIBAULT	8,152	4,196	3,736	220	460 R	51.5%	45.8%	52.9%	47.1%
21,122	FILLMORE	11,234	4,993	5,921	320	928 D	44.4%	52.7%	45.7%	54.3%
32,584	FREEBORN	17,280	6,955	9,915	410	2,960 D	40.2%	57.4%	41.2%	58.8%
44,127	GOODHUE	25,795	12,775	12,420	600	355 R	49.5%	48.1%	50.7%	49.3%
6,289	GRANT	3,605	1,646	1,850	109	204 D	45.7%	51.3%	47.1%	52.9%
1,116,200	HENNEPIN	663,780	231,054	420,958	11.768	189,904 D	34.8%	63.4%	35.4%	64.6%
19,718	HOUSTON	10,883	4,743	5,906	234	1,163 D	43.6%	54.3%	44.5%	55.5%
18,376	HUBBARD	11,638	6,558	4,872	208	1,686 R	56.3%	41.9%	57.4%	42.6%
31,287	ISANTI	20,053	11,324	8,248	481	3,076 R	56.5%	41.1%	57.9%	42.1%
43,992	ITASCA	24,395	10,309	13,460	626	3,151 D	42.3%	55.2%	43.4%	56.6%
11,268	JACKSON	5,623	2,858	2,618	147	240 R	50.8%	46.6%	52.2%	47.8%
14,996	KANABEC	8,499	4,479	3,743	277	736 R	52.7%	44.0%	54.5%	45.5%
41,203	KANDIYOHI	21,895	11,319	10,125	451	1,194 R	51.7%	46.2%	52.8%	47.2%
5,285	KITTSON	2,568	1,016	1,492	60	476 D	39.6%	58.1%	40.5%	59.5%
14,355	KOOCHICHING	6,802	2,962	3,649	191	687 D	43.5%	53.6%	44.8%	55.2%
8,067	LAC QUI PARLE	4,192	1,912	2,160	120	248 D	45.6%	51.5%	47.0%	53.0%
11,058	LAKE	6,969	2,636	4,174	159	1,538 D	37.8%	59.9%	38.7%	61.3%
4,522	LAKE OF THE WOODS	2,313	1,278	971	64	307 R	55.3%	42.0%	56.8%	43.2%
25,426	LE SUEUR	15,009	7,636	6,994	379	642 R	50.9%	46.6%	52.2%	47.8%
6,429	LINCOLN	3,126	1,491	1,517	118	26 D	47.7%	48.5%	49.6%	50.4%
25,425	LYON	12,708	6,315	6,110	283	205 R	49.7%	48.1%	50.8%	49.2%
34,898	MCLEOD	19,029	10,993	7,505	531	3,488 R	57.8%	39.4%	59.4%	40.6%
5,190	MAHNOMEN	2,343	843	1,436	64	593 D	36.0%	61.3%	37.0%	63.0%
10,155	MARSHALL	4,739	2,285	2,311	143	26 D	48.2%	48.8%	49.7%	50.3%
21,802	MARTIN	10,754	6,053	4,413	288	1,640 R	56.3%	41.0%	57.8%	42.2%
22,644	MEEKER	12,545	6,737	5,380	428	1,357 R	53.7%	42.9%	55.6%	44.4%
22,330	MILLE LACS	13,544	7,049	6,072	423	977 R	52.0%	44.8%	53.7%	46.3%
31,712	MORRISON	16,743	9,735	6,547	461	3,188 R	58.1%	39.1%	59.8%	40.2%
38,603	MOWER	19,187	7,075	11,605	507	4,530 D	36.9%	60.5%	37.9%	62.1%

MINNESOTA

PRESIDENT 2008

2000 Census Population	County	Total Vote	Republican	Democratic	Other	Rep.-Dem. Plurality	Percentage			
							Total Vote		Major Vote	
							Rep.	Dem.	Rep.	Dem.
9,165	MURRAY	4,813	2,320	2,345	148	25 D	48.2%	48.7%	49.7%	50.3%
29,771	NICOLLET	18,245	7,968	9,887	390	1,919 D	43.7%	54.2%	44.6%	55.4%
20,832	NOBLES	8,813	4,368	4,244	201	124 R	49.6%	48.2%	50.7%	49.3%
7,442	NORMAN	3,434	1,204	2,129	101	925 D	35.1%	62.0%	36.1%	63.9%
124,277	OLMSTED	76,470	36,202	38,711	1,557	2,509 D	47.3%	50.6%	48.3%	51.7%
57,159	OTTER TAIL	32,687	18,077	13,856	754	4,221 R	55.3%	42.4%	56.6%	43.4%
13,584	PENNINGTON	6,822	3,248	3,394	180	146 D	47.6%	49.8%	48.9%	51.1%
26,530	PINE	14,383	6,862	7,084	437	222 D	47.7%	49.3%	49.2%	50.8%
9,895	PIPESTONE	4,801	2,652	2,023	126	629 R	55.2%	42.1%	56.7%	43.3%
31,369	POLK	15,334	7,148	7,850	336	702 D	46.6%	51.2%	47.7%	52.3%
11,236	POPE	6,536	3,069	3,317	150	248 D	47.0%	50.7%	48.1%	51.9%
511,035	RAMSEY	277,386	88,942	182,974	5,470	94,032 D	32.1%	66.0%	32.7%	67.3%
4,299	RED LAKE	2,191	983	1,120	88	137 D	44.9%	51.1%	46.7%	53.3%
16,815	REDWOOD	7,806	4,308	3,250	248	1,058 R	55.2%	41.6%	57.0%	43.0%
17,154	RENVILLE	8,135	3,956	3,904	275	52 R	48.6%	48.0%	50.3%	49.7%
56,665	RICE	31,799	13,723	17,381	695	3,658 D	43.2%	54.7%	44.1%	55.9%
9,721	ROCK	4,975	2,775	2,079	121	696 R	55.8%	41.8%	57.2%	42.8%
16,338	ROSEAU	7,700	4,438	3,097	165	1,341 R	57.6%	40.2%	58.9%	41.1%
200,528	ST. LOUIS	118,814	38,742	77,351	2,721	38,609 D	32.6%	65.1%	33.4%	66.6%
89,498	SCOTT	67,132	36,724	29,208	1,200	7,516 R	54.7%	43.5%	55.7%	44.3%
64,417	SHERBURNE	44,990	26,140	17,957	893	8,183 R	58.1%	39.9%	59.3%	40.7%
15,356	SIBLEY	7,729	4,492	2,998	239	1,494 R	58.1%	38.8%	60.0%	40.0%
133,166	STEARNS	78,756	41,194	35,690	1,872	5,504 R	52.3%	45.3%	53.6%	46.4%
33,680	STEELE	19,656	10,068	9,016	572	1,052 R	51.2%	45.9%	52.8%	47.2%
10,053	STEVENS	5,634	2,710	2,781	143	71 D	48.1%	49.4%	49.4%	50.6%
11,956	SWIFT	5,244	2,184	2,907	153	723 D	41.6%	55.4%	42.9%	57.1%
24,426	TODD	12,257	6,637	5,277	343	1,360 R	54.1%	43.1%	55.7%	44.3%
4,134	TRAVERSE	2,035	933	1,043	59	110 D	45.8%	51.3%	47.2%	52.8%
21,610	WABASHA	11,893	5,935	5,646	312	289 R	49.9%	47.5%	51.2%	48.8%
13,713	WADENA	7,169	4,128	2,882	159	1,246 R	57.6%	40.2%	58.9%	41.1%
19,526	WASECA	9,888	5,211	4,401	276	810 R	52.7%	44.5%	54.2%	45.8%
201,130	WASHINGTON	137,059	64,334	70,277	2,448	5,943 D	46.9%	51.3%	47.8%	52.2%
11,876	WATONWAN	5,258	2,526	2,562	170	36 D	48.0%	48.7%	49.6%	50.4%
7,138	WILKIN	3,414	1,786	1,550	78	236 R	52.3%	45.4%	53.5%	46.5%
49,985	WINONA	27,935	10,975	16,308	652	5,333 D	39.3%	58.4%	40.2%	59.8%
89,986	WRIGHT	65,578	37,779	26,343	1,456	11,436 R	57.6%	40.2%	58.9%	41.1%
11,080	YELLOW MEDICINE	5,569	2,579	2,816	174	237 D	46.3%	50.6%	47.8%	52.2%
4,919,479	TOTAL	2,910,369	1,275,409	1,573,354	61,606	297,945 D	43.8%	54.1%	44.8%	55.2%

MINNESOTA
SENATOR 2008

2000 Census Population	County	Total Vote	Republican	Democratic	Independence (Barkley)	Other	Plurality		Percentage Rep.	Dem.	Independence
15,301	AITKIN	9,359	3,617	3,893	1,770	79	276	D	38.6%	41.6%	18.9%
298,084	ANOKA	181,067	82,308	66,800	30,504	1,455	15,508	R	45.5%	36.9%	16.8%
30,000	BECKER	16,863	8,437	6,016	2,226	184	2,421	R	50.0%	35.7%	13.2%
39,650	BELTRAMI	22,002	9,454	10,033	2,267	248	579	D	43.0%	45.6%	10.3%
34,226	BENTON	19,207	8,473	6,485	4,071	178	1,988	R	44.1%	33.8%	21.2%
5,820	BIG STONE	2,981	1,211	1,274	476	20	63	D	40.6%	42.7%	16.0%
55,941	BLUE EARTH	34,704	13,660	14,483	6,182	379	823	D	39.4%	41.7%	17.8%
26,911	BROWN	13,554	6,329	4,435	2,684	106	1,894	R	46.7%	32.7%	19.8%
31,671	CARLTON	18,338	6,099	9,521	2,555	163	3,422	D	33.3%	51.9%	13.9%
70,205	CARVER	49,326	26,968	14,102	7,875	381	12,866	R	54.7%	28.6%	16.0%
27,150	CASS	16,217	7,685	5,888	2,504	140	1,797	R	47.4%	36.3%	15.4%
13,088	CHIPPEWA	6,322	2,419	2,559	1,283	61	140	D	38.3%	40.5%	20.3%
41,101	CHISAGO	29,148	13,768	9,833	5,317	230	3,935	R	47.2%	33.7%	18.2%
51,229	CLAY	28,831	13,032	12,067	3,431	301	965	R	45.2%	41.9%	11.9%
8,423	CLEARWATER	4,209	2,109	1,596	460	44	513	R	50.1%	37.9%	10.9%
5,168	COOK	3,327	1,207	1,620	458	42	413	D	36.3%	48.7%	13.8%
12,167	COTTONWOOD	6,017	2,770	2,131	1,051	65	639	R	46.0%	35.4%	17.5%
55,099	CROW WING	34,905	16,107	13,025	5,474	299	3,082	R	46.1%	37.3%	15.7%
355,904	DAKOTA	223,885	102,701	85,298	34,066	1,820	17,403	R	45.9%	38.1%	15.2%
17,731	DODGE	10,125	4,771	3,384	1,853	117	1,387	R	47.1%	33.4%	18.3%
32,821	DOUGLAS	20,801	10,077	6,856	3,723	145	3,221	R	48.4%	33.0%	17.9%
16,181	FARIBAULT	8,105	3,599	2,911	1,509	86	688	R	44.4%	35.9%	18.6%
21,122	FILLMORE	11,131	4,772	4,630	1,604	125	142	R	42.9%	41.6%	14.4%
32,584	FREEBORN	17,119	6,566	7,432	2,920	201	866	D	38.4%	43.4%	17.1%
44,127	GOODHUE	25,675	11,176	9,242	5,047	210	1,934	R	43.5%	36.0%	19.7%
6,289	GRANT	3,597	1,483	1,469	630	15	14	R	41.2%	40.8%	17.5%
1,116,200	HENNEPIN	657,534	237,712	329,616	84,912	5,294	91,904	D	36.2%	50.1%	12.9%
19,718	HOUSTON	10,674	5,027	4,597	942	108	430	R	47.1%	43.1%	8.8%
18,376	HUBBARD	11,572	5,751	4,024	1,692	105	1,727	R	49.7%	34.8%	14.6%
31,287	ISANTI	19,942	9,564	6,557	3,648	173	3,007	R	48.0%	32.9%	18.3%
43,992	ITASCA	24,242	9,263	11,544	3,183	252	2,281	D	38.2%	47.6%	13.1%
11,268	JACKSON	5,621	2,478	2,145	930	68	333	R	44.1%	38.2%	16.5%
14,996	KANABEC	8,454	3,745	2,980	1,631	98	765	R	44.3%	35.2%	19.3%
41,203	KANDIYOHI	21,784	10,246	8,007	3,378	153	2,239	R	47.0%	36.8%	15.5%
5,285	KITTSON	2,553	1,077	1,168	278	30	91	D	42.2%	45.8%	10.9%
14,355	KOOCHICHING	6,725	2,847	3,090	721	67	243	D	42.3%	45.9%	10.7%
8,067	LAC QUI PARLE	4,170	1,611	1,746	779	34	135	D	38.6%	41.9%	18.7%
11,058	LAKE	6,899	2,432	3,549	863	55	1,117	D	35.3%	51.4%	12.5%
4,522	LAKE OF THE WOODS	2,266	1,204	770	258	34	434	R	53.1%	34.0%	11.4%
25,426	LE SUEUR	14,984	6,321	5,270	3,268	125	1,051	R	42.2%	35.2%	21.8%
6,429	LINCOLN	3,109	1,464	1,272	341	32	192	R	47.1%	40.9%	11.0%
25,425	LYON	12,618	6,089	4,410	1,994	125	1,679	R	48.3%	35.0%	15.8%
34,898	MCLEOD	18,967	9,093	5,496	4,147	231	3,597	R	47.9%	29.0%	21.9%
5,190	MAHNOMEN	2,325	858	1,142	299	26	284	D	36.9%	49.1%	12.9%
10,155	MARSHALL	4,713	2,322	1,752	598	41	570	R	49.3%	37.2%	12.7%
21,802	MARTIN	10,670	5,108	3,589	1,369	104	1,519	R	47.9%	33.6%	17.5%
22,644	MEEKER	12,503	5,697	3,870	2,797	139	1,827	R	45.6%	31.0%	22.4%
22,330	MILLE LACS	13,462	5,852	4,801	2,654	155	1,051	R	43.5%	35.7%	19.7%
31,712	MORRISON	16,680	7,826	5,424	3,274	156	2,402	R	46.9%	32.5%	19.6%
38,603	MOWER	19,026	6,844	9,093	2,859	230	2,249	D	36.0%	47.8%	15.0%

MINNESOTA

SENATOR 2008

2000 Census Population	County	Total Vote	Republican	Democratic	Independence (Barkley)	Other	Plurality	Percentage Rep.	Dem.	Independence
9,165	MURRAY	4,796	2,334	1,866	560	36	468 R	48.7%	38.9%	11.7%
29,771	NICOLLET	18,081	7,237	7,384	3,312	148	147 D	40.0%	40.8%	18.3%
20,832	NOBLES	8,724	4,192	3,534	903	95	658 R	48.1%	40.5%	10.4%
7,442	NORMAN	3,410	1,334	1,576	460	40	242 D	39.1%	46.2%	13.5%
124,277	OLMSTED	75,376	35,334	28,589	10,666	787	6,745 R	46.9%	37.9%	14.2%
57,159	OTTER TAIL	32,490	17,199	10,740	4,263	288	6,459 R	52.9%	33.1%	13.1%
13,584	PENNINGTON	6,736	3,239	2,595	822	80	644 R	48.1%	38.5%	12.2%
26,530	PINE	14,345	5,683	6,016	2,489	157	333 D	39.6%	41.9%	17.4%
9,895	PIPESTONE	4,739	2,637	1,681	369	52	956 R	55.6%	35.5%	7.8%
31,369	POLK	15,140	7,353	5,926	1,715	146	1,427 R	48.6%	39.1%	11.3%
11,236	POPE	6,524	2,749	2,559	1,171	45	190 R	42.1%	39.2%	17.9%
511,035	RAMSEY	274,364	92,952	142,251	36,708	2,453	49,299 D	33.9%	51.8%	13.4%
4,299	RED LAKE	2,158	984	834	311	29	150 R	45.6%	38.6%	14.4%
16,815	REDWOOD	7,757	3,642	2,454	1,569	92	1,188 R	47.0%	31.6%	20.2%
17,154	RENVILLE	8,113	3,275	2,909	1,854	75	366 R	40.4%	35.9%	22.9%
56,665	RICE	31,424	12,061	13,680	5,428	255	1,619 D	38.4%	43.5%	17.3%
9,721	ROCK	4,895	2,656	1,750	426	63	906 R	54.3%	35.8%	8.7%
16,338	ROSEAU	7,640	4,394	2,421	743	82	1,973 R	57.5%	31.7%	9.7%
200,528	ST. LOUIS	118,125	38,320	64,531	14,283	991	26,211 D	32.4%	54.6%	12.1%
89,498	SCOTT	66,677	33,839	20,693	11,615	530	13,146 R	50.8%	31.0%	17.4%
64,417	SHERBURNE	44,717	22,887	13,405	8,066	359	9,482 R	51.2%	30.0%	18.0%
15,356	SIBLEY	7,710	3,499	2,158	1,976	77	1,341 R	45.4%	28.0%	25.6%
133,166	STEARNS	78,078	36,224	26,161	15,003	690	10,063 R	46.4%	33.5%	19.2%
33,680	STEELE	19,552	8,647	6,552	4,173	180	2,095 R	44.2%	33.5%	21.3%
10,053	STEVENS	5,613	2,526	2,250	784	53	276 R	45.0%	40.1%	14.0%
11,956	SWIFT	5,229	1,879	2,294	1,007	49	415 D	35.9%	43.9%	19.3%
24,426	TODD	12,175	5,536	4,177	2,346	116	1,359 R	45.5%	34.3%	19.3%
4,134	TRAVERSE	2,027	837	794	381	15	43 R	41.3%	39.2%	18.8%
21,610	WABASHA	11,830	4,959	4,466	2,305	100	493 R	41.9%	37.8%	19.5%
13,713	WADENA	7,152	3,683	2,294	1,107	68	1,389 R	51.5%	32.1%	15.5%
19,526	WASECA	9,861	4,229	3,261	2,285	86	968 R	42.9%	33.1%	23.2%
201,130	WASHINGTON	136,035	63,804	50,562	20,711	958	13,242 R	46.9%	37.2%	15.2%
11,876	WATONWAN	5,239	2,104	2,019	1,065	51	85 R	40.2%	38.5%	20.3%
7,138	WILKIN	3,376	1,814	1,074	453	35	740 R	53.7%	31.8%	13.4%
49,985	WINONA	27,243	11,318	12,761	2,782	382	1,443 D	41.5%	46.8%	10.2%
89,986	WRIGHT	65,219	32,999	18,664	13,010	546	14,335 R	50.6%	28.6%	19.9%
11,080	YELLOW MEDICINE	5,563	2,313	2,174	1,028	48	139 R	41.6%	39.1%	18.5%
	Absentee Ballots	1,205	416	679	101	9	263 D	34.5%	56.3%	8.4%
4,919,479	TOTAL	2,887,646	1,212,317	1,212,629	437,505	25,195	312 D	42.0%	42.0%	15.2%

Note: This table reflects the results certified at the conclusion of a long recount process. Absentee ballots listed on the next to last line were included after the counties had reported their tallies.

MINNESOTA

HOUSE OF REPRESENTATIVES

CD	Year	Total Vote	Republican Vote	Republican Candidate	Democratic Vote	Democratic Candidate	Other Vote	Rep.-Dem. Plurality	Total Vote Rep.	Total Vote Dem.	Major Vote Rep.	Major Vote Dem.
1	2008	332,400	109,453	DAVIS, BRIAN J.	207,753	WALZ, TIMOTHY J.*	15,194	98,300 D	32.9%	62.5%	34.5%	65.5%
1	2006	268,421	126,486	GUTKNECHT, GIL*	141,556	WALZ, TIMOTHY J.	379	15,070 D	47.1%	52.7%	47.2%	52.8%
1	2004	324,055	193,132	GUTKNECHT, GIL*	115,088	POMEROY, LEIGH	15,835	78,044 R	59.6%	35.5%	62.7%	37.3%
1	2002	265,982	163,570	GUTKNECHT, GIL*	92,165	ANDREASEN, STEVE	10,247	71,405 R	61.5%	34.7%	64.0%	36.0%
2	2008	385,656	220,924	KLINE, JOHN*	164,093	SARVI, STEVE	639	56,831 R	57.3%	42.5%	57.4%	42.6%
2	2006	290,540	163,269	KLINE, JOHN*	116,343	ROWLEY, COLEEN	10,928	46,926 R	56.2%	40.0%	58.4%	41.6%
2	2004	365,945	206,313	KLINE, JOHN*	147,527	DALY, TERESA	12,105	58,786 R	56.4%	40.3%	58.3%	41.7%
2	2002	286,860	152,970	KLINE, JOHN	121,121	LUTHER, BILL*	12,769	31,849 R	53.3%	42.2%	55.8%	44.2%
3	2008	369,104	178,932	PAULSEN, ERIK	150,787	MADIA, ASHWIN	39,385	28,145 R	48.5%	40.9%	54.3%	45.7%
3	2006	284,244	184,333	RAMSTAD, JIM*	99,588	WILDE, WENDY	323	84,745 R	64.9%	35.0%	64.9%	35.1%
3	2004	358,892	231,871	RAMSTAD, JIM*	126,665	WATTS, DEBORAH	356	105,206 R	64.6%	35.3%	64.7%	35.3%
3	2002	296,218	213,334	RAMSTAD, JIM*	82,575	STANTON, DARRYL	309	130,759 R	72.0%	27.9%	72.1%	27.9%
4	2008	316,018	98,936	MATTHEWS, ED	216,267	McCOLLUM, BETTY*	815	117,331 D	31.3%	68.4%	31.4%	68.6%
4	2006	247,466	74,797	SIUM, OBI	172,096	McCOLLUM, BETTY*	573	97,299 D	30.2%	69.5%	30.3%	69.7%
4	2004	317,299	105,467	BATAGLIA, PATRICE	182,387	McCOLLUM, BETTY*	29,445	76,920 D	33.2%	57.5%	36.6%	63.4%
4	2002	264,540	89,705	BILLINGTON, CLYDE	164,597	McCOLLUM, BETTY*	10,238	74,892 D	33.9%	62.2%	35.3%	64.7%
5	2008	322,747	71,020	WHITE, BARB DAVIS	228,776	ELLISON, KEITH*	22,951	157,756 D	22.0%	70.9%	23.7%	76.3%
5	2006	244,905	52,263	FINE, ALAN	136,060	ELLISON, KEITH	56,582	83,797 D	21.3%	55.6%	27.8%	72.2%
5	2004	313,526	76,600	MATHIAS, DANIEL	218,434	SABO, MARTIN OLAV*	18,492	141,834 D	24.4%	69.7%	26.0%	74.0%
5	2002	255,982	66,271	MATHIAS, DANIEL	171,572	SABO, MARTIN OLAV*	18,139	105,301 D	25.9%	67.0%	27.9%	72.1%
6	2008	404,725	187,817	BACHMANN, MICHELE*	175,786	TINKLENBERG, EL	41,122	12,031 R	46.4%	43.4%	51.7%	48.3%
6	2006	302,188	151,248	BACHMANN, MICHELE	127,144	WETTERLING, PATTY	23,796	24,104 R	50.1%	42.1%	54.3%	45.7%
6	2004	377,224	203,669	KENNEDY, MARK*	173,309	WETTERLING, PATTY	246	30,360 R	54.0%	45.9%	54.0%	46.0%
6	2002	287,312	164,747	KENNEDY, MARK*	100,738	ROBERT, JANET	21,827	64,009 R	57.3%	35.1%	62.1%	37.9%
7	2008	314,680	87,062	MENZE, GLEN	227,187	PETERSON, COLLIN C.*	431	140,125 D	27.7%	72.2%	27.7%	72.3%
7	2006	257,194	74,557	BARRETT, MICHAEL J.	179,164	PETERSON, COLLIN C.*	3,473	104,607 D	29.0%	69.7%	29.4%	70.6%
7	2004	314,257	106,349	STURROCK, DAVID E.	207,628	PETERSON, COLLIN C.*	280	101,279 D	33.8%	66.1%	33.9%	66.1%
7	2002	260,813	90,342	STEVENS, DAN	170,234	PETERSON, COLLIN C.*	237	79,892 D	34.6%	65.3%	34.7%	65.3%
8	2008	357,284	114,871	CUMMINS, MICHAEL	241,831	OBERSTAR, JAMES L.*	582	126,960 D	32.2%	67.7%	32.2%	67.8%
8	2006	284,016	97,683	GRAMS, ROD	180,670	OBERSTAR, JAMES L.*	5,663	82,987 D	34.4%	63.6%	35.1%	64.9%
8	2004	350,483	112,693	GROETTUM, MARK	228,586	OBERSTAR, JAMES L.*	9,204	115,893 D	32.2%	65.2%	33.0%	67.0%
8	2002	283,931	88,673	LEMEN, BOB	194,909	OBERSTAR, JAMES L.*	349	106,236 D	31.2%	68.6%	31.3%	68.7%
TOTAL	2008	2,802,614	1,069,015		1,612,480		121,119	543,465 D	38.1%	57.5%	39.9%	60.1%
TOTAL	2006	2,178,974	924,636		1,152,621		101,717	227,985 D	42.4%	52.9%	44.5%	55.5%
TOTAL	2004	2,721,681	1,236,094		1,399,624		85,963	163,530 D	45.4%	51.4%	46.9%	53.1%
TOTAL	2002	2,201,638	1,029,612		1,097,911		74,115	68,299 D	46.8%	49.9%	48.4%	51.6%

Note: An asterisk (*) denotes an incumbent.

MINNESOTA

GENERAL AND PRIMARY ELECTIONS

2008 GENERAL ELECTIONS

President   Other vote was 30,152 Independent (Ralph Nader); 9,174 Libertarian (Bob Barr); 6,787 Constitution (Chuck Baldwin); 5,174 Green (Cynthia A. McKinney); 790 Socialist Workers (Roger Calero); 22 write-in (Alan Keyes); 7 write-in (Brian Moore); 3 write-in (Joe Schriner); 1 write-in (Curtis Montgomery); 9,496 scattered write-in.

Senator   Other vote was 13,923 Libertarian (Charles Aldrich); 8,907 Constitution (James Niemackl); 13 write-in (Michael Cavlan); 12 write-in (Anthony Keith Price); 2,340 scattered write-in. The Independence Party candidate, Dean Barkley, received 437,505 votes, 15.2 percent of the total vote. The Independence Party vote is listed in the county table for the 2008 Senate election in Minnesota.

House   Other vote was:

CD 1   14,904 Independence (Gregory Mikkelson); 290 scattered write-in.
CD 2   41 write-in (Kevin Masrud); 1 write-in (Curt Walor); 597 scattered write-in.
CD 3   38,970 Independence (David Dillon); 9 write-in (Harley Swarm Jr.); 406 scattered write-in.
CD 4   1 write-in (Amber Garlan); 814 scattered write-in.
CD 5   22,318 Independence (Bill McGaughey); 633 scattered write-in.
CD 6   40,643 Independence (Bob Anderson); 20 write-in (Aubrey Immelman); 459 scattered write-in.
CD 7   431 scattered write-in.
CD 8   582 scattered write-in.

2008 PRIMARY ELECTIONS

Primary   September 9, 2008   **Registration**   3,119,505   No Party Registration
(as of September 9, 2008)

Primary Type   Open—Any registered voter could participate in the party primary of their choice.

MINNESOTA

GENERAL AND PRIMARY ELECTIONS

	REPUBLICAN PRIMARIES			DEMOCRATIC PRIMARIES		
Senator	Norm Coleman*	130,973	91.3%	Al Franken	164,136	65.3%
	Jack Shepard	12,456	8.7%	Priscilla Lord Faris	74,655	29.7%
				"Dick" Franson	3,923	1.6%
				Bob Larson	3,152	1.3%
				Rob Fitzgerald	3,095	1.2%
				Ole Savior	1,227	0.5%
				Alve Erickson	1,017	0.4%
	TOTAL	*143,429*		*TOTAL*	*251,205*	
Congressional District 1	Brian J. Davis	17,196	67.0%	Timothy J. Walz*	20,998	100.0%
	Dick Day	8,480	33.0%			
	TOTAL	*25,676*				
Congressional District 2	John Kline*	Unopposed		Steve Sarvi	Unopposed	
Congressional District 3	Erik Paulsen	14,187	100.0%	Ashwin Madia	20,830	100.0%
Congressional District 4	Ed Matthews	Unopposed		Betty McCollum*	Unopposed	
Congressional District 5	Barb Davis White	5,284	100.0%	Keith Ellison*	33,988	84.5%
				Gregg A. Iverson	6,251	15.5%
				TOTAL	*40,239*	
Congressional District 6	Michele Bachmann*	19,127	85.9%	El Tinklenberg	17,474	100.0%
	Aubrey Immelman	3,134	14.1%			
	TOTAL	*22,261*				
Congressional District 7	Glen Menze	7,698	51.8%	Collin C. Peterson*	21,791	100.0%
	Alan Roebke	7,172	48.2%			
	TOTAL	*14,87*				
Congressional District 8	Michael Cummins	Unopposed		James L. Oberstar*	Unopposed	

Note: An asterisk (*) denotes incumbent. No votes were tallied for unopposed candidates in districts where none of the parties had a contested primary.

MISSISSIPPI

Congressional districts first established for elections held in 2002
4 members

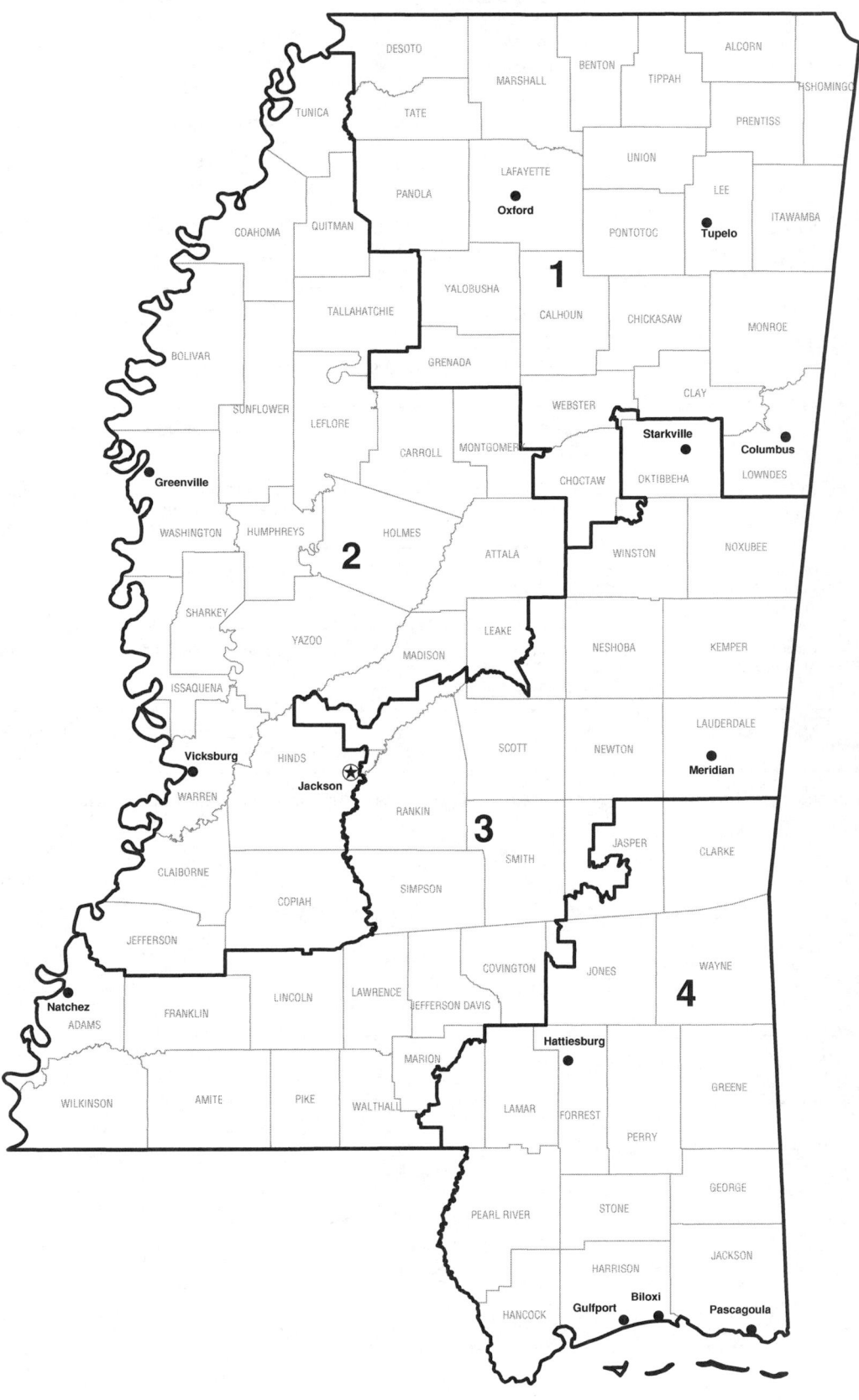

MISSISSIPPI

GOVERNOR
Haley Barbour (R). Reelected 2007 to a four-year term. Previously elected 2003.

SENATORS (2 Republicans)
Thad Cochran (R). Reelected 2008 to a six-year term. Previously elected 2002, 1996, 1990, 1984, 1978.

Roger Wicker (R). Elected 2008 to fill the final four years of the term vacated by the December 2007 resignation of Senator Trent Lott (R). Wicker had been appointed earlier to fill the vacancy and was sworn in as senator on December 31, 2007.

REPRESENTATIVES (3 Democrats, 1 Republican)
1. Travis W. Childers (D)
2. Bennie Thompson (D)
3. Gregg Harper (R)
4. Gene Taylor (D)

POSTWAR VOTE FOR PRESIDENT

		Republican		Democratic				Total Vote		Major Vote	
Year	Total Vote	Vote	Candidate	Vote	Candidate	Other Vote	Plurality	Rep.	Dem.	Rep.	Dem.
2008	1,289,865	724,597	McCain, John	554,662	Obama, Barack	10,606	169,935 R	56.2%	43.0%	56.6%	43.4%
2004	1,152,145	684,981	Bush, George W.	458,094	Kerry, John	9,070	226,887 R	59.5%	39.8%	59.9%	40.1%
2000**	994,184	572,844	Bush, George W.	404,614	Gore, Al	16,726	168,230 R	57.6%	40.7%	58.6%	41.4%
1996**	893,857	439,838	Dole, Bob	394,022	Clinton, Bill	59,997	45,816 R	49.2%	44.1%	52.7%	47.3%
1992**	981,793	487,793	Bush, George	400,258	Clinton, Bill	93,742	87,535 R	49.7%	40.8%	54.9%	45.1%
1988	931,527	557,890	Bush, George	363,921	Dukakis, Michael S.	9,716	193,969 R	59.9%	39.1%	60.5%	39.5%
1984	941,104	582,377	Reagan, Ronald	352,192	Mondale, Walter F.	6,535	230,185 R	61.9%	37.4%	62.3%	37.7%
1980**	892,620	441,089	Reagan, Ronald	429,281	Carter, Jimmy	22,250	11,808 R	49.4%	48.1%	50.7%	49.3%
1976	769,361	366,846	Ford, Gerald R.	381,309	Carter, Jimmy	21,206	14,463 D	47.7%	49.6%	49.0%	51.0%
1972	645,963	505,125	Nixon, Richard M.	126,782	McGovern, George S.	14,056	378,343 R	78.2%	19.6%	79.9%	20.1%
1968**	654,509	88,516	Nixon, Richard M.	150,644	Humphrey, Hubert H.	415,349	264,705 A	13.5%	23.0%	37.0%	63.0%
1964	409,146	356,528	Goldwater, Barry M.	52,618	Johnson, Lyndon B.		303,910 R	87.1%	12.9%	87.1%	12.9%
1960**	298,171	73,561	Nixon, Richard M.	108,362	Kennedy, John F.	116,248	7,886 U	24.7%	36.3%	40.4%	59.6%
1956	248,104	60,685	Eisenhower, Dwight D.	144,453	Stevenson, Adlai E.	42,966	83,768 D	24.5%	58.2%	29.6%	70.4%
1952	285,532	112,966	Eisenhower, Dwight D.	172,566	Stevenson, Adlai E.		59,600 D	39.6%	60.4%	39.6%	60.4%
1948**	192,190	5,043	Dewey, Thomas E.	19,384	Truman, Harry S.	167,763	148,154 SR	2.6%	10.1%	20.6%	79.4%

Notes: **In past elections, the other vote included: 2000 - 8,122 Green (Ralph Nader); 1996 - 52,222 Reform (Ross Perot); 1992 - 85,626 Independent (Perot); 1980 - 12,036 Independent (John Anderson); 1968 - 415,349 American Independent (George Wallace); 1960 - 116,248 Unpledged Independent Democratic electors; 1948 - 167,538 States' Rights (Strom Thurmond). Thurmond won Mississippi in 1948 with 87.2 percent of the vote. The slate of Unpledged Independent Democratic electors carried the state in 1960 with 39.0 percent. Wallace won Mississippi in 1968 with 63.5 percent of the vote.

MISSISSIPPI

POSTWAR VOTE FOR GOVERNOR

Year	Total Vote	Republican Vote	Republican Candidate	Democratic Vote	Democratic Candidate	Other Vote	Rep.-Dem. Plurality	Total Vote Rep.	Total Vote Dem.	Major Vote Rep.	Major Vote Dem.
2007	744,039	430,807	Barbour, Haley	313,232	Eaves, John A.		117,575 R	57.9%	42.1%	57.9%	42.1%
2003	894,487	470,404	Barbour, Haley	409,787	Musgrove, Ronnie	14,296	60,617 R	52.6%	45.8%	53.4%	46.6%
1999**	763,938	370,691	Parker, Mike	379,034	Musgrove, Ronnie	14,213	8,343 D	48.5%	49.6%	49.4%	50.6%
1995	819,471	455,261	Fordice, Kirk	364,210	Molpus, Dick		91,051 R	55.6%	44.4%	55.6%	44.4%
1991	711,188	361,500	Fordice, Kirk	338,435	Mabus, Ray	11,253	23,065 R	50.8%	47.6%	51.6%	48.4%
1987	721,695	336,006	Reed, Jack	385,689	Mabus, Ray		49,683 D	46.6%	53.4%	46.6%	53.4%
1983	742,737	288,764	Bramlett, Leon	409,209	Allain, William A.	44,764	120,445 D	38.9%	55.1%	41.4%	58.6%
1979	677,322	263,702	Carmichael, Gil	413,620	Winter, William F.		149,918 D	38.9%	61.1%	38.9%	61.1%
1975	708,033	319,632	Carmichael, Gil	369,568	Finch, Cliff	18,833	49,936 D	45.1%	52.2%	46.4%	53.6%
1971**	780,537		—	601,122	Waller, William L.	179,415	601,122 D		77.0%		100.0%
1967	448,697	133,379	Phillips, Rubel L.	315,318	Williams, John Bell		181,939 D	29.7%	70.3%	29.7%	70.3%
1963	363,971	138,515	Phillips, Rubel L.	225,456	Johnson, Paul B.		86,941 D	38.1%	61.9%	38.1%	61.9%
1959	57,671		—	57,671	Barnett, Ross R.		57,671 D		100.0%		100.0%
1955	40,707		—	40,707	Coleman, James P.		40,707 D		100.0%		100.0%
1951	43,422		—	43,422	White, Hugh		43,422 D		100.0%		100.0%
1947	166,095		—	161,993	Wright, Fielding L.	4,102	161,993 D		97.5%		100.0%

Notes: **In past elections, the other vote included: 1971 - 172,762 Independent (Charles Evers). The Republican Party did not run a gubernatorial candidate in 1947, 1951, 1955, 1959, and 1971. In 1999 no candidate received a majority of the vote. Democrat Ronnie Musgrove was elected in January 2000 by the Mississippi House of Representatives.

POSTWAR VOTE FOR SENATOR

Year	Total Vote	Republican Vote	Republican Candidate	Democratic Vote	Democratic Candidate	Other Vote	Rep.-Dem. Plurality	Total Vote Rep.	Total Vote Dem.	Major Vote Rep.	Major Vote Dem.
2008	1,247,026	766,111	Cochran, Thad	480,915	Fleming, Erik R.		285,196 R	61.4%	38.6%	61.4%	38.6%
2008S	1,243,473	683,409	Wicker, Roger	560,064	Musgrove, Ronnie		123,345 R	55.0%	45.0%	55.0%	45.0%
2006	610,921	388,399	Lott, Trent	213,000	Fleming, Erik R.	9,522	175,399 R	63.6%	34.9%	64.6%	35.4%
2002**	630,495	533,269	Cochran, Thad		—	97,226	533,269 R	84.6%		100.0%	
2000	994,144	654,941	Lott, Trent	314,090	Brown, Troy	25,113	340,851 R	65.9%	31.6%	67.6%	32.4%
1996	878,662	624,154	Cochran, Thad	240,647	Hunt, James W.	13,861	383,507 R	71.0%	27.4%	72.2%	27.8%
1994	608,085	418,333	Lott, Trent	189,752	Harper, Ken		228,581 R	68.8%	31.2%	68.8%	31.2%
1990	274,244	274,244	Cochran, Thad		—		274,244 R	100.0%		100.0%	
1988	946,719	510,380	Lott, Trent	436,339	Dowdy, Wayne		74,041 R	53.9%	46.1%	53.9%	46.1%
1984	952,240	580,314	Cochran, Thad	371,926	Winter, William F.		208,388 R	60.9%	39.1%	60.9%	39.1%
1982	645,026	230,927	Barbour, Haley	414,099	Stennis, John		183,172 D	35.8%	64.2%	35.8%	64.2%
1978**	583,936	263,089	Cochran, Thad	185,454	Dantin, Maurice	135,393	77,635 R	45.1%	31.8%	58.7%	41.3%
1976	554,433		—	554,433	Stennis, John		554,433 D		100.0%		100.0%
1972	645,746	249,779	Carmichael, Gil	375,102	Eastland, James O.	20,865	125,323 D	38.7%	58.1%	40.0%	60.0%
1970**	324,215		—	286,622	Stennis, John	37,593	286,622 D		88.4%		100.0%
1966	393,900	105,150	Walker, Prentiss	258,248	Eastland, James O.	30,502	153,098 D	26.7%	65.6%	28.9%	71.1%
1964	343,364		—	343,364	Stennis, John		343,364 D		100.0%		100.0%
1960	266,148	21,807	Moore, Joe A.	244,341	Eastland, James O.		222,534 D	8.2%	91.8%	8.2%	91.8%
1958	61,039		—	61,039	Stennis, John		61,039 D		100.0%		100.0%
1954	105,526	4,678	White, James A.	100,848	Eastland, James O.		96,170 D	4.4%	95.6%	4.4%	95.6%
1952	233,919		—	233,919	Stennis, John		233,919 D		100.0%		100.0%
1948	151,478		—	151,478	Eastland, James O.		151,478 D		100.0%		100.0%
1947S	193,709	[See note below]					D				
1946	46,747		—	46,747	Bilbo, Theodore		46,747 D		100.0%		100.0%

Notes: **In past elections, the other vote included: 2002 - 97,226 Reform (Shawn O'Hara); 1978 - 133,646 Independent (Charles Evers); 1970 - 37,593 Independent (William R. Thompson). The 1947 election and one of the 2008 elections were for a short term. Both were held without party designation or nomination. In 1947 John Stennis received 52,068 votes (26.9 percent of the total vote) and won the election with a 6,343-vote plurality. Other candidates included: 45,725 W. M. Colmer; 43,642 Forrest B. Jackson; 27,159 Paul B. Johnson; 24,492 John E. Rankin. The Republican Party did not run a candidate in Senate elections in 1946, 1948, 1952, 1958, 1964, 1970, and 1976. The Democratic Party did not run a candidate in Senate elections in 1990 and 2002.

MISSISSIPPI

PRESIDENT 2008

2000 Census Population	County	Total Vote	Republican	Democratic	Other	Rep.-Dem. Plurality	Percentage Total Vote Rep.	Dem.	Major Vote Rep.	Dem.
34,340	ADAMS	15,696	6,566	9,021	109	2,455 D	41.8%	57.5%	42.1%	57.9%
34,558	ALCORN	15,182	10,805	4,130	247	6,675 R	71.2%	27.2%	72.3%	27.7%
13,599	AMITE	7,650	4,245	3,348	57	897 R	55.5%	43.8%	55.9%	44.1%
19,661	ATTALA	9,183	5,273	3,849	61	1,424 R	57.4%	41.9%	57.8%	42.2%
8,026	BENTON	4,638	2,329	2,227	82	102 R	50.2%	48.0%	51.1%	48.9%
40,633	BOLIVAR	15,381	4,891	10,334	156	5,443 D	31.8%	67.2%	32.1%	67.9%
15,069	CALHOUN	7,034	4,467	2,522	45	1,945 R	63.5%	35.9%	63.9%	36.1%
10,769	CARROLL	5,965	3,902	2,037	26	1,865 R	65.4%	34.1%	65.7%	34.3%
19,440	CHICKASAW	9,058	4,395	4,588	75	193 D	48.5%	50.7%	48.9%	51.1%
9,758	CHOCTAW	4,128	2,624	1,459	45	1,165 R	63.6%	35.3%	64.3%	35.7%
11,831	CLAIBORNE	5,453	748	4,682	23	3,934 D	13.7%	85.9%	13.8%	86.2%
17,955	CLARKE	8,397	5,229	3,121	47	2,108 R	62.3%	37.2%	62.6%	37.4%
21,979	CLAY	11,092	4,466	6,558	68	2,092 D	40.3%	59.1%	40.5%	59.5%
30,622	COAHOMA	10,568	2,917	7,597	54	4,680 D	27.6%	71.9%	27.7%	72.3%
28,757	COPIAH	14,502	6,701	7,710	91	1,009 D	46.2%	53.2%	46.5%	53.5%
19,407	COVINGTON	9,461	5,523	3,852	86	1,671 R	58.4%	40.7%	58.9%	41.1%
107,199	DE SOTO	64,323	44,222	19,627	474	24,595 R	68.7%	30.5%	69.3%	30.7%
72,604	FORREST	27,184	15,296	11,622	266	3,674 R	56.3%	42.8%	56.8%	43.2%
8,448	FRANKLIN	4,685	2,909	1,733	43	1,176 R	62.1%	37.0%	62.7%	37.3%
19,144	GEORGE	9,335	7,700	1,532	103	6,168 R	82.5%	16.4%	83.4%	16.6%
13,299	GREENE	5,789	4,361	1,366	62	2,995 R	75.3%	23.6%	76.1%	23.9%
23,263	GRENADA	11,321	6,234	5,029	58	1,205 R	55.1%	44.4%	55.3%	44.7%
42,967	HANCOCK	17,056	13,020	3,768	268	9,252 R	76.3%	22.1%	77.6%	22.4%
189,601	HARRISON	61,957	38,757	22,673	527	16,084 R	62.6%	36.6%	63.1%	36.9%
250,800	HINDS	108,902	32,949	75,401	552	42,452 D	30.3%	69.2%	30.4%	69.6%
21,609	HOLMES	9,543	1,714	7,765	64	6,051 D	18.0%	81.4%	18.1%	81.9%
11,206	HUMPHREYS	5,126	1,462	3,634	30	2,172 D	28.5%	70.9%	28.7%	71.3%
2,274	ISSAQUENA	950	364	579	7	215 D	38.3%	60.9%	38.6%	61.4%
22,770	ITAWAMBA	9,951	7,663	2,084	204	5,579 R	77.0%	20.9%	78.6%	21.4%
131,420	JACKSON	54,296	35,993	17,781	522	18,212 R	66.3%	32.7%	66.9%	33.1%
18,149	JASPER	9,210	4,135	5,025	50	890 D	44.9%	54.6%	45.1%	54.9%
9,740	JEFFERSON	4,478	551	3,883	44	3,332 D	12.3%	86.7%	12.4%	87.6%
13,962	JEFFERSON DAVIS	7,370	2,871	4,454	45	1,583 D	39.0%	60.4%	39.2%	60.8%
64,958	JONES	29,273	20,157	8,846	270	11,311 R	68.9%	30.2%	69.5%	30.5%
10,453	KEMPER	5,223	1,935	3,256	32	1,321 D	37.0%	62.3%	37.3%	62.7%
38,744	LAFAYETTE	18,460	10,278	7,997	185	2,281 R	55.7%	43.3%	56.2%	43.8%
39,070	LAMAR	23,910	18,497	5,159	254	13,338 R	77.4%	21.6%	78.2%	21.8%
78,161	LAUDERDALE	33,114	19,582	13,332	200	6,250 R	59.1%	40.3%	59.5%	40.5%
13,258	LAWRENCE	7,009	4,369	2,587	53	1,782 R	62.3%	36.9%	62.8%	37.2%
20,940	LEAKE	9,359	5,148	4,151	60	997 R	55.0%	44.4%	55.4%	44.6%
75,755	LEE	34,960	22,694	12,021	245	10,673 R	64.9%	34.4%	65.4%	34.6%
37,947	LEFLORE	13,081	4,105	8,914	62	4,809 D	31.4%	68.1%	31.5%	68.5%
33,166	LINCOLN	16,402	10,781	5,505	116	5,276 R	65.7%	33.6%	66.2%	33.8%
61,586	LOWNDES	27,465	13,994	13,209	262	785 R	51.0%	48.1%	51.4%	48.6%
74,674	MADISON	47,269	27,203	19,831	235	7,372 R	57.5%	42.0%	57.8%	42.2%
25,595	MARION	13,010	8,513	4,422	75	4,091 R	65.4%	34.0%	65.8%	34.2%
34,993	MARSHALL	16,478	6,683	9,685	110	3,002 D	40.6%	58.8%	40.8%	59.2%
38,014	MONROE	17,496	10,184	7,169	143	3,015 R	58.2%	41.0%	58.7%	41.3%
12,189	MONTGOMERY	5,712	3,071	2,609	32	462 R	53.8%	45.7%	54.1%	45.9%
28,684	NESHOBA	11,402	8,209	3,114	79	5,095 R	72.0%	27.3%	72.5%	27.5%

MISSISSIPPI

PRESIDENT 2008

2000 Census Population	County	Total Vote	Republican	Democratic	Other	Rep.-Dem. Plurality	Percentage			
							Total Vote		Major Vote	
							Rep.	Dem.	Rep.	Dem.
21,838	NEWTON	9,855	6,579	3,218	58	3,361 R	66.8%	32.7%	67.2%	32.8%
12,548	NOXUBEE	6,589	1,525	5,030	34	3,505 D	23.1%	76.3%	23.3%	76.7%
42,902	OKTIBBEHA	18,792	9,320	9,326	146	6 D	49.6%	49.6%	50.0%	50.0%
34,274	PANOLA	16,416	7,620	8,690	106	1,070 D	46.4%	52.9%	46.7%	53.3%
48,621	PEARL RIVER	22,443	17,881	4,320	242	13,561 R	79.7%	19.2%	80.5%	19.5%
12,138	PERRY	5,664	4,067	1,533	64	2,534 R	71.8%	27.1%	72.6%	27.4%
38,940	PIKE	18,055	8,651	9,276	128	625 D	47.9%	51.4%	48.3%	51.7%
26,726	PONTOTOC	12,868	9,727	2,982	159	6,745 R	75.6%	23.2%	76.5%	23.5%
25,556	PRENTISS	10,944	7,703	3,020	221	4,683 R	70.4%	27.6%	71.8%	28.2%
10,117	QUITMAN	4,168	1,334	2,803	31	1,469 D	32.0%	67.3%	32.2%	67.8%
115,327	RANKIN	63,103	48,140	14,372	591	33,768 R	76.3%	22.8%	77.0%	23.0%
28,423	SCOTT	11,671	6,584	5,025	62	1,559 R	56.4%	43.1%	56.7%	43.3%
6,580	SHARKEY	2,795	873	1,907	15	1,034 D	31.2%	68.2%	31.4%	68.6%
27,639	SIMPSON	12,610	7,641	4,817	152	2,824 R	60.6%	38.2%	61.3%	38.7%
16,182	SMITH	8,305	6,265	1,968	72	4,297 R	75.4%	23.7%	76.1%	23.9%
13,622	STONE	7,246	5,149	1,996	101	3,153 R	71.1%	27.5%	72.1%	27.9%
34,369	SUNFLOWER	11,193	3,245	7,838	110	4,593 D	29.0%	70.0%	29.3%	70.7%
14,903	TALLAHATCHIE	6,943	2,786	4,105	52	1,319 D	40.1%	59.1%	40.4%	59.6%
25,370	TATE	12,778	7,678	5,003	97	2,675 R	60.1%	39.2%	60.5%	39.5%
20,826	TIPPAH	9,725	6,937	2,623	165	4,314 R	71.3%	27.0%	72.6%	27.4%
19,163	TISHOMINGO	8,419	6,249	1,962	208	4,287 R	74.2%	23.3%	76.1%	23.9%
9,227	TUNICA	4,332	1,017	3,279	36	2,262 D	23.5%	75.7%	23.7%	76.3%
25,362	UNION	12,195	9,072	2,985	138	6,087 R	74.4%	24.5%	75.2%	24.8%
15,156	WALTHALL	7,780	4,253	3,456	71	797 R	54.7%	44.4%	55.2%	44.8%
49,644	WARREN	21,764	11,152	10,489	123	663 R	51.2%	48.2%	51.5%	48.5%
62,977	WASHINGTON	19,583	6,347	13,148	88	6,801 D	32.4%	67.1%	32.6%	67.4%
21,216	WAYNE	10,022	6,070	3,890	62	2,180 R	60.6%	38.8%	60.9%	39.1%
10,294	WEBSTER	5,457	4,072	1,349	36	2,723 R	74.6%	24.7%	75.1%	24.9%
10,312	WILKINSON	5,139	1,560	3,534	45	1,974 D	30.4%	68.8%	30.6%	69.4%
20,160	WINSTON	10,221	5,497	4,653	71	844 R	53.8%	45.5%	54.2%	45.8%
13,051	YALOBUSHA	6,826	3,628	3,151	47	477 R	53.1%	46.2%	53.5%	46.5%
28,149	YAZOO	11,477	5,290	6,116	71	826 D	46.1%	53.3%	46.4%	53.6%
2,844,658	TOTAL	1,289,865	724,597	554,662	10,606	169,935 R	56.2%	43.0%	56.6%	43.4%

MISSISSIPPI
GOVERNOR 2007

2000 Census Population	County	Total Vote	Republican	Democratic	Other	Rep.-Dem. Plurality	Percentage			
							Total Vote		Major Vote	
							Rep.	Dem.	Rep.	Dem.
34,340	ADAMS	8,185	4,487	3,698		789 R	54.8%	45.2%	54.8%	45.2%
34,558	ALCORN	9,058	5,363	3,695		1,668 R	59.2%	40.8%	59.2%	40.8%
13,599	AMITE	4,928	2,589	2,339		250 R	52.5%	47.5%	52.5%	47.5%
19,661	ATTALA	5,463	3,148	2,315		833 R	57.6%	42.4%	57.6%	42.4%
8,026	BENTON	2,293	1,103	1,190		87 D	48.1%	51.9%	48.1%	51.9%
40,633	BOLIVAR	8,630	3,620	5,010		1,390 D	41.9%	58.1%	41.9%	58.1%
15,069	CALHOUN	5,189	2,732	2,457		275 R	52.6%	47.4%	52.6%	47.4%
10,769	CARROLL	4,039	2,550	1,489		1,061 R	63.1%	36.9%	63.1%	36.9%
19,440	CHICKASAW	5,425	2,340	3,085		745 D	43.1%	56.9%	43.1%	56.9%
9,758	CHOCTAW	2,995	1,788	1,207		581 R	59.7%	40.3%	59.7%	40.3%
11,831	CLAIBORNE	3,379	823	2,556		1,733 D	24.4%	75.6%	24.4%	75.6%
17,955	CLARKE	5,657	3,149	2,508		641 R	55.7%	44.3%	55.7%	44.3%
21,979	CLAY	7,512	3,427	4,085		658 D	45.6%	54.4%	45.6%	54.4%
30,622	COAHOMA	4,825	2,359	2,466		107 D	48.9%	51.1%	48.9%	51.1%
28,757	COPIAH	7,779	3,862	3,917		55 D	49.6%	50.4%	49.6%	50.4%
19,407	COVINGTON	7,049	3,651	3,398		253 R	51.8%	48.2%	51.8%	48.2%
107,199	DE SOTO	18,543	14,206	4,337		9,869 R	76.6%	23.4%	76.6%	23.4%
72,604	FORREST	16,071	9,839	6,232		3,607 R	61.2%	38.8%	61.2%	38.8%
8,448	FRANKLIN	2,629	1,472	1,157		315 R	56.0%	44.0%	56.0%	44.0%
19,144	GEORGE	5,288	3,093	2,195		898 R	58.5%	41.5%	58.5%	41.5%
13,299	GREENE	3,525	1,907	1,618		289 R	54.1%	45.9%	54.1%	45.9%
23,263	GRENADA	6,623	3,750	2,873		877 R	56.6%	43.4%	56.6%	43.4%
42,967	HANCOCK	10,089	7,261	2,828		4,433 R	72.0%	28.0%	72.0%	28.0%
189,601	HARRISON	33,582	23,978	9,604		14,374 R	71.4%	28.6%	71.4%	28.6%
250,800	HINDS	60,820	26,746	34,074		7,328 D	44.0%	56.0%	44.0%	56.0%
21,609	HOLMES	5,442	1,574	3,868		2,294 D	28.9%	71.1%	28.9%	71.1%
11,206	HUMPHREYS	3,872	1,436	2,436		1,000 D	37.1%	62.9%	37.1%	62.9%
2,274	ISSAQUENA	796	364	432		68 D	45.7%	54.3%	45.7%	54.3%
22,770	ITAWAMBA	7,265	3,826	3,439		387 R	52.7%	47.3%	52.7%	47.3%
131,420	JACKSON	31,903	22,188	9,715		12,473 R	69.5%	30.5%	69.5%	30.5%
18,149	JASPER	5,389	2,164	3,225		1,061 D	40.2%	59.8%	40.2%	59.8%
9,740	JEFFERSON	2,969	597	2,372		1,775 D	20.1%	79.9%	20.1%	79.9%
13,962	JEFFERSON DAVIS	5,926	2,425	3,501		1,076 D	40.9%	59.1%	40.9%	59.1%
64,958	JONES	19,735	11,928	7,807		4,121 R	60.4%	39.6%	60.4%	39.6%
10,453	KEMPER	3,773	1,578	2,195		617 D	41.8%	58.2%	41.8%	58.2%
38,744	LAFAYETTE	8,315	5,621	2,694		2,927 R	67.6%	32.4%	67.6%	32.4%
39,070	LAMAR	13,314	9,915	3,399		6,516 R	74.5%	25.5%	74.5%	25.5%
78,161	LAUDERDALE	18,189	11,858	6,331		5,527 R	65.2%	34.8%	65.2%	34.8%
13,258	LAWRENCE	4,126	2,276	1,850		426 R	55.2%	44.8%	55.2%	44.8%
20,940	LEAKE	5,824	3,216	2,608		608 R	55.2%	44.8%	55.2%	44.8%
75,755	LEE	20,580	12,191	8,389		3,802 R	59.2%	40.8%	59.2%	40.8%
37,947	LEFLORE	7,623	3,458	4,165		707 D	45.4%	54.6%	45.4%	54.6%
33,166	LINCOLN	9,531	5,673	3,858		1,815 R	59.5%	40.5%	59.5%	40.5%
61,586	LOWNDES	15,801	9,900	5,901		3,999 R	62.7%	37.3%	62.7%	37.3%
74,674	MADISON	26,461	18,207	8,254		9,953 R	68.8%	31.2%	68.8%	31.2%
25,595	MARION	9,166	5,446	3,720		1,726 R	59.4%	40.6%	59.4%	40.6%
34,993	MARSHALL	7,157	3,570	3,587		17 D	49.9%	50.1%	49.9%	50.1%
38,014	MONROE	11,005	5,884	5,121		763 R	53.5%	46.5%	53.5%	46.5%
12,189	MONTGOMERY	4,400	2,289	2,111		178 R	52.0%	48.0%	52.0%	48.0%
28,684	NESHOBA	7,545	4,825	2,720		2,105 R	63.9%	36.1%	63.9%	36.1%

MISSISSIPPI

GOVERNOR 2007

2000 Census Population	County	Total Vote	Republican	Democratic	Other	Rep.-Dem. Plurality	Percentage			
							Total Vote		Major Vote	
							Rep.	Dem.	Rep.	Dem.
21,838	NEWTON	6,171	3,924	2,247		1,677 R	63.6%	36.4%	63.6%	36.4%
12,548	NOXUBEE	3,449	1,180	2,269		1,089 D	34.2%	65.8%	34.2%	65.8%
42,902	OKTIBBEHA	10,596	6,223	4,373		1,850 R	58.7%	41.3%	58.7%	41.3%
34,274	PANOLA	8,097	4,588	3,509		1,079 R	56.7%	43.3%	56.7%	43.3%
48,621	PEARL RIVER	13,081	9,011	4,070		4,941 R	68.9%	31.1%	68.9%	31.1%
12,138	PERRY	3,546	1,881	1,665		216 R	53.0%	47.0%	53.0%	47.0%
38,940	PIKE	10,974	5,594	5,380		214 R	51.0%	49.0%	51.0%	49.0%
26,726	PONTOTOC	8,517	4,676	3,841		835 R	54.9%	45.1%	54.9%	45.1%
25,556	PRENTISS	7,041	3,379	3,662		283 D	48.0%	52.0%	48.0%	52.0%
10,117	QUITMAN	2,352	1,021	1,331		310 D	43.4%	56.6%	43.4%	56.6%
115,327	RANKIN	35,537	27,928	7,609		20,319 R	78.6%	21.4%	78.6%	21.4%
28,423	SCOTT	7,071	4,019	3,052		967 R	56.8%	43.2%	56.8%	43.2%
6,580	SHARKEY	2,082	828	1,254		426 D	39.8%	60.2%	39.8%	60.2%
27,639	SIMPSON	8,627	5,158	3,469		1,689 R	59.8%	40.2%	59.8%	40.2%
16,182	SMITH	5,891	3,640	2,251		1,389 R	61.8%	38.2%	61.8%	38.2%
13,622	STONE	4,713	2,765	1,948		817 R	58.7%	41.3%	58.7%	41.3%
34,369	SUNFLOWER	6,338	2,448	3,890		1,442 D	38.6%	61.4%	38.6%	61.4%
14,903	TALLAHATCHIE	4,742	1,976	2,766		790 D	41.7%	58.3%	41.7%	58.3%
25,370	TATE	6,675	4,508	2,167		2,341 R	67.5%	32.5%	67.5%	32.5%
20,826	TIPPAH	6,950	4,034	2,916		1,118 R	58.0%	42.0%	58.0%	42.0%
19,163	TISHOMINGO	6,518	3,484	3,034		450 R	53.5%	46.5%	53.5%	46.5%
9,227	TUNICA	2,548	1,237	1,311		74 D	48.5%	51.5%	48.5%	51.5%
25,362	UNION	7,126	3,990	3,136		854 R	56.0%	44.0%	56.0%	44.0%
15,156	WALTHALL	4,319	2,378	1,941		437 R	55.1%	44.9%	55.1%	44.9%
49,644	WARREN	13,199	7,894	5,305		2,589 R	59.8%	40.2%	59.8%	40.2%
62,977	WASHINGTON	9,309	4,020	5,289		1,269 D	43.2%	56.8%	43.2%	56.8%
21,216	WAYNE	7,194	3,440	3,754		314 D	47.8%	52.2%	47.8%	52.2%
10,294	WEBSTER	4,018	2,601	1,417		1,184 R	64.7%	35.3%	64.7%	35.3%
10,312	WILKINSON	2,755	1,169	1,586		417 D	42.4%	57.6%	42.4%	57.6%
20,160	WINSTON	7,457	3,678	3,779		101 D	49.3%	50.7%	49.3%	50.7%
13,051	YALOBUSHA	3,645	2,024	1,621		403 R	55.5%	44.5%	55.5%	44.5%
28,149	YAZOO	7,818	4,459	3,359		1,100 R	57.0%	43.0%	57.0%	43.0%
2,844,658	TOTAL	744,039	430,807	313,232		117,575 R	57.9%	42.1%	57.9%	42.1%

MISSISSIPPI

SENATOR 2008 (Full Term)

2000 Census Population	County	Total Vote	Republican	Democratic	Other	Rep.-Dem. Plurality	Percentage Total Vote Rep.	Dem.	Major Vote Rep.	Dem.
34,340	ADAMS	14,921	6,967	7,954		987 D	46.7%	53.3%	46.7%	53.3%
34,558	ALCORN	14,586	10,275	4,311		5,964 R	70.4%	29.6%	70.4%	29.6%
13,599	AMITE	7,353	4,269	3,084		1,185 R	58.1%	41.9%	58.1%	41.9%
19,661	ATTALA	8,923	5,466	3,457		2,009 R	61.3%	38.7%	61.3%	38.7%
8,026	BENTON	4,332	2,408	1,924		484 R	55.6%	44.4%	55.6%	44.4%
40,633	BOLIVAR	14,283	5,756	8,527		2,771 D	40.3%	59.7%	40.3%	59.7%
15,069	CALHOUN	6,847	4,555	2,292		2,263 R	66.5%	33.5%	66.5%	33.5%
10,769	CARROLL	5,801	3,991	1,810		2,181 R	68.8%	31.2%	68.8%	31.2%
19,440	CHICKASAW	8,655	4,512	4,143		369 R	52.1%	47.9%	52.1%	47.9%
9,758	CHOCTAW	3,959	2,715	1,244		1,471 R	68.6%	31.4%	68.6%	31.4%
11,831	CLAIBORNE	5,284	964	4,320		3,356 D	18.2%	81.8%	18.2%	81.8%
17,955	CLARKE	8,188	5,242	2,946		2,296 R	64.0%	36.0%	64.0%	36.0%
21,979	CLAY	10,693	4,772	5,921		1,149 D	44.6%	55.4%	44.6%	55.4%
30,622	COAHOMA	9,792	3,559	6,233		2,674 D	36.3%	63.7%	36.3%	63.7%
28,757	COPIAH	14,016	7,063	6,953		110 R	50.4%	49.6%	50.4%	49.6%
19,407	COVINGTON	9,225	5,758	3,467		2,291 R	62.4%	37.6%	62.4%	37.6%
107,199	DE SOTO	62,632	44,834	17,798		27,036 R	71.6%	28.4%	71.6%	28.4%
72,604	FORREST	26,261	16,926	9,335		7,591 R	64.5%	35.5%	64.5%	35.5%
8,448	FRANKLIN	4,566	2,940	1,626		1,314 R	64.4%	35.6%	64.4%	35.6%
19,144	GEORGE	9,110	7,731	1,379		6,352 R	84.9%	15.1%	84.9%	15.1%
13,299	GREENE	5,685	4,291	1,394		2,897 R	75.5%	24.5%	75.5%	24.5%
23,263	GRENADA	10,885	6,431	4,454		1,977 R	59.1%	40.9%	59.1%	40.9%
42,967	HANCOCK	16,455	13,262	3,193		10,069 R	80.6%	19.4%	80.6%	19.4%
189,601	HARRISON	60,900	43,275	17,625		25,650 R	71.1%	28.9%	71.1%	28.9%
250,800	HINDS	104,588	39,431	65,157		25,726 D	37.7%	62.3%	37.7%	62.3%
21,609	HOLMES	9,043	2,145	6,898		4,753 D	23.7%	76.3%	23.7%	76.3%
11,206	HUMPHREYS	4,860	1,690	3,170		1,480 D	34.8%	65.2%	34.8%	65.2%
2,274	ISSAQUENA	894	397	497		100 D	44.4%	55.6%	44.4%	55.6%
22,770	ITAWAMBA	9,697	7,602	2,095		5,507 R	78.4%	21.6%	78.4%	21.6%
131,420	JACKSON	52,737	38,961	13,776		25,185 R	73.9%	26.1%	73.9%	26.1%
18,149	JASPER	8,997	4,281	4,716		435 D	47.6%	52.4%	47.6%	52.4%
9,740	JEFFERSON	4,341	753	3,588		2,835 D	17.3%	82.7%	17.3%	82.7%
13,962	JEFFERSON DAVIS	7,126	3,088	4,038		950 D	43.3%	56.7%	43.3%	56.7%
64,958	JONES	28,677	21,049	7,628		13,421 R	73.4%	26.6%	73.4%	26.6%
10,453	KEMPER	5,037	2,171	2,866		695 D	43.1%	56.9%	43.1%	56.9%
38,744	LAFAYETTE	17,956	11,826	6,130		5,696 R	65.9%	34.1%	65.9%	34.1%
39,070	LAMAR	23,448	19,384	4,064		15,320 R	82.7%	17.3%	82.7%	17.3%
78,161	LAUDERDALE	31,904	20,679	11,225		9,454 R	64.8%	35.2%	64.8%	35.2%
13,258	LAWRENCE	6,836	4,428	2,408		2,020 R	64.8%	35.2%	64.8%	35.2%
20,940	LEAKE	9,069	5,466	3,603		1,863 R	60.3%	39.7%	60.3%	39.7%
75,755	LEE	34,052	23,736	10,316		13,420 R	69.7%	30.3%	69.7%	30.3%
37,947	LEFLORE	12,365	4,562	7,803		3,241 D	36.9%	63.1%	36.9%	63.1%
33,166	LINCOLN	16,123	10,994	5,129		5,865 R	68.2%	31.8%	68.2%	31.8%
61,586	LOWNDES	26,306	14,966	11,340		3,626 R	56.9%	43.1%	56.9%	43.1%
74,674	MADISON	46,100	29,402	16,698		12,704 R	63.8%	36.2%	63.8%	36.2%
25,595	MARION	12,704	8,640	4,064		4,576 R	68.0%	32.0%	68.0%	32.0%
34,993	MARSHALL	15,467	7,032	8,435		1,403 D	45.5%	54.5%	45.5%	54.5%
38,014	MONROE	16,947	10,478	6,469		4,009 R	61.8%	38.2%	61.8%	38.2%
12,189	MONTGOMERY	5,525	3,174	2,351		823 R	57.4%	42.6%	57.4%	42.6%
28,684	NESHOBA	11,167	8,527	2,640		5,887 R	76.4%	23.6%	76.4%	23.6%

MISSISSIPPI

SENATOR 2008 (Full Term)

2000 Census Population	County	Total Vote	Republican	Democratic	Other	Rep.-Dem. Plurality	Percentage Total Vote Rep.	Total Vote Dem.	Major Vote Rep.	Major Vote Dem.
21,838	NEWTON	9,603	6,820	2,783		4,037 R	71.0%	29.0%	71.0%	29.0%
12,548	NOXUBEE	6,237	1,683	4,554		2,871 D	27.0%	73.0%	27.0%	73.0%
42,902	OKTIBBEHA	18,049	10,466	7,583		2,883 R	58.0%	42.0%	58.0%	42.0%
34,274	PANOLA	15,655	8,137	7,518		619 R	52.0%	48.0%	52.0%	48.0%
48,621	PEARL RIVER	21,525	17,298	4,227		13,071 R	80.4%	19.6%	80.4%	19.6%
12,138	PERRY	5,481	4,233	1,248		2,985 R	77.2%	22.8%	77.2%	22.8%
38,940	PIKE	17,596	9,103	8,493		610 R	51.7%	48.3%	51.7%	48.3%
26,726	PONTOTOC	12,536	9,862	2,674		7,188 R	78.7%	21.3%	78.7%	21.3%
25,556	PRENTISS	10,524	7,504	3,020		4,484 R	71.3%	28.7%	71.3%	28.7%
10,117	QUITMAN	3,858	1,541	2,317		776 D	39.9%	60.1%	39.9%	60.1%
115,327	RANKIN	61,901	49,993	11,908		38,085 R	80.8%	19.2%	80.8%	19.2%
28,423	SCOTT	11,307	6,748	4,559		2,189 R	59.7%	40.3%	59.7%	40.3%
6,580	SHARKEY	2,625	962	1,663		701 D	36.6%	63.4%	36.6%	63.4%
27,639	SIMPSON	12,194	7,915	4,279		3,636 R	64.9%	35.1%	64.9%	35.1%
16,182	SMITH	8,134	6,369	1,765		4,604 R	78.3%	21.7%	78.3%	21.7%
13,622	STONE	7,001	5,390	1,611		3,779 R	77.0%	23.0%	77.0%	23.0%
34,369	SUNFLOWER	10,686	3,906	6,780		2,874 D	36.6%	63.4%	36.6%	63.4%
14,903	TALLAHATCHIE	6,597	3,092	3,505		413 D	46.9%	53.1%	46.9%	53.1%
25,370	TATE	12,193	7,869	4,324		3,545 R	64.5%	35.5%	64.5%	35.5%
20,826	TIPPAH	9,458	6,963	2,495		4,468 R	73.6%	26.4%	73.6%	26.4%
19,163	TISHOMINGO	8,081	6,022	2,059		3,963 R	74.5%	25.5%	74.5%	25.5%
9,227	TUNICA	3,956	1,225	2,731		1,506 D	31.0%	69.0%	31.0%	69.0%
25,362	UNION	11,906	9,242	2,664		6,578 R	77.6%	22.4%	77.6%	22.4%
15,156	WALTHALL	7,488	4,348	3,140		1,208 R	58.1%	41.9%	58.1%	41.9%
49,644	WARREN	21,122	12,183	8,939		3,244 R	57.7%	42.3%	57.7%	42.3%
62,977	WASHINGTON	18,644	7,187	11,457		4,270 D	38.5%	61.5%	38.5%	61.5%
21,216	WAYNE	9,719	6,215	3,504		2,711 R	63.9%	36.1%	63.9%	36.1%
10,294	WEBSTER	5,314	4,139	1,175		2,964 R	77.9%	22.1%	77.9%	22.1%
10,312	WILKINSON	4,774	1,735	3,039		1,304 D	36.3%	63.7%	36.3%	63.7%
20,160	WINSTON	9,965	5,740	4,225		1,515 R	57.6%	42.4%	57.6%	42.4%
13,051	YALOBUSHA	6,644	3,870	2,774		1,096 R	58.2%	41.8%	58.2%	41.8%
28,149	YAZOO	10,935	5,527	5,408		119 R	50.5%	49.5%	50.5%	49.5%
2,844,658	TOTAL	1,247,026	766,111	480,915		285,196 R	61.4%	38.6%	61.4%	38.6%

MISSISSIPPI

SENATOR 2008 (Short Term)

2000 Census Population	County	Total Vote	Republican	Democratic	Other	Rep.-Dem. Plurality	Percentage Total Vote Rep.	Dem.	Major Vote Rep.	Dem.
34,340	ADAMS	14,985	5,942	9,043		3,101 D	39.7%	60.3%	39.7%	60.3%
34,558	ALCORN	14,566	9,624	4,942		4,682 R	66.1%	33.9%	66.1%	33.9%
13,599	AMITE	7,270	3,821	3,449		372 R	52.6%	47.4%	52.6%	47.4%
19,661	ATTALA	8,843	4,922	3,921		1,001 R	55.7%	44.3%	55.7%	44.3%
8,026	BENTON	4,391	2,270	2,121		149 R	51.7%	48.3%	51.7%	48.3%
40,633	BOLIVAR	14,442	5,062	9,380		4,318 D	35.1%	64.9%	35.1%	64.9%
15,069	CALHOUN	6,853	4,386	2,467		1,919 R	64.0%	36.0%	64.0%	36.0%
10,769	CARROLL	5,782	3,704	2,078		1,626 R	64.1%	35.9%	64.1%	35.9%
19,440	CHICKASAW	8,749	4,299	4,450		151 D	49.1%	50.9%	49.1%	50.9%
9,758	CHOCTAW	3,927	2,602	1,325		1,277 R	66.3%	33.7%	66.3%	33.7%
11,831	CLAIBORNE	5,297	1,102	4,195		3,093 D	20.8%	79.2%	20.8%	79.2%
17,955	CLARKE	8,131	4,782	3,349		1,433 R	58.8%	41.2%	58.8%	41.2%
21,979	CLAY	10,628	4,813	5,815		1,002 D	45.3%	54.7%	45.3%	54.7%
30,622	COAHOMA	9,806	3,046	6,760		3,714 D	31.1%	68.9%	31.1%	68.9%
28,757	COPIAH	13,994	6,397	7,597		1,200 D	45.7%	54.3%	45.7%	54.3%
19,407	COVINGTON	9,196	5,033	4,163		870 R	54.7%	45.3%	54.7%	45.3%
107,199	DE SOTO	61,948	41,363	20,585		20,778 R	66.8%	33.2%	66.8%	33.2%
72,604	FORREST	26,195	14,621	11,574		3,047 R	55.8%	44.2%	55.8%	44.2%
8,448	FRANKLIN	4,579	2,604	1,975		629 R	56.9%	43.1%	56.9%	43.1%
19,144	GEORGE	8,975	5,838	3,137		2,701 R	65.0%	35.0%	65.0%	35.0%
13,299	GREENE	5,683	3,479	2,204		1,275 R	61.2%	38.8%	61.2%	38.8%
23,263	GRENADA	10,823	5,993	4,830		1,163 R	55.4%	44.6%	55.4%	44.6%
42,967	HANCOCK	16,354	10,373	5,981		4,392 R	63.4%	36.6%	63.4%	36.6%
189,601	HARRISON	60,065	35,457	24,608		10,849 R	59.0%	41.0%	59.0%	41.0%
250,800	HINDS	105,279	35,743	69,536		33,793 D	34.0%	66.0%	34.0%	66.0%
21,609	HOLMES	8,997	2,145	6,852		4,707 D	23.8%	76.2%	23.8%	76.2%
11,206	HUMPHREYS	4,961	1,593	3,368		1,775 D	32.1%	67.9%	32.1%	67.9%
2,274	ISSAQUENA	898	379	519		140 D	42.2%	57.8%	42.2%	57.8%
22,770	ITAWAMBA	9,702	6,790	2,912		3,878 R	70.0%	30.0%	70.0%	30.0%
131,420	JACKSON	52,296	32,449	19,847		12,602 R	62.0%	38.0%	62.0%	38.0%
18,149	JASPER	8,946	3,816	5,130		1,314 D	42.7%	57.3%	42.7%	57.3%
9,740	JEFFERSON	4,348	826	3,522		2,696 D	19.0%	81.0%	19.0%	81.0%
13,962	JEFFERSON DAVIS	7,103	2,775	4,328		1,553 D	39.1%	60.9%	39.1%	60.9%
64,958	JONES	28,655	18,066	10,589		7,477 R	63.0%	37.0%	63.0%	37.0%
10,453	KEMPER	5,033	1,941	3,092		1,151 D	38.6%	61.4%	38.6%	61.4%
38,744	LAFAYETTE	17,748	10,656	7,092		3,564 R	60.0%	40.0%	60.0%	40.0%
39,070	LAMAR	23,385	17,119	6,266		10,853 R	73.2%	26.8%	73.2%	26.8%
78,161	LAUDERDALE	31,744	18,846	12,898		5,948 R	59.4%	40.6%	59.4%	40.6%
13,258	LAWRENCE	6,770	3,803	2,967		836 R	56.2%	43.8%	56.2%	43.8%
20,940	LEAKE	9,070	4,695	4,375		320 R	51.8%	48.2%	51.8%	48.2%
75,755	LEE	34,449	22,375	12,074		10,301 R	65.0%	35.0%	65.0%	35.0%
37,947	LEFLORE	12,639	4,206	8,433		4,227 D	33.3%	66.7%	33.3%	66.7%
33,166	LINCOLN	16,113	9,768	6,345		3,423 R	60.6%	39.4%	60.6%	39.4%
61,586	LOWNDES	26,216	14,489	11,727		2,762 R	55.3%	44.7%	55.3%	44.7%
74,674	MADISON	45,794	26,920	18,874		8,046 R	58.8%	41.2%	58.8%	41.2%
25,595	MARION	12,716	7,729	4,987		2,742 R	60.8%	39.2%	60.8%	39.2%
34,993	MARSHALL	15,119	7,191	7,928		737 D	47.6%	52.4%	47.6%	52.4%
38,014	MONROE	16,900	9,752	7,148		2,604 R	57.7%	42.3%	57.7%	42.3%
12,189	MONTGOMERY	5,482	2,980	2,502		478 R	54.4%	45.6%	54.4%	45.6%
28,684	NESHOBA	11,157	7,384	3,773		3,611 R	66.2%	33.8%	66.2%	33.8%

MISSISSIPPI

SENATOR 2008 (Short Term)

2000 Census Population	County	Total Vote	Republican	Democratic	Other	Rep.-Dem. Plurality	Percentage			
							Total Vote		Major Vote	
							Rep.	Dem.	Rep.	Dem.
21,838	NEWTON	9,572	6,166	3,406		2,760 R	64.4%	35.6%	64.4%	35.6%
12,548	NOXUBEE	6,298	1,853	4,445		2,592 D	29.4%	70.6%	29.4%	70.6%
42,902	OKTIBBEHA	17,964	9,891	8,073		1,818 R	55.1%	44.9%	55.1%	44.9%
34,274	PANOLA	15,725	7,192	8,533		1,341 D	45.7%	54.3%	45.7%	54.3%
48,621	PEARL RIVER	21,294	13,762	7,532		6,230 R	64.6%	35.4%	64.6%	35.4%
12,138	PERRY	5,444	3,487	1,957		1,530 R	64.1%	35.9%	64.1%	35.9%
38,940	PIKE	17,446	8,139	9,307		1,168 D	46.7%	53.3%	46.7%	53.3%
26,726	PONTOTOC	12,527	9,230	3,297		5,933 R	73.7%	26.3%	73.7%	26.3%
25,556	PRENTISS	10,569	6,652	3,917		2,735 R	62.9%	37.1%	62.9%	37.1%
10,117	QUITMAN	3,848	1,427	2,421		994 D	37.1%	62.9%	37.1%	62.9%
115,327	RANKIN	61,851	45,488	16,363		29,125 R	73.5%	26.5%	73.5%	26.5%
28,423	SCOTT	11,229	6,019	5,210		809 R	53.6%	46.4%	53.6%	46.4%
6,580	SHARKEY	2,684	920	1,764		844 D	34.3%	65.7%	34.3%	65.7%
27,639	SIMPSON	12,113	6,844	5,269		1,575 R	56.5%	43.5%	56.5%	43.5%
16,182	SMITH	8,075	5,480	2,595		2,885 R	67.9%	32.1%	67.9%	32.1%
13,622	STONE	6,948	4,384	2,564		1,820 R	63.1%	36.9%	63.1%	36.9%
34,369	SUNFLOWER	10,769	3,462	7,307		3,845 D	32.1%	67.9%	32.1%	67.9%
14,903	TALLAHATCHIE	6,609	2,788	3,821		1,033 D	42.2%	57.8%	42.2%	57.8%
25,370	TATE	12,112	7,196	4,916		2,280 R	59.4%	40.6%	59.4%	40.6%
20,826	TIPPAH	9,397	6,315	3,082		3,233 R	67.2%	32.8%	67.2%	32.8%
19,163	TISHOMINGO	8,134	5,477	2,657		2,820 R	67.3%	32.7%	67.3%	32.7%
9,227	TUNICA	3,899	1,261	2,638		1,377 D	32.3%	67.7%	32.3%	67.7%
25,362	UNION	11,962	8,082	3,880		4,202 R	67.6%	32.4%	67.6%	32.4%
15,156	WALTHALL	7,465	3,822	3,643		179 R	51.2%	48.8%	51.2%	48.8%
49,644	WARREN	20,953	10,844	10,109		735 R	51.8%	48.2%	51.8%	48.2%
62,977	WASHINGTON	18,475	6,442	12,033		5,591 D	34.9%	65.1%	34.9%	65.1%
21,216	WAYNE	9,673	5,204	4,469		735 R	53.8%	46.2%	53.8%	46.2%
10,294	WEBSTER	5,300	3,800	1,500		2,300 R	71.7%	28.3%	71.7%	28.3%
10,312	WILKINSON	4,613	1,531	3,082		1,551 D	33.2%	66.8%	33.2%	66.8%
20,160	WINSTON	9,949	5,344	4,605		739 R	53.7%	46.3%	53.7%	46.3%
13,051	YALOBUSHA	6,684	3,684	3,000		684 R	55.1%	44.9%	55.1%	44.9%
28,149	YAZOO	10,890	5,254	5,636		382 D	48.2%	51.8%	48.2%	51.8%
2,844,658	TOTAL	1,243,473	683,409	560,064		123,345 R	55.0%	45.0%	55.0%	45.0%

MISSISSIPPI

HOUSE OF REPRESENTATIVES

CD	Year	Total Vote	Republican Vote	Republican Candidate	Democratic Vote	Democratic Candidate	Other Vote	Rep.-Dem. Plurality	Total Vote Rep.	Total Vote Dem.	Major Vote Rep.	Major Vote Dem.
1	2008	341,389	149,818	DAVIS, GREG	185,959	CHILDERS, TRAVIS W.*	5,612	36,141 D	43.9%	54.5%	44.6%	55.4%
1	2006	144,272	95,098	WICKER, ROGER*	49,174	HURT, JAMES K. "KEN"		45,924 R	65.9%	34.1%	65.9%	34.1%
1	2004	277,584	219,328	WICKER, ROGER*	—		58,256	219,328 R	79.0%		100.0%	
1	2002	133,567	95,404	WICKER, ROGER*	32,318	WEATHERS, REX N.	5,845	63,086 R	71.4%	24.2%	74.7%	25.3%
2	2008	291,970	90,364	COOK, RICHARD	201,606	THOMPSON, BENNIE*		111,242 D	30.9%	69.1%	30.9%	69.1%
2	2006	155,832	55,672	BROWN, YVONNE R.	100,160	THOMPSON, BENNIE*		44,488 D	35.7%	64.3%	35.7%	64.3%
2	2004	264,869	107,647	LeSUEUR, CLINTON B.	154,626	THOMPSON, BENNIE*	2,596	46,979 D	40.6%	58.4%	41.0%	59.0%
2	2002	163,050	69,711	LeSUEUR, CLINTON B.	89,913	THOMPSON, BENNIE*	3,426	20,202 D	42.8%	55.1%	43.7%	56.3%
3	2008	340,869	213,171	HARPER, GREGG	127,698	GILL, JOEL L.		85,473 R	62.5%	37.5%	62.5%	37.5%
3	2006	161,480	125,421	PICKERING, CHARLES W. "CHIP" JR.*	—		36,059	125,421 R	77.7%		100.0%	
3	2004	293,368	234,874	PICKERING, CHARLES W. "CHIP" JR.*	76,184	SHOWS, RONNIE*	58,494	234,874 R	80.1%		100.0%	
3	2002	219,151	139,329	PICKERING, CHARLES W. "CHIP" JR.*			3,638	63,145 R	63.6%	34.8%	64.6%	35.4%
4	2008	290,519	73,977	McCAY, JOHN III	216,542	TAYLOR, GENE*		142,565 D	25.5%	74.5%	25.5%	74.5%
4	2006	139,113	28,117	McDONNELL, RANDY	110,996	TAYLOR, GENE*		82,879 D	20.2%	79.8%	20.2%	79.8%
4	2004	280,382	96,740	LOTT, MICHAEL	181,614	TAYLOR, GENE*	2,028	84,874 D	34.5%	64.8%	34.8%	65.2%
4	2002	161,868	34,373	MERTZ, KARL CLEVELAND	121,742	TAYLOR, GENE*	5,753	87,369 D	21.2%	75.2%	22.0%	78.0%
TOTAL	2008	1,264,747	527,330		731,805		5,612	204,475 D	41.7%	57.9%	41.9%	58.1%
TOTAL	2006	600,697	304,308		260,330		36,059	43,978 R	50.7%	43.3%	53.9%	46.1%
TOTAL	2004	1,116,203	658,589		336,240		121,374	322,349 R	59.0%	30.1%	66.2%	33.8%
TOTAL	2002	677,636	338,817		320,157		18,662	18,660 R	50.0%	47.2%	51.4%	48.6%

Note: An asterisk (*) denotes incumbent.

MISSISSIPPI

GENERAL AND PRIMARY ELECTIONS

2008 GENERAL ELECTIONS

President	Other vote was 4,011 Independent (Ralph Nader); 2,551 Constitution (Chuck Baldwin); 2,529 Libertarian (Bob Barr); 1,034 Green (Cynthia A. McKinney); 481 Reform (Ted C. Weill).
Governor 2007	
Senator (Full Term)	
Senator (Short Term)	
House	Other vote was:
CD 1	3,736 Independent (Wally Pang); 1.876 Green (John M. Wages Jr.).
CD 2	
CD 3	
CD 4	

2007-2008 PRIMARY ELECTIONS

Primary	August 7, 2007 (Governor) March 11, 2008	**Registration** (as of May 6, 2006)		1,715,348	No Party Registration
Primary Runoff	April 1, 2008				
Primary Type	Open—Any registered voter could participate in the party primary of their choice. But any voter who participated in the primary of one party could not participate in the runoff of the other party.				

MISSISSIPPI

GENERAL AND PRIMARY ELECTIONS

	REPUBLICAN PRIMARIES			DEMOCRATIC PRIMARIES		
President	John McCain	113,074	78.9%	Barack Obama	265,502	61.2%
	Mike Huckabee	17,943	12.5%	Hillary Clinton	159,221	36.7%
	Ron Paul	5,510	3.8%	John Edwards	3,933	0.9%
	Mitt Romney	2,177	1.5%	Joseph R. Biden Jr.	1,816	0.4%
	Fred Thompson	2,160	1.5%	Bill Richardson	1,396	0.3%
	Rudolph Giuliani	945	0.7%	Dennis J. Kucinich	912	0.2%
	Alan Keyes	842	0.6%	Christopher J. Dodd	739	0.2%
	Duncan Hunter	414	0.3%	Mike Gravel	591	0.1%
	Tom Tancredo	221	0.2%	Undecided	42	
	TOTAL	143,286		TOTAL	434,152	
Governor (2007)	Haley Barbour*	184,036	93.1%	John A. Eaves	314,012	70.3%
	Frederick L. Jones	13,611	6.9%	William Bond Compton Jr.	52,343	11.7%
				Fred T. Smith	49,170	11.0%
				Elmer "Louis" L. Fondren	31,197	7.0%
	TOTAL	197,647		TOTAL	446,722	
Senator (Full Term)	Thad Cochran*	Unopposed		Erik R. Fleming	236,296	65.8%
				Shawn O'Hara	122,803	34.2%
				TOTAL	359,099	
Congressional District 1	Glenn L. McCullough Jr.	17,082	38.9%	Travis W. Childers	40,919	41.4%
	Greg Davis	16,161	36.8%	Steve Holland	30,274	30.6%
	Randy Russell	10,688	24.3%	Marshall Coleman	12,913	13.1%
				Brian Neely	10,624	10.8%
				James "Ken" Hurt	4,095	4.1%
	TOTAL	43,931		TOTAL	98,825	
	PRIMARY RUNOFF			PRIMARY RUNOFF		
	Greg Davis	16,733	50.8%	Travis W. Childers	20,797	56.6%
	Glenn L. McCullough Jr.	16,196	49.2%	Steve Holland	15,958	43.4%
	TOTAL	32,929		TOTAL	36,755	
Congressional District 2	Richard Cook	Unopposed		Bennie Thompson*	111,077	86.2%
				Dorothy "Dot" Benford	17,824	13.8%
				TOTAL	128,901	
Congressional District 3	Charlie Ross	22,254	33.4%	Joel L. Gill	44,313	53.4%
	Gregg Harper	18,892	28.3%	Randy Eads	38,629	46.6%
	David Landrum	17,082	25.6%			
	John Rounsaville	6,949	10.4%			
	Gregory W. Hatcher	748	1.1%			
	James Broadwater	424	0.6%			
	William "Bill" Marcy	344	0.5%			
	TOTAL	66,693		TOTAL	82,942	
	PRIMARY RUNOFF					
	Gregg Harper	29,351	57.0%			
	Charlie Ross	22,178	43.0%			
	TOTAL	51,529				
Congressional District 4	John McCay III	Unopposed		Gene Taylor*	79,807	100.0%

Notes: An asterisk (*) denotes incumbent. If no candidate received a majority of the primary vote, a runoff was held between the top two finishers. The names of unopposed candidates did not have to appear on the primary ballot; therefore, in some races no votes were cast for these candidates. The special Senate election on the November 4 ballot between Republican incumbent Roger Wicker and Democrat Ronnie Musgrove was not preceded by a primary. Candidates in this contest did not have their party affiliation identified on the ballot and there would have been a runoff if no candidate received a majority of the vote.

MISSOURI

Congressional districts first established for elections held in 2002
9 members

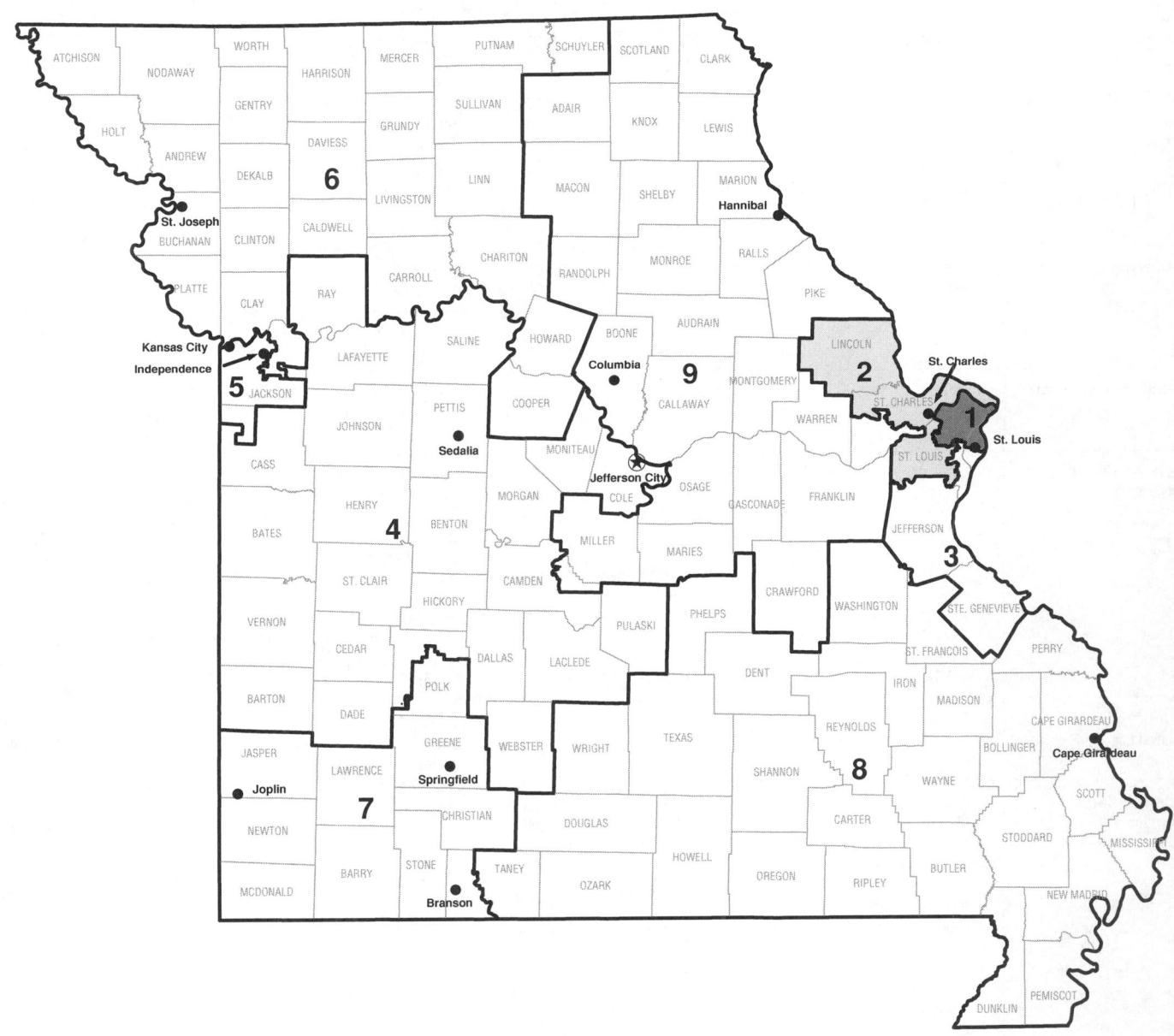

MISSOURI

GOVERNOR
Jeremiah W. "Jay" Nixon (D). Elected 2008 to a four-year term.

SENATORS (1 Democrat, 1 Republican)
Christopher S. Bond (R). Reelected 2004 to a six-year term. Previously elected 1998, 1992, 1986.

Claire McCaskill (D). Elected 2006 to a six-year term.

REPRESENTATIVES (5 Republicans, 4 Democrats)

1. William Lacy Clay (D)
2. Todd Akin (R)
3. Russ Carnahan (D)
4. Ike Skelton (D)
5. Emanuel Cleaver II (D)
6. Sam Graves (R)
7. Roy Blunt (R)
8. Jo Ann Emerson (R)
9. Blaine Luetkemeyer (R)

POSTWAR VOTE FOR PRESIDENT

Year	Total Vote	Republican Vote	Republican Candidate	Democratic Vote	Democratic Candidate	Other Vote	Plurality	Total Vote Rep.	Total Vote Dem.	Major Vote Rep.	Major Vote Dem.
2008	2,925,205	1,445,814	McCain, John	1,441,911	Obama, Barack	37,480	3,903 R	49.4%	49.3%	50.1%	49.9%
2004	2,731,364	1,455,713	Bush, George W.	1,259,171	Kerry, John	16,480	196,542 R	53.3%	46.1%	53.6%	46.4%
2000**	2,359,892	1,189,924	Bush, George W.	1,111,138	Gore, Al	58,830	78,786 R	50.4%	47.1%	51.7%	48.3%
1996**	2,158,065	890,016	Dole, Bob	1,025,935	Clinton, Bill	242,114	135,919 D	41.2%	47.5%	46.5%	53.5%
1992**	2,391,565	811,159	Bush, George	1,053,873	Clinton, Bill	526,533	242,714 D	33.9%	44.1%	43.5%	56.5%
1988	2,093,713	1,084,953	Bush, George	1,001,619	Dukakis, Michael S.	7,141	83,334 R	51.8%	47.8%	52.0%	48.0%
1984	2,122,783	1,274,188	Reagan, Ronald	848,583	Mondale, Walter F.	12	425,605 R	60.0%	40.0%	60.0%	40.0%
1980**	2,099,824	1,074,181	Reagan, Ronald	931,182	Carter, Jimmy	94,461	142,999 R	51.2%	44.3%	53.6%	46.4%
1976	1,953,600	927,443	Ford, Gerald R.	998,387	Carter, Jimmy	27,770	70,944 D	47.5%	51.1%	48.2%	51.8%
1972	1,855,803	1,153,852	Nixon, Richard M.	697,147	McGovern, George S.	4,804	456,705 R	62.2%	37.6%	62.3%	37.7%
1968**	1,809,502	811,932	Nixon, Richard M.	791,444	Humphrey, Hubert H.	206,126	20,488 R	44.9%	43.7%	50.6%	49.4%
1964	1,817,879	653,535	Goldwater, Barry M.	1,164,344	Johnson, Lyndon B.		510,809 D	36.0%	64.0%	36.0%	64.0%
1960	1,934,422	962,221	Nixon, Richard M.	972,201	Kennedy, John F.		9,980 D	49.7%	50.3%	49.7%	50.3%
1956	1,832,562	914,289	Eisenhower, Dwight D.	918,273	Stevenson, Adlai E.		3,984 D	49.9%	50.1%	49.9%	50.1%
1952	1,892,062	959,429	Eisenhower, Dwight D.	929,830	Stevenson, Adlai E.	2,803	29,599 R	50.7%	49.1%	50.8%	49.2%
1948	1,578,628	655,039	Dewey, Thomas E.	917,315	Truman, Harry S.	6,274	262,276 D	41.5%	58.1%	41.7%	58.3%

**In past elections, the other vote included: 2000 - 38,515 Green (Ralph Nader); 1996 - 217,188 Reform (Ross Perot); 1992 - 518,741 Independent (Perot); 1980 - 77,920 Independent (John Anderson); 1968 - 206,126 American Independent (George Wallace).

MISSOURI

POSTWAR VOTE FOR GOVERNOR

Year	Total Vote	Republican Vote	Republican Candidate	Democratic Vote	Democratic Candidate	Other Vote	Rep.-Dem. Plurality	Total Vote Rep.	Total Vote Dem.	Major Vote Rep.	Major Vote Dem.
2008	2,877,778	1,136,364	Hulshof, Kenny	1,680,611	Nixon, Jeremiah W. "Jay"	60,803	544,247 D	39.5%	58.4%	40.3%	59.7%
2004	2,719,599	1,382,419	Blunt, Matt	1,301,442	McCaskill, Claire	35,738	80,977 R	50.8%	47.9%	51.5%	48.5%
2000	2,346,830	1,131,307	Talent, Jim	1,152,752	Holden, Bob	62,771	21,445 D	48.2%	49.1%	49.5%	50.5%
1996	2,142,518	866,268	Kelly, Margaret	1,224,801	Carnahan, Mel	51,449	358,533 D	40.4%	57.2%	41.4%	58.6%
1992	2,344,121	968,574	Webster, William L.	1,375,425	Carnahan, Mel	122	406,851 D	41.3%	58.7%	41.3%	58.7%
1988	2,085,928	1,339,531	Ashcroft, John	724,919	Hearnes, Betty C.	21,478	614,612 R	64.2%	34.8%	64.9%	35.1%
1984	2,108,210	1,194,506	Ashcroft, John	913,700	Rothman, Kenneth J.	4	280,806 R	56.7%	43.3%	56.7%	43.3%
1980	2,088,028	1,098,950	Bond, Christopher S.	981,884	Teasdale, Joseph P.	7,194	117,066 R	52.6%	47.0%	52.8%	47.2%
1976	1,933,575	958,110	Bond, Christopher S.	971,184	Teasdale, Joseph P.	4,281	13,074 D	49.6%	50.2%	49.7%	50.3%
1972	1,865,683	1,029,451	Bond, Christopher S.	832,751	Dowd, Edward L.	3,481	196,700 R	55.2%	44.6%	55.3%	44.7%
1968	1,764,602	691,797	Roos, Lawrence K.	1,072,805	Hearnes, Warren E.		381,008 D	39.2%	60.8%	39.2%	60.8%
1964	1,789,600	678,949	Shepley, Ethan	1,110,651	Hearnes, Warren E.		431,702 D	37.9%	62.1%	37.9%	62.1%
1960	1,887,331	792,131	Farmer, Edward G.	1,095,200	Dalton, John M.		303,069 D	42.0%	58.0%	42.0%	58.0%
1956	1,808,338	866,810	Hocker, Lon	941,528	Blair, James T.		74,718 D	47.9%	52.1%	47.9%	52.1%
1952	1,871,095	886,370	Elliott, Howard	983,166	Donnelly, Phil M.	1,559	96,796 D	47.4%	52.5%	47.4%	52.6%
1948	1,567,338	670,064	Thompson, Murray	893,092	Smith, Forrest	4,182	223,028 D	42.8%	57.0%	42.9%	57.1%

POSTWAR VOTE FOR SENATOR

Year	Total Vote	Republican Vote	Republican Candidate	Democratic Vote	Democratic Candidate	Other Vote	Rep.-Dem. Plurality	Total Vote Rep.	Total Vote Dem.	Major Vote Rep.	Major Vote Dem.
2006	2,128,459	1,006,941	Talent, Jim	1,055,255	McCaskill, Claire	66,263	48,314 D	47.3%	49.6%	48.8%	51.2%
2004	2,706,402	1,518,089	Bond, Christopher S.	1,158,261	Farmer, Nancy	30,052	359,828 R	56.1%	42.8%	56.7%	43.3%
2002S	1,877,620	935,032	Talent, Jim	913,778	Carnahan, Jean	28,810	21,254 R	49.8%	48.7%	50.6%	49.4%
2000**	2,361,586	1,142,852	Ashcroft, John	1,191,812	Carnahan, Mel	26,922	48,960 D	48.4%	50.5%	49.0%	51.0%
1998	1,576,857	830,625	Bond, Christopher S.	690,208	Nixon, Jeremiah W.	56,024	140,417 R	52.7%	43.8%	54.6%	45.4%
1994	1,775,116	1,060,149	Ashcroft, John	633,697	Wheat, Alan	81,270	426,452 R	59.7%	35.7%	62.6%	37.4%
1992	2,354,925	1,221,901	Bond, Christopher S.	1,057,967	Rothman-Serot, Geri	75,057	163,934 R	51.9%	44.9%	53.6%	46.4%
1988	2,078,875	1,407,416	Danforth, John C.	660,045	Nixon, Jeremiah W. "Jay"	11,414	747,371 R	67.7%	31.8%	68.1%	31.9%
1986	1,477,327	777,612	Bond, Christopher S.	699,624	Woods, Harriett	91	77,988 R	52.6%	47.4%	52.6%	47.4%
1982	1,543,521	784,876	Danforth, John C.	758,629	Woods, Harriett	16	26,247 R	50.8%	49.1%	50.9%	49.1%
1980	2,066,965	985,399	McNary, Gene	1,074,859	Eagleton, Thomas F.	6,707	89,460 D	47.7%	52.0%	47.8%	52.2%
1976	1,914,777	1,090,067	Danforth, John C.	813,571	Hearnes, Warren E.	11,139	276,496 R	56.9%	42.5%	57.3%	42.7%
1974	1,224,303	480,900	Curtis, Thomas B.	735,433	Eagleton, Thomas F.	7,970	254,533 D	39.3%	60.1%	39.5%	60.5%
1970	1,283,912	617,903	Danforth, John C.	655,431	Symington, Stuart	10,578	37,528 D	48.1%	51.0%	48.5%	51.5%
1968	1,737,958	850,544	Curtis, Thomas B.	887,414	Eagleton, Thomas F.		36,870 D	48.9%	51.1%	48.9%	51.1%
1964	1,783,043	596,377	Bradshaw, Jean P.	1,186,666	Symington, Stuart		590,289 D	33.4%	66.6%	33.4%	66.6%
1962	1,222,259	555,330	Kemper, Crosby	666,929	Long, Edward V.		111,599 D	45.4%	54.6%	45.4%	54.6%
1960S	1,880,232	880,576	Hocker, Lon	999,656	Long, Edward V.		119,080 D	46.8%	53.2%	46.8%	53.2%
1958	1,173,903	393,847	Palmer, Hazel	780,056	Symington, Stuart		386,209 D	33.6%	66.4%	33.6%	66.4%
1956	1,800,984	785,048	Douglas, Herbert	1,015,936	Hennings, Thomas C.		230,888 D	43.6%	56.4%	43.6%	56.4%
1952	1,868,083	858,170	Kem, James P.	1,008,523	Symington, Stuart	1,390	150,353 D	45.9%	54.0%	46.0%	54.0%
1950	1,279,414	592,922	Donnell, Forrest C.	685,732	Hennings, Thomas C.	760	92,810 D	46.3%	53.6%	46.4%	53.6%
1946	1,084,100	572,556	Kem, James P.	511,544	Briggs, Frank P.		61,012 R	52.8%	47.2%	52.8%	47.2%

Notes: **In 2000 the Democratic candidate, Mel Carnahan, was killed in an airplane crash in October but his name remained on the ballot and he won the election in November. Subsequently, his widow, Jean Carnahan, was appointed to fill the seat until an election could be held in 2002 for the remaining four years of the term. The 1960 election was for a short term to fill a vacancy.

MISSOURI

PRESIDENT 2008

2000 Census Population	County	Total Vote	Republican	Democratic	Other	Rep.-Dem. Plurality	Percentage Total Vote Rep.	Dem.	Major Vote Rep.	Dem.
24,977	ADAIR	11,871	5,891	5,735	245	156 R	49.6%	48.3%	50.7%	49.3%
16,492	ANDREW	8,790	5,279	3,345	166	1,934 R	60.1%	38.1%	61.2%	38.8%
6,430	ATCHISON	2,976	1,936	1,000	40	936 R	65.1%	33.6%	65.9%	34.1%
25,853	AUDRAIN	10,781	6,167	4,434	180	1,733 R	57.2%	41.1%	58.2%	41.8%
34,010	BARRY	14,644	9,758	4,630	256	5,128 R	66.6%	31.6%	67.8%	32.2%
12,541	BARTON	5,948	4,414	1,455	79	2,959 R	74.2%	24.5%	75.2%	24.8%
16,653	BATES	8,283	4,833	3,271	179	1,562 R	58.3%	39.5%	59.6%	40.4%
17,180	BENTON	9,567	5,759	3,629	179	2,130 R	60.2%	37.9%	61.3%	38.7%
12,029	BOLLINGER	5,784	3,972	1,690	122	2,282 R	68.7%	29.2%	70.2%	29.8%
135,454	BOONE	85,251	36,849	47,062	1,340	10,213 D	43.2%	55.2%	43.9%	56.1%
85,998	BUCHANAN	39,040	19,110	19,164	766	54 D	48.9%	49.1%	49.9%	50.1%
40,867	BUTLER	17,338	11,805	5,316	217	6,489 R	68.1%	30.7%	69.0%	31.0%
8,969	CALDWELL	4,564	2,654	1,814	96	840 R	58.2%	39.7%	59.4%	40.6%
40,766	CALLAWAY	19,321	11,389	7,580	352	3,809 R	58.9%	39.2%	60.0%	40.0%
37,051	CAMDEN	22,133	14,074	7,773	286	6,301 R	63.6%	35.1%	64.4%	35.6%
68,693	CAPE GIRARDEAU	37,355	24,768	12,208	379	12,560 R	66.3%	32.7%	67.0%	33.0%
10,285	CARROLL	4,538	2,955	1,535	48	1,420 R	65.1%	33.8%	65.8%	34.2%
5,941	CARTER	2,898	1,840	984	74	856 R	63.5%	34.0%	65.2%	34.8%
82,092	CASS	50,179	29,695	19,844	640	9,851 R	59.2%	39.5%	59.9%	40.1%
13,733	CEDAR	6,354	4,194	2,060	100	2,134 R	66.0%	32.4%	67.1%	32.9%
8,438	CHARITON	4,214	2,339	1,799	76	540 R	55.5%	42.7%	56.5%	43.5%
54,285	CHRISTIAN	37,697	25,382	11,883	432	13,499 R	67.3%	31.5%	68.1%	31.9%
7,416	CLARK	3,456	1,782	1,572	102	210 R	51.6%	45.5%	53.1%	46.9%
184,006	CLAY	109,606	54,516	53,761	1,329	755 R	49.7%	49.0%	50.3%	49.7%
18,979	CLINTON	10,454	5,709	4,545	200	1,164 R	54.6%	43.5%	55.7%	44.3%
71,397	COLE	38,745	24,385	13,959	401	10,426 R	62.9%	36.0%	63.6%	36.4%
16,670	COOPER	8,026	4,902	2,996	128	1,906 R	61.1%	37.3%	62.1%	37.9%
22,804	CRAWFORD	10,085	6,007	3,911	167	2,096 R	59.6%	38.8%	60.6%	39.4%
7,923	DADE	4,112	2,864	1,184	64	1,680 R	69.6%	28.8%	70.8%	29.2%
15,661	DALLAS	7,683	4,895	2,656	132	2,239 R	63.7%	34.6%	64.8%	35.2%
8,016	DAVIESS	3,786	2,263	1,400	123	863 R	59.8%	37.0%	61.8%	38.2%
11,597	DE KALB	4,683	2,889	1,692	102	1,197 R	61.7%	36.1%	63.1%	36.9%
14,927	DENT	6,868	4,655	2,056	157	2,599 R	67.8%	29.9%	69.4%	30.6%
13,084	DOUGLAS	6,712	4,405	2,140	167	2,265 R	65.6%	31.9%	67.3%	32.7%
33,155	DUNKLIN	11,764	7,044	4,540	180	2,504 R	59.9%	38.6%	60.8%	39.2%
93,807	FRANKLIN	49,293	27,355	21,256	682	6,099 R	55.5%	43.1%	56.3%	43.7%
15,342	GASCONADE	7,771	4,763	2,899	109	1,864 R	61.3%	37.3%	62.2%	37.8%
6,861	GENTRY	3,292	1,964	1,235	93	729 R	59.7%	37.5%	61.4%	38.6%
240,391	GREENE	135,695	77,683	56,181	1,831	21,502 R	57.2%	41.4%	58.0%	42.0%
10,432	GRUNDY	4,740	3,006	1,580	154	1,426 R	63.4%	33.3%	65.5%	34.5%
8,850	HARRISON	3,915	2,512	1,287	116	1,225 R	64.2%	32.9%	66.1%	33.9%
21,997	HENRY	11,159	6,095	4,869	195	1,226 R	54.6%	43.6%	55.6%	44.4%
8,940	HICKORY	5,115	2,850	2,171	94	679 R	55.7%	42.4%	56.8%	43.2%
5,351	HOLT	2,633	1,794	802	37	992 R	68.1%	30.5%	69.1%	30.9%
10,212	HOWARD	4,855	2,708	2,036	111	672 R	55.8%	41.9%	57.1%	42.9%
37,238	HOWELL	17,029	10,982	5,736	311	5,246 R	64.5%	33.7%	65.7%	34.3%
10,697	IRON	4,414	2,090	2,213	111	123 D	47.3%	50.1%	48.6%	51.4%
654,880	JACKSON	186,047	92,833	90,722	2,492	2,111 R	49.9%	48.8%	50.6%	49.4%
104,686	JASPER	48,025	31,667	15,730	628	15,937 R	65.9%	32.8%	66.8%	33.2%
198,099	JEFFERSON	105,704	50,804	53,467	1,433	2,663 D	48.1%	50.6%	48.7%	51.3%

MISSOURI

PRESIDENT 2008

2000 Census Population	County	Total Vote	Republican	Democratic	Other	Rep.-Dem. Plurality	Percentage — Total Vote Rep.	Dem.	Major Vote Rep.	Dem.
48,258	JOHNSON	22,080	12,183	9,480	417	2,703 R	55.2%	42.9%	56.2%	43.8%
*See Note	KANSAS CITY	153,219	31,854	120,102	1,263	88,248 D	20.8%	78.4%	21.0%	79.0%
4,361	KNOX	2,024	1,212	759	53	453 R	59.9%	37.5%	61.5%	38.5%
32,513	LACLEDE	16,323	10,875	5,218	230	5,657 R	66.6%	32.0%	67.6%	32.4%
32,960	LAFAYETTE	16,600	9,442	6,902	256	2,540 R	56.9%	41.6%	57.8%	42.2%
35,204	LAWRENCE	16,637	11,263	5,097	277	6,166 R	67.7%	30.6%	68.8%	31.2%
10,494	LEWIS	4,502	2,594	1,837	71	757 R	57.6%	40.8%	58.5%	41.5%
38,944	LINCOLN	23,550	12,924	10,234	392	2,690 R	54.9%	43.5%	55.8%	44.2%
13,754	LINN	5,931	3,140	2,638	153	502 R	52.9%	44.5%	54.3%	45.7%
14,558	LIVINGSTON	6,552	3,993	2,435	124	1,558 R	60.9%	37.2%	62.1%	37.9%
21,681	MCDONALD	8,135	5,499	2,454	182	3,045 R	67.6%	30.2%	69.1%	30.9%
15,762	MACON	7,474	4,586	2,784	104	1,802 R	61.4%	37.2%	62.2%	37.8%
11,800	MADISON	5,028	2,897	2,042	89	855 R	57.6%	40.6%	58.7%	41.3%
8,903	MARIES	4,548	2,853	1,599	96	1,254 R	62.7%	35.2%	64.1%	35.9%
28,289	MARION	12,553	7,705	4,703	145	3,002 R	61.4%	37.5%	62.1%	37.9%
3,757	MERCER	1,748	1,169	519	60	650 R	66.9%	29.7%	69.3%	30.7%
23,564	MILLER	11,535	7,797	3,553	185	4,244 R	67.6%	30.8%	68.7%	31.3%
13,427	MISSISSIPPI	5,356	3,034	2,247	75	787 R	56.6%	42.0%	57.5%	42.5%
14,827	MONITEAU	6,665	4,467	2,084	114	2,383 R	67.0%	31.3%	68.2%	31.8%
9,311	MONROE	4,314	2,533	1,703	78	830 R	58.7%	39.5%	59.8%	40.2%
12,136	MONTGOMERY	5,856	3,428	2,347	81	1,081 R	58.5%	40.1%	59.4%	40.6%
19,309	MORGAN	9,149	5,451	3,565	133	1,886 R	59.6%	39.0%	60.5%	39.5%
19,760	NEW MADRID	8,092	4,593	3,370	129	1,223 R	56.8%	41.6%	57.7%	42.3%
52,636	NEWTON	25,406	17,637	7,450	319	10,187 R	69.4%	29.3%	70.3%	29.7%
21,912	NODAWAY	10,219	5,568	4,493	158	1,075 R	54.5%	44.0%	55.3%	44.7%
10,344	OREGON	4,591	2,652	1,811	128	841 R	57.8%	39.4%	59.4%	40.6%
13,062	OSAGE	7,079	5,062	1,907	110	3,155 R	71.5%	26.9%	72.6%	27.4%
9,542	OZARK	4,686	2,918	1,661	107	1,257 R	62.3%	35.4%	63.7%	36.3%
20,047	PEMISCOT	7,047	3,954	3,029	64	925 R	56.1%	43.0%	56.6%	43.4%
18,132	PERRY	8,647	5,527	3,005	115	2,522 R	63.9%	34.8%	64.8%	35.2%
39,403	PETTIS	18,208	11,018	6,932	258	4,086 R	60.5%	38.1%	61.4%	38.6%
39,825	PHELPS	19,438	11,706	7,394	338	4,312 R	60.2%	38.0%	61.3%	38.7%
18,351	PIKE	7,881	4,268	3,487	126	781 R	54.2%	44.2%	55.0%	45.0%
73,781	PLATTE	46,480	24,460	21,459	561	3,001 R	52.6%	46.2%	53.3%	46.7%
26,992	POLK	13,697	8,956	4,553	188	4,403 R	65.4%	33.2%	66.3%	33.7%
41,165	PULASKI	15,000	9,552	5,249	199	4,303 R	63.7%	35.0%	64.5%	35.5%
5,223	PUTNAM	2,339	1,591	695	53	896 R	68.0%	29.7%	69.6%	30.4%
9,626	RALLS	5,084	2,987	2,041	56	946 R	58.8%	40.1%	59.4%	40.6%
24,663	RANDOLPH	10,624	6,457	3,984	183	2,473 R	60.8%	37.5%	61.8%	38.2%
23,354	RAY	11,053	5,593	5,241	219	352 R	50.6%	47.4%	51.6%	48.4%
6,689	REYNOLDS	3,287	1,782	1,418	87	364 R	54.2%	43.1%	55.7%	44.3%
13,509	RIPLEY	5,363	3,407	1,795	161	1,612 R	63.5%	33.5%	65.5%	34.5%
283,883	ST. CHARLES	188,529	102,550	84,183	1,796	18,367 R	54.4%	44.7%	54.9%	45.1%
9,652	ST. CLAIR	4,988	2,981	1,886	121	1,095 R	59.8%	37.8%	61.2%	38.8%
55,641	ST. FRANCOIS	24,550	12,660	11,540	350	1,120 R	51.6%	47.0%	52.3%	47.7%
1,016,315	ST. LOUIS COUNTY	559,854	221,705	333,123	5,026	111,418 D	39.6%	59.5%	40.0%	60.0%
348,189	ST. LOUIS CITY	158,858	24,662	132,925	1,271	108,263 D	15.5%	83.7%	15.6%	84.4%
17,842	STE. GENEVIEVE	8,825	3,732	4,979	114	1,247 D	42.3%	56.4%	42.8%	57.2%
23,756	SALINE	9,848	4,962	4,712	174	250 R	50.4%	47.8%	51.3%	48.7%
4,170	SCHUYLER	1,983	1,139	775	69	364 R	57.4%	39.1%	59.5%	40.5%

Note: Results from Kansas City used to be included with Jackson County, but in recent years have been listed separately.

MISSOURI

PRESIDENT 2008

2000 Census Population	County	Total Vote	Republican	Democratic	Other	Rep.-Dem. Plurality	Percentage			
							Total Vote		Major Vote	
							Rep.	Dem.	Rep.	Dem.
4,983	SCOTLAND	2,098	1,249	793	56	456 R	59.5%	37.8%	61.2%	38.8%
40,422	SCOTT	18,026	11,563	6,258	205	5,305 R	64.1%	34.7%	64.9%	35.1%
8,324	SHANNON	3,838	2,075	1,637	126	438 R	54.1%	42.7%	55.9%	44.1%
6,799	SHELBY	3,316	2,166	1,114	36	1,052 R	65.3%	33.6%	66.0%	34.0%
29,705	STODDARD	13,262	9,172	3,899	191	5,273 R	69.2%	29.4%	70.2%	29.8%
28,658	STONE	16,387	11,147	5,029	211	6,118 R	68.0%	30.7%	68.9%	31.1%
7,219	SULLIVAN	2,869	1,607	1,173	89	434 R	56.0%	40.9%	57.8%	42.2%
39,703	TANEY	21,664	14,736	6,683	245	8,053 R	68.0%	30.8%	68.8%	31.2%
23,003	TEXAS	10,851	7,215	3,410	226	3,805 R	66.5%	31.4%	67.9%	32.1%
20,454	VERNON	8,878	5,334	3,381	163	1,953 R	60.1%	38.1%	61.2%	38.8%
24,525	WARREN	15,576	8,675	6,705	196	1,970 R	55.7%	43.0%	56.4%	43.6%
23,344	WASHINGTON	9,614	4,706	4,711	197	5 D	48.9%	49.0%	50.0%	50.0%
13,259	WAYNE	6,154	3,784	2,243	127	1,541 R	61.5%	36.4%	62.8%	37.2%
31,045	WEBSTER	16,356	10,431	5,685	240	4,746 R	63.8%	34.8%	64.7%	35.3%
2,382	WORTH	1,174	707	427	40	280 R	60.2%	36.4%	62.3%	37.7%
17,955	WRIGHT	8,514	5,784	2,557	173	3,227 R	67.9%	30.0%	69.3%	30.7%
5,595,211	TOTAL	2,925,205	1,445,814	1,441,911	37,480	3,903 R	49.4%	49.3%	50.1%	49.9%

MISSOURI

GOVERNOR 2008

2000 Census Population	County	Total Vote	Republican	Democratic	Other	Rep.-Dem. Plurality	Percentage			
							Total Vote		Major Vote	
							Rep.	Dem.	Rep.	Dem.
24,977	ADAIR	11,608	5,575	5,771	262	196 D	48.0%	49.7%	49.1%	50.9%
16,492	ANDREW	8,679	4,174	4,313	192	139 D	48.1%	49.7%	49.2%	50.8%
6,430	ATCHISON	2,909	1,336	1,461	112	125 D	45.9%	50.2%	47.8%	52.2%
25,853	AUDRAIN	10,721	5,612	4,951	158	661 R	52.3%	46.2%	53.1%	46.9%
34,010	BARRY	14,463	7,156	6,928	379	228 R	49.5%	47.9%	50.8%	49.2%
12,541	BARTON	5,889	3,661	2,089	139	1,572 R	62.2%	35.5%	63.7%	36.3%
16,653	BATES	8,218	3,431	4,555	232	1,124 D	41.7%	55.4%	43.0%	57.0%
17,180	BENTON	9,543	3,967	5,353	223	1,386 D	41.6%	56.1%	42.6%	57.4%
12,029	BOLLINGER	5,766	3,232	2,425	109	807 R	56.1%	42.1%	57.1%	42.9%
135,454	BOONE	83,788	35,785	46,315	1,688	10,530 D	42.7%	55.3%	43.6%	56.4%
85,998	BUCHANAN	38,621	14,442	23,151	1,028	8,709 D	37.4%	59.9%	38.4%	61.6%
40,867	BUTLER	17,007	9,205	7,459	343	1,746 R	54.1%	43.9%	55.2%	44.8%
8,969	CALDWELL	4,518	2,014	2,361	143	347 D	44.6%	52.3%	46.0%	54.0%
40,766	CALLAWAY	19,277	9,596	9,375	306	221 R	49.8%	48.6%	50.6%	49.4%
37,051	CAMDEN	21,964	10,716	10,795	453	79 D	48.8%	49.1%	49.8%	50.2%
68,693	CAPE GIRARDEAU	36,764	20,672	15,348	744	5,324 R	56.2%	41.7%	57.4%	42.6%
10,285	CARROLL	4,513	2,233	2,201	79	32 R	49.5%	48.8%	50.4%	49.6%
5,941	CARTER	2,845	1,232	1,516	97	284 D	43.3%	53.3%	44.8%	55.2%
82,092	CASS	49,356	22,592	25,754	1,010	3,162 D	45.8%	52.2%	46.7%	53.3%
13,733	CEDAR	6,296	2,970	3,036	290	66 D	47.2%	48.2%	49.5%	50.5%

MISSOURI
GOVERNOR 2008

2000 Census Population	County	Total Vote	Republican	Democratic	Other	Rep.-Dem. Plurality	Percentage Total Vote Rep.	Total Vote Dem.	Major Vote Rep.	Major Vote Dem.
8,438	CHARITON	4,192	1,951	2,166	75	215 D	46.5%	51.7%	47.4%	52.6%
54,285	CHRISTIAN	37,373	18,556	17,840	977	716 R	49.7%	47.7%	51.0%	49.0%
7,416	CLARK	3,452	1,772	1,588	92	184 R	51.3%	46.0%	52.7%	47.3%
184,006	CLAY	107,442	41,518	63,341	2,583	21,823 D	38.6%	59.0%	39.6%	60.4%
18,979	CLINTON	10,366	4,199	5,909	258	1,710 D	40.5%	57.0%	41.5%	58.5%
71,397	COLE	38,673	19,285	18,941	447	344 R	49.9%	49.0%	50.4%	49.6%
16,670	COOPER	7,977	4,170	3,669	138	501 R	52.3%	46.0%	53.2%	46.8%
22,804	CRAWFORD	10,019	4,627	5,204	188	577 D	46.2%	51.9%	47.1%	52.9%
7,923	DADE	4,080	2,049	1,879	152	170 R	50.2%	46.1%	52.2%	47.8%
15,661	DALLAS	7,662	3,212	4,173	277	961 D	41.9%	54.5%	43.5%	56.5%
8,016	DAVIESS	3,756	1,683	1,969	104	286 D	44.8%	52.4%	46.1%	53.9%
11,597	DE KALB	4,652	2,332	2,177	143	155 R	50.1%	46.8%	51.7%	48.3%
14,927	DENT	6,833	3,055	3,583	195	528 D	44.7%	52.4%	46.0%	54.0%
13,084	DOUGLAS	6,658	3,014	3,259	385	245 D	45.3%	48.9%	48.0%	52.0%
33,155	DUNKLIN	11,505	4,792	6,458	255	1,666 D	41.7%	56.1%	42.6%	57.4%
93,807	FRANKLIN	48,899	22,896	25,082	921	2,186 D	46.8%	51.3%	47.7%	52.3%
15,342	GASCONADE	7,722	4,307	3,313	102	994 R	55.8%	42.9%	56.5%	43.5%
6,861	GENTRY	3,257	1,400	1,764	93	364 D	43.0%	54.2%	44.2%	55.8%
240,391	GREENE	134,370	57,565	73,164	3,641	15,599 D	42.8%	54.4%	44.0%	56.0%
10,432	GRUNDY	4,682	2,512	2,042	128	470 R	53.7%	43.6%	55.2%	44.8%
8,850	HARRISON	3,866	2,090	1,696	80	394 R	54.1%	43.9%	55.2%	44.8%
21,997	HENRY	11,022	3,935	6,810	277	2,875 D	35.7%	61.8%	36.6%	63.4%
8,940	HICKORY	5,110	1,820	3,115	175	1,295 D	35.6%	61.0%	36.9%	63.1%
5,351	HOLT	2,583	1,440	1,047	96	393 R	55.7%	40.5%	57.9%	42.1%
10,212	HOWARD	4,843	2,358	2,377	108	19 D	48.7%	49.1%	49.8%	50.2%
37,238	HOWELL	16,895	7,659	8,804	432	1,145 D	45.3%	52.1%	46.5%	53.5%
10,697	IRON	4,434	1,483	2,844	107	1,361 D	33.4%	64.1%	34.3%	65.7%
654,880	JACKSON	182,622	71,781	107,244	3,597	35,463 D	39.3%	58.7%	40.1%	59.9%
104,686	JASPER	47,372	27,764	18,676	932	9,088 R	58.6%	39.4%	59.8%	40.2%
198,099	JEFFERSON	104,425	35,947	66,697	1,781	30,750 D	34.4%	63.9%	35.0%	65.0%
48,258	JOHNSON	21,638	9,367	11,658	613	2,291 D	43.3%	53.9%	44.6%	55.4%
*See Note	KANSAS CITY	149,239	26,316	120,023	2,900	93,707 D	17.6%	80.4%	18.0%	82.0%
4,361	KNOX	2,004	1,180	793	31	387 R	58.9%	39.6%	59.8%	40.2%
32,513	LACLEDE	16,194	7,604	8,242	348	638 D	47.0%	50.9%	48.0%	52.0%
32,960	LAFAYETTE	16,446	7,022	9,060	364	2,038 D	42.7%	55.1%	43.7%	56.3%
35,204	LAWRENCE	16,518	8,118	7,918	482	200 R	49.1%	47.9%	50.6%	49.4%
10,494	LEWIS	4,460	2,533	1,831	96	702 R	56.8%	41.1%	58.0%	42.0%
38,944	LINCOLN	23,307	10,589	12,197	521	1,608 D	45.4%	52.3%	46.5%	53.5%
13,754	LINN	5,912	2,371	3,403	138	1,032 D	40.1%	57.6%	41.1%	58.9%
14,558	LIVINGSTON	6,470	2,830	3,520	120	690 D	43.7%	54.4%	44.6%	55.4%
21,681	MCDONALD	7,978	4,766	2,922	290	1,844 R	59.7%	36.6%	62.0%	38.0%
15,762	MACON	7,421	4,242	3,068	111	1,174 R	57.2%	41.3%	58.0%	42.0%
11,800	MADISON	5,008	2,160	2,719	129	559 D	43.1%	54.3%	44.3%	55.7%
8,903	MARIES	4,542	2,157	2,306	79	149 D	47.5%	50.8%	48.3%	51.7%
28,289	MARION	12,481	7,341	4,964	176	2,377 R	58.8%	39.8%	59.7%	40.3%
3,757	MERCER	1,730	1,043	620	67	423 R	60.3%	35.8%	62.7%	37.3%
23,564	MILLER	11,483	6,414	4,858	211	1,556 R	55.9%	42.3%	56.9%	43.1%
13,427	MISSISSIPPI	5,289	2,659	2,523	107	136 R	50.3%	47.7%	51.3%	48.7%
14,827	MONITEAU	6,667	3,617	2,951	99	666 R	54.3%	44.3%	55.1%	44.9%
9,311	MONROE	4,316	2,459	1,810	47	649 R	57.0%	41.9%	57.6%	42.4%

Note: Results from Kansas City used to be included with Jackson County, but in recent years have been listed separately.

MISSOURI

GOVERNOR 2008

2000 Census Population	County	Total Vote	Republican	Democratic	Other	Rep.-Dem. Plurality	Percentage Total Vote Rep.	Dem.	Major Vote Rep.	Dem.
12,136	MONTGOMERY	5,810	3,215	2,493	102	722 R	55.3%	42.9%	56.3%	43.7%
19,309	MORGAN	9,107	4,333	4,570	204	237 D	47.6%	50.2%	48.7%	51.3%
19,760	NEW MADRID	8,007	3,574	4,313	120	739 D	44.6%	53.9%	45.3%	54.7%
52,636	NEWTON	25,172	15,570	9,134	468	6,436 R	61.9%	36.3%	63.0%	37.0%
21,912	NODAWAY	10,009	4,254	5,418	337	1,164 D	42.5%	54.1%	44.0%	56.0%
10,344	OREGON	4,576	1,742	2,710	124	968 D	38.1%	59.2%	39.1%	60.9%
13,062	OSAGE	7,078	4,212	2,792	74	1,420 R	59.5%	39.4%	60.1%	39.9%
9,542	OZARK	4,632	1,967	2,484	181	517 D	42.5%	53.6%	44.2%	55.8%
20,047	PEMISCOT	6,686	2,491	4,045	150	1,554 D	37.3%	60.5%	38.1%	61.9%
18,132	PERRY	8,468	4,391	3,916	161	475 R	51.9%	46.2%	52.9%	47.1%
39,403	PETTIS	18,001	7,660	9,834	507	2,174 D	42.6%	54.6%	43.8%	56.2%
39,825	PHELPS	19,192	8,485	10,226	481	1,741 D	44.2%	53.3%	45.3%	54.7%
18,351	PIKE	7,843	3,850	3,858	135	8 D	49.1%	49.2%	49.9%	50.1%
73,781	PLATTE	45,677	19,417	25,228	1,032	5,811 D	42.5%	55.2%	43.5%	56.5%
26,992	POLK	13,646	6,244	6,758	644	514 D	45.8%	49.5%	48.0%	52.0%
41,165	PULASKI	12,985	5,627	7,075	283	1,448 D	43.3%	54.5%	44.3%	55.7%
5,223	PUTNAM	2,277	1,467	748	62	719 R	64.4%	32.9%	66.2%	33.8%
9,626	RALLS	5,056	2,717	2,263	76	454 R	53.7%	44.8%	54.6%	45.4%
24,663	RANDOLPH	10,566	5,652	4,700	214	952 R	53.5%	44.5%	54.6%	45.4%
23,354	RAY	10,912	3,899	6,670	343	2,771 D	35.7%	61.1%	36.9%	63.1%
6,689	REYNOLDS	3,241	1,223	1,901	117	678 D	37.7%	58.7%	39.1%	60.9%
13,509	RIPLEY	5,307	2,499	2,640	168	141 D	47.1%	49.7%	48.6%	51.4%
283,883	ST. CHARLES	185,203	82,440	99,705	3,058	17,265 D	44.5%	53.8%	45.3%	54.7%
9,652	ST. CLAIR	4,995	2,093	2,734	168	641 D	41.9%	54.7%	43.4%	56.6%
55,641	ST. FRANCOIS	24,364	8,418	15,468	478	7,050 D	34.6%	63.5%	35.2%	64.8%
1,016,315	ST. LOUIS COUNTY	547,327	180,278	357,649	9,400	177,371 D	32.9%	65.3%	33.5%	66.5%
348,189	ST. LOUIS CITY	155,363	20,205	131,900	3,258	111,695 D	13.0%	84.9%	13.3%	86.7%
17,842	STE. GENEVIEVE	8,704	2,861	5,699	144	2,838 D	32.9%	65.5%	33.4%	66.6%
23,756	SALINE	9,742	3,195	5,540	1,007	2,345 D	32.8%	56.9%	36.6%	63.4%
4,170	SCHUYLER	1,952	1,008	888	56	120 R	51.6%	45.5%	53.2%	46.8%
4,983	SCOTLAND	2,095	1,197	857	41	340 R	57.1%	40.9%	58.3%	41.7%
40,422	SCOTT	17,874	9,494	8,142	238	1,352 R	53.1%	45.6%	53.8%	46.2%
8,324	SHANNON	3,837	1,292	2,327	218	1,035 D	33.7%	60.6%	35.7%	64.3%
6,799	SHELBY	3,316	2,094	1,189	33	905 R	63.1%	35.9%	63.8%	36.2%
29,705	STODDARD	13,092	6,919	5,934	239	985 R	52.8%	45.3%	53.8%	46.2%
28,658	STONE	16,240	8,043	7,708	489	335 R	49.5%	47.5%	51.1%	48.9%
7,219	SULLIVAN	2,870	1,476	1,321	73	155 R	51.4%	46.0%	52.8%	47.2%
39,703	TANEY	21,313	10,903	9,870	540	1,033 R	51.2%	46.3%	52.5%	47.5%
23,003	TEXAS	10,801	4,688	5,848	265	1,160 D	43.4%	54.1%	44.5%	55.5%
20,454	VERNON	8,798	4,095	4,491	212	396 D	46.5%	51.0%	47.7%	52.3%
24,525	WARREN	15,463	7,617	7,587	259	30 R	49.3%	49.1%	50.1%	49.9%
23,344	WASHINGTON	9,629	2,993	6,456	180	3,463 D	31.1%	67.0%	31.7%	68.3%
13,259	WAYNE	6,111	2,727	3,269	115	542 D	44.6%	53.5%	45.5%	54.5%
31,045	WEBSTER	16,241	7,521	8,306	414	785 D	46.3%	51.1%	47.5%	52.5%
2,382	WORTH	1,142	559	548	35	11 R	48.9%	48.0%	50.5%	49.5%
17,955	WRIGHT	8,468	4,198	4,025	245	173 R	49.6%	47.5%	51.1%	48.9%
5,595,211	TOTAL	2,877,778	1,136,364	1,680,611	60,803	544,247 D	39.5%	58.4%	40.3%	59.7%

MISSOURI

HOUSE OF REPRESENTATIVES

CD	Year	Total Vote	Republican Vote	Republican Candidate	Democratic Vote	Democratic Candidate	Other Vote	Rep.-Dem. Plurality	Total Vote Rep.	Total Vote Dem.	Major Vote Rep.	Major Vote Dem.
1	2008	279,277		—	242,570	CLAY, WILLIAM LACY*	36,707	242,570 D		86.9%		100.0%
1	2006	194,235	47,893	BYRNE, MARK J.	141,574	CLAY, WILLIAM LACY*	4,768	93,681 D	24.7%	72.9%	25.3%	74.7%
1	2004	283,771	64,791	FARR, LESLIE L. II	213,658	CLAY, WILLIAM LACY*	5,322	148,867 D	22.8%	75.3%	23.3%	76.7%
1	2002	191,055	51,755	SCHWADRON, RICHARD	133,946	CLAY, WILLIAM LACY*	5,354	82,191 D	27.1%	70.1%	27.9%	72.1%
2	2008	372,972	232,276	AKIN, TODD*	132,068	HAAS, WILLIAM C. "BILL"	8,628	100,208 R	62.3%	35.4%	63.8%	36.2%
2	2006	287,617	176,452	AKIN, TODD*	105,242	WEBER, GEORGE D.	5,923	71,210 R	61.3%	36.6%	62.6%	37.4%
2	2004	349,867	228,725	AKIN, TODD*	115,366	WEBER, GEORGE D.	5,776	113,359 R	65.4%	33.0%	66.5%	33.5%
2	2002	248,828	167,057	AKIN, TODD*	77,223	HOGAN, JOHN	4,548	89,834 R	67.1%	31.0%	68.4%	31.6%
3	2008	305,071	92,759	SANDER, CHRIS	202,470	CARNAHAN, RUSS*	9,842	109,711 D	30.4%	66.4%	31.4%	68.6%
3	2006	221,448	70,189	BERTELSEN, DAVID	145,219	CARNAHAN, RUSS*	6,040	75,030 D	31.7%	65.6%	32.6%	67.4%
3	2004	277,916	125,422	FEDERER, BILL	146,894	CARNAHAN, RUSS	5,600	21,472 D	45.1%	52.9%	46.1%	53.9%
3	2002	206,878	80,551	ENZ, CATHERINE S.	122,181	GEPHARDT, RICHARD A.*	4,146	41,630 D	38.9%	59.1%	39.7%	60.3%
4	2008	303,455	103,446	PARNELL, JEFF	200,009	SKELTON, IKE*		96,563 D	34.1%	65.9%	34.1%	65.9%
4	2006	235,525	69,254	NOLAND, JAMES A. "JIM"	159,303	SKELTON, IKE*	6,968	90,049 D	29.4%	67.6%	30.3%	69.7%
4	2004	288,226	93,334	NOLAND, JAMES A. "JIM"	190,800	SKELTON, IKE*	4,092	97,466 D	32.4%	66.2%	32.8%	67.2%
4	2002	210,238	64,451	NOLAND, JAMES A. "JIM"	142,204	SKELTON, IKE*	3,583	77,753 D	30.7%	67.6%	31.2%	68.8%
5	2008	306,415	109,166	TURK, JACOB	197,249	CLEAVER, EMANUEL II*		88,083 D	35.6%	64.4%	35.6%	64.4%
5	2006	211,919	68,456	TURK, JACOB	136,149	CLEAVER, EMANUEL II*	7,314	67,693 D	32.3%	64.2%	33.5%	66.5%
5	2004	293,025	123,431	PATTERSON, JEANNE	161,727	CLEAVER, EMANUEL II	7,867	38,296 D	42.1%	55.2%	43.3%	56.7%
5	2002	186,167	60,245	GORDON, STEVE	122,645	McCARTHY, KAREN*	3,277	62,400 D	32.4%	65.9%	32.9%	67.1%
6	2008	330,699	196,526	GRAVES, SAM*	121,894	BARNES, KAY	12,279	74,632 R	59.4%	36.9%	61.7%	38.3%
6	2006	244,795	150,882	GRAVES, SAM*	87,477	SHETTLES, SARA JO	6,436	63,405 R	61.6%	35.7%	63.3%	36.7%
6	2004	307,855	196,516	GRAVES, SAM*	106,987	BROOMFIELD, CHARLES S.	4,352	89,529 R	63.8%	34.8%	64.7%	35.3%
6	2002	208,088	131,151	GRAVES, SAM*	73,202	RINEHART, CATHY	3,735	57,949 R	63.0%	35.2%	64.2%	35.8%
7	2008	323,212	219,016	BLUNT, ROY*	91,010	MONROE, RICHARD	13,186	128,006 R	67.8%	28.2%	70.6%	29.4%
7	2006	241,123	160,942	BLUNT, ROY*	72,592	TRUMAN, JACK	7,589	88,350 R	66.7%	30.1%	68.9%	31.1%
7	2004	298,205	210,080	BLUNT, ROY*	84,356	NEWBERRY, JIM	3,769	125,724 R	70.4%	28.3%	71.3%	28.7%
7	2002	199,863	149,519	BLUNT, ROY*	45,964	LAPHAM, RON	4,380	103,555 R	74.8%	23.0%	76.5%	23.5%
8	2008	278,288	198,798	EMERSON, JO ANN*	72,790	ALLEN, JOE	6,700	126,008 R	71.4%	26.2%	73.2%	26.8%
8	2006	217,989	156,164	EMERSON, JO ANN*	57,557	HAMBACKER, VERONICA J.	4,268	98,607 R	71.6%	26.4%	73.1%	26.9%
8	2004	268,711	194,039	EMERSON, JO ANN*	71,543	HENDERSON, DEAN	3,129	122,496 R	72.2%	26.6%	73.1%	26.9%
8	2002	188,321	135,144	EMERSON, JO ANN*	50,686	CURTIS, GENE	2,491	84,458 R	71.8%	26.9%	72.7%	27.3%
9	2008	322,095	161,031	LUETKEMEYER, BLAINE	152,956	BAKER, JUDY	8,108	8,075 R	50.0%	47.5%	51.3%	48.7%
9	2006	242,671	149,114	HULSHOF, KENNY*	87,145	BURGHARD, DUANE N.	6,412	61,969 R	61.4%	35.9%	63.1%	36.9%
9	2004	299,447	193,429	HULSHOF, KENNY*	101,343	JACOBSEN, LINDA	4,675	92,086 R	64.6%	33.8%	65.6%	34.4%
9	2002	214,125	146,032	HULSHOF, KENNY*	61,126	DEICHMAN, DONALD M. "DON"	6,967	84,906 R	68.2%	28.5%	70.5%	29.5%
TOTAL	2008	2,821,484	1,313,018		1,413,016		95,450	99,998 D	46.5%	50.1%	48.2%	51.8%
TOTAL	2006	2,097,322	1,049,346		992,258		55,718	57,088 R	50.0%	47.3%	51.4%	48.6%
TOTAL	2004	2,667,023	1,429,767		1,192,674		44,582	237,093 R	53.6%	44.7%	54.5%	45.5%
TOTAL	2002	1,853,563	985,905		829,177		38,481	156,728 R	53.2%	44.7%	54.3%	45.7%

Note: An asterisk (*) denotes incumbent.

MISSOURI

GENERAL AND PRIMARY ELECTIONS

2008 GENERAL ELECTIONS

President   Other vote was 17,813 Independent (Ralph Nader); 11,386 Libertarian (Bob Barr); 8,201 Constitution (Chuck Baldwin); 80 write-in (Cynthia A. McKinney).

Governor   Other vote was 31,850 Libertarian (Andrew W. Finkenstadt); 28,941 Constitution (Gregory E. Thompson); 8 write-in (Mark Serati); 4 write-in (Theodis "Ted" Brown Sr.).

House   Other vote was:

CD 1   36,700 Libertarian (Robb E. Cunningham); 7 write-in (Damien Johnson).
CD 2   8,628 Libertarian (Thomas L. Knapp).
CD 3   5,518 Libertarian (Kevin C. Babcock); 4,324 Constitution (Cynthia "Cindy" Redburn).
CD 4
CD 5
CD 6   12,279 Libertarian (Dave Browning).
CD 7   6,971 Libertarian (Kevin Craig); 6,166 Constitution (Travis Maddox); 49 write-in (Midge Potts).
CD 8   4,443 Libertarian (Branden C. McCullough); 2,257 Constitution (Richard L. Smith).
CD 9   8,108 Libertarian (Tamara A. Millay).

2008 PRIMARY ELECTIONS

Primary   February 5, 2008 (President)   **Registration**   3,980,105   No Party Registration
August 5, 2008 (Congress)   (as of August 1, 2008)

Primary Type   Open—Any registered voter could participate in the party primary of their choice.

	REPUBLICAN PRIMARIES			DEMOCRATIC PRIMARIES		
President	John McCain	194,053	33.0%	Barack Obama	406,917	49.3%
	Mike Huckabee	185,642	31.5%	Hillary Clinton	395,185	47.9%
	Mitt Romney	172,329	29.3%	John Edwards	16,763	2.0%
	Ron Paul	26,464	4.5%	Uncommitted	3,142	0.4%
	Rudolph Giuliani	3,593	0.6%	Dennis J. Kucinich	820	0.1%
	Fred Thompson	3,102	0.5%	Bill Richardson	689	0.1%
	Uncommitted	2,097	0.4%	Joseph R. Biden Jr.	626	0.1%
	Alan Keyes	892	0.2%	Mike Gravel	438	0.1%
	Duncan Hunter	307	0.1%	Christopher J. Dodd	250	
	Virgil L.R. Wiles	124		Ralph Spelbring	220	
	Tom Tancredo	107				
	Daniel Gilbert	88				
	Hugh Cort	46				
	TOTAL	*588,844*		*TOTAL*	*825,050*	
Governor	Kenny Hulshof	194,616	49.2%	Jeremiah W. "Jay" Nixon	304,181	85.0%
	Sarah Steelman	176,847	44.7%	Daniel Carroll	53,835	15.0%
	Scott Long	18,754	4.7%			
	Jennie Lee "Jen" Sievers	5,668	1.4%			
	TOTAL	*395,885*		*TOTAL*	*358,016*	
Congressional District 1	No Republican candidate			William Lacy Clay*	41,517	100.0%

MISSOURI

GENERAL AND PRIMARY ELECTIONS

	REPUBLICAN PRIMARIES			DEMOCRATIC PRIMARIES		
Congressional District 2	Todd Akin*	46,877	100.0%	William C. "Bill" Haas	9,018	30.7%
				David L. Pentland	6,007	20.5%
				Byron DeLear	5,059	17.2%
				Mike Garman	4,690	16.0%
				John Hogan	4,557	15.5%
				TOTAL	29,331	
Congressional District 3	Chris Sander	7,923	41.7%	Russ Carnahan*	38,020	100.0%
	John Wayne Tucker	5,963	31.4%			
	Greg Zotta	2,576	13.6%			
	Pat Ertmann	2,532	13.3%			
	TOTAL	18,994				
Congressional District 4	Jeff Parnell	31,979	66.8%	Ike Skelton*	37,111	100.0%
	Stanley Plough Jr.	10,324	21.6%			
	Joseph Terrazas	5,568	11.6%			
	TOTAL	47,871				
Congressional District 5	Jacob Turk	9,294	54.2%	Emanuel Cleaver II*	38,260	100.0%
	Chris Knowlton	3,552	20.7%			
	Martin D. Baker	2,647	15.4%			
	Randall D. "Randy" Langkraehr	1,641	9.6%			
	TOTAL	17,134				
Congressional District 6	Sam Graves*	36,131	100.0%	Kay Barnes	36,712	84.5%
				Ali Anon Sherkat	6,714	15.5%
				TOTAL	43,426	
Congressional District 7	Roy Blunt*	64,767	100.0%	Richard Monroe	11,973	77.7%
				L. Gregory Gloeckner	3,439	22.3%
				TOTAL	15,412	
Congressional District 8	Jo Ann Emerson*	51,801	100.0%	Joe Allen	35,418	100.0%
Congressional District 9	Blaine Luetkemeyer	21,543	39.7%	Judy Baker	22,498	44.1%
	Bob Onder	15,752	29.0%	Steve Gaw	15,864	31.1%
	Danielle "Danie" Moore	10,609	19.5%	Lyndon Bode	6,565	12.9%
	Brock Olivo	5,501	10.1%	Ken Jacob	6,060	11.9%
	Dan Bishir	890	1.6%			
	TOTAL	54,295		TOTAL	50,987	

Note: An asterisk (*) denotes incumbent.

MONTANA

One member At Large

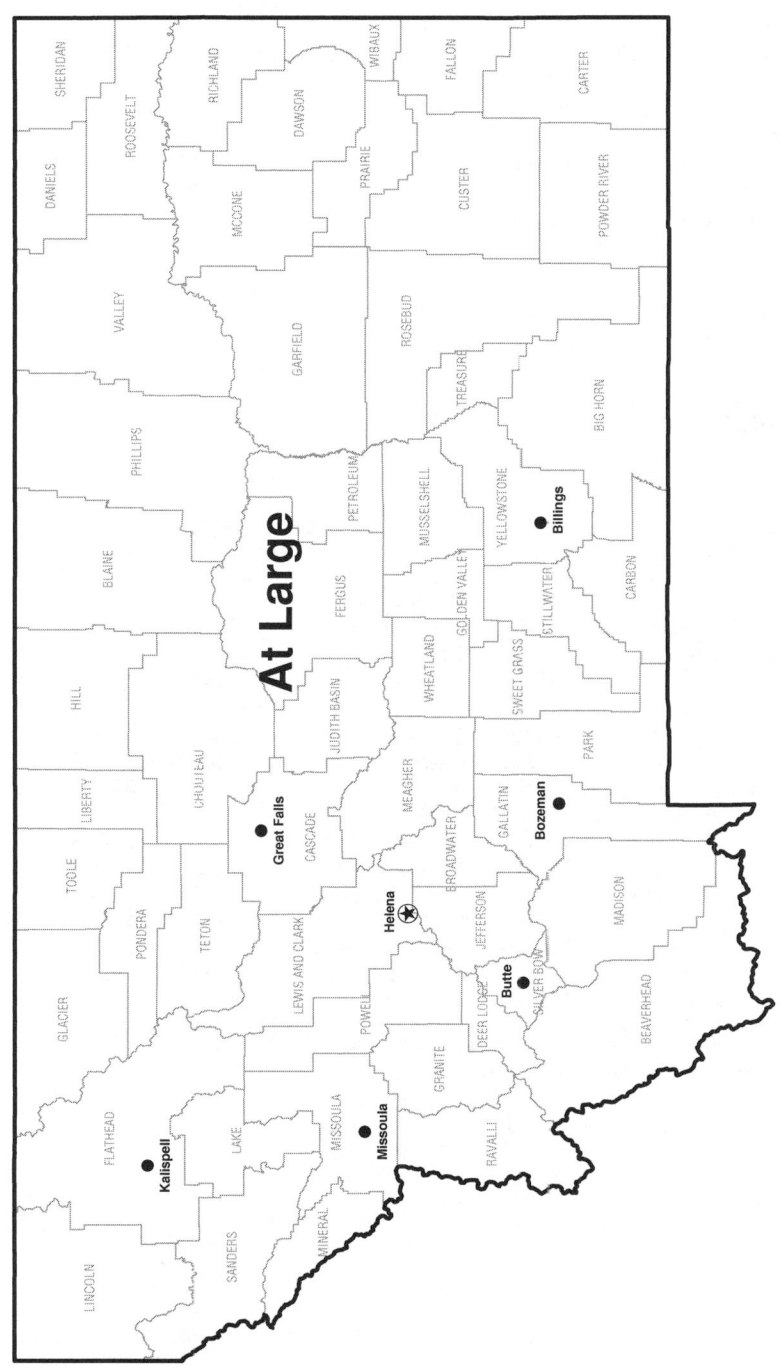

MONTANA

GOVERNOR

Brian Schweitzer (D). Reelected 2008 to a four-year term. Previously elected 2004.

SENATORS (2 Democrats)

Max Baucus (D). Reelected 2008 to a six-year term. Previously elected 2002, 1996, 1990, 1984, 1978.

Jon Tester (D). Elected 2006 to a six-year term.

REPRESENTATIVE (1 Republican)

At Large. Denny Rehberg (R)

POSTWAR VOTE FOR PRESIDENT

| Year | Total Vote | Republican | | Democratic | | Other Vote | Plurality | Percentage | | | |
| | | Vote | Candidate | Vote | Candidate | | | Total Vote | | Major Vote | |
								Rep.	Dem.	Rep.	Dem.
2008	490,302	242,763	McCain, John	231,667	Obama, Barack	15,872	11,096 R	49.5%	47.2%	51.2%	48.8%
2004	450,445	266,063	Bush, George W.	173,710	Kerry, John	10,672	92,353 R	59.1%	38.6%	60.5%	39.5%
2000**	410,997	240,178	Bush, George W.	137,126	Gore, Al	33,693	103,052 R	58.4%	33.4%	63.7%	36.3%
1996**	407,261	179,652	Dole, Bob	167,922	Clinton, Bill	59,687	11,730 R	44.1%	41.2%	51.7%	48.3%
1992**	410,611	144,207	Bush, George	154,507	Clinton, Bill	111,897	10,300 D	35.1%	37.6%	48.3%	51.7%
1988	365,674	190,412	Bush, George	168,936	Dukakis, Michael S.	6,326	21,476 R	52.1%	46.2%	53.0%	47.0%
1984	384,377	232,450	Reagan, Ronald	146,742	Mondale, Walter F.	5,185	85,708 R	60.5%	38.2%	61.3%	38.7%
1980**	363,952	206,814	Reagan, Ronald	118,032	Carter, Jimmy	39,106	88,782 R	56.8%	32.4%	63.7%	36.3%
1976	328,734	173,703	Ford, Gerald R.	149,259	Carter, Jimmy	5,772	24,444 R	52.8%	45.4%	53.8%	46.2%
1972	317,603	183,976	Nixon, Richard M.	120,197	McGovern, George S.	13,430	63,779 R	57.9%	37.8%	60.5%	39.5%
1968**	274,404	138,835	Nixon, Richard M.	114,117	Humphrey, Hubert H.	21,452	24,718 R	50.6%	41.6%	54.9%	45.1%
1964	278,628	113,032	Goldwater, Barry M.	164,246	Johnson, Lyndon B.	1,350	51,214 D	40.6%	58.9%	40.8%	59.2%
1960	277,579	141,841	Nixon, Richard M.	134,891	Kennedy, John F.	847	6,950 R	51.1%	48.6%	51.3%	48.7%
1956	271,171	154,933	Eisenhower, Dwight D.	116,238	Stevenson, Adlai E.		38,695 R	57.1%	42.9%	57.1%	42.9%
1952	265,037	157,394	Eisenhower, Dwight D.	106,213	Stevenson, Adlai E.	1,430	51,181 R	59.4%	40.1%	59.7%	40.3%
1948	224,278	96,770	Dewey, Thomas E.	119,071	Truman, Harry S.	8,437	22,301 D	43.1%	53.1%	44.8%	55.2%

**In past elections, the other vote included: 2000 - 24,437 Green (Ralph Nader); 1996 - 55,229 Reform (Ross Perot); 1992 - 107,225 Independent (Perot); 1980 - 29,281 Independent (John Anderson); 1968 - 20,015 American Independent (George Wallace).

MONTANA

POSTWAR VOTE FOR GOVERNOR

Year	Total Vote	Republican Vote	Republican Candidate	Democratic Vote	Democratic Candidate	Other Vote	Rep.-Dem. Plurality	Total Vote Rep.	Total Vote Dem.	Major Vote Rep.	Major Vote Dem.
2008	486,734	158,268	Brown, Roy	318,670	Schweitzer, Brian	9,796	160,402 D	32.5%	65.5%	33.2%	66.8%
2004	446,146	205,313	Brown, Bob	225,016	Schweitzer, Brian	15,817	19,703 D	46.0%	50.4%	47.7%	52.3%
2000	410,192	209,135	Martz, Judy	193,131	O'Keefe, Mark	7,926	16,004 R	51.0%	47.1%	52.0%	48.0%
1996**	405,175	320,768	Racicot, Marc	84,407	Jacobson, Judy		236,361 R	79.2%	20.8%	79.2%	20.8%
1992	407,842	209,401	Racicot, Marc	198,421	Bradley, Dorothy	20	10,980 R	51.3%	48.7%	51.3%	48.7%
1988	367,021	190,604	Stephens, Stan	169,313	Judge, Thomas L.	7,104	21,291 R	51.9%	46.1%	53.0%	47.0%
1984	378,970	100,070	Goodover, Pat M.	266,578	Schwinden, Ted	12,322	166,508 D	26.4%	70.3%	27.3%	72.7%
1980	360,466	160,892	Ramirez, Jack	199,574	Schwinden, Ted		38,682 D	44.6%	55.4%	44.6%	55.4%
1976	316,720	115,848	Woodahl, Robert	195,420	Judge, Thomas L.	5,452	79,572 D	36.6%	61.7%	37.2%	62.8%
1972	318,754	146,231	Smith, Ed	172,523	Judge, Thomas L.		26,292 D	45.9%	54.1%	45.9%	54.1%
1968	278,112	116,432	Babcock, Tim M.	150,481	Anderson, Forrest H.	11,199	34,049 D	41.9%	54.1%	43.6%	56.4%
1964	280,975	144,113	Babcock, Tim M.	136,862	Renne, Roland		7,251 R	51.3%	48.7%	51.3%	48.7%
1960	279,881	154,230	Nutter, Donald G.	125,651	Cannon, Paul		28,579 R	55.1%	44.9%	55.1%	44.9%
1956	270,366	138,878	Aronson, J. Hugo	131,488	Olsen, Arnold H.		7,390 R	51.4%	48.6%	51.4%	48.6%
1952	263,792	134,423	Aronson, J. Hugo	129,369	Bonner, John W.		5,054 R	51.0%	49.0%	51.0%	49.0%
1948	222,964	97,792	Ford, Sam C.	124,267	Bonner, John W.	905	26,475 D	43.9%	55.7%	44.0%	56.0%

**In 1996 the Democratic vote total included 7,936 absentee ballots cast for the party's initial gubernatorial candidate, Chet Blaylock, who died that October.

POSTWAR VOTE FOR SENATOR

Year	Total Vote	Republican Vote	Republican Candidate	Democratic Vote	Democratic Candidate	Other Vote	Rep.-Dem. Plurality	Total Vote Rep.	Total Vote Dem.	Major Vote Rep.	Major Vote Dem.
2008	477,658	129,369	Kelleher, Bob	348,289	Baucus, Max		218,920 D	27.1%	72.9%	27.1%	72.9%
2006	406,505	196,283	Burns, Conrad	199,845	Tester, Jon	10,377	3,562 D	48.3%	49.2%	49.6%	50.4%
2002	326,537	103,611	Taylor, Mike	204,853	Baucus, Max	18,073	101,242 D	31.7%	62.7%	33.6%	66.4%
2000	411,601	208,082	Burns, Conrad	194,430	Schweitzer, Brian	9,089	13,652 R	50.6%	47.2%	51.7%	48.3%
1996	407,490	182,111	Rehberg, Denny	201,935	Baucus, Max	23,444	19,824 D	44.7%	49.6%	47.4%	52.6%
1994	350,409	218,542	Burns, Conrad	131,845	Mudd, Jack	22	86,697 R	62.4%	37.6%	62.4%	37.6%
1990	319,336	93,836	Kolstad, Allen C.	217,563	Baucus, Max	7,937	123,727 D	29.4%	68.1%	30.1%	69.9%
1988	365,254	189,445	Burns, Conrad	175,809	Melcher, John		13,636 R	51.9%	48.1%	51.9%	48.1%
1984	379,155	154,308	Cozzens, Chuck	215,704	Baucus, Max	9,143	61,396 D	40.7%	56.9%	41.7%	58.3%
1982	321,062	133,789	Williams, Larry	174,861	Melcher, John	12,412	41,072 D	41.7%	54.5%	43.3%	56.7%
1978	287,942	127,589	Williams, Larry	160,353	Baucus, Max		32,764 D	44.3%	55.7%	44.3%	55.7%
1976	321,445	115,213	Burger, Stanley C.	206,232	Melcher, John		91,019 D	35.8%	64.2%	35.8%	64.2%
1972	314,925	151,316	Hibbard, Henry S.	163,609	Metcalf, Lee		12,293 D	48.0%	52.0%	48.0%	52.0%
1970	247,869	97,809	Wallace, Harold E.	150,060	Mansfield, Mike		52,251 D	39.5%	60.5%	39.5%	60.5%
1966	259,863	121,697	Babcock, Tim M.	138,166	Metcalf, Lee		16,469 D	46.8%	53.2%	46.8%	53.2%
1964	280,010	99,367	Blewett, Alex	180,643	Mansfield, Mike		81,276 D	35.5%	64.5%	35.5%	64.5%
1960	276,612	136,281	Fjare, Orvin B.	140,331	Metcalf, Lee		4,050 D	49.3%	50.7%	49.3%	50.7%
1958	229,483	54,573	Welch, Lou W.	174,910	Mansfield, Mike		120,337 D	23.8%	76.2%	23.8%	76.2%
1954	227,454	112,863	D'Ewart, Wesley A.	114,591	Murray, James E.		1,728 D	49.6%	50.4%	49.6%	50.4%
1952	262,297	127,360	Ecton, Zales N.	133,109	Mansfield, Mike	1,823	5,749 D	48.6%	50.7%	48.9%	51.1%
1948	221,003	94,458	David, Tom J.	125,193	Murray, James E.	1,352	30,735 D	42.7%	56.6%	43.0%	57.0%
1946	190,566	101,901	Ecton, Zales N.	86,476	Erickson, Leif	2,189	15,425 R	53.5%	45.4%	54.1%	45.9%

MONTANA

PRESIDENT 2008

2000 Census Population	County	Total Vote	Republican	Democratic	Other	Rep.-Dem. Plurality		Percentage			
								Total Vote		Major Vote	
								Rep.	Dem.	Rep.	Dem.
9,202	BEAVERHEAD	4,763	3,008	1,617	138	1,391	R	63.2%	33.9%	65.0%	35.0%
12,671	BIG HORN	5,219	1,628	3,516	75	1,888	D	31.2%	67.4%	31.6%	68.4%
7,009	BLAINE	2,926	1,139	1,702	85	563	D	38.9%	58.2%	40.1%	59.9%
4,385	BROADWATER	1,149	756	365	28	391	R	65.8%	31.8%	67.4%	32.6%
9,552	CARBON	5,750	3,108	2,443	199	665	R	54.1%	42.5%	56.0%	44.0%
1,360	CARTER	722	573	111	38	462	R	79.4%	15.4%	83.8%	16.2%
80,357	CASCADE	35,396	16,857	17,664	875	807	D	47.6%	49.9%	48.8%	51.2%
5,970	CHOUTEAU	2,861	1,634	1,122	105	512	R	57.1%	39.2%	59.3%	40.7%
11,696	CUSTER	5,452	3,047	2,267	138	780	R	55.9%	41.6%	57.3%	42.7%
2,017	DANIELS	1,073	694	343	36	351	R	64.7%	32.0%	66.9%	33.1%
9,059	DAWSON	4,444	2,639	1,593	212	1,046	R	59.4%	35.8%	62.4%	37.6%
9,417	DEER LODGE	5,074	1,502	3,402	170	1,900	D	29.6%	67.0%	30.6%	69.4%
2,837	FALLON	1,433	1,064	318	51	746	R	74.2%	22.2%	77.0%	23.0%
11,893	FERGUS	6,232	4,108	1,933	191	2,175	R	65.9%	31.0%	68.0%	32.0%
74,471	FLATHEAD	43,744	25,559	16,138	2,047	9,421	R	58.4%	36.9%	61.3%	38.7%
67,831	GALLATIN	48,169	22,578	24,205	1,386	1,627	D	46.9%	50.3%	48.3%	51.7%
1,279	GARFIELD	727	598	110	19	488	R	82.3%	15.1%	84.5%	15.5%
13,247	GLACIER	4,971	1,451	3,423	97	1,972	D	29.2%	68.9%	29.8%	70.2%
1,042	GOLDEN VALLEY	492	343	124	25	219	R	69.7%	25.2%	73.4%	26.6%
2,830	GRANITE	1,718	1,013	601	104	412	R	59.0%	35.0%	62.8%	37.2%
16,673	HILL	6,625	2,787	3,596	242	809	D	42.1%	54.3%	43.7%	56.3%
10,049	JEFFERSON	6,341	3,538	2,582	221	956	R	55.8%	40.7%	57.8%	42.2%
2,329	JUDITH BASIN	1,236	801	397	38	404	R	64.8%	32.1%	66.9%	33.1%
26,507	LAKE	13,919	6,498	6,766	655	268	D	46.7%	48.6%	49.0%	51.0%
55,716	LEWIS AND CLARK	32,873	14,966	17,114	793	2,148	D	45.5%	52.1%	46.7%	53.3%
2,158	LIBERTY	1,001	594	367	40	227	R	59.3%	36.7%	61.8%	38.2%
18,837	LINCOLN	9,227	5,704	3,025	498	2,679	R	61.8%	32.8%	65.3%	34.7%
1,977	MCCONE	1,091	726	321	44	405	R	66.5%	29.4%	69.3%	30.7%
6,851	MADISON	4,568	2,822	1,607	139	1,215	R	61.8%	35.2%	63.7%	36.3%
1,932	MEAGHER	966	624	298	44	326	R	64.6%	30.8%	67.7%	32.3%
3,884	MINERAL	1,997	1,053	845	99	208	R	52.7%	42.3%	55.5%	44.5%
95,802	MISSOULA	59,104	20,743	36,531	1,830	15,788	D	35.1%	61.8%	36.2%	63.8%
4,497	MUSSELSHELL	2,306	1,581	636	89	945	R	68.6%	27.6%	71.3%	28.7%
15,694	PARK	8,898	4,376	4,173	349	203	R	49.2%	46.9%	51.2%	48.8%
493	PETROLEUM	300	227	68	5	159	R	75.7%	22.7%	76.9%	23.1%
4,601	PHILLIPS	2,123	1,423	638	62	785	R	67.0%	30.1%	69.0%	31.0%
6,424	PONDERA	2,885	1,588	1,223	74	365	R	55.0%	42.4%	56.5%	43.5%
1,858	POWDER RIVER	1,038	802	208	28	594	R	77.3%	20.0%	79.4%	20.6%
7,180	POWELL	2,814	1,683	1,021	110	662	R	59.8%	36.3%	62.2%	37.8%
1,199	PRAIRIE	735	503	211	21	292	R	68.4%	28.7%	70.4%	29.6%
36,070	RAVALLI	22,101	13,002	8,400	699	4,602	R	58.8%	38.0%	60.8%	39.2%
9,667	RICHLAND	4,516	3,184	1,203	129	1,981	R	70.5%	26.6%	72.6%	27.4%
10,620	ROOSEVELT	4,153	1,473	2,564	116	1,091	D	35.5%	61.7%	36.5%	63.5%
9,383	ROSEBUD	3,810	1,768	1,919	123	151	D	46.4%	50.4%	48.0%	52.0%
10,227	SANDERS	5,868	3,563	1,970	335	1,593	R	60.7%	33.6%	64.4%	35.6%
4,105	SHERIDAN	2,006	987	953	66	34	R	49.2%	47.5%	50.9%	49.1%
34,606	SILVER BOW	16,969	4,818	11,676	475	6,858	D	28.4%	68.8%	29.2%	70.8%
8,195	STILLWATER	4,667	2,991	1,512	164	1,479	R	64.1%	32.4%	66.4%	33.6%
3,609	SWEET GRASS	2,083	1,494	541	48	953	R	71.7%	26.0%	73.4%	26.6%
6,445	TETON	3,272	1,874	1,294	104	580	R	57.3%	39.5%	59.2%	40.8%

MONTANA

PRESIDENT 2008

2000 Census Population	County	Total Vote	Republican	Democratic	Other	Rep.-Dem. Plurality	Percentage			
							Total Vote		Major Vote	
							Rep.	Dem.	Rep.	Dem.
5,267	TOOLE	2,121	1,317	737	67	580 R	62.1%	34.7%	64.1%	35.9%
861	TREASURE	486	314	156	16	158 R	64.6%	32.1%	66.8%	33.2%
7,675	VALLEY	3,911	2,121	1,645	145	476 R	54.2%	42.1%	56.3%	43.7%
2,259	WHEATLAND	983	657	289	37	368 R	66.8%	29.4%	69.5%	30.5%
1,068	WIBAUX	563	379	146	38	233 R	67.3%	25.9%	72.2%	27.8%
129,352	YELLOWSTONE	70,431	36,483	32,038	1,910	4,445 R	51.8%	45.5%	53.2%	46.8%
902,195	TOTAL	490,302	242,763	231,667	15,872	11,096 R	49.5%	47.2%	51.2%	48.8%

MONTANA

GOVERNOR 2008

2000 Census Population	County	Total Vote	Republican	Democratic	Other	Rep.-Dem. Plurality	Percentage			
							Total Vote		Major Vote	
							Rep.	Dem.	Rep.	Dem.
9,202	BEAVERHEAD	4,722	2,089	2,534	99	445 D	44.2%	53.7%	45.2%	54.8%
12,671	BIG HORN	5,220	1,400	3,724	96	2,324 D	26.8%	71.3%	27.3%	72.7%
7,009	BLAINE	2,916	622	2,242	52	1,620 D	21.3%	76.9%	21.7%	78.3%
4,385	BROADWATER	1,073	452	600	21	148 D	42.1%	55.9%	43.0%	57.0%
9,552	CARBON	5,733	1,961	3,669	103	1,708 D	34.2%	64.0%	34.8%	65.2%
1,360	CARTER	713	443	254	16	189 R	62.1%	35.6%	63.6%	36.4%
80,357	CASCADE	35,391	9,568	25,269	554	15,701 D	27.0%	71.4%	27.5%	72.5%
5,970	CHOUTEAU	2,859	920	1,887	52	967 D	32.2%	66.0%	32.8%	67.2%
11,696	CUSTER	5,413	1,964	3,353	96	1,389 D	36.3%	61.9%	36.9%	63.1%
2,017	DANIELS	1,063	441	601	21	160 D	41.5%	56.5%	42.3%	57.7%
9,059	DAWSON	4,436	1,777	2,576	83	799 D	40.1%	58.1%	40.8%	59.2%
9,417	DEER LODGE	5,153	650	4,419	84	3,769 D	12.6%	85.8%	12.8%	87.2%
2,837	FALLON	1,392	668	696	28	28 D	48.0%	50.0%	49.0%	51.0%
11,893	FERGUS	6,210	2,890	3,209	111	319 D	46.5%	51.7%	47.4%	52.6%
74,471	FLATHEAD	43,150	17,060	24,998	1,092	7,938 D	39.5%	57.9%	40.6%	59.4%
67,831	GALLATIN	47,381	16,879	29,541	961	12,662 D	35.6%	62.3%	36.4%	63.6%
1,279	GARFIELD	722	436	270	16	166 R	60.4%	37.4%	61.8%	38.2%
13,247	GLACIER	4,951	946	3,898	107	2,952 D	19.1%	78.7%	19.5%	80.5%
1,042	GOLDEN VALLEY	496	228	257	11	29 D	46.0%	51.8%	47.0%	53.0%
2,830	GRANITE	1,704	631	1,026	47	395 D	37.0%	60.2%	38.1%	61.9%
16,673	HILL	6,645	1,538	4,983	124	3,445 D	23.1%	75.0%	23.6%	76.4%
10,049	JEFFERSON	6,308	2,328	3,858	122	1,530 D	36.9%	61.2%	37.6%	62.4%
2,329	JUDITH BASIN	1,236	498	705	33	207 D	40.3%	57.0%	41.4%	58.6%
26,507	LAKE	13,813	4,126	9,319	368	5,193 D	29.9%	67.5%	30.7%	69.3%
55,716	LEWIS AND CLARK	32,670	9,509	22,544	617	13,035 D	29.1%	69.0%	29.7%	70.3%
2,158	LIBERTY	994	348	625	21	277 D	35.0%	62.9%	35.8%	64.2%
18,837	LINCOLN	9,116	3,711	5,116	289	1,405 D	40.7%	56.1%	42.0%	58.0%
1,977	MCCONE	1,086	533	538	15	5 D	49.1%	49.5%	49.8%	50.2%
6,851	MADISON	4,535	1,902	2,529	104	627 D	41.9%	55.8%	42.9%	57.1%
1,932	MEAGHER	958	473	468	17	5 R	49.4%	48.9%	50.3%	49.7%

MONTANA

GOVERNOR 2008

2000 Census Population	County	Total Vote	Republican	Democratic	Other	Rep.-Dem. Plurality		Percentage			
								Total Vote		Major Vote	
								Rep.	Dem.	Rep.	Dem.
3,884	MINERAL	1,995	659	1,277	59	618	D	33.0%	64.0%	34.0%	66.0%
95,802	MISSOULA	58,348	12,577	44,558	1,213	31,981	D	21.6%	76.4%	22.0%	78.0%
4,497	MUSSELSHELL	2,295	1,117	1,109	69	8	R	48.7%	48.3%	50.2%	49.8%
15,694	PARK	8,815	3,023	5,590	202	2,567	D	34.3%	63.4%	35.1%	64.9%
493	PETROLEUM	297	151	139	7	12	R	50.8%	46.8%	52.1%	47.9%
4,601	PHILLIPS	2,111	823	1,223	65	400	D	39.0%	57.9%	40.2%	59.8%
6,424	PONDERA	2,874	1,016	1,818	40	802	D	35.4%	63.3%	35.9%	64.1%
1,858	POWDER RIVER	1,007	631	349	27	282	R	62.7%	34.7%	64.4%	35.6%
7,180	POWELL	2,814	1,036	1,716	62	680	D	36.8%	61.0%	37.6%	62.4%
1,199	PRAIRIE	733	347	369	17	22	D	47.3%	50.3%	48.5%	51.5%
36,070	RAVALLI	21,928	8,267	13,237	424	4,970	D	37.7%	60.4%	38.4%	61.6%
9,667	RICHLAND	4,479	2,037	2,362	80	325	D	45.5%	52.7%	46.3%	53.7%
10,620	ROOSEVELT	4,111	866	3,169	76	2,303	D	21.1%	77.1%	21.5%	78.5%
9,383	ROSEBUD	3,811	1,075	2,661	75	1,586	D	28.2%	69.8%	28.8%	71.2%
10,227	SANDERS	5,791	2,199	3,426	166	1,227	D	38.0%	59.2%	39.1%	60.9%
4,105	SHERIDAN	1,999	611	1,353	35	742	D	30.6%	67.7%	31.1%	68.9%
34,606	SILVER BOW	17,024	2,665	14,103	256	11,438	D	15.7%	82.8%	15.9%	84.1%
8,195	STILLWATER	4,638	1,891	2,654	93	763	D	40.8%	57.2%	41.6%	58.4%
3,609	SWEET GRASS	2,063	1,130	898	35	232	R	54.8%	43.5%	55.7%	44.3%
6,445	TETON	3,292	1,253	1,973	66	720	D	38.1%	59.9%	38.8%	61.2%
5,267	TOOLE	2,132	879	1,203	50	324	D	41.2%	56.4%	42.2%	57.8%
861	TREASURE	488	221	251	16	30	D	45.3%	51.4%	46.8%	53.2%
7,675	VALLEY	3,899	1,243	2,590	66	1,347	D	31.9%	66.4%	32.4%	67.6%
2,259	WHEATLAND	981	454	509	18	55	D	46.3%	51.9%	47.1%	52.9%
1,068	WIBAUX	550	223	318	9	95	D	40.5%	57.8%	41.2%	58.8%
129,352	YELLOWSTONE	70,200	24,883	44,107	1,210	19,224	D	35.4%	62.8%	36.1%	63.9%
902,195	TOTAL	486,734	158,268	318,670	9,796	160,402	D	32.5%	65.5%	33.2%	66.8%

MONTANA

SENATOR 2008

2000 Census Population	County	Total Vote	Republican	Democratic	Other	Rep.-Dem. Plurality		Percentage			
								Total Vote		Major Vote	
								Rep.	Dem.	Rep.	Dem.
9,202	BEAVERHEAD	4,751	1,518	3,233		1,715	D	32.0%	68.0%	32.0%	68.0%
12,671	BIG HORN	5,188	888	4,300		3,412	D	17.1%	82.9%	17.1%	82.9%
7,009	BLAINE	2,891	512	2,379		1,867	D	17.7%	82.3%	17.7%	82.3%
4,385	BROADWATER	1,055	405	650		245	D	38.4%	61.6%	38.4%	61.6%
9,552	CARBON	5,587	1,502	4,085		2,583	D	26.9%	73.1%	26.9%	73.1%
1,360	CARTER	701	257	444		187	D	36.7%	63.3%	36.7%	63.3%
80,357	CASCADE	35,107	7,758	27,349		19,591	D	22.1%	77.9%	22.1%	77.9%
5,970	CHOUTEAU	2,805	671	2,134	·	1,463	D	23.9%	76.1%	23.9%	76.1%
11,696	CUSTER	5,336	1,333	4,003		2,670	D	25.0%	75.0%	25.0%	75.0%
2,017	DANIELS	1,033	317	716		399	D	30.7%	69.3%	30.7%	69.3%
9,059	DAWSON	4,369	1,357	3,012		1,655	D	31.1%	68.9%	31.1%	68.9%
9,417	DEER LODGE	5,074	681	4,393		3,712	D	13.4%	86.6%	13.4%	86.6%
2,837	FALLON	1,389	510	879		369	D	36.7%	63.3%	36.7%	63.3%
11,893	FERGUS	6,027	2,088	3,939		1,851	D	34.6%	65.4%	34.6%	65.4%
74,471	FLATHEAD	42,422	15,459	26,963		11,504	D	36.4%	63.6%	36.4%	63.6%

MONTANA

SENATOR 2008

2000 Census Population	County	Total Vote	Republican	Democratic	Other	Rep.-Dem. Plurality	Percentage			
							Total Vote		Major Vote	
							Rep.	Dem.	Rep.	Dem.
67,831	GALLATIN	46,501	13,359	33,142		19,783 D	28.7%	71.3%	28.7%	71.3%
1,279	GARFIELD	707	284	423		139 D	40.2%	59.8%	40.2%	59.8%
13,247	GLACIER	4,939	777	4,162		3,385 D	15.7%	84.3%	15.7%	84.3%
1,042	GOLDEN VALLEY	468	180	288		108 D	38.5%	61.5%	38.5%	61.5%
2,830	GRANITE	1,663	586	1,077		491 D	35.2%	64.8%	35.2%	64.8%
16,673	HILL	6,618	1,285	5,333		4,048 D	19.4%	80.6%	19.4%	80.6%
10,049	JEFFERSON	6,186	1,892	4,294		2,402 D	30.6%	69.4%	30.6%	69.4%
2,329	JUDITH BASIN	1,208	336	872		536 D	27.8%	72.2%	27.8%	72.2%
26,507	LAKE	13,629	3,996	9,633		5,637 D	29.3%	70.7%	29.3%	70.7%
55,716	LEWIS AND CLARK	32,121	7,419	24,702		17,283 D	23.1%	76.9%	23.1%	76.9%
2,158	LIBERTY	966	251	715		464 D	26.0%	74.0%	26.0%	74.0%
18,837	LINCOLN	9,076	3,449	5,627		2,178 D	38.0%	62.0%	38.0%	62.0%
1,977	MCCONE	1,067	386	681		295 D	36.2%	63.8%	36.2%	63.8%
6,851	MADISON	4,466	1,488	2,978		1,490 D	33.3%	66.7%	33.3%	66.7%
1,932	MEAGHER	932	297	635		338 D	31.9%	68.1%	31.9%	68.1%
3,884	MINERAL	1,953	624	1,329		705 D	32.0%	68.0%	32.0%	68.0%
95,802	MISSOULA	57,582	11,961	45,621		33,660 D	20.8%	79.2%	20.8%	79.2%
4,497	MUSSELSHELL	2,239	878	1,361		483 D	39.2%	60.8%	39.2%	60.8%
15,694	PARK	8,659	2,530	6,129		3,599 D	29.2%	70.8%	29.2%	70.8%
493	PETROLEUM	297	114	183		69 D	38.4%	61.6%	38.4%	61.6%
4,601	PHILLIPS	2,089	621	1,468		847 D	29.7%	70.3%	29.7%	70.3%
6,424	PONDERA	2,827	702	2,125		1,423 D	24.8%	75.2%	24.8%	75.2%
1,858	POWDER RIVER	983	385	598		213 D	39.2%	60.8%	39.2%	60.8%
7,180	POWELL	2,771	886	1,885		999 D	32.0%	68.0%	32.0%	68.0%
1,199	PRAIRIE	712	273	439		166 D	38.3%	61.7%	38.3%	61.7%
36,070	RAVALLI	21,513	7,956	13,557		5,601 D	37.0%	63.0%	37.0%	63.0%
9,667	RICHLAND	4,429	1,649	2,780		1,131 D	37.2%	62.8%	37.2%	62.8%
10,620	ROOSEVELT	4,107	766	3,341		2,575 D	18.7%	81.3%	18.7%	81.3%
9,383	ROSEBUD	3,769	895	2,874		1,979 D	23.7%	76.3%	23.7%	76.3%
10,227	SANDERS	5,712	2,350	3,362		1,012 D	41.1%	58.9%	41.1%	58.9%
4,105	SHERIDAN	1,976	508	1,468		960 D	25.7%	74.3%	25.7%	74.3%
34,606	SILVER BOW	16,710	2,265	14,445		12,180 D	13.6%	86.4%	13.6%	86.4%
8,195	STILLWATER	4,496	1,474	3,022		1,548 D	32.8%	67.2%	32.8%	67.2%
3,609	SWEET GRASS	1,982	821	1,161		340 D	41.4%	58.6%	41.4%	58.6%
6,445	TETON	3,242	1,009	2,233		1,224 D	31.1%	68.9%	31.1%	68.9%
5,267	TOOLE	2,101	658	1,443		785 D	31.3%	68.7%	31.3%	68.7%
861	TREASURE	462	126	336		210 D	27.3%	72.7%	27.3%	72.7%
7,675	VALLEY	3,828	864	2,964		2,100 D	22.6%	77.4%	22.6%	77.4%
2,259	WHEATLAND	954	322	632		310 D	33.8%	66.2%	33.8%	66.2%
1,068	WIBAUX	549	183	366		183 D	33.3%	66.7%	33.3%	66.7%
129,352	YELLOWSTONE	67,434	17,308	50,126		32,818 D	25.7%	74.3%	25.7%	74.3%
902,195	TOTAL	477,658	129,369	348,289		218,920 D	27.1%	72.9%	27.1%	72.9%

MONTANA

HOUSE OF REPRESENTATIVES

CD	Year	Total Vote	Republican Vote	Republican Candidate	Democratic Vote	Democratic Candidate	Other Vote	Rep.-Dem. Plurality		Total Vote Rep.	Total Vote Dem.	Major Vote Rep.	Major Vote Dem.
AL	2008	480,900	308,470	REHBERG, DENNY*	155,930	DRISCOLL, JOHN	16,500	152,540	R	64.1%	32.4%	66.4%	33.6%
AL	2006	406,134	239,124	REHBERG, DENNY*	158,916	LINDEEN, MONICA	8,094	80,208	R	58.9%	39.1%	60.1%	39.9%
AL	2004	444,230	286,076	REHBERG, DENNY*	145,606	VELAZQUEZ, TRACY	12,548	140,470	R	64.4%	32.8%	66.3%	33.7%
AL	2002	331,321	214,100	REHBERG, DENNY*	108,233	KELLY, STEVE	8,988	105,867	R	64.6%	32.7%	66.4%	33.6%
AL	2000	410,523	211,418	REHBERG, DENNY	189,971	KEENAN, NANCY	9,134	21,447	R	51.5%	46.3%	52.7%	47.3%
AL	1998	331,551	175,748	HILL, RICK*	147,073	DESCHAMPS, DUSTY	8,730	28,675	R	53.0%	44.4%	54.4%	45.6%
AL	1996	404,426	211,975	HILL, RICK	174,516	YELLOWTAIL, BILL	17,935	37,459	R	52.4%	43.2%	54.8%	45.2%
AL	1994	352,133	148,715	JAMISON, CY	171,372	WILLIAMS, PAT*	32,046	22,657	D	42.2%	48.7%	46.5%	53.5%
AL	1992	403,735	189,570	MARLENEE, RON*	203,711	WILLIAMS, PAT*	10,454	14,141	D	47.0%	50.5%	48.2%	51.8%

Note: An asterisk (*) denotes incumbent.

MONTANA

GENERAL AND PRIMARY ELECTIONS

2008 GENERAL ELECTIONS

President   Other vote was 10,638 Constitution (Ron Paul); 3,686 Independent (Ralph Nader); 1,355 Libertarian (Bob Barr); 143 write-in (Chuck Baldwin); 23 write-in (Cynthia A. McKinney); 12 write-in (RaeDeen Heupel); 10 write-in (Rosa A. Clemente); 3 write-in (Santa Claus); 1 write-in (Jonathan Allen); 1 write-in (Amy Lou Wyatt).

Governor   Other vote was 9,796 Libertarian (Stan Jones).

Senator

House   Other vote was:

At Large   16,500 Libertarian (Mike Fellows).

2008 PRIMARY ELECTIONS

Primary   June 3, 2008   **Registration**   630,633   No Party Registration
                                     (as of June 3, 2008)

Primary Type   Open—Any registered voter could participate in the party primary of their choice.

MONTANA

GENERAL AND PRIMARY ELECTIONS

	REPUBLICAN PRIMARIES			DEMOCRATIC PRIMARIES		
President	John McCain	72,791	76.0%	Barack Obama	103,174	56.6%
	Ron Paul	20,606	21.5%	Hillary Clinton	74,889	41.1%
	No Preference	2,333	2.4%	No Preference	4,358	2.4%
	TOTAL	95,730		TOTAL	182,421	
Governor	Roy Brown	65,883	80.8%	Brian Schweitzer*	159,820	91.3%
	Larry Steele	15,643	19.2%	William Fischer	9,865	5.6%
				Donald Pogreba	5,358	3.1%
	TOTAL	81,526		TOTAL	175,043	
Senator	Bob Kelleher	26,936	36.3%	Max Baucus*	165,050	100.0%
	Michael Lange	17,044	23.0%			
	Kirk Bushman	15,507	20.9%			
	Patty Lovaas	7,632	10.3%			
	Anton Pearson	4,257	5.7%			
	Shay Joshua Garnett	2,788	3.8%			
	TOTAL	74,164				
Congressional At Large	Denny Rehberg*	90,492	100.0%	John Driscoll	70,176	49.2%
				Jim Hunt	59,768	41.9%
				Robert Candee	12,598	8.8%
				TOTAL	142,542	

Note: An asterisk (*) denotes incumbent.

NEBRASKA

Congressional districts first established for elections held in 2002
3 members

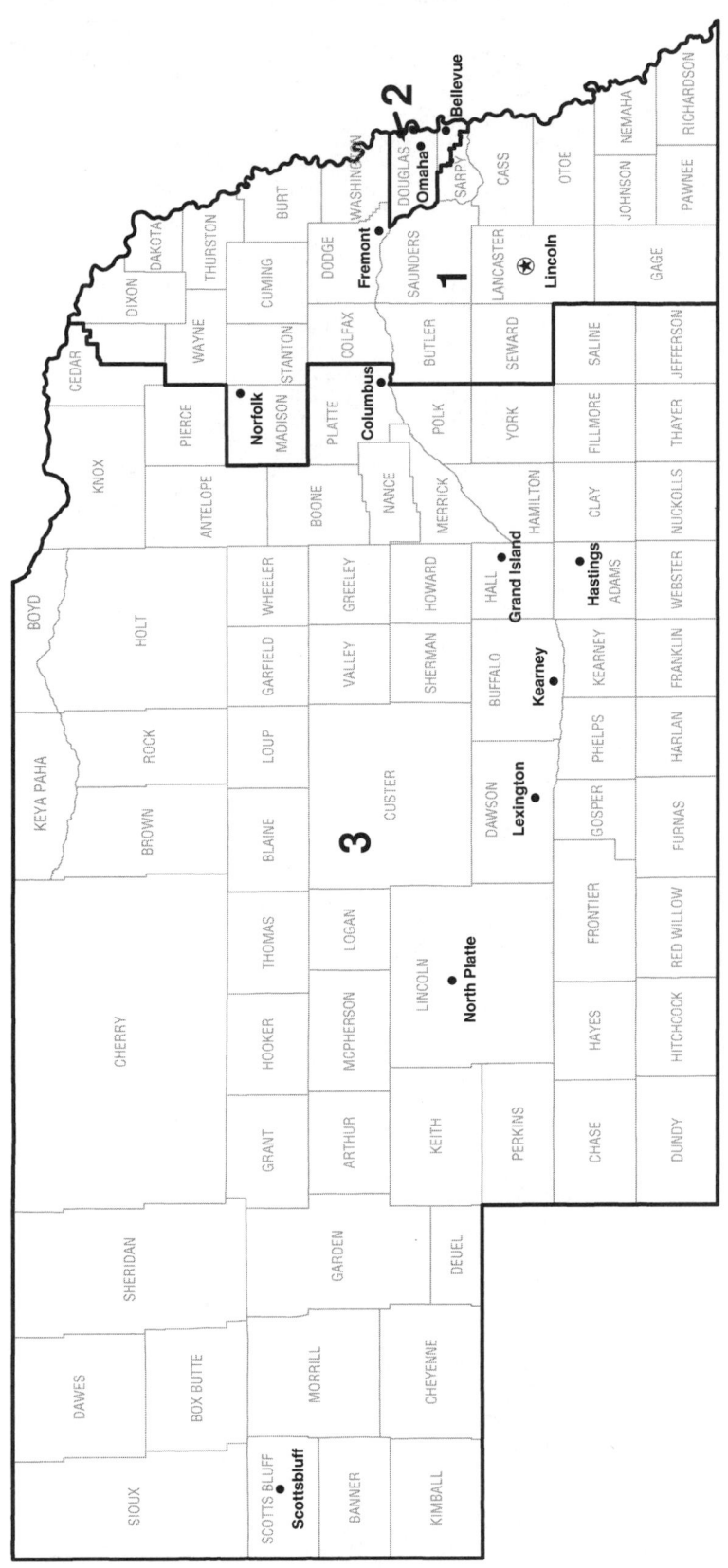

NEBRASKA

GOVERNOR

Dave Heineman (R). Elected 2006 to a four-year term. Became governor January 21, 2005, upon the resignation of Mike Johanns (R) to become U.S. Secretary of Agriculture.

SENATORS (1 Democrat, 1 Republican)

Mike Johanns (R). Elected 2008 to a six-year term.

Ben Nelson (D). Reelected 2006 to a six-year term. Previously elected 2000.

REPRESENTATIVES (3 Republicans)

1. Jeff Fortenberry (R)
2. Lee Terry (R)
3. Adrian Smith (R)

POSTWAR VOTE FOR PRESIDENT

		Republican		Democratic				Total Vote		Major Vote	
Year	Total Vote	Vote	Candidate	Vote	Candidate	Other Vote	Plurality	Rep.	Dem.	Rep.	Dem.
2008	801,281	452,979	McCain, John	333,319	Obama, Barack	14,983	119,660 R	56.5%	41.6%	57.6%	42.4%
2004	778,186	512,814	Bush, George W.	254,328	Kerry, John	11,044	258,486 R	65.9%	32.7%	66.8%	33.2%
2000**	697,019	433,862	Bush, George W.	231,780	Gore, Al	31,377	202,082 R	62.2%	33.3%	65.2%	34.8%
1996**	677,415	363,467	Dole, Bob	236,761	Clinton, Bill	77,187	126,706 R	53.7%	35.0%	60.6%	39.4%
1992**	737,546	343,678	Bush, George	216,864	Clinton, Bill	177,004	126,814 R	46.6%	29.4%	61.3%	38.7%
1988	661,465	397,956	Bush, George	259,235	Dukakis, Michael S.	4,274	138,721 R	60.2%	39.2%	60.6%	39.4%
1984	652,090	460,054	Reagan, Ronald	187,866	Mondale, Walter F.	4,170	272,188 R	70.6%	28.8%	71.0%	29.0%
1980**	640,854	419,937	Reagan, Ronald	166,851	Carter, Jimmy	54,066	253,086 R	65.5%	26.0%	71.6%	28.4%
1976	607,668	359,705	Ford, Gerald R.	233,692	Carter, Jimmy	14,271	126,013 R	59.2%	38.5%	60.6%	39.4%
1972	576,289	406,298	Nixon, Richard M.	169,991	McGovern, George S.		236,307 R	70.5%	29.5%	70.5%	29.5%
1968**	536,851	321,163	Nixon, Richard M.	170,784	Humphrey, Hubert H.	44,904	150,379 R	59.8%	31.8%	65.3%	34.7%
1964	584,154	276,847	Goldwater, Barry M.	307,307	Johnson, Lyndon B.		30,460 D	47.4%	52.6%	47.4%	52.6%
1960	613,095	380,553	Nixon, Richard M.	232,542	Kennedy, John F.		148,011 R	62.1%	37.9%	62.1%	37.9%
1956	577,137	378,108	Eisenhower, Dwight D.	199,029	Stevenson, Adlai E.		179,079 R	65.5%	34.5%	65.5%	34.5%
1952	609,660	421,603	Eisenhower, Dwight D.	188,057	Stevenson, Adlai E.		233,546 R	69.2%	30.8%	69.2%	30.8%
1948	488,940	264,774	Dewey, Thomas E.	224,165	Truman, Harry S.	1	40,609 R	54.2%	45.8%	54.2%	45.8%

**In past elections, the other vote included: 2000 - 24,540 Green (Ralph Nader); 1996 - 71,278 Reform (Ross Perot); 1992 - 174,104 Independent (Perot); 1980 - 44,993 Independent (John Anderson); 1968 - 44,904 American Independent (George Wallace).

NEBRASKA

POSTWAR VOTE FOR GOVERNOR

Year	Total Vote	Republican Vote	Republican Candidate	Democratic Vote	Democratic Candidate	Other Vote	Rep.-Dem. Plurality	Percentage Total Vote Rep.	Percentage Total Vote Dem.	Percentage Major Vote Rep.	Percentage Major Vote Dem.
2006	593,357	435,507	Heineman, Dave	145,115	Hahn, David	12,735	290,392 R	73.4%	24.5%	75.0%	25.0%
2002	480,991	330,349	Johanns, Mike	132,348	Dean, Stormy	18,294	198,001 R	68.7%	27.5%	71.4%	28.6%
1998	545,238	293,910	Johanns, Mike	250,678	Hoppner, Bill	650	43,232 R	53.9%	46.0%	54.0%	46.0%
1994	579,561	148,230	Spence, Gene	423,270	Nelson, Ben	8,061	275,040 D	25.6%	73.0%	25.9%	74.1%
1990	586,542	288,741	Orr, Kay	292,771	Nelson, Ben	5,030	4,030 D	49.2%	49.9%	49.7%	50.3%
1986	564,422	298,325	Orr, Kay	265,156	Boosalis, Helen	941	33,169 R	52.9%	47.0%	52.9%	47.1%
1982	547,902	270,203	Thone, Charles	277,436	Kerrey, Bob	263	7,233 D	49.3%	50.6%	49.3%	50.7%
1978	492,423	275,473	Thone, Charles	216,754	Whelan, Gerald T.	196	58,719 R	55.9%	44.0%	56.0%	44.0%
1974	451,306	159,780	Marvel, Richard D.	267,012	Exon, J. J.	24,514	107,232 D	35.4%	59.2%	37.4%	62.6%
1970	461,619	201,994	Tiemann, Norbert T.	248,552	Exon, J. J.	11,073	46,558 D	43.8%	53.8%	44.8%	55.2%
1966**	486,396	299,245	Tiemann, Norbert T.	186,985	Sorensen, Philip C.	166	112,260 R	61.5%	38.4%	61.5%	38.5%
1964	578,090	231,029	Burney, Dwight W.	347,026	Morrison, Frank B.	35	115,997 D	40.0%	60.0%	40.0%	60.0%
1962	464,585	221,885	Seaton, Fred A.	242,669	Morrison, Frank B.	31	20,784 D	47.8%	52.2%	47.8%	52.2%
1960	598,971	287,302	Cooper, John R.	311,344	Morrison, Frank B.	325	24,042 D	48.0%	52.0%	48.0%	52.0%
1958	421,067	209,705	Anderson, Victor E.	211,345	Brooks, Ralph G.	17	1,640 D	49.8%	50.2%	49.8%	50.2%
1956	567,933	308,293	Anderson, Victor E.	228,048	Sorrell, Frank	31,592	80,245 R	54.3%	40.2%	57.5%	42.5%
1954	414,841	250,080	Anderson, Victor E.	164,753	Ritchie, William	8	85,327 R	60.3%	39.7%	60.3%	39.7%
1952	595,714	366,009	Crosby, Robert B.	229,700	Raecke, Walter R.	5	136,309 R	61.4%	38.6%	61.4%	38.6%
1950	449,720	247,081	Peterson, Val	202,638	Raecke, Walter R.	1	44,443 R	54.9%	45.1%	54.9%	45.1%
1948	476,352	286,119	Peterson, Val	190,214	Sorrell, Frank	19	95,905 R	60.1%	39.9%	60.1%	39.9%
1946	380,835	249,468	Peterson, Val	131,367	Sorrell, Frank		118,101 R	65.5%	34.5%	65.5%	34.5%

**The term of office of Nebraska's governor was increased from two to four years effective with the 1966 election.

POSTWAR VOTE FOR SENATOR

Year	Total Vote	Republican Vote	Republican Candidate	Democratic Vote	Democratic Candidate	Other Vote	Rep.-Dem. Plurality	Percentage Total Vote Rep.	Percentage Total Vote Dem.	Percentage Major Vote Rep.	Percentage Major Vote Dem.
2008	792,511	455,854	Johanns, Mike	317,456	Kleeb, Scott	19,201	138,398 R	57.5%	40.1%	58.9%	41.1%
2006	592,316	213,928	Ricketts, Pete	378,388	Nelson, Ben		164,460 D	36.1%	63.9%	36.1%	63.9%
2002	480,217	397,438	Hagel, Chuck	70,290	Matulka, Charlie A.	12,489	327,148 R	82.8%	14.6%	85.0%	15.0%
2000	692,344	337,967	Stenberg, Don	353,097	Nelson, Ben	1,280	15,130 D	48.8%	51.0%	48.9%	51.1%
1996	676,789	379,933	Hagel, Chuck	281,904	Nelson, Ben	14,952	98,029 R	56.1%	41.7%	57.4%	42.6%
1994	579,205	260,668	Stoney, Jan	317,297	Kerrey, Bob	1,240	56,629 D	45.0%	54.8%	45.1%	54.9%
1990	593,828	243,013	Daub, Harold J.	349,779	Exon, J. J.	1,036	106,766 D	40.9%	58.9%	41.0%	59.0%
1988	667,860	278,250	Karnes, David	378,717	Kerrey, Bob	10,893	100,467 D	41.7%	56.7%	42.4%	57.6%
1984	639,668	307,147	Hoch, Nancy	332,217	Exon, J. J.	304	25,070 D	48.0%	51.9%	48.0%	52.0%
1982	545,647	155,760	Keck, Jim	363,350	Zorinsky, Edward	26,537	207,590 D	28.5%	66.6%	30.0%	70.0%
1978	494,368	159,806	Shasteen, Donald	334,276	Exon, J. J.	286	174,470 D	32.3%	67.6%	32.3%	67.7%
1976	598,314	284,284	McCollister, John Y.	313,809	Zorinsky, Edward	221	29,525 D	47.5%	52.4%	47.5%	52.5%
1972	568,580	301,841	Curtis, Carl T.	265,922	Carpenter, Terry	817	35,919 R	53.1%	46.8%	53.2%	46.8%
1970	458,966	240,894	Hruska, Roman L.	217,681	Morrison, Frank B.	391	23,213 R	52.5%	47.4%	52.5%	47.5%
1966	485,101	296,116	Curtis, Carl T.	187,950	Morrison, Frank B.	1,035	108,166 R	61.0%	38.7%	61.2%	38.8%
1964	563,401	345,772	Hruska, Roman L.	217,605	Arndt, Raymond W.	24	128,167 R	61.4%	38.6%	61.4%	38.6%
1960	598,743	352,748	Curtis, Carl T.	245,837	Conrad, Robert	158	106,911 R	58.9%	41.1%	58.9%	41.1%
1958	417,385	232,227	Hruska, Roman L.	185,152	Morrison, Frank B.	6	47,075 R	55.6%	44.4%	55.6%	44.4%
1954	418,691	255,695	Curtis, Carl T.	162,990	Neville, Keith	6	92,705 R	61.1%	38.9%	61.1%	38.9%
1954S	411,225	250,341	Hruska, Roman L.	160,881	Green, James F.	3	89,460 R	60.9%	39.1%	60.9%	39.1%
1952	591,749	408,971	Butler, Hugh	164,660	Long, Stanley D.	18,118	244,311 R	69.1%	27.8%	71.3%	28.7%
1952S	581,750	369,841	Griswold, Dwight	211,898	Ritchie, William	11	157,943 R	63.6%	36.4%	63.6%	36.4%
1948	471,895	267,575	Wherry, Kenneth S.	204,320	Carpenter, Terry		63,255 R	56.7%	43.3%	56.7%	43.3%
1946	382,958	271,208	Butler, Hugh	111,750	Mekota, John E.		159,458 R	70.8%	29.2%	70.8%	29.2%

Note: S=One each of the 1952 and 1954 elections was for a short term to fill a vacancy.

NEBRASKA

PRESIDENT 2008

2000 Census Population	County	Total Vote	Republican	Democratic	Other	Rep.-Dem. Plurality	Percentage Total Vote Rep.	Dem.	Major Vote Rep.	Dem.
31,151	ADAMS	13,210	8,252	4,685	273	3,567 R	62.5%	35.5%	63.8%	36.2%
7,452	ANTELOPE	3,185	2,383	757	45	1,626 R	74.8%	23.8%	75.9%	24.1%
444	ARTHUR	263	217	39	7	178 R	82.5%	14.8%	84.8%	15.2%
819	BANNER	416	348	62	6	286 R	83.7%	14.9%	84.9%	15.1%
583	BLAINE	316	266	43	7	223 R	84.2%	13.6%	86.1%	13.9%
6,259	BOONE	2,836	2,042	742	52	1,300 R	72.0%	26.2%	73.3%	26.7%
12,158	BOX BUTTE	4,979	2,932	1,886	161	1,046 R	58.9%	37.9%	60.9%	39.1%
2,438	BOYD	1,110	839	250	21	589 R	75.6%	22.5%	77.0%	23.0%
3,525	BROWN	1,567	1,208	311	48	897 R	77.1%	19.8%	79.5%	20.5%
42,259	BUFFALO	19,293	13,097	5,867	329	7,230 R	67.9%	30.4%	69.1%	30.9%
7,791	BURT	3,387	1,907	1,413	67	494 R	56.3%	41.7%	57.4%	42.6%
8,767	BUTLER	3,839	2,557	1,190	92	1,367 R	66.6%	31.0%	68.2%	31.8%
24,334	CASS	12,122	7,120	4,753	249	2,367 R	58.7%	39.2%	60.0%	40.0%
9,615	CEDAR	4,174	2,912	1,190	72	1,722 R	69.8%	28.5%	71.0%	29.0%
4,068	CHASE	1,844	1,477	341	26	1,136 R	80.1%	18.5%	81.2%	18.8%
6,148	CHERRY	3,059	2,360	599	100	1,761 R	77.1%	19.6%	79.8%	20.2%
9,830	CHEYENNE	4,839	3,572	1,173	94	2,399 R	73.8%	24.2%	75.3%	24.7%
7,039	CLAY	3,033	2,177	780	76	1,397 R	71.8%	25.7%	73.6%	26.4%
10,441	COLFAX	3,203	2,018	1,125	60	893 R	63.0%	35.1%	64.2%	35.8%
10,203	CUMING	4,087	2,732	1,274	81	1,458 R	66.8%	31.2%	68.2%	31.8%
11,793	CUSTER	5,578	4,301	1,192	85	3,109 R	77.1%	21.4%	78.3%	21.7%
20,253	DAKOTA	6,396	3,292	2,994	110	298 R	51.5%	46.8%	52.4%	47.6%
9,060	DAWES	3,775	2,376	1,285	114	1,091 R	62.9%	34.0%	64.9%	35.1%
24,365	DAWSON	7,986	5,460	2,399	127	3,061 R	68.4%	30.0%	69.5%	30.5%
2,098	DEUEL	993	732	243	18	489 R	73.7%	24.5%	75.1%	24.9%
6,339	DIXON	2,794	1,785	946	63	839 R	63.9%	33.9%	65.4%	34.6%
36,160	DODGE	15,550	8,557	6,689	304	1,868 R	55.0%	43.0%	56.1%	43.9%
463,585	DOUGLAS	226,701	106,291	116,810	3,600	10,519 D	46.9%	51.5%	47.6%	52.4%
2,292	DUNDY	1,019	783	218	18	565 R	76.8%	21.4%	78.2%	21.8%
6,634	FILLMORE	2,947	1,913	962	72	951 R	64.9%	32.6%	66.5%	33.5%
3,574	FRANKLIN	1,552	1,079	442	31	637 R	69.5%	28.5%	70.9%	29.1%
3,099	FRONTIER	1,404	1,034	349	21	685 R	73.6%	24.9%	74.8%	25.2%
5,324	FURNAS	2,328	1,725	556	47	1,169 R	74.1%	23.9%	75.6%	24.4%
22,993	GAGE	10,160	5,435	4,473	252	962 R	53.5%	44.0%	54.9%	45.1%
2,292	GARDEN	1,138	844	283	11	561 R	74.2%	24.9%	74.9%	25.1%
1,902	GARFIELD	1,030	800	212	18	588 R	77.7%	20.6%	79.1%	20.9%
2,143	GOSPER	1,048	776	260	12	516 R	74.0%	24.8%	74.9%	25.1%
747	GRANT	367	318	41	8	277 R	86.6%	11.2%	88.6%	11.4%
2,714	GREELEY	1,199	715	458	26	257 R	59.6%	38.2%	61.0%	39.0%
53,534	HALL	21,271	12,977	7,855	439	5,122 R	61.0%	36.9%	62.3%	37.7%
9,403	HAMILTON	4,799	3,389	1,332	78	2,057 R	70.6%	27.8%	71.8%	28.2%
3,786	HARLAN	1,766	1,329	402	35	927 R	75.3%	22.8%	76.8%	23.2%
1,068	HAYES	553	461	85	7	376 R	83.4%	15.4%	84.4%	15.6%
3,111	HITCHCOCK	1,379	1,001	346	32	655 R	72.6%	25.1%	74.3%	25.7%
11,551	HOLT	4,974	3,746	1,089	139	2,657 R	75.3%	21.9%	77.5%	22.5%
783	HOOKER	438	355	75	8	280 R	81.1%	17.1%	82.6%	17.4%
6,567	HOWARD	2,996	1,847	1,083	66	764 R	61.6%	36.1%	63.0%	37.0%
8,333	JEFFERSON	3,697	2,103	1,520	74	583 R	56.9%	41.1%	58.0%	42.0%
4,488	JOHNSON	2,110	1,142	914	54	228 R	54.1%	43.3%	55.5%	44.5%
6,882	KEARNEY	3,150	2,224	876	50	1,348 R	70.6%	27.8%	71.7%	28.3%

NEBRASKA

PRESIDENT 2008

2000 Census Population	County	Total Vote	Republican	Democratic	Other	Rep.-Dem. Plurality	Percentage Total Vote Rep.	Total Vote Dem.	Major Vote Rep.	Major Vote Dem.
8,875	KEITH	3,968	2,942	974	52	1,968 R	74.1%	24.5%	75.1%	24.9%
983	KEYA PAHA	533	409	115	9	294 R	76.7%	21.6%	78.1%	21.9%
4,089	KIMBALL	1,811	1,346	439	26	907 R	74.3%	24.2%	75.4%	24.6%
9,374	KNOX	4,084	2,728	1,255	101	1,473 R	66.8%	30.7%	68.5%	31.5%
250,291	LANCASTER	127,490	59,398	65,734	2,358	6,336 D	46.6%	51.6%	47.5%	52.5%
34,632	LINCOLN	16,277	10,817	5,046	414	5,771 R	66.5%	31.0%	68.2%	31.8%
774	LOGAN	416	327	81	8	246 R	78.6%	19.5%	80.1%	19.9%
712	LOUP	393	302	86	5	216 R	76.8%	21.9%	77.8%	22.2%
533	MCPHERSON	293	240	45	8	195 R	81.9%	15.4%	84.2%	15.8%
35,226	MADISON	14,045	9,655	4,142	248	5,513 R	68.7%	29.5%	70.0%	30.0%
8,204	MERRICK	3,431	2,375	986	70	1,389 R	69.2%	28.7%	70.7%	29.3%
5,440	MORRILL	2,351	1,725	557	69	1,168 R	73.4%	23.7%	75.6%	24.4%
4,038	NANCE	1,707	1,116	549	42	567 R	65.4%	32.2%	67.0%	33.0%
7,576	NEMAHA	3,474	2,134	1,240	100	894 R	61.4%	35.7%	63.2%	36.8%
5,057	NUCKOLLS	2,221	1,498	657	66	841 R	67.4%	29.6%	69.5%	30.5%
15,396	OTOE	7,092	4,033	2,915	144	1,118 R	56.9%	41.1%	58.0%	42.0%
3,087	PAWNEE	1,384	859	483	42	376 R	62.1%	34.9%	64.0%	36.0%
3,200	PERKINS	1,420	1,092	310	18	782 R	76.9%	21.8%	77.9%	22.1%
9,747	PHELPS	4,473	3,360	1,050	63	2,310 R	75.1%	23.5%	76.2%	23.8%
7,857	PIERCE	3,226	2,385	783	58	1,602 R	73.9%	24.3%	75.3%	24.7%
31,662	PLATTE	13,420	9,373	3,796	251	5,577 R	69.8%	28.3%	71.2%	28.8%
5,639	POLK	2,543	1,822	668	53	1,154 R	71.6%	26.3%	73.2%	26.8%
11,448	RED WILLOW	5,044	3,735	1,216	93	2,519 R	74.0%	24.1%	75.4%	24.6%
9,531	RICHARDSON	3,968	2,342	1,513	113	829 R	59.0%	38.1%	60.8%	39.2%
1,756	ROCK	801	640	139	22	501 R	79.9%	17.4%	82.2%	17.8%
13,843	SALINE	5,251	2,434	2,674	143	240 D	46.4%	50.9%	47.7%	52.3%
122,595	SARPY	68,022	38,816	28,010	1,196	10,806 R	57.1%	41.2%	58.1%	41.9%
19,830	SAUNDERS	10,212	6,188	3,767	257	2,421 R	60.6%	36.9%	62.2%	37.8%
36,951	SCOTTS BLUFF	14,730	9,708	4,745	277	4,963 R	65.9%	32.2%	67.2%	32.8%
16,496	SEWARD	7,529	4,647	2,703	179	1,944 R	61.7%	35.9%	63.2%	36.8%
6,198	SHERIDAN	2,462	1,941	454	67	1,487 R	78.8%	18.4%	81.0%	19.0%
3,318	SHERMAN	1,572	950	585	37	365 R	60.4%	37.2%	61.9%	38.1%
1,475	SIOUX	732	603	117	12	486 R	82.4%	16.0%	83.8%	16.3%
6,455	STANTON	2,495	1,781	664	50	1,117 R	71.4%	26.6%	72.8%	27.2%
6,055	THAYER	2,659	1,749	860	50	889 R	65.8%	32.3%	67.0%	33.0%
729	THOMAS	390	331	51	8	280 R	84.9%	13.1%	86.6%	13.4%
7,171	THURSTON	2,126	972	1,120	34	148 D	45.7%	52.7%	46.5%	53.5%
4,647	VALLEY	2,423	1,657	706	60	951 R	68.4%	29.1%	70.1%	29.9%
18,780	WASHINGTON	10,320	6,425	3,711	184	2,714 R	62.3%	36.0%	63.4%	36.6%
9,851	WAYNE	3,808	2,503	1,249	56	1,254 R	65.7%	32.8%	66.7%	33.3%
4,061	WEBSTER	1,817	1,233	552	32	681 R	67.9%	30.4%	69.1%	30.9%
886	WHEELER	440	334	96	10	238 R	75.9%	21.8%	77.7%	22.3%
14,598	YORK	6,568	4,848	1,607	113	3,241 R	73.8%	24.5%	75.1%	24.9%
1,711,263	TOTAL	801,281	452,979	333,319	14,983	119,660 R	56.5%	41.6%	57.6%	42.4%

NEBRASKA

SENATOR 2008

2000 Census Population	County	Total Vote	Republican	Democratic	Other	Rep.-Dem. Plurality		Total Vote		Major Vote	
								Rep.	Dem.	Rep.	Dem.
31,151	ADAMS	13,160	6,263	6,665	232	402	D	47.6%	50.6%	48.4%	51.6%
7,452	ANTELOPE	3,180	2,123	983	74	1,140	R	66.8%	30.9%	68.4%	31.6%
444	ARTHUR	250	182	61	7	121	R	72.8%	24.4%	74.9%	25.1%
819	BANNER	407	301	100	6	201	R	74.0%	24.6%	75.1%	24.9%
583	BLAINE	315	188	119	8	69	R	59.7%	37.8%	61.2%	38.8%
6,259	BOONE	2,838	1,706	1,085	47	621	R	60.1%	38.2%	61.1%	38.9%
12,158	BOX BUTTE	4,909	2,966	1,777	166	1,189	R	60.4%	36.2%	62.5%	37.5%
2,438	BOYD	1,079	641	409	29	232	R	59.4%	37.9%	61.0%	39.0%
3,525	BROWN	1,547	1,006	486	55	520	R	65.0%	31.4%	67.4%	32.6%
42,259	BUFFALO	19,198	11,876	7,000	322	4,876	R	61.9%	36.5%	62.9%	37.1%
7,791	BURT	3,338	2,023	1,234	81	789	R	60.6%	37.0%	62.1%	37.9%
8,767	BUTLER	3,837	2,336	1,448	53	888	R	60.9%	37.7%	61.7%	38.3%
24,334	CASS	11,942	7,412	4,210	320	3,202	R	62.1%	35.3%	63.8%	36.2%
9,615	CEDAR	4,109	2,907	1,082	120	1,825	R	70.7%	26.3%	72.9%	27.1%
4,068	CHASE	1,815	1,308	477	30	831	R	72.1%	26.3%	73.3%	26.7%
6,148	CHERRY	2,982	2,093	775	114	1,318	R	70.2%	26.0%	73.0%	27.0%
9,830	CHEYENNE	4,775	3,583	1,040	152	2,543	R	75.0%	21.8%	77.5%	22.5%
7,039	CLAY	3,036	1,770	1,210	56	560	R	58.3%	39.9%	59.4%	40.6%
10,441	COLFAX	3,206	2,057	1,070	79	987	R	64.2%	33.4%	65.8%	34.2%
10,203	CUMING	4,060	2,830	1,170	60	1,660	R	69.7%	28.8%	70.8%	29.3%
11,793	CUSTER	5,615	3,373	2,173	69	1,200	R	60.1%	38.7%	60.8%	39.2%
20,253	DAKOTA	6,292	3,543	2,491	258	1,052	R	56.3%	39.6%	58.7%	41.3%
9,060	DAWES	3,716	2,363	1,173	180	1,190	R	63.6%	31.6%	66.8%	33.2%
24,365	DAWSON	7,982	4,801	3,026	155	1,775	R	60.1%	37.9%	61.3%	38.7%
2,098	DEUEL	979	710	218	51	492	R	72.5%	22.3%	76.5%	23.5%
6,339	DIXON	2,770	1,877	811	82	1,066	R	67.8%	29.3%	69.8%	30.2%
36,160	DODGE	15,396	9,374	5,647	375	3,727	R	60.9%	36.7%	62.4%	37.6%
463,585	DOUGLAS	223,018	123,299	93,667	6,052	29,632	R	55.3%	42.0%	56.8%	43.2%
2,292	DUNDY	1,000	699	258	43	441	R	69.9%	25.8%	73.0%	27.0%
6,634	FILLMORE	2,963	1,610	1,315	38	295	R	54.3%	44.4%	55.0%	45.0%
3,574	FRANKLIN	1,546	734	789	23	55	D	47.5%	51.0%	48.2%	51.8%
3,099	FRONTIER	1,391	873	491	27	382	R	62.8%	35.3%	64.0%	36.0%
5,324	FURNAS	2,335	1,436	860	39	576	R	61.5%	36.8%	62.5%	37.5%
22,993	GAGE	10,172	4,909	5,079	184	170	D	48.3%	49.9%	49.1%	50.9%
2,292	GARDEN	1,112	831	248	33	583	R	74.7%	22.3%	77.0%	23.0%
1,902	GARFIELD	1,027	566	445	16	121	R	55.1%	43.3%	56.0%	44.0%
2,143	GOSPER	1,051	641	394	16	247	R	61.0%	37.5%	61.9%	38.1%
747	GRANT	360	257	91	12	166	R	71.4%	25.3%	73.9%	26.1%
2,714	GREELEY	1,206	522	666	18	144	D	43.3%	55.2%	43.9%	56.1%
53,534	HALL	21,187	11,398	9,419	370	1,979	R	53.8%	44.5%	54.8%	45.2%
9,403	HAMILTON	4,779	2,905	1,824	50	1,081	R	60.8%	38.2%	61.4%	38.6%
3,786	HARLAN	1,761	1,007	724	30	283	R	57.2%	41.1%	58.2%	41.8%
1,068	HAYES	551	353	182	16	171	R	64.1%	33.0%	66.0%	34.0%
3,111	HITCHCOCK	1,362	825	502	35	323	R	60.6%	36.9%	62.2%	37.8%
11,551	HOLT	4,950	3,271	1,570	109	1,701	R	66.1%	31.7%	67.6%	32.4%
783	HOOKER	431	293	130	8	163	R	68.0%	30.2%	69.3%	30.7%
6,567	HOWARD	2,997	1,523	1,419	55	104	R	50.8%	47.3%	51.8%	48.2%
8,333	JEFFERSON	3,698	1,935	1,694	69	241	R	52.3%	45.8%	53.3%	46.7%
4,488	JOHNSON	2,111	1,055	1,014	42	41	R	50.0%	48.0%	51.0%	49.0%
6,882	KEARNEY	3,149	1,888	1,218	43	670	R	60.0%	38.7%	60.8%	39.2%

NEBRASKA
SENATOR 2008

2000 Census Population	County	Total Vote	Republican	Democratic	Other	Rep.-Dem. Plurality	Percentage Total Vote Rep.	Dem.	Major Vote Rep.	Dem.
8,875	KEITH	3,942	2,763	1,085	94	1,678 R	70.1%	27.5%	71.8%	28.2%
983	KEYA PAHA	519	327	180	12	147 R	63.0%	34.7%	64.5%	35.5%
4,089	KIMBALL	1,771	1,243	463	65	780 R	70.2%	26.1%	72.9%	27.1%
9,374	KNOX	4,017	2,524	1,345	148	1,179 R	62.8%	33.5%	65.2%	34.8%
250,291	LANCASTER	126,314	60,805	62,421	3,088	1,616 D	48.1%	49.4%	49.3%	50.7%
34,632	LINCOLN	16,234	9,454	6,442	338	3,012 R	58.2%	39.7%	59.5%	40.5%
774	LOGAN	410	273	133	4	140 R	66.6%	32.4%	67.2%	32.8%
712	LOUP	392	218	172	2	46 R	55.6%	43.9%	55.9%	44.1%
533	MCPHERSON	289	201	77	11	124 R	69.6%	26.6%	72.3%	27.7%
35,226	MADISON	13,908	9,182	4,250	476	4,932 R	66.0%	30.6%	68.4%	31.6%
8,204	MERRICK	3,414	2,023	1,344	47	679 R	59.3%	39.4%	60.1%	39.9%
5,440	MORRILL	2,348	1,627	644	77	983 R	69.3%	27.4%	71.6%	28.4%
4,038	NANCE	1,721	953	743	25	210 R	55.4%	43.2%	56.2%	43.8%
7,576	NEMAHA	3,440	2,119	1,251	70	868 R	61.6%	36.4%	62.9%	37.1%
5,057	NUCKOLLS	2,227	1,231	959	37	272 R	55.3%	43.1%	56.2%	43.8%
15,396	OTOE	7,056	4,111	2,797	148	1,314 R	58.3%	39.6%	59.5%	40.5%
3,087	PAWNEE	1,374	765	578	31	187 R	55.7%	42.1%	57.0%	43.0%
3,200	PERKINS	1,408	993	392	23	601 R	70.5%	27.8%	71.7%	28.3%
9,747	PHELPS	4,494	3,058	1,392	44	1,666 R	68.0%	31.0%	68.7%	31.3%
7,857	PIERCE	3,182	2,259	825	98	1,434 R	71.0%	25.9%	73.2%	26.8%
31,662	PLATTE	13,326	9,166	3,917	243	5,249 R	68.8%	29.4%	70.1%	29.9%
5,639	POLK	2,539	1,579	932	28	647 R	62.2%	36.7%	62.9%	37.1%
11,448	RED WILLOW	5,028	3,269	1,658	101	1,611 R	65.0%	33.0%	66.3%	33.7%
9,531	RICHARDSON	3,916	2,477	1,332	107	1,145 R	63.3%	34.0%	65.0%	35.0%
1,756	ROCK	785	465	307	13	158 R	59.2%	39.1%	60.2%	39.8%
13,843	SALINE	5,241	2,139	3,011	91	872 D	40.8%	57.5%	41.5%	58.5%
122,595	SARPY	66,731	43,116	21,994	1,621	21,122 R	64.6%	33.0%	66.2%	33.8%
19,830	SAUNDERS	10,168	6,266	3,660	242	2,606 R	61.6%	36.0%	63.1%	36.9%
36,951	SCOTTS BLUFF	14,700	9,262	5,117	321	4,145 R	63.0%	34.8%	64.4%	35.6%
16,496	SEWARD	7,520	4,257	3,137	126	1,120 R	56.6%	41.7%	57.6%	42.4%
6,198	SHERIDAN	2,440	1,821	477	142	1,344 R	74.6%	19.5%	79.2%	20.8%
3,318	SHERMAN	1,552	582	943	27	361 D	37.5%	60.8%	38.2%	61.8%
1,475	SIOUX	712	517	180	15	337 R	72.6%	25.3%	74.2%	25.8%
6,455	STANTON	2,464	1,762	632	70	1,130 R	71.5%	25.6%	73.6%	26.4%
6,055	THAYER	2,482	1,303	1,140	39	163 R	52.5%	45.9%	53.3%	46.7%
729	THOMAS	386	238	138	10	100 R	61.7%	35.8%	63.3%	36.7%
7,171	THURSTON	1,981	1,041	818	122	223 R	52.5%	41.3%	56.0%	44.0%
4,647	VALLEY	2,424	1,343	1,043	38	300 R	55.4%	43.0%	56.3%	43.7%
18,780	WASHINGTON	10,170	6,658	3,230	282	3,428 R	65.5%	31.8%	67.3%	32.7%
9,851	WAYNE	3,785	2,626	1,062	97	1,564 R	69.4%	28.1%	71.2%	28.8%
4,061	WEBSTER	1,823	849	939	35	90 D	46.6%	51.5%	47.5%	52.5%
886	WHEELER	429	247	174	8	73 R	57.6%	40.6%	58.7%	41.3%
14,598	YORK	6,559	4,300	2,183	76	2,117 R	65.6%	33.3%	66.3%	33.7%
1,711,263	TOTAL	792,511	455,854	317,456	19,201	138,398 R	57.5%	40.1%	58.9%	41.1%

NEBRASKA

HOUSE OF REPRESENTATIVES

CD	Year	Total Vote	Republican Vote	Republican Candidate	Democratic Vote	Democratic Candidate	Other Vote	Rep.-Dem. Plurality	Total Vote Rep.	Total Vote Dem.	Major Vote Rep.	Major Vote Dem.
1	2008	262,820	184,923	FORTENBERRY, JEFF*	77,897	YASHIRIN, MAX		107,026 R	70.4%	29.6%	70.4%	29.6%
1	2006	207,375	121,015	FORTENBERRY, JEFF*	86,360	MOUL, MAXINE B.		34,655 R	58.4%	41.6%	58.4%	41.6%
1	2004	265,072	143,756	FORTENBERRY, JEFF	113,971	CONNEALY, MATT	7,345	29,785 R	54.2%	43.0%	55.8%	44.2%
1	2002	155,844	133,013	BEREUTER, DOUG*	—		22,831	133,013 R	85.4%		100.0%	
2	2008	274,374	142,473	TERRY, LEE*	131,901	ESCH, JIM		10,572 R	51.9%	48.1%	51.9%	48.1%
2	2006	181,979	99,475	TERRY, LEE*	82,504	ESCH, JIM		16,971 R	54.7%	45.3%	54.7%	45.3%
2	2004	249,764	152,608	TERRY, LEE*	90,292	THOMPSON, NANCY	6,864	62,316 R	61.1%	36.2%	62.8%	37.2%
2	2002	142,014	89,917	TERRY, LEE*	46,843	SIMON, JIM	5,254	43,074 R	63.3%	33.0%	65.7%	34.3%
3	2008	238,204	183,117	SMITH, ADRIAN*	55,087	STODDARD, JAY C.		128,030 R	76.9%	23.1%	76.9%	23.1%
3	2006	206,733	113,687	SMITH, ADRIAN	93,046	KLEEB, SCOTT		20,641 R	55.0%	45.0%	55.0%	45.0%
3	2004	250,136	218,751	OSBORNE, TOM*	26,434	ANDERSON, DONNA J.	4,951	192,317 R	87.5%	10.6%	89.2%	10.8%
3	2002	175,956	163,939	OSBORNE, TOM*	—		12,017	163,939 R	93.2%		100.0%	
TOTAL	2008	775,398	510,513		264,885			245,628 R	65.8%	34.2%	65.8%	34.2%
TOTAL	2006	596,087	334,177		261,910			72,267 R	56.1%	43.9%	56.1%	43.9%
TOTAL	2004	764,972	515,115		230,697		19,160	284,418 R	67.3%	30.2%	69.1%	30.9%
TOTAL	2002	473,814	386,869		46,843		40,102	340,026 R	81.6%	9.9%	89.2%	10.8%

Note: An asterisk (*) denotes incumbent.

NEBRASKA

GENERAL AND PRIMARY ELECTIONS

2008 GENERAL ELECTIONS

President   Other vote was 5,406 By Petition (Ralph Nader); 2,972 Nebraska (Chuck Baldwin); 2,740 Libertarian (Bob Barr); 1,028 Green (Cynthia A. McKinney); 2,837 write-in.

Senator   Other vote was 11,438 Nebraska (Kelly Renee Rosberg); 7,763 Green (Steven R. Larrick).

House   Other vote was:

CD 1
CD 2
CD 3

2008 PRIMARY ELECTIONS

Primary	May 13, 2008	**Registration** (as of May 13, 2008)		
			Republican	550,582
			Democratic	372,866
			Nebraska	8,814
			Green	795
			Nonpartisan	184,438
			TOTAL	1,117,495

Primary Type   Semi-open—Registered Democrats and Republicans could vote only in their party's primary. Voters registered as nonpartisan could participate in either party's primary for the Senate and House (but not for president).

NEBRASKA

GENERAL AND PRIMARY ELECTIONS

	REPUBLICAN PRIMARIES			DEMOCRATIC PRIMARIES		
President	John McCain	118,876	87.0%	Barack Obama	46,670	49.4%
	Ron Paul	17,772	13.0%	Hillary Clinton	43,979	46.5%
				Mike Gravel	3,886	4.1%
	TOTAL	136,648		TOTAL	94,535	
Senator	Mike Johanns	112,191	78.0%	Scott Kleeb	65,582	68.6%
	Pat Flynn	31,560	22.0%	Tony Raimondo	24,141	25.2%
				James Bryan Wilson	3,224	3.4%
				Larry Marvin	2,672	2.8%
	TOTAL	143,751		TOTAL	95,619	
Congressional District 1	Jeff Fortenberry*	46,620	100.0%	Max Yashirin	27,118	100.0%
Congressional District 2	Lee Terry*	23,146	84.4%	Jim Esch	21,197	80.5%
	Steven Laird	4,288	15.6%	Richard N. Carter	5,131	19.5%
	TOTAL	27,434		TOTAL	26,328	
Congressional District 3	Adrian Smith*	55,225	87.4%	Jay C. Stoddard	17,759	74.3%
	Jeremiah Ellison	7,947	12.6%	Paul A. Spatz	6,142	25.7%
	TOTAL	63,172		TOTAL	23,901	

Note: An asterisk (*) denotes incumbent. Ballots cast by nonpartisan voters in primaries for the House and Senate were tallied separately but were combined into an overall total for each candidate, which is listed above.

NEVADA

Congressional districts first established for elections held in 2002
3 members

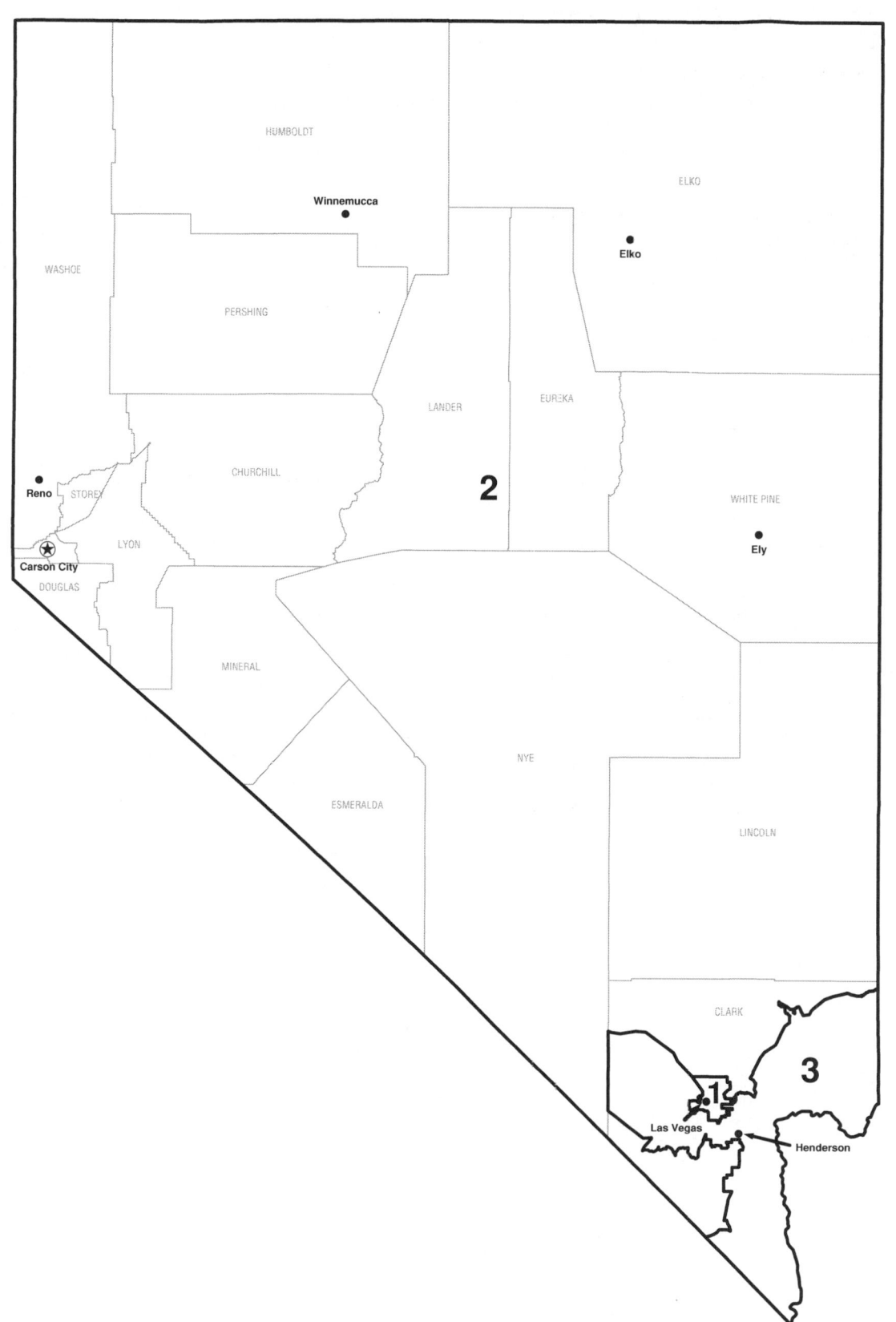

NEVADA

GOVERNOR
Jim Gibbons (R). Elected 2006 to a four-year term.

SENATORS (1 Democrat, 1 Republican)
John Ensign (R). Reelected 2006 to a six-year term. Previously elected 2000.

Harry Reid (D). Reelected 2004 to a six-year term. Previously elected 1998, 1992, 1986.

REPRESENTATIVES (2 Democrats, 1 Republican)
1. Shelley Berkley (D)
2. Dean Heller (R)
3. Dina Titus (D)

POSTWAR VOTE FOR PRESIDENT

Year	Total Vote	Republican Vote	Republican Candidate	Democratic Vote	Democratic Candidate	Other Vote	Plurality		Total Vote Rep.	Total Vote Dem.	Major Vote Rep.	Major Vote Dem.
2008	967,848	412,827	McCain, John	533,736	Obama, Barack	21,285	120,909	D	42.7%	55.1%	43.6%	56.4%
2004	829,587	418,690	Bush, George W.	397,190	Kerry, John	13,707	21,500	R	50.5%	47.9%	51.3%	48.7%
2000**	608,970	301,575	Bush, George W.	279,978	Gore, Al	27,417	21,597	R	49.5%	46.0%	51.9%	48.1%
1996**	464,279	199,244	Dole, Bob	203,974	Clinton, Bill	61,061	4,730	D	42.9%	43.9%	49.4%	50.6%
1992**	506,318	175,828	Bush, George	189,148	Clinton, Bill	141,342	13,320	D	34.7%	37.4%	48.2%	51.8%
1988	350,067	206,040	Bush, George	132,738	Dukakis, Michael S.	11,289	73,302	R	58.9%	37.9%	60.8%	39.2%
1984	286,667	188,770	Reagan, Ronald	91,655	Mondale, Walter F.	6,242	97,115	R	65.8%	32.0%	67.3%	32.7%
1980**	247,885	155,017	Reagan, Ronald	66,666	Carter, Jimmy	26,202	88,351	R	62.5%	26.9%	69.9%	30.1%
1976	201,876	101,273	Ford, Gerald R.	92,479	Carter, Jimmy	8,124	8,794	R	50.2%	45.8%	52.3%	47.7%
1972	181,766	115,750	Nixon, Richard M.	66,016	McGovern, George S.		49,734	R	63.7%	36.3%	63.7%	36.3%
1968**	154,218	73,188	Nixon, Richard M.	60,598	Humphrey, Hubert H.	20,432	12,590	R	47.5%	39.3%	54.7%	45.3%
1964	135,433	56,094	Goldwater, Barry M.	79,339	Johnson, Lyndon B.		23,245	D	41.4%	58.6%	41.4%	58.6%
1960	107,267	52,387	Nixon, Richard M.	54,880	Kennedy, John F.		2,493	D	48.8%	51.2%	48.8%	51.2%
1956	96,689	56,049	Eisenhower, Dwight D.	40,640	Stevenson, Adlai E.		15,409	R	58.0%	42.0%	58.0%	42.0%
1952	82,190	50,502	Eisenhower, Dwight D.	31,688	Stevenson, Adlai E.		18,814	R	61.4%	38.6%	61.4%	38.6%
1948	62,117	29,357	Dewey, Thomas E.	31,291	Truman, Harry S.	1,469	1,934	D	47.3%	50.4%	48.4%	51.6%

**In past elections, the other vote included: 2000 - 15,008 Green (Ralph Nader); 1996 - 43,986 Reform (Ross Perot); 1992 - 132,580 Independent (Perot); 1980 - 17,651 Independent (John Anderson); 1968 - 20,432 American Independent (George Wallace).

NEVADA

POSTWAR VOTE FOR GOVERNOR

Year	Total Vote	Republican Vote	Republican Candidate	Democratic Vote	Democratic Candidate	Other Vote	Rep.-Dem. Plurality	Percentage Total Vote Rep.	Dem.	Major Vote Rep.	Dem.
2006	582,158	279,003	Gibbons, Jim	255,684	Titus, Dina	47,471	23,319 R	47.9%	43.9%	52.2%	47.8%
2002	504,079	344,001	Guinn, Kenny	110,935	Neal, Joe	49,143	233,066 R	68.2%	22.0%	75.6%	24.4%
1998	433,630	223,892	Guinn, Kenny	182,281	Jones, Jan Laverty	27,457	41,611 R	51.6%	42.0%	55.1%	44.9%
1994	379,676	156,875	Gibbons, Jim	200,026	Miller, Robert J.	22,775	43,151 D	41.3%	52.7%	44.0%	56.0%
1990	320,743	95,789	Gallaway, Jim	207,878	Miller, Robert J.	17,076	112,089 D	29.9%	64.8%	31.5%	68.5%
1986	260,375	65,081	Cafferata, Patty	187,268	Bryan, Richard H.	8,026	122,187 D	25.0%	71.9%	25.8%	74.2%
1982	239,751	100,104	List, Robert F.	128,132	Bryan, Richard H.	11,515	28,028 D	41.8%	53.4%	43.9%	56.1%
1978	192,445	108,097	List, Robert F.	76,361	Rose, Robert E.	7,937	31,736 R	56.2%	39.7%	58.6%	41.4%
1974**	169,358	28,959	Crumpler, Shirley	114,114	O'Callaghan, Mike	26,235	85,155 D	17.1%	67.4%	20.2%	79.8%
1970	146,991	64,400	Fike, Ed	70,697	O'Callaghan, Mike	11,894	6,297 D	43.8%	48.1%	47.7%	52.3%
1966	137,677	71,807	Laxalt, Paul	65,870	Sawyer, Grant		5,937 R	52.2%	47.8%	52.2%	47.8%
1962	96,929	32,145	Gragson, Oran K.	64,784	Sawyer, Grant		32,639 D	33.2%	66.8%	33.2%	66.8%
1958	84,889	34,025	Russell, Charles H.	50,864	Sawyer, Grant		16,839 D	40.1%	59.9%	40.1%	59.9%
1954	78,462	41,665	Russell, Charles H.	36,797	Pittman, Vail		4,868 R	53.1%	46.9%	53.1%	46.9%
1950	61,773	35,609	Russell, Charles H.	26,164	Pittman, Vail		9,445 R	57.6%	42.4%	57.6%	42.4%
1946	49,902	21,247	Jepson, Melvin E.	28,655	Pittman, Vail		7,408 D	42.6%	57.4%	42.6%	57.4%

**In past elections, the other vote included: 1974 - 26,285 Independent American (James Ray Houston).

POSTWAR VOTE FOR SENATOR

Year	Total Vote	Republican Vote	Republican Candidate	Democratic Vote	Democratic Candidate	Other Vote	Rep.-Dem. Plurality	Percentage Total Vote Rep.	Dem.	Major Vote Rep.	Dem.
2006	582,572	322,501	Ensign, John	238,796	Carter, Jack	21,275	83,705 R	55.4%	41.0%	57.5%	42.5%
2004	810,068	284,640	Ziser, Richard	494,805	Reid, Harry	30,623	210,165 D	35.1%	61.1%	36.5%	63.5%
2000	600,250	330,687	Ensign, John	238,260	Bernstein, Ed	31,303	92,427 R	55.1%	39.7%	58.1%	41.9%
1998	435,790	208,222	Ensign, John	208,650	Reid, Harry	18,918	428 D	47.8%	47.9%	49.9%	50.1%
1994	380,530	156,020	Furman, Hal	193,804	Bryan, Richard H.	30,706	37,784 D	41.0%	50.9%	44.6%	55.4%
1992	495,887	199,413	Dahl, Demar	253,150	Reid, Harry	43,324	53,737 D	40.2%	51.0%	44.1%	55.9%
1988	349,649	161,336	Hecht, Chic	175,548	Bryan, Richard H.	12,765	14,212 D	46.1%	50.2%	47.9%	52.1%
1986	261,932	116,606	Santini, James	130,955	Reid, Harry	14,371	14,349 D	44.5%	50.0%	47.1%	52.9%
1982	240,394	120,377	Hecht, Chic	114,720	Cannon, Howard W.	5,297	5,657 R	50.1%	47.7%	51.2%	48.8%
1980	246,436	144,224	Laxalt, Paul	92,129	Gojack, Mary	10,083	52,095 R	58.5%	37.4%	61.0%	39.0%
1976	201,980	63,471	Towell, David	127,295	Cannon, Howard W.	11,214	63,824 D	31.4%	63.0%	33.3%	66.7%
1974	169,473	79,605	Laxalt, Paul	78,981	Reid, Harry	10,887	624 R	47.0%	46.6%	50.2%	49.8%
1970	147,768	60,838	Raggio, William J.	85,187	Cannon, Howard W.	1,743	24,349 D	41.2%	57.6%	41.7%	58.3%
1968	152,690	69,068	Fike, Ed	83,622	Bible, Alan		14,554 D	45.2%	54.8%	45.2%	54.8%
1964	134,624	67,288	Laxalt, Paul	67,336	Cannon, Howard W.		48 D	50.0%	50.0%	50.0%	50.0%
1962	97,192	33,749	Wright, William B.	63,443	Bible, Alan		29,694 D	34.7%	65.3%	34.7%	65.3%
1958	84,492	35,760	Malone, George W.	48,732	Cannon, Howard W.		12,972 D	42.3%	57.7%	42.3%	57.7%
1956	96,389	45,712	Young, Clifton	50,677	Bible, Alan		4,965 D	47.4%	52.6%	47.4%	52.6%
1954S	77,513	32,470	Brown, Ernest S.	45,043	Bible, Alan		12,573 D	41.9%	58.1%	41.9%	58.1%
1952	81,090	41,906	Malone, George W.	39,184	Mechling, Thomas B.		2,722 R	51.7%	48.3%	51.7%	48.3%
1950	61,762	25,933	Marshall, George E.	35,829	McCarran, Pat		9,896 D	42.0%	58.0%	42.0%	58.0%
1946	50,354	27,801	Malone, George W.	22,553	Bunker, Berkeley		5,248 R	55.2%	44.8%	55.2%	44.8%

Note: The 1954 election was for a short term to fill a vacancy.

NEVADA

PRESIDENT 2008

| 2000 Census Population | County | Total Vote | Republican | Democratic | Other | Rep.-Dem. Plurality | Percentage | | | |
| | | | | | | | Total Vote | | Major Vote | |
							Rep.	Dem.	Rep.	Dem.
52,457	CARSON CITY	23,680	11,419	11,623	638	204 D	48.2%	49.1%	49.6%	50.4%
23,982	CHURCHILL	10,605	6,832	3,494	279	3,338 R	64.4%	32.9%	66.2%	33.8%
1,375,765	CLARK	651,172	257,078	380,765	13,329	123,687 D	39.5%	58.5%	40.3%	59.7%
41,259	DOUGLAS	25,904	14,648	10,672	584	3,976 R	56.5%	41.2%	57.9%	42.1%
45,291	ELKO	16,019	10,969	4,541	509	6,428 R	68.5%	28.3%	70.7%	29.3%
971	ESMERALDA	439	303	104	32	199 R	69.0%	23.7%	74.4%	25.6%
1,651	EUREKA	745	564	144	37	420 R	75.7%	19.3%	79.7%	20.3%
16,106	HUMBOLDT	5,664	3,586	1,909	169	1,677 R	63.3%	33.7%	65.3%	34.7%
5,794	LANDER	2,102	1,466	577	59	889 R	69.7%	27.5%	71.8%	28.2%
4,165	LINCOLN	2,107	1,498	518	91	980 R	71.1%	24.6%	74.3%	25.7%
34,501	LYON	21,103	12,154	8,405	544	3,749 R	57.6%	39.8%	59.1%	40.9%
5,071	MINERAL	2,307	1,131	1,082	94	49 R	49.0%	46.9%	51.1%	48.9%
32,485	NYE	17,491	9,537	7,226	728	2,311 R	54.5%	41.3%	56.9%	43.1%
6,693	PERSHING	1,836	1,075	673	88	402 R	58.6%	36.7%	61.5%	38.5%
3,399	STOREY	2,418	1,247	1,102	69	145 R	51.6%	45.6%	53.1%	46.9%
339,486	WASHOE	180,414	76,880	99,671	3,863	22,791 D	42.6%	55.2%	43.5%	56.5%
9,181	WHITE PINE	3,842	2,440	1,230	172	1,210 R	63.5%	32.0%	66.5%	33.5%
1,998,257	TOTAL	967,848	412,827	533,736	21,285	120,909 D	42.7%	55.1%	43.6%	56.4%

NEVADA

HOUSE OF REPRESENTATIVES

| CD | Year | Total Vote | Republican Vote | Republican Candidate | Democratic Vote | Democratic Candidate | Other Vote | Rep.-Dem. Plurality | Percentage | | | |
| | | | | | | | | | Total Vote | | Major Vote | |
									Rep.	Dem.	Rep.	Dem.
1	2008	228,922	64,837	WEGNER, KENNETH	154,860	BERKLEY, SHELLEY*	9,225	90,023 D	28.3%	67.6%	29.5%	70.5%
1	2006	131,124	40,917	WEGNER, KENNETH	85,025	BERKLEY, SHELLEY*	5,182	44,108 D	31.2%	64.8%	32.5%	67.5%
1	2004	202,436	63,005	MICKELSON, RUSS	133,569	BERKLEY, SHELLEY*	5,862	70,564 D	31.1%	66.0%	32.1%	67.9%
1	2002	119,714	51,148	BOGGS-McDONALD, LYNETTE MARIA	64,312	BERKLEY, SHELLEY*	4,254	13,164 D	42.7%	53.7%	44.3%	55.7%
2	2008	329,520	170,771	HELLER, DEAN*	136,548	DERBY, JILL	22,201	34,223 R	51.8%	41.4%	55.6%	44.4%
2	2006	232,724	117,168	HELLER, DEAN	104,593	DERBY, JILL	10,963	12,575 R	50.3%	44.9%	52.8%	47.2%
2	2004	291,079	195,466	GIBBONS, JIM*	79,978	COCHRAN, ANGIE G.	15,635	115,488 R	67.2%	27.5%	71.0%	29.0%
2	2002	201,200	149,574	GIBBONS, JIM*	40,189	SOUZA, TRAVIS O.	11,437	109,385 R	74.3%	20.0%	78.8%	21.2%
3	2008	349,812	147,940	PORTER, JON*	165,912	TITUS, Dina	35,960	17,972 D	42.3%	47.4%	47.1%	52.9%
3	2006	210,979	102,232	PORTER, JON*	98,261	HAFEN, TESSA M.	10,486	3,971 R	48.5%	46.6%	51.0%	49.0%
3	2004	297,918	162,240	PORTER, JON*	120,365	GALLAGHER, TOM	15,313	41,875 R	54.5%	40.4%	57.4%	42.6%
3	2002	178,994	100,378	PORTER, JON	66,659	HERRERA, DARIO	11,957	33,719 R	56.1%	37.2%	60.1%	39.9%
TOTAL	2008	908,254	383,548		457,320		67,386	73,772 D	42.2%	50.4%	45.6%	54.4%
TOTAL	2006	574,827	260,317		287,879		26,631	27,562 D	45.3%	50.1%	47.5%	52.5%
TOTAL	2004	791,433	420,711		333,912		36,810	86,799 R	53.2%	42.2%	55.8%	44.2%
TOTAL	2002	499,908	301,100		171,160		27,648	129,940 R	60.2%	34.2%	63.8%	36.2%

Note: An asterisk (*) denotes incumbent.

NEVADA

GENERAL AND PRIMARY ELECTIONS

2008 GENERAL ELECTIONS

President	Other vote was 6,267 "None of these candidates"; 6,150 Independent (Ralph Nader); 4,263 Libertarian (Bob Barr); 3,194 Independent American (Chuck Baldwin); 1,411 Green (Cynthia A. McKinney).
House	Other vote was:

CD 1	4,697 Independent American (Caren Alexander); 4,528 Libertarian (Raymond James Duensing Jr.).
CD 2	11,179 Independent (John Everhart); 5,740 Libertarian (Sean Patrick Morse); 5,282 Green (Craig Bergland).
CD 3	14,922 Independent (Jeffrey C. Reeves); 10,164 Libertarian (Joseph P. Silvestri); 6,937 Independent American (Floyd Fitzgibbons); 3,937 Green (Bob Giaquinta).

2008 PRIMARY ELECTIONS

Primary	August 12, 2008	Registration (as of July 31, 2008—includes 274,895 inactive registrants)		
			Democratic	564,885
			Republican	489,396
			Independent American	53,542
			Libertarian	7,991
			Green	4,189
			Natural Law	390
			Other	5,016
			Nonpartisan	199,724
			TOTAL	1,325,133

Primary Type	Closed—Only registered Democrats and Republicans could vote in their party's primary.

	REPUBLICAN PRIMARIES			DEMOCRATIC PRIMARIES		
Congressional District 1	Kenneth Wegner	4,359	34.7%	Shelley Berkley*	19,444	89.7%
	Russ Mickelson	2,490	19.8%	Mark John Budetich Jr.	2,222	10.3%
	Chris Dyer	1,847	14.7%			
	Eve "No. 1 Mom" Ellingwood	1,137	9.0%			
	Ray J. Kornfeld	1,090	8.7%			
	Mike Powers	896	7.1%			
	Edward "Mr. Clean" Hamilton	761	6.0%			
	TOTAL	12,580		TOTAL	21,666	
Congressional District 2	Dean Heller*	43,112	86.0%	Jill Derby	Unopposed	
	James W. Smack	7,009	14.0%			
	TOTAL	50,121				
Congressional District 3	Jon Porter*	21,955	81.6%	Dina Titus	22,232	84.7%
	Jesse Law	3,030	11.3%	Barry Michaels	2,312	8.8%
	Carl Bunce	1,911	7.1%	Anna Nevenic	1,114	4.2%
				Carlo "Tex" Poliak	587	2.2%
	TOTAL	26,896		TOTAL	26,245	

Note: An asterisk (*) denotes incumbent. The names of unopposed candidates did not appear on the primary ballot; therefore, no votes were cast for these candidates.

NEW HAMPSHIRE

Congressional districts first established for elections held in 2002
2 members

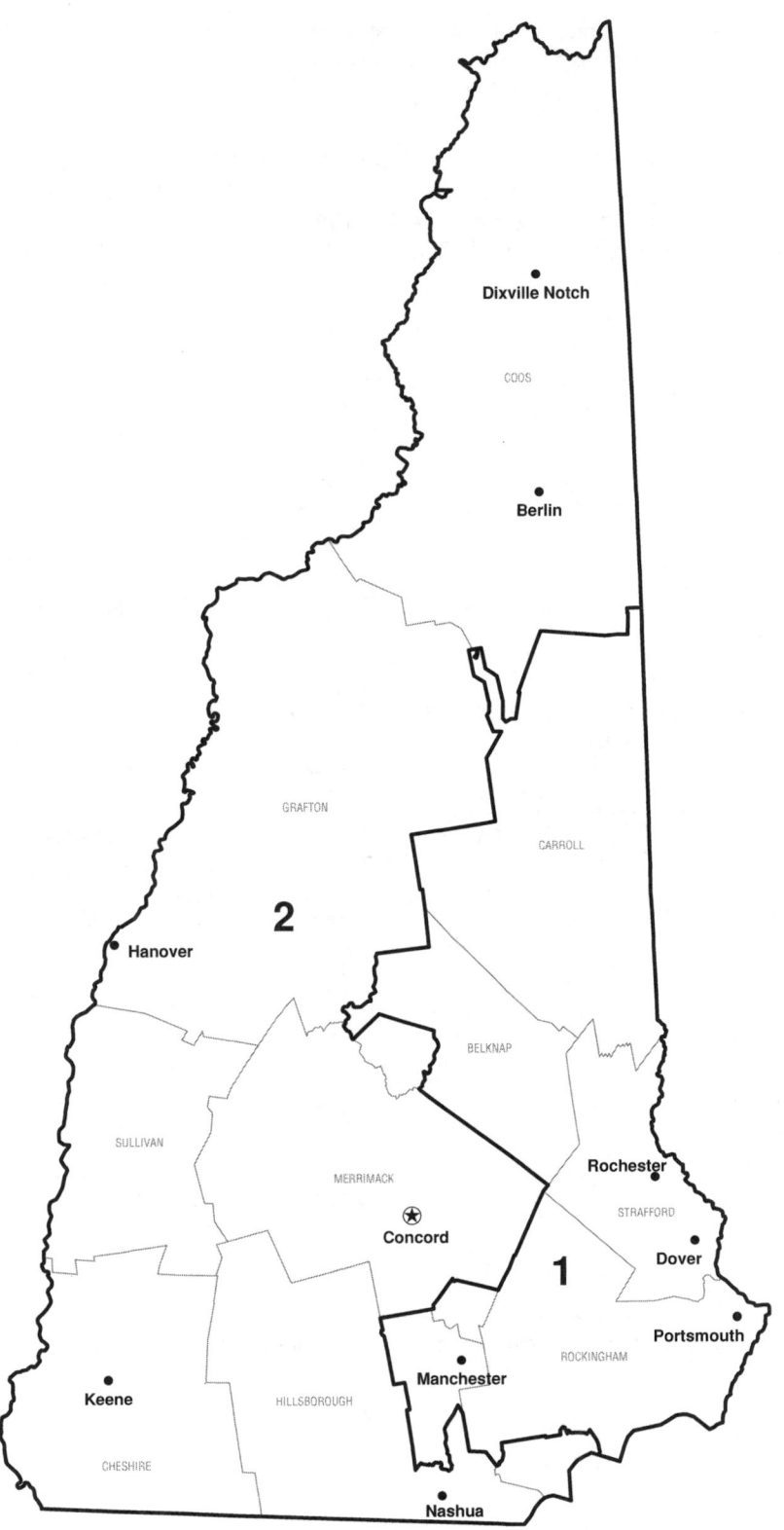

NEW HAMPSHIRE

GOVERNOR
John Lynch (D). Reelected 2008 to a two-year term. Previously elected 2006, 2004.

SENATORS (2 Republicans)
Judd Gregg (R). Reelected 2004 to a six-year term. Previously elected 1998, 1992.

Jeanne Shaheen (D). Elected 2008 to a six-year term.

REPRESENTATIVES (2 Democrats)
1. Carol Shea-Porter (D)   2. Paul W. Hodes (D)

POSTWAR VOTE FOR PRESIDENT

| | | Republican | | Democratic | | | | Percentage | | | |
| | | | | | | | | Total Vote | | Major Vote | |
Year	Total Vote	Vote	Candidate	Vote	Candidate	Other Vote	Plurality	Rep.	Dem.	Rep.	Dem.
2008	710,970	316,534	McCain, John	384,826	Obama, Barack	9,610	68,292 D	44.5%	54.1%	45.1%	54.9%
2004	677,738	331,237	Bush, George W.	340,511	Kerry, John	5,990	9,274 D	48.9%	50.2%	49.3%	50.7%
2000**	569,081	273,559	Bush, George W.	266,348	Gore, Al	29,174	7,211 R	48.1%	46.8%	50.7%	49.3%
1996**	499,175	196,532	Dole, Bob	246,214	Clinton, Bill	56,429	49,682 D	39.4%	49.3%	44.4%	55.6%
1992**	537,943	202,484	Bush, George	209,040	Clinton, Bill	126,419	6,556 D	37.6%	38.9%	49.2%	50.8%
1988	451,074	281,537	Bush, George	163,696	Dukakis, Michael S.	5,841	117,841 R	62.4%	36.3%	63.2%	36.8%
1984	389,066	267,051	Reagan, Ronald	120,395	Mondale, Walter F.	1,620	146,656 R	68.6%	30.9%	68.9%	31.1%
1980**	383,990	221,705	Reagan, Ronald	108,864	Carter, Jimmy	53,421	112,841 R	57.7%	28.4%	67.1%	32.9%
1976	339,618	185,935	Ford, Gerald R.	147,635	Carter, Jimmy	6,048	38,300 R	54.7%	43.5%	55.7%	44.3%
1972	334,055	213,724	Nixon, Richard M.	116,435	McGovern, George S.	3,896	97,289 R	64.0%	34.9%	64.7%	35.3%
1968**	297,298	154,903	Nixon, Richard M.	130,589	Humphrey, Hubert H.	11,806	24,314 R	52.1%	43.9%	54.3%	45.7%
1964	288,093	104,029	Goldwater, Barry M.	184,064	Johnson, Lyndon B.		80,035 D	36.1%	63.9%	36.1%	63.9%
1960	295,761	157,989	Nixon, Richard M.	137,772	Kennedy, John F.		20,217 R	53.4%	46.6%	53.4%	46.6%
1956	266,994	176,519	Eisenhower, Dwight D.	90,364	Stevenson, Adlai E.	111	86,155 R	66.1%	33.8%	66.1%	33.9%
1952	272,950	166,287	Eisenhower, Dwight D.	106,663	Stevenson, Adlai E.		59,624 R	60.9%	39.1%	60.9%	39.1%
1948	231,440	121,299	Dewey, Thomas E.	107,995	Truman, Harry S.	2,146	13,304 R	52.4%	46.7%	52.9%	47.1%

**In past elections, the other vote included: 2000 - 22,198 Green (Ralph Nader); 1996 - 48,390 Reform (Ross Perot); 1992 - 121,337 Independent (Perot); 1980 - 49,693 Independent (John Anderson); 1968 - 11,173 American Independent (George Wallace).

NEW HAMPSHIRE

POSTWAR VOTE FOR GOVERNOR

Year	Total Vote	Republican Vote	Republican Candidate	Democratic Vote	Democratic Candidate	Other Vote	Rep.-Dem. Plurality	Total Vote Rep.	Total Vote Dem.	Major Vote Rep.	Major Vote Dem.
2008	682,910	188,555	Kenney, Joseph D.	479,042	Lynch, John	15,313	290,487 D	27.6%	70.1%	28.2%	71.8%
2006	403,679	104,288	Coburn, Jim	298,760	Lynch, John	631	194,472 D	25.8%	74.0%	25.9%	74.1%
2004	667,020	325,981	Benson, Craig	340,299	Lynch, John	740	14,318 D	48.9%	51.0%	48.9%	51.1%
2002	442,976	259,663	Benson, Craig	169,277	Fernald, Mark	14,036	90,386 R	58.6%	38.2%	60.5%	39.5%
2000	564,953	246,952	Humphrey, Gordon J.	275,038	Shaheen, Jeanne	42,963	28,086 D	43.7%	48.7%	47.3%	52.7%
1998	318,940	98,473	Lucas, Jay	210,769	Shaheen, Jeanne	9,698	112,296 D	30.9%	66.1%	31.8%	68.2%
1996	497,040	196,321	Lamontagne, Ovide	284,175	Shaheen, Jeanne	16,544	87,854 D	39.5%	57.2%	40.9%	59.1%
1994	311,882	218,134	Merrill, Steve	79,686	King, Wayne D.	14,062	138,448 R	69.9%	25.6%	73.2%	26.8%
1992	516,170	289,170	Merrill, Steve	206,232	Arnesen, Deborah A.	20,768	82,938 R	56.0%	40.0%	58.4%	41.6%
1990	295,018	177,773	Gregg, Judd	101,923	Grandmaison, J. Joseph	15,322	75,850 R	60.3%	34.5%	63.6%	36.4%
1988	441,923	267,064	Gregg, Judd	172,543	McEachern, Paul	2,316	94,521 R	60.4%	39.0%	60.8%	39.2%
1986	251,107	134,824	Sununu, John H.	116,142	McEachern, Paul	141	18,682 R	53.7%	46.3%	53.7%	46.3%
1984	383,910	256,574	Sununu, John H.	127,156	Spirou, Chris	180	129,418 R	66.8%	33.1%	66.9%	33.1%
1982	282,588	145,389	Sununu, John H.	132,317	Gallen, Hugh J.	4,882	13,072 R	51.4%	46.8%	52.4%	47.6%
1980	384,031	156,178	Thomson, Meldrim	226,436	Gallen, Hugh J.	1,417	70,258 D	40.7%	59.0%	40.8%	59.2%
1978	269,587	122,464	Thomson, Meldrim	133,133	Gallen, Hugh J.	13,990	10,669 D	45.4%	49.4%	47.9%	52.1%
1976	342,669	197,589	Thomson, Meldrim	145,015	Spanos, Harry V.	65	52,574 R	57.7%	42.3%	57.7%	42.3%
1974	226,665	115,933	Thomson, Meldrim	110,591	Leonard, Richard W.	141	5,342 R	51.1%	48.8%	51.2%	48.8%
1972**	323,102	133,702	Thomson, Meldrim	126,107	Crowley, Roger J.	63,293	7,595 R	41.4%	39.0%	51.5%	48.5%
1970	222,441	102,298	Peterson, Walter R.	98,098	Crowley, Roger J.	22,045	4,200 R	46.0%	44.1%	51.0%	49.0%
1968	285,342	149,902	Peterson, Walter R.	135,378	Bussiere, Emile R.	62	14,524 R	52.5%	47.4%	52.5%	47.5%
1966	233,642	107,259	Gregg, Hugh	125,882	King, John W.	501	18,623 D	45.9%	53.9%	46.0%	54.0%
1964	285,863	94,824	Pillsbury, John	190,863	King, John W.	176	96,039 D	33.2%	66.8%	33.2%	66.8%
1962	230,048	94,567	Pillsbury, John	135,481	King, John W.		40,914 D	41.1%	58.9%	41.1%	58.9%
1960	290,527	161,123	Powell, Wesley	129,404	Boutin, Bernard L.		31,719 R	55.5%	44.5%	55.5%	44.5%
1958	206,745	106,790	Powell, Wesley	99,955	Boutin, Bernard L.		6,835 R	51.7%	48.3%	51.7%	48.3%
1956	258,695	141,578	Dwinell, Lane	117,117	Shaw, John		24,461 R	54.7%	45.3%	54.7%	45.3%
1954	194,631	107,287	Dwinell, Lane	87,344	Shaw, John		19,943 R	55.1%	44.9%	55.1%	44.9%
1952	265,715	167,791	Gregg, Hugh	97,924	Craig, William H.		69,867 R	63.1%	36.9%	63.1%	36.9%
1950	191,239	108,907	Adams, Sherman	82,258	Bingham, Robert P.	74	26,649 R	56.9%	43.0%	57.0%	43.0%
1948	222,571	116,212	Adams, Sherman	105,207	Hill, Herbert W.	1,152	11,005 R	52.2%	47.3%	52.5%	47.5%
1946	163,451	103,204	Dale, Charles M.	60,247	Keefe, F. Clyde		42,957 R	63.1%	36.9%	63.1%	36.9%

**In past elections, the other vote included: 1972 - 63,199 Independent (Malcolm McLane).

NEW HAMPSHIRE

POSTWAR VOTE FOR SENATOR

| | | Republican | | Democratic | | | | Percentage | | | |
| | | | | | | | | Total Vote | | Major Vote | |
Year	Total Vote	Vote	Candidate	Vote	Candidate	Other Vote	Rep.-Dem. Plurality	Rep.	Dem.	Rep.	Dem.
2008	694,787	314,403	Sununu, John E.	358,438	Shaheen, Jeanne	21,946	44,035 D	45.3%	51.6%	46.7%	53.3%
2004	657,086	434,847	Gregg, Judd	221,549	Haddock, Doris Granny D.	690	213,298 R	66.2%	33.7%	66.2%	33.8%
2002	447,135	227,229	Sununu, John E.	207,478	Shaheen, Jeanne	12,428	19,751 R	50.8%	46.4%	52.3%	47.7%
1998	314,956	213,477	Gregg, Judd	88,883	Condodemetraky, George	12,596	124,594 R	67.8%	28.2%	70.6%	29.4%
1996	492,598	242,304	Smith, Robert C.	227,397	Swett, Dick	22,897	14,907 R	49.2%	46.2%	51.6%	48.4%
1992	518,416	249,591	Gregg, Judd	234,982	Rauh, John	33,843	14,609 R	48.1%	45.3%	51.5%	48.5%
1990	291,393	189,792	Smith, Robert C.	91,299	Durkin, John A.	10,302	98,493 R	65.1%	31.3%	67.5%	32.5%
1986	244,797	154,090	Rudman, Warren	79,225	Peabody, Endicott	11,482	74,865 R	62.9%	32.4%	66.0%	34.0%
1984	384,406	225,828	Humphrey, Gordon J.	157,447	D'Amours, Norman E.	1,131	68,381 R	58.7%	41.0%	58.9%	41.1%
1980	375,064	195,563	Rudman, Warren	179,455	Durkin, John A.	46	16,108 R	52.1%	47.8%	52.1%	47.9%
1978	263,779	133,745	Humphrey, Gordon J.	127,945	McIntyre, Thomas J.	2,089	5,800 R	50.7%	48.5%	51.1%	48.9%
1975S	262,682	113,007	Wyman, Louis C.	140,778	Durkin, John A.	8,897	27,771 D	43.0%	53.6%	44.5%	55.5%
1974**	223,363	110,926	Wyman, Louis C.	110,924	Durkin, John A.	1,513	2 R	49.7%	49.7%	50.0%	50.0%
1972	324,354	139,852	Powell, Wesley	184,495	McIntyre, Thomas J.	7	44,643 D	43.1%	56.9%	43.1%	56.9%
1968	286,989	170,163	Cotton, Norris	116,816	King, John W.	10	53,347 R	59.3%	40.7%	59.3%	40.7%
1966	229,305	105,241	Thyng, Harrison R.	123,888	McIntyre, Thomas J.	176	18,647 D	45.9%	54.0%	45.9%	54.1%
1962	224,479	134,035	Cotton, Norris	90,444	Catalfo, Alfred		43,591 R	59.7%	40.3%	59.7%	40.3%
1962S	224,811	107,199	Bass, Perkins	117,612	McIntyre, Thomas J.		10,413 D	47.7%	52.3%	47.7%	52.3%
1960	287,545	173,521	Bridges, Styles	114,024	Hill, Herbert W.		59,497 R	60.3%	39.7%	60.3%	39.7%
1956	251,943	161,424	Cotton, Norris	90,519	Pickett, Laurence M.		70,905 R	64.1%	35.9%	64.1%	35.9%
1954	194,536	117,150	Bridges, Styles	77,386	Morin, Gerard L.		39,764 R	60.2%	39.8%	60.2%	39.8%
1954S	189,558	114,068	Cotton, Norris	75,490	Bentley, Stanley J.		38,578 R	60.2%	39.8%	60.2%	39.8%
1950	190,573	106,142	Tobey, Charles W.	72,473	Kelley, Emmet J.	11,958	33,669 R	55.7%	38.0%	59.4%	40.6%
1948	222,898	129,600	Bridges, Styles	91,760	Fortin, Alfred E.	1,538	37,840 R	58.1%	41.2%	58.5%	41.5%

Notes: **Following the closely contested 1974 election, neither candidate was seated and the 1975 special election was held for the remaining years of that term. One each of the 1954 and 1962 elections were for short terms to fill vacancies.

NEW HAMPSHIRE

PRESIDENT 2008

| 2000 Census Population | County | Total Vote | Republican | Democratic | Other | Rep.-Dem. Plurality | Percentage | | | |
| | | | | | | | Total Vote | | Major Vote | |
							Rep.	Dem.	Rep.	Dem.
56,325	BELKNAP	33,614	16,402	16,796	416	394 D	48.8%	50.0%	49.4%	50.6%
43,666	CARROLL	29,056	13,387	15,221	448	1,834 D	46.1%	52.4%	46.8%	53.2%
73,825	CHESHIRE	42,823	15,205	26,971	647	11,766 D	35.5%	63.0%	36.1%	63.9%
33,111	COOS	16,348	6,558	9,532	258	2,974 D	40.1%	58.3%	40.8%	59.2%
81,743	GRAFTON	49,890	17,687	31,446	757	13,759 D	35.5%	63.0%	36.0%	64.0%
380,841	HILLSBOROUGH	204,709	97,178	104,820	2,711	7,642 D	47.5%	51.2%	48.1%	51.9%
136,225	MERRIMACK	80,106	34,010	45,078	1,018	11,068 D	42.5%	56.3%	43.0%	57.0%
277,359	ROCKINGHAM	167,822	81,917	83,723	2,182	1,806 D	48.8%	49.9%	49.5%	50.5%
112,233	STRAFFORD	63,848	25,021	37,990	837	12,969 D	39.2%	59.5%	39.7%	60.3%
40,458	SULLIVAN	22,754	9,169	13,249	336	4,080 D	40.3%	58.2%	40.9%	59.1%
1,235,786	TOTAL	710,970	316,534	384,826	9,610	68,292 D	44.5%	54.1%	45.1%	54.9%

NEW HAMPSHIRE

PRESIDENT 2008

2000 Census Population	City/Town	Total Vote	Republican	Democratic	Other	Rep.-Dem. Plurality	Percentage Total Vote Rep.	Dem.	Major Vote Rep.	Dem.
10,769	AMHERST	7,464	3,536	3,822	106	286 D	47.4%	51.2%	48.1%	51.9%
6,178	ATKINSON	4,438	2,524	1,853	61	671 R	56.9%	41.8%	57.7%	42.3%
7,475	BARRINGTON	4,784	2,117	2,606	61	489 D	44.3%	54.5%	44.8%	55.2%
18,274	BEDFORD	12,663	7,442	5,115	106	2,327 R	58.8%	40.4%	59.3%	40.7%
6,716	BELMONT	3,528	1,727	1,746	55	19 D	49.0%	49.5%	49.7%	50.3%
10,331	BERLIN	4,419	1,357	2,968	94	1,611 D	30.7%	67.2%	31.4%	68.6%
7,138	BOW	4,863	2,227	2,585	51	358 D	45.8%	53.2%	46.3%	53.7%
13,151	CLAREMONT	5,847	2,236	3,518	93	1,282 D	38.2%	60.2%	38.9%	61.1%
40,687	CONCORD	22,069	7,496	14,302	271	6,806 D	34.0%	64.8%	34.4%	65.6%
8,604	CONWAY	5,263	1,964	3,210	89	1,246 D	37.3%	61.0%	38.0%	62.0%
34,021	DERRY	15,728	7,944	7,527	257	417 R	50.5%	47.9%	51.3%	48.7%
26,884	DOVER	16,181	5,746	10,221	214	4,475 D	35.5%	63.2%	36.0%	64.0%
12,664	DURHAM	7,277	1,838	5,363	76	3,525 D	25.3%	73.7%	25.5%	74.5%
5,476	EPPING	3,332	1,518	1,765	49	247 D	45.6%	53.0%	46.2%	53.8%
14,058	EXETER	8,737	3,365	5,258	114	1,893 D	38.5%	60.2%	39.0%	61.0%
5,774	FARMINGTON	3,049	1,379	1,626	44	247 D	45.2%	53.3%	45.9%	54.1%
8,405	FRANKLIN	3,756	1,600	2,093	63	493 D	42.6%	55.7%	43.3%	56.7%
6,803	GILFORD	4,586	2,292	2,246	48	46 R	50.0%	49.0%	50.5%	49.5%
16,929	GOFFSTOWN	9,031	4,707	4,243	81	464 R	52.1%	47.0%	52.6%	47.4%
8,297	HAMPSTEAD	5,204	2,984	2,161	59	823 R	57.3%	41.5%	58.0%	42.0%
14,937	HAMPTON	9,650	4,506	5,044	100	538 D	46.7%	52.3%	47.2%	52.8%
10,850	HANOVER	7,532	1,328	6,140	64	4,812 D	17.6%	81.5%	17.8%	82.2%
7,015	HOLLIS	5,075	2,475	2,536	64	61 D	48.8%	50.0%	49.4%	50.6%
11,721	HOOKSETT	7,079	3,749	3,277	53	472 R	53.0%	46.3%	53.4%	46.6%
22,928	HUDSON	12,306	6,351	5,807	148	544 R	51.6%	47.2%	52.2%	47.8%
5,476	JAFFREY	2,887	1,290	1,546	51	256 D	44.7%	53.6%	45.5%	54.5%
22,563	KEENE	13,247	3,641	9,427	179	5,786 D	27.5%	71.2%	27.9%	72.1%
5,862	KINGSTON	3,379	1,730	1,585	64	145 R	51.2%	46.9%	52.2%	47.8%
16,411	LACONIA	8,042	3,750	4,218	74	468 D	46.6%	52.4%	47.1%	52.9%
12,568	LEBANON	6,835	2,055	4,680	100	2,625 D	30.1%	68.5%	30.5%	69.5%
7,360	LITCHFIELD	4,567	2,581	1,951	35	630 R	56.5%	42.7%	57.0%	43.0%
5,845	LITTLETON	2,863	1,246	1,582	35	336 D	43.5%	55.3%	44.1%	55.9%
23,236	LONDONDERRY	13,125	6,879	6,107	139	772 R	52.4%	46.5%	53.0%	47.0%
107,006	MANCHESTER	48,354	21,192	26,526	636	5,334 D	43.8%	54.9%	44.4%	55.6%
25,119	MERRIMACK TOWN	15,090	7,558	7,316	216	242 R	50.1%	48.5%	50.8%	49.2%
13,535	MILFORD	7,786	3,660	4,024	102	364 D	47.0%	51.7%	47.6%	52.4%
86,605	NASHUA	40,832	17,325	22,902	605	5,577 D	42.4%	56.1%	43.1%	56.9%
8,027	NEWMARKET	5,107	1,780	3,241	86	1,461 D	34.9%	63.5%	35.5%	64.5%
6,269	NEWPORT	3,015	1,301	1,666	48	365 D	43.2%	55.3%	43.8%	56.2%
10,914	PELHAM	6,979	3,911	2,982	86	929 R	56.0%	42.7%	56.7%	43.3%
6,897	PEMBROKE	3,758	1,721	1,970	67	249 D	45.8%	52.4%	46.6%	53.4%
5,883	PETERBOROUGH	3,907	1,328	2,546	33	1,218 D	34.0%	65.2%	34.3%	65.7%
7,747	PLAISTOW	4,153	2,266	1,827	60	439 R	54.6%	44.0%	55.4%	44.6%
5,892	PLYMOUTH	3,894	1,130	2,703	61	1,573 D	29.0%	69.4%	29.5%	70.5%
20,784	PORTSMOUTH	13,031	3,729	9,147	155	5,418 D	28.6%	70.2%	29.0%	71.0%
9,674	RAYMOND	5,167	2,623	2,460	84	163 R	50.8%	47.6%	51.6%	48.4%
28,461	ROCHESTER	14,630	6,483	7,947	200	1,464 D	44.3%	54.3%	44.9%	55.1%
28,112	SALEM	15,105	8,073	6,838	194	1,235 R	53.4%	45.3%	54.1%	45.9%
7,934	SEABROOK	4,066	2,002	1,991	73	11 R	49.2%	49.0%	50.1%	49.9%
11,477	SOMERSWORTH	5,478	2,054	3,345	79	1,291 D	37.5%	61.1%	38.0%	62.0%
6,800	SWANZEY	3,771	1,485	2,254	32	769 D	39.4%	59.8%	39.7%	60.3%
7,776	WEARE	4,698	2,520	2,109	69	411 R	53.6%	44.9%	54.4%	45.6%
10,709	WINDHAM	7,881	4,644	3,180	57	1,464 R	58.9%	40.4%	59.4%	40.6%

NEW HAMPSHIRE

GOVERNOR 2008

2000 Census Population	County	Total Vote	Republican	Democratic	Other	Rep.-Dem. Plurality	Percentage Total Vote		Percentage Major Vote	
							Rep.	Dem.	Rep.	Dem.
56,325	BELKNAP	32,609	9,858	22,212	539	12,354 D	30.2%	68.1%	30.7%	69.3%
43,666	CARROLL	28,107	10,009	17,488	610	7,479 D	35.6%	62.2%	36.4%	63.6%
73,825	CHESHIRE	40,762	9,827	29,663	1,272	19,836 D	24.1%	72.8%	24.9%	75.1%
33,111	COOS	15,683	3,742	11,588	353	7,846 D	23.9%	73.9%	24.4%	75.6%
81,743	GRAFTON	47,179	11,328	34,564	1,287	23,236 D	24.0%	73.3%	24.7%	75.3%
380,841	HILLSBOROUGH	196,692	56,831	135,189	4,672	78,358 D	28.9%	68.7%	29.6%	70.4%
136,225	MERRIMACK	78,102	18,222	58,410	1,470	40,188 D	23.3%	74.8%	23.8%	76.2%
277,359	ROCKINGHAM	160,721	49,158	108,201	3,362	59,043 D	30.6%	67.3%	31.2%	68.8%
112,233	STRAFFORD	61,333	14,190	45,878	1,265	31,688 D	23.1%	74.8%	23.6%	76.4%
40,458	SULLIVAN	21,722	5,390	15,849	483	10,459 D	24.8%	73.0%	25.4%	74.6%
1,235,786	TOTAL	682,910	188,555	479,042	15,313	290,487 D	27.6%	70.1%	28.2%	71.8%

2000 Census Population	City/Town	Total Vote	Republican	Democratic	Other	Rep.-Dem. Plurality	Percentage Total Vote		Percentage Major Vote	
							Rep.	Dem.	Rep.	Dem.
10,769	AMHERST	7,209	2,285	4,771	153	2,486 D	31.7%	66.2%	32.4%	67.6%
6,178	ATKINSON	4,212	1,524	2,611	77	1,087 D	36.2%	62.0%	36.9%	63.1%
7,475	BARRINGTON	4,613	1,207	3,289	117	2,082 D	26.2%	71.3%	26.8%	73.2%
18,274	BEDFORD	12,258	4,616	7,449	193	2,833 D	37.7%	60.8%	38.3%	61.7%
6,716	BELMONT	3,396	980	2,363	53	1,383 D	28.9%	69.6%	29.3%	70.7%
10,331	BERLIN	4,309	605	3,613	91	3,008 D	14.0%	83.8%	14.3%	85.7%
7,138	BOW	4,750	1,181	3,497	72	2,316 D	24.9%	73.6%	25.2%	74.8%
13,151	CLAREMONT	5,575	1,290	4,164	121	2,874 D	23.1%	74.7%	23.7%	76.3%
40,687	CONCORD	21,604	3,835	17,372	397	13,537 D	17.8%	80.4%	18.1%	81.9%
8,604	CONWAY	5,050	1,449	3,474	127	2,025 D	28.7%	68.8%	29.4%	70.6%
34,021	DERRY	15,004	4,760	9,905	339	5,145 D	31.7%	66.0%	32.5%	67.5%
26,884	DOVER	15,613	3,197	12,106	310	8,909 D	20.5%	77.5%	20.9%	79.1%
12,664	DURHAM	6,716	1,104	5,443	169	4,339 D	16.4%	81.0%	16.9%	83.1%
5,476	EPPING	3,239	873	2,292	74	1,419 D	27.0%	70.8%	27.6%	72.4%
14,058	EXETER	8,372	2,080	6,127	165	4,047 D	24.8%	73.2%	25.3%	74.7%
5,774	FARMINGTON	2,961	823	2,051	87	1,228 D	27.8%	69.3%	28.6%	71.4%
8,405	FRANKLIN	3,674	844	2,765	65	1,921 D	23.0%	75.3%	23.4%	76.6%
6,803	GILFORD	4,446	1,408	2,977	61	1,569 D	31.7%	67.0%	32.1%	67.9%
16,929	GOFFSTOWN	8,823	2,691	6,011	121	3,320 D	30.5%	68.1%	30.9%	69.1%
8,297	HAMPSTEAD	4,956	1,744	3,119	93	1,375 D	35.2%	62.9%	35.9%	64.1%
14,937	HAMPTON	9,311	2,692	6,464	155	3,772 D	28.9%	69.4%	29.4%	70.6%
10,850	HANOVER	6,770	1,029	5,607	134	4,578 D	15.2%	82.8%	15.5%	84.5%
7,015	HOLLIS	4,879	1,606	3,144	129	1,538 D	32.9%	64.4%	33.8%	66.2%
11,721	HOOKSETT	6,977	2,083	4,796	98	2,713 D	29.9%	68.7%	30.3%	69.7%
22,928	HUDSON	11,641	3,741	7,618	282	3,877 D	32.1%	65.4%	32.9%	67.1%
5,476	JAFFREY	2,789	816	1,920	53	1,104 D	29.3%	68.8%	29.8%	70.2%
22,563	KEENE	12,398	2,322	9,647	429	7,325 D	18.7%	77.8%	19.4%	80.6%
5,862	KINGSTON	3,241	1,110	2,061	70	951 D	34.2%	63.6%	35.0%	65.0%
16,411	LACONIA	7,805	2,222	5,488	95	3,266 D	28.5%	70.3%	28.8%	71.2%
12,568	LEBANON	6,502	1,285	5,078	139	3,793 D	19.8%	78.1%	20.2%	79.8%
7,360	LITCHFIELD	4,400	1,439	2,870	91	1,431 D	32.7%	65.2%	33.4%	66.6%
5,845	LITTLETON	2,765	742	1,967	56	1,225 D	26.8%	71.1%	27.4%	72.6%
23,236	LONDONDERRY	12,595	4,207	8,142	246	3,935 D	33.4%	64.6%	34.1%	65.9%
107,006	MANCHESTER	46,927	11,599	34,400	928	22,801 D	24.7%	73.3%	25.2%	74.8%
25,119	MERRIMACK TOWN	14,493	4,228	9,899	366	5,671 D	29.2%	68.3%	29.9%	70.1%

NEW HAMPSHIRE

GOVERNOR 2008

2000 Census Population	City/Town	Total Vote	Republican	Democratic	Other	Rep.-Dem. Plurality	Percentage Total Vote Rep.	Total Vote Dem.	Major Vote Rep.	Major Vote Dem.
13,535	MILFORD	7,535	2,237	5,154	144	2,917 D	29.7%	68.4%	30.3%	69.7%
86,605	NASHUA	38,616	9,911	27,536	1,169	17,625 D	25.7%	71.3%	26.5%	73.5%
8,027	NEWMARKET	4,972	995	3,859	118	2,864 D	20.0%	77.6%	20.5%	79.5%
6,269	NEWPORT	2,898	684	2,154	60	1,470 D	23.6%	74.3%	24.1%	75.9%
10,914	PELHAM	6,607	2,401	4,015	191	1,614 D	36.3%	60.8%	37.4%	62.6%
6,897	PEMBROKE	3,656	862	2,738	56	1,876 D	23.6%	74.9%	23.9%	76.1%
5,883	PETERBOROUGH	3,805	863	2,853	89	1,990 D	22.7%	75.0%	23.2%	76.8%
7,747	PLAISTOW	3,886	1,331	2,438	117	1,107 D	34.3%	62.7%	35.3%	64.7%
5,892	PLYMOUTH	3,607	691	2,781	135	2,090 D	19.2%	77.1%	19.9%	80.1%
20,784	PORTSMOUTH	12,433	2,039	10,122	272	8,083 D	16.4%	81.4%	16.8%	83.2%
9,674	RAYMOND	4,981	1,469	3,374	138	1,905 D	29.5%	67.7%	30.3%	69.7%
28,461	ROCHESTER	14,162	3,686	10,254	222	6,568 D	26.0%	72.4%	26.4%	73.6%
28,112	SALEM	14,118	4,756	9,096	266	4,340 D	33.7%	64.4%	34.3%	65.7%
7,934	SEABROOK	3,992	1,294	2,573	125	1,279 D	32.4%	64.5%	33.5%	66.5%
11,477	SOMERSWORTH	5,254	1,079	4,064	111	2,985 D	20.5%	77.4%	21.0%	79.0%
6,800	SWANZEY	3,658	927	2,623	108	1,696 D	25.3%	71.7%	26.1%	73.9%
7,776	WEARE	4,558	1,374	3,062	122	1,688 D	30.1%	67.2%	31.0%	69.0%
10,709	WINDHAM	7,459	2,908	4,407	144	1,499 D	39.0%	59.1%	39.8%	60.2%

NEW HAMPSHIRE

SENATOR 2008

2000 Census Population	County	Total Vote	Republican	Democratic	Other	Rep.-Dem. Plurality	Percentage Total Vote Rep.	Total Vote Dem.	Major Vote Rep.	Major Vote Dem.
56,325	BELKNAP	32,968	16,166	15,931	871	235 R	49.0%	48.3%	50.4%	49.6%
43,666	CARROLL	28,379	13,965	13,428	986	537 R	49.2%	47.3%	51.0%	49.0%
73,825	CHESHIRE	41,553	15,259	24,788	1,506	9,529 D	36.7%	59.7%	38.1%	61.9%
33,111	COOS	15,949	6,375	9,031	543	2,656 D	40.0%	56.6%	41.4%	58.6%
81,743	GRAFTON	48,334	18,957	27,797	1,580	8,840 D	39.2%	57.5%	40.5%	59.5%
380,841	HILLSBOROUGH	200,143	95,646	97,734	6,763	2,088 D	47.8%	48.8%	49.5%	50.5%
136,225	MERRIMACK	78,854	33,958	42,646	2,250	8,688 D	43.1%	54.1%	44.3%	55.7%
277,359	ROCKINGHAM	164,047	80,051	78,992	5,004	1,059 R	48.8%	48.2%	50.3%	49.7%
112,233	STRAFFORD	62,380	24,503	36,096	1,781	11,593 D	39.3%	57.9%	40.4%	59.6%
40,458	SULLIVAN	22,180	9,523	11,995	662	2,472 D	42.9%	54.1%	44.3%	55.7%
1,235,786	TOTAL	694,787	314,403	358,438	21,946	44,035 D	45.3%	51.6%	46.7%	53.3%

NEW HAMPSHIRE

SENATOR 2008

2000 Census Population	City/Town	Total Vote	Republican	Democratic	Other	Rep.-Dem. Plurality	Percentage			
							Total Vote		Major Vote	
							Rep.	Dem.	Rep.	Dem.
10,769	AMHERST	7,336	3,865	3,309	162	556 R	52.7%	45.1%	53.9%	46.1%
6,178	ATKINSON	4,346	2,362	1,875	109	487 R	54.3%	43.1%	55.7%	44.3%
7,475	BARRINGTON	4,660	2,024	2,470	166	446 D	43.4%	53.0%	45.0%	55.0%
18,274	BEDFORD	12,484	7,781	4,454	249	3,327 R	62.3%	35.7%	63.6%	36.4%
6,716	BELMONT	3,438	1,599	1,749	90	150 D	46.5%	50.9%	47.8%	52.2%
10,331	BERLIN	4,368	1,272	2,966	130	1,694 D	29.1%	67.9%	30.0%	70.0%
7,138	BOW	4,805	2,296	2,408	101	112 D	47.8%	50.1%	48.8%	51.2%
13,151	CLAREMONT	5,706	2,295	3,235	176	940 D	40.2%	56.7%	41.5%	58.5%
40,687	CONCORD	21,789	7,701	13,519	569	5,818 D	35.3%	62.0%	36.3%	63.7%
8,604	CONWAY	5,099	2,102	2,806	191	704 D	41.2%	55.0%	42.8%	57.2%
34,021	DERRY	15,297	7,450	7,313	534	137 R	48.7%	47.8%	50.5%	49.5%
26,884	DOVER	15,875	5,875	9,601	399	3,726 D	37.0%	60.5%	38.0%	62.0%
12,664	DURHAM	6,947	2,129	4,679	139	2,550 D	30.6%	67.4%	31.3%	68.7%
5,476	EPPING	3,275	1,483	1,673	119	190 D	45.3%	51.1%	47.0%	53.0%
14,058	EXETER	8,492	3,454	4,824	214	1,370 D	40.7%	56.8%	41.7%	58.3%
5,774	FARMINGTON	2,979	1,229	1,604	146	375 D	41.3%	53.8%	43.4%	56.6%
8,405	FRANKLIN	3,708	1,466	2,125	117	659 D	39.5%	57.3%	40.8%	59.2%
6,803	GILFORD	4,497	2,371	2,054	72	317 R	52.7%	45.7%	53.6%	46.4%
16,929	GOFFSTOWN	8,903	4,704	3,960	239	744 R	52.8%	44.5%	54.3%	45.7%
8,297	HAMPSTEAD	5,074	2,813	2,130	131	683 R	55.4%	42.0%	56.9%	43.1%
14,937	HAMPTON	9,427	4,408	4,770	249	362 D	46.8%	50.6%	48.0%	52.0%
10,850	HANOVER	7,185	1,813	5,275	97	3,462 D	25.2%	73.4%	25.6%	74.4%
7,015	HOLLIS	4,960	2,603	2,222	135	381 R	52.5%	44.8%	53.9%	46.1%
11,721	HOOKSETT	7,015	3,757	3,117	141	640 R	53.6%	44.4%	54.7%	45.3%
22,928	HUDSON	11,928	5,835	5,701	392	134 R	48.9%	47.8%	50.6%	49.4%
5,476	JAFFREY	2,830	1,221	1,512	97	291 D	43.1%	53.4%	44.7%	55.3%
22,563	KEENE	12,783	3,866	8,448	469	4,582 D	30.2%	66.1%	31.4%	68.6%
5,862	KINGSTON	3,307	1,589	1,568	150	21 R	48.0%	47.4%	50.3%	49.7%
16,411	LACONIA	7,902	3,738	3,991	173	253 D	47.3%	50.5%	48.4%	51.6%
12,568	LEBANON	6,663	2,285	4,232	146	1,947 D	34.3%	63.5%	35.1%	64.9%
7,360	LITCHFIELD	4,470	2,408	1,932	130	476 R	53.9%	43.2%	55.5%	44.5%
5,845	LITTLETON	2,792	1,308	1,390	94	82 D	46.8%	49.8%	48.5%	51.5%
23,236	LONDONDERRY	12,767	6,781	5,670	316	1,111 R	53.1%	44.4%	54.5%	45.5%
107,006	MANCHESTER	47,472	21,236	24,799	1,437	3,563 D	44.7%	52.2%	46.1%	53.9%
25,119	MERRIMACK TOWN	14,700	7,282	6,879	539	403 R	49.5%	46.8%	51.4%	48.6%
13,535	MILFORD	7,622	3,623	3,745	254	122 D	47.5%	49.1%	49.2%	50.8%
86,605	NASHUA	39,613	16,765	21,273	1,575	4,508 D	42.3%	53.7%	44.1%	55.9%
8,027	NEWMARKET	5,048	1,879	3,021	148	1,142 D	37.2%	59.8%	38.3%	61.7%
6,269	NEWPORT	2,920	1,341	1,480	99	139 D	45.9%	50.7%	47.5%	52.5%
10,914	PELHAM	6,792	3,398	3,118	276	280 R	50.0%	45.9%	52.1%	47.9%
6,897	PEMBROKE	3,679	1,668	1,889	122	221 D	45.3%	51.3%	46.9%	53.1%
5,883	PETERBOROUGH	3,848	1,404	2,353	91	949 D	36.5%	61.1%	37.4%	62.6%
7,747	PLAISTOW	4,008	2,020	1,819	169	201 R	50.4%	45.4%	52.6%	47.4%
5,892	PLYMOUTH	3,695	1,221	2,311	163	1,090 D	33.0%	62.5%	34.6%	65.4%
20,784	PORTSMOUTH	12,670	4,147	8,171	352	4,024 D	32.7%	64.5%	33.7%	66.3%
9,674	RAYMOND	5,051	2,404	2,428	219	24 D	47.6%	48.1%	49.8%	50.2%
28,461	ROCHESTER	14,299	6,117	7,808	374	1,691 D	42.8%	54.6%	43.9%	56.1%
28,112	SALEM	14,710	7,390	6,849	471	541 R	50.2%	46.6%	51.9%	48.1%
7,934	SEABROOK	4,105	1,974	1,872	259	102 R	48.1%	45.6%	51.3%	48.7%
11,477	SOMERSWORTH	5,337	1,893	3,289	155	1,396 D	35.5%	61.6%	36.5%	63.5%
6,800	SWANZEY	3,706	1,452	2,115	139	663 D	39.2%	57.1%	40.7%	59.3%
7,776	WEARE	4,618	2,384	1,998	236	386 R	51.6%	43.3%	54.4%	45.6%
10,709	WINDHAM	7,661	4,513	3,037	111	1,476 R	58.9%	39.6%	59.8%	40.2%

NEW HAMPSHIRE

HOUSE OF REPRESENTATIVES

CD	Year	Total Vote	Republican Vote	Republican Candidate	Democratic Vote	Democratic Candidate	Other Vote	Rep.-Dem. Plurality	Total Vote Rep.	Total Vote Dem.	Major Vote Rep.	Major Vote Dem.
1	2008	341,071	156,338	BRADLEY, JEB	176,435	SHEA-PORTER, CAROL*	8,298	20,097 D	45.8%	51.7%	47.0%	53.0%
1	2006	196,377	95,527	BRADLEY, JEB*	100,691	SHEA-PORTER, CAROL	159	5,164 D	48.6%	51.3%	48.7%	51.3%
1	2004	323,372	204,836	BRADLEY, JEB*	118,226	NADEAU, JUSTIN	310	86,610 R	63.3%	36.6%	63.4%	36.6%
1	2002	221,987	128,993	BRADLEY, JEB	85,426	CLARK, MARTHA FULLER	7,568	43,567 R	58.1%	38.5%	60.2%	39.8%
2	2008	333,904	138,222	HORN, JENNIFER	188,332	HODES, PAUL W.*	7,350	50,110 D	41.4%	56.4%	42.3%	57.7%
2	2006	206,292	94,088	BASS, CHARLES*	108,743	HODES, PAUL W.	3,461	14,655 D	45.6%	52.7%	46.4%	53.6%
2	2004	328,194	191,188	BASS, CHARLES*	125,280	HODES, PAUL W.	11,726	65,908 R	58.3%	38.2%	60.4%	39.6%
2	2002	221,456	125,804	BASS, CHARLES*	90,479	SWETT, KATRINA	5,173	35,325 R	56.8%	40.9%	58.2%	41.8%
TOTAL	2008	674,975	294,560		364,767		15,648	70,207 D	43.6%	54.0%	44.7%	55.3%
TOTAL	2006	402,669	189,615		209,434		3,620	19,819 D	47.1%	52.0%	47.5%	52.5%
TOTAL	2004	651,566	396,024		243,506		12,036	152,518 R	60.8%	37.4%	61.9%	38.1%
TOTAL	2002	443,443	254,797		175,905		12,741	78,892 R	57.5%	39.7%	59.2%	40.8%

Note: An asterisk (*) denotes incumbent.

NEW HAMPSHIRE

GENERAL AND PRIMARY ELECTIONS

2008 GENERAL ELECTIONS

President   Other vote was 3,503 Independent (Ralph Nader); 2,217 Libertarian (Bob Barr); 1,124 write-in (Hillary Clinton); 1,092 write-in (Ron Paul); 531 Libertarian (George Phillies); 226 write-in (Chuck Baldwin); 112 write-in (Mitt Romney); 61 write-in (Mike Huckabee); 40 write-in (Cynthia A. McKinney); 18 write-in (Sarah Palin); 13 write-in (Bill Clinton); 673 scattered write-in.

Governor   Other vote was 14,987 Libertarian (Susan M. Newell); 326 scattered write-in.

Senator   Other vote was 21,516 Libertarian ("Ken" Blevens); 430 scattered write-in.

House   Other vote was:

CD 1   8,100 Libertarian (Robert Kingsbury); 198 scattered write-in.
CD 2   7,121 Libertarian (Chester L. Lapointe II); 229 scattered write-in.

2008 PRIMARY ELECTIONS

Primary   January 8, 2008 (President)   **Registration**   Republican   268,108
                  September 9, 2008 (Congress)   (as of August 18, 2008)   Democratic   263,217
                                                                                 Undeclared   332,217

                                                                                 TOTAL   863,542

Primary Type Semi-open—Registered Democrats and Republicans could vote only in their party's primary. "Undeclared" voters could participate in either party's primary.

NEW HAMPSHIRE

GENERAL AND PRIMARY ELECTIONS

	REPUBLICAN PRIMARIES			DEMOCRATIC PRIMARIES		
President	John McCain	88,713	37.0%	Hillary Clinton	112,404	39.1%
	Mitt Romney	75,675	31.6%	Barack Obama	104,815	36.5%
	Mike Huckabee	26,916	11.2%	John Edwards	48,699	16.9%
	Rudolph Giuliani	20,344	8.5%	Bill Richardson	13,269	4.6%
	Ron Paul	18,346	7.7%	Dennis J. Kucinich	3,891	1.4%
	Fred Thompson	2,956	1.2%	Joseph R. Biden Jr.	638	0.2%
	Duncan Hunter	1,192	0.5%	Mike Gravel	404	0.1%
	Alan Keyes	205	0.1%	Richard Edward Caligiuri	253	0.1%
	Stephen W. Marchuk	127	0.1%	Christopher J. Dodd	205	0.1%
	Tom Tancredo	63		Kenneth A. Capalbo	108	
	Cornelius Edward O'Connor	46		D.R. Hunter	95	
	Albert Howard	43		William "Bill" Keefe	51	
	Vermin Supreme	43		"Tom" Laughlin	47	
	John Cox	39		"Randy" Crow	37	
	"Vern" Wuensche	36		Michael Skok	32	
	Hugh Cort	35		O. Savior	30	
	Daniel Gilbert	35		Henry Hewes	17	
	Jack Shepard	28		William C. Hughes	16	
	James Creighton Mitchell Jr.	26		Caroline P. Killeen	11	
	Mark Klein	16		"Tom" Koos	10	
	H. Neal Fendig Jr.	13		Dal LaMagna	8	
	Write-in	4,896	2.0%	Write-in	2,517	0.9%
	TOTAL	*239,793*		*TOTAL*	*287,557*	

Among the Republican write-ins were 1,996 for Barack Obama, 1,828 for Hillary Clinton, 747 for John Edwards, and 210 for Bill Richardson

Among the Democratic write-ins were 932 for John McCain, 611 for Mitt Romney, 267 for Ron Paul, 243 for Mike Huckabee, and 161 for Rudolph Giuliani.

	REPUBLICAN			DEMOCRATIC		
Governor	Joseph D. Kenney	49,235	92.7%	John Lynch*	44,549	90.7%
	John Lynch (D, write-in)	3,352	6.3%	Katy Forry	4,444	9.0%
	Katy Forry (D, write-in)	43	0.1%	Joseph D. Kenney (R, write-in)	49	0.1%
	Scattered write-in	490	0.9%	Scattered write-in	82	0.2%
	TOTAL	53,120		TOTAL	49,124	
Senator	John E. Sununu*	60,852	88.7%	Jeanne Shaheen	42,968	88.3%
	Tom Alciere	7,084	10.3%	Raymond Stebbins	5,281	10.9%
	Jeanne Shaheen (D, write-in)	517	0.8%	John E. Sununu (R, write-in)	235	0.5%
	Raymond Stebbins (D, write-in)	3		Scattered write-in	172	0.4%
	Scattered write-in	165	0.2%			
	TOTAL	68,621		TOTAL	48,656	
Congressional District 1	Jeb Bradley	18,559	51.0%	Carol Shea-Porter*	20,839	98.2%
	John Stephen	16,766	46.1%	Jeb Bradley (R, write-in)	162	0.8%
	Geoff Michael	534	1.5%	John Stephen (R, write-in)	127	0.6%
	Dave Jarvis	414	1.1%	Scattered write-in	89	0.4%
	Carol Shea-Porter (D, write-in)	46	0.1%			
	Scattered write-in	43	0.1%			
	TOTAL	36,362		TOTAL	21,217	
Congressional District 2	Jennifer Horn	12,726	40.1%	Paul W. Hodes*	22,638	98.6%
	Bob Clegg	10,771	33.9%	Bob Clegg (R, write-in)	59	0.3%
	Jim Steiner	4,582	14.4%	Jennifer Horn (R, write-in)	56	0.2%
	Grant Bosse	2,974	9.4%	Jim Steiner (R, write-in)	46	0.2%
	Alfred L'Eplattenier	547	1.7%	Grant Bosse (R, write-in)	18	0.1%
	Paul W. Hodes (D, write-in)	61	0.2%	Scattered write-in	151	0.7%
	Scattered write-in	111	0.3%			
	TOTAL	31,772		TOTAL	22,968	

Note: An asterisk (*) denotes incumbent.

NEW JERSEY

Congressional districts first established for elections held in 2002
13 members

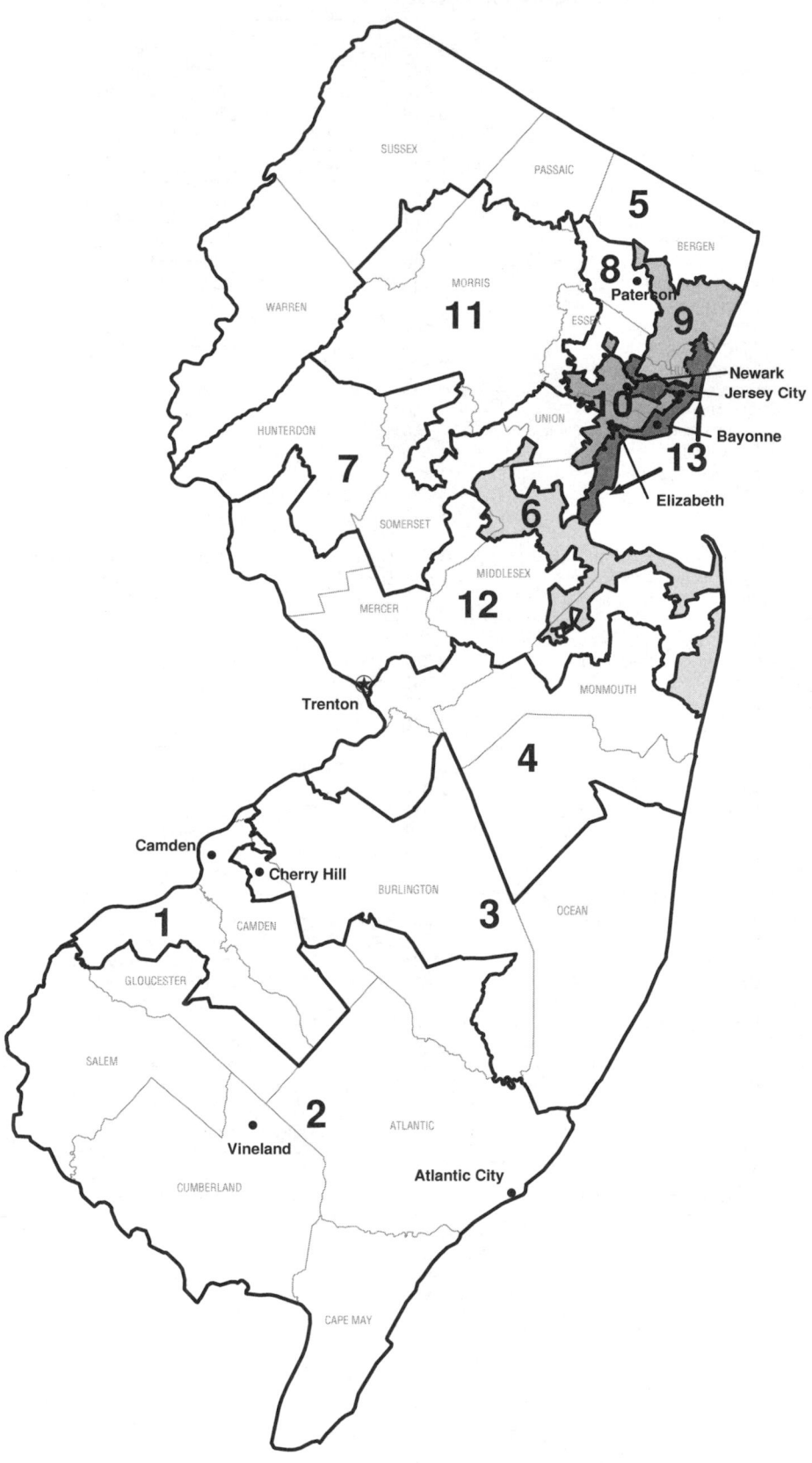

NEW JERSEY

Northern New Jersey Gateway Area

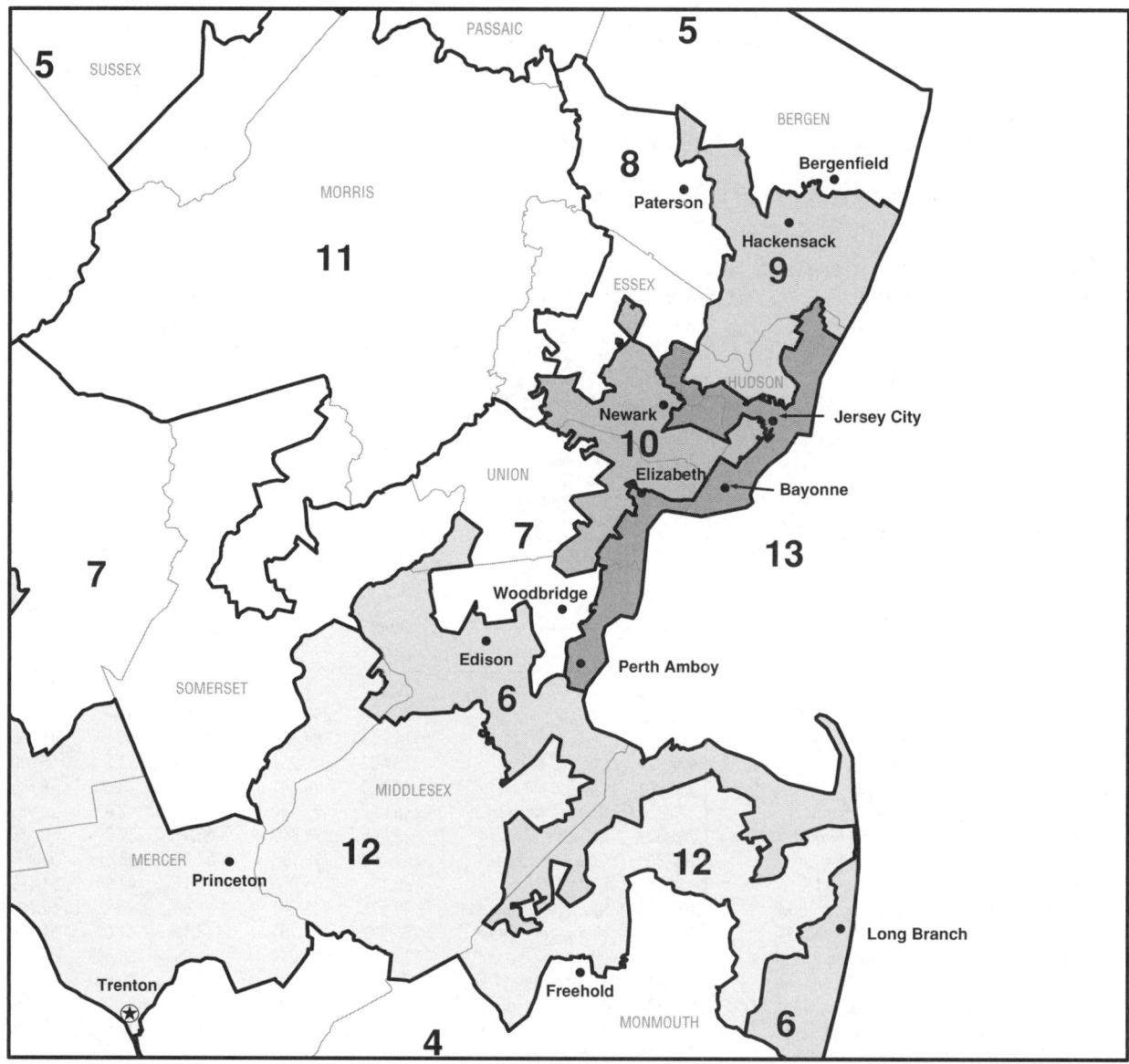

NEW JERSEY

GOVERNOR
Jon Corzine (D). Elected 2005 to a four-year term.

SENATORS (2 Democrats)
Frank R. Lautenberg (D). Reelected 2008 to a six-year term. Previously elected 2002, 1994, 1988, 1982.

Robert Menendez (D). Elected 2006 to a six-year term.

REPRESENTATIVES (8 Democrats, 5 Republicans)

1. Robert E. Andrews (D)
2. Frank A. LoBiondo (R)
3. John H. Adler (D)
4. Christopher H. Smith (R)
5. Scott Garrett (R)
6. Frank Pallone Jr. (D)
7. Leonard Lance (R)
8. Bill Pascrell Jr. (D)
9. Steven R. Rothman (D)
10. Donald M. Payne (D)
11. Rodney Frelinghuysen (R)
12. Rush D. Holt (D)
13. Albio Sires (D)

POSTWAR VOTE FOR PRESIDENT

Year	Total Vote	Republican Vote	Republican Candidate	Democratic Vote	Democratic Candidate	Other Vote	Plurality		Total Vote Rep.	Total Vote Dem.	Major Vote Rep.	Major Vote Dem.
2008	3,868,237	1,613,207	McCain, John	2,215,422	Obama, Barack	39,608	602,215	D	41.7%	57.3%	42.1%	57.9%
2004	3,611,691	1,670,003	Bush, George W.	1,911,430	Kerry, John	30,258	241,427	D	46.2%	52.9%	46.6%	53.4%
2000**	3,187,226	1,284,173	Bush, George W.	1,788,850	Gore, Al	114,203	504,677	D	40.3%	56.1%	41.8%	58.2%
1996**	3,075,807	1,103,078	Dole, Bob	1,652,329	Clinton, Bill	320,400	549,251	D	35.9%	53.7%	40.0%	60.0%
1992**	3,343,594	1,356,865	Bush, George	1,436,206	Clinton, Bill	550,523	79,341	D	40.6%	43.0%	48.6%	51.4%
1988	3,099,553	1,743,192	Bush, George	1,320,352	Dukakis, Michael S.	36,009	422,840	R	56.2%	42.6%	56.9%	43.1%
1984	3,217,862	1,933,630	Reagan, Ronald	1,261,323	Mondale, Walter F.	22,909	672,307	R	60.1%	39.2%	60.5%	39.5%
1980**	2,975,684	1,546,557	Reagan, Ronald	1,147,364	Carter, Jimmy	281,763	399,193	R	52.0%	38.6%	57.4%	42.6%
1976	3,014,472	1,509,688	Ford, Gerald R.	1,444,653	Carter, Jimmy	60,131	65,035	R	50.1%	47.9%	51.1%	48.9%
1972	2,997,229	1,845,502	Nixon, Richard M.	1,102,211	McGovern, George S.	49,516	743,291	R	61.6%	36.8%	62.6%	37.4%
1968**	2,875,395	1,325,467	Nixon, Richard M.	1,264,206	Humphrey, Hubert H.	285,722	61,261	R	46.1%	44.0%	51.2%	48.8%
1964	2,847,663	964,174	Goldwater, Barry M.	1,868,231	Johnson, Lyndon B.	15,258	904,057	D	33.9%	65.6%	34.0%	66.0%
1960	2,773,111	1,363,324	Nixon, Richard M.	1,385,415	Kennedy, John F.	24,372	22,091	D	49.2%	50.0%	49.6%	50.4%
1956	2,484,312	1,606,942	Eisenhower, Dwight D.	850,337	Stevenson, Adlai E.	27,033	756,605	R	64.7%	34.2%	65.4%	34.6%
1952	2,418,554	1,373,613	Eisenhower, Dwight D.	1,015,902	Stevenson, Adlai E.	29,039	357,711	R	56.8%	42.0%	57.5%	42.5%
1948	1,949,555	981,124	Dewey, Thomas E.	895,455	Truman, Harry S.	72,976	85,669	R	50.3%	45.9%	52.3%	47.7%

**In past elections, the other vote included: 2000 - 94,554 Green (Ralph Nader); 1996 - 262,134 Reform (Ross Perot); 1992 - 521,829 Independent (Perot); 1980 - 234,632 Independent (John Anderson); 1968 - 262,187 American Independent (George Wallace).

NEW JERSEY

POSTWAR VOTE FOR GOVERNOR

Year	Total Vote	Republican Vote	Candidate	Democratic Vote	Candidate	Other Vote	Rep.-Dem. Plurality	Total Vote Rep.	Total Vote Dem.	Major Vote Rep.	Major Vote Dem.
2005	2,290,099	985,271	Forrester, Doug	1,224,551	Corzine, Jon	80,277	239,280 D	43.0%	53.5%	44.6%	55.4%
2001	2,227,165	928,174	Schundler, Bret	1,256,853	McGreevey, James E.	42,138	328,679 D	41.7%	56.4%	42.5%	57.5%
1997	2,418,344	1,133,394	Whitman, Christine T.	1,107,968	McGreevey, James E.	176,982	25,426 R	46.9%	45.8%	50.6%	49.4%
1993	2,505,964	1,236,124	Whitman, Christine T.	1,210,031	Florio, James J.	59,809	26,093 R	49.3%	48.3%	50.5%	49.5%
1989	2,253,764	838,553	Courter, James A.	1,379,937	Florio, James J.	35,274	541,384 D	37.2%	61.2%	37.8%	62.2%
1985	1,972,624	1,372,631	Kean, Thomas H.	578,402	Shapiro, Peter	21,591	794,229 R	69.6%	29.3%	70.4%	29.6%
1981	2,317,239	1,145,999	Kean, Thomas H.	1,144,202	Florio, James J.	27,038	1,797 R	49.5%	49.4%	50.0%	50.0%
1977	2,126,264	888,880	Bateman, Raymond H.	1,184,564	Byrne, Brendan T.	52,820	295,684 D	41.8%	55.7%	42.9%	57.1%
1973	2,122,009	676,235	Sandman, Charles W.	1,414,613	Byrne, Brendan T.	31,161	738,378 D	31.9%	66.7%	32.3%	67.7%
1969	2,366,606	1,411,905	Cahill, William T.	911,003	Meyner, Robert B.	43,698	500,902 R	59.7%	38.5%	60.8%	39.2%
1965	2,229,583	915,996	Dumont, Wayne	1,279,568	Hughes, Richard J.	34,019	363,572 D	41.1%	57.4%	41.7%	58.3%
1961	2,152,662	1,049,274	Mitchell, James P.	1,084,194	Hughes, Richard J.	19,194	34,920 D	48.7%	50.4%	49.2%	50.8%
1957	2,018,488	897,321	Forbes, Malcolm S.	1,101,130	Meyner, Robert B.	20,037	203,809 D	44.5%	54.6%	44.9%	55.1%
1953	1,810,812	809,068	Troast, Paul L.	962,710	Meyner, Robert B.	39,034	153,642 D	44.7%	53.2%	45.7%	54.3%
1949**	1,718,788	885,882	Driscoll, Alfred	810,022	Wene, Elmer H.	22,884	75,860 R	51.5%	47.1%	52.2%	47.8%
1946	1,414,527	807,378	Driscoll, Alfred	585,960	Hansen, Lewis G.	21,189	221,418 R	57.1%	41.4%	57.9%	42.1%

**The term of office of New Jersey's governor was increased from three to four years effective with the 1949 election.

POSTWAR VOTE FOR SENATOR

Year	Total Vote	Republican Vote	Candidate	Democratic Vote	Candidate	Other Vote	Rep.-Dem. Plurality	Total Vote Rep.	Total Vote Dem.	Major Vote Rep.	Major Vote Dem.
2008	3,482,445	1,461,025	Zimmer, Dick	1,951,218	Lautenberg, Frank R.	70,202	490,193 D	42.0%	56.0%	42.8%	57.2%
2006	2,250,070	997,775	Kean, Thomas H. Jr.	1,200,843	Menendez, Robert	51,452	203,068 D	44.3%	53.4%	45.4%	54.6%
2002	2,112,604	928,439	Forrester, Doug	1,138,193	Lautenberg, Frank R.	45,972	209,754 D	43.9%	53.9%	44.9%	55.1%
2000	3,015,662	1,420,267	Franks, Bob	1,511,237	Corzine, Jon	84,158	90,970 D	47.1%	50.1%	48.4%	51.6%
1996	2,884,106	1,227,817	Zimmer, Dick	1,519,328	Torricelli, Robert G.	136,961	291,511 D	42.6%	52.7%	44.7%	55.3%
1994	2,054,887	966,244	Haytaian, Garabed	1,033,487	Lautenberg, Frank R.	55,156	67,243 D	47.0%	50.3%	48.3%	51.7%
1990	1,938,454	918,874	Whitman, Christine T.	977,810	Bradley, Bill	41,770	58,936 D	47.4%	50.4%	48.4%	51.6%
1988	2,987,634	1,349,937	Dawkins, Peter M.	1,599,905	Lautenberg, Frank R.	37,792	249,968 D	45.2%	53.6%	45.8%	54.2%
1984	3,096,456	1,080,100	Mochary, Mary V.	1,986,644	Bradley, Bill	29,712	906,544 D	34.9%	64.2%	35.2%	64.8%
1982	2,193,945	1,047,626	Fenwick, Millicent	1,117,549	Lautenberg, Frank R.	28,770	69,923 D	47.8%	50.9%	48.4%	51.6%
1978	1,957,515	844,200	Bell, Jeffrey	1,082,960	Bradley, Bill	30,355	238,760 D	43.1%	55.3%	43.8%	56.2%
1976	2,771,390	1,054,508	Norcross, David F.	1,681,140	Williams, Harrison	35,742	626,632 D	38.0%	60.7%	38.5%	61.5%
1972	2,791,907	1,743,854	Case, Clifford P.	963,573	Krebs, Paul J.	84,480	780,281 R	62.5%	34.5%	64.4%	35.6%
1970	2,142,105	903,026	Gross, Nelson G.	1,157,074	Williams, Harrison	82,005	254,048 D	42.2%	54.0%	43.8%	56.2%
1966	2,131,188	1,279,343	Case, Clifford P.	788,021	Wilentz, Warren W.	63,824	491,322 R	60.0%	37.0%	61.9%	38.1%
1964	2,710,441	1,011,610	Shanley, Bernard M.	1,678,051	Williams, Harrison	20,780	666,441 D	37.3%	61.9%	37.6%	62.4%
1960	2,664,556	1,483,832	Case, Clifford P.	1,151,385	Lord, Thorn	29,339	332,447 R	55.7%	43.2%	56.3%	43.7%
1958	1,881,329	882,287	Kean, Robert W.	966,832	Williams, Harrison	32,210	84,545 D	46.9%	51.4%	47.7%	52.3%
1954	1,770,557	861,528	Case, Clifford P.	858,158	Howell, Charles R.	50,871	3,370 R	48.7%	48.5%	50.1%	49.9%
1952	2,318,232	1,286,782	Smith, H. Alexander	1,011,187	Alexander, Archibald	20,263	275,595 R	55.5%	43.6%	56.0%	44.0%
1948	1,869,882	934,720	Hendrickson, Robert	884,414	Alexander, Archibald	50,748	50,306 R	50.0%	47.3%	51.4%	48.6%
1946	1,367,155	799,808	Smith, H. Alexander	548,458	Brunner, George E.	18,889	251,350 R	58.5%	40.1%	59.3%	40.7%

NEW JERSEY

PRESIDENT 2008

2000 Census Population	County	Total Vote	Republican	Democratic	Other	Rep.-Dem. Plurality	Percentage			
							Total Vote		Major Vote	
							Rep.	Dem.	Rep.	Dem.
252,552	ATLANTIC	119,042	49,902	67,830	1,310	17,928 D	41.9%	57.0%	42.4%	57.6%
884,118	BERGEN	414,733	186,118	225,367	3,248	39,249 D	44.9%	54.3%	45.2%	54.8%
423,394	BURLINGTON	223,174	89,626	131,219	2,329	41,593 D	40.2%	58.8%	40.6%	59.4%
508,932	CAMDEN	235,704	73,819	159,259	2,626	85,440 D	31.3%	67.6%	31.7%	68.3%
102,326	CAPE MAY	50,835	27,288	22,893	654	4,395 R	53.7%	45.0%	54.4%	45.6%
146,438	CUMBERLAND	58,065	22,360	34,919	786	12,559 D	38.5%	60.1%	39.0%	61.0%
793,633	ESSEX	316,183	74,063	240,306	1,814	166,243 D	23.4%	76.0%	23.6%	76.4%
254,673	GLOUCESTER	139,430	60,315	77,267	1,848	16,952 D	43.3%	55.4%	43.8%	56.2%
608,975	HUDSON	211,312	55,360	154,140	1,812	98,780 D	26.2%	72.9%	26.4%	73.6%
121,989	HUNTERDON	69,849	39,092	29,776	981	9,316 R	56.0%	42.6%	56.8%	43.2%
350,761	MERCER	160,039	50,223	107,926	1,890	57,703 D	31.4%	67.4%	31.8%	68.2%
750,162	MIDDLESEX	321,015	123,695	193,812	3,508	70,117 D	38.5%	60.4%	39.0%	61.0%
615,301	MONMOUTH	312,616	160,433	148,737	3,446	11,696 R	51.3%	47.6%	51.9%	48.1%
470,212	MORRIS	246,916	132,331	112,275	2,310	20,056 R	53.6%	45.5%	54.1%	45.9%
510,916	OCEAN	274,298	160,677	110,189	3,432	50,488 R	58.6%	40.2%	59.3%	40.7%
489,049	PASSAIC	187,395	72,552	113,257	1,586	40,705 D	38.7%	60.4%	39.0%	61.0%
64,285	SALEM	31,363	14,816	16,044	503	1,228 D	47.2%	51.2%	48.0%	52.0%
297,490	SOMERSET	151,078	70,085	79,321	1,672	9,236 D	46.4%	52.5%	46.9%	53.1%
144,166	SUSSEX	74,154	44,184	28,840	1,130	15,344 R	59.6%	38.9%	60.5%	39.5%
522,541	UNION	222,097	78,768	141,417	1,912	62,649 D	35.5%	63.7%	35.8%	64.2%
102,437	WARREN	48,939	27,500	20,628	811	6,872 R	56.2%	42.2%	57.1%	42.9%
8,414,350	TOTAL	3,868,237	1,613,207	2,215,422	39,608	602,215 D	41.7%	57.3%	42.1%	57.9%

NEW JERSEY

SENATOR 2008

2000 Census Population	County	Total Vote	Republican	Democratic	Other	Rep.-Dem. Plurality	Percentage			
							Total Vote		Major Vote	
							Rep.	Dem.	Rep.	Dem.
252,552	ATLANTIC	108,691	45,509	61,458	1,724	15,949 D	41.9%	56.5%	42.5%	57.5%
884,118	BERGEN	374,554	159,306	210,799	4,449	51,493 D	42.5%	56.3%	43.0%	57.0%
423,394	BURLINGTON	203,816	85,841	114,781	3,194	28,940 D	42.1%	56.3%	42.8%	57.2%
508,932	CAMDEN	217,310	69,821	144,640	2,849	74,819 D	32.1%	66.6%	32.6%	67.4%
102,326	CAPE MAY	45,055	23,697	20,374	984	3,323 R	52.6%	45.2%	53.8%	46.2%
146,438	CUMBERLAND	50,907	18,498	31,052	1,357	12,554 D	36.3%	61.0%	37.3%	62.7%
793,633	ESSEX	264,800	61,829	198,623	4,348	136,794 D	23.3%	75.0%	23.7%	76.3%
254,673	GLOUCESTER	131,006	55,024	72,990	2,992	17,966 D	42.0%	55.7%	43.0%	57.0%
608,975	HUDSON	171,044	40,573	126,098	4,373	85,525 D	23.7%	73.7%	24.3%	75.7%
121,989	HUNTERDON	65,409	40,309	22,824	2,276	17,485 R	61.6%	34.9%	63.8%	36.2%
350,761	MERCER	146,390	52,298	91,088	3,004	38,790 D	35.7%	62.2%	36.5%	63.5%
750,162	MIDDLESEX	294,363	112,590	175,284	6,489	62,694 D	38.2%	59.5%	39.1%	60.9%
615,301	MONMOUTH	289,461	150,238	132,189	7,034	18,049 R	51.9%	45.7%	53.2%	46.8%
470,212	MORRIS	222,376	124,198	94,558	3,620	29,640 R	55.9%	42.5%	56.8%	43.2%
510,916	OCEAN	253,712	139,480	109,393	4,839	30,087 R	55.0%	43.1%	56.0%	44.0%
489,049	PASSAIC	163,952	59,556	100,598	3,798	41,042 D	36.3%	61.4%	37.2%	62.8%
64,285	SALEM	30,453	12,869	16,132	1,452	3,263 D	42.3%	53.0%	44.4%	55.6%
297,490	SOMERSET	142,022	71,392	66,939	3,691	4,453 R	50.3%	47.1%	51.6%	48.4%
144,166	SUSSEX	71,962	41,660	27,178	3,124	14,482 R	57.9%	37.8%	60.5%	39.5%
522,541	UNION	188,848	69,069	116,201	3,578	47,132 D	36.6%	61.5%	37.3%	62.7%
102,437	WARREN	46,314	27,268	18,019	1,027	9,249 R	58.9%	38.9%	60.2%	39.8%
8,414,350	TOTAL	3,482,445	1,461,025	1,951,218	70,202	490,193 D	42.0%	56.0%	42.8%	57.2%

NEW JERSEY

HOUSE OF REPRESENTATIVES

CD	Year	Total Vote	Republican Vote	Republican Candidate	Democratic Vote	Democratic Candidate	Other Vote	Rep.-Dem. Plurality	Total Vote Rep.	Total Vote Dem.	Major Vote Rep.	Major Vote Dem.
1	2008	285,157	74,001	GLADING, DALE M.	206,453	ANDREWS, ROBERT E.*	4,703	132,452 D	26.0%	72.4%	26.4%	73.6%
1	2006	140,110		—	140,110	ANDREWS, ROBERT E.*		140,110 D		100.0%		100.0%
1	2004	268,203	66,109	HUTCHISON, S. DANIEL	201,163	ANDREWS, ROBERT E.*	931	135,054 D	24.6%	75.0%	24.7%	75.3%
1	2002	131,389		—	121,846	ANDREWS, ROBERT E.*	9,543	121,846 D		92.7%		100.0%
2	2008	283,965	167,701	LoBIONDO, FRANK A.*	110,990	KURKOWSKI, DAVID	5,274	56,711 R	59.1%	39.1%	60.2%	39.8%
2	2006	180,575	111,245	LoBIONDO, FRANK A.*	64,279	THOMAS-HUGHES, VIOLA	5,051	46,966 R	61.6%	35.6%	63.4%	36.6%
2	2004	265,442	172,779	LoBIONDO, FRANK A.*	86,792	ROBB, TIMOTHY J.	5,871	85,987 R	65.1%	32.7%	66.6%	33.4%
2	2002	168,799	116,834	LoBIONDO, FRANK A.*	47,735	FARKAS, STEVEN A.	4,230	69,099 R	69.2%	28.3%	71.0%	29.0%
3	2008	319,512	153,122	MYERS, CHRIS	166,390	ADLER, JOHN H.		13,268 D	47.9%	52.1%	47.9%	52.1%
3	2006	209,851	122,559	SAXTON, H. JAMES*	86,113	SEXTON, RICH	1,179	36,446 R	58.4%	41.0%	58.7%	41.3%
3	2004	308,862	195,938	SAXTON, H. JAMES*	107,034	CONAWAY, HERB	5,890	88,904 R	63.4%	34.7%	64.7%	35.3%
3	2002	189,739	123,375	SAXTON, H. JAMES*	64,364	STRADA, RICHARD	2,000	59,011 R	65.0%	33.9%	65.7%	34.3%
4	2008	306,551	202,972	SMITH, CHRISTOPHER H.*	100,036	ZEITZ, JOSHUA M.	3,543	102,936 R	66.2%	32.6%	67.0%	33.0%
4	2006	189,540	124,482	SMITH, CHRISTOPHER H.*	62,905	GAY, CAROL E.	2,153	61,577 R	65.7%	33.2%	66.4%	33.6%
4	2004	287,553	192,671	SMITH, CHRISTOPHER H.*	92,826	VASQUEZ, AMY	2,056	99,845 R	67.0%	32.3%	67.5%	32.5%
4	2002	174,301	115,293	SMITH, CHRISTOPHER H.*	55,967	BRENNAN, MARY	3,041	59,326 R	66.1%	32.1%	67.3%	32.7%
5	2008	309,007	172,653	GARRETT, SCOTT*	131,033	SHULMAN, DENNIS	5,321	41,620 R	55.9%	42.4%	56.9%	43.1%
5	2006	204,242	112,142	GARRETT, SCOTT*	89,503	ARONSOHN, PAUL	2,597	22,639 R	54.9%	43.8%	55.6%	44.4%
5	2004	297,425	171,220	GARRETT, SCOTT*	122,259	WOLFE, DOROTHEA ANNE	3,946	48,961 R	57.6%	41.1%	58.3%	41.7%
5	2002	199,851	118,881	GARRETT, SCOTT	76,504	SUMERS, ANNE	4,466	42,377 R	59.5%	38.3%	60.8%	39.2%
6	2008	245,077	77,469	McLEOD, ROBERT E.	164,077	PALLONE, FRANK JR *	3,531	86,608 D	31.6%	66.9%	32.1%	67.9%
6	2006	143,773	43,539	BELLEW, LEIGH-ANN	98,615	PALLONE, FRANK JR *	1,619	55,076 D	30.3%	68.6%	30.6%	69.4%
6	2004	230,151	70,942	FERNANDEZ, SYLVESTER	153,981	PALLONE, FRANK JR *	5,228	83,039 D	30.8%	66.9%	31.5%	68.5%
6	2002	137,495	42,479	MEDROW, RIC	91,379	PALLONE, FRANK JR *	3,637	48,900 D	30.9%	66.5%	31.7%	68.3%
7	2008	295,628	148,461	LANCE, LEONARD	124,818	STENDER, LINDA	22,349	23,643 R	50.2%	42.2%	54.3%	45.7%
7	2006	199,075	98,399	FERGUSON, MIKE*	95,454	STENDER, LINDA	5,222	2,945 R	49.4%	47.9%	50.8%	49.2%
7	2004	285,847	162,597	FERGUSON, MIKE*	119,081	BROZAK, STEVE	4,169	43,516 R	56.9%	41.7%	57.7%	42.3%
7	2002	183,002	106,055	FERGUSON, MIKE*	74,879	CARDEN, TIM	2,068	31,176 R	58.0%	40.9%	58.6%	41.4%
8	2008	223,986	63,107	STRATEN, ROLAND	159,279	PASCRELL, BILL JR.*	1,600	96,172 D	28.2%	71.1%	28.4%	71.6%
8	2006	137,639	39,053	SANDOVAL, JOSE M.	97,568	PASCRELL, BILL JR.*	1,018	58,515 D	28.4%	70.9%	28.6%	71.4%
8	2004	218,820	62,747	AJJAN, GEORGE	152,001	PASCRELL, BILL JR.*	4,072	89,254 D	28.7%	69.5%	29.2%	70.8%
8	2002	131,819	40,318	SILVERMAN, JARED	88,101	PASCRELL, BILL JR.*	3,400	47,783 D	30.6%	66.8%	31.4%	68.6%
9	2008	223,885	69,503	MICCO, VINCENT	151,182	ROTHMAN, STEVEN R.*	3,200	81,679 D	31.0%	67.5%	31.5%	68.5%
9	2006	148,095	40,879	MICCO, VINCENT	105,853	ROTHMAN, STEVEN R.*	1,363	64,974 D	27.6%	71.5%	27.9%	72.1%
9	2004	216,251	68,564	TRAWINSKI, EDWARD	146,038	ROTHMAN, STEVEN R.*	1,649	77,474 D	31.7%	67.5%	31.9%	68.1%
9	2002	139,196	42,088	GLASS, JOSEPH	97,108	ROTHMAN, STEVEN R.*		55,020 D	30.2%	69.8%	30.2%	69.8%
10	2008	171,793		—	169,945	PAYNE, DONALD M *	1,848	169,945 D		98.9%		100.0%
10	2006	90,264		—	90,264	PAYNE, DONALD M *		90,264 D		100.0%		100.0%
10	2004	160,713		—	155,697	PAYNE, DONALD M *	5,016	155,697 D		96.9%		100.0%
10	2002	102,346	15,913	WIRTZ, ANDREW	86,433	PAYNE, DONALD M.*		70,520 D	15.5%	84.5%	15.5%	84.5%
11	2008	306,732	189,696	FRELINGHUYSEN, RODNEY*	113,510	WYKA, TOM	3,526	76,186 R	61.8%	37.0%	62.6%	37.4%
11	2006	203,071	126,085	FRELINGHUYSEN, RODNEY*	74,414	WYKA, TOM	2,572	51,671 R	62.1%	36.6%	62.9%	37.1%
11	2004	296,002	200,915	FRELINGHUYSEN, RODNEY*	91,811	BUELL, JAMES W.	3,276	109,104 R	67.9%	31.0%	68.6%	31.4%
11	2002	183,678	132,938	FRELINGHUYSEN, RODNEY*	48,477	PAWAR, VIJ	2,263	84,461 R	72.4%	26.4%	73.3%	26.7%
12	2008	306,934	108,400	BATEMAN, ALAN R.	193,732	HOLT, RUSH D.*	4,802	85,332 D	35.3%	63.1%	35.9%	64.1%
12	2006	190,977	65,509	SINAGRA, JOSEPH S.	125,468	HOLT, RUSH D.*		59,959 D	34.3%	65.7%	34.3%	65.7%
12	2004	289,785	115,014	SPADEA, BILL	171,691	HOLT, RUSH D.*	3,080	56,677 D	39.7%	59.2%	40.1%	59.9%
12	2002	171,713	62,938	SOARIES, DeFOREST "BUSTER"	104,806	HOLT, RUSH D.*	3,969	41,868 D	36.7%	61.0%	37.5%	62.5%

NEW JERSEY

HOUSE OF REPRESENTATIVES

| | | | Republican | | Democratic | | | | Percentage | | | |
| | | | | | | | | | Total Vote | | Major Vote | |
CD	Year	Total Vote	Vote	Candidate	Vote	Candidate	Other Vote	Rep.-Dem. Plurality	Rep.	Dem.	Rep.	Dem.
13	2008	159,753	34,735	TURULA, JOSEPH	120,382	SIRES, ALBIO*	4,636	85,647 D	21.7%	75.4%	22.4%	77.6%
13	2006	99,630	19,284	GUARINI, JOHN J.	77,238	SIRES, ALBIO	3,108	57,954 D	19.4%	77.5%	20.0%	80.0%
13	2004	159,541	35,288	PIATKOWSKI, RICHARD W.	121,018	MENENDEZ, ROBERT*	3,235	85,730 D	22.1%	75.9%	22.6%	77.4%
13	2002	92,731	16,852	GERON, JAMES	72,605	MENENDEZ, ROBERT*	3,274	55,753 D	18.2%	78.3%	18.8%	81.2%
TOTAL	2008	3,437,980	1,461,820		1,911,827		64,333	450,007 D	42.5%	55.6%	43.3%	56.7%
TOTAL	2006	2,136,842	903,176		1,207,784		25,882	304,608 D	42.3%	56.5%	42.8%	57.2%
TOTAL	2004	3,284,595	1,514,784		1,721,392		48,419	206,608 D	46.1%	52.4%	46.8%	53.2%
TOTAL	2002	2,006,059	933,964		1,030,204		41,891	96,240 D	46.6%	51.4%	47.6%	52.4%

Note: An asterisk (*) denotes incumbent.

NEW JERSEY

GENERAL AND PRIMARY ELECTIONS

2008 GENERAL ELECTIONS

President — Other vote was 21,298 Independent (Ralph Nader); 8,441 Libertarian (Bob Barr); 3,956 Constitution (Chuck Baldwin); 3,636 Green (Cynthia A. McKinney); 699 Socialist (Brian Moore); 639 Vote Here (Jeffrey "Jeff" Boss); 523 Socialist Workers (Roger Calero); 416 Socialism and Liberation (Gloria La Riva).

Senator — Other vote was 18,810 Libertarian (Jason Scheurer); 15,935 God We Trust (J.M. Carter); 15,925 Poor People's Campaign (Daryl Mikell Brooks); 10,345 Boss For Senate (Jeffrey Boss); 9,187 Socialist Workers (Sara J. Lobman).

House — Other vote was:

CD 1 — 1,927 Green (Matthew Thieke); 1,258 Back to Basics (Margaret M. Chapman); 1,010 Think Independently (Everitt M. Williams III); 508 Lindsay for Congress (Alvin Lindsay Jr.).

CD 2 — 1,763 Green (Jason M. Glover); 1,551 Constitution (Peter F. Boyce); 1,312 Rock the Boat (Gary Stein); 648 Socialist (Constantino Rizzo).

CD 3 —

CD 4 — 3,543 Green (Steven Welzer).

CD 5 — 5,321 Green (Ed Fanning).

CD 6 — 3,531 Regular Middlesex Independent (Herb Tarbous).

CD 7 — 16,419 Hsing for Congress (Michael P. Hsing); 3,259 All-Day Breakfast Party (Dean Greco); 2,671 Prosperity Not War (Thomas D. Abrams).

CD 8 — 1,600 Libertarian (Derek DeMarco).

CD 9 — 3,200 Independent/Progressive (Michael Perrone Jr.).

CD 10 — 1,848 Socialist Workers (Michael Taber).

CD 11 — 3,526 For the People (Chandler Tedholm).

CD 12 — 4,802 Common Sense Idea (David Corsi).

CD 13 — 3,661 No Slogan Provided (Julio A. Fernandez); 975 Eliminate the Primary (Louis Vernotico).

NEW JERSEY

GENERAL AND PRIMARY ELECTIONS

2008 PRIMARY ELECTIONS

Primary	February 5, 2008 (President) June 3, 2008 (Congress)	Registration (as of May 29, 2008)		
		Democratic	1,682,352	
		Republican	1,030,142	
		Green	794	
		Libertarian	700	
		Constitution	99	
		Reform	65	
		Conservative	45	
		Natural Law	24	
		Unaffiliated	2,238,209	
		TOTAL	4,952,430	

Primary Type Semi-open—Registered Democrats and Republicans could vote only in their party's primary. "Unaffiliated" voters could participate in either party's primary if they were willing to become a member of that party.

	REPUBLICAN PRIMARIES			DEMOCRATIC PRIMARIES		
President	John McCain	313,459	55.4%	Hillary Clinton	613,500	53.8%
	Mitt Romney	160,388	28.3%	Barack Obama	501,372	43.9%
	Mike Huckabee	46,284	8.2%	John Edwards	15,728	1.4%
	Ron Paul	27,301	4.8%	Joseph R. Biden Jr.	4,081	0.4%
	Rudolph Giuliani	15,516	2.7%	Bill Richardson	3,366	0.3%
	Fred Thompson	3,253	0.6%	Dennis J. Kucinich	3,152	0.3%
	TOTAL	566,201		TOTAL	1,141,199	
Senator	Dick Zimmer	84,663	45.8%	Frank R. Lautenberg*	203,012	58.9%
	Joseph Pennacchio	74,546	40.3%	Robert E. Andrews	121,777	35.3%
	Murray Sabrin	25,576	13.8%	Donald Cresitello	19,743	5.7%
	TOTAL	184,785		TOTAL	344,532	
Congressional District 1	Dale M. Glading	5,873	82.3%	Camille S. Andrews	32,108	83.0%
	Fernando Powers	1,266	17.7%	John Caramanna	4,342	11.2%
				Mahdi Ibn-Ziyad	2,222	5.7%
	TOTAL	7,139		TOTAL	38,672	

Camille S. Andrews subsequently withdrew from the race and was replaced on the general election ballot by her husband, Robert E. Andrews, the incumbent. He had run unsuccessfully for the Democratic Senate nomination in the primary.

	REPUBLICAN PRIMARIES			DEMOCRATIC PRIMARIES		
Congressional District 2	Frank A. LoBiondo*	16,026	88.8%	David Kurkowski	16,465	100.0%
	Donna M. Ward	2,025	11.2%			
	TOTAL	18,051				
Congressional District 3	Chris Myers	12,694	49.4%	John H. Adler	18,130	100.0%
	John P. Kelly	6,531	25.4%			
	Justin Michael Murphy	6,494	25.2%			
	TOTAL	25,719				
Congressional District 4	Christopher H. Smith*	16,818	100.0%	Joshua M. Zeitz	13,114	100.0%
Congressional District 5	Scott Garrett*	19,914	100.0%	Dennis Shulman	9,390	61.1%
				Camille M. Abate	4,861	31.6%
				Roger Bacon	1,114	7.3%
				TOTAL	15,365	

NEW JERSEY

GENERAL AND PRIMARY ELECTIONS

	REPUBLICAN PRIMARIES			DEMOCRATIC PRIMARIES		
Congressional District 6	Robert E. McLeod	3,698	55.1%	Frank Pallone Jr.*	18,609	100.0%
	Peter Cerrato	1,946	29.0%			
	James P. Hogan	1,062	15.8%			
	TOTAL	6,706				
Congressional District 7	Leonard Lance	10,094	39.5%	Linda Stender	15,776	100.0%
	Kate Whitman	5,052	19.8%			
	P. Kelly Hatfield	3,902	15.3%			
	Martin Marks	3,211	12.6%			
	Tom Roughneen	1,845	7.2%			
	Darren Young	1,232	4.8%			
	A. D. Amar	241	0.9%			
	TOTAL	25,577				
Congressional District 8	Roland Straten	5,859	100.0%	Bill Pascrell Jr.*	19,948	100.0%
Congressional District 9	Vincent Micco	5,797	100.0%	Steven R. Rothman*	25,418	100.0%
Congressional District 10	No Republican candidate			Donald M. Payne*	30,764	100.0%
Congressional District 11	Rodney Frelinghuysen*	24,304	86.7%	Tom Wyka	10,885	69.7%
	Kate Erber	3,731	13.3%	Ellen Greenberg	2,456	15.7%
				Gary "Harry" Hager	2,271	14.5%
	TOTAL	28,035		TOTAL	15,612	
Congressional District 12	Alan R. Bateman	9,718	100.0%	Rush D. Holt*	23,653	100.0%
Congressional District 13	Joseph Turula	1,739	100.0%	Albio Sires*	26,527	100.0%

Note: An asterisk (*) denotes incumbent.

NEW MEXICO

Congressional districts first established for elections held in 2002
3 members

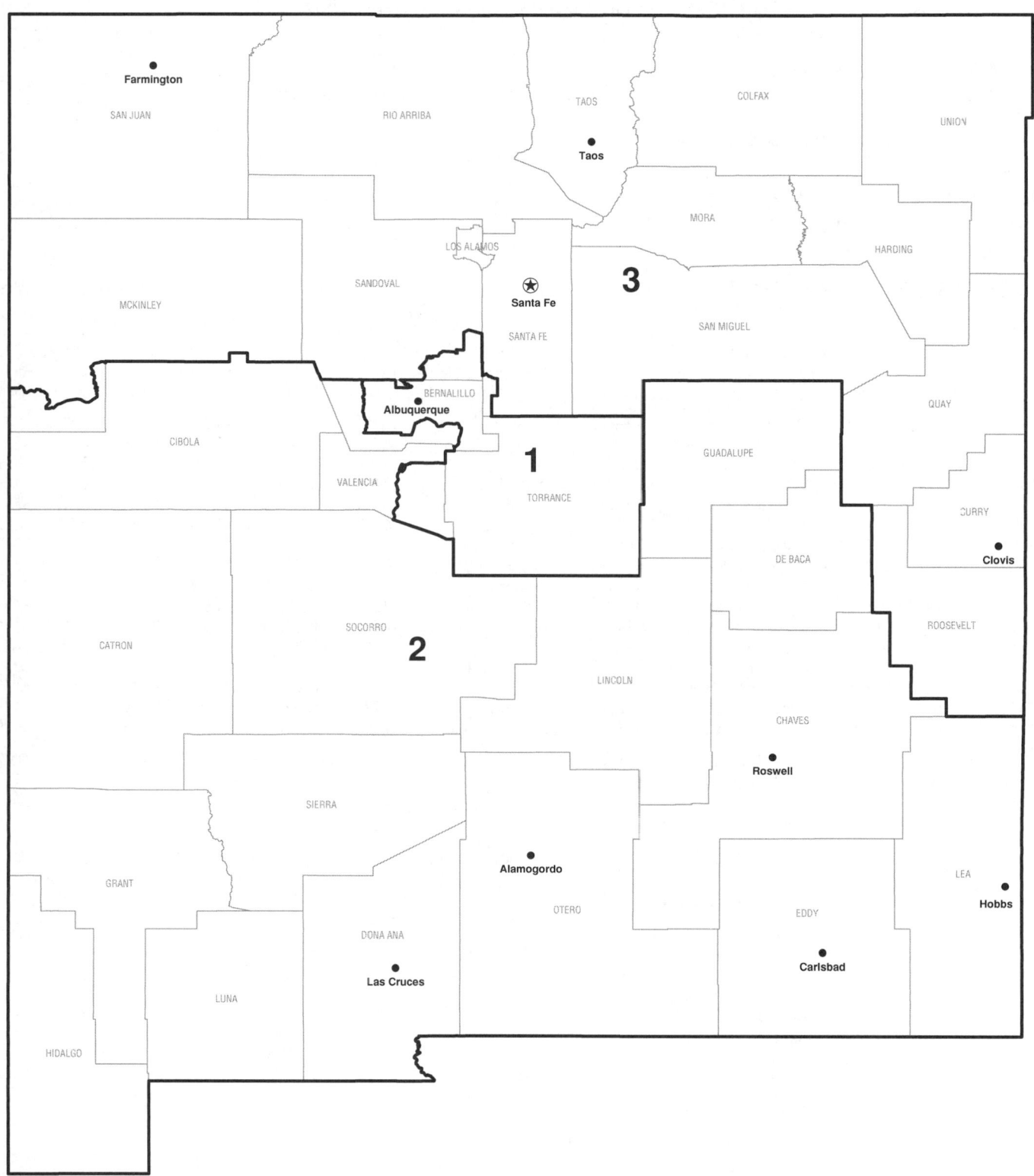

NEW MEXICO

GOVERNOR

Bill Richardson (D). Reelected 2006 to a four-year term. Previously elected 2002.

SENATORS (2 Democrats)

Jeff Bingaman (D). Reelected 2006 to a six-year term. Previously elected 2000, 1994, 1988, 1982.

Tom Udall (D). Elected 2008 to a six-year term.

REPRESENTATIVES (3 Democrats)

1. Martin Heinrich (D)   2. Harry Teague (D)   3. Ben Ray Lujan (D)

POSTWAR VOTE FOR PRESIDENT

| | | Republican | | Democratic | | | | Percentage | | | |
| | | | | | | | | Total Vote | | Major Vote | |
Year	Total Vote	Vote	Candidate	Vote	Candidate	Other Vote	Plurality	Rep.	Dem.	Rep.	Dem.
2008	830,158	346,832	McCain, John	472,422	Obama, Barack	10,904	125,590 D	41.8%	56.9%	42.3%	57.7%
2004	756,304	376,930	Bush, George W.	370,942	Kerry, John	8,432	5,988 R	49.8%	49.0%	50.4%	49.6%
2000**	598,605	286,417	Bush, George W.	286,783	Gore, Al	25,405	366 D	47.8%	47.9%	50.0%	50.0%
1996**	556,074	232,751	Dole, Bob	273,495	Clinton, Bill	49,828	40,744 D	41.9%	49.2%	46.0%	54.0%
1992**	569,986	212,824	Bush, George	261,617	Clinton, Bill	95,545	48,793 D	37.3%	45.9%	44.9%	55.1%
1988	521,287	270,341	Bush, George	244,497	Dukakis, Michael S.	6,449	25,844 R	51.9%	46.9%	52.5%	47.5%
1984	514,370	307,101	Reagan, Ronald	201,769	Mondale, Walter F.	5,500	105,332 R	59.7%	39.2%	60.3%	39.7%
1980**	456,971	250,779	Reagan, Ronald	167,826	Carter, Jimmy	38,366	82,953 R	54.9%	36.7%	59.9%	40.1%
1976	418,409	211,419	Ford, Gerald R.	201,148	Carter, Jimmy	5,842	10,271 R	50.5%	48.1%	51.2%	48.8%
1972	386,241	235,606	Nixon, Richard M.	141,084	McGovern, George S.	9,551	94,522 R	61.0%	36.5%	62.5%	37.5%
1968**	327,350	169,692	Nixon, Richard M.	130,081	Humphrey, Hubert H.	27,577	39,611 R	51.8%	39.7%	56.6%	43.4%
1964	328,645	132,838	Goldwater, Barry M.	194,015	Johnson, Lyndon B.	1,792	61,177 D	40.4%	59.0%	40.6%	59.4%
1960	311,107	153,733	Nixon, Richard M.	156,027	Kennedy, John F.	1,347	2,294 D	49.4%	50.2%	49.6%	50.4%
1956	253,926	146,788	Eisenhower, Dwight D.	106,098	Stevenson, Adlai E.	1,040	40,690 R	57.8%	41.8%	58.0%	42.0%
1952	238,608	132,170	Eisenhower, Dwight D.	105,661	Stevenson, Adlai E.	777	26,509 R	55.4%	44.3%	55.6%	44.4%
1948	187,063	80,303	Dewey, Thomas E.	105,464	Truman, Harry S.	1,296	25,161 D	42.9%	56.4%	43.2%	56.8%

**In past elections, the other vote included: 2000 - 21,251 Green (Ralph Nader); 1996 - 32,257 Reform (Ross Perot); 1992 - 91,895 Independent (Perot); 1980 - 29,459 Independent (John Anderson); 1968 - 25,737 American Independent (George Wallace).

NEW MEXICO

POSTWAR VOTE FOR GOVERNOR

| | | Republican | | Democratic | | | | Percentage | | | |
| | | | | | | | | Total Vote | | Major Vote | |
Year	Total Vote	Vote	Candidate	Vote	Candidate	Other Vote	Rep.-Dem. Plurality	Rep.	Dem.	Rep.	Dem.
2006	559,170	174,364	Dendahl, John	384,806	Richardson, Bill		210,442 D	31.2%	68.8%	31.2%	68.8%
2002	484,233	189,074	Sanchez, John A.	268,693	Richardson, Bill	26,466	79,619 D	39.0%	55.5%	41.3%	58.7%
1998	498,703	271,948	Johnson, Gary E.	226,755	Chavez, Martin J.		45,193 R	54.5%	45.5%	54.5%	45.5%
1994**	467,621	232,945	Johnson, Gary E.	186,686	King, Bruce	47,990	46,259 R	49.8%	39.9%	55.5%	44.5%
1990	411,236	185,692	Bond, Frank M.	224,564	King, Bruce	980	38,872 D	45.2%	54.6%	45.3%	54.7%
1986	394,833	209,455	Carruthers, Garrey E.	185,378	Powell. Ray B.		24,077 R	53.0%	47.0%	53.0%	47.0%
1982	407,466	191,626	Irick, John B.	215,840	Anaya, Toney		24,214 D	47.0%	53.0%	47.0%	53.0%
1978	345,577	170,848	Skeen, Joseph R.	174,631	King, Bruce	98	3,783 D	49.4%	50.5%	49.5%	50.5%
1974	328,742	160,430	Skeen, Joseph R.	164,172	Apodaca, Jerry	4,140	3,742 D	48.8%	49.9%	49.4%	50.6%
1970**	290,375	134,640	Domenici, Pete V.	148,835	King, Bruce	6,900	14,195 D	46.4%	51.3%	47.5%	52.5%
1968	318,975	160,140	Cargo, David F.	157,230	Chavez, Fabian	1,605	2,910 R	50.2%	49.3%	50.5%	49.5%
1966	260,232	134,625	Cargo, David F.	125,587	Lusk, Thomas E.	20	9,038 R	51.7%	48.3%	51.7%	48.3%
1964	318,042	126,540	Tucker, Merle H.	191,497	Campbell, Jack M.	5	64,957 D	39.8%	60.2%	39.8%	60.2%
1962	247,135	116,184	Mechem, Edwin L.	130,933	Campbell, Jack M.	18	14,749 D	47.0%	53.0%	47.0%	53.0%
1960	305,542	153,765	Mechem, Edwin L.	151,777	Burroughs, John		1,988 R	50.3%	49.7%	50.3%	49.7%
1958	205,048	101,567	Mechem, Edwin L.	103,481	Burroughs, John		1,914 D	49.5%	50.5%	49.5%	50.5%
1956	251,751	131,488	Mechem, Edwin L.	120,263	Simms, John F.		11,225 R	52.2%	47.8%	52.2%	47.8%
1954	193,956	83,373	Stockton, Alvin	110,583	Simms, John F.		27,210 D	43.0%	57.0%	43.0%	57.0%
1952	240,150	129,116	Mechem, Edwin L.	111,034	Grantham, Everett		18,082 R	53.8%	46.2%	53.8%	46.2%
1950	180,205	96,846	Mechem, Edwin L.	83,359	Miles, John E.		13,487 R	53.7%	46.3%	53.7%	46.3%
1948	189,992	86,023	Lujan, Manuel	103,969	Mabry, Thomas J.		17,946 D	45.3%	54.7%	45.3%	54.7%
1946	132,930	62,875	Safford, Edward L.	70,055	Mabry, Thomas J.		7,180 D	47.3%	52.7%	47.3%	52.7%

**In past elections, the other vote included: 1994 - 47,990 Green (Roberto Mondragon). The term of New Mexico's governor was increased from two to four years effective with the 1970 election.

POSTWAR VOTE FOR SENATOR

| | | Republican | | Democratic | | | | Percentage | | | |
| | | | | | | | | Total Vote | | Major Vote | |
Year	Total Vote	Vote	Candidate	Vote	Candidate	Other Vote	Rep.-Dem. Plurality	Rep.	Dem.	Rep.	Dem.
2008	823,650	318,522	Pearce, Steve	505,128	Udall, Tom		186,606 D	38.7%	61.3%	38.7%	61.3%
2006	558,550	163,826	McCulloch, Allen W.	394,365	Bingaman, Jeff	359	230,539 D	29.3%	70.6%	29.3%	70.7%
2002	483,340	314,301	Domenici, Pete V.	169,039	Tristani, Gloria		145,262 R	65.0%	35.0%	65.0%	35.0%
2000	589,526	225,517	Redmond, Bill	363,744	Bingaman, Jeff	265	138,227 D	38.3%	61.7%	38.3%	61.7%
1996	551,821	357,171	Domenici, Pete V.	164,356	Trujillo, Art	30,294	192,815 R	64.7%	29.8%	68.5%	31.5%
1994	463,196	213,025	McMillan, Colin R.	249,989	Bingaman, Jeff	182	36,964 D	46.0%	54.0%	46.0%	54.0%
1990	406,938	296,712	Domenici, Pete V.	110,033	Benavides, Tom R.	193	186,679 R	72.9%	27.0%	72.9%	27.1%
1988	508,598	186,579	Valentine, William	321,983	Bingaman, Jeff	36	135,404 D	36.7%	63.3%	36.7%	63.3%
1984	502,634	361,371	Domenici, Pete V.	141,253	Pratt, Judith A.	10	220,118 R	71.9%	28.1%	71.9%	28.1%
1982	404,810	187,128	Schmitt, Harrison	217,682	Bingaman, Jeff		30,554 D	46.2%	53.8%	46.2%	53.8%
1978	343,554	183,442	Domenici, Pete V.	160,045	Anaya, Toney	67	23,397 R	53.4%	46.6%	53.4%	46.6%
1976	413,141	234,681	Schmitt, Harrison	176,382	Montoya, Joseph M.	2,078	58,299 R	56.8%	42.7%	57.1%	42.9%
1972	378,330	204,253	Domenici, Pete V.	173,815	Daniels, Jack	262	30,438 R	54.0%	45.9%	54.0%	46.0%
1970	289,906	135,004	Carter, Anderson	151,486	Montoya, Joseph M.	3,416	16,482 D	46.6%	52.3%	47.1%	52.9%
1966	258,203	120,988	Carter, Anderson	137,205	Anderson, Clinton P.	10	16,217 D	46.9%	53.1%	46.9%	53.1%
1964	325,774	147,562	Mechem, Edwin L.	178,209	Montoya, Joseph M.	3	30,647 D	45.3%	54.7%	45.3%	54.7%
1960	300,551	109,897	Colwes, William F.	190,654	Anderson, Clinton P.		80,757 D	36.6%	63.4%	36.6%	63.4%
1958	203,323	75,827	Atchley, Forrest S.	127,496	Chavez, Dennis		51,669 D	37.3%	62.7%	37.3%	62.7%
1954	194,422	83,071	Mechem, Edwin L.	111,351	Anderson, Clinton P.		28,280 D	42.7%	57.3%	42.7%	57.3%
1952	239,711	117,168	Hurley, Patrick J.	122,543	Chavez, Dennis		5,375 D	48.9%	51.1%	48.9%	51.1%
1948	188,495	80,226	Hurley, Patrick J.	108,269	Anderson, Clinton P.		28,043 D	42.6%	57.4%	42.6%	57.4%
1946	133,282	64,632	Hurley, Patrick J.	68,650	Chavez, Dennis		4,018 D	48.5%	51.5%	48.5%	51.5%

NEW MEXICO
PRESIDENT 2008

2000 Census Population	County	Total Vote	Republican	Democratic	Other	Rep.-Dem. Plurality	Percentage Total Vote Rep.	Dem.	Major Vote Rep.	Dem.
556,678	BERNALILLO	285,778	110,521	171,556	3,701	61,035 D	38.7%	60.0%	39.2%	60.8%
3,543	CATRON	2,112	1,398	664	50	734 R	66.2%	31.4%	67.8%	32.2%
61,382	CHAVES	22,112	13,651	8,197	264	5,454 R	61.7%	37.1%	62.5%	37.5%
25,595	CIBOLA	9,097	3,131	5,827	139	2,696 D	34.4%	64.1%	35.0%	65.0%
14,189	COLFAX	6,384	2,805	3,490	89	685 D	43.9%	54.7%	44.6%	55.4%
45,044	CURRY	14,438	9,599	4,670	169	4,929 R	66.5%	32.3%	67.3%	32.7%
2,240	DE BACA	1,044	676	359	9	317 R	64.8%	34.4%	65.3%	34.7%
174,682	DONA ANA	69,280	28,068	40,282	930	12,214 D	40.5%	58.1%	41.1%	58.9%
51,658	EDDY	20,093	12,500	7,351	242	5,149 R	62.2%	36.6%	63.0%	37.0%
31,002	GRANT	13,755	5,406	8,142	207	2,736 D	39.3%	59.2%	39.9%	60.1%
4,680	GUADALUPE	2,196	620	1,557	19	937 D	28.2%	70.9%	28.5%	71.5%
810	HARDING	626	358	260	8	98 R	57.2%	41.5%	57.9%	42.1%
5,932	HIDALGO	1,951	936	993	22	57 D	48.0%	50.9%	48.5%	51.5%
55,511	LEA	18,645	13,347	5,108	190	8,239 R	71.6%	27.4%	72.3%	27.7%
19,411	LINCOLN	9,696	6,001	3,535	160	2,466 R	61.9%	36.5%	62.9%	37.1%
18,343	LOS ALAMOS	11,069	5,064	5,824	181	760 D	45.7%	52.6%	46.5%	53.5%
25,016	LUNA	8,340	3,870	4,311	159	441 D	46.4%	51.7%	47.3%	52.7%
74,798	MCKINLEY	23,207	6,382	16,572	253	10,190 D	27.5%	71.4%	27.8%	72.2%
5,180	MORA	2,760	569	2,168	23	1,599 D	20.6%	78.6%	20.8%	79.2%
62,298	OTERO	21,766	12,806	8,610	350	4,196 R	58.8%	39.6%	59.8%	40.2%
10,155	QUAY	3,996	2,367	1,547	82	820 R	59.2%	38.7%	60.5%	39.5%
41,190	RIO ARRIBA	16,940	4,086	12,703	151	8,617 D	24.1%	75.0%	24.3%	75.7%
18,018	ROOSEVELT	6,720	4,311	2,303	106	2,008 R	64.2%	34.3%	65.2%	34.8%
89,908	SANDOVAL	58,630	25,193	32,669	768	7,476 D	43.0%	55.7%	43.5%	56.5%
113,801	SAN JUAN	46,511	27,869	18,028	614	9,841 R	59.9%	38.8%	60.7%	39.3%
30,126	SAN MIGUEL	12,941	2,478	10,320	143	7,842 D	19.1%	79.7%	19.4%	80.6%
129,292	SANTA FE	72,223	15,807	55,567	849	39,760 D	21.9%	76.9%	22.1%	77.9%
13,270	SIERRA	5,485	3,017	2,352	116	665 R	55.0%	42.9%	56.2%	43.8%
18,078	SOCORRO	7,895	3,032	4,696	167	1,664 D	38.4%	59.5%	39.2%	60.8%
29,979	TAOS	16,886	2,866	13,816	204	10,950 D	17.0%	81.8%	17.2%	82.8%
16,911	TORRANCE	6,941	3,735	3,087	119	648 R	53.8%	44.5%	54.7%	45.3%
4,174	UNION	1,742	1,227	492	23	735 R	70.4%	28.2%	71.4%	28.6%
66,152	VALENCIA	28,899	13,136	15,366	397	2,230 D	45.5%	53.2%	46.1%	53.9%
1,819,046	TOTAL	830,158	346,832	472,422	10,904	125,590 D	41.8%	56.9%	42.3%	57.7%

NEW MEXICO

SENATOR 2008

2000 Census Population	County	Total Vote	Republican	Democratic	Other	Rep.-Dem. Plurality	Percentage Total Vote Rep.	Percentage Total Vote Dem.	Percentage Major Vote Rep.	Percentage Major Vote Dem.
556,678	BERNALILLO	283,535	102,784	180,751		77,967 D	36.3%	63.7%	36.3%	63.7%
3,543	CATRON	2,096	1,316	780		536 R	62.8%	37.2%	62.8%	37.2%
61,382	CHAVES	22,007	13,398	8,609		4,789 R	60.9%	39.1%	60.9%	39.1%
25,595	CIBOLA	9,059	2,904	6,155		3,251 D	32.1%	67.9%	32.1%	67.9%
14,189	COLFAX	6,354	2,240	4,114		1,874 D	35.3%	64.7%	35.3%	64.7%
45,044	CURRY	14,338	7,218	7,120		98 R	50.3%	49.7%	50.3%	49.7%
2,240	DE BACA	1,042	593	449		144 R	56.9%	43.1%	56.9%	43.1%
174,682	DONA ANA	68,512	26,433	42,079		15,646 D	38.6%	61.4%	38.6%	61.4%
51,658	EDDY	19,947	11,585	8,362		3,223 R	58.1%	41.9%	58.1%	41.9%
31,002	GRANT	13,655	4,932	8,723		3,791 D	36.1%	63.9%	36.1%	63.9%
4,680	GUADALUPE	2,192	596	1,596		1,000 D	27.2%	72.8%	27.2%	72.8%
810	HARDING	624	287	337		50 D	46.0%	54.0%	46.0%	54.0%
5,932	HIDALGO	1,940	855	1,085		230 D	44.1%	55.9%	44.1%	55.9%
55,511	LEA	18,518	13,744	4,774		8,970 R	74.2%	25.8%	74.2%	25.8%
19,411	LINCOLN	9,612	5,787	3,825		1,962 R	60.2%	39.8%	60.2%	39.8%
18,343	LOS ALAMOS	10,903	5,428	5,475		47 D	49.8%	50.2%	49.8%	50.2%
25,016	LUNA	8,231	3,492	4,739		1,247 D	42.4%	57.6%	42.4%	57.6%
74,798	MCKINLEY	23,099	4,742	18,357		13,615 D	20.5%	79.5%	20.5%	79.5%
5,180	MORA	2,748	581	2,167		1,586 D	21.1%	78.9%	21.1%	78.9%
62,298	OTERO	21,526	11,852	9,674		2,178 R	55.1%	44.9%	55.1%	44.9%
10,155	QUAY	3,975	1,761	2,214		453 D	44.3%	55.7%	44.3%	55.7%
41,190	RIO ARRIBA	16,823	4,045	12,778		8,733 D	24.0%	76.0%	24.0%	76.0%
18,018	ROOSEVELT	6,642	3,453	3,189		264 R	52.0%	48.0%	52.0%	48.0%
89,908	SANDOVAL	58,130	22,824	35,306		12,482 D	39.3%	60.7%	39.3%	60.7%
113,801	SAN JUAN	46,259	24,021	22,238		1,783 R	51.9%	48.1%	51.9%	48.1%
30,126	SAN MIGUEL	12,899	2,147	10,752		8,605 D	16.6%	83.4%	16.6%	83.4%
129,292	SANTA FE	71,532	14,782	56,750		41,968 D	20.7%	79.3%	20.7%	79.3%
13,270	SIERRA	5,441	2,769	2,672		97 R	50.9%	49.1%	50.9%	49.1%
18,078	SOCORRO	7,858	3,036	4,822		1,786 D	38.6%	61.4%	38.6%	61.4%
29,979	TAOS	16,751	2,591	14,160		11,569 D	15.5%	84.5%	15.5%	84.5%
16,911	TORRANCE	6,932	3,387	3,545		158 D	48.9%	51.1%	48.9%	51.1%
4,174	UNION	1,723	890	833		57 R	51.7%	48.3%	51.7%	48.3%
66,152	VALENCIA	28,747	12,049	16,698		4,649 D	41.9%	58.1%	41.9%	58.1%
1,819,046	TOTAL	823,650	318,522	505,128		186,606 D	38.7%	61.3%	38.7%	61.3%

NEW MEXICO

HOUSE OF REPRESENTATIVES

CD	Year	Total Vote	Republican Vote	Candidate	Democratic Vote	Candidate	Other Vote	Rep.-Dem. Plurality		Total Vote Rep.	Dem.	Major Vote Rep.	Dem.
1	2008	298,756	132,485	WHITE, DARREN	166,271	HEINRICH, MARTIN		33,786	D	44.3%	55.7%	44.3%	55.7%
1	2006	211,111	105,986	WILSON, HEATHER A.*	105,125	MADRID, PATRICIA A.		861	R	50.2%	49.8%	50.2%	49.8%
1	2004	270,905	147,372	WILSON, HEATHER A.*	123,339	ROMERO, RICHARD M.	194	24,033	R	54.4%	45.5%	54.4%	45.6%
1	2002	172,945	95,711	WILSON, HEATHER A.*	77,234	ROMERO, RICHARD M.		18,477	R	55.3%	44.7%	55.3%	44.7%
2	2008	231,552	101,980	TINSLEY, EDWARD R.	129,572	TEAGUE, HARRY		27,592	D	44.0%	56.0%	44.0%	56.0%
2	2006	155,874	92,620	PEARCE, STEVE*	63,119	KISSLING, ALBERT D.	135	29,501	R	59.4%	40.5%	59.5%	40.5%
2	2004	216,790	130,498	PEARCE, STEVE*	86,292	KING, GARY K.		44,206	R	60.2%	39.8%	60.2%	39.8%
2	2002	141,629	79,631	PEARCE, STEVE	61,916	SMITH, JOHN ARTHUR	82	17,715	R	56.2%	43.7%	56.3%	43.7%
3	2008	284,258	86,618	EAST, DANIEL K.	161,292	LUJAN, BEN RAY	36,348	74,674	D	30.5%	56.7%	34.9%	65.1%
3	2006	194,099	49,219	DOLIN, RONALD M.	144,880	UDALL, TOM*		95,661	D	25.4%	74.6%	25.4%	74.6%
3	2004	255,204	79,935	TUCKER, GREGORY M.	175,269	UDALL, TOM*		95,334	D	31.3%	68.7%	31.3%	68.7%
3	2002	122,950		—	122,950	UDALL, TOM*		122,950	D		100.0%		100.0%
TOTAL	2008	814,566	321,083		457,135		36,348	136,052	D	39.4%	56.1%	41.3%	58.7%
TOTAL	2006	561,084	247,825		313,124		135	65,299	D	44.2%	55.8%	44.2%	55.8%
TOTAL	2004	742,899	357,805		384,900		194	27,095	D	48.2%	51.8%	48.2%	51.8%
TOTAL	2002	437,524	175,342		262,100		82	86,758	D	40.1%	59.9%	40.1%	59.9%

Note: An asterisk (*) denotes incumbent.

NEW MEXICO

GENERAL AND PRIMARY ELECTIONS

2008 GENERAL ELECTIONS

President   Other vote was: 5,327 Independent (Ralph Nader); 2,428 Libertarian (Bob Barr); 1,597 Constitution (Chuck Baldwin); 1,552 Green (Cynthia A. McKinney).

Senator

House   Other vote was:

   CD 1
   CD 2
   CD 3   36,348 Independent (Carol Miller).

2008 PRIMARY ELECTIONS

Primary   June 3, 2008   **Registration** (as of May 23, 2008)

Democratic	543,615
Republican	354,272
Other Parties	26,851
Declined to State	161,116
TOTAL	1,085,854

Primary Type   Closed—Only registered Democrats and Republicans could vote in their party's primary.

NEW MEXICO

GENERAL AND PRIMARY ELECTIONS

	REPUBLICAN PRIMARIES			DEMOCRATIC PRIMARIES		
President	John McCain	95,378	86.0%	No presidential primary		
	Ron Paul	15,561	14.0%			
	TOTAL	110,939				
Senator	Steve Pearce	57,953	51.3%	Tom Udall	141,629	100.0%
	Heather A. Wilson	55,039	48.7%			
	TOTAL	112,992				
Congressional District 1	Darren White	37,060	81.8%	Martin Heinrich	22,341	43.5%
	Joseph J. Carraro	8,246	18.2%	Rebecca D. Vigil-Giron	12,660	24.7%
				Michelle Lujan Grisham	12,074	23.5%
				Robert L. Pidcock	4,273	8.3%
	TOTAL	45,306		TOTAL	51,348	
Congressional District 2	Edward R. Tinsley	11,510	31.6%	Harry Teague	20,281	52.2%
	Monty Newman	7,486	20.6%	Bill McCamley	18,597	47.8%
	Aubrey Dunn	7,341	20.2%			
	Greg Sowards	6,468	17.8%			
	C. Earl Greer	3,614	9.9%			
	TOTAL	36,419		TOTAL	38,878	
Congressional District 3	Daniel K. East	14,767	53.9%	Ben Ray Lujan	26,775	41.5%
	Marco E. Gonzales	12,632	46.1%	Donald H. Wiviott	16,497	25.6%
				Benny J. Shendo Jr.	10,148	15.7%
				Harry B. Montoya	7,234	11.2%
				Jon Adams	1,979	3.1%
				Rudy Martin	1,845	2.9%
	TOTAL	27,399		TOTAL	64,478	

NEW YORK

Congressional districts first established for elections held in 2002
29 members

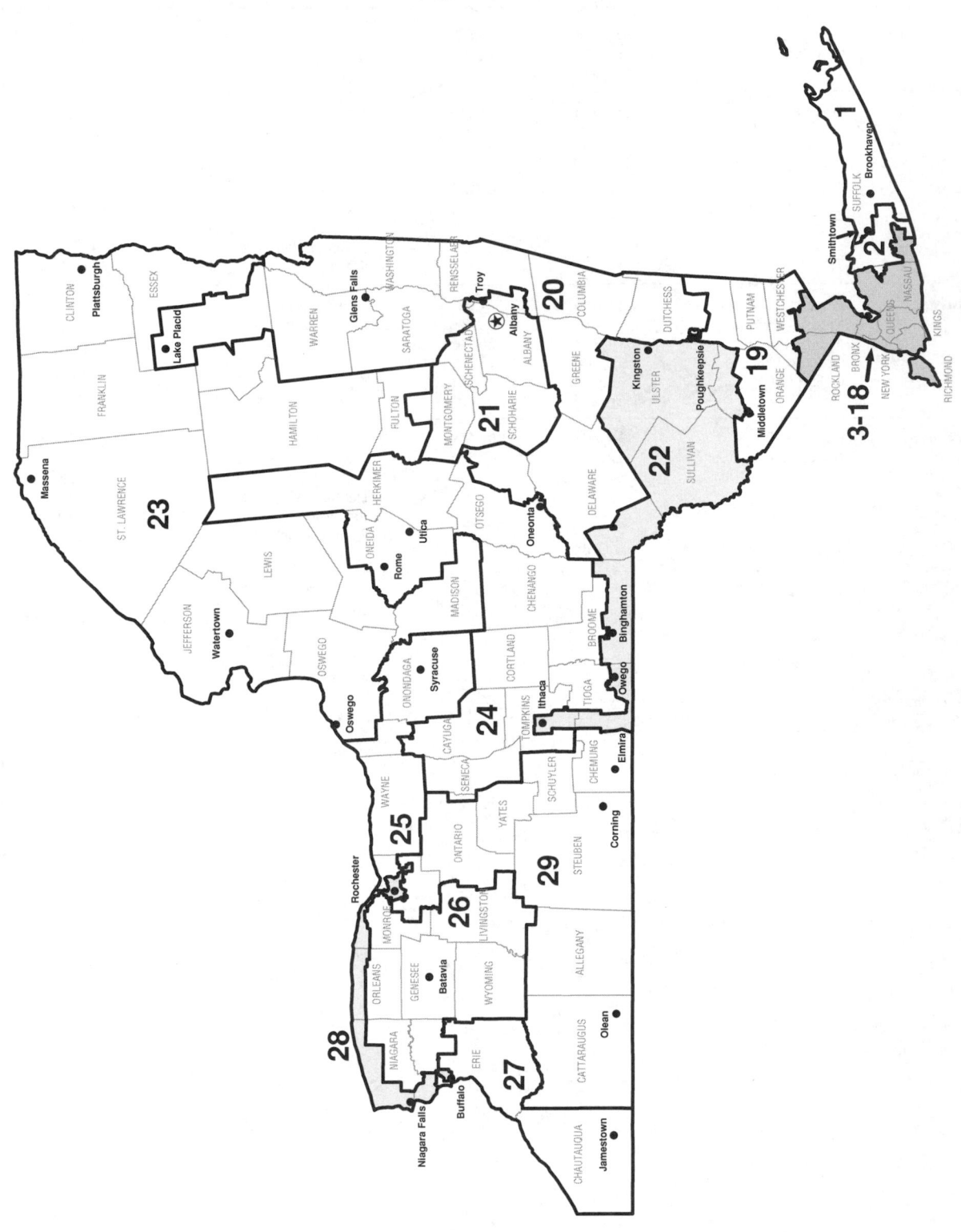

NEW YORK

New York City Area

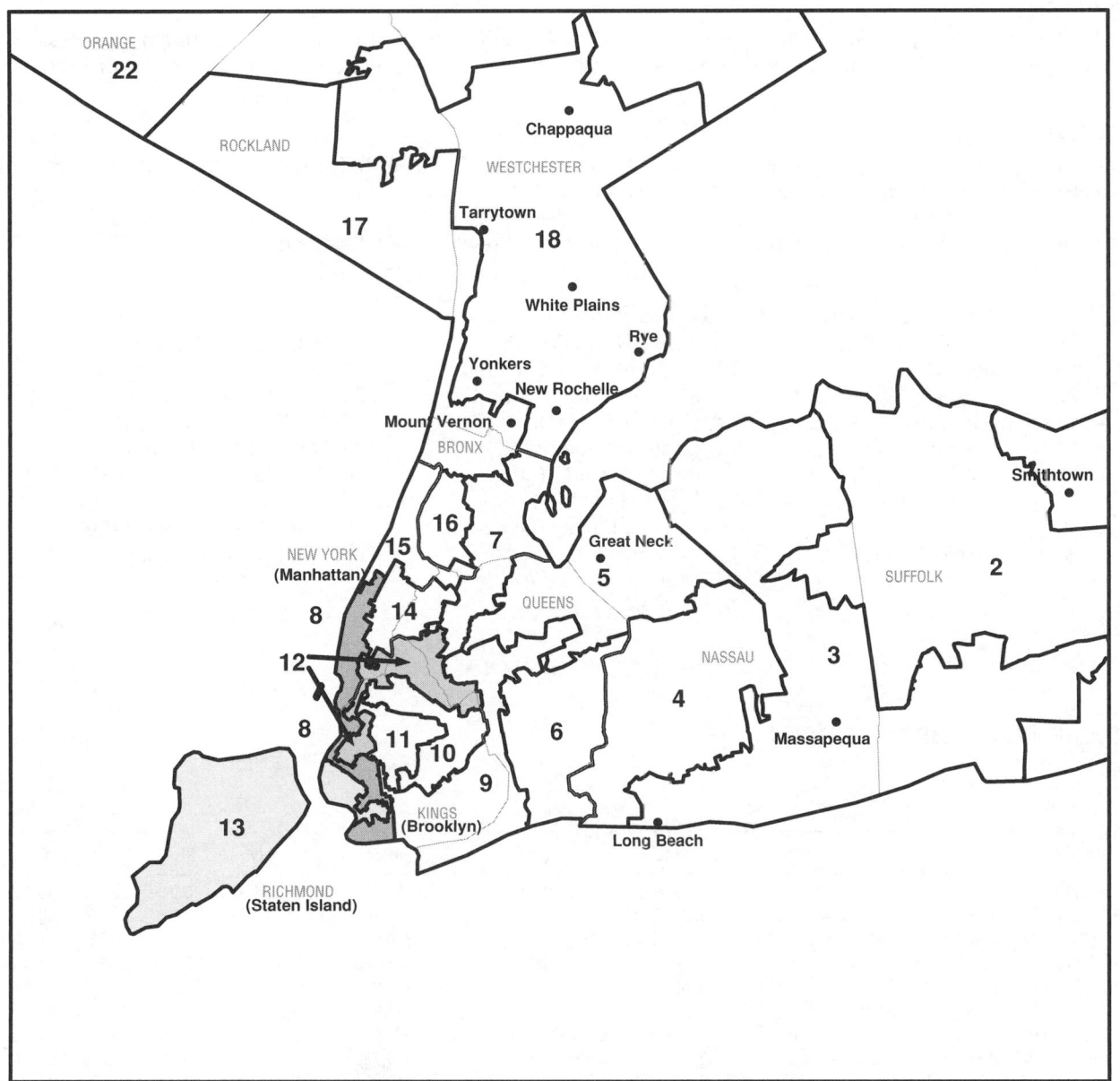

NEW YORK

GOVERNOR

David A. Paterson (D). Sworn in as governor March 17, 2008, to fill the vacancy created by the resignation of Eliot Spitzer (D), who stepped down after acknowledging he had been named as a customer of a prostitution ring.

SENATORS (2 Democrats)

Kirsten E. Gillibrand (D). Sworn in as senator January 27, 2009, to fill the vacancy created by the resignation of Hillary Rodham Clinton (D) to become U.S. Secretary of State.

Charles E. Schumer (D). Reelected 2004 to a six-year term. Previously elected 1998.

REPRESENTATIVES (26 Democrats, 3 Republicans)

1. Timothy H. Bishop (D)
2. Steve Israel (D)
3. Peter T. King (R)
4. Carolyn McCarthy (D)
5. Gary L. Ackerman (D)
6. Gregory W. Meeks (D)
7. Joseph Crowley (D)
8. Jerrold Nadler (D)
9. Anthony Weiner (D)
10. Edolphus Towns (D)
11. Yvette D. Clarke (D)
12. Nydia M. Velázquez (D)
13. Michael E. McMahon (D)
14. Carolyn B. Maloney (D)
15. Charles B. Rangel (D)
16. Jose E. Serrano (D)
17. Eliot L. Engel (D)
18. Nita M. Lowey (D)
19. John Hall (D)
20. Scott Murphy (D)
21. Paul Tonko (D)
22. Maurice D. Hinchey (D)
23. John M. McHugh (R)
24. Michael A. Arcuri (D)
25. Daniel B. Maffei (D)
26. Christopher John Lee (R)
27. Brian Higgins (D)
28. Louise M. Slaughter (D)
29. Eric J.J. Massa (D)

POSTWAR VOTE FOR PRESIDENT

Year	Total Vote	Republican Vote	Candidate	Democratic Vote	Candidate	Other Vote	Plurality	Total Vote Rep.	Dem.	Major Vote Rep.	Dem.
2008	7,640,931	2,752,771	McCain, John	4,804,945	Obama, Barack	83,215	2,052,174 D	36.0%	62.9%	36.4%	63.6%
2004	7,391,036	2,962,567	Bush, George W.	4,314,280	Kerry, John	114,189	1,351,713 D	40.1%	58.4%	40.7%	59.3%
2000**	6,821,999	2,403,374	Bush, George W.	4,107,697	Gore, Al	310,928	1,704,323 D	35.2%	60.2%	36.9%	63.1%
1996**	6,316,129	1,933,492	Dole, Bob	3,756,177	Clinton, Bill	626,460	1,822,685 D	30.6%	59.5%	34.0%	66.0%
1992**	6,926,925	2,346,649	Bush, George	3,444,450	Clinton, Bill	1,135,826	1,097,801 D	33.9%	49.7%	40.5%	59.5%
1988	6,485,683	3,081,871	Bush, George	3,347,882	Dukakis, Michael S.	55,930	266,011 D	47.5%	51.6%	47.9%	52.1%
1984	6,806,810	3,664,763	Reagan, Ronald	3,119,609	Mondale, Walter F.	22,438	545,154 R	53.8%	45.8%	54.0%	46.0%
1980**	6,201,959	2,893,831	Reagan, Ronald	2,728,372	Carter, Jimmy	579,756	165,459 R	46.7%	44.0%	51.5%	48.5%
1976	6,534,170	3,100,791	Ford, Gerald R.	3,389,558	Carter, Jimmy	43,821	288,767 D	47.5%	51.9%	47.8%	52.2%
1972	7,165,919	4,192,778	Nixon, Richard M.	2,951,084	McGovern, George S.	22,057	1,241,694 R	58.5%	41.2%	58.7%	41.3%
1968**	6,791,688	3,007,932	Nixon, Richard M.	3,378,470	Humphrey, Hubert H.	405,286	370,538 D	44.3%	49.7%	47.1%	52.9%
1964	7,166,275	2,243,559	Goldwater, Barry M.	4,913,102	Johnson, Lyndon B.	9,614	2,669,543 D	31.3%	68.6%	31.3%	68.7%
1960	7,291,079	3,446,419	Nixon, Richard M.	3,830,085	Kennedy, John F.	14,575	383,666 D	47.3%	52.5%	47.4%	52.6%
1956	7,095,971	4,345,506	Eisenhower, Dwight D.	2,747,944	Stevenson, Adlai E.	2,521	1,597,562 R	61.2%	38.7%	61.3%	38.7%
1952	7,128,239	3,952,813	Eisenhower, Dwight D.	3,104,601	Stevenson, Adlai E.	70,825	848,212 R	55.5%	43.6%	56.0%	44.0%
1948**	6,177,337	2,841,163	Dewey, Thomas E.	2,780,204	Truman, Harry S.	555,970	60,959 R	46.0%	45.0%	50.5%	49.5%

**In past elections, the other vote included: 2000 - 244,030 Green (Ralph Nader); 1996 - 503,458 Reform (Ross Perot); 1992 - 1,090,721 Independent (Perot); 1980 - 467,801 Independent (John Anderson); 1968 - 358,864 American Independent (George Wallace); 1948 - 509,559 Progressive (Henry Wallace).

NEW YORK

POSTWAR VOTE FOR GOVERNOR

Year	Total Vote	Republican Vote	Republican Candidate	Democratic Vote	Democratic Candidate	Other Vote	Rep.-Dem. Plurality	Total Vote Rep.	Total Vote Dem.	Major Vote Rep.	Major Vote Dem.
2006	4,437,220	1,274,335	Faso, John J.	3,086,709	Spitzer, Eliot	76,176	1,812,374 D	28.7%	69.6%	29.2%	70.8%
2002**	4,579,078	2,262,255	Pataki, George E.	1,534,064	McCall, H. Carl	782,759	728,191 R	49.4%	33.5%	59.6%	40.4%
1998	4,735,236	2,571,991	Pataki, George E.	1,570,317	Vallone, Peter F.	592,928	1,001,674 R	54.3%	33.2%	62.1%	37.9%
1994	5,208,762	2,538,702	Pataki, George E.	2,364,904	Cuomo, Mario M.	305,156	173,798 R	48.7%	45.4%	51.8%	48.2%
1990**	4,056,896	865,948	Rinfret, Pierre A.	2,157,087	Cuomo, Mario M.	1,033,861	1,291,139 D	21.3%	53.2%	28.6%	71.4%
1986	4,294,124	1,363,810	O'Rourke, Andrew P.	2,775,229	Cuomo, Mario M.	155,085	1,411,419 D	31.8%	64.6%	32.9%	67.1%
1982	5,254,891	2,494,827	Lehrman, Lew	2,675,213	Cuomo, Mario M.	84,851	180,386 D	47.5%	50.9%	48.3%	51.7%
1978	4,768,820	2,156,404	Duryea, Perry B.	2,429,272	Carey, Hugh L.	183,144	272,868 D	45.2%	50.9%	47.0%	53.0%
1974	5,293,176	2,219,667	Wilson, Malcolm	3,028,503	Carey, Hugh L.	45,006	808,836 D	41.9%	57.2%	42.3%	57.7%
1970	6,013,064	3,151,432	Rockefeller, Nelson A.	2,421,426	Goldberg, Arthur	440,206	730,006 R	52.4%	40.3%	56.5%	43.5%
1966**	6,031,585	2,690,626	Rockefeller, Nelson A.	2,298,363	O'Connor, Frank D.	1,042,596	392,263 R	44.6%	38.1%	53.9%	46.1%
1962	5,805,631	3,081,587	Rockefeller, Nelson A.	2,552,418	Morgenthau, Robert M.	171,626	529,169 R	53.1%	44.0%	54.7%	45.3%
1958	5,712,665	3,126,929	Rockefeller, Nelson A.	2,553,895	Harriman, Averell	31,841	573,034 R	54.7%	44.7%	55.0%	45.0%
1954	5,161,942	2,549,613	Ives, Irving M.	2,560,738	Harriman, Averell	51,591	11,125 D	49.4%	49.6%	49.9%	50.1%
1950	5,308,889	2,819,523	Dewey, Thomas E.	2,246,855	Lynch, Walter A.	242,511	572,668 R	53.1%	42.3%	55.7%	44.3%
1946	4,964,552	2,825,633	Dewey, Thomas E.	2,138,482	Mead, James M.	437	687,151 R	56.9%	43.1%	56.9%	43.1%

**In past elections, the other vote included: 2002 - 654,016 Independence (B. Thomas Golisano); 1990 - 827,614 Conservative (Herbert I. London); 1966 - 510,023 Conservative (Paul L. Adams); and 507,234 Liberal (Franklin Roosevelt Jr.).

POSTWAR VOTE FOR SENATOR

Year	Total Vote	Republican Vote	Republican Candidate	Democratic Vote	Democratic Candidate	Other Vote	Plurality	Total Vote Rep.	Total Vote Dem.	Major Vote Rep.	Major Vote Dem.
2006	4,490,053	1,392,189	Spencer, John	3,008,428	Clinton, Hillary Rodham	89,436	1,616,239 D	31.0%	67.0%	31.6%	68.4%
2004	6,702,875	1,625,069	Mills, Howard	4,769,824	Schumer, Charles E.	307,982	3,144,755 D	24.2%	71.2%	25.4%	74.6%
2000	6,779,839	2,915,730	Lazio, Rick A.	3,747,310	Clinton, Hillary Rodham	116,799	831,580 D	43.0%	55.3%	43.8%	56.2%
1998	4,670,805	2,058,988	D'Amato, Alfonse M.	2,551,065	Schumer, Charles E.	60,752	492,077 D	44.1%	54.6%	44.7%	55.3%
1994	4,794,601	1,988,308	Castro, Bernadette	2,646,541	Moynihan, Daniel P.	159,752	658,233 D	41.5%	55.2%	42.9%	57.1%
1992	6,458,826	3,166,994	D'Amato, Alfonse M.	3,086,200	Abrams, Robert	205,632	80,794 R	49.0%	47.8%	50.6%	49.4%
1988	6,040,980	1,875,784	McMillan, Robert	4,048,649	Moynihan, Daniel P.	116,547	2,172,865 D	31.1%	67.0%	31.7%	68.3%
1986	4,179,447	2,378,197	D'Amato, Alfonse M.	1,723,216	Green, Mark	78,034	654,981 R	56.9%	41.2%	58.0%	42.0%
1982	4,967,729	1,696,766	Sullivan, Florence M.	3,232,146	Moynihan, Daniel P.	38,817	1,535,380 D	34.2%	65.1%	34.4%	65.6%
1980**	6,014,914	2,699,652	D'Amato, Alfonse M.	2,618,661	Holtzman, Elizabeth	696,601	80,991 R	44.9%	43.5%	50.8%	49.2%
1976	6,319,755	2,836,633	Buckley, James L.	3,422,594	Moynihan, Daniel P.	60,528	585,961 D	44.9%	54.2%	45.3%	54.7%
1974**	5,163,600	2,340,188	Javits, Jacob K.	1,973,781	Clark, Ramsey	849,631	366,407 R	45.3%	38.2%	54.2%	45.8%
1970**	5,904,782	1,434,472	Goodell, Charles	2,171,232	Ottinger, Richard L.	2,299,078	116,958 C	24.3%	36.8%	39.8%	60.2%
1968**	6,581,587	3,269,772	Javits, Jacob K.	2,150,695	O'Dwyer, Paul	1,161,120	1,119,077 R	49.7%	32.7%	60.3%	39.7%
1964	7,151,686	3,104,056	Keating, Kenneth B.	3,823,749	Kennedy, Robert F.	223,881	719,693 D	43.4%	53.5%	44.8%	55.2%
1962	5,700,186	3,269,417	Javits, Jacob K.	2,289,341	Donovan, James B.	141,428	980,076 R	57.4%	40.2%	58.8%	41.2%
1958	5,602,088	2,842,942	Keating, Kenneth B.	2,709,950	Hogan, Frank S.	49,196	132,992 R	50.7%	48.4%	51.2%	48.8%
1956	6,991,136	3,723,933	Javits, Jacob K.	3,265,159	Wagner, Robert F.	2,044	458,774 R	53.3%	46.7%	53.3%	46.7%
1952	6,980,259	3,853,934	Ives, Irving M.	2,521,736	Cashmore, John	604,589	1,332,198 R	55.2%	36.1%	60.4%	39.6%
1950	5,228,403	2,367,353	Hanley, Joe R.	2,632,313	Lehman, Herbert H.	228,737	264,960 D	45.3%	50.3%	47.4%	52.6%
1949S	4,966,878	2,384,381	Dulles, John Foster	2,582,438	Lehman, Herbert H.	59	198,057 D	48.0%	52.0%	48.0%	52.0%
1946	4,867,564	2,559,365	Ives, Irving M.	2,308,112	Lehman, Herbert H.	87	251,253 R	52.6%	47.4%	52.6%	47.4%

Notes: **In past elections, the other vote included: 1980 - 664,544 Liberal (Jacob K. Javits); 1974 - 822,584 Conservative (Barbara A. Keating); 1970 - 2,288,190 Conservative (James L. Buckley); 1968 - 1,139,402 Conservative (Buckley). Buckley won the 1970 election with 38.8 percent of the total vote. The 1949 election was for a short term to fill a vacancy.

NEW YORK

PRESIDENT 2008

2000 Census Population	County	Total Vote	Republican	Democratic	Other	Rep.-Dem. Plurality		Percentage			
								Total Vote		Major Vote	
								Rep.	Dem.	Rep.	Dem.
294,565	ALBANY	147,266	50,586	93,937	2,743	43,351	D	34.4%	63.8%	35.0%	65.0%
49,927	ALLEGANY	18,406	11,013	7,016	377	3,997	R	59.8%	38.1%	61.1%	38.9%
1,332,650	BRONX	381,322	41,683	338,261	1,378	296,578	D	10.9%	88.7%	11.0%	89.0%
200,536	BROOME	88,837	40,077	47,204	1,556	7,127	D	45.1%	53.1%	45.9%	54.1%
83,955	CATTARAUGUS	32,617	17,770	14,307	540	3,463	R	54.5%	43.9%	55.4%	44.6%
81,963	CAYUGA	34,022	15,243	18,128	651	2,885	D	44.8%	53.3%	45.7%	54.3%
139,750	CHAUTAUQUA	58,802	28,579	29,129	1,094	550	D	48.6%	49.5%	49.5%	50.5%
91,070	CHEMUNG	38,695	19,364	18,888	443	476	R	50.0%	48.8%	50.6%	49.4%
51,401	CHENANGO	20,847	10,337	10,100	410	237	R	49.6%	48.4%	50.6%	49.4%
79,894	CLINTON	33,337	12,579	20,216	542	7,637	D	37.7%	60.6%	38.4%	61.6%
63,094	COLUMBIA	31,433	13,337	17,556	540	4,219	D	42.4%	55.9%	43.2%	56.8%
48,599	CORTLAND	21,920	9,678	11,861	381	2,183	D	44.2%	54.1%	44.9%	55.1%
48,055	DELAWARE	20,389	10,524	9,462	403	1,062	R	51.6%	46.4%	52.7%	47.3%
280,150	DUTCHESS	132,302	59,628	71,060	1,614	11,432	D	45.1%	53.7%	45.6%	54.4%
950,265	ERIE	441,985	178,815	256,299	6,871	77,484	D	40.5%	58.0%	41.1%	58.9%
38,851	ESSEX	18,595	7,913	10,390	292	2,477	D	42.6%	55.9%	43.2%	56.8%
51,134	FRANKLIN	17,520	6,676	10,571	273	3,895	D	38.1%	60.3%	38.7%	61.3%
55,073	FULTON	21,824	11,709	9,695	420	2,014	R	53.7%	44.4%	54.7%	45.3%
60,370	GENESEE	26,873	15,705	10,762	406	4,943	R	58.4%	40.0%	59.3%	40.7%
48,195	GREENE	22,335	12,059	9,850	426	2,209	R	54.0%	44.1%	55.0%	45.0%
5,379	HAMILTON	3,411	2,141	1,225	45	916	R	62.8%	35.9%	63.6%	36.4%
64,427	HERKIMER	27,184	14,619	12,094	471	2,525	R	53.8%	44.5%	54.7%	45.3%
111,738	JEFFERSON	38,886	20,220	18,166	500	2,054	R	52.0%	46.7%	52.7%	47.3%
2,465,326	KINGS	759,848	151,872	603,525	4,451	451,653	D	20.0%	79.4%	20.1%	79.9%
26,944	LEWIS	11,138	5,969	4,986	183	983	R	53.6%	44.8%	54.5%	45.5%
64,328	LIVINGSTON	30,149	16,030	13,655	464	2,375	R	53.2%	45.3%	54.0%	46.0%
69,441	MADISON	29,802	14,434	14,692	676	258	D	48.4%	49.3%	49.6%	50.4%
735,343	MONROE	356,424	144,262	207,371	4,791	63,109	D	40.5%	58.2%	41.0%	59.0%
49,708	MONTGOMERY	20,175	10,711	9,080	384	1,631	R	53.1%	45.0%	54.1%	45.9%
1,334,544	NASSAU	635,618	288,776	342,185	4,657	53,409	D	45.4%	53.8%	45.8%	54.2%
1,537,195	NEW YORK	667,885	89,949	572,370	5,566	482,421	D	13.5%	85.7%	13.6%	86.4%
219,846	NIAGARA	95,272	46,348	47,303	1,621	955	D	48.6%	49.7%	49.5%	50.5%
235,469	ONEIDA	94,365	49,256	43,506	1,603	5,750	R	52.2%	46.1%	53.1%	46.9%
458,336	ONONDAGA	218,239	84,972	129,317	3,950	44,345	D	38.9%	59.3%	39.7%	60.3%
100,224	ONTARIO	51,020	25,171	25,103	746	68	R	49.3%	49.2%	50.1%	49.9%
341,367	ORANGE	151,982	72,042	78,326	1,614	6,284	D	47.4%	51.5%	47.9%	52.1%
44,171	ORLEANS	16,584	9,708	6,614	262	3,094	R	58.5%	39.9%	59.5%	40.5%
122,377	OSWEGO	49,349	23,571	24,777	1,001	1,206	D	47.8%	50.2%	48.8%	51.2%
61,676	OTSEGO	26,121	12,026	13,570	525	1,544	D	46.0%	52.0%	47.0%	53.0%
95,745	PUTNAM	47,244	25,145	21,613	486	3,532	R	53.2%	45.7%	53.8%	46.2%
2,229,379	QUEENS	640,137	155,221	480,692	4,224	325,471	D	24.2%	75.1%	24.4%	75.6%
152,538	RENSSELAER	73,986	32,840	39,753	1,393	6,913	D	44.4%	53.7%	45.2%	54.8%
443,728	RICHMOND	166,578	86,062	79,311	1,205	6,751	R	51.7%	47.6%	52.0%	48.0%
286,753	ROCKLAND	132,193	61,752	69,543	898	7,791	D	46.7%	52.6%	47.0%	53.0%
111,931	ST. LAWRENCE	41,326	16,956	23,706	664	6,750	D	41.0%	57.4%	41.7%	58.3%
200,635	SARATOGA	111,387	52,855	56,645	1,887	3,790	D	47.5%	50.9%	48.3%	51.7%
146,555	SCHENECTADY	69,842	29,758	38,611	1,473	8,853	D	42.6%	55.3%	43.5%	56.5%
31,582	SCHOHARIE	14,402	8,071	6,009	322	2,062	R	56.0%	41.7%	57.3%	42.7%
19,224	SCHUYLER	8,600	4,542	3,933	125	609	R	52.8%	45.7%	53.6%	46.4%
33,342	SENECA	14,741	7,038	7,422	281	384	D	47.7%	50.3%	48.7%	51.3%

NEW YORK

PRESIDENT 2008

2000 Census Population	County	Total Vote	Republican	Democratic	Other	Rep.-Dem. Plurality		Percentage			
								Total Vote		Major Vote	
								Rep.	Dem.	Rep.	Dem.
98,726	STEUBEN	41,911	24,203	17,148	560	7,055 R		57.7%	40.9%	58.5%	41.5%
1,419,369	SUFFOLK	659,779	307,021	346,549	6,209	39,528 D		46.5%	52.5%	47.0%	53.0%
73,966	SULLIVAN	31,183	13,900	16,850	433	2,950 D		44.6%	54.0%	45.2%	54.8%
51,784	TIOGA	23,131	12,536	10,172	423	2,364 R		54.2%	44.0%	55.2%	44.8%
96,501	TOMPKINS	42,552	11,927	29,826	799	17,899 D		28.0%	70.1%	28.6%	71.4%
177,749	ULSTER	89,149	33,300	54,320	1,529	21,020 D		37.4%	60.9%	38.0%	62.0%
63,303	WARREN	32,245	15,429	16,281	535	852 D		47.8%	50.5%	48.7%	51.3%
61,042	WASHINGTON	25,730	12,533	12,741	456	208 D		48.7%	49.5%	49.6%	50.4%
93,765	WAYNE	41,045	22,239	18,184	622	4,055 R		54.2%	44.3%	55.0%	45.0%
923,459	WESTCHESTER	413,044	147,824	261,810	3,410	113,986 D		35.8%	63.4%	36.1%	63.9%
43,424	WYOMING	17,667	10,998	6,379	290	4,619 R		62.3%	36.1%	63.3%	36.7%
24,621	YATES	10,280	5,269	4,890	121	379 R		51.3%	47.6%	51.9%	48.1%
18,976,457	TOTAL	7,640,931	2,752,771	4,804,945	83,215	2,052,174 D		36.0%	62.9%	36.4%	63.6%

NEW YORK CITY

2000 Census Population	County	Total Vote	Republican	Democratic	Other	Rep.-Dem. Plurality		Percentage			
								Total Vote		Major Vote	
								Rep.	Dem.	Rep.	Dem.
1,332,650	BRONX	381,322	41,683	338,261	1,378	296,578 D		10.9%	88.7%	11.0%	89.0%
2,465,326	KINGS	759,848	151,872	603,525	4,451	451,653 D		20.0%	79.4%	20.1%	79.9%
1,537,195	NEW YORK	667,885	89,949	572,370	5,566	482,421 D		13.5%	85.7%	13.6%	86.4%
2,229,379	QUEENS	640,137	155,221	480,692	4,224	325,471 D		24.2%	75.1%	24.4%	75.6%
443,728	RICHMOND	166,578	86,062	79,311	1,205	6,751 R		51.7%	47.6%	52.0%	48.0%
8,008,278	TOTAL	2,615,770	524,787	2,074,159	16,824	1,549,372 D		20.1%	79.3%	20.2%	79.8%

NEW YORK

HOUSE OF REPRESENTATIVES

CD	Year	Total Vote	Republican Vote		Republican Candidate	Democratic Vote		Democratic Candidate	Other Vote	Rep.-Dem. Plurality	Percentage Total Vote Rep.	Dem.	Major Vote Rep.	Dem.
1	2008	277,641	115,545	#	ZELDIN, LEE M.	162,083	#	BISHOP, TIMOTHY H.*	13	46,538 D	41.6%	58.4%	41.6%	58.4%
1	2006	167,688	63,328	#	ZANZI, ITALO A.	104,360	#	BISHOP, TIMOTHY H.*		41,032 D	37.8%	62.2%	37.8%	62.2%
1	2004	278,209	121,855	#	MANGER, WILLIAM M. JR.	156,354	#	BISHOP, TIMOTHY H.*		34,499 D	43.8%	56.2%	43.8%	56.2%
1	2002	167,791	81,524	#	GRUCCI, FELIX J. JR.*	84,276	#	BISHOP, TIMOTHY H.	1,991	2,752 D	48.6%	50.2%	49.2%	50.8%
2	2008	240,932	79,641	#	STALZER, FRANK J.	161,279	#	ISRAEL, STEVE*	12	81,638 D	33.1%	66.9%	33.1%	66.9%
2	2006	149,488	44,212	#	BUGLER, JOHN W.	105,276	#	ISRAEL, STEVE*		61,064 D	29.6%	70.4%	29.6%	70.4%
2	2004	242,543	80,950	#	HOFFMANN, RICHARD	161,593	#	ISRAEL, STEVE*		80,643 D	33.4%	66.6%	33.4%	66.6%
2	2002	146,126	59,117	#	FINLEY, JOSEPH P.	85,451	#	ISRAEL, STEVE*	1,558	26,334 D	40.5%	58.5%	40.9%	59.1%
3	2008	270,303	172,774	#	KING, PETER T.*	97,525	#	LONG, GRAHAM E.	4	75,249 R	63.9%	36.1%	63.9%	36.1%
3	2006	181,630	101,787	#	KING, PETER T.*	79,843	#	MEJIAS, DAVID L.		21,944 R	56.0%	44.0%	56.0%	44.0%
3	2004	271,996	171,259	#	KING, PETER T.*	100,737		MATHIES, BLAIR H. JR.		70,522 R	63.0%	37.0%	63.0%	37.0%
3	2002	169,072	121,537	#	KING, PETER T.*	46,022		FINZ, STUART L.	1,513	75,515 R	71.9%	27.2%	72.5%	27.5%
4	2008	256,271	92,242	#	MARTINS, JACK M.	164,028	#	McCARTHY, CAROLYN*	1	71,786 D	36.0%	64.0%	36.0%	64.0%
4	2006	156,911	55,050	#	BLESSINGER, MARTIN W.	101,861	#	McCARTHY, CAROLYN*		46,811 D	35.1%	64.9%	35.1%	64.9%
4	2004	254,110	94,141	#	GARNER, JAMES A.	159,969	#	McCARTHY, CAROLYN*		65,828 D	37.0%	63.0%	37.0%	63.0%
4	2002	168,540	72,882	#	O'GRADY, MARILYN F.	94,806	#	McCARTHY, CAROLYN*	852	21,924 D	43.2%	56.3%	43.5%	56.5%
5	2008	158,778	43,039		BERNEY, ELIZABETH	112,724	#	ACKERMAN, GARY L.*	3,015	69,685 D	27.1%	71.0%	27.6%	72.4%
5	2006	77,190			—	77,190	#	ACKERMAN, GARY L.*		77,190 D		100.0%		100.0%
5	2004	167,841	46,867	#	GRAVES, STEPHEN	119,726	#	ACKERMAN, GARY L.*	1,248	72,859 D	27.9%	71.3%	28.1%	71.9%
5	2002	74,491			—	68,773	#	ACKERMAN, GARY L.*	5,718	68,773 D		92.3%		100.0%
6	2008	141,206			—	141,180		MEEKS, GREGORY W.*	26	141,180 D		100.0%		100.0%
6	2006	69,405			—	69,405		MEEKS, GREGORY W.*		69,405 D		100.0%		100.0%
6	2004	129,688			—	129,688	#	MEEKS, GREGORY W.*		129,688 D		100.0%		100.0%
6	2002	75,431			—	72,799	#	MEEKS, GREGORY W.*	2,632	72,799 D		96.5%		100.0%
7	2008	139,941	21,477	#	BRITT, WILLIAM E. JR.	118,459	#	CROWLEY, JOSEPH*	5	96,982 D	15.3%	84.6%	15.3%	84.7%
7	2006	76,217	12,220	#	BRAWLEY, KEVIN	63,997	#	CROWLEY, JOSEPH*		51,777 D	16.0%	84.0%	16.0%	84.0%
7	2004	128,823	24,548	#	CINQUEMAIN, JOSEPH	104,275	#	CROWLEY, JOSEPH*		79,727 D	19.1%	80.9%	19.1%	80.9%
7	2002	69,539	18,572	#	BRAWLEY, KEVIN	50,967	#	CROWLEY, JOSEPH*		32,395 D	26.7%	73.3%	26.7%	73.3%
8	2008	199,861	39,062	#	LIN, GRACE	160,775	#	NADLER, JERROLD*	24	121,713 D	19.5%	80.4%	19.5%	80.5%
8	2006	127,622	17,413		FRIEDMAN, ELEANOR	108,536	#	NADLER, JERROLD*	1,673	91,123 D	13.6%	85.0%	13.8%	86.2%
8	2004	201,322	39,240	#	HORT, PETER	162,082	#	NADLER, JERROLD*		122,842 D	19.5%	80.5%	19.5%	80.5%
8	2002	106,481	19,674	#	FARRIN, JIM	81,002	#	NADLER, JERROLD*	5,805	61,328 D	18.5%	76.1%	19.5%	80.5%
9	2008	120,589			—	112,205	#	WEINER, ANTHONY*	8,384	112,205 D		93.0%		100.0%
9	2006	71,762			—	71,762	#	WEINER, ANTHONY*		71,762 D		100.0%		100.0%
9	2004	158,476	45,451	#	CRONIN, GERARD J.	113,025	#	WEINER, ANTHONY*		67,574 D	28.7%	71.3%	28.7%	71.3%
9	2002	92,435	31,698	#	DONOHUE, ALFRED F.	60,737	#	WEINER, ANTHONY*		29,039 D	34.3%	65.7%	34.3%	65.7%
10	2008	164,669	9,565	#	GRUPICO, SALVATORE	155,090		TOWNS, EDOLPHUS*	14	145,525 D	5.8%	94.2%	5.8%	94.2%
10	2006	78,307	4,666		ANDERSON, JONATHAN H.	72,171		TOWNS, EDOLPHUS*	1,470	67,505 D	6.0%	92.2%	6.1%	93.9%
10	2004	148,766	11,099		CLARKE, HARVEY R.	136,113	#	TOWNS, EDOLPHUS*	1,554	125,014 D	7.5%	91.5%	7.5%	92.5%
10	2002	75,498			—	73,859	#	TOWNS, EDOLPHUS*	1,639	73,859 D		97.8%		100.0%
11	2008	181,740	11,644		CARR, HUGH C.	168,562	#	CLARKE, YVETTE D.*	1,534	156,918 D	6.4%	92.7%	6.5%	93.5%
11	2006	98,102	7,447	#	FINGER, STEPHEN	88,334	#	CLARKE, YVETTE D.	2,321	80,887 D	7.6%	90.0%	7.8%	92.2%
11	2004	154,198				144,999	#	OWENS, MAJOR R.*	9,199	144,999 D		94.0%		100.0%
11	2002	88,864	11,149	#	CLEARY, SUSAN	76,917	#	OWENS, MAJOR R.*	798	65,768 D	12.5%	86.6%	12.7%	87.3%
12	2008	136,809	13,748	#	ROMAGUERA, ALLAN	123,053	#	VELÁZQUEZ, NYDIA M.*	8	109,305 D	10.0%	89.9%	10.0%	90.0%
12	2006	70,029	7,182	#	ROMAGUERA, ALLAN	62,847	#	VELÁZQUEZ, NYDIA M.*		55,665 D	10.3%	89.7%	10.3%	89.7%
12	2004	124,962	17,166	#	RODRIGUEZ, PAUL A.	107,796	#	VELÁZQUEZ, NYDIA M.*		90,630 D	13.7%	86.3%	13.7%	86.3%
12	2002	50,527			—	48,408	#	VELÁZQUEZ, NYDIA M.*	2,119	48,408 D		95.8%		100.0%

NEW YORK

HOUSE OF REPRESENTATIVES

| | | | Republican | | Democratic | | Other | Rep.-Dem. | Percentage | | | |
| | | Total | | | | | | | Total Vote | | Major Vote | |
CD	Year	Vote	Vote	Candidate	Vote	Candidate	Vote	Plurality	Rep.	Dem.	Rep.	Dem.
13	2008	187,446	62,441	STRANIERE, ROBERT A.	114,219 #	McMAHON, MICHAEL E.	10,786	51,778 D	33.3%	60.9%	35.3%	64.7%
13	2006	104,465	59,334 #	FOSSELLA, VITO J.*	45,131 #	HARRISON, STEPHEN A.		14,203 R	56.8%	43.2%	56.8%	43.2%
13	2004	191,434	112,934 #	FOSSELLA, VITO J.*	78,500 #	BARBARO, FRANK J.		34,434 R	59.0%	41.0%	59.0%	41.0%
13	2002	103,693	72,204 #	FOSSELLA, VITO J.*	29,366 #	MATTSSON, ARNE M.	2,123	42,838 R	69.6%	28.3%	71.1%	28.9%
14	2008	229,308	43,385	HEIM, ROBERT G.	183,239 #	MALONEY, CAROLYN B.*	2,684	139,854 D	18.9%	79.9%	19.1%	80.9%
14	2006	141,551	21,969	MAIO, DANNIEL	119,582 #	MALONEY, CAROLYN B.*		97,613 D	15.5%	84.5%	15.5%	84.5%
14	2004	230,311	43,623 #	SRDANOVIC, ANTON	186,688 #	MALONEY, CAROLYN B.*		143,065 D	18.9%	81.1%	18.9%	81.1%
14	2002	127,479	31,548 #	SRDANOVIC, ANTON	95,931 #	MALONEY, CAROLYN B.*		64,383 D	24.7%	75.3%	24.7%	75.3%
15	2008	198,691	15,676	DANIELS, EDWARD	177,151 #	RANGEL, CHARLES B.*	5,864	161,475 D	7.9%	89.2%	8.1%	91.9%
15	2006	110,508	6,592	DANIELS, EDWARD	103,916 #	RANGEL, CHARLES B.*		97,324 D	6.0%	94.0%	6.0%	94.0%
15	2004	177,051	12,355	JEFFERSON, KENNETH P. JR.	161,351 #	RANGEL, CHARLES B.*	3,345	148,996 D	7.0%	91.1%	7.1%	92.9%
15	2002	95,375	11,008 #	FIELDS, JESSIE A.	84,367 #	RANGEL, CHARLES B.*		73,359 D	11.5%	88.5%	11.5%	88.5%
16	2008	131,669	4,488 #	MOHAMED, ALI	127,179 #	SERRANO, JOSE E.*	2	122,691 D	3.4%	96.6%	3.4%	96.6%
16	2006	58,883	2,759 #	MOHAMED, ALI	56,124 #	SERRANO, JOSE E.*		53,365 D	4.7%	95.3%	4.7%	95.3%
16	2004	117,248	5,610 #	MOHAMED, ALI	111,638 #	SERRANO, JOSE E.*		106,028 D	4.8%	95.2%	4.8%	95.2%
16	2002	55,082	4,366 #	DELLAVALLE, FRANK	50,716 #	SERRANO, JOSE E.*		46,350 D	7.9%	92.1%	7.9%	92.1%
17	2008	202,321	40,707 #	GOODMAN, ROBERT	161,594 #	ENGEL, ELIOT L.*	20	120,887 D	20.1%	79.9%	20.1%	79.9%
17	2006	122,456	28,842 #	FAULKNER, JIM	93,614 #	ENGEL, ELIOT L.*		64,772 D	23.6%	76.4%	23.6%	76.4%
17	2004	184,536	40,524	BRENNAN, MATT I.	140,530 #	ENGEL, ELIOT L.*	3,482	100,006 D	22.0%	76.2%	22.4%	77.6%
17	2002	123,843	42,634 #	VANDERHOEF, C. SCOTT	77,535 #	ENGEL, ELIOT L.*	3,674	34,901 D	34.4%	62.6%	35.5%	64.5%
18	2008	255,311	80,498 #	RUSSELL, JIM	174,791 #	LOWEY, NITA M.*	22	94,293 D	31.5%	68.5%	31.5%	68.5%
18	2006	175,706	51,450	HOFFMAN, RICHARD A.	124,256 #	LOWEY, NITA M.*		72,806 D	29.3%	70.7%	29.3%	70.7%
18	2004	244,690	73,975	HOFFMAN, RICHARD A.	170,715 #	LOWEY, NITA M.*		96,740 D	30.2%	69.8%	30.2%	69.8%
18	2002	107,515		—	98,957 #	LOWEY, NITA M.*	8,558	98,957 D		92.0%		100.0%
19	2008	280,994	116,120 #	LALOR, KIERAN MICHAEL	164,859 #	HALL, JOHN*	15	48,739 D	41.3%	58.7%	41.3%	58.7%
19	2006	195,478	95,359 #	KELLY, SUE W.*	100,119	HALL, JOHN		4,760 D	48.8%	51.2%	48.8%	51.2%
19	2004	262,830	175,401 #	KELLY, SUE W.*	87,429	JALIMAN, MICHAEL		87,972 R	66.7%	33.3%	66.7%	33.3%
19	2002	173,112	121,129 #	KELLY, SUE W.*	44,967	SELENDY, JANINE M.H.	7,016	76,162 R	70.0%	26.0%	72.9%	27.1%
20	2008	311,717	118,031 #	TREADWELL, SANDY	193,651 #	GILLIBRAND, KIRSTEN E.*	35	75,620 D	37.9%	62.1%	37.9%	62.1%
20	2006	235,722	110,554 #	SWEENEY, JOHN E.*	125,168 #	GILLIBRAND, KIRSTEN E.		14,614 D	46.9%	53.1%	46.9%	53.1%
20	2004	286,736	188,753 #	SWEENEY, JOHN E.*	96,630	KELLY, DORIS F.	1,353	92,123 R	65.8%	33.7%	66.1%	33.9%
20	2002	191,278	140,238 #	SWEENEY, JOHN E.*	45,878	STOPPENBACH, FRANK	5,162	94,360 R	73.3%	24.0%	75.3%	24.7%
21	2008	275,872	96,599 #	BUHRMASTER, JAMES R.	171,286 #	TONKO, PAUL	7,987	74,687 D	35.0%	62.1%	36.1%	63.9%
21	2006	214,356	46,752	REDLICH, WARREN	167,604 #	McNULTY, MICHAEL R.*		120,852 D	21.8%	78.2%	21.8%	78.2%
21	2004	274,154	80,121	REDLICH, WARREN	194,033 #	McNULTY, MICHAEL R.*		113,912 D	29.2%	70.8%	29.2%	70.8%
21	2002	214,854	53,525	ROSENSTEIN, CHARLES B.	161,329 #	McNULTY, MICHAEL R.*		107,804 D	24.9%	75.1%	24.9%	75.1%
22	2008	253,718	85,126	PHILLIPS, GEORGE K.	168,558 #	HINCHEY, MAURICE D.*	34	83,432 D	33.6%	66.4%	33.6%	66.4%
22	2006	121,683		—	121,683 #	HINCHEY, MAURICE D.*		121,683 D		100.0%		100.0%
22	2004	249,370	81,881	BRENNER, WILLIAM A.	167,489 #	HINCHEY, MAURICE D.*		85,608 D	32.8%	67.2%	32.8%	67.2%
22	2002	176,484	58,008 #	HALL, ERIC	113,280 #	HINCHEY, MAURICE D.*	5,196	55,272 D	32.9%	64.2%	33.9%	66.1%
23	2008	218,925	143,029 #	McHUGH, JOHN M.*	75,871 #	OOT, MICHAEL P.	25	67,158 R	65.3%	34.7%	65.3%	34.7%
23	2006	169,099	106,781 #	McHUGH, JOHN M.*	62,318	JOHNSON, ROBERT J.		44,463 R	63.1%	36.9%	63.1%	36.9%
23	2004	226,527	160,079 #	McHUGH, JOHN M.*	66,448	JOHNSON, ROBERT J.		93,631 R	70.7%	29.3%	70.7%	29.3%
23	2002	124,682	124,682 #	McHUGH, JOHN M.*		—		124,682 R	100.0%		100.0%	
24	2008	251,692	120,880 #	HANNA, RICHARD L.	130,799 #	ARCURI, MICHAEL A.*	13	9,919 D	48.0%	52.0%	48.0%	52.0%
24	2006	203,324	91,504 #	MEIER, RAYMOND A.	109,686 #	ARCURI, MICHAEL A.	2,134	18,182 D	45.0%	53.9%	45.5%	54.5%
24	2004	251,368	143,000 #	BOEHLERT, SHERWOOD*	85,140	MILLER, JEFFREY A.	23,228	57,860 R	56.9%	33.9%	62.7%	37.3%
24	2002	152,777	108,017	BOEHLERT, SHERWOOD*		—	44,760	108,017 R	70.7%		100.0%	

NEW YORK

HOUSE OF REPRESENTATIVES

| | | | Republican | | Democratic | | | | Percentage | | | |
| | | | | | | | | | Total Vote | | Major Vote | |
CD	Year	Total Vote	Vote	Candidate	Vote	Candidate	Other Vote	Rep.-Dem. Plurality	Rep.	Dem.	Rep.	Dem.
25	2008	287,099	120,217 #	SWEETLAND, DALE A.	157,375 #	MAFFEI, DANIEL B.	9,507	37,158 D	41.9%	54.8%	43.3%	56.7%
25	2006	217,633	110,525 #	WALSH, JAMES T.*	107,108 #	MAFFEI, DANIEL B.		3,417 R	50.8%	49.2%	50.8%	49.2%
25	2004	209,169	189,063 #	WALSH, JAMES T.*	—		20,106	189,063 R	90.4%		100.0%	
25	2002	200,031	144,610 #	WALSH, JAMES T.*	53,290	ALDERSLEY, STEPHANIE	2,131	91,320 R	72.3%	26.6%	73.1%	26.9%
26	2008	270,335	148,607 #	LEE, CHRISTOPHER JOHN	109,615	KRYZAN, ALICE	12,113	38,992 R	55.0%	40.5%	57.6%	42.4%
26	2006	210,171	109,257 #	REYNOLDS, THOMAS M.*	100,914 #	DAVIS, JACK		8,343 R	52.0%	48.0%	52.0%	48.0%
26	2004	283,079	157,466 #	REYNOLDS. THOMAS M.*	125,613 #	DAVIS, JACK		31,853 R	55.6%	44.4%	55.6%	44.4%
26	2002	183,459	135,089 #	REYNOLDS. THOMAS M.*	41,140	NARIMAN, AYESHA F.	7,230	93,949 R	73.6%	22.4%	76.7%	23.3%
27	2008	249,545	56,354 #	HUMISTON, DANIEL J.	185,713 #	HIGGINS, BRIAN*	7,478	129,359 D	22.6%	74.4%	23.3%	76.7%
27	2006	176,641	36,614	McHALE, MICHAEL J.	140,027 #	HIGGINS, BRIAN*		103,413 D	20.7%	79.3%	20.7%	79.3%
27	2004	282,890	139,558 #	NAPLES, NANCY A.	143,332 #	HIGGINS, BRIAN		3,774 D	49.3%	50.7%	49.3%	50.7%
27	2002	173,919	120,117 #	QUINN, JACK*	47,811 #	CROTTY, PETER	5,991	72,306 R	69.1%	27.5%	71.5%	28.5%
28	2008	221,378	48,690 #	CRIMMEN, DAVID W.	172,655 #	SLAUGHTER, LOUISE M.*	33	123,965 D	22.0%	78.0%	22.0%	78.0%
28	2006	152,230	40,844 #	DONNELLY, JOHN E.	111,386 #	SLAUGHTER, LOUISE M.*		70,542 D	26.8%	73.2%	26.8%	73.2%
28	2004	219,876	54,543 #	LABA, MICHAEL D.	159,655 #	SLAUGHTER, LOUISE M.*	5,678	105,112 D	24.8%	72.6%	25.5%	74.5%
28	2002	158,604	59,547 #	WOJTASZEK, HENRY F.	99,057 #	SLAUGHTER, LOUISE M.*		39,510 D	37.5%	62.5%	37.5%	62.5%
29	2008	275,755	135,199 #	KUHL, JOHN R. "RANDY" JR.*	140,529 #	MASSA, ERIC J. J.	27	5,330 D	49.0%	51.0%	49.0%	51.0%
29	2006	206,121	106,077 #	KUHL, JOHN R. "RANDY" JR.*	100,044 #	MASSA, ERIC J. J.		6,033 R	51.5%	48.5%	51.5%	48.5%
29	2004	270,215	136,883 #	KUHL, JOHN R. "RANDY" JR.	110,241 #	BAREND, SAMARA	23,091	26,642 R	50.7%	40.8%	55.4%	44.6%
29	2002	174,631	127,657 #	HOUGHTON, AMO*	37,128	PETERS, KISUN J.	9,846	90,529 R	73.1%	21.3%	77.5%	22.5%
TOTAL	2008	6,390,516	2,034,784		4,286,047		69,685	2,251,263 D	31.8%	67.1%	32.2%	67.8%
TOTAL	2006	4,140,378	1,338,518		2,794,262		7,598	1,455,744 D	32.3%	67.5%	32.4%	67.6%
TOTAL	2004	6,222,418	2,448,345		3,681,789		92,284	1,233,444 D	39.3%	59.2%	39.9%	60.1%
TOTAL	2002	3,821,613	1,770,532		1,924,769		126,312	154,237 D	46.3%	50.4%	47.9%	52.1%

Notes: A pound sign (#) indicates that the candidate received votes on the ballot line of one or more other parties. Each candidate's total vote is listed above. An asterisk (*) denotes incumbent.

NEW YORK

GENERAL AND PRIMARY ELECTIONS

2008 GENERAL ELECTIONS

President   Other vote was 41,249 Populist (Ralph Nader); 19,596 Libertarian (Bob Barr); 12,801 Green (Cynthia A. McKinney); 3,615 Socialist Workers (Roger Calero); 1,639 Socialism and Liberation (Gloria La Riva); 634 write-in (Chuck Baldwin); 35 write-in (Alan Keyes); 18 write-in (Jerome S. White); 10 write-in (Brian Moore); 3 write-in (Lanakila Washington); 1 write-in (Jonathan Allen); 1 write-in (Michael Skok); 3,613 scattered write-in.

House   Other vote was:

CD 1   13 scattered write-in.
CD 2   12 scattered write-in.
CD 3   4 scattered write-in.
CD 4   1 scattered write-in.

NEW YORK

GENERAL AND PRIMARY ELECTIONS

CD 5	3,010 Conservative (Jun Policarpio), 5 scattered write-in.
CD 6	26 scattered write-in.
CD 7	5 scattered write-in.
CD 8	24 scattered write-in.
CD 9	8,378 Conservative (Alfred F. Donohue); 6 scattered wr te-in.
CD 10	14 scattered write-in.
CD 11	1,517 Conservative (Cartrell Gore); 17 scattered write-in.
CD 12	8 scattered write-in.
CD 13	5,799 scattered write-in (Timothy J. Cochrane); 4,947 Independence (Carmine A. Morano); 40 scattered write-in.
CD 14	2,659 Libertarian (Isaiah Matos); 25 scattered write-in.
CD 15	3,708 Vote People Change (Craig Schley); 2,141 Socialist Workers (Martin Koppel); 15 scattered write-in.
CD 16	2 scattered write-in.
CD 17	20 scattered write-in.
CD 18	22 scattered write-in.
CD 19	15 scattered write-in.
CD 20	35 scattered write-in.
CD 21	7,965 Independence (Phillip G. Steck); 22 scattered write-in.
CD 22	34 scattered write-in.
CD 23	25 scattered write-in.
CD 24	13 scattered write-in.
CD 25	9,483 Green Populist (Howie Hawkins); 24 scattered write-in.
CD 26	12,104 Working Families (Jonathan P. Powers); 9 scattered write-in.
CD 27	7,478 Conservative (Harold W. Schroeder).
CD 28	33 scattered write-in.
CD 29	27 scattered write-in.

2008 PRIMARY ELECTIONS

Primary	February 5, 2008 (President) September 9, 2008 (Congress)	**Registration** (as of March 1, 2008—including 1,037,686 inactive registrants)		
			Democratic	5,438,800
			Republican	2,995,982
			Independence	355,934
			Conservative	148,827
			Working Families	37,595
			Green	28,727
			Libertarian	1,175
			Other Parties	10
			Unaffiliated	2,356,128
			TOTAL	*11,363,178*

Primary Type   Closed—Only registered Democrats and Republicans could vote in their party's primary.

Note: Candidates in New York can appear on the ballot line of more than one party. In the 2008 presidential election, Barack Obama received 4,645,332 votes on the Democratic line and 159,613 votes on the Working Families line, for a total of 4,804,945 votes. John McCain received 2,418,323 votes on the Republican line, 170,475 votes on the Conservative line, and 163,973 votes on the Independence line, for a total of 2,752,771 votes. In the New York tables, votes received by each Democratic and Republican candidate on the ballot lines of other parties are combined into one overall vote, which is credited to the major party of which they are a member.

NEW YORK

GENERAL AND PRIMARY ELECTIONS

	REPUBLICAN PRIMARIES			DEMOCRATIC PRIMARIES		
President	John McCain	333,001	51.8%	Hillary Clinton	1,068,496	57.4%
	Mitt Romney	178,043	27.7%	Barack Obama	751,019	40.3%
	Mike Huckabee	68,477	10.7%	John Edwards	21,924	1.2%
	Ron Paul	40,113	6.2%	Dennis J. Kucinich	8,458	0.5%
	Rudolph Giuliani	23,260	3.6%	Bill Richardson	8,227	0.4%
				Joseph R. Biden Jr.	4,321	0.2%
	TOTAL	*642,894*		*TOTAL*	*1,862,445*	
Congressional District 1	Lee M. Zeldin	Unopposed		Timothy H. Bishop*	Unopposed	
Congressional District 2	Frank J. Stalzer	Unopposed		Steve Israel*	Unopposed	
Congressional District 3	Peter T. King*	6,847	88.4%	Graham E. Long	Unopposed	
	Robert Previdi	897	11.6%			
	TOTAL	*7,744*				
Congressional District 4	Jack M. Martins	Unopposed		Carolyn McCarthy*	Unopposed	
Congressional District 5	Elizabeth Berney	Unopposed		Gary L. Ackerman*	Unopposed	
Congressional District 6	No Republican candidate			Gregory W. Meeks*	Unopposed	
Congressional District 7	William E. Britt Jr.	Unopposed		Joseph Crowley*	Unopposed	
Congressional District 8	Grace Lin	Unopposed		Jerrold Nadler*	Unopposed	
Congressional District 9	No Republican candidate			Anthony Weiner*	Unopposed	
Congressional District 10	Salvatore Grupico	Unopposed		Edolphus Towns*	24,405	67.9%
				Kevin Powell	11,558	32.1%
				Write-in	6	
				TOTAL	*35,969*	
Congressional District 11	Hugh C. Carr	Unopposed		Yvette D. Clarke*	Unopposed	
Congressional District 12	Allan Romaguera	Unopposed		Nydia M. Velazquez*	Unopposed	
Congressional District 13	Robert A. Straniere	4,206	56.0%	Michael E. McMahon	12,805	75.7%
	Jamshad I. Wyne	2,702	35.9%	Stephen A. Harrison	3,992	23.6%
	Carmine Morano (write-in)	451	6.0%	Carmine Morano (write-in)	61	0.4%
	Write-in	158	2.1%	Write-in	67	0.4%
	TOTAL	*7,517*		*TOTAL*	*16,925*	
Congressional District 14	Robert G. Heim	Unopposed		Carolyn B. Maloney*	Unopposed	
Congressional District 15	Edward Daniels	Unopposed		Charles B. Rangel*	Unopposed	
Congressional District 16	Ali Mohamed	Unopposed		Jose E. Serrano*	Unopposed	

NEW YORK

GENERAL AND PRIMARY ELECTIONS

	REPUBLICAN PRIMARIES			DEMOCRATIC PRIMARIES		
Congressional District 17	Robert Goodman	Unopposed		Eliot L. Engel*	Unopposed	
Congressional District 18	Jim Russell	Unopposed		Nita M. Lowey*	Unopposed	
Congressional District 19	Kieran Michael Lalor	Unopposed		John Hall*	Unopposed	
Congressional District 20	Sandy Treadwell	Unopposed		Kirsten E. Gillibrand*	Unopposed	
Congressional District 21	James R. Buhrmaster	8,589	70.4%	Paul Tonko	15,932	39.5%
	Steven Vasquez	3,605	29.6%	Tracey Brooks	12,166	30.2%
				Phillip G. Steck	7,498	18.6%
				Darius Shahinfar	4,002	9.9%
				Joseph P. Sullivan	738	1.8%
	TOTAL	12,194		TOTAL	40,336	
Congressional District 22	George K. Phillips	Unopposed		Maurice D. Hinchey*	Unopposed	
Congressional District 23	John M. McHugh*	Unopposed		Michael P. Oot	Unopposed	
Congressional District 24	Richard L. Hanna	Unopposed		Michael A. Arcuri*	Unopposed	
Congressional District 25	Dale A. Sweetland	Unopposed		Daniel B. Maffei	Unopposed	
Congressional District 26	Christopher John Lee	Unopposed		Alice Kryzan	9,792	41.0%
				Jonathan P. Powers	8,500	35.6%
				Jack Davis	5,602	23.4%
				TOTAL	23,894	
Congressional District 27	Daniel J. Humiston	Unopposed		Brian Higgins*	Unopposed	
Congressional District 28	David W. Crimmen	Unopposed		Louise M. Slaughter*	Unopposed	
Congressional District 29	John R. "Randy" Kuhl Jr.*	Unopposed		Eric J. J. Massa	Unopposed	

Notes: An asterisk (*) denotes incumbent. Write-in votes were broken out separately in the official tally from New York City districts but not those in the rest of the state. Names of unopposed candidates did not appear on the primary ballot; therefore, no votes were cast for these candidates.

NORTH CAROLINA

Congressional districts first established for elections held in 2002
13 members

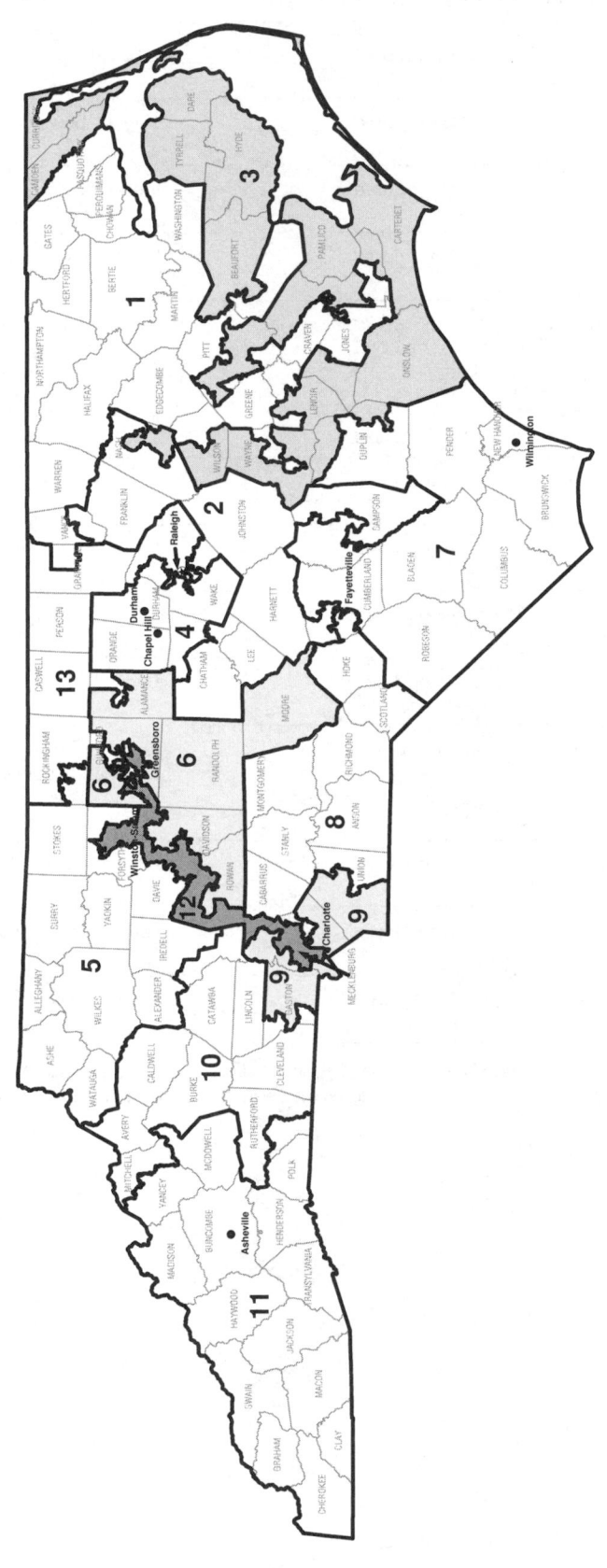

NORTH CAROLINA

Central North Carolina Area

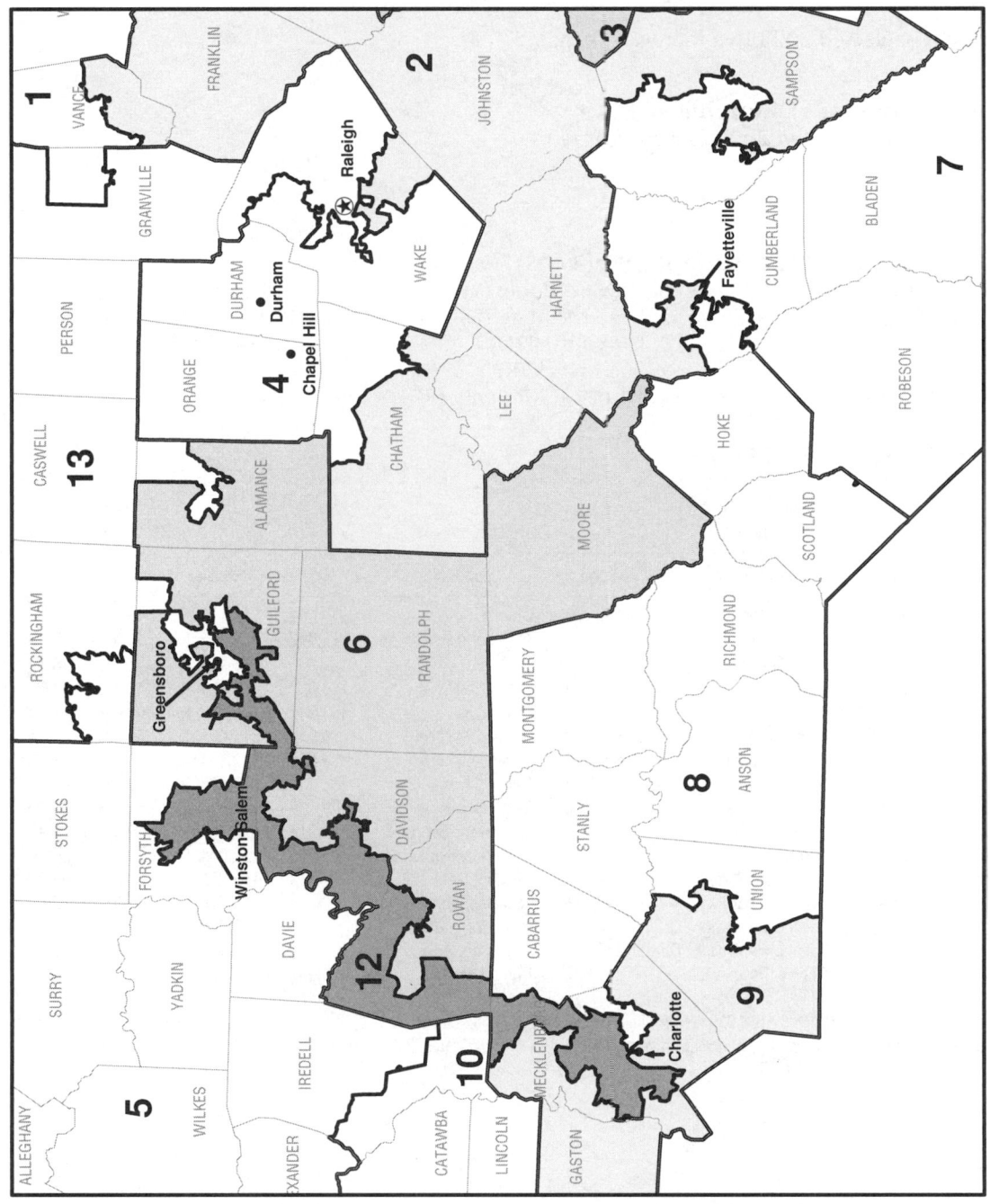

NORTH CAROLINA

GOVERNOR
Bev Perdue (D). Elected 2008 to a four-year term.

SENATORS (1 Democrat, 1 Republican)
Richard M. Burr (R). Elected 2004 to a six-year term.

Kay Hagan (D). Elected 2008 to a six-year term.

REPRESENTATIVES (8 Democrats, 5 Republicans)
1. G.K Butterfield (D)
2. Bob Etheridge (D)
3. Walter B. Jones (R)
4. David E. Price (D)
5. Virginia Foxx (R)
6. Howard Coble (R)
7. Mike McIntyre (D)
8. Larry Kissell (D)
9. Sue Myrick (R)
10. Patrick T. McHenry (R)
11. Heath Shuler (D)
12. Melvin Watt (D)
13. Brad Miller (D)

POSTWAR VOTE FOR PRESIDENT

| | | Republican | | Democratic | | Other | | Percentage | | | |
| | | | | | | | | Total Vote | | Major Vote | |
Year	Total Vote	Vote	Candidate	Vote	Candidate	Vote	Plurality	Rep.	Dem.	Rep.	Dem.
2008	4,310,789	2,128,474	McCain, John	2,142,651	Obama, Barack	39,664	14,177 D	49.4%	49.7%	49.8%	50.2%
2004	3,501,007	1,961,166	Bush, George W.	1,525,849	Kerry, John	13,992	435,317 R	56.0%	43.6%	56.2%	43.8%
2000	2,911,262	1,631,163	Bush, George W.	1,257,692	Gore, Al	22,407	373,471 R	56.0%	43.2%	56.5%	43.5%
1996**	2,515,807	1,225,938	Dole, Bob	1,107,849	Clinton, Bill	182,020	118,089 R	48.7%	44.0%	52.5%	47.5%
1992**	2,611,850	1,134,661	Bush, George	1,114,042	Clinton, Bill	363,147	20,619 R	43.4%	42.7%	50.5%	49.5%
1988	2,134,370	1,237,258	Bush, George	890,167	Dukakis, Michael S.	6,945	347,091 R	58.0%	41.7%	58.2%	41.8%
1984	2,175,361	1,346,481	Reagan, Ronald	824,287	Mondale, Walter F.	4,593	522,194 R	61.9%	37.9%	62.0%	38.0%
1980**	1,855,833	915,018	Reagan, Ronald	875,635	Carter, Jimmy	65,180	39,383 R	49.3%	47.2%	51.1%	48.9%
1976	1,678,914	741,960	Ford, Gerald R.	927,365	Carter, Jimmy	9,589	185,405 D	44.2%	55.2%	44.4%	55.6%
1972	1,518,612	1,054,889	Nixon, Richard M.	438,705	McGovern, George S.	25,018	616,184 R	69.5%	28.9%	70.6%	29.4%
1968**	1,587,493	627,192	Nixon, Richard M.	464,113	Humphrey, Hubert H.	496,188	131,004 R	39.5%	29.2%	57.5%	42.5%
1964	1,424,983	624,844	Goldwater, Barry M.	800,139	Johnson, Lyndon B.		175,295 D	43.8%	56.2%	43.8%	56.2%
1960	1,368,556	655,420	Nixon, Richard M.	713,136	Kennedy, John F.		57,716 D	47.9%	52.1%	47.9%	52.1%
1956	1,165,592	575,062	Eisenhower, Dwight D.	590,530	Stevenson, Adlai E.		15,468 D	49.3%	50.7%	49.3%	50.7%
1952	1,210,910	558,107	Eisenhower, Dwight D.	652,803	Stevenson, Adlai E.		94,696 D	46.1%	53.9%	46.1%	53.9%
1948**	791,209	258,572	Dewey, Thomas E.	459,070	Truman, Harry S.	73,567	200,498 D	32.7%	58.0%	36.0%	64.0%

**In past elections, the other vote included: 1996 - 168,059 Reform (Ross Perot); 1992 - 357,864 Independent (Perot); 1980 - 52,800 Independent (John Anderson); 1968 - 496,188 American Independent (George Wallace), who finished second statewide; 1948 - 69,652 States' Rights (Strom Thurmond).

NORTH CAROLINA

POSTWAR VOTE FOR GOVERNOR

Year	Total Vote	Republican Vote	Republican Candidate	Democratic Vote	Democratic Candidate	Other Vote	Rep.-Dem. Plurality	Total Vote Rep.	Total Vote Dem.	Major Vote Rep.	Major Vote Dem.
2008	4,268,941	2,001,168	McCrory, Pat	2,146,189	Perdue, Bev	121,584	145,021 D	46.9%	50.3%	48.3%	51.7%
2004	3,486,688	1,495,021	Ballantine, Patrick J.	1,939,154	Easley, Michael F.	52,513	444,133 D	42.9%	55.6%	43.5%	56.5%
2000	2,942,062	1,360,960	Vinroot, Richard	1,530,324	Easley, Michael F.	50,778	169,364 D	46.3%	52.0%	47.1%	52.9%
1996	2,566,185	1,097,053	Hayes, Robin	1,436,638	Hunt, James B.	32,494	339,585 D	42.8%	56.0%	43.3%	56.7%
1992	2,595,184	1,121,955	Gardner, James C.	1,368,246	Hunt, James B.	104,983	246,291 D	43.2%	52.7%	45.1%	54.9%
1988	2,180,025	1,222,338	Martin, James G.	957,687	Jordan, Robert B.		264,651 R	56.1%	43.9%	56.1%	43.9%
1984	2,226,727	1,208,167	Martin, James G.	1,011,209	Edmisten, Rufus	7,351	196,958 R	54.3%	45.4%	54.4%	45.6%
1980	1,847,432	691,449	Lake, Beverly	1,143,145	Hunt, James B.	12,838	451,696 D	37.4%	61.9%	37.7%	62.3%
1976	1,663,824	564,102	Flaherty, David T.	1,081,293	Hunt, James B.	18,429	517,191 D	33.9%	65.0%	34.3%	65.7%
1972	1,504,785	767,470	Holshouser, James E.	729,104	Bowles, Hargrove	8,211	38,366 R	51.0%	48.5%	51.3%	48.7%
1968	1,558,308	737,075	Gardner, James C.	821,233	Scott, Robert W.		84,158 D	47.3%	52.7%	47.3%	52.7%
1964	1,396,508	606,165	Gavin, Robert L.	790,343	Moore, Dan K.		184,178 D	43.4%	56.6%	43.4%	56.6%
1960	1,350,360	613,975	Gavin, Robert L.	735,248	Sanford, Terry	1,137	121,273 D	45.5%	54.4%	45.5%	54.5%
1956	1,135,859	375,379	Hayes, Kyle	760,480	Hodges, Luther H.		385,101 D	33.0%	67.0%	33.0%	67.0%
1952	1,179,635	383,329	Seawell, H. F.	796,306	Umstead, William B.		412,977 D	32.5%	67.5%	32.5%	67.5%
1948	780,525	206,166	Pritchard, George	570,995	Scott, William Kerr	3,364	364,829 D	26.4%	73.2%	26.5%	73.5%

POSTWAR VOTE FOR SENATOR

Year	Total Vote	Republican Vote	Republican Candidate	Democratic Vote	Democratic Candidate	Other Vote	Rep.-Dem. Plurality	Total Vote Rep.	Total Vote Dem.	Major Vote Rep.	Major Vote Dem.
2008	4,271,970	1,887,510	Dole, Elizabeth	2,249,311	Hagan, Kay	135,149	361,801 D	44.2%	52.7%	45.6%	54.4%
2004	3,472,082	1,791,450	Burr, Richard M.	1,632,527	Bowles, Erskine	48,105	158,923 R	51.6%	47.0%	52.3%	47.7%
2002	2,331,181	1,248,664	Dole, Elizabeth	1,047,983	Bowles, Erskine	34,534	200,681 R	53.6%	45.0%	54.4%	45.6%
1998	2,012,143	945,943	Faircloth, Lauch	1,029,237	Edwards, John	36,963	83,294 D	47.0%	51.2%	47.9%	52.1%
1996	2,556,456	1,345,833	Helms, Jesse	1,173,875	Gantt, Harvey B.	36,748	171,958 R	52.6%	45.9%	53.4%	46.6%
1992	2,577,891	1,297,892	Faircloth, Lauch	1,194,015	Sanford, Terry	85,984	103,877 R	50.3%	46.3%	52.1%	47.9%
1990	2,069,585	1,087,331	Helms, Jesse	981,573	Gantt, Harvy B.	681	105,758 R	52.5%	47.4%	52.6%	47.4%
1986	1,591,330	767,668	Broyhill, James T.	823,662	Sanford, Terry		55,994 D	48.2%	51.8%	48.2%	51.8%
1984	2,239,051	1,156,768	Helms, Jesse	1,070,488	Hunt, James B.	11,795	86,280 R	51.7%	47.8%	51.9%	48.1%
1980	1,797,665	898,064	East, John P.	887,653	Morgan, Robert	11,948	10,411 R	50.0%	49.4%	50.3%	49.7%
1978	1,135,814	619,151	Helms, Jesse	516,663	Ingram, John		102,488 R	54.5%	45.5%	54.5%	45.5%
1974	1,020,367	377,618	Stevens, William E.	633,775	Morgan, Robert	8,974	256,157 D	37.0%	62.1%	37.3%	62.7%
1972	1,472,541	795,248	Helms, Jesse	677,293	Galifianakis, Nick		117,955 R	54.0%	46.0%	54.0%	46.0%
1968	1,437,340	566,934	Somers, Robert V.	870,406	Ervin, Sam J.		303,472 D	39.4%	60.6%	39.4%	60.6%
1966	901,978	400,502	Shallcross, John S.	501,440	Jordan, B. Everett	36	100,938 D	44.4%	55.6%	44.4%	55.6%
1962	813,155	321,635	Greene, Claude L.	491,520	Ervin, Sam J.		169,885 D	39.6%	60.4%	39.6%	60.4%
1960	1,291,485	497,964	Hayes, Kyle	793,521	Jordan, B. Everett		295,557 D	38.6%	61.4%	38.6%	61.4%
1958S	616,469	184,977	Clarke, Richard C.	431,492	Jordan, B. Everett		246,515 D	30.0%	70.0%	30.0%	70.0%
1956	1,098,828	367,475	Johnson, Joel A.	731,353	Ervin, Sam J.		363,878 D	33.4%	66.6%	33.4%	66.6%
1954	619,634	211,322	West, Paul C.	408,312	Scott, William Kerr		196,990 D	34.1%	65.9%	34.1%	65.9%
1954S	410,574		—	410,574	Ervin, Sam J.		410,574 D		100.0%		100.0%
1950	548,276	171,804	Leavitt, Halsey B.	376,472	Hoey, Clyde R.		204,668 D	31.3%	68.7%	31.3%	68.7%
1950S	544,924	177,753	Gavin, E. L.	364,912	Smith, Willis	2,259	187,159 D	32.6%	67.0%	32.8%	67.2%
1948	764,559	220,307	Wilkinson, John A.	540,762	Broughton, J. M.	3,490	320,455 D	28.8%	70.7%	28.9%	71.1%

Notes: One each of the 1950 and 1954 elections as well as the 1958 election were for short terms to fill vacancies. The Republican Party did not run a Senate candidate in the 1954 election for the short term.

NORTH CAROLINA
PRESIDENT 2008

2000 Census Population	County	Total Vote	Republican	Democratic	Other	Rep.-Dem. Plurality		Total Vote Rep.	Total Vote Dem.	Major Vote Rep.	Major Vote Dem.
130,800	ALAMANCE	64,353	34,859	28,918	576	5,941	R	54.2%	44.9%	54.7%	45.3%
33,603	ALEXANDER	17,254	11,790	5,167	297	6,623	R	68.3%	29.9%	69.5%	30.5%
10,677	ALLEGHANY	5,263	3,124	2,021	118	1,103	R	59.4%	38.4%	60.7%	39.3%
25,275	ANSON	10,733	4,207	6,456	70	2,249	D	39.2%	60.2%	39.5%	60.5%
24,384	ASHE	13,069	7,916	4,872	281	3,044	R	60.6%	37.3%	61.9%	38.1%
17,167	AVERY	7,943	5,681	2,178	84	3,503	R	71.5%	27.4%	72.3%	27.7%
44,958	BEAUFORT	23,010	13,460	9,454	96	4,006	R	58.5%	41.1%	58.7%	41.3%
19,773	BERTIE	9,763	3,376	6,365	22	2,989	D	34.6%	65.2%	34.7%	65.3%
32,278	BLADEN	15,480	7,532	7,853	95	321	D	48.7%	50.7%	49.0%	51.0%
73,143	BRUNSWICK	52,608	30,753	21,331	524	9,422	R	58.5%	40.5%	59.0%	41.0%
206,330	BUNCOMBE	123,795	52,494	69,716	1,585	17,222	D	42.4%	56.3%	43.0%	57.0%
89,148	BURKE	37,443	22,102	14,901	440	7,201	R	59.0%	39.8%	59.7%	40.3%
131,063	CABARRUS	77,994	45,924	31,546	524	14,378	R	58.9%	40.4%	59.3%	40.7%
77,415	CALDWELL	35,155	22,526	12,081	548	10,445	R	64.1%	34.4%	65.1%	34.9%
6,885	CAMDEN	4,821	3,140	1,597	84	1,543	R	65.1%	33.1%	66.3%	33.7%
59,383	CARTERET	34,597	23,131	11,130	336	12,001	R	66.9%	32.2%	67.5%	32.5%
23,501	CASWELL	10,862	5,208	5,545	109	337	D	47.9%	51.0%	48.4%	51.6%
141,685	CATAWBA	69,451	42,993	25,656	802	17,337	R	61.9%	36.9%	62.6%	37.4%
49,329	CHATHAM	32,880	14,668	17,862	350	3,194	D	44.6%	54.3%	45.1%	54.9%
24,298	CHEROKEE	12,586	8,643	3,785	158	4,858	R	68.7%	30.1%	69.5%	30.5%
14,526	CHOWAN	7,512	3,773	3,688	51	85	R	50.2%	49.1%	50.6%	49.4%
8,775	CLAY	5,543	3,707	1,734	102	1,973	R	66.9%	31.3%	68.1%	31.9%
96,287	CLEVELAND	43,835	26,078	17,363	394	8,715	R	59.5%	39.6%	60.0%	40.0%
54,749	COLUMBUS	24,282	12,994	11,076	212	1,918	R	53.5%	45.6%	54.0%	46.0%
91,436	CRAVEN	44,598	24,901	19,352	345	5,549	R	55.8%	43.4%	56.3%	43.7%
302,963	CUMBERLAND	127,575	52,151	74,693	731	22,542	D	40.9%	58.5%	41.1%	58.9%
18,190	CURRITUCK	11,102	7,234	3,737	131	3,497	R	65.2%	33.7%	65.9%	34.1%
29,967	DARE	18,048	9,745	8,074	229	1,671	R	54.0%	44.7%	54.7%	45.3%
147,246	DAVIDSON	68,581	45,419	22,433	729	22,986	R	66.2%	32.7%	66.9%	33.1%
34,835	DAVIE	20,368	13,981	6,178	209	7,803	R	68.6%	30.3%	69.4%	30.6%
49,063	DUPLIN	19,904	10,834	8,958	112	1,876	R	54.4%	45.0%	54.7%	45.3%
223,314	DURHAM	136,897	32,353	103,456	1,088	71,103	D	23.6%	75.6%	23.8%	76.2%
55,606	EDGECOMBE	25,930	8,445	17,403	82	8,958	D	32.6%	67.1%	32.7%	67.3%
306,067	FORSYTH	166,133	73,674	91,085	1,374	17,411	D	44.3%	54.8%	44.7%	55.3%
47,260	FRANKLIN	26,639	13,273	13,085	281	188	R	49.8%	49.1%	50.4%	49.6%
190,365	GASTON	84,402	52,507	31,384	511	21,123	R	62.2%	37.2%	62.6%	37.4%
10,516	GATES	5,420	2,547	2,830	43	283	D	47.0%	52.2%	47.4%	52.6%
7,993	GRAHAM	4,171	2,824	1,265	82	1,559	R	67.7%	30.3%	69.1%	30.9%
48,498	GRANVILLE	24,725	11,447	13,074	204	1,627	D	46.3%	52.9%	46.7%	53.3%
18,974	GREENE	8,103	4,272	3,796	35	476	R	52.7%	46.8%	52.9%	47.1%
421,048	GUILFORD	241,771	97,718	142,101	1,952	44,383	D	40.4%	58.8%	40.7%	59.3%
57,370	HALIFAX	25,091	8,961	16,047	83	7,086	D	35.7%	64.0%	35.8%	64.2%
91,025	HARNETT	40,705	23,579	16,785	341	6,794	R	57.9%	41.2%	58.4%	41.6%
54,033	HAYWOOD	28,067	14,910	12,730	427	2,180	R	53.1%	45.4%	53.9%	46.1%
89,173	HENDERSON	51,614	30,930	20,082	602	10,848	R	59.9%	38.9%	60.6%	39.4%
22,601	HERTFORD	10,650	3,089	7,513	48	4,424	D	29.0%	70.5%	29.1%	70.9%
33,646	HOKE	15,627	6,293	9,227	107	2,934	D	40.3%	59.0%	40.5%	59.5%
5,826	HYDE	2,469	1,212	1,241	16	29	D	49.1%	50.3%	49.4%	50.6%
122,660	IREDELL	73,162	45,148	27,318	696	17,830	R	61.7%	37.3%	62.3%	37.7%
33,121	JACKSON	16,866	7,854	8,766	246	912	D	46.6%	52.0%	47.3%	52.7%

NORTH CAROLINA

PRESIDENT 2008

2000 Census Population	County	Total Vote	Republican	Democratic	Other	Rep.-Dem. Plurality	Percentage Total Vote Rep.	Dem.	Major Vote Rep.	Dem.
121,965	JOHNSTON	71,017	43,622	26,795	600	16,827 R	61.4%	37.7%	61.9%	38.1%
10,381	JONES	5,227	2,817	2,378	32	439 R	53.9%	45.5%	54.2%	45.8%
49,040	LEE	23,788	12,775	10,784	229	1,991 R	53.7%	45.3%	54.2%	45.8%
59,648	LENOIR	26,897	13,401	13,378	118	23 R	49.8%	49.7%	50.0%	50.0%
63,780	LINCOLN	35,798	23,631	11,713	454	11,918 R	66.0%	32.7%	66.9%	33.1%
42,151	MCDOWELL	18,386	11,534	6,571	281	4,963 R	62.7%	35.7%	63.7%	36.3%
29,811	MACON	17,238	10,317	6,620	301	3,697 R	59.9%	38.4%	60.9%	39.1%
19,635	MADISON	10,379	5,192	5,026	161	166 R	50.0%	48.4%	50.8%	49.2%
25,593	MARTIN	12,541	5,957	6,539	45	582 D	47.5%	52.1%	47.7%	52.3%
695,454	MECKLENBURG	410,817	153,848	253,958	3,011	100,110 D	37.4%	61.8%	37.7%	62.3%
15,687	MITCHELL	7,846	5,499	2,238	109	3,261 R	70.1%	28.5%	71.1%	28.9%
26,822	MONTGOMERY	11,210	6,155	4,926	129	1,229 R	54.9%	43.9%	55.5%	44.5%
74,769	MOORE	45,328	27,314	17,624	390	9,690 R	60.3%	38.9%	60.8%	39.2%
87,420	NASH	47,118	23,728	23,099	291	629 R	50.4%	49.0%	50.7%	49.3%
160,307	NEW HANOVER	100,665	50,544	49,145	976	1,399 R	50.2%	48.8%	50.7%	49.3%
22,086	NORTHAMPTON	10,618	3,671	6,903	44	3,232 D	34.6%	65.0%	34.7%	65.3%
150,355	ONSLOW	50,203	30,278	19,499	426	10,779 R	60.3%	38.8%	60.8%	39.2%
118,227	ORANGE	74,910	20,266	53,806	838	33,540 D	27.1%	71.8%	27.4%	72.6%
12,934	PAMLICO	6,712	3,823	2,838	51	985 R	57.0%	42.3%	57.4%	42.6%
34,897	PASQUOTANK	18,180	7,778	10,272	130	2,494 D	42.8%	56.5%	43.1%	56.9%
41,082	PENDER	23,749	13,618	9,907	224	3,711 R	57.3%	41.7%	57.9%	42.1%
11,368	PERQUIMANS	6,501	3,678	2,772	51	906 R	56.6%	42.6%	57.0%	43.0%
35,623	PERSON	18,632	10,030	8,446	156	1,584 R	53.8%	45.3%	54.3%	45.7%
133,798	PITT	74,884	33,927	40,501	456	6,574 D	45.3%	54.1%	45.6%	54.4%
18,324	POLK	10,562	5,990	4,396	176	1,594 R	56.7%	41.6%	57.7%	42.3%
130,454	RANDOLPH	58,147	40,998	16,414	735	24,584 R	70.5%	28.2%	71.4%	28.6%
46,564	RICHMOND	19,327	9,424	9,713	190	289 D	48.8%	50.3%	49.2%	50.8%
123,339	ROBESON	40,834	17,433	23,058	343	5,625 D	42.7%	56.5%	43.1%	56.9%
91,928	ROCKINGHAM	41,612	23,899	17,255	458	6,644 R	57.4%	41.5%	58.1%	41.9%
130,340	ROWAN	61,560	37,451	23,391	718	14,060 R	60.8%	38.0%	61.6%	38.4%
62,899	RUTHERFORD	28,720	18,769	9,641	310	9,128 R	65.4%	33.6%	66.1%	33.9%
60,161	SAMPSON	26,038	14,038	11,836	164	2,202 R	53.9%	45.5%	54.3%	45.7%
35,998	SCOTLAND	14,217	6,005	8,151	61	2,146 D	42.2%	57.3%	42.4%	57.6%
58,100	STANLY	28,506	19,329	8,878	299	10,451 R	67.8%	31.1%	68.5%	31.5%
44,711	STOKES	21,743	14,488	6,875	380	7,613 R	66.6%	31.6%	67.8%	32.2%
71,219	SURRY	29,525	18,730	10,475	320	8,255 R	63.4%	35.5%	64.1%	35.9%
12,968	SWAIN	5,798	2,900	2,806	92	94 R	50.0%	48.4%	50.8%	49.2%
29,334	TRANSYLVANIA	16,909	9,401	7,275	233	2,126 R	55.6%	43.0%	56.4%	43.6%
4,149	TYRRELL	1,910	960	933	17	27 R	50.3%	48.8%	50.7%	49.3%
123,677	UNION	86,089	54,123	31,189	777	22,934 R	62.9%	36.2%	63.4%	36.6%
42,954	VANCE	20,871	7,606	13,166	99	5,560 D	36.4%	63.1%	36.6%	63.4%
627,846	WAKE	442,245	187,001	250,891	4,353	63,890 D	42.3%	56.7%	42.7%	57.3%
19,972	WARREN	10,195	3,063	7,086	46	4,023 D	30.0%	69.5%	30.2%	69.8%
13,723	WASHINGTON	6,454	2,670	3,748	36	1,078 D	41.4%	58.1%	41.6%	58.4%
42,695	WATAUGA	28,372	13,344	14,558	470	1,214 D	47.0%	51.3%	47.8%	52.2%
113,329	WAYNE	49,882	26,952	22,671	259	4,281 R	54.0%	45.4%	54.3%	45.7%
65,632	WILKES	29,724	20,288	8,934	502	11,354 R	68.3%	30.1%	69.4%	30.6%
73,814	WILSON	37,191	17,375	19,652	164	2,277 D	46.7%	52.8%	46.9%	53.1%
36,348	YADKIN	17,147	12,409	4,527	211	7,882 R	72.4%	26.4%	73.3%	26.7%
17,774	YANCEY	9,717	5,045	4,486	186	559 R	51.9%	46.2%	52.9%	47.1%
8,049,313	TOTAL	4,310,789	2,128,474	2,142,651	39,664	14,177 D	49.4%	49.7%	49.8%	50.2%

NORTH CAROLINA
GOVERNOR 2008

2000 Census Population	County	Total Vote	Republican	Democratic	Other	Rep.-Dem. Plurality	Percentage Total Vote Rep.	Dem.	Major Vote Rep.	Dem.
130,800	ALAMANCE	63,742	31,081	30,456	2,205	625 R	48.8%	47.8%	50.5%	49.5%
33,603	ALEXANDER	17,263	11,274	5,673	316	5,601 R	65.3%	32.9%	66.5%	33.5%
10,677	ALLEGHANY	5,277	2,461	2,603	213	142 D	46.6%	49.3%	48.6%	51.4%
25,275	ANSON	10,742	3,832	6,792	118	2,960 D	35.7%	63.2%	36.1%	63.9%
24,384	ASHE	13,111	7,105	5,633	373	1,472 R	54.2%	43.0%	55.8%	44.2%
17,167	AVERY	7,858	5,486	2,179	193	3,307 R	69.8%	27.7%	71.6%	28.4%
44,958	BEAUFORT	22,868	9,856	12,458	554	2,602 D	43.1%	54.5%	44.2%	55.8%
19,773	BERTIE	9,702	2,171	7,411	120	5,240 D	22.4%	76.4%	22.7%	77.3%
32,278	BLADEN	15,133	5,005	9,804	324	4,799 D	33.1%	64.8%	33.8%	66.2%
73,143	BRUNSWICK	51,966	26,360	23,394	2,212	2,966 R	50.7%	45.0%	53.0%	47.0%
206,330	BUNCOMBE	121,936	47,283	69,783	4,870	22,500 D	38.8%	57.2%	40.4%	59.6%
89,148	BURKE	37,430	20,969	15,614	847	5,355 R	56.0%	41.7%	57.3%	42.7%
131,063	CABARRUS	77,891	49,093	27,098	1,700	21,995 R	63.0%	34.8%	64.4%	35.6%
77,415	CALDWELL	35,254	22,096	12,187	971	9,909 R	62.7%	34.6%	64.5%	35.5%
6,885	CAMDEN	4,685	2,354	2,193	138	161 R	50.2%	46.8%	51.8%	48.2%
59,383	CARTERET	34,438	17,534	15,997	907	1,537 R	50.9%	46.5%	52.3%	47.7%
23,501	CASWELL	10,626	4,038	6,310	278	2,272 D	38.0%	59.4%	39.0%	61.0%
141,685	CATAWBA	69,409	44,933	22,987	1,489	21,946 R	64.7%	33.1%	66.2%	33.8%
49,329	CHATHAM	32,659	14,098	17,325	1,236	3,227 D	43.2%	53.0%	44.9%	55.1%
24,298	CHEROKEE	12,277	6,858	5,092	327	1,766 R	55.9%	41.5%	57.4%	42.6%
14,526	CHOWAN	7,298	2,714	4,415	169	1,701 D	37.2%	60.5%	38.1%	61.9%
8,775	CLAY	5,462	3,124	2,171	167	953 R	57.2%	39.7%	59.0%	41.0%
96,287	CLEVELAND	43,554	24,570	18,263	721	6,307 R	56.4%	41.9%	57.4%	42.6%
54,749	COLUMBUS	23,983	7,812	15,572	599	7,760 D	32.6%	64.9%	33.4%	66.6%
91,436	CRAVEN	44,303	18,131	25,174	998	7,043 D	40.9%	56.8%	41.9%	58.1%
302,963	CUMBERLAND	125,441	45,065	77,668	2,708	32,603 D	35.9%	61.9%	36.7%	63.3%
18,190	CURRITUCK	10,705	5,748	4,600	357	1,148 R	53.7%	43.0%	55.5%	44.5%
29,967	DARE	17,627	7,915	9,222	490	1,307 D	44.9%	52.3%	46.2%	53.8%
147,246	DAVIDSON	68,544	39,622	26,401	2,521	13,221 R	57.8%	38.5%	60.0%	40.0%
34,835	DAVIE	20,196	12,422	7,078	696	5,344 R	61.5%	35.0%	63.7%	36.3%
49,063	DUPLIN	19,711	7,638	11,695	378	4,057 D	38.7%	59.3%	39.5%	60.5%
223,314	DURHAM	134,990	34,311	95,338	5,341	61,027 D	25.4%	70.6%	26.5%	73.5%
55,606	EDGECOMBE	25,887	6,749	18,858	280	12,109 D	26.1%	72.8%	26.4%	73.6%
306,067	FORSYTH	164,606	69,408	90,429	4,769	21,021 D	42.2%	54.9%	43.4%	56.6%
47,260	FRANKLIN	26,534	11,849	13,897	788	2,048 D	44.7%	52.4%	46.0%	54.0%
190,365	GASTON	84,281	53,439	29,294	1,548	24,145 R	63.4%	34.8%	64.6%	35.4%
10,516	GATES	5,319	2,035	3,206	78	1,171 D	38.3%	60.3%	38.8%	61.2%
7,993	GRAHAM	4,113	2,145	1,835	133	310 R	52.2%	44.6%	53.9%	46.1%
48,498	GRANVILLE	24,543	10,210	13,681	652	3,471 D	41.6%	55.7%	42.7%	57.3%
18,974	GREENE	8,074	2,965	4,993	116	2,028 D	36.7%	61.8%	37.3%	62.7%
421,048	GUILFORD	238,730	94,409	136,995	7,326	42,586 D	39.5%	57.4%	40.8%	59.2%
57,370	HALIFAX	25,027	6,902	17,789	336	10,887 D	27.6%	71.1%	28.0%	72.0%
91,025	HARNETT	40,567	20,560	18,970	1,037	1,590 R	50.7%	46.8%	52.0%	48.0%
54,033	HAYWOOD	27,874	11,744	15,081	1,049	3,337 D	42.1%	54.1%	43.8%	56.2%
89,173	HENDERSON	50,804	28,006	21,028	1,770	6,978 R	55.1%	41.4%	57.1%	42.9%
22,601	HERTFORD	10,498	2,305	8,108	85	5,803 D	22.0%	77.2%	22.1%	77.9%
33,646	HOKE	15,372	5,184	9,873	315	4,689 D	33.7%	64.2%	34.4%	65.6%
5,826	HYDE	2,449	777	1,620	52	843 D	31.7%	66.1%	32.4%	67.6%
122,660	IREDELL	72,735	47,281	23,863	1,591	23,418 R	65.0%	32.8%	66.5%	33.5%
33,121	JACKSON	16,672	6,554	9,459	659	2,905 D	39.3%	56.7%	40.9%	59.1%

NORTH CAROLINA

GOVERNOR 2008

2000 Census Population	County	Total Vote	Republican	Democratic	Other	Rep.-Dem. Plurality	Percentage			
							Total Vote		Major Vote	
							Rep.	Dem.	Rep.	Dem.
121,965	JOHNSTON	70,619	39,479	29,429	1,711	10,050 R	55.9%	41.7%	57.3%	42.7%
10,381	JONES	5,214	1,851	3,246	117	1,395 D	35.5%	62.3%	36.3%	63.7%
49,040	LEE	23,580	11,169	11,745	666	576 D	47.4%	49.8%	48.7%	51.3%
59,648	LENOIR	26,420	8,975	17,039	406	8,064 D	34.0%	64.5%	34.5%	65.5%
63,780	LINCOLN	35,657	24,193	10,691	773	13,502 R	67.8%	30.0%	69.4%	30.6%
42,151	MCDOWELL	18,277	9,289	8,219	769	1,070 R	50.8%	45.0%	53.1%	46.9%
29,811	MACON	16,961	8,444	7,824	693	620 R	49.8%	46.1%	51.9%	48.1%
19,635	MADISON	10,355	4,334	5,652	369	1,318 D	41.9%	54.6%	43.4%	56.6%
25,593	MARTIN	12,437	3,613	8,644	180	5,031 D	29.1%	69.5%	29.5%	70.5%
695,454	MECKLENBURG	407,251	199,340	199,677	8,234	337 D	48.9%	49.0%	50.0%	50.0%
15,687	MITCHELL	7,716	4,995	2,450	271	2,545 R	64.7%	31.8%	67.1%	32.9%
26,822	MONTGOMERY	11,253	5,364	5,647	242	283 D	47.7%	50.2%	48.7%	51.3%
74,769	MOORE	44,995	26,168	17,585	1,242	8,583 R	58.2%	39.1%	59.8%	40.2%
87,420	NASH	47,034	20,531	25,837	666	5,306 D	43.7%	54.9%	44.3%	55.7%
160,307	NEW HANOVER	98,507	45,625	48,737	4,145	3,112 D	46.3%	49.5%	48.4%	51.6%
22,086	NORTHAMPTON	10,558	2,727	7,697	134	4,970 D	25.8%	72.9%	26.2%	73.8%
150,355	ONSLOW	49,125	22,608	24,552	1,965	1,944 D	46.0%	50.0%	47.9%	52.1%
118,227	ORANGE	73,609	22,288	47,888	3,433	25,600 D	30.3%	65.1%	31.8%	68.2%
12,934	PAMLICO	6,655	2,538	3,962	155	1,424 D	38.1%	59.5%	39.0%	61.0%
34,897	PASQUOTANK	17,759	5,940	11,443	376	5,503 D	33.4%	64.4%	34.2%	65.8%
41,082	PENDER	23,453	11,263	11,009	1,181	254 R	48.0%	46.9%	50.6%	49.4%
11,368	PERQUIMANS	6,321	2,761	3,437	123	676 D	43.7%	54.4%	44.5%	55.5%
35,623	PERSON	18,327	8,243	9,589	495	1,346 D	45.0%	52.3%	46.2%	53.8%
133,798	PITT	74,182	28,611	44,066	1,505	15,455 D	38.6%	59.4%	39.4%	60.6%
18,324	POLK	10,393	5,069	4,917	407	152 R	48.8%	47.3%	50.8%	49.2%
130,454	RANDOLPH	58,002	36,433	19,328	2,241	17,105 R	62.8%	33.3%	65.3%	34.7%
46,564	RICHMOND	19,040	7,862	10,800	378	2,938 D	41.3%	56.7%	42.1%	57.9%
123,339	ROBESON	40,338	11,269	28,480	589	17,211 D	27.9%	70.6%	28.4%	71.6%
91,928	ROCKINGHAM	41,225	19,245	20,428	1,552	1,183 D	46.7%	49.6%	48.5%	51.5%
130,340	ROWAN	61,252	37,309	22,469	1,474	14,840 R	60.9%	36.7%	62.4%	37.6%
62,899	RUTHERFORD	28,135	15,259	11,945	931	3,314 R	54.2%	42.5%	56.1%	43.9%
60,161	SAMPSON	25,936	11,906	13,673	357	1,767 D	45.9%	52.7%	46.5%	53.5%
35,998	SCOTLAND	13,851	4,842	8,770	239	3,928 D	35.0%	63.3%	35.6%	64.4%
58,100	STANLY	28,450	18,872	9,008	570	9,864 R	66.3%	31.7%	67.7%	32.3%
44,711	STOKES	21,780	12,014	8,839	927	3,175 R	55.2%	40.6%	57.6%	42.4%
71,219	SURRY	29,422	15,358	13,148	916	2,210 R	52.2%	44.7%	53.9%	46.1%
12,968	SWAIN	5,778	2,147	3,427	204	1,280 D	37.2%	59.3%	38.5%	61.5%
29,334	TRANSYLVANIA	16,735	8,230	7,844	661	386 R	49.2%	46.9%	51.2%	48.8%
4,149	TYRRELL	1,879	546	1,283	50	737 D	29.1%	68.3%	29.9%	70.1%
123,677	UNION	85,277	58,474	25,145	1,658	33,329 R	68.6%	29.5%	69.9%	30.1%
42,954	VANCE	20,774	6,400	14,066	308	7,666 D	30.8%	67.7%	31.3%	68.7%
627,846	WAKE	437,762	197,244	224,032	16,486	26,788 D	45.1%	51.2%	46.8%	53.2%
19,972	WARREN	9,957	2,693	7,112	152	4,419 D	27.0%	71.4%	27.5%	72.5%
13,723	WASHINGTON	6,455	1,641	4,731	83	3,090 D	25.4%	73.3%	25.8%	74.2%
42,695	WATAUGA	27,764	13,276	13,371	1,117	95 D	47.8%	48.2%	49.8%	50.2%
113,329	WAYNE	49,234	22,621	25,704	909	3,083 D	45.9%	52.2%	46.8%	53.2%
65,632	WILKES	29,545	16,779	11,685	1,081	5,094 R	56.8%	39.5%	58.9%	41.1%
73,814	WILSON	36,700	15,109	21,087	504	5,978 D	41.2%	57.5%	41.7%	58.3%
36,348	YADKIN	17,003	10,361	6,060	582	4,301 R	60.9%	35.6%	63.1%	36.9%
17,774	YANCEY	9,823	4,379	5,207	237	828 D	44.6%	53.0%	45.7%	54.3%
8,049,313	TOTAL	4,268,941	2,001,168	2,146,189	121,584	145,021 D	46.9%	50.3%	48.3%	51.7%

NORTH CAROLINA

SENATOR 2008

2000 Census Population	County	Total Vote	Republican	Democratic	Other	Rep.-Dem. Plurality		Percentage			
								Total Vote		Major Vote	
								Rep.	Dem.	Rep.	Dem.
130,800	ALAMANCE	63,790	30,644	31,101	2,045	457	D	48.0%	48.8%	49.6%	50.4%
33,603	ALEXANDER	17,194	9,956	6,519	719	3,437	R	57.9%	37.9%	60.4%	39.6%
10,677	ALLEGHANY	5,279	2,580	2,456	243	124	R	48.9%	46.5%	51.2%	48.8%
25,275	ANSON	10,709	3,353	7,110	246	3,757	D	31.3%	66.4%	32.0%	68.0%
24,384	ASHE	13,105	6,710	5,805	590	905	R	51.2%	44.3%	53.6%	46.4%
17,167	AVERY	7,845	5,020	2,481	344	2,539	R	64.0%	31.6%	66.9%	33.1%
44,958	BEAUFORT	22,853	11,625	10,523	705	1,102	R	50.9%	46.0%	52.5%	47.5%
19,773	BERTIE	9,667	3,023	6,516	128	3,493	D	31.3%	67.4%	31.7%	68.3%
32,278	BLADEN	15,161	5,873	8,920	368	3,047	D	38.7%	58.8%	39.7%	60.3%
73,143	BRUNSWICK	52,118	24,302	25,554	2,262	1,252	D	46.6%	49.0%	48.7%	51.3%
206,330	BUNCOMBE	122,427	46,855	70,777	4,795	23,922	D	38.3%	57.8%	39.8%	60.2%
89,148	BURKE	37,348	18,618	17,283	1,447	1,335	R	49.9%	46.3%	51.9%	48.1%
131,063	CABARRUS	77,546	40,026	34,441	3,079	5,585	R	51.6%	44.4%	53.7%	46.3%
77,415	CALDWELL	35,143	18,925	14,310	1,908	4,615	R	53.9%	40.7%	56.9%	43.1%
6,885	CAMDEN	4,746	2,995	1,645	106	1,350	R	63.1%	34.7%	64.5%	35.5%
59,383	CARTERET	34,389	20,356	12,926	1,107	7,430	R	59.2%	37.6%	61.2%	38.8%
23,501	CASWELL	10,670	4,371	6,033	266	1,662	D	41.0%	56.5%	42.0%	58.0%
141,685	CATAWBA	69,221	38,473	27,927	2,821	10,546	R	55.6%	40.3%	57.9%	42.1%
49,329	CHATHAM	32,691	13,398	18,316	977	4,918	D	41.0%	56.0%	42.2%	57.8%
24,298	CHEROKEE	12,456	8,020	4,144	292	3,876	R	64.4%	33.3%	65.9%	34.1%
14,526	CHOWAN	7,346	3,478	3,707	161	229	D	47.3%	50.5%	48.4%	51.6%
8,775	CLAY	5,526	3,493	1,901	132	1,592	R	63.2%	34.4%	64.8%	35.2%
96,287	CLEVELAND	43,473	21,136	20,847	1,490	289	R	48.6%	48.0%	50.3%	49.7%
54,749	COLUMBUS	23,976	9,184	14,043	749	4,859	D	38.3%	58.6%	39.5%	60.5%
91,436	CRAVEN	44,254	22,768	20,214	1,272	2,554	R	51.4%	45.7%	53.0%	47.0%
302,963	CUMBERLAND	125,771	46,279	76,509	2,983	30,230	D	36.8%	60.8%	37.7%	62.3%
18,190	CURRITUCK	10,873	7,092	3,513	268	3,579	R	65.2%	32.3%	66.9%	33.1%
29,967	DARE	17,856	9,871	7,538	447	2,333	R	55.3%	42.2%	56.7%	43.3%
147,246	DAVIDSON	68,663	39,221	26,706	2,736	12,515	R	57.1%	38.9%	59.5%	40.5%
34,835	DAVIE	20,228	12,502	7,048	678	5,454	R	61.8%	34.8%	63.9%	36.1%
49,063	DUPLIN	19,741	8,852	10,451	438	1,599	D	44.8%	52.9%	45.9%	54.1%
223,314	DURHAM	135,325	31,808	100,476	3,041	68,668	D	23.5%	74.2%	24.0%	76.0%
55,606	EDGECOMBE	25,897	7,372	18,177	348	10,805	D	28.5%	70.2%	28.9%	71.1%
306,067	FORSYTH	165,037	66,618	93,836	4,583	27,218	D	40.4%	56.9%	41.5%	58.5%
47,260	FRANKLIN	26,520	11,609	14,044	867	2,435	D	43.8%	53.0%	45.3%	54.7%
190,365	GASTON	83,922	45,893	34,934	3,095	10,959	R	54.7%	41.6%	56.8%	43.2%
10,516	GATES	5,352	2,424	2,850	78	426	D	45.3%	53.3%	46.0%	54.0%
7,993	GRAHAM	4,120	2,339	1,599	182	740	R	56.8%	38.8%	59.4%	40.6%
48,498	GRANVILLE	24,537	9,853	13,985	699	4,132	D	40.2%	57.0%	41.3%	58.7%
18,974	GREENE	8,068	3,638	4,281	149	643	D	45.1%	53.1%	45.9%	54.1%
421,048	GUILFORD	239,196	85,152	147,969	6,075	62,817	D	35.6%	61.9%	36.5%	63.5%
57,370	HALIFAX	25,054	7,756	16,929	369	9,173	D	31.0%	67.6%	31.4%	68.6%
91,025	HARNETT	40,562	20,636	18,692	1,234	1,944	R	50.9%	46.1%	52.5%	47.5%
54,033	HAYWOOD	27,990	12,622	14,330	1,038	1,708	D	45.1%	51.2%	46.8%	53.2%
89,173	HENDERSON	50,973	28,022	21,214	1,737	6,808	R	55.0%	41.6%	56.9%	43.1%
22,601	HERTFORD	10,527	2,850	7,590	87	4,740	D	27.1%	72.1%	27.3%	72.7%
33,646	HOKE	15,425	5,539	9,498	388	3,959	D	35.9%	61.6%	36.8%	63.2%
5,826	HYDE	2,458	1,006	1,387	65	381	D	40.9%	56.4%	42.0%	58.0%
122,660	IREDELL	72,497	39,934	29,420	3,143	10,514	R	55.1%	40.6%	57.6%	42.4%
33,121	JACKSON	16,702	6,735	9,298	669	2,563	D	40.3%	55.7%	42.0%	58.0%

NORTH CAROLINA

SENATOR 2008

2000 Census Population	County	Total Vote	Republican	Democratic	Other	Rep.-Dem. Plurality	Percentage			
							Total Vote		Major Vote	
							Rep.	Dem.	Rep.	Dem.
121,965	JOHNSTON	70,594	38,955	29,516	2,123	9,439 R	55.2%	41.8%	56.9%	43.1%
10,381	JONES	5,216	2,461	2,601	154	140 D	47.2%	49.9%	48.6%	51.4%
49,040	LEE	23,607	11,173	11,648	786	475 D	47.3%	49.3%	49.0%	51.0%
59,648	LENOIR	26,387	11,885	14,005	497	2,120 D	45.0%	53.1%	45.9%	54.1%
63,780	LINCOLN	35,523	20,333	13,597	1,593	6,736 R	57.2%	38.3%	59.9%	40.1%
42,151	MCDOWELL	18,359	9,534	7,879	946	1,655 R	51.9%	42.9%	54.8%	45.2%
29,811	MACON	17,070	8,864	7,496	710	1,368 R	51.9%	43.9%	54.2%	45.8%
19,635	MADISON	10,390	4,566	5,436	388	870 D	43.9%	52.3%	45.7%	54.3%
25,593	MARTIN	12,443	4,880	7,342	221	2,462 D	39.2%	59.0%	39.9%	60.1%
695,454	MECKLENBURG	405,556	143,860	249,742	11,954	105,882 D	35.5%	61.6%	36.5%	63.5%
15,687	MITCHELL	7,761	4,898	2,508	355	2,390 R	63.1%	32.3%	66.1%	33.9%
26,822	MONTGOMERY	11,229	5,027	5,850	352	823 D	44.8%	52.1%	46.2%	53.8%
74,769	MOORE	45,020	24,014	19,511	1,495	4,503 R	53.3%	43.3%	55.2%	44.8%
87,420	NASH	47,029	21,234	24,964	831	3,730 D	45.2%	53.1%	46.0%	54.0%
160,307	NEW HANOVER	98,930	42,006	52,958	3,966	10,952 D	42.5%	53.5%	44.2%	55.8%
22,086	NORTHAMPTON	10,563	3,111	7,300	152	4,189 D	29.5%	69.1%	29.9%	70.1%
150,355	ONSLOW	49,267	25,671	21,340	2,256	4,331 R	52.1%	43.3%	54.6%	45.4%
118,227	ORANGE	74,006	19,882	52,037	2,087	32,155 D	26.9%	70.3%	27.6%	72.4%
12,934	PAMLICO	6,649	3,420	3,058	171	362 R	51.4%	46.0%	52.8%	47.2%
34,897	PASQUOTANK	17,860	7,602	9,899	359	2,297 D	42.6%	55.4%	43.4%	56.6%
41,082	PENDER	23,509	11,163	11,186	1,160	23 D	47.5%	47.6%	49.9%	50.1%
11,368	PERQUIMANS	6,365	3,464	2,771	130	693 R	54.4%	43.5%	55.6%	44.4%
35,623	PERSON	18,329	8,599	9,222	508	623 D	46.9%	50.3%	48.3%	51.7%
133,798	PITT	74,227	31,350	41,294	1,583	9,944 D	42.2%	55.6%	43.2%	56.8%
18,324	POLK	10,471	5,051	4,971	449	80 R	48.2%	47.5%	50.4%	49.6%
130,454	RANDOLPH	57,981	35,247	20,031	2,703	15,216 R	60.8%	34.5%	63.8%	36.2%
46,564	RICHMOND	18,999	7,088	11,199	712	4,111 D	37.3%	58.9%	38.8%	61.2%
123,339	ROBESON	40,594	16,161	23,799	634	7,638 D	39.8%	58.6%	40.4%	59.6%
91,928	ROCKINGHAM	41,271	19,729	19,835	1,707	106 D	47.8%	48.1%	49.9%	50.1%
130,340	ROWAN	61,234	32,964	25,790	2,480	7,174 R	53.8%	42.1%	56.1%	43.9%
62,899	RUTHERFORD	28,368	14,639	12,633	1,096	2,006 R	51.6%	44.5%	53.7%	46.3%
60,161	SAMPSON	25,942	12,239	13,223	480	984 D	47.2%	51.0%	48.1%	51.9%
35,998	SCOTLAND	13,956	5,242	8,496	218	3,254 D	37.6%	60.9%	38.2%	61.8%
58,100	STANLY	28,358	16,402	10,802	1,154	5,600 R	57.8%	38.1%	60.3%	39.7%
44,711	STOKES	21,837	12,455	8,335	1,047	4,120 R	57.0%	38.2%	59.9%	40.1%
71,219	SURRY	29,420	15,808	12,615	997	3,193 R	53.7%	42.9%	55.6%	44.4%
12,968	SWAIN	5,782	2,248	3,265	269	1,017 D	38.9%	56.5%	40.8%	59.2%
29,334	TRANSYLVANIA	16,818	8,219	7,919	680	300 R	48.9%	47.1%	50.9%	49.1%
4,149	TYRRELL	1,877	832	983	62	151 D	44.3%	52.4%	45.8%	54.2%
123,677	UNION	84,857	49,185	32,716	2,956	16,469 R	58.0%	38.6%	60.1%	39.9%
42,954	VANCE	20,780	6,519	13,900	361	7,381 D	31.4%	66.9%	31.9%	68.1%
627,846	WAKE	438,358	179,428	245,774	13,156	66,346 D	40.9%	56.1%	42.2%	57.8%
19,972	WARREN	9,985	2,748	7,098	139	4,350 D	27.5%	71.1%	27.9%	72.1%
13,723	WASHINGTON	6,444	2,180	4,123	141	1,943 D	33.8%	64.0%	34.6%	65.4%
42,695	WATAUGA	27,927	12,462	14,253	1,212	1,791 D	44.6%	51.0%	46.6%	53.4%
113,329	WAYNE	49,415	24,377	23,967	1,071	410 R	49.3%	48.5%	50.4%	49.6%
65,632	WILKES	29,620	17,206	11,029	1,385	6,177 R	58.1%	37.2%	60.9%	39.1%
73,814	WILSON	36,705	15,384	20,776	545	5,392 D	41.9%	56.6%	42.5%	57.5%
36,348	YADKIN	17,008	10,557	5,720	731	4,837 R	62.1%	33.6%	64.9%	35.1%
17,774	YANCEY	9,847	4,383	5,126	338	743 D	44.5%	52.1%	46.1%	53.9%
8,049,313	TOTAL	4,271,970	1,887,510	2,249,311	135,149	361,801 D	44.2%	52.7%	45.6%	54.4%

NORTH CAROLINA

HOUSE OF REPRESENTATIVES

CD	Year	Total Vote	Republican Vote	Republican Candidate	Democratic Vote	Democratic Candidate	Other Vote	Rep.-Dem. Plurality	Total Vote Rep.	Total Vote Dem.	Major Vote Rep.	Major Vote Dem.
1	2008	274,271	81,506	STEPHENS, DEAN	192,765	BUTTERFIELD, G.K.*		111,259 D	29.7%	70.3%	29.7%	70.3%
1	2006	82,510		—	82,510	BUTTERFIELD, G.K.*		82,510 D		100.0%		100.0%
1	2004	215,175	77,508	DORITY, GREG	137,667	BUTTERFIELD, G.K.*		60,159 D	36.0%	64.0%	36.0%	64.0%
1	2002	146,157	50,907	DORITY, GREG	93,157	BALANCE, FRANK W. JR.	2,093	42,250 D	34.8%	63.7%	35.3%	64.7%
2	2008	298,430	93,323	MANSELL, DAN	199,730	ETHERIDGE, BOB*	5,377	106,407 D	31.3%	66.9%	31.8%	68.2%
2	2006	129,264	43,271	MANSELL, DAN	85,993	ETHERIDGE, BOB*		42,722 D	33.5%	66.5%	33.5%	66.5%
2	2004	232,890	87,811	CREECH, BILLY J.	145,079	ETHERIDGE, BOB*		57,268 D	37.7%	62.3%	37.7%	62.3%
2	2002	153,184	50,965	ELLEN, JOSEPH L.	100,121	ETHERIDGE, BOB*	2,098	49,156 D	33.3%	65.4%	33.7%	66.3%
3	2008	306,050	201,686	JONES, WALTER B.*	104,364	WEBER, CRAIG		97,322 R	65.9%	34.1%	65.9%	34.1%
3	2006	144,977	99,519	JONES, WALTER B.*	45,458	WEBER, CRAIG		54,061 R	68.6%	31.4%	68.6%	31.4%
3	2004	243,090	171,863	JONES, WALTER B.*	71,227	EATON, ROGER A.		100,636 R	70.7%	29.3%	70.7%	29.3%
3	2002	144,934	131,448	JONES, WALTER B.*		—	13,486	131,448 R	90.7%		100.0%	
4	2008	419,698	153,947	LAWSON, WILLIAM "B.J."	265,751	PRICE, DAVID E.*		111,804 D	36.7%	63.3%	36.7%	63.3%
4	2006	195,939	68,599	ACUFF, STEVE	127,340	PRICE, DAVID E.*		58,741 D	35.0%	65.0%	35.0%	65.0%
4	2004	339,234	121,717	BATCHELOR, TODD A.	217,441	PRICE, DAVID E.*	76	95,724 D	35.9%	64.1%	35.9%	64.1%
4	2002	216,046	78,095	NGUYEN, TUAN A.	132,185	PRICE, DAVID E.*	5,766	54,090 D	36.1%	61.2%	37.1%	62.9%
5	2008	326,923	190,820	FOXX, VIRGINIA*	136,103	CARTER, ROY		54,717 R	58.4%	41.6%	58.4%	41.6%
5	2006	168,199	96,138	FOXX, VIRGINIA*	72,061	SHARPE, ROGER		24,077 R	57.2%	42.8%	57.2%	42.8%
5	2004	284,817	167,546	FOXX, VIRGINIA	117,271	HARRELL, JIM A. JR.		50,275 R	58.8%	41.2%	58.8%	41.2%
5	2002	196,437	137,879	BURR, RICHARD M.*	58,558	CRAWFORD, DAVID		79,321 R	70.2%	29.8%	70.2%	29.8%
6	2008	329,891	221,018	COBLE, HOWARD*	108,873	BRATTON, TERESA SUE		112,145 R	67.0%	33.0%	67.0%	33.0%
6	2006	153,094	108,433	COBLE, HOWARD*	44,661	BLAKE, RORY		63,772 R	70.8%	29.2%	70.8%	29.2%
6	2004	283,623	207,470	COBLE, HOWARD*	76,153	JORDAN, WILLIAM W.		131,317 R	73.1%	26.9%	73.1%	26.9%
6	2002	167,497	151,430	COBLE, HOWARD*		—	16,067	151,430 R	90.4%	0.0%	100.0%	0.0%
7	2008	312,855	97,472	BREAZEALE, WILL	215,383	McINTYRE, MIKE*		117,911 D	31.2%	68.8%	31.2%	68.8%
7	2006	139,820	38,033	DAVIS, SHIRLEY	101,787	McINTYRE, MIKE*		63,754 D	27.2%	72.8%	27.2%	72.8%
7	2004	246,466	66,084	PLONK, KEN	180,382	McINTYRE, MIKE*		114,298 D	26.8%	73.2%	26.8%	73.2%
7	2002	166,654	45,537	ADAMS, JAMES R.	118,543	McINTYRE, MIKE*	2,574	73,006 D	27.3%	71.1%	27.8%	72.2%
8	2008	283,819	126,634	HAYES, ROBIN*	157,185	KISSELL, LARRY		30,551 D	44.6%	55.4%	44.6%	55.4%
8	2006	121,523	60,926	HAYES, ROBIN*	60,597	KISSELL, LARRY		329 R	50.1%	49.9%	50.1%	49.9%
8	2004	225,171	125,070	HAYES, ROBIN*	100,101	TROUTMAN, BETH		24,969 R	55.5%	44.5%	55.5%	44.5%
8	2002	149,736	80,298	HAYES, ROBIN*	66,819	KOURI, CHRIS	2,619	13,479 R	53.6%	44.6%	54.6%	45.4%
9	2008	386,483	241,053	MYRICK, SUE*	138,719	TAYLOR, HARRY	6,711	102,334 R	62.4%	35.9%	63.5%	36.5%
9	2006	159,643	106,206	MYRICK, SUE*	53,437	GLASS, BILL		52,769 R	66.5%	33.5%	66.5%	33.5%
9	2004	300,101	210,783	MYRICK, SUE*	89,318	FLYNN, JACK		121,465 R	70.2%	29.8%	70.2%	29.8%
9	2002	193,443	140,095	MYRICK, SUE*	49,974	McGUIRE, ED	3,374	90,121 R	72.4%	25.8%	73.7%	26.3%
10	2008	298,473	171,774	McHENRY, PATRICK T.*	126,699	JOHNSON, DANIEL		45,075 R	57.6%	42.4%	57.6%	42.4%
10	2006	152,393	94,179	McHENRY, PATRICK T.*	58,214	CARSNER, RICHARD		35,965 R	61.8%	38.2%	61.8%	38.2%
10	2004	246,117	157,884	McHENRY, PATRICK T.	88,233	FISCHER, ANNE N.		69,651 R	64.1%	35.9%	64.1%	35.9%
10	2002	173,292	102,768	BALLENGER, CASS*	65,587	DAUGHERTY, RON	4,937	37,181 R	59.3%	37.8%	61.0%	39.0%
11	2008	340,716	122,087	MUMPOWER, CARL	211,112	SHULER, HEATH*	7,517	89,025 D	35.8%	62.0%	36.6%	63.4%
11	2006	232,314	107,342	TAYLOR, CHARLES H.*	124,972	SHULER, HEATH		17,630 D	46.2%	53.8%	46.2%	53.8%
11	2004	290,897	159,709	TAYLOR, CHARLES H.*	131,188	KEEVER, PATSY		28,521 R	54.9%	45.1%	54.9%	45.1%
11	2002	202,260	112,335	TAYLOR, CHARLES H.*	86,664	NEILL, SAM	3,261	25,671 R	55.5%	42.8%	56.5%	43.5%
12	2008	301,722	85,814	COBB, TY JR.	215,908	WATT, MELVIN*		130,094 D	28.4%	71.6%	28.4%	71.6%
12	2006	106,472	35,127	FISHER, ADA M.	71,345	WATT, MELVIN*		36,218 D	33.0%	67.0%	33.0%	67.0%
12	2004	231,806	76,898	FISHER, ADA M.	154,908	WATT, MELVIN*		78,010 D	33.2%	66.8%	33.2%	66.8%
12	2002	151,239	49,588	KISH, JEFF	98,821	WATT, MELVIN*	2,830	49,233 D	32.8%	65.3%	33.4%	66.6%

NORTH CAROLINA

HOUSE OF REPRESENTATIVES

CD	Year	Total Vote	Republican Vote	Republican Candidate	Democratic Vote	Democratic Candidate	Other Vote	Rep.-Dem. Plurality	Percentage Total Vote Rep.	Total Vote Dem.	Major Vote Rep.	Major Vote Dem.
13	2008	335,762	114,383	WEBSTER, HUGH	221,379	MILLER, BRAD*		106,996 D	34.1%	65.9%	34.1%	65.9%
13	2006	154,660	56,120	JOHNSON, VERNON	98,540	MILLER, BRAD*		42,420 D	36.3%	63.7%	36.3%	63.7%
13	2004	273,684	112,788	JOHNSON, VIRGINIA	160,896	MILLER, BRAD*		48,108 D	41.2%	58.8%	41.2%	58.8%
13	2002	183,270	77,688	GRANT, CAROLYN W.	100,287	MILLER, BRAD	5,295	22,599 D	42.4%	54.7%	43.7%	56.3%
TOTAL	2008	4,215,093	1,901,517		2,293,971		19,605	392,454 D	45.1%	54.4%	45.3%	54.7%
TOTAL	2006	1,940,808	913,893		1,026,915			113,022 D	47.1%	52.9%	47.1%	52.9%
TOTAL	2004	3,413,071	1,743,131		1,669,864		76	73,267 R	51.1%	48.9%	51.1%	48.9%
TOTAL	2002	2,244,149	1,209,033		970,716		64,400	238,317 R	53.9%	43.3%	55.5%	44.5%

Note: An asterisk (*) denotes incumbent.

NORTH CAROLINA

GENERAL AND PRIMARY ELECTIONS

2008 GENERAL ELECTIONS

President   Other vote was 25,722 Libertarian (Bob Barr); 1,448 write-in (Ralph Nader); 158 write-in (Cynthia A. McKinney); 38 write-in (Brian Moore); 12,298 scattered write-in.

Governor   Other vote was 121,584 Libertarian (Michael C. Munger).

Senator   Other vote was 133,430 Libertarian (Christopher Cole); 64 write-in (Walker Fry Rucker); 1,655 scattered write-in.

House   Other vote was:

CD 1
CD 2   5,377 Libertarian (Will Adkins).
CD 3
CD 4
CD 5
CD 6
CD 7
CD 8
CD 9   6,711 Libertarian (Andy Grum).
CD 10
CD 11   7,517 Libertarian (Keith Smith).
CD 12
CD 13

2008 PRIMARY ELECTIONS

Primary   May 6, 2008

Registration (as of March 1, 2008)

Democratic	2,536,180
Republican	1,930,856
Unaffiliated	1,196,083
TOTAL	5,663,119

Primary Runoff   June 24, 2008

Primary Type   Semi-open—Registered Democrats and Republicans could vote only in their party's primary. Unaffiliated voters could participate in the primary of either party.

NORTH CAROLINA

GENERAL AND PRIMARY ELECTIONS

	REPUBLICAN PRIMARIES			DEMOCRATIC PRIMARIES		
President	John McCain	383,085	74.0%	Barack Obama	887,391	56.1%
	Mike Huckabee	63,018	12.2%	Hillary Clinton	657,669	41.6%
	Ron Paul	37,260	7.2%	No Preference	23,214	1.5%
	No Preference	20,624	4.0%	Mike Gravel	12,452	0.8%
	Alan Keyes	13,596	2.6%			
	TOTAL	517,583		TOTAL	1,580,726	
Governor	Pat McCrory	232,818	46.1%	Bev Perdue	840,342	56.2%
	Fred Smith	186,843	37.0%	Richard H. Moore	594,028	39.7%
	Bill Graham	46,861	9.3%	Dennis Nielsen	60,628	4.1%
	Robert F. "Bob" Orr	34,007	6.7%			
	E. Powers	4,444	0.9%			
	TOTAL	504,973		TOTAL	1,494,998	
Senator	Elizabeth Dole*	460,665	90.0%	Kay Hagan	801,920	60.1%
	Pete Di Lauro	51,406	10.0%	Jim Neal	239,623	17.9%
				Marcus W. Williams	170,970	12.8%
				Duskin C. Lassiter	62,136	4.7%
				Howard Staley	60,403	4.5%
	TOTAL	512,071		TOTAL	1,335,052	
Congressional District 1	Dean Stephens	Unopposed		G.K. Butterfield*	Unopposed	
Congressional District 2	Dan Mansell	Unopposed		Bob Etheridge*	Unopposed	
Congressional District 3	Walter B. Jones*	23,699	59.0%	Craig Weber	54,366	69.2%
	Joe McLaughlin	16,491	41.0%	Marshall Adame	24,181	30.8%
	TOTAL	40,190		TOTAL	78,547	
Congressional District 4	William "B.J." Lawson	23,373	70.6%	David E. Price*	Unopposed	
	Augustus Cho	9,756	29.4%			
	TOTAL	33,129				
Congressional District 5	Virginia Foxx*	Unopposed		Roy Carter	40,101	50.3%
				Diane Hamby	39,624	49.7%
				TOTAL	79,725	
Congressional District 6	Howard Coble*	Unopposed		Teresa Sue Bratton	42,687	61.2%
				Johnny J. Carter	19,817	28.4%
				Jay Ovittore	7,294	10.5%
				TOTAL	69,798	
Congressional District 7	Will Breazeale	Unopposed		Mike McIntyre*	Unopposed	
Congressional District 8	Robin Hayes*	Unopposed		Larry Kissell	Unopposed	
Congressional District 9	Sue Myrick*	51,402	92.2%	Harry Taylor	45,329	58.5%
	Jack Stratton	4,370	7.8%	Ross Overby	32,197	41.5%
	TOTAL	55,772		TOTAL	77,526	
Congressional District 10	Patrick T. McHenry*	34,457	67.1%	Daniel Johnson	41,076	60.1%
	Lance Sigmon	16,892	32.9%	Steve Ivester	27,216	39.9%
	TOTAL	51,349		TOTAL	68,292	
Congressional District 11	Carl Mumpower	19,678	48.2%	Heath Shuler*	Unopposed	
	Spence Campbell	17,266	42.3%			
	John C. Armor	3,911	9.6%			
	TOTAL	40,855				
Congressional District 12	Ty Cobb Jr.	Unopposed		Melvin Watt*	Unopposed	
Congressional District 13	Hugh Webster	Unopposed		Brad Miller*	113,254	88.5%
				Derald Hafner	14,744	11.5%
				TOTAL	127,998	

Notes: An asterisk (*) denotes incumbent. The names of unopposed candidates did not appear on the primary ballot; therefore, no votes were cast for these candidates. A runoff was triggered if the leading candidate received less than 40 percent of the primary vote and the second-place candidate called for a runoff. No runoffs for governor or Congress were required in 2008.

NORTH DAKOTA

One member At Large

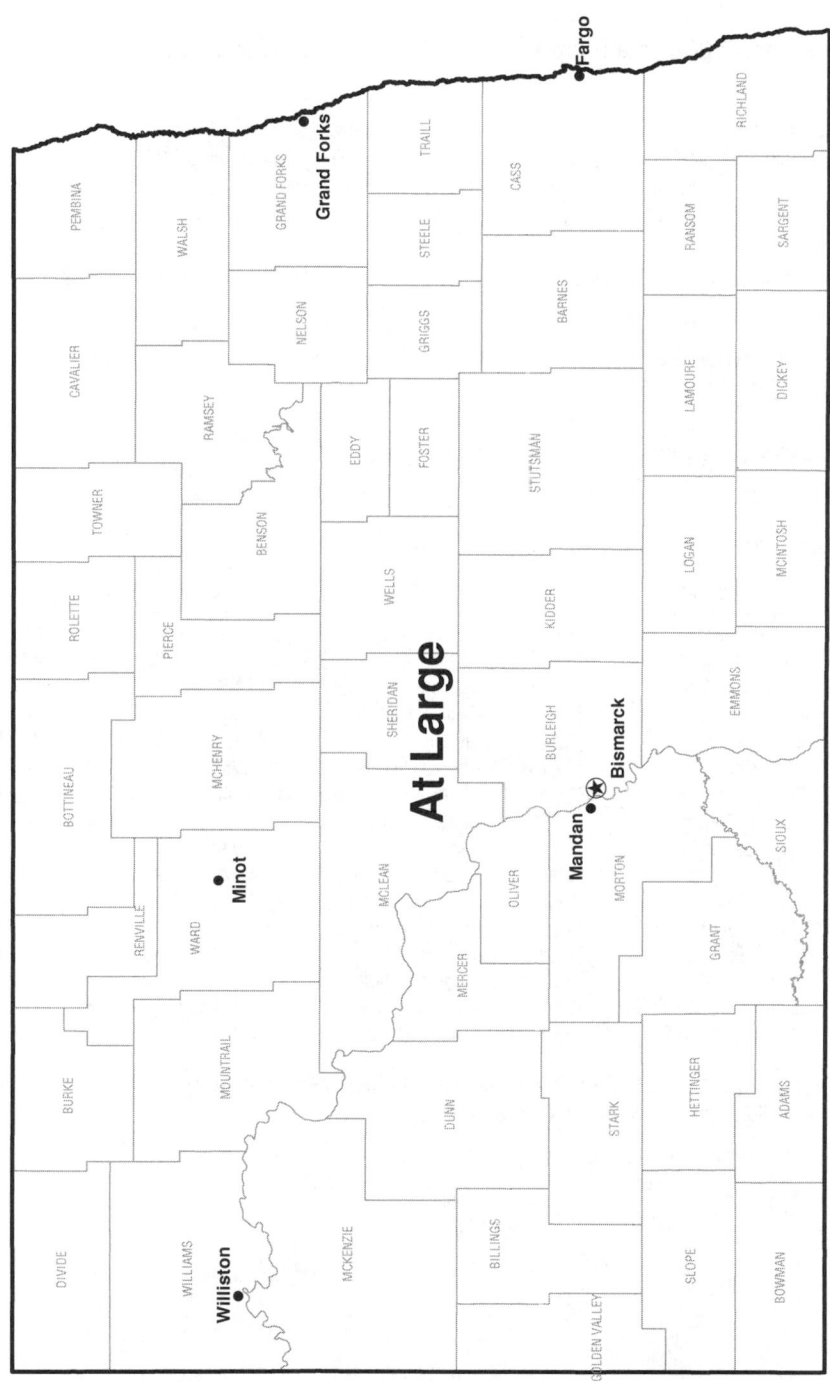

NORTH DAKOTA

GOVERNOR
John Hoeven (R). Reelected 2008 to a four-year term. Previously elected 2004, 2000.

SENATORS (2 Democrats)
Kent Conrad (D). Reelected 2006 to a six-year term. Previously elected 2000, 1994, and in a special election in December 1992 to fill the remaining two years of the term vacated by the death of Senator Quentin N. Burdick (D), who died in September 1992; elected 1986 to a six-year term.

Byron L. Dorgan (D). Reelected 2004 to a six-year term. Previously elected 1998, 1992.

REPRESENTATIVES (1 Democrat)
At Large. Earl Pomeroy (D)

POSTWAR VOTE FOR PRESIDENT

| | | Republican | | Democratic | | | | Percentage | | | |
| | | | | | | | | Total Vote | | Major Vote | |
Year	Total Vote	Vote	Candidate	Vote	Candidate	Other Vote	Plurality	Rep.	Dem.	Rep.	Dem.
2008	316,621	168,601	McCain, John	141,278	Obama, Barack	6,742	27,323 R	53.3%	44.6%	54.4%	45.6%
2004	312,833	196,651	Bush, George W.	111,052	Kerry, John	5,130	85,599 R	62.9%	35.5%	63.9%	36.1%
2000**	288,256	174,852	Bush, George W.	95,284	Gore, Al	18,120	79,568 R	60.7%	33.1%	64.7%	35.3%
1996**	266,411	125,050	Dole, Bob	106,905	Clinton, Bill	34,456	18,145 R	46.9%	40.1%	53.9%	46.1%
1992**	308,133	136,244	Bush, George	99,168	Clinton, Bill	72,721	37,076 R	44.2%	32.2%	57.9%	42.1%
1988	297,261	166,559	Bush, George	127,739	Dukakis, Michael S.	2,963	38,820 R	56.0%	43.0%	56.6%	43.4%
1984	308,971	200,336	Reagan, Ronald	104,429	Mondale, Walter F.	4,206	95,907 R	64.8%	33.8%	65.7%	34.3%
1980**	301,545	193,695	Reagan, Ronald	79,189	Carter, Jimmy	28,661	114,506 R	64.2%	26.3%	71.0%	29.0%
1976	297,188	153,470	Ford, Gerald R.	136,078	Carter, Jimmy	7,640	17,392 R	51.6%	45.8%	53.0%	47.0%
1972	280,514	174,109	Nixon, Richard M.	100,384	McGovern, George S.	6,021	73,725 R	62.1%	35.8%	63.4%	36.6%
1968**	247,882	138,669	Nixon, Richard M.	94,769	Humphrey, Hubert H.	14,444	43,900 R	55.9%	38.2%	59.4%	40.6%
1964	258,389	108,207	Goldwater, Barry M.	149,784	Johnson, Lyndon B.	398	41,577 D	41.9%	58.0%	41.9%	58.1%
1960	278,431	154,310	Nixon, Richard M.	123,963	Kennedy, John F.	158	30,347 R	55.4%	44.5%	55.5%	44.5%
1956	253,991	156,766	Eisenhower, Dwight D.	96,742	Stevenson, Adlai E.	483	60,024 R	61.7%	38.1%	61.8%	38.2%
1952	270,127	191,712	Eisenhower, Dwight D.	76,694	Stevenson, Adlai E.	1,721	115,018 R	71.0%	28.4%	71.4%	28.6%
1948	220,716	115,139	Dewey, Thomas E.	95,812	Truman, Harry S.	9,765	19,327 R	52.2%	43.4%	54.6%	45.4%

**In past elections, the other vote included: 2000 - 9,486 Green (Ralph Nader); 1996 - 32,515 Reform (Ross Perot); 1992 - 71,084 Independent (Perot); 1980 - 23,640 Independent (John Anderson); 1968 - 14,244 American Independent (George Wallace).

NORTH DAKOTA

POSTWAR VOTE FOR GOVERNOR

Year	Total Vote	Republican Vote	Republican Candidate	Democratic Vote	Democratic Candidate	Other Vote	Rep.-Dem. Plurality	Total Vote Rep.	Total Vote Dem.	Major Vote Rep.	Major Vote Dem.
2008	315,692	235,009	Hoeven, John	74,279	Mathern, Tim	6,404	160,730 R	74.4%	23.5%	76.0%	24.0%
2004	309,873	220,803	Hoeven, John	84,877	Satrom, Joseph A.	4,193	135,926 R	71.3%	27.4%	72.2%	27.8%
2000	289,412	159,255	Hoeven, John	130,144	Heitkamp, Heidi	13	29,111 R	55.0%	45.0%	55.0%	45.0%
1996	264,298	174,937	Schafer, Edward T.	89,349	Kaldor, Lee	12	85,588 R	66.2%	33.8%	66.2%	33.8%
1992	304,861	176,398	Schafer, Edward T.	123,845	Spaeth, Nicholas	4,618	52,553 R	57.9%	40.6%	58.8%	41.2%
1988	299,080	119,986	Mallberg, Leon L.	179,094	Sinner, George		59,108 D	40.1%	59.9%	40.1%	59.9%
1984	314,382	140,460	Olson, Allen I.	173,922	Sinner, George		33,462 D	44.7%	55.3%	44.7%	55.3%
1980	302,621	162,230	Olson, Allen I.	140,391	Link, Arthur A.		21,839 R	53.6%	46.4%	53.6%	46.4%
1976	297,249	138,321	Elkin, Richard	153,309	Link, Arthur A.	5,619	14,988 D	46.5%	51.6%	47.4%	52.6%
1972	281,931	138,032	Larsen, Richard	143,899	Link, Arthur A.		5,867 D	49.0%	51.0%	49.0%	51.0%
1968	248,000	108,382	McCarney, Robert P.	135,955	Guy, William L.	3,663	27,573 D	43.7%	54.8%	44.4%	55.6%
1964**	262,661	116,247	Halcrow, Donald M.	146,414	Guy, William L.		30,167 D	44.3%	55.7%	44.3%	55.7%
1962	228,509	113,251	Andrews, Mark	115,258	Guy, William L.		2,007 D	49.6%	50.4%	49.6%	50.4%
1960	275,375	122,486	Dahl, C. P.	136,148	Guy, William L.	16,741	13,662 D	44.5%	49.4%	47.4%	52.6%
1958	210,599	111,836	Davis, John E.	98,763	Lord, John F.		13,073 R	53.1%	46.9%	53.1%	46.9%
1956	252,435	147,566	Davis, John E.	104,869	Warner, Wallace E.		42,697 R	58.5%	41.5%	58.5%	41.5%
1954	193,501	124,253	Brunsdale, C. Norman	69,248	Bymers, Cornelius		55,005 R	64.2%	35.8%	64.2%	35.8%
1952	253,934	199,944	Brunsdale, C. Norman	53,990	Johnson, Ole C.		145,954 R	78.7%	21.3%	78.7%	21.3%
1950	183,772	121,822	Brunsdale, C. Norman	61,950	Byerly, Clyde G.		59,872 R	66.3%	33.7%	66.3%	33.7%
1948	214,858	131,764	Aandahl, Fred G.	80,555	Henry, Howard	2,539	51,209 R	61.3%	37.5%	62.1%	37.9%
1946	169,391	116,672	Aandahl, Fred G.	52,719	Burdick, Quentin N.		63,953 R	68.9%	31.1%	68.9%	31.1%

**The term of office of North Dakota's governor was increased from two to four years effective with the 1964 election.

POSTWAR VOTE FOR SENATOR

Year	Total Vote	Republican Vote	Republican Candidate	Democratic Vote	Democratic Candidate	Other Vote	Plurality	Total Vote Rep.	Total Vote Dem.	Major Vote Rep.	Major Vote Dem.
2006	218,152	64,417	Grotberg, Dwight	150,146	Conrad, Kent	3,589	85,729 D	29.5%	68.8%	30.0%	70.0%
2004	310,696	98,553	Liffrig, Mike	212,143	Dorgan, Byron L.		113,590 D	31.7%	68.3%	31.7%	68.3%
2000	287,539	111,069	Sand, Duane	176,470	Conrad, Kent		65,401 D	38.6%	61.4%	38.6%	61.4%
1998	213,358	75,013	Nalewaja, Donna	134,747	Dorgan, Byron L.	3,598	59,734 D	35.2%	63.2%	35.8%	64.2%
1994	236,547	99,390	Clayburg, Ben	137,157	Conrad, Kent		37,767 D	42.0%	58.0%	42.0%	58.0%
1992	303,957	118,162	Sydness, Steve	179,347	Dorgan, Byron L.	6,448	61,185 D	38.9%	59.0%	39.7%	60.3%
1992S	163,311	55,194	Dalrymple, Jack	103,246	Conrad, Kent	4,871	48,052 D	33.8%	63.2%	34.8%	65.2%
1988	289,170	112,937	Striden, Earl	171,899	Burdick, Quentin N.	4,334	58,962 D	39.1%	59.4%	39.6%	60.4%
1986	288,998	141,797	Andrews, Mark	143,932	Conrad, Kent	3,269	2,135 D	49.1%	49.8%	49.6%	50.4%
1982	262,465	89,304	Knorr, Gene	164,873	Burdick, Quentin N.	8,288	75,569 D	34.0%	62.8%	35.1%	64.9%
1980	299,272	210,347	Andrews, Mark	86,658	Johanneson, Kent	2,267	123,689 R	70.3%	29.0%	70.8%	29.2%
1976	283,062	103,466	Stroup, Richard	175,772	Burdick, Quentin N.	3,824	72,306 D	36.6%	62.1%	37.1%	62.9%
1974	235,661	114,117	Young, Milton R.	113,931	Guy, William L.	7,613	186 R	48.4%	48.3%	50.0%	50.0%
1970	219,560	82,996	Kleppe, Tom	134,519	Burdick, Quentin N.	2,045	51,523 D	37.8%	61.3%	38.2%	61.8%
1968	239,776	154,968	Young, Milton R.	80,815	Lashkowitz, Herschel	3,993	74,153 R	64.6%	33.7%	65.7%	34.3%
1964	258,945	109,681	Kleppe, Tom	149,264	Burdick, Quentin N.		39,583 D	42.4%	57.6%	42.4%	57.6%
1962	223,737	135,705	Young, Milton R.	88,032	Lanier, William		47,673 R	60.7%	39.3%	60.7%	39.3%
1960S	210,349	103,475	Davis, John E.	104,593	Burdick, Quentin N.	2,281	1,118 D	49.2%	49.7%	49.7%	50.3%
1958	204,635	117,070	Langer, William	84,892	Vendsel, Raymond	2,673	32,178 R	57.2%	41.5%	58.0%	42.0%
1956	244,161	155,305	Young, Milton R.	87,919	Burdick, Quentin N.	937	67,386 R	63.6%	36.0%	63.9%	36.1%
1952**	237,995	157,907	Langer, William	55,347	Morrison, Harold A.	24,741	102,560 R	66.3%	23.3%	74.0%	26.0%
1950	186,716	126,209	Young, Milton R.	60,507	O'Brien, Harry		65,702 R	67.6%	32.4%	67.6%	32.4%
1946**	165,382	88,210	Langer, William	38,368	Larson, Abner B.	38,804	49,406 R	53.3%	23.2%	69.7%	30.3%
1946S**	136,852	75,998	Young, Milton R.	37,507	Lanier, William	23,347	38,491 R	55.5%	27.4%	67.0%	33.0%

Notes: **In past elections, the other vote included: 1952 - 24,741 Independent (Fred G. Aandahl); 1946 - 38,804 Independent (Arthur E. Thompson), who finished second; 1946 Special - 20,848 Independent (Gerald P. Nye). One of the 1992 elections was for a short term to fill a vacancy and the special election was held in December. The 1946 and 1960 special elections were held in June for short terms to fill vacancies.

NORTH DAKOTA
PRESIDENT 2008

2000 Census Population	County	Total Vote	Republican	Democratic	Other	Rep.-Dem. Plurality	Percentage Total Vote Rep.	Percentage Total Vote Dem.	Percentage Major Vote Rep.	Percentage Major Vote Dem.
2,593	ADAMS	1,271	788	435	48	353 R	62.0%	34.2%	64.4%	35.6%
11,775	BARNES	5,694	2,826	2,741	127	85 R	49.6%	48.1%	50.8%	49.2%
6,964	BENSON	2,374	773	1,569	32	796 D	32.6%	66.1%	33.0%	67.0%
888	BILLINGS	499	375	114	10	261 R	75.2%	22.8%	76.7%	23.3%
7,149	BOTTINEAU	3,516	2,059	1,387	70	672 R	58.6%	39.4%	59.8%	40.2%
3,242	BOWMAN	1,640	1,107	478	55	629 R	67.5%	29.1%	69.8%	30.2%
2,242	BURKE	943	640	286	17	354 R	67.9%	30.3%	69.1%	30.9%
69,416	BURLEIGH	41,772	25,443	15,600	729	9,843 R	60.9%	37.3%	62.0%	38.0%
123,138	CASS	71,419	32,566	37,622	1,231	5,056 D	45.6%	52.7%	46.4%	53.6%
4,831	CAVALIER	2,130	1,128	930	72	198 R	53.0%	43.7%	54.8%	45.2%
5,757	DICKEY	2,620	1,525	1,044	51	481 R	58.2%	39.8%	59.4%	40.6%
2,283	DIVIDE	1,131	630	464	37	166 R	55.7%	41.0%	57.6%	42.4%
3,600	DUNN	1,644	1,080	527	37	553 R	65.7%	32.1%	67.2%	32.8%
2,757	EDDY	1,165	548	583	34	35 D	47.0%	50.0%	48.5%	51.5%
4,331	EMMONS	1,837	1,230	546	61	684 R	67.0%	29.7%	69.3%	30.7%
3,759	FOSTER	1,651	914	687	50	227 R	55.4%	41.6%	57.1%	42.9%
1,924	GOLDEN VALLEY	875	642	210	23	432 R	73.4%	24.0%	75.4%	24.6%
66,109	GRAND FORKS	31,153	14,520	16,104	529	1,584 D	46.6%	51.7%	47.4%	52.6%
2,841	GRANT	1,329	587	280	462	307 R	44.2%	21.1%	67.7%	32.3%
2,754	GRIGGS	1,314	682	598	34	84 R	51.9%	45.5%	53.3%	46.7%
2,715	HETTINGER	1,348	893	406	49	487 R	66.2%	30.1%	68.7%	31.3%
2,753	KIDDER	1,228	752	422	54	330 R	61.2%	34.4%	64.1%	35.9%
4,701	LA MOURE	2,241	1,310	868	63	442 R	58.5%	38.7%	60.1%	39.9%
2,308	LOGAN	1,057	726	299	32	427 R	68.7%	28.3%	70.8%	29.2%
5,987	MCHENRY	2,416	1,374	981	61	393 R	56.9%	40.6%	58.3%	41.7%
3,390	MCINTOSH	1,532	916	579	37	337 R	59.8%	37.8%	61.3%	38.7%
5,737	MCKENZIE	2,715	1,740	933	42	807 R	64.1%	34.4%	65.1%	34.9%
9,311	MCLEAN	4,736	2,767	1,867	102	900 R	58.4%	39.4%	59.7%	40.3%
8,644	MERCER	4,397	2,789	1,476	132	1,313 R	63.4%	33.6%	65.4%	34.6%
25,303	MORTON	13,264	7,869	5,079	316	2,790 R	59.3%	38.3%	60.8%	39.2%
6,631	MOUNTRAIL	2,938	1,406	1,477	55	71 D	47.9%	50.3%	48.8%	51.2%
3,715	NELSON	1,752	800	907	45	107 D	45.7%	51.8%	46.9%	53.1%
2,065	OLIVER	1,040	682	332	26	350 R	65.6%	31.9%	67.3%	32.7%
8,585	PEMBINA	3,307	1,722	1,494	91	228 R	52.1%	45.2%	53.5%	46.5%
4,675	PIERCE	2,139	1,301	792	46	509 R	60.8%	37.0%	62.2%	37.8%
12,066	RAMSEY	4,762	2,361	2,314	87	47 R	49.6%	48.6%	50.5%	49.5%
5,890	RANSOM	2,433	998	1,371	64	373 D	41.0%	56.4%	42.1%	57.9%
2,610	RENVILLE	1,346	799	505	42	294 R	59.4%	37.5%	61.3%	38.7%
17,998	RICHLAND	7,563	3,900	3,513	150	387 R	51.6%	46.4%	52.6%	47.4%
13,674	ROLETTE	4,534	1,045	3,403	86	2,358 D	23.0%	75.1%	23.5%	76.5%
4,366	SARGENT	1,927	778	1,115	34	337 D	40.4%	57.9%	41.1%	58.9%
1,710	SHERIDAN	803	555	229	19	326 R	69.1%	28.5%	70.8%	29.2%
4,044	SIOUX	1,378	215	1,145	18	930 D	15.6%	83.1%	15.8%	84.2%
767	SLOPE	411	297	106	8	191 R	72.3%	25.8%	73.7%	26.3%
22,636	STARK	11,070	7,024	3,802	244	3,222 R	63.5%	34.3%	64.9%	35.1%
2,258	STEELE	1,032	404	614	14	210 D	39.1%	59.5%	39.7%	60.3%
21,908	STUTSMAN	9,784	5,499	4,056	229	1,443 R	56.2%	41.5%	57.6%	42.4%
2,876	TOWNER	1,197	536	621	40	85 D	44.8%	51.9%	46.3%	53.7%
8,477	TRAILL	4,041	1,845	2,136	60	291 D	45.7%	52.9%	46.3%	53.7%
12,389	WALSH	4,882	2,415	2,325	142	90 R	49.5%	47.6%	50.9%	49.1%
58,795	WARD	25,621	15,061	10,144	416	4,917 R	58.8%	39.6%	59.8%	40.2%
5,102	WELLS	2,377	1,468	841	68	627 R	61.8%	35.4%	63.6%	36.4%
19,761	WILLIAMS	9,373	6,291	2,921	161	3,370 R	67.1%	31.2%	68.3%	31.7%
642,200	TOTAL	316,621	168,601	141,278	6,742	27,323 R	53.3%	44.6%	54.4%	45.6%

Note: The presidential results from Grant County are suspect. More votes were recorded for Libertarian candidate Bob Barr (297) than for Democrat Barack Obama (280). The county results, however, are listed as certified by state election officials.

NORTH DAKOTA
GOVERNOR 2008

2000 Census Population	County	Total Vote	Republican	Democratic	Other	Rep.-Dem. Plurality	Percentage			
							Total Vote		Major Vote	
							Rep.	Dem.	Rep.	Dem.
2,593	ADAMS	1,289	989	266	34	723 R	76.7%	20.6%	78.8%	21.2%
11,775	BARNES	5,704	4,187	1,384	133	2,803 R	73.4%	24.3%	75.2%	24.8%
6,964	BENSON	2,360	1,470	847	43	623 R	62.3%	35.9%	63.4%	36.6%
888	BILLINGS	509	424	70	15	354 R	83.3%	13.8%	85.8%	14.2%
7,149	BOTTINEAU	3,514	2,802	663	49	2,139 R	79.7%	18.9%	80.9%	19.1%
3,242	BOWMAN	1,645	1,346	258	41	1,088 R	81.8%	15.7%	83.9%	16.1%
2,242	BURKE	958	802	140	16	662 R	83.7%	14.6%	85.1%	14.9%
69,416	BURLEIGH	41,691	32,398	8,379	914	24,019 R	77.7%	20.1%	79.5%	20.5%
123,138	CASS	70,719	49,741	19,598	1380	30,143 R	70.3%	27.7%	71.7%	28.3%
4,831	CAVALIER	2,146	1,713	405	28	1,308 R	79.8%	18.9%	80.9%	19.1%
5,757	DICKEY	2,609	1,964	599	46	1,365 R	75.3%	23.0%	76.6%	23.4%
2,283	DIVIDE	1,142	882	251	9	631 R	77.2%	22.0%	77.8%	22.2%
3,600	DUNN	1,670	1,292	332	46	960 R	77.4%	19.9%	79.6%	20.4%
2,757	EDDY	1,172	838	315	19	523 R	71.5%	26.9%	72.7%	27.3%
4,331	EMMONS	1,863	1,412	408	43	1,004 R	75.8%	21.9%	77.6%	22.4%
3,759	FOSTER	1,673	1,327	317	29	1,010 R	79.3%	18.9%	80.7%	19.3%
1,924	GOLDEN VALLEY	876	730	127	19	603 R	83.3%	14.5%	85.2%	14.8%
66,109	GRAND FORKS	30,506	22,619	7,268	619	15,351 R	74.1%	23.8%	75.7%	24.3%
2,841	GRANT	1,358	1,052	276	30	776 R	77.5%	20.3%	79.2%	20.8%
2,754	GRIGGS	1,322	989	317	16	672 R	74.8%	24.0%	75.7%	24.3%
2,715	HETTINGER	1,364	1,071	270	23	801 R	78.5%	19.8%	79.9%	20.1%
2,753	KIDDER	1,247	895	317	35	578 R	71.8%	25.4%	73.8%	26.2%
4,701	LA MOURE	2,261	1,543	650	68	893 R	68.2%	28.7%	70.4%	29.6%
2,308	LOGAN	1,081	801	258	22	543 R	74.1%	23.9%	75.6%	24.4%
5,987	MCHENRY	2,470	1,841	579	50	1,262 R	74.5%	23.4%	76.1%	23.9%
3,390	MCINTOSH	1,545	1,241	282	22	959 R	80.3%	18.3%	81.5%	18.5%
5,737	MCKENZIE	2,701	2,115	525	61	1,590 R	78.3%	19.4%	80.1%	19.9%
9,311	MCLEAN	4,743	3,527	1,097	119	2,430 R	74.4%	23.1%	76.3%	23.7%
8,644	MERCER	4,438	3,374	957	107	2,417 R	76.0%	21.6%	77.9%	22.1%
25,303	MORTON	13,320	9,939	3,067	314	6,872 R	74.6%	23.0%	76.4%	23.6%
6,631	MOUNTRAIL	2,944	1,949	892	103	1,057 R	66.2%	30.3%	68.6%	31.4%
3,715	NELSON	1,774	1,308	444	22	864 R	73.7%	25.0%	74.7%	25.3%
2,065	OLIVER	1,049	805	213	31	592 R	76.7%	20.3%	79.1%	20.9%
8,585	PEMBINA	3,347	2,695	614	38	2,081 R	80.5%	18.3%	81.4%	18.6%
4,675	PIERCE	2,164	1,666	465	33	1,201 R	77.0%	21.5%	78.2%	21.8%
12,066	RAMSEY	4,779	3,674	1,035	70	2,639 R	76.9%	21.7%	78.0%	22.0%
5,890	RANSOM	2,444	1,553	853	38	700 R	63.5%	34.9%	64.5%	35.5%
2,610	RENVILLE	1,351	1,067	249	35	818 R	79.0%	18.4%	81.1%	18.9%
17,998	RICHLAND	7,549	5,641	1,762	146	3,879 R	74.7%	23.3%	76.2%	23.8%
13,674	ROLETTE	4,523	1,820	2,610	93	790 D	40.2%	57.7%	41.1%	58.9%
4,366	SARGENT	1,958	1,278	658	22	620 R	65.3%	33.6%	66.0%	34.0%
1,710	SHERIDAN	803	636	148	19	488 R	79.2%	18.4%	81.1%	18.9%
4,044	SIOUX	1,372	689	653	30	36 R	50.2%	47.6%	51.3%	48.7%
767	SLOPE	419	339	65	15	274 R	80.9%	15.5%	83.9%	16.1%
22,636	STARK	11,036	8,857	1,949	230	6,908 R	80.3%	17.7%	82.0%	18.0%
2,258	STEELE	1,047	663	372	12	291 R	63.3%	35.5%	64.1%	35.9%
21,908	STUTSMAN	9,746	7,390	2,162	194	5,228 R	75.8%	22.2%	77.4%	22.6%
2,876	TOWNER	1,214	883	302	29	581 R	72.7%	24.9%	74.5%	25.5%
8,477	TRAILL	4,048	2,951	1,048	49	1,903 R	72.9%	25.9%	73.8%	26.2%
12,389	WALSH	4,946	3,919	972	55	2,947 R	79.2%	19.7%	80.1%	19.9%
58,795	WARD	25,521	20,355	4,607	559	15,748 R	79.8%	18.1%	81.5%	18.5%
5,102	WELLS	2,403	1,839	509	55	1,330 R	76.5%	21.2%	78.3%	21.7%
19,761	WILLIAMS	9,359	7,708	1,475	176	6,233 R	82.4%	15.8%	83.9%	16.1%
642,200	TOTAL	315,692	235,009	74,279	6,404	160,730 R	74.4%	23.5%	76.0%	24.0%

NORTH DAKOTA

HOUSE OF REPRESENTATIVES

| | | | Republican | | Democratic | | | | Percentage | | | |
| | | Total | | | | | Other | Rep.-Dem. | Total Vote | | Major Vote | |
CD	Year	Vote	Vote	Candidate	Vote	Candidate	Vote	Plurality	Rep.	Dem.	Rep.	Dem.
AL	2008	313,965	119,388	SAND, DUANE	194,577	POMEROY, EARL*		75,189 D	38.0%	62.0%	38.0%	62.0%
AL	2006	217,621	74,687	MECHTEL, MATT	142,934	POMEROY, EARL*		68,247 D	34.3%	65.7%	34.3%	65.7%
AL	2004	310,814	125,684	SAND, DUANE	185,130	POMEROY, EARL*		59,446 D	40.4%	59.6%	40.4%	59.6%
AL	2002	231,030	109,957	CLAYBURGH, RICK	121,073	POMEROY, EARL*		11,116 D	47.6%	52.4%	47.6%	52.4%
AL	2000	285,658	127,251	DORSO, JOHN	151,173	POMEROY, EARL*	7,234	23,922 D	44.5%	52.9%	45.7%	54.3%
AL	1998	215,469	75,013	CRAMER, KEVIN	134,747	POMEROY, EARL*	5,709	59,734 D	34.8%	62.5%	35.8%	64.2%
AL	1996	263,010	113,684	CRAMER, KEVIN	144,833	POMEROY, EARL*	4,493	31,149 D	43.2%	55.1%	44.0%	56.0%
AL	1994	235,389	105,988	PORTER, GARY	123,134	POMEROY, EARL*	6,267	17,146 D	45.0%	52.3%	46.3%	53.7%
AL	1992	297,898	117,442	KORSMO, JOHN T.	169,273	POMEROY, EARL	11,183	51,831 D	39.4%	56.8%	41.0%	59.0%
AL	1990	233,979	81,443	SCHAFER, EDWARD	152,530	DORGAN, BYRON L.*	6	71,087 D	34.8%	65.2%	34.8%	65.2%
AL	1988	299,982	84,475	SYDNESS, STEVE	212,583	DORGAN, BYRON L.*	2,924	128,108 D	28.2%	70.9%	28.4%	71.6%
AL	1986	286,361	66,989	VINJE, SYVER	216,258	DORGAN, BYRON L.*	3,114	149,269 D	23.4%	75.5%	23.7%	76.3%
AL	1984	308,729	65,761	ALTENBURG, LOIS I.	242,968	DORGAN, BYRON L.*		177,207 D	21.3%	78.7%	21.3%	78.7%
AL	1982	260,499	72,241	JONES, KENT	186,534	DORGAN, BYRON L.*	1,724	114,293 D	27.7%	71.6%	27.9%	72.1%
AL	1980	293,076	124,707	SMYKOWSKI, JIM	166,437	DORGAN, BYRON L.	1,932	41,730 D	42.6%	56.8%	42.8%	57.2%
AL	1978	220,348	147,746	ANDREWS, MARK*	68,016	HAGEN, BRUCE	4,586	79,730 R	67.1%	30.9%	68.5%	31.5%
AL	1976	289,881	181,018	ANDREWS, MARK*	104,263	OMDAHL, LLOYD B.	4,600	76,755 R	62.4%	36.0%	63.5%	36.5%
AL	1974	233,688	130,184	ANDREWS, MARK*	103,504	DORGAN, BYRON L.		26,680 R	55.7%	44.3%	55.7%	44.3%
AL	1972	268,721	195,360	ANDREWS, MARK*	72,850	ISTA, RICHARD	511	122,510 R	72.7%	27.1%	72.8%	27.2%

Notes: An asterisk (*) denotes incumbent. North Dakota had two House seats before 1972.

NORTH DAKOTA

GENERAL AND PRIMARY ELECTIONS

2008 GENERAL ELECTIONS

President Other vote was 4,189 Independent (Ralph Nader); 1,354 Libertarian (Bob Barr); 1,199 Constitution (Chuck Baldwin).

Governor Other vote was 6,404 Independent (DuWayne Hendrickson).

House

At Large

2008 PRIMARY ELECTIONS

Primary June 10, 2008   **Registration**   No Formal Registration

Primary Type Open—Any person of voting age (18 years old at the time of the primary election) could participate in the primary of either party. As of June 10, 2008, North Dakota's estimated voting-age population was 496,906.

	REPUBLICAN PRIMARIES			DEMOCRATIC PRIMARIES		
Governor	John Hoeven*	50,226	100.0%	Tim Mathern	38,784	100.0%
House At Large	Duane Sand	46,785	100.0%	Earl Pomeroy*	43,293	100.0%

Note: An asterisk (*) denotes incumbent.

379

OHIO

Congressional districts first established for elections held in 2002
18 members

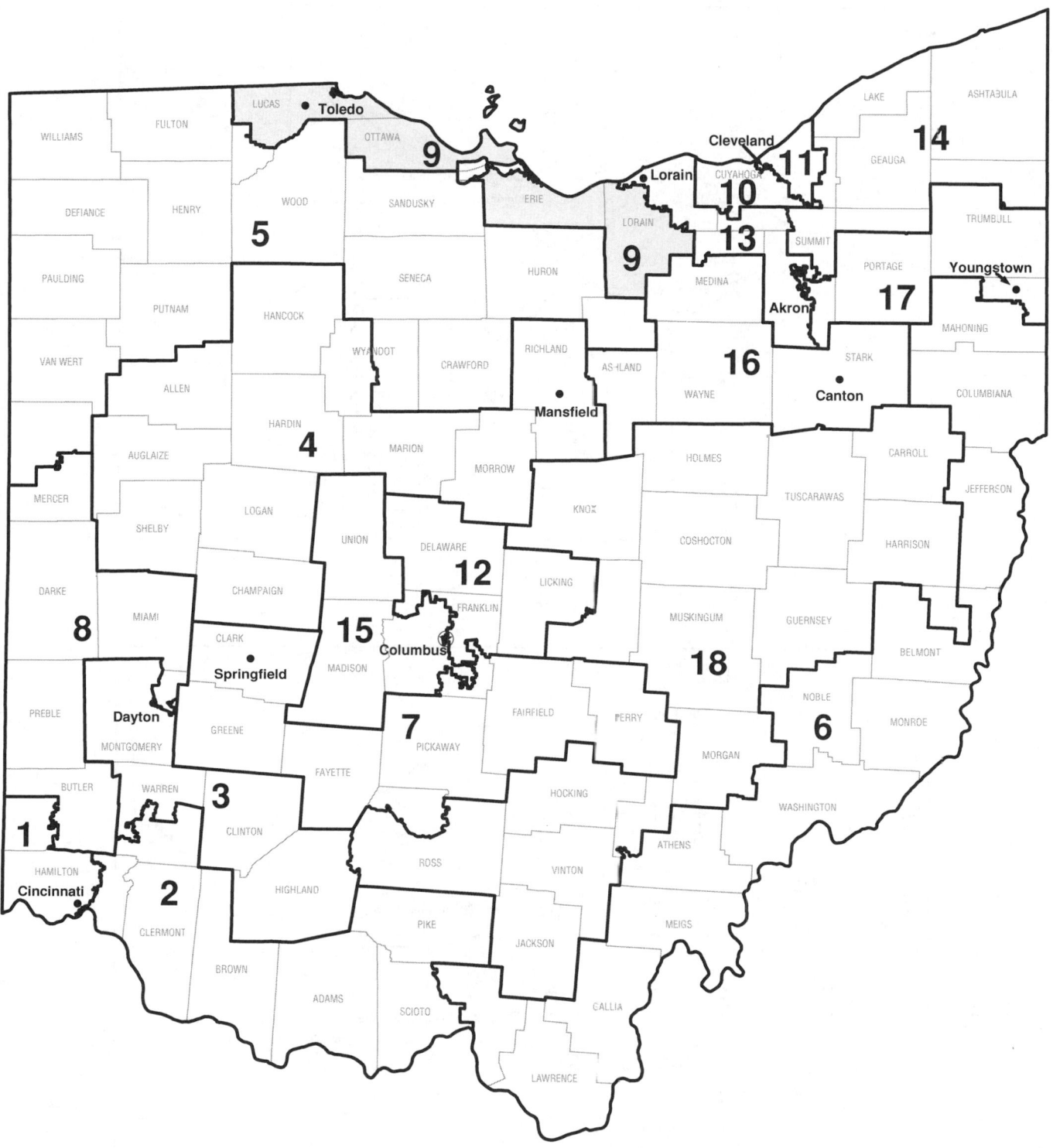

OHIO

Cleveland Area

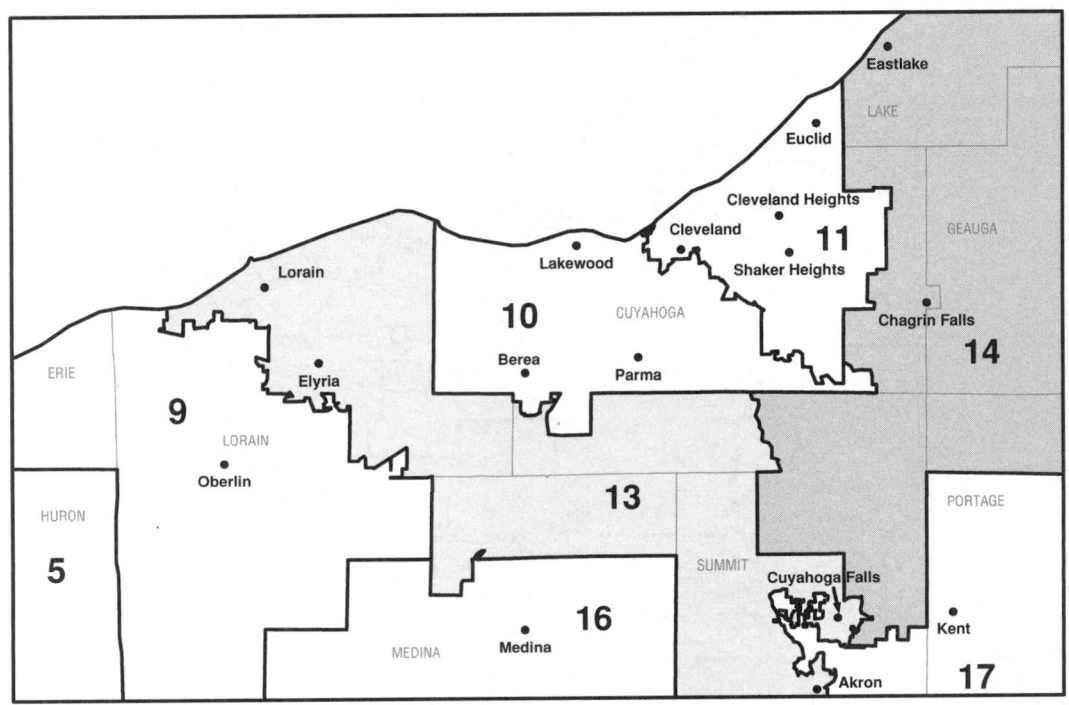

Columbus Area

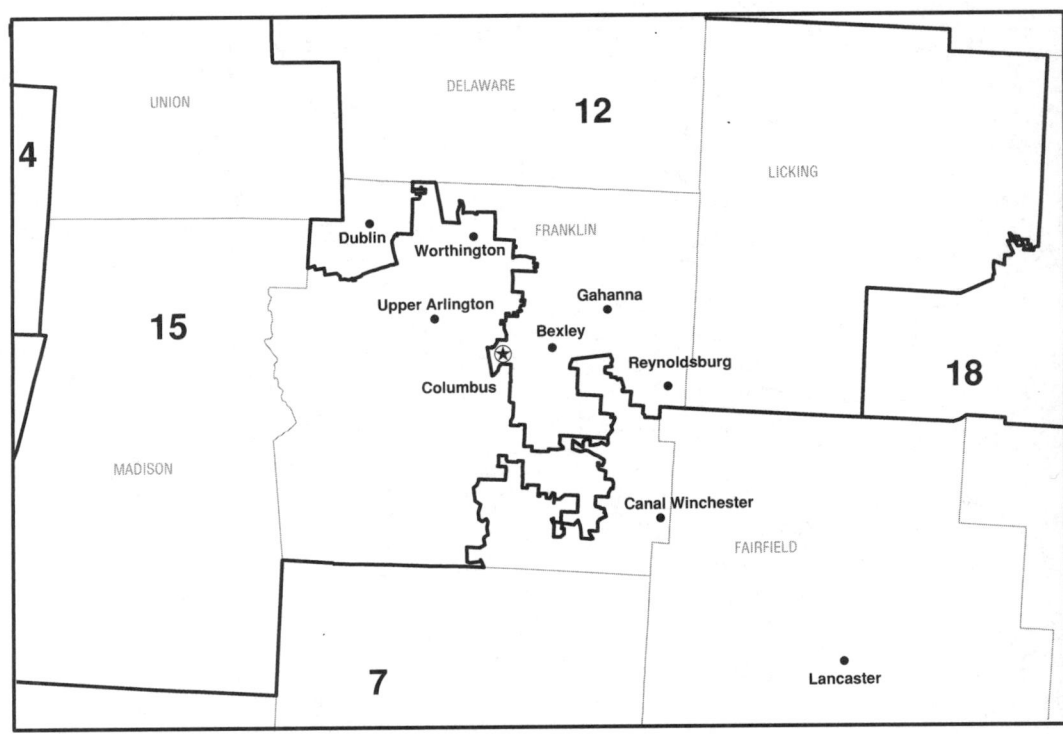

OHIO

GOVERNOR
Ted Strickland (D). Elected 2006 to a four-year term.

SENATORS (1 Democrat, 1 Republican)
Sherrod Brown (D). Elected 2006 to a six-year term.

George V. Voinovich (R). Reelected 2004 to a six-year term. Previously elected 1998.

REPRESENTATIVES (10 Democrats, 8 Republicans)

1. Steve Driehaus (D)
2. Jean Schmidt (R)
3. Michael R. Turner (R)
4. Jim Jordan (R)
5. Robert E. Latta (R)
6. Charles A. Wilson (D)
7. Steve Austria (R)
8. John A. Boehner (R)
9. Marcy Kaptur (D)
10. Dennis J. Kucinich (D)
11. Marcia L. Fudge (D)
12. Pat Tiberi (R)
13. Betty Sutton (D)
14. Steven C. LaTourette (R)
15. Mary Jo Kilroy (D)
16. John A. Boccieri (D)
17. Tim Ryan (D)
18. Zack Space (D)

POSTWAR VOTE FOR PRESIDENT

		Republican		Democratic				Total Vote		Major Vote	
Year	Total Vote	Vote	Candidate	Vote	Candidate	Other Vote	Plurality	Rep.	Dem.	Rep.	Dem.
2008	5,708,350	2,677,820	McCain, John	2,940,044	Obama, Barack	90,486	262,224 D	46.9%	51.5%	47.7%	52.3%
2004	5,627,903	2,859,764	Bush, George W.	2,741,165	Kerry, John	26,974	118,599 R	50.8%	48.7%	51.1%	48.9%
2000**	4,701,998	2,350,363	Bush, George W.	2,183,628	Gore, Al	168,007	166,735 R	50.0%	46.4%	51.8%	48.2%
1996**	4,534,434	1,859,883	Dole, Bob	2,148,222	Clinton, Bill	526,329	288,339 D	41.0%	47.4%	46.4%	53.6%
1992**	4,939,967	1,894,310	Bush, George	1,984,942	Clinton, Bill	1,060,715	90,632 D	38.3%	40.2%	48.8%	51.2%
1988	4,393,699	2,416,549	Bush, George	1,939,629	Dukakis, Michael S.	37,521	476,920 R	55.0%	44.1%	55.5%	44.5%
1984	4,547,619	2,678,560	Reagan, Ronald	1,825,440	Mondale, Walter F.	43,619	853,120 R	58.9%	40.1%	59.5%	40.5%
1980**	4,283,603	2,206,545	Reagan, Ronald	1,752,414	Carter, Jimmy	324,644	454,131 R	51.5%	40.9%	55.7%	44.3%
1976	4,111,873	2,000,505	Ford, Gerald R.	2,011,621	Carter, Jimmy	99,747	11,116 D	48.7%	48.9%	49.9%	50.1%
1972	4,094,787	2,441,827	Nixon, Richard M.	1,558,889	McGovern, George S.	94,071	882,938 R	59.6%	38.1%	61.0%	39.0%
1968**	3,959,698	1,791,014	Nixon, Richard M.	1,700,586	Humphrey, Hubert H.	468,098	90,428 R	45.2%	42.9%	51.3%	48.7%
1964	3,969,196	1,470,865	Goldwater, Barry M.	2,498,331	Johnson, Lyndon B.		1,027,466 D	37.1%	62.9%	37.1%	62.9%
1960	4,161,859	2,217,611	Nixon, Richard M.	1,944,248	Kennedy, John F.		273,363 R	53.3%	46.7%	53.3%	46.7%
1956	3,702,265	2,262,610	Eisenhower, Dwight D.	1,439,655	Stevenson, Adlai E.		822,955 R	61.1%	38.9%	61.1%	38.9%
1952	3,700,758	2,100,391	Eisenhower, Dwight D.	1,600,367	Stevenson, Adlai E.		500,024 R	56.8%	43.2%	56.8%	43.2%
1948	2,936,071	1,445,684	Dewey, Thomas E.	1,452,791	Truman, Harry S.	37,596	7,107 D	49.2%	49.5%	49.9%	50.1%

**In past elections, the other vote included: 2000 - 117,799 Green (Ralph Nader); 1996 - 483,207 Reform (Ross Perot); 1992 - 1,036,426 Independent (Perot); 1980 - 254,472 Independent (John Anderson); 1968 - 467,495 American Independent (George Wallace).

OHIO

POSTWAR VOTE FOR GOVERNOR

Year	Total Vote	Republican Vote	Republican Candidate	Democratic Vote	Democratic Candidate	Other Vote	Rep.-Dem. Plurality	Total Vote Rep.	Total Vote Dem.	Major Vote Rep.	Major Vote Dem.
2006	4,022,754	1,474,285	Blackwell, J. Kenneth	2,435,384	Strickland, Ted	113,085	961,099 D	36.6%	60.5%	37.7%	62.3%
2002	3,228,992	1,865,007	Taft, Bob	1,236,924	Hagan, Timothy	127,061	628,083 R	57.8%	38.3%	60.1%	39.9%
1998	3,354,213	1,678,721	Taft, Bob	1,498,956	Fisher, Lee	176,536	179,765 R	50.0%	44.7%	52.8%	47.2%
1994	3,346,238	2,401,572	Voinovich, George V.	835,849	Burch, Robert L.	108,817	1,565,723 R	71.8%	25.0%	74.2%	25.8%
1990	3,477,650	1,938,103	Voinovich, George V.	1,539,416	Celebrezze, Anthony J.	131	398,687 R	55.7%	44.3%	55.7%	44.3%
1986	3,066,611	1,207,264	Rhodes, James A.	1,858,372	Celeste, Richard F.	975	651,108 D	39.4%	60.6%	39.4%	60.6%
1982	3,356,721	1,303,962	Brown, Clarence, Jr.	1,981,882	Celeste, Richard F.	70,877	677,920 D	38.8%	59.0%	39.7%	60.3%
1978	2,843,351	1,402,167	Rhodes, James A.	1,354,631	Celeste, Richard F.	86,553	47,536 R	49.3%	47.6%	50.9%	49.1%
1974	3,072,010	1,493,679	Rhodes, James A.	1,482,191	Gilligan, John J.	96,140	11,488 R	48.6%	48.2%	50.2%	49.8%
1970	3,184,133	1,382,659	Cloud, Roger	1,725,560	Gilligan, John J.	75,914	342,901 D	43.4%	54.2%	44.5%	55.5%
1966	2,887,331	1,795,277	Rhodes, James A.	1,092,054	Reams, Frazier, Jr.		703,223 R	62.2%	37.8%	62.2%	37.8%
1962	3,116,711	1,836,190	Rhodes, James A.	1,280,521	DiSalle, Michael V.		555,669 R	58.9%	41.1%	58.9%	41.1%
1958**	3,284,134	1,414,874	O'Neill, C. William	1,869,260	DiSalle, Michael V.		454,386 D	43.1%	56.9%	43.1%	56.9%
1956	3,542,091	1,984,988	O'Neill, C. William	1,557,103	DiSalle, Michael V.		427,885 R	56.0%	44.0%	56.0%	44.0%
1954	2,597,790	1,192,528	Rhodes, James A.	1,405,262	Lausche, Frank J.		212,734 D	45.9%	54.1%	45.9%	54.1%
1952	3,605,168	1,590,058	Taft, Charles P.	2,015,110	Lausche, Frank J.		425,052 D	44.1%	55.9%	44.1%	55.9%
1950	2,892,819	1,370,570	Ebright, Don H.	1,522,249	Lausche, Frank J.		151,679 D	47.4%	52.6%	47.4%	52.6%
1948	3,018,289	1,398,514	Herbert, Thomas J.	1,619,775	Lausche, Frank J.		221,261 D	46.3%	53.7%	46.3%	53.7%
1946	2,303,750	1,166,550	Herbert, Thomas J.	1,125,997	Lausche, Frank J.	11,203	40,553 R	50.6%	48.9%	50.9%	49.1%

**The term of office of Ohio's governor was increased from two to four years effective with the 1958 election.

POSTWAR VOTE FOR SENATOR

Year	Total Vote	Republican Vote	Republican Candidate	Democratic Vote	Democratic Candidate	Other Vote	Rep.-Dem. Plurality	Total Vote Rep.	Total Vote Dem.	Major Vote Rep.	Major Vote Dem.
2006	4,019,236	1,761,037	DeWine, Mike	2,257,369	Brown, Sherrod	830	496,332 D	43.8%	56.2%	43.8%	56.2%
2004	5,425,823	3,464,356	Voinovich, George V.	1,961,171	Fingerhut, Eric D.	296	1,503,185 R	63.8%	36.1%	63.9%	36.1%
2000	4,448,801	2,665,512	DeWine, Mike	1,595,066	Celeste, Ted	188,223	1,070,446 R	59.9%	35.9%	62.6%	37.4%
1998	3,404,351	1,922,087	Voinovich, George V.	1,482,054	Boyle, Mary O.	210	440,033 R	56.5%	43.5%	56.5%	43.5%
1994	3,436,884	1,836,556	DeWine, Mike	1,348,213	Hyatt, Joel	252,115	488,343 R	53.4%	39.2%	57.7%	42.3%
1992	4,793,953	2,028,300	DeWine, Mike	2,444,419	Glenn, John H.	321,234	416,119 D	42.3%	51.0%	45.3%	54.7%
1988	4,352,905	1,872,716	Voinovich, George V.	2,480,038	Metzenbaum, Howard	151	607,322 D	43.0%	57.0%	43.0%	57.0%
1986	3,121,189	1,171,893	Kindness, Thomas N.	1,949,208	Glenn, John H.	88	777,315 D	37.5%	62.5%	37.5%	62.5%
1982	3,395,463	1,396,790	Pfeifer, Paul E.	1,923,767	Metzenbaum, Howard	74,906	526,977 D	41.1%	56.7%	42.1%	57.9%
1980	4,027,303	1,137,695	Betts, James E.	2,770,786	Glenn, John H.	118,822	1,633,091 D	28.2%	68.8%	29.1%	70.9%
1976	3,920,613	1,823,774	Taft, Robert A., Jr.	1,941,113	Metzenbaum, Howard	155,726	117,339 D	46.5%	49.5%	48.4%	51.6%
1974	2,987,951	918,133	Perk, Ralph J.	1,930,670	Glenn, John H.	139,148	1,012,537 D	30.7%	64.6%	32.2%	67.8%
1970	3,151,274	1,565,682	Taft, Robert A., Jr.	1,495,262	Metzenbaum, Howard	90,330	70,420 R	49.7%	47.4%	51.2%	48.8%
1968	3,743,121	1,928,964	Saxbe, William B.	1,814,152	Gilligan, John J.	5	114,812 R	51.5%	48.5%	51.5%	48.5%
1964	3,830,389	1,906,781	Taft, Robert A., Jr.	1,923,608	Young, Stephen M.		16,827 D	49.8%	50.2%	49.8%	50.2%
1962	2,994,986	1,151,173	Briley, John M.	1,843,813	Lausche, Frank J.		692,640 D	38.4%	61.6%	38.4%	61.6%
1958	3,149,410	1,497,199	Bricker, John W.	1,652,211	Young, Stephen M.		155,012 D	47.5%	52.5%	47.5%	52.5%
1956	3,525,499	1,660,910	Bender, George H.	1,864,589	Lausche, Frank J.		203,679 D	47.1%	52.9%	47.1%	52.9%
1954S	2,512,778	1,257,874	Bender, George H.	1,254,904	Burke, Thomas A.		2,970 R	50.1%	49.9%	50.1%	49.9%
1952	3,442,291	1,878,961	Bricker, John W.	1,563,330	DiSalle, Michael V.		315,631 R	54.6%	45.4%	54.6%	45.4%
1950	2,860,102	1,645,643	Taft, Robert A.	1,214,459	Ferguson, Joseph T.		431,184 R	57.5%	42.5%	57.5%	42.5%
1946	2,237,269	1,275,774	Bricker, John W.	947,610	Huffman, James W.	13,885	328,164 R	57.0%	42.4%	57.4%	42.6%

Note: The 1954 election was for a short term to fill a vacancy.

OHIO

PRESIDENT 2008

2000 Census Population	County	Total Vote	Republican	Democratic	Other	Rep.-Dem. Plurality	Percentage			
							Total Vote		Major Vote	
							Rep.	Dem.	Rep.	Dem.
27,330	ADAMS	11,388	6,914	4,170	304	2,744 R	60.7%	36.6%	62.4%	37.6%
108,473	ALLEN	50,263	29,940	19,522	801	10,418 R	59.6%	38.8%	60.5%	39.5%
52,523	ASHLAND	25,168	15,158	9,300	710	5,858 R	60.2%	37.0%	62.0%	38.0%
102,728	ASHTABULA	44,874	18,949	25,027	898	6,078 D	42.2%	55.8%	43.1%	56.9%
62,223	ATHENS	31,098	9,742	20,722	634	10,980 D	31.3%	66.6%	32.0%	68.0%
46,611	AUGLAIZE	23,516	16,414	6,738	364	9,676 R	69.8%	28.7%	70.9%	29.1%
70,226	BELMONT	32,411	15,422	16,302	687	880 D	47.6%	50.3%	48.6%	51.4%
42,285	BROWN	20,113	12,192	7,503	418	4,689 R	60.6%	37.3%	61.9%	38.1%
332,807	BUTLER	173,777	105,341	66,030	2,406	39,311 R	60.6%	38.0%	61.5%	38.5%
28,836	CARROLL	13,953	7,097	6,423	433	674 R	50.9%	46.0%	52.5%	47.5%
38,890	CHAMPAIGN	18,887	11,141	7,385	361	3,756 R	59.0%	39.1%	60.1%	39.9%
144,742	CLARK	66,770	33,634	31,958	1,178	1,676 R	50.4%	47.9%	51.3%	48.7%
177,977	CLERMONT	95,480	62,559	31,611	1,310	30,948 R	65.5%	33.1%	66.4%	33.6%
40,543	CLINTON	19,305	12,409	6,558	338	5,851 R	64.3%	34.0%	65.4%	34.6%
112,075	COLUMBIANA	48,487	25,585	21,882	1,020	3,703 R	52.8%	45.1%	53.9%	46.1%
36,655	COSHOCTON	16,863	8,675	7,689	499	986 R	51.4%	45.6%	53.0%	47.0%
46,966	CRAWFORD	21,174	12,316	8,289	569	4,027 R	58.2%	39.1%	59.8%	40.2%
1,393,978	CUYAHOGA	665,352	199,880	458,422	7,050	258,542 D	30.0%	68.9%	30.4%	69.6%
53,309	DARKE	25,793	17,290	7,964	539	9,326 R	67.0%	30.9%	68.5%	31.5%
39,500	DEFIANCE	19,197	10,407	8,399	391	2,008 R	54.2%	43.8%	55.3%	44.7%
109,989	DELAWARE	92,419	54,778	36,653	988	18,125 R	59.3%	39.7%	59.9%	40.1%
79,551	ERIE	41,229	17,432	23,148	649	5,716 D	42.3%	56.1%	43.0%	57.0%
122,759	FAIRFIELD	71,946	41,580	29,250	1,116	12,330 R	57.8%	40.7%	58.7%	41.3%
28,433	FAYETTE	11,694	7,102	4,401	191	2,701 R	60.7%	37.6%	61.7%	38.3%
1,068,978	FRANKLIN	560,325	218,486	334,709	7,130	116,223 D	39.0%	59.7%	39.5%	60.5%
42,084	FULTON	21,973	11,689	9,900	384	1,789 R	53.2%	45.1%	54.1%	45.9%
31,069	GALLIA	13,318	8,247	4,777	294	3,470 R	61.9%	35.9%	63.3%	36.7%
90,895	GEAUGA	51,102	29,096	21,250	756	7,846 R	56.9%	41.6%	57.8%	42.2%
147,886	GREENE	83,589	48,936	33,540	1,113	15,396 R	58.5%	40.1%	59.3%	40.7%
40,792	GUERNSEY	17,325	9,197	7,625	503	1,572 R	53.1%	44.0%	54.7%	45.3%
845,303	HAMILTON	425,086	195,530	225,213	4,343	29,683 D	46.0%	53.0%	46.5%	53.5%
71,295	HANCOCK	36,981	22,420	13,870	691	8,550 R	60.6%	37.5%	61.8%	38.2%
31,945	HARDIN	13,114	7,749	5,013	352	2,736 R	59.1%	38.2%	60.7%	39.3%
15,856	HARRISON	7,787	3,872	3,683	232	189 R	49.7%	47.3%	51.3%	48.7%
29,210	HENRY	14,840	8,239	6,320	281	1,919 R	55.5%	42.6%	56.6%	43.4%
40,875	HIGHLAND	19,186	11,907	6,856	423	5,051 R	62.1%	35.7%	63.5%	36.5%
28,241	HOCKING	12,961	6,364	6,259	338	105 R	49.1%	48.3%	50.4%	49.6%
38,943	HOLMES	11,113	7,720	3,141	252	4,579 R	69.5%	28.3%	71.1%	28.9%
59,487	HURON	25,582	12,884	12,076	622	808 R	50.4%	47.2%	51.6%	48.4%
32,641	JACKSON	13,993	8,219	5,397	377	2,822 R	58.7%	38.6%	60.4%	39.6%
73,894	JEFFERSON	35,939	17,559	17,635	745	76 D	48.9%	49.1%	49.9%	50.1%
54,500	KNOX	28,231	16,640	11,014	577	5,626 R	58.9%	39.0%	60.2%	39.8%
227,511	LAKE	121,335	59,142	60,155	2,038	1,013 D	48.7%	49.6%	49.6%	50.4%
62,319	LAWRENCE	27,194	15,415	11,262	517	4,153 R	56.7%	41.4%	57.8%	42.2%
145,491	LICKING	82,356	46,918	33,932	1,506	12,986 R	57.0%	41.2%	58.0%	42.0%
46,005	LOGAN	22,217	13,848	7,936	433	5,912 R	62.3%	35.7%	63.6%	36.4%
284,664	LORAIN	146,859	59,068	85,276	2,515	26,208 D	40.2%	58.1%	40.9%	59.1%
455,054	LUCAS	219,831	73,706	142,852	3,273	69,146 D	33.5%	65.0%	34.0%	66.0%
40,213	MADISON	17,454	10,606	6,532	316	4,074 R	60.8%	37.4%	61.9%	38.1%
257,555	MAHONING	127,203	45,319	79,173	2,711	33,854 D	35.6%	62.2%	36.4%	63.6%

OHIO

PRESIDENT 2008

2000 Census Population	County	Total Vote	Republican	Democratic	Other	Rep.-Dem. Plurality	Percentage Total Vote Rep.	Dem.	Major Vote Rep.	Dem.
66,217	MARION	29,017	15,454	12,870	693	2,584 R	53.3%	44.4%	54.6%	45.4%
151,095	MEDINA	90,451	48,189	40,924	1,338	7,265 R	53.3%	45.2%	54.1%	45.9%
23,072	MEIGS	10,354	6,015	4,094	245	1,921 R	58.1%	39.5%	59.5%	40.5%
40,924	MERCER	21,271	15,100	5,853	318	9,247 R	71.0%	27.5%	72.1%	27.9%
98,868	MIAMI	52,807	33,417	18,372	1,018	15,045 R	63.3%	34.8%	64.5%	35.5%
15,180	MONROE	6,982	3,066	3,705	211	639 D	43.9%	53.1%	45.3%	54.7%
559,062	MONTGOMERY	278,511	128,679	145,997	3,835	17,318 D	46.2%	52.4%	46.8%	53.2%
14,897	MORGAN	6,608	3,440	2,966	202	474 R	52.1%	44.9%	53.7%	46.3%
31,628	MORROW	16,643	10,067	6,177	399	3,890 R	60.5%	37.1%	62.0%	38.0%
84,585	MUSKINGUM	39,071	20,549	17,730	792	2,819 R	52.6%	45.4%	53.7%	46.3%
14,058	NOBLE	6,172	3,450	2,474	248	976 R	55.9%	40.1%	58.2%	41.8%
40,985	OTTAWA	23,090	10,624	12,064	402	1,440 D	46.0%	52.2%	46.8%	53.2%
20,293	PAULDING	9,769	5,317	4,165	287	1,152 R	54.4%	42.6%	56.1%	43.9%
34,078	PERRY	15,404	7,721	7,261	422	460 R	50.1%	47.1%	51.5%	48.5%
52,727	PICKAWAY	23,726	14,228	9,077	421	5,151 R	60.0%	38.3%	61.1%	38.9%
27,695	PIKE	12,506	6,162	6,033	311	129 R	49.3%	48.2%	50.5%	49.5%
152,061	PORTAGE	78,206	34,822	41,856	1,528	7,034 D	44.5%	53.5%	45.4%	54.6%
42,337	PREBLE	21,002	13,562	6,999	441	6,563 R	64.6%	33.3%	66.0%	34.0%
34,726	PUTNAM	18,680	13,072	5,281	327	7,791 R	70.0%	28.3%	71.2%	28.8%
128,852	RICHLAND	61,122	34,034	25,727	1,361	8,307 R	55.7%	42.1%	57.0%	43.0%
73,345	ROSS	31,840	16,759	14,455	626	2,304 R	52.6%	45.4%	53.7%	46.3%
61,792	SANDUSKY	30,377	14,192	15,602	583	1,410 D	46.7%	51.4%	47.6%	52.4%
79,195	SCIOTO	32,571	16,994	14,926	651	2,068 R	52.2%	45.8%	53.2%	46.8%
58,683	SENECA	27,449	13,823	13,087	539	736 R	50.4%	47.7%	51.4%	48.6%
47,910	SHELBY	23,667	15,924	7,316	427	8,608 R	67.3%	30.9%	68.5%	31.5%
378,098	STARK	187,545	86,743	96,990	3,812	10,247 D	46.3%	51.7%	47.2%	52.8%
542,899	SUMMIT	277,685	113,284	160,858	3,543	47,574 D	40.8%	57.9%	41.3%	58.7%
225,116	TRUMBULL	106,911	40,164	64,145	2,602	23,981 D	37.6%	60.0%	38.5%	61.5%
90,914	TUSCARAWAS	42,950	20,454	21,498	998	1,044 D	47.6%	50.1%	48.8%	51.2%
40,909	UNION	24,928	15,744	8,761	423	6,983 R	63.2%	35.1%	64.2%	35.8%
29,659	VAN WERT	14,652	9,168	5,178	306	3,990 R	62.6%	35.3%	63.9%	36.1%
12,806	VINTON	5,646	3,021	2,463	162	558 R	53.5%	43.6%	55.1%	44.9%
158,383	WARREN	106,216	71,691	33,398	1,127	38,293 R	67.5%	31.4%	68.2%	31.8%
63,251	WASHINGTON	29,932	17,019	12,368	545	4,651 R	56.9%	41.3%	57.9%	42.1%
111,564	WAYNE	52,142	29,342	21,712	1,088	7,630 R	56.3%	41.6%	57.5%	42.5%
39,188	WILLIAMS	18,396	9,879	8,174	343	1,705 R	53.7%	44.4%	54.7%	45.3%
121,065	WOOD	65,023	29,648	34,285	1,090	4,637 D	45.6%	52.7%	46.4%	53.6%
22,908	WYANDOT	10,977	6,270	4,461	246	1,809 R	57.1%	40.6%	58.4%	41.6%
11,353,140	TOTAL	5,708,350	2,677,820	2,940,044	90,486	262,224 D	46.9%	51.5%	47.7%	52.3%

OHIO

HOUSE OF REPRESENTATIVES

| | | | Republican | | Democratic | | | | Percentage | | | |
| | | | | | | | Other | Rep.-Dem. | Total Vote | | Major Vote | |
CD	Year	Total Vote	Vote	Candidate	Vote	Candidate	Vote	Plurality	Rep.	Dem.	Rep.	Dem.
1	2008	296,290	140,683	CHABOT, STEVE*	155,455	DRIEHAUS, STEVE	152	14,772 D	47.5%	52.5%	47.5%	52.5%
1	2006	202,264	105,680	CHABOT, STEVE*	96,584	CRANLEY, JOHN		9,096 R	52.2%	47.8%	52.2%	47.8%
1	2004	289,863	173,430	CHABOT, STEVE*	116,235	HARRIS, GREG	198	57,195 R	59.8%	40.1%	59.9%	40.1%
1	2002	170,928	110,760	CHABOT, STEVE*	60,168	HARRIS, GREG		50,592 R	64.8%	35.2%	64.8%	35.2%
2	2008	331,624	148,671	SCHMIDT, JEAN*	124,213	WULSIN, VICTORIA	58,740	24,458 R	44.8%	37.5%	54.5%	45.5%
2	2006	238,081	120,112	SCHMIDT, JEAN*	117,595	WULSIN, VICTORIA	374	2,517 R	50.5%	49.4%	50.5%	49.5%
2	2004	316,760	227,102	PORTMAN, ROB*	89,598	SANDERS, CHARLES	60	137,504 R	71.7%	28.3%	71.7%	28.3%
2	2002	188,016	139,218	PORTMAN, ROB*	48,785	SANDERS, CHARLES	13	90,433 R	74.0%	25.9%	74.1%	25.9%
3	2008	316,180	200,204	TURNER, MICHAEL R.*	115,976	MITAKIDES, JANE		84,228 R	63.3%	36.7%	63.3%	36.7%
3	2006	218,628	127,978	TURNER, MICHAEL R.*	90,650	CHEMA, RICHARD		37,328 R	58.5%	41.5%	58.5%	41.5%
3	2004	316,738	197,290	TURNER, MICHAEL R.*	119,448	MITAKIDES, JANE		77,842 R	62.3%	37.7%	62.3%	37.7%
3	2002	189,951	111,630	TURNER, MICHAEL R.	78,307	CARNE, RICK	14	33,323 R	58.8%	41.2%	58.8%	41.2%
4	2008	285,653	186,154	JORDAN, JIM*	99,499	CARROLL, MIKE		86,655 R	65.2%	34.8%	65.2%	34.8%
4	2006	216,636	129,958	JORDAN, JIM	86,678	SIFERD, RICHARD E.		43,280 R	60.0%	40.0%	60.0%	40.0%
4	2004	286,345	167,807	OXLEY, MICHAEL G.*	118,538	KONOP, BEN		49,269 R	58.6%	41.4%	58.6%	41.4%
4	2002	177,727	120,001	OXLEY, MICHAEL G.*	57,726	CLARK, JIM		62,275 R	67.5%	32.5%	67.5%	32.5%
5	2008	294,745	188,905	LATTA, ROBERT E.*	105,840	MAYS, GEORGE F.		83,065 R	64.1%	35.9%	64.1%	35.9%
5	2006	228,357	129,813	GILLMOR, PAUL E.*	98,544	WEIRAUCH, ROBIN		31,269 R	56.8%	43.2%	56.8%	43.2%
5	2004	293,305	196,649	GILLMOR, PAUL E.*	96,656	WEIRAUCH, ROBIN		99,993 R	67.0%	33.0%	67.0%	33.0%
5	2002	188,254	126,286	GILLMOR, PAUL E.*	51,872	ANDERSON, ROGER	10,096	74,414 R	67.1%	27.6%	70.9%	29.1%
6	2008	283,110	92,968	STOBBS, RICHARD D.	176,330	WILSON, CHARLES A.*	13,812	83,362 D	32.8%	62.3%	34.5%	65.5%
6	2006	218,476	82,848	BLASDEL, CHUCK	135,628	WILSON, CHARLES A.		52,780 D	37.9%	62.1%	37.9%	62.1%
6	2004	223,989		—	223,844	STRICKLAND, TED*	145	223,844 D		99.9%		100.0%
6	2002	191,615	77,643	HALLECK, MIKE	113,972	STRICKLAND, TED*		36,329 D	40.5%	59.5%	40.5%	59.5%
7	2008	300,462	174,915	AUSTRIA, STEVE	125,547	NEUHARDT, SHAREN SWARTZ		49,368 R	58.2%	41.8%	58.2%	41.8%
7	2006	227,478	137,899	HOBSON, DAVID L.*	89,579	CONNER, WILLIAM R.		48,320 R	60.6%	39.4%	60.6%	39.4%
7	2004	287,151	186,534	HOBSON, DAVID L.*	100,617	ANASTASIO, KARA		85,917 R	65.0%	35.0%	65.0%	35.0%
7	2002	167,632	113,252	HOBSON, DAVID L.*	45,568	ANASTASIO, KARA	8,812	67,684 R	67.6%	27.2%	71.3%	28.7%
8	2008	297,573	202,063	BOEHNER, JOHN A.*	95,510	VON STEIN, NICHOLAS A.		106,553 R	67.9%	32.1%	67.9%	32.1%
8	2006	214,503	136,863	BOEHNER, JOHN A.*	77,640	MEIER, MORT		59,223 R	63.8%	36.2%	63.8%	36.2%
8	2004	292,249	201,675	BOEHNER, JOHN A.*	90,574	HARDENBROOK, JEFF		111,101 R	69.0%	31.0%	69.0%	31.0%
8	2002	169,391	119,947	BOEHNER, JOHN A.*	49,444	HARDENBROOK, JEFF		70,503 R	70.8%	29.2%	70.8%	29.2%
9	2008	298,566	76,512	LEAVITT, BRADLEY S.	222,054	KAPTUR, MARCY*		145,542 D	25.6%	74.4%	25.6%	74.4%
9	2006	208,999	55,119	LEAVITT, BRADLEY S.	153,880	KAPTUR, MARCY*		98,761 D	26.4%	73.6%	26.4%	73.6%
9	2004	301,132	95,983	KACZALA, LARRY A.	205,149	KAPTUR, MARCY*		109,166 D	31.9%	68.1%	31.9%	68.1%
9	2002	178,717	46,481	EMERY, ED	132,236	KAPTUR, MARCY*		85,755 D	26.0%	74.0%	26.0%	74.0%
10	2008	275,809	107,918	TRAKAS, JIM	157,268	KUCINICH, DENNIS J.*	10,623	49,350 D	39.1%	57.0%	40.7%	59.3%
10	2006	208,389	69,996	DOVILLA, MICHAEL D.	138,393	KUCINICH, DENNIS J.*		68,397 D	33.6%	66.4%	33.6%	66.4%
10	2004	287,212	96,463	HERMAN, EDWARD FITZPATRICK	172,406	KUCINICH, DENNIS J.*	18,343	75,943 D	33.6%	60.0%	35.9%	64.1%
10	2002	175,536	41,778	HEBEN, JON	129,997	KUCINICH, DENNIS J.*	3,761	88,219 D	23.8%	74.1%	24.3%	75.7%
11	2008	249,542	36,708	PEKAREK, THOMAS	212,667	FUDGE, MARCIA L.	167	175,959 D	14.7%	85.2%	14.7%	85.3%
11	2006	175,924	29,125	STRING, LINDSEY N.	146,799	JONES, STEPHANIE TUBBS*		117,674 D	16.6%	83.4%	16.6%	83.4%
11	2004	222,371		—	222,371	JONES, STEPHANIE TUBBS*		222,371 D		100.0%		100.0%
11	2002	152,736	36,146	PAPPANO, PATRICK	116,590	JONES, STEPHANIE TUBBS*		80,444 D	23.7%	76.3%	23.7%	76.3%
12	2008	360,388	197,447	TIBERI, PAT*	152,234	ROBINSON, DAVID	10,707	45,213 R	54.8%	42.2%	56.5%	43.5%
12	2006	254,689	145,943	TIBERI, PAT*	108,746	SHAMANSKY, BOB		37,197 R	57.3%	42.7%	57.3%	42.7%
12	2004	321,046	198,912	TIBERI, PAT*	122,109	BROWN, EDWARD	25	76,803 R	62.0%	38.0%	62.0%	38.0%
12	2002	181,689	116,982	TIBERI, PAT*	64,707	BROWN, EDWARD		52,275 R	64.4%	35.6%	64.4%	35.6%

OHIO

HOUSE OF REPRESENTATIVES

CD	Year	Total Vote	Republican		Democratic		Other Vote	Rep.-Dem. Plurality	Percentage			
									Total Vote		Major Vote	
			Vote	Candidate	Vote	Candidate			Rep.	Dem.	Rep.	Dem.
13	2008	297,680	105,050	POTTER, DAVID S.	192,593	SUTTON, BETTY*	37	87,543 D	35.3%	64.7%	35.3%	64.7%
13	2006	221,561	85,922	FOLTIN, CRAIG	135,639	SUTTON, BETTY		49,717 D	38.8%	61.2%	38.8%	61.2%
13	2004	298,094	97,090	LUCAS, ROBERT	201,004	BROWN, SHERROD*		103,914 D	32.6%	67.4%	32.6%	67.4%
13	2002	178,382	55,357	OLIVEROS, ED	123,025	BROWN, SHERROD*		67,668 D	31.0%	69.0%	31.0%	69.0%
14	2008	323,213	188,488	LaTOURETTE, STEVEN C.*	125,214	O'NEILL, BILL	9,511	63,274 R	58.3%	38.7%	60.1%	39.9%
14	2006	250,322	144,069	LaTOURETTE, STEVEN C.*	97,753	KATZ, LEWIS R.	8,500	46,316 R	57.6%	39.1%	59.6%	40.4%
14	2004	321,366	201,652	LaTOURETTE, STEVEN C.*	119,714	CAFARO, CAPRI S.		81,938 R	62.7%	37.3%	62.7%	37.3%
14	2002	186,372	134,413	LaTOURETTE, STEVEN C.*	51,846	BLANCHARD, DALE	113	82,567 R	72.1%	27.8%	72.2%	27.8%
15	2008	303,838	137,272	STIVERS, STEVE	139,584	KILROY, MARY JO	26,982	2,312 D	45.2%	45.9%	49.6%	50.4%
15	2006	220,567	110,714	PRYCE, DEBORAH*	109,659	KILROY, MARY JO	194	1,055 R	50.2%	49.7%	50.2%	49.8%
15	2004	277,435	166,520	PRYCE, DEBORAH*	110,915	BROWN, MARK		55,605 R	60.0%	40.0%	60.0%	40.0%
15	2002	162,479	108,193	PRYCE, DEBORAH*	54,286	BROWN, MARK		53,907 R	66.6%	33.4%	66.6%	33.4%
16	2008	305,337	136,293	SCHURING, KIRK	169,044	BOCCIERI, JOHN A.		32,751 D	44.6%	55.4%	44.6%	55.4%
16	2006	235,122	137,167	REGULA, RALPH*	97,955	SHAW, THOMAS		39,212 R	58.3%	41.7%	58.3%	41.7%
16	2004	304,361	202,544	REGULA, RALPH*	101,817	SEEMANN, JEFF		100,727 R	66.5%	33.5%	66.5%	33.5%
16	2002	188,378	129,734	REGULA, RALPH*	58,644	RICE, JIM		71,090 R	68.9%	31.1%	68.9%	31.1%
17	2008	280,112	61,216	GRASSELL, DUANE V.	218,896	RYAN, TIM*		157,680 D	21.9%	78.1%	21.9%	78.1%
17	2006	212,294	41,925	MANNING, DON III	170,369	RYAN, TIM*		128,444 D	19.7%	80.3%	19.7%	80.3%
17	2004	275,671	62,871	CUSIMANO, FRANK V.	212,800	RYAN, TIM*		149,929 D	22.8%	77.2%	22.8%	77.2%
17	2002	184,674	62,188	BENJAMIN, ANN WOMER	94,441	RYAN, TIM	28,045	32,253 D	33.7%	51.1%	39.7%	60.3%
18	2008	274,218	110,031	DAILEY, FRED	164,187	SPACE, ZACK*		54,156 D	40.1%	59.9%	40.1%	59.9%
18	2006	208,905	79,259	PADGETT, JOY	129,646	SPACE, ZACK		50,387 D	37.9%	62.1%	37.9%	62.1%
18	2004	268,420	177,600	NEY, BOB*	90,820	THOMAS, BRIAN R.		86,780 R	66.2%	33.8%	66.2%	33.8%
18	2002	125,546	125,546	NEY, BOB*		—		125,546 R	100.0%		100.0%	
TOTAL	2008	5,374,340	2,491,498		2,752,111		130,731	260,613 D	46.4%	51.2%	47.5%	52.5%
TOTAL	2006	3,961,195	1,870,390		2,081,737		9,068	211,347 D	47.2%	52.6%	47.3%	52.7%
TOTAL	2004	5,183,508	2,650,122		2,514,615		18,771	135,507 R	51.1%	48.5%	51.3%	48.7%
TOTAL	2002	3,158,023	1,775,555		1,331,614		50,854	443,941 R	56.2%	42.2%	57.1%	42.9%

Note: An asterisk (*) denotes incumbent.

OHIO

GENERAL AND PRIMARY ELECTIONS

2008 GENERAL ELECTIONS

President Other vote was 42,337 Independent (Ralph Nader); 19,917 Libertarian (Bob Barr); 12,565 Constitution (Chuck Baldwin); 8,518 Green (Cynthia A. McKinney); 3,905 Independent (Richard Duncan); 2,735 Socialist (Brian Moore); 212 Independent write-in (Donald Allen); 160 Independent write-in (Alan Keyes); 71 Independent write-in (Joe Schriner); 63 Independent write-in (Platt Robertson); 2 Independent write-in (Jonathan Allen); 1 Independent write-in (James Germalic).

House Other vote was:

CD 1 85 Independent write-in (Eric Wilson); 67 Independent write-in (Rich Stevenson).
CD 2 58,710 Independent (David Krikorian); 30 Independent write-in (James Condit).
CD 3
CD 4
CD 5
CD 6 13,812 Green (Dennis Spisak).
CD 7
CD 8
CD 9
CD 10 10,623 Libertarian (Paul Conroy).
CD 11 144 Independent write-in (Craig Willis); 23 Independent write-in (Eric Johnson).
CD 12 10,707 Libertarian (Steven Linnabary).
CD 13 37 Independent write-in (Robert Crow).
CD 14 9,511 Libertarian (David Macko).
CD 15 14,061 Libertarian (Mark Noble); 12,915 Independent (Don Eckhart); 6 Independent write-in (Travis Casper).
CD 16
CD 17
CD 18

2008 PRIMARY ELECTIONS

Primary March 4, 2008 **Registration** (as of March 4, 2008) 7,826,480 No Formal System of Party Registration

Primary Type Open—Any registered voter could participate in the primary of either party. However, records are kept of voter participation in recent primaries, and voters who have recently cast a ballot in one party's primary could be challenged if they attempted to participate in the other party's primary. They could be asked to sign an affidavit affirming the fact that they were voting in the opposing party's primary and would become identified with that party because of their primary ballot cast.

OHIO

GENERAL AND PRIMARY ELECTIONS

	REPUBLICAN PRIMARIES			DEMOCRATIC PRIMARIES		
President	John McCain	656,687	59.9%	Hillary Clinton	1,259,620	53.5%
	Mike Huckabee	335,356	30.6%	Barack Obama	1,055,769	44.8%
	Ron Paul	50,964	4.7%	John Edwards	39,332	1.7%
	Mitt Romney	36,031	3.3%			
	Fred Thompson	16,879	1.5%			
	TOTAL	1,095,917		TOTAL	2,354,721	
Congressional District 1	Steve Chabot*	46,408	100.0%	Steve Driehaus	60,454	100.0%
Congressional District 2	Jean Schmidt*	41,987	57.5%	Victoria Wulsin	57,673	57.8%
	Tom Brinkman	28,897	39.6%	Stephen L. Black	29,616	29.7%
	Nathan W. Bailey	2,126	2.9%	William R. Smith	12,455	12.5%
	TOTAL	73,010		TOTAL	99,744	
Congressional District 3	Michael R. Turner*	61,915	100.0%	Jane Mitakides	51,416	53.6%
				Charles W. Sanders	33,268	34.7%
				David Esrati	11,164	11.6%
				TOTAL	95,848	
Congressional District 4	Jim Jordan*	66,771	100.0%	Mike Carroll	59,693	100.0%
Congressional District 5	Robert E. Latta*	54,093	74.8%	George F. Mays	64,450	100.0%
	Scott B. Radcliffe	12,347	17.1%			
	Michael L. Reynolds	5,873	8.1%			
	TOTAL	72,313				
Congressional District 6	Richard D. Stobbs	38,401	100.0%	Charles A. Wilson*	114,409	100.0%
Congressional District 7	Steve Austria	42,499	55.0%	Sharen Swartz Neuhardt	32,826	37.1%
	Ron Hood	25,984	33.6%	Bill Conner	30,029	33.9%
	Dan Harkins	4,817	6.2%	Dave Woolever	9,243	10.4%
	John Mitchel	4,030	5.2%	Jack D. Null	6,118	6.9%
				Richard J. Wyderski	5,236	5.9%
				Thomas L. Scrivens	5,024	5.7%
	TOTAL	77,330		TOTAL	88,476	
Congressional District 8	John A. Boehner*	65,271	100.0%	Nicholas A. Von Stein	52,602	100.0%
Congressional District 9	Bradley S. Leavitt	14,703	55.7%	Marcy Kaptur*	118,814	100.0%
	Ed Emery	11,693	44.3%			
	TOTAL	26,396				
Congressional District 10	Jim Trakas	22,401	79.3%	Dennis J. Kucinich*	72,646	50.3%
	Jason Werner	5,844	20.7%	Joe Cimperman	50,760	35.2%
				Barbara Anne Ferris	9,362	6.5%
				Thomas E. O'Grady	7,264	5.0%
				Rosemary A. Palmer	4,339	3.0%
	TOTAL	28,245		TOTAL	144,371	
Congressional District 11	Thomas Pekarek	9,123	100.0%	Stephanie Tubbs Jones*	131,857	100.0%

Stephanie Tubbs Jones died in August 2008. Marcia L. Fudge was subsequently chosen by Cuyahoga County Democratic officials to replace her on the general election ballot.

	REPUBLICAN PRIMARIES			DEMOCRATIC PRIMARIES		
Congressional District 12	Pat Tiberi*	63,450	90.5%	David Robinson	48,873	51.1%
	David Ryon	6,681	9.5%	Russ Goodwin	32,836	34.4%
				Aaron J. Dagres	13,868	14.5%
	TOTAL	70,131		TOTAL	95,577	

OHIO

GENERAL AND PRIMARY ELECTIONS

	REPUBLICAN PRIMARIES			DEMOCRATIC PRIMARIES		
Congressional District 13	David S. Potter	12,064	40.2%	Betty Sutton*	105,802	100.0%
	Frank Chestney	10,093	33.6%			
	Frances L. Kalapodis	7,852	26.2%			
	TOTAL	30,009				
Congressional District 14	Steven C. LaTourette*	53,036	100.0%	Bill O'Neill	62,263	62.3%
				John H. Greene Jr.	21,352	21.4%
				Dale Virgil Blanchard	16,339	16.3%
				TOTAL	99,954	
Congressional District 15	Steve Stivers	33,838	65.9%	Mary Jo Kilroy	85,840	100.0%
	Robert Wagner	17,499	34.1%			
	TOTAL	51,337				
Congressional District 16	Kirk Schuring	33,534	47.4%	John A. Boccieri	71,038	63.7%
	Matt Miller	29,735	42.0%	Mary M. Cirelli	40,429	36.3%
	Paul R. Schiffer	7,448	10.5%			
	TOTAL	70,717		TOTAL	111,467	
Congressional District 17	Duane V. Grassell	18,683	100.0%	Tim Ryan*	138,610	100.0%
Congressional District 18	Fred Dailey	23,598	39.1%	Zack Space*	87,503	84.6%
	Jeannette Moll	18,612	30.9%	Mark Pitrone	15,980	15.4%
	Paul Phillips	13,483	22.4%			
	Beau M. Bromberg	4,620	7.7%			
	TOTAL	60,313		TOTAL	103,483	

Note: An asterisk (*) denotes incumbent.

OKLAHOMA

Congressional districts first established for elections held in 2002
5 members

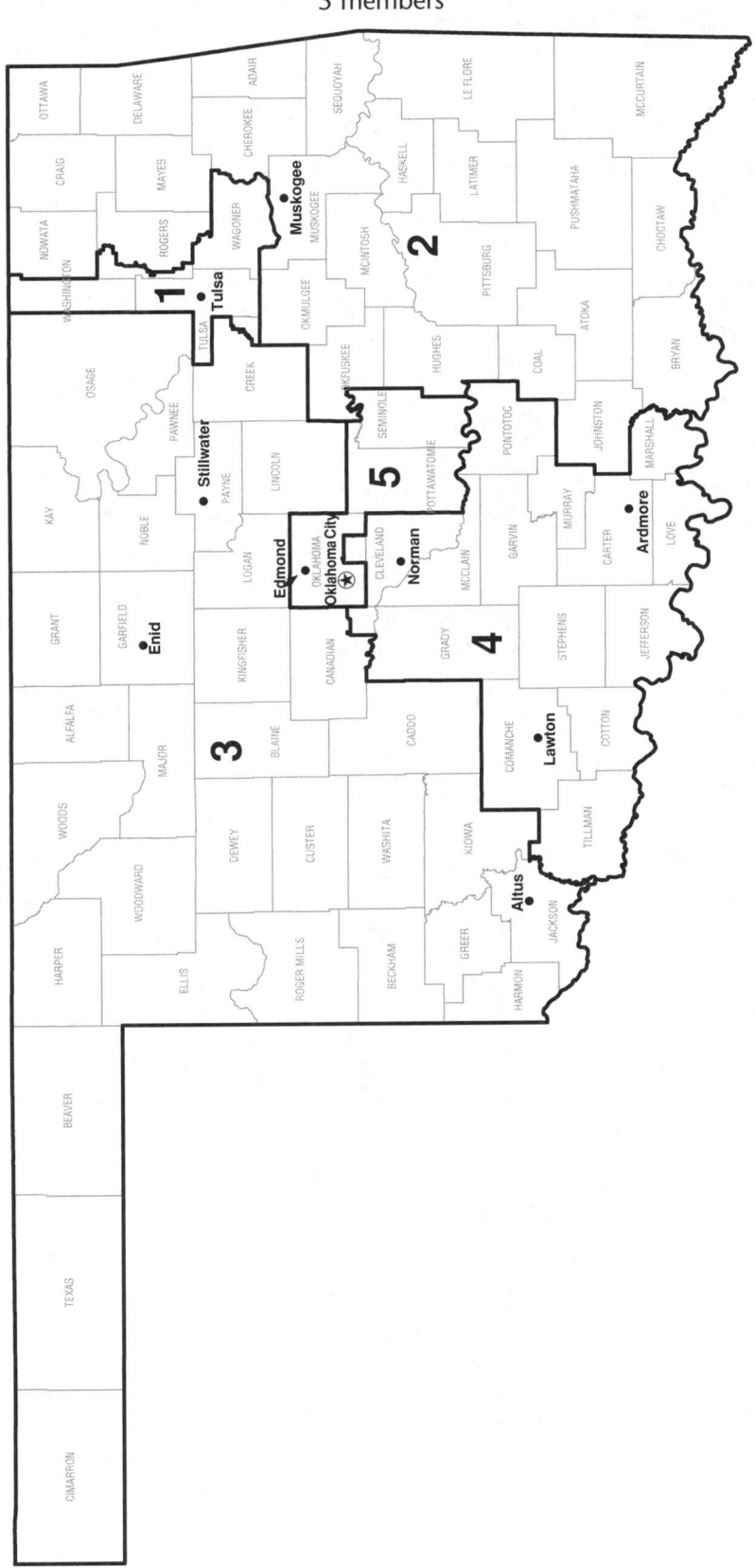

OKLAHOMA

GOVERNOR
Brad Henry (D). Reelected 2006 to a four-year term. Previously elected 2002.

SENATORS (2 Republicans)
Tom Coburn (R). Elected 2004 to a six-year term.

James M. Inhofe (R). Reelected 2008 to a six-year term. Previously elected 2002, 1996, and 1994 to fill out the remaining two years of the term vacated when David L. Boren (D) resigned to become president of the University of Oklahoma.

REPRESENTATIVES (4 Republicans, 1 Democrat)
1. John Sullivan (R)
2. Dan Boren (D)
3. Frank D. Lucas (R)
4. Tom Cole (R)
5. Mary Fallin (R)

POSTWAR VOTE FOR PRESIDENT

Year	Total Vote	Republican Vote	Republican Candidate	Democratic Vote	Democratic Candidate	Other Vote	Plurality	Total Vote Rep.	Total Vote Dem.	Major Vote Rep.	Major Vote Dem.
2008	1,462,661	960,165	McCain, John	502,496	Obama, Barack		457,669 R	65.6%	34.4%	65.6%	34.4%
2004	1,463,758	959,792	Bush, George W.	503,966	Kerry, John		455,826 R	65.6%	34.4%	65.6%	34.4%
2000	1,234,229	744,337	Bush, George W.	474,276	Gore, Al	15,616	270,061 R	60.3%	38.4%	61.1%	38.9%
1996**	1,206,713	582,315	Dole, Bob	488,105	Clinton, Bill	136,293	94,210 R	48.3%	40.4%	54.4%	45.6%
1992**	1,390,359	592,929	Bush, George	473,066	Clinton, Bill	324,364	119,863 R	42.6%	34.0%	55.6%	44.4%
1988	1,171,036	678,367	Bush, George	483,423	Dukakis, Michael S.	9,246	194,944 R	57.9%	41.3%	58.4%	41.6%
1984	1,255,676	861,530	Reagan, Ronald	385,080	Mondale, Walter F.	9,066	476,450 R	68.6%	30.7%	69.1%	30.9%
1980**	1,149,708	695,570	Reagan, Ronald	402,026	Carter, Jimmy	52,112	293,544 R	60.5%	35.0%	63.4%	36.6%
1976	1,092,251	545,708	Ford, Gerald R.	532,442	Carter, Jimmy	14,101	13,266 R	50.0%	48.7%	50.6%	49.4%
1972	1,029,900	759,025	Nixon, Richard M.	247,147	McGovern, George S.	23,728	511,878 R	73.7%	24.0%	75.4%	24.6%
1968**	943,086	449,697	Nixon, Richard M.	301,658	Humphrey, Hubert H.	191,731	148,039 R	47.7%	32.0%	59.9%	40.1%
1964	932,499	412,665	Goldwater, Barry M.	519,834	Johnson, Lyndon B.		107,169 D	44.3%	55.7%	44.3%	55.7%
1960	903,150	533,039	Nixon, Richard M.	370,111	Kennedy, John F.		162,928 R	59.0%	41.0%	59.0%	41.0%
1956	859,350	473,769	Eisenhower, Dwight D.	385,581	Stevenson, Adlai E.		88,188 R	55.1%	44.9%	55.1%	44.9%
1952	948,984	518,045	Eisenhower, Dwight D.	430,939	Stevenson, Adlai E.		87,106 R	54.6%	45.4%	54.6%	45.4%
1948	721,599	268,817	Dewey, Thomas E.	452,782	Truman, Harry S.		183,965 D	37.3%	62.7%	37.3%	62.7%

**In past elections, the other vote included: 1996 - 130,788 Reform (Ross Perot); 1992 - 319,878 Independent (Perot); 1980 - 38,284 Independent (John Anderson); 1968 - 191,731 American Independent (George Wallace).

OKLAHOMA

POSTWAR VOTE FOR GOVERNOR

Year	Total Vote	Republican Vote	Republican Candidate	Democratic Vote	Democratic Candidate	Other Vote	Rep.-Dem. Plurality	Total Vote Rep.	Total Vote Dem.	Major Vote Rep.	Major Vote Dem.
2006	926,462	310,327	Istook, Ernest	616,135	Henry, Brad		305,808 D	33.5%	66.5%	33.5%	66.5%
2002**	1,035,620	441,277	Largent, Steve	448,143	Henry, Brad	146,200	6,866 D	42.6%	43.3%	49.6%	50.4%
1998	873,585	505,498	Keating, Frank	357,552	Boyd, Laura	10,535	147,946 R	57.9%	40.9%	58.6%	41.4%
1994**	995,012	466,740	Keating, Frank	294,936	Mildren, Jack	233,336	171,804 R	46.9%	29.6%	61.3%	38.7%
1990	911,314	297,584	Price, Bill	523,196	Walters, David	90,534	225,612 D	32.7%	57.4%	36.3%	63.7%
1986	909,925	431,762	Bellmon, Henry	405,295	Walters, David	72,868	26,467 R	47.5%	44.5%	51.6%	48.4%
1982	883,130	332,207	Daxon, Tom	548,159	Nigh, George	2,764	215,952 D	37.6%	62.1%	37.7%	62.3%
1978	777,414	367,055	Shotts, Ron	402,240	Nigh, George	8,119	35,185 D	47.2%	51.7%	47.7%	52.3%
1974	804,848	290,459	Inhofe, James M.	514,389	Boren, David L.		223,930 D	36.1%	63.9%	36.1%	63.9%
1970	698,790	336,157	Bartlett, Dewey F.	338,338	Hall, David	24,295	2,181 D	48.1%	48.4%	49.8%	50.2%
1966	677,258	377,078	Bartlett, Dewey F.	296,328	Moore, Preston J.	3,852	80,750 R	55.7%	43.8%	56.0%	44.0%
1962	709,763	392,316	Bellmon, Henry	315,357	Atkinson, W. P.	2,090	76,959 R	55.3%	44.4%	55.4%	44.6%
1958	538,839	107,495	Ferguson, Phil	399,504	Edmondson, J. Howard	31,840	292,009 D	19.9%	74.1%	21.2%	78.8%
1954	609,194	251,808	Sparks, Reuben K.	357,386	Gary, Raymond		105,578 D	41.3%	58.7%	41.3%	58.7%
1950	644,276	313,205	Ferguson, Jo O.	329,308	Murray, Johnston	1,763	16,103 D	48.6%	51.1%	48.7%	51.3%
1946	494,599	227,426	Flynn, Olney F.	259,491	Turner, Roy J.	7,682	32,065 D	46.0%	52.5%	46.7%	53.3%

**In past elections, the other vote included: 2002 - 146,200 Independent (Gary L. Richardson); 1994 - 233,336 Independent (Wes Watkins).

POSTWAR VOTE FOR SENATOR

Year	Total Vote	Republican Vote	Republican Candidate	Democratic Vote	Democratic Candidate	Other Vote	Rep.-Dem. Plurality	Total Vote Rep.	Total Vote Dem.	Major Vote Rep.	Major Vote Dem.
2008	1,346,819	763,375	Inhofe, James M.	527,736	Rice, Andrew	55,708	235,639 R	56.7%	39.2%	59.1%	40.9%
2004	1,446,846	763,433	Coburn, Tom	596,750	Carson, Brad	86,663	166,683 R	52.8%	41.2%	43.9%	56.1%
2002	1,018,424	583,579	Inhofe, James M.	369,789	Walters, David	65,056	213,790 R	57.3%	36.3%	61.2%	38.8%
1998	859,713	570,682	Nickles, Don	268,898	Carroll, Don E.	20,133	301,784 R	66.4%	31.3%	68.0%	32.0%
1996	1,183,150	670,610	Inhofe, James M.	474,162	Boren, Jim	38,378	196,448 R	56.7%	40.1%	58.6%	41.4%
1994S	982,430	542,390	Inhofe, James M.	392,488	McCurdy, Dave	47,552	149,902 R	55.2%	40.0%	58.0%	42.0%
1992	1,294,423	757,876	Nickles, Don	494,350	Lewis, Steve	42,197	263,526 R	58.5%	38.2%	60.5%	39.5%
1990	884,498	148,814	Jones, Stephen	735,684	Boren, David L.		586,870 D	16.8%	83.2%	16.8%	83.2%
1986	893,666	493,436	Nickles, Don	400,230	Jones, James R.		93,206 R	55.2%	44.8%	55.2%	44.8%
1984	1,197,937	280,638	Crozier, Will E.	906,131	Boren, David L.	11,168	625,493 D	23.4%	75.6%	23.6%	76.4%
1980	1,098,294	587,252	Nickles, Don	478,283	Coats, Andrew	32,759	108,969 R	53.5%	43.5%	55.1%	44.9%
1978	754,264	247,857	Kamm, Robert B.	493,953	Boren, David L.	12,454	246,096 D	32.9%	65.5%	33.4%	66.6%
1974	791,809	390,997	Bellmon, Henry	387,162	Edmondson, Ed	13,650	3,835 R	49.4%	48.9%	50.2%	49.8%
1972	1,005,148	516,934	Bartlett, Dewey F.	478,212	Edmondson, Ed	10,002	38,722 R	51.4%	47.6%	51.9%	48.1%
1968	909,119	470,120	Bellmon, Henry	419,658	Monroney, A. S. Mike	19,341	50,462 R	51.7%	46.2%	52.8%	47.2%
1966	638,742	295,585	Patterson, Pat J.	343,157	Harris, Fred R.		47,572 D	46.3%	53.7%	46.3%	53.7%
1964S	912,174	445,392	Wilkinson, Bud	466,782	Harris, Fred R.		21,390 D	48.8%	51.2%	48.8%	51.2%
1962	664,712	307,966	Crawford, B. Hayden	353,890	Monroney, A. S. Mike	2,856	45,924 D	46.3%	53.2%	46.5%	53.5%
1960	864,475	385,646	Crawford, B. Hayden	474,116	Kerr, Robert S.	4,713	88,470 D	44.6%	54.8%	44.9%	55.1%
1956	831,142	371,146	McKeever, Douglas	459,996	Monroney, A. S. Mike		88,850 D	44.7%	55.3%	44.7%	55.3%
1954	600,120	262,013	Mock, Fred M.	335,127	Kerr, Robert S.	2,980	73,114 D	43.7%	55.8%	43.9%	56.1%
1950	631,177	285,224	Alexander, W. H.	345,953	Monroney, A. S. Mike		60,729 D	45.2%	54.8%	45.2%	54.8%
1948	708,931	265,169	Rizley, Ross	441,654	Kerr, Robert S.	2,108	176,485 D	37.4%	62.3%	37.5%	62.5%

Note: The 1964 and 1994 elections were for short terms to fill vacancies.

OKLAHOMA

PRESIDENT 2008

2000 Census Population	County	Total Vote	Republican	Democratic	Other	Rep.-Dem. Plurality	Percentage			
							Total Vote		Major Vote	
							Rep.	Dem.	Rep.	Dem.
21,038	ADAIR	6,690	4,638	2,052		2,586 R	69.3%	30.7%	69.3%	30.7%
6,105	ALFALFA	2,434	2,023	411		1,612 R	83.1%	16.9%	83.1%	16.9%
13,879	ATOKA	4,881	3,511	1,370		2,141 R	71.9%	28.1%	71.9%	28.1%
5,857	BEAVER	2,464	2,199	265		1,934 R	89.2%	10.8%	89.2%	10.8%
19,799	BECKHAM	7,397	5,772	1,625		4,147 R	78.0%	22.0%	78.0%	22.0%
11,976	BLAINE	4,112	3,101	1,011		2,090 R	75.4%	24.6%	75.4%	24.6%
36,534	BRYAN	13,733	9,307	4,426		4,881 R	67.8%	32.2%	67.8%	32.2%
30,150	CADDO	9,817	6,413	3,404		3,009 R	65.3%	34.7%	65.3%	34.7%
87,697	CANADIAN	47,854	36,428	11,426		25,002 R	76.1%	23.9%	76.1%	23.9%
45,621	CARTER	18,844	13,241	5,603		7,638 R	70.3%	29.7%	70.3%	29.7%
42,521	CHEROKEE	16,380	9,186	7,194		1,992 R	56.1%	43.9%	56.1%	43.9%
15,342	CHOCTAW	5,590	3,730	1,860		1,870 R	66.7%	33.3%	66.7%	33.3%
3,148	CIMARRON	1,271	1,119	152		967 R	88.0%	12.0%	88.0%	12.0%
208,016	CLEVELAND	104,430	64,749	39,681		25,068 R	62.0%	38.0%	62.0%	38.0%
6,031	COAL	2,272	1,672	600		1,072 R	73.6%	26.4%	73.6%	26.4%
114,996	COMANCHE	34,247	20,127	14,120		6,007 R	58.8%	41.2%	58.8%	41.2%
6,614	COTTON	2,483	1,793	690		1,103 R	72.2%	27.8%	72.2%	27.8%
14,950	CRAIG	5,931	3,858	2,073		1,785 R	65.0%	35.0%	65.0%	35.0%
67,367	CREEK	28,505	20,187	8,318		11,869 R	70.8%	29.2%	70.8%	29.2%
26,142	CUSTER	10,502	7,842	2,660		5,182 R	74.7%	25.3%	74.7%	25.3%
37,077	DELAWARE	15,362	10,277	5,085		5,192 R	66.9%	33.1%	66.9%	33.1%
4,743	DEWEY	2,203	1,857	346		1,511 R	84.3%	15.7%	84.3%	15.7%
4,075	ELLIS	1,909	1,627	282		1,345 R	85.2%	14.8%	85.2%	14.8%
57,813	GARFIELD	22,612	17,067	5,545		11,522 R	75.5%	24.5%	75.5%	24.5%
27,210	GARVIN	10,738	7,710	3,028		4,682 R	71.8%	28.2%	71.8%	28.2%
45,516	GRADY	20,715	15,195	5,520		9,675 R	73.4%	26.6%	73.4%	26.6%
5,144	GRANT	2,350	1,836	514		1,322 R	78.1%	21.9%	78.1%	21.9%
6,061	GREER	2,114	1,548	566		982 R	73.2%	26.8%	73.2%	26.8%
3,283	HARMON	1,090	757	333		424 R	69.4%	30.6%	69.4%	30.6%
3,562	HARPER	1,563	1,342	221		1,121 R	85.9%	14.1%	85.9%	14.1%
11,792	HASKELL	4,681	3,207	1,474		1,733 R	68.5%	31.5%	68.5%	31.5%
14,154	HUGHES	4,843	3,134	1,709		1,425 R	64.7%	35.3%	64.7%	35.3%
28,439	JACKSON	8,983	6,719	2,264		4,455 R	74.8%	25.2%	74.8%	25.2%
6,818	JEFFERSON	2,457	1,652	805		847 R	67.2%	32.8%	67.2%	32.8%
10,513	JOHNSTON	3,957	2,708	1,249		1,459 R	68.4%	31.6%	68.4%	31.6%
48,080	KAY	18,693	13,230	5,463		7,767 R	70.8%	29.2%	70.8%	29.2%
13,926	KINGFISHER	6,381	5,372	1,009		4,363 R	84.2%	15.8%	84.2%	15.8%
10,227	KIOWA	3,763	2,537	1,226		1,311 R	67.4%	32.6%	67.4%	32.6%
10,692	LATIMER	4,173	2,860	1,313		1,547 R	68.5%	31.5%	68.5%	31.5%
48,109	LE FLORE	16,741	11,605	5,136		6,469 R	69.3%	30.7%	69.3%	30.7%
32,080	LINCOLN	13,974	10,470	3,504		6,966 R	74.9%	25.1%	74.9%	25.1%
33,924	LOGAN	18,273	12,556	5,717		6,839 R	68.7%	31.3%	68.7%	31.3%
8,831	LOVE	3,846	2,589	1,257		1,332 R	67.3%	32.7%	67.3%	32.7%
27,740	MCCLAIN	14,744	11,193	3,551		7,642 R	75.9%	24.1%	75.9%	24.1%
34,402	MCCURTAIN	10,539	7,745	2,794		4,951 R	73.5%	26.5%	73.5%	26.5%
19,456	MCINTOSH	8,223	4,903	3,320		1,583 R	59.6%	40.4%	59.6%	40.4%
7,545	MAJOR	3,471	2,956	515		2,441 R	85.2%	14.8%	85.2%	14.8%
13,184	MARSHALL	5,373	3,730	1,643		2,087 R	69.4%	30.6%	69.4%	30.6%
38,369	MAYES	15,983	10,234	5,749		4,485 R	64.0%	36.0%	64.0%	36.0%
12,623	MURRAY	5,338	3,746	1,592		2,154 R	70.2%	29.8%	70.2%	29.8%

.

OKLAHOMA

PRESIDENT 2008

2000 Census Population	County	Total Vote	Republican	Democratic	Other	Rep.-Dem. Plurality	Percentage Total Vote Rep.	Dem.	Major Vote Rep.	Dem.
69,451	MUSKOGEE	26,583	15,289	11,294		3,995 R	57.5%	42.5%	57.5%	42.5%
11,411	NOBLE	5,055	3,881	1,174		2,707 R	76.8%	23.2%	76.8%	23.2%
10,569	NOWATA	4,442	3,031	1,411		1,620 R	68.2%	31.8%	68.2%	31.8%
11,814	OKFUSKEE	4,123	2,643	1,480		1,163 R	64.1%	35.9%	64.1%	35.9%
660,448	OKLAHOMA	279,354	163,172	116,182		46,990 R	58.4%	41.6%	58.4%	41.6%
39,685	OKMULGEE	14,918	8,727	6,191		2,536 R	58.5%	41.5%	58.5%	41.5%
44,437	OSAGE	19,658	12,160	7,498		4,662 R	61.9%	38.1%	61.9%	38.1%
33,194	OTTAWA	11,173	6,905	4,268		2,637 R	61.8%	38.2%	61.8%	38.2%
16,612	PAWNEE	6,596	4,533	2,063		2,470 R	68.7%	31.3%	68.7%	31.3%
68,190	PAYNE	29,036	18,435	10,601		7,834 R	63.5%	36.5%	63.5%	36.5%
43,953	PITTSBURG	17,209	11,752	5,457		6,295 R	68.3%	31.7%	68.3%	31.7%
35,143	PONTOTOC	14,262	9,750	4,512		5,238 R	68.4%	31.6%	68.4%	31.6%
65,521	POTTAWATOMIE	25,663	17,753	7,910		9,843 R	69.2%	30.8%	69.2%	30.8%
11,667	PUSHMATAHA	4,473	3,208	1,265		1,943 R	71.7%	28.3%	71.7%	28.3%
3,436	ROGER MILLS	1,789	1,502	287		1,215 R	84.0%	16.0%	84.0%	16.0%
70,641	ROGERS	38,515	27,743	10,772		16,971 R	72.0%	28.0%	72.0%	28.0%
24,894	SEMINOLE	8,577	5,600	2,977		2,623 R	65.3%	34.7%	65.3%	34.7%
38,972	SEQUOYAH	13,920	9,466	4,454		5,012 R	68.0%	32.0%	68.0%	32.0%
43,182	STEPHENS	18,932	14,394	4,538		9,856 R	76.0%	24.0%	76.0%	24.0%
20,107	TEXAS	6,259	5,336	923		4,413 R	85.3%	14.7%	85.3%	14.7%
9,287	TILLMAN	3,237	2,195	1,042		1,153 R	67.8%	32.2%	67.8%	32.2%
563,299	TULSA	254,496	158,363	96,133		62,230 R	62.2%	37.8%	62.2%	37.8%
57,491	WAGONER	30,251	21,441	8,810		12,631 R	70.9%	29.1%	70.9%	29.1%
48,996	WASHINGTON	22,765	16,457	6,308		10,149 R	72.3%	27.7%	72.3%	27.7%
11,508	WASHITA	4,776	3,724	1,052		2,672 R	78.0%	22.0%	78.0%	22.0%
9,089	WOODS	3,916	3,043	873		2,170 R	77.7%	22.3%	77.7%	22.3%
18,486	WOODWARD	7,754	6,404	1,350		5,054 R	82.6%	17.4%	82.6%	17.4%
3,450,654	TOTAL	1,462,661	960,165	502,496		457,669 R	65.6%	34.4%	65.6%	34.4%

OKLAHOMA

SENATOR 2008

2000 Census Population	County	Total Vote	Republican	Democratic	Other	Rep.-Dem. Plurality	Percentage			
							Total Vote		Major Vote	
							Rep.	Dem.	Rep.	Dem.
21,038	ADAIR	6,319	3,488	2,575	256	913 R	55.2%	40.8%	57.5%	42.5%
6,105	ALFALFA	2,339	1,571	618	150	953 R	67.2%	26.4%	71.8%	28.2%
13,879	ATOKA	4,452	2,515	1,757	180	758 R	56.5%	39.5%	58.9%	41.1%
5,857	BEAVER	2,232	1,804	328	100	1,476 R	80.8%	14.7%	84.6%	15.4%
19,799	BECKHAM	6,953	4,444	2,209	300	2,235 R	63.9%	31.8%	66.8%	33.2%
11,976	BLAINE	3,896	2,504	1,242	150	1,262 R	64.3%	31.9%	66.8%	33.2%
36,534	BRYAN	12,593	7,166	4,893	534	2,273 R	56.9%	38.9%	59.4%	40.6%
30,150	CADDO	9,222	4,821	3,999	402	822 R	52.3%	43.4%	54.7%	45.3%
87,697	CANADIAN	43,055	28,701	12,513	1,841	16,188 R	66.7%	29.1%	69.6%	30.4%
45,621	CARTER	17,103	10,306	6,092	705	4,214 R	60.3%	35.6%	62.8%	37.2%
42,521	CHEROKEE	15,637	6,939	7,997	701	1,058 D	44.4%	51.1%	46.5%	53.5%
15,342	CHOCTAW	5,037	2,570	2,233	234	337 R	51.0%	44.3%	53.5%	46.5%
3,148	CIMARRON	1,163	909	191	63	718 R	78.2%	16.4%	82.6%	17.4%
208,016	CLEVELAND	93,756	51,283	38,332	4,141	12,951 R	54.7%	40.9%	57.2%	42.8%
6,031	COAL	2,128	1,167	870	91	297 R	54.8%	40.9%	57.3%	42.7%
114,996	COMANCHE	31,018	16,984	12,727	1,307	4,257 R	54.8%	41.0%	57.2%	42.8%
6,614	COTTON	2,315	1,442	769	104	673 R	62.3%	33.2%	65.2%	34.8%
14,950	CRAIG	5,609	2,877	2,477	255	400 R	51.3%	44.2%	53.7%	46.3%
67,367	CREEK	26,451	15,986	9,370	1,095	6,616 R	60.4%	35.4%	63.0%	37.0%
26,142	CUSTER	10,015	6,568	3,069	378	3,499 R	65.6%	30.6%	68.2%	31.8%
37,077	DELAWARE	14,269	7,902	5,662	705	2,240 R	55.4%	39.7%	58.3%	41.7%
4,743	DEWEY	2,077	1,486	505	86	981 R	71.5%	24.3%	74.6%	25.4%
4,075	ELLIS	1,808	1,323	394	91	929 R	73.2%	21.8%	77.1%	22.9%
57,813	GARFIELD	20,628	13,963	5,819	846	8,144 R	67.7%	28.2%	70.6%	29.4%
27,210	GARVIN	10,006	5,813	3,680	513	2,133 R	58.1%	36.8%	61.2%	38.8%
45,516	GRADY	19,357	11,715	6,662	980	5,053 R	60.5%	34.4%	63.7%	36.3%
5,144	GRANT	2,228	1,486	624	118	862 R	66.7%	28.0%	70.4%	29.6%
6,061	GREER	1,914	1,130	696	88	434 R	59.0%	36.4%	61.9%	38.1%
3,283	HARMON	999	576	389	34	187 R	57.7%	38.9%	59.7%	40.3%
3,562	HARPER	1,471	1,109	305	57	804 R	75.4%	20.7%	78.4%	21.6%
11,792	HASKELL	4,349	2,119	2,030	200	89 R	48.7%	46.7%	51.1%	48.9%
14,154	HUGHES	4,578	2,255	2,114	209	141 R	49.3%	46.2%	51.6%	48.4%
28,439	JACKSON	8,224	5,652	2,260	312	3,392 R	68.7%	27.5%	71.4%	28.6%
6,818	JEFFERSON	2,219	1,233	870	116	363 R	55.6%	39.2%	58.6%	41.4%
10,513	JOHNSTON	3,663	1,970	1,536	157	434 R	53.8%	41.9%	56.2%	43.8%
48,080	KAY	17,126	10,512	5,700	914	4,812 R	61.4%	33.3%	64.8%	35.2%
13,926	KINGFISHER	5,968	4,454	1,285	229	3,169 R	74.6%	21.5%	77.6%	22.4%
10,227	KIOWA	3,511	1,922	1,463	126	459 R	54.7%	41.7%	56.8%	43.2%
10,692	LATIMER	3,945	1,937	1,803	205	134 R	49.1%	45.7%	51.8%	48.2%
48,109	LE FLORE	15,314	8,190	6,305	819	1,885 R	53.5%	41.2%	56.5%	43.5%
32,080	LINCOLN	13,090	8,107	4,339	644	3,768 R	61.9%	33.1%	65.1%	34.9%
33,924	LOGAN	16,795	10,287	5,787	721	4,500 R	61.3%	34.5%	64.0%	36.0%
8,831	LOVE	3,464	2,010	1,349	105	661 R	58.0%	38.9%	59.8%	40.2%
27,740	MCCLAIN	13,594	8,658	4,307	629	4,351 R	63.7%	31.7%	66.8%	33.2%
34,402	MCCURTAIN	9,517	5,140	3,820	557	1,320 R	54.0%	40.1%	57.4%	42.6%
19,456	MCINTOSH	7,707	3,417	3,970	320	553 D	44.3%	51.5%	46.3%	53.7%
7,545	MAJOR	3,241	2,391	695	155	1,696 R	73.8%	21.4%	77.5%	22.5%
13,184	MARSHALL	4,858	2,934	1,722	202	1,212 R	60.4%	35.4%	63.0%	37.0%
38,369	MAYES	15,192	7,751	6,827	614	924 R	51.0%	44.9%	53.2%	46.8%
12,623	MURRAY	4,991	2,810	1,942	239	868 R	56.3%	38.9%	59.1%	40.9%

OKLAHOMA

SENATOR 2008

2000 Census Population	County	Total Vote	Republican	Democratic	Other	Rep.-Dem. Plurality	Percentage Total Vote Rep.	Dem.	Major Vote Rep.	Dem.
69,451	MUSKOGEE	24,973	11,079	12,833	1,061	1,754 D	44.4%	51.4%	46.3%	53.7%
11,411	NOBLE	4,801	3,120	1,436	245	1,684 R	65.0%	29.9%	68.5%	31.5%
10,569	NOWATA	4,211	2,390	1,605	216	785 R	56.8%	38.1%	59.8%	40.2%
11,814	OKFUSKEE	3,844	1,960	1,729	155	231 R	51.0%	45.0%	53.1%	46.9%
660,448	OKLAHOMA	254,726	132,338	112,418	9,970	19,920 R	52.0%	44.1%	54.1%	45.9%
39,685	OKMULGEE	14,128	6,521	7,093	514	572 D	46.2%	50.2%	47.9%	52.1%
44,437	OSAGE	18,055	9,339	8,007	709	1,332 R	51.7%	44.3%	53.8%	46.2%
33,194	OTTAWA	10,124	5,215	4,383	526	832 R	51.5%	43.3%	54.3%	45.7%
16,612	PAWNEE	6,264	3,478	2,485	301	993 R	55.5%	39.7%	58.3%	41.7%
68,190	PAYNE	27,007	15,235	10,440	1,332	4,795 R	56.4%	38.7%	59.3%	40.7%
43,953	PITTSBURG	16,140	8,892	6,536	712	2,356 R	55.1%	40.5%	57.6%	42.4%
35,143	PONTOTOC	13,348	7,442	5,261	645	2,181 R	55.8%	39.4%	58.6%	41.4%
65,521	POTTAWATOMIE	23,816	13,826	8,823	1,167	5,003 R	58.1%	37.0%	61.0%	39.0%
11,667	PUSHMATAHA	4,089	2,263	1,611	215	652 R	55.3%	39.4%	58.4%	41.6%
3,436	ROGER MILLS	1,730	1,176	484	70	692 R	68.0%	28.0%	70.8%	29.2%
70,641	ROGERS	36,398	22,099	12,816	1,483	9,283 R	60.7%	35.2%	63.3%	36.7%
24,894	SEMINOLE	8,089	4,335	3,384	370	951 R	53.6%	41.8%	56.2%	43.8%
38,972	SEQUOYAH	12,692	6,462	5,663	567	799 R	50.9%	44.6%	53.3%	46.7%
43,182	STEPHENS	17,771	11,457	5,472	842	5,985 R	64.5%	30.8%	67.7%	32.3%
20,107	TEXAS	5,671	4,334	1,019	318	3,315 R	76.4%	18.0%	81.0%	19.0%
9,287	TILLMAN	2,906	1,691	1,085	130	606 R	58.2%	37.3%	60.9%	39.1%
563,299	TULSA	234,104	133,010	93,495	7,599	39,515 R	56.8%	39.9%	58.7%	41.3%
57,491	WAGONER	28,164	17,108	10,009	1,047	7,099 R	60.7%	35.5%	63.1%	36.9%
48,996	WASHINGTON	20,860	13,592	6,451	817	7,141 R	65.2%	30.9%	67.8%	32.2%
11,508	WASHITA	4,520	2,883	1,427	210	1,456 R	63.8%	31.6%	66.9%	33.1%
9,089	WOODS	3,620	2,493	940	187	1,553 R	68.9%	26.0%	72.6%	27.4%
18,486	WOODWARD	7,372	5,340	1,710	322	3,630 R	72.4%	23.2%	75.7%	24.3%
3,450,654	TOTAL	1,346,819	763,375	527,736	55,708	235,639 R	56.7%	39.2%	59.1%	40.9%

OKLAHOMA

HOUSE OF REPRESENTATIVES

CD	Year	Total Vote	Republican Vote	Republican Candidate	Democratic Vote	Democratic Candidate	Other Vote	Rep.-Dem. Plurality	Total Vote Rep.	Total Vote Dem.	Major Vote Rep.	Major Vote Dem.
1	2008	292,294	193,404	SULLIVAN, JOHN*	98,890	OLIVER, GEORGIANNA W.		94,514 R	66.2%	33.8%	66.2%	33.8%
1	2006	183,729	116,920	SULLIVAN, JOHN*	56,724	GENTGES, ALAN	10,085	60,196 R	63.6%	30.9%	67.3%	32.7%
1	2004	310,934	187,145	SULLIVAN, JOHN*	116,731	DODD, DOUG	7,058	70,414 R	60.2%	37.5%	61.6%	38.4%
1	2002	214,955	119,566	SULLIVAN, JOHN*	90,649	DODD, DOUG	4,740	28,917 R	55.6%	42.2%	56.9%	43.1%
2	2008	246,572	72,815	WICKSON, RAYMOND J.	173,757	BOREN, DAN*		100,942 D	29.5%	70.5%	29.5%	70.5%
2	2006	168,208	45,861	MILLER, PATRICK	122,347	BOREN, DAN*		76,486 D	27.3%	72.7%	27.3%	72.7%
2	2004	272,542	92,963	SMALLEY, WAYLAND	179,579	BOREN, DAN		86,616 D	34.1%	65.9%	34.1%	65.9%
2	2002	197,982	51,234	PHAROAH, KENT	146,748	CARSON, BRAD*		95,514 D	25.9%	74.1%	25.9%	74.1%
3	2008	264,359	184,306	LUCAS, FRANK D.*	62,297	ROBBINS, FRANKIE	17,756	122,009 R	69.7%	23.6%	74.7%	25.3%
3	2006	189,791	128,042	LUCAS, FRANK D.*	61,749	BARTON, SUE		66,293 R	67.5%	32.5%	67.5%	32.5%
3	2004	262,131	215,510	LUCAS, FRANK D.*		—	46,621	215,510 R	82.2%		100.0%	
3	2002	196,090	148,206	LUCAS, FRANK D.*		—	47,884	148,206 R	75.6%		100.0%	
4	2008	272,781	180,080	COLE, TOM*	79,674	CUMMINGS, BLAKE	13,027	100,406 R	66.0%	29.2%	69.3%	30.7%
4	2006	183,041	118,266	COLE, TOM*	64,775	SPAKE, HAL		53,491 R	64.6%	35.4%	64.6%	35.4%
4	2004	255,854	198,985	COLE, TOM*		—	56,869	198,985 R	77.8%		100.0%	
4	2002	197,774	106,452	COLE, TOM	91,322	ROBERTS, DARRYL		15,130 R	53.8%	46.2%	53.8%	46.2%
5	2008	260,921	171,925	FALLIN, MARY*	88,996	PERRY, STEVEN L.		82,929 R	65.9%	34.1%	65.9%	34.1%
5	2006	180,425	108,936	FALLIN, MARY	67,293	HUNTER, DAVID	4,196	41,643 R	60.4%	37.3%	61.8%	38.2%
5	2004	273,149	180,430	ISTOOK, ERNEST*	92,719	SMITH, BERT		87,711 R	66.1%	33.9%	66.1%	33.9%
5	2002	195,051	121,374	ISTOOK, ERNEST*	63,208	BARLOW, LOU	10,469	58,166 R	62.2%	32.4%	65.8%	34.2%
TOTAL	2008	1,336,927	802,530		503,614		30,783	298,916 R	60.0%	37.7%	61.4%	38.6%
TOTAL	2006	905,194	518,025		372,888		14,281	145,137 R	57.2%	41.2%	58.1%	41.9%
TOTAL	2004	1,374,610	875,033		389,029		110,548	486,004 R	63.7%	28.3%	69.2%	30.8%
TOTAL	2002	1,001,852	546,832		391,927		63,093	154,905 R	54.6%	39.1%	58.3%	41.7%

Note: An asterisk (*) denotes incumbent.

OKLAHOMA

GENERAL AND PRIMARY ELECTIONS

2008 GENERAL ELECTIONS

President

Senator   Other vote was 55,708 Independent (Stephen P. Wallace).

House   Other vote was:

CD 1
CD 2
CD 3   17,756 Independent (Forrest Michael).
CD 4   13,027 Independent (David E. Joyce).
CD 5

2008 PRIMARY ELECTIONS

Primary	February 5, 2008 (President)	**Registration**	Democratic	1,012,594
	July 29, 2008 (Congress)	(as of January 15, 2008)	Republican	790,713
Primary Runoff	August 26, 2008		Independent	219,230
			TOTAL	2,022,537

Primary Type   Closed—Only registered Democrats and Republicans could vote in their party's primary.

OKLAHOMA

GENERAL AND PRIMARY ELECTIONS

	REPUBLICAN PRIMARIES			DEMOCRATIC PRIMARIES		
President	John McCain	122,772	36.6%	Hillary Clinton	228,480	54.8%
	Mike Huckabee	111,899	33.4%	Barack Obama	130,130	31.2%
	Mitt Romney	83,030	24.8%	John Edwards	42,725	10.2%
	Ron Paul	11,183	3.3%	Bill Richardson	7,078	1.7%
	Rudolph Giuliani	2,412	0.7%	Jim Rogers	3,905	0.9%
	Fred Thompson	1,924	0.6%	Christopher J. Dodd	2,511	0.6%
	Alan Keyes	817	0.2%	Dennis J. Kucinich	2,378	0.6%
	Jerry R. Curry	387	0.1%			
	Duncan Hunter	317	0.1%			
	Tom Tancredo	189	0.1%			
	Daniel Gilbert	124				
	TOTAL	*335,054*		*TOTAL*	*417,207*	
Senator	James M. Inhofe*	116,371	84.2%	Andrew Rice	113,795	59.6%
	Evelyn L. Rogers	10,770	7.8%	Jim Rogers	76,981	40.4%
	Ted Ryals	7,306	5.3%			
	Dennis Lopez	3,800	2.7%			
	TOTAL	*138,247*		*TOTAL*	*190,776*	
Congressional District 1	John Sullivan*	33,563	91.7%	Georgianna W. Oliver	11,116	55.7%
	Fran Mo-Ghaddam	3,025	8.3%	Mark Manley	8,842	44.3%
	TOTAL	*36,588*		*TOTAL*	*19,958*	
Congressional District 2	Raymond J. Wickson	Unopposed		Dan Boren*	66,041	85.2%
				Kevin Coleman	11,438	14.8%
				TOTAL	*77,479*	
Congressional District 3	Frank D. Lucas*	Unopposed		Frankie Robbins	Unopposed	
Congressional District 4	Tom Cole*	Unopposed		Blake Cummings	Unopposed	
Congressional District 5	Mary Fallin*	Unopposed		Steven L. Perry	12,902	58.9%
				Bert Smith	9,003	41.1%
				TOTAL	*21,905*	

Notes: An asterisk (*) denotes incumbent. The names of unopposed candidates did not appear on the primary ballot; therefore, no votes were cast for these candidates. A runoff was triggered if the leading candidate received less than 50 percent of the primary vote. No runoffs for Congress were required in 2008.

OREGON

Congressional districts first established for elections held in 2002
5 members

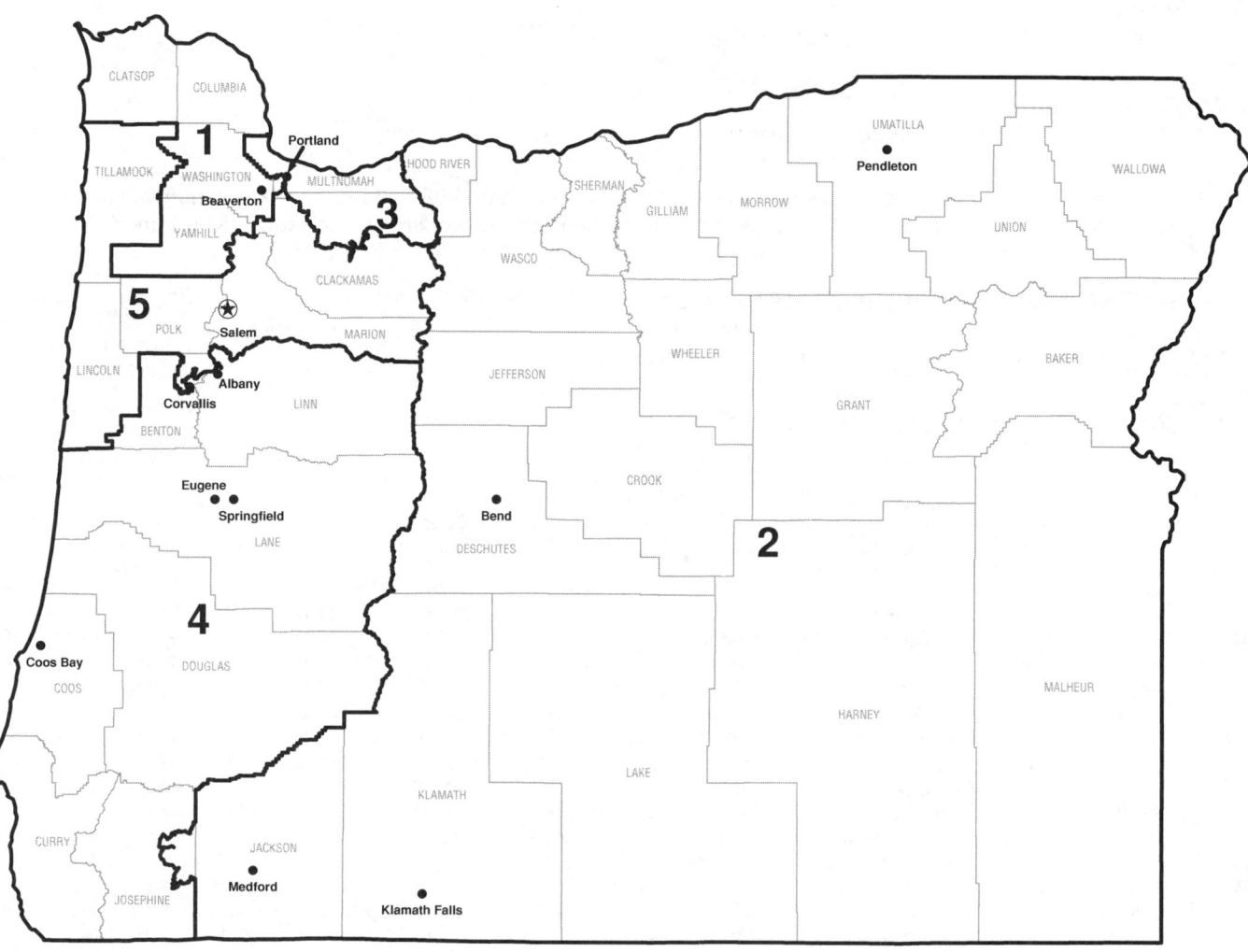

OREGON

GOVERNOR
Theodore R. Kulongoski (D). Reelected 2006 to a four-year term. Previously elected 2002.

SENATORS (2 Democrats)
Jeff Merkley (D). Elected 2008 to a six-year term.

Ron Wyden (D). Reelected 2004 to a six-year term. Previously elected 1998 and in a special election January 30, 1996, to serve the remaining three years of the term vacated when Senator Robert W. Packwood (R) resigned.

REPRESENTATIVES (4 Democrats, 1 Republican)
1. David Wu (D)
2. Greg Walden (R)
3. Earl Blumenauer (D)
4. Peter A. DeFazio (D)
5. Kurt Schrader (D)

POSTWAR VOTE FOR PRESIDENT

		Republican		Democratic				Total Vote		Major Vote	
Year	Total Vote	Vote	Candidate	Vote	Candidate	Other Vote	Plurality	Rep.	Dem.	Rep.	Dem.
2008	1,827,864	738,475	McCain, John	1,037,291	Obama, Barack	52,098	298,816 D	40.4%	56.7%	41.6%	58.4%
2004	1,836,782	866,831	Bush, George W.	943,163	Kerry, John	26,788	76,332 D	47.2%	51.3%	47.9%	52.1%
2000**	1,533,968	713,577	Bush, George W.	720,342	Gore, Al	100,049	6,765 D	46.5%	47.0%	49.8%	50.2%
1996**	1,377,760	538,152	Dole, Bob	649,641	Clinton, Bill	189,967	111,489 D	39.1%	47.2%	45.3%	54.7%
1992**	1,462,643	475,757	Bush, George	621,314	Clinton, Bill	365,572	145,557 D	32.5%	42.5%	43.4%	56.6%
1988	1,201,694	560,126	Bush, George	616,206	Dukakis, Michael S.	25,362	56,080 D	46.6%	51.3%	47.6%	52.4%
1984	1,226,527	685,700	Reagan, Ronald	536,479	Mondale, Walter F.	4,348	149,221 R	55.9%	43.7%	56.1%	43.9%
1980**	1,181,516	571,044	Reagan, Ronald	456,890	Carter, Jimmy	153,582	114,154 R	48.3%	38.7%	55.6%	44.4%
1976	1,029,876	492,120	Ford, Gerald R.	490,407	Carter, Jimmy	47,349	1,713 R	47.8%	47.6%	50.1%	49.9%
1972	927,946	486,686	Nixon, Richard M.	392,760	McGovern, George S.	48,500	93,926 R	52.4%	42.3%	55.3%	44.7%
1968**	819,622	408,433	Nixon, Richard M.	358,866	Humphrey, Hubert H.	52,323	49,567 R	49.8%	43.8%	53.2%	46.8%
1964	786,305	282,779	Goldwater, Barry M.	501,017	Johnson, Lyndon B.	2,509	218,238 D	36.0%	63.7%	36.1%	63.9%
1960	776,421	408,060	Nixon, Richard M.	367,402	Kennedy, John F.	959	40,658 R	52.6%	47.3%	52.6%	47.4%
1956	736,132	406,393	Eisenhower, Dwight D.	329,204	Stevenson, Adlai E.	535	77,189 R	55.2%	44.7%	55.2%	44.8%
1952	695,059	420,815	Eisenhower, Dwight D.	270,579	Stevenson, Adlai E.	3,665	150,236 R	60.5%	38.9%	60.9%	39.1%
1948	524,080	260,904	Dewey, Thomas E.	243,147	Truman, Harry S.	20,029	17,757 R	49.8%	46.4%	51.8%	48.2%

**In past elections, the other vote included: 2000 - 77,357 Green (Ralph Nader); 1996 - 121,221 Reform (Ross Perot); 1992 - 354,091 Independent (Perot); 1980 - 112,389 Independent (John Anderson); 1968 - 49,683 American Independent (George Wallace).

OREGON

POSTWAR VOTE FOR GOVERNOR

Year	Total Vote	Republican Vote	Republican Candidate	Democratic Vote	Democratic Candidate	Other Vote	Rep.-Dem. Plurality	Total Vote Rep.	Total Vote Dem.	Major Vote Rep.	Major Vote Dem.
2006	1,379,475	589,748	Saxton, Ron	699,786	Kulongoski, Theodore R.	89,941	110,038 D	42.8%	50.7%	45.7%	54.3%
2002	1,260,497	581,785	Mannix, Kevin L.	618,004	Kulongoski, Theodore R.	60,708	36,219 D	46.2%	49.0%	48.5%	51.5%
1998	1,113,098	334,001	Sizemore, Bill	717,061	Kitzhaber, John	62,036	383,060 D	30.0%	64.4%	31.8%	68.2%
1994	1,221,010	517,874	Smith, Denny	622,083	Kitzhaber, John	81,053	104,209 D	42.4%	50.9%	45.4%	54.6%
1990**	1,112,847	444,646	Frohnmayer, Dave	508,749	Roberts, Barbara	159,452	64,103 D	40.0%	45.7%	46.6%	53.4%
1986	1,059,630	506,986	Paulus, Norma	549,456	Goldschmidt, Neil	3,188	42,470 D	47.8%	51.9%	48.0%	52.0%
1982	1,042,009	639,841	Atiyeh, Victor	374,316	Kulongoski, Theodore R.	27,852	265,525 R	61.4%	35.9%	63.1%	36.9%
1978	911,143	498,452	Atiyeh, Victor	409,411	Straub, Robert W.	3,280	89,041 R	54.7%	44.9%	54.9%	45.1%
1974	770,574	324,751	Atiyeh, Victor	444,812	Straub, Robert W.	1,011	120,061 D	42.1%	57.7%	42.2%	57.8%
1970	666,394	369,964	McCall, Tom	293,892	Straub, Robert W.	2,538	76,072 R	55.5%	44.1%	55.7%	44.3%
1966	682,862	377,346	McCall, Tom	305,008	Straub, Robert W.	508	72,338 R	55.3%	44.7%	55.3%	44.7%
1962	637,407	345,497	Hatfield, Mark	265,359	Thornton, Robert Y.	26,551	80,138 R	54.2%	41.6%	56.6%	43.4%
1958	599,994	331,900	Hatfield, Mark	267,934	Holmes, Robert D.	160	63,966 R	55.3%	44.7%	55.3%	44.7%
1956S	731,279	361,840	Smith, Elmo E.	369,439	Holmes, Robert D.		7,599 D	49.5%	50.5%	49.5%	50.5%
1954	566,701	322,522	Patterson, Paul	244,179	Carson, Joseph K.		78,343 R	56.9%	43.1%	56.9%	43.1%
1950	505,910	334,160	McKay, Douglas	171,750	Flegel, Austin F.		162,410 R	66.1%	33.9%	66.1%	33.9%
1948S	509,633	271,295	McKay, Douglas	226,958	Wallace, Lew	11,380	44,337 R	53.2%	44.5%	54.4%	45.6%
1946	344,155	237,681	Snell, Earl	106,474	Donaugh, Carl C.		131,207 R	69.1%	30.9%	69.1%	30.9%

Notes: **In past elections, the other vote included: 1990 - 144,062 Independent (Al Mobley). The 1948 and 1956 elections were for short terms to fill vacancies.

POSTWAR VOTE FOR SENATOR

Year	Total Vote	Republican Vote	Republican Candidate	Democratic Vote	Democratic Candidate	Other Vote	Rep.-Dem. Plurality	Total Vote Rep.	Total Vote Dem.	Major Vote Rep.	Major Vote Dem.
2008	1,767,504	805,159	Smith, Gordon H.	864,392	Merkley, Jeff	97,953	59,233 D	45.6%	48.9%	48.2%	51.8%
2004	1,780,550	565,254	King, Al	1,128,728	Wyden, Ron	86,568	563,474 D	31.7%	63.4%	33.4%	66.6%
2002	1,267,221	712,287	Smith, Gordon H.	501,898	Bradbury, Bill	53,036	210,389 R	56.2%	39.6%	58.7%	41.3%
1998	1,117,747	377,739	Lim, John	682,425	Wyden, Ron	57,583	304,686 D	33.8%	61.1%	35.6%	64.4%
1996	1,360,230	677,336	Smith, Gordon H.	624,370	Bruggere, Tom	58,524	52,966 R	49.8%	45.9%	52.0%	48.0%
1996S	1,196,608	553,519	Smith, Gordon H.	571,739	Wyden, Ron	71,350	18,220 D	46.3%	47.8%	49.2%	50.8%
1992	1,376,033	717,455	Packwood, Robert W.	639,851	AuCoin, Les	18,727	77,604 R	52.1%	46.5%	52.9%	47.1%
1990	1,099,255	590,095	Hatfield, Mark	507,743	Lonsdale, Harry	1,417	82,352 R	53.7%	46.2%	53.8%	46.2%
1986	1,042,555	656,317	Packwood, Robert W.	375,735	Bauman, Rick	10,503	280,582 R	63.0%	36.0%	63.6%	36.4%
1984	1,214,735	808,152	Hatfield, Mark	406,122	Hendriksen, Margie	461	402,030 R	66.5%	33.4%	66.6%	33.4%
1980	1,140,494	594,290	Packwood, Robert W.	501,963	Kulongoski, Theodore R.	44,241	92,327 R	52.1%	44.0%	54.2%	45.8%
1978	892,518	550,165	Hatfield, Mark	341,616	Cook, Vernon	737	208,549 R	61.6%	38.3%	61.7%	38.3%
1974	766,414	420,984	Packwood, Robert W.	338,591	Roberts, Betty	6,839	82,393 R	54.9%	44.2%	55.4%	44.6%
1972	920,833	494,671	Hatfield, Mark	425,036	Morse, Wayne L.	1,126	69,635 R	53.7%	46.2%	53.8%	46.2%
1968	814,176	408,646	Packwood, Robert W.	405,353	Morse, Wayne L.	177	3,293 R	50.2%	49.8%	50.2%	49.8%
1966	685,067	354,391	Hatfield, Mark	330,374	Duncan, Robert B.	302	24,017 R	51.7%	48.2%	51.8%	48.2%
1962	636,558	291,587	Unander, Sig	344,716	Morse, Wayne L.	255	53,129 D	45.8%	54.2%	45.8%	54.2%
1960	755,875	343,009	Smith, Elmo E.	412,757	Neuberger, Maurine	109	69,748 D	45.4%	54.6%	45.4%	54.6%
1956	732,254	335,405	McKay, Douglas	396,849	Morse, Wayne L.		61,444 D	45.8%	54.2%	45.8%	54.2%
1954	569,088	283,313	Cordon, Guy	285,775	Neuberger, Richard L.		2,462 D	49.8%	50.2%	49.8%	50.2%
1950	503,455	376,510	Morse, Wayne L.	116,780	Latourette, Howard	10,165	259,730 R	74.8%	23.2%	76.3%	23.7%
1948	498,570	299,295	Cordon, Guy	199,275	Wilson, Manley J.		100,020 R	60.0%	40.0%	60.0%	40.0%

Note: The January 1996 election was for a short term to fill a vacancy.

OREGON

PRESIDENT 2008

2000 Census Population	County	Total Vote	Republican	Democratic	Other	Rep.-Dem. Plurality		Percentage			
								Total Vote		Major Vote	
								Rep.	Dem.	Rep.	Dem.
16,741	BAKER	8,777	5,650	2,805	322	2,845	R	64.4%	32.0%	66.8%	33.2%
78,153	BENTON	46,478	15,264	29,901	1,313	14,637	D	32.8%	64.3%	33.8%	66.2%
338,391	CLACKAMAS	191,878	83,595	103,476	4,807	19,881	D	43.6%	53.9%	44.7%	55.3%
35,630	CLATSOP	18,548	7,192	10,701	655	3,509	D	38.8%	57.7%	40.2%	59.8%
43,560	COLUMBIA	24,768	10,413	13,390	965	2,977	D	42.0%	54.1%	43.7%	56.3%
62,779	COOS	30,951	15,354	14,401	1,196	953	R	49.6%	46.5%	51.6%	48.4%
19,182	CROOK	10,352	6,371	3,632	349	2,739	R	61.5%	35.1%	63.7%	36.3%
21,137	CURRY	12,332	6,646	5,230	456	1,416	R	53.9%	42.4%	56.0%	44.0%
115,367	DESCHUTES	79,782	39,064	38,819	1,899	245	R	49.0%	48.7%	50.2%	49.8%
100,399	DOUGLAS	52,937	30,919	20,298	1,720	10,621	R	58.4%	38.3%	60.4%	39.6%
1,915	GILLIAM	1,110	648	430	32	218	R	58.4%	38.7%	60.1%	39.9%
7,935	GRANT	3,909	2,785	1,006	118	1,779	R	71.2%	25.7%	73.5%	26.5%
7,609	HARNEY	3,683	2,595	950	138	1,645	R	70.5%	25.8%	73.2%	26.8%
20,411	HOOD RIVER	9,830	3,265	6,302	263	3,037	D	33.2%	64.1%	34.1%	65.9%
181,269	JACKSON	101,047	49,043	49,090	2,914	47	D	48.5%	48.6%	50.0%	50.0%
19,009	JEFFERSON	8,318	4,402	3,682	234	720	R	52.9%	44.3%	54.5%	45.5%
75,726	JOSEPHINE	42,049	22,973	17,412	1,664	5,561	R	54.6%	41.4%	56.9%	43.1%
63,775	KLAMATH	29,399	19,113	9,370	916	9,743	R	65.0%	31.9%	67.1%	32.9%
7,422	LAKE	3,688	2,638	957	93	1,681	R	71.5%	25.9%	73.4%	26.6%
322,959	LANE	182,910	63,835	114,037	5,038	50,202	D	34.9%	62.3%	35.9%	64.1%
44,479	LINCOLN	23,889	8,791	14,258	840	5,467	D	36.8%	59.7%	38.1%	61.9%
103,069	LINN	51,982	28,071	22,163	1,748	5,908	R	54.0%	42.6%	55.9%	44.1%
31,615	MALHEUR	10,433	7,157	2,949	327	4,208	R	68.6%	28.3%	70.8%	29.2%
284,834	MARION	124,563	59,059	61,816	3,688	2,757	D	47.4%	49.6%	48.9%	51.1%
10,995	MORROW	4,058	2,509	1,410	139	1,099	R	61.8%	34.7%	64.0%	36.0%
660,486	MULTNOMAH	364,710	75,171	279,696	9,843	204,525	D	20.6%	76.7%	21.2%	78.8%
62,380	POLK	36,207	17,714	17,536	957	178	R	48.9%	48.4%	50.3%	49.7%
1,934	SHERMAN	1,047	634	385	28	249	R	60.6%	36.8%	62.2%	37.8%
24,262	TILLAMOOK	13,297	5,757	7,072	468	1,315	D	43.3%	53.2%	44.9%	55.1%
70,548	UMATILLA	25,523	15,254	9,484	785	5,770	R	59.8%	37.2%	61.7%	38.3%
24,530	UNION	12,594	7,581	4,613	400	2,968	R	60.2%	36.6%	62.2%	37.8%
7,226	WALLOWA	4,465	2,836	1,492	137	1,344	R	63.5%	33.4%	65.5%	34.5%
23,791	WASCO	11,380	5,103	5,906	371	803	D	44.8%	51.9%	46.4%	53.6%
445,342	WASHINGTON	236,632	89,185	141,544	5,903	52,359	D	37.7%	59.8%	38.7%	61.3%
1,547	WHEELER	812	498	281	33	217	R	61.3%	34.6%	63.9%	36.1%
84,992	YAMHILL	43,526	21,390	20,797	1,339	593	R	49.1%	47.8%	50.7%	49.3%
3,421,399	TOTAL	1,827,864	738,475	1,037,291	52,098	298,816	D	40.4%	56.7%	41.6%	58.4%

OREGON

SENATOR 2008

2000 Census Population	County	Total Vote	Republican	Democratic	Other	Rep.-Dem. Plurality	Percentage			
							Total Vote		Major Vote	
							Rep.	Dem.	Rep.	Dem.
16,741	BAKER	8,531	5,662	2,203	666	3,459 R	66.4%	25.8%	72.0%	28.0%
78,153	BENTON	44,574	17,933	24,911	1,730	6,978 D	40.2%	55.9%	41.9%	58.1%
338,391	CLACKAMAS	185,668	92,780	83,558	9,330	9,222 R	50.0%	45.0%	52.6%	47.4%
35,630	CLATSOP	17,848	7,939	8,795	1,114	856 D	44.5%	49.3%	47.4%	52.6%
43,560	COLUMBIA	24,031	10,679	11,166	2,186	487 D	44.4%	46.5%	48.9%	51.1%
62,779	COOS	29,845	14,838	12,621	2,386	2,217 R	49.7%	42.3%	54.0%	46.0%
19,182	CROOK	10,007	6,436	2,735	836	3,701 R	64.3%	27.3%	70.2%	29.8%
21,137	CURRY	11,957	6,679	4,410	868	2,269 R	55.9%	36.9%	60.2%	39.8%
115,367	DESCHUTES	76,442	41,108	31,024	4,310	10,084 R	53.8%	40.6%	57.0%	43.0%
100,399	DOUGLAS	51,112	29,969	17,387	3,756	12,582 R	58.6%	34.0%	53.3%	36.7%
1,915	GILLIAM	1,081	699	302	80	397 R	64.7%	27.9%	59.8%	30.2%
7,935	GRANT	3,806	2,821	748	237	2,073 R	74.1%	19.7%	79.0%	21.0%
7,609	HARNEY	3,576	2,574	755	247	1,819 R	72.0%	21.1%	77.3%	22.7%
20,411	HOOD RIVER	9,536	4,070	5,045	421	975 D	42.7%	52.9%	44.7%	55.3%
181,269	JACKSON	97,420	49,225	41,828	6,367	7,397 R	50.5%	42.9%	54.1%	45.9%
19,009	JEFFERSON	8,079	4,788	2,705	586	2,083 R	59.3%	33.5%	63.9%	36.1%
75,726	JOSEPHINE	40,477	22,790	14,153	3,534	8,637 R	56.3%	35.0%	61.7%	38.3%
63,775	KLAMATH	28,502	19,241	7,005	2,256	12,236 R	67.5%	24.6%	73.3%	26.7%
7,422	LAKE	3,606	2,697	668	241	2,029 R	74.8%	18.5%	80.1%	19.9%
322,959	LANE	178,409	66,936	103,631	7,842	36,695 D	37.5%	58.1%	39.2%	60.8%
44,479	LINCOLN	23,206	9,464	12,097	1,645	2,633 D	40.8%	52.1%	43.9%	56.1%
103,069	LINN	49,822	27,047	18,403	4,372	8,644 R	54.3%	36.9%	59.5%	40.5%
31,615	MALHEUR	10,047	7,355	2,218	474	5,137 R	73.2%	22.1%	76.8%	23.2%
284,834	MARION	120,986	62,560	49,626	8,800	12,934 R	51.7%	41.0%	55.8%	44.2%
10,995	MORROW	4,012	2,751	988	273	1,763 R	68.6%	24.6%	73.6%	26.4%
660,486	MULTNOMAH	352,162	95,950	242,518	13,694	146,568 D	27.2%	68.9%	28.3%	71.7%
62,380	POLK	34,966	18,718	13,906	2,342	4,812 R	53.5%	39.8%	57.4%	42.6%
1,934	SHERMAN	1,023	685	277	61	408 R	67.0%	27.1%	71.2%	28.8%
24,262	TILLAMOOK	12,918	6,516	5,540	862	976 R	50.4%	42.9%	54.0%	46.0%
70,548	UMATILLA	24,996	17,933	5,948	1,115	11,985 R	71.7%	23.8%	75.1%	24.9%
24,530	UNION	12,260	8,230	3,329	701	4,901 R	67.1%	27.2%	71.2%	28.8%
7,226	WALLOWA	4,348	3,226	940	182	2,286 R	74.2%	21.6%	77.4%	22.6%
23,791	WASCO	11,089	5,762	4,586	741	1,176 R	52.0%	41.4%	55.7%	44.3%
445,342	WASHINGTON	228,045	106,114	111,367	10,564	5,253 D	46.5%	48.8%	48.8%	51.2%
1,547	WHEELER	791	509	212	70	297 R	64.3%	26.8%	70.6%	29.4%
84,992	YAMHILL	42,326	22,475	16,787	3,064	5,688 R	53.1%	39.7%	57.2%	42.8%
3,421,399	TOTAL	1,767,504	805,159	864,392	97,953	59,233 D	45.6%	48.9%	48.2%	51.8%

OREGON

HOUSE OF REPRESENTATIVES

CD	Year	Total Vote	Republican Vote	Republican Candidate	Democratic Vote	Democratic Candidate	Other Vote	Rep.-Dem. Plurality	Total Vote Rep.	Total Vote Dem.	Major Vote Rep.	Major Vote Dem.
1	2008	332,248		—	237,567	WU, DAVID*	94,681	237,567 D		71.5%		100.0%
1	2006	269,627	90,904	KITTS, DERRICK	169,409	WU, DAVID*	9,314	78,505 D	33.7%	62.8%	34.9%	65.1%
1	2004	354,338	135,164	GOLI, AMERI	203,771	WU, DAVID*	15,403	68,607 D	38.1%	57.5%	39.9%	60.1%
1	2002	238,036	80,917	GREENFIELD, JIM	149,215	WU, DAVID*	7,904	68,298 D	34.0%	62.7%	35.2%	64.8%
2	2008	340,379	236,560	WALDEN, GREG*	87,649	LEMAS, NOAH	16,170	148,911 R	69.5%	25.8%	73.0%	27.0%
2	2006	271,719	181,529	WALDEN, GREG*	82,484	VOISON, CAROL	7,706	99,045 R	66.8%	30.4%	68.8%	31.2%
2	2004	346,865	248,461	WALDEN, GREG*	88,914	McCOLGAN, JOHN C.	9,490	159,547 R	71.6%	25.6%	73.6%	26.4%
2	2002	252,284	181,295	WALDEN, GREG*	64,991	BUCKLEY, PETER	5,998	116,304 R	71.9%	25.8%	73.6%	26.4%
3	2008	341,062	71,063	LOPEZ, DELIA	254,235	BLUMENAUER, EARL*	15,764	183,172 D	20.8%	74.5%	21.8%	78.2%
3	2006	253,610	59,529	BROUSSARD, BRUCE	186,380	BLUMENAUER, EARL*	7,701	126,851 D	23.5%	73.5%	24.2%	75.8%
3	2004	346,560	82,045	MARS, TAMI	245,559	BLUMENAUER, EARL*	18,956	163,514 D	23.7%	70.9%	25.0%	75.0%
3	2002	234,977	62,821	SEALE, SARAH	156,851	BLUMENAUER, EARL*	15,305	94,030 D	26.7%	66.8%	28.6%	71.4%
4	2008	334,146		—	275,143	DeFAZIO, PETER A.*	59,003	275,143 D		82.3%		100.0%
4	2006	290,244	109,105	FELDKAMP, JIM	180,607	DeFAZIO, PETER A.*	532	71,502 D	37.6%	62.2%	37.7%	62.3%
4	2004	374,909	140,882	FELDKAMP, JIM	228,611	DeFAZIO, PETER A.*	5,416	87,729 D	37.6%	61.0%	38.1%	61.9%
4	2002	263,481	90,523	VanLEEUWEN, LIZ	168,150	DeFAZIO, PETER A.*	4,808	77,627 D	34.4%	63.8%	35.0%	65.0%
5	2008	334,674	128,297	ERICKSON, MIKE	181,577	SCHRADER, KURT	24,800	53,280 D	38.3%	54.3%	41.4%	58.6%
5	2006	272,234	116,424	ERICKSON, MIKE	146,973	HOOLEY, DARLENE*	8,837	30,549 D	42.8%	54.0%	44.2%	55.8%
5	2004	349,634	154,993	ZUPANCIC, JIM	184,833	HOOLEY, DARLENE*	9,808	29,840 D	44.3%	52.9%	45.6%	54.4%
5	2002	251,537	113,441	BOQUIST, BRIAN J.	137,713	HOOLEY, DARLENE*	383	24,272 D	45.1%	54.7%	45.2%	54.8%
TOTAL	2008	1,682,509	435,920		1,036,171		210,418	600,251 D	25.9%	61.6%	29.6%	70.4%
TOTAL	2006	1,357,434	557,491		765,853		34,090	208,362 D	41.1%	56.4%	42.1%	57.9%
TOTAL	2004	1,772,306	761,545		951,688		59,073	190,143 D	43.0%	53.7%	44.5%	55.5%
TOTAL	2002	1,240,315	528,997		676,920		34,398	147,923 D	42.7%	54.6%	43.9%	56.1%

Note: An asterisk (*) denotes incumbent.

OREGON

GENERAL AND PRIMARY ELECTIONS

2008 GENERAL ELECTIONS

President   Other vote was 18,614 Peace (Ralph Nader); 7,693 Constitution (Chuck Baldwin); 7,635 Libertarian (Bob Barr); 4,543 Pacific Green (Cynthia A. McKinney); 13,613 scattered write-in.

Senator   Other vote was 92,565 Constitution (Dave Brownlow); 5,388 scattered write-in.

House   Other vote was:

CD 1   58,279 Independent Party (Joel Haugen); 14,172 Constitution (Scott Semrau); 10,992 Libertarian (H. Joe Tabor); 7,128 Pacific Green (Chris Henry); 4,110 scattered write-in.

CD 2   9,668 Pacific Green (Tristin Mock); 5,817 Constitution (Richard D. Hake); 685 scattered write-in.

CD 3   15,063 Pacific Green (Michael Meo); 701 scattered write-in.

CD 4   43,133 Constitution (Jaynee Germond); 13,162 Pacific Green (Mike Beilstein); 2,708 scattered write-in.

CD 5   6,830 Independent Party (Sean Bates); 6,558 Constitution (Douglas Patterson); 5,272 Pacific Green (Alex Polikoff); 4,814 Libertarian (Steve Milligan); 1,326 scattered write-in.

2008 PRIMARY ELECTIONS

Primary   May 20, 2008

Registration (as of May 20, 2008)		
Democratic	861,998
Republican	669,636
Others	72,399
Non-Affiliated	404,924
TOTAL	*2,008,957*

Primary Type   Closed—Only registered Democrats and Republicans could vote in their party's primary.

OREGON

GENERAL AND PRIMARY ELECTIONS

	REPUBLICAN PRIMARIES			DEMOCRATIC PRIMARIES		
President	John McCain	285,881	80.9%	Barack Obama	375,385	58.5%
	Ron Paul	51,100	14.5%	Hillary Clinton	259,825	40.5%
	Scattered write-in	16,495	4.7%	Scattered write-in	6,289	1.0%
	TOTAL	*353,476*		*TOTAL*	*641,499*	
Senator	Gordon H. Smith*	296,330	85.4%	Jeff Merkley	246,482	44.8%
	Gordon Leitch	48,560	14.0%	Steve Novick	230,889	42.0%
	Scattered write-in	2,068	0.6%	Candy Neville	38,367	7.0%
				Roger S. Obrist	12,647	2.3%
				Pavel Goberman	12,056	2.2%
				David Loera	6,127	1.1%
				Scattered write-in	3,398	0.6%
	TOTAL	*346,958*		*TOTAL*	*549,966*	
Congressional District 1	Joel Haugen	29,658	69.0%	David Wu*	91,466	77.9%
	Claude William Chappell IV	12,525	29.1%	Will Hobbs	19,659	16.7%
	Scattered write-in	829	1.9%	Mark Welyczko	5,982	5.1%
				Scattered write-in	285	0.2%
	TOTAL	*43,012*		*TOTAL*	*117,392*	
	Joel Haugen subsequently withdrew as the Republican nominee in order to run in the general election as the candidate of the Independent Party.					
Congressional District 2	Greg Walden*	83,087	99.1%	Noah Lemas	56,980	97.9%
	Scattered write-in	721	0.9%	Scattered write-in	1,247	2.1%
	TOTAL	*83,808*		*TOTAL*	*58,227*	
Congressional District 3	Delia Lopez	22,114	96.9%	Earl Blumenauer*	121,176	86.7%
	Scattered write-in	712	3.1%	John Sweeney	9,389	6.7%
				Joseph Walsh (Lone Vet)	8,783	6.3%
				Scattered write-in	343	0.2%
	TOTAL	*22,826*		*TOTAL*	*139,691*	
Congressional District 4	*No Republican candidate filed for the primary. Democratic Rep. Peter A. DeFazio received 906 write-in votes. There were also 2,345 scattered write-in votes cast in the GOP primary.*			Peter A. DeFazio*	119,366	99.2%
				Scattered write-in	955	0.8%
				TOTAL	*120,321*	
Congressional District 5	Mike Erickson	37,217	47.9%	Kurt Schrader	51,980	53.8%
	Kevin Mannix	36,005	46.4%	Nancy Moran	18,597	19.3%
	Richard "RJ" Wilson	4,110	5.3%	Steve Marks	17,643	18.3%
	Scattered write-in	302	0.4%	Andrew Foster	6,104	6.3%
				Richard Nathe	1,748	1.8%
				Scattered write-in	482	0.5%
	TOTAL	*77,634*		*TOTAL*	*96,554*	

Notes: An asterisk (*) denotes incumbent. The primary and general elections were conducted entirely by mail.

PENNSYLVANIA

Congressional districts first established for elections held in 2004
19 members

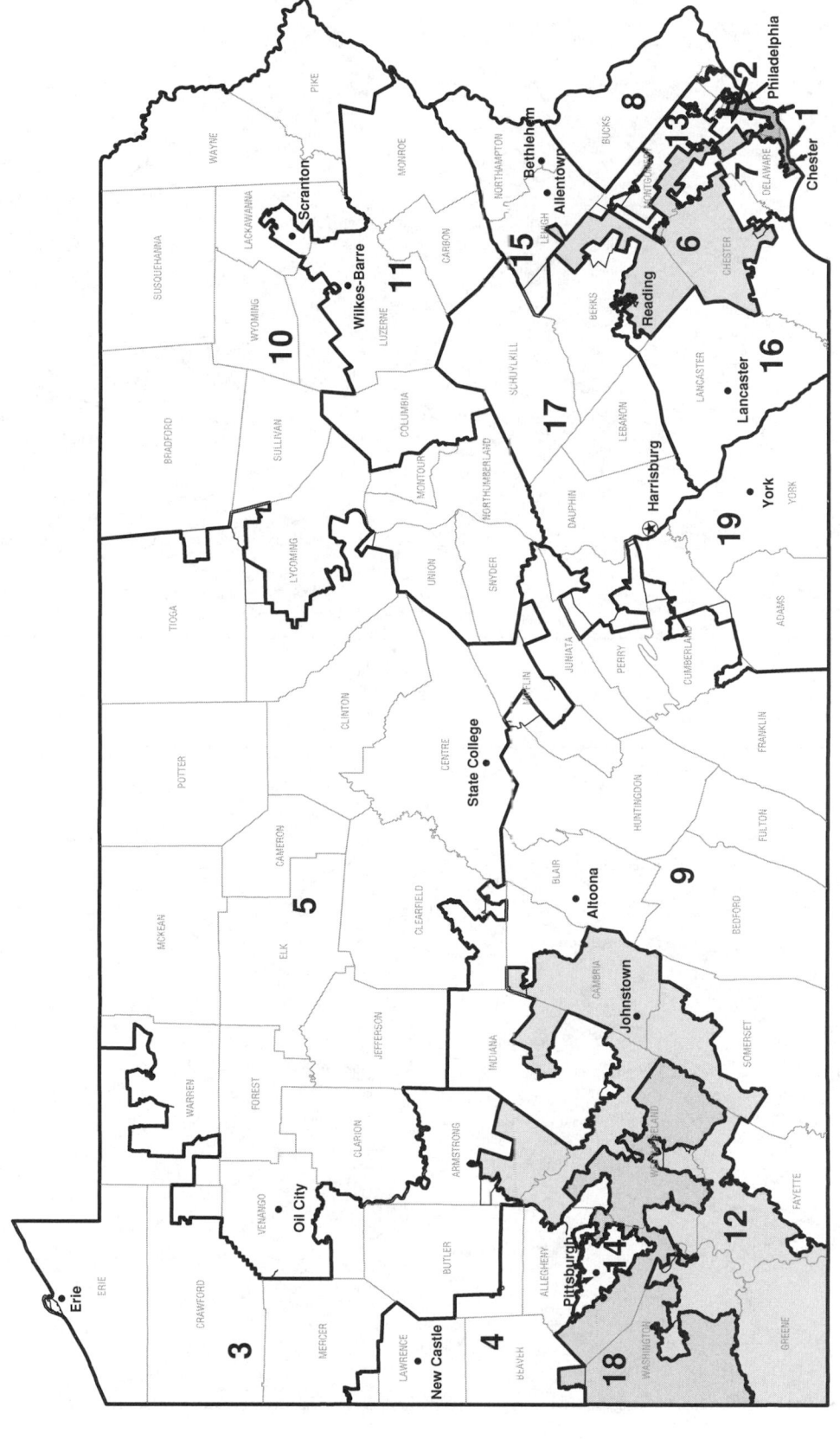

PENNSYLVANIA

Philadelphia Area

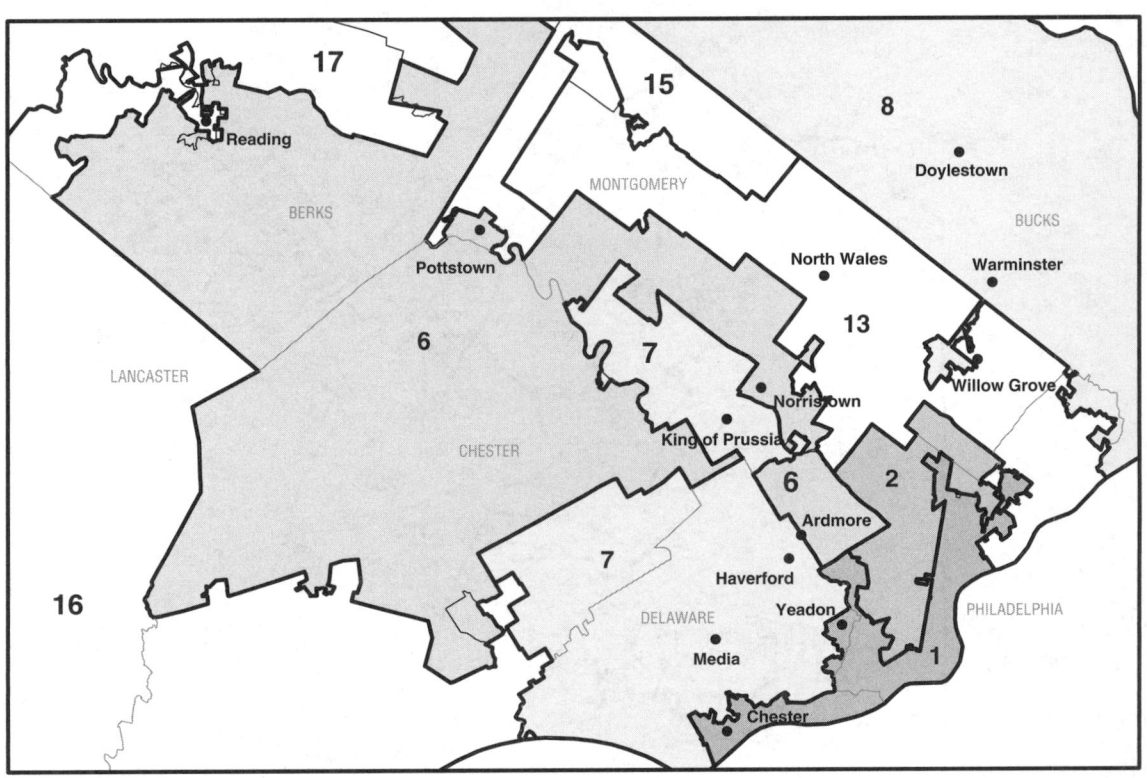

Pittsburgh Area

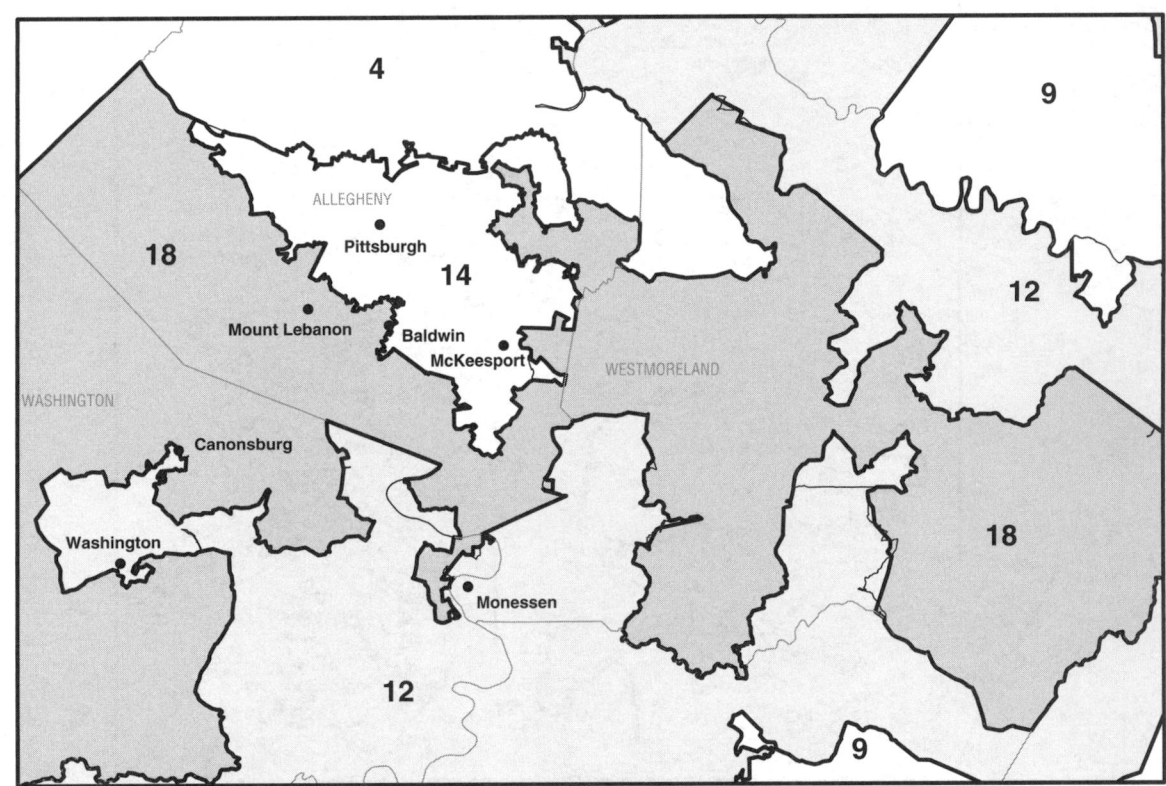

PENNSYLVANIA

GOVERNOR
Edward G. Rendell (D). Reelected 2006 to a four-year term. Previously elected 2002.

SENATORS (2 Democrats)
Bob Casey Jr. (D). Elected 2006 to a six-year term.

Arlen Specter (D). Reelected 2004 to a six-year term. Previously e ected 1998, 1992, 1986, 1980. Announced switch in party affiliation from Republican to Democrat April 28, 2008, which became effective April 30, 2008.

REPRESENTATIVES (12 Democrats, 7 Republicans)
1. Robert A. Brady (D)
2. Chaka Fattah (D)
3. Kathleen A. Dahlkemper (D)
4. Jason Altmire (D)
5. Glenn Thompson (R)
6. Jim Gerlach (R)
7. Joe Sestak (D)
8. Patrick J. Murphy (D)
9. Bill Shuster (R)
10. Christopher P. Carney (D)
11. Paul E. Kanjorski (D)
12. John P. Murtha (D)
13. Allyson Y. Schwartz (D)
14. Mike Doyle (D)
15. Charlie Dent (R)
16. Joe Pitts (R)
17. Tim Holden (D)
18. Tim Murphy (R)
19. Todd R. Platts (R)

POSTWAR VOTE FOR PRESIDENT

Year	Total Vote	Republican Vote	Republican Candidate	Democratic Vote	Democratic Candidate	Other Vote	Plurality	Total Vote Rep.	Total Vote Dem.	Major Vote Rep.	Major Vote Dem.
2008	6,013,272	2,655,885	McCain, John	3,276,363	Obama, Barack	81,024	620,478 D	44.2%	54.5%	44.8%	55.2%
2004	5,769,590	2,793,847	Bush, George W.	2,938,095	Kerry, John	37,648	144,248 D	48.4%	50.9%	48.7%	51.3%
2000**	4,913,119	2,281,127	Bush, George W.	2,485,967	Gore, Al	146,025	204,840 D	46.4%	50.6%	47.9%	52.1%
1996**	4,506,118	1,801,169	Dole, Bob	2,215,819	Clinton, Bill	489,130	414,650 D	40.0%	49.2%	44.8%	55.2%
1992**	4,959,810	1,791,841	Bush, George	2,239,164	Clinton, Bill	928,805	447,323 D	36.1%	45.1%	44.5%	55.5%
1988	4,536,251	2,300,087	Bush, George	2,194,944	Dukakis, Michael S.	41,220	105,143 R	50.7%	48.4%	51.2%	48.8%
1984	4,844,903	2,584,323	Reagan, Ronald	2,228,131	Mondale, Walter F.	32,449	356,192 R	53.3%	46.0%	53.7%	46.3%
1980**	4,561,501	2,261,872	Reagan, Ronald	1,937,540	Carter, Jimmy	362,089	324,332 R	49.6%	42.5%	53.9%	46.1%
1976	4,620,787	2,205,604	Ford, Gerald R.	2,328,677	Carter, Jimmy	86,506	123,073 D	47.7%	50.4%	48.6%	51.4%
1972	4,592,106	2,714,521	Nixon, Richard M.	1,796,951	McGovern, George S.	80,634	917,570 R	59.1%	39.1%	60.2%	39.8%
1968**	4,747,928	2,090,017	Nixon, Richard M.	2,259,405	Humphrey, Hubert H.	398,506	169,388 D	44.0%	47.6%	48.1%	51.9%
1964	4,822,690	1,673,657	Goldwater, Barry M.	3,130,954	Johnson, Lyndon B.	18,079	1,457,297 D	34.7%	64.9%	34.8%	65.2%
1960	5,006,541	2,439,956	Nixon, Richard M.	2,556,282	Kennedy, John F.	10,303	116,326 D	48.7%	51.1%	48.8%	51.2%
1956	4,576,503	2,585,252	Eisenhower, Dwight D.	1,981,769	Stevenson, Adlai E.	9,482	603,483 R	56.5%	43.3%	56.6%	43.4%
1952	4,580,969	2,415,789	Eisenhower, Dwight D.	2,146,269	Stevenson, Adlai E.	18,911	269,520 R	52.7%	46.9%	53.0%	47.0%
1948	3,735,348	1,902,197	Dewey, Thomas E.	1,752,426	Truman, Harry S.	80,725	149,771 R	50.9%	46.9%	52.0%	48.0%

**In past elections, the other vote included: 2000 - 103,392 Green (Ralph Nader); 1996 - 430,984 Reform (Ross Perot); 1992 - 902,667 Independent (Perot); 1980 - 292,921 Independent (John Anderson); 1968 - 378,582 American Independent (George Wallace).

PENNSYLVANIA

POSTWAR VOTE FOR GOVERNOR

Year	Total Vote	Republican Vote	Republican Candidate	Democratic Vote	Democratic Candidate	Other Vote	Rep.-Dem. Plurality	Total Vote Rep.	Total Vote Dem.	Major Vote Rep.	Major Vote Dem.
2006	4,096,077	1,622,135	Swann, Lynn	2,470,517	Rendell, Edward G.	3,425	848,382 D	39.6%	60.3%	39.6%	60.4%
2002	3,583,179	1,589,408	Fisher, Mike	1,913,235	Rendell, Edward G.	80,536	323,827 D	44.4%	53.4%	45.4%	54.6%
1998**	3,025,152	1,736,844	Ridge, Thomas J.	938,745	Itkin, Ivan	349,563	798,099 R	57.4%	31.0%	64.9%	35.1%
1994**	3,585,526	1,627,976	Ridge, Thomas J.	1,430,099	Singel, Mark S.	527,451	197,877 R	45.4%	39.9%	53.2%	46.8%
1990	3,052,760	987,516	Hafer, Barbara	2,065,244	Casey, Robert		1,077,728 D	32.3%	67.7%	32.3%	67.7%
1986	3,388,275	1,638,268	Scranton, William W., III	1,717,484	Casey, Robert	32,523	79,216 D	48.4%	50.7%	48.8%	51.2%
1982	3,683,985	1,872,784	Thornburgh, Richard L.	1,772,353	Ertel, Allen E.	38,848	100,431 R	50.8%	48.1%	51.4%	48.6%
1978	3,741,969	1,966,042	Thornburgh, Richard L.	1,737,888	Flaherty, Peter	38,039	228,154 R	52.5%	46.4%	53.1%	46.9%
1974	3,491,234	1,578,917	Lewis, Andrew L.	1,878,252	Shapp, Milton	34,065	299,335 D	45.2%	53.8%	45.7%	54.3%
1970	3,700,060	1,542,854	Broderick, Raymond	2,043,029	Shapp, Milton	114,177	500,175 D	41.7%	55.2%	43.0%	57.0%
1966	4,050,668	2,110,349	Shafer, Raymond P.	1,868,719	Shapp, Milton	71,600	241,630 R	52.1%	46.1%	53.0%	47.0%
1962	4,378,042	2,424,918	Scranton, William W.	1,938,627	Dilworth, Richardson	14,497	486,291 R	55.4%	44.3%	55.6%	44.4%
1958	3,986,918	1,948,769	McGonigle, A. T.	2,024,852	Lawrence, David	13,297	76,083 D	48.9%	50.8%	49.0%	51.0%
1954	3,720,457	1,717,070	Wood, Lloyd H.	1,996,266	Leader, George M.	7,121	279,196 D	46.2%	53.7%	46.2%	53.8%
1950	3,540,059	1,796,119	Fine, John S.	1,710,355	Dilworth, Richardson	33,585	85,764 R	50.7%	48.3%	51.2%	48.8%
1946	3,123,994	1,828,462	Duff, James H.	1,270,947	Rice, John S.	24,585	557,515 R	58.5%	40.7%	59.0%	41.0%

**In past elections, the other vote included: 1998 - 315,761 Constitutional (Peg Luksik); 1994 - 460,269 Constitutional (Luksik).

POSTWAR VOTE FOR SENATOR

Year	Total Vote	Republican Vote	Republican Candidate	Democratic Vote	Democratic Candidate	Other Vote	Rep.-Dem. Plurality	Total Vote Rep.	Total Vote Dem.	Major Vote Rep.	Major Vote Dem.
2006	4,081,043	1,684,778	Santorum, Rick	2,392,984	Casey, Bob Jr.	3,281	708,206 D	41.3%	58.6%	41.3%	58.7%
2004	5,559,105	2,925,080	Specter, Arlen	2,334,126	Hoeffel, Joseph M.	299,899	590,954 R	52.6%	42.0%	55.6%	44.4%
2000	4,735,504	2,481,962	Santorum, Rick	2,154,908	Klink, Ron	98,634	327,054 R	52.4%	45.5%	53.5%	46.5%
1998	2,957,772	1,814,180	Specter, Arlen	1,028,839	Lloyd, Bill	114,753	785,341 R	61.3%	34.8%	63.8%	36.2%
1994	3,513,361	1,735,691	Santorum, Rick	1,648,481	Wofford, Harris	129,189	87,210 R	49.4%	46.9%	51.3%	48.7%
1992	4,802,410	2,358,125	Specter, Arlen	2,224,966	Yeakel, Lynn	219,319	133,159 R	49.1%	46.3%	51.5%	48.5%
1991S	3,382,746	1,521,986	Thornburgh, Richard	1,860,760	Wofford, Harris		338,774 D	45.0%	55.0%	45.0%	55.0%
1988	4,366,598	2,901,715	Heinz, H. John	1,416,764	Vignola, Joseph C.	48,119	1,484,951 R	66.5%	32.4%	67.2%	32.8%
1986	3,378,226	1,906,537	Specter, Arlen	1,448,219	Edgar, Robert W.	23,470	458,318 R	56.4%	42.9%	56.8%	43.2%
1982	3,604,108	2,136,418	Heinz, H. John	1,412,965	Wecht, Cyril H.	54,725	723,453 R	59.3%	39.2%	60.2%	39.8%
1980	4,418,042	2,230,404	Specter, Arlen	2,122,391	Flaherty, Peter	65,247	108,013 R	50.5%	48.0%	51.2%	48.8%
1976	4,546,353	2,381,891	Heinz, H. John	2,126,977	Green, William J., III	37,485	254,914 R	52.4%	46.8%	52.8%	47.2%
1974	3,477,812	1,843,317	Schweiker, Richard S.	1,596,121	Flaherty, Peter	38,374	247,196 R	53.0%	45.9%	53.6%	46.4%
1970	3,644,305	1,874,106	Scott, Hugh	1,653,774	Sesler, William G.	116,425	220,332 R	51.4%	45.4%	53.1%	46.9%
1968	4,624,218	2,399,762	Schweiker, Richard S.	2,117,662	Clark, Joseph S.	106,794	282,100 R	51.9%	45.8%	53.1%	46.9%
1964	4,803,835	2,429,858	Scott, Hugh	2,359,223	Blatt, Genevieve	14,754	70,635 R	50.6%	49.1%	50.7%	49.3%
1962	4,383,475	2,134,649	Van Zandt, James E.	2,238,383	Clark, Joseph S.	10,443	103,734 D	48.7%	51.1%	48.8%	51.2%
1958	3,988,622	2,042,586	Scott, Hugh	1,929,821	Leader, George M.	16,215	112,765 R	51.2%	48.4%	51.4%	48.6%
1956	4,529,874	2,250,671	Duff, James H.	2,268,641	Clark, Joseph S.	10,562	17,970 D	49.7%	50.1%	49.8%	50.2%
1952	4,519,761	2,331,034	Martin, Edward	2,168,546	Bard, Guy Kurtz	20,181	162,488 R	51.6%	48.0%	51.8%	48.2%
1950	3,548,703	1,820,400	Duff, James H.	1,694,076	Myers, Francis J.	34,227	126,324 R	51.3%	47.7%	51.8%	48.2%
1946	3,127,860	1,853,458	Martin, Edward	1,245,338	Guffey, Joseph F.	29,064	608,120 R	59.3%	39.8%	59.8%	40.2%

Note: The 1991 election was for a short term to fill a vacancy.

PENNSYLVANIA

PRESIDENT 2008

2000 Census Population	County	Total Vote	Republican	Democratic	Other	Rep.-Dem. Plurality	Percentage Total Vote Rep.	Dem.	Major Vote Rep.	Dem.
91,292	ADAMS	44,491	26,349	17,633	509	8,716 R	59.2%	39.6%	59.9%	40.1%
1,281,666	ALLEGHENY	651,436	272,347	373,153	5,936	100,806 D	41.8%	57.3%	42.2%	57.8%
72,392	ARMSTRONG	30,081	18,542	11,138	401	7,404 R	61.6%	37.0%	62.5%	37.5%
181,412	BEAVER	84,488	42,895	40,499	1,094	2,396 R	50.8%	47.9%	51.4%	48.6%
49,984	BEDFORD	22,443	16,124	6,059	260	10,065 R	71.8%	27.0%	72.7%	27.3%
373,638	BERKS	180,000	80,513	97,047	2,440	16,534 D	44.7%	53.9%	45.3%	54.7%
129,144	BLAIR	53,102	32,708	19,813	581	12,895 R	61.6%	37.3%	62.3%	37.7%
62,761	BRADFORD	25,787	15,057	10,306	424	4,751 R	58.4%	40.0%	59.4%	40.6%
597,635	BUCKS	332,924	150,248	179,031	3,645	28,783 D	45.1%	53.8%	45.6%	54.4%
174,083	BUTLER	90,425	57,074	32,260	1,091	24,814 R	63.1%	35.7%	63.9%	36.1%
152,598	CAMBRIA	65,670	31,995	32,451	1,224	456 D	48.7%	49.4%	49.6%	50.4%
5,974	CAMERON	2,245	1,323	879	43	444 R	58.9%	39.2%	60.1%	39.9%
58,802	CARBON	26,923	12,957	13,464	502	507 D	48.1%	50.0%	49.0%	51.0%
135,758	CENTRE	75,763	32,992	41,950	821	8,958 D	43.5%	55.4%	44.0%	56.0%
433,501	CHESTER	254,354	114,421	137,833	2,100	23,412 D	45.0%	54.2%	45.4%	54.6%
41,765	CLARION	17,766	10,737	6,756	273	3,981 R	60.4%	38.0%	61.4%	38.6%
83,382	CLEARFIELD	33,813	18,662	14,555	596	4,107 R	55.2%	43.0%	56.2%	43.8%
37,914	CLINTON	14,791	7,504	7,097	190	407 R	50.7%	48.0%	51.4%	48.6%
64,151	COLUMBIA	28,063	14,477	13,230	356	1,247 R	51.6%	47.1%	52.3%	47.7%
90,366	CRAWFORD	38,134	20,750	16,780	604	3,970 R	54.4%	44.0%	55.3%	44.7%
213,674	CUMBERLAND	113,304	63,739	48,306	1,259	15,433 R	56.3%	42.6%	56.9%	43.1%
251,798	DAUPHIN	129,529	58,238	69,975	1,316	11,737 D	45.0%	54.0%	45.4%	54.6%
550,864	DELAWARE	297,004	115,273	178,870	2,861	63,597 D	38.8%	60.2%	39.2%	60.8%
35,112	ELK	14,271	6,676	7,290	305	614 D	46.8%	51.1%	47.8%	52.2%
280,843	ERIE	127,691	50,351	75,775	1,565	25,424 D	39.4%	59.3%	39.9%	60.1%
148,644	FAYETTE	52,560	26,081	25,866	613	215 R	49.6%	49.2%	50.2%	49.8%
4,946	FOREST	2,444	1,366	1,038	40	328 R	55.9%	42.5%	56.8%	43.2%
129,313	FRANKLIN	63,641	41,906	21,169	566	20,737 R	65.8%	33.3%	66.4%	33.6%
14,261	FULTON	6,306	4,642	1,576	88	3,066 R	73.6%	25.0%	74.7%	25.3%
40,672	GREENE	15,976	7,889	7,829	258	60 R	49.4%	49.0%	50.2%	49.8%
45,586	HUNTINGDON	18,632	11,745	6,621	266	5,124 R	63.0%	35.5%	63.9%	36.1%
89,605	INDIANA	37,302	19,727	17,065	510	2,662 R	52.9%	45.7%	53.6%	46.4%
45,932	JEFFERSON	18,802	12,057	6,447	298	5,610 R	64.1%	34.3%	65.2%	34.8%
22,821	JUNIATA	9,711	6,484	3,068	159	3,416 R	66.8%	31.6%	67.9%	32.1%
213,295	LACKAWANNA	107,876	39,488	67,520	868	28,032 D	36.6%	62.6%	36.9%	63.1%
470,658	LANCASTER	228,137	126,568	99,586	1,983	26,982 R	55.5%	43.7%	56.0%	44.0%
94,643	LAWRENCE	42,103	21,851	19,711	541	2,140 R	51.9%	46.8%	52.6%	47.4%
120,327	LEBANON	58,297	34,314	23,310	673	11,004 R	58.9%	40.0%	59.5%	40.5%
312,090	LEHIGH	152,473	63,382	87,089	2,002	23,707 D	41.6%	57.1%	42.1%	57.9%
319,250	LUZERNE	135,175	61,127	72,492	1,556	11,365 D	45.2%	53.6%	45.7%	54.3%
120,044	LYCOMING	49,237	30,280	18,381	576	11,899 R	61.5%	37.3%	62.2%	37.8%
45,936	MCKEAN	15,947	9,224	6,465	258	2,759 R	57.8%	40.5%	58.8%	41.2%
120,293	MERCER	53,821	26,565	26,411	845	154 R	49.4%	49.1%	50.1%	49.9%
46,486	MIFFLIN	16,502	10,929	5,375	198	5,554 R	66.2%	32.6%	67.0%	33.0%
138,687	MONROE	68,443	28,293	39,453	697	11,160 D	41.3%	57.6%	41.8%	58.2%
750,097	MONTGOMERY	422,419	165,552	253,393	3,474	87,841 D	39.2%	60.0%	39.5%	60.5%
18,236	MONTOUR	8,023	4,574	3,364	85	1,210 R	57.0%	41.9%	57.6%	42.4%
267,066	NORTHAMPTON	135,587	58,551	75,255	1,781	16,704 D	43.2%	55.5%	43.8%	56.2%
94,556	NORTHUMBERLAND	33,939	19,018	14,329	592	4,689 R	56.0%	42.2%	57.0%	43.0%
43,602	PERRY	19,745	13,058	6,396	291	6,662 R	66.1%	32.4%	67.1%	32.9%

PENNSYLVANIA

PRESIDENT 2008

2000 Census Population	County	Total Vote	Republican	Democratic	Other	Rep.-Dem. Plurality	Percentage			
							Total Vote		Major Vote	
							Rep.	Dem.	Rep.	Dem.
1,517,550	PHILADELPHIA	717,329	117,221	595,980	4,128	478,759 D	16.3%	83.1%	16.4%	83.6%
46,302	PIKE	24,284	12,518	11,493	273	1,025 R	51.5%	47.3%	52.1%	47.9%
18,080	POTTER	7,507	5,109	2,300	98	2,809 R	68.1%	30.6%	69.0%	31.0%
150,336	SCHUYLKILL	63,057	33,767	28,300	990	5,467 R	53.5%	44.9%	54.4%	45.6%
37,546	SNYDER	15,479	9,900	5,382	197	4,518 R	64.0%	34.8%	64.8%	35.2%
80,023	SOMERSET	35,168	21,686	12,878	604	8,808 R	61.7%	36.6%	62.7%	37.3%
6,556	SULLIVAN	3,120	1,841	1,233	46	608 R	59.0%	39.5%	59.9%	40.1%
42,238	SUSQUEHANNA	19,286	10,633	8,381	272	2,252 R	55.1%	43.5%	55.9%	44.1%
41,373	TIOGA	17,984	11,326	6,390	268	4,936 R	63.0%	35.5%	63.9%	36.1%
41,624	UNION	17,400	9,859	7,333	208	2,526 R	56.7%	42.1%	57.3%	42.7%
57,565	VENANGO	23,307	13,718	9,238	351	4,480 R	58.9%	39.6%	59.8%	40.2%
43,863	WARREN	18,517	9,685	8,537	295	1,148 R	52.3%	46.1%	53.2%	46.8%
202,897	WASHINGTON	98,047	50,752	46,122	1,173	4,630 R	51.8%	47.0%	52.4%	47.6%
47,722	WAYNE	22,835	12,702	9,892	241	2,810 R	55.6%	43.3%	56.2%	43.8%
369,993	WESTMORELAND	176,873	102,294	72,721	1,858	29,573 R	57.8%	41.1%	58.4%	41.6%
28,080	WYOMING	13,138	6,983	5,985	170	998 R	53.2%	45.6%	53.8%	46.2%
381,751	YORK	194,210	109,268	82,839	2,103	26,429 R	56.3%	42.7%	56.9%	43.1%
12,281,054	TOTAL	6,013,272	2,655,885	3,276,363	81,024	620,478 D	44.2%	54.5%	44.8%	55.2%

Note: The statewide totals for "Total Vote" and "Other" include 18,135 write-in votes that were not part of the county-by-county returns.

PENNSYLVANIA

HOUSE OF REPRESENTATIVES

CD	Year	Total Vote	Republican Vote	Republican Candidate	Democratic Vote	Democratic Candidate	Other Vote	Rep.-Dem. Plurality	Total Vote Rep.	Total Vote Dem.	Major Vote Rep.	Major Vote Dem.
1	2008	267,513	24,714	MUHAMMAD, MIKE	242,799	BRADY, ROBERT A.*		218,085 D	9.2%	90.8%	9.2%	90.8%
1	2006	137,999		—	137,987	BRADY, ROBERT A.*	12	137,987 D		100.0%		100.0%
1	2004	248,587	33,266	WILLIAMS, DEBORAH L.	214,462	BRADY, ROBERT A.*	859	181,196 D	13.4%	86.3%	13.4%	86.6%
1	2002	140,090	17,444	DELANEY, MARIE G.	121,076	BRADY, ROBERT A.*	1,570	103,632 D	12.5%	86.4%	12.6%	87.4%
2	2008	311,336	34,466	LANG, ADAM A.	276,870	FATTAH, CHAKA*		242,404 D	11.1%	88.9%	11.1%	88.9%
2	2006	187,283	17,291	GESSNER, MICHAEL	165,867	FATTAH, CHAKA*	4,125	148,576 D	9.2%	88.6%	9.4%	90.6%
2	2004	287,637	34,411	BOLNO, STEWART	253,226	FATTAH, CHAKA*		218,815 D	12.0%	88.0%	12.0%	88.0%
2	2002	171,611	20,988	DOUGHERTY, THOMAS G.	150,623	FATTAH, CHAKA*		129,635 D	12.2%	87.8%	12.2%	87.8%
3	2008	286,603	139,757	ENGLISH, PHIL*	146,846	DAHLKEMPER, KATHLEEN A.		7,089 D	48.8%	51.2%	48.8%	51.2%
3	2006	202,518	108,525	ENGLISH, PHIL*	85,110	PORTER, STEVEN	8,883	23,415 R	53.6%	42.0%	56.0%	44.0%
3	2004	277,323	166,580	ENGLISH, PHIL*	110,684	PORTER, STEVEN	59	55,896 R	60.1%	39.9%	60.1%	39.9%
3	2002	150,329	116,763	ENGLISH, PHIL*		—	33,566	116,763 R	77.7%		100.0%	
4	2008	333,947	147,411	HART, MELISSA A.	186,536	ALTMIRE, JASON*		39,125 D	44.1%	55.9%	44.1%	55.9%
4	2006	254,084	122,049	HART, MELISSA A.*	131,847	ALTMIRE, JASON	188	9,798 D	48.0%	51.9%	48.1%	51.9%
4	2004	323,945	204,329	HART, MELISSA A.*	116,303	DROBAC, STEVAN JR.	3,313	88,026 R	63.1%	35.9%	63.7%	36.3%
4	2002	202,218	130,534	HART, MELISSA A.*	71,674	DROBAC, STEVAN JR.	10	58,860 R	64.6%	35.4%	64.6%	35.4%
5	2008	274,177	155,513	THOMPSON, GLENN	112,509	McCRACKEN, MARK B	6,155	43,004 R	56.7%	41.0%	58.0%	42.0%
5	2006	191,727	115,126	PETERSON, JOHN E.*	76,456	HILLIARD, DONALD L.	145	38,670 R	60.0%	39.9%	60.1%	39.9%
5	2004	219,198	192,852	PETERSON, JOHN E.*		—	26,346	192,852 R	88.0%		100.0%	
5	2002	143,211	124,942	PETERSON, JOHN E.*		—	18,269	124,942 R	87.2%		100.0%	
6	2008	344,375	179,423	GERLACH, JIM*	164,952	ROGGIO, BOB		14,471 R	52.1%	47.9%	52.1%	47.9%
6	2006	238,939	121,047	GERLACH, JIM*	117,892	MURPHY, LOIS		3,155 R	50.7%	49.3%	50.7%	49.3%
6	2004	314,386	160,348	GERLACH, JIM*	153,977	MURPHY, LOIS	61	6,371 R	51.0%	49.0%	51.0%	49.0%
6	2002	201,791	103,648	GERLACH, JIM	98,128	WOFFORD, DAN	15	5,520 R	51.4%	48.6%	51.4%	48.6%
7	2008	352,317	142,362	WILLIAMS, W. CRAIG	209,955	SESTAK, JOE*		67,593 D	40.4%	59.6%	40.4%	59.6%
7	2006	262,434	114,426	WELDON, CURT*	147,898	SESTAK, JOE	110	33,472 D	43.6%	56.4%	43.6%	56.4%
7	2004	334,547	196,556	WELDON, CURT*	134,932	SCOLES, PAUL	3,059	61,624 R	58.8%	40.3%	59.3%	40.7%
7	2002	221,351	146,296	WELDON, CURT*	75,055	LENNON, PETER A.		71,241 R	66.1%	33.9%	66.1%	33.9%
8	2008	348,515	145,103	MANION, TOM	197,869	MURPHY, PATRICK J.*	5,543	52,766 D	41.6%	56.8%	42.3%	57.7%
8	2006	249,817	124,138	FITZPATRICK, MICHAEL G.*	125,656	MURPHY, PATRICK J.	23	1,518 D	49.7%	50.3%	49.7%	50.3%
8	2004	331,276	183,229	FITZPATRICK, MICHAEL G.	143,427	SCHRADER, VIRGINIA WATERS	4,620	39,802 R	55.3%	43.3%	56.1%	43.9%
8	2002	203,687	127,475	GREENWOOD, JAMES C.*	76,178	REECE, TIMOTHY T.	34	51,297 R	62.6%	37.4%	62.6%	37.4%
9	2008	273,686	174,951	SHUSTER, BILL*	98,735	BARR, TONY		76,216 R	63.9%	36.1%	63.9%	36.1%
9	2006	200,820	121,069	SHUSTER, BILL*	79,610	BARR, TONY	141	41,459 R	60.3%	39.6%	60.3%	39.7%
9	2004	265,272	184,320	SHUSTER, BILL*	80,787	POLITIS, PAUL I.	165	103,533 R	69.5%	30.5%	69.5%	30.5%
9	2002	174,849	124,184	SHUSTER, BILL*	50,558	HENRY, JOHN R.	107	73,626 R	71.0%	28.9%	71.1%	28.9%
10	2008	285,518	124,681	HACKETT, CHRIS	160,837	CARNEY, CHRISTOPHER P.*		36,156 D	43.7%	56.3%	43.7%	56.3%
10	2006	208,173	97,862	SHERWOOD, DON*	110,115	CARNEY, CHRISTOPHER P.	196	12,253 D	47.0%	52.9%	47.1%	52.9%
10	2004	206,839	191,967	SHERWOOD, DON*		—	14,872	191,967 R	92.8%		100.0%	
10	2002	164,159	152,017	#SHERWOOD, DON*		—	12,142	152,017 R	92.6%		100.0%	
11	2008	283,530	137,151	BARLETTA, LOU	146,379	KANJORSKI, PAUL E.*		9,228 D	48.4%	51.6%	48.4%	51.6%
11	2006	185,413	51,033	LEONARDI, JOSEPH F.	134,340	KANJORSKI, PAUL E.*	40	83,307 D	27.5%	72.5%	27.5%	72.5%
11	2004	181,285		—	171,147	KANJORSKI, PAUL E.*	10,138	171,147 D		94.4%		100.0%
11	2002	168,615	71,543	BARLETTA, LOU	93,758	KANJORSKI, PAUL E.*	3,314	22,215 D	42.4%	55.6%	43.3%	56.7%
12	2008	268,388	113,120	RUSSELL, WILLIAM	155,268	MURTHA, JOHN P.*		42,148 D	42.1%	57.9%	42.1%	57.9%
12	2006	203,163	79,612	IREY, DIANA	123,472	MURTHA, JOHN P.*	79	43,860 D	39.2%	60.8%	39.2%	60.8%
12	2004	204,710		—	204,504	MURTHA, JOHN P.*	206	204,504 D		99.9%		100.0%
12	2002	169,028	44,818	CHOBY, BILL	124,201	MURTHA, JOHN P.*	9	79,383 D	26.5%	73.5%	26.5%	73.5%

PENNSYLVANIA

HOUSE OF REPRESENTATIVES

			Republican		Democratic				Percentage			
									Total Vote		Major Vote	
CD	Year	Total Vote	Vote	Candidate	Vote	Candidate	Other Vote	Rep.-Dem. Plurality	Rep.	Dem.	Rep.	Dem.
13	2008	313,513	108,271	KATS, MARINA	196,868	SCHWARTZ, ALLYSON Y.*	8,374	88,597 D	34.5%	62.8%	35.5%	64.5%
13	2006	222,860	75,492	BHAKTA, RAJ PETER	147,368	SCHWARTZ, ALLYSON Y.*		71,876 D	33.9%	66.1%	33.9%	66.1%
13	2004	308,124	127,205	BROWN, MELISSA	171,763	SCHWARTZ, ALLYSON Y.	9,156	44,558 D	41.3%	55.7%	42.5%	57.5%
13	2002	211,867	100,295	BROWN, MELISSA	107,945	HOEFFEL, JOSEPH M.*	3,627	7,650 D	47.3%	50.9%	48.2%	51.8%
14	2008	265,540		—	242,326	DOYLE, MIKE*	23,214	242,326 D		91.3%		100.0%
14	2006	179,401		—	161,075	DOYLE, MIKE*	18,326	161,075 D		89.8%		100.0%
14	2004	220,299		—	220,139	DOYLE, MIKE*	160	220,139 D		99.9%		100.0%
14	2002	123,412		—	123,323	DOYLE, MIKE*	89	123,323 D		99.9%		100.0%
15	2008	309,766	181,433	DENT, CHARLIE*	128,333	BENNETT, SAM		53,100 R	58.6%	41.4%	58.6%	41.4%
15	2006	198,173	106,153	DENT, CHARLIE*	86,186	DERTINGER, CHARLES	5,834	19,967 R	53.6%	43.5%	55.2%	44.8%
15	2004	291,147	170,634	DENT, CHARLIE	114,646	DRISCOLL, JOE	5,867	55,988 R	58.6%	39.4%	59.8%	40.2%
15	2002	171,713	98,493	TOOMEY, PATRICK J.*	73,212	O'BRIEN, EDWARD J.	8	25,281 R	57.4%	42.6%	57.4%	42.6%
16	2008	305,167	170,329	PITTS, JOE*	120,193	SLATER, BRUCE A.	14,645	50,136 R	55.8%	39.4%	58.6%	41.4%
16	2006	204,669	115,741	PITTS, JOE*	80,915	HERR, LOIS K.	8,013	34,826 R	56.6%	39.5%	58.9%	41.1%
16	2004	285,313	183,620	PITTS, JOE*	98,410	HERR, LOIS K.	3,283	85,210 R	64.4%	34.5%	65.1%	34.9%
16	2002	134,597	119,046	PITTS, JOE*		—	15,551	119,046 R	88.4%		100.0%	
17	2008	302,608	109,909	GILHOOLEY, TONI	192,699	HOLDEN, TIM*		82,790 D	36.3%	63.7%	36.3%	63.7%
17	2006	212,777	75,455	WERTZ, MATTHEW A.	137,253	HOLDEN, TIM*	69	61,798 D	35.5%	64.5%	35.5%	64.5%
17	2004	291,793	113,592	PATERNO, SCOTT	172,412	HOLDEN, TIM*	5,789	58,820 D	38.9%	59.1%	39.7%	60.3%
17	2002	201,291	97,802	GEKAS, GEORGE W.*	103,483	HOLDEN, TIM*	6	5,681 D	48.6%	51.4%	48.6%	51.4%
18	2008	333,010	213,349	MURPHY, TIM*	119,661	O'DONNELL, STEVE		93,688 R	64.1%	35.9%	64.1%	35.9%
18	2006	250,240	144,632	MURPHY, TIM*	105,419	KLUKO, CHAD	189	39,213 R	57.8%	42.1%	57.8%	42.2%
18	2004	315,342	197,894	MURPHY, TIM*	117,420	BOLES, MARK G.	28	80,474 R	62.8%	37.2%	62.8%	37.2%
18	2002	199,349	119,885	MURPHY, TIM	79,451	MACHEK, JACK	13	40,434 R	60.1%	39.9%	60.1%	39.9%
19	2008	328,395	218,862	PLATTS, TODD R.*	109,533	AVILLO, PHILIP J. JR.		109,329 R	66.6%	33.4%	66.6%	33.4%
19	2006	222,898	142,512	PLATTS, TODD R.*	74,625	AVILLO, PHILIP J. JR.	5,761	67,887 R	63.9%	33.5%	65.6%	34.4%
19	2004	245,251	224,274	PLATTS, TODD R.*		—	20,977	224,274 R	91.4%		100.0%	
19	2002	157,145	143,097	PLATTS, TODD R.*		—	14,048	143,097 R	91.1%		100.0%	
TOTAL	2008	5,791,284	2,520,805		3,209,168		61,311	688,363 D	43.5%	55.4%	44.0%	56.0%
TOTAL	2006	4,013,388	1,732,163		2,229,091		52,134	496,928 D	43.2%	55.5%	43.7%	56.3%
TOTAL	2004	5,152,274	2,565,077		2,478,239		108,958	86,838 R	49.8%	48.1%	50.9%	49.1%
TOTAL	2002	3,310,313	1,859,270		1,348,665		102,378	510,605 R	56.2%	40.7%	58.0%	42.0%

Notes: The aggregate totals in 2008 for "Total Vote" and "Other Vote" include 3,380 write-in votes that were not part of the district-by-district returns. An asterisk (*) denotes incumbent. A pound sign (#) indicates that the candidate had the endorsement of more than one party. Some of the congressional district lines underwent revision before the 2004 election, but the changes were minor in nature.

PENNSYLVANIA

GENERAL AND PRIMARY ELECTIONS

2008 GENERAL ELECTIONS

President — Other vote was 42,977 Independent (Ralph Nader); 19,912 Libertarian (Bob Barr); 3,849 write-in (Ron Paul); 1,092 write-in (Chuck Baldwin); 13,194 scattered write-in.

House — Other vote was:

CD 1

CD 2

CD 3

CD 4

CD 5 — 6,155 Libertarian (James Fryman).

CD 6

CD 7

CD 8 — 5,543 Independent (Tom Lingenfelter).

CD 9

CD 10

CD 11

CD 12

CD 13 — 8,374 Constitution (John P. McDermott).

CD 14 — 23,214 Green (Titus North).

CD 15

CD 16 — 11,768 Independent (John A. Murphy); 2,877 Constitution (Daniel Frank).

CD 17

CD 18

CD 19

Note: There was also a statewide total of 3,380 scattered write-in votes that were not part of the district-by-district returns.

2008 PRIMARY ELECTIONS

Primary — April 22, 2008

Registration (as of April 17, 2008)

Democratic	4,200,109
Republican	3,186,057
Other	567,607
No Affiliation	374,350
TOTAL	*8,328,123*

Primary Type — Closed—Only registered Democrats and Republicans could vote in their party's primary.

	REPUBLICAN PRIMARIES			DEMOCRATIC PRIMARIES		
President	John McCain	595,175	72.9%	Hillary Clinton	1,275,039	54.6%
	Ron Paul	129,323	15.8%	Barack Obama	1,061,441	45.4%
	Mike Huckabee	92,430	11.3%			
	TOTAL	*816,928*		*TOTAL*	*2,336,480*	
Congressional District 1	Mike Muhammad	4,637	100.0%	Robert A. Brady*	116,334	100.0%
Congressional District 2	Michael Livingston	4,521	100.0%	Chaka Fattah*	161,022	100.0%
	Michael Livingston subsequently withdrew from the race and was replaced on the general election ballot by Adam A. Lang.					

PENNSYLVANIA

GENERAL AND PRIMARY ELECTIONS

	REPUBLICAN PRIMARIES			DEMOCRATIC PRIMARIES		
Congressional District 3	Phil English*	42,636	100.0%	Kathleen A. Dahlkemper	43,858	44.9%
				Kyle W. Foust	24,672	25.3%
				Tom Myers	18,584	19.0%
				Mike Waltner	10,532	10.8%
				TOTAL	97,646	
Congressional District 4	Melissa A. Hart	42,854	100.0%	Jason Altmire*	112,049	100.0%
Congressional District 5	Glenn Thompson	13,988	19.2%	Mark B. McCracken	30,358	40.9%
	Derek A. Walker	13,153	18.0%	Bill Cahir	25,920	34.9%
	Matt Shaner	12,860	17.6%	Richard P. Vilello Jr.	17,921	24.2%
	Jeffrey J. Stroehmann	9,921	13.6%			
	Keith Richardson	7,094	9.7%			
	Lou Radkowski	5,083	7.0%			
	John Rea Stroup	4,550	6.2%			
	Chris Exarchos	4,376	6.0%			
	John T. Krupa	1,916	2.6%			
	TOTAL	72,941		TOTAL	74,199	
Congressional District 6	Jim Gerlach*	39,232	100.0%	Bob Roggio	82,540	100.0%
Congressional District 7	W. Craig Williams	52,733	100.0%	Joe Sestak*	91,272	100.0%
Congressional District 8	Tom Manion	35,610	100.0%	Patrick J. Murphy*	100,788	100.0%
Congressional District 9	Bill Shuster*	57,890	100.0%	Tony Barr	58,522	100.0%
Congressional District 10	Chris Hackett	34,129	52.3%	Christopher P. Carney*	71,988	100.0%
	Dan Meuser	31,102	47.7%			
	TOTAL	65,231				
Congressional District 11	Lou Barletta	27,710	100.0%	Paul E. Kanjorski*	93,120	100.0%
Congressional District 12	William Russell (write-in)	3,165	100.0%	John P. Murtha*	112,082	100.0%
Congressional District 13	Marina Kats	27,169	100.0%	Allyson Y. Schwartz*	98,696	100.0%
Congressional District 14	No Republican candidate			Mike Doyle*	134,298	100.0%
Congressional District 15	Charlie Dent*	27,875	100.0%	Sam Bennett	73,734	100.0%
Congressional District 16	Joe Pitts*	49,740	100.0%	Bruce A. Slater	59,246	100.0%
Congressional District 17	Toni Gilhooley	49,123	100.0%	Tim Holden*	79,551	100.0%
Congressional District 18	Tim Murphy*	39,780	100.0%	Steve O'Donnell	52,247	45.0%
				Beth Hafer	48,224	41.5%
				Brien Wall	15,733	13.5%
				TOTAL	116,204	
Congressional District 19	Todd R. Platts*	57,198	100.0%	Philip J. Avillo Jr.	69,068	100.0%

Note: An asterisk (*) denotes incumbent.

RHODE ISLAND

Congressional districts first established for elections held in 2002
2 members

PROVIDENCE

1

Pawtucket

Providence

Cranston

BRISTOL

Warwick

Bristol

KENT

2

NEWPORT

1

WASHINGTON

Newport

Kingston

Westerly

New Shoreham

2

RHODE ISLAND

GOVERNOR
Donald L. Carcieri (R). Reelected 2006 to a four-year term. Previously elected 2002.

SENATORS (2 Democrats)
Jack Reed (D). Reelected 2008 to a six-year term. Previously elected 2002, 1996.

Sheldon Whitehouse (D). Elected 2006 to a six-year term.

REPRESENTATIVES (2 Democrats)
1. Patrick J. Kennedy (D)   2. Jim Langevin (D)

POSTWAR VOTE FOR PRESIDENT

| | | Republican | | Democratic | | | | Percentage | | | |
| | | | | | | | | Total Vote | | Major Vote | |
Year	Total Vote	Vote	Candidate	Vote	Candidate	Other Vote	Plurality	Rep.	Dem.	Rep.	Dem.
2008	471,766	165,391	McCain, John	296,571	Obama, Barack	9,804	131,180 D	35.1%	62.9%	35.8%	64.2%
2004	437,134	169,046	Bush, George W.	259,760	Kerry, John	8,328	90,714 D	38.7%	59.4%	39.4%	60.6%
2000**	409,047	130,555	Bush, George W.	249,508	Gore, Al	28,984	118,953 D	31.9%	61.0%	34.4%	65.6%
1996**	390,284	104,683	Dole, Bob	233,050	Clinton, Bill	52,551	128,367 D	26.8%	59.7%	31.0%	69.0%
1992**	453,477	131,601	Bush, George	213,299	Clinton, Bill	108,577	81,698 D	29.0%	47.0%	38.2%	61.8%
1988	404,620	177,761	Bush, George	225,123	Dukakis, Michael S.	1,736	47,362 D	43.9%	55.6%	44.1%	55.9%
1984	410,492	212,080	Reagan, Ronald	197,106	Mondale, Walter F.	1,306	14,974 R	51.7%	48.0%	51.8%	48.2%
1980**	416,072	154,793	Reagan, Ronald	198,342	Carter, Jimmy	62,937	43,549 D	37.2%	47.7%	43.8%	56.2%
1976	411,170	181,249	Ford, Gerald R.	227,636	Carter, Jimmy	2,285	46,387 D	44.1%	55.4%	44.3%	55.7%
1972	415,808	220,383	Nixon, Richard M.	194,645	McGovern, George S.	780	25,738 R	53.0%	46.8%	53.1%	46.9%
1968**	385,000	122,359	Nixon, Richard M.	246,518	Humphrey, Hubert H.	16,123	124,159 D	31.8%	64.0%	33.2%	66.8%
1964	390,091	74,615	Goldwater, Barry M.	315,463	Johnson, Lyndon B.	13	240,848 D	19.1%	80.9%	19.1%	80.9%
1960	405,535	147,502	Nixon, Richard M.	258,032	Kennedy, John F.	1	110,530 D	36.4%	63.6%	36.4%	63.6%
1956	387,609	225,819	Eisenhower, Dwight D.	161,790	Stevenson, Adlai E.		64,029 R	58.3%	41.7%	58.3%	41.7%
1952	414,498	210,935	Eisenhower, Dwight D.	203,293	Stevenson, Adlai E.	270	7,642 R	50.9%	49.0%	50.9%	49.1%
1948	327,702	135,787	Dewey, Thomas E.	188,736	Truman, Harry S.	3,179	52,949 D	41.4%	57.6%	41.8%	58.2%

**In past elections, the other vote included: 2000 - 25,052 Green (Ralph Nader); 1996 - 43,723 Reform (Ross Perot); 1992 - 105,045 Independent (Perot); 1980 - 59,819 Independent (John Anderson); 1968 - 15,678 American Independent (George Wallace).

RHODE ISLAND

POSTWAR VOTE FOR GOVERNOR

Year	Total Vote	Republican Vote	Republican Candidate	Democratic Vote	Democratic Candidate	Other Vote	Rep.-Dem. Plurality	Total Vote Rep.	Total Vote Dem.	Major Vote Rep.	Major Vote Dem.
2006	387,010	197,366	Carcieri, Donald L.	189,562	Fogarty, Charles J.	82	7,804 R	51.0%	49.0%	51.0%	49.0%
2002	332,655	181,827	Carcieri, Donald L.	150,229	York, Myrth	599	31,598 R	54.7%	45.2%	54.8%	45.2%
1998	306,445	156,180	Almond, Lincoln C.	129,105	York, Myrth	21,160	27,075 R	51.0%	42.1%	54.7%	45.3%
1994**	361,377	171,194	Almond, Lincoln C.	157,361	York, Myrth	32,822	13,833 R	47.4%	43.5%	52.1%	47.9%
1992	425,026	145,590	Leonard, Elizabeth Ann	261,484	Sundlun, Bruce G.	17,952	115,894 D	34.3%	61.5%	35.8%	64.2%
1990	356,672	92,177	DiPrete, Edward	264,411	Sundlun, Bruce G.	84	172,234 D	25.8%	74.1%	25.8%	74.2%
1988	400,516	203,550	DiPrete, Edward	196,936	Sundlun, Bruce G.	30	6,614 R	50.8%	49.2%	50.8%	49.2%
1986	322,724	208,822	DiPrete, Edward	104,508	Sundlun, Bruce G.	9,394	104,314 R	64.7%	32.4%	66.6%	33.4%
1984	408,375	245,059	DiPrete, Edward	163,311	Solomon, Anthony J.	5	81,748 R	60.0%	40.0%	60.0%	40.0%
1982	337,259	79,602	Marzullo, Vincent	247,208	Garrahy, J. Joseph	10,449	167,606 D	23.6%	73.3%	24.4%	75.6%
1980	405,916	106,729	Cianci, Vincent A.	299,174	Garrahy, J. Joseph	13	192,445 D	26.3%	73.7%	26.3%	73.7%
1978	314,363	96,596	Almond, Lincoln C.	197,386	Garrahy, J. Joseph	20,381	100,790 D	30.7%	62.8%	32.9%	67.1%
1976	398,683	178,254	Taft, James L.	218,561	Garrahy, J. Joseph	1,868	40,307 D	44.7%	54.8%	44.9%	55.1%
1974	321,660	69,224	Nugent, James W.	252,436	Noel, Philip W.		183,212 D	21.5%	78.5%	21.5%	78.5%
1972	412,866	194,315	DeSimone, Herbert F.	216,953	Noel, Philip W.	1,598	22,638 D	47.1%	52.5%	47.2%	52.8%
1970	346,342	171,549	DeSimone, Herbert F.	173,420	Licht, Frank	1,373	1,871 D	49.5%	50.1%	49.7%	50.3%
1968	383,725	187,958	Chafee, John H.	195,766	Licht, Frank	1	7,808 D	49.0%	51.0%	49.0%	51.0%
1966	332,064	210,202	Chafee, John H.	121,862	Hobbs, Horace E.		88,340 R	63.3%	36.7%	63.3%	36.7%
1964	391,668	239,501	Chafee, John H.	152,165	Gallogly, Edward P.	2	87,336 R	61.1%	38.9%	61.1%	38.9%
1962	327,506	163,952	Chafee, John H.	163,554	Notte, John A.		398 D	50.1%	49.9%	50.1%	49.9%
1960	401,362	174,044	Del Sesto, Christopher	227,318	Notte, John A.		53,274 D	43.4%	56.6%	43.4%	56.6%
1958	346,780	176,505	Del Sesto, Christopher	170,275	Roberts, Dennis J.		6,230 R	50.9%	49.1%	50.9%	49.1%
1956	383,919	191,604	Del Sesto, Christopher	192,315	Roberts, Dennis J.		711 D	49.9%	50.1%	49.9%	50.1%
1954	328,670	137,131	Lewis, Dean J.	189,595	Roberts, Dennis J.	1,944	52,464 D	41.7%	57.7%	42.0%	58.0%
1952	409,689	194,102	Archambault, Raoul	215,587	Roberts, Dennis J.		21,485 D	47.4%	52.6%	47.4%	52.6%
1950	296,809	120,684	Lachapelle, E. T.	176,125	Roberts, Dennis J.		55,441 D	40.7%	59.3%	40.7%	59.3%
1948	323,863	124,441	Ruerat, Albert P.	198,056	Pastore, John O.	1,366	73,615 D	38.4%	61.2%	38.6%	61.4%
1946	275,341	126,456	Murphy, John G.	148,885	Pastore, John O.		22,429 D	45.9%	54.1%	45.9%	54.1%

**The term of office of Rhode Island's governor was increased from two to four years effective with the 1994 election.

POSTWAR VOTE FOR SENATOR

Year	Total Vote	Republican Vote	Republican Candidate	Democratic Vote	Democratic Candidate	Other Vote	Rep.-Dem. Plurality	Total Vote Rep.	Total Vote Dem.	Major Vote Rep.	Major Vote Dem.
2008	438,812	116,174	Tingle, Robert G.	320,644	Reed, Jack	1,994	204,470 D	26.5%	73.1%	26.6%	73.4%
2006	385,451	179,001	Chafee, Lincoln	206,110	Whitehouse, Sheldon	340	27,109 D	46.4%	53.5%	46.5%	53.5%
2002	323,912	69,881	Tingle, Robert G.	253,922	Reed, Jack	109	184,041 D	21.6%	78.4%	21.6%	78.4%
2000	391,537	222,588	Chafee, Lincoln	161,023	Weygand, Bob	7,926	61,565 R	56.8%	41.1%	58.0%	42.0%
1996	363,378	127,368	Mayer, Nancy	230,676	Reed, Jack	5,334	103,308 D	35.1%	63.5%	35.6%	64.4%
1994	345,388	222,856	Chafee, John H.	122,532	Kushner, Linda J.		100,324 R	64.5%	35.5%	64.5%	35.5%
1990	364,062	138,947	Schneider, Claudine	225,105	Pell, Claiborne	10	86,158 D	38.2%	61.8%	38.2%	61.8%
1988	397,996	217,273	Chafee, John H.	180,717	Licht, Richard A.	6	36,556 R	54.6%	45.4%	54.6%	45.4%
1984	395,285	108,492	Leonard, Barbara	286,780	Pell, Claiborne	13	178,288 D	27.4%	72.6%	27.4%	72.6%
1982	342,779	175,495	Chafee, John H.	167,283	Michaelson, Julius C.	1	8,212 R	51.2%	48.8%	51.2%	48.8%
1978	305,618	76,061	Reynolds, James G.	229,557	Pell, Claiborne		153,496 D	24.9%	75.1%	24.9%	75.1%
1976	398,906	230,329	Chafee, John H.	167,665	Lorber, Richard P.	912	62,664 R	57.7%	42.0%	57.9%	42.1%
1972	413,432	188,990	Chafee, John H.	221,942	Pell, Claiborne	2,500	32,952 D	45.7%	53.7%	46.0%	54.0%
1970	341,222	107,351	McLaughlin, John	230,469	Pastore, John O.	3,402	123,118 D	31.5%	67.5%	31.8%	68.2%
1966	324,173	104,838	Briggs, Ruth M.	219,331	Pell, Claiborne	4	114,493 D	32.3%	67.7%	32.3%	67.7%
1964	386,322	66,715	Lagueux, Ronald R.	319,607	Pastore, John O.		252,892 D	17.3%	82.7%	17.3%	82.7%
1960	399,983	124,408	Archambault, Raoul	275,575	Pell, Claiborne		151,167 D	31.1%	68.9%	31.1%	68.9%
1958	344,519	122,353	Ewing, Bayard	222,166	Pastore, John O.		99,813 D	35.5%	64.5%	35.5%	64.5%
1954	326,624	132,970	Sundlun, Walter I.	193,654	Green, Theodore F.		60,684 D	40.7%	59.3%	40.7%	59.3%
1952	410,978	185,850	Ewing, Bayard	225,128	Pastore, John O.		39,278 D	45.2%	54.8%	45.2%	54.8%
1950S	297,909	114,184	Levy, Austin T.	183,725	Pastore, John O.		69,541 D	38.3%	61.7%	38.3%	61.7%
1948	320,420	130,262	Hazard, Thomas P.	190,158	Green, Theodore F.		59,896 D	40.7%	59.3%	40.7%	59.3%
1946	273,528	122,780	Dyer, W. Gurnee	150,748	McGrath, J. Howard		27,968 D	44.9%	55.1%	44.9%	55.1%

Note: The 1950 election was for a short term to fill a vacancy.

RHODE ISLAND

PRESIDENT 2008

2000 Census Population	County	Total Vote	Republican	Democratic	Other	Rep.-Dem. Plurality		Percentage			
								Total Vote		Major Vote	
								Rep.	Dem.	Rep.	Dem.
50,648	BRISTOL	25,905	9,260	16,162	483	6,902	D	35.7%	62.4%	36.4%	63.6%
167,090	KENT	84,074	33,780	48,406	1,888	14,626	D	40.2%	57.6%	41.1%	58.9%
85,433	NEWPORT	41,997	15,717	25,479	801	9,762	D	37.4%	60.7%	38.2%	61.8%
621,602	PROVIDENCE	253,630	81,010	167,442	5,178	86,432	D	31.9%	66.0%	32.6%	67.4%
123,546	WASHINGTON	66,160	25,624	39,082	1,454	13,458	D	38.7%	59.1%	39.6%	60.4%
1,048,319	TOTAL	471,766	165,391	296,571	9,804	131,180	D	35.1%	62.9%	35.8%	64.2%

2000 Census Population	City/Town	Total Vote	Republican	Democratic	Other	Rep.-Dem. Plurality		Percentage			
								Total Vote		Major Vote	
								Rep.	Dem.	Rep.	Dem.
16,819	BARRINGTON	9,905	3,666	6,075	164	2,409	D	37.0%	61.3%	37.6%	62.4%
22,469	BRISTOL TOWN	10,869	3,834	6,833	202	2,999	D	35.3%	62.9%	35.9%	64.1%
15,796	BURRILLVILLE	7,091	3,160	3,730	201	570	D	44.6%	52.6%	45.9%	54.1%
18,928	CENTRAL FALLS	3,901	661	3,191	49	2,530	D	16.9%	81.8%	17.2%	82.8%
7,859	CHARLESTOWN	4,476	1,693	2,670	113	977	D	37.8%	59.7%	38.8%	61.2%
33,668	COVENTRY	17,389	7,367	9,622	400	2,255	D	42.4%	55.3%	43.4%	56.6%
79,269	CRANSTON	37,219	13,981	22,520	718	8,539	D	37.6%	60.5%	38.3%	61.7%
31,840	CUMBERLAND	17,007	6,941	9,707	359	2,766	D	40.8%	57.1%	41.7%	58.3%
12,948	EAST GREENWICH	7,630	3,570	3,916	144	346	D	46.8%	51.3%	47.7%	52.3%
48,688	EAST PROVIDENCE	22,067	6,216	15,380	471	9,164	D	28.2%	69.7%	28.8%	71.2%
6,045	EXETER	3,286	1,447	1,763	76	316	D	44.0%	53.7%	45.1%	54.9%
4,274	FOSTER	2,578	1,155	1,337	86	182	D	44.8%	51.9%	46.3%	53.7%
9,948	GLOCESTER	5,292	2,498	2,639	155	141	D	47.2%	49.9%	48.6%	51.4%
7,836	HOPKINTON	4,063	1,691	2,247	125	556	D	41.6%	55.3%	42.9%	57.1%
5,622	JAMESTOWN	3,698	1,300	2,316	82	1,016	D	35.2%	62.6%	36.0%	64.0%
28,195	JOHNSTON	14,183	6,066	7,763	354	1,697	D	42.8%	54.7%	43.9%	56.1%
20,898	LINCOLN	11,324	4,831	6,264	229	1,433	D	42.7%	55.3%	43.5%	56.5%
3,593	LITTLE COMPTON	2,288	911	1,327	50	416	D	39.8%	58.0%	40.7%	59.3%
17,334	MIDDLETOWN	7,727	2,964	4,631	132	1,667	D	38.4%	59.9%	39.0%	61.0%
16,361	NARRAGANSETT	8,311	3,170	4,983	158	1,813	D	38.1%	60.0%	38.9%	61.1%
26,475	NEWPORT CITY	10,385	3,215	6,989	181	3,774	D	31.0%	67.3%	31.5%	68.5%
1,010	NEW SHOREHAM	1,062	285	758	19	473	D	26.8%	71.4%	27.3%	72.7%
26,326	NORTH KINGSTOWN	15,162	6,285	8,562	315	2,277	D	41.5%	56.5%	42.3%	57.7%
32,411	NORTH PROVIDENCE	16,212	5,933	9,954	325	4,021	D	36.6%	61.4%	37.3%	62.7%
10,618	NORTH SMITHFIELD	6,279	2,839	3,290	150	451	D	45.2%	52.4%	46.3%	53.7%
72,958	PAWTUCKET	25,129	6,098	18,486	545	12,388	D	24.3%	73.6%	24.8%	75.2%
17,149	PORTSMOUTH	9,917	4,276	5,464	177	1,188	D	43.1%	55.1%	43.9%	56.1%
173,618	PROVIDENCE CITY	55,635	8,548	46,276	811	37,728	D	15.4%	83.2%	15.6%	84.4%
7,222	RICHMOND	4,032	1,654	2,273	105	619	D	41.0%	56.4%	42.1%	57.9%
10,324	SCITUATE	5,965	3,025	2,763	177	262	R	50.7%	46.3%	52.3%	47.7%
20,613	SMITHFIELD	10,394	4,660	5,464	270	804	D	44.8%	52.6%	46.0%	54.0%
27,921	SOUTH KINGSTOWN	14,328	4,689	9,336	303	4,647	D	32.7%	65.2%	33.4%	66.6%
15,260	TIVERTON	7,982	3,051	4,752	179	1,701	D	38.2%	59.5%	39.1%	60.9%
11,360	WARREN	5,131	1,760	3,254	117	1,494	D	34.3%	63.4%	35.1%	64.9%
85,808	WARWICK	43,327	16,541	25,802	984	9,261	D	38.2%	59.6%	39.1%	60.9%
22,966	WESTERLY	11,440	4,710	6,490	240	1,780	D	41.2%	56.7%	42.1%	57.9%
5,085	WEST GREENWICH	3,243	1,567	1,591	85	24	D	48.3%	49.1%	49.6%	50.4%
29,581	WEST WARWICK	12,485	4,735	7,475	275	2,740	D	37.9%	59.9%	38.8%	61.2%
43,224	WOONSOCKET	13,354	4,398	8,678	278	4,280	D	32.9%	65.0%	33.6%	66.4%
1,048,319	TOTAL	471,766	165,391	296,571	9,804	131,180	D	35.1%	62.9%	35.8%	64.2%

RHODE ISLAND

SENATOR 2008

2000 Census Population	County	Total Vote	Republican	Democratic	Other	Rep.-Dem. Plurality	Total Vote Rep.	Total Vote Dem.	Major Vote Rep.	Major Vote Dem.
50,648	BRISTOL	24,248	6,657	17,507	84	10,850 D	27.5%	72.2%	27.5%	72.5%
167,090	KENT	79,929	23,885	55,643	401	31,758 D	29.9%	69.6%	30.0%	70.0%
85,433	NEWPORT	39,216	11,121	27,981	114	16,860 D	28.4%	71.4%	28.4%	71.6%
621,602	PROVIDENCE	233,020	55,607	176,273	1,140	120,666 D	23.9%	75.6%	24.0%	76.0%
123,546	WASHINGTON	62,399	18,904	43,240	255	24,336 D	30.3%	69.3%	30.4%	69.6%
1,048,319	TOTAL	438,812	116,174	320,644	1,994	204,470 D	26.5%	73.1%	26.6%	73.4%

2000 Census Population	City/Town	Total Vote	Republican	Democratic	Other	Rep.-Dem. Plurality	Total Vote Rep.	Total Vote Dem.	Major Vote Rep.	Major Vote Dem.
16,819	BARRINGTON	9,472	2,816	6,627	29	3,811 D	29.7%	70.0%	29.8%	70.2%
22,469	BRISTOL TOWN	9,943	2,638	7,272	33	4,634 D	26.5%	73.1%	26.6%	73.4%
15,796	BURRILLVILLE	6,701	1,942	4,744	15	2,802 D	29.0%	70.8%	29.0%	71.0%
18,928	CENTRAL FALLS	3,294	385	2,902	7	2,517 D	11.7%	88.1%	11.7%	88.3%
7,859	CHARLESTOWN	4,235	1,262	2,953	20	1,691 D	29.8%	69.7%	29.9%	70.1%
33,668	COVENTRY	16,587	5,104	11,410	73	6,306 D	30.8%	68.8%	30.9%	69.1%
79,269	CRANSTON	35,037	9,665	25,186	186	15,521 D	27.6%	71.9%	27.7%	72.3%
31,840	CUMBERLAND	15,967	4,853	11,047	67	6,194 D	30.4%	69.2%	30.5%	69.5%
12,948	EAST GREENWICH	7,290	2,818	4,435	37	1,617 D	38.7%	60.8%	38.9%	61.1%
48,688	EAST PROVIDENCE	20,541	4,528	15,916	97	11,388 D	22.0%	77.5%	22.1%	77.9%
6,045	EXETER	3,100	1,120	1,960	20	840 D	36.1%	63.2%	36.4%	63.6%
4,274	FOSTER	2,440	862	1,562	16	700 D	35.3%	64.0%	35.6%	64.4%
9,948	GLOCESTER	5,021	1,713	3,290	18	1,577 D	34.1%	65.5%	34.2%	65.8%
7,836	HOPKINTON	3,774	1,238	2,519	17	1,281 D	32.8%	66.7%	33.0%	67.0%
5,622	JAMESTOWN	3,545	913	2,616	16	1,703 D	25.8%	73.8%	25.9%	74.1%
28,195	JOHNSTON	13,320	3,809	9,413	98	5,604 D	28.6%	70.7%	28.8%	71.2%
20,898	LINCOLN	10,765	3,344	7,376	45	4,032 D	31.1%	68.5%	31.2%	68.8%
3,593	LITTLE COMPTON	2,197	819	1,369	9	550 D	37.3%	62.3%	37.4%	62.6%
17,334	MIDDLETOWN	7,162	1,938	5,208	16	3,270 D	27.1%	72.7%	27.1%	72.9%
16,361	NARRAGANSETT	7,808	2,355	5,413	40	3,058 D	30.2%	69.3%	30.3%	69.7%
26,475	NEWPORT CITY	9,470	2,267	7,182	21	4,915 D	23.9%	75.8%	24.0%	76.0%
1,010	NEW SHOREHAM	1,014	200	813	1	613 D	19.7%	80.2%	19.7%	80.3%
26,326	NORTH KINGSTOWN	14,477	4,661	9,754	62	5,093 D	32.2%	67.4%	32.3%	67.7%
32,411	NORTH PROVIDENCE	15,074	4,067	10,898	109	6,831 D	27.0%	72.3%	27.2%	72.8%
10,618	NORTH SMITHFIELD	5,926	1,874	4,034	18	2,160 D	31.6%	68.1%	31.7%	68.3%
72,958	PAWTUCKET	22,815	4,219	18,496	100	14,277 D	18.5%	81.1%	18.6%	81.4%
17,149	PORTSMOUTH	9,299	2,975	6,306	18	3,331 D	32.0%	67.8%	32.1%	67.9%
173,618	PROVIDENCE CITY	48,239	5,991	42,018	230	36,027 D	12.4%	87.1%	12.5%	87.5%
7,222	RICHMOND	3,833	1,240	2,572	21	1,332 D	32.4%	67.1%	32.5%	67.5%
10,324	SCITUATE	5,716	2,287	3,394	35	1,107 D	40.0%	59.4%	40.3%	59.7%
20,613	SMITHFIELD	9,963	3,344	6,559	60	3,215 D	33.6%	65.8%	33.8%	66.2%
27,921	SOUTH KINGSTOWN	13,498	3,674	9,771	53	6,097 D	27.2%	72.4%	27.3%	72.7%
15,260	TIVERTON	7,543	2,209	5,300	34	3,091 D	29.3%	70.3%	29.4%	70.6%
11,360	WARREN	4,833	1,203	3,608	22	2,405 D	24.9%	74.7%	25.0%	75.0%
85,808	WARWICK	41,247	11,676	29,363	208	17,687 D	28.3%	71.2%	28.5%	71.5%
22,966	WESTERLY	10,660	3,154	7,485	21	4,331 D	29.6%	70.2%	29.6%	70.4%
5,085	WEST GREENWICH	3,051	1,168	1,871	12	703 D	38.3%	61.3%	38.4%	61.6%
29,581	WEST WARWICK	11,754	3,119	8,564	71	5,445 D	26.5%	72.9%	26.7%	73.3%
43,224	WOONSOCKET	12,201	2,724	9,438	39	6,714 D	22.3%	77.4%	22.4%	77.6%
1,048,319	TOTAL	438,812	116,174	320,644	1,994	204,470 D	26.5%	73.1%	26.6%	73.4%

RHODE ISLAND

HOUSE OF REPRESENTATIVES

| | | | Republican | | Democratic | | | | Percentage | | | |
| | | | | | | | | | Total Vote | | Major Vote | |
CD	Year	Total Vote	Vote	Candidate	Vote	Candidate	Other Vote	Rep.-Dem. Plurality	Rep.	Dem.	Rep.	Dem.
1	2008	211,998	51,340	SCOTT, JONATHAN P.	145,254	KENNEDY, PATRICK J.*	15,404	93,914 D	24.2%	68.5%	26.1%	73.9%
1	2006	180,185	41,856	SCOTT, JONATHAN P.	124,676	KENNEDY, PATRICK J.*	13,653	82,820 D	23.2%	69.2%	25.1%	74.9%
1	2004	195,010	69,819	ROGERS, DAVID W.	124,923	KENNEDY, PATRICK J.*	268	55,104 D	35.8%	64.1%	35.9%	64.1%
1	2002	159,066	59,370	ROGERS, DAVID W.	95,286	KENNEDY, PATRICK J.*	4,410	35,916 D	37.3%	59.9%	38.4%	61.6%
2	2008	226,234	67,433	ZACCARIA, MARK S.	158,416	LANGEVIN, JIM*	385	90,983 D	29.8%	70.0%	29.9%	70.1%
2	2006	193,197		—	140,352	LANGEVIN, JIM*	52,845	140,352 D		72.6%		100.0%
2	2004	207,165	43,139	BARTON, ARTHUR CHUCK III	154,392	LANGEVIN, JIM*	9,634	111,253 D	20.8%	74.5%	21.8%	78.2%
2	2002	169,580	37,767	MATSON, JOHN O.	129,390	LANGEVIN, JIM*	2,423	91,623 D	22.3%	76.3%	22.6%	77.4%
TOTAL	2008	438,232	118,773		303,670		15,789	184,897 D	27.1%	69.3%	28.1%	71.9%
TOTAL	2006	373,382	41,856		265,028		66,498	223,172 D	11.2%	71.0%	13.6%	86.4%
TOTAL	2004	402,175	112,958		279,315		9,902	166,357 D	28.1%	69.5%	28.8%	71.2%
TOTAL	2002	328,646	97,137		224,676		6,833	127,539 D	29.6%	68.4%	30.2%	69.8%

Note: An asterisk (*) denotes incumbent.

RHODE ISLAND

GENERAL AND PRIMARY ELECTIONS

2008 GENERAL ELECTIONS

President Other vote was 4,829 Independent (Ralph Nader); 1,382 Libertarian (Bob Barr); 797 Green (Cynthia A. McKinney); 675 Constitution (Chuck Baldwin); 122 Socialism and Liberation (Gloria La Riva); 472 write-in (Ron Paul); 5 write-in (Alan Keyes); 1,522 scattered write-in.

Senator Other vote was 1,994 scattered write-in.

House Other vote was:

CD 1 15,108 Independent (Kenneth A. Capalbo); 296 scattered write-in.
CD 2 385 scattered write-in.

2008 PRIMARY ELECTIONS

Primary March 4, 2008 (President)
September 9, 2008 (Congress)

Registration (as of August 9, 2008)

Democratic	279,148
Republican	75,469
Unaffiliated	330,127
TOTAL	684,744

Primary Type Semi-open—Registered Democrats and Republicans could vote only in their party's primary. Unaffiliated voters could participate in either party's primary if they were willing to remain a member of that party for a period of at least 90 days.

RHODE ISLAND

GENERAL AND PRIMARY ELECTIONS

	REPUBLICAN PRIMARIES			DEMOCRATIC PRIMARIES		
President	John McCain	17,480	64.8%	Hillary Clinton	108,949	58.4%
	Mike Huckabee	5,847	21.7%	Barack Obama	75,316	40.4%
	Ron Paul	1,777	6.6%	John Edwards	1,133	0.6%
	Mitt Romney	1,181	4.4%	Uncommitted	1,041	0.6%
	Uncommitted	570	2.1%			
	Alan Keyes	117	0.4%			
	Hugh Cort	24	0.1%			
	TOTAL	*26,996*		*TOTAL*	*186,439*	
Senator	Robert G. Tingle	1,068	100.0%	Jack Reed*	48,038	86.8%
				Christopher F. Young	7,277	13.2%
				TOTAL	*55,315*	
Congressional District 1	Jonathan P. Scott	44	100.0%	Patrick J. Kennedy*	25,427	100.0%
Congressional District 2	Mark S. Zaccaria	1,030	100.0%	Jim Langevin*	20,007	100.0%

Note: An asterisk (*) denotes incumbent.

SOUTH CAROLINA

Congressional districts first established for elections held in 2002
6 members

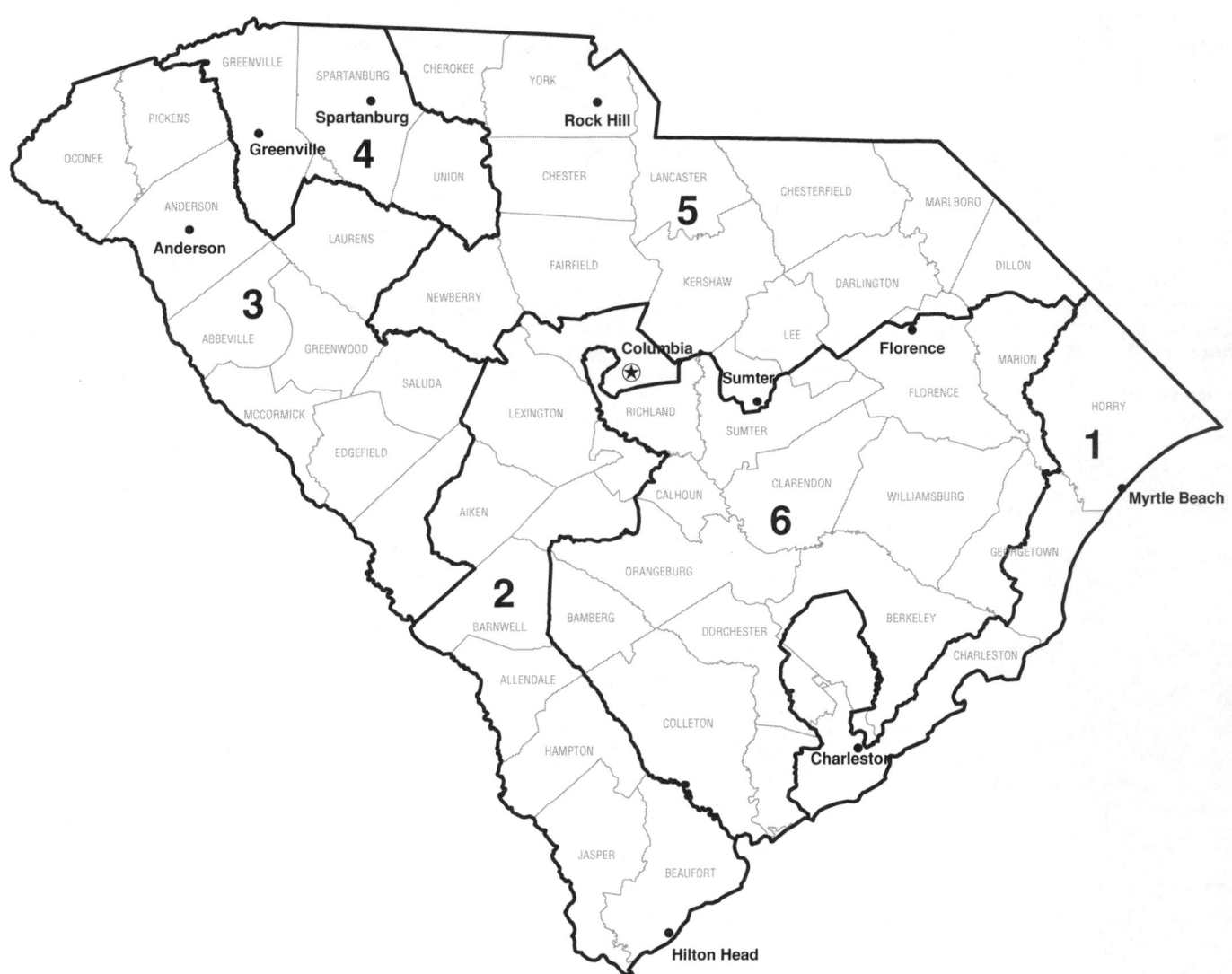

SOUTH CAROLINA

GOVERNOR
Mark Sanford (R). Reelected 2006 to a four-year term. Previously elected 2002.

SENATORS (2 Republicans)
Jim DeMint (R). Elected 2004 to a six-year term.

Lindsey Graham (R). Reelected 2008 to a six-year term. Previously elected 2002.

REPRESENTATIVES (4 Republicans, 2 Democrats)
1. Henry E. Brown Jr. (R)
2. Joe Wilson (R)
3. J. Gresham Barrett (R)
4. Bob Inglis (R)
5. John M. Spratt Jr. (D)
6. James E. Clyburn (D)

POSTWAR VOTE FOR PRESIDENT

Year	Total Vote	Republican Vote	Republican Candidate	Democratic Vote	Democratic Candidate	Other Vote	Plurality	Total Vote Rep.	Total Vote Dem.	Major Vote Rep.	Major Vote Dem.
2008	1,920,969	1,034,896	McCain, John	862,449	Obama, Barack	23,624	172,447 R	53.9%	44.9%	54.5%	45.5%
2004	1,617,730	937,974	Bush, George W.	661,699	Kerry, John	18,057	276,275 R	58.0%	40.9%	58.6%	41.4%
2000**	1,382,717	785,937	Bush, George W.	565,561	Gore, Al	31,219	220,376 R	56.8%	40.9%	58.2%	41.8%
1996**	1,151,689	573,458	Dole, Bob	506,283	Clinton, Bill	71,948	67,175 R	49.8%	44.0%	53.1%	46.9%
1992**	1,202,527	577,507	Bush, George	479,514	Clinton, Bill	145,506	97,993 R	48.0%	39.9%	54.6%	45.4%
1988	986,009	606,443	Bush, George	370,554	Dukakis, Michael S.	9,012	235,889 R	61.5%	37.6%	62.1%	37.9%
1984	968,529	615,539	Reagan, Ronald	344,459	Mondale, Walter F.	8,531	271,080 R	63.6%	35.6%	64.1%	35.9%
1980**	894,071	441,841	Reagan, Ronald	430,385	Carter, Jimmy	21,845	11,456 R	49.4%	48.1%	50.7%	49.3%
1976	802,583	346,149	Ford, Gerald R.	450,807	Carter, Jimmy	5,627	104,658 D	43.1%	56.2%	43.4%	56.6%
1972	673,960	477,044	Nixon, Richard M.	186,824	McGovern, George S.	10,092	290,220 R	70.8%	27.7%	71.9%	28.1%
1968**	666,978	254,062	Nixon, Richard M.	197,486	Humphrey, Hubert H.	215,430	38,632 R	38.1%	29.6%	56.3%	43.7%
1964	524,779	309,048	Goldwater, Barry M.	215,723	Johnson, Lyndon B.	8	93,325 R	58.9%	41.1%	58.9%	41.1%
1960	386,688	188,558	Nixon, Richard M.	198,129	Kennedy, John F.	1	9,571 D	48.8%	51.2%	48.8%	51.2%
1956**	300,583	75,700	Eisenhower, Dwight D.	136,372	Stevenson, Adlai E.	88,511	47,863 D	25.2%	45.4%	35.7%	64.3%
1952	341,087	168,082	Eisenhower, Dwight D.	173,004	Stevenson, Adlai E.	1	4,922 D	49.3%	50.7%	49.3%	50.7%
1948**	142,571	5,386	Dewey, Thomas E.	34,423	Truman, Harry S.	102,762	68,184 SR	3.8%	24.1%	13.5%	86.5%

**In past elections, the other vote included: 2000 - 20,200 Green (Ralph Nader); 1996 - 64,386 Reform (Ross Perot); 1992 - 138,872 Independent (Perot); 1980 - 14,153 Independent (John Anderson); 1968 - 215,430 American Independent (George Wallace), who finished second in South Carolina; 1956 - 88,509 Uncommitted States' Rights electors, which placed second; 1948 - 102,607 States' Rights (Strom Thurmond), who won South Carolina with 72.0 percent of the total vote.

SOUTH CAROLINA

POSTWAR VOTE FOR GOVERNOR

| | | Republican | | Democratic | | Other | Rep.-Dem. | Percentage | | | |
| | Total | | | | | | | Total Vote | | Major Vote | |
Year	Vote	Vote	Candidate	Vote	Candidate	Vote	Plurality	Rep.	Dem.	Rep.	Dem.
2006	1,091,952	601,868	Sanford, Mark	489,076	Moore, Tommy	1,008	112,792 R	55.1%	44.8%	55.2%	44.8%
2002	1,107,725	585,422	Sanford, Mark	521,140	Hodges, Jim	1,163	64,282 R	52.8%	47.0%	52.9%	47.1%
1998	1,070,869	484,088	Beasley, David	570,070	Hodges, Jim	16,711	85,982 D	45.2%	53.2%	45.9%	54.1%
1994	933,850	470,756	Beasley, David	447,002	Theodore, Nick A.	16,092	23,754 R	50.4%	47.9%	51.3%	48.7%
1990	760,965	528,831	Campbell, Carroll	212,034	Mitchell, Theo	20,100	316,797 R	69.5%	27.9%	71.4%	28.6%
1986	753,751	384,565	Campbell, Carroll	361,325	Daniel, Mike	7,861	23,240 R	51.0%	47.9%	51.6%	48.4%
1982	671,625	202,806	Workman, W. D.	468,819	Riley, Richard W.		266,013 D	30.2%	69.8%	30.2%	69.8%
1978	627,182	236,946	Young, Edward L.	384,898	Riley, Richard W.	5,338	147,952 D	37.8%	61.4%	38.1%	61.9%
1974	523,199	266,109	Edwards, James B.	248,938	Dorn, W. J. Bryan	8,152	17,171 R	50.9%	47.6%	51.7%	48.3%
1970	484,857	221,233	Watson, Albert W.	250,551	West, John C.	13,073	29,318 D	45.6%	51.7%	46.9%	53.1%
1966	439,942	184,088	Rogers, Joseph O.	255,854	McNair, Robert E.		71,766 D	41.8%	58.2%	41.8%	58.2%
1962	253,721	—		253,704	Russell, Donald S.	17	253,704 D		100.0%		100.0%
1958	77,740	—		77,714	Hollings, Ernest F.	26	77,714 D		100.0%		100.0%
1954	214,212	—		214,204	Timmerman, George B.	8	214,204 D		100.0%		100.0%
1950	50,642	—		50,633	Byrnes, James F.	9	50,633 D		100.0%		100.0%
1946	26,520	—		26,520	Thurmond, Strom		26,520 D		100.0%		100.0%

Note: The Republican Party did not run a candidate in the gubernatorial elections of 1946, 1950, 1954, 1958, and 1962.

POSTWAR VOTE FOR SENATOR

| | | Republican | | Democratic | | Other | | Percentage | | | |
| | Total | | | | | | | Total Vote | | Major Vote | |
Year	Vote	Vote	Candidate	Vote	Candidate	Vote	Plurality	Rep.	Dem.	Rep.	Dem.
2008	1,871,431	1,076,534	Graham, Lindsey	790,621	Conley, Bob	4,276	285,913 R	57.5%	42.2%	57.7%	42.3%
2004	1,597,221	857,167	DeMint, Jim	704,384	Tenenbaum, Inez	35,670	152,783 R	53.7%	44.1%	54.9%	45.1%
2002	1,102,948	600,010	Graham, Lindsey	487,359	Sanders, Alex	15,579	112,651 R	54.4%	44.2%	55.2%	44.8%
1998	1,068,367	488,132	Inglis, Bob	562,791	Hollings, Ernest F.	17,444	74,659 D	45.7%	52.7%	46.4%	53.6%
1996	1,161,372	619,859	Thurmond, Strom	510,951	Close, Elliott Springs	30,562	108,908 R	53.4%	44.0%	54.8%	45.2%
1992	1,180,438	554,175	Hartnett, Thomas F.	591,030	Hollings, Ernest F.	35,233	36,855 D	46.9%	50.1%	48.4%	51.6%
1990	750,716	482,032	Thurmond, Strom	244,112	Cunningham, Bob	24,572	237,920 R	64.2%	32.5%	66.4%	33.6%
1986	737,962	262,886	McMaster, Henry D.	465,500	Hollings, Ernest F.	9,576	202,614 D	35.6%	63.1%	36.1%	63.9%
1984	965,130	644,815	Thurmond, Strom	306,982	Purvis, Melvin	13,333	337,833 R	66.8%	31.8%	67.7%	32.3%
1980	870,594	257,946	Mays, Marshall T.	612,554	Hollings, Ernest F.	94	354,608 D	29.6%	70.4%	29.6%	70.4%
1978	632,852	351,733	Thurmond, Strom	281,119	Ravenel, Charles D.		70,614 R	55.6%	44.4%	55.6%	44.4%
1974	512,397	146,645	Bush, Gwenyfred	356,126	Hollings, Ernest F.	9,626	209,481 D	28.6%	69.5%	29.2%	70.8%
1972	672,246	426,601	Thurmond, Strom	245,457	Zeigler, Eugene N.	188	181,144 R	63.5%	36.5%	63.5%	36.5%
1968	652,855	248,780	Parker, Marshall	404,060	Hollings, Ernest F.	15	155,280 D	38.1%	61.9%	38.1%	61.9%
1966	436,252	271,297	Thurmond, Strom	164,955	Morrah, Bradley		106,342 R	62.2%	37.8%	62.2%	37.8%
1966S	435,822	212,032	Parker, Marshall	223,790	Hollings, Ernest F.		11,758 D	48.7%	51.3%	48.7%	51.3%
1962	312,647	133,930	Workman, W.D.	178,712	Johnston, Olin D.	5	44,782 D	42.8%	57.2%	42.8%	57.2%
1960	330,266	—		330,164	Thurmond, Strom	102	330,164 D		100.0%		100.0%
1956	279,845	49,695	Crawford, Leon P.	230,150	Johnston, Olin D.		180,455 D	17.8%	82.2%	17.8%	82.2%
1956S	251,907	—		251,907	Thurmond, Strom		251,907 D		100.0%		100.0%
1954**	227,232	—		83,525	Brown, Edgar A.	143,707	59,919 ID		36.8%		100.0%
1950	50,277	—		50,240	Johnston, Olin D.	37	50,240 D		99.9%		100.0%
1948	141,006	5,008	Gerald, J. Bates	135,998	Maybank, Burnet R.		130,990 D	3.6%	96.4%	3.6%	96.4%

Notes: **In past elections, the other vote included: 1954 - 143,444 Independent Democratic (Strom Thurmond). Thurmond ran as a write-in candidate and won with 63.1 percent of the total vote. One each of the 1956 and 1966 elections was for a short term to fill a vacancy. The Republican Party did not run a Senate candidate in 1950, 1954, 1956 (for the short term), and 1960.

SOUTH CAROLINA

PRESIDENT 2008

2000 Census Population	County	Total Vote	Republican	Democratic	Other	Rep.-Dem. Plurality	Total Vote Rep.	Total Vote Dem.	Major Vote Rep.	Major Vote Dem.
26,167	ABBEVILLE	11,001	6,264	4,593	144	1,671 R	56.9%	41.8%	57.7%	42.3%
142,552	AIKEN	69,770	42,849	26,101	820	16,748 R	61.4%	37.4%	62.1%	37.9%
11,211	ALLENDALE	4,024	947	3,029	48	2,082 D	23.5%	75.3%	23.8%	76.2%
165,740	ANDERSON	73,787	48,690	24,132	965	24,558 R	66.0%	32.7%	66.9%	33.1%
16,658	BAMBERG	6,814	2,309	4,426	79	2,117 D	33.9%	65.0%	34.3%	65.7%
23,478	BARNWELL	9,798	4,769	4,931	98	162 D	48.7%	50.3%	49.2%	50.8%
120,937	BEAUFORT	68,870	37,821	30,396	653	7,425 R	54.9%	44.1%	55.4%	44.6%
142,651	BERKELEY	64,781	36,205	27,755	821	8,450 R	55.9%	42.8%	56.6%	43.4%
15,185	CALHOUN	7,738	3,695	3,970	73	275 D	47.8%	51.3%	48.2%	51.8%
309,969	CHARLESTON	154,434	69,822	82,698	1,914	12,876 D	45.2%	53.5%	45.8%	54.2%
52,537	CHEROKEE	20,766	13,305	7,215	246	6,090 R	64.1%	34.7%	64.8%	35.2%
34,068	CHESTER	13,981	6,318	7,478	185	1,160 D	45.2%	53.5%	45.8%	54.2%
42,768	CHESTERFIELD	16,359	8,325	7,842	192	483 R	50.9%	47.9%	51.5%	48.5%
32,502	CLARENDON	15,552	6,758	8,673	121	1,915 D	43.5%	55.8%	43.8%	56.2%
38,264	COLLETON	17,321	8,525	8,616	180	91 D	49.2%	49.7%	49.7%	50.3%
67,394	DARLINGTON	29,334	14,544	14,505	285	39 R	49.6%	49.4%	50.1%	49.9%
30,722	DILLON	13,417	5,874	7,408	135	1,534 D	43.8%	55.2%	44.2%	55.8%
96,413	DORCHESTER	52,405	29,929	21,806	670	8,123 R	57.1%	41.6%	57.9%	42.1%
24,595	EDGEFIELD	11,520	6,334	5,075	111	1,259 R	55.0%	44.1%	55.5%	44.5%
23,454	FAIRFIELD	11,619	3,912	7,591	116	3,679 D	33.7%	65.3%	34.0%	66.0%
125,761	FLORENCE	58,373	29,861	28,012	500	1,849 R	51.2%	48.0%	51.6%	48.4%
55,797	GEORGETOWN	30,290	15,790	14,199	301	1,591 R	52.1%	46.9%	52.7%	47.3%
379,616	GREENVILLE	190,657	116,363	70,886	3,408	45,477 R	61.0%	37.2%	62.1%	37.9%
66,271	GREENWOOD	29,667	16,995	12,348	324	4,647 R	57.3%	41.6%	57.9%	42.1%
21,386	HAMPTON	9,350	3,439	5,816	95	2,377 D	36.8%	62.2%	37.2%	62.8%
196,629	HORRY	104,798	64,609	38,879	1,310	25,730 R	61.7%	37.1%	62.4%	37.6%
20,678	JASPER	8,854	3,365	5,389	100	2,024 D	38.0%	60.9%	38.4%	61.6%
52,647	KERSHAW	27,985	16,466	11,226	293	5,240 R	58.8%	40.1%	59.5%	40.5%
61,351	LANCASTER	28,921	16,441	12,139	341	4,302 R	56.8%	42.0%	57.5%	42.5%
69,567	LAURENS	26,282	15,334	10,578	370	4,756 R	58.3%	40.2%	59.2%	40.8%
20,119	LEE	9,153	3,074	5,960	119	2,886 D	33.6%	65.1%	34.0%	66.0%
216,014	LEXINGTON	109,512	74,960	33,303	1,249	41,657 R	68.4%	30.4%	69.2%	30.8%
9,958	MCCORMICK	5,232	2,437	2,755	40	318 D	46.6%	52.7%	46.9%	53.1%
35,466	MARION	15,174	5,416	9,608	150	4,192 D	35.7%	63.3%	36.0%	64.0%
28,818	MARLBORO	10,876	3,996	6,794	86	2,798 D	36.7%	62.5%	37.0%	63.0%
36,108	NEWBERRY	16,524	9,616	6,708	200	2,908 R	58.2%	40.6%	58.9%	41.1%
66,215	OCONEE	31,132	21,164	9,481	487	11,683 R	68.0%	30.5%	69.1%	30.9%
91,582	ORANGEBURG	39,754	12,115	27,263	376	15,148 D	30.5%	68.6%	30.8%	69.2%
110,757	PICKENS	45,128	32,552	11,691	885	20,861 R	72.1%	25.9%	73.6%	26.4%
320,677	RICHLAND	165,037	57,941	105,656	1,440	47,715 D	35.1%	64.0%	35.4%	64.6%
19,181	SALUDA	8,603	5,191	3,323	89	1,868 R	60.3%	38.6%	61.0%	39.0%
253,791	SPARTANBURG	108,328	65,042	41,632	1,654	23,410 R	60.0%	38.4%	61.0%	39.0%
104,646	SUMTER	44,358	18,581	25,431	346	6,850 D	41.9%	57.3%	42.2%	57.8%
29,881	UNION	13,551	7,449	5,935	167	1,514 R	55.0%	43.8%	55.7%	44.3%
37,217	WILLIAMSBURG	16,443	5,004	11,279	160	6,275 D	30.4%	68.6%	30.7%	69.3%
164,614	YORK	93,696	54,500	37,918	1,278	16,582 R	58.2%	40.5%	59.0%	41.0%
4,012,012	TOTAL	1,920,969	1,034,896	862,449	23,624	172,447 R	53.9%	44.9%	54.5%	45.5%

SOUTH CAROLINA
SENATOR 2008

2000 Census Population	County	Total Vote	Republican	Democratic	Other	Rep.-Dem. Plurality	Percentage Total Vote Rep.	Dem.	Major Vote Rep.	Dem.
26,167	ABBEVILLE	10,791	6,226	4,558	7	1,668 R	57.7%	42.2%	57.7%	42.3%
142,552	AIKEN	68,129	43,555	24,412	162	19,143 R	63.9%	35.8%	64.1%	35.9%
11,211	ALLENDALE	3,849	1,042	2,805	2	1,763 D	27.1%	72.9%	27.1%	72.9%
165,740	ANDERSON	72,254	48,323	23,759	172	24,564 R	66.9%	32.9%	67.0%	33.0%
16,658	BAMBERG	6,569	2,521	4,045	3	1,524 D	38.4%	61.6%	38.4%	61.6%
23,478	BARNWELL	9,517	4,850	4,657	10	193 R	51.0%	48.9%	51.0%	49.0%
120,937	BEAUFORT	66,939	39,932	26,879	128	13,053 R	59.7%	40.2%	59.8%	40.2%
142,651	BERKELEY	63,181	37,540	25,494	147	12,046 R	59.4%	40.4%	59.6%	40.4%
15,185	CALHOUN	7,594	3,924	3,664	6	260 R	51.7%	48.2%	51.7%	48.3%
309,969	CHARLESTON	149,479	78,424	70,463	592	7,961 R	52.5%	47.1%	52.7%	47.3%
52,537	CHEROKEE	20,240	12,462	7,744	34	4,718 R	61.6%	38.3%	61.7%	38.3%
34,068	CHESTER	13,475	6,297	7,168	10	871 D	46.7%	53.2%	46.8%	53.2%
42,768	CHESTERFIELD	15,876	8,557	7,306	13	1,251 R	53.9%	46.0%	53.9%	46.1%
32,502	CLARENDON	15,312	6,996	8,313	3	1,317 D	45.7%	54.3%	45.7%	54.3%
38,264	COLLETON	16,941	9,052	7,876	13	1,176 R	53.4%	46.5%	53.5%	46.5%
67,394	DARLINGTON	28,669	15,490	13,161	18	2,329 R	54.0%	45.9%	54.1%	45.9%
30,722	DILLON	12,113	6,315	5,784	14	531 R	52.1%	47.8%	52.2%	47.8%
96,413	DORCHESTER	51,221	31,255	19,836	130	11,419 R	61.0%	38.7%	61.2%	38.8%
24,595	EDGEFIELD	11,307	6,390	4,889	28	1,501 R	56.5%	43.2%	56.7%	43.3%
23,454	FAIRFIELD	11,216	4,472	6,737	7	2,265 D	39.9%	60.1%	39.9%	60.1%
125,761	FLORENCE	57,329	32,680	24,589	60	8,091 R	57.0%	42.9%	57.1%	42.9%
55,797	GEORGETOWN	29,549	16,769	12,753	27	4,016 R	56.7%	43.2%	56.8%	43.2%
379,616	GREENVILLE	185,834	112,522	72,205	1,107	40,317 R	60.5%	38.9%	60.9%	39.1%
66,271	GREENWOOD	29,059	17,911	11,104	44	6,807 R	61.6%	38.2%	61.7%	38.3%
21,386	HAMPTON	8,840	3,609	5,225	6	1,616 D	40.8%	59.1%	40.9%	59.1%
196,629	HORRY	102,019	67,215	34,678	126	32,537 R	65.9%	34.0%	66.0%	34.0%
20,678	JASPER	8,573	3,367	5,203	3	1,836 D	39.3%	60.7%	39.3%	60.7%
52,647	KERSHAW	27,365	17,344	9,999	22	7,345 R	63.4%	36.5%	63.4%	36.6%
61,351	LANCASTER	27,906	16,295	11,585	26	4,710 R	58.4%	41.5%	58.4%	41.6%
69,567	LAURENS	25,873	15,448	10,377	48	5,071 R	59.7%	40.1%	59.8%	40.2%
20,119	LEE	8,912	3,418	5,489	5	2,071 D	38.4%	61.6%	38.4%	61.6%
216,014	LEXINGTON	107,645	78,255	29,255	135	49,000 R	72.7%	27.2%	72.8%	27.2%
9,958	MCCORMICK	5,118	2,521	2,592	5	71 D	49.3%	50.6%	49.3%	50.7%
35,466	MARION	14,557	5,951	8,599	7	2,648 D	40.9%	59.1%	40.9%	59.1%
28,818	MARLBORO	10,571	4,256	6,306	9	2,050 D	40.3%	59.7%	40.3%	59.7%
36,108	NEWBERRY	16,183	10,064	6,111	8	3,953 R	62.2%	37.8%	62.2%	37.8%
66,215	OCONEE	30,574	22,305	8,236	33	14,069 R	73.0%	26.9%	73.0%	27.0%
91,582	ORANGEBURG	38,502	13,346	25,129	27	11,783 D	34.7%	65.3%	34.7%	65.3%
110,757	PICKENS	44,446	32,158	12,121	167	20,037 R	72.4%	27.3%	72.6%	27.4%
320,677	RICHLAND	160,814	72,654	87,891	269	15,237 D	45.2%	54.7%	45.3%	54.7%
19,181	SALUDA	8,454	5,282	3,163	9	2,119 R	62.5%	37.4%	62.5%	37.5%
253,791	SPARTANBURG	105,509	61,117	43,966	426	17,151 R	57.9%	41.7%	58.2%	41.8%
104,646	SUMTER	43,556	19,906	23,625	25	3,719 D	45.7%	54.2%	45.7%	54.3%
29,881	UNION	13,251	6,881	6,349	21	532 R	51.9%	47.9%	52.0%	48.0%
37,217	WILLIAMSBURG	15,809	5,662	10,137	10	4,475 D	35.8%	64.1%	35.8%	64.2%
164,614	YORK	90,511	55,975	34,384	152	21,591 R	61.8%	38.0%	61.9%	38.1%
4,012,012	TOTAL	1,871,431	1,076,534	790,621	4,276	285,913 R	57.5%	42.2%	57.7%	42.3%

SOUTH CAROLINA

HOUSE OF REPRESENTATIVES

CD	Year	Total Vote	Republican		Democratic		Other Vote	Rep.-Dem. Plurality	Percentage			
			Vote	Candidate	Vote	Candidate			Total Vote		Major Vote	
									Rep.	Dem.	Rep.	Dem.
1	2008	341,879	177,540	BROWN, HENRY E. JR.*	163,724	KETNER, LINDA	615	13,816 R	51.9%	47.9%	52.0%	48.0%
1	2006	193,375	115,766	BROWN, HENRY E. JR.*	73,218	#MAATTA, RANDY	4,391	42,548 R	59.9%	37.9%	61.3%	38.7%
1	2004	212,308	186,448	BROWN, HENRY E. JR.*	—		25,860	186,448 R	87.8%		100.0%	
1	2002	142,425	127,562	BROWN, HENRY E. JR.*	—		14,863	127,562 R	89.6%		100.0%	
2	2008	343,486	184,583	WILSON, JOE*	158,627	MILLER, ROB	276	25,956 R	53.7%	46.2%	53.8%	46.2%
2	2006	204,052	127,811	WILSON, JOE*	76,090	ELLISOR, MICHAEL R.	151	51,721 R	62.6%	37.3%	62.7%	37.3%
2	2004	279,870	181,862	WILSON, JOE*	93,249	ELLISOR, MICHAEL R.	4,759	88,613 R	65.0%	33.3%	66.1%	33.9%
2	2002	171,359	144,149	WILSON, JOE*	—		27,210	144,149 R	84.1%		100.0%	
3	2008	288,741	186,799	BARRETT, J. GRESHAM*	101,724	DYER, JANE BALLARD	218	85,075 R	64.7%	35.2%	64.7%	35.3%
3	2006	177,988	111,882	BARRETT, J. GRESHAM*	66,039	#BALLENGER, LEE	67	45,843 R	62.9%	37.1%	62.9%	37.1%
3	2004	191,999	191,052	BARRETT, J. GRESHAM*	—		947	191,052 R	99.5%		100.0%	
3	2002	178,195	119,644	BARRETT, J. GRESHAM	55,743	BRIGHTHARP, GEORGE L.	2,808	63,901 R	67.1%	31.3%	68.2%	31.8%
4	2008	306,928	184,440	INGLIS, BOB*	113,291	CORDEN, PAUL	9,197	71,149 R	60.1%	36.9%	61.9%	38.1%
4	2006	179,931	115,553	INGLIS, BOB*	57,490	GRIFFITH, WILLIAM GRIFF	6,888	58,063 R	64.2%	32.0%	66.8%	33.2%
4	2004	270,594	188,795	INGLIS, BOB	78,376	BROWN, BRANDON P.	3,423	110,419 R	69.8%	29.0%	70.7%	29.3%
4	2002	177,417	122,422	DeMINT, JIM*	52,635	#ASHY, PETER J.	2,360	69,787 R	69.0%	29.7%	69.9%	30.1%
5	2008	306,285	113,282	SPENCER, ALBERT F.	188,785	SPRATT, JOHN M. JR.*	4,218	75,503 D	37.0%	61.6%	37.5%	62.5%
5	2006	175,154	75,422	NORMAN, RALPH	99,669	SPRATT, JOHN M. JR.*	63	24,247 D	43.1%	56.9%	43.1%	56.9%
5	2004	242,518	89,568	SPENCER, ALBERT F.	152,867	SPRATT, JOHN M. JR.*	83	63,299 D	36.9%	63.0%	36.9%	63.1%
5	2002	141,972		—	121,912	SPRATT, JOHN M. JR.*	20,060	121,912 D		85.9%		100.0%
6	2008	286,571	93,059	HARRELSON, NANCY	193,378	CLYBURN, JAMES E.*	134	100,319 D	32.5%	67.5%	32.5%	67.5%
6	2006	155,706	53,181	McLEOD, GARY	100,213	CLYBURN, JAMES E.*	2,312	47,032 D	34.2%	64.4%	34.7%	65.3%
6	2004	241,829	79,600	#McLEOD, GARY	161,987	CLYBURN, JAMES E.*	242	82,387 D	32.9%	67.0%	32.9%	67.1%
6	2002	174,066	55,760	McLEOD, GARY	116,586	CLYBURN, JAMES E.*	1,720	60,826 D	32.0%	67.0%	32.4%	67.6%
TOTAL	2008	1,873,890	939,703		919,529		14,658	20,174 R	50.1%	49.1%	50.5%	49.5%
TOTAL	2006	1,086,206	599,615		472,719		13,872	126,896 R	55.2%	43.5%	55.9%	44.1%
TOTAL	2004	1,439,118	917,325		486,479		35,314	430,846 R	63.7%	33.8%	65.3%	34.7%
TOTAL	2002	985,434	569,537		346,876		69,021	222,661 R	57.8%	35.2%	62.1%	37.9%

Notes: An asterisk (*) denotes incumbent. A pound sign (#) indicates that the candidate received votes on the ballot line of another party.

SOUTH CAROLINA

GENERAL AND PRIMARY ELECTIONS

2008 GENERAL ELECTIONS

President   Other vote was 7,283 Libertarian (Bob Barr); 6,827 Constitution (Chuck Baldwin); 5,053 Nominated by Petition (Ralph Nader); 4,461 Green (Cynthia A. McKinney).

Senator   Other vote was 4,276 scattered write-in.

House   Other vote was:

CD 1   615 scattered write-in.
CD 2   276 scattered write-in.
CD 3   218 scattered write-in.
CD 4   7,332 Green (C. Faye Walters); 1,865 scattered write-in.
CD 5   4,093 Constitution (Frank Waggoner); 125 scattered write-in.
CD 6   134 scattered write-in.

SOUTH CAROLINA

GENERAL AND PRIMARY ELECTIONS

2008 PRIMARY ELECTIONS

Primary	January 19, 2008 (President–Rep.) January 26, 2008 (President-Dem.) June 10, 2008 (Congress)	**Registration** (as of June 10, 2008)	2,340,771 No Party Registration

Primary Runoff   June 24, 2008

Primary Type   Open—Any registered voter could participate in either the Democratic or Republican primary, although any voter who participated in one party's primary could not vote in a primary runoff of the other party.

	REPUBLICAN PRIMARIES			DEMOCRATIC PRIMARIES		
President	John McCain	147,686	33.2%	Barack Obama	294,898	55.4%
	Mike Huckabee	132,943	29.8%	Hillary Clinton	140,990	26.5%
	Fred Thompson	69,651	15.6%	John Edwards	93,801	17.6%
	Mitt Romney	68,142	15.3%	Bill Richardson	726	0.1%
	Ron Paul	16,154	3.6%	Joseph R. Biden Jr.	693	0.1%
	Rudolph Giuliani	9,557	2.1%	Dennis J. Kucinich	551	0.1%
	Duncan Hunter	1,051	0.2%	Christopher J. Dodd	247	
	Tom Tancredo	121		Mike Gravel	245	
	Hugh Cort	88				
	John Cox	83				
	Cap Fendig	23				
	TOTAL	*445,499*		*TOTAL*	*532,151*	
Senator	Lindsey Graham*	187,736	66.8%	Bob Conley	74,185	50.4%
	Buddy Witherspoon	93,125	33.2%	Michael Cone	73,127	49.6%
	TOTAL	*280,861*		*TOTAL*	*147,312*	
Congressional District 1	Henry E. Brown Jr.*	42,588	70.1%	Linda Ketner	9,107	65.2%
	Katherine Jenerette	11,488	18.9%	Ben Frasier	4,871	34.8%
	Paul V. Norris	6,718	11.1%			
	TOTAL	*60,794*		*TOTAL*	*13,978*	
Congressional District 2	Joe Wilson*	44,783	85.1%	Rob Miller	16,911	67.3%
	Phil Black	7,831	14.9%	Blaine Lotz	8,219	32.7%
	TOTAL	*52,614*		*TOTAL*	*25,130*	
Congressional District 3	J. Gresham Barrett*	Unopposed		Jane Ballard Dyer	Unopposed	100.0%
Congressional District 4	Bob Inglis*	37,571	67.0%	Paul Corden	6,189	41.3%
	Charles Jeter	18,545	33.0%	Ted Christian	4,900	32.7%
				Bryan McCanless	3,879	25.9%
	TOTAL	*56,116*		*TOTAL*	*14,968*	
				PRIMARY RUNOFF		
				Paul Corden	5,312	68.2%
				Ted Christian	2,479	31.8%
				TOTAL	*7,791*	
Congressional District 5	Albert F. Spencer	Unopposed		John M. Spratt Jr.*	Unopposed	
Congressional District 6	Nancy Harrelson	Unopposed		James E. Clyburn*	Unopposed	

Notes: An asterisk (*) denotes incumbent. The names of unopposed candidates did not appear on the primary ballot; therefore, no votes were cast for these candidates. A runoff was triggered if the leading candidate received less than a majority of the primary vote.

SOUTH DAKOTA

One member At Large

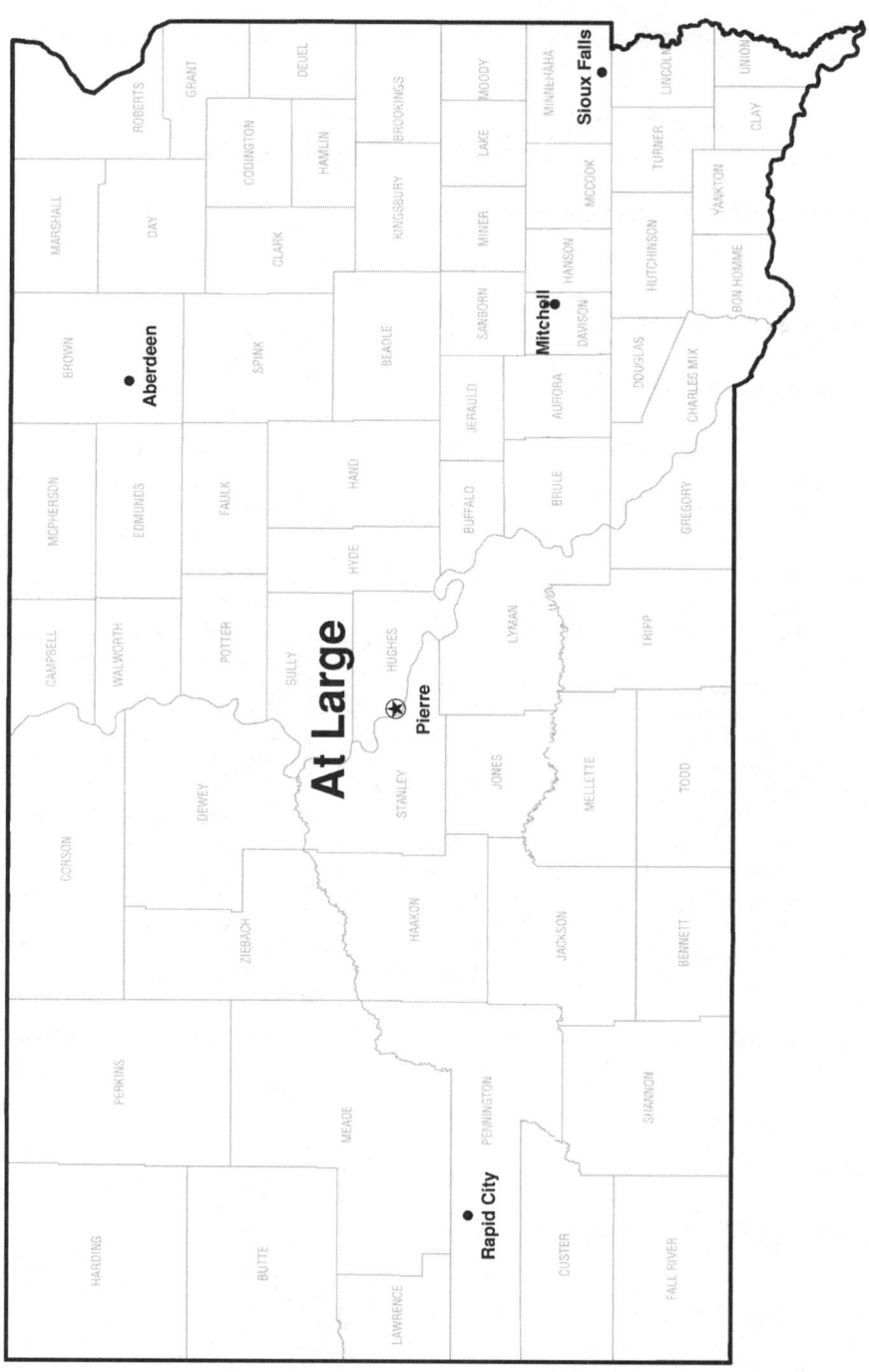

SOUTH DAKOTA

GOVERNOR

Michael Rounds (R). Reelected 2006 to a four-year term. Previously elected 2002.

SENATORS (1 Democrat, 1 Republican)

Tim Johnson (D). Reelected 2008 to a six-year term. Previously elected 2002, 1996.

John Thune (R). Elected 2004 to a six-year term.

REPRESENTATIVE (1 Democrat)

At Large. Stephanie Herseth Sandlin (D)

POSTWAR VOTE FOR PRESIDENT

| | | Republican | | Democratic | | | | Percentage | | | |
| | | | | | | | | Total Vote | | Major Vote | |
Year	Total Vote	Vote	Candidate	Vote	Candidate	Other Vote	Plurality	Rep.	Dem.	Rep.	Dem.
2008	381,975	203,054	McCain, John	170,924	Obama, Barack	7,997	32,130 R	53.2%	44.7%	54.3%	45.7%
2004	388,215	232,584	Bush, George W.	149,244	Kerry, John	6,387	83,340 R	59.9%	38.4%	60.9%	39.1%
2000	316,269	190,700	Bush, George W.	118,804	Gore, Al	6,765	71,896 R	60.3%	37.6%	61.6%	38.4%
1996**	323,826	150,543	Dole, Bob	139,333	Clinton, Bill	33,950	11,210 R	46.5%	43.0%	51.9%	48.1%
1992**	336,254	136,718	Bush, George	124,888	Clinton, Bill	74,648	11,830 R	40.7%	37.1%	52.3%	47.7%
1988	312,991	165,415	Bush, George	145,560	Dukakis, Michael S.	2,016	19,855 R	52.8%	46.5%	53.2%	46.8%
1984	317,867	200,267	Reagan, Ronald	116,113	Mondale, Walter F.	1,487	84,154 R	63.0%	36.5%	63.3%	36.7%
1980**	327,703	198,343	Reagan, Ronald	103,855	Carter, Jimmy	25,505	94,488 R	60.5%	31.7%	65.6%	34.4%
1976	300,678	151,505	Ford, Gerald R.	147,068	Carter, Jimmy	2,105	4,437 R	50.4%	48.9%	50.7%	49.3%
1972	307,415	166,476	Nixon, Richard M.	139,945	McGovern, George S.	994	26,531 R	54.2%	45.5%	54.3%	45.7%
1968**	281,264	149,841	Nixon, Richard M.	118,023	Humphrey, Hubert H.	13,400	31,818 R	53.3%	42.0%	55.9%	44.1%
1964	293,118	130,108	Goldwater, Barry M.	163,010	Johnson, Lyndon B.		32,902 D	44.4%	55.6%	44.4%	55.6%
1960	306,487	178,417	Nixon, Richard M.	128,070	Kennedy, John F.		50,347 R	58.2%	41.8%	58.2%	41.8%
1956	293,857	171,569	Eisenhower, Dwight D.	122,288	Stevenson, Adlai E.		49,281 R	58.4%	41.6%	58.4%	41.6%
1952	294,283	203,857	Eisenhower, Dwight D.	90,426	Stevenson, Adlai E.		113,431 R	69.3%	30.7%	69.3%	30.7%
1948	250,105	129,651	Dewey, Thomas E.	117,653	Truman, Harry S.	2,801	11,998 R	51.8%	47.0%	52.4%	47.6%

**In past elections, the other vote included: 1996 - 31,250 Reform (Ross Perot); 1992 - 73,295 Independent (Perot); 1980 - 21,431 Independent (John Anderson); 1968 - 13,400 American Independent (George Wallace).

SOUTH DAKOTA

POSTWAR VOTE FOR GOVERNOR

Year	Total Vote	Republican Vote	Republican Candidate	Democratic Vote	Democratic Candidate	Other Vote	Rep.-Dem. Plurality	Percentage Total Vote Rep.	Total Vote Dem.	Major Vote Rep.	Major Vote Dem.
2006	335,508	206,990	Rounds, Michael	121,226	Billion, Jack	7,292	85,764 R	61.7%	36.1%	63.1%	36.9%
2002	334,559	189,920	Rounds, Michael	140,263	Abbott, Jim	4,376	49,657 R	56.8%	41.9%	57.5%	42.5%
1998	260,187	166,621	Janklow, Bill	85,473	Hunhoff, Bernie	8,093	81,148 R	64.0%	32.9%	66.1%	33.9%
1994	311,613	172,515	Janklow, Bill	126,273	Beddow, Jim	12,825	46,242 R	55.4%	40.5%	57.7%	42.3%
1990	256,723	151,198	Mickelson, George S.	105,525	Samuelson, Bob L.		45,673 R	58.9%	41.1%	58.9%	41.1%
1986	294,441	152,543	Mickelson, George S.	141,898	Herseth, R. Lars		10,645 R	51.8%	48.2%	51.8%	48.2%
1982	278,562	197,426	Janklow, Bill	81,136	O'Connor, Michael J.		116,290 R	70.9%	29.1%	70.9%	29.1%
1978	259,795	147,116	Janklow, Bill	112,679	McKellips, Roger		34,437 R	56.6%	43.4%	56.6%	43.4%
1974**	278,228	129,077	Olson, John E.	149,151	Kneip, Richard F.		20,074 D	46.4%	53.6%	46.4%	53.6%
1972	308,177	123,165	Thompson, Carveth	185,012	Kneip, Richard F.		61,847 D	40.0%	60.0%	40.0%	60.0%
1970	239,963	108,347	Farrar, Frank	131,616	Kneip, Richard F.		23,269 D	45.2%	54.8%	45.2%	54.8%
1968	276,906	159,646	Farrar, Frank	117,260	Chamberlin, Robert		42,386 R	57.7%	42.3%	57.7%	42.3%
1966	228,214	131,710	Boe, Nils A.	96,504	Chamberlin, Robert		35,206 R	57.7%	42.3%	57.7%	42.3%
1964	290,570	150,151	Boe, Nils A.	140,419	Lindley, John F.		9,732 R	51.7%	48.3%	51.7%	48.3%
1962	256,120	143,682	Gubbrud, Archie M.	112,438	Herseth, Ralph		31,244 R	56.1%	43.9%	56.1%	43.9%
1960	304,625	154,530	Gubbrud, Archie M.	150,095	Herseth, Ralph		4,435 R	50.7%	49.3%	50.7%	49.3%
1958	258,281	125,520	Saunders, Phil	132,761	Herseth, Ralph		7,241 D	48.6%	51.4%	48.6%	51.4%
1956	292,017	158,819	Foss, Joe J.	133,198	Herseth, Ralph		25,621 R	54.4%	45.6%	54.4%	45.6%
1954	236,255	133,878	Foss, Joe J.	102,377	Martin, Ed C.		31,501 R	56.7%	43.3%	56.7%	43.3%
1952	289,515	203,102	Anderson, Sigurd	86,413	Iverson, Sherman A.		116,689 R	70.2%	29.8%	70.2%	29.8%
1950	253,316	154,254	Anderson, Sigurd	99,062	Robbie, Joseph		55,192 R	60.9%	39.1%	60.9%	39.1%
1948	245,372	149,883	Mickelson, George	95,489	Volz, Harold J.		54,394 R	61.1%	38.9%	61.1%	38.9%
1946	162,292	108,998	Mickelson, George	53,294	Haeder, Richard		55,704 R	67.2%	32.8%	67.2%	32.8%

**The term of office of South Dakota's governor was increased from two to four years effective with the 1974 election.

POSTWAR VOTE FOR SENATOR

Year	Total Vote	Republican Vote	Republican Candidate	Democratic Vote	Democratic Candidate	Other Vote	Rep.-Dem. Plurality	Percentage Total Vote Rep.	Total Vote Dem.	Major Vote Rep.	Major Vote Dem.
2008	380,673	142,784	Dykstra, Joel	237,889	Johnson, Tim		95,105 D	37.5%	62.5%	37.5%	62.5%
2004	391,188	197,848	Thune, John	193,340	Daschle, Tom		4,508 R	50.6%	49.4%	50.6%	49.4%
2002	337,508	166,957	Thune, John	167,481	Johnson, Tim	3,070	524 D	49.5%	49.6%	49.9%	50.1%
1998	262,111	95,431	Schmidt, Ron	162,884	Daschle, Tom	3,796	67,453 D	36.4%	62.1%	36.9%	63.1%
1996	324,487	157,954	Pressler, Larry	166,533	Johnson, Tim		8,579 D	48.7%	51.3%	48.7%	51.3%
1992	334,495	108,733	Haar, Charlene	217,095	Daschle, Tom	8,667	108,362 D	32.5%	64.9%	33.4%	66.6%
1990	258,976	135,682	Pressler, Larry	116,727	Muenster, Ted	6,567	18,955 R	52.4%	45.1%	53.8%	46.2%
1986	295,830	143,173	Abdnor, James	152,657	Daschle, Tom		9,484 D	48.4%	51.6%	48.4%	51.6%
1984	315,713	235,176	Pressler, Larry	80,537	Cunningham, George V.		154,639 R	74.5%	25.5%	74.5%	25.5%
1980	327,478	190,594	Abdnor, James	129,018	McGovern, George S.	7,866	61,576 R	58.2%	39.4%	59.6%	40.4%
1978	255,599	170,832	Pressler, Larry	84,767	Barnett, Don		86,065 R	66.8%	33.2%	66.8%	33.2%
1974	278,884	130,955	Thorsness, Leo K.	147,929	McGovern, George S.		16,974 D	47.0%	53.0%	47.0%	53.0%
1972	306,386	131,613	Hirsch, Robert W.	174,773	Abourezk, James		43,160 D	43.0%	57.0%	43.0%	57.0%
1968	279,912	120,951	Gubbrud, Archie M.	158,961	McGovern, George S.		38,010 D	43.2%	56.8%	43.2%	56.8%
1966	227,080	150,517	Mundt, Karl E.	76,563	Wright, Donn H.		73,954 R	66.3%	33.7%	66.3%	33.7%
1962	254,319	126,861	Bottum, Joe H.	127,458	McGovern, George S.		597 D	49.9%	50.1%	49.9%	50.1%
1960	305,442	160,181	Mundt, Karl E.	145,261	McGovern, George S.		14,920 R	52.4%	47.6%	52.4%	47.6%
1956	290,622	147,621	Case, Francis	143,001	Holum, Kenneth		4,620 R	50.8%	49.2%	50.8%	49.2%
1954	235,745	135,071	Mundt, Karl E.	100,674	Holum, Kenneth		34,397 R	57.3%	42.7%	57.3%	42.7%
1950	251,362	160,670	Case, Francis	90,692	Engel, John A.		69,978 R	63.9%	36.1%	63.9%	36.1%
1948	242,833	144,084	Mundt, Karl E.	98,749	Engel, John A.		45,335 R	59.3%	40.7%	59.3%	40.7%

SOUTH DAKOTA

PRESIDENT 2008

2000 Census Population	County	Total Vote	Republican	Democratic	Other	Rep.-Dem. Plurality	Percentage			
							Total Vote		Major Vote	
							Rep.	Dem.	Rep.	Dem.
3,058	AURORA	1,495	794	655	46	139 R	53.1%	43.8%	54.8%	45.2%
17,023	BEADLE	7,714	4,054	3,493	167	561 R	52.6%	45.3%	53.7%	46.3%
3,574	BENNETT	1,208	614	557	37	57 R	50.8%	46.1%	52.4%	47.6%
7,260	BON HOMME	3,175	1,712	1,367	96	345 R	53.9%	43.1%	55.6%	44.4%
28,220	BROOKINGS	13,945	6,431	7,207	307	776 D	46.1%	51.7%	47.2%	52.8%
35,460	BROWN	17,426	8,067	9,041	318	974 D	46.3%	51.9%	47.2%	52.8%
5,364	BRULE	2,439	1,407	965	67	442 R	57.7%	39.6%	59.3%	40.7%
2,032	BUFFALO	619	156	454	9	298 D	25.2%	73.3%	25.6%	74.4%
9,094	BUTTE	4,256	2,821	1,306	129	1,515 R	66.3%	30.7%	68.4%	31.6%
1,782	CAMPBELL	854	591	243	20	348 R	69.2%	28.5%	70.9%	29.1%
9,350	CHARLES MIX	3,978	2,109	1,807	62	302 R	53.0%	45.4%	53.9%	46.1%
4,143	CLARK	1,940	1,065	830	45	235 R	54.9%	42.8%	56.2%	43.8%
13,537	CLAY	6,242	2,296	3,808	138	1,512 D	36.8%	61.0%	37.6%	62.4%
25,897	CODINGTON	12,185	6,374	5,595	216	779 R	52.3%	45.9%	53.3%	46.7%
4,181	CORSON	1,406	535	837	34	302 D	38.1%	59.5%	39.0%	61.0%
7,275	CUSTER	4,507	2,909	1,475	123	1,434 R	64.5%	32.7%	66.4%	33.6%
18,741	DAVISON	8,455	4,731	3,554	170	1,177 R	56.0%	42.0%	57.1%	42.9%
6,267	DAY	3,205	1,372	1,785	48	413 D	42.8%	55.7%	43.5%	56.5%
4,498	DEUEL	2,218	1,088	1,054	76	34 R	49.1%	47.5%	50.8%	49.2%
5,972	DEWEY	2,019	659	1,328	32	669 D	32.6%	65.8%	33.2%	66.8%
3,458	DOUGLAS	1,756	1,293	424	39	869 R	73.6%	24.1%	75.3%	24.7%
4,367	EDMUNDS	2,076	1,213	819	44	394 R	58.4%	39.5%	59.7%	40.3%
7,453	FALL RIVER	3,809	2,348	1,338	123	1,010 R	61.6%	35.1%	63.7%	36.3%
2,640	FAULK	1,192	739	426	27	313 R	62.0%	35.7%	63.4%	36.6%
7,847	GRANT	3,830	1,951	1,786	93	165 R	50.9%	46.6%	52.2%	47.8%
4,792	GREGORY	2,247	1,423	771	53	652 R	63.3%	34.3%	64.9%	35.1%
2,196	HAAKON	1,153	939	187	27	752 R	81.4%	16.2%	83.4%	16.6%
5,540	HAMLIN	2,787	1,661	1,043	83	618 R	59.6%	37.4%	61.4%	38.6%
3,741	HAND	2,011	1,247	718	46	529 R	62.0%	35.7%	63.5%	36.5%
3,139	HANSON	2,431	1,426	961	44	465 R	58.7%	39.5%	59.7%	40.3%
1,353	HARDING	734	575	135	24	440 R	78.3%	18.4%	81.0%	19.0%
16,481	HUGHES	8,468	5,298	3,037	133	2,261 R	62.6%	35.9%	63.6%	36.4%
8,075	HUTCHINSON	3,608	2,285	1,242	81	1,043 R	63.3%	34.4%	64.8%	35.2%
1,671	HYDE	785	547	226	12	321 R	69.7%	28.8%	70.8%	29.2%
2,930	JACKSON	1,133	668	435	30	233 R	59.0%	38.4%	60.6%	39.4%
2,295	JERAULD	1,105	546	542	17	4 R	49.4%	49.0%	50.2%	49.8%
1,193	JONES	627	463	147	17	316 R	73.8%	23.4%	75.9%	24.1%
5,815	KINGSBURY	2,784	1,435	1,277	72	158 R	51.5%	45.9%	52.9%	47.1%
11,276	LAKE	6,157	2,993	3,033	131	40 D	48.6%	49.3%	49.7%	50.3%
21,802	LAWRENCE	12,055	6,787	4,932	336	1,855 R	56.3%	40.9%	57.9%	42.1%
24,131	LINCOLN	20,767	11,803	8,642	322	3,161 R	56.8%	41.6%	57.7%	42.3%
3,895	LYMAN	1,641	894	710	37	184 R	54.5%	43.3%	55.7%	44.3%
5,832	MCCOOK	2,945	1,646	1,219	80	427 R	55.9%	41.4%	57.5%	42.5%
2,904	MCPHERSON	1,375	915	441	19	474 R	66.5%	32.1%	67.5%	32.5%
4,576	MARSHALL	2,191	900	1,261	30	361 D	41.1%	57.6%	41.6%	58.4%
24,253	MEADE	11,606	7,515	3,751	340	3,764 R	64.8%	32.3%	66.7%	33.3%
2,083	MELLETTE	843	445	373	25	72 R	52.8%	44.2%	54.4%	45.6%
2,884	MINER	1,218	577	605	36	28 D	47.4%	49.7%	48.8%	51.2%
148,281	MINNEHAHA	80,552	39,251	39,838	1,463	587 D	48.7%	49.5%	49.6%	50.4%
6,595	MOODY	3,254	1,508	1,663	83	155 D	46.3%	51.1%	47.6%	52.4%

SOUTH DAKOTA

PRESIDENT 2008

2000 Census Population	County	Total Vote	Republican	Democratic	Other	Rep.-Dem. Plurality	Percentage			
							Total Vote		Major Vote	
							Rep.	Dem.	Rep.	Dem.
88,565	PENNINGTON	46,280	27,603	17,802	875	9,801 R	59.6%	38.5%	60.8%	39.2%
3,363	PERKINS	1,686	1,102	499	85	603 R	65.4%	29.6%	68.8%	31.2%
2,693	POTTER	1,440	937	482	21	455 R	65.1%	33.5%	66.0%	34.0%
10,016	ROBERTS	4,536	1,781	2,672	83	891 D	39.3%	58.9%	40.0%	60.0%
2,675	SANBORN	1,207	669	500	38	169 R	55.4%	41.4%	57.2%	42.8%
12,466	SHANNON	3,350	331	2,971	48	2,640 D	9.9%	88.7%	10.0%	90.0%
7,454	SPINK	3,269	1,660	1,550	59	110 R	50.8%	47.4%	51.7%	48.3%
2,772	STANLEY	1,553	1,017	510	26	507 R	65.5%	32.8%	66.6%	33.4%
1,556	SULLY	833	581	233	19	348 R	69.7%	28.0%	71.4%	28.6%
9,050	TODD	2,828	571	2,208	49	1,637 D	20.2%	78.1%	20.5%	79.5%
6,430	TRIPP	2,839	1,859	914	66	945 R	65.5%	32.2%	67.0%	33.0%
8,849	TURNER	4,352	2,538	1,681	133	857 R	58.3%	38.6%	60.2%	39.8%
12,584	UNION	7,701	4,310	3,244	147	1,066 R	56.0%	42.1%	57.1%	42.9%
5,974	WALWORTH	2,650	1,668	923	59	745 R	62.9%	34.8%	64.4%	35.6%
21,652	YANKTON	10,134	5,039	4,838	257	201 R	49.7%	47.7%	51.0%	49.0%
2,519	ZIEBACH	891	312	554	25	242 D	35.0%	62.2%	36.0%	64.0%
754,844	TOTAL	381,975	203,054	170,924	7,997	32,130 R	53.2%	44.7%	54.3%	45.7%

SOUTH DAKOTA

SENATOR 2008

2000 Census Population	County	Total Vote	Republican	Democratic	Other	Rep.-Dem. Plurality	Percentage			
							Total Vote		Major Vote	
							Rep.	Dem.	Rep.	Dem.
3,058	AURORA	1,499	484	1,015		531 D	32.3%	67.7%	32.3%	67.7%
17,023	BEADLE	7,726	2,589	5,137		2,548 D	33.5%	66.5%	33.5%	66.5%
3,574	BENNETT	1,201	418	783		365 D	34.8%	65.2%	34.8%	65.2%
7,260	BON HOMME	3,199	1,070	2,129		1,059 D	33.4%	66.6%	33.4%	66.6%
28,220	BROOKINGS	13,839	4,485	9,354		4,869 D	32.4%	67.6%	32.4%	67.6%
35,460	BROWN	17,475	4,993	12,482		7,489 D	28.6%	71.4%	28.6%	71.4%
5,364	BRULE	2,457	885	1,572		687 D	36.0%	64.0%	36.0%	64.0%
2,032	BUFFALO	620	108	512		404 D	17.4%	82.6%	17.4%	82.6%
9,094	BUTTE	4,235	2,034	2,201		167 D	48.0%	52.0%	48.0%	52.0%
1,782	CAMPBELL	857	392	465		73 D	45.7%	54.3%	45.7%	54.3%
9,350	CHARLES MIX	4,028	1,422	2,606		1,184 D	35.3%	64.7%	35.3%	64.7%
4,143	CLARK	1,973	641	1,332		691 D	32.5%	67.5%	32.5%	67.5%
13,537	CLAY	6,182	1,545	4,637		3,092 D	25.0%	75.0%	25.0%	75.0%
25,897	CODINGTON	12,217	4,253	7,964		3,711 D	34.8%	65.2%	34.8%	65.2%
4,181	CORSON	1,394	394	1,000		606 D	28.3%	71.7%	28.3%	71.7%
7,275	CUSTER	4,504	2,217	2,287		70 D	49.2%	50.8%	49.2%	50.8%
18,741	DAVISON	8,482	3,107	5,375		2,268 D	36.6%	63.4%	36.6%	63.4%
6,267	DAY	3,224	823	2,401		1,578 D	25.5%	74.5%	25.5%	74.5%
4,498	DEUEL	2,229	659	1,570		911 D	29.6%	70.4%	29.6%	70.4%
5,972	DEWEY	2,019	353	1,666		1,313 D	17.5%	82.5%	17.5%	82.5%

SOUTH DAKOTA

SENATOR 2008

2000 Census Population	County	Total Vote	Republican	Democratic	Other	Rep.-Dem. Plurality	Percentage Total Vote Rep.	Total Vote Dem.	Major Vote Rep.	Major Vote Dem.
3,458	DOUGLAS	1,753	848	905		57 D	48.4%	51.6%	48.4%	51.6%
4,367	EDMUNDS	2,083	758	1,325		567 D	36.4%	63.6%	36.4%	63.6%
7,453	FALL RIVER	3,778	1,710	2,068		358 D	45.3%	54.7%	45.3%	54.7%
2,640	FAULK	1,202	439	763		324 D	36.5%	63.5%	36.5%	63.5%
7,847	GRANT	3,826	1,208	2,618		1,410 D	31.6%	68.4%	31.6%	68.4%
4,792	GREGORY	2,272	1,004	1,268		264 D	44.2%	55.8%	44.2%	55.8%
2,196	HAAKON	1,159	608	551		57 R	52.5%	47.5%	52.5%	47.5%
5,540	HAMLIN	2,793	1,200	1,593		393 D	43.0%	57.0%	43.0%	57.0%
3,741	HAND	2,011	775	1,236		461 D	38.5%	61.5%	38.5%	61.5%
3,139	HANSON	2,318	1,107	1,211		104 D	47.8%	52.2%	47.8%	52.2%
1,353	HARDING	736	452	284		168 R	61.4%	38.6%	61.4%	38.6%
16,481	HUGHES	8,461	3,406	5,055		1,649 D	40.3%	59.7%	40.3%	59.7%
8,075	HUTCHINSON	3,608	1,448	2,160		712 D	40.1%	59.9%	40.1%	59.9%
1,671	HYDE	798	335	463		128 D	42.0%	58.0%	42.0%	58.0%
2,930	JACKSON	1,134	448	686		238 D	39.5%	60.5%	39.5%	60.5%
2,295	JERAULD	1,115	341	774		433 D	30.6%	69.4%	30.6%	69.4%
1,193	JONES	621	318	303		15 R	51.2%	48.8%	51.2%	48.8%
5,815	KINGSBURY	2,807	798	2,009		1,211 D	28.4%	71.6%	28.4%	71.6%
11,276	LAKE	6,107	2,021	4,086		2,065 D	33.1%	66.9%	33.1%	66.9%
21,802	LAWRENCE	11,970	5,294	6,676		1,382 D	44.2%	55.8%	44.2%	55.8%
24,131	LINCOLN	20,696	8,817	11,879		3,062 D	42.6%	57.4%	42.6%	57.4%
3,895	LYMAN	1,647	571	1,076		505 D	34.7%	65.3%	34.7%	65.3%
5,832	MCCOOK	2,960	1,051	1,909		858 D	35.5%	64.5%	35.5%	64.5%
2,904	MCPHERSON	1,373	633	740		107 D	46.1%	53.9%	46.1%	53.9%
4,576	MARSHALL	2,199	585	1,614		1,029 D	26.6%	73.4%	26.6%	73.4%
24,253	MEADE	11,491	5,402	6,089		687 D	47.0%	53.0%	47.0%	53.0%
2,083	MELLETTE	839	279	560		281 D	33.3%	66.7%	33.3%	66.7%
2,884	MINER	1,243	328	915		587 D	26.4%	73.6%	26.4%	73.6%
148,281	MINNEHAHA	79,882	29,189	50,693		21,504 D	36.5%	63.5%	36.5%	63.5%
6,595	MOODY	3,284	947	2,337		1,390 D	28.8%	71.2%	28.8%	71.2%
88,565	PENNINGTON	45,793	20,980	24,813		3,833 D	45.8%	54.2%	45.8%	54.2%
3,363	PERKINS	1,702	877	825		52 R	51.5%	48.5%	51.5%	48.5%
2,693	POTTER	1,439	593	846		253 D	41.2%	58.8%	41.2%	58.8%
10,016	ROBERTS	4,568	1,321	3,247		1,926 D	28.9%	71.1%	28.9%	71.1%
2,675	SANBORN	1,214	367	847		480 D	30.2%	69.8%	30.2%	69.8%
12,466	SHANNON	3,362	172	3,190		3,018 D	5.1%	94.9%	5.1%	94.9%
7,454	SPINK	3,294	945	2,349		1,404 D	28.7%	71.3%	28.7%	71.3%
2,772	STANLEY	1,551	637	914		277 D	41.1%	58.9%	41.1%	58.9%
1,556	SULLY	836	379	457		78 D	45.3%	54.7%	45.3%	54.7%
9,050	TODD	2,834	415	2,419		2,004 D	14.6%	85.4%	14.6%	85.4%
6,430	TRIPP	2,854	1,234	1,620		386 D	43.2%	56.8%	43.2%	56.8%
8,849	TURNER	4,359	1,556	2,803		1,247 D	35.7%	64.3%	35.7%	64.3%
12,584	UNION	7,630	3,337	4,293		956 D	43.7%	56.3%	43.7%	56.3%
5,974	WALWORTH	2,665	1,131	1,534		403 D	42.4%	57.6%	42.4%	57.6%
21,652	YANKTON	10,145	3,451	6,694		3,243 D	34.0%	66.0%	34.0%	66.0%
2,519	ZIEBACH	901	197	704		507 D	21.9%	78.1%	21.9%	78.1%
754,844	TOTAL	380,673	142,784	237,889		95,105 D	37.5%	62.5%	37.5%	62.5%

SOUTH DAKOTA

HOUSE OF REPRESENTATIVES

| | | | Republican | | Democratic | | Other | Rep.-Dem. | Percentage | | | |
| | | Total | | | | | | | Total Vote | | Major Vote | |
CD	Year	Vote	Vote	Candidate	Vote	Candidate	Vote	Plurality	Rep.	Dem.	Rep.	Dem.
AL	2008	379,007	122,966	LIEN, CHRIS	256,041	HERSETH SANDLIN, STEPHANIE*		133,075 D	32.4%	67.6%	32.4%	67.6%
AL	2006	333,562	97,864	WHALEN, BRUCE W.	230,468	HERSETH, STEPHANIE*	5,230	132,604 D	29.3%	69.1%	29.8%	70.2%
AL	2004	389,468	178,823	DIEDRICH, LARRY	207,837	HERSETH, STEPHANIE*	2,808	29,014 D	45.9%	53.4%	46.2%	53.8%
AL	2002	336,807	180,023	JANKLOW, BILL	153,656	HERSETH, STEPHANIE	3,128	26,367 R	53.4%	45.6%	54.0%	46.0%
AL	2000	314,761	231,083	THUNE, JOHN*	78,321	HOHN, CURT	5,357	152,762 R	73.4%	24.9%	74.7%	25.3%
AL	1998	258,590	194,157	THUNE, JOHN*	64,433	MOSER, JEFF		129,724 R	75.1%	24.9%	75.1%	24.9%
AL	1996	323,203	186,393	THUNE, JOHN	119,547	WEILAND, RICK	17,263	66,846 R	57.7%	37.0%	60.9%	39.1%
AL	1994	305,922	112,054	BERKHOUT, JAN	183,036	JOHNSON, TIM*	10,832	70,982 D	36.6%	59.8%	38.0%	62.0%
AL	1992	332,902	89,375	TIMMER, JOHN	230,070	JOHNSON, TIM*	13,457	140,695 D	26.8%	69.1%	28.0%	72.0%
AL	1990	257,298	83,484	FRANKENFELD, DON	173,814	JOHNSON, TIM*		90,330 D	32.4%	67.6%	32.4%	67.6%
AL	1988	311,916	88,157	VOLK, DAVID	223,759	JOHNSON, TIM*		135,602 D	28.3%	71.7%	28.3%	71.7%
AL	1986	289,723	118,261	BELL, DALE	171,462	JOHNSON, TIM		53,201 D	40.8%	59.2%	40.8%	59.2%
AL	1984	316,222	134,821	BELL, DALE	181,401	DASCHLE, TOM*		46,580 D	42.6%	57.4%	42.6%	57.4%
AL	1982	275,652	133,530	ROBERTS, CLINT	142,122	DASCHLE, TOM*		8,592 D	48.4%	51.6%	48.4%	51.6%

Notes: An asterisk (*) denotes incumbent. South Dakota had two House seats before 1982.

SOUTH DAKOTA

GENERAL AND PRIMARY ELECTIONS

2008 GENERAL ELECTIONS

President   Other vote was 4,267 Independent (Ralph Nader); 1,895 Constitution (Chuck Baldwin); 1,835 Independent (Bob Barr).

Senator

House   Other vote was:

   At Large

2008 PRIMARY ELECTIONS

Primary   June 3, 2008   **Registration**
(active registrants as of May 19, 2008)

Republican	235,388
Democratic	195,063
Libertarian	1,002
Constitution	297
Other	596
Independent	75,894
TOTAL	*508,240*

Primary Type   Closed—Only registered Democrats and Republicans could vote in their party's primary. In addition to the active registered voters, there were 46,285 inactive voters at the time of the 2008 primary.

SOUTH DAKOTA

GENERAL AND PRIMARY ELECTIONS

	REPUBLICAN PRIMARIES			DEMOCRATIC PRIMARIES		
President	John McCain	42,788	70.2%	Hillary Clinton	54,128	55.3%
	Ron Paul	10,072	16.5%	Barack Obama	43,669	44.7%
	Mike Huckabee	4,328	7.1%			
	Mitt Romney	1,990	3.3%			
	Uncommitted	1,786	2.9%			
	TOTAL	60,964		TOTAL	97,797	
Senator	Joel Dykstra	34,598	65.7%	Tim Johnson*	Unopposed	
	Sam Kephart	13,047	24.8%			
	Charles Lyonel Gonyo	4,983	9.5%			
	TOTAL	52,628				
House At Large	Chris Lien	Unopposed		Stephanie Herseth Sandlin*	Unopposed	

Notes: An asterisk (*) denotes incumbent. The names of unopposed candidates did not appear on the primary ballot; therefore, no votes were cast for these candidates. A runoff was triggered if the leading candidate received less than 35 percent of the primary vote. No runoffs for Congress were required in 2008.

TENNESSEE

Congressional districts first established for elections held in 2002
9 members

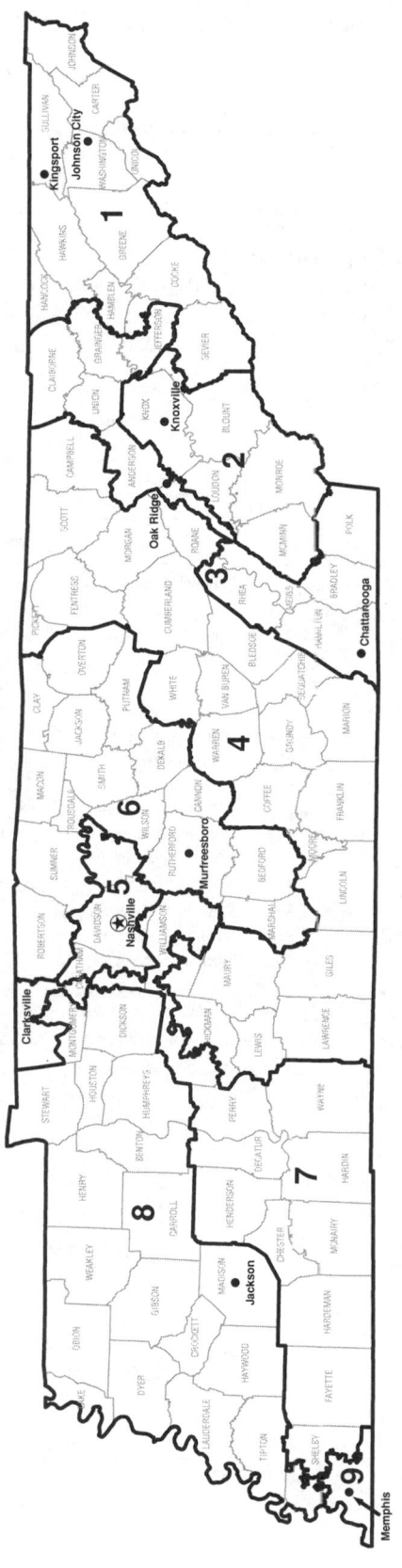

TENNESSEE

GOVERNOR

Phil Bredesen (D). Reelected 2006 to a four-year term. Previously elected 2002.

SENATORS (2 Republicans)

Lamar Alexander (R). Reelected 2008 to a six-year term. Previously elected 2002.

Bob Corker (R). Elected 2006 to a six-year term.

REPRESENTATIVES (5 Democrats, 4 Republicans)

1. Phil Roe (R)
2. John J. "Jimmy" Duncan Jr. (R)
3. Zach Wamp (R)
4. Lincoln Davis (D)
5. Jim Cooper (D)
6. Bart Gordon (D)
7. Marsha Blackburn (R)
8. John Tanner (D)
9. Steve Cohen (D)

POSTWAR VOTE FOR PRESIDENT

Year	Total Vote	Republican Vote	Republican Candidate	Democratic Vote	Democratic Candidate	Other Vote	Plurality	Total Vote Rep.	Total Vote Dem.	Major Vote Rep.	Major Vote Dem.
2008	2,599,749	1,479,178	McCain, John	1,087,437	Obama, Barack	33,134	391,741 R	56.9%	41.8%	57.6%	42.4%
2004	2,437,319	1,384,375	Bush, George W.	1,036,477	Kerry, John	16,467	347,898 R	56.8%	42.5%	57.2%	42.8%
2000**	2,076,181	1,061,949	Bush, George W.	981,720	Gore, Al	32,512	80,229 R	51.1%	47.3%	52.0%	48.0%
1996**	1,894,105	863,530	Dole, Bob	909,146	Clinton, Bill	121,429	45,616 D	45.6%	48.0%	48.7%	51.3%
1992**	1,982,638	841,300	Bush, George	933,521	Clinton, Bill	207,817	92,221 D	42.4%	47.1%	47.4%	52.6%
1988	1,636,250	947,233	Bush, George	679,794	Dukakis, Michael S.	9,223	267,439 R	57.9%	41.5%	58.2%	41.8%
1984	1,711,994	990,212	Reagan, Ronald	711,714	Mondale, Walter F.	10,068	278,498 R	57.8%	41.6%	58.2%	41.8%
1980**	1,617,616	787,761	Reagan, Ronald	783,051	Carter, Jimmy	46,804	4,710 R	48.7%	48.4%	50.1%	49.9%
1976	1,476,345	633,969	Ford, Gerald R.	825,879	Carter, Jimmy	16,497	191,910 D	42.9%	55.9%	43.4%	56.6%
1972	1,201,182	813,147	Nixon, Richard M.	357,293	McGovern, George S.	30,742	455,854 R	67.7%	29.7%	69.5%	30.5%
1968**	1,248,617	472,592	Nixon, Richard M.	351,233	Humphrey, Hubert H.	424,792	47,800 R	37.8%	28.1%	57.4%	42.6%
1964	1,143,946	508,965	Goldwater, Barry M.	634,947	Johnson, Lyndon B.	34	125,982 D	44.5%	55.5%	44.5%	55.5%
1960	1,051,792	556,577	Nixon, Richard M.	481,453	Kennedy, John F.	13,762	75,124 R	52.9%	45.8%	53.6%	46.4%
1956	939,404	462,288	Eisenhower, Dwight D.	456,507	Stevenson, Adlai E.	20,609	5,781 R	49.2%	48.6%	50.3%	49.7%
1952	892,553	446,147	Eisenhower, Dwight D.	443,710	Stevenson, Adlai E.	2,696	2,437 R	50.0%	49.7%	50.1%	49.9%
1948**	550,283	202,914	Dewey, Thomas E.	270,402	Truman, Harry S.	76,967	67,488 D	36.9%	49.1%	42.9%	57.1%

**In past elections, the other vote included: 2000 - 19,781 Green (Ralph Nader); 1996 - 105,918 Reform (Ross Perot); 1992 - 199,968 Independent (Perot); 1980 - 35,991 Independent (John Anderson); 1968 - 424,792 American Independent (George Wallace), who finished second; 1948 - 73,815 States' Rights (Strom Thurmond).

TENNESSEE

POSTWAR VOTE FOR GOVERNOR

Year	Total Vote	Republican		Democratic		Other Vote	Rep.-Dem. Plurality	Percentage			
		Vote	Candidate	Vote	Candidate			Total Vote		Major Vote	
								Rep.	Dem.	Rep.	Dem.
2006	1,818,549	540,853	Bryson, Jim	1,247,491	Bredesen, Phil	30,205	706,638 D	29.7%	68.6%	30.2%	69.8%
2002	1,653,167	786,803	Hilleary, Van	837,284	Bredesen, Phil	29,080	50,481 D	47.6%	50.6%	48.4%	51.6%
1998	976,236	669,973	Sundquist, Don	287,750	Hooker, John J.	18,513	382,223 R	68.6%	29.5%	70.0%	30.0%
1994	1,487,130	807,104	Sundquist, Don	664,252	Bredesen, Phil	15,774	142,852 R	54.3%	44.7%	54.9%	45.1%
1990	790,441	289,348	Henry, Dwight	480,885	McWherter, Ned	20,208	191,537 D	36.6%	60.8%	37.6%	62.4%
1986	1,210,339	553,449	Dunn, Winfield	656,602	McWherter, Ned	288	103,153 D	45.7%	54.2%	45.7%	54.3%
1982	1,238,927	737,963	Alexander, Lamar	500,937	Tyree, Randy	27	237,026 R	59.6%	40.4%	59.6%	40.4%
1978	1,189,695	661,959	Alexander, Lamar	523,495	Butcher, Jake	4,241	138,464 R	55.6%	44.0%	55.8%	44.2%
1974	1,040,714	455,467	Alexander, Lamar	576,833	Blanton, Ray	8,414	121,366 D	43.8%	55.4%	44.1%	55.9%
1970	1,108,247	575,777	Dunn, Winfield	509,521	Hooker, John J.	22,949	66,256 R	52.0%	46.0%	53.1%	46.9%
1966	656,566		—	532,998	Ellington, Buford	123,568	532,998 D		81.2%		100.0%
1962**	621,064	100,190	Patty, Hubert D.	315,648	Clement, Frank G.	205,226	215,458 D	16.1%	50.8%	24.1%	75.9%
1958**	432,545	35,938	Wall, Thomas P.	248,874	Ellington, Buford	147,733	212,936 D	8.3%	57.5%	12.6%	87.4%
1954**	322,586		—	281,291	Clement, Frank G.	41,295	281,291 D		87.2%		100.0%
1952	806,771	166,377	Witt, R. Beecher	640,290	Clement, Frank G.	104	473,913 D	20.6%	79.4%	20.6%	79.4%
1950**	236,194		—	184,437	Browning, Gordon	51,757	184,437 D		78.1%		100.0%
1948	543,881	179,957	Acuff, Roy	363,903	Browning, Gordon	21	183,946 D	33.1%	66.9%	33.1%	66.9%
1946	229,456	73,222	Lowe, W. O.	149,937	McCord, Jim Nance	6,297	76,715 D	31.9%	65.3%	32.8%	67.2%

Notes: **In past elections, the other vote included: 1962 - 203,765 Independent (William R. Anderson), who finished second; 1958 - 136,399 Independent (Jim Nance McCord), who finished second; 1954 - 39,574 Independent (John R. Neal); 1950 - 51,757 Independent (Neal). The Republican Party did not run a gubernatorial candidate in 1950, 1954, and 1966. The term of office of Tennessee's governor was increased from two to four years effective with the 1954 election.

POSTWAR VOTE FOR SENATOR

Year	Total Vote	Republican		Democratic		Other Vote	Rep.-Dem. Plurality	Percentage			
		Vote	Candidate	Vote	Candidate			Total Vote		Major Vote	
								Rep.	Dem.	Rep.	Dem.
2008	2,424,585	1,579,477	Alexander, Lamar	767,236	Tuke, Robert D.	77,872	812,241 R	65.1%	31.6%	67.3%	32.7%
2006	1,833,695	929,911	Corker, Bob	879,976	Ford, Harold E. Jr.	23,808	49,935 R	50.7%	48.0%	51.4%	48.6%
2002	1,642,421	891,420	Alexander, Lamar	728,295	Clement, Bob	22,706	163,125 R	54.3%	44.3%	55.0%	45.0%
2000	1,928,613	1,255,444	Frist, Bill	621,152	Clark, Jeff	52,017	634,292 R	65.1%	32.2%	66.9%	33.1%
1996	1,778,664	1,091,554	Thompson, Fred	654,937	Gordon, Houston	32,173	436,617 R	61.4%	36.8%	62.5%	37.5%
1994	1,480,391	834,226	Frist, Bill	623,164	Sasser, James R.	23,001	211,062 R	56.4%	42.1%	57.2%	42.8%
1994S	1,465,862	885,998	Thompson, Fred	565,930	Cooper, Jim	13,934	320,068 R	60.4%	38.6%	61.0%	39.0%
1990	783,922	233,703	Hawkins, William R.	530,898	Gore, Al	19,321	297,195 D	29.8%	67.7%	30.6%	69.4%
1988	1,567,181	541,033	Anderson, Bill	1,020,061	Sasser, James R.	6,087	479,028 D	34.5%	65.1%	34.7%	65.3%
1984	1,648,064	557,016	Ashe, Victor	1,000,607	Gore, Al	90,441	443,591 D	33.8%	60.7%	35.8%	64.2%
1982	1,259,785	479,642	Beard, Robin L.	780,113	Sasser, James R.	30	300,471 D	38.1%	61.9%	38.1%	61.9%
1978	1,157,094	642,644	Baker, Howard H., Jr.	466,228	Eskind, Jane	48,222	176,416 R	55.5%	40.3%	58.0%	42.0%
1976	1,432,046	673,231	Brock, William E.	751,180	Sasser, James R.	7,635	77,949 D	47.0%	52.5%	47.3%	52.7%
1972	1,164,195	716,539	Baker, Howard H., Jr.	440,599	Blanton, Ray	7,057	275,940 R	61.5%	37.8%	61.9%	38.1%
1970	1,097,041	562,645	Brock, William E.	519,858	Gore, Albert	14,538	42,787 R	51.3%	47.4%	52.0%	48.0%
1966	866,961	483,063	Baker, Howard H., Jr.	383,843	Clement, Frank G.	55	99,220 R	55.7%	44.3%	55.7%	44.3%
1964	1,064,018	493,475	Kuykendall, Daniel H.	570,542	Gore, Albert	1	77,067 D	46.4%	53.6%	46.4%	53.6%
1964S	1,091,093	517,330	Baker, Howard H., Jr.	568,905	Bass, Ross	4,858	51,575 D	47.4%	52.1%	47.6%	52.4%
1960	828,519	234,053	Frazier, A. Bradley	594,460	Kefauver, Estes	6	360,407 D	28.2%	71.7%	28.2%	71.8%
1958	401,666	76,371	Atkins, Hobart F.	317,324	Gore, Albert	7,971	240,953 D	19.0%	79.0%	19.4%	80.6%
1954	356,094	106,971	Wall, Thomas P.	249,121	Kefauver, Estes	2	142,150 D	30.0%	70.0%	30.0%	70.0%
1952	735,219	153,479	Atkins, Hobart F.	545,432	Gore, Albert	36,308	391,953 D	20.9%	74.2%	22.0%	78.0%
1948	499,218	166,947	Reece, B. Carroll	326,142	Kefauver, Estes	6,129	159,195 D	33.4%	65.3%	33.9%	66.1%
1946	218,714	57,238	Ladd, William B.	145,654	McKellar, Kenneth	15,822	88,416 D	26.2%	66.6%	28.2%	71.8%

Note: One each of the 1964 and 1994 elections was for a short term to fill a vacancy.

TENNESSEE

PRESIDENT 2008

2000 Census Population	County	Total Vote	Republican	Democratic	Other	Rep.-Dem. Plurality	Total Vote Rep.	Total Vote Dem.	Major Vote Rep.	Major Vote Dem.
71,330	ANDERSON	31,570	19,675	11,396	499	8,279 R	62.3%	36.1%	63.3%	36.7%
37,586	BEDFORD	15,507	10,217	5,027	263	5,190 R	65.9%	32.4%	67.0%	33.0%
16,537	BENTON	6,479	3,696	2,645	138	1,051 R	57.0%	40.8%	58.3%	41.7%
12,367	BLEDSOE	4,784	3,166	1,517	101	1,649 R	66.2%	31.7%	67.6%	32.4%
105,823	BLOUNT	51,645	35,571	15,253	821	20,318 R	68.9%	29.5%	70.0%	30.0%
87,965	BRADLEY	38,191	28,333	9,357	501	18,976 R	74.2%	24.5%	75.2%	24.8%
39,854	CAMPBELL	12,628	8,535	3,867	226	4,668 R	67.6%	30.6%	68.8%	31.2%
12,826	CANNON	5,457	3,322	2,011	124	1,311 R	60.9%	36.9%	62.3%	37.7%
29,475	CARROLL	11,646	7,455	3,980	211	3,475 R	64.0%	34.2%	65.2%	34.8%
56,742	CARTER	21,769	15,852	5,587	330	10,265 R	72.8%	25.7%	73.9%	26.1%
35,912	CHEATHAM	16,428	10,702	5,498	228	5,204 R	65.1%	33.5%	66.1%	33.9%
15,540	CHESTER	6,459	4,587	1,797	75	2,790 R	71.0%	27.8%	71.9%	28.1%
29,862	CLAIBORNE	10,420	7,175	3,078	167	4,097 R	68.9%	29.5%	70.0%	30.0%
7,976	CLAY	2,994	1,676	1,248	70	428 R	56.0%	41.7%	57.3%	42.7%
33,565	COCKE	12,481	8,945	3,340	196	5,605 R	71.7%	26.8%	72.8%	27.2%
48,014	COFFEE	20,790	13,250	7,132	408	6,118 R	63.7%	34.3%	65.0%	35.0%
14,532	CROCKETT	6,037	3,994	1,967	76	2,027 R	66.2%	32.6%	67.0%	33.0%
46,802	CUMBERLAND	25,712	17,436	7,889	387	9,547 R	67.8%	30.7%	68.8%	31.2%
569,891	DAVIDSON	264,486	102,915	158,423	3,148	55,508 D	38.9%	59.9%	39.4%	60.6%
11,731	DECATUR	4,763	3,101	1,566	96	1,535 R	65.1%	32.9%	66.4%	33.6%
17,423	DE KALB	7,065	4,085	2,832	148	1,253 R	57.8%	40.1%	59.1%	40.9%
43,156	DICKSON	19,519	11,677	7,506	336	4,171 R	59.8%	38.5%	60.9%	39.1%
37,279	DYER	14,450	9,859	4,411	180	5,448 R	68.2%	30.5%	69.1%	30.9%
28,806	FAYETTE	19,254	12,173	6,892	189	5,281 R	63.2%	35.8%	63.8%	36.2%
16,625	FENTRESS	6,739	4,789	1,831	119	2,958 R	71.1%	27.2%	72.3%	27.7%
39,270	FRANKLIN	17,432	10,539	6,613	280	3,926 R	60.5%	37.9%	61.4%	38.6%
48,152	GIBSON	21,253	13,516	7,406	331	6,110 R	63.6%	34.8%	64.6%	35.4%
29,447	GILES	11,689	6,902	4,614	173	2,288 R	59.0%	39.5%	59.9%	40.1%
20,659	GRAINGER	7,503	5,297	2,066	140	3,231 R	70.6%	27.5%	71.9%	28.1%
62,909	GREENE	24,670	17,151	7,110	409	10,041 R	69.5%	28.8%	70.7%	29.3%
14,332	GRUNDY	4,632	2,563	1,971	98	592 R	55.3%	42.6%	56.5%	43.5%
58,128	HAMBLEN	22,669	15,508	6,807	354	8,701 R	68.4%	30.0%	69.5%	30.5%
307,896	HAMILTON	147,520	81,702	64,246	1,572	17,456 R	55.4%	43.6%	56.0%	44.0%
6,786	HANCOCK	2,241	1,588	604	49	984 R	70.9%	27.0%	72.4%	27.6%
28,105	HARDEMAN	11,237	5,225	5,919	93	694 D	46.5%	52.7%	46.9%	53.1%
25,578	HARDIN	10,035	7,077	2,794	164	4,283 R	70.5%	27.8%	71.7%	28.3%
53,563	HAWKINS	21,040	14,756	5,930	354	8,826 R	70.1%	28.2%	71.3%	28.7%
19,797	HAYWOOD	8,121	3,165	4,893	63	1,728 D	39.0%	60.3%	39.3%	60.7%
25,522	HENDERSON	10,834	7,669	3,021	144	4,648 R	70.8%	27.9%	71.7%	28.3%
31,115	HENRY	13,545	8,182	5,153	210	3,029 R	60.4%	38.0%	61.4%	38.6%
22,295	HICKMAN	8,498	4,784	3,563	151	1,221 R	56.3%	41.9%	57.3%	42.7%
8,088	HOUSTON	3,354	1,608	1,678	68	70 D	47.9%	50.0%	48.9%	51.1%
17,929	HUMPHREYS	7,580	3,818	3,600	162	218 R	50.4%	47.5%	51.5%	48.5%
10,984	JACKSON	4,501	2,185	2,224	92	39 D	48.5%	49.4%	49.6%	50.4%
44,294	JEFFERSON	18,532	13,092	5,178	262	7,914 R	70.6%	27.9%	71.7%	28.3%
17,499	JOHNSON	6,591	4,621	1,837	133	2,784 R	70.1%	27.9%	71.6%	28.4%
382,032	KNOX	186,086	113,015	70,215	2,856	42,800 R	60.7%	37.7%	61.7%	38.3%
7,954	LAKE	2,238	1,175	1,024	39	151 R	52.5%	45.8%	53.4%	46.6%
27,101	LAUDERDALE	9,338	4,933	4,322	83	611 R	52.8%	46.3%	53.3%	46.7%
39,926	LAWRENCE	16,020	10,566	5,161	293	5,405 R	66.0%	32.2%	67.2%	32.8%

TENNESSEE

PRESIDENT 2008

2000 Census Population	County	Total Vote	Republican	Democratic	Other	Rep.-Dem. Plurality	Percentage Total Vote Rep.	Total Vote Dem.	Major Vote Rep.	Major Vote Dem.
11,367	LEWIS	4,834	2,951	1,804	79	1,147 R	61.0%	37.3%	62.1%	37.9%
31,340	LINCOLN	13,130	9,231	3,695	204	5,536 R	70.3%	28.1%	71.4%	28.6%
39,086	LOUDON	22,184	15,815	6,058	311	9,757 R	71.3%	27.3%	72.3%	27.7%
49,015	MCMINN	18,789	12,989	5,541	259	7,448 R	69.1%	29.5%	70.1%	29.9%
24,653	MCNAIRY	10,422	7,135	3,131	156	4,004 R	68.5%	30.0%	69.5%	30.5%
20,386	MACON	7,360	5,145	2,060	155	3,085 R	69.9%	28.0%	71.4%	28.6%
91,837	MADISON	43,846	23,290	20,209	347	3,081 R	53.1%	46.1%	53.5%	46.5%
27,776	MARION	11,437	6,746	4,506	185	2,240 R	59.0%	39.4%	60.0%	40.0%
26,767	MARSHALL	11,289	6,755	4,320	214	2,435 R	59.8%	38.3%	61.0%	39.0%
69,498	MAURY	33,767	20,288	13,058	421	7,230 R	60.1%	38.7%	60.8%	39.2%
11,086	MEIGS	4,237	2,797	1,372	68	1,425 R	66.0%	32.4%	67.1%	32.9%
38,961	MONROE	16,777	11,484	5,053	240	6,431 R	68.5%	30.1%	69.4%	30.6%
134,768	MONTGOMERY	56,518	30,175	25,716	627	4,459 R	53.4%	45.5%	54.0%	46.0%
5,740	MOORE	2,952	2,010	881	61	1,129 R	68.1%	29.8%	69.5%	30.5%
19,757	MORGAN	6,822	4,717	1,969	136	2,748 R	69.1%	28.9%	70.6%	29.4%
32,450	OBION	13,392	8,873	4,308	211	4,565 R	66.3%	32.2%	67.3%	32.7%
20,118	OVERTON	8,092	4,497	3,419	176	1,078 R	55.6%	42.3%	56.8%	43.2%
7,631	PERRY	3,000	1,596	1,329	75	267 R	53.2%	44.3%	54.6%	45.4%
4,945	PICKETT	2,671	1,786	854	31	932 R	66.9%	32.0%	67.7%	32.3%
16,050	POLK	6,501	4,267	2,124	110	2,143 R	65.6%	32.7%	66.8%	33.2%
62,315	PUTNAM	27,316	17,101	9,739	476	7,362 R	62.6%	35.7%	63.7%	36.3%
28,400	RHEA	11,106	8,042	2,907	157	5,135 R	72.4%	26.2%	73.4%	26.6%
51,910	ROANE	23,276	15,658	7,224	394	8,434 R	67.3%	31.0%	68.4%	31.6%
54,433	ROBERTSON	27,614	17,903	9,318	393	8,585 R	64.8%	33.7%	65.8%	34.2%
182,023	RUTHERFORD	101,737	59,892	40,460	1,385	19,432 R	58.9%	39.8%	59.7%	40.3%
21,127	SCOTT	6,783	4,931	1,720	132	3,211 R	72.7%	25.4%	74.1%	25.9%
11,370	SEQUATCHIE	5,437	3,610	1,717	110	1,893 R	66.4%	31.6%	67.8%	32.2%
71,170	SEVIER	33,941	24,922	8,604	415	16,318 R	73.4%	25.3%	74.3%	25.7%
897,472	SHELBY	404,180	145,458	256,297	2,425	110,839 D	36.0%	63.4%	36.2%	63.8%
17,712	SMITH	7,741	4,563	2,992	186	1,571 R	58.9%	38.7%	60.4%	39.6%
12,370	STEWART	5,507	2,956	2,470	81	486 R	53.7%	44.9%	54.5%	45.5%
153,048	SULLIVAN	63,997	44,808	18,354	835	26,454 R	70.0%	28.7%	70.9%	29.1%
130,449	SUMNER	67,228	44,949	21,487	792	23,462 R	66.9%	32.0%	67.7%	32.3%
51,271	TIPTON	25,316	17,165	7,931	220	9,234 R	67.8%	31.3%	68.4%	31.6%
7,259	TROUSDALE	3,239	1,688	1,475	76	213 R	52.1%	45.5%	53.4%	46.6%
17,667	UNICOI	7,223	5,011	2,107	105	2,904 R	69.4%	29.2%	70.4%	29.6%
17,808	UNION	6,399	4,467	1,829	103	2,638 R	69.8%	28.6%	70.9%	29.1%
5,508	VAN BUREN	2,206	1,294	849	63	445 R	58.7%	38.5%	60.4%	39.6%
38,276	WARREN	14,400	8,562	5,515	323	3,047 R	59.5%	38.3%	60.8%	39.2%
107,198	WASHINGTON	48,982	32,341	15,941	700	16,400 R	66.0%	32.5%	67.0%	33.0%
16,842	WAYNE	5,527	4,076	1,355	96	2,721 R	73.7%	24.5%	75.1%	24.9%
34,895	WEAKLEY	13,690	8,855	4,596	239	4,259 R	64.7%	33.6%	65.8%	34.2%
23,102	WHITE	9,647	6,103	3,372	172	2,731 R	63.3%	35.0%	64.4%	35.6%
126,638	WILLIAMSON	93,646	64,858	27,886	902	36,972 R	69.3%	29.8%	69.9%	30.1%
88,809	WILSON	51,159	34,595	15,886	678	18,709 R	67.6%	31.1%	68.5%	31.5%
5,689,283	TOTAL	2,599,749	1,479,178	1,087,437	33,134	391,741 R	56.9%	41.8%	57.6%	42.4%

TENNESSEE

SENATOR 2008

2000 Census Population	County	Total Vote	Republican	Democratic	Other	Rep.-Dem. Plurality	Total Vote Rep.	Total Vote Dem.	Major Vote Rep.	Major Vote Dem.
71,330	ANDERSON	29,923	21,365	7,675	883	13,690 R	71.4%	25.6%	73.6%	26.4%
37,586	BEDFORD	13,808	9,717	3,548	543	6,169 R	70.4%	25.7%	73.3%	26.7%
16,537	BENTON	6,053	3,614	2,217	222	1,397 R	59.7%	36.6%	62.0%	38.0%
12,367	BLEDSOE	4,508	3,105	1,252	151	1,853 R	68.9%	27.8%	71.3%	28.7%
105,823	BLOUNT	49,218	38,961	8,664	1,593	30,297 R	79.2%	17.6%	81.8%	18.2%
87,965	BRADLEY	36,291	28,820	6,485	986	22,335 R	79.4%	17.9%	81.6%	18.4%
39,854	CAMPBELL	11,484	8,264	2,790	430	5,474 R	72.0%	24.3%	74.8%	25.2%
12,826	CANNON	4,853	3,125	1,433	295	1,692 R	64.4%	29.5%	68.6%	31.4%
29,475	CARROLL	10,695	7,254	3,075	366	4,179 R	67.8%	28.8%	70.2%	29.8%
56,742	CARTER	20,249	16,148	3,448	653	12,700 R	79.7%	17.0%	82.4%	17.6%
35,912	CHEATHAM	15,369	10,665	4,160	544	6,505 R	69.4%	27.1%	71.9%	28.1%
15,540	CHESTER	5,951	4,403	1,344	204	3,059 R	74.0%	22.6%	76.6%	23.4%
29,862	CLAIBORNE	9,671	7,095	2,246	330	4,849 R	73.4%	23.2%	76.0%	24.0%
7,976	CLAY	2,576	1,623	852	101	771 R	63.0%	33.1%	65.6%	34.4%
33,565	COCKE	11,298	8,742	2,231	325	6,511 R	77.4%	19.7%	79.7%	20.3%
48,014	COFFEE	20,008	13,173	5,985	850	7,188 R	65.8%	29.9%	68.8%	31.2%
14,532	CROCKETT	5,189	3,766	1,274	149	2,492 R	72.6%	24.6%	74.7%	25.3%
46,802	CUMBERLAND	23,722	17,094	5,730	898	11,364 R	72.1%	24.2%	74.9%	25.1%
569,891	DAVIDSON	244,049	119,996	115,354	8,699	4,642 R	49.2%	47.3%	51.0%	49.0%
11,731	DECATUR	4,584	2,958	1,488	138	1,470 R	64.5%	32.5%	66.5%	33.5%
17,423	DE KALB	6,063	3,914	1,861	288	2,053 R	64.6%	30.7%	67.8%	32.2%
43,156	DICKSON	18,116	11,264	6,053	799	5,211 R	62.2%	33.4%	65.0%	35.0%
37,279	DYER	12,999	9,533	2,995	471	6,538 R	73.3%	23.0%	76.1%	23.9%
28,806	FAYETTE	17,787	12,457	4,925	405	7,532 R	70.0%	27.7%	71.7%	28.3%
16,625	FENTRESS	5,849	4,469	1,167	213	3,302 R	76.4%	20.0%	79.3%	20.7%
39,270	FRANKLIN	16,108	10,461	5,064	583	5,397 R	64.9%	31.4%	67.4%	32.6%
48,152	GIBSON	19,014	13,208	5,172	634	8,036 R	69.5%	27.2%	71.9%	28.1%
29,447	GILES	10,246	6,355	3,433	458	2,922 R	62.0%	33.5%	64.9%	35.1%
20,659	GRAINGER	6,924	5,229	1,445	250	3,784 R	75.5%	20.9%	78.3%	21.7%
62,909	GREENE	23,869	18,468	4,788	613	13,680 R	77.4%	20.1%	79.4%	20.6%
14,332	GRUNDY	4,088	2,368	1,571	149	797 R	57.9%	38.4%	60.1%	39.9%
58,128	HAMBLEN	21,178	16,191	4,426	561	11,765 R	76.5%	20.9%	78.5%	21.5%
307,896	HAMILTON	142,304	91,563	47,754	2,987	43,809 R	64.3%	33.6%	65.7%	34.3%
6,786	HANCOCK	1,989	1,537	386	66	1,151 R	77.3%	19.4%	79.9%	20.1%
28,105	HARDEMAN	9,927	5,144	4,476	307	668 R	51.8%	45.1%	53.5%	46.5%
25,578	HARDIN	9,362	6,770	2,304	288	4,466 R	72.3%	24.6%	74.6%	25.4%
53,563	HAWKINS	20,330	15,260	4,437	633	10,823 R	75.1%	21.8%	77.5%	22.5%
19,797	HAYWOOD	7,507	3,402	3,969	136	567 D	45.3%	52.9%	46.2%	53.8%
25,522	HENDERSON	10,052	7,367	2,356	329	5,011 R	73.3%	23.4%	75.8%	24.2%
31,115	HENRY	12,106	8,084	3,667	355	4,417 R	66.8%	30.3%	68.8%	31.2%
22,295	HICKMAN	7,868	4,738	2,735	395	2,003 R	60.2%	34.8%	63.4%	36.6%
8,088	HOUSTON	2,969	1,572	1,293	104	279 R	52.9%	43.6%	54.9%	45.1%
17,929	HUMPHREYS	7,141	3,965	2,927	249	1,038 R	55.5%	41.0%	57.5%	42.5%
10,984	JACKSON	3,967	2,097	1,672	198	425 R	52.9%	42.1%	55.6%	44.4%
44,294	JEFFERSON	17,581	13,542	3,395	644	10,147 R	77.0%	19.3%	80.0%	20.0%
17,499	JOHNSON	6,069	4,620	1,191	258	3,429 R	76.1%	19.6%	79.5%	20.5%
382,032	KNOX	178,008	126,776	45,844	5,388	80,932 R	71.2%	25.8%	73.4%	26.6%
7,954	LAKE	1,838	1,038	685	115	353 R	56.5%	37.3%	60.2%	39.8%
27,101	LAUDERDALE	8,139	5,256	2,630	253	2,626 R	64.6%	32.3%	66.6%	33.4%
39,926	LAWRENCE	14,347	10,115	3,761	471	6,354 R	70.5%	26.2%	72.9%	27.1%

TENNESSEE

SENATOR 2008

2000 Census Population	County	Total Vote	Republican	Democratic	Other	Rep.-Dem. Plurality	Percentage Total Vote Rep.	Dem.	Major Vote Rep.	Dem.
11,367	LEWIS	4,483	2,857	1,431	195	1,426 R	63.7%	31.9%	66.6%	33.4%
31,340	LINCOLN	12,372	8,653	3,197	522	5,456 R	69.9%	25.8%	73.0%	27.0%
39,086	LOUDON	21,312	17,110	3,658	544	13,452 R	80.3%	17.2%	82.4%	17.6%
49,015	MCMINN	17,868	13,464	3,832	572	9,632 R	75.4%	21.4%	77.8%	22.2%
24,653	MCNAIRY	9,970	6,908	2,783	279	4,125 R	69.3%	27.9%	71.3%	28.7%
20,386	MACON	6,459	4,665	1,382	412	3,283 R	72.2%	21.4%	77.1%	22.9%
91,837	MADISON	40,390	23,890	15,333	1,167	8,557 R	59.1%	38.0%	60.9%	39.1%
27,776	MARION	10,940	6,803	3,803	334	3,000 R	62.2%	34.8%	64.1%	35.9%
26,767	MARSHALL	10,335	6,675	3,172	488	3,503 R	64.6%	30.7%	67.8%	32.2%
69,498	MAURY	32,823	20,330	11,355	1,138	8,975 R	61.9%	34.6%	64.2%	35.8%
11,086	MEIGS	3,881	2,807	951	123	1,856 R	72.3%	24.5%	74.7%	25.3%
38,961	MONROE	16,224	12,198	3,541	485	8,657 R	75.2%	21.8%	77.5%	22.5%
134,768	MONTGOMERY	49,497	31,012	16,337	2,148	14,675 R	62.7%	33.0%	65.5%	34.5%
5,740	MOORE	2,841	1,989	751	101	1,238 R	70.0%	26.4%	72.6%	27.4%
19,757	MORGAN	6,256	4,746	1,334	176	3,412 R	75.9%	21.3%	78.1%	21.9%
32,450	OBION	11,815	8,056	3,385	374	4,671 R	68.2%	28.7%	70.4%	29.6%
20,118	OVERTON	6,786	4,220	2,309	257	1,911 R	62.2%	34.0%	64.6%	35.4%
7,631	PERRY	2,686	1,559	1,026	101	533 R	58.0%	38.2%	60.3%	39.7%
4,945	PICKETT	2,454	1,805	575	74	1,230 R	73.6%	23.4%	75.8%	24.2%
16,050	POLK	6,241	4,233	1,794	214	2,439 R	67.8%	28.7%	70.2%	29.8%
62,315	PUTNAM	24,680	16,629	6,990	1,061	9,639 R	67.4%	28.3%	70.4%	29.6%
28,400	RHEA	10,313	7,907	2,102	304	5,805 R	76.7%	20.4%	79.0%	21.0%
51,910	ROANE	22,291	16,617	5,042	632	11,575 R	74.5%	22.6%	76.7%	23.3%
54,433	ROBERTSON	25,161	17,485	6,744	932	10,741 R	69.5%	26.8%	72.2%	27.8%
182,023	RUTHERFORD	95,454	62,464	28,906	4,084	33,558 R	65.4%	30.3%	68.4%	31.6%
21,127	SCOTT	5,790	4,501	1,099	190	3,402 R	77.7%	19.0%	80.4%	19.6%
11,370	SEQUATCHIE	4,958	3,553	1,238	167	2,315 R	71.7%	25.0%	74.2%	25.8%
71,170	SEVIER	32,721	26,021	5,539	1,161	20,482 R	79.5%	16.9%	82.4%	17.6%
897,472	SHELBY	373,139	189,851	173,924	9,364	15,927 R	50.9%	46.6%	52.2%	47.8%
17,712	SMITH	6,948	4,458	2,136	354	2,322 R	64.2%	30.7%	67.6%	32.4%
12,370	STEWART	5,021	3,006	1,779	236	1,227 R	59.9%	35.4%	62.8%	37.2%
153,048	SULLIVAN	61,856	47,721	12,906	1,229	34,815 R	77.1%	20.9%	78.7%	21.3%
130,449	SUMNER	62,563	44,945	15,134	2,484	29,811 R	71.8%	24.2%	74.8%	25.2%
51,271	TIPTON	23,116	17,157	5,299	660	11,858 R	74.2%	22.9%	76.4%	23.6%
7,259	TROUSDALE	2,749	1,725	890	134	835 R	62.8%	32.4%	66.0%	34.0%
17,667	UNICOI	6,702	5,251	1,257	194	3,994 R	78.3%	18.8%	80.7%	19.3%
17,808	UNION	5,640	4,276	1,139	225	3,137 R	75.8%	20.2%	79.0%	21.0%
5,508	VAN BUREN	1,964	1,223	661	80	562 R	62.3%	33.7%	64.9%	35.1%
38,276	WARREN	12,847	8,225	4,045	577	4,180 R	64.0%	31.5%	67.0%	33.0%
107,198	WASHINGTON	45,563	34,592	9,715	1,256	24,877 R	75.9%	21.3%	78.1%	21.9%
16,842	WAYNE	4,837	3,685	1,035	117	2,650 R	76.2%	21.4%	78.1%	21.9%
34,895	WEAKLEY	12,814	8,546	3,809	459	4,737 R	66.7%	29.7%	69.2%	30.8%
23,102	WHITE	9,016	5,969	2,620	427	3,349 R	66.2%	29.1%	69.5%	30.5%
126,638	WILLIAMSON	90,422	68,258	19,405	2,759	48,853 R	75.5%	21.5%	77.9%	22.1%
88,809	WILSON	49,143	34,781	12,240	2,122	22,541 R	70.8%	24.9%	74.0%	26.0%
5,689,283	TOTAL	2,424,585	1,579,477	767,236	77,872	812,241 R	65.1%	31.6%	67.3%	32.7%

TENNESSEE

HOUSE OF REPRESENTATIVES

CD	Year	Total Vote	Republican Vote	Republican Candidate	Democratic Vote	Democratic Candidate	Other Vote	Rep.-Dem. Plurality	Total Vote Rep.	Total Vote Dem.	Major Vote Rep.	Major Vote Dem.
1	2008	234,381	168,343	ROE, PHIL	57,525	RUSSELL, ROB	8,513	110,818 R	71.8%	24.5%	74.5%	25.5%
1	2006	177,278	108,336	DAVIS, DAVID	65,538	TRENT, RICK	3,404	42,798 R	61.1%	37.0%	62.3%	37.7%
1	2004	233,560	172,543	JENKINS, BILL*	56,361	LEONARD, GRAHAM	4,656	116,182 R	73.9%	24.1%	75.4%	24.6%
1	2002	128,886	127,300	JENKINS, BILL*	—		1,586	127,300 R	98.8%		100.0%	
2	2008	290,759	227,120	DUNCAN, JOHN J. "JIMMY" JR.*	63,639	SCOTT, BOB		163,481 R	78.1%	21.9%	78.1%	21.9%
2	2006	202,120	157,095	DUNCAN, JOHN J. "JIMMY" JR.*	45,025	GREENE, JOHN		112,070 R	77.7%	22.3%	77.7%	22.3%
2	2004	272,928	215,795	DUNCAN, JOHN J. "JIMMY" JR.*	52,155	GREENE, JOHN	4,978	163,640 R	79.1%	19.1%	80.5%	19.5%
2	2002	185,981	146,887	DUNCAN, JOHN J. "JIMMY" JR.*	37,035	GREENE, JOHN	2,059	109,852 R	79.0%	19.9%	79.9%	20.1%
3	2008	266,628	184,964	WAMP, ZACH*	73,059	VANDAGRIFF, DOUG	8,605	111,905 R	69.4%	27.4%	71.7%	28.3%
3	2006	199,115	130,791	WAMP, ZACH*	68,324	BENEDICT, BRENT		62,467 R	65.7%	34.3%	65.7%	34.3%
3	2004	256,636	166,154	WAMP, ZACH*	84,295	WOLFE, JOHN	6,187	81,859 R	64.7%	32.8%	66.3%	33.7%
3	2002	173,921	112,254	WAMP, ZACH*	58,824	WOLFE, JOHN	2,843	53,430 R	64.5%	33.8%	65.6%	34.4%
4	2008	249,805	94,447	LANKFORD, MONTY J.	146,776	DAVIS, LINCOLN*	8,582	52,329 D	37.8%	58.8%	39.2%	60.8%
4	2006	186,115	62,449	MARTIN, KENNETH	123,666	DAVIS, LINCOLN*		61,217 D	33.6%	66.4%	33.6%	66.4%
4	2004	252,646	109,993	BOWLING, JANICE	138,459	DAVIS, LINCOLN*	4,194	28,466 D	43.5%	54.8%	44.3%	55.7%
4	2002	184,300	85,680	BOWLING, JANICE	95,989	DAVIS, LINCOLN	2,631	10,309 D	46.5%	52.1%	47.2%	52.8%
5	2008	275,602	85,471	DONOVAN, GERARD	181,467	COOPER, JIM*	8,664	95,996 D	31.0%	65.8%	32.0%	68.0%
5	2006	178,142	49,702	KOVACH, THOMAS F.	122,919	COOPER, JIM*	5,521	73,217 D	27.9%	69.0%	28.8%	71.2%
5	2004	243,963	74,978	KNAPP, SCOTT	168,970	COOPER, JIM*	15	93,992 D	30.7%	69.3%	30.7%	69.3%
5	2002	170,886	56,825	DUVALL, ROBERT	108,903	COOPER, JIM	5,158	52,078 D	33.3%	63.7%	34.3%	65.7%
6	2008	261,028		—	194,264	GORDON, BART*	66,764	194,264 D		74.4%		100.0%
6	2006	192,380	60,392	DAVIS, DAVID R.	129,069	GORDON, BART*	2,919	68,677 D	31.4%	67.1%	31.9%	68.1%
6	2004	260,642	87,523	DEMAS, NICK	167,448	GORDON, BART*	5,671	79,925 D	33.6%	64.2%	34.3%	65.7%
6	2002	177,547	57,401	GARRISON, ROBERT L.	117,034	GORDON, BART*	3,112	59,633 D	32.3%	65.9%	32.9%	67.1%
7	2008	316,881	217,332	BLACKBURN, MARSHA*	99,549	MORRIS, RANDY G.		117,783 R	68.6%	31.4%	68.6%	31.4%
7	2006	230,582	152,288	BLACKBURN, MARSHA*	73,369	MORRISON, BILL	4,925	78,919 R	66.0%	31.8%	67.5%	32.5%
7	2004	232,404	232,404	BLACKBURN, MARSHA*	—			232,404 R	100.0%		100.0%	
7	2002	195,558	138,314	BLACKBURN, MARSHA	51,790	BARRON, TIM	5,454	86,524 R	70.7%	26.5%	72.8%	27.2%
8	2008	180,519		—	180,465	TANNER, JOHN*	54	180,465 D		100.0%		100.0%
8	2006	177,108	47,492	FARMER, JOHN	129,610	TANNER, JOHN*	6	82,118 D	26.8%	73.2%	26.8%	73.2%
8	2004	233,567	59,853	HART, JAMES L.	173,623	TANNER, JOHN*	91	113,770 D	25.6%	74.3%	25.6%	74.4%
8	2002	167,970	45,853	McCLAIN, MAT	117,811	TANNER, JOHN*	4,306	71,958 D	27.3%	70.1%	28.0%	72.0%
9	2008	226,282		—	198,798	COHEN, STEVE*	27,484	198,798 D		87.9%		100.0%
9	2006	172,586	31,002	WHITE, MARK	103,341	COHEN, STEVE	38,243	72,339 D	18.0%	59.9%	23.1%	76.9%
9	2004	232,392	41,578	FORT, RUBEN M.	190,648	FORD, HAROLD E. JR.*	166	149,070 D	17.9%	82.0%	17.9%	82.1%
9	2002	144,260		—	120,904	FORD, HAROLD E. JR.*	23,356	120,904 D		83.8%		100.0%
TOTAL	2008	2,301,885	977,677		1,195,542		128,666	217,865 D	42.5%	51.9%	45.0%	55.0%
TOTAL	2006	1,715,426	799,547		860,861		55,018	61,314 D	46.6%	50.2%	48.2%	51.8%
TOTAL	2004	2,218,738	1,160,821		1,031,959		25,958	128,862 R	52.3%	46.5%	52.9%	47.1%
TOTAL	2002	1,529,309	770,514		708,290		50,505	62,224 R	50.4%	46.3%	52.1%	47.9%

Note: An asterisk (*) denotes incumbent.

TENNESSEE

GENERAL AND PRIMARY ELECTIONS

2008 GENERAL ELECTIONS

President Other vote was 11,560 Independent (Ralph Nader); 8,547 Independent (Bob Barr); 8,191 Independent (Chuck Baldwin); 2,499 Independent (Cynthia A. McKinney); 1,326 Independent (Brian Moore); 1,011 Independent (Charles Jay).

Senator Other vote was 31,631 Independent (Edward L. Buck); 11,073 Independent (Christopher G. Fenner); 9,367 Independent (Daniel Towers Lewis); 9,170 Independent (Chris Lugo); 8,986 Independent (Ed Lawhorn); 7,645 Independent (David Gatchell).

House Other vote was:

CD 1 3,988 Independent (Joel Goodman); 2,544 Independent (James W. Reeves); 1,981 Independent (Thomas "T.K." Owens).

CD 2

CD 3 4,848 Independent (Jean Howard-Hill); 3,750 Independent (Ed Choate); 7 write-in (June Griffin).

CD 4 4,869 Independent (James Anthony Gray); 3,713 Independent (Kevin Ragsdale).

CD 5 5,464 Independent (Jon Jackson); 3,196 Independent (John P. Miglietta); 4 write-in (Thomas F. Kovach).

CD 6 66,764 Independent (Chris Baker).

CD 7

CD 8 54 write-in (James Hart).

CD 9 11,003 Independent (Jake Ford); 10,047 Independent (Dewey Clark); 6,434 Independent (Mary "Taylor Shelby" Wright).

Note: In Tennessee all third-party candidates are listed as Independent regardless of party affiliation.

2008 PRIMARY ELECTIONS

Primary February 5, 2008 (President) **Registration** 3,791,861 No Party Registration
August 7, 2008 (Congress) (as of June 12, 2008—includes 391,585 inactive registrants)

Primary Type Open—Any registered voter could participate in either the Democratic or Republican primary.

	REPUBLICAN PRIMARIES			DEMOCRATIC PRIMARIES		
President	Mike Huckabee	190,904	34.5%	Hillary Clinton	336,245	53.8%
	John McCain	176,091	31.8%	Barack Obama	252,874	40.5%
	Mitt Romney	130,632	23.6%	John Edwards	27,820	4.5%
	Ron Paul	31,026	5.6%	Uncommitted	3,158	0.5%
	Fred Thompson	16,263	2.9%	Joseph R. Biden Jr.	1,531	0.2%
	Rudolph Giuliani	5,159	0.9%	Bill Richardson	1,178	0.2%
	Uncommitted	1,830	0.3%	Dennis J. Kucinich	971	0.2%
	Alan Keyes	978	0.2%	Christopher J. Dodd	526	0.1%
	Duncan Hunter	738	0.1%	Mike Gravel	461	0.1%
	Tom Tancredo	194				
	TOTAL	*553,815*		*TOTAL*	*624,764*	
Senator	Lamar Alexander*	244,222	100.0%	Robert D. Tuke	59,050	32.2%
				Gary G. Davis	39,119	21.3%
				Wm Mike Padgett	33,471	18.3%
				Mark E. Clayton	32,309	17.6%
				Kenneth Eaton	14,702	8.0%
				Leonard D. Ladner	4,697	2.6%
				TOTAL	*183,348*	

TENNESSEE

GENERAL AND PRIMARY ELECTIONS

	REPUBLICAN PRIMARIES			DEMOCRATIC PRIMARIES		
Congressional District 1	Phil Roe	25,993	50.1%	Rob Russell	4,123	67.7%
	David Davis*	25,511	49.2%	Michael Donihe	1,968	32.3%
	Mahmood "Michael" Sabri	329	0.6%			
	TOTAL	51,833		TOTAL	6,091	
Congressional District 2	John J. "Jimmy" Duncan Jr.*	50,722	100.0%	Bob Scott	10,006	59.7%
				David Ryan Hancock	6,765	40.3%
				TOTAL	16,771	
Congressional District 3	Zach Wamp*	31,782	91.0%	Doug Vandagriff	13,122	100.0%
	Teresa Sheppard	3,125	9.0%			
	TOTAL	34,907				
Congressional District 4	Monty J. Lankford	13,363	62.7%	Lincoln Davis*	30,487	90.4%
	Don Strong	4,199	19.7%	Bert Mason	3,233	9.6%
	Kent Greenough	3,749	17.6%			
	TOTAL	21,311		TOTAL	33,720	
Congressional District 5	Gerard Donovan	5,482	71.1%	Jim Cooper*	17,985	100.0%
	Vijay A. Kumar	2,225	28.9%			
	TOTAL	7,707				
Congressional District 6	No candidate filed for the primary. Steven L. Edmondson received 723 write-in votes.			Bart Gordon*	21,752	100.0%
Congressional District 7	Marsha Blackburn*	30,997	62.0%	Randy G. Morris	12,003	77.2%
	Tom Leatherwood	19,025	38.0%	James Tomasik	3,535	22.8%
	TOTAL	50,022		TOTAL	15,538	
Congressional District 8	No candidate filed for the primary. James Hart received 23 write-in votes.			John Tanner*	24,844	100.0%
Congressional District 9	No Republican candidate			Steve Cohen*	50,306	79.4%
				Nikki Tinker	11,817	18.6%
				Joe Towns Jr.	914	1.4%
				James Gregory	180	0.3%
				Isaac Richmond	172	0.3%
				TOTAL	63,389	

Note: An asterisk (*) denotes incumbent.

TEXAS

Congressional districts first established for elections held in 2004
32 members

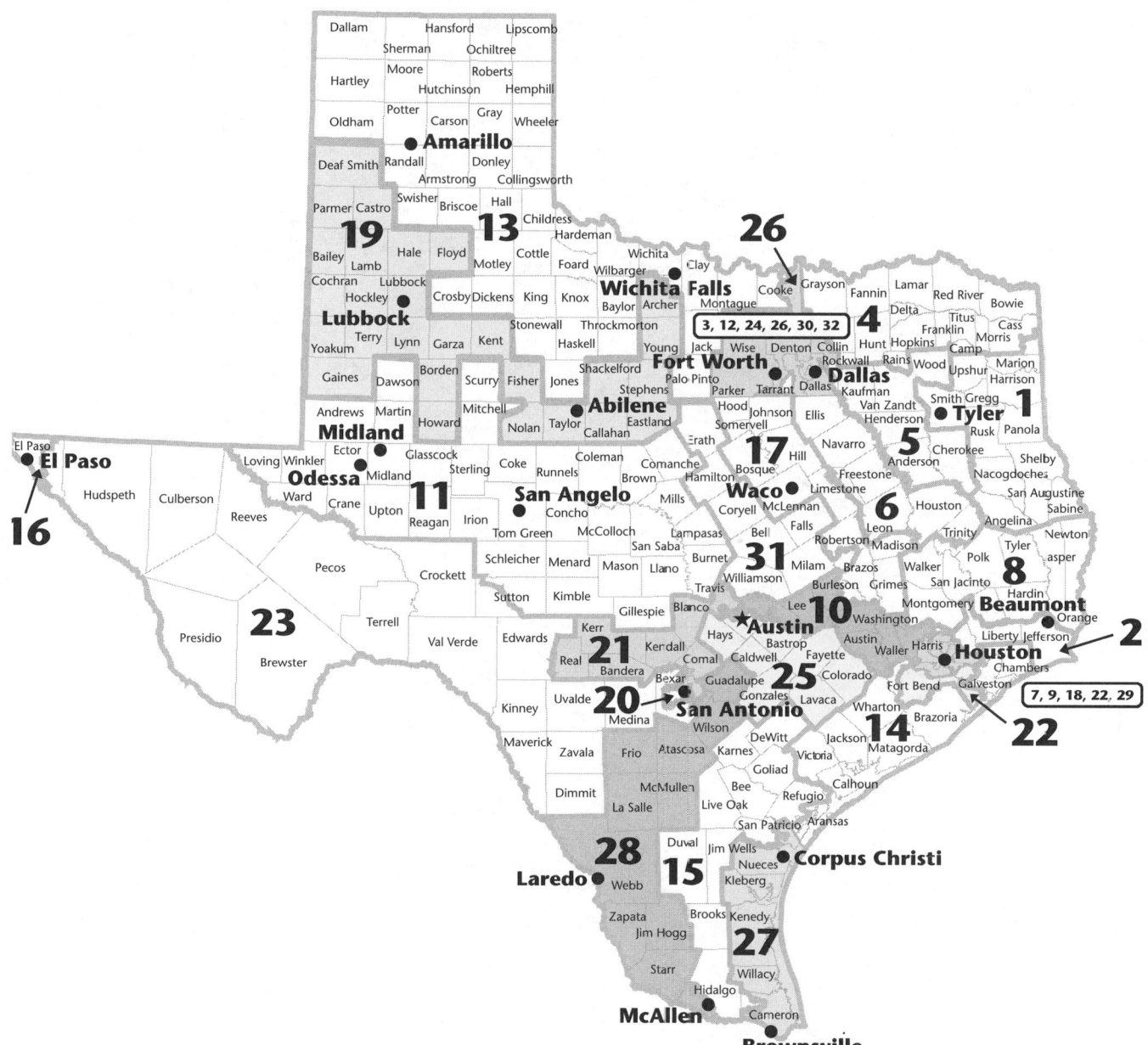

TEXAS

Houston Area

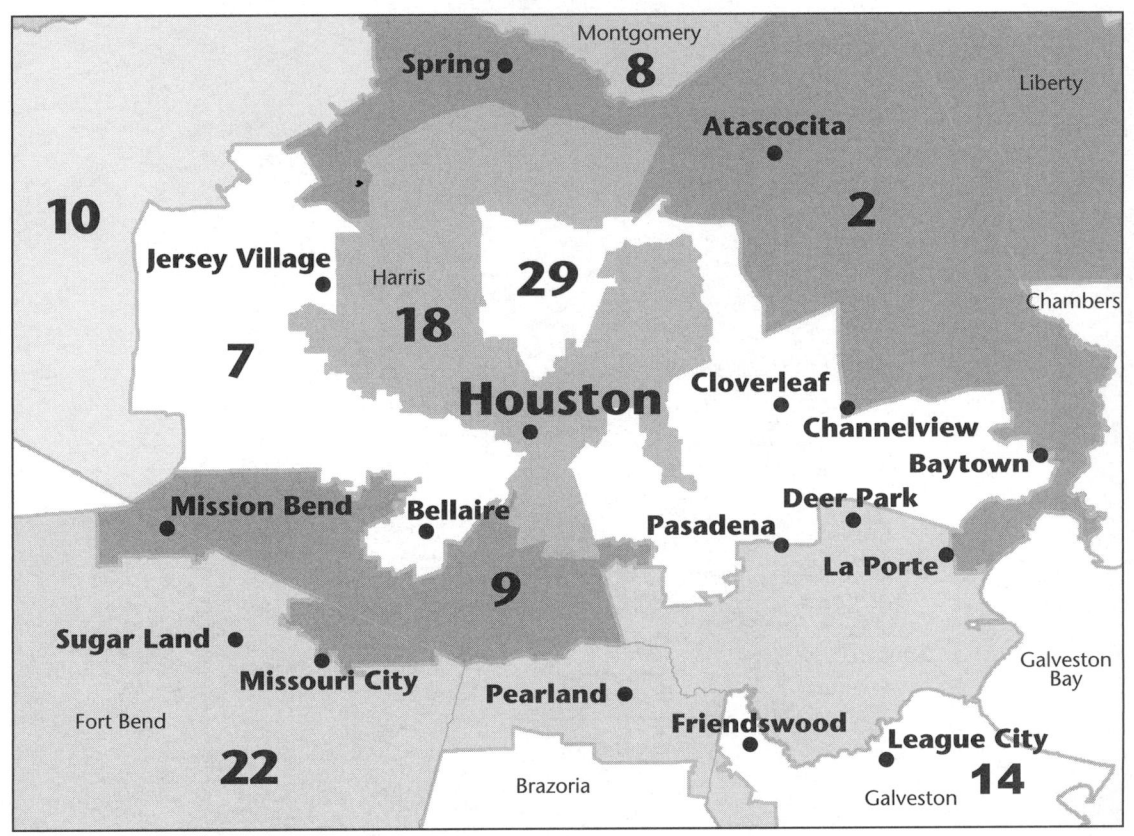

TEXAS

Dallas-Fort Worth Area

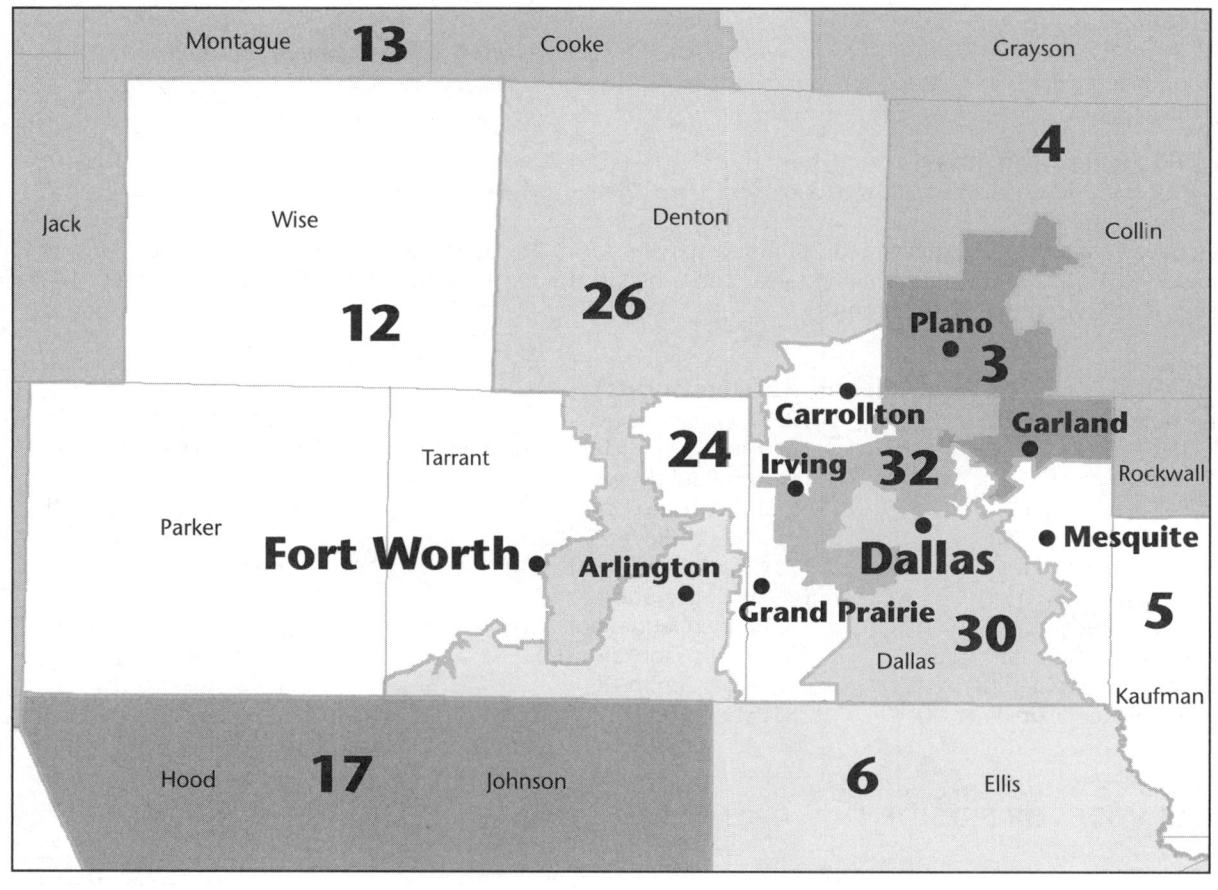

TEXAS

GOVERNOR

Rick Perry (R). Reelected 2006 to a four-year term. Previously elected 2002. Assumed office December 21, 2000, following the resignation of president-elect George W. Bush.

SENATORS (2 Republicans)

John Cornyn (R). Reelected 2008 to a six-year term. Previously elected 2002.

Kay Bailey Hutchison (R). Reelected 2006 to a six-year term. Previously elected 2000, 1994, and in a special election June 5, 1993, to fill out the remaining year and a half of the term vacated when Sen. Lloyd Bentsen (D) resigned to become U.S. Secretary of the Treasury.

REPRESENTATIVES (20 Republicans, 12 Democrats)

1. Louie Gohmert (R)
2. Ted Poe (R)
3. Sam Johnson (R)
4. Ralph M. Hall (R)
5. Jeb Hensarling (R)
6. Joe L. Barton (R)
7. John Culberson (R)
8. Kevin Brady (R)
9. Al Green (D)
10. Michael McCaul (R)
11. K. Michael Conaway (R)
12. Kay Granger (R)
13. William M. "Mac" Thornberry (R)
14. Ron Paul (R)
15. Ruben Hinojosa (D)
16. Silvestre Reyes (D)
17. Chet Edwards (D)
18. Sheila Jackson-Lee (D)
19. Randy Neugebauer (R)
20. Charlie Gonzalez (D)
21. Lamar Smith (R)
22. Pete Olson (R)
23. Ciro D. Rodriguez (D)
24. Kenny Marchant (R)
25. Lloyd Doggett (D)
26. Michael C. Burgess (R)
27. Solomon P. Ortiz (D)
28. Henry Cuellar (D)
29. Gene Green (D)
30. Eddie Bernice Johnson (D)
31. John Carter (R)
32. Pete Sessions (R)

POSTWAR VOTE FOR PRESIDENT

Year	Total Vote	Republican Vote	Republican Candidate	Democratic Vote	Democratic Candidate	Other Vote	Plurality	Rep. (Total)	Dem. (Total)	Rep. (Major)	Dem. (Major)
2008	8,077,795	4,479,328	McCain, John	3,528,633	Obama, Barack	69,834	950,695 R	55.5%	43.7%	55.9%	44.1%
2004	7,410,765	4,526,917	Bush, George W.	2,832,704	Kerry, John	51,144	1,694,213 R	61.1%	38.2%	61.5%	38.5%
2000**	6,407,637	3,799,639	Bush, George W.	2,433,746	Gore, Al	174,252	1,365,893 R	59.3%	38.0%	61.0%	39.0%
1996**	5,611,644	2,736,167	Dole, Bob	2,459,683	Clinton, Bill	415,794	276,484 R	48.8%	43.8%	52.7%	47.3%
1992**	6,154,018	2,496,071	Bush, George	2,281,815	Clinton, Bill	1,376,132	214,256 R	40.6%	37.1%	52.2%	47.8%
1988	5,427,410	3,036,829	Bush, George	2,352,748	Dukakis, Michael S.	37,833	684,081 R	56.0%	43.3%	56.3%	43.7%
1984	5,397,571	3,433,428	Reagan, Ronald	1,949,276	Mondale, Walter F.	14,867	1,484,152 R	63.6%	36.1%	63.8%	36.2%
1980**	4,541,636	2,510,705	Reagan, Ronald	1,881,147	Carter, Jimmy	149,784	629,558 R	55.3%	41.4%	57.2%	42.8%
1976	4,071,884	1,953,300	Ford, Gerald R.	2,082,319	Carter, Jimmy	36,265	129,019 D	48.0%	51.1%	48.4%	51.6%
1972	3,471,281	2,298,896	Nixon, Richard M.	1,154,289	McGovern, George S.	18,096	1,144,607 R	66.2%	33.3%	66.6%	33.4%
1968**	3,079,216	1,227,844	Nixon, Richard M.	1,266,804	Humphrey, Hubert H.	584,568	38,960 D	39.9%	41.1%	49.2%	50.8%
1964	2,626,811	958,566	Goldwater, Barry M.	1,663,185	Johnson, Lyndon B.	5,060	704,619 D	36.5%	63.3%	36.6%	63.4%
1960	2,311,084	1,121,310	Nixon, Richard M.	1,167,567	Kennedy, John F.	22,207	46,257 D	48.5%	50.5%	49.0%	51.0%
1956	1,955,168	1,080,619	Eisenhower, Dwight D.	859,958	Stevenson, Adlai E.	14,591	220,661 R	55.3%	44.0%	55.7%	44.3%
1952	2,075,946	1,102,878	Eisenhower, Dwight D.	969,228	Stevenson, Adlai E.	3,840	133,650 R	53.1%	46.7%	53.2%	46.8%
1948**	1,249,577	303,467	Dewey, Thomas E.	824,235	Truman, Harry S.	121,875	520,768 D	24.3%	66.0%	26.9%	73.1%

**In past elections, the other vote included: 2000 - 137,994 Green (Ralph Nader); 1996 - 378,537 Reform (Ross Perot); 1992 - 1,354,781 Independent (Perot); 1980 - 111,613 Independent (John Anderson); 1968 - 584,269 American Independent (George Wallace); 1948 - 113,920 States' Rights (Strom Thurmond).

TEXAS

POSTWAR VOTE FOR GOVERNOR

Year	Total Vote	Republican		Democratic		Other Vote	Rep.-Dem. Plurality	Percentage			
		Vote	Candidate	Vote	Candidate			Total Vote		Major Vote	
								Rep.	Dem.	Rep.	Dem.
2006**	4,399,116	1,716,792	Perry, Rick	1,310,337	Bell, Chris	1,371,987	406,455 R	39.0%	29.8%	56.7%	43.3%
2002	4,553,987	2,632,591	Perry, Rick	1,819,798	Sanchez, Tony	101,598	812,793 R	57.8%	40.0%	59.1%	40.9%
1998	3,738,483	2,551,454	Bush, George W.	1,165,444	Mauro, Garry	21,585	1,386,010 R	68.2%	31.2%	68.6%	31.4%
1994	4,396,242	2,350,994	Bush, George W.	2,016,928	Richards, Ann	28,320	334,066 R	53.5%	45.9%	53.8%	46.2%
1990	3,892,746	1,826,431	Williams, Clayton	1,925,670	Richards, Ann	140,645	99,239 D	46.9%	49.5%	48.7%	51.3%
1986	3,441,460	1,813,779	Clements, William P.	1,584,515	White, Mark	43,166	229,264 R	52.7%	46.0%	53.4%	46.6%
1982	3,191,091	1,465,937	Clements, William P.	1,697,870	White, Mark	27,284	231,933 D	45.9%	53.2%	46.3%	53.7%
1978	2,369,764	1,183,839	Clements, William P.	1,166,979	Hill, John	18,946	16,860 R	50.0%	49.2%	50.4%	49.6%
1974**	1,654,984	514,725	Granberry, Jim	1,016,334	Briscoe, Dolph	123,925	501,609 D	31.1%	61.4%	33.6%	66.4%
1972	3,410,128	1,534,060	Grover, Henry C.	1,633,970	Briscoe, Dolph	242,098	99,910 D	45.0%	47.9%	48.4%	51.6%
1970	2,235,847	1,037,723	Eggers, Paul W.	1,197,726	Smith, Preston	398	160,003 D	46.4%	53.6%	46.4%	53.6%
1968	2,916,509	1,254,333	Eggers, Paul W.	1,662,019	Smith, Preston	157	407,686 D	43.0%	57.0%	43.0%	57.0%
1966	1,425,861	368,025	Kennerly, T. E.	1,037,517	Connally, John B.	20,319	669,492 D	25.8%	72.8%	26.2%	73.8%
1964	2,544,753	661,675	Crichton, Jack	1,877,793	Connally, John B.	5,285	1,216,118 D	26.0%	73.8%	26.1%	73.9%
1962	1,569,181	715,025	Cox, Jack	847,036	Connally, John B.	7,120	132,011 D	45.6%	54.0%	45.8%	54.2%
1960	2,250,718	612,963	Steger, William M.	1,637,755	Daniel, Price		1,024,792 D	27.2%	72.8%	27.2%	72.8%
1958	789,133	94,098	Mayer, Edwin S.	695,035	Daniel, Price		600,937 D	11.9%	88.1%	11.9%	88.1%
1956	1,828,161	271,088	Bryant, William R.	1,433,051	Daniel, Price	124,022	1,161,963 D	14.8%	78.4%	15.9%	84.1%
1954	636,892	66,154	Adams, Tod R.	569,533	Shivers, Allan	1,205	503,379 D	10.4%	89.4%	10.4%	89.6%
1952	1,881,202		—	1,844,530	Shivers, Allan	36,672	1,844,530 D		98.1%		100.0%
1950	394,747	39,737	Currie, Ralph W.	355,010	Shivers, Allan		315,273 D	10.1%	89.9%	10.1%	89.9%
1948	1,208,860	177,399	Lane, Alvin H.	1,024,160	Jester, Beauford	7,301	846,761 D	14.7%	84.7%	14.8%	85.2%
1946	378,744	33,231	Nolte, Eugene	345,513	Jester, Beauford		312,282 D	8.8%	91.2%	8.8%	91.2%

**In past elections, the other vote included: 2006 - 796,851 Independent (Carole Keeton Strayhorn); 547,674 Independent (Richard "Kinky" Friedman). The term of office of Texas's governor was increased from two to four years effective with the 1974 election. The Republican Party did not run a candidate in the 1952 gubernatorial election.

TEXAS

POSTWAR VOTE FOR SENATOR

Year	Total Vote	Republican Vote	Republican Candidate	Democratic Vote	Democratic Candidate	Other Vote	Rep.-Dem. Plurality		Total Vote Rep.	Total Vote Dem.	Major Vote Rep.	Major Vote Dem.
2008	7,912,075	4,337,469	Cornyn, John	3,389,365	Noriega, Richard J. "Rick"	185,241	948,104	R	54.8%	42.8%	56.1%	43.9%
2006	4,314,663	2,661,789	Hutchison, Kay Bailey	1,555,202	Radnofsky, Barbara Ann	97,672	1,106,587	R	61.7%	36.0%	63.1%	36.9%
2002	4,514,012	2,496,243	Cornyn, John	1,955,758	Kirk, Ron	62,011	540,485	R	55.3%	43.3%	56.1%	43.9%
2000	6,276,652	4,082,091	Hutchison, Kay Bailey	2,030,315	Kelly, Gene	164,246	2,051,776	R	65.0%	32.3%	66.8%	33.2%
1996	5,527,441	3,027,680	Gramm, Phil	2,428,776	Morales, Victor M.	70,985	598,904	R	54.8%	43.9%	55.5%	44.5%
1994	4,279,940	2,604,218	Hutchison, Kay Bailey	1,639,615	Fisher, Richard	36,107	964,603	R	60.8%	38.3%	61.4%	38.6%
1993S	1,765,254	1,188,716	Hutchison, Kay Bailey	576,538	Krueger, Robert		612,178	R	67.3%	32.7%	67.3%	32.7%
1990	3,822,157	2,302,357	Gramm, Phil	1,429,986	Parmer, Hugh	89,814	872,371	R	60.2%	37.4%	61.7%	38.3%
1988	5,323,606	2,129,228	Boulter, Beau	3,149,806	Bentsen, Lloyd	44,572	1,020,578	D	40.0%	59.2%	40.3%	59.7%
1984	5,319,178	3,116,348	Gramm, Phil	2,202,557	Doggett, Lloyd	273	913,791	R	58.6%	41.4%	58.6%	41.4%
1982	3,103,167	1,256,759	Collins, James M.	1,818,223	Bentsen, Lloyd	28,185	561,464	D	40.5%	58.6%	40.9%	59.1%
1978	2,312,540	1,151,376	Tower, John G.	1,139,149	Krueger, Robert	22,015	12,227	R	49.8%	49.3%	50.3%	49.7%
1976	3,874,516	1,636,370	Steelman, Alan	2,199,956	Bentsen, Lloyd	38,190	563,586	D	42.2%	56.8%	42.7%	57.3%
1972	3,413,903	1,822,877	Tower, John G.	1,511,985	Sanders, Barefoot	79,041	310,892	R	53.4%	44.3%	54.7%	45.3%
1970	2,231,671	1,035,794	Bush, George	1,194,069	Bentsen, Lloyd	1,808	158,275	D	46.4%	53.5%	46.5%	53.5%
1966	1,493,182	842,501	Tower, John G.	643,855	Carr, Waggoner	6,826	198,646	R	56.4%	43.1%	56.7%	43.3%
1964	2,603,856	1,134,337	Bush, George	1,463,958	Yarborough, Ralph	5,561	329,621	D	43.6%	56.2%	43.7%	56.3%
1961S	886,091	448,217	Tower, John G.	437,874	Blakley, William A.		10,343	R	50.6%	49.4%	50.6%	49.4%
1960	2,253,784	926,653	Tower, John G.	1,306,625	Johnson, Lyndon B.	20,506	379,972	D	41.1%	58.0%	41.5%	58.5%
1958	787,128	185,926	Whittenburg, Roy	587,030	Yarborough, Ralph	14,172	401,104	D	23.6%	74.6%	24.1%	75.9%
1957S	957,298		[See note below]					D				
1954	636,475	94,131	Watson, Carlos G.	539,319	Johnson, Lyndon B.	3,025	445,188	D	14.8%	84.7%	14.9%	85.1%
1952	1,895,192		—	1,895,192	Daniel, Price		1,895,192	D		100.0%		100.0%
1948	1,061,563	349,665	Porter, Jack	702,985	Johnson, Lyndon B.	8,913	353,320	D	32.9%	66.2%	33.2%	66.8%
1946	380,681	43,750	Sells, Murray C.	336,931	Connally, Tom		293,181	D	11.5%	88.5%	11.5%	88.5%

Notes: The June 1993 election was for a short term to fill a vacancy; the vote above was for the special election runoff. The April 1957 and May 1961 elections were also for short terms to fill vacancies. Although neither vote was held with official party designations, the 1961 vote above reflected the result of a runoff between unofficial party candidates. In 1957 there was a single ballot without a runoff and Democrat Ralph Yarborough polled 364,605 votes (38.1 percent of the total vote) and won the election with a 73,802 vote plurality over Democrat Martin Dies. The Republican Party did not run a candidate in the 1952 Senate election.

TEXAS

PRESIDENT 2008

2000 Census Population	County	Total Vote	Republican	Democratic	Other	Rep.-Dem. Plurality	Percentage			
							Total Vote		Major Vote	
							Rep.	Dem.	Rep.	Dem.
55,109	ANDERSON	16,655	11,884	4,630	141	7,254 R	71.4%	27.8%	72.0%	28.0%
13,004	ANDREWS	4,629	3,816	790	23	3,026 R	82.4%	17.1%	82.8%	17.2%
80,130	ANGELINA	29,153	19,569	9,379	205	10,190 R	67.1%	32.2%	67.6%	32.4%
22,497	ARANSAS	9,778	6,693	3,006	79	3,687 R	68.4%	30.7%	69.0%	31.0%
8,854	ARCHER	4,365	3,595	740	30	2,855 R	82.4%	17.0%	82.9%	17.1%
2,148	ARMSTRONG	990	856	128	6	728 R	86.5%	12.9%	87.0%	13.0%
38,628	ATASCOSA	9,938	5,462	4,415	61	1,047 R	55.0%	44.4%	55.3%	44.7%
23,590	AUSTIN	11,721	8,786	2,821	114	5,965 R	75.0%	24.1%	75.7%	24.3%
6,594	BAILEY	2,316	1,618	682	16	936 R	69.9%	29.4%	70.3%	29.7%
17,645	BANDERA	9,297	6,935	2,250	112	4,685 R	74.6%	24.2%	75.5%	24.5%
57,733	BASTROP	25,918	13,817	11,687	414	2,130 R	53.3%	45.1%	54.2%	45.8%
4,093	BAYLOR	1,643	1,262	366	15	896 R	76.8%	22.3%	77.5%	22.5%
32,359	BEE	8,157	4,471	3,645	41	826 R	54.8%	44.7%	55.1%	44.9%
237,974	BELL	90,334	49,242	40,413	679	8,829 R	54.5%	44.7%	54.9%	45.1%
1,392,931	BEXAR	525,715	246,275	275,527	3,913	29,252 D	46.8%	52.4%	47.2%	52.8%
8,418	BLANCO	4,939	3,418	1,467	54	1,951 R	69.2%	29.7%	70.0%	30.0%
729	BORDEN	361	316	40	5	276 R	87.5%	11.1%	88.8%	11.2%
17,204	BOSQUE	7,646	5,762	1,797	87	3,965 R	75.4%	23.5%	76.2%	23.8%
89,306	BOWIE	35,186	24,162	10,815	209	13,347 R	68.7%	30.7%	69.1%	30.9%
241,767	BRAZORIA	104,940	67,515	36,480	945	31,035 R	64.3%	34.8%	64.9%	35.1%
152,415	BRAZOS	58,673	37,465	20,502	706	16,963 R	63.9%	34.9%	64.6%	35.4%
8,866	BREWSTER	3,900	1,855	1,970	75	115 D	47.6%	50.5%	48.5%	51.5%
1,790	BRISCOE	830	617	205	8	412 R	74.3%	24.7%	75.1%	24.9%
7,976	BROOKS	2,309	556	1,747	6	1,191 D	24.1%	75.7%	24.1%	75.9%
37,674	BROWN	15,015	12,052	2,822	141	9,230 R	80.3%	18.8%	81.0%	19.0%
16,470	BURLESON	6,665	4,547	2,053	65	2,494 R	68.2%	30.8%	68.9%	31.1%
34,147	BURNET	16,893	12,059	4,608	226	7,451 R	71.4%	27.3%	72.4%	27.6%
32,194	CALDWELL	11,648	6,107	5,403	138	704 R	52.4%	46.4%	53.1%	46.9%
20,647	CALHOUN	6,879	4,106	2,729	44	1,377 R	59.7%	39.7%	60.1%	39.9%
12,905	CALLAHAN	5,716	4,589	1,063	64	3,526 R	80.3%	18.6%	81.2%	18.8%
335,227	CAMERON	75,657	26,671	48,480	506	21,809 D	35.3%	64.1%	35.5%	64.5%
11,549	CAMP	4,567	2,798	1,734	35	1,064 R	61.3%	38.0%	61.7%	38.3%
6,516	CARSON	2,980	2,548	406	26	2,142 R	85.5%	13.6%	86.3%	13.7%
30,438	CASS	11,846	8,279	3,490	77	4,789 R	69.9%	29.5%	70.3%	29.7%
8,285	CASTRO	2,291	1,562	719	10	843 R	68.2%	31.4%	68.5%	31.5%
26,031	CHAMBERS	13,292	9,988	3,188	116	6,800 R	75.1%	24.0%	75.8%	24.2%
46,659	CHEROKEE	16,417	11,695	4,610	112	7,085 R	71.2%	28.1%	71.7%	28.3%
7,688	CHILDRESS	2,296	1,782	497	17	1,285 R	77.6%	21.6%	78.2%	21.8%
11,006	CLAY	5,339	4,213	1,085	41	3,128 R	78.9%	20.3%	79.5%	20.5%
3,730	COCHRAN	1,057	758	284	15	474 R	71.7%	26.9%	72.7%	27.3%
3,864	COKE	1,569	1,252	299	18	953 R	79.8%	19.1%	80.7%	19.3%
9,235	COLEMAN	3,702	3,011	643	48	2,368 R	81.3%	17.4%	82.4%	17.6%
491,675	COLLIN	296,583	184,897	109,047	2,639	75,850 R	62.3%	36.8%	62.9%	37.1%
3,206	COLLINGSWORTH	1,195	943	234	18	709 R	78.9%	19.6%	80.1%	19.9%
20,390	COLORADO	8,353	5,795	2,508	50	3,287 R	69.4%	30.0%	69.8%	30.2%
78,021	COMAL	48,158	35,233	12,384	541	22,849 R	73.2%	25.7%	74.0%	26.0%
14,026	COMANCHE	5,217	3,813	1,334	70	2,479 R	73.1%	25.6%	74.1%	25.9%
3,966	CONCHO	1,077	807	257	13	550 R	74.9%	23.9%	75.8%	24.2%
36,363	COOKE	15,032	11,871	3,051	110	8,820 R	79.0%	20.3%	79.6%	20.4%
74,978	CORYELL	18,332	11,550	6,619	163	4,931 R	63.0%	36.1%	63.6%	36.4%

TEXAS

PRESIDENT 2008

2000 Census Population	County	Total Vote	Republican	Democratic	Other	Rep.-Dem. Plurality	Total Vote Rep.	Total Vote Dem.	Major Vote Rep.	Major Vote Dem.
1,904	COTTLE	705	509	187	9	322 R	72.2%	26.5%	73.1%	26.9%
3,996	CRANE	1,454	1,119	319	16	800 R	77.0%	21.9%	77.8%	22.2%
4,099	CROCKETT	1,545	1,026	512	7	514 R	66.4%	33.1%	66.7%	33.3%
7,072	CROSBY	1,914	1,221	684	9	537 R	63.8%	35.7%	64.1%	35.9%
2,975	CULBERSON	759	257	492	10	235 D	33.9%	64.8%	34.3%	65.7%
6,222	DALLAM	1,589	1,269	302	18	967 R	79.9%	19.0%	80.8%	19.2%
2,218,899	DALLAS	738,463	310,000	422,989	5,474	112,989 D	42.0%	57.3%	42.3%	57.7%
14,985	DAWSON	4,096	2,906	1,152	38	1,754 R	70.9%	28.1%	71.6%	28.4%
18,561	DEAF SMITH	4,744	3,466	1,247	31	2,219 R	73.1%	26.3%	73.5%	26.5%
5,327	DELTA	2,187	1,580	589	18	991 R	72.2%	26.9%	72.8%	27.2%
432,976	DENTON	243,263	149,935	91,160	2,168	58,775 R	61.6%	37.5%	62.2%	37.8%
20,013	DE WITT	6,626	4,888	1,716	22	3,172 R	73.8%	25.9%	74.0%	26.0%
2,762	DICKENS	972	730	234	8	496 R	75.1%	24.1%	75.7%	24.3%
10,248	DIMMIT	3,587	874	2,692	21	1,818 D	24.4%	75.0%	24.5%	75.5%
3,828	DONLEY	1,690	1,374	291	25	1,083 R	81.3%	17.2%	82.5%	17.5%
13,120	DUVAL	4,409	1,076	3,298	35	2,222 D	24.4%	74.8%	24.6%	75.4%
18,297	EASTLAND	6,509	5,165	1,271	73	3,894 R	79.4%	19.5%	80.3%	19.7%
121,123	ECTOR	35,606	26,199	9,123	284	17,076 R	73.6%	25.6%	74.2%	25.8%
2,162	EDWARDS	1,035	673	346	16	327 R	65.0%	33.4%	66.0%	34.0%
111,360	ELLIS	53,853	38,078	15,333	442	22,745 R	70.7%	28.5%	71.3%	28.7%
679,622	EL PASO	185,233	61,783	122,021	1,429	60,238 D	33.4%	65.9%	33.6%	66.4%
33,001	ERATH	14,019	10,768	3,128	123	7,640 R	76.8%	22.3%	77.5%	22.5%
18,576	FALLS	5,599	3,328	2,225	46	1,103 R	59.4%	39.7%	59.9%	40.1%
31,242	FANNIN	11,694	8,092	3,464	138	4,628 R	69.2%	29.6%	70.0%	30.0%
21,804	FAYETTE	10,714	7,582	3,014	118	4,568 R	70.8%	28.1%	71.6%	28.4%
4,344	FISHER	1,784	1,083	687	14	396 R	60.7%	38.5%	61.2%	38.8%
7,771	FLOYD	2,521	1,784	730	7	1,054 R	70.8%	29.0%	71.0%	29.0%
1,622	FOARD	538	327	198	13	129 R	60.8%	36.8%	62.3%	37.7%
354,452	FORT BEND	202,822	103,206	98,368	1,248	4,838 R	50.9%	48.5%	51.2%	48.8%
9,458	FRANKLIN	4,491	3,392	1,036	63	2,356 R	75.5%	23.1%	76.6%	23.4%
17,867	FREESTONE	7,288	5,205	2,034	49	3,171 R	71.4%	27.9%	71.9%	28.1%
16,252	FRIO	4,062	1,644	2,405	13	761 D	40.5%	59.2%	40.6%	59.4%
14,467	GAINES	4,067	3,385	650	32	2,735 R	83.2%	16.0%	83.9%	16.1%
250,158	GALVESTON	105,004	62,258	41,805	941	20,453 R	59.3%	39.8%	59.8%	40.2%
4,872	GARZA	1,750	1,356	375	19	981 R	77.5%	21.4%	78.3%	21.7%
20,814	GILLESPIE	12,338	9,563	2,576	199	6,987 R	77.5%	20.9%	78.8%	21.2%
1,406	GLASSCOCK	557	502	52	3	450 R	90.1%	9.3%	90.6%	9.4%
6,928	GOLIAD	3,655	2,298	1,329	28	969 R	62.9%	36.4%	63.4%	36.6%
18,628	GONZALES	6,287	4,076	2,167	44	1,909 R	64.8%	34.5%	65.3%	34.7%
22,744	GRAY	8,133	6,924	1,153	56	5,771 R	85.1%	14.2%	85.7%	14.3%
110,595	GRAYSON	45,477	31,136	13,900	441	17,236 R	68.5%	30.6%	69.1%	30.9%
111,379	GREGG	42,610	29,203	13,166	241	16,037 R	68.5%	30.9%	68.9%	31.1%
23,552	GRIMES	8,322	5,562	2,704	56	2,858 R	66.8%	32.5%	67.3%	32.7%
89,023	GUADALUPE	47,461	30,869	16,156	436	14,713 R	65.0%	34.0%	65.6%	34.4%
36,602	HALE	9,943	7,171	2,708	64	4,463 R	72.1%	27.2%	72.6%	27.4%
3,782	HALL	1,264	930	324	10	606 R	73.6%	25.6%	74.2%	25.8%
8,229	HAMILTON	3,778	2,876	863	39	2,013 R	76.1%	22.8%	76.9%	23.1%
5,369	HANSFORD	2,102	1,847	240	15	1,607 R	87.9%	11.4%	88.5%	11.5%
4,724	HARDEMAN	1,595	1,199	373	23	826 R	75.2%	23.4%	76.3%	23.7%
48,073	HARDIN	20,702	16,603	3,939	160	12,664 R	80.2%	19.0%	80.8%	19.2%

TEXAS

PRESIDENT 2008

2000 Census Population	County	Total Vote	Republican	Democratic	Other	Rep.-Dem. Plurality	Percentage Total Vote Rep.	Total Vote Dem.	Major Vote Rep.	Major Vote Dem.
3,400,578	HARRIS	1,171,472	571,883	590,982	8,607	19,099 D	48.8%	50.4%	49.2%	50.8%
62,110	HARRISON	26,158	17,103	8,887	168	8,216 R	65.4%	34.0%	65.8%	34.2%
5,537	HARTLEY	1,985	1,711	250	24	1,461 R	86.2%	12.6%	87.3%	12.7%
6,093	HASKELL	2,116	1,388	699	29	689 R	65.6%	33.0%	66.5%	33.5%
97,589	HAYS	59,052	29,638	28,431	983	1,207 R	50.2%	48.1%	51.0%	49.0%
3,351	HEMPHILL	1,570	1,345	216	9	1,129 R	85.7%	13.8%	86.2%	13.8%
73,277	HENDERSON	28,993	20,857	7,913	223	12,944 R	71.9%	27.3%	72.5%	27.5%
569,463	HIDALGO	130,784	39,668	90,261	855	50,593 D	30.3%	69.0%	30.5%	69.5%
32,321	HILL	13,188	9,264	3,811	113	5,453 R	70.2%	28.9%	70.9%	29.1%
22,716	HOCKLEY	7,645	5,795	1,797	53	3,998 R	75.8%	23.5%	76.3%	23.7%
41,100	HOOD	22,596	17,299	5,087	210	12,212 R	76.6%	22.5%	77.3%	22.7%
31,960	HOPKINS	12,919	9,299	3,530	90	5,769 R	72.0%	27.3%	72.5%	27.5%
23,185	HOUSTON	8,624	5,872	2,656	96	3,216 R	68.1%	30.8%	68.9%	31.1%
33,627	HOWARD	9,689	7,029	2,545	115	4,484 R	72.5%	26.3%	73.4%	26.6%
3,344	HUDSPETH	898	458	430	10	28 R	51.0%	47.9%	51.6%	48.4%
76,596	HUNT	29,524	20,573	8,594	357	11,979 R	69.7%	29.1%	70.5%	29.5%
23,857	HUTCHINSON	8,761	7,361	1,322	78	6,039 R	84.0%	15.1%	84.8%	15.2%
1,771	IRION	817	644	164	9	480 R	78.8%	20.1%	79.7%	20.3%
8,763	JACK	3,023	2,528	470	25	2,058 R	83.6%	15.5%	84.3%	15.7%
14,391	JACKSON	5,057	3,723	1,301	33	2,422 R	73.6%	25.7%	74.1%	25.9%
35,604	JASPER	12,776	9,022	3,658	96	5,364 R	70.6%	28.6%	71.2%	28.8%
2,207	JEFF DAVIS	1,236	749	468	19	281 R	60.6%	37.9%	61.5%	38.5%
252,051	JEFFERSON	88,296	42,905	44,888	503	1,983 D	48.6%	50.8%	48.9%	51.1%
5,281	JIM HOGG	1,815	472	1,336	7	864 D	26.0%	73.6%	26.1%	73.9%
39,326	JIM WELLS	11,612	4,841	6,706	65	1,865 D	41.7%	57.8%	41.9%	58.1%
126,811	JOHNSON	50,050	36,685	12,912	453	23,773 R	73.3%	25.8%	74.0%	26.0%
20,785	JONES	5,808	4,203	1,528	77	2,675 R	72.4%	26.3%	73.3%	26.7%
15,446	KARNES	4,527	2,736	1,760	31	976 R	60.4%	38.9%	60.9%	39.1%
71,313	KAUFMAN	35,145	23,735	11,161	249	12,574 R	67.5%	31.8%	68.0%	32.0%
23,743	KENDALL	16,746	12,971	3,599	176	9,372 R	77.5%	21.5%	78.3%	21.7%
414	KENEDY	202	94	108		14 D	46.5%	53.5%	46.5%	53.5%
859	KENT	448	342	99	7	243 R	76.3%	22.1%	77.6%	22.4%
43,653	KERR	22,556	16,752	5,570	234	11,182 R	74.3%	24.7%	75.0%	25.0%
4,468	KIMBLE	1,843	1,487	342	14	1,145 R	80.7%	18.6%	81.3%	18.7%
356	KING	163	151	8	4	143 R	92.6%	4.9%	95.0%	5.0%
3,379	KINNEY	1,551	907	633	11	274 R	58.5%	40.8%	58.9%	41.1%
31,549	KLEBERG	9,876	4,540	5,256	80	716 D	46.0%	53.2%	46.3%	53.7%
4,253	KNOX	1,368	986	367	15	619 R	72.1%	26.8%	72.9%	27.1%
48,499	LAMAR	18,362	12,952	5,243	167	7,709 R	70.5%	28.6%	71.2%	28.8%
14,709	LAMB	4,525	3,344	1,156	25	2,188 R	73.9%	25.5%	74.3%	25.7%
17,762	LAMPASAS	7,634	5,651	1,903	80	3,748 R	74.0%	24.9%	74.8%	25.2%
5,866	LA SALLE	1,776	714	1,052	10	338 D	40.2%	59.2%	40.4%	59.6%
19,210	LAVACA	8,223	6,293	1,869	61	4,424 R	76.5%	22.7%	77.1%	22.9%
15,657	LEE	6,377	4,312	2,000	65	2,312 R	67.6%	31.4%	68.3%	31.7%
15,335	LEON	7,041	5,566	1,418	57	4,148 R	79.1%	20.1%	79.7%	20.3%
70,154	LIBERTY	21,626	15,448	5,991	187	9,457 R	71.4%	27.7%	72.1%	27.9%
22,051	LIMESTONE	7,652	5,079	2,516	57	2,563 R	66.4%	32.9%	66.9%	33.1%
3,057	LIPSCOMB	1,256	1,093	155	8	938 R	87.0%	12.3%	87.6%	12.4%
12,309	LIVE OAK	4,176	3,095	1,048	33	2,047 R	74.1%	25.1%	74.7%	25.3%
17,044	LLANO	9,629	7,281	2,250	98	5,031 R	75.6%	23.4%	76.4%	23.6%
67	LOVING	79	67	12		55 R	84.8%	15.2%	84.8%	15.2%
242,628	LUBBOCK	97,534	66,304	30,486	744	35,818 R	68.0%	31.3%	68.5%	31.5%
6,550	LYNN	2,116	1,473	627	16	846 R	69.6%	29.6%	70.1%	29.9%
8,205	MCCULLOCH	3,010	2,263	728	19	1,535 R	75.2%	24.2%	75.7%	24.3%
213,517	MCLENNAN	79,674	49,044	29,998	632	19,046 R	61.6%	37.7%	62.0%	38.0%

TEXAS

PRESIDENT 2008

2000 Census Population	County	Total Vote	Republican	Democratic	Other	Rep.-Dem. Plurality	Percentage Total Vote Rep.	Dem.	Major Vote Rep.	Dem.
851	MCMULLEN	537	400	132	5	268 R	74.5%	24.6%	75.2%	24.8%
12,940	MADISON	4,074	2,891	1,146	37	1,745 R	71.0%	28.1%	71.6%	28.4%
10,941	MARION	4,252	2,567	1,644	41	923 R	60.4%	38.7%	61.0%	39.0%
4,746	MARTIN	1,715	1,389	314	12	1,075 R	81.0%	18.3%	81.6%	18.4%
3,738	MASON	2,121	1,544	546	31	998 R	72.8%	25.7%	73.9%	26.1%
37,957	MATAGORDA	12,373	7,835	4,440	98	3,395 R	63.3%	35.9%	63.8%	36.2%
47,297	MAVERICK	10,939	2,316	8,554	69	6,238 D	21.2%	78.2%	21.3%	78.7%
39,304	MEDINA	15,737	10,480	5,147	110	5,333 R	66.6%	32.7%	67.1%	32.9%
2,360	MENARD	1,018	712	295	11	417 R	69.9%	29.0%	70.7%	29.3%
116,009	MIDLAND	46,216	36,155	9,691	370	26,464 R	78.2%	21.0%	78.9%	21.1%
24,238	MILAM	8,357	5,217	3,044	96	2,173 R	62.4%	36.4%	63.2%	36.8%
5,151	MILLS	2,177	1,753	398	26	1,355 R	80.5%	18.3%	81.5%	18.5%
9,698	MITCHELL	2,431	1,815	586	30	1,229 R	74.7%	24.1%	75.6%	24.4%
19,117	MONTAGUE	7,950	6,245	1,597	108	4,648 R	78.6%	20.1%	79.6%	20.4%
293,768	MONTGOMERY	157,847	119,884	36,703	1,260	83,181 R	75.9%	23.3%	76.6%	23.4%
20,121	MOORE	5,437	4,282	1,123	32	3,159 R	78.8%	20.7%	79.2%	20.8%
13,048	MORRIS	5,248	3,158	2,055	35	1,103 R	60.2%	39.2%	60.6%	39.4%
1,426	MOTLEY	594	522	67	5	455 R	87.9%	11.3%	88.6%	11.4%
59,203	NACOGDOCHES	23,391	14,828	8,393	170	6,435 R	63.4%	35.9%	63.9%	36.1%
45,124	NAVARRO	16,321	10,810	5,400	111	5,410 R	66.2%	33.1%	66.7%	33.3%
15,072	NEWTON	5,260	3,446	1,751	63	1,695 R	65.5%	33.3%	66.3%	33.7%
15,802	NOLAN	5,063	3,485	1,521	57	1,964 R	68.8%	30.0%	69.6%	30.4%
313,645	NUECES	101,230	52,391	47,912	927	4,479 R	51.8%	47.3%	52.2%	47.8%
9,006	OCHILTREE	3,109	2,851	243	15	2,608 R	91.7%	7.8%	92.1%	7.9%
2,185	OLDHAM	920	813	102	5	711 R	88.4%	11.1%	88.9%	11.1%
84,966	ORANGE	29,406	21,509	7,646	251	13,863 R	73.1%	26.0%	73.8%	26.2%
27,026	PALO PINTO	9,890	7,264	2,499	127	4,765 R	73.4%	25.3%	74.4%	25.6%
22,756	PANOLA	10,216	7,582	2,586	48	4,996 R	74.2%	25.3%	74.6%	25.4%
88,495	PARKER	47,951	36,974	10,502	475	26,472 R	77.1%	21.9%	77.9%	22.1%
10,016	PARMER	3,713	2,969	719	25	2,250 R	80.0%	19.4%	80.5%	19.5%
16,809	PECOS	4,010	2,480	1,476	54	1,004 R	61.8%	36.8%	62.7%	37.3%
41,133	POLK	20,149	13,731	6,230	188	7,501 R	68.1%	30.9%	68.8%	31.2%
113,546	POTTER	30,013	20,761	8,939	313	11,822 R	69.2%	29.8%	69.9%	30.1%
7,304	PRESIDIO	1,757	489	1,252	16	763 D	27.8%	71.3%	28.1%	71.9%
9,139	RAINS	4,236	3,146	1,048	42	2,098 R	74.3%	24.7%	75.0%	25.0%
104,312	RANDALL	51,832	41,948	9,468	416	32,480 R	80.9%	18.3%	81.6%	18.4%
3,326	REAGAN	994	795	197	2	598 R	80.0%	19.8%	80.1%	19.9%
3,047	REAL	1,628	1,238	375	15	863 R	76.0%	23.0%	76.8%	23.2%
14,314	RED RIVER	5,052	3,461	1,539	52	1,922 R	68.5%	30.5%	69.2%	30.8%
13,137	REEVES	3,077	1,445	1,606	26	161 D	47.0%	52.2%	47.4%	52.6%
7,828	REFUGIO	3,261	1,855	1,382	24	473 R	56.9%	42.4%	57.3%	42.7%
887	ROBERTS	518	477	41		436 R	92.1%	7.9%	92.1%	7.9%
16,000	ROBERTSON	6,710	3,980	2,675	55	1,305 R	59.3%	39.9%	59.8%	40.2%
43,080	ROCKWALL	32,066	23,300	8,492	274	14,808 R	72.7%	26.5%	73.3%	26.7%
11,495	RUNNELS	3,867	3,118	720	29	2,398 R	80.6%	18.6%	81.2%	18.8%
47,372	RUSK	18,722	13,646	4,983	93	8,663 R	72.9%	26.6%	73.3%	26.7%
10,469	SABINE	4,874	3,749	1,077	48	2,672 R	76.9%	22.1%	77.7%	22.3%
8,946	SAN AUGUSTINE	3,715	2,342	1,328	45	1,014 R	63.0%	35.7%	63.8%	36.2%
22,246	SAN JACINTO	8,958	6,151	2,721	86	3,430 R	68.7%	30.4%	69.3%	30.7%
67,138	SAN PATRICIO	21,396	12,404	8,854	138	3,550 R	58.0%	41.4%	58.3%	41.7%

TEXAS

PRESIDENT 2008

2000 Census Population	County	Total Vote	Republican	Democratic	Other	Rep.-Dem. Plurality	Percentage Total Vote Rep.	Dem.	Major Vote Rep.	Dem.
6,186	SAN SABA	2,457	1,941	487	29	1,454 R	79.0%	19.8%	79.9%	20.1%
2,935	SCHLEICHER	1,304	970	324	10	646 R	74.4%	24.8%	75.0%	25.0%
16,361	SCURRY	5,569	4,414	1,088	67	3,326 R	79.3%	19.5%	80.2%	19.8%
3,302	SHACKELFORD	1,505	1,284	208	13	1,076 R	85.3%	13.8%	86.1%	13.9%
25,224	SHELBY	9,220	6,630	2,548	42	4,082 R	71.9%	27.6%	72.2%	27.8%
3,186	SHERMAN	1,020	884	127	9	757 R	86.7%	12.5%	87.4%	12.6%
174,706	SMITH	79,561	55,187	23,726	648	31,461 R	69.4%	29.8%	69.9%	30.1%
6,809	SOMERVELL	3,533	2,677	799	57	1,878 R	75.8%	22.6%	77.0%	23.0%
53,597	STARR	9,792	1,492	8,274	26	6,782 D	15.2%	84.5%	15.3%	84.7%
9,674	STEPHENS	3,526	2,869	626	31	2,243 R	81.4%	17.8%	82.1%	17.9%
1,393	STERLING	619	520	97	2	423 R	84.0%	15.7%	84.3%	15.7%
1,693	STONEWALL	735	524	206	5	318 R	71.3%	28.0%	71.8%	28.2%
4,077	SUTTON	1,578	1,189	381	8	808 R	75.3%	24.1%	75.7%	24.3%
8,378	SWISHER	2,535	1,683	813	39	870 R	66.4%	32.1%	67.4%	32.6%
1,446,219	TARRANT	628,553	348,420	274,880	5,253	73,540 R	55.4%	43.7%	55.9%	44.1%
126,555	TAYLOR	47,439	34,317	12,690	432	21,627 R	72.3%	26.8%	73.0%	27.0%
1,081	TERRELL	519	323	186	10	137 R	62.2%	35.8%	63.5%	36.5%
12,761	TERRY	4,280	2,879	1,379	22	1,500 R	67.3%	32.2%	67.6%	32.4%
1,850	THROCKMORTON	838	671	166	1	505 R	80.1%	19.8%	80.2%	19.8%
28,118	TITUS	9,245	6,028	3,145	72	2,883 R	65.2%	34.0%	65.7%	34.3%
104,010	TOM GREEN	38,861	27,362	11,158	341	16,204 R	70.4%	28.7%	71.0%	29.0%
812,280	TRAVIS	397,714	136,981	254,017	6,716	117,036 D	34.4%	63.9%	35.0%	65.0%
13,779	TRINITY	6,077	4,095	1,925	57	2,170 R	67.4%	31.7%	68.0%	32.0%
20,871	TYLER	7,910	5,644	2,166	100	3,478 R	71.4%	27.4%	72.3%	27.7%
35,291	UPSHUR	15,164	11,222	3,790	152	7,432 R	74.0%	25.0%	74.8%	25.2%
3,404	UPTON	1,197	898	288	11	610 R	75.0%	24.1%	75.7%	24.3%
25,926	UVALDE	8,766	4,590	4,126	50	464 R	52.4%	47.1%	52.7%	47.3%
44,856	VAL VERDE	12,820	5,752	6,982	86	1,230 D	44.9%	54.5%	45.2%	54.8%
48,140	VAN ZANDT	20,395	15,734	4,505	156	11,229 R	77.1%	22.1%	77.7%	22.3%
84,088	VICTORIA	29,931	19,878	9,832	221	10,046 R	66.4%	32.8%	66.9%	33.1%
61,758	WALKER	19,146	11,623	7,334	189	4,289 R	60.7%	38.3%	61.3%	38.7%
32,663	WALLER	15,508	8,265	7,153	90	1,112 R	53.3%	46.1%	53.6%	46.4%
10,909	WARD	3,602	2,667	899	36	1,768 R	74.0%	25.0%	74.8%	25.2%
30,373	WASHINGTON	14,377	10,176	4,034	167	6,142 R	70.8%	28.1%	71.6%	28.4%
193,117	WEBB	46,821	13,119	33,452	250	20,333 D	28.0%	71.4%	28.2%	71.8%
41,188	WHARTON	14,418	9,431	4,937	50	4,494 R	65.4%	34.2%	65.6%	34.4%
5,284	WHEELER	2,245	1,918	314	13	1,604 R	85.4%	14.0%	85.9%	14.1%
131,664	WICHITA	45,982	31,731	13,868	383	17,863 R	69.0%	30.2%	69.6%	30.4%
14,676	WILBARGER	4,509	3,283	1,196	30	2,087 R	72.8%	26.5%	73.3%	26.7%
20,082	WILLACY	4,903	1,456	3,409	38	1,953 D	29.7%	69.5%	29.9%	70.1%
249,967	WILLIAMSON	158,403	88,323	67,691	2,389	20,632 R	55.8%	42.7%	56.6%	43.4%
32,408	WILSON	16,366	10,904	5,362	100	5,542 R	66.6%	32.8%	67.0%	33.0%
7,173	WINKLER	2,032	1,529	477	26	1,052 R	75.2%	23.5%	76.2%	23.8%
48,793	WISE	20,639	15,973	4,471	195	11,502 R	77.4%	21.7%	78.1%	21.9%
36,752	WOOD	17,784	13,658	4,010	116	9,648 R	76.8%	22.5%	77.3%	22.7%
7,322	YOAKUM	2,458	1,989	450	19	1,539 R	80.9%	18.3%	81.5%	18.5%
17,943	YOUNG	7,305	5,942	1,303	60	4,639 R	81.3%	17.8%	82.0%	18.0%
12,182	ZAPATA	2,866	919	1,939	8	1,020 D	32.1%	67.7%	32.2%	67.8%
11,600	ZAVALA	3,876	596	3,263	17	2,667 D	15.4%	84.2%	15.4%	84.6%
20,851,820	TOTAL	8,077,795	4,479,328	3,528,633	69,834	950,695 R	55.5%	43.7%	55.9%	44.1%

TEXAS

SENATOR 2008

2000 Census Population	County	Total Vote	Republican	Democratic	Other	Rep.-Dem. Plurality	Percentage Total Vote Rep.	Dem.	Major Vote Rep.	Dem.
55,109	ANDERSON	16,391	11,093	5,027	271	6,066 R	67.7%	30.7%	68.8%	31.2%
13,004	ANDREWS	4,497	3,658	734	105	2,924 R	81.3%	16.3%	83.3%	16.7%
80,130	ANGELINA	28,555	18,508	9,623	424	8,885 R	64.8%	33.7%	65.8%	34.2%
22,497	ARANSAS	9,576	6,449	2,793	334	3,656 R	67.3%	29.2%	69.8%	30.2%
8,854	ARCHER	4,208	3,378	761	69	2,617 R	80.3%	18.1%	81.6%	18.4%
2,148	ARMSTRONG	970	821	130	19	691 R	84.6%	13.4%	86.3%	13.7%
38,628	ATASCOSA	9,717	5,012	4,518	187	494 R	51.6%	46.5%	52.6%	47.4%
23,590	AUSTIN	11,540	8,403	2,947	190	5,456 R	72.8%	25.5%	74.0%	26.0%
6,594	BAILEY	2,254	1,586	627	41	959 R	70.4%	27.8%	71.7%	28.3%
17,645	BANDERA	9,184	6,709	2,175	300	4,534 R	73.1%	23.7%	75.5%	24.5%
57,733	BASTROP	25,611	13,478	11,094	1,039	2,384 R	52.6%	43.3%	54.9%	45.1%
4,093	BAYLOR	1,577	1,173	367	37	806 R	74.4%	23.3%	76.2%	23.8%
32,359	BEE	7,965	4,042	3,746	177	296 R	50.7%	47.0%	51.9%	48.1%
237,974	BELL	88,348	50,118	35,936	2,294	14,182 R	56.7%	40.7%	58.2%	41.8%
1,392,931	BEXAR	514,105	233,983	265,311	14,811	31,328 D	45.5%	51.6%	46.9%	53.1%
8,418	BLANCO	4,888	3,390	1,324	174	2,066 R	69.4%	27.1%	71.9%	28.1%
729	BORDEN	353	300	48	5	252 R	85.0%	13.6%	86.2%	13.8%
17,204	BOSQUE	7,542	5,400	1,977	165	3,423 R	71.6%	26.2%	73.2%	26.8%
89,306	BOWIE	34,259	22,471	11,252	536	11,219 R	65.6%	32.8%	66.6%	33.4%
241,767	BRAZORIA	102,971	63,342	36,993	2,636	26,349 R	61.5%	35.9%	63.1%	36.9%
152,415	BRAZOS	57,067	37,818	17,701	1,548	20,117 R	66.3%	31.0%	68.1%	31.9%
8,866	BREWSTER	3,809	1,809	1,861	139	52 D	47.5%	48.9%	49.3%	50.7%
1,790	BRISCOE	785	586	187	12	399 R	74.6%	23.8%	75.8%	24.2%
7,976	BROOKS	2,258	408	1,817	33	1,409 D	18.1%	80.5%	18.3%	81.7%
37,674	BROWN	14,791	11,457	2,973	361	8,484 R	77.5%	20.1%	79.4%	20.6%
16,470	BURLESON	6,530	4,377	2,003	150	2,374 R	67.0%	30.7%	68.6%	31.4%
34,147	BURNET	16,774	11,964	4,288	522	7,676 R	71.3%	25.6%	73.6%	26.4%
32,194	CALDWELL	11,522	5,932	5,244	346	688 R	51.5%	45.5%	53.1%	46.9%
20,647	CALHOUN	6,791	3,825	2,806	160	1,019 R	56.3%	41.3%	57.7%	42.3%
12,905	CALLAHAN	5,582	4,410	1,039	133	3,371 R	79.0%	18.6%	80.9%	19.1%
335,227	CAMERON	74,122	24,223	48,020	1,879	23,797 D	32.7%	64.8%	33.5%	66.5%
11,549	CAMP	4,461	2,705	1,695	61	1,010 R	60.6%	38.0%	61.5%	38.5%
6,516	CARSON	2,945	2,467	409	69	2,058 R	83.8%	13.9%	85.8%	14.2%
30,438	CASS	11,464	7,466	3,816	182	3,650 R	65.1%	33.3%	66.2%	33.8%
8,285	CASTRO	2,226	1,526	671	29	855 R	68.6%	30.1%	69.5%	30.5%
26,031	CHAMBERS	12,744	9,053	3,416	275	5,637 R	71.0%	26.8%	72.6%	27.4%
46,659	CHEROKEE	16,113	11,324	4,569	220	6,755 R	70.3%	28.4%	71.3%	28.7%
7,688	CHILDRESS	2,194	1,668	475	51	1,193 R	76.0%	21.6%	77.8%	22.2%
11,006	CLAY	5,103	3,837	1,158	108	2,679 R	75.2%	22.7%	76.8%	23.2%
3,730	COCHRAN	1,030	750	259	21	491 R	72.8%	25.1%	74.3%	25.7%
3,864	COKE	1,473	1,194	231	48	963 R	81.1%	15.7%	83.8%	16.2%
9,235	COLEMAN	3,573	2,858	651	64	2,207 R	80.0%	18.2%	81.4%	18.6%
491,675	COLLIN	287,090	184,000	96,094	6,996	87,906 R	64.1%	33.5%	65.7%	34.3%
3,206	COLLINGSWORTH	1,121	864	234	23	630 R	77.1%	20.9%	78.7%	21.3%
20,390	COLORADO	8,137	5,389	2,628	120	2,761 R	66.2%	32.3%	67.2%	32.8%
78,021	COMAL	47,179	34,392	11,373	1,414	23,019 R	72.9%	24.1%	75.1%	24.9%
14,026	COMANCHE	5,095	3,498	1,509	88	1,989 R	68.7%	29.6%	69.9%	30.1%
3,966	CONCHO	1,059	794	248	17	546 R	75.0%	23.4%	76.2%	23.8%
36,363	COOKE	14,788	11,259	3,239	290	8,020 R	76.1%	21.9%	77.7%	22.3%
74,978	CORYELL	18,022	11,642	5,914	466	5,728 R	64.6%	32.8%	66.3%	33.7%

TEXAS

SENATOR 2008

2000 Census Population	County	Total Vote	Republican	Democratic	Other	Rep.-Dem. Plurality		Percentage			
								Total Vote		Major Vote	
								Rep.	Dem.	Rep.	Dem.
1,904	COTTLE	640	440	182	18	258	R	68.8%	28.4%	70.7%	29.3%
3,996	CRANE	1,354	990	319	45	671	R	73.1%	23.6%	75.6%	24.4%
4,099	CROCKETT	1,462	877	569	16	308	R	60.0%	38.9%	60.7%	39.3%
7,072	CROSBY	1,837	1,184	638	15	546	R	64.5%	34.7%	65.0%	35.0%
2,975	CULBERSON	665	239	401	25	162	D	35.9%	60.3%	37.3%	62.7%
6,222	DALLAM	1,554	1,245	259	50	986	R	80.1%	16.7%	82.8%	17.2%
2,218,899	DALLAS	723,613	312,781	396,354	14,478	83,573	D	43.2%	54.8%	44.1%	55.9%
14,985	DAWSON	3,883	2,742	1,064	77	1,678	R	70.6%	27.4%	72.0%	28.0%
18,561	DEAF SMITH	4,634	3,382	1,175	77	2,207	R	73.0%	25.4%	74.2%	25.8%
5,327	DELTA	2,128	1,409	684	35	725	R	66.2%	32.1%	67.3%	32.7%
432,976	DENTON	238,839	150,389	81,939	6,511	68,450	R	63.0%	34.3%	64.7%	35.3%
20,013	DE WITT	6,492	4,767	1,619	106	3,148	R	73.4%	24.9%	74.6%	25.4%
2,762	DICKENS	913	699	202	12	497	R	76.6%	22.1%	77.6%	22.4%
10,248	DIMMIT	3,448	751	2,651	46	1,900	D	21.8%	76.9%	22.1%	77.9%
3,828	DONLEY	1,648	1,333	270	45	1,063	R	80.9%	16.4%	83.2%	16.8%
13,120	DUVAL	4,247	773	3,386	88	2,613	D	18.2%	79.7%	18.6%	81.4%
18,297	EASTLAND	6,382	4,859	1,360	163	3,499	R	76.1%	21.3%	78.1%	21.9%
121,123	ECTOR	35,176	25,356	8,933	887	16,423	R	72.1%	25.4%	73.9%	26.1%
2,162	EDWARDS	957	635	305	17	330	R	66.4%	31.9%	67.6%	32.4%
111,360	ELLIS	53,107	36,186	15,491	1,430	20,695	R	68.1%	29.2%	70.0%	30.0%
679,622	EL PASO	179,804	56,692	118,284	4,828	61,592	D	31.5%	65.8%	32.4%	67.6%
33,001	ERATH	13,866	10,374	3,198	294	7,176	R	74.8%	23.1%	76.4%	23.6%
18,576	FALLS	5,453	3,253	2,115	85	1,138	R	59.7%	38.8%	60.6%	39.4%
31,242	FANNIN	11,509	7,345	3,925	239	3,420	R	63.8%	34.1%	65.2%	34.8%
21,804	FAYETTE	10,505	7,311	2,971	223	4,340	R	69.6%	28.3%	71.1%	28.9%
4,344	FISHER	1,745	1,037	684	24	353	R	59.4%	39.2%	60.3%	39.7%
7,771	FLOYD	2,380	1,700	654	26	1,046	R	71.4%	27.5%	72.2%	27.8%
1,622	FOARD	499	283	203	13	80	R	56.7%	40.7%	58.2%	41.8%
354,452	FORT BEND	199,615	101,563	94,909	3,143	6,654	R	50.9%	47.5%	51.7%	48.3%
9,458	FRANKLIN	4,372	3,315	964	93	2,351	R	75.8%	22.0%	77.5%	22.5%
17,867	FREESTONE	7,120	4,808	2,170	142	2,638	R	67.5%	30.5%	68.9%	31.1%
16,252	FRIO	3,923	1,500	2,369	54	869	D	38.2%	60.4%	38.8%	61.2%
14,467	GAINES	3,901	3,184	653	64	2,531	R	81.6%	16.7%	83.0%	17.0%
250,158	GALVESTON	102,754	57,291	43,107	2,356	14,184	R	55.8%	42.0%	57.1%	42.9%
4,872	GARZA	1,760	1,308	421	31	887	R	74.3%	23.9%	75.7%	24.3%
20,814	GILLESPIE	12,210	9,612	2,256	342	7,356	R	78.7%	18.5%	81.0%	19.0%
1,406	GLASSCOCK	537	481	46	10	435	R	89.6%	8.6%	91.3%	8.7%
6,928	GOLIAD	3,493	2,157	1,233	103	924	R	61.8%	35.3%	63.6%	36.4%
18,628	GONZALES	6,101	3,799	2,187	115	1,612	R	62.3%	35.8%	63.5%	36.5%
22,744	GRAY	8,026	6,777	1,085	164	5,692	R	84.4%	13.5%	86.2%	13.8%
110,595	GRAYSON	44,501	30,180	13,377	944	16,803	R	67.8%	30.1%	69.3%	30.7%
111,379	GREGG	41,955	29,176	12,211	568	16,965	R	69.5%	29.1%	70.5%	29.5%
23,552	GRIMES	8,207	5,234	2,803	170	2,431	R	63.8%	34.2%	65.1%	34.9%
89,023	GUADALUPE	46,202	29,752	15,293	1,157	14,459	R	64.4%	33.1%	66.0%	34.0%
36,602	HALE	9,706	6,905	2,632	169	4,273	R	71.1%	27.1%	72.4%	27.6%
3,782	HALL	1,196	847	327	22	520	R	70.8%	27.3%	72.1%	27.9%
8,229	HAMILTON	3,707	2,688	945	74	1,743	R	72.5%	25.5%	74.0%	26.0%
5,369	HANSFORD	2,043	1,806	207	30	1,599	R	88.4%	10.1%	89.7%	10.3%
4,724	HARDEMAN	1,551	1,116	397	38	719	R	72.0%	25.6%	73.8%	26.2%
48,073	HARDIN	20,239	15,534	4,361	344	11,173	R	76.8%	21.5%	78.1%	21.9%

TEXAS

SENATOR 2008

2000 Census Population	County	Total Vote	Republican	Democratic	Other	Rep.-Dem. Plurality	Percentage			
							Total Vote		Major Vote	
							Rep.	Dem.	Rep.	Dem.
3,400,578	HARRIS	1,151,174	544,857	583,782	22,535	38,925 D	47.3%	50.7%	48.3%	51.7%
62,110	HARRISON	25,150	16,310	8,465	375	7,845 R	64.9%	33.7%	65.8%	34.2%
5,537	HARTLEY	1,965	1,695	243	27	1,452 R	86.3%	12.4%	87.5%	12.5%
6,093	HASKELL	2,058	1,311	709	38	602 R	63.7%	34.5%	64.9%	35.1%
97,589	HAYS	58,105	30,071	25,688	2,346	4,383 R	51.8%	44.2%	53.9%	46.1%
3,351	HEMPHILL	1,535	1,294	218	23	1,076 R	84.3%	14.2%	85.6%	14.4%
73,277	HENDERSON	28,620	19,699	8,384	537	11,315 R	68.8%	29.3%	70.1%	29.9%
569,463	HIDALGO	126,422	35,720	88,539	2,163	52,819 D	28.3%	70.0%	28.7%	71.3%
32,321	HILL	13,002	8,640	4,112	250	4,528 R	66.5%	31.6%	67.8%	32.2%
22,716	HOCKLEY	7,500	5,771	1,587	142	4,184 R	76.9%	21.2%	78.4%	21.6%
41,100	HOOD	22,294	16,523	5,239	532	11,284 R	74.1%	23.5%	75.9%	24.1%
31,960	HOPKINS	12,524	8,380	3,876	268	4,504 R	66.9%	30.9%	68.4%	31.6%
23,185	HOUSTON	8,326	5,513	2,677	136	2,836 R	66.2%	32.2%	67.3%	32.7%
33,627	HOWARD	9,447	6,562	2,609	276	3,953 R	69.5%	27.6%	71.6%	28.4%
3,344	HUDSPETH	827	392	393	42	1 D	47.4%	47.5%	49.9%	50.1%
76,596	HUNT	29,063	19,752	8,592	719	11,160 R	68.0%	29.6%	69.7%	30.3%
23,857	HUTCHINSON	8,640	7,245	1,191	204	6,054 R	83.9%	13.8%	85.9%	14.1%
1,771	IRION	793	623	150	20	473 R	78.6%	18.9%	80.6%	19.4%
8,763	JACK	2,954	2,333	567	54	1,766 R	79.0%	19.2%	80.4%	19.6%
14,391	JACKSON	4,817	3,420	1,320	77	2,100 R	71.0%	27.4%	72.2%	27.8%
35,604	JASPER	12,356	8,170	3,961	225	4,209 R	66.1%	32.1%	67.3%	32.7%
2,207	JEFF DAVIS	1,170	645	480	45	165 R	55.1%	41.0%	57.3%	42.7%
252,051	JEFFERSON	85,758	40,800	43,820	1,138	3,020 D	47.6%	51.1%	48.2%	51.8%
5,281	JIM HOGG	1,785	308	1,456	21	1,148 D	17.3%	81.6%	17.5%	82.5%
39,326	JIM WELLS	11,324	4,117	6,948	259	2,831 D	36.4%	61.4%	37.2%	62.8%
126,811	JOHNSON	49,542	34,512	13,830	1,200	20,682 R	69.7%	27.9%	71.4%	28.6%
20,785	JONES	5,660	4,013	1,495	152	2,518 R	70.9%	26.4%	72.9%	27.1%
15,446	KARNES	4,393	2,581	1,709	103	872 R	58.8%	38.9%	60.2%	39.8%
71,313	KAUFMAN	34,704	22,527	11,499	678	11,028 R	64.9%	33.1%	66.2%	33.8%
23,743	KENDALL	16,449	12,765	3,224	460	9,541 R	77.6%	19.6%	79.8%	20.2%
414	KENEDY	192	90	101	1	11 D	46.9%	52.6%	47.1%	52.9%
859	KENT	423	317	98	8	219 R	74.9%	23.2%	76.4%	23.6%
43,653	KERR	22,209	16,249	5,391	569	10,858 R	73.2%	24.3%	75.1%	24.9%
4,468	KIMBLE	1,805	1,436	328	41	1,108 R	79.6%	18.2%	81.4%	18.6%
356	KING	133	121	10	2	111 R	91.0%	7.5%	92.4%	7.6%
3,379	KINNEY	1,503	868	615	20	253 R	57.8%	40.9%	58.5%	41.5%
31,549	KLEBERG	9,695	3,896	5,569	230	1,673 D	40.2%	57.4%	41.2%	58.8%
4,253	KNOX	1,335	923	399	13	524 R	69.1%	29.9%	69.8%	30.2%
48,499	LAMAR	17,972	11,612	6,027	333	5,585 R	64.6%	33.5%	65.8%	34.2%
14,709	LAMB	4,396	3,262	1,060	74	2,202 R	74.2%	24.1%	75.5%	24.5%
17,762	LAMPASAS	7,537	5,616	1,699	222	3,917 R	74.5%	22.5%	76.8%	23.2%
5,866	LA SALLE	1,674	592	1,055	27	463 D	35.4%	63.0%	35.9%	64.1%
19,210	LAVACA	7,949	5,769	2,044	136	3,725 R	72.6%	25.7%	73.8%	26.2%
15,657	LEE	6,075	4,088	1,838	149	2,250 R	67.3%	30.3%	69.0%	31.0%
15,335	LEON	6,817	5,251	1,442	124	3,809 R	77.0%	21.2%	78.5%	21.5%
70,154	LIBERTY	21,142	13,903	6,770	469	7,133 R	65.8%	32.0%	67.3%	32.7%
22,051	LIMESTONE	7,496	4,831	2,552	113	2,279 R	64.4%	34.0%	65.4%	34.6%
3,057	LIPSCOMB	1,229	1,060	150	19	910 R	86.2%	12.2%	87.6%	12.4%
12,309	LIVE OAK	4,067	2,864	1,086	117	1,778 R	70.4%	26.7%	72.5%	27.5%
17,044	LLANO	9,543	7,163	2,102	278	5,061 R	75.1%	22.0%	77.3%	22.7%

TEXAS

SENATOR 2008

2000 Census Population	County	Total Vote	Republican	Democratic	Other	Rep.-Dem. Plurality	Percentage Total Vote Rep.	Percentage Total Vote Dem.	Percentage Major Vote Rep.	Percentage Major Vote Dem.
67	LOVING	73	55	16	2	39 R	75.3%	21.9%	77.5%	22.5%
242,628	LUBBOCK	95,667	67,267	26,246	2,154	41,021 R	70.3%	27.4%	71.9%	28.1%
6,550	LYNN	2,100	1,488	578	34	910 R	70.9%	27.5%	72.0%	28.0%
8,205	MCCULLOCH	2,947	2,207	676	64	1,531 R	74.9%	22.9%	76.6%	23.4%
213,517	MCLENNAN	78,524	48,995	28,197	1,332	20,798 R	62.4%	35.9%	63.5%	36.5%
851	MCMULLEN	471	347	109	15	238 R	73.7%	23.1%	76.1%	23.9%
12,940	MADISON	3,985	2,680	1,226	79	1,454 R	67.3%	30.8%	68.6%	31.4%
10,941	MARION	4,101	2,436	1,584	81	852 R	59.4%	38.6%	60.6%	39.4%
4,746	MARTIN	1,632	1,252	343	37	909 R	76.7%	21.0%	78.5%	21.5%
3,738	MASON	2,031	1,516	451	64	1,065 R	74.6%	22.2%	77.1%	22.9%
37,957	MATAGORDA	12,107	7,142	4,676	289	2,466 R	59.0%	38.6%	60.4%	39.6%
47,297	MAVERICK	9,809	1,849	7,759	201	5,910 D	18.9%	79.1%	19.2%	80.8%
39,304	MEDINA	15,543	10,120	5,095	328	5,025 R	65.1%	32.8%	66.5%	33.5%
2,360	MENARD	966	695	245	26	450 R	71.9%	25.4%	73.9%	26.1%
116,009	MIDLAND	45,468	35,514	8,798	1,156	26,716 R	78.1%	19.3%	80.1%	19.9%
24,238	MILAM	8,212	5,012	3,054	146	1,958 R	61.0%	37.2%	62.1%	37.9%
5,151	MILLS	2,101	1,620	414	67	1,206 R	77.1%	19.7%	79.6%	20.4%
9,698	MITCHELL	2,342	1,657	628	57	1,029 R	70.8%	26.8%	72.5%	27.5%
19,117	MONTAGUE	7,725	5,751	1,765	209	3,986 R	74.4%	22.8%	76.5%	23.5%
293,768	MONTGOMERY	155,938	116,003	36,699	3,236	79,304 R	74.4%	23.5%	76.0%	24.0%
20,121	MOORE	5,320	4,154	1,078	88	3,076 R	78.1%	20.3%	79.4%	20.6%
13,048	MORRIS	5,094	2,885	2,134	75	751 R	56.6%	41.9%	57.5%	42.5%
1,426	MOTLEY	576	494	76	6	418 R	85.8%	13.2%	86.7%	13.3%
59,203	NACOGDOCHES	22,755	14,493	7,845	417	6,648 R	63.7%	34.5%	64.9%	35.1%
45,124	NAVARRO	15,928	9,996	5,658	274	4,338 R	62.8%	35.5%	63.9%	36.1%
15,072	NEWTON	5,124	2,986	2,007	131	979 R	58.3%	39.2%	59.8%	40.2%
15,802	NOLAN	4,942	3,359	1,481	102	1,878 R	68.0%	30.0%	69.4%	30.6%
313,645	NUECES	99,210	48,179	48,299	2,732	120 D	48.6%	48.7%	49.9%	50.1%
9,006	OCHILTREE	3,049	2,768	243	38	2,525 R	90.8%	8.0%	91.9%	8.1%
2,185	OLDHAM	888	777	85	26	692 R	87.5%	9.6%	90.1%	9.9%
84,966	ORANGE	29,028	19,885	8,593	550	11,292 R	68.5%	29.6%	69.8%	30.2%
27,026	PALO PINTO	9,687	6,714	2,782	191	3,932 R	69.3%	28.7%	70.7%	29.3%
22,756	PANOLA	9,920	7,123	2,661	136	4,462 R	71.8%	26.8%	72.8%	27.2%
88,495	PARKER	47,707	35,486	11,132	1,089	24,354 R	74.4%	23.3%	76.1%	23.9%
10,016	PARMER	3,617	2,894	667	56	2,227 R	80.0%	18.4%	81.3%	18.7%
16,809	PECOS	3,836	2,268	1,467	101	801 R	59.1%	38.2%	60.7%	39.3%
41,133	POLK	19,252	12,254	6,502	496	5,752 R	63.7%	33.8%	65.3%	34.7%
113,546	POTTER	29,424	20,361	8,197	866	12,164 R	69.2%	27.9%	71.3%	28.7%
7,304	PRESIDIO	1,549	396	1,132	21	736 D	25.6%	73.1%	25.9%	74.1%
9,139	RAINS	4,133	2,820	1,220	93	1,600 R	68.2%	29.5%	69.8%	30.2%
104,312	RANDALL	51,430	41,718	8,501	1,211	33,217 R	81.1%	16.5%	83.1%	16.9%
3,326	REAGAN	951	752	179	20	573 R	79.1%	18.8%	80.8%	19.2%
3,047	REAL	1,586	1,192	346	48	846 R	75.2%	21.8%	77.5%	22.5%
14,314	RED RIVER	4,824	3,000	1,750	74	1,250 R	62.2%	36.3%	63.2%	36.8%
13,137	REEVES	2,893	1,171	1,651	71	480 D	40.5%	57.1%	41.5%	58.5%
7,828	REFUGIO	3,059	1,643	1,353	63	290 R	53.7%	44.2%	54.8%	45.2%
887	ROBERTS	509	471	31	7	440 R	92.5%	6.1%	93.8%	6.2%
16,000	ROBERTSON	6,553	3,758	2,667	128	1,091 R	57.3%	40.7%	58.5%	41.5%
43,080	ROCKWALL	31,581	22,875	8,002	704	14,873 R	72.4%	25.3%	74.1%	25.9%
11,495	RUNNELS	3,716	2,952	683	81	2,269 R	79.4%	18.4%	81.2%	18.8%
47,372	RUSK	18,163	13,159	4,752	252	8,407 R	72.4%	26.2%	73.5%	26.5%
10,469	SABINE	4,690	3,300	1,266	124	2,034 R	70.4%	27.0%	72.3%	27.7%
8,946	SAN AUGUSTINE	3,514	2,114	1,332	68	782 R	60.2%	37.9%	61.3%	38.7%
22,246	SAN JACINTO	8,733	5,418	3,091	224	2,327 R	62.0%	35.4%	63.7%	36.3%
67,138	SAN PATRICIO	20,763	11,277	8,956	530	2,321 R	54.3%	43.1%	55.7%	44.3%

TEXAS

SENATOR 2008

2000 Census Population	County	Total Vote	Republican	Democratic	Other	Rep.-Dem. Plurality	Percentage			
							Total Vote		Major Vote	
							Rep.	Dem.	Rep.	Dem.
6,186	SAN SABA	2,357	1,849	458	50	1,391 R	78.4%	19.4%	80.1%	19.9%
2,935	SCHLEICHER	1,218	838	346	34	492 R	68.8%	28.4%	70.8%	29.2%
16,361	SCURRY	5,416	4,210	1,086	120	3,124 R	77.7%	20.1%	79.5%	20.5%
3,302	SHACKELFORD	1,457	1,227	210	20	1,017 R	84.2%	14.4%	85.4%	14.6%
25,224	SHELBY	8,867	6,146	2,598	123	3,548 R	69.3%	29.3%	70.3%	29.7%
3,186	SHERMAN	988	849	113	26	736 R	85.9%	11.4%	88.3%	11.7%
174,706	SMITH	78,146	54,252	22,613	1,281	31,639 R	69.4%	28.9%	70.6%	29.4%
6,809	SOMERVELL	3,436	2,433	920	83	1,513 R	70.8%	26.8%	72.6%	27.4%
53,597	STARR	9,214	1,220	7,910	84	6,690 D	13.2%	85.8%	13.4%	86.6%
9,674	STEPHENS	3,440	2,668	706	66	1,962 R	77.6%	20.5%	79.1%	20.9%
1,393	STERLING	576	482	86	8	396 R	83.7%	14.9%	84.9%	15.1%
1,693	STONEWALL	700	472	212	16	260 R	67.4%	30.3%	69.0%	31.0%
4,077	SUTTON	1,554	1,113	417	24	696 R	71.6%	26.8%	72.7%	27.3%
8,378	SWISHER	2,492	1,580	861	51	719 R	63.4%	34.6%	64.7%	35.3%
1,446,219	TARRANT	618,227	341,772	262,870	13,585	78,902 R	55.3%	42.5%	56.5%	43.5%
126,555	TAYLOR	46,602	34,144	11,392	1,066	22,752 R	73.3%	24.4%	75.0%	25.0%
1,081	TERRELL	482	283	183	16	100 R	58.7%	38.0%	60.7%	39.3%
12,761	TERRY	4,122	2,852	1,181	89	1,671 R	69.2%	28.7%	70.7%	29.3%
1,850	THROCKMORTON	763	593	162	8	431 R	77.7%	21.2%	78.5%	21.5%
28,118	TITUS	9,079	5,619	3,308	152	2,311 R	61.9%	36.4%	62.9%	37.1%
104,010	TOM GREEN	38,257	27,296	9,937	1,024	17,359 R	71.3%	26.0%	73.3%	26.7%
812,280	TRAVIS	390,404	145,520	228,620	16,264	83,100 D	37.3%	58.6%	38.9%	61.1%
13,779	TRINITY	5,883	3,637	2,114	132	1,523 R	61.8%	35.9%	63.2%	36.8%
20,871	TYLER	7,645	5,102	2,336	207	2,766 R	66.7%	30.6%	68.6%	31.4%
35,291	UPSHUR	14,886	10,677	3,920	289	6,757 R	71.7%	26.3%	73.1%	26.9%
3,404	UPTON	1,109	830	255	24	575 R	74.8%	23.0%	76.5%	23.5%
25,926	UVALDE	8,623	4,206	4,281	136	75 D	48.8%	49.6%	49.6%	50.4%
44,856	VAL VERDE	12,477	5,170	7,062	245	1,892 D	41.4%	56.6%	42.3%	57.7%
48,140	VAN ZANDT	20,068	14,601	5,086	381	9,515 R	72.8%	25.3%	74.2%	25.8%
84,088	VICTORIA	29,231	19,590	9,036	605	10,554 R	67.0%	30.9%	68.4%	31.6%
61,758	WALKER	18,818	11,080	7,235	503	3,845 R	58.9%	38.4%	60.5%	39.5%
32,663	WALLER	15,387	7,995	7,167	225	828 R	52.0%	46.6%	52.7%	47.3%
10,909	WARD	3,486	2,466	912	108	1,554 R	70.7%	26.2%	73.0%	27.0%
30,373	WASHINGTON	14,126	9,894	3,960	272	5,934 R	70.0%	28.0%	71.4%	28.6%
193,117	WEBB	46,063	9,626	35,802	635	26,176 D	20.9%	77.7%	21.2%	78.8%
41,188	WHARTON	14,107	8,681	5,215	211	3,466 R	61.5%	37.0%	62.5%	37.5%
5,284	WHEELER	2,157	1,800	327	30	1,473 R	83.4%	15.2%	84.6%	15.4%
131,664	WICHITA	44,371	30,354	12,946	1,071	17,408 R	68.4%	29.2%	70.1%	29.9%
14,676	WILBARGER	4,300	3,032	1,178	90	1,854 R	70.5%	27.4%	72.0%	28.0%
20,082	WILLACY	4,690	1,358	3,242	90	1,884 D	29.0%	69.1%	29.5%	70.5%
249,967	WILLIAMSON	155,388	91,115	58,250	6,023	32,865 R	58.6%	37.5%	61.0%	39.0%
32,408	WILSON	16,135	10,431	5,322	382	5,109 R	64.6%	33.0%	66.2%	33.8%
7,173	WINKLER	1,967	1,452	464	51	988 R	73.8%	23.6%	75.8%	24.2%
48,793	WISE	20,454	15,035	4,974	445	10,061 R	73.5%	24.3%	75.1%	24.9%
36,752	WOOD	17,535	13,280	3,928	327	9,352 R	75.7%	22.4%	77.2%	22.8%
7,322	YOAKUM	2,390	1,877	474	39	1,403 R	78.5%	19.8%	79.8%	20.2%
17,943	YOUNG	7,111	5,598	1,368	145	4,230 R	78.7%	19.2%	80.4%	19.6%
12,182	ZAPATA	2,740	626	2,082	32	1,456 D	22.8%	76.0%	23.1%	76.9%
11,600	ZAVALA	3,618	506	3,064	48	2,558 D	14.0%	84.7%	14.2%	85.8%
20,851,820	TOTAL	7,912,075	4,337,469	3,389,365	185,241	948,104 R	54.8%	42.8%	56.1%	43.9%

TEXAS

HOUSE OF REPRESENTATIVES

CD	Year	Total Vote	Republican Vote	Republican Candidate	Democratic Vote	Democratic Candidate	Other Vote	Rep.-Dem. Plurality	Total Vote Rep.	Total Vote Dem.	Major Vote Rep.	Major Vote Dem.
1	2008	215,826	189,012	GOHMERT, LOUIE*	—		26,814	189,012 R	87.6%		100.0%	
1	2006	153,070	104,099	GOHMERT, LOUIE*	46,303	OWEN, ROGER L.	2,668	57,796 R	68.0%	30.2%	69.2%	30.8%
1	2004	255,507	157,068	GOHMERT, LOUIE	96,281	SANDLIN, MAX*	2,158	60,787 R	61.5%	37.7%	62.0%	38.0%
2	2008	196,914	175,101	POE, TED*	—		21,813	175,101 R	88.9%		100.0%	
2	2006	137,865	90,490	POE, TED*	45,080	BINDERIM, GARY E.	2,295	45,410 R	65.6%	32.7%	66.7%	33.3%
2	2004	252,038	139,951	POE, TED	108,156	LAMPSON, NICK*	3,931	31,795 R	55.5%	42.9%	56.4%	43.6%
3	2008	285,783	170,742	JOHNSON, SAM*	108,693	DALEY, TOM	6,348	62,049 R	59.7%	38.0%	61.1%	38.9%
3	2006	141,881	88,690	JOHNSON, SAM*	49,529	DODD, DAN	3,662	39,161 R	62.5%	34.9%	64.2%	35.8%
3	2004	210,352	180,099	JOHNSON, SAM*	—		30,253	180,099 R	85.6%		100.0%	
4	2008	300,744	206,906	HALL, RALPH M.*	88,067	MELANCON, GLENN	5,771	118,839 R	68.8%	29.3%	70.1%	29.9%
4	2006	165,269	106,495	HALL, RALPH M.*	55,278	MELANCON, GLENN	3,496	51,217 R	64.4%	33.4%	65.8%	34.2%
4	2004	267,942	182,866	HALL, RALPH M.*	81,585	NICKERSON, JIM	3,491	101,281 R	68.2%	30.4%	69.1%	30.9%
5	2008	194,861	162,894	HENSARLING, JEB*	—		31,967	162,894 R	83.6%		100.0%	
5	2006	143,252	88,478	HENSARLING, JEB*	50,983	THOMPSON, CHARLIE	3,791	37,495 R	61.8%	35.6%	63.4%	36.6%
5	2004	230,845	148,816	HENSARLING, JEB*	75,911	BERNSTEIN, EILL	6,118	72,905 R	64.5%	32.9%	66.2%	33.8%
6	2008	280,582	174,008	BARTON, JOE L.*	99,919	OTTO, LUDWIG	6,655	74,089 R	62.0%	35.6%	63.5%	36.5%
6	2006	152,036	91,927	BARTON, JOE L.*	56,369	HARRIS, DAVID T.	3,740	35,558 R	60.5%	37.1%	62.0%	38.0%
6	2004	255,627	168,767	BARTON, JOE L.*	83,609	MEYER, MORRIS	3,251	85,158 R	66.0%	32.7%	66.9%	33.1%
7	2008	290,934	162,635	CULBERSON, JOHN*	123,242	SKELLY, MICHAEL	5,057	39,393 R	55.9%	42.4%	56.9%	43.1%
7	2006	167,785	99,318	CULBERSON, JOHN*	64,514	HENLEY, JIM	3,953	34,804 R	59.2%	38.5%	60.6%	39.4%
7	2004	273,651	175,440	CULBERSON, JOHN*	91,126	MARTINEZ, JOHN	7,085	84,314 R	64.1%	33.3%	65.8%	34.2%
8	2008	285,451	207,128	BRADY, KEVIN*	70,758	HARGETT, KENT	7,565	136,370 R	72.6%	24.8%	74.5%	25.5%
8	2006	157,058	105,665	BRADY, KEVIN*	51,393	WRIGHT, JAMES "JIM"		54,272 R	67.3%	32.7%	67.3%	32.7%
8	2004	260,628	179,599	BRADY, KEVIN*	77,324	WRIGHT, JAMES "JIM"	3,705	102,275 R	68.9%	29.7%	69.9%	30.1%
9	2008	153,628		—	143,868	GREEN, AL*	9,760	143,868 D		93.6%		100.0%
9	2006	60,253		—	60,253	GREEN, AL*		60,253 D		100.0%		100.0%
9	2004	158,566	42,132	MOLINA, ARLETTE	114,462	GREEN, AL	1,972	72,330 D	26.6%	72.2%	26.9%	73.1%
10	2008	333,083	179,493	McCAUL, MICHAEL*	143,719	DOHERTY, LARRY JOE	9,871	35,774 R	53.9%	43.1%	55.5%	44.5%
10	2006	176,755	97,726	McCAUL, MICHAEL*	71,415	ANKRUM, TED	7,614	26,311 R	55.3%	40.4%	57.8%	42.2%
10	2004	231,643	182,113	McCAUL, MICHAEL	—		49,530	182,113 R	78.6%		100.0%	
11	2008	214,676	189,625	CONAWAY, K. MICHAEL*	—		25,051	189,625 R	88.3%		100.0%	
11	2006	107,268	107,268	CONAWAY, K. MICHAEL*	—			107,268 R	100.0%		100.0%	
11	2004	230,977	177,291	CONAWAY, K. MICHAEL	50,339	RAASCH, WAYNE	3,347	126,952 R	76.8%	21.8%	77.9%	22.1%
12	2008	268,754	181,662	GRANGER, KAY*	82,250	SMITH, TRACEY	4,842	99,412 R	67.6%	30.6%	68.8%	31.2%
12	2006	146,935	98,371	GRANGER, KAY*	45,676	MORRIS, JOHN R.	2,888	52,695 R	66.9%	31.1%	68.3%	31.7%
12	2004	239,538	173,222	GRANGER, KAY*	66,316	ALVARADO, FELIX		106,906 R	72.3%	27.7%	72.3%	27.7%
13	2008	231,919	180,078	THORNBERRY, WILLIAM M. "MAC"*	51,841	WAUN, ROGER JAMES		128,237 R	77.6%	22.4%	77.6%	22.4%
13	2006	145,396	108,107	THORNBERRY, WILLIAM M. "MAC"*	33,460	WAUN, ROGER JAMES	3,829	74,647 R	74.4%	23.0%	76.4%	23.6%
13	2004	205,241	189,448	THORNBERRY, WILLIAM M. "MAC"*	—		15,793	189,448 R	92.3%		100.0%	
14	2008	191,293	191,293	PAUL, RON*	—			191,293 R	100.0%		100.0%	
14	2006	156,809	94,380	PAUL, RON*	62,429	SKLAR, SHANE		31,951 R	60.2%	39.8%	60.2%	39.8%
14	2004	173,668	173,668	PAUL, RON*	—			173,668 R	100.0%		100.0%	
15	2008	163,708	52,303	ZAMORA, EDDIE	107,578	HINOJOSA, RUBEN*	3,827	55,275 D	31.9%	65.7%	32.7%	67.3%
15	2006	69,987	26,751	HARING/ZAMORA	43,236	HINOJOSA, RUBEN*		26,635 D	38.2%	61.8%	38.2%	61.8%
16	2008	158,723		—	130,375	REYES, SILVESTRE*	28,348	130,375 D		82.1%		100.0%
16	2006	77,688		—	61,116	REYES, SILVESTRE*	16,572	61,116 D		78.7%		100.0%
16	2004	160,773	49,972	BRIGHAM, DAVID	108,577	REYES, SILVESTRE*	2,224	58,605 D	31.1%	67.5%	31.5%	68.5%
17	2008	254,022	115,581	CURNOCK, ROB	134,592	EDWARDS, CHET*	3,849	19,011 D	45.5%	53.0%	46.2%	53.8%
17	2006	159,124	64,142	TAYLOR, VAN	92,478	EDWARDS, CHET*	2,504	28,336 D	40.3%	58.1%	41.0%	59.0%
17	2004	244,748	116,049	WOHLGEMUTH, ARLENE	125,309	EDWARDS, CHET*	3,390	9,260 D	47.4%	51.2%	48.1%	51.9%

TEXAS

HOUSE OF REPRESENTATIVES

CD	Year	Total Vote	Republican Vote	Republican Candidate	Democratic Vote	Democratic Candidate	Other Vote	Rep.-Dem. Plurality	Total Vote Rep.	Total Vote Dem.	Major Vote Rep.	Major Vote Dem.
18	2008	192,198	39,095	FAULK, JOHN	148,617	JACKSON-LEE, SHEILA*	4,486	109,522 D	20.3%	77.3%	20.8%	79.2%
18	2006	86,051	16,448	HASSAN, AHMAD	65,936	JACKSON-LEE, SHEILA*	3,667	49,488 D	19.1%	76.6%	20.0%	80.0%
18	2004	152,988		—	136,018	JACKSON-LEE, SHEILA*	16,970	136,018 D		88.9%		100.0%
19	2008	232,611	168,501	NEUGEBAUER, RANDY*	58,030	FULLINGIM, DWIGHT	6,080	110,471 R	72.4%	24.9%	74.4%	25.6%
19	2006	140,007	94,785	NEUGEBAUER, RANDY*	41,676	RICKETTS, ROBERT	3,546	53,109 R	67.7%	29.8%	69.5%	30.5%
19	2004	233,514	136,459	NEUGEBAUER, RANDY*	93,531	STENHOLM, CHARLES W.*	3,524	42,928 R	58.4%	40.1%	59.3%	40.7%
20	2008	177,055	44,585	LITOFF, ROBERT	127,298	GONZALEZ, CHARLIE*	5,172	82,713 D	25.2%	71.9%	25.9%	74.1%
20	2006	78,245		—	68,348	GONZALEZ, CHARLIE*	9,897	68,348 D		87.4%		100.0%
20	2004	171,804	54,976	SCOTT, ROGER	112,480	GONZALEZ, CHARLIE*	4,348	57,504 D	32.0%	65.5%	32.8%	67.2%
21	2008	304,350	243,471	SMITH, LAMAR*		—	60,879	243,471 R	80.0%		100.0%	
21	2006	203,782	122,486	SMITH, LAMAR*	68,312	COURAGE/KELLY	12,984	72,529 R	60.1%	33.5%	64.2%	35.8%
22	2008	308,995	161,996	OLSON, PETE	140,160	LAMPSON, NICK*	6,839	21,836 R	52.4%	45.4%	53.6%	46.4%
22	2006	148,239	61,938	GIBBS, SHELLEY SEKULA	76,775	LAMPSON, NICK	9,526	14,837 D	41.8%	51.8%	44.7%	55.3%
22	2004	272,620	150,386	DeLAY, TOM*	112,034	MORRISON, RICHARD R.	10,200	38,352 R	55.2%	41.1%	57.3%	42.7%
23	2008	240,470	100,799	LARSON, LYLE	134,090	RODRIGUEZ, CIRO D.*	5,581	33,291 D	41.9%	55.8%	42.9%	57.1%
23	2006	70,473	32,217	BONILLA, HENRY*	38,256	RODRIGUEZ, CIRO D.		6,039 D	45.7%	54.3%	45.7%	54.3%
24	2008	270,495	151,434	MARCHANT, KENNY*	111,089	LOVE, TOM	7,972	40,345 R	56.0%	41.1%	57.7%	42.3%
24	2006	140,138	83,835	MARCHANT, KENNY*	52,075	PAGE, GARY R.	4,228	31,760 R	59.8%	37.2%	61.7%	38.3%
24	2004	241,374	154,435	MARCHANT, KENNY	82,599	PAGE, GARY R.	4,340	71,836 R	64.0%	34.2%	65.2%	34.8%
25	2008	291,296	88,693	MOROVICH, GEORGE L.	191,755	DOGGETT, LLOYD*	10,848	103,062 D	30.4%	65.8%	31.6%	68.4%
25	2006	163,424	42,975	ROSTIG, GRANT	109,911	DOGGETT, LLOYD*	10,538	66,936 D	26.3%	67.3%	28.1%	71.9%
26	2008	324,376	195,181	BURGESS, MICHAEL C.*	118,167	LEACH, KEN	11,028	77,014 R	60.2%	36.4%	62.3%	37.7%
26	2006	156,483	94,219	BURGESS, MICHAEL C.*	58,271	BARNWELL, TIM	3,993	35,948 R	60.2%	37.2%	61.8%	38.2%
26	2004	274,539	180,519	BURGESS, MICHAEL C.*	89,809	REYES, LICO	4,211	90,710 R	65.8%	32.7%	66.8%	33.2%
27	2008	180,951	69,458	VADEN, WILLIAM "WILLIE"	104,864	ORTIZ, SOLOMON P.*	6,629	35,406 D	38.4%	58.0%	39.8%	60.2%
27	2006	109,314	42,538	VADEN, WILLIAM "WILLIE"	62,058	ORTIZ, SOLOMON P.*	4,718	19,520 D	38.9%	56.8%	40.7%	59.3%
27	2004	177,536	61,955	VADEN, WILLIAM "WILLIE"	112,081	ORTIZ, SOLOMON P.*	3,500	50,126 D	34.9%	63.1%	35.6%	64.4%
28	2008	179,740	52,524	FISH, JIM	123,494	CUELLAR, HENRY*	3,722	70,970 D	29.2%	68.7%	29.8%	70.2%
28	2006	77,755		—	68,372	Cuellar*/Enriquez	9,383	36,776 D		87.9%		100.0%
29	2008	106,794	25,512	STORY, ERIC	79,718	GREEN, GENE*	1,564	54,206 D	23.9%	74.6%	24.2%	75.8%
29	2006	50,550	12,347	STORY, ERIC	37,174	GREEN, GENE*	1,029	24,827 D	24.4%	73.5%	24.9%	75.1%
29	2004	83,124		—	78,256	GREEN, GENE*	4,868	78,256 D		94.1%		100.0%
30	2008	203,976	32,361	WOOD, FRED	168,249	JOHNSON, EDDIE BERNICE*	3,366	135,888 D	15.9%	82.5%	16.1%	83.9%
30	2006	101,448	17,850	AURBACH, WILSON	81,348	JOHNSON, EDDIE BERNICE*	2,250	63,498 D	17.6%	80.2%	18.0%	82.0%
30	2004	155,334		—	144,513	JOHNSON, EDDIE BERNICE*	10,821	144,513 D		93.0%		100.0%
31	2008	291,304	175,563	CARTER, JOHN*	106,559	RUIZ, BRIAN P.	9,182	69,004 R	60.3%	36.6%	62.2%	37.8%
31	2006	155,383	90,869	CARTER, JOHN*	60,293	HARRELL, MARY BETH	4,221	30,576 R	58.5%	38.8%	60.1%	39.9%
31	2004	247,427	160,247	CARTER, JOHN*	80,292	PORTER, JON	6,888	79,955 R	64.8%	32.5%	66.6%	33.4%
32	2008	203,110	116,283	SESSIONS, PETE*	82,406	ROBERSON, ERIC	4,421	33,877 R	57.3%	40.6%	58.5%	41.5%
32	2006	126,652	71,461	SESSIONS, PETE*	52,269	PRYOR, WILL	2,922	19,192 R	56.4%	41.3%	57.8%	42.2%
32	2004	202,236	109,859	SESSIONS, PETE*	89,030	FROST, MARTIN*	3,347	20,829 R	54.3%	44.0%	55.2%	44.8%
TOTAL	2008	7,528,622	4,203,917		2,979,398		345,307	1,224,519 R	55.8%	39.6%	58.5%	41.5%
TOTAL	2006	4,179,701	2,183,833		1,852,613		143,255	331,220 R	52.2%	44.3%	54.1%	45.9%
TOTAL	2004	6,958,603	4,012,534		2,713,968		232,101	1,298,566 R	57.7%	39.0%	59.7%	40.3%
TOTAL	2002	4,295,210	2,290,723		1,885,178		119,309	405,545 R	53.3%	43.9%	54.9%	45.1%

Notes: An asterisk (*) denotes incumbent. Congressional district lines in Texas were redrawn between the elections of 2002 and 2004, and for Districts 15, 21, 23, 25, and 28 between the 2006 primary and general elections. In each of these five districts, candidates of all parties ran together in a special election on the November ballot, with the plurality measured as the difference between the vote for the winner and the vote for the runner-up, regardless of party. The designated Republican candidate in the 22nd District in 2006 was a write-in candidate, Shelley Sekula Gibbs. The results listed for the 23rd District are from a December runoff, required when no candidate won a majority of the vote in November voting. The statewide vote totals represent the aggregate vote for all House candidates of each party in the November balloting. The results from 2002, and a map of the Texas congressional district lines that year, can be found in *America Votes 25*. The results from 2004, and a map of the Texas congressional district lines that year, can be found in *America Votes 26*.

TEXAS

GENERAL AND PRIMARY ELECTIONS

2008 GENERAL ELECTIONS

President Other vote was 56,116 Libertarian (Bob Barr); 5,751 write-in (Ralph Nader); 5,708 write-in (Chuck Baldwin); 909 write-in (Cynthia A. McKinney); 895 write-in (Alan Keyes); 216 write-in (Thaddaus Hill); 135 write-in (Brian Moore); 104 write-in (Jonathan Allen).

Senator Other vote was 185,241 Libertarian (Yvonne Adams Schick).

House Other vote was:

CD 1	26,814 Independent (Roger L. Owen).
CD 2	21,813 Libertarian (Craig Wolfe).
CD 3	6,348 Libertarian (Christopher J. Claytor).
CD 4	5,771 Libertarian (Fred Annett).
CD 5	31,967 Libertarian (Ken Ashby).
CD 6	6,655 Libertarian (Max W. Koch III).
CD 7	5,057 Libertarian (Drew Parks).
CD 8	7,565 Libertarian (Brian Stevens).
CD 9	9,760 Libertarian (Brad Walters).
CD 10	9,871 Libertarian (Matt Finkel).
CD 11	25,051 Libertarian (John R. Strohm).
CD 12	4,842 Libertarian (Shiloh Sidney Shambaugh).
CD 13	
CD 14	
CD 15	3,827 Libertarian (Gricha Raether).
CD 16	16,348 Independent (Benjamin Eloy "Ben" Mendoza); 12,000 Libertarian (Mette A. Baker).
CD 17	3,849 Libertarian (Gardner C. Osborne).
CD 18	4,486 Libertarian (Mike Taylor).
CD 19	6,080 Libertarian (Richard "Chip" Peterson).
CD 20	5,172 Libertarian (Michael Idrogo).
CD 21	60,879 Libertarian (James Arthur Strohm).
CD 22	6,839 Libertarian (John Wieder).
CD 23	5,581 Libertarian (Lani Connolly).
CD 24	7,972 Libertarian (David A. Casey).
CD 25	10,848 Libertarian (Jim Stutsman).
CD 26	11,028 Libertarian (Stephanie B. Weiss).
CD 27	6,629 Libertarian (Robert E. Powell).
CD 28	3,722 Libertarian (Ross Lynn Leone).
CD 29	1,564 Libertarian (Joel Grace).
CD 30	3,366 Libertarian (Jarrett Woods).
CD 31	9,182 Libertarian (Barry N. Cooper).
CD 32	4,421 Libertarian (Alex Bischoff).

2008 PRIMARY ELECTIONS

Primary	March 4, 2008	**Registration**		12,752,417	No Party Registration
Primary Runoff	April 8, 2008	(as of March 4, 2008)			

Primary Type Open—Any registered voter could participate in the Democratic or Republican primary, although if they voted in the primary of one party they could not vote in the runoff of the other party.

TEXAS

GENERAL AND PRIMARY ELECTIONS

	REPUBLICAN PRIMARIES			DEMOCRATIC PRIMARIES		
President	John McCain	697,767	51.2%	Hillary Clinton	1,462,734	50.9%
	Mike Huckabee	518,002	38.0%	Barack Obama	1,362,476	47.4%
	Ron Paul	66,360	4.9%	John Edwards	29,936	1.0%
	Mitt Romney	27,264	2.0%	Bill Richardson	10,773	0.4%
	Uncommitted	17,574	1.3%	Joseph R. Biden Jr.	5,290	0.2%
	Fred Thompson	11,503	0.8%	Christopher J. Dodd	3,777	0.1%
	Alan Keyes	8,260	0.6%			
	Duncan Hunter	8,222	0.6%			
	Rudolph Giuliani	6,038	0.4%			
	Hugh Cort	728	0.1%			
	Hoa Tran	604				
	TOTAL	1,362,322		TOTAL	2,874,986	
Senator	John Cornyn*	997,216	81.5%	Richard J. "Rick" Noriega	1,110,579	51.0%
	Larry Kilgore	226,649	18.5%	Gene Kelly	584,966	26.9%
				Ray McMurrey	269,402	12.4%
				Rhett R. Smith	212,305	9.8%
	TOTAL	1,223,865		TOTAL	2,177,252	
Congressional District 1	Louie Gohmert*	49,035	100.0%	No Democratic candidate		
Congressional District 2	Ted Poe*	36,562	100.0%	No Democratic candidate		
Congressional District 3	Sam Johnson*	36,050	86.9%	Tom Daley	33,592	71.6%
	Harry Pierce	3,466	8.4%	Ronald E. "Ron" Minkow	13,305	28.4%
	Wayne Avellanet	1,952	4.7%			
	TOTAL	41,468		TOTAL	46,897	
Congressional District 4	Ralph M. Hall*	41,764	73.4%	Glenn Melancon	37,416	57.4%
	Kathy Seei	5,835	10.3%	VaLinda Hathcox	27,766	42.6%
	Gene Christensen	5,492	9.7%			
	Kevin George	2,965	5.2%			
	Joshua Kowert	852	1.5%			
	TOTAL	56,908		TOTAL	65,182	
Congressional District 5	Jeb Hensarling*	45,803	100.0%	No Democratic candidate		
Congressional District 6	Joe L. Barton*	42,054	100.0%	Ludwig Otto	33,021	50.8%
				Steve Bush	31,959	49.2%
				TOTAL	64,980	
Congressional District 7	John Culberson*	44,477	100.0%	Michael Skelly	55,771	100.0%
Congressional District 8	Kevin Brady*	51,011	100.0%	Kent Hargett	55,817	100.0%
Congressional District 9	No Republican candidate			Al Green*	73,657	100.0%
Congressional District 10	Michael McCaul*	44,214		Larry Joe Doherty	51,977	61.1%
				Dan Grant	33,072	38.9%
				TOTAL	85,049	
Congressional District 11	K. Michael Conaway*	61,409	100.0%	No Democratic candidate		
Congressional District 12	Kay Granger*	49,374	100.0%	Tracey Smith	48,975	100.0%

TEXAS

GENERAL AND PRIMARY ELECTIONS

	REPUBLICAN PRIMARIES			DEMOCRATIC PRIMARIES		
Congressional District 13	William M. "Mac" Thornberry*	56,807	100.0%	Roger James Waun	35,649	100.0%
Congressional District 14	Ron Paul* W. Chris Peden TOTAL	37,777 15,859 53,636	70.4% 29.6%	No Democratic candidate		
Congressional District 15	Eddie Zamora	8,370	100.0%	Ruben Hinojosa*	77,227	100.0%
Congressional District 16	No Republican candidate			Silvestre Reyes* Jorge Artalejo TOTAL	75,058 18,274 93,332	80.4% 19.6%
Congressional District 17	Rob Curnock	44,448	100.0%	Chet Edwards*	60,557	100.0%
Congressional District 18	John Faulk TJ Baker Holm TOTAL	5,638 1,539 7,177	78.6% 21.4%	Sheila Jackson-Lee*	78,161	100.0%
Congressional District 19	Randy Neugebauer*	54,099	100.0%	Dwight Fullingim Rufus Mark TOTAL	26,966 16,786 43,752	61.6% 38.4%
Congressional District 20	Robert Litoff	10,409	100.0%	Charlie Gonzalez*	52,245	100.0%
Congressional District 21	Lamar Smith*	64,350	100.0%	No Democratic candidate		
Congressional District 22	Shelley Sekula Gibbs Pete Olson John Manlove Robert Talton Dean Hrbacek Cynthia Dunbar Brian Klock Jim Squier Kevyn Bazzy Ryan Rowley TOTAL PRIMARY RUNOFF Pete Olson Shelley Sekula Gibbs TOTAL	16,697 11,634 8,399 8,169 5,864 2,116 992 989 880 424 56,164 15,511 7,125 22,636	29.7% 20.7% 15.0% 14.5% 10.4% 3.8% 1.8% 1.8% 1.6% 0.8% 68.5% 31.5%	Nick Lampson*	73,831	100.0%
Congressional District 23	Lyle Larson Quico Canseco TOTAL	18,681 11,671 30,352	61.5% 38.5%	Ciro D. Rodriguez*	71,716	100.0%
Congressional District 24	Kenny Marchant*	30,378	100.0%	Tom Love	49,166	100.0%
Congressional District 25	George L. Morovich	23,213	100.0%	Lloyd Doggett*	110,108	100.0%
Congressional District 26	Michael C. Burgess*	41,328	100.0%	Ken Leach	54,417	100.0%
Congressional District 27	William "Willie" Vaden George Benavidez TOTAL	9,292 7,236 16,528	56.2% 43.8%	Solomon P. Ortiz*	77,513	100.0%

TEXAS

GENERAL AND PRIMARY ELECTIONS

	REPUBLICAN PRIMARIES			DEMOCRATIC PRIMARIES		
Congressional District 28	Jim Fish	14,073	100.0%	Henry Cuellar*	84,819	100.0%
Congressional District 29	Eric Story	5,302	100.0%	Gene Green*	42,222	100.0%
Congressional District 30	Fred Wood	5,366	100.0%	Eddie Bernice Johnson*	90,425	100.0%
Congressional District 31	John Carter*	46,388	100.0%	Brian P. Ruiz	58,792	100.0%
Congressional District 32	Pete Sessions*	28,736	100.0%	Eric Roberson	20,043	44.9%
				Steve Love	14,929	33.4%
				Dennis C. Burns	9,705	21.7%
				TOTAL	44,677	
				PRIMARY RUNOFF		
				Eric Roberson	1,981	72.5%
				Steve Long	753	27.5%
				TOTAL	2,734	

Notes: An asterisk (*) denotes incumbent. A runoff was triggered if the leading vote-getter in the primary received less than a majority of the primary vote.

UTAH

Congressional districts first established for elections held in 2002
3 members

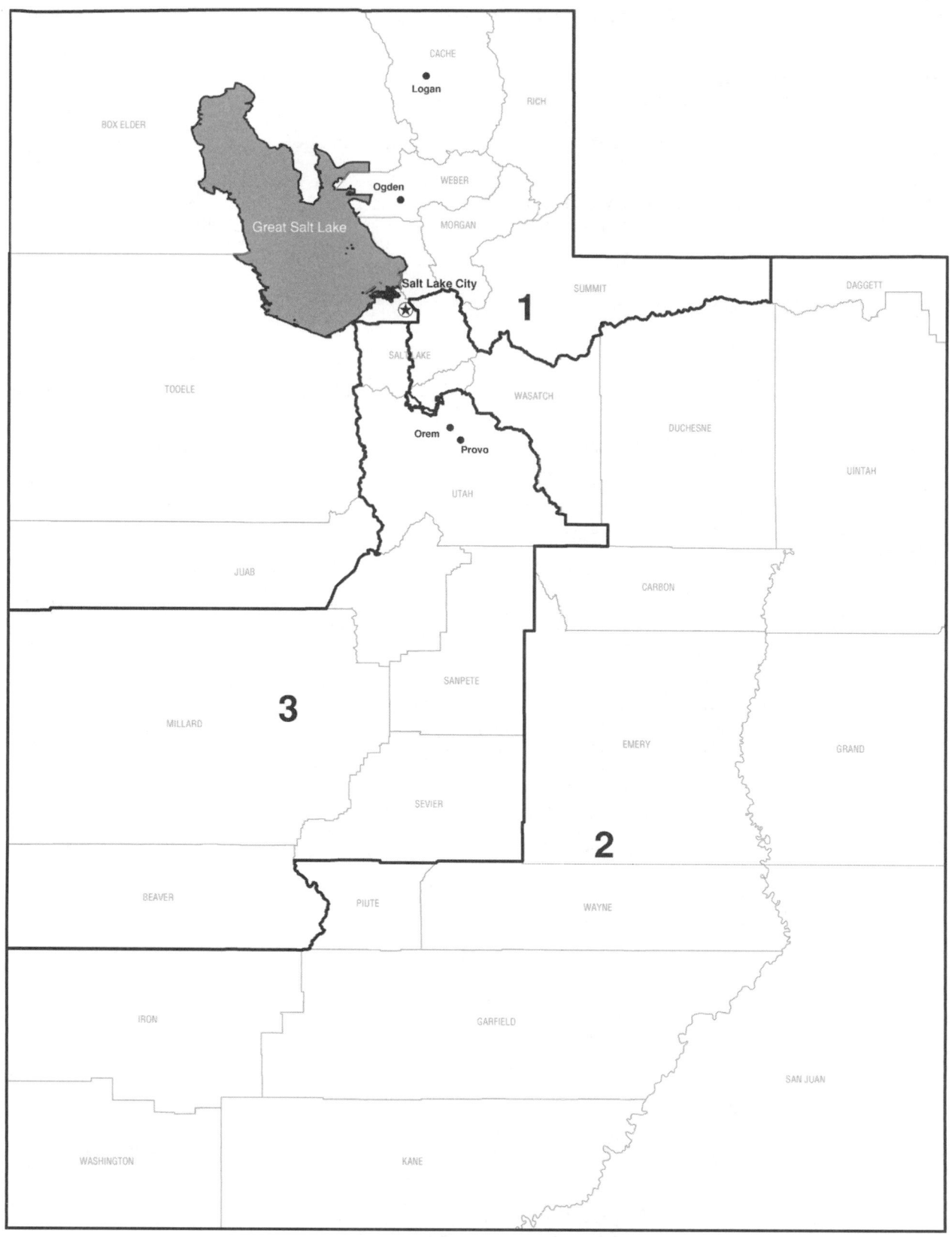

UTAH

GOVERNOR
Jon Huntsman Jr. (R). Reelected 2008 to a four-year term. Previously elected 2004.

SENATORS (2 Republicans)
Robert F. Bennett (R). Reelected 2004 to a six-year term. Previously elected 1998, 1992.

Orrin G. Hatch (R). Reelected 2006 to a six-year term. Previously elected 2000, 1994, 1988, 1982, 1976.

REPRESENTATIVES (2 Republicans, 1 Democrat)
1. Rob Bishop (R)   2. Jim Matheson (D)   3. Jason Chaffetz (R)

POSTWAR VOTE FOR PRESIDENT

Year	Total Vote	Republican Vote	Republican Candidate	Democratic Vote	Democratic Candidate	Other Vote	Plurality	Total Vote Rep.	Total Vote Dem.	Major Vote Rep.	Major Vote Dem.
2008	952,370	596,030	McCain, John	327,670	Obama, Barack	28,670	268,360 R	62.6%	34.4%	64.5%	35.5%
2004	927,844	663,742	Bush, George W.	241,199	Kerry, John	22,903	422,543 R	71.5%	26.0%	73.3%	26.7%
2000**	770,754	515,096	Bush, George W.	203,053	Gore, Al	52,605	312,043 R	66.8%	26.3%	71.7%	28.3%
1996**	665,629	361,911	Dole, Bob	221,633	Clinton, Bill	82,085	140,278 R	54.4%	33.3%	62.0%	38.0%
1992**	743,999	322,632	Bush, George	183,429	Clinton, Bill	237,938	119,232 R	43.4%	24.7%	63.8%	36.2%
1988	647,008	428,442	Bush, George	207,343	Dukakis, Michael S.	11,223	221,099 R	66.2%	32.0%	67.4%	32.6%
1984	629,656	469,105	Reagan, Ronald	155,369	Mondale, Walter F.	5,182	313,736 R	74.5%	24.7%	75.1%	24.9%
1980**	604,222	439,687	Reagan, Ronald	124,266	Carter, Jimmy	40,269	315,421 R	72.8%	20.6%	78.0%	22.0%
1976	541,198	337,908	Ford, Gerald R.	182,110	Carter, Jimmy	21,180	155,798 R	62.4%	33.6%	65.0%	35.0%
1972	478,476	323,643	Nixon, Richard M.	126,284	McGovern, George S.	28,549	197,359 R	67.6%	26.4%	71.9%	28.1%
1968**	422,568	238,728	Nixon, Richard M.	156,665	Humphrey, Hubert H.	27,175	82,063 R	56.5%	37.1%	60.4%	39.6%
1964	401,413	181,785	Goldwater, Barry M.	219,628	Johnson, Lyndon B.		37,843 D	45.3%	54.7%	45.3%	54.7%
1960	374,709	205,361	Nixon, Richard M.	169,248	Kennedy, John F.	100	36,113 R	54.8%	45.2%	54.8%	45.2%
1956	333,995	215,631	Eisenhower, Dwight D.	118,364	Stevenson, Adlai E.		97,267 R	64.6%	35.4%	64.6%	35.4%
1952	329,554	194,190	Eisenhower, Dwight D.	135,364	Stevenson, Adlai E.		58,826 R	58.9%	41.1%	58.9%	41.1%
1948	276,306	124,402	Dewey, Thomas E.	149,151	Truman, Harry S.	2,753	24,749 D	45.0%	54.0%	45.5%	54.5%

**In past elections, the other vote included: 2000 - 35,850 Green (Ralph Nader); 1996 - 66,461 Reform (Ross Perot); 1992 - 203,400 Independent (Perot), who finished second; 1980 - 30,284 Independent (John Anderson); 1968 - 26,906 American Independent (George Wallace).

UTAH

POSTWAR VOTE FOR GOVERNOR

Year	Total Vote	Republican Vote	Republican Candidate	Democratic Vote	Democratic Candidate	Other Vote	Rep.-Dem. Plurality	Total Vote Rep.	Total Vote Dem.	Major Vote Rep.	Major Vote Dem.
2008	945,525	734,049	Huntsman, Jon Jr.	186,503	Springmeyer, Bob	24,973	547,546 R	77.6%	19.7%	79.7%	20.3%
2004	919,960	531,190	Huntsman, Jon Jr.	380,359	Matheson, Scott M. Jr.	8,411	150,831 R	57.7%	41.3%	58.3%	41.7%
2000	761,806	424,837	Leavitt, Michael O.	321,979	Orton, Bill	14,990	102,858 R	55.8%	42.3%	56.9%	43.1%
1996	671,879	503,693	Leavitt, Michael O.	156,616	Bradley, Jim	11,570	347,077 R	75.0%	23.3%	76.3%	23.7%
1992**	762,549	321,713	Leavitt, Michael O.	177,181	Hanson, Stewart	263,655	65,960 R	42.2%	23.2%	64.5%	35.5%
1988**	649,114	260,462	Bangerter, Norman H.	249,321	Wilson, Ted	139,331	11,141 R	40.1%	38.4%	51.1%	48.9%
1984	629,619	351,792	Bangerter, Norman H.	275,669	Owens, Wayne	2,158	76,123 R	55.9%	43.8%	56.1%	43.9%
1980	600,019	266,578	Wright, Bob	330,974	Matheson, Scott M.	2,467	64,396 D	44.4%	55.2%	44.6%	55.4%
1976	539,649	248,027	Romney, Vernon B.	280,706	Matheson, Scott M.	10,916	32,679 D	46.0%	52.0%	46.9%	53.1%
1972	476,447	144,449	Strike, Nicholas L.	331,998	Rampton, Calvin L.		187,549 D	30.3%	69.7%	30.3%	69.7%
1968	421,012	131,729	Buehner, Carl W.	289,283	Rampton, Calvin L.		157,554 D	31.3%	68.7%	31.3%	68.7%
1964	398,256	171,300	Melich, Mitchell	226,956	Rampton, Calvin L.		55,656 D	43.0%	57.0%	43.0%	57.0%
1960	371,489	195,634	Clyde, George D.	175,855	Barlocker, W. A.		19,779 R	52.7%	47.3%	52.7%	47.3%
1956**	332,889	127,164	Clyde, George D.	111,297	Romney, L. C.	94,428	15,867 R	38.2%	33.4%	53.3%	46.7%
1952	327,704	180,516	Lee, J. Bracken	147,188	Glade, Earl J.		33,328 R	55.1%	44.9%	55.1%	44.9%
1948	275,067	151,253	Lee, J. Bracken	123,814	Maw, Herbert B.		27,439 R	55.0%	45.0%	55.0%	45.0%

**In past elections, the other vote included: 1992 - 255,753 Independent (Merrill Cook), who finished second; 1988 - 136,651 Independent (Cook); 1956 - 94,428 Independent (J. Bracken Lee).

POSTWAR VOTE FOR SENATOR

Year	Total Vote	Republican Vote	Republican Candidate	Democratic Vote	Democratic Candidate	Other Vote	Rep.-Dem. Plurality	Total Vote Rep.	Total Vote Dem.	Major Vote Rep.	Major Vote Dem.
2006	571,252	356,238	Hatch, Orrin G.	177,459	Ashdown, Pete	37,555	178,779 R	62.4%	31.1%	66.7%	33.3%
2004	911,726	626,640	Bennett, Robert F.	258,955	Van Dam, R. Paul	26,131	367,685 R	68.7%	28.4%	70.8%	29.2%
2000	769,704	504,803	Hatch, Orrin G.	242,569	Howell, Scott N.	22,332	262,234 R	65.6%	31.5%	67.5%	32.5%
1998	494,909	316,652	Bennett, Robert F.	163,172	Leckman, Scott	15,085	153,480 R	64.0%	33.0%	66.0%	34.0%
1994	519,323	357,297	Hatch, Orrin G.	146,938	Shea, Patrick A.	15,088	210,359 R	68.8%	28.3%	70.9%	29.1%
1992	758,479	420,069	Bennett, Robert F.	301,228	Owens, Wayne	37,182	118,841 R	55.4%	39.7%	58.2%	41.8%
1988	640,702	430,089	Hatch, Orrin G.	203,364	Moss, Brian H.	7,249	226,725 R	67.1%	31.7%	67.9%	32.1%
1986	435,111	314,608	Garn, E. J.	115,523	Oliver, Craig	4,980	199,085 R	72.3%	26.6%	73.1%	26.9%
1982	530,802	309,332	Hatch, Orrin G.	219,482	Wilson, Ted	1,988	89,850 R	58.3%	41.3%	58.5%	41.5%
1980	594,298	437,675	Garn, E. J.	151,454	Berman, Dan	5,169	286,221 R	73.6%	25.5%	74.3%	25.7%
1976	540,108	290,221	Hatch, Orrin G.	241,948	Moss, Frank E.	7,939	48,273 R	53.7%	44.8%	54.5%	45.5%
1974	420,642	210,299	Garn, E. J.	185,377	Owens, Wayne	24,966	24,922 R	50.0%	44.1%	53.1%	46.9%
1970	374,303	159,004	Burton, Laurence J.	210,207	Moss, Frank E.	5,092	51,203 D	42.5%	56.2%	43.1%	56.9%
1968	419,262	225,075	Bennett, Wallace F.	192,168	Weilenmann, Milton	2,019	32,907 R	53.7%	45.8%	53.9%	46.1%
1964	397,384	169,562	Wilkinson, Ernest L.	227,822	Moss, Frank E.		58,260 D	42.7%	57.3%	42.7%	57.3%
1962	318,411	166,755	Bennett, Wallace F.	151,656	King, David S.		15,099 R	52.4%	47.6%	52.4%	47.6%
1958**	291,311	101,471	Watkins, Arthur V.	112,827	Moss, Frank E.	77,013	11,356 D	34.8%	38.7%	47.4%	52.6%
1956	330,381	178,261	Bennett, Wallace F.	152,120	Hopkin, Alonzo F.		26,141 R	54.0%	46.0%	54.0%	46.0%
1952	327,033	177,435	Watkins, Arthur V.	149,598	Granger, Walter K.		27,837 R	54.3%	45.7%	54.3%	45.7%
1950	264,440	142,427	Bennett, Wallace F.	121,198	Thomas, Elbert D.	815	21,229 R	53.9%	45.8%	54.0%	46.0%
1946	197,399	101,142	Watkins, Arthur V.	96,257	Murdock, Abe		4,885 R	51.2%	48.8%	51.2%	48.8%

**In past elections, the other vote included: 1958 - 77,013 Independent (J. Bracken Lee).

UTAH

PRESIDENT 2008

2000 Census Population	County	Total Vote	Republican	Democratic	Other	Rep.-Dem. Plurality	Percentage			
							Total Vote		Major Vote	
							Rep.	Dem.	Rep.	Dem.
6,005	BEAVER	2,509	1,902	542	65	1,360 R	75.8%	21.6%	77.8%	22.2%
42,745	BOX ELDER	19,058	15,228	3,311	519	11,917 R	79.9%	17.4%	82.1%	17.9%
91,391	CACHE	41,332	29,127	10,294	1,911	18,833 R	70.5%	24.9%	73.9%	26.1%
20,422	CARBON	7,777	4,091	3,468	218	623 R	52.6%	44.6%	54.1%	45.9%
921	DAGGETT	439	297	131	11	166 R	67.7%	29.8%	69.4%	30.6%
238,994	DAVIS	110,902	77,341	30,477	3,084	46,864 R	69.7%	27.5%	71.7%	28.3%
14,371	DUCHESNE	5,744	4,689	911	144	3,778 R	81.6%	15.9%	83.7%	16.3%
10,860	EMERY	4,448	3,358	973	117	2,385 R	75.5%	21.9%	77.5%	22.5%
4,735	GARFIELD	2,159	1,710	405	44	1,305 R	79.2%	18.8%	80.9%	19.1%
8,485	GRAND	4,077	1,871	2,067	139	196 D	45.9%	50.7%	47.5%	52.5%
33,779	IRON	16,450	12,518	3,258	674	9,260 R	76.1%	19.8%	79.3%	20.7%
8,238	JUAB	3,616	2,683	741	192	1,942 R	74.2%	20.5%	78.4%	21.6%
6,046	KANE	3,154	2,212	856	86	1,356 R	70.1%	27.1%	72.1%	27.9%
12,405	MILLARD	4,739	3,653	758	328	2,895 R	77.1%	16.0%	82.8%	17.2%
7,129	MORGAN	4,161	3,311	689	161	2,622 R	79.6%	16.6%	82.8%	17.2%
1,435	PIUTE	798	635	141	22	494 R	79.6%	17.7%	81.8%	18.2%
1,961	RICH	1,006	831	154	21	677 R	82.6%	15.3%	84.4%	15.6%
898,387	SALT LAKE	363,749	176,692	176,988	10,069	296 D	48.6%	48.7%	50.0%	50.0%
14,413	SAN JUAN	5,130	2,638	2,406	86	232 R	51.4%	46.9%	52.3%	47.7%
22,763	SANPETE	8,771	6,664	1,631	476	5,033 R	76.0%	18.6%	80.3%	19.7%
18,842	SEVIER	8,007	6,394	1,359	254	5,035 R	79.9%	17.0%	82.5%	17.5%
29,736	SUMMIT	16,809	6,956	9,532	321	2,576 D	41.4%	56.7%	42.2%	57.8%
40,735	TOOELE	17,337	10,998	5,830	509	5,168 R	63.4%	33.6%	65.4%	34.6%
25,224	UINTAH	10,151	8,441	1,462	248	6,979 R	83.2%	14.4%	85.2%	14.8%
368,536	UTAH	157,279	122,224	29,567	5,488	92,657 R	77.7%	18.8%	80.5%	19.5%
15,215	WASATCH	8,531	5,430	2,892	209	2,538 R	63.7%	33.9%	65.2%	34.8%
90,354	WASHINGTON	49,529	37,311	10,826	1,392	26,485 R	75.3%	21.9%	77.5%	22.5%
2,509	WAYNE	1,314	940	335	39	605 R	71.5%	25.5%	73.7%	26.3%
196,533	WEBER	73,394	45,885	25,666	1,843	20,219 R	62.5%	35.0%	64.1%	35.9%
2,233,169	TOTAL	952,370	596,030	327,670	28,670	268,360 R	62.6%	34.4%	64.5%	35.5%

UTAH

GOVERNOR 2008

2000 Census Population	County	Total Vote	Republican	Democratic	Other	Rep.-Dem. Plurality	Total Vote Rep.	Total Vote Dem.	Major Vote Rep.	Major Vote Dem.
6,005	BEAVER	2,475	2,038	386	51	1,652 R	82.3%	15.6%	84.1%	15.9%
42,745	BOX ELDER	18,889	16,619	1,681	589	14,938 R	88.0%	8.9%	90.8%	9.2%
91,391	CACHE	40,924	34,909	4,967	1,048	29,942 R	85.3%	12.1%	87.5%	12.5%
20,422	CARBON	7,588	4,943	2,412	233	2,531 R	65.1%	31.8%	67.2%	32.8%
921	DAGGETT	442	357	79	6	278 R	80.8%	17.9%	81.9%	18.1%
238,994	DAVIS	109,879	90,998	16,103	2,778	74,895 R	82.8%	14.7%	85.0%	15.0%
14,371	DUCHESNE	5,683	4,961	586	136	4,375 R	87.3%	10.3%	89.4%	10.6%
10,860	EMERY	4,399	3,418	854	127	2,564 R	77.7%	19.4%	80.0%	20.0%
4,735	GARFIELD	2,141	1,834	251	56	1,583 R	85.7%	11.7%	88.0%	12.0%
8,485	GRAND	3,949	2,505	1,295	149	1,210 R	63.4%	32.8%	65.9%	34.1%
33,779	IRON	16,260	14,060	1,702	498	12,358 R	86.5%	10.5%	89.2%	10.8%
8,238	JUAB	3,162	2,464	542	156	1,922 R	77.9%	17.1%	82.0%	18.0%
6,046	KANE	3,104	2,447	575	82	1,872 R	78.8%	18.5%	81.0%	19.0%
12,405	MILLARD	4,674	3,743	676	255	3,067 R	80.1%	14.5%	84.7%	15.3%
7,129	MORGAN	4,112	3,615	374	123	3,241 R	87.9%	9.1%	90.6%	9.4%
1,435	PIUTE	783	662	95	26	567 R	84.5%	12.1%	87.5%	12.5%
1,961	RICH	986	878	89	19	789 R	89.0%	9.0%	90.8%	9.2%
898,387	SALT LAKE	362,663	250,311	103,290	9,062	147,021 R	69.0%	28.5%	70.8%	29.2%
14,413	SAN JUAN	5,068	3,050	1,879	139	1,171 R	60.2%	37.1%	61.9%	38.1%
22,763	SANPETE	8,646	7,125	1,182	339	5,943 R	82.4%	13.7%	85.8%	14.2%
18,842	SEVIER	7,826	6,488	1,074	264	5,414 R	82.9%	13.7%	85.8%	14.2%
29,736	SUMMIT	16,609	11,771	4,469	369	7,302 R	70.9%	26.9%	72.5%	27.5%
40,735	TOOELE	17,254	13,442	3,276	536	10,166 R	77.9%	19.0%	80.4%	19.6%
25,224	UINTAH	9,949	8,697	995	257	7,702 R	87.4%	10.0%	89.7%	10.3%
368,536	UTAH	157,030	136,753	15,801	4,476	120,952 R	87.1%	10.1%	89.6%	10.4%
15,215	WASATCH	8,423	6,834	1,407	182	5,427 R	81.1%	16.7%	82.9%	17.1%
90,354	WASHINGTON	48,841	41,254	6,445	1,142	34,809 R	84.5%	13.2%	86.5%	13.5%
2,509	WAYNE	1,282	1,018	234	30	784 R	79.4%	18.3%	81.3%	18.7%
196,533	WEBER	72,484	56,855	13,784	1,845	43,071 R	78.4%	19.0%	80.5%	19.5%
2,233,169	TOTAL	945,525	734,049	186,503	24,973	547,546 R	77.6%	19.7%	79.7%	20.3%

UTAH

HOUSE OF REPRESENTATIVES

CD	Year	Total Vote	Republican Vote	Republican Candidate	Democratic Vote	Democratic Candidate	Other Vote	Rep.-Dem. Plurality	Total Vote Rep.	Total Vote Dem.	Major Vote Rep.	Major Vote Dem.
1	2008	303,445	196,799	BISHOP, ROB*	92,469	BOWEN, MORGAN	14,177	104,330 R	64.9%	30.5%	68.0%	32.0%
1	2006	178,474	112,546	BISHOP, ROB*	57,922	OLSEN, STEVEN	8,006	54,624 R	63.1%	32.5%	66.0%	34.0%
1	2004	293,961	199,615	BISHOP, ROB*	85,630	THOMPSON, STEVEN	8,716	113,985 R	67.9%	29.1%	70.0%	30.0%
1	2002	179,412	109,265	BISHOP, ROB	66,104	THOMAS, DAVE	4,043	43,161 R	60.9%	36.8%	62.3%	37.7%
2	2008	348,325	120,083	DEW, BILL	220,666	MATHESON, JIM*	7,576	100,583 D	34.5%	63.4%	35.2%	64.8%
2	2006	225,818	84,234	CHRISTENSEN, LAVAR	133,231	MATHESON, JIM*	8,353	48,997 D	37.3%	59.0%	38.7%	61.3%
2	2004	341,968	147,778	SWALLOW, JOHN	187,250	MATHESON, JIM*	6,940	39,472 D	43.2%	54.8%	44.1%	55.9%
2	2002	224,098	109,123	SWALLOW, JOHN	110,764	MATHESON, JIM*	4,211	1,641 D	48.7%	49.4%	49.6%	50.4%
3	2008	285,069	187,035	CHAFFETZ, JASON	80,626	SPENCER, BENNION L.	17,408	106,409 R	65.6%	28.3%	69.9%	30.1%
3	2006	165,398	95,455	CANNON, CHRIS*	53,330	BURRIDGE, CHRISTIAN	16,613	42,125 R	57.7%	32.2%	64.2%	35.8%
3	2004	272,928	173,010	CANNON, CHRIS*	88,748	BABKA, BEAU	11,170	84,262 R	63.4%	32.5%	66.1%	33.9%
3	2002	153,643	103,598	CANNON, CHRIS*	44,533	WOODSIDE, NANCY JANE	5,512	59,065 R	67.4%	29.0%	69.9%	30.1%
TOTAL	2008	936,839	503,917		393,761		39,161	110,156 R	53.8%	42.0%	56.1%	43.9%
TOTAL	2006	569,690	292,235		244,483		32,972	47,752 R	51.3%	42.9%	54.4%	45.6%
TOTAL	2004	908,857	520,403		361,628		26,826	158,775 R	57.3%	39.8%	59.0%	41.0%
TOTAL	2002	557,153	321,986		221,401		13,766	100,585 R	57.8%	39.7%	59.3%	40.7%

Note: An asterisk (*) denotes incumbent.

UTAH

GENERAL AND PRIMARY ELECTIONS

2008 GENERAL ELECTIONS

President	Other vote was 12,012 Constitution (Chuck Baldwin); 8,416 Peace and Freedom (Ralph Nader); 6,966 Libertarian (Bob Barr); 982 Green (Cynthia A. McKinney); 262 Socialism and Liberation (Gloria La Riva); 25 write-in (Alan Keyes); 3 write-in (Frank Moore); 2 write-in (Jonathan Allen); 1 write-in (Charles Jay); 1 write-in (David Jon Sponheim).
Governor	Other vote was 24,820 Libertarian ("SUPERDELL" Dell Schanze); 153 write-in (Bob Doughton).
House	Other vote was:
CD 1	7,397 Constitution (Kirk D. Pearson); 6,780 Libertarian (Joseph G. Buchman).
CD 2	4,576 Libertarian (Matthew Arndt); 3,000 Constitution (Dennis Ray Emery).
CD 3	17,408 Constitution (Jim Noorlander).

2008 PRIMARY ELECTIONS

Primary	February 5, 2008 (President) June 24, 2008 (Congress)	Registration (as of June 24, 2008)	1,359,597	In process of instituting registration by party
Primary Type	Registered Democrats and unaffiliated voters could participate in the Democratic primary. Registered Republicans and unaffiliated voters who chose to change their registration to Republican on primary day could vote in the Republican primary. (As of June 2009, there were 653,614 registered Republicans in Utah and 152,245 registered Democrats.)			

	REPUBLICAN PRIMARIES			DEMOCRATIC PRIMARIES		
President	Mitt Romney	264,956	89.5%	Barack Obama	74,538	56.7%
	John McCain	15,931	5.4%	Hillary Clinton	51,333	39.1%
	Ron Paul	8,846	3.0%	John Edwards	3,758	2.9%
	Mike Huckabee	4,252	1.4%	Bill Richardson	549	0.4%
	Rudolph Giuliani	988	0.3%	Joseph R. Biden Jr.	462	0.4%
	Fred Thompson	613	0.2%	Dennis J. Kucinich	408	0.3%
	Alan Keyes	261	0.1%	Mike Gravel	166	0.1%
	Duncan Hunter	211	0.1%	Christopher J. Dodd	117	0.1%
	Tom Tancredo	3		Frank Lynch	72	0.1%
	TOTAL	296,061		TOTAL	131,403	
Governor	Jon Huntsman Jr.*	Nominated by convention		Bob Springmeyer	Nominated by convention	
Congressional District 1	Rob Bishop*	Nominated by convention		Morgan Bowen	Nominated by convention	
Congressional District 2	Bill Dew	Nominated by convention		Jim Matheson*	Nominated by convention	
Congressional District 3	Jason Chaffetz	28,618	59.8%	Bennion L. Spencer	Nominated by convention	
	Chris Cannon*	19,255	40.2%			
	TOTAL	47,873				

Note: An asterisk (*) denotes incumbent. Candidates in Utah are usually nominated by convention. It is up to each party to determine the percentage of the convention vote that is needed to force a primary.

VERMONT

One member At Large

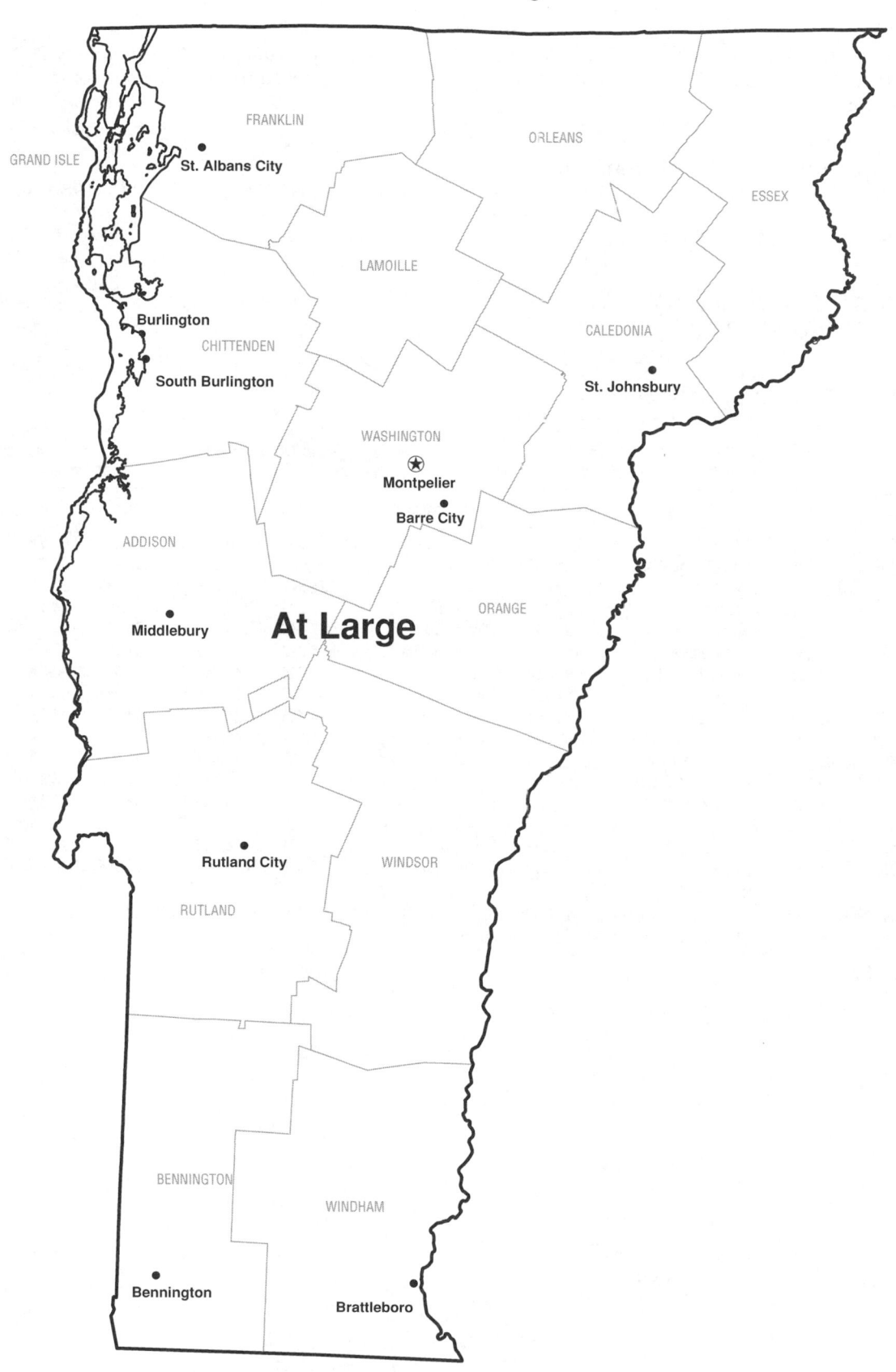

GRAND ISLE

FRANKLIN

ORLEANS

ESSEX

- St. Albans City

LAMOILLE

CALEDONIA

- Burlington

CHITTENDEN

- St. Johnsbury

- South Burlington

WASHINGTON

⭐ Montpelier

- Barre City

ADDISON

ORANGE

At Large

- Middlebury

- Rutland City

WINDSOR

RUTLAND

BENNINGTON

WINDHAM

- Bennington

- Brattleboro

VERMONT

GOVERNOR
Jim Douglas (R). Reelected 2008 to a two-year term. Previously elected 2006, 2004, and January 2003 by the state legislature. Douglas had finished first in the 2002 general election but failed to win a majority of the vote as required by Vermont law.

SENATORS (1 Democrat, 1 Independent)
Patrick J. Leahy (D). Reelected 2004 to a six-year term. Previously elected 1998, 1992, 1986, 1980, 1974.

Bernard Sanders (I). Elected 2006 to a six-year term.

REPRESENTATIVE (1 Democrat)
At Large. Peter Welch (D)

POSTWAR VOTE FOR PRESIDENT

Year	Total Vote	Republican		Democratic		Other Vote	Plurality	Percentage			
								Total Vote		Major Vote	
		Vote	Candidate	Vote	Candidate			Rep.	Dem.	Rep.	Dem.
2008	325,046	98,974	McCain, John	219,262	Obama, Barack	6,810	120,288 D	30.4%	67.5%	31.1%	68.9%
2004	312,309	121,180	Bush, George W.	184,067	Kerry, John	7,062	62,887 D	38.8%	58.9%	39.7%	60.3%
2000**	294,308	119,775	Bush, George W.	149,022	Gore, Al	25,511	29,247 D	40.7%	50.6%	44.6%	55.4%
1996**	258,449	80,352	Dole, Bob	137,894	Clinton, Bill	40,203	57,542 D	31.1%	53.4%	36.8%	63.2%
1992**	289,701	88,122	Bush, George	133,592	Clinton, Bill	67,987	45,470 D	30.4%	46.1%	39.7%	60.3%
1988	243,328	124,331	Bush, George	115,775	Dukakis, Michael S.	3,222	8,556 R	51.1%	47.6%	51.8%	48.2%
1984	234,561	135,865	Reagan, Ronald	95,730	Mondale, Walter F.	2,966	40,135 R	57.9%	40.8%	58.7%	41.3%
1980**	213,299	94,628	Reagan, Ronald	81,952	Carter, Jimmy	36,719	12,676 R	44.4%	38.4%	53.6%	46.4%
1976	187,765	102,085	Ford, Gerald R.	80,954	Carter, Jimmy	4,726	21,131 R	54.4%	43.1%	55.8%	44.2%
1972	186,947	117,149	Nixon, Richard M.	68,174	McGovern, George S.	1,624	48,975 R	62.7%	36.5%	63.2%	36.8%
1968**	161,404	85,142	Nixon, Richard M.	70,255	Humphrey, Hubert H.	6,007	14,887 R	52.8%	43.5%	54.8%	45.2%
1964	163,089	54,942	Goldwater, Barry M.	108,127	Johnson, Lyndon B.	20	53,185 D	33.7%	66.3%	33.7%	66.3%
1960	167,324	98,131	Nixon, Richard M.	69,186	Kennedy, John F.	7	28,945 R	58.6%	41.3%	58.6%	41.4%
1956	152,978	110,390	Eisenhower, Dwight D.	42,549	Stevenson, Adlai E.	39	67,841 R	72.2%	27.8%	72.2%	27.8%
1952	153,557	109,717	Eisenhower, Dwight D.	43,355	Stevenson, Adlai E.	485	66,362 R	71.5%	28.2%	71.7%	28.3%
1948	123,382	75,926	Dewey, Thomas E.	45,557	Truman, Harry S.	1,899	30,369 R	61.5%	36.9%	62.5%	37.5%

**In past elections, the other vote included: 2000 - 20,374 Green (Ralph Nader); 1996 - 31,024 Reform (Ross Perot); 1992 - 65,991 Independent (Perot); 1980 - 31,761 Independent (John Anderson); 1968 - 5,104 American Independent (George Wallace).

VERMONT

POSTWAR VOTE FOR GOVERNOR

Year	Total Vote	Republican Vote	Republican Candidate	Democratic Vote	Democratic Candidate	Other Vote	Plurality		Percentage Total Vote Rep.	Percentage Total Vote Dem.	Percentage Major Vote Rep.	Percentage Major Vote Dem.
2008**	319,085	170,492	Douglas, Jim	69,534	Symington, Gaye	79,059	100,701	R	53.4%	21.8%	71.0%	29.0%
2006	262,524	148,014	Douglas, Jim	108,090	Parker, Scudder	6,420	39,924	R	56.4%	41.2%	57.8%	42.2%
2004	309,285	181,540	Douglas, Jim	117,327	Clavelle, Peter	10,418	64,213	R	58.7%	37.9%	60.7%	39.3%
2002**	230,161	103,436	Douglas, Jim	97,565	Racine, Doug	29,160	5,871	R	44.9%	42.4%	51.5%	48.5%
2000	293,473	111,359	Dwyer, Ruth	148,059	Dean, Howard B.	34,055	36,700	D	37.9%	50.5%	42.9%	57.1%
1998	218,120	89,726	Dwyer, Ruth	121,425	Dean, Howard B.	6,969	31,699	D	41.1%	55.7%	42.5%	57.5%
1996	254,648	57,161	Gropper, John L.	179,544	Dean, Howard B.	17,943	122,383	D	22.4%	70.5%	24.1%	75.9%
1994	212,046	40,292	Kelley, David F.	145,661	Dean, Howard B.	26,093	105,369	D	19.0%	68.7%	21.7%	78.3%
1992	285,728	65,837	McClaughry, John	213,523	Dean, Howard B.	6,368	147,686	D	23.0%	74.7%	23.6%	76.4%
1990	211,422	109,540	Snelling, Richard A.	97,321	Welch, Peter	4,561	12,219	R	51.8%	46.0%	53.0%	47.0%
1988	243,130	105,319	Bernhardt, Michael	134,594	Kunin, Madeleine M.	3,253	29,275	D	43.3%	55.4%	43.9%	56.1%
1986**	196,716	75,162	Smith, Peter	92,379	Kunin, Madeleine M.	29,175	17,217	D	38.2%	47.0%	44.9%	55.1%
1984	233,753	113,264	Easton, John J.	116,938	Kunin, Madeleine M.	3,551	3,674	D	48.5%	50.0%	49.2%	50.8%
1982	169,251	93,111	Snelling, Richard A.	74,394	Kunin, Madeleine M.	1,746	18,717	R	55.0%	44.0%	55.6%	44.4%
1980	210,381	123,229	Snelling, Richard A.	77,363	Diamond, J. Jerome	9,789	45,866	R	58.6%	36.8%	61.4%	38.6%
1978	124,482	78,181	Snelling, Richard A.	42,482	Granai, Edwin C.	3,819	35,699	R	62.8%	34.1%	64.8%	35.2%
1976	185,929	99,268	Snelling, Richard A.	75,262	Hackel, Stella B.	11,399	24,006	R	53.4%	40.5%	56.9%	43.1%
1974	141,156	53,672	Kennedy, Walter L.	79,842	Salmon, Thomas P.	7,642	26,170	D	38.0%	56.6%	40.2%	59.8%
1972	189,237	82,491	Hackett, Luther F.	104,533	Salmon, Thomas P.	2,213	22,042	D	43.6%	55.2%	44.1%	55.9%
1970	153,528	87,458	Davis, Deane C.	66,028	O'Brien, Leo	42	21,430	R	57.0%	43.0%	57.0%	43.0%
1968	161,089	89,387	Davis, Deane C.	71,656	Daley, John J.	46	17,731	R	55.5%	44.5%	55.5%	44.5%
1966	136,262	57,577	Snelling, Richard A.	78,669	Hoff, Philip H.	16	21,092	D	42.3%	57.7%	42.3%	57.7%
1964	164,199	57,576	Foote, Ralph A.	106,611	Hoff, Philip H.	12	49,035	D	35.1%	64.9%	35.1%	64.9%
1962	121,422	60,035	Keyser, F. Ray	61,383	Hoff, Philip H.	4	1,348	D	49.4%	50.6%	49.4%	50.6%
1960	164,632	92,861	Keyser, F. Ray	71,755	Niquette, Russell F.	16	21,106	R	56.4%	43.6%	56.4%	43.6%
1958	123,728	62,222	Stafford, Robert T.	61,503	Leddy, Bernard J.	3	719	R	50.3%	49.7%	50.3%	49.7%
1956	153,809	88,379	Johnson, Joseph B.	65,420	Branon, E. Frank	10	22,959	R	57.5%	42.5%	57.5%	42.5%
1954	114,360	59,778	Johnson, Joseph B.	54,554	Branon, E. Frank	28	5,224	R	52.3%	47.7%	52.3%	47.7%
1952	150,862	78,338	Emerson, Lee E.	60,051	Larrow, Robert W.	12,473	18,287	R	51.9%	39.8%	56.6%	43.4%
1950	87,155	64,915	Emerson, Lee E.	22,227	Moran, J. Edward	13	42,688	R	74.5%	25.5%	74.5%	25.5%
1948	120,183	86,394	Gibson, Ernest W., Jr.	33,588	Ryan, Charles F.	201	52,806	R	71.9%	27.9%	72.0%	28.0%
1946	72,044	57,849	Gibson, Ernest W., Jr.	14,096	Coburn, Berthold	99	43,753	R	80.3%	19.6%	80.4%	19.6%

**In past elections, the other vote included: 2008 - 69,791 Independent (Anthony Pollina), who finished second; 1986 - 28,430 Independent (Bernard Sanders). In 1986 and 2002, in the absence of a majority for any candidate, the state legislature elected the governor — Democrat Madeleine M. Kunin in January 1987 and Republican Jim Douglas in January 2003 .

VERMONT

POSTWAR VOTE FOR SENATOR

Year	Total Vote	Republican Vote	Republican Candidate	Democratic Vote	Democratic Candidate	Other Vote	Plurality		Percentage Total Vote Rep.	Dem.	Major Vote Rep.	Dem.
2006**	262,419	84,924	Tarrant, Rich	—		177,495	86,714	I	32.4%		100.0%	
2004	307,208	75,398	McMullen, Jack	216,972	Leahy, Patrick J.	14,838	141,574	D	24.5%	70.6%	25.8%	74.2%
2000	288,500	189,133	Jeffords, James M.	73,352	Flanagan, Ed	26,015	115,781	R	65.6%	25.4%	72.1%	27.9%
1998	214,036	48,051	Tuttle, Fred H.	154,567	Leahy, Patrick J.	11,418	106,516	D	22.4%	72.2%	23.7%	76.3%
1994	211,672	106,505	Jeffords, James M.	85,868	Backus, Jan	19,299	20,637	R	50.3%	40.6%	55.4%	44.6%
1992	285,739	123,854	Douglas, Jim	154,762	Leahy, Patrick J.	7,123	30,908	D	43.3%	54.2%	44.5%	55.5%
1988	240,111	163,203	Jeffords, James M.	71,469	Gray, William	5,439	91,736	R	68.0%	29.8%	69.5%	30.5%
1986	196,532	67,798	Snelling, Richard A.	124,123	Leahy, Patrick J.	4,611	56,325	D	34.5%	63.2%	35.3%	64.7%
1982	168,003	84,450	Stafford, Robert T.	79,340	Guest, James A.	4,213	5,110	R	50.3%	47.2%	51.6%	48.4%
1980	209,124	101,421	Ledbetter, Stewart M.	104,176	Leahy, Patrick J.	3,527	2,755	D	48.5%	49.8%	49.3%	50.7%
1976	189,060	94,481	Stafford, Robert T.	85,682	Salmon, Thomas P.	8,897	8,799	R	50.0%	45.3%	52.4%	47.6%
1974	142,772	66,223	Mallary, Richard W.	70,629	Leahy, Patrick J.	5,920	4,406	D	46.4%	49.5%	48.4%	51.6%
1972S	71,348	45,888	Stafford, Robert T.	23,842	Major, Randolph T.	1,618	22,046	R	64.3%	33.4%	65.8%	34.2%
1970	154,899	91,198	Prouty, Winston L.	62,271	Hoff, Philip H.	1,430	28,927	R	58.9%	40.2%	59.4%	40.6%
1968**	157,375	157,154	Aiken, George D.		—	221	157,154	R	99.9%		100.0%	
1964	164,350	87,879	Prouty, Winston L.	76,457	Fayette, Frederick J.	14	11,422	R	53.5%	46.5%	53.5%	46.5%
1962	121,571	81,241	Aiken, George D.	40,134	Johnson, W. Robert	196	41,107	R	66.8%	33.0%	66.9%	33.1%
1958	124,442	64,900	Prouty, Winston L.	59,536	Fayette, Frederick J.	6	5,364	R	52.2%	47.8%	52.2%	47.8%
1956	155,289	103,101	Aiken, George D.	52,184	O'Shea, Bernard G.	4	50,917	R	66.4%	33.6%	66.4%	33.6%
1952	154,052	111,406	Flanders, Ralph E.	42,630	Johnston, Allan R.	16	68,776	R	72.3%	27.7%	72.3%	27.7%
1950	89,171	69,543	Aiken, George D.	19,608	Bigelow, James E.	20	49,935	R	78.0%	22.0%	78.0%	22.0%
1946	73,340	54,729	Flanders, Ralph E.	18,594	McDevitt, Charles P.	17	36,135	R	74.6%	25.4%	74.6%	25.4%

Notes: **In past elections, the other vote included: 2006 - 171,638 Independent (Bernard Sanders). Sanders received 65.4 percent of the total vote and was elected with a 86,714 vote plurality. Sanders also won the Democratic primary in 2006, but declined the nomination in order to run as an independent. The January 1972 election was for a short term to fill a vacancy. In 1968 the Republican candidate won both major party nominations.

VERMONT

PRESIDENT 2008

2000 Census Population	County	Total Vote	Republican	Democratic	Other	Rep.-Dem. Plurality	Total Vote Rep.	Total Vote Dem.	Major Vote Rep.	Major Vote Dem.
35,974	ADDISON	19,238	5,667	13,202	369	7,535 D	29.5%	68.6%	30.0%	70.0%
36,994	BENNINGTON	19,129	6,133	12,524	472	6,391 D	32.1%	65.5%	32.9%	67.1%
29,702	CALEDONIA	14,728	5,472	8,900	356	3,428 D	37.2%	60.4%	38.1%	61.9%
146,571	CHITTENDEN	83,440	22,237	59,611	1,592	37,374 D	26.7%	71.4%	27.2%	72.8%
6,459	ESSEX	3,101	1,284	1,733	84	449 D	41.4%	55.9%	42.6%	57.4%
45,417	FRANKLIN	21,460	7,853	13,179	428	5,326 D	36.6%	61.4%	37.3%	62.7%
6,901	GRAND ISLE	4,269	1,490	2,694	85	1,204 D	34.9%	63.1%	35.6%	64.4%
23,233	LAMOILLE	12,668	3,515	8,914	239	5,399 D	27.7%	70.4%	28.3%	71.7%
28,226	ORANGE	15,179	5,047	9,799	333	4,752 D	33.2%	64.6%	34.0%	66.0%
26,277	ORLEANS	12,771	4,482	7,998	291	3,516 D	35.1%	62.6%	35.9%	64.1%
63,400	RUTLAND	31,617	11,584	19,355	678	7,771 D	36.6%	61.2%	37.4%	62.6%
58,039	WASHINGTON	32,200	9,129	22,324	747	13,195 D	28.4%	69.3%	29.0%	71.0%
44,216	WINDHAM	24,081	5,997	17,585	499	11,588 D	24.9%	73.0%	25.4%	74.6%
57,418	WINDSOR	31,165	9,084	21,444	637	12,360 D	29.1%	68.8%	29.8%	70.2%
608,827	TOTAL	325,046	98,974	219,262	6,810	120,288 D	30.4%	67.5%	31.1%	68.9%

2000 Census Population	City/Town	Total Vote	Republican	Democratic	Other	Rep.-Dem. Plurality	Total Vote Rep.	Total Vote Dem.	Major Vote Rep.	Major Vote Dem.
9,291	BARRE CITY	3,703	1,263	2,339	101	1,076 D	34.1%	63.2%	35.1%	64.9%
7,602	BARRE TOWN	4,374	1,868	2,437	69	569 D	42.7%	55.7%	43.4%	56.6%
15,737	BENNINGTON	6,812	1,941	4,702	169	2,761 D	28.5%	69.0%	29.2%	70.8%
12,005	BRATTLEBORO	6,316	1,098	5,077	141	3,979 D	17.4%	80.4%	17.8%	82.2%
38,889	BURLINGTON	20,878	3,086	17,257	535	14,171 D	14.8%	82.7%	15.2%	84.8%
16,986	COLCHESTER	8,048	2,692	5,217	139	2,525 D	33.4%	64.8%	34.0%	66.0%
4,604	DERBY	2,314	870	1,392	52	522 D	37.6%	60.2%	38.5%	61.5%
18,626	ESSEX	10,914	3,660	7,083	171	3,423 D	33.5%	64.9%	34.1%	65.9%
10,367	HARTFORD	5,194	1,517	3,585	92	2,068 D	29.2%	69.0%	29.7%	70.3%
5,015	JERICHO	3,189	981	2,151	57	1,170 D	30.8%	67.5%	31.3%	68.7%
5,448	LYNDON	2,310	920	1,344	46	424 D	39.8%	58.2%	40.6%	59.4%
4,180	MANCHESTER	2,516	862	1,600	54	738 D	34.3%	63.6%	35.0%	65.0%
8,183	MIDDLEBURY	3,509	685	2,772	52	2,087 D	19.5%	79.0%	19.8%	80.2%
9,479	MILTON	4,947	2,056	2,789	102	733 D	41.6%	56.4%	42.4%	57.6%
8,035	MONTPELIER	4,810	810	3,901	99	3,091 D	16.8%	81.1%	17.2%	82.8%
5,139	MORRISTOWN	2,696	724	1,920	52	1,196 D	26.9%	71.2%	27.4%	72.6%
5,791	NORTHFIELD	2,433	867	1,491	75	624 D	35.6%	61.3%	36.8%	63.2%
4,853	RANDOLPH	2,354	733	1,560	61	827 D	31.1%	66.3%	32.0%	68.0%
4,090	RICHMOND	2,532	675	1,816	41	1,141 D	26.7%	71.7%	27.1%	72.9%
5,309	ROCKINGHAM	2,448	619	1,756	73	1,137 D	25.3%	71.7%	26.1%	73.9%
17,292	RUTLAND CITY	7,752	2,659	4,950	143	2,291 D	34.3%	63.9%	34.9%	65.1%
4,038	RUTLAND TOWN	2,510	1,048	1,415	47	367 D	41.8%	56.4%	42.5%	57.5%
6,944	SHELBURNE	4,615	1,217	3,347	51	2,130 D	26.4%	72.5%	26.7%	73.3%
15,814	SOUTH BURLINGTON	9,918	2,772	6,971	175	4,199 D	27.9%	70.3%	28.5%	71.5%
9,078	SPRINGFIELD	4,286	1,436	2,746	104	1,310 D	33.5%	64.1%	34.3%	65.7%
7,650	ST. ALBANS CITY	2,741	840	1,844	57	1,004 D	30.6%	67.3%	31.3%	68.7%
5,086	ST. ALBANS TOWN	3,000	1,160	1,792	48	632 D	38.7%	59.7%	39.3%	60.7%
7,571	ST. JOHNSBURY	3,140	1,183	1,889	58	706 D	37.7%	60.2%	38.5%	61.5%
2,548	SWANTON	2,665	1,036	1,596	33	560 D	38.9%	59.9%	39.4%	60.6%
4,915	WATERBURY	2,892	696	2,146	50	1,450 D	24.1%	74.2%	24.5%	75.5%
7,650	WILLISTON	5,236	1,645	3,507	34	1,862 D	31.4%	67.0%	31.9%	68.1%
6,561	WINOOSKI	2,876	670	2,142	64	1,472 D	23.3%	74.5%	23.8%	76.2%
3,232	WOODSTOCK	2,024	531	1,461	32	930 D	26.2%	72.2%	26.7%	73.3%
608,827	TOTAL	325,046	98,974	219,262	6,810	120,288 D	30.4%	67.5%	31.1%	68.9%

VERMONT

GOVERNOR 2008

2000 Census Population	County	Total Vote	Republican	Democratic	Independent (Pollina)	Other	Plurality	Rep.	Dem.	Ind.
								Percentage of Total Vote		
35,974	ADDISON	19,046	10,558	3,706	4,442	340	6,116 R	55.4%	19.5%	23.3%
36,994	BENNINGTON	18,628	9,847	5,802	2,143	836	4,045 R	52.9%	31.1%	11.5%
29,702	CALEDONIA	14,535	9,009	2,069	2,917	540	6,092 R	62.0%	14.2%	20.1%
146,571	CHITTENDEN	81,574	42,163	18,865	18,968	1,578	23,195 R	51.7%	23.1%	23.3%
6,459	ESSEX	3,032	1,992	486	405	149	1,506 R	65.7%	16.0%	13.4%
45,417	FRANKLIN	21,278	13,840	3,004	3,996	438	9,844 R	65.0%	14.1%	18.8%
6,901	GRAND ISLE	4,230	2,523	721	904	82	1,619 R	59.6%	17.0%	21.4%
23,233	LAMOILLE	12,475	6,722	2,043	3,407	303	3,315 R	53.9%	16.4%	27.3%
28,226	ORANGE	14,972	8,101	2,991	3,464	416	4,637 R	54.1%	20.0%	23.1%
26,277	ORLEANS	12,624	7,331	1,743	2,705	845	4,626 R	58.1%	13.8%	21.4%
63,400	RUTLAND	31,163	18,170	5,927	6,212	854	11,958 R	58.3%	19.0%	19.9%
58,039	WASHINGTON	31,705	15,820	5,798	9,363	724	6,457 R	49.9%	18.3%	29.5%
44,216	WINDHAM	23,329	8,693	8,570	4,906	1,160	123 R	37.3%	36.7%	21.0%
57,418	WINDSOR	30,494	15,723	7,809	5,959	1,003	7,914 R	51.6%	25.6%	19.5%
608,827	TOTAL	319,085	170,492	69,534	69,791	9,268	100,701 R	53.4%	21.8%	21.9%

Note: In each county, as well as statewide, the plurality is based on the winner's margin over the second-place finisher. An independent candidate, Anthony Pollina, placed second in 10 counties and statewide.

2000 Census Population	City/Town	Total Vote	Republican	Democratic	Independent (Pollina)	Other	Plurality	Rep.	Dem.	Ind.
								Percentage of Total Vote		
9,291	BARRE CITY	3,651	2,119	536	919	77	1,200 R	58.0%	14.7%	25.2%
7,602	BARRE TOWN	4,349	2,965	484	823	77	2,142 R	68.2%	11.1%	18.9%
15,737	BENNINGTON	6,626	3,195	2,421	709	301	774 R	48.2%	36.5%	10.7%
12,005	BRATTLEBORO	6,105	1,709	2,360	1,746	290	614 D	28.0%	38.7%	28.6%
38,889	BURLINGTON	19,929	6,884	6,119	6,238	688	646 R	34.5%	30.7%	31.3%
16,986	COLCHESTER	7,899	4,834	1,415	1,507	143	3,327 R	61.2%	17.9%	19.1%
4,604	DERBY	2,297	1,419	292	452	134	967 R	61.8%	12.7%	19.7%
18,626	ESSEX	10,754	6,714	1,854	2,036	150	4,678 R	62.4%	17.2%	18.9%
10,367	HARTFORD	5,057	2,772	1,344	776	165	1,428 R	54.8%	26.6%	15.3%
5,015	JERICHO	3,167	1,619	955	562	31	664 R	51.1%	30.2%	17.7%
5,448	LYNDON	2,268	1,513	277	384	94	1,129 R	66.7%	12.2%	16.9%
4,180	MANCHESTER	2,455	1,545	538	294	78	1,007 R	62.9%	21.9%	12.0%
8,183	MIDDLEBURY	3,423	1,656	860	861	46	795 R	48.4%	25.1%	25.2%
9,479	MILTON	4,893	3,357	666	793	77	2,564 R	68.6%	13.6%	16.2%
8,035	MONTPELIER	4,743	1,642	1,242	1,754	105	112 I	34.6%	26.2%	37.0%
5,139	MORRISTOWN	2,653	1,411	441	743	58	668 R	53.2%	16.6%	28.0%
5,791	NORTHFIELD	2,394	1,475	375	490	54	985 R	61.6%	15.7%	20.5%
4,853	RANDOLPH	2,329	1,242	402	629	56	613 R	53.3%	17.3%	27.0%
4,090	RICHMOND	2,519	1,260	606	620	33	640 R	50.0%	24.1%	24.6%
5,309	ROCKINGHAM	2,360	926	958	326	150	32 D	39.2%	40.6%	13.8%
17,292	RUTLAND CITY	7,602	4,365	1,572	1,474	191	2,793 R	57.4%	20.7%	19.4%
4,038	RUTLAND TOWN	2,482	1,648	384	403	47	1,245 R	66.4%	15.5%	16.2%
6,944	SHELBURNE	4,534	2,462	1,079	932	61	1,383 R	54.3%	23.8%	20.6%
15,814	SOUTH BURLINGTON	9,742	5,471	2,141	1,998	132	3,330 R	56.2%	22.0%	20.5%
9,078	SPRINGFIELD	4,218	2,324	1,036	678	180	1,288 R	55.1%	24.6%	16.1%

VERMONT

GOVERNOR 2008

2000 Census Population	City/Town	Total Vote	Republican	Democratic	Independent (Pollina)	Other	Plurality	Percentage of Total Vote		
								Rep.	Dem.	Ind.
7,650	ST. ALBANS CITY	2,702	1,670	475	492	65	1,178 R	61.8%	17.6%	18.2%
5,086	ST. ALBANS TOWN	2,977	2,060	398	470	49	1,590 R	69.2%	13.4%	15.8%
7,571	ST. JOHNSBURY	3,127	2,004	484	531	108	1,473 R	64.1%	15.5%	17.0%
2,548	SWANTON	2,658	1,831	366	423	38	1,408 R	68.9%	13.8%	15.9%
4,915	WATERBURY	2,854	1,437	551	813	53	624 R	50.4%	19.3%	28.5%
7,650	WILLISTON	5,179	3,155	980	986	58	2,169 R	60.9%	18.9%	19.0%
6,561	WINOOSKI	2,798	1,349	655	734	60	615 R	48.2%	23.4%	26.2%
3,232	WOODSTOCK	1,978	1,011	589	325	53	422 R	51.1%	29.8%	16.4%
608,827	TOTAL	319,085	170,492	69,534	69,791	9,268	100,701 R	53.4%	21.8%	21.9%

Note: In each city/town, the plurality is based on the winner's margin over the second-place finisher.

VERMONT

HOUSE OF REPRESENTATIVES

CD	Year	Total Vote	Republican Vote	Republican Candidate	Democratic Vote	Democratic Candidate	Other Vote	Plurality**	Total Vote Rep.	Total Vote Dem.	Major Vote Rep.	Major Vote Dem.
AL	2008	298,151	—		248,203	#Welch, Peter*	49,948	248,203 D		83.2%		100.0%
AL	2006	262,726	117,023	Rainville, Martha	139,815	Welch, Peter	5,888	22,792 D	44.5%	53.2%	45.6%	54.4%
AL	2004	305,008	74,271	Parke, Greg	21,684	Drown, Larry	209,053	131,503 I	24.4%	67.5% (I)		
AL	2002	225,476	72,813	Meub, William "Bill"	—		152,663	72,067 I	32.3%	64.3% (I)		
AL	2000	283,366	51,977	Kerin, Karen Ann	14,918	#Diamondstone, Pete	216,471	144,141 I	18.3%	69.2% (I)		
AL	1998	215,133	70,740	Candon, Mark	—		144,393	65,663 I	32.9%	63.4% (I)		
AL	1996	254,706	83,021	Sweetser, Susan W.	23,830	Long, Jack	147,855	57,657 I	32.6%	55.2% (I)		
AL	1994	211,449	98,523	Carroll, John	—		112,926	6,979 I	46.6%	49.9% (I)		
AL	1992	281,626	86,901	Philbin, Timothy	22,279	Young, Lewis E.	172,446	75,823 I	30.9%	57.8% (I)		
AL	1990	209,856	82,938	Smith, Peter*	6,315	Sandoval, Dolores	120,603	34,584 I	39.5%	56.0% (I)		
AL	1988	240,131	98,937	Smith, Peter	45,330	Poirier, Paul N.	95,864	53,607 R	41.2%	18.9%	68.6%	31.4%
AL	1986	188,954	168,403	#Jeffords, James M.*	—		20,551	168,403 R	89.1%		100.0%	
AL	1984	226,297	148,025	Jeffords, James M.*	60,360	Pollina, Anthony	17,912	87,665 R	65.4%	26.7%	71.0%	29.0%
AL	1982	164,951	114,191	Jeffords, James M.*	38,296	Kaplan, Mark A.	12,464	75,895 R	69.2%	23.2%	74.9%	25.1%
AL	1980	194,697	154,274	Jeffords, James M.*	—		40,423	154,274 R	79.2%		100.0%	
AL	1978	120,502	90,688	Jeffords, James M.*	23,228	Dietz, S. Marie	6,586	67,460 R	75.3%	19.3%	79.6%	20.4%
AL	1976	184,783	124,458	Jeffords, James M.*	60,202	#Burgess, John A.	123	64,256 R	67.4%	32.6%	67.4%	32.6%
AL	1974	140,899	74,561	Jeffords, James M.	56,342	#Cain, Francis J.	9,996	18,219 R	52.9%	40.0%	57.0%	43.0%
AL	1972	186,028	120,924	Mallary, Richard W.	65,062	Meyer, William H.	42	55,862 R	65.0%	35.0%	65.0%	35.0%
AL	1970	152,557	103,806	Stafford, Robert T.*	44,415	O'Shea, Bernard G.	4,336	59,391 R	68.0%	29.1%	70.0%	30.0%
AL	1968	157,133	156,956	#Stafford, Robert T.*	—		177	156,956 R	99.9%		100.0%	
AL	1966	135,748	89,097	Stafford, Robert T.*	46,643	Ryan, William J.	8	42,454 R	65.6%	34.4%	65.6%	34.4%
AL	1964	163,452	92,252	Stafford, Robert T.*	71,193	O'Shea, Bernard G.	7	21,059 R	56.4%	43.6%	56.4%	43.6%
AL	1962	121,381	68,822	Stafford, Robert T.*	52,535	Raynolds, Harold	24	16,287 R	56.7%	43.3%	56.7%	43.3%
AL	1960	166,035	94,905	Stafford, Robert T.	71,111	Meyer, William H.	19	23,794 R	57.2%	42.8%	57.2%	42.8%
AL	1958	122,702	59,536	Arthur, Harold J.	63,131	Meyer, William H.	35	3,595 D	48.5%	51.5%	48.5%	51.5%
AL	1956	154,536	103,736	Prouty, Winston L.*	50,797	St. Amour, Camille	3	52,939 R	67.1%	32.9%	67.1%	32.9%
AL	1954	114,289	70,143	Prouty, Winston L.*	44,141	Baylan, John J.	5	26,002 R	61.4%	38.6%	61.4%	38.6%
AL	1952	153,060	109,871	Prouty, Winston L.*	43,187	Comings, Herbert B.	2	66,684 R	71.8%	28.2%	71.8%	28.2%
AL	1950	88,851	65,248	Prouty, Winston L.	22,709	Comings, Herbert B.	894	42,539 R	73.4%	25.6%	74.2%	25.8%
AL	1948	121,968	74,076	Plumley, Charles A.*	47,767	Ready, Robert W.	125	26,309 R	60.7%	39.2%	60.8%	39.2%
AL	1946	73,066	46,985	Plumley, Charles A.*	26,056	Caldbeck, Matthew J.	25	20,929 R	64.3%	35.7%	64.3%	35.7%

Notes: An asterisk (*) denotes incumbent. Seat was won in 1990, 1992, 1994, 1996, 1998, 2000, 2002, and 2004 by Bernard Sanders, an independent. "Other Vote" for those years includes the total for Sanders and other independent and third party candidates. A double asterisk (**) indicates the plurality and percentage of total vote figures from 1990 through 2004 compare the Republican candidate and Sanders. For other years, the plurality reflects the difference between the votes for the Republican and Democratic candidates. A pound sign (#) indicates that a candidate received the nomination of another party. Democratic candidates from 1990 through 2004 received the following share of the total vote: 2004 - Larry Drown, 7.1 percent; 2000 - Pete Diamondstone, 5.3 percent; 1996 - Jack Long, 9.4 percent; 1992 - Lewis E. Young, 7.9 percent; 1990 - Dolores Sandoval, 3.0 percent.

VERMONT

GENERAL AND PRIMARY ELECTIONS

2008 GENERAL ELECTIONS

President   Other vote was 3,339 Independent (Ralph Nader); 1,067 Libertarian (Bob Barr); 500 Constitution (Chuck Baldwin); 150 Socialist Workers (Roger Calero); 149 Socialism and Liberation (Gloria La Riva); 141 Liberty Union (Brian Moore); 66 write-in (Cynthia A. McKinney); 1,398 scattered write-in.

Governor   Other vote was 3,106 Cheap Renewable Energy (Tony O'Connor); 2,490 Independent (Sam Young); 1,710 Liberty Union (Pete Diamondstone); 1,704 Independent (Cris Ericson); 258 scattered write-in. (Independent Anthony Pollina received 69,791 votes, 21.9 percent of the total vote. Pollina's vote is listed in the county and city/town tables for the 2008 gubernatorial election in Vermont.)

House   Other vote was:

At Large   14,349 Independent (Mike Bethel); 10,818 Energy Independence (Jerry Trudell); 9,081 Progressive (Thomas James Hermann); 7,841 Independent (Cris Ericson); 5,307 Liberty Union (Jane Newton); 2,552 scattered write-in.

2008 PRIMARY ELECTIONS

Primary	March 4, 2008 (President)	**Registration**	431,631	No Party Registration
	September 9, 2008 (Congress)	(as of September 9, 2008)		

Primary Type   Open—Any registered voter could participate in the primary of any recognized party.

	REPUBLICAN PRIMARIES			DEMOCRATIC PRIMARIES		
President	John McCain	28,417	71.3%	Barack Obama	91,901	59.3%
	Mike Huckabee	5,698	14.3%	Hillary Clinton	59,806	38.6%
	Ron Paul	2,635	6.6%	John Edwards	1,936	1.2%
	Mitt Romney	1,809	4.5%	Dennis J. Kucinich	1,010	0.7%
	Rudolph Giuliani	931	2.3%	Scattered write-in	307	0.2%
	Scattered write-in	353	0.9%			
	TOTAL	39,843		TOTAL	154,960	
Governor	Jim Douglas*	11,605	98.4%	Gaye Symington	17,263	91.6%
	Scattered write-in	193	1.6%	Scattered write-in	1,588	8.4%
	TOTAL	11,798		TOTAL	18,851	
House **At Large**	*No candidate filed for the primary. Democratic Rep. Peter Welch received 600 write-in votes to capture the Republican nomination. There were also 609 scattered write-in votes.*			Peter Welch*	19,566	87.7%
				Craig Barclay Hill	2,635	11.8%
				Scattered write-in	98	0.4%
				TOTAL	22,299	

Note: An asterisk (*) denotes incumbent.

VIRGINIA

Congressional districts first established for elections held in 2002
11 members

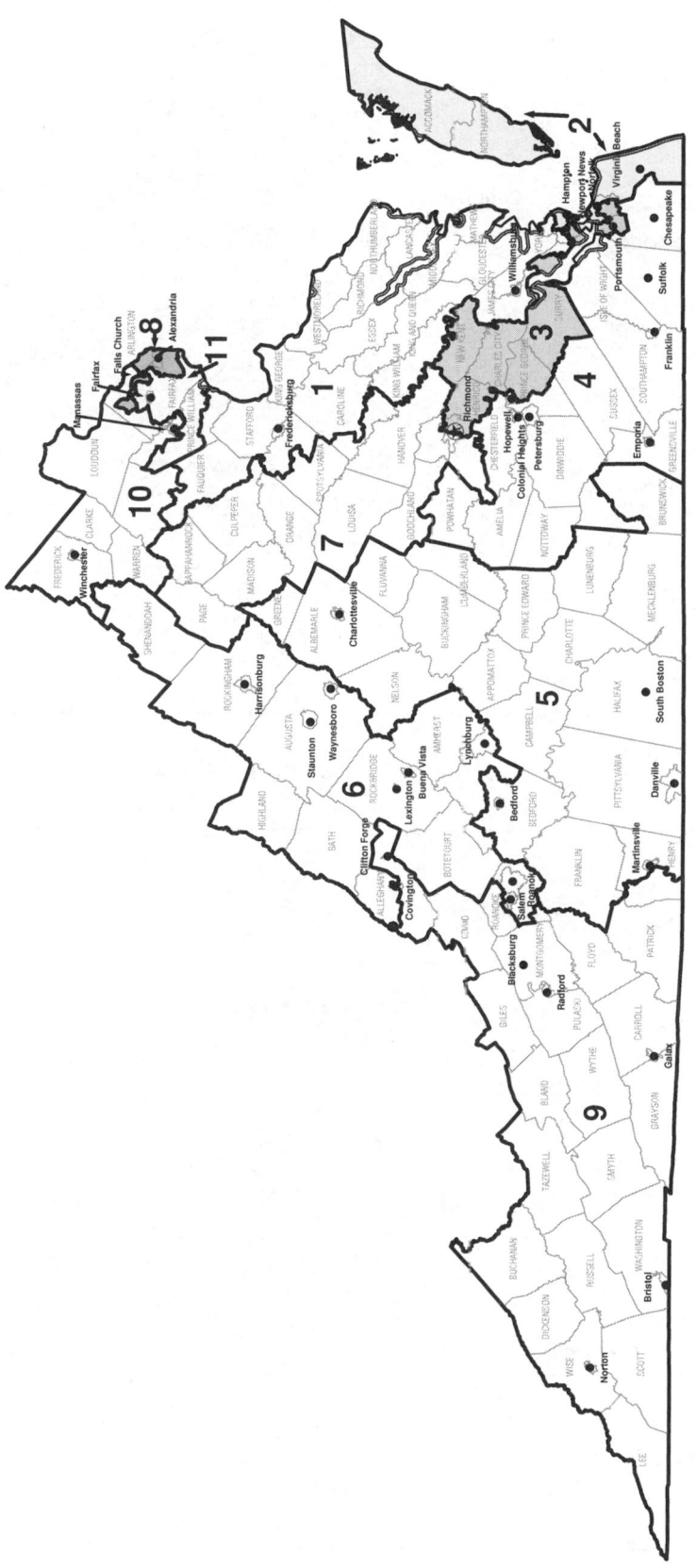

VIRGINIA

Northern Virginia Area

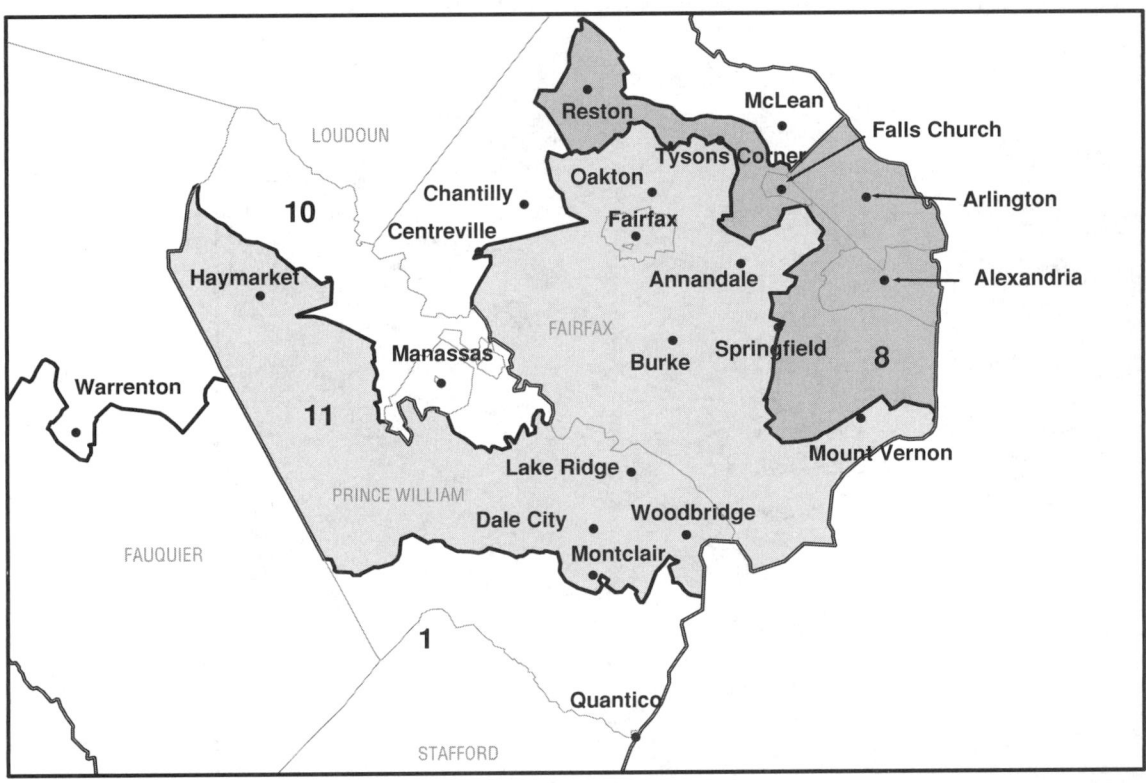

Hampton Roads, Virginia Beach Area

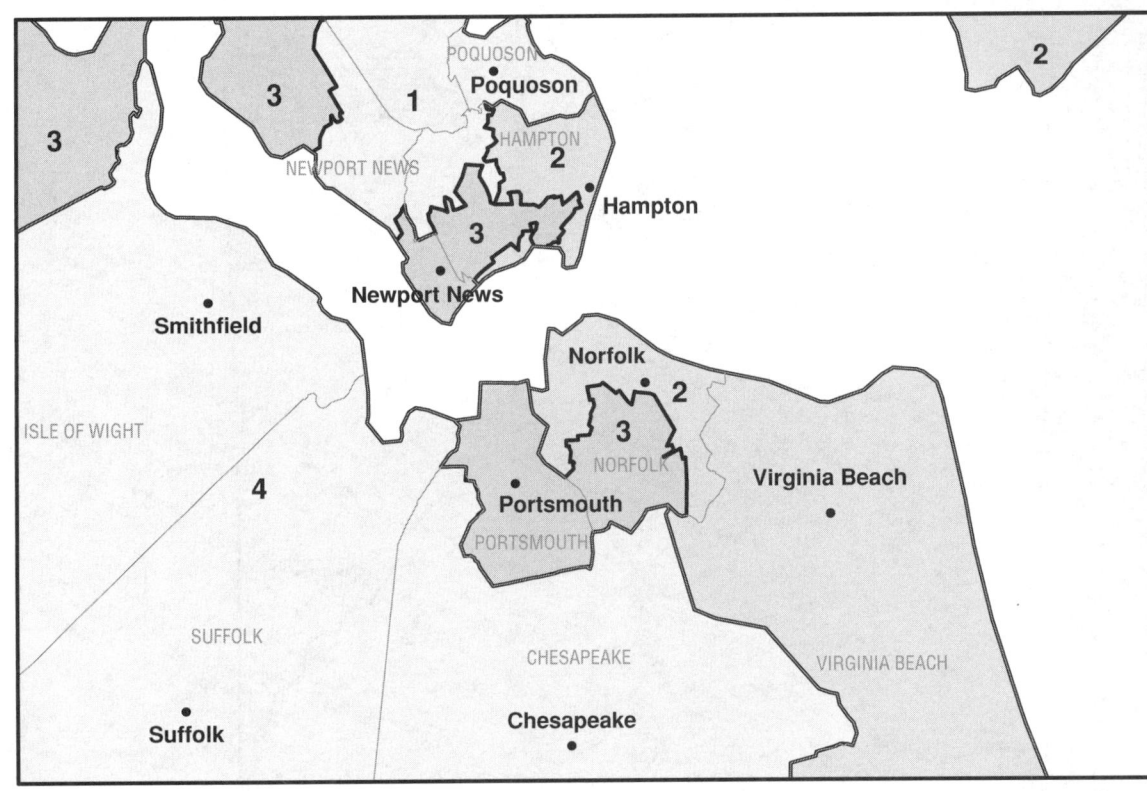

VIRGINIA

GOVERNOR
Timothy M. Kaine (D). Elected 2005 to a four-year term.

SENATORS (2 Democrats)
Mark R. Warner (D). Elected 2008 to a six-year term.

James Webb (D). Elected 2006 to a six-year term.

REPRESENTATIVES (6 Democrats, 5 Republicans)
1. Robert J. Wittman (R)
2. Glenn C. Nye (D)
3. Robert C. Scott (D)
4. J. Randy Forbes (R)
5. Thomas S. P. Perriello (D)
6. Robert W. Goodlatte (R)
7. Eric Cantor (R)
8. James P. Moran (D)
9. Rick Boucher (D)
10. Frank R. Wolf (R)
11. Gerald E. Connolly (D)

POSTWAR VOTE FOR PRESIDENT

Year	Total Vote	Republican Vote	Candidate	Democratic Vote	Candidate	Other Vote	Plurality	Total Vote Rep.	Total Vote Dem.	Major Vote Rep.	Major Vote Dem.
2008	3,723,260	1,725,005	McCain, John	1,959,532	Obama, Barack	38,723	234,527 D	46.3%	52.6%	46.8%	53.2%
2004	3,198,367	1,716,959	Bush, George W.	1,454,742	Kerry, John	26,666	262,217 R	53.7%	45.5%	54.1%	45.9%
2000**	2,739,447	1,437,490	Bush, George W.	1,217,290	Gore, Al	84,667	220,200 R	52.5%	44.4%	54.1%	45.9%
1996**	2,416,642	1,138,350	Dole, Bob	1,091,060	Clinton, Bill	187,232	47,290 R	47.1%	45.1%	51.1%	48.9%
1992**	2,558,665	1,150,517	Bush, George	1,038,650	Clinton, Bill	369,498	111,867 R	45.0%	40.6%	52.6%	47.4%
1988	2,191,609	1,309,162	Bush, George	859,799	Dukakis, Michael S.	22,648	449,363 R	59.7%	39.2%	60.4%	39.6%
1984	2,146,635	1,337,078	Reagan, Ronald	796,250	Mondale, Walter F.	13,307	540,828 R	62.3%	37.1%	62.7%	37.3%
1980**	1,866,032	989,609	Reagan, Ronald	752,174	Carter, Jimmy	124,249	237,435 R	53.0%	40.3%	56.8%	43.2%
1976	1,697,094	836,554	Ford, Gerald R.	813,896	Carter, Jimmy	46,644	22,658 R	49.3%	48.0%	50.7%	49.3%
1972	1,457,019	988,493	Nixon, Richard M.	438,887	McGovern, George S.	29,639	549,606 R	67.8%	30.1%	69.3%	30.7%
1968**	1,361,491	590,319	Nixon, Richard M.	442,387	Humphrey, Hubert H.	328,785	147,932 R	43.4%	32.5%	57.2%	42.8%
1964	1,042,267	481,334	Goldwater, Barry M.	558,038	Johnson, Lyndon B.	2,895	76,704 D	46.2%	53.5%	46.3%	53.7%
1960	771,449	404,521	Nixon, Richard M.	362,327	Kennedy, John F.	4,601	42,194 R	52.4%	47.0%	52.8%	47.2%
1956	697,978	386,459	Eisenhower, Dwight D.	267,760	Stevenson, Adlai E.	43,759	118,699 R	55.4%	38.4%	59.1%	40.9%
1952	619,689	349,037	Eisenhower, Dwight D.	268,677	Stevenson, Adlai E.	1,975	80,360 R	56.3%	43.4%	56.5%	43.5%
1948**	419,256	172,070	Dewey, Thomas E.	200,786	Truman, Harry S.	46,400	28,716 D	41.0%	47.9%	46.1%	53.9%

**In past elections, the other vote included: 2000 - 59,398 Green (Ralph Nader); 1996 - 159,861 Reform (Ross Perot); 1992 - 348,639 Independent (Perot); 1980 - 95,418 Independent (John Anderson); 1968 - 321,833 American Independent (George Wallace); 1948 - 43,393 States' Rights (Strom Thurmond).

VIRGINIA

POSTWAR VOTE FOR GOVERNOR

Year	Total Vote	Republican Vote	Republican Candidate	Democratic Vote	Democratic Candidate	Other Vote	Plurality	Total Vote Rep.	Total Vote Dem.	Major Vote Rep.	Major Vote Dem.
2005	1,983,778	912,327	Kilgore, Jerry W.	1,025,942	Kaine, Timothy M.	45,509	113,615 D	46.0%	51.7%	47.1%	52.9%
2001	1,886,721	887,234	Earley, Mark L.	984,177	Warner, Mark R.	15,310	96,943 D	47.0%	52.2%	47.4%	52.6%
1997	1,736,314	969,062	Gilmore, James S. "Jim" III	738,971	Beyer, Donald S., Jr.	28,281	230,091 R	55.8%	42.6%	56.7%	43.3%
1993	1,793,916	1,045,319	Allen, George	733,527	Terry, Mary Sue	15,070	311,792 R	58.3%	40.9%	58.8%	41.2%
1989	1,789,078	890,195	Coleman, J. Marshall	896,936	Wilder, L. Douglas	1,947	6,741 D	49.8%	50.1%	49.8%	50.2%
1985	1,343,243	601,652	Durrette, Wyatt B.	741,438	Baliles, Gerald L.	153	139,786 D	44.8%	55.2%	44.8%	55.2%
1981	1,420,611	659,398	Coleman, J. Marshall	760,357	Robb, Charles S.	856	100,959 D	46.4%	53.5%	46.4%	53.6%
1977	1,250,940	699,302	Dalton, John	541,319	Howell, Henry	10,319	157,983 R	55.9%	43.3%	56.4%	43.6%
1973**	1,035,495	525,075	Godwin, Mills E.	—		510,420	14,972 R	50.7%		100.0%	
1969	915,764	480,869	Holton, Linwood	415,695	Battle, William C.	19,200	65,174 R	52.5%	45.4%	53.6%	46.4%
1965**	562,789	212,207	Holton, Linwood	269,526	Godwin, Mills E.	81,056	57,319 D	37.7%	47.9%	44.1%	55.9%
1961	394,490	142,567	Pearson, H. Clyde	251,861	Harrison, Albertis	62	109,294 D	36.1%	63.8%	36.1%	63.9%
1957	517,655	188,628	Dalton, Ted	326,921	Almond, J. Lindsay	2,106	138,293 D	36.4%	63.2%	36.6%	63.4%
1953	414,025	183,328	Dalton, Ted	226,998	Stanley, Thomas B.	3,699	43,670 D	44.3%	54.8%	44.7%	55.3%
1949	262,350	71,991	Johnson, Walter	184,772	Battle, John S.	5,587	112,781 D	27.4%	70.4%	28.0%	72.0%
1945	168,783	52,386	Landreth, S. Floyd	112,355	Tuck, William M.	4,042	59,969 D	31.0%	66.6%	31.8%	68.2%

**In past elections, the other vote included: 1973 - 510,103 Independent (Henry Howell); 1965 - 75,307 Conservative (William J. Story Jr.). In 1973 the plurality reflects the difference in the vote for the Republican candidate and Henry Howell. In other elections, the plurality is the difference between the Republican and Democratic vote. The Democratic Party did not run a candidate in the 1973 gubernatorial election.

POSTWAR VOTE FOR SENATOR

Year	Total Vote	Republican Vote	Republican Candidate	Democratic Vote	Democratic Candidate	Other Vote	Rep.-Dem. Plurality	Total Vote Rep.	Total Vote Dem.	Major Vote Rep.	Major Vote Dem.
2008	3,643,294	1,228,830	Gilmore, James S. "Jim" III	2,369,327	Warner, Mark R.	45,137	1,140,497 D	33.7%	65.0%	34.2%	65.8%
2006	2,370,445	1,166,277	Allen, George	1,175,606	Webb, James	28,562	9,329 D	49.2%	49.6%	49.8%	50.2%
2002	1,489,422	1,229,894	Warner, John W.	—		259,528	1,229,894 R	82.6%		100.0%	
2000	2,718,301	1,420,460	Allen, George	1,296,093	Robb, Charles S.	1,748	124,367 R	52.3%	47.7%	52.3%	47.7%
1996	2,354,715	1,235,744	Warner, John W.	1,115,982	Warner, Mark R.	2,989	119,762 R	52.5%	47.4%	52.5%	47.5%
1994**	2,057,463	882,213	North, Oliver L.	938,376	Robb, Charles S.	236,874	56,163 D	42.9%	45.6%	48.5%	51.5%
1990**	1,083,690	876,782	Warner, John W.	—		206,908	876,782 R	80.9%		100.0%	
1988	2,068,897	593,652	Dawkins, Maurice A.	1,474,086	Robb, Charles S.	1,159	880,434 D	28.7%	71.2%	28.7%	71.3%
1984	2,007,487	1,406,194	Warner, John W.	601,142	Harrison, Edythe C.	151	805,052 R	70.0%	29.9%	70.1%	29.9%
1982	1,415,622	724,571	Trible, Paul	690,839	Davis, Richard	212	33,732 R	51.2%	48.8%	51.2%	48.8%
1978	1,222,256	613,232	Warner, John W.	608,511	Miller, Andrew P.	513	4,721 R	50.2%	49.8%	50.2%	49.8%
1976**	1,557,500	—		596,009	Zumwalt, Elmo R.	961,491	294,769 I		38.3%		100.0%
1972	1,396,268	718,337	Scott, William L.	643,963	Spong, William B.	33,968	74,374 R	51.4%	46.1%	52.7%	47.3%
1970**	946,751	145,031	Garland, Ray	295,057	Rawlings, George C.	506,663	211,576 I	15.3%	31.2%	33.0%	67.0%
1966	733,879	245,681	Ould, James P.	429,855	Spong, William B.	58,343	184,174 D	33.5%	58.6%	36.4%	63.6%
1966S	729,839	272,804	Traylor, Lawrence M.	389,028	Byrd, Harry Flood, Jr.	68,007	116,224 D	37.4%	53.3%	41.2%	58.8%
1964**	928,363	176,624	May, Richard A.	592,260	Byrd, Harry Flood	159,479	415,636 D	19.0%	63.8%	23.0%	77.0%
1960**	622,820	—		506,169	Robertson, A. Willis	116,651	506,169 D		81.3%		100.0%
1958**	457,640	—		317,221	Byrd, Harry Flood	140,419	317,221 D		69.3%		100.0%
1954**	306,510	—		244,844	Robertson, A. Willis	61,666	244,844 D		79.9%		100.0%
1952**	543,516	—		398,677	Byrd, Harry Flood	144,839	398,677 D		73.4%		100.0%
1948	386,178	118,546	Woods, Robert	253,865	Robertson, A. Willis	13,767	135,319 D	30.7%	65.7%	31.8%	68.2%
1946	252,863	77,005	Parsons, Lester S.	163,960	Byrd, Harry Flood	11,898	86,955 D	30.5%	64.8%	32.0%	68.0%
1946S	248,962	72,253	Woods, Robert	169,680	Robertson, A. Willis	7,029	97,427 D	29.0%	68.2%	29.9%	70.1%

Notes: **In past elections, the other vote included: 1994 - 235,324 Independent (J. Marshall Coleman); 1990 - 196,755 Independent (Nancy Spannaus); 1976 - 890,778 Independent (Harry Flood Byrd Jr.), who won the election with 57.2 percent of the total vote; 1970 - 506,633 Independent (Harry Flood Byrd Jr.), who won the election with 53.5 percent of the total vote; 1964 - 95,526 Independent (James W. Respess); 1960 - 88,718 Independent Democrat (Stuart D. Baker); 1958 - 120,224 Independent (Louis Wensel); 1954 - 32,681 Independent Democrat (Charles William Lewis Jr.); 1952 - 69,133 Independent Democrat (H. M. Vise Sr.); and 67,281 Social Democrat (Clarke T. Robb). In the 1970 and 1976 elections Byrd's plurality is compared with the Democratic candidate, who in each case finished second. In other elections the plurality is the difference between the Republican and Democratic vote. One each of the 1946 and 1966 elections was for a short term to fill a vacancy. The Democratic Party did not run a candidate in the Senate elections of 1990 and 2002. The Republican Party did not run a candidate in the Senate elections of 1952, 1954, 1958, 1960, and 1976.

VIRGINIA

PRESIDENT 2008

2000 Census Population	County	Total Vote	Republican	Democratic	Other	Rep.-Dem. Plurality	Percentage Total Vote Rep.	Dem.	Major Vote Rep.	Dem.
38,305	ACCOMACK	15,623	7,833	7,607	183	226 R	50.1%	48.7%	50.7%	49.3%
79,236	ALBEMARLE	50,984	20,576	29,792	616	9,216 D	40.4%	58.4%	40.9%	59.1%
17,215	ALLEGHANY	7,369	3,715	3,553	101	162 R	50.4%	48.2%	51.1%	48.9%
11,400	AMELIA	6,529	3,970	2,488	71	1,482 R	60.8%	38.1%	61.5%	38.5%
31,894	AMHERST	14,700	8,470	6,094	136	2,376 R	57.6%	41.5%	58.2%	41.8%
13,705	APPOMATTOX	7,630	4,903	2,641	86	2,262 R	64.3%	34.6%	65.0%	35.0%
189,453	ARLINGTON	110,153	29,876	78,994	1,283	49,118 D	27.1%	71.7%	27.4%	72.6%
65,615	AUGUSTA	33,338	23,120	9,825	393	13,295 R	69.4%	29.5%	70.2%	29.8%
5,048	BATH	2,432	1,349	1,043	40	306 R	55.5%	42.9%	56.4%	43.6%
60,371	BEDFORD COUNTY	35,830	24,420	11,017	393	13,403 R	68.2%	30.7%	68.9%	31.1%
6,871	BLAND	2,959	2,031	864	64	1,167 R	68.6%	29.2%	70.2%	29.8%
30,496	BOTETOURT	17,406	11,471	5,693	242	5,778 R	65.9%	32.7%	66.8%	33.2%
18,419	BRUNSWICK	7,914	2,877	4,973	64	2,096 D	36.4%	62.8%	36.6%	63.4%
26,978	BUCHANAN	8,734	4,541	4,063	130	478 R	52.0%	46.5%	52.8%	47.2%
15,623	BUCKINGHAM	6,994	3,428	3,489	77	61 D	49.0%	49.9%	49.6%	50.4%
51,078	CAMPBELL	25,814	17,444	8,091	279	9,353 R	67.6%	31.3%	68.3%	31.7%
22,121	CAROLINE	12,919	5,617	7,163	139	1,546 D	43.5%	55.4%	44.0%	56.0%
29,245	CARROLL	12,579	8,187	4,109	283	4,078 R	65.1%	32.7%	66.6%	33.4%
6,926	CHARLES CITY	4,153	1,288	2,838	27	1,550 D	31.0%	68.3%	31.2%	68.8%
12,472	CHARLOTTE	6,157	3,372	2,705	80	667 R	54.8%	43.9%	55.5%	44.5%
259,903	CHESTERFIELD	162,088	86,413	74,310	1,365	12,103 R	53.3%	45.8%	53.8%	46.2%
12,652	CLARKE	7,431	3,840	3,457	134	383 R	51.7%	46.5%	52.6%	47.4%
5,091	CRAIG	2,621	1,695	877	49	818 R	64.7%	33.5%	65.9%	34.1%
34,262	CULPEPER	19,741	10,711	8,802	228	1,909 R	54.3%	44.6%	54.9%	45.1%
9,017	CUMBERLAND	4,724	2,418	2,255	51	163 R	51.2%	47.7%	51.7%	48.3%
16,395	DICKENSON	6,753	3,324	3,278	151	46 R	49.2%	48.5%	50.3%	49.7%
24,533	DINWIDDIE	12,892	6,526	6,246	120	280 R	50.6%	48.4%	51.1%	48.9%
9,989	ESSEX	5,364	2,379	2,934	51	555 D	44.4%	54.7%	44.8%	55.2%
969,749	FAIRFAX COUNTY	516,254	200,994	310,359	4,901	109,365 D	38.9%	60.1%	39.3%	60.7%
55,139	FAUQUIER	34,219	19,227	14,616	376	4,611 R	56.2%	42.7%	56.8%	43.2%
13,874	FLOYD	7,516	4,441	2,937	138	1,504 R	59.1%	39.1%	60.2%	39.8%
20,047	FLUVANNA	12,735	6,420	6,185	130	235 R	50.4%	48.6%	50.9%	49.1%
47,286	FRANKLIN COUNTY	25,401	15,414	9,618	369	5,796 R	60.7%	37.9%	61.6%	38.4%
59,209	FREDERICK	33,612	20,149	12,961	502	7,188 R	59.9%	38.6%	60.9%	39.1%
16,657	GILES	7,795	4,462	3,192	141	1,270 R	57.2%	40.9%	58.3%	41.7%
34,780	GLOUCESTER	19,222	12,089	6,916	217	5,173 R	62.9%	36.0%	63.6%	36.4%
16,863	GOOCHLAND	12,562	7,643	4,813	106	2,830 R	60.8%	38.3%	61.4%	38.6%
17,917	GRAYSON	7,220	4,540	2,480	200	2,060 R	62.9%	34.3%	64.7%	35.3%
15,244	GREENE	8,260	4,980	3,174	106	1,806 R	60.3%	38.4%	61.1%	38.9%
11,560	GREENSVILLE	4,887	1,729	3,122	36	1,393 D	35.4%	63.9%	35.6%	64.4%
37,355	HALIFAX	16,850	8,600	8,126	124	474 R	51.0%	48.2%	51.4%	48.6%
86,320	HANOVER	56,248	37,344	18,447	457	18,897 R	66.4%	32.8%	66.9%	33.1%
262,300	HENRICO	154,966	67,381	86,323	1,262	18,942 D	43.5%	55.7%	43.8%	56.2%
57,930	HENRY	25,215	13,758	11,118	339	2,640 R	54.6%	44.1%	55.3%	44.7%
2,536	HIGHLAND	1,554	930	590	34	340 R	59.8%	38.0%	61.2%	38.8%
29,728	ISLE OF WIGHT	19,997	11,258	8,573	166	2,685 R	56.3%	42.9%	56.8%	43.2%
48,102	JAMES CITY	38,603	20,912	17,352	339	3,560 R	54.2%	44.9%	54.7%	45.3%
6,630	KING AND QUEEN	3,705	1,763	1,918	24	155 D	47.6%	51.8%	47.9%	52.1%
16,803	KING GEORGE	10,474	5,888	4,473	113	1,415 R	56.2%	42.7%	56.8%	43.2%
13,146	KING WILLIAM	8,388	4,966	3,344	78	1,622 R	59.2%	39.9%	59.8%	40.2%

VIRGINIA
PRESIDENT 2008

2000 Census Population	County	Total Vote	Republican	Democratic	Other	Rep.-Dem. Plurality	Percentage Total Vote Rep.	Dem.	Major Vote Rep.	Dem.
11,567	LANCASTER	6,938	3,647	3,235	56	412 R	52.6%	46.6%	53.0%	47.0%
23,589	LEE	9,227	5,825	3,219	183	2,606 R	63.1%	34.9%	64.4%	35.6%
169,599	LOUDOUN	139,459	63,336	74,845	1,278	11,509 D	45.4%	53.7%	45.8%	54.2%
25,627	LOUISA	15,353	8,182	6,978	193	1,204 R	53.3%	45.5%	54.0%	46.0%
13,146	LUNENBURG	5,650	2,900	2,703	47	197 R	51.3%	47.8%	51.8%	48.2%
12,520	MADISON	6,699	3,758	2,862	79	896 R	56.1%	42.7%	56.8%	43.2%
9,207	MATHEWS	5,440	3,456	1,934	50	1,522 R	63.5%	35.6%	64.1%	35.9%
32,380	MECKLENBURG	15,082	7,817	7,127	138	690 R	51.8%	47.3%	52.3%	47.7%
9,932	MIDDLESEX	6,006	3,545	2,391	70	1,154 R	59.0%	39.8%	59.7%	40.3%
83,629	MONTGOMERY	40,653	19,028	21,031	594	2,003 D	46.8%	51.7%	47.5%	52.5%
14,445	NELSON	8,133	3,647	4,391	95	744 D	44.8%	54.0%	45.4%	54.6%
13,462	NEW KENT	9,991	6,385	3,493	113	2,892 R	63.9%	35.0%	64.6%	35.4%
13,093	NORTHAMPTON	6,586	2,713	3,800	73	1,087 D	41.2%	57.7%	41.7%	58.3%
12,259	NORTHUMBERLAND	7,406	4,041	3,312	53	729 R	54.6%	44.7%	55.0%	45.0%
15,725	NOTTOWAY	6,988	3,499	3,413	76	86 R	50.1%	48.8%	50.6%	49.4%
25,881	ORANGE	15,801	8,506	7,107	188	1,399 R	53.8%	45.0%	54.5%	45.5%
23,177	PAGE	10,389	6,041	4,235	113	1,806 R	58.1%	40.8%	58.8%	41.2%
19,407	PATRICK	8,531	5,491	2,879	161	2,612 R	64.4%	33.7%	65.6%	34.4%
61,745	PITTSYLVANIA	30,433	18,730	11,415	288	7,315 R	61.5%	37.5%	62.1%	37.9%
22,377	POWHATAN	14,456	10,088	4,237	131	5,851 R	69.8%	29.3%	70.4%	29.6%
19,720	PRINCE EDWARD	9,388	4,174	5,101	113	927 D	44.5%	54.3%	45.0%	55.0%
33,047	PRINCE GEORGE	16,006	8,752	7,130	124	1,622 R	54.7%	44.5%	55.1%	44.9%
280,813	PRINCE WILLIAM	162,446	67,621	93,435	1,390	25,814 D	41.6%	57.5%	42.0%	58.0%
35,127	PULASKI	15,050	8,857	5,918	275	2,939 R	58.9%	39.3%	59.9%	40.1%
6,983	RAPPAHANNOCK	4,405	2,227	2,105	73	122 R	50.6%	47.8%	51.4%	48.6%
8,809	RICHMOND COUNTY	3,745	2,092	1,618	35	474 R	55.9%	43.2%	56.4%	43.6%
85,778	ROANOKE COUNTY	50,975	30,571	19,812	592	10,759 R	60.0%	38.9%	60.7%	39.3%
20,808	ROCKBRIDGE	10,195	5,732	4,347	116	1,385 R	56.2%	42.6%	56.9%	43.1%
67,725	ROCKINGHAM	33,334	22,468	10,453	413	12,015 R	67.4%	31.4%	68.2%	31.8%
30,308	RUSSELL	11,494	6,389	4,932	173	1,457 R	55.6%	42.9%	56.4%	43.6%
23,403	SCOTT	9,875	6,980	2,725	170	4,255 R	70.7%	27.6%	71.9%	28.1%
35,075	SHENANDOAH	19,223	12,005	6,912	306	5,093 R	62.5%	36.0%	63.5%	36.5%
33,081	SMYTH	12,302	7,817	4,239	246	3,578 R	63.5%	34.5%	64.8%	35.2%
17,482	SOUTHAMPTON	9,067	4,583	4,402	82	181 R	50.5%	48.5%	51.0%	49.0%
90,395	SPOTSYLVANIA	54,069	28,610	24,897	562	3,713 R	52.9%	46.0%	53.5%	46.5%
92,446	STAFFORD	55,455	29,221	25,716	518	3,505 R	52.7%	46.4%	53.2%	46.8%
6,829	SURRY	4,325	1,663	2,626	36	963 D	38.5%	60.7%	38.8%	61.2%
12,504	SUSSEX	5,363	2,026	3,301	36	1,275 D	37.8%	61.6%	38.0%	62.0%
44,598	TAZEWELL	17,061	11,201	5,596	264	5,605 R	65.7%	32.8%	66.7%	33.3%
31,584	WARREN	16,126	8,879	6,997	250	1,882 R	55.1%	43.4%	55.9%	44.1%
51,103	WASHINGTON	24,500	16,077	8,063	360	8,014 R	65.6%	32.9%	66.6%	33.4%
16,718	WESTMORELAND	8,377	3,719	4,577	81	858 D	44.4%	54.6%	44.8%	55.2%
40,123	WISE	14,138	8,914	4,995	229	3,919 R	63.0%	35.3%	64.1%	35.9%
27,599	WYTHE	12,491	8,207	4,107	177	4,100 R	65.7%	32.9%	66.6%	33.4%
56,297	YORK	33,897	19,833	13,700	364	6,133 R	58.5%	40.4%	59.1%	40.9%
7,078,515	TOTAL	3,723,260	1,725,005	1,959,532	38,723	234,527 D	46.3%	52.6%	46.8%	53.2%

VIRGINIA

PRESIDENT 2008

2000 Census Population	City/Town	Total Vote	Republican	Democratic	Other	Rep.-Dem. Plurality	Percentage			
							Total Vote		Major Vote	
							Rep.	Dem.	Rep.	Dem.
128,283	ALEXANDRIA	70,364	19,181	50,473	710	31,292 D	27.3%	71.7%	27.5%	72.5%
6,299	BEDFORD CITY	2,734	1,497	1,208	29	289 R	54.8%	44.2%	55.3%	44.7%
17,367	BRISTOL	7,359	4,579	2,665	115	1,914 R	62.2%	36.2%	63.2%	36.8%
6,349	BUENA VISTA	2,423	1,282	1,108	33	174 R	52.9%	45.7%	53.6%	46.4%
45,049	CHARLOTTESVILLE	20,044	4,078	15,705	261	11,627 D	20.3%	78.4%	20.6%	79.4%
199,184	CHESAPEAKE	107,521	52,625	53,994	902	1,369 D	48.9%	50.2%	49.4%	50.6%
16,897	COLONIAL HEIGHTS	8,849	6,161	2,562	126	3,599 R	69.6%	29.0%	70.6%	29.4%
6,303	COVINGTON	2,354	1,020	1,304	30	284 D	43.3%	55.4%	43.9%	56.1%
48,411	DANVILLE	20,890	8,361	12,352	177	3,991 D	40.0%	59.1%	40.4%	59.6%
5,665	EMPORIA	2,617	897	1,702	18	805 D	34.3%	65.0%	34.5%	65.5%
21,498	FAIRFAX CITY	11,398	4,691	6,575	132	1,884 D	41.2%	57.7%	41.6%	58.4%
10,377	FALLS CHURCH	6,750	1,970	4,695	85	2,725 D	29.2%	69.6%	29.6%	70.4%
8,346	FRANKLIN CITY	4,427	1,576	2,819	32	1,243 D	35.6%	63.7%	35.9%	64.1%
19,279	FREDERICKSBURG	9,677	3,413	6,155	109	2,742 D	35.3%	63.6%	35.7%	64.3%
6,837	GALAX	2,402	1,317	1,052	33	265 R	54.8%	43.8%	55.6%	44.4%
146,437	HAMPTON	67,943	20,476	46,917	550	26,441 D	30.1%	69.1%	30.4%	69.6%
40,468	HARRISONBURG	14,675	6,048	8,444	183	2,396 D	41.2%	57.5%	41.7%	58.3%
22,354	HOPEWELL	9,524	4,149	5,285	90	1,136 D	43.6%	55.5%	44.0%	56.0%
6,867	LEXINGTON	2,479	914	1,543	22	629 D	36.9%	62.2%	37.2%	62.8%
65,269	LYNCHBURG	34,341	17,638	16,269	434	1,369 R	51.4%	47.4%	52.0%	48.0%
35,135	MANASSAS	13,627	5,975	7,518	134	1,543 D	43.8%	55.2%	44.3%	55.7%
10,290	MANASSAS PARK	4,140	1,634	2,463	43	829 D	39.5%	59.5%	39.9%	60.1%
15,416	MARTINSVILLE	6,520	2,311	4,139	70	1,828 D	35.4%	63.5%	35.8%	64.2%
180,150	NEWPORT NEWS	81,295	28,667	51,972	656	23,305 D	35.3%	63.9%	35.5%	64.5%
234,403	NORFOLK	88,446	24,814	62,819	813	38,005 D	28.1%	71.0%	28.3%	71.7%
3,904	NORTON	1,512	744	743	25	1 R	49.2%	49.1%	50.0%	50.0%
33,740	PETERSBURG	15,540	1,583	13,774	183	12,191 D	10.2%	88.6%	10.3%	89.7%
11,566	POQUOSON	7,065	5,229	1,748	88	3,481 R	74.0%	24.7%	74.9%	25.1%
100,565	PORTSMOUTH	46,665	13,984	32,327	354	18,343 D	30.0%	69.3%	30.2%	69.8%
15,859	RADFORD	5,429	2,418	2,930	81	512 D	44.5%	54.0%	45.2%	54.8%
197,790	RICHMOND CITY	93,085	18,649	73,623	813	54,974 D	20.0%	79.1%	20.2%	79.8%
94,911	ROANOKE CITY	40,772	15,394	24,934	444	9,540 D	37.8%	61.2%	38.2%	61.8%
24,747	SALEM	12,406	7,088	5,164	154	1,924 R	57.1%	41.6%	57.9%	42.1%
23,853	STAUNTON	11,015	5,330	5,569	116	239 D	48.4%	50.6%	48.9%	51.1%
63,677	SUFFOLK	39,908	17,165	22,446	297	5,281 D	43.0%	56.2%	43.3%	56.7%
425,257	VIRGINIA BEACH	201,249	100,319	98,885	2,045	1,434 R	49.8%	49.1%	50.4%	49.6%
19,520	WAYNESBORO	8,860	4,815	3,906	139	909 R	54.3%	44.1%	55.2%	44.8%
11,998	WILLIAMSBURG	6,787	2,353	4,328	106	1,975 D	34.7%	63.8%	35.2%	64.8%
23,585	WINCHESTER	10,126	4,725	5,268	133	543 D	46.7%	52.0%	47.3%	52.7%
7,078,515	TOTAL	3,723,260	1,725,005	1,959,532	38,723	234,527 D	46.3%	52.6%	46.8%	53.2%

VIRGINIA
SENATOR 2008

2000 Census Population	County	Total Vote	Republican	Democratic	Other	Rep.-Dem. Plurality		Percentage			
								Total Vote		Major Vote	
								Rep.	Dem.	Rep.	Dem.
38,305	ACCOMACK	15,202	5,379	9,594	229	4,215	D	35.4%	63.1%	35.9%	64.1%
79,236	ALBEMARLE	50,239	15,076	34,603	560	19,527	D	30.0%	68.9%	30.3%	69.7%
17,215	ALLEGHANY	7,257	1,794	5,397	66	3,603	D	24.7%	74.4%	24.9%	75.1%
11,400	AMELIA	6,454	3,163	3,219	72	56	D	49.0%	49.9%	49.6%	50.4%
31,894	AMHERST	14,283	5,895	8,152	236	2,257	D	41.3%	57.1%	42.0%	58.0%
13,705	APPOMATTOX	7,543	2,921	4,551	71	1,630	D	38.7%	60.3%	39.1%	60.9%
189,453	ARLINGTON	108,104	24,232	82,119	1,753	57,887	D	22.4%	76.0%	22.8%	77.2%
65,615	AUGUSTA	32,176	16,750	14,963	463	1,787	R	52.1%	46.5%	52.8%	47.2%
5,048	BATH	2,390	821	1,544	25	723	D	34.4%	64.6%	34.7%	65.3%
60,371	BEDFORD COUNTY	35,225	17,084	17,862	279	778	D	48.5%	50.7%	48.9%	51.1%
6,871	BLAND	2,798	1,232	1,517	49	285	D	44.0%	54.2%	44.8%	55.2%
30,496	BOTETOURT	17,221	7,811	9,230	180	1,419	D	45.4%	53.6%	45.8%	54.2%
18,419	BRUNSWICK	7,694	1,961	5,655	78	3,694	D	25.5%	73.5%	25.7%	74.3%
26,978	BUCHANAN	8,599	2,533	6,017	49	3,484	D	29.5%	70.0%	29.6%	70.4%
15,623	BUCKINGHAM	6,904	2,229	4,581	94	2,352	D	32.3%	66.4%	32.7%	67.3%
51,078	CAMPBELL	24,841	11,499	13,016	326	1,517	D	46.3%	52.4%	46.9%	53.1%
22,121	CAROLINE	12,705	3,780	8,799	126	5,019	D	29.8%	69.3%	30.1%	69.9%
29,245	CARROLL	12,178	5,247	6,737	194	1,490	D	43.1%	55.3%	43.8%	56.2%
6,926	CHARLES CITY	4,111	967	3,105	39	2,138	D	23.5%	75.5%	23.7%	76.3%
12,472	CHARLOTTE	5,816	2,115	3,616	85	1,501	D	36.4%	62.2%	36.9%	63.1%
259,903	CHESTERFIELD	159,846	63,950	93,910	1,986	29,960	D	40.0%	58.8%	40.5%	59.5%
12,652	CLARKE	7,337	2,745	4,495	97	1,750	D	37.4%	61.3%	37.9%	62.1%
5,091	CRAIG	2,633	1,006	1,585	42	579	D	38.2%	60.2%	38.8%	61.2%
34,262	CULPEPER	19,017	7,727	11,031	259	3,304	D	40.6%	58.0%	41.2%	58.8%
9,017	CUMBERLAND	4,590	1,665	2,866	59	1,201	D	36.3%	62.4%	36.7%	63.3%
16,395	DICKENSON	6,580	2,105	4,415	60	2,310	D	32.0%	67.1%	32.3%	67.7%
24,533	DINWIDDIE	12,467	4,747	7,561	159	2,814	D	38.1%	60.6%	38.6%	61.4%
9,989	ESSEX	5,249	1,633	3,565	51	1,932	D	31.1%	67.9%	31.4%	68.6%
969,749	FAIRFAX COUNTY	509,473	157,286	345,978	6,209	188,692	D	30.9%	67.9%	31.3%	68.7%
55,139	FAUQUIER	33,796	14,707	18,725	364	4,018	D	43.5%	55.4%	44.0%	56.0%
13,874	FLOYD	7,365	2,649	4,597	119	1,948	D	36.0%	62.4%	36.6%	63.4%
20,047	FLUVANNA	12,565	4,811	7,635	119	2,824	D	38.3%	60.8%	38.7%	61.3%
47,286	FRANKLIN COUNTY	24,953	9,292	15,391	270	6,099	D	37.2%	61.7%	37.6%	62.4%
59,209	FREDERICK	33,176	14,647	18,168	361	3,521	D	44.1%	54.8%	44.6%	55.4%
16,657	GILES	7,578	2,353	5,108	117	2,755	D	31.1%	67.4%	31.5%	68.5%
34,780	GLOUCESTER	18,923	8,039	10,622	262	2,583	D	42.5%	56.1%	43.1%	56.9%
16,863	GOOCHLAND	12,396	5,472	6,777	147	1,305	D	44.1%	54.7%	44.7%	55.3%
17,917	GRAYSON	6,975	2,743	4,121	111	1,378	D	39.3%	59.1%	40.0%	60.0%
15,244	GREENE	8,101	3,711	4,293	97	582	D	45.8%	53.0%	46.4%	53.6%
11,560	GREENSVILLE	4,715	1,155	3,507	53	2,352	D	24.5%	74.4%	24.8%	75.2%
37,355	HALIFAX	15,837	5,769	9,881	187	4,112	D	36.4%	62.4%	36.9%	63.1%
86,320	HANOVER	55,519	27,559	27,218	742	341	R	49.6%	49.0%	50.3%	49.7%
262,300	HENRICO	152,375	48,286	102,465	1,624	54,179	D	31.7%	67.2%	32.0%	68.0%
57,930	HENRY	24,551	6,551	17,753	247	11,202	D	26.7%	72.3%	27.0%	73.0%
2,536	HIGHLAND	1,568	640	905	23	265	D	40.8%	57.7%	41.4%	58.6%
29,728	ISLE OF WIGHT	19,667	7,849	11,579	239	3,730	D	39.9%	58.9%	40.4%	59.6%
48,102	JAMES CITY	38,077	14,908	22,682	487	7,774	D	39.2%	59.6%	39.7%	60.3%
6,630	KING AND QUEEN	3,585	1,204	2,340	41	1,136	D	33.6%	65.3%	34.0%	66.0%
16,803	KING GEORGE	10,263	4,112	6,026	125	1,914	D	40.1%	58.7%	40.6%	59.4%
13,146	KING WILLIAM	8,249	3,436	4,719	94	1,283	D	41.7%	57.2%	42.1%	57.9%

VIRGINIA

SENATOR 2008

2000 Census Population	County	Total Vote	Republican	Democratic	Other	Rep.-Dem. Plurality	Percentage Total Vote Rep.	Dem.	Major Vote Rep.	Dem.
11,567	LANCASTER	6,741	2,602	4,072	57	1,470 D	38.6%	60.4%	39.0%	61.0%
23,589	LEE	9,000	3,411	5,507	82	2,096 D	37.9%	61.2%	38.2%	61.8%
169,599	LOUDOUN	137,034	50,962	84,470	1,632	33,508 D	37.2%	61.6%	37.6%	62.4%
25,627	LOUISA	15,080	5,859	9,020	201	3,161 D	38.9%	59.8%	39.4%	60.6%
13,146	LUNENBURG	5,540	1,932	3,542	66	1,610 D	34.9%	63.9%	35.3%	64.7%
12,520	MADISON	6,454	2,657	3,701	96	1,044 D	41.2%	57.3%	41.8%	58.2%
9,207	MATHEWS	5,351	2,228	3,070	53	842 D	41.6%	57.4%	42.1%	57.9%
32,380	MECKLENBURG	14,422	5,747	8,445	230	2,698 D	39.8%	58.6%	40.5%	59.5%
9,932	MIDDLESEX	5,906	2,510	3,325	71	815 D	42.5%	56.3%	43.0%	57.0%
83,629	MONTGOMERY	39,920	11,767	27,564	589	15,797 D	29.5%	69.0%	29.9%	70.1%
14,445	NELSON	8,056	2,412	5,581	63	3,169 D	29.9%	69.3%	30.2%	69.8%
13,462	NEW KENT	9,845	4,713	4,989	143	276 D	47.9%	50.7%	48.6%	51.4%
13,093	NORTHAMPTON	6,475	1,583	4,803	89	3,220 D	24.4%	74.2%	24.8%	75.2%
12,259	NORTHUMBERLAND	7,287	2,928	4,285	74	1,357 D	40.2%	58.8%	40.6%	59.4%
15,725	NOTTOWAY	6,364	2,123	4,142	99	2,019 D	33.4%	65.1%	33.9%	66.1%
25,881	ORANGE	15,513	6,050	9,275	188	3,225 D	39.0%	59.8%	39.5%	60.5%
23,177	PAGE	10,235	4,327	5,797	111	1,470 D	42.3%	56.6%	42.7%	57.3%
19,407	PATRICK	7,957	3,221	4,580	156	1,359 D	40.5%	57.6%	41.3%	58.7%
61,745	PITTSYLVANIA	29,009	11,557	17,092	360	5,535 D	39.8%	58.9%	40.3%	59.7%
22,377	POWHATAN	14,302	7,774	6,363	165	1,411 R	54.4%	44.5%	55.0%	45.0%
19,720	PRINCE EDWARD	8,791	2,767	5,881	143	3,114 D	31.5%	66.9%	32.0%	68.0%
33,047	PRINCE GEORGE	15,713	6,570	8,876	267	2,306 D	41.8%	56.5%	42.5%	57.5%
280,813	PRINCE WILLIAM	159,999	53,545	104,517	1,937	50,972 D	33.5%	65.3%	33.9%	66.1%
35,127	PULASKI	14,745	5,113	9,467	165	4,354 D	34.7%	64.2%	35.1%	64.9%
6,983	RAPPAHANNOCK	4,364	1,675	2,632	57	957 D	38.4%	60.3%	38.9%	61.1%
8,809	RICHMOND COUNTY	3,668	1,337	2,297	34	960 D	36.5%	62.6%	36.8%	63.2%
85,778	ROANOKE COUNTY	50,429	20,113	29,783	533	9,670 D	39.9%	59.1%	40.3%	59.7%
20,808	ROCKBRIDGE	9,986	3,771	6,098	117	2,327 D	37.8%	61.1%	38.2%	61.8%
67,725	ROCKINGHAM	32,934	17,156	15,475	303	1,681 R	52.1%	47.0%	52.6%	47.4%
30,308	RUSSELL	11,314	3,773	7,472	69	3,699 D	33.3%	66.0%	33.6%	66.4%
23,403	SCOTT	9,601	4,255	5,241	105	986 D	44.3%	54.6%	44.8%	55.2%
35,075	SHENANDOAH	18,888	8,938	9,686	264	748 D	47.3%	51.3%	48.0%	52.0%
33,081	SMYTH	12,035	4,703	7,199	133	2,496 D	39.1%	59.8%	39.5%	60.5%
17,482	SOUTHAMPTON	8,886	2,906	5,884	96	2,978 D	32.7%	66.2%	33.1%	66.9%
90,395	SPOTSYLVANIA	53,290	21,025	31,660	605	10,635 D	39.5%	59.4%	39.9%	60.1%
92,446	STAFFORD	54,522	21,695	32,150	677	10,455 D	39.8%	59.0%	40.3%	59.7%
6,829	SURRY	3,803	1,029	2,732	42	1,703 D	27.1%	71.8%	27.4%	72.6%
12,504	SUSSEX	5,159	1,281	3,817	61	2,536 D	24.8%	74.0%	25.1%	74.9%
44,598	TAZEWELL	16,002	6,583	9,194	225	2,611 D	41.1%	57.5%	41.7%	58.3%
31,584	WARREN	15,833	6,766	8,862	205	2,096 D	42.7%	56.0%	43.3%	56.7%
51,103	WASHINGTON	23,962	10,835	12,929	198	2,094 D	45.2%	54.0%	45.6%	54.4%
16,718	WESTMORELAND	7,988	2,395	5,485	108	3,090 D	30.0%	68.7%	30.4%	69.6%
40,123	WISE	13,849	5,114	8,605	130	3,491 D	36.9%	62.1%	37.3%	62.7%
27,599	WYTHE	12,367	4,899	7,325	143	2,426 D	39.6%	59.2%	40.1%	59.9%
56,297	YORK	33,399	14,599	18,389	411	3,790 D	43.7%	55.1%	44.3%	55.7%
7,078,515	TOTAL	3,643,294	1,228,830	2,369,327	45,137	1,140,497 D	33.7%	65.0%	34.2%	65.8%

VIRGINIA

SENATOR 2008

2000 Census Population	City/Town	Total Vote	Republican	Democratic	Other	Rep.-Dem. Plurality	Percentage			
							Total Vote		Major Vote	
							Rep.	Dem.	Rep.	Dem.
128,283	ALEXANDRIA	69,211	14,756	53,472	983	38,716 D	21.3%	77.3%	21.6%	78.4%
6,299	BEDFORD CITY	2,667	894	1,748	25	854 D	33.5%	65.5%	33.8%	66.2%
17,367	BRISTOL	7,179	3,031	4,060	88	1,029 D	42.2%	56.6%	42.7%	57.3%
6,349	BUENA VISTA	2,381	769	1,591	21	822 D	32.3%	66.8%	32.6%	67.4%
45,049	CHARLOTTESVILLE	19,678	2,923	16,470	285	13,547 D	14.9%	83.7%	15.1%	84.9%
199,184	CHESAPEAKE	104,873	38,304	65,527	1,042	27,223 D	36.5%	62.5%	36.9%	63.1%
16,897	COLONIAL HEIGHTS	8,623	4,405	4,076	142	329 R	51.1%	47.3%	51.9%	48.1%
6,303	COVINGTON	2,314	474	1,817	23	1,343 D	20.5%	78.5%	20.7%	79.3%
48,411	DANVILLE	19,573	5,069	14,294	210	9,225 D	25.9%	73.0%	26.2%	73.8%
5,665	EMPORIA	2,538	598	1,907	33	1,309 D	23.6%	75.1%	23.9%	76.1%
21,498	FAIRFAX CITY	11,218	3,515	7,527	176	4,012 D	31.3%	67.1%	31.8%	68.2%
10,377	FALLS CHURCH	6,674	1,550	5,022	102	3,472 D	23.2%	75.2%	23.6%	76.4%
8,346	FRANKLIN CITY	4,220	958	3,217	45	2,259 D	22.7%	76.2%	22.9%	77.1%
19,279	FREDERICKSBURG	9,486	2,233	7,100	153	4,867 D	23.5%	74.8%	23.9%	76.1%
6,837	GALAX	2,281	726	1,534	21	808 D	31.8%	67.3%	32.1%	67.9%
146,437	HAMPTON	66,214	14,149	51,193	872	37,044 D	21.4%	77.3%	21.7%	78.3%
40,468	HARRISONBURG	14,335	4,268	9,867	200	5,599 D	29.8%	68.8%	30.2%	69.8%
22,354	HOPEWELL	8,821	2,849	5,844	128	2,995 D	32.3%	66.3%	32.8%	67.2%
6,867	LEXINGTON	2,411	588	1,796	27	1,208 D	24.4%	74.5%	24.7%	75.3%
65,269	LYNCHBURG	33,723	13,489	19,852	382	6,363 D	40.0%	58.9%	40.5%	59.5%
35,135	MANASSAS	11,940	4,167	7,624	149	3,457 D	34.9%	63.9%	35.3%	64.7%
10,290	MANASSAS PARK	4,070	1,264	2,743	63	1,479 D	31.1%	67.4%	31.5%	68.5%
15,416	MARTINSVILLE	6,390	1,089	5,261	40	4,172 D	17.0%	82.3%	17.1%	82.9%
180,150	NEWPORT NEWS	79,170	20,469	57,654	1,047	37,185 D	25.9%	72.8%	26.2%	73.8%
234,403	NORFOLK	86,832	16,660	69,102	1,070	52,442 D	19.2%	79.6%	19.4%	80.6%
3,904	NORTON	1,495	398	1,076	21	678 D	26.6%	72.0%	27.0%	73.0%
33,740	PETERSBURG	15,090	1,276	13,605	209	12,329 D	8.5%	90.2%	8.6%	91.4%
11,566	POQUOSON	6,973	3,562	3,324	87	238 R	51.1%	47.7%	51.7%	48.3%
100,565	PORTSMOUTH	45,530	9,597	35,371	562	25,774 D	21.1%	77.7%	21.3%	78.7%
15,859	RADFORD	5,370	1,460	3,853	57	2,393 D	27.2%	71.8%	27.5%	72.5%
197,790	RICHMOND CITY	90,634	12,517	76,593	1,524	64,076 D	13.8%	84.5%	14.0%	86.0%
94,911	ROANOKE CITY	40,075	9,823	29,823	429	20,000 D	24.5%	74.4%	24.8%	75.2%
24,747	SALEM	12,287	4,550	7,617	120	3,067 D	37.0%	62.0%	37.4%	62.6%
23,853	STAUNTON	10,669	3,656	6,897	116	3,241 D	34.3%	64.6%	34.6%	65.4%
63,677	SUFFOLK	36,777	12,260	24,069	448	11,809 D	33.3%	65.4%	33.7%	66.3%
425,257	VIRGINIA BEACH	194,995	67,886	124,517	2,592	56,631 D	34.8%	63.9%	35.3%	64.7%
19,520	WAYNESBORO	8,691	3,549	5,039	103	1,490 D	40.8%	58.0%	41.3%	58.7%
11,998	WILLIAMSBURG	6,676	1,630	4,875	171	3,245 D	24.4%	73.0%	25.1%	74.9%
23,585	WINCHESTER	10,026	3,017	6,896	113	3,879 D	30.1%	68.8%	30.4%	69.6%
7,078,515	TOTAL	3,643,294	1,228,830	2,369,327	45,137	1,140,497 D	33.7%	65.0%	34.2%	65.8%

VIRGINIA

HOUSE OF REPRESENTATIVES

CD	Year	Total Vote	Republican		Democratic		Other Vote	Rep.-Dem. Plurality	Percentage			
									Total Vote		Major Vote	
			Vote	Candidate	Vote	Candidate			Rep.	Dem.	Rep.	Dem.
1	2008	360,292	203,839	WITTMAN, ROBERT J.*	150,432	DAY, BILL S. JR.	6,021	53,407 R	56.6%	41.8%	57.5%	42.5%
1	2006	228,534	143,889	DAVIS, JO ANN*	81,083	O'DONNELL, SHAWN M.	3,562	62,806 R	63.0%	35.5%	64.0%	36.0%
1	2004	286,534	225,071	DAVIS, JO ANN*	—		61,463	225,071 R	78.5%		100.0%	
1	2002	117,997	113,168	DAVIS, JO ANN*	—		4,829	113,168 R	95.9%		100.0%	
2	2008	270,711	128,486	DRAKE, THELMA*	141,857	NYE, GLENN C.	368	13,371 D	47.5%	52.4%	47.5%	52.5%
2	2006	173,159	88,777	DRAKE, THELMA*	83,901	KELLAM, PHILIP J.	481	4,876 R	51.3%	48.5%	51.4%	48.6%
2	2004	241,380	132,946	DRAKE, THELMA	108,180	ASHE, DAVID B.	254	24,766 R	55.1%	44.8%	55.1%	44.9%
2	2002	124,846	103,807	SCHROCK, ED*			21,039	103,807 R	83.1%		100.0%	
3	2008	247,288		—	239,911	SCOTT, ROBERT C.*	7,377	239,911 D		97.0%		100.0%
3	2006	138,994			133,546	SCOTT, ROBERT C.*	5,448	133,546 D		96.1%		100.0%
3	2004	229,892	70,194	SEARS, WINSOME E.	159,373	SCOTT, ROBERT C.*	325	89,179 D	30.5%	69.3%	30.6%	69.4%
3	2002	91,073		—	87,521	SCOTT, ROBERT C.*	3,552	87,521 D		96.1%		100.0%
4	2008	334,521	199,075	FORBES, J. RANDY*	135,041	MILLER, ANDREA R.	405	64,034 R	59.5%	40.4%	59.6%	40.4%
4	2006	198,340	150,967	FORBES, J. RANDY*	—		47,373	150,967 R	76.1%		100.0%	
4	2004	283,027	182,444	FORBES, J. RANDY*	100,413	MENEFEE, JONATHAN R.	170	82,031 R	64.5%	35.5%	64.5%	35.5%
4	2002	111,041	108,733	FORBES, J. RANDY*	—		2,308	108,733 R	97.9%		100.0%	
5	2008	317,076	158,083	GOODE, VIRGIL H. JR.*	158,810	PERRIELLO, THOMAS S. P.	183	727 D	49.9%	50.1%	49.9%	50.1%
5	2006	212,079	125,370	GOODE, VIRGIL H. JR.*	84,682	WEED, AL C. II	2,027	40,688 R	59.1%	39.9%	59.7%	40.3%
5	2004	270,758	172,431	GOODE, VIRGIL H. JR.*	98,237	WEED, AL C. II	90	74,194 R	63.7%	36.3%	63.7%	36.3%
5	2002	150,233	95,360	GOODE, VIRGIL H. JR.*	54,805	RICHARDS, MEREDITH M.	68	40,555 R	63.5%	36.5%	63.5%	36.5%
6	2008	312,392	192,350	GOODLATTE, ROBERT W.*	114,367	RASOUL, S. "SAM"	5,675	77,983 R	61.6%	36.6%	62.7%	37.3%
6	2006	203,995	153,187	GOODLATTE, ROBERT W.*	—		50,808	153,187 R	75.1%		100.0%	
6	2004	213,648	206,560	GOODLATTE, ROBERT W.*	—		7,088	206,560 R	96.7%		100.0%	
6	2002	108,732	105,530	GOODLATTE, ROBERT W.*	—		3,202	105,530 R	97.1%		100.0%	
7	2008	372,337	233,531	CANTOR, ERIC*	138,123	HARTKE, ANITA	683	95,408 R	62.7%	37.1%	62.8%	37.2%
7	2006	256,397	163,706	CANTOR, ERIC*	88,206	NACHMAN, JAMES M.	4,485	75,500 R	63.8%	34.4%	65.0%	35.0%
7	2004	305,658	230,765	CANTOR, ERIC*	—		74,893	230,765 R	75.5%		100.0%	
7	2002	163,665	113,658	CANTOR, ERIC*	49,854	JONES, BEN L. "COOTER"	153	63,804 R	69.4%	30.5%	69.5%	30.5%
8	2008	328,197	97,425	ELLMORE, MARK W.	222,986	MORAN, JAMES P.*	7,786	125,561 D	29.7%	67.9%	30.4%	69.6%
8	2006	217,909	66,639	O'DONOGHUE, TOM M.	144,700	MORAN, JAMES P.*	6,570	78,061 D	30.6%	66.4%	31.5%	68.5%
8	2004	287,919	106,231	CHENEY, LISA MARIE	171,986	MORAN, JAMES P.*	9,702	65,755 D	36.9%	59.7%	38.2%	61.8%
8	2002	171,799	64,121	TATE, SCOTT C.	102,759	MORAN, JAMES P.*	4,919	38,638 D	37.3%	59.8%	38.4%	61.6%
9	2008	213,570		—	207,306	BOUCHER, RICK*	6,264	207,306 D		97.1%		100.0%
9	2006	191,415	61,574	CARRICO, C.W. "BILL"	129,705	BOUCHER, RICK*	136	68,131 D	32.2%	67.8%	32.2%	67.8%
9	2004	252,947	98,499	TRIPLETT, KEVIN R.	150,039	BOUCHER, RICK*	4,409	51,540 D	38.9%	59.3%	39.6%	60.4%
9	2002	152,183	52,076	KATZEN, JAY K.	100,075	BOUCHER, RICK*	32	47,999 D	34.2%	65.8%	34.2%	65.8%
10	2008	379,480	223,140	WOLF, FRANK R.*	147,357	FEDER, JUDY M.	8,983	75,783 R	58.8%	38.8%	60.2%	39.8%
10	2006	241,134	138,213	WOLF, FRANK R.*	98,769	FEDER, JUDY M.	4,152	39,444 R	57.3%	41.0%	58.3%	41.7%
10	2004	323,011	205,982	WOLF, FRANK R.*	116,654	SOCAS, JAMES R.	375	89,328 R	63.8%	36.1%	63.8%	36.2%
10	2002	161,615	115,917	WOLF, FRANK R.*	45,464	STEVENS, JOHN B. JR.	234	70,453 R	71.7%	28.1%	71.8%	28.2%
11	2008	359,491	154,758	FIMIAN, KEITH S.	196,598	CONNOLLY, GERALD E.	8,135	41,840 D	43.0%	54.7%	44.0%	56.0%
11	2006	235,280	130,468	DAVIS, THOMAS M. III*	102,511	HURST, ANDREW L.	2,301	27,957 R	55.5%	43.6%	56.0%	44.0%
11	2004	309,233	186,299	DAVIS, THOMAS M. III*	118,305	LONGMYER, KEN	4,629	67,994 R	60.2%	38.3%	61.2%	38.8%
11	2002	163,298	135,379	DAVIS, THOMAS M. III*	—		27,919	135,379 R	82.9%		100.0%	
TOTAL	2008	3,495,355	1,590,687		1,852,788		51,880	262,101 D	45.5%	53.0%	46.2%	53.8%
TOTAL	2006	2,297,236	1,222,790		947,103		127,343	275,687 R	53.2%	41.2%	56.4%	43.6%
TOTAL	2004	3,004,007	1,817,422		1,023,187		163,398	794,235 R	60.5%	34.1%	64.0%	36.0%
TOTAL	2002	1,516,482	1,007,749		440,478		68,255	567,271 R	66.5%	29.0%	69.6%	30.4%

Note: An asterisk (*) denotes incumbent.

VIRGINIA

GENERAL AND PRIMARY ELECTIONS

2008 GENERAL ELECTIONS

President   Other vote was 11,483 Independent (Ralph Nader); 11,067 Libertarian (Bob Barr); 7,474 Independent Green (Chuck Baldwin); 2,344 Green (Cynthia A. McKinney); 38 write-in (Alan Keyes); 13 write-in (Brian Moore); 2 write-in (Jonathan Allen); 1 write-in (Keith Russell Judd); 6,301 scattered write-in.

Senator   Other vote was 21,690 Independent Green (Glenda Gail Parker); 20,269 Libertarian (William B. Redpath); 3,178 scattered write-in.

House   Other vote was:

CD 1	5,265 Independent (Nathan D. Larson); 756 scattered write-in.
CD 2	368 scattered write-in.
CD 3	7,377 scattered write-in.
CD 4	405 scattered write-in.
CD 5	183 scattered write-in.
CD 6	5,413 Independent (Janice Lee Allen); 262 scattered write-in.
CD 7	683 scattered write-in.
CD 8	6,829 Independent Green (J. Ron Fisher); 957 scattered write-in.
CD 9	6,264 scattered write-in.
CD 10	8,457 Independent (Neeraj C. Nigam); 526 scattered write-in.
CD 11	7,271 Independent Green (Joseph P. Oddo); 864 scattered write-in.

2008 PRIMARY ELECTIONS

Primary   February 12, 2008 (President)   **Registration**   4,698,385   No Party Registration
June 10, 2008 (Congress)   (as of May 31, 2008)

Primary Type   Open—Any registered voter could participate in the primary of either party.

	REPUBLICAN PRIMARIES			DEMOCRATIC PRIMARIES		
President	John McCain	244,829	50.0%	Barack Obama	627,820	63.7%
	Mike Huckabee	199,003	40.7%	Hillary Clinton	349,766	35.5%
	Ron Paul	21,999	4.5%	John Edwards	5,206	0.5%
	Mitt Romney	18,002	3.7%	Dennis J. Kucinich	1,625	0.2%
	Fred Thompson	3,395	0.7%	Bill Richardson	991	0.1%
	Rudolph Giuliani	2,024	0.4%	Joseph R. Biden Jr.	795	0.1%
	TOTAL	489,252		TOTAL	986,203	
Senator	James S. "Jim" Gilmore III	Nominated by convention		Mark R. Warner	Unopposed	
Congressional District 1	Robert J. Wittman*	Unopposed		Bill S. Day Jr.	Nominated by convention	
Congressional District 2	Thelma Drake*	Unopposed		Glenn C. Nye	Unopposed	
Congressional District 3	No Republican candidate	Robert C. Scott*		Unopposed		
Congressional District 4	J. Randy Forbes*	Unopposed		Andrea R. Miller	Nominated by convention	
Congressional District 5	Virgil H. Goode Jr.*	Unopposed		Tom S. P. Perriello	Nominated by convention	

VIRGINIA

GENERAL AND PRIMARY ELECTIONS

	REPUBLICAN PRIMARIES			DEMOCRATIC PRIMARIES		
Congressional District 6	Robert W. Goodlatte*	Unopposed		S. "Sam" Rasoul	Nominated by convention	
Congressional District 7	Eric Cantor*	Unopposed		Anita Hartke	Unopposed	
Congressional District 8	Mark W. Ellmore	3,286	56.0%	James P. Moran*	11,792	87.0%
	Amit K. Singh	2,577	44.0%	Matthew T. Famiglietti	1,764	13.0%
	TOTAL	5,863		TOTAL	13,556	
Congressional District 9	No Republican candidate			Rick Boucher*	Nominated by convention	
Congressional District 10	Frank R. Wolf*	16,726	91.7%	Judy M. Feder	5,462	61.8%
	Vern P. McKinley	1,506	8.3%	Mike R. Turner	3,377	38.2%
	TOTAL	18,232		TOTAL	8,839	
Congressional District 11	Keith S. Fimian	Unopposed		Gerald E. Connolly	14,233	57.9%
				Leslie L. Byrne	8,196	33.4%
				Douglas J. Denneny	1,508	6.1%
				Lori P. Alexander	638	2.6%
				TOTAL	24,575	

Note: An asterisk (*) denotes incumbent. The state parties and local party committees traditionally have the option of holding a primary or nominating candidates by convention or committee. If a primary was called and only one candidate filed to run in it, then ro primary was held.

WASHINGTON

Congressional districts first established for elections held in 2002
9 members

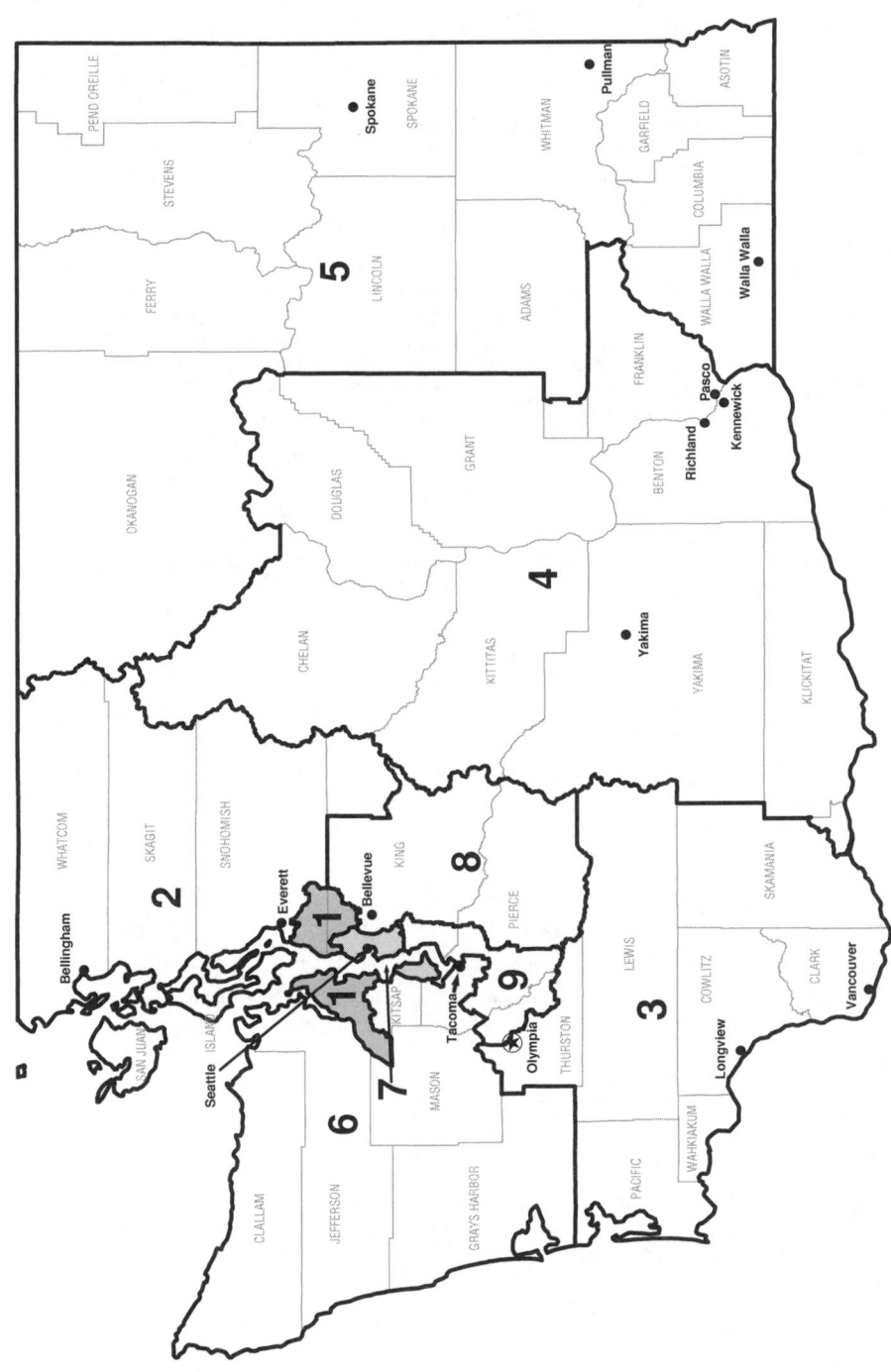

WASHINGTON

Seattle, Puget Sound Area

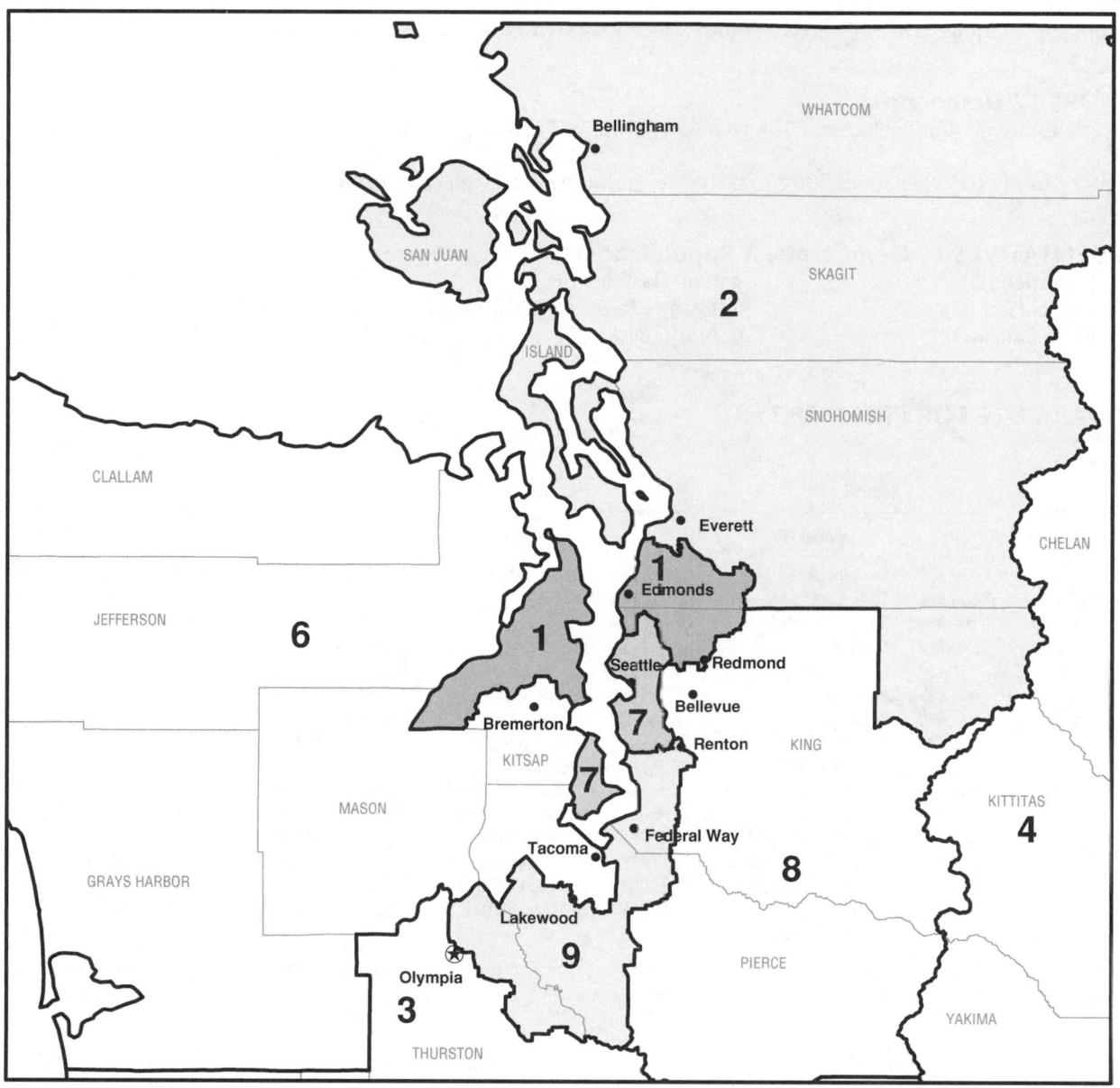

WASHINGTON

GOVERNOR
Christine Gregoire (D). Reelected 2008 to a four-year term. Previously elected 2004.

SENATORS (2 Democrats)
Maria Cantwell (D). Reelected 2006 to a six-year term. Previously elected 2000.

Patty Murray (D). Reelected 2004 to a six-year term. Previously elected 1998, 1992.

REPRESENTATIVES (6 Democrats, 3 Republicans)
1. Jay Inslee (D)
2. Rick Larsen (D)
3. Brian Baird (D)
4. Doc Hastings (R)
5. Cathy McMorris Rodgers (R)
6. Norm Dicks (D)
7. Jim McDermott (D)
8. Dave Reichert (R)
9. Adam Smith (D)

POSTWAR VOTE FOR PRESIDENT

		Republican		Democratic				Total Vote		Major Vote	
Year	Total Vote	Vote	Candidate	Vote	Candidate	Other Vote	Plurality	Rep.	Dem.	Rep.	Dem.
2008	3,036,878	1,229,216	McCain, John	1,750,848	Obama, Barack	56,814	521,632 D	40.5%	57.7%	41.2%	58.8%
2004	2,859,084	1,304,894	Bush, George W.	1,510,201	Kerry, John	43,989	205,307 D	45.6%	52.8%	46.4%	53.6%
2000**	2,487,433	1,108,864	Bush, George W.	1,247,652	Gore, Al	130,917	138,788 D	44.6%	50.2%	47.1%	52.9%
1996**	2,253,837	840,712	Dole, Bob	1,123,323	Clinton, Bill	289,802	282,611 D	37.3%	49.8%	42.8%	57.2%
1992**	2,288,230	731,234	Bush, George	993,037	Clinton, Bill	563,959	261,803 D	32.0%	43.4%	42.4%	57.6%
1988	1,865,253	903,835	Bush, George	933,516	Dukakis, Michael S.	27,902	29,681 D	48.5%	50.0%	49.2%	50.8%
1984	1,883,910	1,051,670	Reagan, Ronald	807,352	Mondale, Walter F.	24,888	244,318 R	55.8%	42.9%	56.6%	43.4%
1980**	1,742,394	865,244	Reagan, Ronald	650,193	Carter, Jimmy	226,957	215,051 R	49.7%	37.3%	57.1%	42.9%
1976	1,555,534	777,732	Ford, Gerald R.	717,323	Carter, Jimmy	60,479	60,409 R	50.0%	46.1%	52.0%	48.0%
1972	1,470,847	837,135	Nixon, Richard M.	568,334	McGovern, George S.	65,378	268,801 R	56.9%	38.6%	59.6%	40.4%
1968**	1,304,281	588,510	Nixon, Richard M.	616,037	Humphrey, Hubert H.	99,734	27,527 D	45.1%	47.2%	48.9%	51.1%
1964	1,258,556	470,366	Goldwater, Barry M.	779,881	Johnson, Lyndon B.	8,309	309,515 D	37.4%	62.0%	37.6%	62.4%
1960	1,241,572	629,273	Nixon, Richard M.	599,298	Kennedy, John F.	13,001	29,975 R	50.7%	48.3%	51.2%	48.8%
1956	1,150,889	620,430	Eisenhower, Dwight D.	523,002	Stevenson, Adlai E.	7,457	97,428 R	53.9%	45.4%	54.3%	45.7%
1952	1,102,708	599,107	Eisenhower, Dwight D.	492,845	Stevenson, Adlai E.	10,756	106,262 R	54.3%	44.7%	54.9%	45.1%
1948	905,058	386,314	Dewey, Thomas E.	476,165	Truman, Harry S.	42,579	89,851 D	42.7%	52.6%	44.8%	55.2%

**In past elections, the other vote included: 2000 - 103,002 Green (Ralph Nader); 1996 - 201,003 Reform (Ross Perot); 1992 - 541,780 Independent (Perot); 1980 - 185,073 Independent (John Anderson); 1968 - 96,990 American Independent (George Wallace).

WASHINGTON

POSTWAR VOTE FOR GOVERNOR

Year	Total Vote	Republican Vote	Candidate	Democratic Vote	Candidate	Other Vote	Rep.-Dem. Plurality	Total Vote Rep.	Dem.	Major Vote Rep.	Dem.
2008	3,002,862	1,404,124	Rossi, Dino	1,598,738	Gregoire, Christine		194,614 D	46.8%	53.2%	46.8%	53.2%
2004**	2,810,058	1,373,232	Rossi, Dino	1,373,361	Gregoire, Christine	63,465	129 D	48.9%	48.9%	50.0%	50.0%
2000	2,469,852	980,060	Carlson, John	1,441,973	Locke, Gary	47,819	461,913 D	39.7%	58.4%	40.5%	59.5%
1996	2,237,030	940,538	Craswell, Ellen	1,296,492	Locke, Gary		355,954 D	42.0%	58.0%	42.0%	58.0%
1992	2,270,826	1,086,216	Eikenberry, Ken	1,184,315	Lowry, Mike	295	98,099 D	47.8%	52.2%	47.8%	52.2%
1988	1,874,929	708,481	Williams, Bob	1,166,448	Gardner, Booth		457,967 D	37.8%	62.2%	37.8%	62.2%
1984	1,888,987	881,994	Spellman, John D.	1,006,993	Gardner, Booth		124,999 D	46.7%	53.3%	46.7%	53.3%
1980	1,730,896	981,083	Spellman, John D.	749,813	McDermott, James A.		231,270 R	56.7%	43.3%	56.7%	43.3%
1976	1,546,382	687,039	Spellman, John D.	821,797	Ray, Dixy Lee	37,546	134,758 D	44.4%	53.1%	45.5%	54.5%
1972	1,472,542	747,825	Evans, Daniel J.	630,613	Rosellini, Albert D.	94,104	117,212 R	50.8%	42.8%	54.3%	45.7%
1968	1,265,355	692,378	Evans, Daniel J.	560,262	O'Connell, John J.	12,715	132,116 R	54.7%	44.3%	55.3%	44.7%
1964	1,250,274	697,256	Evans, Daniel J.	548,692	Rosellini, Albert D.	4,326	148,564 R	55.8%	43.9%	56.0%	44.0%
1960	1,215,748	594,122	Andrews, Lloyd J.	611,987	Rosellini, Albert D.	9,639	17,865 D	48.9%	50.3%	49.3%	50.7%
1956	1,128,977	508,041	Anderson, Emmett T.	616,773	Rosellini, Albert D.	4,163	108,732 D	45.0%	54.6%	45.2%	54.8%
1952	1,078,497	567,822	Langlie, Arthur B.	510,675	Mitchell, Hugh B.		57,147 R	52.6%	47.4%	52.6%	47.4%
1948	883,141	445,958	Langlie, Arthur B.	417,035	Wallgren, Mon C.	20,148	28,923 R	50.5%	47.2%	51.7%	48.3%

**In 2004, the initial official vote count put Republican Dino Rossi ahead by 261 votes. A machine recount reduced Rossi's margin to 42 votes. A subsequent manual recount gave Democrat Christine Gregoire the election by a margin of 129 votes, and she was inaugurated governor.

POSTWAR VOTE FOR SENATOR

Year	Total Vote	Republican Vote	Candidate	Democratic Vote	Candidate	Other Vote	Rep.-Dem. Plurality	Total Vote Rep.	Dem.	Major Vote Rep.	Dem.
2006	2,083,734	832,106	McGavick, Mike	1,184,659	Cantwell, Maria	66,969	352,553 D	39.9%	56.9%	41.3%	58.7%
2004	2,818,651	1,204,584	Nethercutt, George	1,549,708	Murray, Patty	64,359	345,124 D	42.7%	55.0%	43.7%	56.3%
2000	2,461,379	1,197,208	Gorton, Slade	1,199,437	Cantwell, Maria	64,734	2,229 D	48.6%	48.7%	50.0%	50.0%
1998	1,888,561	785,377	Smith, Linda	1,103,184	Murray, Patty		317,807 D	41.6%	58.4%	41.6%	58.4%
1994	1,700,173	947,821	Gorton, Slade	752,352	Sims, Ron		195,469 R	55.7%	44.3%	55.7%	44.3%
1992	2,219,162	1,020,829	Chandler, Rod	1,197,973	Murray, Patty	360	177,144 D	46.0%	54.0%	46.0%	54.0%
1988	1,848,542	944,359	Gorton, Slade	904,183	Lowry, Mike		40,176 R	51.1%	48.9%	51.1%	48.9%
1986	1,337,367	650,931	Gorton, Slade	677,471	Adams, Brock	8,965	26,540 D	48.7%	50.7%	49.0%	51.0%
1983S	1,213,307	672,326	Evans, Daniel J.	540,981	Lowry, Mike		131,345 R	55.4%	44.6%	55.4%	44.6%
1982	1,368,476	332,273	Jewett, Doug	943,655	Jackson, Henry M.	92,548	611,382 D	24.3%	69.0%	26.0%	74.0%
1980	1,728,369	936,317	Gorton, Slade	792,052	Magnuson, Warren G.		144,265 R	54.2%	45.8%	54.2%	45.8%
1976	1,491,111	361,546	Brown, George M.	1,071,219	Jackson, Henry M.	58,346	709,673 D	24.2%	71.8%	25.2%	74.8%
1974	1,007,847	363,626	Metcalf, Jack	611,811	Magnuson, Warren G.	32,410	248,185 D	36.1%	60.7%	37.3%	62.7%
1970	1,066,807	170,790	Elicker, Charles W.	879,385	Jackson, Henry M.	16,632	708,595 D	16.0%	82.4%	16.3%	83.7%
1968	1,236,063	435,894	Metcalf, Jack	796,183	Magnuson, Warren G.	3,986	360,289 D	35.3%	64.4%	35.4%	64.6%
1964	1,213,088	337,138	Andrews, Lloyd J.	875,950	Jackson, Henry M.		538,812 D	27.8%	72.2%	27.8%	72.2%
1962	943,229	446,204	Christensen, Richard G.	491,365	Magnuson, Warren G.	5,660	45,161 D	47.3%	52.1%	47.6%	52.4%
1958	886,822	278,271	Bantz, William B.	597,040	Jackson, Henry M.	11,511	318,769 D	31.4%	67.3%	31.8%	68.2%
1956	1,122,217	436,652	Langlie, Arthur B.	685,565	Magnuson, Warren G.		248,913 D	38.9%	61.1%	38.9%	61.1%
1952	1,058,735	460,884	Cain, Harry P.	595,288	Jackson, Henry M.	2,563	134,404 D	43.5%	56.2%	43.6%	56.4%
1950	744,783	342,464	Williams, Walter	397,719	Magnuson, Warren G.	4,600	55,255 D	46.0%	53.4%	46.3%	53.7%
1946	660,342	358,847	Cain, Harry P.	298,683	Mitchell, Hugh B.	2,812	60,164 R	54.3%	45.2%	54.6%	45.4%

Note: The 1983 election was for a short term to fill a vacancy.

WASHINGTON

PRESIDENT 2008

2000 Census Population	County	Total Vote	Republican	Democratic	Other	Rep.-Dem. Plurality	Percentage Total Vote Rep.	Dem.	Major Vote Rep.	Dem.
16,428	ADAMS	4,858	3,222	1,552	84	1,670 R	66.3%	31.9%	67.5%	32.5%
20,551	ASOTIN	9,780	5,451	4,139	190	1,312 R	55.7%	42.3%	56.8%	43.2%
142,475	BENTON	72,911	45,345	26,288	1,278	19,057 R	62.2%	36.1%	63.3%	36.7%
66,616	CHELAN	31,958	17,605	13,781	572	3,824 R	55.1%	43.1%	56.1%	43.9%
64,525	CLALLAM	38,519	18,199	19,470	850	1,271 D	47.2%	50.5%	48.3%	51.7%
345,238	CLARK	182,764	84,212	95,356	3,196	11,144 D	46.1%	52.2%	46.9%	53.1%
4,064	COLUMBIA	2,228	1,499	686	43	813 R	67.3%	30.8%	68.6%	31.4%
92,948	COWLITZ	45,229	19,554	24,597	1,078	5,043 D	43.2%	54.4%	44.3%	55.7%
32,603	DOUGLAS	15,209	9,098	5,848	263	3,250 R	59.8%	38.5%	60.9%	39.1%
7,260	FERRY	3,501	1,916	1,467	118	449 R	54.7%	41.9%	56.6%	43.4%
49,347	FRANKLIN	19,696	12,037	7,361	298	4,676 R	61.1%	37.4%	62.1%	37.9%
2,397	GARFIELD	1,373	968	385	20	583 R	70.5%	28.0%	71.5%	28.5%
74,698	GRANT	27,438	17,153	9,601	684	7,552 R	62.5%	35.0%	64.1%	35.9%
67,194	GRAYS HARBOR	29,184	12,104	16,354	726	4,250 D	41.5%	56.0%	42.5%	57.5%
71,558	ISLAND	42,159	19,426	22,058	675	2,632 D	46.1%	52.3%	46.8%	53.2%
25,953	JEFFERSON	19,991	6,330	13,252	409	6,922 D	31.7%	66.3%	32.3%	67.7%
1,737,034	KING	922,032	259,716	648,230	14,086	388,514 D	28.2%	70.3%	28.6%	71.4%
231,969	KITSAP	124,337	53,297	68,624	2,416	15,327 D	42.9%	55.2%	43.7%	56.3%
33,362	KITTITAS	17,868	9,471	8,030	367	1,441 R	53.0%	44.9%	54.1%	45.9%
19,161	KLICKITAT	10,164	4,944	4,965	255	21 D	48.6%	48.8%	49.9%	50.1%
68,600	LEWIS	34,705	20,278	13,624	803	6,654 R	58.4%	39.3%	59.8%	40.2%
10,184	LINCOLN	5,977	3,803	2,032	142	1,771 R	63.6%	34.0%	65.2%	34.8%
49,405	MASON	28,306	12,600	15,050	656	2,450 D	44.5%	53.2%	45.6%	54.4%
39,564	OKANOGAN	16,870	8,798	7,613	459	1,185 R	52.2%	45.1%	53.6%	46.4%
20,984	PACIFIC	10,937	4,555	6,094	288	1,539 D	41.6%	55.7%	42.8%	57.2%
11,732	PEND OREILLE	6,552	3,717	2,562	273	1,155 R	56.7%	39.1%	59.2%	40.8%
700,820	PIERCE	329,520	141,673	181,824	6,023	40,151 D	43.0%	55.2%	43.8%	56.2%
14,077	SAN JUAN	10,531	2,958	7,374	199	4,416 D	28.1%	70.0%	28.6%	71.4%
102,979	SKAGIT	55,886	24,687	30,053	1,146	5,366 D	44.2%	53.8%	45.1%	54.9%
9,872	SKAMANIA	5,490	2,524	2,817	149	293 D	46.0%	51.3%	47.3%	52.7%
606,024	SNOHOMISH	320,333	126,722	187,294	6,317	60,572 D	39.6%	58.5%	40.4%	59.6%
417,939	SPOKANE	219,511	108,314	105,786	5,411	2,528 R	49.3%	48.2%	50.6%	49.4%
40,066	STEVENS	22,341	13,132	8,499	710	4,633 R	58.8%	38.0%	60.7%	39.3%
207,355	THURSTON	126,709	48,366	75,882	2,461	27,516 D	38.2%	59.9%	38.9%	61.1%
3,824	WAHKIAKUM	2,294	1,105	1,121	68	16 D	48.2%	48.9%	49.6%	50.4%
55,180	WALLA WALLA	24,727	14,182	10,081	464	4,101 R	57.4%	40.8%	58.5%	41.5%
166,814	WHATCOM	100,339	40,205	58,236	1,898	18,031 D	40.1%	58.0%	40.8%	59.2%
40,740	WHITMAN	17,589	8,104	9,070	415	966 D	46.1%	51.6%	47.2%	52.8%
222,581	YAKIMA	77,062	41,946	33,792	1,324	8,154 R	54.4%	43.9%	55.4%	44.6%
5,894,121	TOTAL	3,036,878	1,229,216	1,750,848	56,814	521,632 D	40.5%	57.7%	41.2%	58.8%

WASHINGTON
GOVERNOR 2008

2000 Census Population	County	Total Vote	Republican	Democratic	Other	Rep.-Dem. Plurality	Percentage Total Vote Rep.	Dem.	Major Vote Rep.	Dem.
16,428	ADAMS	4,816	3,363	1,453		1,910 R	69.8%	30.2%	69.8%	30.2%
20,551	ASOTIN	9,686	5,432	4,254		1,178 R	56.1%	43.9%	56.1%	43.9%
142,475	BENTON	72,603	50,635	21,968		28,667 R	69.7%	30.3%	69.7%	30.3%
66,616	CHELAN	31,817	19,730	12,087		7,643 R	62.0%	38.0%	62.0%	38.0%
64,525	CLALLAM	38,418	19,431	18,987		444 R	50.6%	49.4%	50.6%	49.4%
345,238	CLARK	178,984	91,301	87,683		3,618 R	51.0%	49.0%	51.0%	49.0%
4,064	COLUMBIA	2,243	1,537	706		831 R	68.5%	31.5%	68.5%	31.5%
92,948	COWLITZ	44,677	23,954	20,723		3,231 R	53.6%	46.4%	53.6%	46.4%
32,603	DOUGLAS	15,141	10,013	5,128		4,885 R	66.1%	33.9%	66.1%	33.9%
7,260	FERRY	3,470	2,140	1,330		810 R	61.7%	38.3%	61.7%	38.3%
49,347	FRANKLIN	19,641	13,276	6,365		6,911 R	67.6%	32.4%	67.6%	32.4%
2,397	GARFIELD	1,356	922	434		488 R	68.0%	32.0%	68.0%	32.0%
74,698	GRANT	27,336	18,604	8,732		9,872 R	68.1%	31.9%	68.1%	31.9%
67,194	GRAYS HARBOR	29,136	13,407	15,729		2,322 D	46.0%	54.0%	46.0%	54.0%
71,558	ISLAND	41,579	20,688	20,891		203 D	49.8%	50.2%	49.8%	50.2%
25,953	JEFFERSON	19,788	7,200	12,588		5,388 D	36.4%	63.6%	36.4%	63.6%
1,737,034	KING	909,177	325,820	583,357		257,537 D	35.8%	64.2%	35.8%	64.2%
231,969	KITSAP	123,134	60,656	62,478		1,822 D	49.3%	50.7%	49.3%	50.7%
33,362	KITTITAS	17,720	10,732	6,988		3,744 R	60.6%	39.4%	60.6%	39.4%
19,161	KLICKITAT	9,992	5,454	4,538		916 R	54.6%	45.4%	54.6%	45.4%
68,600	LEWIS	34,630	22,347	12,283		10,064 R	64.5%	35.5%	64.5%	35.5%
10,184	LINCOLN	5,920	3,868	2,052		1,816 R	65.3%	34.7%	65.3%	34.7%
49,405	MASON	28,123	14,181	13,942		239 R	50.4%	49.6%	50.4%	49.6%
39,564	OKANOGAN	16,743	10,168	6,575		3,593 R	60.7%	39.3%	60.7%	39.3%
20,984	PACIFIC	10,893	5,198	5,695		497 D	47.7%	52.3%	47.7%	52.3%
11,732	PEND OREILLE	6,483	3,912	2,571		1,341 R	60.3%	39.7%	60.3%	39.7%
700,820	PIERCE	325,925	159,363	166,562		7,199 D	48.9%	51.1%	48.9%	51.1%
14,077	SAN JUAN	10,400	3,356	7,044		3,688 D	32.3%	67.7%	32.3%	67.7%
102,979	SKAGIT	55,460	27,545	27,915		370 D	49.7%	50.3%	49.7%	50.3%
9,872	SKAMANIA	5,377	2,813	2,564		249 R	52.3%	47.7%	52.3%	47.7%
606,024	SNOHOMISH	317,380	150,205	167,175		16,970 D	47.3%	52.7%	47.3%	52.7%
417,939	SPOKANE	216,939	112,570	104,369		8,201 R	51.9%	48.1%	51.9%	48.1%
40,066	STEVENS	22,189	14,418	7,771		6,647 R	65.0%	35.0%	65.0%	35.0%
207,355	THURSTON	125,532	52,880	72,652		19,772 D	42.1%	57.9%	42.1%	57.9%
3,824	WAHKIAKUM	2,290	1,330	960		370 R	58.1%	41.9%	58.1%	41.9%
55,180	WALLA WALLA	24,542	15,137	9,405		5,732 R	61.7%	38.3%	61.7%	38.3%
166,814	WHATCOM	99,224	44,975	54,249		9,274 D	45.3%	54.7%	45.3%	54.7%
40,740	WHITMAN	17,259	8,896	8,363		533 R	51.5%	48.5%	51.5%	48.5%
222,581	YAKIMA	76,839	46,667	30,172		16,495 R	60.7%	39.3%	60.7%	39.3%
5,894,121	TOTAL	3,002,862	1,404,124	1,598,738		194,614 D	46.8%	53.2%	46.8%	53.2%

WASHINGTON

HOUSE OF REPRESENTATIVES

CD	Year	Total Vote	Republican Vote	Republican Candidate	Democratic Vote	Democratic Candidate	Other Vote	Rep.-Dem. Plurality	Total Vote Rep.	Total Vote Dem.	Major Vote Rep.	Major Vote Dem.
1	2008	345,020	111,240	ISHMAEL, LARRY W.	233,780	INSLEE, JAY*		122,540 D	32.2%	67.8%	32.2%	67.8%
1	2006	241,937	78,105	ISHMAEL, LARRY W.	163,832	INSLEE, JAY*		85,727 D	32.3%	67.7%	32.3%	67.7%
1	2004	327,769	117,850	EASTWOOD, RANDY	204,121	INSLEE, JAY*	5,798	86,271 D	36.0%	62.3%	36.6%	63.4%
1	2002	205,034	84,696	MARINE, JOE	114,087	INSLEE, JAY*	6,251	29,391 D	41.3%	55.6%	42.6%	57.4%
2	2008	348,467	131,051	BART, RICK	217,416	LARSEN, RICK*		86,365 D	37.6%	62.4%	37.6%	62.4%
2	2006	244,794	87,730	ROULSTONE, DOUG	157,064	LARSEN, RICK*		69,334 D	35.8%	64.2%	35.8%	64.2%
2	2004	316,682	106,333	SINCLAIR, SUZANNE	202,383	LARSEN, RICK*	7,966	96,050 D	33.6%	63.9%	34.4%	65.6%
2	2002	202,150	92,528	SMITH, NORMA	101,219	LARSEN, RICK*	8,403	8,691 D	45.8%	50.1%	47.8%	52.2%
3	2008	338,529	121,828	DELAVAR, MICHAEL	216,701	BAIRD, BRIAN*		94,873 D	36.0%	64.0%	36.0%	64.0%
3	2006	232,980	85,915	MESSMORE, MICHAEL	147,065	BAIRD, BRIAN*		61,150 D	36.9%	63.1%	36.9%	63.1%
3	2004	312,653	119,027	CROWSON, THOMAS A.	193,626	BAIRD, BRIAN*		74,599 D	38.1%	61.9%	38.1%	61.9%
3	2002	193,329	74,065	ZARELLI, JOSEPH	119,264	BAIRD, BRIAN*		45,199 D	38.3%	61.7%	38.3%	61.7%
4	2008	269,370	169,940	HASTINGS, DOC*	99,430	FEARING, GEORGE		70,510 R	63.1%	36.9%	63.1%	36.9%
4	2006	192,300	115,246	HASTINGS, DOC*	77,054	WRIGHT, RICHARD		38,192 R	59.9%	40.1%	59.9%	40.1%
4	2004	247,113	154,627	HASTINGS, DOC*	92,486	MATHESON, SANDY		62,141 R	62.6%	37.4%	62.6%	37.4%
4	2002	161,829	108,257	HASTINGS, DOC*	53,572	MASON, CRAIG		54,685 R	66.9%	33.1%	66.9%	33.1%
5	2008	323,687	211,305	McMORRIS RODGERS, CATHY*	112,382	MAYS, MARK		98,923 R	65.3%	34.7%	65.3%	34.7%
5	2006	239,324	134,967	McMORRIS, CATHY*	104,357	GOLDMARK, PETER J.		30,610 R	56.4%	43.6%	56.4%	43.6%
5	2004	300,933	179,600	McMORRIS, CATHY	121,333	BARBIERI, DON		58,267 R	59.7%	40.3%	59.7%	40.3%
5	2002	202,282	126,757	NETHERCUTT, GEORGE*	65,146	HAGGIN, BART	10,379	61,611 R	62.7%	32.2%	66.1%	33.9%
6	2008	308,072	102,081	CLOUD, DOUG	205,991	DICKS, NORM*		103,910 D	33.1%	66.9%	33.1%	66.9%
6	2006	224,085	65,883	CLOUD, DOUG	158,202	DICKS, NORM*		92,319 D	29.4%	70.6%	29.4%	70.6%
6	2004	294,147	91,228	CLOUD, DOUG	202,919	DICKS, NORM*		111,691 D	31.0%	69.0%	31.0%	69.0%
6	2002	196,444	61,584	LAWRENCE, BOB	126,116	DICKS, NORM*	8,744	64,532 D	31.3%	64.2%	32.8%	67.2%
7	2008	349,017	57,054	BEREN, STEVE	291,963	McDERMOTT, JIM*		234,909 D	16.3%	83.7%	16.3%	83.7%
7	2006	246,133	38,715	BEREN, STEVE	195,462	McDERMOTT, JIM*	11,956	156,747 D	15.7%	79.4%	16.5%	83.5%
7	2004	337,528	65,226	CASSADY, CAROL	272,302	McDERMOTT, JIM*		207,076 D	19.3%	80.7%	19.3%	80.7%
7	2002	211,003	46,256	CASSADY, CAROL	156,300	McDERMOTT, JIM*	8,447	110,044 D	21.9%	74.1%	22.8%	77.2%
8	2008	362,926	191,568	REICHERT, DAVE*	171,358	BURNER, DARCY		20,210 R	52.8%	47.2%	52.8%	47.2%
8	2006	251,383	129,362	REICHERT, DAVE*	122,021	BURNER, DARCY		7,341 R	51.5%	48.5%	51.5%	48.5%
8	2004	336,499	173,298	REICHERT, DAVE	157,148	ROSS, DAVE	6,053	16,150 R	51.5%	46.7%	52.4%	47.6%
8	2002	203,335	121,633	DUNN, JENNIFER*	75,931	BEHRENS-BENEDICT, HEIDI	5,771	45,702 R	59.8%	37.3%	61.6%	38.4%
9	2008	269,375	93,080	POSTMA, JAMES	176,295	SMITH, ADAM*		83,215 D	34.6%	65.4%	34.6%	65.4%
9	2006	181,120	62,082	COFCHIN, STEVEN C.	119,038	SMITH, ADAM*		56,956 D	34.3%	65.7%	34.3%	65.7%
9	2004	256,671	88,304	LORD, PAUL J.	162,433	SMITH, ADAM*	5,934	74,129 D	34.4%	63.3%	35.2%	64.8%
9	2002	163,710	63,146	CASADA, SARAH	95,805	SMITH, ADAM*	4,759	32,659 D	38.6%	58.5%	39.7%	60.3%
TOTAL	2008	2,914,463	1,189,147		1,725,316			536,169 D	40.8%	59.2%	40.8%	59.2%
TOTAL	2006	2,054,056	798,005		1,244,095		11,956	446,090 D	38.9%	60.6%	39.1%	60.9%
TOTAL	2004	2,729,995	1,095,493		1,608,751		25,751	513,258 D	40.1%	58.9%	40.5%	59.5%
TOTAL	2002	1,739,116	778,922		907,440		52,754	128,518 D	44.8%	52.2%	46.2%	53.8%

Note: An asterisk (*) denotes incumbent.

WASHINGTON

GENERAL AND PRIMARY ELECTIONS

2008 GENERAL ELECTIONS

President   Other vote was 29,489 Independent (Ralph Nader); 12,728 Libertarian (Bob Barr); 9,432 Constitution (Chuck Baldwin); 3,819 Green (Cynthia A. McKinney); 705 Socialism and Liberation (Gloria La Riva); 641 Socialist Workers (James E. Harris).

Governor

House   Other vote was:

CD 1
CD 2
CD 3
CD 4
CD 5
CD 6
CD 7
CD 8
CD 9

2008 PRIMARY ELECTIONS

Primary   February 19, 2008 (President)   Registration   3,417,355   No Party Registration
August 19, 2008 (Congress)   (as of August 19, 2008)

Primary Type   Open—Any registered voter could participate in the primary.

	REPUBLICAN PRIMARIES			DEMOCRATIC PRIMARIES		
President	John McCain	262,304	49.5%	Barack Obama	354,112	51.2%
	Mike Huckabee	127,657	24.1%	Hillary Clinton	315,744	45.7%
	Mitt Romney	86,140	16.3%	John Edwards	11,892	1.7%
	Ron Paul	40,539	7.6%	Dennis J. Kucinich	4,021	0.6%
	Rudolph Giuliani	5,145	1.0%	Bill Richardson	2,040	0.3%
	Fred Thompson	4,865	0.9%	Joseph R. Biden Jr.	1,883	0.3%
	Alan Keyes	2,226	0.4%	Mike Gravel	1,071	0.2%
	Duncan Hunter	1,056	0.2%	Christopher J. Dodd	618	0.1%
	TOTAL	*529,932*		*TOTAL*	*691,381*	

	ALL-PARTY PRIMARIES		
Governor	Christine Gregoire (D)*#	696,306	48.3%
	Dino Rossi (R)#	668,571	46.3%
	John W. Aiken Jr. (R)	21,564	1.5%
	Christian Pierre Joubert (D)	16,646	1.2%
	James White (Independent Party)	10,884	0.8%
	Duff Badgley (Green)	9,702	0.7%
	Christopher A. Tudor (No Party)	5,600	0.4%
	Will Baker (Reform)	5,201	0.4%
	Javier O. Lopez (R)	4,981	0.3%
	Mohammad Hasan Said (No Party)	3,002	0.2%
	TOTAL	*1,442,457*	
Congressional District 1	Jay Inslee (D)*#	104,342	66.4%
	Larry W. Ishmael (R)#	52,700	33.6%
	TOTAL	*157,042*	

WASHINGTON

GENERAL AND PRIMARY ELECTIONS

ALL-PARTY PRIMARIES

Congressional District 2	Rick Larsen (D)*#	98,304	54.3%
	Rick Bart (R)#	68,189	37.7%
	Doug Schaffer (D)	8,857	4.9%
	Glen S. Johnson	5,590	3.1%
	TOTAL	180,940	
Congressional District 3	Brian Baird (D)*#	83,409	50.6%
	Michael Delavar (R)#	32,372	19.6%
	Christine Webb (R)	27,738	16.8%
	Cheryl Crist (D)	21,356	13.0%
	TOTAL	164,875	
Congressional District 4	Doc Hastings (R)*#	93,241	62.2%
	George Fearing (D)#	49,841	33.2%
	Gordon Allen Pross (GOP)	6,842	4.6%
	TOTAL	149,924	
Congressional District 5	Cathy McMorris Rodgers (R)*#	96,584	56.3%
	Mark Mays (D)#	34,251	20.0%
	Barbara Lampert (D)	19,645	11.4%
	Kurt Erickson (R)	12,155	7.1%
	Randall Yearout (Constitution)	5,268	3.1%
	John H. Beck (Libertarian)	3,673	2.1%
	TOTAL	171,576	
Congressional District 6	Norm Dicks (D)*#	96,862	57.3%
	Doug Cloud (R)#	51,300	30.3%
	Paul Richmond (D)	14,983	8.9%
	Gary Murrell (Green)	6,014	3.6%
	TOTAL	169,159	
Congressional District 7	Jim McDermott (D)*#	95,344	73.8%
	Steve Beren (R)#	19,307	14.9%
	Donovan Rivers (D)	6,685	5.2%
	Mark A. Goldman (No Party)	3,410	2.6%
	Goodspaceguy Nelson (D)	3,199	2.5%
	Al Schaefer (No Party)	1,216	0.9%
	TOTAL	129,161	
Congressional District 8	Dave Reichert (R)*#	74,140	48.5%
	Darcy Burner (D)#	68,010	44.5%
	James E. Vaughn (D)	5,051	3.3%
	Richard Todd (No Party)	2,116	1.4%
	Keith Arnold (D)	1,886	1.2%
	Boleslaw "John" Orlinski (No Party)	1,523	1.0%
	TOTAL	152,726	
Congressional District 9	Adam Smith (D)*#	81,503	64.7%
	James Postma (R)#	44,472	35.3%
	TOTAL	125,975	

Notes: An asterisk (*) denotes incumbent. In 2008 Washington held an all-party primary, in which candidates of all parties ran together on a single ballot. The top two vote-getters, regardless of party, advanced to the November general election. They are indicated by a pound sign (#).

WEST VIRGINIA

Congressional districts first established for elections held in 2002
3 members

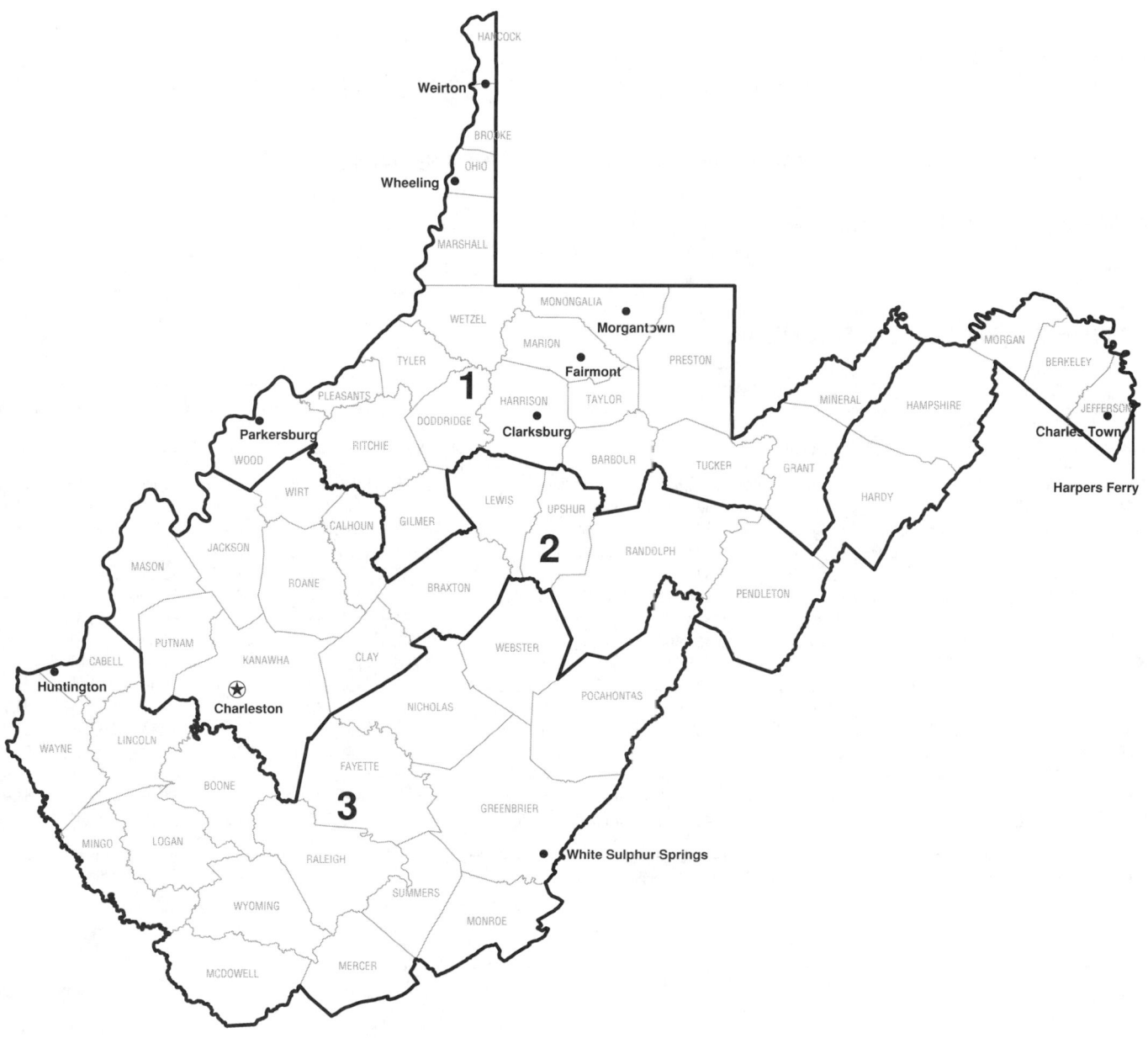

508

WEST VIRGINIA

GOVERNOR
Joe Manchin III (D). Reelected 2008 to a four-year term. Previously elected 2004.

SENATORS (2 Democrats)
Robert C. Byrd (D). Reelected 2006 to a six-year term. Previously elected 2000, 1994, 1988, 1982, 1976, 1970, 1964, 1958.

John D. Rockefeller IV (D). Reelected 2008 to a six-year term. Previously elected 2002, 1996, 1990, 1984.

REPRESENTATIVES (2 Democrats, 1 Republican)
1. Alan B. Mollohan (D)   2. Shelley Moore Capito (R)   3. Nick J. Rahall II (D)

POSTWAR VOTE FOR PRESIDENT

Year	Total Vote	Republican Vote	Republican Candidate	Democratic Vote	Democratic Candidate	Other Vote	Plurality	Rep. Total	Dem. Total	Rep. Major	Dem. Major
2008	713,451	397,466	McCain, John	303,857	Obama, Barack	12,128	93,609 R	55.7%	42.6%	56.7%	43.3%
2004	755,887	423,778	Bush, George W.	326,541	Kerry, John	5,568	97,237 R	56.1%	43.2%	56.5%	43.5%
2000**	648,124	336,475	Bush, George W.	295,497	Gore, Al	16,152	40,978 R	51.9%	45.6%	53.2%	46.8%
1996**	636,459	233,946	Dole, Bob	327,812	Clinton, Bill	74,701	93,866 D	36.8%	51.5%	41.6%	58.4%
1992**	683,762	241,974	Bush, George	331,001	Clinton, Bill	110,787	89,027 D	35.4%	48.4%	42.2%	57.8%
1988	653,311	310,065	Bush, George	341,016	Dukakis, Michael S.	2,230	30,951 D	47.5%	52.2%	47.6%	52.4%
1984	735,742	405,483	Reagan, Ronald	328,125	Mondale, Walter F.	2,134	77,358 R	55.1%	44.6%	55.3%	44.7%
1980**	737,715	334,206	Reagan, Ronald	367,462	Carter, Jimmy	36,047	33,256 D	45.3%	49.8%	47.6%	52.4%
1976	750,964	314,760	Ford, Gerald R.	435,914	Carter, Jimmy	290	121,154 D	41.9%	58.0%	41.9%	58.1%
1972	762,399	484,964	Nixon, Richard M.	277,435	McGovern, George S.		207,529 R	63.6%	36.4%	63.6%	36.4%
1968**	754,206	307,555	Nixon, Richard M.	374,091	Humphrey, Hubert H.	72,560	66,536 D	40.8%	49.6%	45.1%	54.9%
1964	792,040	253,953	Goldwater, Barry M.	538,087	Johnson, Lyndon B.		284,134 D	32.1%	67.9%	32.1%	67.9%
1960	837,781	395,995	Nixon, Richard M.	441,786	Kennedy, John F.		45,791 D	47.3%	52.7%	47.3%	52.7%
1956	830,831	449,297	Eisenhower, Dwight D.	381,534	Stevenson, Adlai E.		67,763 R	54.1%	45.9%	54.1%	45.9%
1952	873,548	419,970	Eisenhower, Dwight D.	453,578	Stevenson, Adlai E.		33,608 D	48.1%	51.9%	48.1%	51.9%
1948	748,750	316,251	Dewey, Thomas E.	429,188	Truman, Harry S.	3,311	112,937 D	42.2%	57.3%	42.4%	57.6%

**In past elections, the other vote included: 2000 - 10,680 Green (Ralph Nader); 1996 - 71,639 Reform (Ross Perot); 1992 - 108,829 Independent (Perot); 1980 - 31,691 Independent (John Anderson); 1968 - 72,560 American Independent (George Wallace).

WEST VIRGINIA

POSTWAR VOTE FOR GOVERNOR

Year	Total Vote	Republican Vote	Republican Candidate	Democratic Vote	Democratic Candidate	Other Vote	Plurality	Total Vote Rep.	Total Vote Dem.	Major Vote Rep.	Major Vote Dem.
2008	706,046	181,612	Weeks, Russ	492,697	Manchin, Joe III	31,737	311,085 D	25.7%	69.8%	26.9%	73.1%
2004	744,433	253,131	Warner, Monty	472,758	Manchin, Joe III	18,544	219,627 D	34.0%	63.5%	34.9%	65.1%
2000	648,047	305,926	Underwood, Cecil H.	324,822	Wise, Bob	17,299	18,896 D	47.2%	50.1%	48.5%	51.5%
1996	628,559	324,518	Underwood, Cecil H.	287,870	Pritt, Charlotte	16,171	36,648 R	51.6%	45.8%	53.0%	47.0%
1992	657,193	240,390	Benedict, Cleveland K.	368,302	Caperton, Gaston	48,501	127,912 D	36.6%	56.0%	39.5%	60.5%
1988	649,593	267,172	Moore, Arch A.	382,421	Caperton, Gaston		115,249 D	41.1%	58.9%	41.1%	58.9%
1984	741,502	394,937	Moore, Arch A.	346,565	See, Clyde M.		48,372 R	53.3%	46.7%	53.3%	46.7%
1980	742,150	337,240	Moore, Arch A.	401,863	Rockefeller, John D. IV	3,047	64,623 D	45.4%	54.1%	45.6%	54.4%
1976	749,270	253,420	Underwood, Cecil H.	495,661	Rockefeller, John D. IV	189	242,241 D	33.8%	66.2%	33.8%	66.2%
1972	774,279	423,817	Moore, Arch A.	350,462	Rockefeller, John D. IV		73,355 R	54.7%	45.3%	54.7%	45.3%
1968	743,845	378,315	Moore, Arch A.	365,530	Sprouse, James M.		12,785 R	50.9%	49.1%	50.9%	49.1%
1964	788,582	355,559	Underwood, Cecil H.	433,023	Smith, Hulett C.		77,464 D	45.1%	54.9%	45.1%	54.9%
1960	827,420	380,665	Neely, Harold E.	446,755	Barron, W. W.		66,090 D	46.0%	54.0%	46.0%	54.0%
1956	817,623	440,502	Underwood, Cecil H.	377,121	Mollohan, Robert H.		63,381 R	53.9%	46.1%	53.9%	46.1%
1952	882,527	427,629	Holt, Rush D.	454,898	Marland, William C.		27,269 D	48.5%	51.5%	48.5%	51.5%
1948	768,061	329,309	Boreman, Herbert	438,752	Patteson, Okey L.		109,443 D	42.9%	57.1%	42.9%	57.1%

POSTWAR VOTE FOR SENATOR

Year	Total Vote	Republican Vote	Republican Candidate	Democratic Vote	Democratic Candidate	Other Vote	Plurality	Total Vote Rep.	Total Vote Dem.	Major Vote Rep.	Major Vote Dem.
2008	702,308	254,629	Wolfe, Jay	447,560	Rockefeller, John D. IV	119	192,931 D	36.3%	63.7%	36.3%	63.7%
2006	459,884	155,043	Raese, John R.	296,276	Byrd, Robert C.	8,565	141,233 D	33.7%	64.4%	34.4%	65.6%
2002	436,183	160,902	Wolfe, Jay	275,281	Rockefeller, John D. IV		114,379 D	36.9%	63.1%	36.9%	63.1%
2000	603,477	121,635	Gallaher, David T.	469,215	Byrd, Robert C.	12,627	347,580 D	20.2%	77.8%	20.6%	79.4%
1996	595,614	139,088	Burks, Betty A.	456,526	Rockefeller, John D. IV		317,438 D	23.4%	76.6%	23.4%	76.6%
1994	420,936	130,441	Klos, Stan	290,495	Byrd, Robert C.		160,054 D	31.0%	69.0%	31.0%	69.0%
1990	404,305	128,071	Yoder, John	276,234	Rockefeller, John D. IV		148,163 D	31.7%	68.3%	31.7%	68.3%
1988	634,547	223,564	Wolfe, Jay	410,983	Byrd, Robert C.		187,419 D	35.2%	64.8%	35.2%	64.8%
1984	722,212	344,680	Raese, John R.	374,233	Rockefeller, John D. IV	3,299	29,553 D	47.7%	51.8%	47.9%	52.1%
1982	565,314	173,910	Benedict, Cleveland K.	387,170	Byrd, Robert C.	4,234	213,260 D	30.8%	68.5%	31.0%	69.0%
1978	493,351	244,317	Moore, Arch A.	249,034	Randolph, Jennings		4,717 D	49.5%	50.5%	49.5%	50.5%
1976	566,790		—	566,423	Byrd, Robert C.	367	566,423 D		99.9%		100.0%
1972	731,841	245,531	Leonard, Louise	486,310	Randolph, Jennings		240,779 D	33.5%	66.5%	33.5%	66.5%
1970	445,623	99,658	Dodson, Elmer H.	345,965	Byrd, Robert C.		246,307 D	22.4%	77.6%	22.4%	77.6%
1966	491,216	198,891	Love, Francis J.	292,325	Randolph, Jennings		93,434 D	40.5%	59.5%	40.5%	59.5%
1964	761,087	246,072	Benedict, Cooper P.	515,015	Byrd, Robert C.		268,943 D	32.3%	67.7%	32.3%	67.7%
1960	828,292	369,935	Underwood, Cecil H.	458,355	Randolph, Jennings	2	88,420 D	44.7%	55.3%	44.7%	55.3%
1958	644,917	263,172	Revercomb, Chapman	381,745	Byrd, Robert C.		118,573 D	40.8%	59.2%	40.8%	59.2%
1958S	630,677	256,510	Hoblitzell, John D.	374,167	Randolph, Jennings		117,657 D	40.7%	59.3%	40.7%	59.3%
1956S	805,174	432,123	Revercomb, Chapman	373,051	Marland, William C.		59,072 R	53.7%	46.3%	53.7%	46.3%
1954	593,329	268,066	Sweeney, Tom	325,263	Neely, Matthew M.		57,197 D	45.2%	54.8%	45.2%	54.8%
1952	876,573	406,554	Revercomb, Chapman	470,019	Kilgore, Harley M.		63,465 D	46.4%	53.6%	46.4%	53.6%
1948	763,888	328,534	Revercomb, Chapman	435,354	Neely, Matthew M.		106,820 D	43.0%	57.0%	43.0%	57.0%
1946	542,768	269,617	Sweeney, Tom	273,151	Kilgore, Harley M.		3,534 D	49.7%	50.3%	49.7%	50.3%

Notes: The 1956 election and one of the 1958 elections were for short terms to fill vacancies. The Republican Party did not run a candidate in the 1976 Senate election.

WEST VIRGINIA

PRESIDENT 2008

2000 Census Population	County	Total Vote	Republican	Democratic	Other	Rep.-Dem. Plurality	Percentage Total Vote Rep.	Dem.	Major Vote Rep.	Dem.
15,557	BARBOUR	6,232	3,685	2,419	128	1,266 R	59.1%	38.8%	60.4%	39.6%
75,905	BERKELEY	37,292	20,841	15,994	457	4,847 R	55.9%	42.9%	56.6%	43.4%
25,535	BOONE	8,370	3,632	4,529	209	897 D	43.4%	54.1%	44.5%	55.5%
14,702	BRAXTON	5,409	2,629	2,704	76	75 D	48.6%	50.0%	49.3%	50.7%
25,447	BROOKE	9,857	4,961	4,717	179	244 R	50.3%	47.9%	51.3%	48.7%
96,784	CABELL	34,592	18,793	15,292	507	3,501 R	54.3%	44.2%	55.1%	44.9%
7,582	CALHOUN	2,429	1,366	993	70	373 R	56.2%	40.9%	57.9%	42.1%
10,330	CLAY	3,265	1,755	1,421	89	334 R	53.8%	43.5%	55.3%	44.7%
7,403	DODDRIDGE	3,018	2,218	735	65	1,483 R	73.5%	24.4%	75.1%	24.9%
47,579	FAYETTE	15,194	7,658	7,242	294	416 R	50.4%	47.7%	51.4%	48.6%
7,160	GILMER	2,521	1,445	1,004	72	441 R	57.3%	39.8%	59.0%	41.0%
11,299	GRANT	4,218	3,166	997	55	2,169 R	75.1%	23.6%	76.1%	23.9%
34,453	GREENBRIER	13,732	7,567	5,881	284	1,686 R	55.1%	42.8%	56.3%	43.7%
20,203	HAMPSHIRE	8,347	5,222	2,983	142	2,239 R	62.6%	35.7%	63.6%	36.4%
32,667	HANCOCK	13,220	7,518	5,504	198	2,014 R	56.9%	41.6%	57.7%	42.3%
12,669	HARDY	5,407	3,376	1,901	130	1,475 R	62.4%	35.2%	64.0%	36.0%
68,652	HARRISON	31,872	17,824	13,582	466	4,242 R	55.9%	42.6%	56.8%	43.2%
28,000	JACKSON	12,236	7,148	4,861	227	2,287 R	58.4%	39.7%	59.5%	40.5%
42,190	JEFFERSON	22,545	10,600	11,687	258	1,087 D	47.0%	51.8%	47.6%	52.4%
200,073	KANAWHA	82,484	40,952	40,594	938	358 R	49.6%	49.2%	50.2%	49.8%
16,919	LEWIS	6,606	4,335	2,109	162	2,226 R	65.6%	31.9%	67.3%	32.7%
22,108	LINCOLN	6,835	3,637	3,029	169	608 R	53.2%	44.3%	54.6%	45.4%
37,710	LOGAN	13,465	7,326	5,873	266	1,453 R	54.4%	43.6%	55.5%	44.5%
27,329	MCDOWELL	6,430	2,882	3,430	118	548 D	44.8%	53.3%	45.7%	54.3%
56,598	MARION	23,607	11,501	11,618	488	117 D	48.7%	49.2%	49.7%	50.3%
35,519	MARSHALL	14,001	7,759	5,996	246	1,763 R	55.4%	42.8%	56.4%	43.6%
25,957	MASON	10,603	5,853	4,484	266	1,369 R	55.2%	42.3%	56.6%	43.4%
62,980	MERCER	21,022	13,246	7,450	326	5,796 R	63.0%	35.4%	64.0%	36.0%
27,078	MINERAL	11,547	7,616	3,750	181	3,866 R	66.0%	32.5%	67.0%	33.0%
28,253	MINGO	8,338	4,587	3,582	169	1,005 R	55.0%	43.0%	56.2%	43.8%
81,866	MONONGALIA	33,379	15,775	17,060	544	1,285 D	47.3%	51.1%	48.0%	52.0%
14,583	MONROE	5,575	3,397	2,014	164	1,383 R	60.9%	36.1%	62.8%	37.2%
14,943	MORGAN	7,276	4,428	2,721	127	1,707 R	60.9%	37.4%	61.9%	38.1%
26,562	NICHOLAS	9,361	4,804	4,357	200	447 R	51.3%	46.5%	52.4%	47.6%
47,427	OHIO	19,540	10,694	8,593	253	2,101 R	54.7%	44.0%	55.4%	44.6%
8,196	PENDLETON	3,395	2,035	1,310	50	725 R	59.9%	38.6%	60.8%	39.2%
7,514	PLEASANTS	2,975	1,772	1,142	61	630 R	59.6%	38.4%	60.8%	39.2%
9,131	POCAHONTAS	3,642	2,011	1,548	83	463 R	55.2%	42.5%	56.5%	43.5%
29,334	PRESTON	11,796	7,325	4,205	266	3,120 R	62.1%	35.6%	63.5%	36.5%
51,589	PUTNAM	24,780	15,162	9,334	284	5,828 R	61.2%	37.7%	61.9%	38.1%
79,220	RALEIGH	28,259	17,548	10,237	474	7,311 R	62.1%	36.2%	63.2%	36.8%
28,262	RANDOLPH	10,833	6,060	4,539	234	1,521 R	55.9%	41.9%	57.2%	42.8%
10,343	RITCHIE	3,846	2,781	998	67	1,783 R	72.3%	25.9%	73.6%	26.4%
15,446	ROANE	5,563	2,943	2,511	109	432 R	52.9%	45.1%	54.0%	46.0%
12,999	SUMMERS	5,316	2,891	2,290	135	601 R	54.4%	43.1%	55.8%	44.2%
16,089	TAYLOR	6,203	3,605	2,462	136	1,143 R	58.1%	39.7%	59.4%	40.6%
7,321	TUCKER	3,507	2,123	1,288	96	835 R	60.5%	36.7%	62.2%	37.8%
9,592	TYLER	3,741	2,415	1,241	85	1,174 R	64.6%	33.2%	66.1%	33.9%
23,404	UPSHUR	8,971	5,911	2,925	135	2,986 R	65.9%	32.6%	66.9%	33.1%
42,903	WAYNE	15,430	8,947	6,137	346	2,810 R	58.0%	39.8%	59.3%	40.7%
9,719	WEBSTER	3,057	1,386	1,552	119	166 D	45.3%	50.8%	47.2%	52.8%
17,693	WETZEL	6,454	3,342	2,942	170	400 R	51.8%	45.6%	53.2%	46.8%
5,873	WIRT	2,326	1,496	782	48	714 R	64.3%	33.6%	65.7%	34.3%
87,986	WOOD	36,002	22,896	12,573	533	10,323 R	63.6%	34.9%	64.6%	35.4%
25,708	WYOMING	7,530	4,621	2,735	174	1,886 R	61.4%	36.3%	62.8%	37.2%
1,808,344	TOTAL	713,451	397,466	303,857	12,128	93,609 R	55.7%	42.6%	56.7%	43.3%

WEST VIRGINIA

GOVERNOR 2008

2000 Census Population	County	Total Vote	Republican	Democratic	Other	Rep.-Dem. Plurality	Percentage Total Vote Rep.	Total Vote Dem.	Major Vote Rep.	Major Vote Dem.
15,557	BARBOUR	6,255	1,426	4,613	216	3,187 D	22.8%	73.7%	23.6%	76.4%
75,905	BERKELEY	36,371	13,288	21,545	1,538	8,257 D	36.5%	59.2%	38.1%	61.9%
25,535	BOONE	8,342	1,729	6,124	489	4,395 D	20.7%	73.4%	22.0%	78.0%
14,702	BRAXTON	5,303	1,111	4,083	109	2,972 D	21.0%	77.0%	21.4%	78.6%
25,447	BROOKE	9,771	1,686	7,793	292	6,107 D	17.3%	79.8%	17.8%	82.2%
96,784	CABELL	34,668	6,651	26,970	1,047	20,319 D	19.2%	77.8%	19.8%	80.2%
7,582	CALHOUN	2,423	635	1,612	176	977 D	26.2%	66.5%	28.3%	71.7%
10,330	CLAY	3,267	782	2,316	159	1,534 D	23.9%	70.9%	25.2%	74.8%
7,403	DODDRIDGE	3,015	1,021	1,868	126	847 D	33.9%	62.0%	35.3%	64.7%
47,579	FAYETTE	15,248	4,306	10,305	637	5,999 D	28.2%	67.6%	29.5%	70.5%
7,160	GILMER	2,506	595	1,728	133	1,133 D	23.7%	69.0%	25.6%	74.4%
11,299	GRANT	4,051	1,508	2,425	118	917 D	37.2%	59.9%	38.3%	61.7%
34,453	GREENBRIER	13,700	3,606	9,521	573	5,915 D	26.3%	69.5%	27.5%	72.5%
20,203	HAMPSHIRE	8,254	2,491	5,465	298	2,974 D	30.2%	66.2%	31.3%	68.7%
32,667	HANCOCK	13,013	2,580	10,069	364	7,489 D	19.8%	77.4%	20.4%	79.6%
12,669	HARDY	5,292	1,278	3,777	237	2,499 D	24.1%	71.4%	25.3%	74.7%
68,652	HARRISON	31,580	7,514	22,746	1,320	15,232 D	23.8%	72.0%	24.8%	75.2%
28,000	JACKSON	12,250	3,392	8,233	625	4,841 D	27.7%	67.2%	29.2%	70.8%
42,190	JEFFERSON	21,918	7,010	13,563	1,345	6,553 D	32.0%	61.9%	34.1%	65.9%
200,073	KANAWHA	81,040	20,595	55,129	5,316	34,534 D	25.4%	68.0%	27.2%	72.8%
16,919	LEWIS	6,609	1,921	4,434	254	2,513 D	29.1%	67.1%	30.2%	69.8%
22,108	LINCOLN	6,904	1,755	4,776	373	3,021 D	25.4%	69.2%	26.9%	73.1%
37,710	LOGAN	13,243	2,591	10,101	551	7,510 D	19.6%	76.3%	20.4%	79.6%
27,329	MCDOWELL	6,394	933	5,323	138	4,390 D	14.6%	83.2%	14.9%	85.1%
56,598	MARION	23,503	4,610	17,849	1,044	13,239 D	19.6%	75.9%	20.5%	79.5%
35,519	MARSHALL	13,928	2,915	10,555	458	7,640 D	20.9%	75.8%	21.6%	78.4%
25,957	MASON	10,753	1,806	8,605	342	6,799 D	16.8%	80.0%	17.3%	82.7%
62,980	MERCER	20,874	5,687	14,654	533	8,967 D	27.2%	70.2%	28.0%	72.0%
27,078	MINERAL	11,431	3,061	8,100	270	5,039 D	26.8%	70.9%	27.4%	72.6%
28,253	MINGO	8,210	1,525	6,353	332	4,828 D	18.6%	77.4%	19.4%	80.6%
81,866	MONONGALIA	32,268	9,064	19,546	3,658	10,482 D	28.1%	60.6%	31.7%	68.3%
14,583	MONROE	5,596	1,589	3,824	183	2,235 D	28.4%	68.3%	29.4%	70.6%
14,943	MORGAN	7,078	2,432	4,318	328	1,886 D	34.4%	61.0%	36.0%	64.0%
26,562	NICHOLAS	9,431	2,027	7,080	324	5,053 D	21.5%	75.1%	22.3%	77.7%
47,427	OHIO	19,324	4,422	14,225	677	9,803 D	22.9%	73.6%	23.7%	76.3%
8,196	PENDLETON	3,319	1,127	2,056	135	929 D	34.0%	61.9%	35.4%	64.6%
7,514	PLEASANTS	2,981	658	2,235	88	1,577 D	22.1%	75.0%	22.7%	77.3%
9,131	POCAHONTAS	3,646	902	2,479	265	1,577 D	24.7%	68.0%	26.7%	73.3%
29,334	PRESTON	11,656	3,782	7,078	796	3,296 D	32.4%	60.7%	34.8%	65.2%
51,589	PUTNAM	24,628	6,622	16,995	1,011	10,373 D	26.9%	69.0%	28.0%	72.0%
79,220	RALEIGH	28,019	11,645	15,736	638	4,091 D	41.6%	56.2%	42.5%	57.5%
28,262	RANDOLPH	10,775	2,084	8,149	542	6,065 D	19.3%	75.6%	20.4%	79.6%
10,343	RITCHIE	3,793	1,153	2,503	137	1,350 D	30.4%	66.0%	31.5%	68.5%
15,446	ROANE	5,587	1,494	3,798	295	2,304 D	26.7%	68.0%	28.2%	71.8%
12,999	SUMMERS	5,296	1,573	3,535	188	1,962 D	29.7%	66.7%	30.8%	69.2%
16,089	TAYLOR	6,163	1,477	4,419	267	2,942 D	24.0%	71.7%	25.1%	74.9%
7,321	TUCKER	3,469	748	2,554	167	1,806 D	21.6%	73.6%	22.7%	77.3%
9,592	TYLER	3,705	1,001	2,567	137	1,566 D	27.0%	69.3%	28.1%	71.9%
23,404	UPSHUR	9,016	2,253	6,498	265	4,245 D	25.0%	72.1%	25.7%	74.3%
42,903	WAYNE	15,304	3,132	11,793	379	8,661 D	20.5%	77.1%	21.0%	79.0%
9,719	WEBSTER	3,086	555	2,361	170	1,806 D	18.0%	76.5%	19.0%	81.0%
17,693	WETZEL	6,398	1,162	4,975	261	3,813 D	18.2%	77.8%	18.9%	81.1%
5,873	WIRT	2,322	581	1,652	89	1,071 D	25.0%	71.1%	26.0%	74.0%
87,986	WOOD	35,525	7,658	26,769	1,098	19,111 D	21.6%	75.4%	22.2%	77.8%
25,708	WYOMING	7,545	2,463	4,917	165	2,454 D	32.6%	65.2%	33.4%	66.6%
1,808,344	TOTAL	706,046	181,612	492,697	31,737	311,085 D	25.7%	69.8%	26.9%	73.1%

WEST VIRGINIA

SENATOR 2008

2000 Census Population	County	Total Vote	Republican	Democratic	Other	Rep.-Dem. Plurality		Percentage Total Vote Rep.	Dem.	Major Vote Rep.	Dem.
15,557	BARBOUR	6,205	2,405	3,798	2	1,393	D	38.8%	61.2%	38.8%	61.2%
75,905	BERKELEY	36,208	16,234	19,967	7	3,733	D	44.8%	55.1%	44.8%	55.2%
25,535	BOONE	8,347	2,155	6,192		4,037	D	25.8%	74.2%	25.8%	74.2%
14,702	BRAXTON	5,124	1,363	3,761		2,398	D	26.6%	73.4%	26.6%	73.4%
25,447	BROOKE	9,714	2,396	7,318		4,922	D	24.7%	75.3%	24.7%	75.3%
96,784	CABELL	34,136	12,488	21,644	4	9,156	D	36.6%	63.4%	36.6%	63.4%
7,582	CALHOUN	2,393	908	1,484	1	576	D	37.9%	62.0%	38.0%	62.0%
10,330	CLAY	3,251	911	2,340		1,429	D	28.0%	72.0%	28.0%	72.0%
7,403	DODDRIDGE	2,992	1,829	1,161	2	668	R	61.1%	38.8%	61.2%	38.8%
47,579	FAYETTE	15,179	4,649	10,529	1	5,880	D	30.6%	69.4%	30.6%	69.4%
7,160	GILMER	2,507	925	1,582		657	D	36.9%	63.1%	36.9%	63.1%
11,299	GRANT	4,063	2,281	1,782		499	R	56.1%	43.9%	56.1%	43.9%
34,453	GREENBRIER	13,584	4,853	8,731		3,878	D	35.7%	64.3%	35.7%	64.3%
20,203	HAMPSHIRE	8,247	3,852	4,394	1	542	D	46.7%	53.3%	46.7%	53.3%
32,667	HANCOCK	12,945	3,805	9,140		5,335	D	29.4%	70.6%	29.4%	70.6%
12,669	HARDY	5,314	2,069	3,245		1,176	D	38.9%	61.1%	38.9%	61.1%
68,652	HARRISON	31,738	13,153	18,574	11	5,421	D	41.4%	58.5%	41.5%	58.5%
28,000	JACKSON	12,156	4,574	7,582		3,008	D	37.6%	62.4%	37.6%	62.4%
42,190	JEFFERSON	22,006	8,411	13,592	3	5,181	D	38.2%	61.8%	38.2%	61.8%
200,073	KANAWHA	81,493	27,087	54,402	4	27,315	D	33.2%	66.8%	33.2%	66.8%
16,919	LEWIS	6,636	2,944	3,691	1	747	D	44.4%	55.6%	44.4%	55.6%
22,108	LINCOLN	6,786	2,252	4,534	-	2,282	D	33.2%	66.8%	33.2%	66.8%
37,710	LOGAN	12,964	3,814	9,148	2	5,334	D	29.4%	70.6%	29.4%	70.6%
27,329	MCDOWELL	6,373	1,113	5,260		4,147	D	17.5%	82.5%	17.5%	82.5%
56,598	MARION	23,484	7,316	16,156	12	8,840	D	31.2%	68.8%	31.2%	68.8%
35,519	MARSHALL	13,801	3,849	9,950	2	6,101	D	27.9%	72.1%	27.9%	72.1%
25,957	MASON	10,568	3,113	7,455		4,342	D	29.5%	70.5%	29.5%	70.5%
62,980	MERCER	20,502	8,161	12,341		4,180	D	39.8%	60.2%	39.8%	60.2%
27,078	MINERAL	11,433	4,911	6,520	2	1,609	D	43.0%	57.0%	43.0%	57.0%
28,253	MINGO	8,029	2,170	5,859		3,689	D	27.0%	73.0%	27.0%	73.0%
81,866	MONONGALIA	32,606	10,292	22,308	6	12,016	D	31.6%	68.4%	31.6%	68.4%
14,583	MONROE	5,528	2,147	3,381		1,234	D	38.8%	61.2%	38.8%	61.2%
14,943	MORGAN	6,981	3,109	3,868	4	759	D	44.5%	55.4%	44.6%	55.4%
26,562	NICHOLAS	9,391	2,688	6,697	6	4,009	D	28.6%	71.3%	28.6%	71.4%
47,427	OHIO	19,266	5,617	13,647	2	8,030	D	29.2%	70.8%	29.2%	70.8%
8,196	PENDLETON	3,345	1,259	2,086		827	D	37.6%	62.4%	37.6%	62.4%
7,514	PLEASANTS	2,976	1,188	1,787	1	599	D	39.9%	60.0%	39.9%	60.1%
9,131	POCAHONTAS	3,603	1,317	2,286		969	D	36.6%	63.4%	36.6%	63.4%
29,334	PRESTON	11,634	4,801	6,825	8	2,024	D	41.3%	58.7%	41.3%	58.7%
51,589	PUTNAM	24,622	10,236	14,386		4,150	D	41.6%	58.4%	41.6%	58.4%
79,220	RALEIGH	27,626	11,408	16,213	5	4,805	D	41.3%	58.7%	41.3%	58.7%
28,262	RANDOLPH	10,680	3,493	7,180	7	3,687	D	32.7%	67.2%	32.7%	67.3%
10,343	RITCHIE	3,796	2,156	1,639	1	517	R	56.8%	43.2%	56.8%	43.2%
15,446	ROANE	5,535	1,843	3,691	1	1,848	D	33.3%	66.7%	33.3%	66.7%
12,999	SUMMERS	5,214	1,792	3,422		1,630	D	34.4%	65.6%	34.4%	65.6%
16,089	TAYLOR	6,148	2,325	3,820	3	1,495	D	37.8%	62.1%	37.8%	62.2%
7,321	TUCKER	3,506	1,246	2,260		1,014	D	35.5%	64.5%	35.5%	64.5%
9,592	TYLER	3,692	1,644	2,048		404	D	44.5%	55.5%	44.5%	55.5%
23,404	UPSHUR	8,932	3,686	5,241	5	1,555	D	41.3%	58.7%	41.3%	58.7%
42,903	WAYNE	14,890	5,437	9,450	3	4,013	D	36.5%	63.5%	36.5%	63.5%
9,719	WEBSTER	3,087	752	2,333	2	1,581	D	24.4%	75.6%	24.4%	75.6%
17,693	WETZEL	6,367	1,928	4,432	7	2,504	D	30.3%	69.6%	30.3%	69.7%
5,873	WIRT	2,296	1,004	1,292		288	D	43.7%	56.3%	43.7%	56.3%
87,986	WOOD	34,985	14,954	20,029	2	5,075	D	42.7%	57.3%	42.7%	57.3%
25,708	WYOMING	7,424	2,316	5,107	1	2,791	D	31.2%	68.8%	31.2%	68.8%
1,808,344	TOTAL	702,308	254,629	447,560	119	192,931	D	36.3%	63.7%	36.3%	63.7%

WEST VIRGINIA

HOUSE OF REPRESENTATIVES

CD	Year	Total Vote	Republican Vote	Republican Candidate	Democratic Vote	Democratic Candidate	Other Vote	Rep.-Dem. Plurality	Total Vote Rep.	Total Vote Dem.	Major Vote Rep.	Major Vote Dem.
1	2008	187,864		—	187,734	MOLLOHAN, ALAN B.*	130	187,734 D		99.9%		100.0%
1	2006	157,000	55,963	WAKIM, CHRIS	100,939	MOLLOHAN, ALAN B.*	98	44,976 D	35.6%	64.3%	35.7%	64.3%
1	2004	245,779	79,196	PARKS, ALAN LEE	166,583	MOLLOHAN, ALAN B.*		87,387 D	32.2%	67.8%	32.2%	67.8%
1	2002	111,261		—	110,941	MOLLOHAN, ALAN B.*	320	110,941 D		99.7%		100.0%
2	2008	258,169	147,334	CAPITO, SHELLEY MOORE*	110,819	BARTH, ANNE	16	36,515 R	57.1%	42.9%	57.1%	42.9%
2	2006	164,580	94,110	CAPITO, SHELLEY MOORE*	70,470	CALLAGHAN, MIKE		23,640 R	57.2%	42.8%	57.2%	42.8%
2	2004	257,025	147,676	CAPITO, SHELLEY MOORE*	106,131	WELLS, ERIK	3,218	41,545 R	57.5%	41.3%	58.2%	41.8%
2	2002	163,676	98,276	CAPITO, SHELLEY MOORE*	65,400	HUMPHREYS, JIM		32,876 R	60.0%	40.0%	60.0%	40.0%
3	2008	199,527	66,005	GEARHEART, MARTY	133,522	RAHALL, NICK J. II*		67,517 D	33.1%	66.9%	33.1%	66.9%
3	2006	133,233	40,820	WOLFE, KIM	92,413	RAHALL, NICK J. II*		51,593 D	30.6%	69.4%	30.6%	69.4%
3	2004	218,852	76,170	SNUFFER, RICK	142,682	RAHALL, NICK J. II*		66,512 D	34.8%	65.2%	34.8%	65.2%
3	2002	125,012	37,229	CHAPMAN, PAUL E.	87,783	RAHALL, NICK J. II*		50,554 D	29.8%	70.2%	29.8%	70.2%
TOTAL	2008	645,560	213,339		432,075		146	218,736 D	33.0%	66.9%	33.1%	66.9%
TOTAL	2006	454,813	190,893		263,822		98	72,929 D	42.0%	58.0%	42.0%	58.0%
TOTAL	2004	721,656	303,042		415,396		3,218	112,354 D	42.0%	57.6%	42.2%	57.8%
TOTAL	2002	399,949	135,505		264,124		320	128,619 D	33.9%	66.0%	33.9%	66.1%

Note: An asterisk (*) denotes incumbent.

WEST VIRGINIA

GENERAL AND PRIMARY ELECTIONS

2008 GENERAL ELECTIONS

President Other vote was 7,219 No Party (Ralph Nader); 2,465 Constitution (Chuck Baldwin); 2,355 Mountain (Cynthia A. McKinney); 59 write-in (Santa Claus); 18 write-in (David L. Rice); 4 write-in (Donald K. Allen); 3 write-in (Robert Brown); 3 write-in (Charles G. "Bud' Railey); 1 write-in (Ron Hobbs); 1 write-in (Frank Moore).

Governor Other vote was 31,486 Mountain (Jesse Johnson); 234 write-in (Butch Paugh); 17 write-in (James Davis).

Senator Other vote was 83 write-in (John R. "Rick" Bartlett); 36 write-in (Chad Shaffer).

House Other vote was:

CD 1 69 write-in (Ted Osgood); 61 write-in (R.J. Smith).
CD 2 16 write-in (Aaron Mills).
CD 3

2008 PRIMARY ELECTIONS

Primary May 13, 2008

Registration
(as of April 25, 2008)

Democratic	665,234
Republican	347,760
Mountain	931
Other Parties	13,371
No Party	156,199
TOTAL	1,183,495

Primary Type Semi-open—Registered Democrats and registered Republicans could vote only in their party's primary. Those voters registered with no party could participate in either the Democratic or Republican primary.

WEST VIRGINIA

GENERAL AND PRIMARY ELECTIONS

	REPUBLICAN PRIMARIES			DEMOCRATIC PRIMARIES		
President	John McCain	90,469	76.0%	Hillary Clinton	240,890	66.9%
	Mike Huckabee	12,310	10.3%	Barack Obama	92,736	25.8%
	Ron Paul	5,969	5.0%	John Edwards	26,284	7.3%
	Mitt Romney	5,242	4.4%			
	Rudolph Giuliani	2,875	2.4%			
	Alan Keyes	1,441	1.2%			
	Jerry Curry	728	0.6%			
	TOTAL	119,034		TOTAL	359,910	
Governor	Russ Weeks	81,019	100.0%	Joe Manchin III*	264,775	74.6%
				Melvin "Mel" Kessler	90,074	25.4%
				TOTAL	354,849	
Senator	Jay Wolfe	81,702	100.0%	John D. Rockefeller IV*	271,425	77.1%
				Sheirl L. Fletcher	51,073	14.5%
				Billy Hendricks Jr.	29,707	8.4%
				TOTAL	352,205	
Congressional District 1	No Republican candidate			Alan B. Mollohan*	95,674	100.0%
Congressional District 2	Shelley Moore Capito*	42,476	100.0%	Anne Barth	66,112	62.8%
				Richard A. Robb	30,177	28.6%
				Thornton Cooper	9,068	8.6%
				TOTAL	105,357	
Congressional District 3	Marty Gearheart	15,919	100.0%	Nick J. Rahall II*	100,845	100.0%

Note: An asterisk (*) denotes incumbent.

WISCONSIN

Congressional districts first established for elections held in 2002
8 members

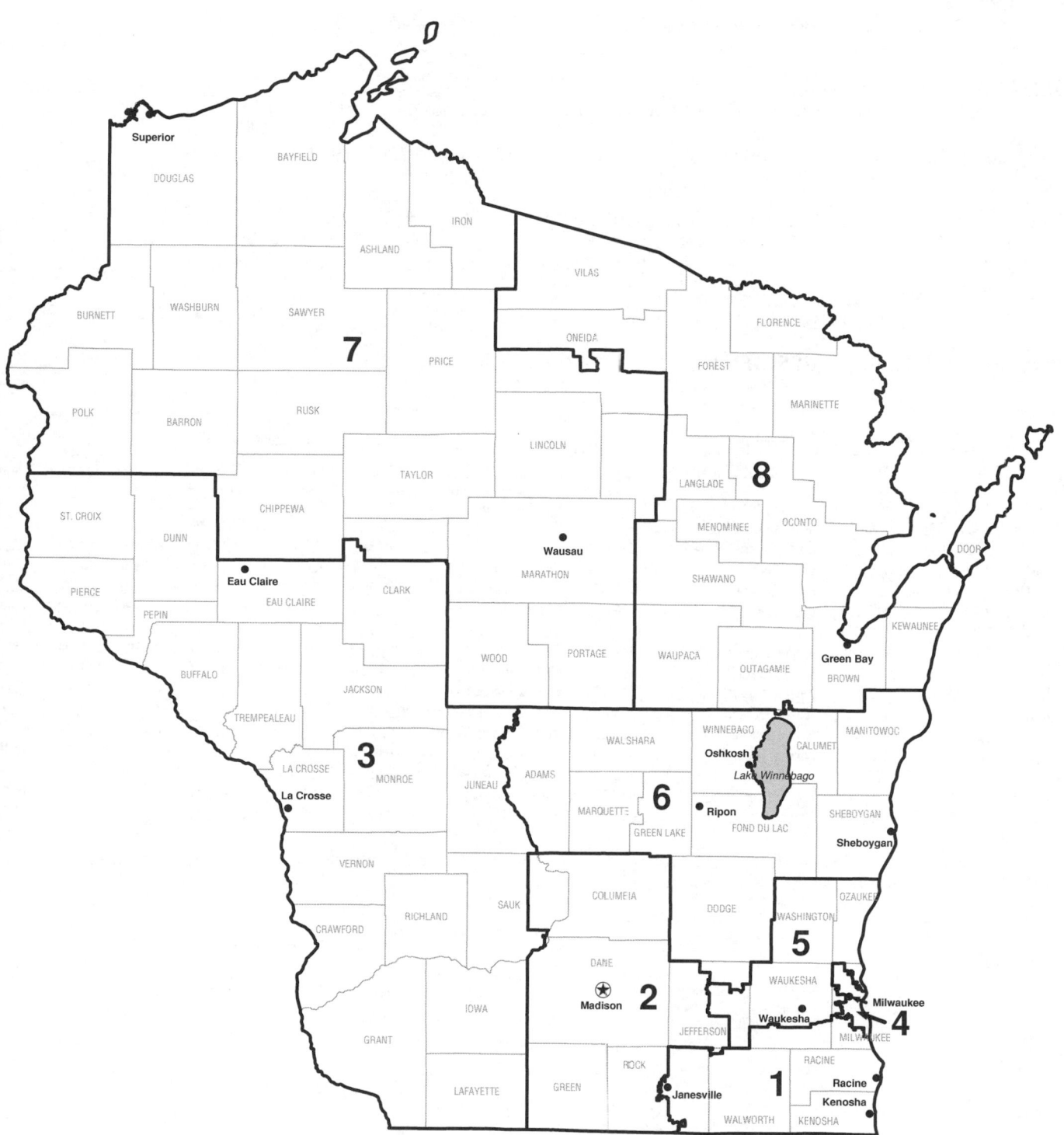

WISCONSIN

GOVERNOR
James E. Doyle (D). Reelected 2006 to a four-year term. Previously elected 2002.

SENATORS (2 Democrats)
Russell D. Feingold (D). Reelected 2004 to a six-year term. Previously elected 1998, 1992.

Herb Kohl (D). Reelected 2006 to a six-year term. Previously elected 2000, 1994, 1988.

REPRESENTATIVES (5 Democrats, 3 Republicans)
1. Paul D. Ryan (R)
2. Tammy Baldwin (D)
3. Ron Kind (D)
4. Gwen Moore (D)
5. F. James Sensenbrenner Jr. (R)
6. Tom Petri (R)
7. David R. Obey (D)
8. Steven Kagen (D)

POSTWAR VOTE FOR PRESIDENT

Year	Total Vote	Republican Vote	Republican Candidate	Democratic Vote	Democratic Candidate	Other Vote	Plurality	Total Vote Rep.	Total Vote Dem.	Major Vote Rep.	Major Vote Dem.
2008	2,983,417	1,262,393	McCain, John	1,677,211	Obama, Barack	43,813	414,818 D	42.3%	56.2%	42.9%	57.1%
2004	2,997,007	1,478,120	Bush, George W.	1,489,504	Kerry, John	29,383	11,384 D	49.3%	49.7%	49.8%	50.2%
2000**	2,598,607	1,237,279	Bush, George W.	1,242,987	Gore, Al	118,341	5,708 D	47.6%	47.8%	49.9%	50.1%
1996**	2,196,169	845,029	Dole, Bob	1,071,971	Clinton, Bill	279,169	226,942 D	38.5%	48.8%	44.1%	55.9%
1992**	2,531,114	930,855	Bush, George	1,041,066	Clinton, Bill	559,193	110,211 D	36.8%	41.1%	47.2%	52.8%
1988	2,191,608	1,047,499	Bush, George	1,126,794	Dukakis, Michael S.	17,315	79,295 D	47.8%	51.4%	48.2%	51.8%
1984	2,211,689	1,198,584	Reagan, Ronald	995,740	Mondale, Walter F.	17,365	202,844 R	54.2%	45.0%	54.6%	45.4%
1980**	2,273,221	1,088,845	Reagan, Ronald	981,584	Carter, Jimmy	202,792	107,261 R	47.9%	43.2%	52.6%	47.4%
1976	2,104,175	1,004,987	Ford, Gerald R.	1,040,232	Carter, Jimmy	58,956	35,245 D	47.8%	49.4%	49.1%	50.9%
1972	1,852,890	989,430	Nixon, Richard M.	810,174	McGovern, George S.	53,286	179,256 R	53.4%	43.7%	55.0%	45.0%
1968**	1,691,538	809,997	Nixon, Richard M.	748,804	Humphrey, Hubert H.	132,737	61,193 R	47.9%	44.3%	52.0%	48.0%
1964	1,691,815	638,495	Goldwater, Barry M.	1,050,424	Johnson, Lyndon B.	2,896	411,929 D	37.7%	62.1%	37.8%	62.2%
1960	1,729,082	895,175	Nixon, Richard M.	830,805	Kennedy, John F.	3,102	64,370 R	51.8%	48.0%	51.9%	48.1%
1956	1,550,558	954,844	Eisenhower, Dwight D.	586,768	Stevenson, Adlai E.	8,946	368,076 R	61.6%	37.8%	61.9%	38.1%
1952	1,607,370	979,744	Eisenhower, Dwight D.	622,175	Stevenson, Adlai E.	5,451	357,569 R	61.0%	38.7%	61.2%	38.8%
1948	1,276,800	590,959	Dewey, Thomas E.	647,310	Truman, Harry S.	38,531	56,351 D	46.3%	50.7%	47.7%	52.3%

**In past elections, the other vote included: 2000 - 94,070 Green (Ralph Nader); 1996 - 227,339 Reform (Ross Perot); 1992 - 544,479 Independent (Perot); 1980 - 160,657 Independent (John Anderson); 1968 - 127,835 American Independent (George Wallace).

WISCONSIN

POSTWAR VOTE FOR GOVERNOR

Year	Total Vote	Republican Vote	Republican Candidate	Democratic Vote	Democratic Candidate	Other Vote	Rep.-Dem. Plurality	Total Vote Rep.	Total Vote Dem.	Major Vote Rep.	Major Vote Dem.
2006	2,161,700	979,427	Green, Mark	1,139,115	Doyle, James E.	43,158	159,688 D	45.3%	52.7%	46.2%	53.8%
2002**	1,775,349	734,779	McCallum, Scott	800,515	Doyle, James E.	240,055	65,736 D	41.4%	45.1%	47.9%	52.1%
1998	1,756,014	1,047,716	Thompson, Tommy G.	679,553	Garvey, Edward R.	28,745	368,163 R	59.7%	38.7%	60.7%	39.3%
1994	1,563,835	1,051,326	Thompson, Tommy G.	482,850	Chvala, Chuck	29,659	568,476 R	67.2%	30.9%	68.5%	31.5%
1990	1,379,727	802,321	Thompson, Tommy G.	576,280	Loftus, Thomas	1,126	226,041 R	58.2%	41.8%	58.2%	41.8%
1986	1,526,960	805,090	Thompson, Tommy G.	705,578	Earl, Anthony S.	16,292	99,512 R	52.7%	46.2%	53.3%	46.7%
1982	1,580,344	662,838	Kohler, Terry J.	896,812	Earl, Anthony S.	20,694	233,974 D	41.9%	56.7%	42.5%	57.5%
1978	1,500,996	816,056	Dreyfus, Lee S.	673,813	Schreiber, Martin J.	11,127	142,243 R	54.4%	44.9%	54.8%	45.2%
1974	1,181,976	497,195	Dyke, William D.	628,639	Lucey, Patrick J.	56,142	131,444 D	42.1%	53.2%	44.2%	55.8%
1970**	1,343,160	602,617	Olson, Jack B.	728,403	Lucey, Patrick J.	12,140	125,786 D	44.9%	54.2%	45.3%	54.7%
1968	1,689,738	893,463	Knowles, Warren P.	791,100	LaFollette, Bronson C.	5,175	102,363 R	52.9%	46.8%	53.0%	47.0%
1966	1,170,173	626,041	Knowles, Warren P.	539,258	Lucey, Patrick J.	4,874	86,783 R	53.5%	46.1%	53.7%	46.3%
1964	1,694,887	856,779	Knowles, Warren P.	837,901	Reynolds, John W.	207	18,878 R	50.6%	49.4%	50.6%	49.4%
1962	1,265,900	625,536	Kuehn, Philip G.	637,491	Reynolds, John W.	2,873	11,955 D	49.4%	50.4%	49.5%	50.5%
1960	1,728,009	837,123	Kuehn, Philip G.	890,868	Nelson, Gaylord A.	18	53,745 D	48.4%	51.6%	48.4%	51.6%
1958	1,202,219	556,391	Thomson, Vernon W.	644,296	Nelson, Gaylord A.	1,532	87,905 D	46.3%	53.6%	46.3%	53.7%
1956	1,557,788	808,273	Thomson, Vernon W.	749,421	Proxmire, William	94	58,852 R	51.9%	48.1%	51.9%	48.1%
1954	1,158,666	596,158	Kohler, Walter J.	560,747	Proxmire, William	1,761	35,411 R	51.5%	48.4%	51.5%	48.5%
1952	1,615,214	1,009,171	Kohler, Walter J.	601,844	Proxmire, William	4,199	407,327 R	62.5%	37.3%	62.6%	37.4%
1950	1,138,148	605,649	Kohler, Walter J.	525,319	Thompson, Carl W.	7,180	80,330 R	53.2%	46.2%	53.6%	46.4%
1948	1,266,139	684,839	Rennebohm, Oscar	558,497	Thompson, Carl W.	22,803	126,342 R	54.1%	44.1%	55.1%	44.9%
1946	1,040,444	621,970	Goodland, Walter	406,499	Hoan, Daniel W.	11,975	215,471 R	59.8%	39.1%	60.5%	39.5%

**In past elections, the other vote included: 2002 - 185,455 Libertarian (Ed Thompson). The term of office of Wisconsin's governor was increased from two to four years effective with the 1970 election.

POSTWAR VOTE FOR SENATOR

Year	Total Vote	Republican Vote	Republican Candidate	Democratic Vote	Democratic Candidate	Other Vote	Rep.-Dem. Plurality	Total Vote Rep.	Total Vote Dem.	Major Vote Rep.	Major Vote Dem.
2006	2,138,297	630,299	Lorge, Robert Gerald	1,439,214	Kohl, Herb	68,784	808,915 D	29.5%	67.3%	30.5%	69.5%
2004	2,949,743	1,301,183	Michels, Tim	1,632,697	Feingold, Russell D.	15,863	331,514 D	44.1%	55.4%	44.4%	55.6%
2000	2,540,083	940,744	Gillespie, John	1,563,238	Kohl, Herb	36,101	622,494 D	37.0%	61.5%	37.6%	62.4%
1998	1,760,836	852,272	Neumann, Mark W.	890,059	Feingold, Russell D.	18,505	37,787 D	48.4%	50.5%	48.9%	51.1%
1994	1,565,628	636,989	Welch, Robert T.	912,662	Kohl, Herb	15,977	175,673 D	40.7%	58.3%	41.1%	58.9%
1992	2,455,124	1,129,599	Kasten, Robert W.	1,290,662	Feingold, Russell D.	34,863	161,063 D	46.0%	52.6%	46.7%	53.3%
1988	2,168,190	1,030,440	Engeleiter, Susan	1,128,625	Kohl, Herb	9,125	98,185 D	47.5%	52.1%	47.7%	52.3%
1986	1,483,174	754,573	Kasten, Robert W.	702,963	Garvey, Edward R.	25,638	51,610 R	50.9%	47.4%	51.8%	48.2%
1982	1,544,981	527,355	McCallum, Scott	983,311	Proxmire, William	34,315	455,956 D	34.1%	63.6%	34.9%	65.1%
1980	2,204,202	1,106,311	Kasten, Robert W.	1,065,487	Nelson, Gaylord A.	32,404	40,824 R	50.2%	48.3%	50.9%	49.1%
1976	1,935,183	521,902	York, Stanley	1,396,970	Proxmire, William	16,311	875,068 D	27.0%	72.2%	27.2%	72.8%
1974	1,199,495	429,327	Petri, Tom	740,700	Nelson, Gaylord A.	29,468	311,373 D	35.8%	61.8%	36.7%	63.3%
1970	1,338,967	381,297	Erickson, John E.	948,445	Proxmire, William	9,225	567,148 D	28.5%	70.8%	28.7%	71.3%
1968	1,654,861	633,910	Leonard, Jerris	1,020,931	Nelson, Gaylord A.	20	387,021 D	38.3%	61.7%	38.3%	61.7%
1964	1,673,776	780,116	Renk, Wilbur N.	892,013	Proxmire, William	1,647	111,897 D	46.6%	53.3%	46.7%	53.3%
1962	1,260,168	594,846	Wiley, Alexander	662,342	Nelson, Gaylord A.	2,980	67,496 D	47.2%	52.6%	47.3%	52.7%
1958	1,194,678	510,398	Steinle, Roland J.	682,440	Proxmire, William	1,840	172,042 D	42.7%	57.1%	42.8%	57.2%
1957S	772,620	312,931	Kohler, Walter J.	435,985	Proxmire, William	23,704	123,054 D	40.5%	56.4%	41.8%	58.2%
1956	1,523,356	892,473	Wiley, Alexander	627,903	Maier, Henry W.	2,980	264,570 R	58.6%	41.2%	58.7%	41.3%
1952	1,605,228	870,444	McCarthy, Joseph R.	731,402	Fairchild, Thomas E.	3,382	139,042 R	54.2%	45.6%	54.3%	45.7%
1950	1,116,135	595,283	Wiley, Alexander	515,539	Fairchild, Thomas E.	5,313	79,744 R	53.3%	46.2%	53.6%	46.4%
1946	1,014,594	620,430	McCarthy, Joseph R.	378,772	McMurray, Howard J.	15,392	241,658 R	61.2%	37.3%	62.1%	37.9%

Note: The August 1957 election was for a short term to fill a vacancy.

WISCONSIN

PRESIDENT 2008

2000 Census Population	County	Total Vote	Republican	Democratic	Other	Rep.-Dem. Plurality	Percentage Total Vote Rep.	Percentage Total Vote Dem.	Percentage Major Vote Rep.	Percentage Major Vote Dem.
18,643	ADAMS	9,986	3,974	5,806	206	1,832 D	39.8%	58.1%	40.6%	59.4%
16,866	ASHLAND	8,574	2,634	5,818	122	3,184 D	30.7%	67.9%	31.2%	68.8%
44,963	BARRON	22,886	10,457	12,078	351	1,621 D	45.7%	52.8%	46.4%	53.6%
15,013	BAYFIELD	9,468	3,365	5,972	131	2,607 D	35.5%	63.1%	36.0%	64.0%
226,778	BROWN	124,754	55,854	67,269	1,631	11,415 D	44.8%	53.9%	45.4%	54.6%
13,804	BUFFALO	7,000	2,923	3,949	128	1,026 D	41.8%	56.4%	42.5%	57.5%
15,674	BURNETT	8,688	4,200	4,337	151	137 D	48.3%	49.9%	49.2%	50.8%
40,631	CALUMET	26,474	12,722	13,295	457	573 D	48.1%	50.2%	48.9%	51.1%
55,195	CHIPPEWA	30,231	13,492	16,239	500	2,747 D	44.6%	53.7%	45.4%	54.6%
33,557	CLARK	14,187	6,383	7,454	350	1,071 D	45.0%	52.5%	46.1%	53.9%
52,468	COLUMBIA	29,272	12,193	16,661	418	4,468 D	41.7%	56.9%	42.3%	57.7%
17,243	CRAWFORD	7,981	2,830	4,987	164	2,157 D	35.5%	62.5%	36.2%	63.8%
426,526	DANE	282,939	73,065	205,984	3,890	132,919 D	25.8%	72.8%	26.2%	73.8%
85,897	DODGE	42,823	23,015	19,183	625	3,832 R	53.7%	44.8%	54.5%	45.5%
27,961	DOOR	17,481	7,112	10,142	227	3,030 D	40.7%	58.0%	41.2%	58.8%
43,287	DOUGLAS	24,066	7,835	15,830	401	7,995 D	32.6%	65.8%	33.1%	66.9%
39,858	DUNN	22,989	9,566	13,002	421	3,436 D	41.6%	56.6%	42.4%	57.6%
93,142	EAU CLAIRE	55,010	20,959	33,146	905	12,187 D	38.1%	60.3%	38.7%	61.3%
5,088	FLORENCE	2,685	1,512	1,134	39	378 R	56.3%	42.2%	57.1%	42.9%
97,296	FOND DU LAC	52,323	28,164	23,463	696	4,701 R	53.8%	44.8%	54.6%	45.4%
10,024	FOREST	4,683	1,963	2,673	47	710 D	41.9%	57.1%	42.3%	57.7%
49,597	GRANT	24,320	9,068	14,875	377	5,807 D	37.3%	61.2%	37.9%	62.1%
33,647	GREEN	18,534	6,730	11,502	302	4,772 D	36.3%	62.1%	36.9%	63.1%
19,105	GREEN LAKE	9,536	5,393	4,000	143	1,393 R	56.6%	41.9%	57.4%	42.6%
22,780	IOWA	11,969	3,829	7,987	153	4,158 D	32.0%	66.7%	32.4%	67.6%
6,861	IRON	3,432	1,464	1,914	54	450 D	42.7%	55.8%	43.3%	56.7%
19,100	JACKSON	9,251	3,552	5,572	127	2,020 D	38.4%	60.2%	38.9%	61.1%
74,021	JEFFERSON	43,166	21,096	21,448	622	352 D	48.9%	49.7%	49.6%	50.4%
24,316	JUNEAU	11,530	5,148	6,186	196	1,038 D	44.6%	53.7%	45.4%	54.6%
149,577	KENOSHA	78,789	31,609	45,836	1,344	14,227 D	40.1%	58.2%	40.8%	59.2%
20,187	KEWAUNEE	10,787	4,711	5,902	174	1,191 D	43.7%	54.7%	44.4%	55.6%
107,120	LA CROSSE	63,218	23,701	38,524	993	14,823 D	37.5%	60.9%	38.1%	61.9%
16,137	LAFAYETTE	7,831	2,984	4,732	115	1,748 D	38.1%	60.4%	38.7%	61.3%
20,740	LANGLADE	10,402	5,081	5,182	139	101 D	48.8%	49.8%	49.5%	50.5%
29,641	LINCOLN	15,268	6,519	8,424	325	1,905 D	42.7%	55.2%	43.6%	56.4%
82,887	MANITOWOC	42,414	19,234	22,428	752	3,194 D	45.3%	52.9%	46.2%	53.8%
125,834	MARATHON	67,940	30,345	36,367	1,228	6,022 D	44.7%	53.5%	45.5%	54.5%
43,384	MARINETTE	21,255	9,726	11,195	334	1,469 D	45.8%	52.7%	46.5%	53.5%
15,832	MARQUETTE	7,846	3,654	4,068	124	414 D	46.6%	51.8%	47.3%	52.7%
4,562	MENOMINEE	1,448	185	1,257	6	1,072 D	12.8%	86.8%	12.8%	87.2%
940,164	MILWAUKEE	475,192	149,445	319,819	5,928	170,374 D	31.4%	67.3%	31.8%	68.2%
40,899	MONROE	19,152	8,666	10,198	288	1,532 D	45.2%	53.2%	45.9%	54.1%
35,634	OCONTO	18,968	8,755	9,927	286	1,172 D	46.2%	52.3%	46.9%	53.1%
36,776	ONEIDA	21,927	9,630	11,907	390	2,277 D	43.9%	54.3%	44.7%	55.3%
160,971	OUTAGAMIE	91,563	39,677	50,294	1,592	10,617 D	43.3%	54.9%	44.1%	55.9%
82,317	OZAUKEE	53,365	32,172	20,579	614	11,593 R	60.3%	38.6%	61.0%	39.0%
7,213	PEPIN	3,771	1,616	2,102	53	486 D	42.9%	55.7%	43.5%	56.5%
36,804	PIERCE	22,107	9,812	11,803	492	1,991 D	44.4%	53.4%	45.4%	54.6%
41,319	POLK	22,643	11,282	10,876	485	406 R	49.8%	48.0%	50.9%	49.1%
67,182	PORTAGE	39,422	13,810	24,817	795	11,007 D	35.0%	63.0%	35.8%	64.2%

WISCONSIN
PRESIDENT 2008

2000 Census Population	County	Total Vote	Republican	Democratic	Other	Rep.-Dem. Plurality	Percentage			
							Total Vote		Major Vote	
							Rep.	Dem.	Rep.	Dem.
15,822	PRICE	8,194	3,461	4,559	174	1,098 D	42.2%	55.6%	43.2%	56.8%
188,831	RACINE	100,642	45,954	53,408	1,28C	7,454 D	45.7%	53.1%	46.2%	53.8%
17,924	RICHLAND	8,450	3,298	5,041	111	1,743 D	39.0%	59.7%	39.5%	60.5%
152,307	ROCK	79,169	27,364	50,529	1,276	23,165 D	34.6%	63.8%	35.1%	64.9%
15,347	RUSK	7,272	3,253	3,855	164	602 D	44.7%	53.0%	45.8%	54.2%
63,155	ST. CROIX	44,821	22,837	21,177	807	1,660 R	51.0%	47.2%	51.9%	48.1%
55,225	SAUK	30,626	11,562	18,617	447	7,055 D	37.8%	60.8%	38.3%	61.7%
16,196	SAWYER	9,085	4,199	4,765	121	566 D	46.2%	52.4%	46.8%	53.2%
40,664	SHAWANO	20,089	9,538	10,259	292	721 D	47.5%	51.1%	48.2%	51.8%
112,646	SHEBOYGAN	62,107	30,801	30,395	911	406 R	49.6%	48.9%	50.3%	49.7%
19,680	TAYLOR	9,346	4,586	4,563	197	23 R	49.1%	48.8%	50.1%	49.9%
27,010	TREMPEALEAU	13,314	4,808	8,321	185	3,513 D	36.1%	62.5%	36.6%	63.4%
28,056	VERNON	14,075	5,367	8,463	245	3,096 D	38.1%	60.1%	38.8%	61.2%
21,033	VILAS	13,750	7,055	6,491	204	564 R	51.3%	47.2%	52.1%	47.9%
93,759	WALWORTH	50,422	25,485	24,177	760	1,308 R	50.5%	47.9%	51.3%	48.7%
16,036	WASHBURN	9,112	4,303	4,693	116	390 D	47.2%	51.5%	47.8%	52.2%
117,493	WASHINGTON	74,411	47,729	25,719	963	22,010 R	64.1%	34.6%	65.0%	35.0%
360,767	WAUKESHA	232,897	145,152	85,339	2,406	59,813 R	62.3%	36.6%	63.0%	37.0%
51,731	WAUPACA	25,511	12,232	12,952	327	720 D	47.9%	50.8%	48.6%	51.4%
23,154	WAUSHARA	11,849	5,770	5,868	211	98 D	48.7%	49.5%	49.6%	50.4%
156,763	WINNEBAGO	87,677	37,946	48,167	1,564	10,221 D	43.3%	54.9%	44.1%	55.9%
75,555	WOOD	39,052	16,581	21,710	761	5,129 D	42.5%	55.6%	43.3%	56.7%
5,363,675	TOTAL	2,983,417	1,262,393	1,677,211	43,813	414,818 D	42.3%	56.2%	42.9%	57.1%

WISCONSIN

HOUSE OF REPRESENTATIVES

CD	Year	Total Vote	Republican Vote	Republican Candidate	Democratic Vote	Democratic Candidate	Other Vote	Rep.-Dem. Plurality		Total Vote Rep.	Total Vote Dem.	Major Vote Rep.	Major Vote Dem.
1	2008	361,107	231,009	RYAN, PAUL D.*	125,268	KRUPP, MARGE	4,830	105,741	R	64.0%	34.7%	64.8%	35.2%
1	2006	257,596	161,320	RYAN, PAUL D.*	95,761	THOMAS, JEFFREY C.	515	65,559	R	62.6%	37.2%	62.8%	37.2%
1	2004	356,976	233,372	RYAN, PAUL D.*	116,250	THOMAS, JEFFREY C.	7,354	117,122	R	65.4%	32.6%	66.7%	33.3%
1	2002	208,613	140,176	RYAN, PAUL D.*	63,895	THOMAS, JEFFREY C.	4,542	76,281	R	67.2%	30.6%	68.7%	31.3%
2	2008	400,841	122,513	THERON, PETER	277,914	BALDWIN, TAMMY*	414	155,401	D	30.6%	69.3%	30.6%	69.4%
2	2006	304,688	113,015	MAGNUM, DAVE	191,414	BALDWIN, TAMMY*	259	78,399	D	37.1%	62.8%	37.1%	62.9%
2	2004	397,724	145,810	MAGNUM, DAVE	251,637	BALDWIN, TAMMY*	277	105,827	D	36.7%	63.3%	36.7%	63.3%
2	2002	247,410	83,694	GREER, RON	163,313	BALDWIN, TAMMY*	403	79,619	D	33.8%	66.0%	33.9%	66.1%
3	2008	356,400	122,760	STARK, PAUL	225,208	KIND, RON*	8,432	102,448	D	34.4%	63.2%	35.3%	64.7%
3	2006	252,087	88,523	NELSON, PAUL R.	163,322	KIND, RON*	242	74,799	D	35.1%	64.8%	35.1%	64.9%
3	2004	363,008	157,866	SCHULTZ, DALE W.	204,856	KIND, RON*	286	46,990	D	43.5%	56.4%	43.5%	56.5%
3	2002	208,581	69,955	ARNDT, BILL	131,038	KIND, RON*	7,588	61,083	D	33.5%	62.8%	34.8%	65.2%
4	2008	254,179		—	222,728	MOORE, GWEN*	31,451	222,728	D		87.6%		100.0%
4	2006	191,742	54,486	RIVERA, PERFECTO	136,735	MOORE, GWEN*	521	82,249	D	28.4%	71.3%	28.5%	71.5%
4	2004	305,142	85,928	BOYLE, GERALD H.	212,382	MOORE, GWEN	6,832	126,454	D	28.2%	69.6%	28.8%	71.2%
4	2002	141,367		—	122,031	KLECZKA, GERALD D.*	19,336	122,031	D		86.3%		100.0%
5	2008	345,899	275,271	SENSENBRENNER, F. JAMES JR.*		—	70,628	275,271	R	79.6%		100.0%	
5	2006	315,180	194,669	SENSENBRENNER, F. JAMES JR.*	112,451	KENNEDY, BRYAN	8,060	82,218	R	61.8%	35.7%	63.4%	36.6%
5	2004	407,291	271,153	SENSENBRENNER, F. JAMES JR.*	129,384	KENNEDY, BRYAN	6,754	141,769	R	66.6%	31.8%	67.7%	32.3%
5	2002	222,012	191,224	SENSENBRENNER, F. JAMES JR.*		—	30,788	191,224	R	86.1%		100.0%	
6	2008	348,264	221,875	PETRI, TOM*	126,090	KITTELSON, ROGER A.	299	95,785	R	63.7%	36.2%	63.8%	36.2%
6	2006	203,557	201,367	PETRI, TOM*		—	2,190	201,367	R	98.9%		100.0%	
6	2004	355,995	238,620	PETRI, TOM*	107,209	HALL, JEF	10,166	131,411	R	67.0%	30.1%	69.0%	31.0%
6	2002	171,161	169,834	PETRI, TOM*		—	1,327	169,834	R	99.2%		100.0%	
7	2008	349,837	136,938	MIELKE, DAN	212,666	OBEY, DAVID R.*	233	75,728	D	39.1%	60.8%	39.2%	60.8%
7	2006	260,428	91,069	REID, NICK	161,903	OBEY, DAVID R.*	7,456	70,834	D	35.0%	62.2%	36.0%	64.0%
7	2004	281,752		—	241,306	OBEY, DAVID R.*	40,446	241,306	D		85.6%		100.0%
7	2002	227,955	81,518	ROTHBAUER, JOE	146,364	OBEY, DAVID R.*	73	64,846	D	35.8%	64.2%	35.8%	64.2%
8	2008	358,647	164,621	GARD, JOHN	193,662	KAGEN, STEVE	364	29,041	D	45.9%	54.0%	45.9%	54.1%
8	2006	278,135	135,622	GARD, JOHN	141,570	KAGEN, STEVE	943	5,948	D	48.8%	50.9%	48.9%	51.1%
8	2004	353,725	248,070	GREEN, MARK*	105,513	LE CLAIR, DOTTIE	142	142,557	R	70.1%	29.8%	70.2%	29.8%
8	2002	210,447	152,745	GREEN, MARK*	50,284	BECKER, ANDREW M.	7,418	102,461	R	72.6%	23.9%	75.2%	24.8%
TOTAL	2008	2,775,174	1,274,987		1,383,536		116,651	108,549	D	45.9%	49.9%	48.0%	52.0%
TOTAL	2006	2,063,413	1,040,071		1,003,156		20,186	36,915	R	50.4%	48.6%	50.9%	49.1%
TOTAL	2004	2,821,613	1,380,819		1,368,537		72,257	12,282	R	48.9%	48.5%	50.2%	49.8%
TOTAL	2002	1,637,546	889,146		676,925		71,475	212,221	R	54.3%	41.3%	56.8%	43.2%

Note: An asterisk (*) denotes incumbent.

WISCONSIN
GENERAL AND PRIMARY ELECTIONS

2008 GENERAL ELECTIONS

President Other vote was 17,605 Independent (Ralph Nader); 8,858 Libertarian (Bob Barr); 5,072 Independent (Chuck Baldwin); 4,216 Wisconsin Green (Cynthia A. McKinney); 764 Independent (Jeffrey J. Wamboldt); 540 Independent (Brian Moore); 237 Independent (Gloria La Riva); 6,521 scattered write-in.

House Other vote was:

CD 1 4,606 Libertarian (Joseph Kexel); 224 scattered write-in.
CD 2 414 scattered write-in.
CD 3 8,236 Libertarian (Kevin Barrett); 196 scattered write-in.
CD 4 29,282 Independent (Michael D. LaForest); 2,169 scattered write-in.
CD 5 69,715 Independent (Robert R. Raymond); 913 scattered write-in.
CD 6 299 scattered write-in.
CD 7 233 scattered write-in.
CD 8 364 scattered write-in.

2008 PRIMARY ELECTIONS

Primary February 19, 2008 (President) **Registration** 3,416,675 No Party Registration
September 9, 2008 (Congress) (as of September 9, 2008)

Primary Type Open—Any registered voter could participate in the party primary of their choice.

	REPUBLICAN PRIMARIES			DEMOCRATIC PRIMARIES		
President	John McCain	224,755	54.7%	Barack Obama	646,851	58.1%
	Mike Huckabee	151,707	36.9%	Hillary Clinton	453,954	40.8%
	Ron Paul	19,090	4.6%	John Edwards	6,693	0.6%
	Mitt Romney	8,080	2.0%	Dennis J. Kucinich	2,625	0.2%
	Fred Thompson	2,709	0.7%	Uninstructed Delegation	861	0.1%
	Rudolph Giuliani	1,935	0.5%	Joseph R. Biden Jr.	755	0.1%
	Uninstructed Delegation	850	0.2%	Bill Richardson	528	
	Duncan Hunter	799	0.2%	Mike Gravel	517	
	Tom Tancredo	185		Christopher J. Dodd	501	
	Scattered write-in	497	0.1%	Scattered write-in	468	
	TOTAL	410,607		TOTAL	1,113,753	
Congressional District 1	Paul D. Ryan*	11,718	99.8%	Marge Krupp	6,015	36.5%
	Scattered write-in	24	0.2%	Paulette Garin	5,221	31.7%
				Mike Hebert	4,511	27.4%
				John Mogk	689	4.2%
				Scattered write-in	49	0.3%
	TOTAL	11,742		TOTAL	16,485	
Congressional District 2	Peter Theron	7,407	99.7%	Tammy Baldwin*	18,414	99.3%
	Scattered write-in	22	0.3%	Scattered write-in	132	0.7%
	TOTAL	7,429		TOTAL	18,546	
Congressional District 3	Paul Stark	17,841	99.6%	Ron Kind*	18,039	99.7%
	Scattered write-in	63	0.4%	Scattered write-in	62	0.3%
	TOTAL	17,904		TOTAL	18,101	
Congressional District 4	No Republican candidate			Gwen Moore*	18,342	96.4%
				Scattered write-in	694	3.6%
				TOTAL	19,036	

WISCONSIN

GENERAL AND PRIMARY ELECTIONS

	REPUBLICAN PRIMARIES			DEMOCRATIC PRIMARIES		
Congressional District 5	F. James Sensenbrenner Jr.*	47,144	78.3%	*No Democratic candidate filed for the primary. There were 691 scattered write-in votes.*		
	Jim Burkee	13,078	21.7%			
	Scattered write-in	14				
	TOTAL	60,236				
Congressional District 6	Tom Petri*	21,839	99.6%	Roger A. Kittelson	7,441	62.0%
	Scattered write-in	82	0.4%	Mark Wollum	4,548	37.9%
				Scattered write-in	22	0.2%
	TOTAL	21,921		TOTAL	12,011	
Congressional District 7	Dan Mielke	8,208	99.6%	David R. Obey*	25,100	99.5%
	Scattered write-in	35	0.4%	Scattered write-in	129	0.5%
	TOTAL	8,243		TOTAL	25,229	
Congressional District 8	John Gard	16,569	99.4%	Steve Kagen*	14,500	99.8%
	Scattered write-in	93	0.6%	Scattered write-in	26	0.2%
	TOTAL	16,662		TOTAL	14,526	

Note: An asterisk (*) denotes incumbent.

WYOMING

One member At Large

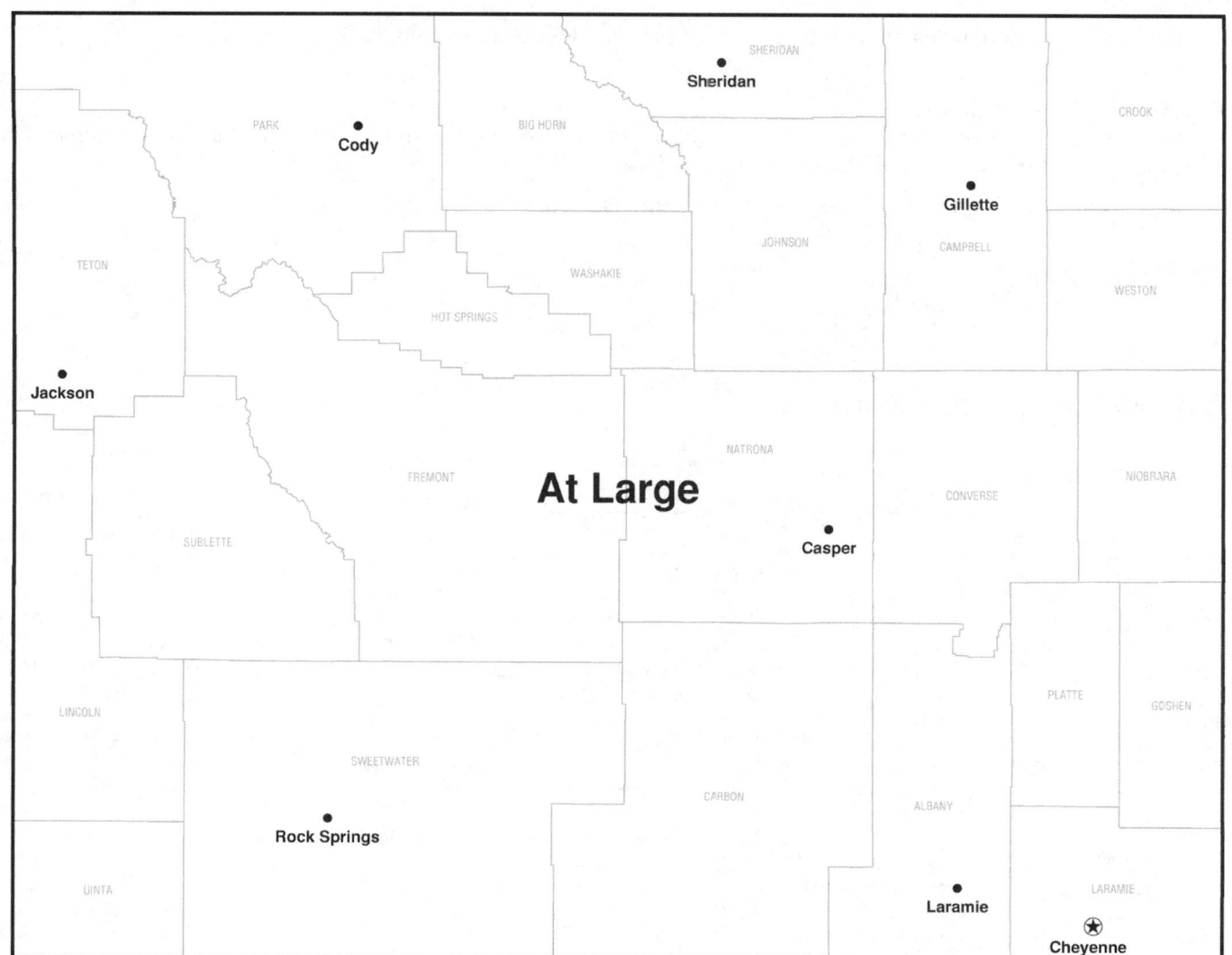

WYOMING

GOVERNOR
Dave Freudenthal (D). Reelected 2006 to a four-year term. Previously elected 2002.

SENATORS (2 Republicans)
John Barrasso (R). Elected 2008 to fill out the remaining four years of the term vacated by the June 2007 death of Sen. Craig Thomas (R); sworn in as Thomas's successor June 25, 2007.

Michael B. Enzi (R). Reelected 2008 to a six-year term. Previously elected 2002, 1996.

REPRESENTATIVE (1 Republican)
At Large. Cynthia M. Lummis (R)

POSTWAR VOTE FOR PRESIDENT

		Republican		Democratic				Total Vote		Major Vote	
Year	Total Vote	Vote	Candidate	Vote	Candidate	Other Vote	Plurality	Rep.	Dem.	Rep.	Dem.
2008	254,658	164,958	McCain, John	82,868	Obama, Barack	6,832	82,090 R	64.8%	32.5%	66.6%	33.4%
2004	243,428	167,629	Bush, George W.	70,776	Kerry, John	5,023	96,853 R	68.9%	29.1%	70.3%	29.7%
2000**	218,351	147,947	Bush, George W.	60,481	Gore, Al	9,923	87,466 R	67.8%	27.7%	71.0%	29.0%
1996**	211,571	105,388	Dole, Bob	77,934	Clinton, Bill	28,249	27,454 R	49.8%	36.8%	57.5%	42.5%
1992**	200,598	79,347	Bush, George	68,160	Clinton, Bill	53,091	11,187 R	39.6%	34.0%	53.8%	46.2%
1988	176,551	106,867	Bush, George	67,113	Dukakis, Michael S.	2,571	39,754 R	60.5%	38.0%	61.4%	38.6%
1984	188,968	133,241	Reagan, Ronald	53,370	Mondale, Walter F.	2,357	79,871 R	70.5%	28.2%	71.4%	28.6%
1980**	176,713	110,700	Reagan, Ronald	49,427	Carter, Jimmy	16,586	61,273 R	62.6%	28.0%	69.1%	30.9%
1976	156,343	92,717	Ford, Gerald R.	62,239	Carter, Jimmy	1,387	30,478 R	59.3%	39.8%	59.8%	40.2%
1972	145,570	100,464	Nixon, Richard M.	44,358	McGovern, George S.	748	56,106 R	69.0%	30.5%	69.4%	30.6%
1968**	127,205	70,927	Nixon, Richard M.	45,173	Humphrey, Hubert H.	11,105	25,754 R	55.8%	35.5%	61.1%	38.9%
1964	142,716	61,998	Goldwater, Barry M.	80,718	Johnson, Lyndon B.		18,720 D	43.4%	56.6%	43.4%	56.6%
1960	140,782	77,451	Nixon, Richard M.	63,331	Kennedy, John F.		14,120 R	55.0%	45.0%	55.0%	45.0%
1956	124,127	74,573	Eisenhower, Dwight D.	49,554	Stevenson, Adlai E.		25,019 R	60.1%	39.9%	60.1%	39.9%
1952	129,253	81,049	Eisenhower, Dwight D.	47,934	Stevenson, Adlai E.	270	33,115 R	62.7%	37.1%	62.8%	37.2%
1948	101,425	47,947	Dewey, Thomas E.	52,354	Truman, Harry S.	1,124	4,407 D	47.3%	51.6%	47.8%	52.2%

**In past elections, the other vote included: 2000 - 4,625 Green (Ralph Nader); 1996 - 25,928 Reform (Ross Perot); 1992 - 51,263 Independent (Perot); 1980 - 12,072 Independent (John Anderson); 1968 - 11,105 American Independent (George Wallace).

WYOMING

POSTWAR VOTE FOR GOVERNOR

Year	Total Vote	Republican Vote	Candidate	Democratic Vote	Candidate	Other Vote	Rep.-Dem. Plurality	Rep.	Dem.	Rep.	Dem.
2006	193,892	58,100	Hunkins, Ray	135,516	Freudenthal, Dave	276	77,416 D	30.0%	69.9%	30.0%	70.0%
2002	185,459	88,873	Bebout, Eli	92,662	Freudenthal, Dave	3,924	3,789 D	47.9%	50.0%	49.0%	51.0%
1998	174,888	97,235	Geringer, Jim	70,754	Vinich, John P.	6,899	26,481 R	55.6%	40.5%	57.9%	42.1%
1994	200,990	118,016	Geringer, Jim	80,747	Karpan, Kathy	2,227	37,269 R	58.7%	40.2%	59.4%	40.6%
1990	160,109	55,471	Mead, Mary	104,638	Sullivan, Mike		49,167 D	34.6%	65.4%	34.6%	65.4%
1986	164,720	75,841	Simpson, Peter	88,879	Sullivan, Mike		13,038 D	46.0%	54.0%	46.0%	54.0%
1982	168,555	62,128	Morton, Warren A.	106,427	Herschler, Ed		44,299 D	36.9%	63.1%	36.9%	63.1%
1978	137,567	67,595	Ostlund, John C.	69,972	Herschler, Ed		2,377 D	49.1%	50.9%	49.1%	50.9%
1974	128,386	56,645	Jones, Dick	71,741	Herschler, Ed		15,096 D	44.1%	55.9%	44.1%	55.9%
1970	118,257	74,249	Hathaway, Stan	44,008	Rooney, John J.		30,241 R	62.8%	37.2%	62.8%	37.2%
1966	120,873	65,624	Hathaway, Stan	55,249	Wilkerson, Ernest		10,375 R	54.3%	45.7%	54.3%	45.7%
1962	119,268	64,970	Hansen, Clifford P.	54,298	Gage, Jack R.		10,672 R	54.5%	45.5%	54.5%	45.5%
1958	112,537	52,488	Simpson, Milward L.	55,070	Hickey, J. J.	4,979	2,582 D	46.6%	48.9%	48.8%	51.2%
1954	111,438	56,275	Simpson, Milward L.	55,163	Jack, William		1,112 R	50.5%	49.5%	50.5%	49.5%
1950	96,959	54,441	Barrett, Frank A.	42,518	McIntyre, John J.		11,923 R	56.1%	43.9%	56.1%	43.9%
1946	81,353	38,333	Wright, Earl	43,020	Hunt, Lester C.		4,687 D	47.1%	52.9%	47.1%	52.9%

POSTWAR VOTE FOR SENATOR

Year	Total Vote	Republican Vote	Candidate	Democratic Vote	Candidate	Other Vote	Rep.-Dem. Plurality	Rep.	Dem.	Rep.	Dem.
2008	249,946	189,046	Enzi, Michael B.	60,631	Rothfuss, Chris	269	128,415 R	75.6%	24.3%	75.7%	24.3%
2008S	249,558	183,063	Barrasso, John	66,202	Carter, Nick	293	116,861 R	73.4%	26.5%	73.4%	26.6%
2006	193,136	135,174	Thomas, Craig	57,671	Groutage, Dale	291	77,503 R	70.0%	29.9%	70.1%	29.9%
2002	183,280	133,710	Enzi, Michael B.	49,570	Corcoran, Joyce Jansa		84,140 R	73.0%	27.0%	73.0%	27.0%
2000	213,659	157,622	Thomas, Craig	47,087	Logan, Mel	8,950	110,535 R	73.8%	22.0%	77.0%	23.0%
1996	211,077	114,116	Enzi, Michael B.	89,103	Karpan, Kathy	7,858	25,013 R	54.1%	42.2%	56.2%	43.8%
1994	201,710	118,754	Thomas, Craig	79,287	Sullivan, Mike	3,669	39,467 R	58.9%	39.3%	60.0%	40.0%
1990	157,632	100,784	Simpson, Alan K.	56,848	Helling, Kathy		43,936 R	63.9%	36.1%	63.9%	36.1%
1988	180,964	91,143	Wallop, Malcolm	89,821	Vinich, John P.		1,322 R	50.4%	49.6%	50.4%	49.6%
1984	186,898	146,373	Simpson, Alan K.	40,525	Ryan, Victor A.		105,848 R	78.3%	21.7%	78.3%	21.7%
1982	167,191	94,725	Wallop, Malcolm	72,466	McDaniel, Rodger		22,259 R	56.7%	43.3%	56.7%	43.3%
1978	133,364	82,908	Simpson, Alan K.	50,456	Whitaker, Raymond B.		32,452 R	62.2%	37.8%	62.2%	37.8%
1976	155,368	84,810	Wallop, Malcolm	70,558	McGee, Gale		14,252 R	54.6%	45.4%	54.6%	45.4%
1972	142,067	101,314	Hansen, Clifford P.	40,753	Vinich, Mike		60,561 R	71.3%	28.7%	71.3%	28.7%
1970	120,486	53,279	Wold, John S.	67,207	McGee, Gale		13,928 D	44.2%	55.8%	44.2%	55.8%
1966	122,689	63,548	Hansen, Clifford P.	59,141	Roncalio, Teno		4,407 R	51.8%	48.2%	51.8%	48.2%
1964	141,670	65,185	Wold, John S.	76,485	McGee, Gale		11,300 D	46.0%	54.0%	46.0%	54.0%
1962S	119,372	69,043	Simpson, Milward L.	50,329	Hickey, J. J.		18,714 R	57.8%	42.2%	57.8%	42.2%
1960	138,550	78,103	Thomson, E. Keith	60,447	Whitaker, Ray		17,656 R	56.4%	43.6%	56.4%	43.6%
1958	114,157	56,122	Barrett, Frank A.	58,035	McGee, Gale		1,913 D	49.2%	50.8%	49.2%	50.8%
1954	112,252	54,407	Harrison, William H.	57,845	O'Mahoney, Joseph C.		3,438 D	48.5%	51.5%	48.5%	51.5%
1952	130,097	67,176	Barrett, Frank A.	62,921	O'Mahoney, Joseph C.		4,255 R	51.6%	48.4%	51.6%	48.4%
1948	101,480	43,527	Robertson, Edward V.	57,953	Hunt, Lester C.		14,426 D	42.9%	57.1%	42.9%	57.1%
1946	81,557	35,714	Henderson, Harry B.	45,843	O'Mahoney, Joseph C.		10,129 D	43.8%	56.2%	43.8%	56.2%

Note: The 1962 election and one of the 2008 elections were for a short term to fill a vacancy.

WYOMING

PRESIDENT 2008

2000 Census Population	County	Total Vote	Republican	Democratic	Other	Rep.-Dem. Plurality	Percentage Total Vote		Percentage Major Vote	
							Rep.	Dem.	Rep.	Dem.
32,014	ALBANY	17,117	7,936	8,644	537	708 D	46.4%	50.5%	47.9%	52.1%
11,461	BIG HORN	5,310	4,045	1,108	157	2,937 R	76.2%	20.9%	78.5%	21.5%
33,698	CAMPBELL	16,320	13,011	2,990	319	10,021 R	79.7%	18.3%	81.3%	18.7%
15,639	CARBON	6,854	4,331	2,336	187	1,995 R	63.2%	34.1%	65.0%	35.0%
12,052	CONVERSE	6,451	4,922	1,380	149	3,542 R	76.3%	21.4%	78.1%	21.9%
5,887	CROOK	3,683	2,967	612	104	2,355 R	80.6%	16.6%	82.9%	17.1%
35,804	FREMONT	17,592	11,083	6,016	493	5,067 R	63.0%	34.2%	64.8%	35.2%
12,538	GOSHEN	5,912	3,942	1,832	138	2,110 R	66.7%	31.0%	68.3%	31.7%
4,882	HOT SPRINGS	2,546	1,834	619	93	1,215 R	72.0%	24.3%	74.8%	25.2%
7,075	JOHNSON	4,354	3,334	908	112	2,426 R	76.6%	20.9%	78.6%	21.4%
81,607	LARAMIE	41,625	24,549	16,072	1,004	8,477 R	59.0%	38.6%	60.4%	39.6%
14,573	LINCOLN	8,568	6,485	1,823	260	4,662 R	75.7%	21.3%	78.1%	21.9%
66,533	NATRONA	33,267	21,906	10,475	886	11,431 R	65.8%	31.5%	67.7%	32.3%
2,407	NIOBRARA	1,293	1,017	244	32	773 R	78.7%	18.9%	80.7%	19.3%
25,786	PARK	14,985	10,839	3,757	389	7,082 R	72.3%	25.1%	74.3%	25.7%
8,807	PLATTE	4,560	3,002	1,407	151	1,595 R	65.8%	30.9%	68.1%	31.9%
26,560	SHERIDAN	14,981	10,177	4,458	346	5,719 R	67.9%	29.8%	69.5%	30.5%
5,920	SUBLETTE	4,356	3,316	936	104	2,380 R	76.1%	21.5%	78.0%	22.0%
37,613	SWEETWATER	16,703	10,360	5,762	581	4,598 R	62.0%	34.5%	64.3%	35.7%
18,251	TETON	12,316	4,565	7,472	279	2,907 D	37.1%	60.7%	37.9%	62.1%
19,742	UINTA	8,383	5,763	2,317	303	3,446 R	68.7%	27.6%	71.3%	28.7%
8,289	WASHAKIE	4,089	2,956	1,042	91	1,914 R	72.3%	25.5%	73.9%	26.1%
6,644	WESTON	3,393	2,618	658	117	1,960 R	77.2%	19.4%	79.9%	20.1%
493,782	TOTAL	254,658	164,958	82,868	6,832	82,090 R	64.8%	32.5%	66.6%	33.4%

WYOMING

SENATOR 2006 (Full Term)

2000 Census Population	County	Total Vote	Republican	Democratic	Other	Rep.-Dem. Plurality	Percentage Total Vote		Percentage Major Vote	
							Rep.	Dem.	Rep.	Dem.
32,014	ALBANY	16,676	10,481	6,170	25	4,311 R	62.9%	37.0%	62.9%	37.1%
11,461	BIG HORN	5,278	4,590	682	6	3,908 R	87.0%	12.9%	87.1%	12.9%
33,698	CAMPBELL	16,145	14,191	1,938	16	12,253 R	87.9%	12.0%	88.0%	12.0%
15,639	CARBON	6,719	4,951	1,760	8	3,191 R	73.7%	26.2%	73.8%	26.2%
12,052	CONVERSE	6,385	5,393	990	2	4,403 R	84.5%	15.5%	84.5%	15.5%
5,887	CROOK	3,647	3,202	437	8	2,765 R	87.8%	12.0%	88.0%	12.0%
35,804	FREMONT	17,154	12,927	4,212	15	8,715 R	75.4%	24.6%	75.4%	24.6%
12,538	GOSHEN	5,815	4,603	1,210	2	3,393 R	79.2%	20.8%	79.2%	20.8%
4,882	HOT SPRINGS	2,523	2,097	423	3	1,674 R	83.1%	16.8%	83.2%	16.8%
7,075	JOHNSON	4,319	3,733	577	9	3,156 R	86.4%	13.4%	86.6%	13.4%
81,607	LARAMIE	40,760	28,871	11,845	44	17,026 R	70.8%	29.1%	70.9%	29.1%
14,573	LINCOLN	8,443	7,001	1,430	12	5,571 R	82.9%	16.9%	83.0%	17.0%
66,533	NATRONA	32,606	24,724	7,848	34	16,876 R	75.8%	24.1%	75.9%	24.1%
2,407	NIOBRARA	1,284	1,107	177		930 R	86.2%	13.8%	86.2%	13.8%
25,786	PARK	14,766	12,105	2,645	16	9,460 R	82.0%	17.9%	82.1%	17.9%

WYOMING

SENATOR 2006 (Full Term)

2000 Census Population	County	Total Vote	Republican	Democratic	Other	Rep.-Dem. Plurality	Percentage Total Vote Rep.	Dem.	Major Vote Rep.	Dem.
8,807	PLATTE	4,524	3,418	1,104	2	2,314 R	75.6%	24.4%	75.6%	24.4%
26,560	SHERIDAN	14,785	11,674	3,105	6	8,569 R	79.0%	21.0%	79.0%	21.0%
5,920	SUBLETTE	4,244	3,555	680	9	2,875 R	83.8%	16.0%	83.9%	16.1%
37,613	SWEETWATER	16,438	11,479	4,937	22	6,542 R	69.8%	30.0%	69.9%	30.1%
18,251	TETON	11,789	6,348	5,423	18	925 R	53.8%	46.0%	53.9%	46.1%
19,742	UINTA	8,252	6,305	1,941	6	4,364 R	76.4%	23.5%	76.5%	23.5%
8,289	WASHAKIE	4,033	3,427	602	4	2,825 R	85.0%	14.9%	85.1%	14.9%
6,644	WESTON	3,361	2,864	495	2	2,369 R	85.2%	14.7%	85.3%	14.7%
493,782	TOTAL	249,946	189,046	60,631	269	128,415 R	75.6%	24.3%	75.7%	24.3%

WYOMING

SENATOR 2006 (Short Term)

2000 Census Population	County	Total Vote	Republican	Democratic	Other	Rep.-Dem. Plurality	Percentage Total Vote Rep.	Dem.	Major Vote Rep.	Dem.
32,014	ALBANY	16,563	9,786	6,745	32	3,041 R	59.1%	40.7%	59.2%	40.8%
11,461	BIG HORN	5,261	4,543	714	4	3,829 R	86.4%	13.6%	86.4%	13.6%
33,698	CAMPBELL	16,046	12,277	3,751	18	8,526 R	76.5%	23.4%	76.6%	23.4%
15,639	CARBON	6,702	4,901	1,795	6	3,106 R	73.1%	26.8%	73.2%	26.8%
12,052	CONVERSE	6,397	5,407	984	6	4,423 R	84.5%	15.4%	84.6%	15.4%
5,887	CROOK	3,634	3,016	612	6	2,404 R	83.0%	16.8%	83.1%	16.9%
35,804	FREMONT	17,318	12,823	4,483	12	8,340 R	74.0%	25.9%	74.1%	25.9%
12,538	GOSHEN	5,803	4,559	1,239	5	3,320 R	78.6%	21.4%	78.6%	21.4%
4,882	HOT SPRINGS	2,532	2,095	436	1	1,659 R	82.7%	17.2%	82.8%	17.2%
7,075	JOHNSON	4,302	3,654	640	8	3,014 R	84.9%	14.9%	85.1%	14.9%
81,607	LARAMIE	40,713	27,582	13,086	45	14,496 R	67.7%	32.1%	67.8%	32.2%
14,573	LINCOLN	8,397	6,914	1,472	11	5,442 R	82.3%	17.5%	82.4%	17.6%
66,533	NATRONA	32,699	24,489	8,171	39	16,318 R	74.9%	25.0%	75.0%	25.0%
2,407	NIOBRARA	1,281	1,126	153	2	973 R	87.9%	11.9%	88.0%	12.0%
25,786	PARK	14,722	11,799	2,898	25	8,901 R	80.1%	19.7%	80.3%	19.7%
8,807	PLATTE	4,510	3,358	1,149	3	2,209 R	74.5%	25.5%	74.5%	25.5%
26,560	SHERIDAN	14,719	11,199	3,503	17	7,696 R	76.1%	23.8%	76.2%	23.8%
5,920	SUBLETTE	4,241	3,554	679	8	2,875 R	83.8%	16.0%	84.0%	16.0%
37,613	SWEETWATER	16,403	11,360	5,025	18	6,335 R	69.3%	30.6%	69.3%	30.7%
18,251	TETON	11,697	6,266	5,417	14	849 R	53.6%	46.3%	53.6%	46.4%
19,742	UINTA	8,222	6,183	2,032	7	4,151 R	75.2%	24.7%	75.3%	24.7%
8,289	WASHAKIE	4,033	3,383	646	4	2,737 R	83.9%	16.0%	84.0%	16.0%
6,644	WESTON	3,363	2,789	572	2	2,217 R	82.9%	17.0%	83.0%	17.0%
493,782	TOTAL	249,558	183,063	66,202	293	116,861 R	73.4%	26.5%	73.4%	26.6%

WYOMING

HOUSE OF REPRESENTATIVES

CD	Year	Total Vote	Republican Vote	Republican Candidate	Democratic Vote	Democratic Candidate	Other Vote	Rep.-Dem. Plurality	Total Vote Rep.	Total Vote Dem.	Major Vote Rep.	Major Vote Dem.
AL	2008	249,395	131,244	Lummis, Cynthia M.	106,758	Trauner, Gary	11,393	24,486 R	52.6%	42.8%	55.1%	44.9%
AL	2006	193,369	93,336	Cubin, Barbara*	92,324	Trauner, Gary	7,709	1,012 R	48.3%	47.7%	50.3%	49.7%
AL	2004	239,034	132,107	Cubin, Barbara*	99,989	Ladd, Ted	6,938	32,118 R	55.3%	41.8%	56.9%	43.1%
AL	2002	182,152	110,229	Cubin, Barbara*	65,961	Akin, Ron	5,962	44,268 R	60.5%	36.2%	62.6%	37.4%
AL	2000	212,312	141,848	Cubin, Barbara*	60,638	Green, Michael Allen	9,826	81,210 R	66.8%	28.6%	70.1%	29.9%
AL	1998	174,219	100,687	Cubin, Barbara*	67,399	Farris, Scott	6,133	33,288 R	57.8%	38.7%	59.9%	40.1%
AL	1996	209,983	116,004	Cubin, Barbara*	85,724	Maxfield, Pete	8,255	30,280 R	55.2%	40.8%	57.5%	42.5%
AL	1994	196,197	104,426	Cubin, Barbara	81,022	Schuster, Bob	10,749	23,404 R	53.2%	41.3%	56.3%	43.7%
AL	1992	196,977	113,882	Thomas, Craig*	77,418	Herschler, Jon	5,677	36,464 R	57.8%	39.3%	59.5%	40.5%
AL	1990	158,055	87,078	Thomas, Craig*	70,977	Maxfield, Pete		16,101 R	55.1%	44.9%	55.1%	44.9%
AL	1988	177,651	118,350	Cheney, Richard*	56,527	Sharratt, Bryan	2,774	61,823 R	66.6%	31.8%	67.7%	32.3%
AL	1986	159,787	111,007	Cheney, Richard*	48,780	Gilmore, Rick		62,227 R	69.5%	30.5%	69.5%	30.5%
AL	1984	187,904	138,234	Cheney, Richard*	45,857	McFadden, Hugh B.	3,813	92,377 R	73.6%	24.4%	75.1%	24.9%
AL	1982	159,277	113,236	Cheney, Richard*	46,041	Hommel, Theodore H.		67,195 R	71.1%	28.9%	71.1%	28.9%
AL	1980	169,699	116,361	Cheney, Richard*	53,338	Rogers, Jim		63,023 R	68.6%	31.4%	68.6%	31.4%
AL	1978	129,377	75,855	Cheney, Richard	53,522	Bagley, Bill		22,333 R	58.6%	41.4%	58.6%	41.4%
AL	1976	151,868	66,147	Hart, Larry	85,721	Roncalio, Teno*		19,574 D	43.6%	56.4%	43.6%	56.4%
AL	1974	126,933	57,499	Strook, Tom	69,434	Roncalio, Teno*		11,935 D	45.3%	54.7%	45.3%	54.7%
AL	1972	146,299	70,667	Kidd, William	75,632	Roncalio, Teno*		4,965 D	48.3%	51.7%	48.3%	51.7%
AL	1970	116,304	57,848	Roberts, Harry	58,456	Roncalio, Teno		608 D	49.7%	50.3%	49.7%	50.3%
AL	1968	123,313	77,363	Wold, John S.	45,950	Linford, Velma		31,413 R	62.7%	37.3%	62.7%	37.3%
AL	1966	119,426	62,984	Harrison, William H.	56,442	Christian, Al		6,542 R	52.7%	47.3%	52.7%	47.3%
AL	1964	139,175	68,482	Harrison, William H.*	70,693	Roncalio, Teno		2,211 D	49.2%	50.8%	49.2%	50.8%
AL	1962	116,474	71,489	Harrison, William H.*	44,985	Mankus, Louis A.		26,504 R	61.4%	38.6%	61.4%	38.6%
AL	1960	134,331	70,241	Harrison, William H.	64,090	Armstong, H.T.		6,151 R	52.3%	47.7%	52.3%	47.7%
AL	1958	111,780	59,894	Thomson, E. Keith*	51,886	Whitaker, Ray		8,008 R	53.6%	46.4%	53.6%	46.4%
AL	1956	120,128	69,903	Thomson, E. Keith*	50,225	O'Callaghan, Jerry		19,678 R	58.2%	41.8%	58.2%	41.8%
AL	1954	108,771	61,111	Thomson, E. Keith	47,660	Tully, Sam		13,451 R	56.2%	43.8%	56.2%	43.8%
AL	1952	126,720	76,161	Harrison, William H.*	50,559	Rose, Robert R.		25,602 R	60.1%	39.9%	60.1%	39.9%
AL	1950	93,348	50,865	Harrison, William H.	42,483	Clark, John B.		8,382 R	54.5%	45.5%	54.5%	45.5%
AL	1948	97,464	50,218	Barrett, Frank A.*	47,246	Flannery, L. G.		2,972 R	51.5%	48.5%	51.5%	48.5%
AL	1946	79,438	44,482	Barrett, Frank A.*	34,956	McIntyre, John J.		9,526 R	56.0%	44.0%	56.0%	44.0%

Note: An asterisk (*) denotes incumbent.

WYOMING

GENERAL AND PRIMARY ELECTIONS

2008 GENERAL ELECTIONS

President Other vote was 2,525 Independent (Ralph Nader); 1,594 Libertarian (Bob Barr); 1,192 Independent (Chuck Baldwin); 1,521 scattered write-in.

Senator (Full Term) Other vote was 269 scattered write-in.

Senator (Short Term) Other vote was 293 scattered write-in.

House Other vote was:

  At Large 11,030 Libertarian (W. David Herbert); 363 scattered write-in.

WYOMING

GENERAL AND PRIMARY ELECTIONS

2008 PRIMARY ELECTIONS

Primary	August 19, 2008	**Registration** (active registrants as of August 19, 2008)	Republican 138,234
			Democratic 60,736
			Libertarian 655
			Other 45
			Unaffiliated 22,930
			TOTAL 222,600

Primary Type   Only registered Democrats and Republicans could vote in their party's primary, although on primary day any new voter could register with the party of their choice and any previously registered voter could participate in another party's primary by changing their registration to that party.

	REPUBLICAN PRIMARIES			DEMOCRATIC PRIMARIES		
Senator (Full Term)	Michael B. Enzi*	69,195	99.3%	Craig Rothfuss	14,221	61.9%
	Scattered write-in	463	0.7%	Al Hamburg	8,578	37.3%
				Scattered write-in	181	0.8%
	TOTAL	*69,658*		*TOTAL*	*22,980*	
Senator (Short Term)	John Barrasso*	68,194	99.2%	Nick Carter	12,316	50.5%
	Scattered write-in	566	0.8%	Keith B. Goodenough	11,984	49.1%
				Scattered write-in	86	0.4%
	TOTAL	*68,760*		*TOTAL*	*24,386*	
House **At Large**	Cynthia M. Lummis	33,149	46.2%	Gary Trauner	24,741	99.4%
	Mark Gordon	26,827	37.4%	Scattered write-in	147	0.6%
	Bill Winney	8,537	11.9%			
	Michael S. Holland	3,171	4.4%			
	Scattered write-in	139	0.2%			
	TOTAL	*71,823*		*TOTAL*	*24,888*	

Note: An asterisk (*) denotes incumbent.

DISTRICT OF COLUMBIA

WARD 4

WARD 3

Western Ave

Eastern Ave

Spring Road

Harewood Road

Park Pl

Connecticut Ave

WARD 1

2nd St

1st St

WARD 5

W ST

White Haven Pkwy

New Jersey Ave

Florida Ave

Benning Road

WARD 2

6th St

WARD 6

WARD 7

S Capitol St

Anacostia River

WARD 6

Morris Road

Naylor Road

Potomac River

Southern Ave

WARD 8

DISTRICT OF COLUMBIA

DELEGATE

Eleanor Holmes Norton (D). Reelected 2008 to a two-year term. Previously elected 2006, 2004, 2002, 2000, 1998, 1996, 1994, 1992, 1990.

POSTWAR VOTE FOR PRESIDENT

Year	Total Vote	Republican		Democratic		Other Vote	Plurality	Percentage			
								Total Vote		Major Vote	
		Vote	Candidate	Vote	Candidate			Rep.	Dem.	Rep.	Dem.
2008	265,853	17,367	McCain, John	245,800	Obama, Barack	2,686	228,433 D	6.5%	92.5%	6.6%	93.4%
2004	227,586	21,256	Bush, George W.	202,970	Kerry, John	3,360	181,714 D	9.3%	89.2%	9.5%	90.5%
2000**	201,894	18,073	Bush, George W.	171,923	Gore, Al	11,898	153,850 D	9.0%	85.2%	9.5%	90.5%
1996**	185,726	17,339	Dole, Bob	158,220	Clinton, Bill	10,167	140,881 D	9.3%	85.2%	9.9%	90.1%
1992**	227,572	20,698	Bush, George	192,619	Clinton, Bill	14,255	171,921 D	9.1%	84.6%	9.7%	90.3%
1988	192,877	27,590	Bush, George	159,407	Dukakis, Michael S.	5,880	131,817 D	14.3%	82.6%	14.8%	85.2%
1984	211,288	29,009	Reagan, Ronald	180,408	Mondale, Walter F.	1,871	151,399 D	13.7%	85.4%	13.9%	86.1%
1980**	175,237	23,545	Reagan, Ronald	131,113	Carter, Jimmy	20,579	107,568 D	13.4%	74.8%	15.2%	84.8%
1976	168,830	27,873	Ford, Gerald R.	137,818	Carter, Jimmy	3,139	109,945 D	16.5%	81.6%	16.8%	83.2%
1972	163,421	35,226	Nixon, Richard M.	127,627	McGovern, George S.	568	92,401 D	21.6%	78.1%	21.6%	78.4%
1968	170,578	31,012	Nixon, Richard M.	139,566	Humphrey, Hubert H.		108,554 D	18.2%	81.8%	18.2%	81.8%
1964**	198,597	28,801	Goldwater, Barry M.	169,796	Johnson, Lyndon B.		140,995 D	14.5%	85.5%	14.5%	85.5%

**In past elections, the other vote included: 2000 - 10,576 Green (Ralph Nader); 1996 - 3,611 Reform (Ross Perot); 1992 - 9,681 Independent (Perot); 1980 - 16,337 Independent (John Anderson). Under the Twenty-third Amendment to the Constitution, the District of Columbia could choose presidential electors beginning with the 1964 election.

POSTWAR VOTE FOR DELEGATE

Year	Total Vote	Republican		Democratic		Other Vote	Rep.-Dem. Plurality	Percentage			
								Total Vote		Major Vote	
		Vote	Candidate	Vote	Candidate			Rep.	Dem.	Rep.	Dem.
2008	247,471		—	228,376	Norton, Eleanor Holmes	19,095	228,376 D		92.3%		100.0%
2006	114,777		—	111,726	Norton, Eleanor Holmes	3,051	111,726 D		97.3%		100.0%
2004	221,213	18,296	Monroe, Michael Andrew	202,027	Norton, Eleanor Holmes	890	183,731 D	8.3%	91.3%	8.3%	91.7%
2002	128,233		—	119,268	Norton, Eleanor Holmes	8,965	119,268 D		93.0%		100.0%
2000	175,631	10,258	Wolterbeek, Edward	158,824	Norton, Eleanor Holmes	6,549	148,566 D	5.8%	90.4%	6.1%	93.9%
1998	136,359	8,610	Wolterbeek, Edward	122,228	Norton, Eleanor Holmes	5,221	113,618 D	6.3%	89.6%	6.6%	93.4%
1996	149,998	11,306	Simonds, Sprague	134,996	Norton, Eleanor Holmes	3,696	123,690 D	7.5%	90.0%	7.7%	92.3%
1994	173,664	13,828	Saltz, Donald	154,988	Norton, Eleanor Holmes	4,848	141,160 D	8.0%	89.2%	8.2%	91.8%
1992	196,754	20,108	Emerson, Susan	166,808	Norton, Eleanor Holmes	9,838	146,700 D	10.2%	84.8%	10.8%	89.2%
1990	159,627	41,999	Singleton, Harry M.	98,442	Norton, Eleanor Holmes	19,186	56,443 D	26.3%	61.7%	29.9%	70.1%
1988	170,933	22,936	Reed, William	121,817	Fauntroy, Walter E.	26,180	98,881 D	13.4%	71.3%	15.8%	84.2%
1986	126,855	17,643	King, Mary L. H.	101,604	Fauntroy, Walter E.	7,608	83,961 D	13.9%	80.1%	14.8%	85.2%
1984	161,771		—	154,583	Fauntroy, Walter E.	7,188	154,583 D		95.6%		100.0%
1982	112,543	17,242	West, John	93,422	Fauntroy, Walter E.	1,879	76,180 D	15.3%	83.0%	15.6%	84.4%
1980	151,046	21,245	Roehr, Robert J.	112,339	Fauntroy, Walter E.	17,462	91,094 D	14.1%	74.4%	15.9%	84.1%
1978	96,306	11,677	Champion, Jackson R.	76,557	Fauntroy, Walter E.	8,072	64,880 D	12.1%	79.5%	13.2%	86.8%
1976	159,790	21,699	Hall, Daniel L.	123,464	Fauntroy, Walter E.	14,627	101,765 D	13.6%	77.3%	14.9%	85.1%
1974	104,014	9,166	Phillips, William R.	66,337	Fauntroy, Walter E.	28,511	57,171 D	8.8%	63.8%	12.1%	87.9%
1972	159,612	39,487	Chin-Lee, William	95,300	Fauntroy, Walter E.	24,825	55,813 D	24.7%	59.7%	29.3%	70.7%
1971S	116,635	29,249	Nevius, John A.	68,166	Fauntroy, Walter E.	19,220	38,917 D	25.1%	58.4%	30.0%	70.0%

Note: The 1971 election was held in March for a short term until the end of the 92nd Congress.

DISTRICT OF COLUMBIA

PRESIDENT 2008

2000 Census Population	Ward	Total Vote	Republican	Democratic	Other	Rep.-Dem. Plurality	Percentage			
							Total Vote		Major Vote	
							Rep.	Dem.	Rep.	Dem.
73,364	Ward 1	31,029	1,599	28,977	453	27,378 D	5.2%	93.4%	5.2%	94.8%
68,869	Ward 2	28,952	3,619	24,865	468	21,246 D	12.5%	85.9%	12.7%	87.3%
73,718	Ward 3	36,831	5,737	30,491	603	24,754 D	15.6%	82.8%	15.8%	84.2%
74,092	Ward 4	36,395	1,395	34,720	280	33,325 D	3.8%	95.4%	3.9%	96.1%
72,527	Ward 5	34,379	887	33,259	233	32,372 D	2.6%	96.7%	2.6%	97.4%
68,035	Ward 6	35,006	3,518	31,031	457	27,513 D	10.0%	88.6%	10.2%	89.8%
70,540	Ward 7	34,100	312	33,663	125	33,351 D	0.9%	98.7%	0.9%	99.1%
70,914	Ward 8	27,665	210	27,394	61	27,184 D	0.8%	99.0%	0.8%	99.2%
	Federal ballots	1,496	90	1,400	6	1,310 D	6.0%	93.6%	6.0%	94.0%
572,059	TOTAL	265,853	17,367	245,800	2,686	228,433 D	6.5%	92.5%	6.6%	93.4%

Note: Federal ballots were cast for president only in the form of an absentee vote and were not attributed to any particular ward.

DISTRICT OF COLUMBIA

GENERAL ELECTIONS

2008 GENERAL ELECTIONS

President   Other vote was 958 Independent (Ralph Nader); 590 Statehood Green (Cynthia A. McKinney); 1,138 scattered write-in.

Delegate   Other vote was 16,693 Statehood Green (Maude Louise Hills); 2,402 scattered write-in.